P9-DNR-405

Southern Africa in Perspective

ESSAYS IN REGIONAL POLITICS

EDITED BY
CHRISTIAN P. POTHOLM
AND
RICHARD DALE

THE FREE PRESS NEW YORK
Collier-Macmillan Limited LONDON

TO OUR PARENTS
Harold C. and Ella D. Potholm,
and Edgar and Elizabeth K. Dale,
IN GRATEFUL APPRECIATION

Printed in the United States of America

THE FREE PRESS
A DIVISION OF THE MACMILLAN COMPANY
866 Third Avenue, New York, New York 10022

Collier-Macmillan Canada Ltd., Toronto, Ontario

Library of Congress Catalog Card Number: 79-143520

printing number
1 2 3 4 5 6 7 8 9 10

Contents

PREFACE vii

BIOGRAPHICAL SKETCHES x

PART ONE. INTRODUCTION

1 RICHARD DALE — Southern Africa: Research Frontiers in Political Science 3

PART TWO. THE SOUTH AFRICAN NEXUS

Country Profiles 18

1 DENIS J. WORRALL — Afrikaner Nationalism: A Contemporary Analysis 19

2 INEZ SMITH REID — African Nationalism in South Africa and Zimbabwe 31

3 J. E. SPENCE — South African Foreign Policy: The "Outward Movement" 46

4 CHRISTOPHER R. HILL — The Future of Separate Development in South Africa 59

5 PAUL S. VAN DER MERWE — South Africa and South West Africa 69

6 HIDIPO L. HAMUTENYA AND GOTTFRIED H. GEINGOB — African Nationalism in Namibia 85

PART THREE. THE FORMER HIGH COMMISSION TERRITORIES

Country Profiles 96

1 RICHARD P. STEVENS — The History of the Anglo-South African Conflict over the Proposed Incorporation of the High Commission Territories 97

2 RICHARD DALE — Botswana 110

3 RICHARD F. WEISFELDER — Lesotho 125

4 CHRISTIAN P. POTHOLM — Swaziland 141

PART FOUR. ANGOLA AND MOZAMBIQUE — *Country Profiles* 156

1 ANTONIO DA SILVA REGO — Portugal and Africa: A Historical Survey (1482–1961) 157

2 DOUGLAS L. WHEELER — Portugal in Angola: A Living Colonialism? 172

3 RONALD H. CHILCOTE — Mozambique: The African Nationalist Response to Portuguese Imperialism and Underdevelopment 183

4 MAINA D. KAGOMBE — African Nationalism and Guerrilla Warfare in Angola and Mozambique 196

PART FIVE. THE FORMER CENTRAL AFRICAN FEDERATION AND SOUTHERN AFRICA — *Country Profiles* 206

1 SAMUEL W. SPECK, JR. — Malawi and the Southern African Complex 207

2 JAMES P. BARBER — Rhodesia and Interstate Relationships in Southern Africa 219

3 VERNON J. MWAANGA — Zambia's Policy toward Southern Africa 234

PART SIX. INFLUENCE VECTORS

1 YASHPAL TANDON — The Organization of African Unity and the Liberation of Southern Africa 245

2 JOHN A. MARCUM — The Exile Condition and Revolutionary Effectiveness: Southern African Liberation Movements 262

3 ESCHEL M. RHOODIE — Southern Africa: Towards a New Commonwealth? 276

4 CHARLES W. PETERSEN — The Military Balance in Southern Africa 298

PART SEVEN. CONCLUSION

1 Toward the Millennium 321
CHRISTIAN P. POTHOLM

NOTES 333

Suggested Readings on Southern Africa 398
Compiled by DORIS CRUGER DALE

INDEX 407

Preface

During the course of their teaching on and research in Southern Africa, the editors have been concerned about four principal shortcomings in the literature on this region of Africa. First, despite the large number of books, monographs, and articles on each of the nine component units in the Southern African subsystem (which includes South Africa, South West Africa, Malawi, Rhodesia, Angola, Mozambique, Botswana, Swaziland, and Lesotho), one can seldom find works which include a balanced presentation of the differing (and often antagonistic) views of African nationalist spokesmen, government officials, and scholars on the politics of Southern Africa. Such views are rarely expressed in the same forum, and thus one must search for them in the debates of national parliaments, in the records of the United Nations and/or the Organization of African Unity, and among the often ephemeral literature of African nationalist groups, particularly those operating in exile. Second, all too often one finds that works by single authors on one or more units of the Southern African subsystem are tendentious, apologetic, polemical, or purely descriptive; dispassionate and analytical works are usually the exception, rather than the rule, particularly when they treat the twin topics of nationalism and race. Third, because of the recent independence of Botswana, Lesotho, Swaziland, and Malawi, much of the literature on these nations is rather out of date and refers primarily to the colonial era. Finally, even when there is no paucity of literature (as is true in the case of South Africa), the individual units are customarily treated as discrete, disjointed entities which interact with units outside the subsystem rather than with those inside the subsystem. Such a view can be myopic indeed since it may preclude the application of techniques of crossnational comparison and subsystemic analysis.

In organizing the format of *Southern Africa in Perspective: Essays in Regional Politics*, the editors kept the above four criticisms in mind, and it was their purpose to try to improve the state of the literature on this very crucial region in Africa, a region which will become increasingly significant with the passage of time. In the first place, they have attempted to provide a forum for African nationalist spokesmen, government officials, and university professors with acknowledged expertise on certain aspects of Southern Africa. Owing to limitations of space and the exigencies of time, it was not possible for every conceivable shade of opinion to be represented in this volume; still, the editors have attempted to include proponents as well as opponents of the established order in much of Southern Africa. Like John Stuart Mill, who in his essay *On Liberty* recognized that no one individual or group had a monopoly on truth, the editors trust that the readers will find the presentation of differing perspectives on Southern Africa an invitation to draw their own tentative conclusions as to the advantages or disadvantages of certain controversial policies. The editors assumed responsibility for inviting the contributors to submit their essays and for ensuring that these essays met certain commonly accepted academic standards. Like the readers, the editors do not necessarily find themselves in agreement on all matters with all the contributors, but they do feel that all the contributors have important points to make and questions to raise.

Second, the editors have invited several university faculty members from Western Europe, the United States, and Africa to contribute essays on particular subjects, and in many instances their essays concern topics on which they have recently written their doctoral dissertations or have subsequently published scholarly works. The editors especially wanted to provide an opportunity for the younger generation of scholars of Southern Africa to share with readers the results of their most recent research in Southern Africa, for it is the responsibility of these young faculty members to advance the research frontiers of Southern Africa in cooperation with their colleagues in Africa and elsewhere. Naturally, it is to such persons that the editors have turned for analytical sophistication, logical rigor, and command of the literature of both their subfields and their academic disciplines. Although they have concentrated on the empirical approach to a particular nation or problem, such an approach does not necessarily preclude normative preferences and judgments.

In the third place, the editors have attempted to keep the readers as up to date as possible on the latest developments in the newly emerging black-led nations of Southern Africa. They are fully aware that there will always be a gap between the submission of a book manuscript and the publication of that book some months later, and they acknowledge that this book, in turn, would be out of date as soon as it is published if it concentrated solely on current events. Consequently, the authors of these essays have been more concerned about patterns of political development than with all the minutiae of such development.

With respect to the fourth criticism, the editors have chosen to treat Southern Africa as a subsystem of the international political system in order to facilitate crossnational comparisons among the nine component units and in order to adumbrate present and future patterns of conflict and cooperation among the nine units of the subsystem. Such an approach is both heuristic and analytical and is by no means the only way to consider the whole and/or parts of Southern Africa. The editors did not wish to repeat previous studies which dealt with bilateral relations between one of the component units of the subsystem and one of the Great Powers. Rather, they preferred to focus attention on inter-African relations, a sorely neglected field of study, and thus one of the essays in this volume examines in detail the nature of the interaction between the subsystem and a transnational, continental organization, the Organization of African Unity. Such an approach, the editors hope, will suggest to the readers the range of possibilities for future research on inter-African diplomacy within a regional framework. The contributors have not neglected to draw attention to the ties between the new African-run states and the former metropole (the United Kingdom in all four cases), and one must not underestimate the significance of such bilateral relationships, particularly with respect to patterns of international trade. But, again, the emphasis has been upon the political ramifications of geographical propinquity in Southern Africa.

It is not the intention of the introductory chapter of this book to provide the readers with a preview of what follows in the remaining chapters, nor is it the intention of the concluding chapter to summarize the findings of the previous chapters. The introductory chapter analyzes some of the rather extensive literature on Southern Africa and suggests what topics in Southern Africa still remain to be treated adequately by scholars. Because this first chapter is in effect a bibliographic essay and because the editors have encouraged the contributors to make extensive use of footnotes in their chapters, they have not appended a conventional, exhaustive bibliography at the end of this book. Rather, they have included a selective bibliography which takes into account those works that the contributors regard as most germane to their topic or that set forth a point of view with which the contributors closely identify.

The concluding chapter deals principally with the future of the Southern African subsystem and is, perforce, speculative in nature. It asks: What will the subsystem look like at the end of the twentieth century? It then attempts to provide nine separate answers to this seminal question. It stipulates the number and type of variables involved, the possible and probable combinations and permutations of the variables, and makes explicit the assumptions involved in this type of exercise. Such answers (or scenarios) are by no means definitive or exhaustive and deal principally with empirical data rather than with normative concerns. The editors hope that such an exercise in political prognostication will, in turn, stimulate the readers to probe their own assumptions and value preferences, as well as those of the contributors, and so begin to think seriously about the future of a very crucial and complex region of Africa.

The editors are most appreciative of the unlimited patience and unfailing support of their editor, Mr. James M. Cron, vice president of The Free Press, and they would also like to thank the Research Committee of Vassar College, the Department of Political Science of Vassar College, the Office of Research and Projects of Southern Illinois University, and the Department of Government of Southern Illinois University for financial and professional support in preparing the manuscript. Both editors are deeply grateful to Miss Gig Babson and Miss Darcy Kirk of Vassar College, and Miss C. Daphne Saul, former Librarian of the South African Institute of International Affairs, who served as their conscientious research assistants. They are equally beholden and grateful to the students in their courses on African politics for their interest and cooperation in this joint venture, and they would also like to thank the Shell Companies, Inc., for a predoctoral fellowship for Professor Potholm to travel to

Southern Africa in 1965–1966 and the American Philosophical Society for a postdoctoral grant for Professor Dale to undertake a second trip to Southern Africa in the summer of 1970. Finally, the editors would like to acknowledge that very special debt they owe to their wives, Sandra Q. Potholm and Doris Cruger Dale, for their constant help, forbearance, and encouragement.

CHRISTIAN P. POTHOLM
Brunswick, Maine

RICHARD DALE
Carbondale, Illinois

Biographical Sketches

EDITORS

CHRISTIAN P. POTHOLM, born in Hartford, Conn., 1940, received his A.B. degree from Bowdoin College, and his M.A., M.A.L.D., and Ph.D. degrees from the Fletcher School of Law and Diplomacy. Presently an associate professor of government at Bowdoin College, he previously taught at Dartmouth and Vassar colleges. He has traveled and done research work in East, West, and Southern Africa during 1965–1966 and 1969, and is the author of *Four African Political Systems* (1970). His articles have appeared in *The Journal of Developing Areas, The Journal of Modern African Studies, Africa Report, Africa Today, Journal of Asian and African Studies*, and *International Journal*. He wrote his doctoral dissertation at the Fletcher School on political development in Swaziland, and he received a Shell Fellowship for his field research in Southern Africa.

RICHARD DALE, born in Columbus, Ohio, 1932, received his A.B. degree from Bowdoin College, his M.A. degree from the Ohio State University, and his M.A. and Ph.D. degrees from Princeton University. He is currently associate professor of government and secretary of the African studies committee at Southern Illinois University. Previously he had taught at the University of New Hampshire and Northern Illinois University. He has also studied at the University of California, Los Angeles, where he was a National Defense Foreign Language Fellow in Afrikaans in the summer of 1964. He has undertaken field research in Southern Africa in 1966–1967 and in the summer of 1970, when he received a travel grant from the American Philosophical Society for a study of relations between the Bechuanaland Protectorate and South Africa, 1945–1966. He is the author of a monograph, *Botswana and Its Southern Neighbor* (1970), and he has published articles and review articles in *Africa Report, Africa Today, SAIPA: Journal for Public Administration*, and *World Politics*. He wrote his doctoral dissertation at Princeton University on the South West African dispute at the United Nations.

CONTRIBUTORS

JAMES P. BARBER, born in Liverpool, England, 1931, received his B.A. and Ph.D. degrees from Cambridge University. He is currently reader in political science at the Open University and has recently received a Nuffield Research Grant for a study of Anglo-South African relations since 1945. He was lecturer in politics and government at the University of Exeter from 1967–1969. In 1965–1967, he was the acting head of the Department of Government at the University College of Rhodesia, and he had previously been a lecturer in history at the University of New South Wales in Australia. He served as a district officer, a clerk to the cabinet, and secretary in the office of the prime minister in Uganda from 1956 to 1962. He is the author of *Rhodesia: Road to Rebellion* (1967) and *Imperial Frontier: A Study of the Relations between the British Administration and the Pastoral Tribes of North-East Uganda* (1968).

RONALD H. CHILCOTE, born in Cleveland, Ohio, 1935, received his A.B. degree from Dartmouth College and his M.B.A., M.A., and Ph.D. degrees from Stanford University. Presently, he is associate professor of political science at the University of California at Riverside. He has also studied at the University of Lisbon and done field research in both Latin America and Africa. He is the author of *Portuguese Africa* (1967) and *Emerging Nationalism in Portuguese Africa: A Bibliography of Documentary Ephemera through 1965* (1969). He has published articles in *African Studies Bulletin, The World Today, Africa Today, The New Republic, Contemporary Review, The*

Nation, The Journal of Modern African Studies, Le Mois en Afrique, Comparative Political Studies, Journal of Inter-American Affairs, Geographical Review, Latin American Research Review, and *International Affairs*.

GOTTFRIED H. GEINGOB, born in Otjiwarongo, Namibia (South West Africa), 1941, received his B.A. degree from Fordham University. He is currently the official representative of SWAPO (South West Africa People's Organization) to the United States and to the United Nations. He had previously been a SWAPO representative in Kimshasa, the Congo, and Francistown, Botswana. Prior to that, he had taught primary school at the Rhenish Mission School in Tsumeb, Namibia. He is vice president of the New York chapter of the Pan-African Students Organization in the Americas, editor of the *SWAPO Information Bulletin*, and has contributed a chapter to *South West Africa: Travesty of Trust*, edited by Ronald Segal and Ruth First (1967).

HIDIPO L. HAMUTENYA was born at Onengali, Namibia in 1939. He is deputy representative of the South West Africa People's Organization (SWAPO) to the United Nations and has presented petitions to the United Nations on behalf of Namibia. He received his B.A. degree from Lincoln University where he was chapter president of the Pan-African Students Organization in the Americas (PASOA). He is currently studying for his M.A. degree at McGill University.

CHRISTOPHER R. HILL, born in London, 1935, received his B.A. and M.A. degrees from Cambridge University. He is presently lecturer in politics at the University of York, and he had previously been lecturer in government at the University College of Rhodesia, a member of the British Foreign Service, and assistant director of the Institute of Race Relations in London. He has traveled in both Southern and Eastern Africa and is the author of *Bantustans: The Fragmentation of South Africa* (1964), and editor of *Rights and Wrongs: Some Essays on Human Rights* (1969). He has contributed a chapter to *Africa South of the Congo* (1968) and has published articles in *The World Today* and *The Journal of Commonwealth Political Studies*.

MAINA D. KAGOMBE, born in Weithaga, Kenya, 1940, received his B.A. degree from Eastern Nazarene College, and his M.A. degree from Northeastern University. He is the Editor-in-Chief of the *Pan-African Journal*, a member of the Executive Board and Publicity Secretary of the African Heritage Studies Association, formerly assistant professor of history and politics at Jersey City State College, and is presently the Director of Black and Puerto Rican Studies at Borough of Manhattan Community College and associate professor, The City University of New York.

JOHN A. MARCUM, born in San Jose, California, 1927, received his A.B. and Ph.D. degrees from Stanford University and his M.A. degree from Columbia University. From 1952 until 1954 he was a Fulbright scholar at the Institute of Political Studies of the University of Paris. His research in Africa has been supported by a Ford International Relations Grant in 1958–1959 and by a Fulbright-Hays Grant in 1966–1967. He has taught at Colgate University and at Lincoln University, where he served as director of the African program. During 1969–1970, he was visiting professor of politics at Merrill College of the University of California at Santa Cruz. Dr. Marcum is currently visiting professor at the Graduate School of International Studies of the University of Denver and executive editor of *Africa Today*. He is the author of *The Angolan Revolution: Anatomy of an Explosion (1950–1962)* (1969) and his articles have been published in *Africa Report, Africa Today, Western Political Quarterly*, and *The New Leader*.

VERNON J. MWAANGA, born in Choma, Zambia, 1939, is the Permanent Representative of the Republic of Zambia to the United Nations, as well as a member of the United Nations Security Council and the United Nations Council for Namibia. In December, 1969 he was the president of the United Nations Security Council and was the youngest person ever to hold that post. He attended the Livingstone Technical College from 1957 to 1960, and in 1963 and 1964 he studied at Stanford University and at the Institute of Commonwealth Studies of Oxford University, respectively. He has served as regional secretary of the United National Independence party from 1960 to 1963, and the subsequent year he was an administrative officer in the office of the prime minister. Later he served as deputy high commissioner in London and as ambassador to Moscow.

CHARLES W. PETERSEN, born in Portland, Maine, 1939, received his A.B. degree from Bowdoin College after serving with the Third Infantry Division, United States Army, in the Federal Republic of Germany. He later received his M.S. degree from Danbury State College, and presently he is a doctoral candidate at the University of Maine. He has been awarded a George C. Marshall Fellowship by the Danish business community to undertake research in Copenhagen in 1970–1971 dealing with the Danish navy.

INEZ SMITH REID, born in New Orleans, Louisiana, received her B.A. degree from Tufts University, her LL.B. degree from Yale University Law School, her M.A. degree from the University of California at Los Angeles, and her Ph.D. degree from Columbia University. She is presently an associate professor of political science at Brooklyn College. Previously she has taught at the National School of Law and Administration in Kinshasa, the Congo, Hunter College, the State University of New York at New Paltz, the New School for Social Research, and Barnard College. She is the editor of *The Black Prism: Perspectives on the Black Experience* (1970), and has published articles and bibliographic essays in *Southern California Law Review*, *Pan-African Journal*, *African Forum*, and *Afro-American Studies*.

ESCHEL M. RHOODIE, born in Caledon, South Africa, 1933, received his B.A., M.A., and Ph.D. degrees from the University of Pretoria. Currently he is counsellor of the South African Embassy at The Hague, Netherlands. A former journalist, he served on the staff of *Commando* and *Die Vaderland* and later was a member of the parliamentary staff of the Department of Information. He was attached to the South African embassies in Canberra and Washington, D.C., and was a delegate to the International Labor Organization in 1962. In addition, he served with the South African Information Service in New York from 1963 to 1965, returning to South Africa to head the American desk at the Department of Information from 1965 to 1967. His books include *Penal Systems of the Commonwealth* (1965), *South West: The Last Frontier in Africa* (1967), *The Third Africa* (1968), and *The Paper Curtain* (1969).

ANTONIO da SILVA REGO, born in Braga, Portugal, 1905, was ordained as a Roman Catholic priest in 1927 and received his *Licence en Sciences Historiques* from Louvain University, Belgium. He is presently professor at the *Instituto Superior de Ciências Sociais e Politica Ultramarina* and president of the *Centro de Estudos Históricos Ultramarinos*. He is the author of a dozen books and monographs as well as over 50 articles, most dealing with Portuguese overseas history and missionary activities.

SAMUEL W. SPECK, JR., born in Canton, Ohio, 1937, received his B.A. degree from Muskingum College and his M.A. and Ph.D. degrees from Harvard University. He is presently an associate professor of political science and chairman of the department of political science at Muskingum College. He studied at the University College of Rhodesia as a Rotary Fellow in 1961 and did field research in Malawi in 1963. He has published in *Africa Report*, and he wrote his doctoral dissertation at Harvard on local government in Malawi.

J. E. SPENCE, born in Krugersdorp, South Africa, 1931, received his B.A. and B.A. (Hons.) degrees from the University of the Witwatersrand and his B.S. degree from the London School of Economics, where he was a Rockefeller Junior Research Fellow in 1960–1961. At present he is senior lecturer in international politics at University College, Swansea, Wales. Previously, he had taught at the University of Natal and at the University of California at Los Angeles. He is the author of *Republic under Pressure: A Study of South African Foreign Policy* (1965) and *Lesotho: The Politics of Dependence* (1968). He has contributed a chapter to *Africa South of the Congo* (1968), and his articles have appeared in *The Journal of Modern African Studies*, *Government and Opposition*, *Race*, *The World Today*, and *The Journal of Commonwealth Political Studies*. He is also the co-author of the monograph, *South Africa's Defense: The Problem of Internal Control* (1966).

RICHARD P. STEVENS, born in New Castle, Pennsylvania, 1931, received his B.A. degree from Notre Dame University and his M.A. and Ph.D. degrees from Georgetown University. Presently, he is professor of political science and chairman of the department of political science, as well as director of the African studies program, at Lincoln University. Previously he taught at King's College and at the University College of Botswana, Lesotho, and Swaziland, and was a Fulbright scholar in the United Arab Republic in the summer of 1965 and a Visiting Fellow at Princeton University in the spring of 1968. He has traveled and done field research in Eastern, Western, Northern, Central, and Southern Africa and in the Middle East. He is the author of *American Zionism and U.S. Foreign Policy, 1942–1947* (1962) and *Lesotho, Botswana, and Swaziland: The Former High Commission Territories in Southern Africa* (1967). His articles have appeared in *Africa Report*, *Africa Today*, *The Journal of Modern African Studies*, and *The Arab World*.

YASHPAL TANDON, born in Kaberamaido, Uganda, 1939, received his B.Sc. and Ph.D. degrees from the London School of Economics. Presently he is a senior lecturer in international relations at Makerere University College and has served as executive director of the Makerere Institute in Diplomacy. In 1967 he held a Senior Research Fellowship at the Columbia University

School of International Relations. He has published articles in *International Relations*, *Minerva*, *Africa Quarterly*, and *International Organization*. He has contributed a chapter to *Portrait of a Minority*, edited by D. Ghai (1965) and to *Protest and Power in Black Africa*, edited by Robert I. Rotberg and Ali A. Mazrui (1970), and is the author of *Primitive Peacekeeping: A Generation of Peacekeeping by the United Nations* (1970).

PAUL S. VAN DER MERWE, born in Humpata, Angola, 1922, moved to South West Africa in 1928. He received his B.A., B.A. (Hons.), and M.A. degrees from the University of South Africa and his D. Phil. degree from the University of Pretoria. Since 1958 he has been a member of Parliament for Middelland, South West Africa, and he is presently a member of the Federal Council of the National party as well as a whip of the Parliamentary National party and chairman of the Foreign Affairs Group of the National party. Prior to his election to the House of Assembly, he served as editor of the Windhoek newspaper, *Die Suidwester*, from 1950 until 1958 and was president of the Scientific Society of South West Africa in 1956–1957. His master's thesis dealt with the development of self-government in South West Africa. He recently visited the United States as a member of a South African parliamentary group.

RICHARD F. WEISFELDER, born in Bronxville, New York, 1939, received his B.A. degree from Amherst College and his M.A. from Harvard. Presently he is instructor of government at Ohio University, Athens, Ohio, and is a Ph.D. candidate at Harvard. He spent the Fall of 1964 in London studying Sesotho and 1965–1966 in Lesotho. He is the author of the monograph *Defining National Purpose in Lesotho* (1969) and has contributed to *Africa Report*.

DOUGLAS L. WHEELER, born in St. Louis, Missouri, 1937, received his A.B. degree from Dartmouth College and his M.A. and Ph.D. degrees from Boston University. He is presently an associate professor of history at the University of New Hampshire and he has also taught at the University College of Rhodesia. In 1961–1962 he was a Fulbright Scholar in Portugal, and he has traveled and done field research in Southern Africa as well. His articles have been published in *The Journal of African History*, *The Journal of Modern African Studies*, *Foreign Affairs*, *Africa Report*, and *African Historical Studies*, and he has contributed a chapter to *Leadership in Eastern Africa: Six Political Biographies*, edited by Norman R. Bennett (1968), and to *Protest and Power in Black Africa*, edited by Robert I. Rotberg and Ali A. Mazrui (1970). His doctoral dissertation dealt with the history of nineteenth-century Angola.

DENIS J. WORRALL, born in Benoni, South Africa, 1935, received his B.A., B.A. (Hons.), and M.A. degrees from the University of Cape Town and his Ph.D. from Cornell University. Presently, he is senior lecturer in international relations at the University of the Witwatersrand, and he has previously taught at the University of Ibadan, the University of California at Los Angeles, the University of South Africa, and the University of Natal. He has published in *Africa Report*, and since 1966 he has been a political columnist for the Sunday South African newspaper, *Die Beeld*. He is also the editor of the monthly South African political and literary review, *New Nation*.

PART ONE

Introduction

1

Southern Africa: Research Frontiers in Political Science

RICHARD DALE*

All notes appear at end of text in a separate section beginning on p. 333.

Introduction

This introductory chapter is intended to serve two purposes. In the first place, it will attempt to suggest the kinds of practical and theoretical problems that beset political scientists whose principal research interests lie in Southern Africa. There are often vexing problems in collecting, creating, processing, classifying, storing, and retrieving data, and many, if not most, of these problems political scientists working on Southern African affairs share with their colleagues who undertake research on other non-Western areas. One of the most difficult obstacles to the collection and creation of data in Southern Africa is in connection with research on matters of internal security, exile politics, and unconventional (as well as conventional) warfare. Here one faces frustrations in coping with security measures, censorship, unverifiable data, classified or secret (and perforce unobtainable) data, and covert or overt threats to the research worker, and so forth. And there is also the moral dilemma of how to protect the scholar's informants from possible retribution, on the one hand, and the deeply felt professional ethics concerning full identification of sources, on the other hand. Professor John A. Marcum, one of the contributors to this volume, has had long experience in coping with these difficulties in his research work on African nationalist movements in Angola and discusses them in his own work.[1]

The second purpose of this chapter is, within the limits available, to survey some of the institutions in Southern Africa, the United Kingdom, and the United States where research on Southern Africa is being undertaken. This discussion of the institutional sponsorship of research and publications is followed by an analysis of the types of questions with which political scientists, including those writing in this volume, have concerned themselves and which still await answers. These questions are germane both to Southern Africa and to

* The author wishes to express his gratitude to his co-editor, Professor Christian P. Potholm, and to both Professor Edward Feit of the Department of Government of the University of Massachusetts and Mr. Hans E. Panofsky, Curator of Africana at Northwestern University, for reading and commenting upon an earlier draft of this chapter.

the fields of comparative and international politics, and therefore it is necessary to view Southern Africa in the perspective of these two important subfields of political science.

Data Collection and Storage

Southern Africa presents the contemporary student of its affairs with the extremes of both a surfeit and a paucity of data. In some fields, there is a richness of material, whereas in others there is scarcity. The quality and consistency of data are particularly distressing in those countries where there may be a restricted access to the country itself either because of travel (especially visa) regulations or because of limited access to archives and potential interviewees resulting from research restrictions—such as prior cabinet approval of a research design. If a scholar can secure access to data of high quality and consistency in spite of such travel and/or research regulations, his or her task is correspondingly easier. Indeed, a great deal of the documentary research[2] on Southern Africa, especially on those nations once under British rule or associated with the Commonwealth of Nations, can be done in the United States and in the United Kingdom by means of interlibrary loan, microfilming, microprinting, and Xeroxing procedures.

Presently, the Cooperative Africana Microform Project (CAMP), sponsored by the Center for Research Libraries in Chicago,[3] has been making larger and larger numbers of Southern African materials, such as newspapers and non-American unpublished theses and dissertations, available to research students in both American and non-American universities and institutions. Because of technological advances in the microprinting field, the scholar will be able to work not only with greater speed but also with greater accuracy. At present, the major drawback of CAMP is that the printed catalogue of the Center for Research Libraries is neither complete (only six volumes have been issued so far) nor does it list these dissertations and theses. Presumably, these lacunae will be filled in the near future.

The State Library in Pretoria, Republic of South Africa, has also been active in this field, particularly in terms of collating and microfilming South African newspapers as well as reprinting some extremely valuable Africana, such as eight volumes of the South African House of Assembly debates as reported in the *Cape Times* from 1915 until 1923.[4] Unfortunately, no official reports of these debates (known as Hansards, following the British terminology) were issued during these years, and thus the only published record of the debates would be the South African press, especially that of Cape Town (the site of the Parliament).

Also involved in the newspaper microfilming field is a commercial firm, Microfile Limited of Johannesburg, which has microfilmed a considerable number of important documents pertaining to politically significant trials in the Union and Republic of South Africa. An exegesis of such documents is often a necessary step in the analysis of African nationalism in South Africa and South West Africa (Namibia), especially when the documents include oral testimony and written pleadings and evidence of both plaintiffs and defendants.[5] Just as the 12 volumes of written and oral testimony in the South West Africa cases at the International Court of Justice are an unparalleled source of material on the political development of the territory of South West Africa, so too are the records of these South African trials indispensable for studies of African nationalism in the Republic of South Africa, especially when they are combined with a search of those South African newspapers which are (or were) primarily designed to cater to the interests, needs, and tastes of their African readers, such as the *Guardian* (and its successors, the *Clarion*, the *People's World*, *Advance*, *New Age*, and *Spark*) and *The World*.[6]

Another rich source of published material which is not yet exhausted by students of Southern African politics is the entire gamut of United Nations documents, particularly those concerning the trusteeship system and the collation of material (under the provisions of Article 73(e) of the United Nations Charter) relating to nonself-governing territories. Especially important are studies prepared by the Secretariat of the United Nations and the plethora of petitions to the various organs of the United Nations.[7] A content analysis of petitions to the United Nations from African nationalist groups in Southern Africa would be especially useful when coupled with an examination of other types of African protest literature; such an analysis would suggest the types and frequency of symbol manipulation and broaden our understanding of African nationalism[8]

For those interested in a comparative analysis of decolonization in Southern Africa, the announcement that the League of Nations archives in Geneva are in the process of being catalogued is most encouraging.[9] Access to these archives, as well as to the British ones (where the closed period has been reduced from fifty to thirty years)[10] will facilitate transnational studies of colonial administration, the comparative analysis of the role of the League of Nations and of the United Nations in the Africans' quest for self-determination and the corresponding response of the British, Portuguese, Rhodesian, and South African governments to the growth of African nationalism. Such studies could be interdisciplinary and could involve Africanists of many nationalities. In the case of South West Africa, for example, it is likely that access to British, League of Nations, and United Nations archives would be easier to secure than comparable access to the archives of the imperial German regime located in Potsdam, East Germany, and/or the archives of that regime left in Windhoek, South West Africa.[11]

One of the most intriguing and challenging fields in which there can be mutually beneficial cooperation between political scientists and librarians of several nationalities concerns the collection, cataloguing, and preservation (often by means of microfilming) of African electoral campaign literature, clandestine journals and newspapers, broadsheets, correspondence, manuscripts, and other priceless material. At present, considerable efforts are being made in the United States by the Hoover Institution and Northwestern University Library, in conjunction with CAMP, to make this kind of data more readily available to the academic community. Professor Ronald H. Chilcote, one of the contributors to this volume, has been interested in such an endeavor and has worked closely with the Hoover Institution on collecting such material from Angola and Mozambique.[12] Plans are now under way to catalogue the unusually fine holdings of African nationalist literature at the Africa Bureau in London, an institution which long befriended African nationalists from Southern Africa; eventually, some or all of that collection may be microfilmed by CAMP, provided the Africa Bureau gives its permission.[13]

The exchange of publications between various African institutes throughout the world and the use of consortium techniques to retrieve and store data are encouraging signs for those concerned about the study of Southern African affairs. Such close cooperation will be of long-range benefit for Africans and non-Africans from Southern Africa studying in the United States and/or the United Kingdom since they will have access to a wealth of data from their own and neighboring nations without having to go to the expense (and, in some cases, political risk) of returning home or going to Southern Africa to gather published data. In addition, such cooperation on an institutional basis may open doors once closed to all Africanists except the most favored, and it should enable American or British scholars to complete more of certain types of research projects at home and perhaps to reduce the necessity and/or length of a costly research trip to Southern Africa.[14]

Data Retrieval

As we suggested earlier, there are often obvious deficiencies and inadequacies in the quantity and quality of data which have been collected and stored. These difficulties are slowly being overcome by political scientists and other social scientists working in close cooperation with librarians and others responsible for data storage and classification. A closely related problem (which has been solved much more readily, thanks to librarians and archivists) is how to retrieve the data once they have been stored. The research worker can do so in part by taking advantage of many bibliographies, indexes, news summaries, and press translations that are now readily available. We would like to draw attention to some of the most useful bibliographic and research tools for students of Southern African affairs.

The Program of Eastern African Studies of the Maxwell Graduate School of Citizenship of Syracuse has sponsored bibliographies of Botswana, Lesotho, Malawi, and Swaziland.[15] In addition, the School of Librarianship of the University of Cape Town and the Department of Bibliography, Librarianship, and Typography of the University of the Witwatersrand in Johannesburg have issued bibliographies of Angola, Botswana, the former Central African Federation, Rhodesia, South Africa, South West Africa, and Swaziland.[16] At the official level, the Botswana National Library Service is now issuing the *National Bibliography of Botswana*, which is an annual list of all works published in Botswana, and the National Archives of Rhodesia in Salisbury publishes the comparable *Rhodesia National Bibliography* annually.

Frequently bibliographic essays appear in the *African Studies Bulletin*, published by the African Studies Center of Boston University for the African Studies Association. In recent years, such essays have covered Angola, Malawi, Mozambique, and South Africa.[17] For those whose research deals with South Africa, there are a number of reference guides, such as the *Guide to South Africa Reference Books* by Reuben Musiker of Rhodes University,[18] the *Union Catalogue of Theses and Dissertations of South African Universities* with accompanying annual supplements,[19] and *A Select Bibliography of South African History: A Guide for Historical Research*, edited by C. F. J. Muller, F. A. van Jaarsveld, and Theo van Wyk.[20] Some of the South African theses and dissertations in history and political science are published in the *Archives Year Book for South African History*, issued annually by the Office of the Director of the South African Archives.

Particularly valuable for the specialist in South

African studies are review articles by Professor Monica Wilson of the University of Cape Town[21] and Professor Pierre L. van den Berghe of the University of Washington.[22] Other review articles in the field of South African history have also been written by Professor Leonard M. Thompson of Yale University[23] and by Deryck van der H. Schreuder of New College, Oxford University.[24] Professor Leslie Rubin of Howard University has written a review of the literature on South West Africa and the former High Commission Territories.[25] Two other research tools widely used by students of South African politics—particularly by those who do not have complete access to the full array of primary sources and by those who are not fluent in the Afrikaans language—are *A Survey of Race Relations in South Africa*, issued annually by the South African Institute of Race Relations in Johannesburg, and the *Press Digest*, published weekly by the Jewish Board of Deputies in Johannesburg. In addition to providing a summary and a translation of selected articles published in the Afrikaans newspapers, this *Press Digest* also surveys both the English-language press and those newspapers which especially cater to the needs of nonwhites in the Republic.

One of the greatest difficulties research workers experience in utilizing the South African press is that there are no published indexes to any South African newspapers. Therefore, it is often necessary to have access both to the clipping files of the libraries of these newspapers in South Africa and to the actual newspapers themselves, most of which are available at the State Library in Pretoria and at the British Museum Newspaper Library in London. Such a situation, which limits access to a valuable source of data to those able to travel to South Africa and/or the United Kingdom, would work great hardships on many who would like to undertake research on the Republic. Some of the hardships can be alleviated by a more active program of microfilming South African newspapers and the use of interlibrary loan procedures. It should also be noted that some of the South African press is summarized in the *Africa Research Bulletin* (in both the political, social, and cultural series and the economic, financial, and technical series), published monthly by Africa Research Limited in Exeter, England and in the *International Defence and Aid Fund Information Service* (in both the political and social series and the economic series), published by the International Defense and Aid Fund for Southern Africa in London.

Fortunately, there is little difficulty in working with South African periodicals because of the very thorough system of indexing. The Johannesburg Public Library has sponsored the *Index to South African Periodicals*, which covers periodicals back to 1940. And for parliamentary documents, there is the *Index to the Manuscript Annexures and Printed Papers of the House of Assembly*, published by the House of Assembly in 1963. It covers the period from 1910 until 1960 and also includes Select Committee reports, commission reports, bills, motions, and resolutions. The principal drawback to using materials cited in this index is that one needs the permission of a Member of Parliament to have access to the manuscript papers. However, the printed papers referred to in the index are readily available and may be secured with little or no difficulty. For those interested in Rhodesian parliamentary documents, there is the *Catalogue of the Parliamentary Papers of Southern Rhodesia, 1899–1953* by F. M. G. Willson and Gloria C. Passmore.[26] Two other guides to Rhodesian source materials are *The Rhodesias and Nyasaland: A Guide to Official Publications*[27] and *A Guide to the Public Records of Southern Rhodesia under the Regime of the British South Africa Company, 1890–1923.*[28]

Libraries and librarians in the United Kingdom have undertaken some extremely fine bibliographic work on Southern Africa which is of considerable interest to those doing research, particularly on the Anglophone countries of that region. One of the most valuable research tools is the *United Kingdom Publications and Theses on Africa*, which has been published annually since 1963 under the aegis of the Standing Conference on Library Materials on Africa (SCOLMA).[29] These British publications list theses and dissertations written for British universities, articles on Africa appearing in British periodicals, and new books on Africa published in the United Kingdom, and they also provide references to African topics in the debates of the House of Commons and House of Lords. Moreover, SCOLMA has issued a directory of African collections in British libraries.[30] Those who are fortunate enough to undertake part or all of their Southern African research in British libraries and archives should consult the recently published guide to the *Manuscript Collections of Africana in Rhodes House Library, Oxford* compiled by Louis B. Frewer[31] and the *Guide to Resources for Commonwealth Studies in London, Oxford, and Cambridge with Bibliographical and Other Information* by A. R. Hewitt.[32]

In the United States, the Hoover Institution on War, Revolution, and Peace at Stanford University publishes annual lists of Africana which are somewhat comparable to those published by SCOLMA in the United Kingdom.[33] The director of the African Program at the Hoover Institution, Dr. Peter Duignan, recently wrote the *Handbook of American Resources for African Studies* as a part of the Hoover Institution bibliographical series. Other useful bibliographical guides have been issued by the Library of Congress,[34] the African Bibliographic Center in Washington, D.C.,[35] and Boston University.[36]

Recently, a number of libraries with outstanding African collections—such as Boston University and Northwestern University in the United States and the School of Oriental and African Studies of the University of London and the British Colonial Office—have had their card catalogues reproduced and bound in several volumes, and this will facilitate research where interlibrary loan and photoduplication services are readily available. Indeed, in some areas there may be such a wealth of published material that techniques of data storage and retrieval will need to be improved to the point where, at some future date, computer techniques can be economically employed. In fact, specialists on Africana have recently been studying the possibilities of using such techniques.[37]

Institutional Sponsorship of Research and Publications

In addition to rapid advances in the technology of data storage and retrieval, progress has also been made in the field of institutional sponsorship of, and support for, research and publications on Southern African affairs. At present, a considerable amount of the research on Southern Africa which is of interest to political scientists is done by individuals with institutional sponsorship. These institutions either have their own full-time research staffs or arrange for research to be done under contract. This is particularly the case in the Republic of South Africa, the United Kingdom, and the United States. The following survey of some of the activities of several of these organizations in South Africa, the United Kingdom, and the United States is intended to be suggestive of the range of such research, rather than to be conclusive or exhaustive.

Two important research centers in South Africa are the South Africa Institute of Race Relations in Johannesburg and the African Institute in Pretoria. The former is perhaps better known outside the Republic than the latter, primarily because it is older and since 1948 has been generally regarded as being both outspoken and sophisticated in its criticism of apartheid. The Africa Institute has a different focus from that of the South Africa Institute of Race Relations, which devotes most of its attention to conditions in the Republic itself; the Africa Institute is more concerned with the Republic's relations with the rest of the continent, especially with its neighbors.[38]

The Africa Institute has a much closer relation-

ship with the government than does the Institute of Race Relations. Its patron is the state president (Mr. J. J. Fouché), and its honorary members include the prime minister (Mr. B. J. Vorster), the minister of foreign affairs (Dr. Hilgard Muller), the former ambassador to the United States (Mr. Wentzel C. du Plesis), a former senator from South West Africa (Dr. Heinrich Vedder), a former minister of Bantu administration and development (Mr. M. D. C. de Wet Nel), and the president of the South African Senate (Mr. Jan de Klerk). None of its honorary members is a member of any political party other than the National party, and neither the leader of the Opposition (Sir de Villiers Graaff) nor the lone representative of the Progressive party in Parliament, Mrs. Helen Suzman, is an honorary member of the Institute or a member of its council. However, the council does include among its members the presidents of two English-medium universities (the universities of the Witwatersrand and Cape Town) in addition to those of two Afrikaans-medium universities (the universities of Pretoria and of Stellenbosch) and the nonresidential University of South Africa. The council appears to exclude Africans and other nonwhites as members.

Founded on April 7, 1960, the Institute began publishing its regular *Bulletin* in February 1963, and it now has a rather active publications program, ranging from popular journalism to scholarly monographs. It publishes a series of short data sheets on different African nations, entitled *Africa at a Glance*, and it has issued an atlas, sponsored and published the results of several symposia on various topics, and recently undertaken the publication of a serial known as *Southern Africa Data*. It has been particularly energetic in supporting research and publications on the kingdoms of Lesotho and Swaziland, although it has also published material on Rhodesia, Botswana, and Malawi.[39] In addition, it has its own library and library staff, publications staff, director, secretary, and research staff.

Another well-known research center of interest to political scientists is the South African Institute of Race Relations, which has its head office in Johannesburg and additional offices in Cape Town and Durban.[40] It is considerably older than the Africa Institute, dating back to 1929, and it would appear to have a much larger membership than the Africa Institute, for in 1967–1968 the South African Institute of Race Relations claimed a membership of 3,604 persons.

Like the Africa Institute, it disclaims any links to South African political parties but, unlike the Africa Institute, a number of the notables in the leadership of the institute have been connected with the now defunct Liberal party (Mr. Alan Paton and Dr. Edgar H. Brookes), the Progressive party (Mrs. Helen Suzman, M.P.), and the United party (Mr. Arthur Hopewell, M.P.). In addition, a number of African organizations, Catholic, Jewish, and Protestant religious groups, and educational institutions are affiliated with the Institute. Moreover, the Institute provides administrative and secretarial services for some social welfare organizations and for the South African Voluntary Service (which is comparable to the United States Peace Corps volunteer program).

The Institute of Race Relations has its own library and, like the Africa Institute in Pretoria, a newspaper clipping file also. The portion of the file from 1957 to 1967 has been microfilmed, which should prove valuable to research students working in the United States and the United Kingdom. These files are utilized in the compilation of the annual serial issued by the Institute. *A Survey of Race Relations in South Africa*. This *Survey* does include some material on South African foreign relations, but its principal focus is on domestic affairs, especially as they concern interracial affairs. The publications program of the institute is one of the most vigorous, if not the most vigorous, in the Republic.[41] In addition to the *Survey*, it issues a number of short essays known as *Topical Talks* on a variety of subjects by different authors, a monthly periodical entitled *Race Relations News*, a number of memoranda, and several monographs on various racial groups in the Republic and on different aspects of apartheid. Some of the monographs are of high quality and are well documented and footnoted. Three examples of such monographs are Professor A. L. Müller's study of the Indian and colored communities in the Republic, Miss Muriel Horrell's monograph on South African trade unionism, and Miss Horrell's analysis of the African reserves in the Republic.[42]

Several other South African organizations are significant for political scientists. The South African Institute of International Affairs,[43] which has its headquarters in Johannesburg and is associated to some extent with the University of the Witwatersrand there (just as the Africa Institute is associated with the University of South Africa in Pretoria), was founded in 1934 and thus is considerably older than the Africa Institute. Unlike the Africa Institute, the Institute of International Affairs apparently has no systematic publications program, even though it has sponsored the publication of several research papers and monographs dealing with the former High Commission Territories, the South African foreign service, Southern African problems, South West Africa, South African policy toward Basutoland, and South Africa and the United Nations.[44] The Institute does not publish a regular journal, although it does have a library and library staff, and it does not have as large an administrative, publications, and research staff as the Africa Institute.

A relatively new organization is the *Sentrum vir Internasionale Politiek* (Center for International Politics), affiliated to the Political Science Department of the Afrikaans-medium Potchefstroom University at Potchefstroom in the Transvaal Province of South Africa. Its publications include a monthly mimeographed newsletter, *Die Wêreld in Oënskou* (The World in Review), published accounts of two symposia on international politics, a monograph on South African relations with Africa, and one on the "outward policy" of the South African Government.[45] Judging from the articles appearing in the newsletter, as well as from those in the published symposia, it would appear that the principal concern of this Center seems to be the dissemination of factual material about world affairs (and not just about South African foreign policy) rather than the support of research in the areas of empirical and normative theory in international politics.

Another significant organization is the South African Institute for Public Administration, which has its headquarters in Pretoria and which has published a quarterly journal, *SAIPA: Journal for Public Administration*, since January 1965. Obviously, its main area of interest is public administration, and thus it appeals both to university-trained civil servants in the Republic and to those who teach courses in and/or do research in public administration there. The orientation of the institute is primarily to the South African civil service and is reflected in the composition of the council of the institute, which includes the chairman and deputy chairman of the Public Service Commission, representatives of civil servants in the national, provincial, and local levels of administration, and representatives from six South African universities.[46] Thus the Institute for Public Administration is a useful point of contact for those concerned with analyzing bureaucratic structures, policies, and personnel in the Republic and South West Africa.

For those whose research focus is the study of elites, the Abe Bailey Institute of Interracial Studies in Cape Town is important. This institute[47] is one of the newest in the Republic, dating back only to April 1968 when it established an informal link with the University of Cape Town (comparable to the one existing between the South African Institute of International Affairs and the University of the Witwatersrand). The present director of the institute, Dr. Hendrik W. van der Merwe, is in charge of a research project analyzing the white elite in the Republic with particular emphasis on the attitude structure and socio-economic background of that elite. This research had begun in 1966 under the aegis of the Institute of Social and Economic Research at Rhodes University in Grahamstown, South Africa, and is funded by a grant from the South African Human Sciences Research Council. The institute has awarded research grants to American doctoral students in sociology (at Yale University and the University of California at Berkeley) and to a British doctoral student in history (at Oxford University) and has aided in a study of young businessmen in the Western Cape Province, race relations in the Transkei in the late nineteenth century, intergroup relations in Rhodesia, and the political and cultural development of the colored community in South Africa. The institute staff have done a considerable amount of survey research and have access to a computer for processing the data.

Survey research in Southern Africa, however, has not been restricted to the Abe Bailey Institute and three South African commercial firms (Media and Communications Research, International Consumer Research, and Market Research Africa [Pty.] Limited) have undertaken projects dealing with the attitudes of South African whites[48] and Africans.[49] Naturally, such data will be all the more significant when compared with previous attitudinal studies among the African[50] and white[51] inhabitants of the Republic. Perhaps all the results of the various surveys conducted in the Republic (and in Rhodesia as well)[52] will be collated and published at some future date and/or placed in a data bank. The publication of such data and/or the creation of a data bank (presumably with overseas links) would greatly facilitate a fuller investigation of the nature of the South African (or any other nation in Southern Africa for which survey data would be available) political culture, perhaps along the lines set forth for some other nations by Professors Almond and Verba.[53]

Additional research on racial matters in the Republic is conducted by the South African Bureau of Racial Affairs, located in Pretoria and founded in 1948.[54] Unlike the South African Institute of Race Relations, the Bureau endorses the policy of apartheid and appeals to many Afrikaner intellectuals. The Bureau undertakes research projects, has sponsored several surveys on the colored and African communities in the Republic, and also concerns itself with problems affecting the various African tribal homelands. The Bureau often works in close cooperation with some faculty members from the Afrikaans-medium universities and the chairman of the Bureau, Dr. Gerrit Viljoen, is the rector of the newly created Rand Afrikaans University in Johannesburg. The Bureau has its own quarterly

periodical, the *Journal of Racial Affairs*, and it published an annual known as *Triomf* (Triumph).

Turning to the United Kingdom, a well-known center for research on Southern Africa is the Institute of Race Relations in London.[55] Usually in cooperation with Oxford University Press, the Institute has sponsored the publication of quite a number of studies on Southern Africa. These studies have dealt with Angola, South West Africa, South Africa, Rhodesia, Bechuanaland, Lesotho, and the erstwhile Central African Federation.[56] Like its South African counterpart in Johannesburg, the Institute maintains a library as well as a newspaper clipping file (which has been microfilmed by CAMP). Its quarterly journal, *Race*, carries articles as well as reviews of books on Southern Africa. The Institute was founded only in 1958, but from 1952 until 1958 it was associated with the Royal Institute of International Affairs (more commonly known as Chatham House). Chatham House, in turn, sponsored three publications on Southern Africa,[57] although its primary focus is not Africa, much less Southern Africa.

Another British organization which conducts research that has some bearing on Southern Africa—even though its main concerns lie elsewhere—is the Institute of Strategic Studies in London. This institute has published a series of *Adelphi Papers*, some of which contain material relevant to the nations of Southern Africa,[58] and it also publishes an annual summation of the military capabilities of the nations of the world, known as the *Military Balance*, a valuable guide for those specializing in strategic studies relating to Southern Africa.

Perhaps of greater significance for the political scientist, London is the site of significant numbers of Southern African anti-apartheid exile groups as well as groups which are deeply committed to the continuation of white rule in Southern Africa. For example, the African National Congress of South Africa (ANC) and the South West African People's Organization (SWAPO) have offices in London. The former office issues a weekly mimeographed news digest, *Spotlight on South Africa*, and a monthly magazine entitled *Sechaba*, while the latter from time to time issues a mimeographed newsletter called *Namibia News*. In addition, the Anti-Apartheid Movement has its headquarters in London, along with the International Defense and Aid Fund. The Anti-Apartheid Movement distributes and publishes material on Rhodesia, South Africa, Angola, Mozambique, and South West Africa, and it also publishes its own monthly newspaper, *Anti-Apartheid News*.[59] The International Defense and Aid Fund issues the *International Defence and Aid Fund Information*

Service (essentially an abstract of the South African press) and has recently undertaken the publication of several pamphlets about South Africa and Rhodesia.[60] The activities of these and similar groups are countered by the South Africa Foundation[61] which (although it has its headquarters in Johannesburg) has an office in London whose staff distribute material which for the most part constitutes a defense of the Republic's policies. None of the three aforementioned groups in London (the Anti-Apartheid Movement, the International Defense and Aid Fund, and the South Africa Foundation) can be properly classified as a disinterested research body; nevertheless, they are some of the better known Southern African interest or pressure groups operating in London whose activities and literature are of considerable importance.

Another significant organization in London concerned with Southern Africa is the Africa Bureau.[62] Dating back to 1952, the Bureau has worked closely with those who have championed the cause of both Sir Seretse Khama and his uncle (the late Tshekedi Khama) during the Bamangwato leadership difficulties in Botswana in the 1950s and has unmistakably aligned itself against continued white rule in Southern Africa. The biographer of the late Tshekedi Khama, Miss Mary Benson, once served as its secretary, and the Reverend Michael Scott, an oral petitioner at the United Nations in the South West Africa controversy, was the first director of the Bureau. It publishes an African press summary entitled *Africa Digest* and has sponsored publications on Lesotho, Bechuanaland, and the High Commission Territories in general.[63]

Two other similar organizations in London are the Fabian Society[64] and Christian Action,[65] both active in publishing pamphlets which are rather critical of the policies of the South African government. Finally, the Committee for Freedom in Mozambique, Angola, and Guiné has an office in London which serves to mobilize support for the African nationalist groups in these three countries and to distribute material favoring the cause of these groups. Organizations such as the Africa Bureau, Christian Action, and International Defense and Aid are focal points for many clerics, British peers and Members of Parliament, journalists, publicists, African nationalists, and South African expatriates who attempt to neutralize or to offset the activities of the South Africa Foundation, South Africa House (the South African Embassy) in London, and those who have vested emotional, social, political, or economic interests in the Republic and in the continuance of white rule in this and other parts of Southern Africa.

In the United States, organizations comparable to those found in the United Kingdom engage in scholarly or promotional type activities relating to Southern Africa. The counterpart of Chatham House, the Council on Foreign Relations in New York, has sponsored only one study of Southern Africa.[66] In addition, the Foreign Policy Association in New York has published a pamphlet on South Africa by a former member of the staff of the United States Embassy in South Africa.[67] Another New York-based organization, the Carnegie Endowment for International Peace, has been somewhat more active than either the Council on Foreign Relations or the Foreign Policy Association; it has been responsible for the publication of studies dealing with Portuguese Africa, Rhodesia, and the Republic of South Africa.[68]

At the official level, the United States Army has authorized the publication of studies of Angola, Mozambique, South Africa, and Zambia,[69] while the Subcommittee on Africa of the Committee on Foreign Affairs of the United States House of Representatives has sponsored reports and held hearings on American policy in South Africa and Rhodesia.[70] The published reports of this subcommittee (headed by the late Honorable Barratt O'Hara of Illinois and his successor, the Honorable Charles C. Diggs, Jr., of Michigan) are especially illuminating from the perspective of American interest groups concerned about Southern Africa.

In addition, some research has been done at various institutes throughout the United States, including those which are closely linked with universities. The bibliographic work sponsored by the Hoover Institution on War, Revolution, and Peace at Stanford University has already been mentioned. Other important institutions are the Center for Strategic and International Studies at Georgetown University in Washington, D.C., which undertook the publication of a full-scale handbook on Portuguese Africa,[71] and the Center for International Studies at Ohio University, which has issued monographs on Lesotho, Zambia, Malawi, and Botswana.[72] The Washington Center of Foreign Policy Research of the Johns Hopkins University School of Advanced International Studies has undertaken the publication of a study dealing with Rhodesia,[73] while the Program of Eastern African Studies at the Maxwell School of Citizenship and Public Affairs of Syracuse University has issued a monograph on South Africa[74] as well as the bibliographies mentioned earlier.

The noted African Studies Center at the University of California at Los Angeles has published a monograph on South West Africa as well as one on South Africa.[75] Similarly, the African Studies Center of Michigan State University sponsored the publication of a work on Swaziland.[76] Other university-related American research centers which have sponsored publications on Southern Africa include the Institute of International and Area Studies of Western Michigan University,[77] the Center on International Race Relations at the University of Denver,[78] the Food Research Institute at Stanford University,[79] the Commonwealth Studies Center of Duke University,[80] and the Industrial Relations Section of the Department of Economics at Princeton University.[81]

Outside the academic community, research dealing with Southern Africa has been undertaken by the Rand Corporation in Santa Monica, California,[82] and the Hudson Institute at Hudson-on-Croton, New York.[83] In addition to these two organizations, the American-African Affairs Association[84] in New York City, which is principally an interest group rather than a research corporation, has sponsored the publication of several reports dealing with Southern African affairs.[85] This association, which was founded in 1965, publishes a newsletter called *Spotlight on Africa*, reprints articles, finances the publication of monographs, and concerns itself with making an impact on decision-making elites and opinion leaders in the United States and abroad. In general, it may be said that the association supports the policies of the present governments in Rhodesia, South Africa, South West Africa, and Portugal.

An important and vigorous interest group dealing with Southern Africa is the American Committee on Africa, with headquarters in New York City. It published *Africa Today* from 1953 until 1966 (this journal is now published in association with the Center of International Race Relations at the University of Denver) and it sponsors the publication and distribution of a considerable amount of literature on Southern Africa.[86] Unlike the American-African Affairs Association, the committee is an articulate critic of continued white rule in South Africa, South West Africa, Rhodesia, Angola, and Mozambique, and its executive director (Mr. George M. Houser) has put forth the views of this committee before the O'Hara subcommittee on United States–South African relations as well as before the Diggs subcommittee on United States–Rhodesian relations.[87]

Finally, there is the African-American Institute, which has published a monthly journal, *Africa Report*, ever since July 1956. Its president (Mr. Waldemar A. Nielsen) has also appeared before the O'Hara subcommittee, but has not yet spoken on the matter of Rhodesia before the Diggs subcommittee.[88] It has published two very useful reports on Southern Africa stemming from conferences which the Institute had sponsored on economic development in two of the erstwhile High Commission Territories and on refugee

students from Southern Africa.[89] Perhaps the Institute may be said to occupy the middle political ground between the Association and the Committee, although it would seem to lean more toward the Committee than toward the Association.

Research Frontiers

Now that we have briefly examined data collection, storage, and retrieval as well as the institutional sponsorship of research and publications, we may turn to the research itself. Because excellent surveys have been written about the work political scientists have already done in African affairs[90] and the problems they have faced in their field research in Africa,[91] it would be appropriate to reflect on the prospects for future research on, and in, Southern Africa. What unfinished business is there for political scientists whose area specialty is Southern Africa?

For those whose principal focus is international politics, Southern Africa can be analyzed in terms of a regional subsystem which depends heavily upon the Republic of South Africa. Mr. Larry W. Bowman of the University of Connecticut has aptly described this region as a "subordinate state system,"[92] and this imaginative construct allows one to investigate the region in a comparative manner and thus to draw upon the findings and insights of those political scientists who have already analyzed other such international subsystems.[93] In particular, much more data on intra-regional trade, balance of payments, private investments, labor migration, currency flows, and transportation will be necessary—especially if one wishes to do a longitudinal study[94] of Southern Africa.

Such a study would need to address itself to questions on whether centrifugal or centripetal forces were paramount, what type(s) of subsystem is/are likely to emerge under conditions of extreme stress and violence (as characterized by guerrilla warfare in Angola, Mozambique, and Rhodesia), what types of inducements are required or demanded to reinforce (or to redirect) flows of goods, services, and persons, and what types of relations are likely to emerge between landlocked and coastal states. Indeed, of the nine component units in the Southern African subsystem, five (the three former High Commission Territories, Malawi, and Rhodesia) are landlocked and this, in turn, has a bearing on the types and strengths of linkages that have been established in the region.[95] The political scientist will find some of the concepts of geopolitics and of geographers most valuable, particularly in a region such as Southern Africa, which has a marked industrial core and a less well developed economic periphery.[96] Some of the questions we have asked in this book are answered in the chapter by Dr. Eschel M. Rhoodie and in Professor Potholm's concluding chapter.

Quite naturally, the units within the subsystem interact with one another, but to varying degrees both in terms of scope and depth and in terms of the partners involved. In addition to longitudinal analyses of regional integration or disintegration (entailing the use of quantitative techniques in political science), it would be necessary to include an attitudinal dimension to such analyses. Particularly among the governments with African majority rule—such as Malawi, Botswana, and Swaziland—political factors may well take precedence over economic ones, especially when it comes to matters of sovereignty and territorial integrity. Consequently, how the decision makers in these countries perceive their neighbors in Southern Africa can be of the utmost importance. The same may be said of the Republic of South Africa which, in its present foreign policy, hopes to make friends—if not allies—of its neighbors. Thus what the political scientist needs to investigate is how the elites of each of the units perceive the other members of the subsystem. Survey research would be necessary, of course, and fortunately there are antecedents for just such a study.[97]

Perhaps the Abe Bailey Institute, which was mentioned earlier, could supervise such a survey in South Africa. If such research were conducted by this Institute, it would be particularly revealing if the white elite in the Republic were to be queried on their attitudes toward both Africans in the Republic, on the one hand, and toward Africans from Lesotho, Malawi, Swaziland, and Botswana, on the other hand. Would the white respondents perceive Africans from the Republic differently from the latter four (whose governments are independent)? This is an especially important psychological dimension for the conduct of South African policy, which must take into account the change in political status of these four nations.

Conversely, it is important to conduct survey research in these four African-led nations regarding the attitude of the African elites to the whites in South Africa, South West Africa, Rhodesia, Angola, and Mozambique. Obviously, the research would have to be undertaken by an organization which enjoyed the trust and respect of the governments and elites of Malawi and the three former High Commission Territories. This survey research is all the more meaningful when one recalls the words written by the American student of politics, Walter Lippmann, about half a century earlier. He contended that "For the most part we do not first see, and then define, we define first and then see."[98] The question, then, would be: Who defines whom and what and, correspondingly, who sees whom and what? Such a survey could use previous data as a basis for comparison,[99] could involve an interdisciplinary research team,[100] and thus could be a most stimulating longitudinal study.

Hopefully, such survey research would explore the psychological dimension to the political problem of whether to form a more integrated subsystem between white- and African-dominated states in the subsystem and the equally important problem of the timing of further integration (or disengagement, if so desired). Such research would suggest the dimensions of consensus on the matter of integration or disengagement and would do so more accurately than election returns in Southern African states—provided that the proper questions were posed and the sample were properly constructed. Such data would be of considerable interest to the governments and decision makers concerned.

From the standpoint of subsystemic analysis, additional research could be carried out on bloc voting behavior in the United Nations General Assembly and the Organization of African Unity with particular reference to the refractory and emotionally charged issues of South African racial practices, the political future of South West Africa and Rhodesia, and the continued Portuguese presence in Angola and Mozambique. Some of these data are presented in Professor Tandon's chapter on the Organization of African Unity. A voting behavior study would help to operationalize and to quantify the extent to which Malawi and the former High Commission Territories can be designated client or vassal states and also the extent to which they are completely free agents politically. Furthermore, the investigator could then place these four nations in rank order in terms of their dependence on and/or subservience to the Republic of South Africa. Particularly revealing would be the frequency with which these four small powers' delegates either abstained on, or were absent from, roll call votes on Southern Africa in the United Nations and the Organization of African Unity.

Of course, such studies would have to take into consideration the work already done on small state diplomacy and on ministates, and thus they could test some of the hypotheses advanced in these studies.[101] It would be instructive to know, for example, what the costs-benefits ratio is for these four nations on voting for, against, or abstaining on issues which the South African and Portuguese delegations at the United Nations General Assembly regard as essential to the security and well-being of their respective nations. What, then, is the nature of the inducements and deprivations that South Africa and Portugal can and do, in fact, use with their black neighboring states? Conversely, what is the costs-benefits ratio for these four small nations for cooperating with, and endorsing the position of the majority of the members of, the Organization of African Unity?

The Organization of African Unity, the United Nations, Portugal, and the Republic of South Africa are four of the important variables involved in small state diplomacy, and the existence of an unrecognized, albeit powerful, government in Rhodesia is a fifth major variable in the statecraft of Botswana, Lesotho, Malawi, and Swaziland. The critical question is: How are these variables fitted together into patterns of diplomacy? Thus questions need to be posed and hypotheses formulated about the different types of diplomacy that are open to the decision makers in these small nations. Just as the conflict between the *verligtes* and the *verkramptes* in the South African National party has shown that there are options in South African foreign policy, the *coup d'état* of 1970 in Lesotho has clearly suggested the existence of alternative patterns of statecraft (as advocated by the opposition Congress party of Mr. Ntsu Mokhehle).

Thus an obvious need in the field of Southern African politics is a series of foreign policy studies of each of the subsystem units. There have been some studies in South African diplomacy in the past,[102] but much more thorough and rigorous research needs to be undertaken on South African diplomacy,[103] and on the foreign policies of Portugal, Rhodesia, Malawi, Lesotho,[104] Botswana, and Swaziland. Such studies should provide an analysis of the relationships of the given unit within the subsystem in addition to its relationships with exogenous powers and/or organizations. Particularly important among the exogenous powers and/or organizations are the United Kingdom, the United States, the United Nations, and the Organization of African Unity. To date, some research has been undertaken on Anglo–South African relations,[105] United States–South African relations,[106] and the relations between South Africa and the United Nations with respect to the political future of South West Africa.[107] But much more extensive and intensive studies could and should be undertaken which focus not only on South Africa but also on the other units in the subsystem. Moreover, consideration could and should be given to the question of how exogenous powers and/or organizations perceive the units of the subsystem and vice versa. Some research has already been done on this problem with respect to the Republic of South Africa and the outside world.[108]

An especially important facet of studies dealing with foreign policies of the units of the Southern African subsystem should be the role of indigenous and exogenous interest groups, including exile groups. These interest groups would appear to be significant in Anglo–Rhodesian, Anglo–South African, American–Rhodesian, American–South African, and African–Rhodesian and African–South African relations since these relations entail divergent racial attitudes and investment practices. Thus, for example, questions such as the following come to mind. To what extent, and in what instances, has British policy toward South Africa been affected by, say, the Anti-Apartheid Movement, the Africa Bureau, the South Africa Foundation, the Institute of Race Relations, and so forth? What types of access do these groups have to British M.P.s and peers and to members of the Foreign Office (or, previously, the Commonwealth Relations Office)? Who spoke to whom with what effect? Moreover, what are the most (and least) powerful indigenous and exogenous interest groups in terms of the conduct of South African, Rhodesian, American, and African diplomacy? There are, of course, published accounts of both the anti- and the pro-South African lobbies based in the United Kingdom,[109] yet what is needed is a more thorough investigation of the role of these indigenous and exogenous interest groups in the decision-making process in the United Kingdom, for example.[110] Case studies of individual decisions affecting the bilateral and multilateral relationships would seem to be in order. Case studies would be valuable, though, only to the extent that they could be used to test hypotheses which had already been developed elsewhere, to refine these hypotheses, or to create new data for the comparative study of foreign policy.

From the perspective of comparative politics as well, until quite recently interest groups in Southern Africa have not been examined with particular care.[111] The role of the Dutch Reformed Churches in Afrikaner politics has still to be analyzed with sufficient care, and the same might be said of the various mining concerns and agricultural societies in South Africa, South West Africa, and Rhodesia. In the kingdom of Lesotho, Angola, and Mozambique, for example, what type of access does the Roman Catholic Church have to the political elite? How does it affect the political socialization process? Similar questions may also be posed about the missionaries, South African organizations for the recruitment of African labor for the mines on the Witwatersrand, South African and South West African exiles, and the teachers in the elementary and secondary schools in Botswana, Swaziland, and Malawi. In Swaziland and Botswana, for instance, questions could also be asked about the political role of the white agricultural community, many of whom were and are South African by birth, if not by nationality now. Again, case studies of decision making in these nations, with particular regard to interest groups, would help to generate data and would be all the more valuable if the research design had transnational utility.

Research projects such as the one undertaken by the Abe Bailey Institute at Cape Town on the white elite are welcome additions to the literature of political sociology of Southern Africa. It would be equally important to use a comparable research design for the African elite in the Republic, although some of the research on the African middle class in South Africa has already been completed by Professor Leo Kuper of the University of California at Los Angeles.[112] At some future date such research could and should extend to the rest of the units in Southern Africa. Often the only way a research student can sometimes locate any biographical information about these elites is through newspaper clipping files, even in South Africa where an annual *Who's Who of Southern Africa* is published but which restricts its biographies to whites.[113] For studies concerned with the socioeconomic, ethnic, racial, linguistic, and educational backgrounds of the elites of Southern Africa, the construction of data banks would be invaluable.

Data banks of this sort would be especially helpful in another area of political science which so far has generally been treated unsystematically namely, electoral studies. To date, no full-length studies of South African elections comparable to those undertaken at Nuffield College, Oxford, have been published. Only one such study modeled after the Nuffield College ones has been published; it constituted only part of a book on South African politics.[114] What is really needed is a uniform set of analyses of elections in as many of the units of the Southern African subsystem as possible. There are works which include one or more of these elections in South Africa, Rhodesia, and South West Africa as well, but no single volumes on single elections.[115]

A fruitful area of investigation and concern is the process of political recruitment and socialization in Southern Africa, especially in the youngest and oldest nations in the region. The political implications of Christian national education and of single-medium (that is, unilingual) schools and universities in the Republic of South Africa have been examined.[116] Other inquiries have dealt with the student politics in South Africa[117] and with what is termed Bantu education in South Africa.[118] Yet the subject is far from exhausted in the other parts of Southern Africa, and it would be especially rewarding to do research on the role of South Africa, Rhodesia, and Lesotho in training future African leaders from other parts of Southern Africa. Fort Hare College in the Cape Province,[119] for instance, is the alma mater for many members of the African elite in South Africa and elsewhere in Africa, and the same may be said of Tiger Kloof,[120] a secondary school run by the London Missionary Society in the northern Cape Province which a great many of the current elite in Botswana attended in the 1930s and 1940s. Other important institutions are the University College of Rhodesia in Salisbury, the nonresidential University of South Africa in Pretoria, and the University of Botswana, Lesotho, and Swaziland in Roma, Lesotho.

A topic closely related to those of political recruitment and socialization is the growth of African nationalism in the units of the subsystem. At present, quite a number of works (of varying quality) have been written on the subject of African nationalism in Rhodesia,[121] Angola,[122] Mozambique,[123] South Africa,[124] South West Africa,[125] the three former High Commission Territories,[126] Malawi, and Zambia.[127] However new vistas of research could be opened by the use of comparative techniques so that the political scientist could begin to develop typologies and to build empirical theory about African nationalism in Southern Africa, which now has the largest number of permanently settled whites and which thus has proved to be the most difficult bastion for the African nationalists to secure. Indeed, some of the African nationalist movement in some of the nations of Southern Africa consists of expatriates living in African-run states of Southern Africa, other parts of Africa, the United Kingdom, Western and Eastern Europe, and the United States. The problems of African refugees and exiles are now being analyzed by political scientists and other Africanists,[128] and Professor John A. Marcum's chapter in this book examines some of those problems in considerable detail.

Some of these refugees have become full- or part-time students, full- or part-time political organizers and leaders, while others have become officers and men in insurgent armies. The struggle for paramountcy has escalated into violence in Southern Africa, beginning with the onset of the guerrilla war in Angola in early 1961. Yet there does not seem to be enough reliable published material about insurgency or counterinsurgency warfare in Southern Africa. Although some valuable studies have been undertaken so far,[129] a great deal remains to be done. Several chapters in this volume deal with insurgency operations in Southern Africa. This is an area in which comparative analysis would yield rather rich insights and would allow political scientists to develop and to refine further their understanding of the great complexities of unconventional warfare.[130]

An ancillary subject is the role of the armed

forces and of the police forces in Southern Africa, especially in those units of the subsystem that still remain under white rule. In the case of South Africa, which is the strongest military power in the entire subsystem and one of the strongest in the entire continent, very little has been published other than mere profiles of force levels, equipment, and defense spending. Indeed, there has been little or no attempt to relate South Africa to the rest of the continent and/or extracontinental nations. There have been no rigorous, scholarly studies of the role of the South African armed forces, the relationship of those forces to the body politic, the socialization and recruitment of officers and noncommissioned officers, the politics of defense budgets, and other customary matters.[131] Such studies would entail a thorough examination of the debates on defense in both houses of Parliament as well as of other official reports and publications, such as *Paratus*, the monthly bilingual journal of the armed forces.

It is significant that two of the prime ministers of South Africa, Louis Botha and Jan Christiaan Smuts, were soldiers as well as political leaders and that neither had undergone any specialized military training equivalent, for example, to that offered at the United States Military Academy at West Point or at the Royal Military Academy at Sandhurst. Since South Africa has had a military tradition dating back at least to World War I, it would be useful to examine the role of the retired officer in South Africa. Moreover, one would want to know whether the role of the South African armed forces is comparable to that which once characterized the armed forces of the Third French Republic—namely, that of *la grande muette*.[132] How highly politicized are the armed forces? What type of access do the higher echelons of the officer cadre have to government? Is there a so-called military-industrial complex in South Africa? If so, what is the nature of the interlocking directorate? Naturally, *mutatis mutandis*, the same questions can and should be asked with respect to the armed forces of Rhodesia[133] and Portugal,[134] and related questions could be asked about the unconventional armed forces of the African nationalist groups operating in Angola and Mozambique. Again, one would be well advised to take into account comparable analyses of other conventional and unconventional armed forces, African as well as Western.

In those nations such as the erstwhile High Commission Territories, where there are no armed forces, the police forces are responsible for securing internal order and for patrolling the borders of the nation. Here, again, more research needs to be done on the role of paramilitary units in those Southern African states without customary armed forces. The police units do have functions which differ from those of the armed forces and some of which are of direct import for the process of political modernization.[135] The armed forces, in turn, may also have nonmilitary roles which must be considered as well.[136]

Finally, the Southern African subsystem presents the research worker with ample opportunity to build, and to test, theories concerned with the etiology of violence in political life, the utility and disutility of violence in promoting socioeconomic and political change, the durability and future types of plural societies composed of often antagonistic racial and/or linguistic groups, and the growth of political consciousness among component parts of plural societies. Such complexities require rather sophisticated research designs and these designs should maximize—if at all possible—subsystemic comparison. Such comparison can be within the subsystem and also between relatively similar subsystems elsewhere in the world.

These, then, are some of the items of unfinished business on the research agenda for Southern Africa. This research will entail team projects, crossnational comparisons, interdisciplinary approaches, and the formulation and testing of hypotheses in a multiethnic and multinational context. Southern Africa is a region in flux, an international subsystem subjected to severe internal and external strains, a region in which different ideologies and leaders compete for both allegiance and tribute, a region with strong affinities and animosities, and a region of fear and hope. Its fears, hopes, achievements, and failures are both parochial and universal.

It is the hope of the editors that this volume will not only faithfully reflect the diversity of convictions and outlooks on Southern Africa but also that it will help to clarify, rather than to obscure, some of the complex and refractory realities of Southern Africa. They would be most gratified if the kaleidoscopic images of Southern Africa which the contributors present in the various essays will stimulate the readers and others interested in Southern Africa to begin to cope with some of the unfinished business there.

PART TWO

The South African Nexus

Country Profiles

REPUBLIC OF SOUTH AFRICA

Political situation

Since May 1961 South Africa has been a republic with a bicameral parliament, cabinet, president, and prime minister. There are four white representatives for the coloreds in the national parliament and none who represent the Africans and Asians.

The president is Mr. J. J. Fouche, the prime minister is Balthazar Johannes Vorster. The ruling party is the National party. The United party and the Progressive party, provide the legal opposition.

Most of the African parties have been outlawed. The African National Congress and the Pan-African Congress were banned in 1960, making organized protest by Africans virtually impossible.

Demographic situation

Area: 471,445 square miles
Population: 18,773,000 (1967), including 3,563,000 whites, 1,859,000 coloreds, 561,000 Asians
Capital: Pretoria (administrative, 517,000 inhabitants (1967) Cape Town (legislative), 914,000 inhabitants (1967)

Economic situation

Gross national product: $12.3 billion (including South West Africa)
Per capita income: $366
Currency: South African rand, 1R = $1.40
Principal products: gold, diamonds, platinum, antimony, uranium, coal

---

SOUTH WEST AFRICA (NAMIBIA)

Political situation

South West Africa is administered as an internal part of South Africa. In 1966 the United Nations General Assembly passed a resolution stating that South Africas' mandate was terminated, but South Africa continues to administer the country. South West African voters sent 18 representatives to their Legislative Assembly, 6 to the South African House of Assembly, and 4 senators to the South African Senate.

The National party of South West Africa is a part of South Africa's National party and supports the South African aim of incorporating into the Republic. The United National South West party (UNSWP) is the primary opposition although it holds no seats.

African opposition has centered around two exile movements: the South West Africa People's Organization (SWAPO) and the South West African National Union (SWANU).

Demographic situation

Area: 318,261 square miles
Population: 610,000 (1966), including 96,000 whites and 15,000 coloreds
Capital: Windhoek, 61,000 inhabitants (1967)

Economic situation

Gross national product: included within South Africa's total of $12.3 billion
Per capita income: since 1955 the statistics of South West Africa have been incorporated into South Africa's
Currency: South African Rand, 1R = $1.40
Principal products: fish, dairy products, diamonds, copper

1

Afrikaner Nationalism: A Contemporary Analysis

DENIS J. WORRALL

The modern political history of South Africa is the story of the Afrikaner's rise to dominance and the steady but certain molding of constitutional and political relations to suit his thinking. Afrikaner thought has impressed itself on the constitutional character of South Africa; it has influenced the nature of the relationship between Afrikaners, on the one hand, and the rest of white South Africa, on the other hand; and it has profoundly changed, and continues to change, relations between the white minority and the nonwhite majority.[1]

This is not to say that the Afrikaners themselves have remained immune to change. On the contrary, their development as a community reflects the great economic, social, and political changes which have affected South Africa in particular and Southern Africa in general. At times this change has assumed crisis dimensions. In fact, as Afrikanerdom enters the seventies it is in the midst of such a crisis.

It is rather easy to describe the development of Afrikaner nationalism in historical terms.[2] It is much more difficult to explain the role of Afrikaner nationalism within the greater South African white political system. In the first part of this chapter we shall discuss the development of Afrikaner nationalism and its ideology, and then we shall attempt to explain in theoretical terms the relationship of Afrikaner nationalism to the South African white political system.

I

The distinction between nationalism[3] as a phenomenon and nationalism as an ideology is important in the South African context. The ingredients of nationalism—a common historical background, a single language, a distinctive religion, the experience of military defeat, and the frustration of economic inferiority—were all present at the close of the nineteenth century. But that complex of group interests which, when formulated into specific economic and political interests and articulated as demands, constitutes a program of political action or an ideology did not develop until some thirty years later.

The two outstanding forces of Afrikaner nationalism were and still are language[4] and economics, and some consideration of them is necessary if one is to understand the character of Afrikaner nationalism and its main political objectives. Dr. J. P. Meyer, presently chairman of the South African Broadcasting Corporation (in South Africa radio is controlled and operated by a public corporation which, theoretically, is supposed to insulate it from party political pressures) and an Afrikaans cultural leader of prominence, has pointed out that Afrikaner

> nationalism finds its most direct and comprehensive expression in the Afrikaans language.
>
> . . . .
>
> When a child acquires his mother-tongue, he simultaneously acquires his nation's style of life and work as it has developed during its long history and assumed a fixed form. . . .
>
> A distinct yet common language is the most important condition for the origin and existence of a nation as a distinctive nation among the nations of the world. The maintenance of your mother-tongue is for this reason still the most important reason for the fulfillment of national self-determination in all social spheres.[5]

Dr. Meyer is expressing here the general sentiment of Afrikaners toward their language, although there is considerable disagreement among them regarding the vigor with which they should (or indeed need to) campaign for the use of Afrikaans today.

Afrikaans was a distinct language by the beginning of the nineteenth century and early in the eighteenth century, long before a viable Afrikaner group consciousness had emerged, Afrikaans speakers were vigorously pressing the claims of their language against the Dutch. After 1806, when the British occupied the Cape, Afrikaans faced a more determined challenge. English became the language of the civil service, of commerce, and of the towns. The language laws of 1823, 1825, and 1827 were intended to ensure this. The use of Dutch and Afrikaans was forbidden in the Cape Parliament in 1854, and in 1865 it was abolished as a medium of instruction in state schools.[6]

Professor F. A. van Jaarsveld of the Rand Afrikaans University admits that these efforts at anglicization were somewhat successful. But they also triggered a reaction. For one thing, the language policy of the British administration contributed to the exodus of Afrikaners in the Great Trek (and the colonizing of the interior) which started in 1834; and, for another, it led to increasing demands for the recognition of Afrikaans as an official language. This was accompanied by a vague sense of Afrikaner group consciousness. Real *national* consciousness developed during the period 1868–1881. According to Professor van Jaarsveld,

> This was the period when they, the Afrikaners, became aware as a community of the obvious fact that individuals felt themselves to be members of one nation and one country. It was only then that the nationally conscious Afrikaners regarded themselves as a group, from which they experienced interests and for which they were prepared to make sacrifices.[7]

Organized campaigns for the recognition of Afrikaans as an official and formal language started in the 1870s in the Cape, where the threat of English was strongest. Thus in 1875 *Di Genootskap van Regte Afrikaners* (The Association of True Afrikaners) was established "to stand up for our language, our nation and our people."[8] The first Afrikaans newspaper, *Di Afrikaanse Patriot*, published appeals for the Afrikaners to arise. "Afrikaners! Do you not know where you want to go? It's time that you arise. Believe in Africa's future—our own nationality," wrote the Reverend S. J. du Toit, an early Cape Afrikaner patriot.[9]

Thus the Afrikaner *national* consciousness, a phenomenon based on a common historical experience, a common language, and a common religion, was an established fact by 1880. However, it took the second Anglo-Boer War of 1899–1902 and a common enemy to unite the Afrikaner people, and another three decades before an ideology of Afrikaner nationalism emerged. This was a nationalism which was largely language-centered and culturally oriented. It lacked an ideology mainly because the political and economic interests of Afrikaners in the Cape and elsewhere were different. So, for example, whereas by the end of the nineteenth century anti-British feeling was rampant among Afrikaners elsewhere, Cape Afrikaners drew a clear distinction between the British, toward whom they felt increasing hostility, and English-speaking South Africans. In fact, the term *Afrikaner* was used by the Reverend Mr. du Toit and others to include English-speaking South Africans—the important qualification was that they identified with South Africa and felt that South Africa was their only home.[10]

Neither did Cape Afrikaners share in any clearly articulated way the republicanism of their fellow Afrikaners to the north. This is not to say that they did not have a distinct political consciousness, because by 1872 an Afrikaner point of view was being advocated in the Cape parliament. However, its main thrust related to language.

There can be no question that, according to the late Professor William H. Vatcher,

> a national language is a fundamental ingredient of nationalism. The emergence of Afrikaans as a formal language heightened the Afrikaner's sense of belonging to a unique group, while the development of a language different from any other marked the group with a singular identity.[11]

The Afrikaans language was an important root of Afrikaner nationalism, and it contributed later to the development of the ideology of Afrikaner nationalism.

The importance of economics as a factor in the development of nationalism is, in general, widely recognized,[12] and Afrikaner nationalism is no exception in this regard. Economic considerations have also greatly influenced Afrikaner nationalist ideology. By tradition, the Afrikaners have been the farmers of South Africa. They benefited only indirectly from the discovery of diamonds and gold in the second half of the nineteenth century, and by the turn of the century their economic backwardness *vis-à-vis* the rest of white South Africa was a noticeable feature of the society. Starting in 1893, the Afrikaans churches in particular addressed themselves to their community's plight and to finding ways to alleviate that poverty.

The second Anglo-Boer War of 1899–1902, which ruined thousands of Afrikaners, added to their misery.[13] Ramsay MacDonald, who was later to become prime minister of Great Britain, visited South Africa soon after the war and observed that "the devastation of house and home, the wholesale destruction of property, the absolute clearing away of stock will have to be paid for in cash, in racial estrangement, and in sullen acquiescence in our rule."[14] Following the war came one of the worst droughts in living memory and a depression which crippled the domestic economy. Poor farming methods and the practice of dividing farms into uneconomic units to provide each son with his own farm added to the impoverishment of the Afrikaners. The trickle of Afrikaners from the farms to the towns became a flood after union in 1910. In that year 20 percent of all Afrikaners were town dwellers; by 1936 this percentage had grown to 40.

The phenomenon of rural depopulation and all its consequences is a well-known concomitant of industrialization. But the point is that among white South Africans it was primarily the Afrikaners who were affected. Some of the grief this caused Afrikaner leaders is expressed in an editorial that Dr. Daniel F. Malan, at the time editor of *Die Burger*, wrote in 1923:

> This stream to the cities is a flight. To where? The fugitive himself can't say. He knows only that he is fleeing imminent hunger or barbarousness or both, and this is enough for him. Alas, the bitter, bitter sorrow of the untrained, landless white man in South Africa, of our flesh and blood, of the children of the Geuse and the Huguenots![15]

The "untrained, landless" Afrikaner had to find his place on the lower rungs of industry, of the civil service, and of the mines, often in competition with black Africans.

Awareness of the plight of the poor Afrikaner expressed itself in a series of people's conferences (*volks* conferences) on the problem of the "poor whites." A strong spirit of self-help developed, and all over the country Afrikaner businessmen were launched to mobilize Afrikaner capital for the immediate purpose of the economic advancement of the Afrikaners. Less positively, the plight of the Afrikaner expressed itself in resentment of English-speaking South Africa and, later, in virulent anti-Semitism.[16] It also expressed itself as opposition to the capitalist system and in agitation for the introduction of legislative protection against "unfair" competition with black workers.[17]

II

Although there was considerable support among Cape Afrikaners for the Boer cause during the second Anglo-Boer War, prior to 1910 united Afrikaans political activity was not possible because Afrikaners were involved in different political systems with different issues and problems. Even in the years immediately following union, it was some time before most Afrikaners were grouped in one party and before a distinct Afrikaner nationalist ideology evolved. The spirit of the National party program of principles, adopted in January 1914, was one of "South Africa first."[18] The national unity they sought was a unity of all white South Africans. Even the term *Afrikaner* was used as it had been used in Cape politics toward the end of the nineteenth century to refer to South Africans of European descent, regardless of their mother language.[19]

There is also no hint of republicanism in the National party's program of principles of 1914. In fact, Article 4 declared that "the position of the Union in regard to its relationship towards the United Kingdom, resting on the good faith of two nations, is unequivocally recognised by the party," and this particular article, however, went on to say that the party

> is convinced that the maintenance of a cordial

> understanding between the Union and the Empire depends on a meticulous avoidance of any act whereby the political liberty of the people of the Union might be curtailed or restricted or whereby any of the liberties of the country or its Government might be withdrawn from the immediate supervision or control of the people of the Union.[20]

When the National party came to power in coalition with the Labor party in 1924, it strove to spell out the constitutional implications of its "South Africa first" policy, and as a consequence South Africa played a leading role in the development of dominion status and in the events which led up to the Statute of Westminster in 1931.[21]

The emergence of a full-fledged ideology of Afrikaner nationalism occurred after the Hertzog–Smuts decision of 1933 to fuse their respective parties (the South Africa party and the National party) and thus to form the United party, and the refusal of the right wing of the National party to follow General Hertzog. A year later the Purified National party was established under Dr. Daniel F. Malan, and between 1934 and 1961 (the year South Africa became a republic and left the Commonwealth), Afrikaners increasingly perceived their interests as a group to fall within the ideology of Afrikaner nationalism as interpreted by the National party. Essentially, the progress of the National party in successive general elections is due to the desertion of Afrikaners from the United party and the crystallization of political allegiances along language lines. The table below illustrates this:

Parliamentary Representation: 1943–1966

	1943	*1948*	*1953*	*1958*	*1961*	*1966*
National Party	43	70	94	103	105	126
United Party	89	65	57	53	50	39

In a letter to General Hertzog dated September 16, 1933, Dr. Malan wrote that

> I am concerned with the preservation and propagation of Nationalism. I therefore feel that the National Party, which so far has been the best embodiment of that principle, may be surrendered for something else only if Nationalism is completely safe within such a new party and can maintain its fullest evolution.[22]

In the spirit of this passage, Dr. Malan's Purified National party committed itself to the promotion of Afrikaner interests and ideals; and the major issues around which white South African politics revolved from that time until 1948 related to the nature of white unity, the practical implementation of language equality, and South Africa's constitutional status. These issues were more important than the policies of the major parties with regard to race relations, which in any event differed only slightly; both were committed to the maintenance of white supremacy and advocated essentially segregationist policies; neither disapproved of the discrimination on grounds of color which was inherent in the "South African way of life."[23] Color policies figured more prominently after 1948, as white South African politics began to reflect the independence movement elsewhere on the continent. Even so, the main driving force of Afrikaner nationalism during the fifties was republicanism.

The republican ideal occupied a central place in Afrikaner nationalist ideology and, from its inception, the Purified National party committed itself to the achievement of a republic. By 1936 the National party in all the provinces had adopted the republican ideal, and the program of principles was amended on this point to read:

> The Party is convinced that the republican constitutional form, divorced from the British Crown, fits in best with the traditions, the circumstances, and the aspirations of the South African nation, and therefore this Party will preserve the republican ideal and work for the establishment of a republic in South Africa.[24]

During the fifties the Afrikaners substituted symbols of their own choosing for the symbols of state in South Africa, a process which culminated in the realization of a republic in 1961 and South Africa's departure from the Commonwealth of Nations. These events were the clearest indication that the Afrikaner had arrived—politically, at any rate.

III

If the Republic signified the fulfillment of probably the strongest aspiration in Afrikaner ideology, and hence the exhaustion of a major emotional source of Afrikaner nationalism, it also signified the removal of an important component of Afrikaner unity at a time when economic developments were generating a much wider range of interests within Afrikanerdom and when differences within the white community regarding race relations and the National party's policies in particular were growing.

Despite the appearance of unity and harmony in the years immediately after the achievement of the Republic, there were deep undercurrents of discontent within Afrikaner nationalism, which only an unassailable leader like Dr. Hendrik F. Verwoerd could have kept in check. His domination of Afrikanerdom was total from about the time of the establishment of the Republic until his assassination in 1966. The attempt on his life in April 1960, when he was shot twice in the head at point-blank range by David Pratt, a deranged white man, and his dignified and generally impressive performance (as seen from South Africa) at the Commonwealth conference in London the following year generated a confidence in the near infallibility of his leadership among white South Africans in general and Afrikaners in particular.[25] Once the Republic was established, he had an unchallengeable monopoly over ideology and tactics within the National party and was without doubt the leading theorist of separate development.[26]

Once the republican issue was played out, the only conceivable threat to Dr. Verwoerd's leadership could have come from the right wing.[27] With the introduction of the Bantu homeland concept[28] in 1959, separate development had become a reformist (as opposed to a status quo) ideology, the ultimate objectives of which exceeded anything rank-and-file nationalists would support. Significantly, the several right-wing miniparties established among Afrikaners at one time or another during the last fifteen years all advocated a tougher brand of white supremacy, championed white lower socioeconomic interests, and contested exclusively working class constituencies. However, no strong National Party leader need have feared "out" groups which had no respectable press support and no access to the legitimizing organs within Afrikanerdom—the churches, cultural bodies, and universities. Moreover, most of these parties projected an image of political crankiness.

There is considerable evidence of mounting right-wing grievances during the last six years of Dr. Verwoerd's premiership.[29] But such grievances were never articulated in the form of criticism of the leadership or in the form of ideological demands. Within weeks of Mr. B. J. Vorster's election as prime minister, however, a major conflict had come to the surface.

IV

Mr. Vorster was elected leader of the National party and prime minister on September 13, 1966. On October 4, less than a month later, Professor W. J. de Klerk of the Department of Philosophy at Potchefstroom University delivered an address which had far-reaching consequences. He described two kinds of extreme Afrikaners: the *verkrampte* (narrow-minded), who were opposed to change in general and to any change in the existing pattern of race relations in particular; and the *verligte* (enlightened), whom he judged to be too hasty in their advocacy of change. Both were at fault, and he counseled a middle course between "standpattism" and precipitate action.

There was nothing profound about this speech, but its timing and the taxonomy which it developed set in motion a process of polarization climaxed three years later in a rupture within Afrikaner nationalist ranks. On the surface the dispute seemed purely ideological—a form of the revisionist-orthodox phenomenon. However, it had important socioeconomic dimensions. Urbanization, education, and the greatly improved standard of living of Afrikaners have changed the sociology of Afrikaner nationalism. Its authority structure has changed. The churches have lost a great deal of their influence and the immense success and glamor of individual Afrikaner capitalists, such as the industrialist Albert Wessels, the banker Jan Marais, and the tobacco tycoon Anton Rupert, have not been lost on the younger generation of Afrikaners, while the attractiveness of politics as a career and the appeal of politicians have declined.

The relative socioeconomic uniformity of Afrikaners is a thing of the past.[30] They fill out the white South African middle class and spill over into the upper income brackets. As a result, the range of interests represented within the National party has been greatly widened and new ideological demands have been made which the leadership has found increasingly difficult to accommodate.

At least six years before the *verligte-verkrampte* dispute began and the fight to capture the leadership of the National party started, what can only be called reactionary right-wing grievances appeared regularly in a little monthly publication called the *South African Observer*, which paradoxically was the only organ of Afrikaner right-wing opinion until the establishment of the Pretoria newspaper *Hoofstad* in April 1968.[31] The *South African Observer*'s theme has consistently been that

> Afrikaner solidarity on all planes—political, financial, cultural, and religious—is the prerequisite of Western survival, which means White survival. . . . If we have offended certain Afrikaners it is only because we have consistently drawn their attention to a previous heritage of values which they have seemed inclined to abandon.[32]

In April 1963 the *South African Observer* wrote of a "liberal/conservative disjunction" within Afrikanerdom, and from this point on, leading Afrikaner businessmen who associated with their English-speaking counterparts or with organizations like the South Africa Foundation and the United States–South Africa Leadership Exchange Program were singled out for attack. Thus, in

September 1964, Mr. S. E. D. Brown, the editor of this self-designated "Journal for Realists" declared that

> in recent issues of *The S.A. Observer* it has been considered necessary to turn the spotlight of public attention on the activities of a group of Afrikaner businessmen and financiers, mainly centred in the Western Cape, all animated, so it seems, by an anxious desire to establish a basis of mutually profitable co-existence with South Africa's traditional critics and enemies.[33]

For its part, the *South African Observer* purports to speak for the "conservative Afrikaner" who is judged to be

> not the big businessmen or industrialist or the new-rich, nor is he a person who hob-nobs with the mighty. He is the little man, whether he be an Afrikaans teacher, worker, clergyman, farmer or professional man, and he is and will always remain the backbone of the White nation.[34]

On the ideological level this intra-Afrikaner dispute has revolved around four issues: first, the inclusion of nonwhites on visiting national sports teams; second, immigration; third, the terms on which South Africa should enter diplomatic relations with its black neighbors; and, fourth, Afrikaner–English relations. The last is undoubtedly the most important.

At its simplest level, the dispute represents uncertainty and insecurity in the face of the changes which have confronted Afrikanerdom and the National party. But, on a more sophisticated level, it involves the terms on which English–Afrikaans-speaking cooperation should occur and the nature of the white South African nation. On the one side have been those led by Dr. Albert Hertzog, a son of the former prime minister, General J. B. M. Hertzog. Dr. Hertzog's view has been that there is no such entity as the South African "nation"; there are only two *volkere* (peoples). Therefore, talk of nation-building is anathema to the interests of the Afrikaner because it entails a weakening of his sense of identity. In the view of Dr. Hertzog, the National party is intended to be the *volksfront* of Afrikanerdom and as such it has a primary duty to the Afrikaner.

The contrasting point of view asserts that an important principle of National party policy is its commitment, in the words of the editor of *Die Beeld* (one of the biggest Afrikaans newspapers),

> to a genuine striving towards the growth of a South African nation composed of both Afrikaans- and English-speakers. . . . The policy is clear. There is in South Africa a South African nation, whose interests rise above any sectional interest. And this greater interest guarantees in terms of Party policy and the Party constitution, every legitimate interest of every constituent of our nation. *The National Party government cannot, does not, and will not, govern South Africa as if only Afrikaners lived in this land.*[35]

Here, as will be seen presently, the editor of *Die Beeld* was touching on the most basic aspect of the dispute.

From late 1966 until about the middle of 1967, the battle between the revisionists and the hardliners was largely restricted to Afrikaans cultural circles. The main issues were the position of the Afrikaans language and culture in the face of European immigration and the conditions of English–Afrikaans cooperation. The prime minister, after first minimizing the conflict (in July 1967 he described it as a "holiday squabble") and appealing to the two factions to exercise restraint, intervened directly with a speech strongly attacking the *South African Observer* and its editor as well as those nationalists who supported him. The conflict then inevitably spread to the various policymaking bodies of the National party (most notably the provincial congresses and the parliamentary caucus), and a right-wing breakaway became unavoidable when Prime Minister Vorster actually sacked Dr. Hertzog—who refused to resign when requested to do so—from the cabinet in February 1969.[36]

From this point on the Afrikaans newspapers, most of which advocated a revisionist line[37] and supported the prime minister, pressed for the expulsion of the leading dissidents. Matters came to a head at the congress of the Transvaal National party held in Pretoria during September 1969, when a motion of confidence in the leadership was proposed and party delegates were asked to affirm their support of party policy with respect to (1) English-Afrikaans cooperation; (2) diplomatic relations with black states; (3) immigration; and (4) the government's policy with respect to visiting national sports teams which might include nonwhites.[38] The dissidents, led by Dr. Hertzog, balked on the matter of visiting sports teams and subsequently either resigned from the party or were expelled. Soon afterward, they gave public notice that they intended to establish a new political party and Prime Minister Vorster, no doubt as a counterploy, announced on September 20, 1969, that a general election would be held early in 1970—more than a year before it was constitutionally due.[39]

Dr. Hertzog and his followers held a meeting over the weekend of October 24–25 and established the *Herstigte* (Reconstituted) National party.

Without greatly deviating from the National party policy on race relations (it is committed to racial separation in all facets of social life), the new party stands for complete Afrikaner hegemony in South Africa, the relegation of English to a "second language" status, the abolition of the present "monarchical" parliamentary system and its replacement by a presidential-cabinet system, and very strongly reflects lower socioeconomic class interests.[40]

V

The problem of relating Afrikaner nationalism and these recent developments to the wider South African political system is compounded by the fact that scholars have tended to treat South Africa as *sui generis*. With the exception of one study which considers South Africa from the "politics of diversity" point of view (and even then there is very little theoretical underpinning),[41] and another which analyzes the South African political system in functional terms,[42] for the most part studies of South African government and politics have tended to focus on race relations.[43] While this is certainly the most salient feature of the South African polity, political scientists need to understand the structure and working of the South African political system in contemporary behavioral terms.

Professor James S. Coleman's characterization of the political system as "European oligarchic" is essentially correct. Analyzed in functional terms, direct participation in the political system is limited to the white minority. However, Professor Coleman's description does not tell all that we should know. For example, the unenfranchised majority participates in the decision-making process on the "input" side in an indirect and negative way. Participation is indirect in that, simply by its presence, the nonwhite majority arouses a mixture of realism, fear, paternalism, Negrophilic sentimentalism, and racial arrogance.[44] It participates indirectly also in that the more important issues of white politics relate to policies regarding nonwhites.

Nonwhite participation is negative in that the majority's alienation from the political system is basically responsible for the considerable security apparatus which has been built up over the last twenty years and the incursions into democratic procedure, and privileges which have increasingly occurred during the last fifteen years.[45] Professor Coleman's characterization is also unsatisfactory in that it tells us very little about possible directions of change inherent within the South African political system.[46]

For the purposes of this analysis of Afrikaner nationalism, Professor David E. Apter's typology

has been found very helpful.[47] He distinguishes three types of political regimes in developing countries. South Africa, with some qualifications, can be treated as a developing country—taking into account the per capita income of its entire population, sources of its gross national product, distribution of occupations, and the four major problems it faces: the training of skilled personnel, economic development, and the related problems of nation-building and political integration. The first type of political regime is the mobilization system; the second is the reconciliation system; and the third is the modernizing autocracy. Each type is defined in terms of five categories: (1) patterns of legitimacy; (2) loyalty; (3) decisional autonomy; (4) distribution of authority; and (5) ideological expression.[48]

The mobilization system tries "to rebuild society in such a way that both the instrumentalities and the values associated with change are remarkably altered."[49] The characteristics of the mobilization system, defined in terms of the five categories enumerated above, are (1) hierarchical authority; (2) total allegiance; (3) tactical flexibility; (4) unitarianism; and (5) ideological specialization.[50] Professor Apter admits that the reconciliation system is more difficult to describe.

> Its outstanding characteristic is the high value it places on compromises between groups which express prevailing political objectives and views. As we are using the term, the reconciliation system evolves with the formation of a single political unit from constituent political units which do not lose their political identity or unity.[51]

In terms of the five categories, the reconciliation system is characterized by (1) pyramidal authority; (2) multiple loyalties; (3) necessity for compromise; (4) pluralism; and (5) ideological diffuseness.[52]

The modernizing autocracy

> manifests a profound internal solidarity based on ethnicity or religion, by means of which support is retained for the political leaders or king who makes claims on the members of the system and controls them.[53]

Its five characteristics are (1) hierarchical authority; (2) exclusiveness; (3) strategic flexibility; (4) (4) unitarianism; and (5) neotraditionalism.[54]

Of particular relevance for the South African situation are the reconciliation and the mobilization types. The South African political system from its inception in 1910 can be classified as a reconciliation type. However, Afrikaner nationalism from about 1934 until the early 1960s has constituted a mobilization type of subsystem within the South African policy. If, in simple historical terms, the main theme of South African politics has been the steady rise to dominance of Afrikaner nationalism, in theoretical terms it has been the development of tension between the reconciliation and mobilization types of political regimes and the final sublimation of the latter in the former as Afrikaner nationalism has realized most of its ideological goals, exhausted its primary emotional sources, and reshaped the symbols of the South African polity in its own image.

VI

South Africa was established in 1910 as a result of a union of several peoples of different historical backgrounds, cultures, and political traditions. Furthermore, this union occurred while bitter memories of the second Anglo-Boer War were still fresh. The spirit which dominated the conference proceedings leading up to Union of South Africa as well as the constitutional arrangements of the Union themselves was one of reconciliation.[55] Thus to satisfy the advocates of both unitarianism and federalism a quasi-federal constitution was adopted.

The equal status of both English and Dutch (and later Afrikaans) as the official languages of the country was entrenched in the constitution; and in the years which followed immediately after union, dedication to the unity of English- and Afrikaans-speakers was a *sine qua non* of South African white politics. A spirit of compromise was reflected in the symbols of statehood—the use of two anthems and the South African flag itself—and in the acknowledgment of loyalty to the British crown.

Moreover, relations between white South Africans as well as those between white and nonwhite South Africans were cast in an essentially nonideological mold. In fact, the South African political system from the very beginning manifested all the characteristics of the reconciliation type. The goal of all white political parties from 1910 was a broad South Africanism which retained the very salient cultural, linguistic, and racial diversity of the South African society.

The circumstances surrounding the establishment of Dr. Malan's Purified National party in 1934 and the emergence of an ideology of Afrikaner nationalism in the following years have already been described. In contrast to the reconciliation character of the South African political system, Afrikaner nationalism from 1934 until well into the 1950s formed a subsystem within the South African polity which organized on mobilization lines.

Professor Gwendolen M. Carter of Northwestern University correctly speaks of a "new withdrawal of the Afrikaner people from the community as a whole" after 1934.[56] A phalanx of new, specifically Afrikaans, interest groups which reflected the ethnocentrism of Dr. Malan's Purified National party came into being. So, for example, an Afrikaans equivalent of the Boy Scout movement (known as the *Voortrekkers*) was established; and Afrikaans-speaking students broke away from the National Union of South African Students to form their own organization. The 1938 centennial commemoration of the Great Trek was turned into an exclusively Afrikaner affair. Various proposals for a republican form of government disregarded altogether the interests and sentiments of English-speaking South Africans; and the principle of language equality for which General Hertzog had so fervently campaigned was replaced by advocacy of the supremacy of Afrikaans.

Afrikaans organizations which had been created at an earlier date, such as the *Broederbond* (founded in 1918)[57] and the Federation of Afrikaans Cultural Organizations (founded in 1929), now gained momentum. Afrikaans schools, Afrikaans teachers' colleges, Afrikaans universities, and other educational institutions energetically promoted the Afrikaans language.

Afrikaner intellectuals reaffirmed more clearly than ever before the Calvinist principles underlying the Afrikaner's political conceptions, thus setting Afrikaners even further apart from the rest of the society. The Calvinist theory of politics assumes that all aspects of life are subordinated to God's will; and basic to the Calvinist concept of nation is the principle of what is known as "sovereignty in one's own circle." Dr. Malan was himself a leading proponent of this position and, in his farewell sermon before leaving the ministry in 1915 to take up the editorship of the newly established Cape Town Afrikaans newspaper *Die Burger*, he spelled out the implications of Calvinism for the Afrikaner's political pursuits:

> Is there behind the existence of our nation an eternal idea of God which gives a national life destiny and a vocation, or is it all purposeless, blind fate? The nation which truly acknowledges God in its own creation and worships him and therefore attaches great importance to its own continued existence will for this reason also be prepared to bow to God's ordaining. Ask the nation to lose its identity in another existing nation or one that does not yet exist, and it will answer: in the name of God, definitely not.[58]

Professor J. Albert Coetzee, a member of Parliament, explained Dr. Malan's refusal to follow General Hertzog into coalition with General Smuts in terms of this pronouncement.[59]

On another occasion in 1916, Dr. Malan said that

> the Calvinist maintains that freedom and own existence of every nation.. . . Sovereign is the Calvinist in home and state, and freedom is his characteristic.[60]

In terms of concrete political demands, this philosophy gave rise to the demand for the establishment of a Christian national republic in South Africa. This became the central symbolic goal of Afrikaner nationalism in the 1930s, and it was a goal which Dr. Malan and his party pursued without concern for English-speaking support. The symbolic trek of 1938 reinforced Afrikaner nationalism. In Professor D. W. Krüger's words,

> The renewed interest in the heroic past found its emotional and dramatic expression in the ox-wagon, the Republican flags, the voortrekker dress, the muzzle-loader, all objects to be venerated.[61]

The role of economics as a factor in the development of Afrikaner nationalism was discussed earlier. In the economic sphere as well as in the political one, the Afrikaner isolated himself from the remainder of white society, and he regarded the essentially capitalistic economic system prevailing in South Africa as an import and something foreign to his national character. At one conference in the 1930s, Professor L. J. du Plessis, one of the leading exponents of Afrikaner Calvinism, declared that the purpose of the new Afrikaans nationalist movement was not to enable the Afrikaner nation to survive economically by adapting to the alien capitalist system, but rather to mobilize this nation to control the system and to transform it into something more compatible with the Afrikaner character.[62]

To achieve this goal, Afrikaner businesses were to be established. Thus Dr. T. E. Dönges, in a paper he delivered on "The Mobilisation of Afrikaner Capital and Savings Power," called for

> the creation and support of different kinds of Afrikaner enterprises which could provide saving facilities and through which accumulated capital could be invested with an eye towards the realisation of our main goal, namely, the establishment of thrift and national banks, of insurance companies and building societies.[63]

So in 1935 an Afrikaans bank opened its doors for the first time. Significantly, it was called *Volkskas*. In 1936 and 1937 two department stores financed by Afrikaners (*Uniewinkels* in Pretoria and *Sonop* in Bloemfontein) were founded, and a publishing company (*Voortrekkerpers*) was established in Johannesburg.

The salient point is that both politically and economically Afrikaner nationalism opted out of the South African polity after 1934. The ideological goals Afrikaners set themselves in this period were too ethnocentric to warrant hope even of some support from English-speaking South Africans; and their economic activity was primarily directed at raising the standards of their own people. To the Afrikaner nationalists whom Dr. Malan represented, the real conflict in South African politics during the 1930s was between those whose aspirations were determined by the mobilization system and those who, like General Hertzog, continued in the larger reconciliation system.

Organizationally, Afrikaner nationalism was well structured during this period. The different organs and institutions had relatively clearly demarcated roles.[64] There was a single loyalty to the ideals and goals of Afrikaner nationalism which, in turn, were defined by the National party. The Afrikaans newspapers at this time were party organs in all but name and proprietorship, and they rarely deviated from the party line.[65]

The alienation of those Afrikaners in the mobilization subsystem from the South African system was most acute after South Africa entered World War II. As early as 1938 Afrikanerdom showed signs of Nazi influence.[66] Many Afrikaners believed that a German victory, which many of them regarded as imminent in the early 1940s, would bring about the republic Dr. Malan and his followers wanted. This republic was to be a purely Afrikaner one which would include English-speaking South Africans in a subordinate status but would exclude Jews.[67]

After Prime Minister Hertzog had broken with General Smuts over South Africa's participation in the war in September 1939,[68] he rejoined Dr. Malan and became leader of the now Reunited National party, while Dr. Malan became the deputy leader. Nothing illustrates so well the conflict between the beliefs and political styles of the reconciliationist General Hertzog and the mobilizationist Dr. Malan. They experienced the greatest difficulty in finding common ground. According to Professor D. W. Krüger,

> The followers of Malan had a deeply-rooted suspicion that Hertzog was lukewarm in his adherence to nationalist principles. This suspicion was strengthened when he declared that he still believed in his oft proclaimed principle of equality between Afrikaans and English-speaking South Africans. The Malan-nationalists, setting store by Afrikaner unity, could not understand why Hertzog was prepared to jeopardise this ideal in favour of those who had left him in the lurch in September, 1939.[69]

Matters came to a head in November 1940 when the Orange Free State congress of the Reunited National party rejected the principle of equality between English- and Afrikaans-speaking whites (as proposed by General Hertzog) in favor of a program which, while guaranteeing the equality of the English language and culture, specifically omitted reference to civil and political rights. One month later, General Hertzog resigned from this party and retired from politics, thus ending an association which had lasted no longer than sixteen months. Those of the general's supporters who followed him out of the Reunited National party subsequently established the Afrikaner party in January 1941. But nothing much ever came of this party, and just before the general election of 1948 it coalesced with the National party. "The decisive fact" at the time, as Professor Carter has remarked, "was that the extremists of the HNP [the Reunited National party] had won their struggle to keep that party 'pure.' "[70] In terms of the theoretical framework utilized in the present analysis, the mobilization system took precedence over the reconciliation one.

During the next two years Afrikaner nationalism further alienated itself from the South African polity. Various constitutional and political programs circulated among Afrikaners during 1941 and 1942; they favored a Christian national republic, the denial of citizenship to Jews, and the abolition of the British parliamentary system. However, by early 1943 the German retreat had begun, and in the general election campaign of June and July 1943 the National party dropped all talk of a republic, and for the most part adopted a generally moderate platform. The war issue dominated this election and the National party's parliamentary representation was further reduced.[71]

The 1943 general election marks a turning point in Afrikaner nationalism's relationship to the rest of the South African polity. From 1934 until 1943 Afrikaner nationalism constituted a subsystem, organized on mobilization lines. While its alienation from the reconciliation-oriented South African system increased over the years, this trend began to reverse itself after 1943. The immediate reason for this was the course World War II was taking. Just as Paul Kruger and his Transvaal republicans were encouraged by the possibility of German support in their struggle against the British at the turn of the century, so a significant section of Afrikaners pinned their hopes for favorable constitutional changes on a German victory. By 1943 these hopes had largely been shattered. The success of the Allies and the outcome of the general election in that year made it clear to Afrikaner leaders like Dr. Malan that the only way to power was through Parliament,[72] which meant that the National party had to widen its electoral appeal. To do this, the party had to jettison, or at least to soft-pedal, some of the more important of Afrikaner nationalism's ideological objectives.

This may be illustrated in terms of the National party's policy with regard to the republican ideal. Dr. Malan and other National party leaders realized that the various radical republican institutions which had been proposed during the early 1940s had shocked English-speaking South Africans. After the 1943 general election, they not only specifically dissociated themselves from these proposals but actually played down the republic as a political objective. The republican issue was not one of the National party's campaign issues in the general election of 1948, and Dr. Malan did not refer to it in his victory message. A republican form of state was made an objective of the National party in its revised program of principles adopted in 1952. However, one principle of that revised program stated that

> while the Party thus declares itself in favour of the attainment of this form of state, it recognises at the same time, however, that a republic can be established only on the broad basis of the national will, and with the faithful observance of the equal language and cultural rights of the two sections of the European population. Accordingly it stipulates that this constitutional change can be brought about only as the result of a special and definite mandate from the European electorate, and not merely by a parliamentary majority obtained as the result of an ordinary election.[73]

Despite India's successful application to be allowed to remain a member of the Commonwealth of Nations—clearly a prececent for South Africa—the National party did not make an issue of the republic in the 1953 election. Dr. Malan softpedaled the matter[74] and his successor, Prime Minister Strijdom, who had the reputation of being the leading republican within the party, hedged its realization with conditions. In his view, South Africa would become a republic "when we are economically strong enough, when we have satisfactorily solved the coloured problem, and when we have obtained sufficient support for it."[75]

This statement illustrates the great change which had occurred within Afrikaner politics since the late 1930s, when Afrikaner nationalist politicians seemed oblivious to the reactions of the English-speaking whites. Neither did the republic figure as an issue in the 1958 general election. It was only in 1960 that Dr. Verwoerd announced the government's decision to hold a referendum on the matter. But even then it was to be a republic within the Commonwealth, and the only really important constitutional change was that a president would be substituted for the existing governor-general as the ceremonial head of state.[76]

VII

What this change in attitude toward the republic signifies is the Afrikaner leaders' new appreciation of the role of their nationalism in, and the nature of its relationship to, the South African polity. For after the National party's victory in the 1948 election, Afrikaner nationalism steadily shed its mobilization features and increasingly manifested features of a reconciliational system. This is not to suggest that Afrikaner nationalism completely identified itself with the South African polity. To some extent it did, yet one cannot ignore the important changes in the South African polity which the National party induced after 1948.

In the 1950s the Afrikaners substituted symbols of their choosing for the symbols of state in South Africa. Thus, soon after the 1948 general election, the National party government introduced military insignia and designations of rank with a specifically South African flavor. Until that time they had been closely modeled on the British armed forces. An amendment to the Citizenship Act in 1949 introduced an exclusively South African citizenship. In 1950 the right of appeal to the Judicial Committee of the British Privy Council was abolished. Legislation in 1957 declared the Union flag to be the only national flag, and use of the British union jack was ended. Later in the same year the government declared that in future South Africa would have one anthem, "The Call of South Africa," and "God Save the Queen" was discontinued. In 1958 the words "On Her Majesty's Service," which appeared on government correspondence, were replaced with "Official." This process culminated in republican status.

A second important consideration is that after 1948 Afrikaner nationalism was in a position to reshape relations between whites and nonwhites in terms of its beliefs and concepts, which the National party, under the influence of Dr. Verwoerd (who was appointed minister of native affairs, as the portfolio was called in 1952), quickly proceeded to do.[77]

But the third and possibly most important reason for the altered character of Afrikaner nationalism and its relationship to the South African polity refers to the considerable socioeconomic changes which occurred within Afrikaner nationalism itself. Some details of the Afrikaner's progress in the economy were given earlier. However, this improvement has had three important consequences which affect the nature of the relationship of Afrikaner nationalism to the rest of South African society.

First, it has reconciled Afrikaners to the free enterprise system. Thus the chairman of the *Afrikaanse Handelsinstituut* (Afrikaans Institute of Commerce), in a speech delivered during March 1969, dealt with those Afrikaners who, because of their economic backwardness, demand greater governmental intervention in the economy. After warning against the adverse consequences of such an attitude, he said: "It is time that the Afrikaner broke away from this historical pattern of development. He should consciously prepare himself to enthusiastically move into that part of the domestic economy [the private sector] which is still largely foreign to him."[78] Second, the ethnocentric orientation of Afrikaans businesses is a thing of the past. This is reflected in the policies of older established concerns which were launched on Afrikaner sentiment. They now spurn the carefully calculated community appeal used before and vigorously canvass the whole market. New institutions avoid from the outset the (now limiting) specific Afrikaner association. Third, Afrikaner businessmen have become less concerned about identifying with their English-speaking and Jewish counterparts. The association between Federale Mynbou and Anglo-American in 1964 was the first significant development of this kind. However, joint ventures are common occurrences today.

Primarily for these reasons, Afrikaner nationalism today is very different from what it was in the 1930s or from what it was even fifteen years ago. The authority structure is less clearly defined. The churches have lost a great deal of their influence and the politicians no longer command the authority they once did.[79] Gone too is the ideological uniformity of Afrikaner nationalism. Afrikaner political opinion spreads more widely across the white political spectrum than does English-speaking opinion,[80] and within Afrikanerdom the ideological preeminence of the politicians has been challenged by editors and academicians. The difference in the leadership provided by Dr. Verwoerd and Mr. Vorster has had a great deal to do with this.[81] Economically, not only are Afrikaans businesses involved in the whole economy, but some of the keenest competition in South Africa occurs between Afrikaans concerns.

Naturally, there has been resistance to these developments from the ranks of Afrikaner nationalism. Conditioned to the values and ways of the mobilization system, a section of Afrikanerdom has balked at adjusting to the new role of Afrikaner nationalism within the South African polity. As we pointed out earlier, in the beginning of the 1960s this reaction was largely limited to the pages of the *South African Observer*. But it is now fully articulated by the *Herstigte* (Reconstituted) National party of Dr. Albert Hertzog, a party that espouses the following goals:

1. To serve as the political *volksfront* of the Afrikaner nation (*volk*) and to ensure that its principles are applied on all levels of national life.

2. To develop a strong sense of white identity and a "powerful" realization of the need to expand national independence and freedom; to cooperate with those English-speakers who are undivided in their loyalty and dedication to the Republic and who identify with the Afrikaners' history, struggle, and vocation.

3. To fight liberalism and communism on all levels of social life.[82]

Possibly more interesting than the goals themselves are the claims which the HNP makes. Thus

> for the first time the Afrikaner has a party which is unashamedly Afrikaans; for the first time we have a party which is based on the infallible word of God; for the first time the Afrikaner now has a Christian-National party; for the first time the Afrikaans language is accepted as the language of the Republic of South Africa; and for the first time the Afrikaner is now first in his own land.[83]

The parallel between the HNP's brand of Afrikaner nationalism and the Afrikaner nationalism of Dr. Malan in the 1930s is striking. There are the same ethnocentric values and goals, the same exclusiveness, the same introspection. What is also clear is that the pattern of white South African politics during the 1970s—depending on the strength of the HNP—will resemble the politics of the 1930s. The real struggle will be between Afrikaners and, like the politics of the 1930s, the struggle will assume a reconciliationist-mobilizationist form.

Whether the parallel can be taken further and a mobilizationist victory postulated is doubtful. The circumstances are so different, considering the greatly improved material conditions of the Afrikaners, the assurance which they have regarding their culture and language, and the confidence which twenty-one years of uninterrupted rule must impart. These considerations aside, there is the great change which has occurred on the African continent during the last two decades. A significant proportion of Afrikaners realize that the survival of the Afrikaner nation depends on whether it can work out a mutually acceptable basis of coexistence with black Africa: and we would hazard the opinion that these Afrikaners are sufficiently strong to prevent the kind of retrogression which the HNP represents.

2

African Nationalism in South Africa and Zimbabwe

INEZ SMITH REID

In 1963 Jean Ziegler wrote a book entitled *La Contre-Révolution en Afrique*[1] which endeavored to show that in the face of rapid independence for the African majorities in West, East, and Central Africa, Southern African resistance to liberation movements was increasing on economic, political, and military fronts. It is with this general reminder of a counterrevolution that one must approach an analysis of African nationalism in Zimbabwe (Rhodesia) and South Africa. For pitted against the fledgling and often uncertain movements of African nationalists in Southern Africa are the military might, economic strength, and political machinations of the Portuguese-South African-Rhodesian "alliance" supported covertly and sometimes overtly by Western powers and at least one African country, Malawi.

Two phases of the African nationalist movements in Zimbabwe and South Africa have been noticeable since the early 1920s. The first, characterized by reform and peaceful transition, extended from the early twentieth century to approximately 1960; the second, reflecting the necessity of a forceful transition to African government, began approximately in 1960 and continues to the present day.

The reform and peaceful transition aspect of the nationalist movement was recognizable in voters' and "native" associations, the efforts of industrial and commercial workers' unions in Zimbabwe and South Africa, and fledgling political associations. Conservative, elitist, and dependent on the goodwill of Europeans were the Rhodesian Bantu Voters' Association, created in Bulawayo in 1920, the Rhodesian Native Association, formed in Mashonaland also in 1920, and the Union Bantu Vigilance Association, founded earlier in South Africa. Reflecting attitudes and influences of colonial powers and missionaries, the Rhodesian Bantu Voters' Association described itself as

> a constructive and co-operative society, . . .

> desiring to work for the general uplift of the Bantus irrespective of tribe and status. We pledge ourselves to conserve the rights of our people and do all in our power to develop their dormant potentialities by means of practical education and industry. . . We believe that justice must be done to our people and their legitimate rights respected; we believe that only by means of industrial education, a test of Christianity our people will rise gradually in the scale of civilization and that religion must be fostered to grow as the true foundation of a man's character [*sic*].
>
> Work shall be effected by constitutional resolutions and peaceful propaganda, and by consulting the Native Affairs Department, MPs and Missionaries.[2]

During a period of ineffectualness of traditional political groups, leadership of the reform endeavor fell temporarily to an organization of trade unionists, the Industrial and Commercial Workers Union, which appeared first in South Africa and then in Zimbabwe.[3] It was this union (also known later in Zimbabwe as the Reformed Industrial and Commercial Workers Union) which battled for improved working conditions in urban areas. The early political organizations in South Africa and Zimbabwe proved effective only periodically and were often beset by internal divisions. Formed in 1912 by professionals (such as teachers, lawyers, clergymen, and journalists), the African National Congress (ANC), based in South Africa, resorted to normal redress-of-grievance procedures and nonviolent tactics such as petitions, deputations, and a peaceful-pass protest campaign in 1919. It was quite active in the second decade of the twentieth century, froze into inaction during the 1920s and early thirties, revived itself in 1936 when one of the early South African control laws was passed (the Representation of Natives Act of 1936), and tapered off until the post-World War II period.

The ANC in Zimbabwe was founded in 1934 by Aaron Jacha and proved to be more ineffective than the South African ANC, having bouts of dormancy from its inception until its extinction by governmental fiat in 1959. According to Nathan Shamuyarira, the ANC's "inactivity was due to personal quarrels among the top office holders."[4] This charge is verified by the passage of Zimbabwe ANC leadership from Aaron Jacha to Thompson Samkange, a religious leader, to Joshua Nkomo, and the establishment in 1955 of the City Youth League (led by Dunduzu Chisiza, Edson Sithole, and James Chikerema) in response to youthful dissatisfaction with the direction of the ANC and the desire to launch direct action tactics. The Youth League was modeled on one created earlier (1943) in South Africa in which Anton Lembede, Nelson Mandela, Walter Sislu, and Oliver Tambo were active.[5]

The youthful enthusiasts of the League offered a contrast to the more conservative, professional membership of the ANC. Three of the early South African Youth League leaders, Lembede, Tambo, and Sislu, came from economically poor homes but managed to obtain some formal education. Lembede's parents worked on a farm in Natal as manual laborers and reportedly were very poor. Despite the poverty of his parents, Lembede enrolled at the Adams Teacher Training College, where his mind was shaped by a professional staff which included Chief Albert Luthuli and Professor Z. K. Matthews who had studied at Yale University and the London School of Economics. Following his studies at Adams, Lembede taught in the Orange Free State and worked for his B.A. in philosophy and Roman-Dutch law through correspondence courses; he had an untimely death at the age of 33.[6]

Oliver Tambo, who today heads the ANC-in-exile, was born to peasant parents. He studied at the St. Peter's School and later won a scholarship to Fort Hare College where he majored in science. His studies were interrupted due to his expulsion from Fort Hare for participation in student strikes. He later taught science at the St. Peter's School but eventually switched his interest from science to law through the influence of Walter Sislu.[7]

Walter Sislu's early days were not as poverty-stricken as those of Lembede and Tambo since the uncle who raised him was a respected village headman in the Transkei. His uncle died in 1928, however, when Sislu was sixteen and Walter was forced to work to help support the family. He experienced a variety of occupations—mineworker in Johannesburg, "kitchen boy" for a private family in East London, bakery worker, and factory worker. Inevitably, Sislu encountered some conflict with his employers. For example, he lost his job at the bakery when he went on strike in complaint against working conditions. He achieved his junior certificate through correspondence courses and then gained admission to the technical college. Following his studies, he became active in the ANC and also founded a real estate agency with five friends which eventually ran into difficulties and had to be salvaged by the help of others.[8]

By far one of the most perceptive, skillful, and dynamic leaders of the African struggle in South Africa was the fourth key member of the ANC Youth League, Nelson Rolihlahla Mandela, who later became known as the Black Pimpernel during the days when he was forced underground by the South African government. Even then, he was "a tall, handsome, athletic young man with natural authority."[9] Although born into a traditional family, Mandela himself escaped efforts of the South African government to coopt or corrupt traditional leaders. On his father's death in 1930, responsibility for the twelve-year-old Nelson passed to his cousin, then acting paramount chief of the Tembu. His higher education started at Fort Hare College where he soon became involved in college politics. When he joined a boycott of the students' representative council protesting that organization's loss of power to the college administration, Mandela was suspended. Not only was he confronted with suspension from the college, but he also faced a personal problem because of his opposition to a traditional marriage arranged for him by his cousin. To avoid the marriage, Mandela set out for Johannesburg where he became a mine policeman for two days. The brief duration of his job was attributed to his cousin's determination to find Mandela so that the marriage ceremonies could take place. With the assistance of Walter Sislu, Mandela was given a position in a law firm after he had spent some time working as a government clerk. He completed his B.A. by correspondence and one year later, in 1943, enrolled at the University of the Witwatersrand to become a lawyer.[10]

These four—Lembede, Sislu, Tambo, and Mandela—were determined to mold the ANC more into their image of a nationalist organization. One of the major areas of concentration for realization of this objective was the leadership position within ANC. During the decade of the forties, Dr. A. B. Xuma headed the ANC.[11] Dr. Xuma, a resident of the Transkei, had studied medicine first in the United States, then in Hungary and Great Britain where he specialized in surgery and gynecology. Dr. Xuma rose to the top ANC office in December 1940, and during the latter part of the decade, he decided to take the Congress campaign to the United Nations. While in New York in 1946, he encountered Prime Minister Jan Christiaan Smuts when both men sought to advance and to defend their respective positions before that international body.

Despite Dr. Xuma's work in behalf of the Congress, the Youth League was dissatisfied with progress in the nationalist movement and in 1949, when elections were to be held for ANC president, a delegation of youth leaguers approached Dr. Xuma and asked his approval of their program of action which they defined as one embodying "African nationalism" through a boycott of all mock forms of representation such as the Natives' Representative Council (NRC) and Advisory Board.[12] Dr. Xuma balked at turning the ANC into an all-African, nonallied organization and said to the Youth Leaguers: "We should be careful about Africa for the Africans because we can make ourselves isolationists like the government we are opposing."[13] He reminded the youth leaguers that his success at the United Nations in 1946 was attributable in part to the assistance of Indians and the South African Indian Congress. On the issue of a boycott of NRC, Dr. Xuma considered such a step a tactical error in that ambitious but weaker or less qualified individuals would ignore the wishes of the Youth League and stand for election. As the meeting between Dr. Xuma and the Youth League representatives proceeded, fundamental differences concerning the issues of alliances and the boycott of the legislative council were apparent. In a heated moment, Dr. Xuma shouted to the youth leaguers: "I don't want your vote, I don't want to be dictated to by any clique."[14] Mary Benson interprets Dr. Xuma's outcry as an assertion of independence in that "He felt insulted, as if they were looking for someone whom they could influence and manipulate, and he regarded their action as 'bribery and corruption.' "[15]

Although they had not persuaded Dr. Xuma to their point of view, the youth leaguers entered the 1949 ANC election with the clear intent of supporting Dr. Xuma for lack of a better candidate. At the meeting, however, a middle-aged, wealthy physician, Dr. James Moroka, who had played a key role in a 1936 deputation sent to Prime Minister Hertzog, spoke out strongly in behalf of the Youth League's "Program of Action" and gave it his clear endorsement. Even though youth leaguers were not fully briefed on Dr. Moroka's background, they decided to throw their support to him on the spur of the moment, thus enabling Dr. Moroka to beat Dr. Xuma. Later the youth leaguers were to reject Dr. Moroka because of his failure to secure the objectives of the Youth League. Having successfully placed "their man" in office, the youth leaguers sought to implement their program whose immediate objective was "freedom from White domination and the attainment of political independence."[16] The program was to be part of the ANC's post-World War II concentration on reforms in political and civil liberties and was designed to gain acceptance not only for the "one adult, one vote" or "one man, one vote" formula, but also for a more equitable land distribution, the elimination of pass laws, and revisions in the judicial process. In essence, the program represented one of pressure tactics, or a pattern of direct action, which included boycotts, demonstrations, and strikes. At a later point in time, during a treason trial, Nelson Mandela explained the *raison d'être* of the "Program of Action" in the following terms:

> My Lord, up to 1949 the leaders of the ANC had always acted in the hope that by merely pleading their cause, placing it before the

> authorities, they, the authorities, would change their hearts and extend to them all the rights that they were demanding. But the forms of political action which are set out in the Programme of Action meant that the ANC was not going to rely on a change of heart. It was going to exert pressure to compel the authorities to grant its demands.[17]

Similar to, and a continuation of, the 1949 Program of Action was the "Campaign of Defiance of Unjust Laws" organized from 1951 to 1952 in collaboration with the South African Indian Congress. It was designed to force the withdrawal of six repressive laws from the statute books: the Pass Laws, the Group Areas Act, the Separate Representation of Voters Act, the Suppression of Communism Act, the Bantu Authorities Act, and the Compulsory Cattle Culling Policy.[18] Some eight thousand volunteers participated in the campaign by violating laws, submitting themselves to arrest, and rejecting bail in favor of serving time in prison.[19]

In Zimbabwe, activity in the reform and peaceful phase of the nationalist movement increased following World War II and during the existence of the Federation of Northern Rhodesia, Southern Rhodesia, and Nyasaland, the latter being formed after some initial flirtation by Southern Rhodesia with the idea of amalgamation with South Africa. Leadership of the Zimbabwe ANC fell into the hands of Joshua Nkomo in 1957. He received his education at Adams College in Natal, South Africa, and at the Jan Hofmeyr School of Social Work in Johannesburg. Following his studies he was employed as a social worker among African railway laborers. In addition, he spent some time as general secretary of the Railway African Employees' Union. Joshua Nkomo envisioned "a society of equals" in which African and European alike would collaborate for a better Rhodesia in accordance with the policy of partnership.[20] During the era of Garfield Todd's premiership, and even after the rise to power of Sir Edgar Whitehead, the ANC had hopes for ". . .direct participation in the territorial legislature and government."[21] The Whitehead government, not appreciating the efforts of Nkomo's ANC, banned the party in February 1959.

Like the Zimbabwean ANC, the sister organization in South Africa subscribed to a moderate philosophy pointing toward a multiracial society in which each person would be accorded the same basic rights. To emphasize this philosophy, a Congress of People convened at Kliptown (not far from Johannesburg) in June 1955 to draft a "Freedom Charter." Gathered from all walks of life, the three thousand delegates at this multiracial congress included professionals, students, taxi drivers, trade unionists, and others. One of the essential provisions of the Freedom Charter stated: "South Africa belongs to all who live in it, black and white."[22] The idea of black/white cooperation was espoused by one of the architects of the South African ANC, Chief Albert Luthuli, who became president of the organization after the fall from favor of Dr. James Moroka who criticized and disassociated himself from the defiance campaign of 1952. "What we have aimed to do in South Africa," Luthuli wrote, "is to bring the white man to his senses, not slaughter him. Our desire has been that he should cooperate with us, and we with him."[23]

Joshua Nkomo did not abandon his hopes of seeing "a society of equals" implemented even though the ANC was banned in 1959. A new party emerged in January 1960, the National Democratic party (NDP). In reality, the NDP was a continuation of the ANC under a different name. It sought to attract to membership a wide cross-section of the African population. Among its estimated two hundred thousand members in 1961 were "intellectuals, workers, and rural villagers."[24] The party's major efforts in 1961 were directed toward constitutional reform. Insisting upon the formula "one man one vote," the NDP pushed for a constitutional conference which would lead toward a more equitable distribution of power in Zimbabwe. When Sir Edgar Whitehead decided to call a conference in December 1960, his first inclination was to ignore the NDP almost totally by not inviting Joshua Nkomo, the NDP president but requesting instead the presence, in his individual capacity, of Herbert Chitepo, a lawyer and NDP adherent. Due to the application of British pressure, NDP delegates were invited to a January 1961 constitutional conference held in Salisbury. Representing the NDP were Joshua Nkomo and the Reverend Ndabaningi Sithole, along with their advisers Herbert Chitepo and George Silundika. Duncan Sandys, then British Secretary of State for Commonwealth Affairs, chaired the conference which numerous United Federal party (UFP) delegates also attended.

The conference was an attempt to reach agreement on the composition of a Rhodesian parliament, especially the distribution of seats to Africans and Europeans. Apparently, one key to the conference was the introduction of a plan for parliamentary elections by Dr. M. I. Hirsch of the UFP. According to John Day the plan, with modifications, consisted of the following:

> Fifty members would be elected in constituencies with mainly upper-roll (predominantly European) electors, and ten members would be elected in constituencies with mainly lower-roll (predominantly African) electors.

> Lower-roll electors could vote in upper-roll constituencies: but if the lower-roll votes exceeded 20 per cent of the upper-roll votes, then each lower-roll vote would be reduced in value so that their total was equivalent to a prescribed maximum of 20 per cent of the upper-roll votes. A similar arrangement would devalue upper-roll votes in lower roll constituencies. . . .
> On 29 January, the day before the conference was to start . . . Dr Hirsch presented this scheme to Whitehead, who welcomed it, with certain modifications: that there should be 15 lower-roll seats instead of ten, and that the "cross-voting" maximum should be 25 not 20 per cent.[25]

When the conference ended, European delegates thought that the NDP had given its accord to the Hirsch plan and its revisions. Later, however, the NDP clearly discounted this belief. As Mtshali has stated:

> On February 17, 1961, Nkomo and Sithole announced their total rejection of the constitutional proposals on the grounds that the terms offered for African participation in government did not, as they had been led to believe, form a basis for working toward majority rule.[26]

Day traces the later, overt opposition of Nkomo and Sithole to internal NDP pressures. A strongly worded telegram was sent from the London Office signed by Leopold Takawira, a former NDP president and then Secretary of Pan-African and External Affairs, and supported by Michael Mawema, also a former NDP president. The telegram read:

> We totally reject Southern Rhodesia constitutional conference agreement as treacherous to the future of three million Africans. Agreement diabolical and disastrous. Outside world shocked by N.D.P.'s docile agreement.[27]

Whatever face Nkomo or Sithole had lost by confusion over their positions during the 1961 constitutional conference had been regained by March 18–19 and June 17–18 when special congresses of the NDP were held. At the later congress the NDP adopted a special "program of positive action" designed to undermine the proposed constitutional arrangement. As part of the positive action program, the NDP decided to boycott the government referendum on the constitution and to organize its own. While the white minority approved the new constitutional formula during its referendum, Africans overwhelmingly rejected it by a vote of 467,189 to 584.[28]

The 1961 Salisbury constitutional conference revealed quite clearly the inability of Europeans and Africans to agree peacefully on the key issue of representation. A European minority, fearful of an erosion of its power, could never agree to a formula allowing for any meaningful evolution to African political power, whereas an African majority could not be satisfied with a few seats of power in a system dominated by a European minority.

The first phase of African nationalist movements in Zimbabwe and South Africa, then, represented dedication to a policy of peaceful reform and change in collaboration with—or at least not in antagonism toward—Europeans in the respective societies. It was essentially the failure to stir white consciences to the need to redress previous wrongs that gave rise to the second thrust of the nationalist movement.

Increasingly, Africans in Zimbabwe and South Africa came to realize that despite rapid multiplication of independent African states to the north, they would have to face determined and intense white resistance to any form of African nationalism. This determined attitude of whites called for a reevaluation of the nationalist struggle. Many, reassessing the situation, concluded that a peaceful transition to African rule was not only a luxury but a fruitless tactic which could only result in maintenance of the white power structure. Waldemar Nielsen, in his book *African Battleline*, reports that

> a recent survey of 150 middle-class Africans conducted by the South African Institute of Race Relations found that most of them are now prepared to accept violence as a method of political action, and nearly half believe that the use of force has become inevitable.[29]

Increasingly, the movement came under the influence of the "Bambata School"—an ideology that insisted " . . . that Africans can only regain their freedom on the battlefield where they lost it."[30] The Bambata rebellion constituted a systematic and persistent resistance to payment of a poll tax imposed by the government.[31] In 1905 the government of Natal passed legislation calling for a tax on all men over eighteen. The tax was designed to raise money and to force Africans to work. Immediately after its imposition unrest began to set in as the government urged payment. One white farmer, Harry Smith, journeyed to a nearby town in January 1906 to pay his tax. He insisted that his African workers accompany him in order to pay theirs. Later, Smith was found murdered—stabbed with an assegai. In an effort to counteract opposition to the poll tax, the government published reports that Africans voluntarily were paying their taxes and cited as a primary illustration the case of Dinizulu, paramount chief of the Zulus. Simultaneously, however, came word that another chief, Chief Mveli, would not pay his taxes, nor would the members of his tribe. Policemen assigned to force payment were killed.

The height of the movement against the poll tax came when Bambata, the chief of a small group living on the edge of Zululand, repeatedly refused to pay. European discontent with Bambata soon was expressed through the press; for example, the *Natal Mercury* of February 20, 1906, urged the dismissal of Bambata from his post as chief:

> Some surprise is created here at the Government not acting more promptly in the removal of Chief Bambata, whose repulsive presence and control near Greytown is not inviting to the local European population.[32]

Newspaper opposition to Bambata increased and he was referred to as "cheeky" and an "Insolent Chief." As a result of these pressures Bambata was dethroned from his chieftainship and a relative, Magwababa, was appointed acting chief.

Following his dismissal, Bambata sought the advice of the paramount chief, Dinizulu, who suggested that he, Bambata, return to his homeland, commit an act of rebellion, and immediately flee the territory for his own safety. On March 31, 1906, Bambata returned to his Greytown District, seized Magwababa, and commenced his rebellion. European and "loyal" African troops, called to roust Bambata and his followers, were ambushed on April 3. In May 1906 a magistrate, sent to collect taxes in Zululand, was assassinated. Bambata penetrated further into the interior and joined forces with another strong opponent of the poll tax, Sigananda, a ninety-six-year-old local chief. The major battle of the resistance occurred in Mome Gorge with victory going to a better armed European force. As Roux has related:

> In a thickly-wooded mountain valley the followers of Bambata and Sigananda tried to defend themselves. One section of the Government forces drove the rebels up the valley, while another section cut off their retreat and mowed them down unmercifully with machine guns. About 500 Africans were killed in the fight, among them Bambata himself.[33]

Although Dinizulu cleverly had written the government on April 18, 1906, offering his services to apprehend Bambata, this subterfuge eventually proved unsuccessful as the paramount chief was charged in 1908 ". . . with high treason, public violence, sedition, rebellion, and with being responsible for the death of certain persons killed during the rebellion."[34] A guilty verdict was handed down and a sentence of four years in prison was imposed in addition to a fine of £100 or another twelve months in prison. In 1911 Dinizulu was exiled to the Transvaal.

The final statistics of the Bambata rebellion are reminiscent of those stemming from the Mau Mau movement; that is to say, the cost in lives proved greater to Africans than Europeans. The total number of Africans estimated to have lost their lives in the poll tax rebellion stood at four thousand whereas government forces lost twenty-five Europeans and six Africans.[35]

The message of the Bambata rebellion was clear: overt opposition accompanied by violence is perhaps the only way of ending European imposition of unwanted laws. In that respect the Bambata rebellion bore a resemblance to a phenomenon which occurred later, for the occupation of Cornell University's student union building by black students and their subsequent emergence from the seized building with rifles in hand did more for instant change in conditions than deputations, petitions, and negotiating sessions could have accomplished.

Not only has "force" become an important new component of African nationalism in the second phase but also the emphasis on "African." During the first phase collaboration with, and the assistance of, whites was sought. The shift away from white influence became noticeable in 1958–1959 in South Africa when the South African ANC lost part of its membership to a new organization, the Pan-Africanist Congress (PAC), formed in part because of a rejection of white "domination" of an African struggle.

White domination often took the form of Communist party activity.[36] As early as the 1920s the Communist party of South Africa attempted to infiltrate the African nationalist movement. At times there was an effort to coopt the entire struggle by asserting its legitimacy in behalf of the "black masses." The party concentrated upon influencing the thinking of J. T. Gumede, one of the early ANC presidents. In 1927, for example, at the urging of the South African Communists, Gumede attended a conference in Brussels organized by the League Against Imperialism. As a part of the trip he also visited Russia. On his return to South Africa in February 1928, Gumede espoused the cause of Communism in a series of meetings.[37] Rather than welcoming his efforts with open arms, ANC members strongly opposed Gumede and tried to remove him from office. During the Easter 1928 Bloemfontein Conference, a group of chiefs passed a motion disapproving the growing "fraternisation" between the ANC and the Communist party.

Undaunted by these rebuffs, the Communist party continued its recruitment of Africans and proved successful in the Transvaal area among semirural people, but failed miserably with respect to intellectuals.[38] In 1929 the Communist party established a League of African Rights which was designed to play a major role in the liberation struggle. Heading the organization was J. T. Gumede. In its charter the League of African Rights demanded "abolition of the pass laws and land laws, extension of the vote and free education for the Bantu."[39] The familiar black, green, and red colors, now an integral part of the American Black Power movement, constituted those of the League's flag. Adopted as the league's slogan was the phrase "*Mayiby' i Afrika*" (Let Africa return). This theme appeared in the league's official song "*Mayibuye*":

> Let it come back!
> We the people who are brown bless Africa,
> which was taken from our fathers
> when they were in darkness.
> Let it return, let it return,
> let Africa return to us!
> Down with passes
> We demand freedom.[40]

Throughout its first approach to African nationalism—that is, the attempt to coopt the movement—the Communist party sought to discredit the ANC with familiar slogans designed to arouse the resentment of peasants and the working class. These included "bourgeois nationalist movement" and "enemy of the working-class."[41] When the approach of cooptation did not prove eminently successful, the Communist party adopted a policy of cooperation or alliance which meant that Africans would lead the nationalist struggle with the assistance of Communists. Cooperation was to be realized through a series of joint projects between the African nationalists and the Communist party or communist-front organizations such as the Congress of Democrats.

Although some of the African nationalist leaders traveled to Communist countries, few were deeply influenced by the ideology of Marx, Lenin, or Mao. Among those who visited Communist countries were Walter Sislu and Duma Nokwe. Traveling in the mid-fifties the two visited China, the USSR, Poland, and other Communist countries. These two appeared to have been influenced more by the style of dress in Communist countries than by the ideology of those areas as Sislu returned sporting a "high-buttoned Chinese jacket" and Nokwe a "peace cap."[42]

An overwhelming percentage of African nationalists firmly opposed a Communist role in the nationalist movement. They were aided in this attitude by ANC membership requirements which precluded the possibility of white Communists becoming attached to the organization. And, outside of Gumede, Albert Nzula, Moses Kotane, and J. B. Marks, few key African nationalists sympathized with or worked for the Communist cause. On the contrary, in the ANC Youth League, for example, feelings against the Communist party ran so high in 1951 that Nelson Mandela and others "campaigned furiously" against the party. The Youth League, fearing a Communist party takeover of nationalist activity, began to attend party meetings for the purpose of disrupting them and urging Africans to repulse Communists, their ideology and their tactics.[43]

Even during the early stages of his association with the Youth League, Nelson Mandela had argued for the purging of Communists from ANC ranks.[44] His disagreement with the Communists seems to rest with his perception of a difference in objectives on the part of the Communists and the African nationalists. Whereas the ultimate task of the ANC is "for the African people to win unity and full political rights,"[45] according to Mandela, "The Communist Party's main aim . . . was to remove the capitalists and to replace them with a working-class government."[46] Moreover, "The Communist Party sought to emphasize class distinctions whilst the ANC seeks to harmonize them."[47] Yet, even though Mandela's antagonism to the Communist party was well known—especially in terms of white Communist membership in the ANC or a central role for Communists in the African nationalist struggle—during the Rivonia trial he sought to explain why African nationalists could not wash their hands completely of Communists but rather allowed a certain degree of interaction between the two groups:

> It is perhaps difficult for white South Africans, with an ingrained prejudice against communism, to understand why experienced African politicians so readily accept communists as their friends. But to us the reason is obvious. Theoretical differences amongst those fighting against oppression is a luxury we cannot afford at this stage. What is more, for many decades communists were the only political group in South Africa who were prepared to treat Africans as human beings and their equals; who were prepared to eat with us, live with us, and work with us.[48]

Like Mandela, Robert Sobukwe rejected the classical Marxist analysis of society. Sobukwe, one of the leaders of PAC, denied that the existence of a class struggle in South Africa should be given prominent weight. Rather, he interpreted the South African society as evidencing a struggle between black and white. White workers could not be accepted as friends to black workers or be seen as collaborators with black workers to terminate a class struggle. Indeed, to Sobukwe, white workers were the very enemies of black workers in South Africa. Following Mandela's thinking,

Sobukwe too rejected any major role for Communists in ANC affairs.[49]

Despite the internal fight against communism within the ANC and the attitudes of the leading nationalists toward the Communist party, part of the 1956 indictment against those involved in the famous treason trials alleged involvement in a "conspiracy inspired by international communism" and designed "to overthrow the South African state by violence."[50] This allegation, however, was no doubt reflective of a South African governmental tendency to brand its opposition as Communists arbitrarily. Commenting on this 1956 accusation during the Rivonia trial, Nelson Mandela stated:

> We were acquitted on all counts, which included a count that the ANC sought to set up a communist state in place of the existing régime. The Government has always sought to label all its opponents as communists. This allegation has been repeated in the present case, but as I will show, the ANC is not, and never has been, a communist organization.[51]

The Legums have written: "The Communists' role in the African nationalist struggle has always been strongly divisive."[52] The truth of this statement could be seen in the 1960 split in the ANC culminating in the creation of the Pan Africanist Congress.

Leadership of PAC fell to Robert Mangaliso (Wonderful) Sobukwe who was born in 1925. In contrast to Nelson Mandela's family background, Sobukwe's father was a Methodist lay minister. Like Mandela, however, Sobukwe studied first at a mission school—in his case, Healdtown Institute—and then enrolled at Fort Hare College as a result of financial assistance from the principal of Healdtown Institute and others. As was the fate of other young African students, Sobukwe became enmeshed in politics at Fort Hare, rising to the presidency of the students' union and serving as editor of a student journal as well as secretary-general of the ANC Youth League. In 1949, the year Dr. Xuma was rejected for leadership of ANC, Sobukwe was selected to head the action program of the Youth League. In his last year at Fort Hare, Sobukwe lost his scholarship because of his activism in student politics. Nonetheless, with the assistance of friends, he managed to scrape together enough money to complete his studies. For two years, following his graduation from Fort Hare, he taught at Standerton but lost his position when he joined the defiance campaign in 1952. He then acquired a language assistantship at the University of the Witwatersrand in Johannesburg where he was able to earn a diploma in languages.

The PAC, under the leadership of Sobukwe, castigated the ANC alliance with the (white) Congress of Democrats, the South African Indian Congress, and the South African Colored Peoples Congress. PAC deemphasized and indeed rejected any policy of multiracialism in favor of a purely African nationalism. Explaining his position on alliances, Sobukwe said:

> Our contention is that the Africans are the only people who, because of their material position, can be interested in the complete overhaul of the present structure of society. We have admitted that there are Europeans who are intellectual converts to the Africans' cause, but because they benefit materially from the present set-up, they cannot completely identify themselves with that cause.[53]

It was Sobukwe who led PAC's 1959 Positive action campaign, designed "to overthrow white domination and to attain freedom and independence,"[54] But the first significant activity of PAC was the March 1960 anti-pass campaign. The drive against the pass laws was to be a sustained one culminating in arrests and bloodshed. The response to the campaign was enormous and bore parallels to the 1963 civil rights march on Washington—at least in terms of numbers participating. By March 30 "hundreds of people" were under detention and a state of emergency had been proclaimed.[55] Those in the Transvaal area known as Sharpeville received the most brutal and shocking treatment of all when unarmed citizens were massacred by members of the South African police. In other areas, too, demonstrators were met with South African armed police. For example, at Langa where some thirty thousand individuals were led by Philip Kgosana, "crowds were dispersed by baton charges and then machine-gun fire; they retaliated by burning property and throwing stones."[56] As part of the anti-pass campaign of 1960 many resorted to a work stoppage or a "stay-at-home" movement. This was most effective in Cape Town where an estimated sixty thousand Africans worked at that time. According to Friedmann: "For nearly three weeks, building and engineering projects, deliveries of food, coal and newspapers came to a standstill and goods piled up at the docks. Meanwhile the police went berserk with batons and home-made whips and wherever Africans were encountered, blood flowed."[57]

Sickened and startled by this police violence, some individuals organized underground wings of PAC and ANC since both organizations were banned in 1960. *Poqo* (meaning pure or only), an offshoot of PAC, allegedly consisted of a one hundred and fifty thousand-man army whose target was the white population of South Africa and those African chiefs who collaborated with government authorities. *Poqo* adherents were recruited from "the less sophisticated group of urban Africans in the Western Cape"—particularly ". . . the chronically 'illegal' and the unemployed. . . ."[58] It has been characterized as "a spontaneous, atavistic movement."[59] The tactics of *Poqo* were assault and murder, not unlike the stated objectives of Mau Mau. In terms of application of terror tactics and violence, *Poqo* was charged with killing three African policemen in 1962, five whites in 1963, and a white girl and white man during a combination protest and attack on a police station, stores, and houses in retaliation against the murder of some five Africans and three coloreds in the Mbekini area.[60]

ANC produced the Spear of the Nation (*Umkonto We Sizwe*), headed by Nelson Mandela. The specific purposes of this group were to disrupt the white society and to cause chaos through a policy of interrupting communications by tampering with power lines, destruction of government offices, and the inauguration of guerrilla tactics. At the time of the Rivonia trial, Nelson Mandela conceded his organizational role in *Umkonto*. Explaining the reasons behind the formation of *Umkonto*, Mandela asserted:

> I, and the others who started the organization [*Umkonto*], did so for two reasons. Firstly, we believed that as a result of Government policy, violence by the African people had become inevitable, and that unless responsible leadership was given to canalize and control the feelings of our people, there would be outbreaks of terrorism which would produce an intensity of bitterness and hostility between the various races of this country which is not produced even by war. Secondly, we felt that without violence there would be no way open to the African people to succeed in their struggle against the principle of White supremacy.[61]

The manifesto of *Umkonto* clearly reflected an increasing sentiment that recourse to violence was inevitable.

> The time comes in the life of any nation when there remain only two choices—submit or fight. That time has now come to South Africa. We shall not submit and we have no choice but to hit back by all means in our power in defence of our people, our future, and our freedom.[62]

Mandela has admitted openly his belief in the necessity of sabotage and violence against the South African government for African nationalism to achieve its objective of political control. At the Rivonia trial he stated:

> I do not . . . deny that I planned sabotage. I did not plan it in a spirit of recklessness, nor because I have any love of violence. I planned it as a result of a calm and sober assessment of the political situation that had arisen after many years of tyranny, exploitation, and oppression of my people by the Whites.[63]

Although he acknowledged his contributions to sabotage activities in South Africa, he was careful to note his rejection of terrorism and assassination as tactics: "Umkonto was to perform sabotage, and strict instructions were given to its members right from the start, that on no account were they to injure or kill people in planning or carrying out operations."[64]

A more forceful phase of the African nationalist movement also occurred in Zimbabwe, beginning in the early 1960s. The NDP became the victim of a governmental ban on December 9, 1962, as a result of civil disobedience and sabotage. The Zimbabwe African People's Union (ZAPU), which was formed ten days after the NDP suffered the stamp of illegality, continued the struggle. Among ZAPU adherents, too, could be found "a growing conviction . . . that their struggle would have to involve bloodshed and violence."[65] But the factional and divisive forces within ZAPU, which ultimately resulted in two rival parties—ZAPU (or PCC, Peoples Caretaker Council) and ZANU (Zimbabwe African National Union) in 1963—hampered the continuation of the campaign against the colonial government because both groups turned inward and sometimes waged a vicious competitive struggle for leadership of the independence movement.[66] The Rhodesian government, asserting its duty to maintain internal security, banned both ZAPU and ZANU. After the unilateral declaration of independence in November 1965, the leaders of both parties—Reverend Sithole of ZANU and Joshua Mkomo of ZAPU—were placed under detention.

When both the Rhodesian and South African governments clamped down on African nationalist activities, an increasing number of young men fled each country and some of them received training in guerrilla warfare.[67] Camps were organized in Tanzania, the Congo (Kinshasa), Zambia, Algeria, and the United Arab Republic on the continent. In addition, some individuals were sent off to Cuba, Czechoslovakia, the Soviet Union, and China for training. Tanzania became a crucial, pivotal country and now plays host to the ANC, which is headed by Oliver Tambo, and to branches of PAC, ZAPU, and ZANU. Tanzania not only has served as an organizational zone where policy decisions are made and young men assigned to various training grounds, but it also has played an important role in "political indoctrination." The main guerrilla bases in Tanzania allegedly may be found at Ilala, close to the capital and at Feira, not far from the borders of Malawi and Rhodesia.[68] ZAPU's exile contingent is directed by James Chikerema and based mainly in Lusaka, Zambia, where President Kenneth Kaunda has tried to give support to the greatest extent possible. Herbert Chitepo heads ZANU's exile group which has branches in Lusaka as well as in Dar es Salaam.

With forces from Zimbabwe, South Africa, Namibia, South West Africa, Mozambique, and Angola all in exile and training together with a grim determination to liberate their respective countries, a crucial decision occurred in 1967. In August of that year there were reports of an alliance between ANC and ZAPU, an alliance which, according to one writer, may have marked a ". . . new stage in practical revolutionary consciousness."[69] Abandoning the "my country first" or "my country only" approach, ANC and ZAPU leaders decided to concentrate on the West Zambezi Valley in Rhodesia under two probable assumptions: one, once Rhodesia is liberated, all forces can be directed toward South Africa; or two, without the combined operation of ANC and ZAPU there is very little possibility of African political independence in Rhodesia within the next few years.

Apparently, not all freedom fighters welcomed the ZAPU-ANC alliance. Some insisted on the validity of the "my country only" or "my country first" approach. Matthew Nkoana reported ". . . defections from ANC and disaffection with the ZAPU leadership . . ." because of the alliance.[70] Furthermore, by citing an article printed in an unidentified issue of the *Zimbabwe News*, he drew attention to the position on alliances allegedly assumed by ZANU.

> The historical fact, if we must be honest with outselves [*sic*], does not allow us at this point to pretend that a South African, even though he may be black, can automatically find acceptance among the people of Zimbabwe. . . . In guerrilla warfare we must strive to spread the enemy forces so that we can wipe them out one by one. The greatest help we can get from ANC is for ANC to wage intensive guerrilla warfare in South Africa. If ANC can pin down the whole South African force inside South Africa, then Zimbabweans shall be left with Smith alone without South African aid. . . . As it is now, the ANC and PCC (SAPU) [*sic*] alliance has made it easy for Smith and Vorster to unite and concentrate their forces to slaughter Zimbabweans. . . [*sic*].[71]

Despite some opposition to and discontent with the alliance, it continues and has produced some favorable results. The initial encounter in the Zambezi Valley reportedly met with success.[72] Attention now has been turned to the northeastern part of Rhodesia, where the lands are particularly favorable for cultivation and resemble the fertile area in Kenya's so-called White Highlands. According to Russell Warren Howe, who managed to get a firsthand glimpse of the war, two major aims have been stated by ZAPU-ANC:

> First, to establish "reactivable" bases and arms caches, and to build a network of resistance supporters among whom the liberation forces can work in the later "direct action" phase; and secondly, to guide and interpret for the South Africans until they reach the Limpopo River at the South African border.[73]

ANC objectives in South Africa are "the establishment of bases" and the continuation of "resistance" efforts in the form of sabotage. ZANU has not stood by idly since the ZAPU-ANC alliance was forged, and it has organized sabotage efforts in the north, center and southeastern part of Zimbabwe.

During 1968 a major initiative took place in March and April in Zimbabwe which "Mr. Ian Smith said . . . would be over quickly, as had all previous attacks."[74] Yet South African aid had to be sought as the battle continued into the second month and the minister of justice, Desmond Lardner-Burke, was compelled to admit "that these guerrillas were much better armed and trained than the previous ones."[75] Rhodesian deaths in the guerrilla warfare exceed those of ZANU-ZAPU-ANC, a fact which the Smith regime tries to conceal "by conducting military funerals at night, by cordoning off roads when mortuary convoys pass and by the orthodox lies of wars."[76] The necessity for a military appeal to South Africa may be attributed in large measure to the inferiority of Rhodesian troops in guerrilla warfare despite their modern weapons system. The South African minister of police, Mr. S. L. Muller, explained the rationale behind South Africa's decision to aid the Rhodesian government in its effort to control guerrilla incursions:

> During 1967 the terrorist threat took a new turn when the Rhodesian security forces which had clashed with a group of terrorists, found that amongst those who had been caught and killed there were also members of the South African ANC movement. These African National Congress members were identified as South African Bantu who had unlawfully left the Republic during 1962 for military training abroad. In addition it soon became apparent that the ANC and the Rhodesian ZAPU had joined forces for the purpose of making onslaughts primarily on

> Rhodesia but with South Africa as the ultimate target. These events resulted in our Prime Minister offering to Rhodesia the services of the S.A. Police Force in their territory, to assist in resisting the common enemy and in that way to ensure our own security as well.[77]

David Smock interprets the South African decision to give military assistance to Rhodesia as indicative of its leaders belief in the domino theory:

> A major concern of Vorster is the guerrilla activity in Rhodesia. As an advocate of the domino theory, his sending of military support to Rhodesia is based on the fear that guerrilla successes in Rhodesia would pave the way for guerrilla attacks on South Africa.[78]

The important point, however, is that without South African assistance to the Rhodesian government the guerrilla movement might prove more effective than it is. As Ronald Segal stated in his testimony before the United Nations Committee on Apartheid:

> If South African troops had not come to Rhodesia's assistance, the army of the Zimbabwe liberation movement would already have reduced the Smith regime to a seriously embarrassing position.[79]

Of invaluable assistance to the guerrilla forces has been the response of the African populace. In spite of repeated accusations of apathy among Zimbabweans, what little information is available points to general cooperation and sustenance of troops by villagers. Hasan Chimutengwende, who saw action in Zimbabwe, stated

> I stayed at large for eight whole months in Rhodesia moving from village to village, and I learnt that if a freedom fighter can convince a villager that he is genuine he will be helped, whether he is ZAPU or ZANU.[80]

This report coincides with one made by another Zimbabwean guerrilla which was printed in *AfricAsia*. In it he recounts the support he received from the head of a village, the headman's wife, and others. The guerrillas had approached a village cautiously, saying that they were lost fishermen who were hungry and whose supplies had been exhausted. When they requested something to eat the village headman admonished them not to lie. He informed the group that he had heard of the war and that they should identify themselves if they were freedom fighters. When they did so the headman gave them a warm welcome and supplied them with food. For his assistance the headman was later killed but his wife assumed the role of supporter until the governmental authorities made her a useless contact by strict surveillance. In her place rose another villager. As the guerrilla who recounted the story attempted to escape the pursuing Rhodesian troops, he was wounded in the leg by a grenade. A villager cared for him until his leg had healed sufficiently for him to move on. He summarizes his experiences as follows:

> We know now that we can proceed with confidence, strong from the support of our millions of oppressed brothers and from the active aid of thousands of men like the "old man," his widow, the new "old man" and all the others, the people of our villages.[81]

And Russell Howe, too, noted:

> Guerrilla reports, which seek to impress the sedentary leadership with their problems, only rarely complain of villagers' disloyalty to the African cause. . . . This rural identification with the liberation struggle has probably increased South African reluctance to participate.[82]

If these reports are accurate, if in fact villagers are beginning to assist guerrillas, then one of the first conditions of guerrilla warfare is well on the way to being met.[83]

One estimate of the ratio of Zimbabwean guerrillas to governmental troops is two thousand to ten thousand.[84] While the exact number of all guerrillas in training is impossible to discover, some guesses range from two thousand all the way to nine thousand.[85] If a few thousand more guerrillas are sent into Rhodesia and if there is an intensification of village support, then it is very likely that the war will become a prolonged and bloody one. Moreover, it is interesting to speculate whether the eruption of internal Detroit-like riots in Salisbury or Newark-like riots in Bulawayo, combined with the guerrilla offensive, would be sufficient to overthrow the white-dominated Rhodesian government.

It can be seen, then, that the nationalist struggle in Zimbabwe and South Africa has moved into a forceful phase. In other words, peaceful, direct-action tactics have now been abandoned for the most part. Despite some limited success on the battlefield, an extremely optimistic view is unwarranted. Several obstacles confront the African nationalists. These include reprisals by white governments, de facto alliances, increased military expenditures by the South African and Rhodesian governments, and internal struggles within the African nationalist movement.

Subjection to the judicial process has been a favored tactic of control used successfully by the Rhodesian and South African governments. In 1956, for example, the South African government moved to neutralize or destroy the effectiveness of the ANC and the entire nationalist struggle by arresting some 156 persons on charges of "treasonable conspiracy inspired by international communism to overthrow the South African State by violence."[86] In many instances justice is an aggravatingly slow process; cases may lag for long periods of time. The 1956 treason trial lasted for an unbelievable four and one half years. It began with the December 1956 arrests of a wide cross-section of those involved in the nationalist movement. The preparatory examination (or preliminary hearing) lasted for a whole year. In January 1958 charges were dismissed against sixty-five of the accused and ninety-one were ordered to stand trial. The trial began on August 1, 1958. It was interrupted on October 13 when the indictment was withdrawn as a result of legal arguments pointing out its invalidity. On January 19, 1959, a shorter indictment was handed down against some thirty individuals charging them with high treason. Later, on April 20, the remaining sixty-one accused were released and in August 1959 the trial against the thirty began. The prosecution did not complete its case until March 10, 1960. In the midst of the defense presentation, the Sharpeville massacre occurred leading to the proclamation of a state of emergency and the recess of the trial on April 1, 1960.

Prior to the recess, the trial had been marked by considerable harassment of defense counsel, so much so that the defense attorneys resigned from the case. This left the burden of the defense upon several of the accused, including Nelson Mandela (himself an attorney), Walter Sislu, Duma Nokwe, Robert Resha, and Ahmed Kathrada. Mandela and the others continued the presentation of the defense case from April 26 to October 7, 1960. The summations of counsel proved to be quite lengthy; the prosecution began its summary argument on November 7 and ended in March 1961. In comparison, the defense summary argument lasted a much shorter period of time—three weeks. Eventually, a verdict of acquittal was handed down for Mandela and others, but the trial managed to occupy the minds and drain the energies of some of the leading nationalists for an inordinate amount of time. Despite this, as we have seen, the ANC and PAC managed to wage an anti-pass campaign. The South African government, however, once again invoked the judicial process in an effort to terminate nationalist activities.

In March 1961 at Pietermaritzburg, the site of an All-in-African Conference designed to map a "peaceful scheme of opposition to apartheid," six African nationalists and their allies were arrested: Duma Nokwe, Reverend Rajuili (member of the Progressive party), Reverend Tantsi, Jordan Ngubane, Hyacinth Bhangu, and Julius Malie of the Liberal party. The six were charged specifically with having "printed, circulated, distributed and published circulars which set out the objects of the All-in-African Conference. These objects were said to be 'calculated' to further the objects of the banned African National Congress and the banned Pan-African Congress."[87] The proceedings against the six are so striking because of the two statutes under which they were tried. One of the statutes, S. 381 (vii) of the South African Criminal Code provided:

> When a member of an association of persons, other than a corporate body, has, in carrying on the business or affairs of that association or in furthering or endeavouring to further its interests, committed an offence, any person who was at the time of the commission of the offence a member of that association, shall be deemed to be guilty of the said offence unless it is proved that he did not take part in the commission of the offence and that he could not have prevented it.[88]

In essence, S. 381 (vii) is a conspiracy statute which makes every individual responsible for the acts of another. Yet S. 381 (vii) is even more severe in that the onus of prevention is placed on the shoulders of an organizational member; for an individual to escape punishment under S. 381 (vii), he must demonstrate that he could not have prevented the offense. The second statute, S. 263, of the Criminal Code made it unnecessary to establish, by way of membership lists or dues records, the affiliation of any individual to a particular organization.[89] One merely had to show a name on any document discovered on any person or at any office during the time of arrest. Presumably, then, if one had met a person on the street and jotted his name on a circular, that person would have been liable to prosecution under S. 381 (vii) and S. 263.

In late 1962 Nelson Mandela was indicted for "inciting African workers to strike . . . ; and leaving South Africa without a valid travel document."[90] He was given three years in prison on the first count and two years on the second. In the same year Duma Nokwe, an African barrister, was arrested for "furthering the aims of an unlawful organization."[91] Nokwe, who had attended missionary school with Oliver Tambo and collaborated with Nelson Mandela and Walter Sislu in nationalist activities, had had a history of brushes with the government prior to his 1962 arrest. Although he held a B.Sc. degree from Fort Hare College and a law degree from the University of the Witwatersrand, he had considerable difficulty finding a job. He became a lawyer but because he had been banned to Johannesburg under the Riotous Assemblies Act during his student days, he could not take cases outside of the immediate

Johannesburg area. For example, he could not make a trip to Pretoria to defend a client without special permission. Nowke fled the country before his court appearance on the 1962 charge had been scheduled. His bitterness at being harassed by the South African judicial process to the extent of being unable to conduct a decent law practice is apparent from some of his writings.[92] At one point he stated:

> In South Africa we have been turned into criminals because we demand dignity and to be treated as human beings with a right to a future, hopes and success if we work for it.[93]

Still not satisfied that the judicial process had been as effective as it should have been, the South African government staged its most famous trial to date, the Rivonia trial (named for the suburb housing the underground office of the arrested nationalist leaders). Those arrested in June 1963 included Walter Sislu, Govan Mbeki, Raymond Mlangani, Dennis Goldberg, and Lionel Bernstein. They, and Nelson Mandela as well (who was still serving time on his 1962 sentence), were charged with "sabotage and . . . conspiracy to overthrow the Government by revolution and by assisting an armed invasion of South Africa by foreign troops."[94] Only Lionel Bernstein was acquitted; the others were handed life imprisonment terms.

Robert Sobukwe, another leading nationalist, was also taken before the South African courts, tried, convicted, and sentenced to three years' imprisonment for "incitement" as a result of his role in the anti-pass campaign of 1960. When time for his release finally came, the South African government put yet another of its techniques of control into affect: detainment under the General Laws Amendment Act. Sobukwe's stay on Robben Island exceeded his original sentence by some six years. When he was finally released from detention on May 14, 1969, Robert Sobukwe was placed under house arrest in Kimberley with the following conditions: that he not

> leave the municipal area of Kimberley; attend or address gatherings; leave his residence between 6 P.M. and 6 A.M.; communicate with listed or restricted persons; give educational instruction at an educational institution; or take a hand in publications of a particular type or with particular objectives.[95]

A number of individuals were arrested in 1968 and 1969 and accused of being members of *Poqo*. On September 3, 1968, some twenty-six Africans were indicted under the Sabotage Act for having "conspired to attack and murder the police of the small town of Victoria West, murder the white inhabitants of the town, seize control of the power station and cut off the town's electricity supply, and tamper with drugs, poison and medical supplies at a hospital at King William's Town near East London."[96] Ten other alleged members of *Poqo* were arrested in October 1968, tried, convicted, and sentenced to three years under the Suppression of Communism Act. Eventually, these sentences were reversed on procedural and evidentiary grounds. Thirteen others were tried and convicted in July 1969 for their alleged membership in *Poqo*. These persons were given varying sentences ranging from one to seven years in prison.[97]

In January 1969 the South African government commenced yet another trial of African nationalists. This time twelve, including one woman, were tried at Pietermaritzburg in violation of the Terrorism and Suppression of Communism Acts. Specifically, they were accused of having

> wrongfully and unlawfully and with intent endangered the maintenance of law and order in South Africa and conspired to commit acts to encourage discontent, violence, and revolution and to overthrow the order in the country by means of subversion, terrorism, violent revolution and warfare.[98]

It was further alleged that they had attempted to find a landing site for a foreign submarine, received guerrilla training in the Soviet Union, Algeria, Tanzania, and Ethiopia, prepared to launch a series of attacks against South Africa, and established contacts with the illegal South African Communist party. The trial revealed that the Rhodesian and South African governments were collaborating not only on the military front to stop the guerrilla movements, but also in the judicial arena. Several of the defendants were arrested in Rhodesia and extradited to South Africa. During the trial of the twelve, Rhodesian policemen testified in behalf of the prosecution.[99] A variety of sentences were imposed: one person was condemned to twenty years' imprisonment, six to eighteen years, one to fifteen years, two to ten years, one to five years; and one was acquitted.[100]

In the Spring of 1969 some twenty-two Africans including Mrs. Winnie Mandela, wife of Nelson Mandela, were held under the Suppression of Communism Act. In February 1970 charges were dropped but the accused were reindicted under the Terrorism Act. The arrests stemmed from the alleged involvement of the accused in the African National Congress. Specifically they were accused of having searched for train and railway targets for sabotage, having given financial help to the ANC, having planned to contact ANC guerrillas, and having "encouraged feelings of hostility between the races."[101] The Terrorism Act allows the government to detain accused persons, without the benefit of bail or trial, for an indefinite period of time.

It can be seen, then, that the judicial process in South Africa has been quite effective as a technique of control, especially since it has been aided by a series of repressive laws. Particularly useful have been the Sabotage Act, the Suppression of Communism Act, the Unlawful Organizations Act, and the Terrorism Act. In 1968 alone, 374 Africans were serving sentences under the Sabotage Act, 34 under the Suppression of Communism Act, 527 under the Unlawful Organizations Act, and 31 under the Terrorism Act.[102] Besides these more serious acts, Africans have been arrested for violation of pass laws. The 1966–1967 Annual Report of the Commissioner of the South African Police revealed that in 1966–1967 there were 315,756 cases sent to trial regarding registration and production of documents by Africans compared with 241,698 such cases for the previous year.[103] When the Commissioner's Report was released, the *Rand Daily Mail* commented:

> These figures are appalling. What is more they are probably even higher by now: if the rate of increase has been maintained since 1967—and there is no reason to suppose it has not—then there must be something like 2,500 men, women and teenagers bundled into police vans every day for these offences.[104]

The policy of the Rhodesian government is quite similar to that of the South African government with respect to the utilization of legislation and the judicial process as techniques of control. In 1963 approximately 1,168 persons were arrested under the Law and Maintenance Act. By the end of 1964 some 1,980 Africans were in detention or under restriction.[105] Several guerrillas have been arrested and sentenced. Nine were captured and tried in Salisbury in July 1968; forty-five others were condemned to life imprisonment for their activities in the Zambezi Valley; and Ndabaningi Sithole himself was sentenced to six years of hard labor for conspiracy to murder Ian Smith, Desmond Lardner-Burke, and Jack Howman, minister of defense and foreign affairs.[106]

Another obstacle to the growth of African nationalism in South Africa and Zimbabwe is internal disagreement. There is probably no nationalist movement which at one time or another has not been confronted with internal crises, factions, and splits, and this has been the case in Mozambique, Angola, South Africa, Zimbabwe, and Namibia. Undoubtedly, factionalization and in-fighting are counterproductive. Nathan Shamuyarira has commented on the intense, bitter fight for control of the nationalist movement in Zimbabwe:

> It was tragic to see so much of the time and the energy of the nationalists dissipated in fighting the rival party after the split.[107]

Such internal splits are certainly counterproductive; yet they are probably inevitable and a reality with which the nationalists will have to cope. It is difficult to see, for example, how the ZAPU-ZANU split of 1963 could have been avoided, given the apparent deceit and dishonesty displayed by Joshua Nkomo in dealing with Julius Nyerere, president of Tanzania, and other African leaders on the question of a Zimbabwean government-in-exile. African leaders insisted that ZAPU should remain in Zimbabwe and wage the struggle domestically. Despite this clearly stated position, Nkomo convinced the top leadership of ZAPU that they should go immediately to Dar Es Salaam in accordance with the advice of certain African leaders. According to Mtshali, Nkomo wanted to go to Dar because he believed that "arrests would cripple the work of ZAPU at a time when UDI was pending."[108] Moreover, a fundamental difference emerged concerning tactics as what later became ZANU eschewed the "policy of circumvention" being implemented by Nkoma and insisted instead upon a "policy of confrontation." In other words, there was a disagreement with Nkomo's "policy of fighting from outside" or "circumvention" instead of "facing the government squarely" or "confrontation."[109] Those who split from the ranks of ZAPU were Reverend Sithole, Robert Mugabe, Leopold Takawira, and Washington Malianga. These men formed ZANU with the slogan *Chimurenga* or "liberation war". Reverend Sithole was elected president and Leopold Takawira eventually emerged as his deputy.[110]

In the South African situation, too, disagreements have led to splits in the nationalist groups. For example, some ANC adherents broke away in 1960 to form PAC because of opposition to Communist involvement in ANC and because of a belief that the ANC was dominated by whites.[111] And with the imprisonment of Robert Sobukwe, PAC was beset by internal conflict. Currently, there is a PAC splinter group based in the Congo (Kinshasa) and the report of the Special Study Mission to Southern Africa made the following observation on PAC:

> The Party was expelled from Zambia in the summer of 1968 following the arrest of Tsepo Letlaka and some other leaders by their own soldiers near Livingstone.[112]

Presently, the OAU recognized leader of PAC is Potlako Leballo, a former United States Information Service employee in Johannesburg.[113]

Part of the internal conflict, especially in Zimbabwe, may be traceable to the fact that no single person who may be labeled as "charismatic" has been able to capture the emotions and devotions of the Zimbabweans. As one recalls the strategies and patterns of nationalist struggles in many African countries which are now independent, a charismatic figure assumed a pivotal organizational role. Yet the leadership problem among Zimbabweans seems to have become more severe than anywhere else. As Waldemar Nielsen has written:

> The decline in influence of the nationalist movement may have been due in part to the low quality of its leadership and to fundamental errors of judgment on crucial occasions.[114]

In South Africa the most effective leaders and those who are candidates for the charismatic label—for example, Mandela, Sislu, Sobukwe—are separated from their people by virtue of prison, detention, or house arrest.

Despite the various divisions and splits within the nationalist movement the struggle continues. In addition to the various groups struggling to liberate "Portuguese" Africa, ZAPU and ZANU continue raids and sabotage in Zimbabwe, and ANC and PAC have not given up in South Africa even though their efforts seem to have been directed toward Zimbabwe. Thus, though these splits may be counterproductive, inevitable, and may, in fact, prolong the rule of the white-dominated governments, they are nevertheless not crippling. As Richard Gibson has written:

> However divided the liberation movements may sometimes seem to the casual observer, however, bogged down in exile politics and intrigue, no one, least of all Afro-Americans, should underestimate the profound commitment of African people, particularly the young to the elimination of white-minority rule from the continent. Africans are now well aware that this can only be achieved by a bloody and costly liberation war which would last a decade and that the price in human lives, especially African lives, will be great.[115]

3

*South African Foreign Policy: The "Outward Movement"**

J. E. SPENCE

* This rather clumsy phrase is a literal translation of the Afrikaans *uitwaartse beweging.* Its use is justified on the grounds that some of its more ardent exponents claim that the phrase refers to more than a change in *official* policy insofar as it also suggests a new mood of confidence and optimism among influential elites after nearly two decades of isolation and "inward-looking" preoccupations.

The Historical Background

For much of the postwar period, South African diplomacy was exclusively concerned at the public and ideological level with defending the principles and practical application of apartheid. In the General Assembly of the United Nations, at successive Commonwealth conferences, and in foreign policy debates in the South African Parliament, government spokesmen reacted bitterly to criticism of their country's policies, interpreting such attacks as improper interference with the rights afforded to South Africa by the Charter of the United Nations, especially the provision precluding intervention in domestic affairs (Article 2, paragraph 7). Judged solely in terms of formal votes of censure at the United Nations and elsewhere, South Africa was isolated—an object of contempt and derision in a world which refused to recognize the morality of any claims for the sanctity of domestic jurisdiction as a defense for a state which ordered its affairs on the basis of racial discrimination.

South Africa withstood this criticism with little if any damage to its political and economic stability, concentrating the day-to-day operation of its foreign policy on the extension of its traditional economic and political ties with the Western Powers. At this stage—from 1948 to 1960—these states were by and large prepared to refrain from joining the ranks of those who condemned South Africa in resolution after resolution at the United Nations and were willing to stand firm on a narrow interpretation of the Charter forbidding any intervention in South Africa's domestic affairs. Their reasons for doing so need not detain us; suffice to say that their governments were indisposed to take "prophylactic" action against a state which seemed more stable than many created in the postwar period and in which they all, in varying degree, retained valuable economic interests. Nor were South Africa's most vociferous critics among the Afro-Asian group in any position to weaken the power base of the dominant white minority, and this remained the case even after 1960, despite the large increase in the number of independent African states. Militarily speaking, these states lacked the resources for any conventional operation against the Republic which had always enjoyed the protection of a vast buffer strip of white-ruled territory between its own boundaries and those of potential enemies to the north. Second, in the absence of any significant trade links, their leaders were unable to utilize economic pressures on a scale sufficient to weaken the confidence of the white electorate in the rightness of its government's policies.[1]

Thus the hard facts of geography and economics, coupled with the critical inability of South Africa's major critics to translate verbal assault into concrete action, gave the government a degree of security which was less evident to those for whom ideological isolation was a symbol of real and damaging insecurity. Indeed, it could be argued that South Africa's external position seemed more precarious than it really was precisely because its policies were exposed to continuous public scrutiny at the United Nations, at Commonwealth conferences, and in the world's press. Nor did the public response of South African spokesmen to these attacks do very much to dispel the image of a small embattled power desperately trying to keep its opponents at bay. This was the peculiar contribution of the late Mr. Eric Louw, the minister of external affairs from 1955 to 1963, whose diplomatic style combined an aggressive defense of his country's policies with vigorous counterattacks on the shortcomings of his critics. His widely reported confrontations with his opponents at the United Nations and elsewhere might be described as an overreaction to the prevailing ideological climate, rather than a strict barometer of South Africa's capacity to hold its own course despite the abuse heaped upon its domestic policies. Moreover, in view of the events that followed the Sharpeville shootings in March 1960 and the circumstances surrounding South Africa's withdrawal from the Commonwealth a year later, the contemporary observer could be excused for believing that the days of the apartheid regime were numbered and that progressive isolation in the external sphere would inevitably have damaging repercussions internally. Indeed, the British prime minister, Harold Macmillan, contributed to this mood of impending apocalypse with his "wind of change" speech in Cape Town a month before Sharpeville occurred, stessing the need for white South Africa to come to terms with the fact of African nationalism within and beyond its borders. At the same time he implied that in the future Britain would increasingly be forced to withdraw its traditional support for South Africa in the world's forums.

South Africa's departure form the Commonwealth, however, did not have the damaging consequences which the government's opponents had predicted in the early 1960s. As Professor D. W. Krüger has aptly remarked, "Not everyone grasped at once that the links with Whitehall would be severed, but those with Manchester and Stratford-upon-Avon maintained intact."[2] The new Republic might appear more isolated than before, but the fact remained that the termination of the "special relationship" with Britain had important implications for South Africa's role in the southern third of the African continent. On the domestic front, a contentious issue of long standing was at last settled as both English- and Afrikaans-speaking South Africans began to recognize that a degree of national unity was essential to cope with a difficult future in which they could no longer rely upon British support.[3] As Britain withdrew from its remaining responsibilities in Southern Africa, white South Africans began to realize, however dimly, that their country was, for better or worse, an African power and no longer the "offshoot of a European-dominated continent."[4] The words of a perceptive South African commentator summarize the dawning recognition of the new role the Republic saw for itself in the very different circumstances of the 1960s:

> The White man's status and authority in South Africa had their origin in, and until the revolution of the last two derived support from, Western European hegemony.
>
> This is now past. In less than twenty years European influence and European institutions have disappeared north of the Zambesi, leaving little more than a street name here or there to bear witness to their erstwhile presence. And we have remained behind. Have remained behind in Africa. We have become, whatever the history of colonialism may have been, an African plant whose existence and future will depend on how we adapt ourselves to Africa.[5]

Yet it would be a mistake to overemphasize the novelty of this particular aspiration to be a regional power. In the interwar period, General Jan C. Smuts had nursed a vague ambition to project South Africa's influence beyond the Limpopo River but, following the abortive campaign to entice Rhodesia into the Union of South Africa in the early 1920s, little had been achieved beyond a modest degree of technical and economic cooperation with British-ruled Central Africa. In the 1950s, however, Mr. Eric Louw returned to this theme on a number of occasions, stressing the advantages that would accrue to independent Africa from a policy of coexistence with the Republic.[6] The latter, it was argued, was well placed to make a major contribution to the economic progress of the new states. South Africa possessed the resources and expertise necessary for the task and, more important, a unique fund of experience derived from decades of involvement with the administration and development of the Bantu "homelands."

At this stage, however, a policy of cooperation with independent Africa south of the Sahara was primarily viewed in the wider framework of South Africa's traditional links with the Western nations on the grounds that it "would enable the Union to act as a permanent link between the Western nations, on the one hand, and the populations of Africa South of the Sahara on the other."[7] It was never very clear, however, how this "link" was to operate in practice; it is possible that what Mr. Louw and others had in mind was a role in terms of which South Africa, acting as an "informal" member of the Western Alliance, would pose as the guardian of Western interests in the area as a whole, guaranteeing its military security from Communist infiltration, and partly relieving the West of its commitment to develop the region economically. In this way South Africa would, it was believed, make an indispensable contribution to the effective prosecution of the cold war and in the process enhance its value as a partner in the global task of countering Communist expansion.

Yet, despite constant reiteration of South Africa's willingness to help in the work of developing the economies of its poorer neighbors, the "Africa" policy which Mr. Louw enunciated achieved little in practice. Its rhetorical overtones had, however, some value in the domestic context to the extent that the rejection of this policy by opponents in the independent African states of the early 1960s was interpreted by white opinion as additional evidence of the outside world's blind and unreasoning refusal to recognize the merits of South Africa's policies. Nor were the Western Powers prepared to encourage South Africa's aspirations to become a regional power; throughout the 1950s and the early 1960s these states were locked in a struggle with the Communist bloc for the support of the Third World, and any overt support for South Africa in this context was deemed counterproductive and likely to weaken Western influence and prestige in the uncommitted states. By contrast, South Africa, despite protestations of its indispensability to the West, could not turn this to bargaining advantage, for its government, given its pronounced anti-Communist bias, was hardly in a position to opt for a more neutralist stance in foreign policy.

The Change in the Internal and External Environment

By the mid 1960s, however, the isolation of the Republic's position on the continent of Africa began to break down. A number of factors contributed to this change in South Africa's position, confirming for many the wisdom of Mr. Louw's belief, expressed on many occasions in the 1950s and early 1960s, that the hostile attitude of the African states was "a passing phase and [that] improvement would come in time."[8] First, the high expectations of radical change in the white South entertained by critics of South Africa, which reached a climax in 1960, were rapidly dissipated as many of the African states began to show signs of increasing instability.[9] The military governments that succeeded to power in several of these states were more inward-looking than their civilian predecessors; similarly, their foreign policies tended to be conservative, deemphasizing the revolutionary and Pan-African sentiment characteristic of the immediate postindependence period. In Western capitals, a disillusion with the haphazard pace of African advance strengthened the conviction of those who had always been skeptical about the efficacy of tough measures against the Republic and made the maintenance of the status quo in South Africa seem all the more attractive to governments which had heretofore resisted the pressure of the Afro-Asian states to embark on sanctions and similar policies. The bargaining position of independent Africa was weakened still further by the slackening of cold war tension between the Soviet Union and the United States following the resolution of the Cuban missile crisis in 1962, and the traditional competition for the allegiance of the Third World declined in priority for decision makers of both superpowers. America's growing involvement in Vietnam appears to have diverted attention and concern from Africa's problems, while the failure to resolve the worsening Middle East crisis and the continued closure of the Suez Canal greatly enhanced the value of the Republic's ports and harbors to Western shipping interests.

Second, the granting of independence to the three former High Commission Territories meant, in effect, that the "imperial factor"—which had for so long bedeviled relations between Britain and South Africa whenever the future of the Territories was discussed—was at last removed. The Republic was now presented with the long-awaited opportunity to demonstrate in a practical way its commitment to coexistence and its willingness to aid the social and economic development of its poorer neighbors. A third and compelling factor was the Unilateral Declaration of Independence by the Smith regime in Rhodesia on November 11, 1965. This, as we shall see later in this chapter, was to affect the smooth implementation of the "outward-looking" policy in the long term. In the short term, however, the failure of sanctions to bring the relatively weak economy of Rhodesia to its knees in "weeks rather than months" (as the British prime minister expressed it) was interpreted as a highly favorable portent for the Republic. Finally, we must mention South Africa's "technical" victory in the long-drawn-out South West Africa case at the International Court of Justice. This was interpreted by government spokesmen as providing yet further evidence of the Republic's immunity from the threat of intervention; moreover, it enhanced the prestige of the government in the eyes of the white electorate. Against all odds, South Africa appeared to have gambled and won, and the UN stood revealed as impotent.

But perhaps more important than these four changes in South Africa's external environment were a number of internal developments which by 1966 had combined to produce a mood of confidence and optimism on the part of the electorate. First, the economy had by this time amply demonstrated its powers of recovery after the dark months of 1960, and a boom of major proportions, involving an annual growth rate of 8 percent, bore striking testimony to the efficiency of the government's management in this respect. Second, the internal security of the state had been enhanced by a series of crippling blows struck at the nonwhite opposition movements whose sporadic attempts at sabotage and terrorism in the early 1960s had provided the government with the justification for its harsh and repressive legislation, irrespective of the damage this might inflict on an already weakened structure of civil liberties. Supplementing this policy of intimidation was a thoroughgoing reorganization and expansion of South Africa's armed forces involving the introduction of conscription, the adoption of a counter insurgency strategy, and a considerable increase in defense expenditure.[10] The optimism of the government was shared by the electorate and, in effect, the visible evidence of stability and prosperity confirmed its view that "guns and butter" need not be mutually exclusive alternatives.

This combination of internal and external factors, together with the removal of the republican issue from domestic interparty strife accelerated the decline of the traditional animosity between Boer and Briton, as both language groups supported their government's policy of capitalizing upon this new-found flexibility in the field of foreign policy. South Africa, it was claimed, was now in an admirable position to jettison its defensive position and to adopt a policy more in keeping with its real status as a power on the African continent. The time had come to exert the authority and influence which was the Republic's objec-

tive—indeed, its right—as an African power.[11]

At this point we turn to a detailed analysis of the extent to which South Africa has succeeded in establishing economic and political links with independent Africa. Given this analysis, it will then be possible to examine the assumptions on which the policy is based, the chances of its long-term success, the domestic implications of such a policy within the Republic, and the degree to which military developments in Rhodesia, Angola, and Mozambique have proved to be assets or liabilities to the implementation of such a policy.

The "Outward" Policy in Practice

RELATIONS WITH THE FORMER HIGH COMMISSION TERRITORIES

The formal inauguration of a new phase in South Africa's foreign policy was marked by a visit by Prime Minister Leabua Jonathan of Lesotho to Pretoria on September 3, 1966—a month before his country achieved independence from colonial rule. The South African government reciprocated by sending representatives to the independence celebrations of all three territories and, in the case of Botswana, withdrew its ban on Sir Seretse Khama, the new president, as a prohibited immigrant. President Khama, however, has tended to be circumspect in his dealings with the South African government as distinct from private interests such as the Anglo-American Company, which is currently involved with Roan Selection Trust, a British-based company, in preparatory exploration of Botswana's mineral resources. His caution and discretion in official contact with the South African authorities contrasts markedly with Prime Minister Jonathan's zealousness, despite vigorous protests from the opposition Lesotho Congress party, in encouraging a wide range of private and public contacts with the Republic.

It is quite significant that there are a number of senior South African civil servants on loan to the Lesotho government, filling key posts such as those of chief justice, attorney general, and chief electoral officer. Other examples of official support include donations of grain for famine relief, technical assistance from the South African Wool Board, and use of the South African air force to airlift food and fodder to areas affected by drought. On the unofficial level, the Orange Free State farmers have plowed the fields of their counterparts in Lesotho, the South African Volunteer Service has been active in Lesotho, and Dr. Anton Rupert (a prominent Afrikaner industrialist) has been appointed to act as economic adviser to the Lesotho government. But the most important development has been the Republic's agreement in principle to the construction of the Oxbow hydroelectric scheme for the exploitation of Lesotho's considerable water supplies; these supplies are Lesotho's only national resource of any significance. The sale of water and power to the Republic would clearly make a valuable contribution to Lesotho's revenue, and the funds made available could be used to promote development in other sectors of the Lesotho economy.[12]

By contrast, Swaziland has far more raw materials than the other two former High Commission Territories; indeed, the contribution of private South African capital to the exploitation of the asbestos and iron ore deposits has been a marked feature of the postwar period. The role of white farmers there, many of them South African, has been of critical importance in the modernization of the country's agriculture.[13] Official assistance to date has included an agreement with the Republic in terms of which South African experts will participate in the local administration. As the richest of the three new states in Southern Africa, Swaziland has marginally more room to maneuver than either Lesotho or Botswana. Less dependent on the Republic, especially with regard to labor migration, the Swaziland government has attempted to diversify its trading pattern, and Kenya and Zambia have already agreed to take a proportion of the country's beef and sugar production.[14] Botswana, too, sends a small amount of its beef exports to Zambia and the Congo (Kinshasa), and Sir Seretse is determined to widen the range of aid donors for his country's development. Scandinavia, Canada, and Nationalist China have all made aid contributions, but the general effect of these efforts to reduce significantly the dependence on South Africa must not be exaggerated. It is true that, although none of the three states has so far exchanged diplomatic representatives with its powerful neighbor, official visits to Pretoria at the civil servant and ministerial level have been assiduously cultivated and maximum publicity is given to both formal and informal contacts.

Yet were all these developments really so very surprising? After all, the economic integration of these states with South Africa has been a brutal, inescapable fact of life ever since the creation of the Union in 1910; their admission to formal independent status could not significantly affect this critical dependence and, given Britain's traditional indifference to their poverty and backwardness, their leaders have had little alternative but to bargain for the best terms of coexistence they could get. Thus, as enclaves within white-dominated South Africa, Lesotho, and Swaziland, in particular, have served as useful testing grounds for the implementation of the "outward-looking" policy of the Republic. This is particularly true in the case of Lesotho, where Prime Minister Jonathan's welcome for South Africa's assistance, symbolized by his state visit of early 1967, must be seen as the long-delayed, but inevitable, political expression of a traditional and well-established economic relationship. Thus the benefits that accrued to the Republic were ideological rather than political—at least in the short term. They were ideological because the spectacle in the early months of 1967 of an African prime minister being received on South African soil with the elaborate trappings of a great state occasion was interpreted as a major breakthrough for South African diplomacy. The wall of isolation surrounding the Republic had at last been dented and Jonathan's enthusiasm for closer links with Pretoria was hailed as tangible proof of South Africa's willingness to live in peace with its black neighbors, cooperating with them in matters of common concern, despite the very real differences of principle underlying the political and social organization of their societies.

Moreover, in the domestic arena the ruling National party was quick to capitalize on its new initiatives as both opposition parties and the English-language press praised the achievement of the government in taking the diplomatic offensive.[15] Henceforth foreign policy, it was claimed, need no longer be exclusively concerned with keeping the apocalypse at bay, with a negative and rigid defense of apartheid at the international level. Rather, there was the possibility of restoring foreign relations to a more normal and orthodox basis, as had existed before 1948.

At this early stage in implementation of the new policy, welcome support came from Dr. Robert Gardiner, the Ghanian executive secretary of the United Nations Economic Commission for Africa (ECA). Shortly after a visit to the former High Commission Territories in March 1967, he argued in a press conference at Addis Ababa that the "economic integration" of these states with the Republic was "necessary and desirable" provided that it was based on mutual respect. He also suggested that the Republic be invited to rejoin the ECA, from which it had been suspended in 1963.[16]

RELATIONS WITH MALAWI

The most dramatic manifestation of the "outward-looking" policy came in March 1967, with the visit to Pretoria of three Malawian cabinet ministers and the signing of a trade pact between Malawi and South Africa.[17] This was followed shortly by an agreement to exchange diplomatic representatives. This link with a Central African state is the cornerstone of the new policy and its creation obviously owes much to Dr. Kamuzu Banda's belief that

> being a good African does not mean cutting your economic throat. . . . I have to be realistic. Colonial geography and history are against us. We cannot boycott South Africa, Rhodesia, or Portuguese Mozambique—that would mean the breakdown of Malawi's economy.[18]

This display of economic realism by an African head of state reinforced the traditional South African belief that economic self-interest of the African states would ultimately triumph over ideological considerations.[19]

In Dr. Banda's case, the conversion from being a vigorous opponent of colonialism to the friend and trading partner of the apartheid regime occurred within two years after his country had received its independence. In 1966 his government accepted a $8.4 million contribution from the Republic of South Africa for the financing of a sugar mill; other agreements followed in 1968. Malawi accepted a South African loan of $11.2 million to build a new capital at Lilongwe in the northern part of the country. Underlying this decision to transfer the capital was the belief that a new growth point was required to stimulate economic development in the central region of Malawi. In addition, South African assistance in the form of $15.4 million grant has been forthcoming for the construction of a railway line to give Malawi a second outlet to the sea at the Mozambique port of Nacala.[20] Agreement on these major items of aid has stimulated assistance at the unofficial level in a variety of ways, including visits by South Africa chambers of commerce and so forth.

Apart from the material advantages that South Africa anticipates from the economic penetration of a friendly African state, there is the added implicit expectation that President Banda will defend the interests of the Republic in international forums, such as the Organization of African Unity and the United Nations. Denied access to the former, the South African government gains a marginal diplomatic advantage when Dr. Banda extolls the positive advantages to be gained from cooperation with the Republic; moreover, its isolation in the General Assembly of the United Nations has been somewhat offset by the willingness of Malawi and the three former High Commission Territories to vote against, or at least abstain on, resolutions hostile to South African interests.[21] In this context, Larry Bowman's observation is particularly apposite. Referring to Pretoria's relations with these four African states and the embryonic structure of diplomatic and economic cooperation emerging in the region as a whole, he noted that

> because of South Africa's long-standing position as the pariah of the world community,

> both her friends and enemies have generally been reluctant to be publicly associated with her. It is a political change worthy of some comment that neighboring countries (both black and white) are now prepared to interact more openly with the South African government.[22]

Yet, granting that the evolving relationship with Malawi represents an important coup for South African diplomacy and one which ten years ago would have been considered highly improbable by many political analysts, it should be stressed that, as in the case of the former high Commission Territories, the Republic's success should be interpreted as political manipulation of its economic dominance in the region as a whole.[23] That the Republic has at least been able to take advantage of this dominance is, as we suggested earlier, an indication of the favorable changes that have occurred within its immediate and global environment.

RELATIONS WITH PORTUGUESE AFRICA

Traditionally, South Africa and Portugal have always maintained friendly relations, although, in the case of Angola, this has entailed minimal economic cooperation.[24] From the political standpoint, South Africa could always count on Portugal's vote at the United Nations, especially during the lonely years of the 1950s, but beyond this demonstration of diplomatic solidarity there was very little attempt to coordinate policy within the region. This was hardly surprising given the ideological gulf which—in formal terms, at any rate—separated the two governments in respect to their policies for African advancement.

Following the outbreak of revolutionary war against the Portuguese in Angola in 1961, South Africa's relative indifference to developments in Angola and Mozambique changed dramatically. The possible loss of Angola and Mozambique to nationalist African control was regarded as a direct threat to the security of the Republic's strategic perimeter and meant, in effect, the possible conquest of the buffer area traditionally protecting South Africa from continental African nationalist envelopment. This meant that the Republic's control of South West Africa would be jeopardized, although African control of Angola was less dangerous than that of Mozambique, the boundaries of which are shared with the Eastern Transvaal, Swaziland, and the predominantly African areas of northern Natal.

As the Portuguese poured men and resources into their struggle to defeat the insurgents in both territories, the identification of the South African national interest with that of the Salazar regime in Lisbon became increasingly evident in ministerial pronouncements. In 1964, for instance, the South African foreign minister, Dr. Hilgard Muller, stated that both countries shared the same attachment to Africa and had an unbreakable determination to remain there for the good of the local population and in defense of Western interests generally. Likewise, the Portuguese foreign minister, Dr. Franco Nogueira, observed that "the two countries have considerable opportunities for technical and economic development [which] . . . call for collaboration in a determined spirit."[25] By 1969 there was considerable evidence of this "collaboration," particularly in the economic sphere; Portugal's efforts to stimulate economic development in Angola and Mozambique offered South African entrepreneurs innumerable tempting opportunities. Thus both governments have agreed to participate in the construction of three major hydroelectric projects: Cabora Bassa in northern Mozambique; Ruacana Falls on the Angola–South West Africa border; and the Kunene River scheme in the same area. South Africa has promised to take the entire initial output of 1,200 megawatts from the first of these projects, the building of which will be the responsibility of the Anglo-American Corporation at a cost estimated to be $231 million for the first phase of construction. The scheme is likely to bring considerable economic benefits to Mozambique. The effects of the recession, induced by the application of United Nations sanctions against Rhodesia, will, it is hoped, be overcome as the Cabora Bassa development makes possible the settlement of a million new settlers in the area, a vast expansion of the land under cultivation, and the exploitation of iron, coal, and other mineral resources. Similar benefits are alleged to be likely from the other two projects.[26]

Apart from this cooperation in the hydroelectric sphere, South Africa has also been attracted by the lure of Angolan oil, produced in Cabinda, a Portuguese enclave north of the Congo River. Current estimates suggest that by 1970 some 7.5 million tons will be produced, sufficient to meet 40 percent of Southern Africa's total requirements.[27] The importance of this commercial link cannot be underestimated, given South Africa's present vulnerability to world sanctions and the desperate search which the government encouraged throughout the 1960s to make the Republic as self-sufficient as possible in this crucial raw material. Finally, the growing cooperation between the two countries was given symbolic recognition by the opening of an underwater cable between Cape Town and Lisbon on February 18, 1969, which Prime Minister Vorster —perhaps echoing the language of Dr. Christian Barnard—described as reducing "the six thousand miles that separates South Africa from Portugal to the space of a heartbeat."[28]

Despite pressure from certain elements within the South African military elite, so far there has been no attempt to underpin the Republic's economic links with Portuguese Africa with large-scale military assistance against the insurgents. The establishment of an "Unholy Alliance" between the three white regimes of Southern Africa—the Republic, Portugal, and Rhodesia—has often been predicted by their opponents, although the evidence of a specific military commitment to Portugal by the Republic has been impressionistic, or at least partisan.[29] South Africa's hesitation to offer Portugal military support in Angola in the early 1960s was explicable on the grounds that at the time it was commonly believed that Portugal could not sustain a lengthy counterinsurgency campaign without crippling effects on its domestic economy. If the French were not able to hold Algeria, what guarantee was there that Portugal, a much weaker power in military terms and a nation plagued with severe economic problems at home, could maintain its grip on the overseas provinces? On the basis of a rational calculation of its interests as construed at that time, South Africa could derive no advantage from assisting a government militarily weaker and likely to be forced into a settlement as Pan-African pressure was increased and the drain on Portuguese resources became acute. Furthermore, direct military intervention by the Republic would be construed by its enemies as the start of a "race war" and would provide them with legal and moral justification for the assertion that apartheid was indeed a threat to international peace and security.

Since 1967, however, Pretoria's lack of confidence in Portuguese efforts has been replaced by an optimistic belief that the latter's judicious combination of military and economic skills will in the long run suffice to crush the liberation movement. Hence the Republic's willingness to support and underwrite Portugal's development of Angola and Mozambique on the assumption that this will be an effective substitute for direct military aid. Yet in recent years South African spokesmen have been far less inhibited about discussing the security implications of a struggle in the Portuguese colonies. Part of the explanation for this change in the mood of Pretoria lies in the fact that the investment projects the government is backing in Angola and Mozambique are conceivably vulnerable to African nationalist assaults. Especially is this true of Cabora Bassa, which lies seventy miles from the Zambian border in an area which has already suffered severely from guerrilla attack; the projected eight hundred-mile stretch of power line is, therefore, an obvious target for the FRELIMO forces.[30] By the same token, the Cabinda oilfield might be similarly threatened.

The concern felt by some members of the ruling elite in South Africa was well expressed in a statement by Mr. Theo Gerdener, the former administrator of Natal, in November 1967. He contrasted the massive Portuguese expenditure in men and resources to hold its empire intact with South African military preparations, pointing out that "the Portuguese had to keep five soldiers in the field for every one soldier in the whole of the South African Permanent Force."[31] Shortly after visiting Mozambique in July 1968, Mr. Gerdener argued that the Republic would have to do far more in the future to show its appreciation to those who were "throwing everything into the struggle to free Southern Africa of terrorists."[32] These words were echoed by Sir de Villiers Graaff, leader of the United party opposition, in April 1968; he claimed that "Portugal was fighting South Africa's battles" and stressed the need for nonmilitary help from the Republic.[33]

Government spokesmen were quick to respond to these accusations of indifference. In May 1968, Prime Minister Vorster emphasized his government's recognition of the fact that the guerrillas' ultimate target was the Republic, while Mr. P. W. Botha, the minister of defense, was quick to point out that

> South Africa has an interest in what happens in Angola and Mozambique. . . . The onslaughts there are aimed at the Republic in the final instance. About that we can have no illusions. In the words already said by myself and the Prime Minister, I say "true friends need no signed treaties."[34]

Finally, the possibility that formal military links might be established was suggested by both the tour Lt. General C. A. Fraser of the Joint South African Combat Forces took to the combat areas of Mozambique in January 1969 and the discussion that took place in Pretoria in February 1969 between General Rebelo, the Portuguese minister of defense, and his opposite number in South Africa. "Matters of importance to both countries" were discussed and stress was laid on the contribution of both countries to the defense of the Free World in guaranteeing "the gateway to the East."[35]

RELATIONS WITH RHODESIA AND ZAMBIA

These relationships have been transformed by the Unilateral Declaration of Independence (UDI) of Mr. Ian Smith's government on November 11, 1965. In the years before this critical event, Rhodesia and South Africa had been closely linked by ties of trade and commerce but, as in the case of the Portuguese territories, there was a notable reluctance to extend these links by military or

political means. Closer political union with a predominantly English-speaking territory had never had much attraction for Afrikaner nationalists in the interwar period, and this aversion was reinforced in the years after 1945 by the seemingly different pattern of race relations that appeared to be emerging in South Africa's northern neighbor. Doctrines of multiracialism and "partnership" ran contrary to the Union's commitment to segregation as an instrument of social and political control and, apart from these ideological differences, South Africa had little to gain in either strategic or political terms from the incorporation of a tiny white minority. Certainly the government had no wish to increase the size of the large African majority already under its jurisdiction.

Since UDI, however, the Republic's economic and military links with a beleaguered Rhodesia have been considerably strengthened. Public sympathy with the plight of their fellow whites across the Limpopo, coupled with a hardheaded appreciation of the dangerous precedent that a successful sanctions campaign against the Smith regime would constitute for the Republic, compelled its leaders to extend their economic links beyond the maintenance of "normal" trade as asserted by Mr. Vorster in the early stages of the crisis. South African middlemen handle the great bulk of Rhodesian trade. In 1965 South Africa and Mozambique accepted 26 percent of Rhodesia's exports; in 1969 the proportion was estimated to be as high as 85 percent.[36] In addition, throughout the period since UDI the South African Central Bank has made several loans of foreign exchange available to the Smith regime. And, with the closing of the Beira-Rhodesia import route following the imposition of sanctions in December 1965, Rhodesia has had to rely increasingly on oil supplies by road from the Republic and by rail from Lourenço Marques. South Africa's economic goodwill is, therefore, crucial to Rhodesia's continued survival.

Late in 1967, however, South African policy toward Rhodesia moved beyond economic assistance with the decision of the government to send police units to help the Rhodesian security forces in their campaign against African guerrilla forces operating in the Zambesi Valley. The effect of this move was to exacerbate the already strained relations between South Africa and Zambia. It is clear from official announcements that the Republic's leaders in the past have envisaged an important role for Zambia, both in the context of regional economic cooperation and security needs of Southern Africa as a whole.[37] After South Africa, Zambia is the most economically powerful state in the area, while South Africa has always been an important source of imports and a supplier of the capital required to extract the copper and mineral resources of Zambia. Moreover, Zambian dependence on the Republic increased dramatically after UDI; for example, its imports from the latter rose from $58 million in 1965 to $120 million in 1967 as Zambia attempted to reduce its traditional dependence upon Rhodesia.[38] Before 1965 Zambia's reliance on its southern neighbor was almost complete. Its copper was exported by Rhodesia, its coal was exclusively imported from Rhodesia, the power it required for its industries was produced by the Kariba hydroelectric scheme, and altogether some 40 percent of all its import requirements (excluding oil) were supplied by Rhodesia.[39]

The effect of the crisis was to reinforce President Kaunda's determination to avoid becoming an economic hostage of the white South. His government, therefore, began to seek alternative sources of supply for Zambia's raw material needs and to devise new communication links to bypass those that traditionally operated via Rhodesia and South Africa. Oil, for example, was initially imported by road and air from Dar es Salaam, but a new pipeline has recently been completed. UDI also stimulated the exploitation of local coal resources and Zambia's power needs, it is hoped, will be met by the construction of the Kafue hydroelectric project. Imports from Rhodesia have been cut from 98 percent in 1964 to 75 percent in 1968, while over two-thirds of Zambian exports of copper by 1967 were being rerouted through Angola, Mozambique, and Tanzania.[40] Obviously, the construction of the much-discussed Tanzam railroad would make an enormous difference to the pattern of Zambian trade, especially if this were followed by membership in the East African Economic Community.

Notwithstanding the increased dependence of Zambia on the Republic since UDI, which has encouraged the South African government to believe that it is only a matter of time before President Kaunda eschews ideology to follow the realistic line of President Banda, the Rhodesian counterinsurgency operation in which South African units are engaged has tended to diminish the political and diplomatic value of the network of economic links that at present bind the two countries. In the long term it may indeed negate it altogether. There is no sign of any willingness on President Kaunda's part to transform these links with South Africa from short-term expedients into the full-scale diplomatic and economic cooperation that exists between Malawi and the Republic. Nor is the prospect of mutual accommodation enhanced by the periodic threats of South African cabinet ministers to retaliate against Zambia for harboring guerrillas and for encouraging instability throughout the region.[41] There can be no doubt that President Kaunda, whose country has already experienced Portuguese air raids on border villages, feels vulnerable to an "Israeli-type" reaction from the Republic. This explains his attempt in July 1968 to purchase a ground-to-air missile system from the United Kingdom.[42]

RELATIONS WITH OTHER AFRICAN STATES

In the last three years the Republic has attempted to extend its range of contacts with several African states beyond those in its immediate locale. Dr. Hilgard Muller, the South African foreign minister, pointed out in a speech to the House of Assembly on May 30th, 1968, that:

> . . . persons from quite a number of African states are continually paying visits here. I want to point out that as far as official visits are concerned, an average of more than three such official visits from various African states were paid to South Africa per month in the past 12 months, while an average of more than four official visits from South Africa were paid to various African states per month. However, that is not all. During the past 12 months there were no fewer than 136 cases of Ministers from African states either visiting or passing through the Republic and making contact with us.[43]

The government of Malagasay sent an official delegation to Pretoria in 1968, and the air lines of both countries agreed to establish a link between Tananarive and Johannesburg in 1969. In the same year a team of South African experts visited Malagasay to report on the feasibility of constructing a major tourist resort development scheme. The promotion of formal diplomatic and economic links with Malagasay would clearly ease the way to the establishment of similar links with other Francophone states, and Gabon, Chad, and Upper Volta have been mentioned as possibilities.[44]

The Risks and Rewards of the "Outward-Looking" Policy

South Africa's foreign policy—like that of any other state in international society—tends to combine ideological justification with a realistic appreciation of the security needs of the state and the opportunities available for their satisfaction. The new policy toward independent Africa has been presented by the government as an expression of its deeply felt concern with the plight of its poorer neighboring states for whose welfare South Africa, because it is already highly industrialized and has considerable reserves of capital and technical skills, has a special responsibility. At times official pronouncements have a missionary, if not old-fashioned imperialist, ring about them.

Prime Minister Vorster, speaking in Nigel, South Africa, in early November 1968, declared that:

> We have a measure of self-interest—and I do not attempt to hide this—in the development and prosperity of Africa, but it is not self-interest alone that motivates us.
>
> We have a sense of mission in respect of Africa. In addition, providence has been very good to us in Africa and we want to return to Africa something of this.
>
> This is the spirit that inspires us—and this is the spirit that will conquer Africa.[45]

Phrased in these terms, the policy has clearly made an appeal to the younger generation of Afrikaner nationalists, many of whom are attracted by the prospect of voluntary work in nations such as Lesotho. More important, however, in the government's calculations (and one reason for the ideological connotation given to the policy) has been the necessity of explaining the new policy to its rank-and-file supporters. In the 1950s these supporters were repeatedly offered an interpretation of events north of the Limpopo which stressed the political and economic inadequacy of the new states, their role as pawns in the Communist conspiracy against South Africa, and the corruption of their leaders. The recent defection of the *verkrampte* (inward-looking) wing of the National party is indicative of a profound dissatisfaction with the "outward" foreign policy among at least a minority of government supporters. For these the "liberalism" of the late Dr. Verwoerd and his successor has always been suspect. Nor are they likely to be mollified by the construction of diplomatic suburbs in Cape Town and Pretoria to insulate black envoys against the indignities of apartheid because the presence of nonwhite representatives from the outside world —whether visiting Maori rugby players or African diplomats—is regarded by the *verkrampte* Afrikaner as a fundamental departure from traditional South African mores. Thus the *verkramptes* acknowledge no distinction between the assumptions underlying domestic policy, on the one hand, and the claims of foreign policy, on the other hand. Mr. Vorster's attempts to befriend black African states are seen as ill-conceived efforts to apply the pernicious doctrine of multiracialism in the external realm, a deviation from past practice which in their view will inevitably have damaging repercussions on domestic policy.

On a more mundane level of ideological justification, however, the emphasis is laid on the notion of harmonious relations with African states on the basis of "tolerance and mutual respect, the recognition of the sovereign independence of all states and non-interference in each other's domestic affairs."[46] Superficially, this appears to be a repetition of the language employed by South African delegates at the United Nations in the 1950s when there was little alternative to a reliance on legal nostrums, such as the sanctity of domestic jurisdiction. In the context of the late 1960s, however, these statements of principle have acquired a new and practical significance. Crucial to the success of the new policy must be a recognition on the part of the Republic's African neighbors that differences in domestic policy—involving as they do in this case fundamentally opposed views on the moral validity of racial discrimination and the right to self-determination on a majority rule basis—need not constitute a major impediment to economic and diplomatic cooperation.

"Liberalism abroad, repression at home" may seem a rather tendentious description of South Africa's new stance in external relations, but it is a convenient shorthand description of current policy and in particular the emphasis on the need for "tolerance and mutual respect" between the various states in the region. For obvious reasons if South Africa is to survive in its present form, it cannot afford any massive relaxation of the apartheid system and the bureaucratic and military structures underpinning it. Although the merits of the Bantustan policy as a long-term solution to the political and economic aspirations of the nonwhite population are examined in another chapter, it should be stressed here that a central feature of such a policy is the assumption that the increasing number of Africans living in the urban and rural areas of "white South Africa" cannot expect a change in their status as "temporary sojourners" with all that this particular phrase implies in terms of racial discrimination coupled with intensive government regulation of their everyday existence.

Moreover, the stress laid on the "recognition of the sovereign independence of all states" suggests South Africa's concern for gaining recognition for its peculiarly constituted statehood—a claim which, by implication, has never been accepted by South Africa's hostile critics at the United Nations and elsewhere. To comply with the demands of these critics to end apartheid has always been regarded by the white majority as constituting an invitation to commit national suicide. Hence the importance attached to obtaining that degree of elementary recognition by the world community, the lack of which in the past has given South Africa a unique position in international politics. Viewed in this light, it is not surprising that Mr. Vortser's foreign policy achievements—limited as they are at this stage to friendly, yet cautious cooperation with states with a long tradition of "client" status—have been hailed by the South African press and public alike as a "dramatic breakthrough" after nearly two decades of isolation.

The potential rewards have been construed as more than purely ideological, however. In the local context of Southern Africa, acceptance of the Republic's "legitimacy"—symbolized by a continuous process of diplomatic and economic interaction—will, it is claimed, lead in time to even greater recognition both by Africa and the world as a whole of the Republic's role as a regional power, guaranteeing the security of the area and actively promoting its economic development. Success on these terms would remove the specter of external intervention against South Africa on the grounds that a higher degree of economic integration among the units of the system would make it difficult to isolate the Republic for punitive action without doing damage to the economies of neighboring states.[47] Finally, the stress placed upon "sovereign independence" illustrates South Africa's obvious interest in avoiding accusations of neocolonial behavior in its relations with the new states. As Prime Minister Vorster emphasized in an interview in 1966, "We wish to avoid the dangers of neo-colonialism in any pattern of assistance which may be agreed upon, but we expect in return a recognition of our own sovereignty within our borders."[48]

The assertion of the principle of "non-interference in each other's domestic affairs" has been a traditional response of South Africa's foreign policymakers in the postwar period, but it has acquired a peculiar relevance in the context of an "outward-looking" policy. "Non-interference" in this context means more than abstaining from criticism of each other's domestic arrangements; it implies a tacit agreement not to encourage the subversion and ultimate destruction of neighboring states. Hence the welcome given to the cooperative attitude of the governments of the former High Commission Territories in dealing with refugee elements, who are alleged to be using the territory of these states as bases for infiltration and violent action against the Republic;[49] hence the hostility directed at the Zambian government for permitting guerrilla forces to operate from within its borders against the white regimes in the South.

In accordance with this principle, the South African government has emphasized that its military forces will operate on the territory of a neighboring state only when requested to do so by the government of that state. Referring to the African nationalist guerrilla threat in Rhodesia and the Portuguese colonies, Prime Minister Vorster stated categorically that "we are good friends and good friends do not need an agreement to combat murderers. Good friends know what their duty is when their neighbour's house is on fire. . . . We shall act in any country where we are asked to act by the government of that country."[50] However, a recent exchange between President Kaunda and Prime Minister Vorster over the vexed question of Zambian sanctuary for guerrilla forces suggests that in certain circumstances the Republic would ignore its self-imposed rule of noninterference without invitation from the host state.[51] Nevertheless, Prime Minister Vorster has been careful not to define the limits beyond which the principle of noninterference would no longer apply and military retaliation undertaken because of hostile acts committed by a neighboring state. It is reasonable to infer that South Africa would retaliate only in circumstances of the direst necessity; clearly the guerrilla threat to South Africa, serious as it may be, has so far not developed to a stage justifying a preemptive attack on the Zambian sanctuary.

Moreover, given the assumptions of the outward policy, it could be argued that South Africa's real interest lies in cooperation with Zambia rather than in perpetuating the "cold war" atmosphere that characterizes their present relations.[52] The continuation of the Rhodesia impasse reduces the possibility of realizing this particular goal and in the long term may even jeopardize the success of the Republic's attempts to build a stable, prosperous regional bloc. From Prime Minister Vorster's point of view, it could plausibly be argued that a peaceful settlement of the Rhodesian issue—even if this meant an African government coming to power in Salisbury under British tutelage—might be regarded as preferable to an indefinite period of uncertainty about Rhodesia's future. The prospect is all the more attractive if the alternative is an escalation in the conflict between the Smith regime and the African insurgents, requiring an open-ended military commitment by Pretoria to protect the white minority there from those who ultimately have their sights set on the downfall of the Republic.

It is true that a settlement of the Rhodesian problem would not necessarily predispose the Zambian government to pursue a policy of friendly economic and diplomatic cooperation with the Republic, as the Malawian government has done. As we argued earlier, President Kaunda's government is making determined efforts to reduce its dependence on its white neighbors in the South and it might be difficult, if not impossible, to reverse this policy both on ideological and practical grounds—even if it were thought desirable to do so.[53] Thus the prolongation of the Rhodesian crisis, in the long run, may cost South Africa the loss of Zambia as a potential partner in the Republic's attempts to build a stable, integrated network of political and economic relations. Yet this does not make a "settlement" of the crisis any less desirable in the short run if only because of the possibility that the burden and the dangers involved in being Rhodesia's sole support might substantially diminish. That this is a possibility and no more indicates the complexity of the problems which support for Rhodesia has forced upon South Africa. A settlement on Mr. Smith's terms might well encourage, rather than discourage, guerrilla raids against Rhodesia and require an even greater military commitment by the Republic than is the case at present; a settlement on Mr. Nkomo's terms, however, might present the Republic with another candidate for inclusion in the "outward movement" or, conversely, act as a stimulus for the work of "liberating" the last remaining bastion of white supremacy.

To date, however, the Republic has successfully managed to follow a forward-looking policy in the area as a whole, combining the use of both economic and military instruments. On the assumption that prevention is better than cure, the economic development of the region is regarded as the best long-term policy for providing security, although it is recognized, as in the case of Rhodesia, that in the short term military intervention may be necessary from time to time.[54] Thus the aid offered to Malawi and to the former High Commission Territories can be interpreted as an attempt to help stabilize the region as a whole, thereby making South Africa's strategic perimeter more secure and thus avoiding the danger that conflict within these states might otherwise spill over into the Republic. Small and weak though these peripheral states are, their leaders can probably count on military assistance as well should domestic unrest get beyond their control. Indeed, it could be argued, despite South Africa's claims to the contrary, that in certain circumstances its forces would intervene without an invitation from the government concerned if, in Pretoria's view, local unrest or external intervention directly threatened its own security.[55]

However, the use of military force is a technique of last resort to be used as sparingly as possible and only in those situations where the legitimate government of a friendly state is clearly unable to contain or, preferably, to prevent threats to its integrity. This assumption has clearly operated in the context of the Republic's relations with Portuguese Africa, where the Portuguese forces have so far proved able to contain the insurgent threat without South African assistance. Many observers have been surprised by the fact that the Republic's increasing involvement in the economies of Angola and Mozambique has not led to a correspondingly military participation in the counterinsurgency campaigns in both territories. Yet South Africa's economic assistance does have a strategic dimension insofar as it might be interpreted as the political and ideological component

of a major counterinsurgency campaign, the military burden of which is borne exclusively at this stage by the Portuguese ally. At the same time it enables Pretoria to demonstrate both to the Portuguese and to its own more vociferous supporters at home that the Portuguese are not being left isolated to defend "white civilization" in Southern Africa.

Moreover, the economic links binding the two countries have the long-term aim of promoting effective regional economic cooperation in terms of which South Africa as well as neighboring states like Malawi will gain tangible material benefits.[56] In the Republic's case, these benefits would be measured in terms of access to hitherto untapped sources of water, power, outlets for investment capital and, ultimately vast new markets for its exports.

Conclusion

In the last analysis, though, the success of this policy within Portuguese Africa or elsewhere assumes that there will be no major extension of the insurgency campaign in Rhodesia and the Portuguese colonies requiring a proportionately larger and perhaps ever-increasing military commitment. This is not an unreasonable assumption in view of the success with which the insurgent threat has been countered so far. But the implications of a change in the guerrillas' fortunes could be serious for the Republic, whose military involvement to date has been small and without any serious repercussions for its "outward" policy in general. By contrast, a running battle against guerrillas on several fronts would have profoundly damaging effects on the attempt to build a Southern African Economic Community, the ultimate success of which depends on the creation and maintenance of political stability in the area. A black-white military confrontation across the northern perimeter of the Republic—apart from entailing the threat of external intervention—would effectively force it into the posture of a garrison state, intent on survival at all costs. In these circumstances white power might indeed preserve itself within South Africa, but an ever-widening military commitment to keep black insurgency at bay would cut across and ultimately destroy the aspiration to be the guarantor of a *Pax Africana* in the southern third of the continent and also demonstrate to the world that "race groups with different views and . . . nations following different policies . . . [can] live in peace alongside one another in the same geographic area."[57]

These reflections, admittedly speculative, have been prompted by an alternative hypothesis put forward with considerable skill by Mr. Larry Bowman who has raised this critical question:

> Is internal stability of member states necessary for systemic maintenance? Here we must, as we have in other places, make a sharp distinction between South Africa and the other states of the system. Malawi, Lesotho, Swaziland, and Botswana can be endemically unstable without greatly affecting the overall stability of Southern Africa. Angola, Mozambique, Rhodesia, and even South Africa have all sustained periods of internal unrest without endangering the nature of the system as it now exists. Containable instability does not affect the system but what would be the effect of revolutionary change?
>
> Here we can only speculate. One could presume, though not with complete certainty, that if one Portuguese territory was lost, the others would quickly follow. Angola under an African government could cause serious trouble for South-West Africa, because South Africa's controls over Angola are very limited and the defense of South-West Africa would be a distant and difficult problem. Mozambique under an African government would ease the geographical dependence of Malawi and Swaziland on the white countries, but Mozambique's important labor and transport ties to Rhodesia and South Africa would probably prevent overt hostility toward white governments in Rhodesia and South Africa. If Rhodesia became black before Mozambique, its militance would necessarily be tempered by its transport needs. If Mozambique and Rhodesia were *both* African-governed, they could over time reduce their own and their neighbor's vulnerability vis-à-vis South Africa. In the last analysis, however, it is my conclusion that internal stability, up to and including internal revolution, could be sustained within the system for all countries other than South Africa.[58]

This is an impressive analysis, but it rests on the assumption that instability can be contained—presumably by the local governments, though the analysis does not make this clear. If, however, the work of containment is to involve military intervention by the South Africans, then, in our view (assuming the guerrillas in Mozambique, for example, gather strength and force the Portuguese into desperate straits), he is underestimating the effects that a progressively larger commitment by the Republic would have on the general stability of the area. He also underestimates the extent to which this would undermine the Republic's efforts to maintain and to extend its influence by economic means; such efforts require the maintenance of a peaceful status quo throughout the area as a whole.

As far as the effects of revolutionary change are concerned, Mr. Bowman is rightly cautious, though his conclusion that "internal stability, up to and including internal revolution, could be sustained within the system for all countries other than South Africa" seems questionable to us. The analysis appears to assume that the South Africans would permit the emergence of a black Mozambique and Rhodesia by revolutionary means, putting their faith in economic considerations to determine these nations' future relations with the Republic. Yet the current presence of South African police units in Rhodesia seems to indicate a determination—in the short term, at any rate—to prevent this eventuality from occurring; a compulsion to step up this commitment, if and when guerrilla activity escalated, would make it difficult, if not impossible, to operate the "outward" policy along the lines of economic aid within the framework of peaceful coexistence as defined by its most ardent supporters. And if, in spite of South Africa's military support, revolution, were to triumph in Angola, Mozambique, and Rhodesia, one could not so readily assume, as Mr. Bowman appears to do, that South Africa's standing as a power in the area and the prospects of the outward policy would remain unaffected.

He correctly stresses the point that the ultimate aspiration is to establish "an economically and militarily strong South Africa, surrounded by client states, befriended by the Great Powers, and geographically isolated from any significant political enemy."[59] Thus our disagreement with him is not whether the Republic can achieve this objective, but rather about the likely effects that "internal unrest" and "revolutionary change"—if they occur—would have on its attempts to do so.

Whether the insurgents in Portuguese Africa and Rhodesia will remain insignificant is a speculative question beyond the scope of this particular analysis. Such evidence as we have suggests that in Rhodesia the guerrilla forces operating from Zambia have so far achieved little.[60] Clearly, if they are to achieve their long-term political objectives, a cardinal aim of their military strategy must be to involve South Africa on the widest possible front, thus compelling the government to substitute military force for economic aid as the instrument of its policy to safeguard and to promote security in the Southern African region. That there appears to be no prospect of this happening in the foreseeable future is evidence both of the guerrillas' weakness and South African confidence that time and resources are on its side in the struggle for mastery in the white South.

4

The Future of Separate Development in South Africa

CHRISTOPHER R. HILL

It is sometimes suggested that the policy of separate development is so obviously bound to fail that those who support it must be insincere or hypocritical. This is to ignore facts—above all, the fact of the undoubted intelligence of many of the most devoted supporters of the policy. The British may have acquired an empire in a fit of absence of mind and dissolved it with self-deluding pride in the success of their mission, but the Afrikaners are not people to base a whole national policy on conscious self-delusion.

To assess—or, more correctly, to guess at—the future requires some attempt to understand both the present and the past. Specifically, we should ask why a nation (there is no need to dispute that the Afrikaners are indeed a nation) whose intelligence there is no compelling reason to doubt should pursue goals which are apparently unattainable—by means which seem impractical and often cruel and in defense of values which repel many, are incomprehensible to others, yet which elicit a purely visceral response of fellow feeling from many.

Supporters of the policy of separate development (or apartheid, as we may call it for the sake of brevity) believe that the different races in South Africa should be separated territorially as well as socially, and that each should be free to develop "along its own lines." Small states, which may eventually become independent (the Transkei already has limited self-government), are being set up in the old African reserves. These embryo states are often referred to as Bantustans, *Bantu* being the word used by the South African government as a synonym for *African*. The term *Bantustan* was originally used derisively, but has now become common parlance. The African areas are also often referred to as *homelands*.

The white African's value system (and, according to some accounts, his dreams) centers upon a set of deeply ingrained attitudes toward black Africans.[1] Race matters more than any other single subject: in his conversational cosmology it is the sun round which all lesser stars revolve.

The white man born in South Africa knows the black one in a very special way—and is not slow to say so. But when he reproaches the foreign critic by saying "You'll never know the African as I do," he makes the very point the foreigner ought to be making himself. That is, foreigners (except those concerned with certain disciplines like literature or social psychology) have little interest in knowing the black African in anything like the way his white compatriot does. The latter knows the African in terms of very few roles; he has highly stylized expectations of African behavior, and if those expectations are not met he will experience consternation, confusion, anger, even disgust. The politically oriented foreign observer may also be interested in a few African roles, but these roles are generally quite different ones. He is less concerned about servants and farm laborers and more interested in the African as political agitator, potential voter, consumer, and so on. Moreover, his expectations are more open, his identification of the roles an African may reasonably play is less secure. His mind, in other words, stays open—or should do so; many social scientists' minds, of course, do not. Thus, broadly speaking, the white South African feels at home with Africans when the latter are in subordinate roles. He may indeed (as Mannoni has suggested in another connection)[2] enjoy the feeling of being depended upon. The visitor, on the other hand, will not be shocked if he finds Africans occupying roles of potential equality.

It is not only indigenous whites whose range of vision is so narrow. The immigrant white man seems to acquire with extraordinary ease the attitudes appropriate to his status. For example, a study in Rhodesia[3] has shown a significant relation between length of residence and development of "conservative" attitudes (though this is not to say that the responses elicited were not symptomatic of values latent long before the immigrants had left home).

The belief from which the policy of separate development derives its strength and which it, in turn, legitimizes is the belief in the essential difference of the races. No more than this is necessary; indeed, the sophisticated proponents of apartheid take pains to stress that the policy entails no belief in the inferiority of nonwhites. Nevertheless, it seems reasonable to suppose that, whatever the intellectual may say, most white South Africans would regard nonwhites (and particularly Africans) not only as different, but as inferior.

Fear runs alongside the feeling of superiority. "Black is the badge of hell. The hue of dungeons and the scowl of night,"[4] and denizens of hell provoke more than contempt, for most of us have been afraid of the dark at one time or another. From fear the apartheid policy also derives strength—though it is a source of strength which could prove difficult to handle should the Bantustans ever appear strong enough to be perceived as a threat. Furthermore, if too much is spent on the Bantustans, the presently muted cries from the white electorate that "the kaffirs are being pampered" could gain in force. It was jealousy of this kind which apparently motivated the assassin of Dr. Hendrik F. Verwoerd, the late Prime Minister of South Africa.

The policy of separate development, then, is presented to the white electorate as one of self-protection. White civilization, it is said, must be protected, and for it to be protected the races must be kept apart. Then Christianity, the values of the West, and national purity will be preserved. It is important to be clear about what these terms mean.

It is easy enough to see what national purity means: the fear is of interracial sexual intercourse (whether or not children result). We cannot go into the subject in depth here, but we may notice in passing that there is a certain ambiguity about this fear. It has often been suggested that the South African laws forbidding sexual activity across the color line are designed as much to restrain the guilty desires of the white man as to protect white women from what used to be called the "black peril." Indeed, if statistics are a reliable indication, black and colored, rather than white, women are in need of protection, because in the twelve months ending June 30, 1967, 349 white men, 180 black women, and 126 colored women were convicted under the Immorality Act, and only 5 black men and 5 colored men.[5] It is interesting, too, to note Roger Bastide's argument that so far as the male partner is concerned, these sexual encounters may be more appropriately identified as expressions of hate than of love or uncomplicated lust.[6]

It is less easy to see what essentially Western values are being preserved. Certainly few of the traditional freedoms, won at such cost in the West, are available to Africans and many of them are slipping, perhaps almost unnoticed, through the fingers of whites. It would be dreary and otiose to reiterate here the long list of laws which have been introduced in recent years and whose function is very seriously to limit the freedom of all individuals—particularly the black ones.

As for Christianity, churchmen outside South Africa have devoted much thought and charity to the analysis of the South African situation. The conclusion reached in 1964 by a distinguished working party of the British Council of Churches that "apartheid is a blasphemy against the Holy

Spirit'' has been echoed in many similar documents in different countries.[7] But, of course, comment of this kind does not come only from outside. In the Republic itself many Anglican and Roman Catholic bishops and clergy have said what they think, at considerable risk to their personal freedom.

Nevertheless, there are also in South Africa many devout churchmen—mostly Afrikaner members of the Dutch Reformed Churches—who genuinely believe that the apartheid policy is right and Christian. Upon this kind of belief it is difficult, perhaps presumptuous, for the outsider to offer any judgment. Clearly, it would be a facile impertinence to say that those who hold such beliefs are simply dishonest. It may be reasonable though, to suggest that conscience cannot operate properly without information and that many white South African consciences seem not adequately informed. This, indeed, is what that much reviled dissident pressure group within Afrikanerdom, the Christian Institute, does say with great courage and persistence.[8]

This digression has indicated some of the dimensions of white men's fear; what black men fear is obvious enough. Fear is the rock upon which the policy of separate development is based but that, of course, is not its only foundation. The other main pillar is the conviction, which started among the elite of white South Africans and is gradually spreading among the masses, that South Africa ought not to remain in self-conscious isolation at the southern tip of Africa but expand its influence throughout the African-ruled portions of the continent.

In this expansionist policy lies the chief difference between the *verligtes* (enlightened) and *verkramptes* (bigoted) in the National Party (there are nuances of opinion dividing the factions regarding internal policy, but they are not of great importance). The prime minister, Mr. B. J. Vorster, and most of his cabinet are firmly set on a course of extended contact with African states, leading to increased trade and possibly even the establishment of formal diplomatic relations—as with Malawi. The aim of this *verligte* policy is to secure peaceful coexistence, leaving the African states free to develop in their own ways and South Africa itself free to increase in prosperity and to maintain its own social system indefinitely. Nothing in this vision is inconsistent with current National party policy, since, as we have seen, it is an axiom of the Bantustan policy that nations should be allowed to "develop along their own lines," and there is no reason why the African states should not be regarded as outlying Bantustans. It must be admitted, however, that the analysis of the position of non-African minorities in those states requires some ideological juggling.

The *verkramptes*, however, are scared by this whole line of thought because it may lead to social mixing between the races, which the entire apartheid policy is designed to avoid. Though many have no objection to mixing outside South Africa (it has often been observed that even the most orthodox whites are able to behave cordially to Africans they meet abroad) they regard it as an intolerable danger within the Republic itself. The problem is, in a sense, not severe, since there are not likely to be many nonwhite diplomats in South Africa in the foreseeable future, but their presence can be seen as the thin end of the wedge.

To allay such fears, Mr. Vorster has to show that there is no intention to relax apartheid at home—and of this he has given ample demonstration. Indeed, during his premiership there has been a tightening of repressive legislation and a general increase of state control over the life of the individual. This affects white as well as black, National party supporters as well as the Opposition. The recent establishment of BOSS (Bureau of State Security) is an important step forward in the process of general surveillance, for it is widely assumed that the new organization will maintain agents within civil service departments and even within the party itself to ensure that full information is available even on government supporters (in case they show any tendency to stray from the path of strict orthodoxy).

Against this background we may turn to these two questions. First, what would it mean to say that the policy of separate development was a success? Second, what would it mean to say it was a failure? We may then conclude with some guesses about the future.

Internally the policy must, to be a success, satisfy certain minimum conditions. First, it must keep the races apart. Second, it must, by keeping the various African groups apart, ensure that they continue to perceive each other as separate and distinct groups and so inhibit the growth of a single African nationalism. Third, it must be presented in a way acceptable to the white electorate. Fourth, the policy can be regarded as a success outside the Republic if it is presented as a sufficiently plausible attempt to solve South Africa's racial problems[9] and thus allow foreign governments (particularly those of the United Kingdom and the United States) to maintain with an easier conscience their present close relations with South Africa. This does not mean that foreign governments or officials actually need to believe that the Bantustans policy will work—or even that it has a chance of working, or is seriously intended to work—but they must be able to make at least one of these assertions without appearing foolish. Somewhat similar considerations apply to businessmen: they must be persuaded that trade with and investment in South Africa are safe, and some of them also feel the need for some argument to support the view that these activities are not immoral. Finally, insofar as external affairs are concerned, the policy will be successful if it creates a general feeling among the inexpert public that black Africans are not ill treated in South Africa but that, on the contrary, great attention and a great deal of money are devoted to their welfare.

In the last of these aims the extremely efficient propaganda conducted by the South African government does seem to have an effect, though it is to some extent offset by organizations like the Anti-Apartheid Movement in Britain. The effect of the Bantustan policy on the deliberations of foreign governments and businessmen is more debatable, but my overall impression is that it is barely relevant to real decision making, though it may be useful for public rhetoric. In other words, the British and American governments are interested in keeping the peace in Southern Africa, in continuing to trade with the Republic, and in avoiding a situation in which they are obliged to choose between black or white Africa. In the short term the policy of separate development is relevant to the pursuit of these governmental aims only to the degree that it promotes or damps down African unrest. In the long run, the Bantustans do at least provide training grounds for administrators, and to that extent are useful if eventual African equality is foreseen.

Businessmen contemplating investment in South Africa are obliged to take account of the political risk—that is, the possibility, however remote, of successful African rebellion. Direct investment may sometimes be the result of government pressure, to which a firm yields in order to protect the market it already has, or it may be prompted by the vision of an expanding market covering the whole of Southern Africa. Portfolio investment is a slightly different matter; it is often argued that there is no strong case for investment in South African industrial stocks, but a very strong case for investment in mining concerns. In the latter, the political risk is diminished by their diversification of activities outside the Republic.[10]

All types of investors have an interest in the maintenance of peace. On the one hand, it is perfectly obvious that South Africa is able, for the foreseeable future, to deal with any military measures likely to be taken by other African states. On the other hand, South African police are committed in Southern Rhodesia and at least intermittently in the Portuguese territories. So far as can be foreseen, this commitment is open-ended, likely to end only when Rhodesia and the Portuguese territories fall to African governments. In terms of men the commitment is not great,[11] and they receive useful training in combating guerrilla operations, but the psychological insecurity induced by the knowledge that guerrilla warfare must from now on be a part of the South African way of life is likely to grow, and can hardly fail to affect business confidence.

The policy of separate development—if this is taken in the limited, constitutional sense to mean the setting up of African states within the Republic—does not seem of direct relevance to businessmen. What matters to them is peace and the maintenance of the labor supply. There are many related factors, however, such as the devolution of industry away from the four main existing industrial centers, and various impediments to the free movement of capital and labor which are of obvious relevance to business decisions. We must now consider factors of this kind to ascertain what it would mean to say the policy was a success *internally*.

The first objective of separate development has been stated as the maintenance of physical separation of the races. In other words, Africans are to remain in the areas set aside for them, where they are to *exist* in rural obscurity and *develop* "along their own lines." What these lines are, in the minds of National party theoreticians, is not always easy to determine. One strand of thought is that Africans have institutions and values peculiar to themselves, which are characterized as "tribal" and ought to be preserved. There are obvious connections here with the thought of Lugard and Lyautey, and the whole philosophy of indirect rule.

There are, though, a great many questions to be asked. Some of them are: What exactly are these institutions and values? Are they tribally based? What exactly is meant by the term *tribe*? Are these institutions and values relevant to all classes of Africans? Why and for whom ought they to be preserved? Does the present-day policy tend to preserve them?

If it were the intention of the South African government to preserve African societies as museum pieces these questions would be easier to answer. But separate *development* is the term the government employs and this seems to mean both political and economic development. The central question then is: In a developing society to what extent can, and should, traditional values be retained? This is not a problem peculiar to South Africa, but it is to be found in one form or another throughout the developing world—as well, indeed, as in many advanced societies.

A major institution of the tribal system is the chieftainship, and the central traditional imperative of collective morality is to respect the chief, provided he acts in accordance with established law and custom. Very broadly speaking, this means that he should not behave in an authoritarian way. Although his pronouncements are authoritative, they owe their legitimacy to the very full consultation and discussion which precedes them; this procedure results in a collective view of what should be done. The chief will naturally have a council of close advisers, very often including members of his own family, but any adult in the tribe will have the right to be heard in debate. This, of course, is a highly stylized picture of how a chief is expected to behave in traditional society. Clearly, many chiefs have succeeded in breaking the rules; others have tried and failed, and the penalty of failure has been death, banishment, or fission within the tribe.

Though the picture is stylized, the view of African decision making as the product of an exhaustive process of discussion leading to something like the discovery of Rousseau's "General Will" is very close to the picture presented by such proponents of African socialism as President Julius Nyerere of Tanzania. The difficulty about this kind of decision making is, as many commentators have observed,[12] that while it sounds plausible enough at the level of the small group, it is difficult to envisage the practical means by which it may be extended to the whole nation.

In the Eastern Cape in the last century, the British decided to rely mainly on location headmen and break the power of the chiefs. The South African government in 1951 gave their power back to them in the Promotion of Bantu Self-Government Act, but it gave it back in a somewhat different form. Instead of the composition of a chief's council being a matter of customary evolution, the act specifically stated how many councillors were to be appointed in accordance with local law and custom, how many by the chief, and how many by the Bantu affairs commissioner. Tribal authorities, as they were called, were to have paid secretaries who tend, very naturally, to be educated men. This is necessary because they have to know how to keep accounts, prepare agendas, and write minutes, and in general they must have a grasp of a variety of skills required in modern local government.

It is this modernity which lies at the heart of the problem. On the one hand Africans have resented the departure from tradition entailed by the Promotion of Bantu Self-Government Act. Many chiefs have been placed in the classical dilemma of those who must occupy an intercalary role. Are they to please the government by enforcing unpopular modernizing policies like cattle culling and land conservation, but run the risk of retaining their positions only because they have government support? Or are they to please their people and perhaps be deposed by higher authority? The problem is a familiar one in other parts of Africa (it also faces prefects in British public schools and foremen in factories[13]) and only the most subtle chiefs can retain the approbation of both sides.

On the other hand, Africans, particularly those who have received some education, resent the assumption that white man should impose upon them a culture whose outline, at least, is tribal rather than Western. This resentment does not mean that Africans reject their past, or regard their own traditions as necessarily inferior. They do, however, wish to be free to practice the eclecticism so noticeable elsewhere in Africa; free, that is, to retain certain aspects of the past, while gladly accepting those aspects of what has been brought from Europe which they perceive as relevant. The point is that the choice should be made by Africans, not by the minister of Bantu administration and development—and this is a view held, though perhaps not articulated, by Africans at all educational levels. For evidence, one has only to look back to the acclamation with which the abandonment of Bantu education was received in the Transkei.[14]

The return to tribal institutions has, then, attracted opposition from many directions though, ironically, the institutions as now set up differ from the traditional model and so are no longer really "tribal." It is possible that government has only itself to thank for much of the execration the policy has received. If the constant references to "development along their own lines" were dropped, the recomposition of chiefs' councils as Tribal Authorities might be seen as one perfectly tenable kind of answer to some of the problems of modernization. The solution is not novel, the problem itself is not novel, but what is unique to South Africa is the racial ideology whose rhetoric so obfuscates what is being done in the Bantustans.

Similarly, most commentators have paid too much attention to the composition of the Transkeian Legislative Assembly (TLA). Of course, the majority of chiefs over elected members in the TLA means that the Transkei government is almost certain to have a majority in the House sympathetic (at least on the surface) to the policies of the government in Pretoria. But some answer has to be found to the question of what to do with the chiefs. The other possible answer, which has been adopted, for example, in Botswana, is to have an Upper House of Chiefs that would become essentially apolitical.[15] This solution has been repeatedly suggested by the opposition Democratic party (DP) in the TLA and strenuously resisted by the Transkei National Independence party (TNIP) government. It is hard to predict what will happen; if the TNIP continues to increase its electoral support,[16] it might well be prepared to endorse the idea of an entirely elected lower

House. It should be remembered that the South African government, as long ago as 1962, was not opposed to this, but insisted that if any chiefs were members of the TLA, then all sixty-four should be included to avoid invidious choices.[17] This principle has since been abandoned, as new chiefs have been created, though only sixty-four (as before) sit in the TLA. If chiefs are not removed to an Upper House, the younger generation of chiefs being educated at the School for the Sons of Chiefs and Headmen in the Transkei (in practice a sizable number of pupils are *not* the sons of chiefs and headmen) will in due course come into the TLA. They will not only be chiefs, but educated men, and their presence will inevitably alter the whole style of debate and government in the Transkei.

Thus the current of politics will be determined not so much by the formal composition of the assembly as by the training of those in power. At present the Transkei ministers are educated men (some are also chiefs): the African civil servants in the Transkei are also educated and some are related to chiefly families. What matters is that the society is being modernized: the developmental problems are twentieth-century problems, and the men who have to find the answers are (at least in their role as decision makers) modern men. This kind of pattern must persist whether or not commoners come to control the assembly, and to lay too much stress upon formal structures obscures the most interesting questions. In whose interest is the policy of separate development being pursued? How relevant is it to the African population?

The second question is particularly relevant to the broader inquiry as to the success or failure of the policy as a whole. In answering it the network analysis employed by, for example, Professor Philip Mayer[18] is most helpful. Professor Mayer points out that to say a man is "urbanized" just because he lives in a town is inadequate. What has to be done is to investigate his network of relationships, and if most of those which have what Mayer calls "moral content" remain in the rural areas, it is more sensible to regard the subject as a countryman who has temporarily migrated to town, rather than as a full-fledged townsman. Thus the man who has left his wife and children behind and who still has land and cattle in the rural area is likely to return there, and while he is in town the majority of his contacts outside work will probably be with people of his own tribe—indeed, of his own village or location. For the migrant, tribal values and institutions remain primary, while for the townsman they have been replaced by transtribal ties of a specifically urban kind. For the townsman, traditional values may be entirely foreign or, if he still pays occasional visits to what was once his home, they will at most be secondary—in the sense that he may temporarily slip into those roles appropriate to the rural area for the duration of his visit, but abandon them as soon as he returns to town.

The South African government's policy is to stabilize, and ultimately to reduce, the urban African population as far as possible. Attempts are being made[19] to oblige employers in the Western Cape to reduce their African labor force by 5 percent annually and to replace Africans with coloreds. Naturally, these attempts are unpopular with the employers and execeedingly difficult to administer; whether or not they are ultimately successful, it does nevertheless seem perfectly clear that, in the Republic as a whole, the reliance on African labor is unlikely to be reduced to any significant extent for a very long time. Automation may help, as may such measures as official limitations on employment of domestic servants, but by and large the policy must be to reduce the established urban African population outside the reserves rather than to reduce the African population of the white areas as a whole. In other words, migrants must replace townsmen; if possible, existing townsmen must be turned into migrants, and any future African labor must be obliged to remain as migrants and prevented from acquiring the ties characteristic of townsmen.

It is worth mentioning, though not describing in great detail, various aspects of the policy. First, those Africans who already are townsmen have had their security reduced by a series of legislative enactments to the point where no African can be certain of his right to live in town at all. Although regulations governing the residence of wives and children are strictly administered, South African administrators are no less fallible than others, and it appears that a good many Africans do slip through the net.[20]

Second, all new labor entering the white areas must pass through labor bureaus, which, in theory at least direct to any given area the type and quantity of labor it requires. This should mean that all Africans, except the permanent townsmen, are in the white areas on contract to specific employers and are obliged to return home at the end of their contracts. That this does not always work is shown by the number of "pass" offences sent for trial—no less than 479,114 in the twelve months ending June 30, 1966.[21]

Third, African employees in town are as far as possible segregated in certain streets according to tribe. This is difficult to administer in long-established African towns, but relatively easy in the newer ones. Furthermore, the system is now gaining some momentum by which Territorial Authorities and some major chiefs send "ambassadors" to the urban areas to keep contact with their people. The maintenance of tribal discipline, or at least the threat of it, helps support migrant status and prevents the growth of a community of townsmen.

The "grand design," then, is to produce a situation in which the African population outside the reserves remains as small as possible, and in which all Africans regard themselves as temporary visitors to the European area, with their real homes in the reserves. Some supporters of apartheid recognize that such a situation may be impossible to produce, but can see no other solution to the racial problems they have created for themselves; the more far-seeing recognize, too, that there must be some positive attraction about life in a Bantustan if the cooperation of urban Africans is to be secured. The "push" effect to the reserves from the European areas is created by influx control, endorsing out,* and all the other regulations to which Africans are subject, but to create a "pull" is more difficult.

If Africans are to wish to live in the Bantustans, there must be a sufficiency of land and jobs and both present formidable difficulties. To some extent the problem of jobs is solved by administrative juggling. That is, townships are built (for example, near Durban) to house part of the labor force for the Durban industrial complex. The townships, instead of being formally part of the white area and administered by the municipality, are designated as part of the Bantu Homeland (or Bantustan) and fall under the control of the Ministry of Bantu Administration and Development. Thus, though these townships fulfill precisely the same function for the European economy as do the older municipal ones, it is possible to say that they do not lie within the European area, and hence that their inhabitants do not form part of the urban African population within that area.

This ingenious expedient does not, however, affect the situation in those reserves which are not near an industrial area, except insofar as migrants' remittances contribute to their families' subsistence. The principal problem of the reserves is the problem of land and its animal and human carrying capacity. There is excellent land to be found in the homelands, as well as much very poor land. Some areas have been greatly improved in recent years by betterment schemes. But the problem is that the total area set aside for Africans is under 14 percent of the area of the Republic and could not possibly provide an agricultural livelihood for anything approaching the total African population, every one of whose members, the government hopes, will eventually regard himself or herself as rooted in the reserves. Furthermore, a betterment scheme, if properly carried out, requires the strict division of the land into economic units and the removal to "rural townships" of the population for whom no land is available. According to the Tomlinson Commission,[22] this would mean removing half the agricultural population. Since operations on this scale would be impracticable and inhumane, improved areas do in fact carry more than their appropriate population and half, or even quarter, economic units are allocated to households in some areas.

Whatever advances are made in agricultural production (and there is enormous scope for such improvement) there will in any foreseeable circumstances be a surplus population for whom jobs must be found. Some can be accommodated in the "rural townships," a few of which (those growing up round developing administrative centers) have a fair chance of economic viability. For the others, though it is too soon to predict with any confidence, the economic future does not look bright.

Clearly, commerce and industry must be brought to the reserves. To this end most praiseworthy attempts are being made by the Bantu Investment Corporation to train Africans to run trading stores, and a number of stores have been bought from their European owners. Most of this activity is going on in the Transkei, where many white families have been established as traders for generations. There has been considerable bitterness among the whites in the Transkei because of the government's failure to state promptly when, and at what prices, it will purchase the many trading stations offered for sale; this dilatoriness is, however, fully understandable from the government's point of view, since it does not wish the exodus of European traders to disrupt the territory's commercial life by out-stripping the supply of trained Africans.

In any case commerce—whether in the country districts or in the small towns which have grown up during the last century round the various magisterial headquarters—cannot provide large-scale employment. To cope with this problem, the government has adopted a policy of establishing small-scale industries within the Bantustans—of which the best known is the Vulindlela furniture factory outside Umtata in the Transkei. Progress, though, is slow. The minister of Bantu administration and development said in February 1968 that 35 industries employing 945 Africans had been established in the homelands between 1960 and 1966.[23] To some extent ideological scruples prevent the more rapid growth of industry within the reserves since the direct investment of European-owned capital is forbidden on the grounds that it would promote interracial contact.

* Influx control is the control of African movement into the white areas. Those who have not complied with regulations governing residence are sent back to the reserves; that is, endorsed out of white areas.

White industrialists are, however, very strongly encouraged to invest on the *borders* of the reserves and considerable inducements have been offered them to do so. Yet it cannot be said that industrialists have shown any great enthusiasm to take part in the decentralization of industry, though from the point of view of the economy as a whole there are good reasons for encouragement of this process. Nor have they been quick to set up remote border industries. There are a number of reasons for this reluctance. For example, some industrialists fear that if the Bantustans themselves eventually generate industries on any significant scale, the border industries would lose their supplies of skilled African labor. Again, I have heard it argued that if the Bantustans ultimately acquire independence, there will be considerable difficulties in controlling a labor force which commutes from a foreign country.

So far new industrial areas are popular with industrialists if, like Rosslyn (near Pretoria), they lie near the existing industrial complexes. The government has expended very great sums ($260.4 million by the end of 1967) on the border industries program, but by the same date only about 49,000 new jobs had been created for Africans.[24]

Though the prospects for the large-scale absorption of African labor do not look promising, there is no shortage of high status employment in the Bantustans. In these areas, even if little is happening to disturb the economic calm, there is considerable development of administrative services, and eventually all jobs are to be filled by Africans. In the Transkei, the most developed of the Bantustans, the civil service fixed establishment increased from 2,446 to 3,394 between 1963 and 1967; there were still 365 European civil servants at the end of 1967 but the number is being reduced every year.[25] As other Bantustans achieve the limited self-government already conferred upon the Transkei, there will be a similar proliferation of civil service posts and correspondingly increased opportunities for Africans.

Judging by the experience in the Transkei, these opportunities do not attract Africans from the urban areas of the Republic, but they do provide employment for educated young men who have grown up in the territory and are prepared to stay there. These young men, together with the staffs of the tribal, regional, and territorial authorities, constitute a new and growing African bureaucracy. So long as they do not publicly oppose the ideals of separate development they have much to gain from operating the system and they must realize that, should an African government ever come to power in the Republic as a whole, their services will still be essential.

These bureaucrats, some chiefs, and perhaps some elected members of the TLA (and the similar bodies developing in some other Bantustans)[26] are the Africans who may be said to benefit positively from the policy of separate development. The settled rural population (those who have land) are unlikely to be at a disadvantage and may even derive some satisfaction from the contemplation of the apparatus of embryo statehood. But for urban Africans there are no advantages at all; instead there is a considerable price to be paid in the increasing insecurity of urban life. As H. Bhengu observed as long ago as 1958:

> To the African, to be an urban African means to be a tree without roots because of the many laws and regulations that dog you all your conscious life. The only time you are allowed to forget your humble and insecure role in the white man's area is when you are asleep, or engrossed in your work, if you are fortunate to be in a type of work which can command your full attention without a constant reminder that you do not belong.[27]

Nor does separate development seem to have any relevance for the Africans living on European farms (who will not be considered in this chapter) except perhaps to increase their insecurity.

Separate development is, however, very much in the interest of the white population as a whole. This does not mean that all sections of the white population approve of this policy. Leaving aside the Progressive party and the now-dissolved Liberal party, there are also considerable misgivings within the main opposition party, the United party (UP). The UP is as opposed to social mixing between the races as are the nationalists, but many of its members regard the granting of limited self-government to the Bantustans as dangerous and unnecessary. It is dangerous because, if the Bantustans eventually achieve independence, they may be used as guerrilla bases and the labor supply may be threatened. It is unnecessary because the UP sees no difficulty in maintaining white control of the Republic without setting up the apparatus of statehood in the reserves.

This is an argument about methods, not ends. The Nationalists' insistence that the reserves should be developed as "homelands" and not merely labor dormitories rests upon the view that if Africans are to be regarded as migrants, or visitors, to the European areas, they must have some territory of their own from which to migrate. Furthermore, because the Africans will eventually be able to make whatever laws they like in their own areas the laws to which Africans must submit if they choose to enter the European areas are, it is said, justified. In the moral overtones of this argument may be perceived the vestiges of lip service to the idea of human rights, mixed with the desire to demonstrate to the outside world that South Africa's policy of separate development is a serious attempt to cope with the racial problem.

It is often forgotten that apartheid theoreticians do indeed see their policy as a rational attempt to solve a problem. The outsider might be tempted to agree with Jonty Driver, who wrote: "Indeed, no one man, however great, could solve the problems which South Africa now faces. It is as though the country were in the grip of some irrational fate, which has as much to do with the exposed entrails of slaughtered birds as with human reason."[28] To this the theoretician replies that the road may be difficult and long, but that no other offers even the prospect of success.

In this chapter attention is focused on development in the Transkei because that is the reserve whose eventual statehood looks least implausible and upon whose progress most stress has been laid by the South African government. It is a relatively large area, containing few "white spots" and with good prospects of agricultural development if methods can be improved and the rural population reduced.

Meanwhile, in the other Bantustans, there is also constitutional progress. The Zulus have accepted the principle of Bantu Authorities: even Vendaland now has a Territorial Authority. Though progress may be slower than in the Transkei, there is no reason to suppose that there will not eventually be a number of Bantustans enjoying the same measure of self-government as the Transkei. But, to an even greater extent than the Transkei, their prospects of any genuine independent or semi-independent statehood are limited by poverty and fragmentation of the land between black and white. All the arguments adduced to demonstrate the impracticability of the policy of separate development and its irrelevance to the interest of the mass of Africans apply to the other Bantustans with even greater force than to the Transkei. Therefore, I am not discussing Zululand, the Ciskei, Tswanaland, and so on in any detail, but using the Transkei to illustrate the general principles which I believe to be relevant to an assessment of the future of apartheid.

What, then, to return to an earlier question, is "success"? It will be recalled that the minimum conditions were stated as: keeping the races apart; maintaining and promoting the feeling of "otherness" between different African groups; presenting the policy in a manner acceptable to the white electorate; and providing a justification of apartheid for external consumption.

From what has already been said, it is clear that no policy could separate the races completely, given white South Africa's dependence on black labor and the lack of opportunities in the reserves. On the other hand, it is hard to conceive of any policy which would be more successful in this respect.

It seems, too, that at least among the poorly educated masses separate development does strengthen, for example, the Zulu's perception of the Venda as "other," partly by keeping them apart and partly by promoting a feeling of nationalism in the different Bantustans. This growth of nationalist feeling, which seems to lie behind the increased popularity of the TNIP, does have its dangers since with it goes a growing desire in the predominantly Xhosa Transkei for union with the Ciskei, which is also primarily Xhosa. But the growth of petty nationalisms is seen as a reasonable price to pay for the avoidance of a single all-embracing African nationalism.

The presentation of the policy in a way acceptable to the electorate gives rise to problems, as we have seen. It is feared by the United party, by businessmen, by Europeans in the Transkei and Natal, and various other groups. Nevertheless, on the whole, the electorate appears to accept the necessity of separate development, with its attendant inconveniences. The National party continues to grow in strength at the expense of the Opposition, and discordant elements within the National party itself can, for the present at least, be contained, or if necessary purged. Yet it would be extraordinarily difficult for Mr. Vorster to give way to the pressure from what is often called the "liberal" wing of his party and allow some more equitable division of land between the races.[29]

Finally, what of the effect of South African propaganda upon the outside world? It seems to me that the propaganda attack has two aspects. On the one hand, it is made clear that South African trade is essential to, at least, the United Kingdom and highly desirable to a number of other countries. With this goes the assurance that foreign investment in South Africa is safe, because the republic's armed forces are capable of dealing with any likely demands upon them. On the other hand, the world is told, black South Africans are not ill treated, but are prosperous, well provided with social services, and being given states of their own which may eventually achieve independence. If they are given independence, so the argument runs, they will have been properly prepared for it—unlike most other African countries.

Speaking again in very general terms, the information effort seems successful. Trade and investment continue and even some of those who find South African practices unappealing wonder whether they are not preferable to events such as those in Nigeria, the Congo, and elsewhere. There remains, of course, a small public which is still unconvinced. Many of its members continue to irritate the South African government, but they are a small and not very powerful minority, and those in South Africa itself are often dealt with ruthlessly.[30]

Put in the simplest terms, the white man's problem in South Africa is to retain his dominant position, and his leaders have chosen separate development as the means by which he does it. We have distinguished a number of conditions this policy must meet if it is to be termed "successful" and we have seen that the most important of these, the physical separation of the races, is virtually impossible. This is because there is little employment in the Reserves for the growing African population and little willingness or ability in the European areas to do without African labor.

It may, however, be argued that even though all but the most starry-eyed theorists believe economic interdependence must continue, social mixing is effectively prevented, and that this is what really matters if national purity is to be maintained. It is true that loopholes remain, so that occasional interracial contact of a noneconomic kind takes place, but there is no reason in principle why such gaps should not be stopped. Similarly, while there may be a few Africans who still have a right to reside in the European area, it seems that in a few years the entire black population outside the Reserves will be there by grace of the Europeans; this will be the culmination of a policy steadfastly pursued over many years.

Such a policy necessarily carries disadvantages with it. If labor is on contract, there is a high turnover; migrants without wives will be discontented; there is a shortage of white skilled labor, and job reservation (that is, the reservation of certain jobs in the white area for white people) inhibits the training of Africans for skilled jobs. These and other inefficiencies are not welcomed by businessmen, and job reservation is increasingly evaded by the redefinition of jobs. But by the white society as a whole, it seems they are accepted as not too high a price for safety, and the preservation of a way of life.

There is an argument among economists as to the future, summarized by Professor Blumer of the University of Califronia (Berkeley) in an important article.[31] He first states the orthodox view that industrialization by its very nature changes the societies in which it occurs. For example, jobs are allocated on the basis of merit rather than traditional standing, and there is no reason why "rational" business practices of this kind should not cut across racial lines. The business of the entrepreneur is not to kowtow to prejudice, but to make money.

Against this view, Professor Blumer argues that while industrialization may be what he calls an *incitant* to change, political factors *bring about* change. Industry, he contends, fits itself into the racial mold of the society in which it operates. If, for example, management selection ignores racial differences in a society where they are entrenched, customers may be lost and governmental disfavor earned. The rational decision here is to accommodate to the prevailing prejudice. If political conditions change, then industry will change its practices.[32]

Of South Africa, Blumer says:

> The official policy of *apartheid* seeks to harden the traditional racial order, to sharpen and cement racial lines, and to place the whites in an unassailable position of control in the white areas of the nation. Despite occasional minor compromises this policy is being followed logically and with stubborn determination towards its objective. There is no question that industry, like other areas of life, is being brought firmly under the control of the official *apartheid* policy despite apparent disfavour shown by many industrialists to many portions of the programme. This development . . . is a striking instance of the shaping and solidification of a racial order in industry in response to a demanding policy from the outside.[33]

If this interpretation is correct, there is little comfort for those economists and businessmen who believe that increasing prosperity will of itself bring the barriers crashing down. Nor is it encouraging for those who look for a change of political climate. To me there seems no reason whatever why white South Africans should abandon the imperative of survival, nor is any power likely to force them to do so.

The pattern of the future, then, is likely to be one of developing relations with black African states, increasing devolution of power to the Bantustan governments, very likely leading to independence (for the Transkei at least), and to offset these "liberal" tendencies, continuing and increasing repression of Africans in the white area. This will be accompanied by continuing guerrilla warfare in Rhodesia until an African government is installed there (it is, I believe, reasonable to suppose that such a government would not allow its territory to be used as a base by the African National Congress for operations against South Africa). One may expect, too, the continuance of a very high crime rate and a strikingly high execution rate.[34]

Though the policy of separate development does not solve white South Africans' problems, it is hard to see any other policy which could be more effective. But at the same time it is difficult for the outsider to see the policy as anything more than a palliative at best—at worst an irrelevance.

5

South Africa and South West Africa

PAUL S. VAN DER MERWE

Since the opening of the first plenary session of the United Nations General Assembly more than twenty-three years ago on January 10, 1946, the subject of South West Africa has occupied much time and energy of this world organization with monotonous regularity and persistency, and it has filled voluminous records—completely out of proportion with its importance, since it is one of the most arid, thinly populated, and ostensibly insignificant countries in the world today. During two decades of acrimonious maneuver and intrigue more than seventy resolutions have been passed on this issue by the General Assembly, several ad hoc committees were appointed, many volumes of hearsay and unsubstantiated evidence were collected, more than nine hundred meetings of various committees and subcommittees were called, numerous petitioners were interviewed, and no less than four times were issues related to South West Africa considered by the International Court of Justice. On three occasions advisory opinions were requested and on one occasion, the recent marathon case which lasted from 1960 to 1966, contentious proceedings were instituted against South Africa. The records in the latter instance comprised about six thousand pages. The oral proceedings lasted one year.

The student of international affairs is immediately struck by the preoccupation of the United Nations with South West Africa, especially in view of the inability of this organization to solve any of the real major world problems. One of them is the dire food shortage which threatens modern civilization. The inhabitants of the earth now number three billion and, at the present rate of increase, will number six billion by the end of this century. More than half the world's population suffers from varying degrees of malnutrition, while the increase of food production is not keeping pace with the population growth, and some of the world's natural resources are nearing depletion. Another problem is the production of armaments. Since 1946 there has been no diminution of the arms race, and little progress in evolving agreed forms of international security. In 1966 the world collectively spent $150 billion on arms and at that stage the United States of America alone had at its disposal more than sixty-thousand megaton bombs—that is a sufficient amount to wipe out in a fraction of a second six thousand cities the size of London.[1]

The future of the half-million peaceful and economically developing whites and nonwhites in South West Africa has featured more prominently in the world press in recent years than the 266 tribal clashes that occurred in one region in Uganda during one single month, where (according to the August 7, 1965, issue of the *Times of Zambia*) members of an international Peace Corps were threatened with being eaten, or the massacre in Nigeria, where in one year two hundred thousand people (equal to nearly half of the entire population of South West Africa) were killed in combat. According to press reports, two million Biafrans were dying of hunger, and there is an atrocious war of attrition in the Sudan, where some twelve million people were given "independence" in January 1956. During years of increasing economic privation, violent dissension, and relentless political eruptions in the Sudan, more than the entire population of South West Africa was exterminated during the course of one single year.

Ironically, massive international attention was focused on South West Africa when, legally speaking, the political future of the people of this semidesert country was of no international concern. No less a body than the International Court of Justice found explicitly that no individual state has any legal right or interest in the manner in which South Africa fulfills its obligations toward the inhabitants of the territory. In addition, the Court suggested very strongly that no entity, such as the United Nations, possesses any such right or interest.[2]

If the Court was correct in its judgment—and no evidence has since been adduced that it erred—why had the South West Africa issue been blown up to such an extent that even the Western Powers were tempted to indulge in precipitate action and voted for a resolution terminating South Africa's administration of the territory? What considerations shelter behind the cynicism and ruthlessness with which the matter has been pursued by the Afro-Asian and Communist bloc? What are the real issues at stake, and will South Africa ever be prepared to surrender the territory? In this chapter the salient factors of the South West Africa issue will be briefly considered and the prospects for the future analyzed.

The Legal Aspects

It is true that the detractors of South Africa did everything in their power to disparage the 1966 judgment of the International Court of Justice. Some described it as "meaningless," while others thought it was only a victory for South Africa "on a technical point." Let there be no doubt about it: the judgment of 1966 constituted a major triumph for South Africa which cannot be denied. Conversely, the judgment marked the most devastating defeat ever suffered by South Africa's enemies, the more so because the battlefield was of their own choice.

One of the questions was whether the mandate had survived the dissolution of the League of Nations. Either the mandate came to an end with the demise of the League or the mandate remained in existence. Even if the mandate survived the dissolution of the League, the more important question is whether the control formerly exercised by the League has passed to the United Nations as the successor of the League. In 1950 the International Court of Justice in its advisory opinion found that South West Africa was still a mandated territory. In the 1966 judgment no finding was made on this question. In fact, the judgment explicitly stated that

> . . . it should be made clear [that the judgment is given] . . . without pronouncing upon, and wholly without prejudice to, the question of whether that Mandate is still in force. The Court moreover thinks it necessary to state that its 1962 decision on the question of competence was equally given without prejudice to that of the survival of the Mandate. . . .[3]

Whatever the reason might have been for the explicit inclusion of these cautious remarks, they leave the impression that a finding that the mandate has lapsed was at least a realistic possibility. Therefore, the question of the existence of the mandate is today, legally speaking, just as open as it was before the advisory opinion of 1950. Without getting absorbed in the details of legal arguments, the question can be rightly posed whether the mandates system was not in fact so closely and inseparably tied up with the League of Nations that its existence was vitally and entirely dependent on the existence of the League. It should be admitted that the system was not evolved to create rights and obligations between the mandatory power and the mandate, the latter not being a *persona* in the community of nations, but between the mandatory and the League of Nations. The system could never function without the League, and when the latter was dissolved the other must have ceased to exist. The majority of the judges in 1950 conceded that there was no express provision for the transfer of the League's functions to the United Nations, but relied heavily on the resolution of the League dated April 18, 1946, which recognized that its functions with respect to the mandated territories would come to an end and took into account "the expressed intentions of the Members of the League now administering territories under Mandate to continue to administer them. . .in accordance with the obligations contained in the respective Mandates, until other arrangements have been agreed to between the United Nations and the respective mandatory Powers."[4]

The judges of 1950 were apparently not aware of the fact that a draft proposal by the Chinese representatives to the League just prior to its dissolution in April 1946 would have had the effect of placing mandated territories under the United Nations; however, this proposal was rejected. Moreover, in the Preparatory Commission of the United Nations proposals had been made to provide for United Nations supervision of those mandates which were not converted into trust territories. The inescapable conclusion is that there was indeed no express or even tacit transfer of functions by the League of Nations. No provision whatsoever was made in the Charter for United Nations' supervision of mandates, unless a mandatory voluntarily agreed to place its mandated territory under UN supervision.

In its 1966 judgment, the Court did not pronounce on this point but there are passages in the reasoning in the judgment which suggest that the majority of judges was of the opinion that there was no longer any entity vested with supervisory power in respect of the mandate.[5] The Court, in fact, did not name the "entities" it had in mind. It is common knowledge that it was decided at a conference of the Organization of African Unity at Addis Ababa in June 1960 that Ethiopia and Liberia, because of their membership in the former League of Nations, were elected to institute legal proceedings against South Africa in the International Court of Justice.[6] Furthermore, the records of the United Nations bear sufficient testimony to the fact that the South West Africa case constituted but one aspect of a much larger plan to transform the political order of the states and territories in the southern part of the African continent. The general strategy of this plan is shown in the various programs of action initiated and consistently maintained against the Republic of South Africa by a group of Afro-Asian and Communist countries in the various organs and specialized agencies of the United Nations. In the mind of every reasonable person there cannot be any doubt whatsoever as to the "entities" which would most likely claim the so-called "due performance" of the mandate.

The most disappointing feature of the judgment, however, as far as the critics of South Africa are concerned, is that it does not constitute a decision in terms of Article 94 of the Charter of the United Nations. In terms of this article, each member of the organization undertakes to comply with the decision of the Court in any case to which it is a party, and if it fails to perform the obligations incumbent upon it under a judgment, the other party may have recourse to the Security Council for enforcement. This leaves now only one other possible basis for intervention by the United Nations—that is, a threat to international peace and security, which has probably also been frustrated by the findings of dissenting judges Tanaka (Japan) and Jessup (United States) who found that there exists no evidence of militarization in the mandated territory.[7]

Political Aspects

While the learned judges of the International Court of Justice were absorbed since 1950 in the extremely complicated legal aspects of the South West African dispute, every knowledgeable person realized that the real issues at stake were the policies of apartheid of the Republic of South Africa. Ethiopia and Liberia claimed, *inter alia*, that the Republic has violated the mandate by deliberately oppressing the nonwhite population groups.

Although the Court did not pronounce on this issue, it probably constitutes—as far as South Africa was concerned—the most vital and important part of the legal proceedings. For the first time in history the detractors of South Africa were afforded the opportunity (in the exalted and dignified atmosphere of the highest tribunal in the world) to state and prove their case against separate development, to call their own witnesses to support their case abundantly, to cross-examine, shatter, and expose to public contempt the witnesses called by South Africa, and in no uncertain manner to reveal in the face of the entire civilized world the so-called "wickedness" of the policy they detest. But did they make use of this golden opportunity? A distinguished authority on international law, Mr. Clifford J. Hynning, vice-chairman of the Division of Comparative Law of the American Bar Association, said:

> I was really startled when Mr. Ernest Gross declined to call any witnesses. Here we had had debates within the General Assembly of the U.N. stretching from 1946 until yesterday or today, and there has been a complaint they haven't had a forum in which to make charges against South Africa and to controvert the denials by South Africa that the maximum

interests of the indigenous population were not being promoted. Here was a tailor-made opportunity in an international forum to present witnesses, to give oral testimony, to cross-examine. What a magnificent opportunity for the African states to make a case against South Africa! . . .

The implication of course, is that the African states did not have the evidence to show that the indigenous population of South [West] Africa was being oppressed or treated in a manner differently from certain indigenous populations in other parts of Africa.[8]

They even failed badly when South Africa presented fourteen witnesses, including three professors from the United States and one from the United Kingdom. But perhaps the most significant feature of this part of the litigation is that the world press, an ardent opponent of South African policies and a great champion of universal freedom and fundamental human rights, equally failed to report on the course of events in the World Court and in particular on the oral evidence given by South Africa's witnesses.

Knowing that the charges rested on an emotional basis rather than on any attempt at an objective assessment or analysis of facts, South Africa was so keen to expose the gross distortions of the truth in the charges that it went so far as to indicate it would consider, if the applicant states should wish to call the petitioners as witnesses, offering to pay their witness fees to allow South Africa the privilege of cross-examining them before the International Court of Justice.[9] Inasmuch as the original charges of the African states against the Republic were largely instigated by petitioners at the United Nations who claimed firsthand knowledge of conditions in the territory, the applicants could have availed themselves of no better opportunity to obtain "expert evidence" free of charge. Very wisely, however, they refused to accept this generous offer.

South Africa went even further and invited the Court to visit the territory for inspection purposes to let them see "anything which the inspecting body itself may wish to see, or which the Applicants may wish to bring to its attention."[10] South Africa also suggested, but without making it a condition, that South Africa as well as Ethiopia and Liberia and even a number of other African countries also be visited, not as a matter "of introducing policies and their application in the African States for adjudication by this Court" but as a matter "of assisting the Court in properly fulfilling its task in regard to adjudication and evaluation of the policies applied in South West Africa."[11] Here another opportunity was offered the applicants to expose the so-called "atrocious conditions" existing under the policy of separate development. One would expect that they would have grasped this ideal opportunity with both hands and done their utmost to persuade the Court to accept this proposal. Instead, they vigorously opposed it and said that

> the proposal for the inspection *in loco* is unnecessary, expensive, dilatory, cumbersome and unwarranted, that the weighing of the proposal and its asserted reasons in the scale of justice, alongside the length of time which this litigation has consumed, in respect of the antecedents of this legislation, in respect of the voluminous pleadings which, for more than four years, have been prepared, collated, and are now submitted in unusually bulky form—that in the light of all these considerations the Court should reject the proposal.[12]

In a formal notification conveyed to the parties on May 24, 1965, the Court indicated that it would not consider an on-the-spot inspection until after it had received all the evidence and the parties had finished their pleadings.[13] Later, on November 29, 1965, the Court, by a vote of 8 to 6, rejected the inspection proposal.[14]

A further triumph was scored by South Africa when the applicants suddenly decided to retreat from the factual issue on the pleadings by accepting as true all the averments of fact in South Africa's pleadings, including South Africa's controversions of allegations which the applicants had made in their own pleadings. They categorically stated:

> The Applicants have advised [the] Respondent as well as this honourable Court that all and any averments of fact in [the] Respondent's written pleadings will be and are accepted as true, unless specifically denied. And the Applicants have not found it necessary and do not find it necessary to controvert any such averments of fact. Hence, for the purposes of these proceedings, such averments of fact, although made by [the] Respondent in a copious and unusually voluminous record, may be treated as if incorporated by reference into the Applicants' pleadings.[15]

From this point on, the case of Ethiopia and Liberia rested solely on their contention that South Africa's policies and practices violated an international norm and standard of "non-discrimination or non-separation". Even here the applicants could not accomplish anything spectacular. Three expert witnesses, Professor C. A. W. Manning (for more than thirty-two years professor of international relations at the University of London), Dr. E. van den Haag (professor of social philosophy at New York University), and Professor S. T. Possony (director of the International Political Studies Program at the Hoover Institution on War, Revolution, and Peace at Stanford University) testified exhaustively on the contemporary practices of differentiation in fifty countries in which status, rights, duties, and burdens were allotted by both law and official practice on the basis of membership of a group, class, or race. Forty of these states were members of the United Nations and they included even Liberia and Ethiopia. The evidence dealt with the legislation and practices in Asian systems of pluralistic societies, certain systems on the eastern Meditettanean, pluralistic systems in Islamic countries, and systems in various countries making distinctions between groups.

Moreover, South Africa submitted that such a norm had to satisfy two requirements. Firstly, the applicants had to establish that it was a rule of law binding upon South Africa and, secondly, that it was part of the mandate. The mandate itself, however, contained clear provisions not only allowing but also establishing differentiation between groups, particularly as far as land, military training, and the supply of liquor were concerned. Such a norm clearly did not exist as a rule of international law.

The Political Aftermath of the International Court's Decision

If those eminent men who laid the foundation stones of international law, such as Grotius and many others, could have had a bird's-eye view of the modern world, they would have been flabbergasted and humiliated by the tendency of caucus meetings of the different groups of "blocs" at the United Nations to assume greater importance than the meetings of the General Assembly, the various General Assembly committees, and the International Court of Justice. Exactly 101 days after the International Court of Justice delivered its judgment, the Afro-Asian caucus in an emotional storm succeeded in stampeding the General Assembly into adopting Resolution 2145 (XXI) of October 27, 1966, by which South Africa's administration of South West Africa was "terminated" and the territory placed under the direct responsibility of the United Nations. Less than a year later on May 19, 1967, at a special session of the General Assembly, a further resolution was rushed through the Assembly establishing a "United Nations Council for South West Africa" comprising eleven members to " . . . administer South West Africa until independence . . ." and to " . . . promulgate such laws, decrees and administrative regulations as are necessary for the administration of the Territory until a legislative assembly is established following elections conducted on the basis of universal suffrage."[16] When, at a later stage, the council was composed of Chile, Colombia, Guyana, India, Indonesia, Nigeria, Pakistan, Turkey, Yugoslavia, and Zambia, nearly half of these members were striking examples of states where there was differential treatment by law of different groups and religions in respect of land, rights, legal status, and universal suffrage. In one of them, Nigeria, thousands of innocent men, women, and children died as a direct result of group differences.

The abuse and manipulation of the United Nations for political purposes indicates the ominous direction in which the world is now moving. Indeed, it may already be too late to return to a state where the rule of law has significant meaning any longer. The editor of the *Chicago Tribune* wrote on October 14, 1966:

> The real question is why on earth we must inject ourselves into another African dispute which is basically a matter of power politics and which, if Mr. Goldberg succeeds, will probably result in the withdrawal of South Africa from the U.N., the intensification of the Rhodesian dispute, the distinct possibility of war in Africa, the breakup of the British commonwealth [*sic*] and the wreckage of the economy of all southern Africa.[17]

The caucus of the Afro-Asians was quite determined to "overrule" the existing law, and the most tragic feature of the aftermath of the judgment is that some of the leading Western countries, including the United States of America, have condoned the lawlessness. This fact certainly indicates considerable danger for the future, inasmuch as such support mainly encourages the young irresponsible countries to continue along illegal lines in their international relations with others and even among themselves.

The basis for the two resolutions in question was said to be the "inhuman, unjust and oppressive" policies applied to the territory—the same sort of emotional charges that have been so exhaustively argued before the International Court of Justice and withdrawn by the applicants. The judicial tribune and its impartial judges have been replaced by a political "tribunal" where the applicants are simultaneously the prosecutors, judges, witnesses, and executioners. They have conveniently ensconced themselves behind the proverbial heads-I-win-and-tails-you-lose-barricade—and that with the support of responsible states which should know better.

The Subsequent Attack on the World Court

The judges of the International Court who constituted the Court in 1966 included some of the most eminent jurists of the world. They were elected by the United Nations. The way they were criticized, however, and the language used affords some insight into the mentality and philosophy of those members of the United Nations who campaign against South Africa. The following extracts from the debate in the General Assembly demonstrate the intention of some countries to "pack" the Court in future with judges prepared to support their views:

> Mr. Yifru (Ethiopia): We have also been taught one cardinal lesson, that is, we have to take an active part in all the organs of the United Nations, including the International Court of Justice. To this end, we shall demand equitable representation on the bench of the Court, a representation commensurate with our role in the United Nations. . . .[18]
>
> Mr. Mgonja (United Republic of Tanzania); We believe that this experience—the most recent Judgment of the International Court—sad as it is, has been a salutary lesson to the newly independent countries in their struggle for effective representation in all international bodies.[19]
>
> Mr. Arkhurst (Ghana): Furthermore, and this is extremely important, since the Court is the foremost body for the development of international law and justice, judges elected to the Court must be men of agile mind and with the courage to adapt to the evolving norms of the international community. . . . It is, therefore, in this spirit that my delegation will vote in the forthcoming elections to the International Court of Justice.[20]
>
> Mr. Ilboudo (Upper Volta): Established at a time when the world was altogether different from the world of today, the International Court of Justice, so far as its composition is concerned, is no longer consistent with current reality. To revise its composition could not but benefit the entire United Nations.[21]
>
> Mr. Gallin-Douathe (Central African Republic): The Court has fully justified our previous expressed reservations concerning its membership, which fails to reflect the current range of legal and political trends in the United Nations.[22]
>
> Mr. Banjar (Mongolia): In this connexion, the delegation of Mongolia shares the view that serious consideration should be given to the need to make the structure of the Court reflect the changes which have occurred in the alignment of forces in the world and within the United Nations itself.[23]
>
> Mr. Ake (Ivory Coast): . . . we have good reason to question its impartiality. I feel that the Member States should seriously consider altering the Court's composition so as to assure more equitable representation for all the different cultures.[24]
>
> Mr. Bakala (Congo [Brazzaville]): My delegation believes, as do many others, that it is high time to change the Court so that it will no longer reflect the obsolete concepts of an outdated era. . . .[25]
>
> Mr. Taieb Slim (Tunisia): Two decades ago, when it was established, the Court reflected the world as it was after the last war. . . . In its present composition, the Court cannot exercise its basic function.[26]

Thus a new feature, entirely foreign to the International Court of Justice and its predecessors has been introduced in international arbitration. Member states are now determined not only to select judges whose political views are beyond any doubt proved to be in accordance with their own, but also in future international disputes member states will most likely be prepared to submit their case to the International Court of Justice only after "heads had been counted" and the result had indicated a clear majority for their own views. Any judge of such a court will then be a mere pawn, and those judges who dare dissent will run the risk of exposure to severe slander and ridicule. This would, in fact, be commensurate with the role of certain states at the United Nations. The following quotations indicate how the Court and the individual judges were degraded by certain delegations at the United Nations:

> Mr. Grimes (Liberia): Thus, . . . transparent justice was denied and seven men perverted justice and brought upon the International Court the greatest opprobrium in its history.[27]
> Mr. Pirzada (Pakistan): Such a perverse result could not but be a setback to all those who reposed faith in the judicial organ of the United Nations. . . .[28]
> Mr. Achkar (Guinea): It is enough to see that these Judges are from Greece, Italy, the United Kingdom and France—all countries that give unqualified support to the rash policies of South Africa and secretly uphold that country because of the enormous profits that their economies derive from the pitiless implementation of the policy of economic and social slavery known as apartheid. As for the Australian Judge, Sir Percy Spender, whose name, I think, means "spendthrift"—he needs money—his deciding vote and his

conduct throughout the proceedings show that he is now worthy of the confidence which the General Assembly placed in him in electing him and which his colleagues expressed in raising him to the high office of President of the Court. . . . As for the Polish Judge, whose behaviour has been denounced by his own Government, we can only wish for him that in the golden exile he will no doubt arrange for himself in a country in which he will claim to have "chosen freedom," he may quietly enjoy the money he has been able to amass, to the extent to which his conscience will be able to bear the heavy burden that he is now helping to impose on the unfortunate African people of South West Africa.[29]

Mr. El Kony (United Arab Republic): My delegation was greatly surprised and disappointed by the judgement of the International Court of Justice. We believe that the reasons on which the Court based its judgement are of dubious validity. It is to be deeply regretted that that world institution, by failing in its duty, has shaken our trust.[30]

Mr. Auguste (Haiti): Is this the language of the law? Is this in keeping with what we have been told about the judges, those supposed supermen? Is this in accordance with the respect we have for them and their decisions?[31]

Mr. Kapwepwe (Zambia): Indeed, the International Court of Justice at the Hague took six long years . . . only to frustrate finally the wishes of the indigenous people of South West Africa, only to disgrace this our own Organization, by cowardly shirking its responsibility to the peoples of the world, by shamelessly judging not to judge. . . .[32]

Mr. Ilboudo (Upper Volta): Was it necessary to spend 336 hours in order to pronounce judgement on procedure alone? Were 3,756 pages of evidence required to state that Ethiopia and Liberia had not established any interest in the case? Lastly, did the Court need 112 sittings to accept a system—I refer to apartheid—which had been rejected by the United Nations as contrary to its Charter? Was so much time, so much evidence really needed in order to put us off with such a fallacious excuse?[33]

Mr. El Mufti (Sudan): The Judgement of the Court represents to us an abdication of responsibility.[34]

Mr. Ake (Ivory Coast): It is our feeling that the Court's judgement of 18 July 1966 is a scandal without precedent in the annals of law.[35]

Mr. Ba (Mali): . . .the Judgment of the International Court of Justice was dictated more by the desire to safeguard the interests of imperialist financial groups than by the

desire to free this region from the yoke of apartheid.[36]

Mr. Kironde (Uganda): Augustine has described a state without justice as no better than a band of robber-thieves, and this equally applies to an international organization, the members of which refuse to be guided by principles of justice and prefer to hide behind specious arguments and legalistic terms.[37]

The scathing attack on the integrity of the Court was soon followed up by a rejection of an increase in the budget for the International Court. This, perhaps, has been the most severe blow directed at the United Nations during its existence; the eventual destruction of this institution will undoubtedly be more detrimental to the young, economically undeveloped nations of Africa than to any other states.

Under these tragic circumstances, would South Africa ever again be a party before the International Court of Justice? I firmly believe that those Western countries which have maintained a high standard of justice over past centuries would promptly admit that their own enthusiasm for the settlement of disputes by the type of tribunal the quoted delegates had in mind must have cooled off. Such a "court" would resemble the so-called "People's Tribunals" which are so prevalent in some areas of the world as "instruments of the revolution."

South African Membership in the United Nations

It has often been stated that South Africa might under certain circumstances decide to withdraw from the United Nations. In South Africa itself there is a very strong feeling that the country should walk out, and the sooner the better. Proponents of this view look upon the organization as a purely political institution where there remains very little room for rational thinking, and they regard it as powerless to solve the real problems of the world, such as the Vietnam conflict, the Middle East situation, and the war in Nigeria —not to speak of poverty, disease, famine, and illiteracy in so many parts of the world. During the past twenty-six years South Africa has quietly gone its way—developing economically, creating conditions of peace and progress for all her peoples, and living in peace with all countries, including her black neighbors. And she yet has been continuously the victim of unrestrained vituperation within the United Nations.

Nevertheless, South Africa has always acted in the correct and proper way that can be expected from any civilized country. She is sometimes accused of having acted in a contumacious manner in the case of South West Africa. In fact, the contrary is true. She left the door open for negotiations, but it became clear that nothing short of surrender to the wild, irresponsible demands of the Afro-Asian group at the United Nations would be acceptable. In 1951 South Africa proposed that a new agreement be entered into with the remaining principal allied and associated powers of World War I. This did not satisfy the majority of the General Assembly. Toward the end of 1952 the United Nations' Committee on South West Africa could report agreement in principle on five points. The committee itself expressed its appreciation of South Africa's efforts, but regarded itself so bound by its terms of reference that it could not accept anything less than the surrender of the territory. In 1958 South Africa invited the members of the United Nations Good Offices Committee to visit South West Africa, and the committee eventually suggested a form of partition. This idea, however, was summarily rejected by the extremists at the world organization. In 1962 the Carpio–De Alva mission was sent to South Africa and South West Africa, and at the conclusion of their visit these two officials eventually subscribed to a joint communiqué which was, from the point of view of the majority of the United Nations members, too partial to South Africa.[38]

In the meantime South Africa proved time and again that it had nothing to hide or to be ashamed of concerning its administration, policies, or objectives in the territory. Full and detailed information was given to the International Court in the pleadings and extensive expert testimony, and an invitation had been tendered the Court to inspect the territory. The *South West Africa Survey*, an extensive analysis of all matters concerning the territory, was published and distributed to governments and international organizations, and the envoys of all governments accredited to South Africa were invited to visit all parts of the territory. From time to time the South African representatives participated in the debates in the various organs of the United Nations and furnished information on the territory. In fact, it was invariably proved that any information and findings favorable to South Africa were summarily rejected and ignored by the United Nations. Similarly, mere assertions, mostly uninformed and often reckless, were eagerly accepted, provided this furthered the objectives of the majority. One example will suffice to illustrate this point. General S. L. A. Marshall, an American military expert, told the World Court that he had inspected a particular facility in the territory which had been described by petitioners as a "nuclear station." When he went to South West Africa, however, he had found that it was nothing other than an establishment of the Max Planck Institute for Aeronomy, one of two hundred similar stations all over the world concerned with ionospheric research for the benefit of almost all countries of the world. Two dissenting judges, in fact, found that there was no truth in the charge of "militarization." When the discussion of South West Africa was resumed in the General Assembly, however, South Africa was again accused of "militarizing" the territory.

All these events contributed to South Africa's losing faith in the United Nations. Even a report submitted by UN committee members was not accepted unless it condemned South Africa, as was the case with the De Alva report, and the judgment of the International Court of Justice was relegated to the wastepaper basket. After a Liberian motion to expunge the speech of Dr. Eric H. Louw (the South African minister of foreign affairs) on October 11, 1961, from the records of the General Assembly was withdrawn, another Liberian motion was adopted to censure South Africa for a statement which was "offensive, fictitious and erroneous."[39] Whenever a minister of foreign affairs of South Africa would go to the rostrum to participate in the debates a walkout would be staged. This is the treatment that South Africa receives as an original member of both the League of Nations and the United Nations organization, and whose distinguished prime minister, the late Field Marshal J. C. Smuts, was not only the author of the preamble to the charter of the organization but also contributed extensively toward the foundation of this international body. South Africa has never occupied a seat in the Security Council and has been suspended from various agencies of the organization but, ironically, has always paid her contributions to the United Nations budget.

South Africa believes that if the United Nations could be induced to face the truth, many of the misunderstandings and misrepresentations might disappear. She remains willing to enlighten those who are genuinely interested in South West Africa. But she is not prepared to expose the peoples committed to her care to the ruthless demands of certain states. On October 12, 1966, the minister of foreign affairs, Dr. Hilgard Muller, not only challenged the legality of the resolution terminating South Africa's administration of the territory, but told the General Assembly in no uncertain terms that "dire consequences" would follow an attempt by the organization to take over the territory and that South Africa was prepared to "resist with all the power at its disposal any attempts which endanger the safety of our country or of the peoples committed to our care. And my Government knows that it will have the support of peoples equally determined to resist—meaning thereby, most certainly, not only the white people."[40]

In this issue the South African minister of foreign affairs, in fact, can depend on the support of all the peoples of South West Africa. A referendum conducted by the Smuts government in 1946 indicated that only 11 percent of the territory's nonwhite population voted against a political association with the Republic.[41] The chief minister of the Transkei (Mr. Kaiser Matanzima),[42] the paramount chief of the Damaras in South West Africa (Mr. David Goraseb),[43] and the colored people of the territory[44] recently reiterated their violent opposition toward United Nations interference in South West African affairs.

The prime minister of South Africa, Mr. B. J. Vorster, decided to caution the United Nations in a public address at Beaufort West in June 1967, when he stated that South Africa was not prepared to pay for the "picnics" of the United Nations—the frequent symposia held to discuss South Africa's race policies, which took place under the auspices of this organization (to which South Africa has to contribute considerable amounts of money). He also stated that a serious reappraisal should be made of South Africa's position in the United Nations and that the Western countries should decide whether South Africa was still worth anything to them. "If they decided South Africa was no longer of use to them, South Africa would no longer regard herself as being under any obligation towards them. Then South Africa would have to give careful consideration to whether it was still worthwhile remaining a member of the United Nations."[45] The prime minister also made it quite clear that South Africa had reached the stage where the government would not allow any interference in her affairs by the United Nations. Later, in Pretoria, Prime Minister Vorster said that South Africa would withdraw from the United Nations "when and if it is of no importance to her to belong to the Organization."[46]

South Africa has, therefore, come to a stage where her membership in the United Nations is continuously under consideration, and the question could rightly be posed: What factors would eventually determine whether she would remain a member? I submit that the outbursts and tirades of the Afro-Asian and Communist countries would not be the determining factor, but rather the attitudes of countries like the United States, France, the United Kingdom, and other Western powers. I firmly believe that South Africa is destined to play a substantial role in world politics in general, but more particularly in the economic development of Africa, a part she can fulfill more effectively if she remains an active member of the United Nations. Furthermore, I believe the Western powers are heavily burdened with great problems that also concern South Africa and South Africa can contribute to the solution of these problems. It is also in the interests of these powers that South Africa should remain a member of the United Nations. They should ask themselves whether they would rather appease South Africa's enemies and thereby help to create chaos and revolution in Africa, or assume an attitude of responsibility and thereby engender more respect for law and order and provide a meaningful role for the United Nations. If the latter is true, then I am confident that South Africa will remain in the United Nations; if the former proves to be the case, the next two years will be decisive as far as South Africa's membership is concerned.

South West Africa's Strategic Position

A glance at the map of Southern Africa will show that South West Africa is located between Angola in the north, Zambia in the northeast, Botswana in the east, and the Republic of South Africa in the south and southeast, and that it is bounded by a long stretch of over nine hundred miles of the Atlantic Ocean in the west. It thus flanks the vital sea route to the Republic and the Far East. Should the territory be occupied by an enemy, the threat of air or sea attack on shipping would be phenomenal. Moreover, apart from its potentialities as a base for a direct attack by land, air warfare has placed vital centers like Cape Town and Johannesburg within an easy range of less than five hundred miles.

Geographically and economically, the territory cannot exist without the Republic of South Africa. Mr. G. L. Beer, head of the Colonial Division of the American delegation at Versailles after World War I has pointed out that

> the development of this Territory would be gravely handicapped if it were administered entirely apart from the adjoining Union of South Africa with distinctive native, fiscal and railroad policies and systems.[47]

The territory's political and economic future is so inextricably bound up with that of the Republic that a formal incorporation would mainly be a recognition of a unity that existed since 1920 and just another phase in the process of coordination of human destinies throughout the great geographic entities of the world. The budgetary history of the territory shows recurring heavy deficits with their consequent effects on economic development. The main sources of revenue are agriculture, mining, and fishing, and they all need the stimulus of a secure future. Because of the low and irregular rainfall, agriculture cannot be relied upon, and the scope for economic expansion without the expenditure of large capital sums is very limited.

Despite the demands for her own capital development, South Africa spent some $230 million in the territory between 1920 and 1963, with no provision for interest or recovery. This did not include capital outlays on the railways of more than $196 million and an accumulated operating loss on railroads and air services of over $56 million. In all, South Africa has contributed financial aid to South West Africa amounting to $420 per capita, an achievement that is unequaled by any other mandatory power. This does not include "invisible" expenditure. This fabulous development has been achieved in spite of the formidable obstacle that has, like the proverbial sword of Damocles, hung continuously over the territory—namely, the uncertainty about the country's future since 1920. Even today, the largest deterrent to the influx of overseas capital and subsequent economic development is the sporadic discussions of the territory's future at the United Nations. Only a few years ago South Africa embarked on a new program of development costing more than $346 million which, in terms of the United States population of approximately four hundred times that of South West Africa, is the equivalent of $138 billion—almost the entire U.S. budget for one year.

As the major economic market and industrial state within a radius of some six thousand miles, the only producer of coal (so vital for the future industries and mining operations) in near proximity, and the major source of capital investment, the Republic is most vital for the very existence of the territory. As Ray Vicker recently wrote in the *Wall Street Journal*, "Separating the two in economic terms would be about like trying to separate Alaska from North America."[48]

Without the harbor of Walvis Bay, which belongs to the Republic, the whole territory would suffer tremendously since the only other possible harbor, Luderitz, is situated in the far south, nearly a thousand miles away from the fertile north where most of the development is likely to take place. The southern part of the country is semidesert, only suitable for the raising of sheep, and it has very scant possibilities for industrial development.

In view of the inseparability of the two countries, it would be most unwise to assess the strategic value of South West Africa without taking into consideration the enormous impact the Republic has made on the economic development of Southern Africa and the ultimate role it can play in the balance of power, which is so essential for the maintenance of world peace. I firmly believe that Africa with all her potentialities of minerals, electric power, raw materials, and other inexhaustible natural resources will play a decisive part in the race between Communism and the Western world. Communist infiltration in Africa is imminent. Significantly, those petitioners raising vigorous objections against the proposed incorporation of South West Africa in 1946 by the Republic were often of Communist sympathies—for example, the Port Elizabeth section of the former South African Communist Party, the former Communist Party of Transvaal, the former League of South African Communist Youth, the former Communist Party of South Africa, and the former Communist Party of the City of Johannesburg.[49]

The Soviet Union refused to support the African states on the critical issue of South West Africa in 1967 only because it does not want an effective United Nations peacekeeping military body in Southern Africa. If the United Nations however, should decide to send a military force to South West Africa, Communist penetration would be inevitable. In the Congo in 1960, the Soviet Union had not opposed the original Security Council resolution which authorized the sending of a United Nations force to the Congo, but increasingly it pursued a policy of sending aid, including arms and ammunition, direct to Prime Minister Lumumba.[50] This was accompanied by the introduction of Communist agents into the Congo under the guise of a massive buildup of the Soviet and Czech embassies, which ultimately resulted in a long internecine war, killing and scattering large sections of the population of that country. Any United Nations intervention will no doubt be pursued by similar repercussions with even more tragic results. "It took the Communists twenty years to conquer China," writes Dr. Eschel M. Rhoodie, "and with mineral resources elsewhere in the world being slowly but surely exhausted, it seems unlikely that they are going to be put off by temporary setbacks in their efforts to capture mineral rich Africa."[51] He refers to an address by Dean Rusk in 1965, confirming "that the Russians and Chinese have funneled some R700,000,000 [$980 million] in aid to new African nations since 1960 and have assigned 5,000 technical advisers in an effort to woo Africa's emergent states. In addition some 6–8,000 African students are in Communist countries."[52]

Active Communist infiltration in Africa involves another imminent threat to Western civilization in Africa, and that is the phenomenal Chinese interest in this subcontinent. At the end of his first African tour, Chou En-lai announced that "an excellent revolutionary situation exists in Africa today."[53] The only comfort for the Western powers is that Communist efforts in Africa have been limited by the lack of relevance of Communist doctrines to actual African problems and needs and also by the unwillingness of Africans to be made use of by either side in the East-West conflict.[54] However, one wonders whether the nonalignment policy of the African states at this stage is not really due to their greediness to collect financial aid from both sides and to maintain the financial competition between the East and the West. The Chinese are building the $16.8 million Zambian railway line, and in return Zambia has just appointed her first ambassador to China.

All these events constitute a prelude to larger Chinese and Communist penetration in Africa and suggest that greater consideration of, and a more realistic approach to, African affairs are needed by the Western powers. The time for conjecture and child's play have passed. The gravity of the situation requires a reappraisal of the South West African issue. Western powers should not use it as an instrument to appease certain extravagant states, which in the end might prove to be lost to the Western cause. Rather, they should seriously consider the real issues at stake.

The Future of the Territory

Apart from the legal aspect which has indisputably been proved to be in favor of South Africa, there is also the element of moral obligation under the original mandate which South Africa cannot summarily dispose of and which—for economic, social, and strategic reasons—can best be performed by South Africa. We can by no means yield to illegal resolutions of the majority at the United Nations merely because they represent "world opinion." The United States turned a deaf ear toward "world opinion" in the Vietnam issue because she realized only too well that there were other matters at stake. Israel ignores world opinion because she has to survive. Other countries assume similar attitudes from time to time. It is deceptive to pander to "world opinion," which is usually subject to emotional manipulation and is sometimes based on total ignorance of the real situation. In fact, regional and national interests as well as other covert prejudices are sometimes termed "world opinion." History has proved that no country in the world, however small, has voluntarily surrendered its self-respect, and South Africa will be no exception.

A committee of the Swedish Ministries of Foreign Affairs and Trade found that if total economic sanctions were imposed on South Africa, along with a fully effective ban on both imports and exports applied by the rest of the world, the Republic's economy would be seriously damaged, but it would not be destroyed.[55] The committee did not accept the oft-made contention that an oil embargo would paralyze the economy. It pointed out that the main national system of transport is the railways, which are powered by coal. In addition, most South African industry uses electricity generated by coal as a source of power. For those nations considering economic sanctions against South Africa, perhaps the situation in Rhodesia could be a warning. Since UDI in 1965, the gross national product in Rhodesia increased by $78 million and the value of building plans (perhaps a better yardstick of progress) jumped from $16.24 million to $56.56 million in the first nine months of 1968.[56]

A more favorable situation for South Africa recently occurred when, in an atmosphere of jubilation and excitement, the South African minister of mines (Dr. Carel de Wet) announced in Parliament on March 25, 1969, that South Africa's first gas, yielding 25 million cubic feet a day, was struck forty miles from the coast off Plettenberg Bay. While the editor of *The Cape Argus* wrote that because of this huge petroleum gas strike the "costs of planning for the eventuality of a cold war directed at South Africa will no doubt be considerably reduced in the coming years, and the country may be able to afford to relax with a feeling of economic security and greater self-dependence,"[57] the newspaper's staff reporter anticipated "an era of political immunity from international pressures."[58]

A lively topic among those specializing in the field of international politics is the possibility of military intervention in pursuance of Article 42 of the Charter of the United Nations. The Carnegie Endowment for International Peace recently published an intensive study on this[59] which, I maintain, signifies only an alarming amount of prematurity. In my opinion, an armed invasion of South West Africa can generally be ruled out; in any event it will never succeed. Those who might desire action of that nature could not risk it.

Admittedly, the United States of America at one stage seriously considered the mustering of a massive fleet on the west coast of the territory in an attempt to exert pressure on South Africa, but the main impression I gained from informed circles on a recent two months' tour in the United States is that a military action by U.S. armed forces in Southern Africa is extremely unlikely.

Field Marshal Lord Montgomery conducted a study of a possible invasion of South West Africa and arrived at this conclusion: "My own opinion is that any United Nations force which attempted 'to liberate' South-West Africa would have a very rough passage, and would suffer total defeat."[60]

His survey was completed in 1964. Since that

date the South African budget for defense matters has been substantially increased, and thus it is not necessary to pursue this matter any further.

I firmly believe that the ultimate destiny of South West Africa will not be determined at the United Nations but, rather, by the inhabitants of the territory of South West Africa, in close consultation with the Republic of South Africa. What can be its ultimate destiny?

There are two reasons why the Republic will not accede to any proposal for the administration of South West Africa by the United Nations. The first is that the United Nations cannot afford the massive financial and technical means to develop the territory. The political and economic development of this arid country calls for an annual outlay of capital sufficient to finance the entire United Nations administration for a full year.[61] Yet at this stage the United Nations can hardly raise enough funds to maintain itself. In 1965 South Africa and eight other countries had to pay the membership fees in advance to save the organization from financial difficulties. Moreover, in 1968 six countries were deprived of their vote because they were more than two years in arrears with the payment of their dues. In the event of a takeover by the United Nations, more than 90 percent of the approximately one hundred thousand whites in the territory would immediately leave the country with their capital and technical skills, and this would result in a major disaster as far as the economy of the country was concerned. Furthermore, there would be the anomaly that South Africa would still control Walvis Bay, the only deep-sea port in the territory. The second reason why the Republic will not accede to any proposal of a takeover by the United Nations requires no elaboration at all. It would be illegal.

One could safely assume that future political, economic, and social development in South West Africa will take place on the lines laid down by the *Report of the Commission of Enquiry into South West Africa Affairs* (Odendaal Commission Report).[62] The commission, which consisted of experts from outside the political field, was appointed to inquire thoroughly into the means of further promoting the material and moral welfare and the social progress of the inhabitants of South West Africa, especially the nonwhite inhabitants. It proposed a tremendous development plan to be implemented over three five-year plans, the first of which would entail the considerable amount of $210 million.

Nonwhite Homelands: The commission recommended that homelands be constituted as self-governing areas for the eight nonwhite nations in the territory. For this purpose enormous areas had to be purchased from white farmers to be added to the original African reserves. The land allocated to the nonwhites amounts to an average of 182.9 acres per capita of the population. In reply to a question in the House of Assembly on February 27, 1968, Prime Minister B. J. Vorster announced that up to that date 410 farms, covering an area of 7.5 million acres, and 68 erven in towns had been purchased at a cost of $34 million from white farmers to be added to the nonwhite homelands.[63] The government endorses the view of the commission that, as far as practicable, it should be the aim to develop a homeland for each nonwhite nation in South West Africa, in which it can attain self-determination and self-realization.

This was further pursued in 1968 when the South African Parliament passed the Development of Self-Government for Native Nations in South West Africa Act (Act no. 54 of 1968), which established specific areas for the different nonwhite nations in the territory—namely, Damaraland, Hereroland, Kaokoland, Okavangoland, Eastern Caprivi, Ovamboland, and "such other land or area as may after the commencement of this Act be reserved and set apart for the exclusive use of and occupation by any native nation."[64] The act provides for the fundamental principles of self-government for each nation through a system of central government, consisting of a legislative council and an executive council, and a system of local government through subordinate authorities, the details of which are to be determined after consultation by proclamation in respect of each nation.[65] The members of a nation working outside their home area are linked with the central government by representatives in urban areas and in other centers where there are large numbers of these members; the representatives are nominated by their respective executive councils.[66] The central government will assume a leading role in connection with matters affecting the material, moral, and social welfare of the nation in question, and it will be vested with legislative powers concerning economic development in the homelands, agricultural education (so that all rights over and responsibilities for their own lands may be assigned to them), welfare services, the establishment of medical clinics, the control of business and trading establishments, industries, mining, roads, bridges, afforestation, and markets, the administration of justice, employment offices, public works, and taxation.[67] The white administrative and professional officers will gradually and systematically be replaced by qualified and competent members of the nation concerned.

In October 1968 the Legislative Council for Ovamboland was constituted with headquarters at Oshakati; it consists of forty-two members elected by the seven tribes of Ovamboland in accordance with their tribal tradition. The Executive Council is composed of seven members, one elected by each tribe. Mr. Ushona Shiimi, paramount chief of the Ogandjera tribe, was elected chief councillor (practically prime minister) of the Ovambo nation.

Economic Progress: The Odendaal Commission recommended a massive economic development of South West Africa and the Republic decided that these projects be undertaken immediately. The main schemes, most of which had progressed very rapidly by the end of 1968 and thus changed the entire territory, will be discussed below.

Water and Electricity: The Kunene River scheme, which will cost $70 million, will supply the northern and central areas of the territory with electric power. While the Etaka section of the canal scheme for the supply of water in Ovamboland has been completed, an additional water supply scheme (linked with the Kunene scheme) is in progress, traversing the more densely populated areas with canals and pipelines. In the south of the territory, an enormous irrigation scheme in the Orange River will be developed for the colored group. In the central homelands a number of dam projects for the supply of water to the Namas, Damaras, and Hereros are being planned at a cost of $22.4 million. This does not include hundreds of dams and boreholes (some of which have already been completed) contemplated for several homelands.

Transport: The Commission recommended considerable development of roads, air services, and railroads. In addition to the roads which are to be constructed in the normal course of development by the administration of the territory, the government of South Africa has embarked on a large-scale development of the main roads (at a cost of $45.5 million) as well as the construction of seven hundred miles of roads as internal connecting links in the nonwhite areas (at a total cost of $11.76 million). The tarred road has now been completed from the Orange River in the south (a distance of nearly one thousand miles) up to the Kunene River in the north and from Windhoek to the west coast. A new tarred road from Windhoek to Gobabis in the east is well under way. Owing to the vast distances in the territory, sixteen principal airfields, thirty-one secondary airfields, and sixty private airfields and emergency landing strips are being developed simultaneously. The Commission found that the territory had adequate rail and road transport services. During the previous ten years, $100.8 million was spent on modernizing and improving the railway system, which had accumulated a loss of approximately $72 million since 1922. The government, however, decided to abolish the "split tariff" formerly applicable to the territory, thus incurring the additional expenditure of $3.54 million.[68]

Mining: The Commission pointed out that there were possibilities for the greater development of mining in the territory. The government accordingly decided to organize the exploration and mapping of the whole territory and to assist the inhabitants of the nonwhite areas in prospecting and exploiting the mineral resources in the homelands.

Industries: It was decided that, with the assistance of the Bantu Investment Corporation, special attention should be given to the efficient marketing of livestock from the northern areas and the establishment of a meat canning factory, a furniture factory, a clothing factory, a jute factory, and other suitable industries in Ovamboland.

Agriculture: In addition to the large-scale water supply schemes, professional research, education, and guidance are being extended. The cultivation of groundnuts and jute is being expanded, while quarantine and abattoir facilities are established to assist in the campaign against cattle diseases. A large number of agricultural officers have been appointed to advise and assist nonwhite farmers.

Education and Health Services: The Commission found an exceptionally good rate of growth in education and health services. Forty-six percent of the indigenous children between the ages of five and nineteen years attended school in 1962, as compared with 29 percent in Botswana, 13 percent in Ethiopia, 28 percent in Ghana, 12 percent in Liberia, 9 percent in Sudan and 4 percent in Somalia, for example.[69] Because education will necessarily play an important part in future development, the government decided to provide for still more advanced and more numerous schools, dormitories, and centers for the training of teachers. Today the Augustineum training school for nonwhite teachers in Windhoek is one of the most modern in the world. White students in South West Africa do not have the privilege of attending such a fine establishment.

The health services for indigenous inhabitants of the territory also compare favorably with those in other African states. In South West Africa there was one medical practitioner for 5,500 people in the African areas. In Botswana the figure was one for 20,000; in Liberia one for 40,000; in Nigeria one for 40,000; and in Senegal one for 50,000.[70] The government, nevertheless, decided to embark on a further program of development, including the erection of a huge tuberculosis and general hospital at Okatana (Ovamboland) at a total cost of $2 million. This hospital has already been completed. Twenty more hospitals and clinics will be built in a comprehensive campaign to combat malaria, tuberculosis, and other diseases.

Financial Arrangements: In view of the large-scale development contemplated by the Odendaal

Commission, the commission proposed a rearrangement of administrative and financial relations between the Republic and South West Africa which would be worked out in detail by a committee of financial experts. These experts completed their report in 1966, and the government of South Africa subsequently resolved to embody their recommendations in legislation. But the government announced that, despite its view that the mandate had lapsed, its administration of the territory would continue to be based on the following principles which are compatible with the provisions of the mandate agreement:

> (a) the Government of South Africa has full power of administration and legislation over the Territory, as an integral portion of South Africa, and may apply the laws of South Africa to the Territory, subject to such local modifications as circumstances may require; and
> (b) the administrative and legislative powers of the Government of South Africa are exercised with a view to promoting to the utmost the material and moral well-being and social progress of all the population groups of the Territory.[71]

The government also emphasized that the sole aim of the proposed financial and administrative rearrangements is to promote the welfare and security of the territory and its various nations as well as to meet the requirements of the new large-scale developments in the territory by making greater contributions in the financial and administrative fields available to South West Africa from the Republic. The magnitude of the new developments is such that the overlapping of functions and responsibilities between the territory and the Republic will have to be eliminated as far as possible and that greater use should be made of the Republic's facilities in the fields of expert guidance, technical knowledge, and efficient planning. The aim is to promote better public administration.

When Prime Minister B. J. Vorster announced the proposed reorganization in Windhoek in August 1967, he emphasized that it was completely legal and in accordance with the spirit of the former mandate, which granted the government of South Africa full powers of administration and legislation over the territory as an integral portion of the mandatory power. Therefore, he said that there could "be no question of incorporation or a change in the territory's separate international status."[72] All taxes derived from the territory will be kept separately and utilized solely for the benefit of the territory. The administration of South West Africa will have sufficient sources of revenue at its disposal to finance those responsibilities which it still retains.

Accordingly, the Parliament of the Republic of South Africa passed the South West Africa Affairs Act (Act No. 25 of 1969) which provided for the readjustment of administrative, legislative, and financial relations between the territory and the Republic and the amendment of the South West Africa Constitution Act of 1949. It came into operation on April 1, 1969. In addition to those departments concerned with South West African affairs which were administered by South Africa herself since 1920, the better equipped, more experienced and technically more advanced departments of the Republic have, in terms of this act, now assumed responsibility for the following branches of the territory's administration: Labor, African Education, Interior, Prisons, Commerce, Industries, Justice, Colored Affairs, Agriculture, Mines, Cultural Affairs, Public Works, Post and Telegraphs, Transport, Social Welfare and Pensions, and Water Affairs.

This reorganization will no doubt provide the greatest impetus for economic development in the territory since the inception of the mandate in 1920. Although this new act does not mean incorporation of the territory into the Republic of South Africa, the territory in future will enjoy all the privileges of a province. Indeed, the territory will be envied because it will have all the advantages and benefits of the provincial system but yet in contrast to the provinces retain authority over individual taxation. In Parliament the territory already enjoys greater proportionate representation than the provinces; there are 11,503 constituents in the Republic for each representative in the House of Assembly, as compared with the 6,402 in South West Africa. This means that a voter in the territory has the same representation as two voters in the Republic in the South African House of Assembly.

Furthermore, the vulnerable economy of the territory (which is based on precarious assets like the diamond and fishing industries, both of which could be exhausted any day) will be closely linked with that of the Republic, which today could rightly lay claim to one of the most stable and progressive economies in the world. During the years of prosperity all the revenue of the territory will be ploughed back into the economy, and during the years of adversity the territory will be subsidized by the Republic. Under these circumstances South West Africa can not lose, it can only win.

Conclusions

In concluding this chapter on South West Africa, reference should briefly be made to two further issues which are very closely related to the future of the country—namely, the question of self-determination and the threat of terrorist infiltration.

Self-Determination: The critics of the policy of separate development often advance the argument that the homelands in South West Africa will not be viable and that therefore they could not attain sovereignty. From this premise they infer that the policy must fail. The question whether the nonwhite homelands are viable could no doubt be argued at length. Viability is a relative term. It largely depends on factors like natural resources, the development of these resources and the availability of capital, and the ability and skill to utilize this capital. The potentialities of the nonwhite homelands in South West Africa are only beginning to be developed. But apart from this, let it be abundantly clear that South Africa's policy of separate development does not necessarily imply sovereignty for each and every group in the territory. The ultimate aim is self-determination; once this has been attained sovereign independence is merely one of several future possibilities.

No criticism has ever been leveled against self-determination. In fact, it constitutes one of the purposes and principles of the United Nations. Article 1, Paragraph 2 of the UN Charter states that the purpose of the organization is "to develop friendly relations among nations based on respect for the principle of equal rights and self-determination of peoples."

With respect to the various nonwhite nations in South West Africa which are characterized by traditional diversity of language, customs, culture, and religion, the first step should be to organize them by establishing representative (executive, judicial, and legislative) organs to enable them to utilize their democratic rights and express themselves. The second step should be to afford them opportunity to determine their future by means of the established democratic institutions. At that juncture several possible futures could be explored. First, they might wish to retain that particular form of government. Second, they might want provincial status or to become a member of a federation. Third, they might decide to amalgamate with another black, colored, or white homeland—provided that the homeland concerned has achieved self-government and agrees to enter into such an arrangement. Fourth, they might amalgamate with some other independent country. Fifth, they might themselves become independent. All these rights of the nonwhite nations in South West Africa could likewise be exercised by the whites in the territory. If this is not the ultimate meaning of self-determination as accepted in a civilized world and as implied

in the spirit of the mandatory system, then I do not know what other meaning self-determination has.

Terrorist Infiltration: The infiltration of terrorists in the territory constitutes a serious threat to the future of South West Africa. The first group of six terrorists infiltrated into Ovamboland in September 1965. By September 1966 a total of twenty-three terrorists had been rounded up by the police, largely as a result of the close cooperation between the Ovambo people and the South African police force. On September 28, 1966, terrorists set fire to two houses occupied by white officials on the Angolan border, but the only casualty was an Ovambo watchman who was seriously injured. In November of that year terrorists attacked two Ovambo chiefs, assaulted them, and stole their firearms. The next month the offices of a senior Ovambo chief were raided and one of the chief's subjects killed. Two others were wounded.

The Parliament of South Africa passed the Terrorism Act (Act No. 83 of 1967) to deal with persons who employ ruthless methods of violence to coerce innocent members of the public and who recklessly attempt to sow murder, arson, and terror. Section 2 of the Act defines terrorist activity as one which includes, in general, any deed committed for the purpose of undermining the maintenance of law and order; this includes guerrilla training and the possession of explosives, ammunition, and firearms used in terrorist activities.

On September 11, 1967, the trial against thirty-seven terrorists commenced in Pretoria. A total of eighty witnesses testified for the Republic, including thirteen terrorists who were treated as accomplices.[73] One of the latter testified that he was given military training in the use of explosives in Cairo by Arab officers and that he later returned to Kongwa (Tanzania), where he received further training for a year in the use of carbines and submachine guns.[74] Another witness told the court that he and nine others had gone to Moscow for general military training.[75] An expert witness testified that, judging by documents found in the possession of some of the accused, they had received highly effective training designed to make them guerrilla fighters.[76]

Judgment in the case was delivered on January 26, 1968, and sentence passed on February 9, 1968. After having convicted thirty of the accused on the main charge brought against them under the Terrorism Act, as well as three of the accused on charges under the Suppression of Communism Act (to which they pleaded guilty) the judge stated:

> In my view it has been proved that the Accused, because of the level of their civilisation, became the easy misguided dupes of communist indoctrination. Had it not been for the active financial and practical assistance which the Accused received from the Governments of Moscow and Peking and other countries, they would never have found themselves in their present predicament.[77]

Inasmuch as this was the first trial of persons convicted under this retrospective act, the judge decided not to impose the death penalty. He took into account the common law crimes which they were proved to have committed in arriving at an appropriate sentence. Nineteen were sentenced to life imprisonment and nine others were jailed for twenty years each. Two were sent to prison for five years.

When I attended the sessions of the United Nations in November 1968, I was stunned by a decision of the chairman of one of the subcommittees that these terrorists should be referred to as "freedom fighters." What the world does not realize is that these so-called freedom fighters are trained in the Soviet Union, Cuba, the United Arab Republic, Tunisia, Ethiopia, and Tanzania and that a large number of them are trained soldiers of these countries. In the Pretoria trial the judge stated that

> one cannot conceive of conduct against civilians which is more clearly criminal. Here, the terrorists committed arson and tried to commit murder in a well thought-out and planned attempt, which is something far removed from heroic freedom fighters fighting as soldiers (this they also call themselves) against soldiers in order to free their country. Like cowards in the night they attempted to kill innocent people, White and non-White, and then like cowards they fled from the scene when the return fire became too hot.[78]

These infiltrators are indeed well armed. Two caches of arms found in the Zambezi valley on March 27, 1968, yielded 54 Russian, Red Chinese, and Czechoslovakian automatic weapons, 77,090 rounds of ammunition, 6 Russian and Chinese bazooka shells, 169 Russian, American, and Chinese hand grenades, and 3 pairs of East German binoculars.[79]

Since World War II Communist infiltration has undoubtedly led to various wars in countries like Korea, Algeria, Cuba, and Vietnam; therefore, it should be closely watched in Southern Africa. The most alarming phenomenon is that countries not very far from South West Africa's borders harbor the terrorists and blatantly aid their training by allowing them to establish training camps. The South African Minister of Defense (Mr. P. W. Botha) recently referred to such a practice and stated that

> making a country available as a base for terrorists constitutes provocation of a nature which gradually becomes so serious that it turns into guerrilla warfare. Such a situation recently arose for Israel. It then becomes necessary for a country to take sterner action against those threats. I want to say. . .that it will be a good thing if the people who are inciting terrorism and guerrilla warfare against South Africa come to realize that provocation may eventually lead to severe retaliation for the sake of self-respect and peace.[80]

One can only hope that the United Nations will urge its members to refrain from becoming involved in conduct which would invite such retaliation. I firmly believe that terrorism today constitutes one of the major threats to world peace. In fact, the growth of Communism in Africa is one of the reasons why politics in Angola, Mozambique, Rhodesia, South Africa, Malawi, Botswana, Lesotho, and Swaziland have moved to the right in recent years.

The Communist world probably realizes the overwhelming economic and strategic importance of the territory of South West Africa. The tragedy, however, is that the Western world obviously ignores Communist infiltration in Southern Africa and assumes such an indifferent attitude that it can only endanger South Africa's solitary battle against Communism in this part of the world.

6

African Nationalism in Namibia

HIDIPO L. HAMUTENYA
AND
GOTTFRIED H. GEINGOB

The Origins of the Name Namibia

The country of Namibia has been variously named and renamed by foreigners. Early in the 1760s white settlers of the Cape Colony referred to this territory as the "Transgariep," meaning the territory north of the Orange River. Charles John Andersson, a Swedish-born adventurer, was the first person to term the area north of the Orange River "South West Africa." Following the raising of the German flag at Luderitz Bay on August 7, 1884, the territory became known as "German South West Africa." From that date up to the end of World War I, the territory remained known as German South West Africa. After the German defeat during World War I, the territory was declared a League of Nations mandate under the Treaty of Versailles. It was to be administered by the Union of South Africa on behalf of the British government. Thereafter, the territory has been referred to simply as South West Africa. As Dr. Eschel M. Rhoodie has observed,

> Every square mile of land is part of a nation state with a name, except this huge slice of Africa which is simply called South West Africa. It shares the distinction with South Africa and Central African Republic. . .of being the only country [*sic*] in the world with a name which is a purely geographical designation.[1]

We of the South West Africa People's Organization (SWAPO) have adopted Namibia as the name of our country because of some important attributes of the country. Namibia is derived from the word *!Namib* (the coastal desert of this territory), a Nama-Damara word which literally means the "enclosure." The "!" represents the click stress in pronunciation (in another form—that is, Na-ḿib—it means mirage).

Stretching 850 miles from the Kunene River on

the Namibia–Angola border to the Orange River on the South African–Namibia border, with a width varying from thirty to eighty miles, the Namib constitutes a natural shield to this country. Running along the entire length of the shore, this coastal desert or "enclosure" had for centuries protected the interior and those who lived there from the prying intruders such as the Portuguese slave hunters. As the late Professor J. P. van S. Bruwer of the University of Port Elizabeth put it:

> For centuries sea-farers braved the dangers of the coast. But the waterless barrier of the Namib Desert guarded the entrance to the hinterland. None ever endeavoured to venture inland, but proceeded on their trade route to the distant East, leaving fabulous riches untouched beneath the surface of sand. . . . For ages . . . the hinterland remained hidden beyond the towering sand-dunes . . . of the Namib Desert. Only since the seventeenth century information had been gathered about the vast inland region and its peoples.[2]

Similarly, Ruth First has remarked: "The Portuguese expedition must have stepped ashore just long enough to be deterred by the same sight that discourages sea travellers today: those endless high sand-dunes along the dreary desert coastline of the Namib."[3]

The Namib might also be described as the real treasure house of South West Africa. The Luderitz district in the southern part of the Namib is known as the "Diamond Coast" and it is indeed one of the world's richest alluvial sources of diamonds in Africa. Here diamonds are extensively found loose in sand gravel on the ground. Furthermore, the Namib rolls down to a freezing sea chilled by the cold Benguela Current which comes up from the Antarctic to form one of the world's richest fishing grounds off this coast. Here whales, seals, and penguins come ashore from the icy waters of the Antarctic to walk on the Namibian coast. The numerous varieties of fish which run off the coast and the tens of thousands of guano-producing birds which cloud the sky constitute a majestic panorama of the Namib. The country's two important harbors, Walvis Bay and Luderitz, are both situated on the Namib. Although it is a desert region covering only 15 percent of the total area of the country which is three hundred and eighteen thousand square miles with approximately a million people, the Namib nonetheless accommodates 6 percent of this total population, concentrated mainly in the coastal towns of Oranjemund, Luderitz Bay, and Walvis Bay. People are attracted to these towns by diamond deposits and the flourishing pilchard, lobster, and whaling industries, and Swakopmund is a popular vacation resort.[4]

Thus the natural defense shield (or the "enclosure"), the teeming marine life, and the diamond fields are valuable attributes which make the Namib a very great asset to the country's economic potential. Hence SWAPO proposed that it be called "Namibia"—the land of the Namib. We of the South West Africa People's Organization have adopted the name Namibia as a part of our comprehensive program for both national liberation and eradication of all the negative consequences of white minority rule. The nationalist affirmation regarding this name was aptly expressed by one of SWAPO's founding leaders, Toivo H. ja Toivo, in his statement delivered under oath during the trial of thirty-seven African nationalists in Pretoria, South Africa, on February 1, 1968. He proclaimed:

> We are Namibians and not South Africans. We do not now, and will not in the future recognise your right to govern us; to make laws for us in which we had no say; to treat our country as if it were your property and us as if you were our masters.[5]

The South African government and other forces of reaction naturally prefer John Charles Andersson's label to Namibia. However, the United Nations and the Organization of African Unity (OAU) have both adopted Namibia as the name of this country. The use of this name by the African states and by the United Nations is in accordance with the principle of self-determination, for it is the people of Namibia who must determine their own destiny and identity.

African Nationalism in Namibia

In its efforts to rationalize the continuation of its racist policy of white supremacy, the South African government is currently advancing a myth which postulates that deep-seated ethnic enmities, as well as cultural and linguistic differences, preclude any possibility of a collective action for national purpose among the Africans of Namibia. The myth further asserts that ethnic hostilities would break out in Namibia if the African population were allowed to form a single political community. In his latest policy statement, Dr. Hilgard Muller, the South African foreign minister, claimed:

> It is precisely to avoid friction and a recurrence of the internecine warfare of the previous century that the South African government has adopted the approach of political self-determination for each population group.

> It is precisely because of the struggle which would inevitably follow should an attempt be made to force the peoples against their will into artificial unity, that the South African government is not prepared to abandon its responsibilities and to leave the peoples of South West Africa to a fate which is not so difficult to imagine in the light of events elsewhere.[6]

But these theories of ethnic determinism have no empirical basis. The South African government allegation that the precolonial history of Namibia is a history of "internecine tribal warfare" is not supported by the evidence now available. The government stresses only those events which, when taken out of context, seem to support the conclusion the South African government has already drawn before examining the evidence. To put matters in their proper perspective, we of SWAPO would like to draw attention to several points about the nineteenth-century history of Namibia before we analyze the nature of African Nationalism in Namibia.

The known ethnic rivalry in the history of Namibia was mainly between the Herero and Nama communities. Essentially, however, this rivalry was a nineteenth-century phenomenon resulting from exogenous changes in values and environment in both the Herero and Nama areas. Dr. Eschel Rhoodie has pointed out that, although these sporadic outbreaks of violence were not unknown when the white settlers first arrived in the country, the major force of the rivalry between the Hereros and the Namas did not flare up until the middle of the nineteenth century.[7] Professor J. H. Wellington of the University of the Witwatersrand also observed:

> The tribes and their chiefs considered themselves independent of one another, to the extent that there were rivalries and fairly frequent raids on each other's territory, quarrels over succession and other matters. But the territory was large enough to allow such causes of strain to be held largely in suspension. . . .[8]

Thus, following the European settlement in the late 1760s, items such as liquor, tobacco, and guns were supplied by European traders in exchange for African cattle and land. As substantial portions of African land and herds increasingly fell into European hands, both economic and social pressures were exerted on the cattle-complex cultures of both the central and southern areas of Namibia. Specifically, the acquisition of substantial amounts of firearms and horses from the Cape Province by the Orlams (who were a part of the Namas) created political disequilibrium between the Hereros and the Namas. It was against this background that frictions between the two communities developed as one or the other tried to claim what was left of their land and cattle.

The general tensions and pressures resulting from white settlement were further exacerbated by the settlers' interference in interethnic politics. There had been many instances in which white traders managed successfully to pit one ethnic group against another. For instance, in 1864 the Swedish adventurer, Charles Andersson, along with two British traders (Green and Heybittel), organized and led a Herero expedition against the Namas who had raided Andersson's trading post.[9] Then in 1880 Benjamin Musgrave, a special commissioner of the Cape administration stationed at Walvis Bay, engaged in supplying the Rehoboth community with ammunition and sided with the Namas in the conflict between the Namas and Hereros that broke out that year [10]

But the sporadic skirmishes fought between the Hereros and the Namas were insignificant when compared to the bitter hostilities between the Afrikaners and the British which culminated in the Anglo-Boer War of 1899–1902. Notwithstanding these historic enmities, some Afrikaners and the British joined together in a common effort against Germany during World War I. Remarking upon this fact, the *Cape Times* declared: "The conquest of German South-West Africa by troops of British and Dutch birth . . . in a land where we have too often been busily engaged in cutting each other's throats, actually and metaphorically, has struck the imagination of the world."[11] After having cut one another's throats, the Afrikaners, Britons, and Germans in Namibia then joined forces to dominate and to exploit the African population. These groups submerged their traditional enmities and redefined their common interest in terms of a white race.

Similarly, it is important to recall that by 1903 the Damaras, Hereros, and Namas had resolved to submerge their local quarrels and had joined forces against their common enemy—the German colonizers. During the 1903–1907 historic war against the Germans, Chief Maharero, the Herero leader, addressed a letter urging coordination of action against the Germans to Chief Hendrik Witbooi, leader of the Namas. He wrote: "Rather let us die together and not die as a result of ill-treatment, prison or all the other ways."[12] Moreover, it is also significant that when the Damaras, Hereros, and Namas were fighting against the Germans in the southern and central areas of Namibia, the Ovambos in the north had simultaneously launched an attack on the Germans' military outpost at Namutoni in January 1904.[13]

At present, ethnic animosities in Namibia are

being encouraged by the South West African administration by means of what the administration terms separate development schemes which deliberately ignore the right of the Africans to national independence on the pretext that to grant such independence would necessarily lead to anarchy. Thus each ethnic community must be legally and physically barred from social, economic, or political interaction with other indigenous groups. All this is done to stifle the growth of African nationalism, which represents the collective desire of the Namibian people to govern themselves and to live under laws of their own choosing. Today quite a lot is known about the techniques of colonial administration and about the sophistry the colonial powers used to continue their rule. These powers employed ethnic and linguistic differences as excuses to deny the nationalist aspirations of colonial peoples. Professor Karl Deutsch of Harvard University made some insightful observations when he noted that

> In the days when British wanted to point out that India could not be independent, it was a favorite device of language surveys to say that India had 212 languages and dialects. On closer inspection it turns out that almost 200 of these are lesser known dialects . . . with little or no political or economic significance, and that something like 80 or 90 per cent of the Indian people are covered by fourteen languages. . . . Now we are getting statement after statement that an African country has twenty or thirty . . . languages or dialects. Upon investigation of frequency distributions it turns out that four to six languages cover more than one half the population, and that bilingualism is often present.[14]

Indeed, in the case of Namibia, South Africa lists no less than ten languages,[15] whereas in actual fact over 90 percent of the indigenous population is covered by four main languages—Herero, Nama, Ovambo, and Silozi—and their respective local dialects.

However, African nationalism in Namibia, as in many other countries of Africa and Asia, does not seek to build a nation-state along lines of common languages and cultures. Rather, it seeks to create a progressive, independent state and government in Namibia and to foster a spirit of collective purpose among all the people of Namibia. This nationalism also aims at the reconciliation of whatever rival allegiances might exist among ethnic groups of Namibia and thus rejects the South West African administration policy of "tribal homelands." Moreover, the Namibian African nationalists have never claimed that there will be an absence of conflicts in an independent Namibia. On the contrary, we not only accept the fact that social and political conflicts among the people are inevitable, but also that such conflicts serve a function. Conflicts only threaten the equilibrium of a social and political system in which class or racial oppression leave no room for peaceful solution to such conflicts.

That ethnic hostility would "inevitably" break out in Namibia if the indigenous people are allowed to form a single political entity is, as we mentioned earlier, a myth. The fact is that, in the face of white-minority rule, the Africans in Namibia have acquired not only a sense of shared plight but also a consciousness of common purpose. The proper way to expose this myth is for the South African government to allow a free and internationally supervised referendum to enable the people of Namibia, not a tiny clique of government-appointed and politically malleable chiefs, to choose between national independence and continued white domination. This is a challenge which the South African government fears most.

Throughout the 1950s African nationalism had manifested itself in various ways in Namibia. Early in the 1950s a group of African students from Namibia who were attending various schools and colleges in South Africa organized themselves into the South West Africa Student Body. Because the student body was comprised of those students who were able to attend South African schools, its membership was very small. Organizationally, the South West Africa Student Body did very little to extend its influence to African schools in Namibia, and thus its support in Namibia was very marginal. However, by 1956 the South West Africa Student Body evolved into the South West Africa Progressive Association (SWAPA), a culturally oriented organization. One of SWAPA's objectives was to campaign for better education for African children and to advise African students about how to secure admission to African schools and colleges in South Africa. Unlike Namibia, South Africa has long-established institutions of education for Africans, some of which have retained their educational qualities even under the present government-imposed system of Bantu education. However, like the South West Africa Student Body, the South West Africa Progressive Association was a small club of teachers, clerical workers, and other quasi-intellectuals in Windhoek, the capital of Namibia.[16]

By 1959 some members of SWAPA founded an African newspaper, *The South West News*, which appeared in both English and Afrikaans.[17] By reporting favorably the struggles for independence in other parts of Africa and the world, the *South West News* sought to foster the growth of nationalism among Namibia's urban African youth. However, by 1960 the white administration banned this paper.

The labor movement was another organizational activity in which African nationalism found its initial expression in Namibia. By 1950 the African contract workers at Luderitz Bay organized themselves into a labor union which led a large strike in 1952. Recognizing the effectiveness of their organized power, these workers carried out a more protracted strike in 1953 which temporarily paralyzed the lobster industry at Luderitz Bay. To suppress the power of organized workers, the South African police resorted to violence and in 1953 the police opened fire on the strikers, killing three African workers and wounding many others.[18]

In spite of this suppression of labor organization, the occurrence of strikes at the industrial centers (such as the American Metal Climax and Newmont-owned Tsumeb Corporation, and the fishing industries of Walvis Bay and Luderitz Bay) is a manifestation of labor unrest in the country. Against this background, a second attempt at a workers' movement was launched by a group of Namibians employed in Cape Town and in mining industries in other parts of South Africa. They formed the Ovamboland People's Organization (OPO) in 1958. The primary aim of the OPO was to end the system of contract labor which is so common in Ovamboland. The leaders of the OPO, like those of the Progressive Association, inspired by the goals of nationalism, felt that the oppressive and exploitative conditions and long-standing abuse to which the Africans were subjected in the contract system were the most immediate and burning issues around which the African workers in Namibia could be organized and politicized.

Since the German era, Namibia has been divided into two principal zones, and this division has been central to the contract labor system. The first zone, known as the Police Zone, comprises the entire southern two-thirds of Namibia. Except for the remote, tiny, and widely scattered enclaves carved out on the edge of the Police Zone as the "Damara homeland," "Herero homeland," "Nama homeland," "Tswana homeland," and "Rehoboth homeland," the Police Zone is an exclusive "homeland" for white settlers. It contains virtually all the important natural resources of the country and, therefore, all the industrial centers. The second zone consists of the remaining northern third, referred to as the "Northern Bantu Areas." In these "Bantu Areas" almost half the total population live at a subsistence level. Even to reach subsistence, African men from these "Bantu homelands" must seek employment in the Police Zone, the area to which, by law, they have no free entry.

Under the South West African administration's Extra-Territorial and Northern Natives Control Proclamation of 1935 (which was devised to regulate the movements of Africans from the northern areas into and from the Police Zone), the only way Africans in these areas can obtain work in the Police Zone is through the South West African Native Labor Association (SWANLA), a very efficient government-supported organization. To enter the urban areas in the "white homeland" as migratory laborers, these Africans must first procure permits from SWANLA's local recruiting offices in the northern "Bantu Areas." From there they must carry with them fingerprinted duplicates of their contract services as identification passes. Upon their arrival at the place of work in the Police Zone, the African laborers are issued passes by their employers. These passes, of course, confine the movements of these African laborers within a few miles' radius of the town or farm in which they are employed. For the eighteen or twenty months of his contract services, each African lives a bachelor's life in a compound with barbed-wire fence. Labor organization or strikes constitute a criminal offense.

The OPO was initially an urban organization, concerned with this specific problem. Since this issue was perceived by many to be genuine, the OPO was formed with the support of nearly all the Namibians who were in Cape Town where the OPO was founded. A number of the individuals who participated in framing its constitution were non-Ovambo Namibians who were in the Cape either as workers or as students. By the end of 1958 Herman Toivo ja Toivo, the leading member of the OPO, was arrested and deported from Cape Town to Ovamboland where he was kept under house arrest until 1967 when he was rearrested and sent to Robben Island prison for twenty years.

However, by the time of ja Toivo's first arrest, the OPO had already gained support in Namibia. In that same year Sam Nujoma assumed the leadership of this movement in Windhoek and immediately became its full-time organizer. Through Nujoma's personal efforts a number of branches were established in all the industrial areas of Namibia. The OPO membership was open to all Namibians who agreed with its anti-contract labor aims. It forged good working relations with other anti-apartheid groups in the country, such as the late Chief Hosea Kutako's Herero Council and the South West African National Union (SWANU) which was formed in Windhoek in 1959 by elements of the South West Africa Progressive Association.

In December 1959 these three nationalist groups —Chief Hosea Kutako's council, the OPO, and SWANU—jointly organized a mass campaign against the forced removal of the African residential township in Windhoek by the South West

African administration. The campaign first took the form of boycotts of public buses, municipal movie theater, and beer halls, and demonstrations. However, on December 11–12, 1959, the police opened fire on the African crowd, killing eleven and wounding fifty-four.[19] As the police began shooting Africans, the demonstrators fought back by setting fire to the administration's beer halls and movie theater, burning municipal and police vehicles, and opening jails to release prisoners.[20] The Windhoek uprising was followed by a student revolt at Augustineum Teachers' Training School at Okahandja in 1960. Augustineum, the largest educational institution for Africans in Namibia, has a multiethnic student body. It has become the scene of nationalist ferment characterized by frequent crises and continued mass expulsions.

In an attempt to curb African nationalist activity in the urban areas, the South West African administration began to issue banishment and deportation orders against most of the leaders of emerging nationalist organizations. By that time, however, African nationalism had gained a popular base, and no amount of intimidation and victimization could stop it. By 1960 the OPO transformed itself into the South West Africa People's Organization (SWAPO) in order to emphasize national, as contrasted with regional, aspirations and in order to broaden the base for popular participation.

Thus by 1959–1960 there were three manifestly anticolonial groups in the country, each with a somewhat distinct orientation. The Herero Council of Chief Hosea Kutako remained under traditionalist yet anticolonial leadership. Constitutionally, it remained confined to a single ethnic group, the Herero. By opting to retain this character, Kutako's council has sought to protect the traditional institutions of authority. Essentially, the South West Africa National Union (SWANU) was an outgrowth of both the elitist South West Africa Student Body and the Progressive Association. In its earlier days, SWANU looked mostly to Augustineum (at Okahandja). and Dubra Teachers' Training School (at Windhoek) for its new recruits. Hence its self-image was that of an intellectual organization. SWAPO, however, sought its support chiefly among rural and urban workers employed in the mines, fisheries, karakul farms, railways and harbors, in construction, and in domestic services.

The emergence of SWANU and SWAPO introduced an element of organizational rivalry which was later to find its focus in the personality conflict between Jariretundu F. Kozonguizi and Mburumba G. Kerina. Kerina and Kozonguizi were the first two Namibian petitioners at the United Nations on behalf of Chief Hosea Kutako's Herero Council. They were also the first college-educated Namibians on the nationalist political scene at that time. Kerina and Kozonguizi, therefore, saw themselves as the sole competitors for national leadership, and their rivalry was sharpened by the illusion of an imminent independence to be achieved under the auspices of the United Nations. This illusion was nurtured by the innumerable resolutions of the United Nations General Assembly which created the impression that it would not be long before South Africa was forced out of Namibia. Following the formation of SWANU in Namibia in 1959, Kozonguizi, who was then abroad, was elected president of the newly founded organization. As far as Kerina was concerned, it was humiliating that his rival was now a spokesman of a nationalist movement in Namibia rather than merely a representative of the Herero Council, and he quickly ingratiated himself with both ja Toivo and Nujoma, the leaders of OPO and later SWAPO.

Superficial commentaries have been written on the rivalry between these two organizations. Ruth First, for instance, feels that the East-West orientation underlies this rivalry, and she claims:

> The leadership quarrels, reflecting some differences in policy, remain. Kozonguizi, disillusioned with the U.N.'s dilatory handling of the South West African issue, expressed his disappointment over Peking radio while on a visit to China. This exposed S.W.A.N.U. to criticisms of abandoning the West and seeking an alignment with the Communist world. S.W.A.N.U. leaders replied by attacking S.W.A.P.O. for its close connexions with the American Metal Climax Corporation, which has allocated bursaries to S.W.A.P.O. members abroad and has substantial economic interests in South West Africa through the Tsumeb mines. S.W.A.P.O. leaders objected to Kozonguizi's Peking speech because it was strongly anti-imperialist in tone, and delivered before a Communist audience. They claim that any South West African identification with the Communist countries would damage the South West African cause throughout the West.[21]

The East-West implications of the rivalry are, however, misleading. SWAPO, as an organization, had never opposed identification with socialist countries. In fact, by the time Kozonguizi made his statement in Peking, SWAPO had already sent students, including some of its top leadership, to study in these countries. It was actually Kerina who unilaterally took it upon himself to criticize Kozonguizi's Peking speech. With regard to the American Metal Climax Corporation, there was never any cooperation between that corporation and SWAPO, and the scholarships allegedly allocated to SWAPO students were entirely fictional. SWAPO's denunciation of the activities of the American Metal Climax are well known. It should be emphasized that at the time she wrote her book entitled *South West Africa*, Ruth First was under the impression that SWANU was *the* progressive organization in Namibia. She no longer holds this view.

Apart from the difference in backgrounds, there was no genuine evidence of either an ideological or a policy split between SWAPO and SWANU in the period between 1960 and 1962. During this time the two movements organized side by side in the country. Their policies were both characteristic of protest politics, based on petitioning to the United Nations. Both organizations placed their hopes in United Nations intervention in Namibia.

By 1962, however, SWAPO had come to the realization that to rely on the United Nations' intervention to liberate Namibia was to leave this liberation to mere chance. SWAPO decided that political and military efforts in pursuit of national liberation were not contradictory, but rather they were complementary and should be pursued concurrently. In accordance with this decision, SWAPO started a military training program. Cadres were recruited and sent for military training to other African, Asian, and Eastern European nations.

In the ensuing years SWAPO has attempted to build up a force of trained cadres as a nucleus of a people's liberation army. The need to pay closer attention to guerrilla strategy in Namibia became even more urgent when the African nationalist movements were forbidden to hold public meetings in Namibia in 1963.[22] This ban by the South West African administration was obviously aimed at curbing the political activities of the African nationalist movements. It became apparent that the struggle would have to be carried on outside the regular political channels and the SWAPO leadership decided to combine its military and political efforts.

The trained cadres are intended to serve as the major organizational core in the underground mobilization of the African population for participation in the liberation struggle. Moreover, in accordance with the basic principles of guerrilla warfare, the initial activities of the guerrillas had to be concentrated in the areas where the logistics of food and other personal needs of an underground movement are relatively easy; and these activities also had to begin where the underdeveloped nature of communications affords the guerrillas an advantage over the South African police and regular military units which are highly mechanized and thus dependent on more complex logistics.

In October 1964 a regional organization in the Caprivi Zipfel, known as the Caprivi African National Union (CANU), formed early that year under the leadership of Bredan K. Simbwaye, relinquished its independent status and joined SWAPO. This link closed one regional gap and also broadened the base for mobilization. The Caprivi Zipfel—which lies between Botswana, Zambia, and Angola and forms Namibia's eastern boundary—has become South Africa's most sensitive military frontier and the scene of armed encounters between SWAPO freedom fighters and South African ground and air units.[23]

When the International Court of Justice took so long to determine whether South Africa has the legal right to continue its racist policies in Namibia, many Namibian African nationalists felt that the Court was searching for legal technicalities in order to avoid passing judgment on the substantive issue in the case—namely, the legality of apartheid in Namibia. These speculations were based on the belief that even in the event of an anti-South African verdict, the major Western powers would not support a United Nations Security Council resolution calling for the use of coercive measures to compel South Africa to comply with such a verdict. Indeed, on July 18, 1966, the case was dismissed by the International Court, and its evasion of substantive issues led to a victory for the South African government. At this stage the prospects for international action to end apartheid in Namibia began to look very bleak, and internal action in the form of armed resistance began to loom large as an alternative strategy in the anti-apartheid campaign.

By August 1966 the advance party of SWAPO's guerrilla forces went into action against South African forces. Since then SWAPO has launched selective attacks on the South African military and administrative posts in the Okavango, Caprivi Zipfel, Grootfontein, and Ovamboland regions. SWAPO has also suffered some setbacks in the initial efforts during the last three years. The biggest blow of all was the capture of the Ongulumbashe training camp in Ovamboland in 1966. This camp was the first SWAPO base in Namibia, and it was equipped and fortified over a period of eleven months prior to the first armed clash between the freedom fighters and South African forces on August 26, 1966. Its capture led to the arrests of some of the thirty-seven Namibians who were brought to trial in a Pretoria court in February 1968. Some of these nationalists are now serving terms ranging from twenty years to life imprisonment on Robben Island.

These setbacks, however, have forced the nationalists to search for new methods of operation in accordance with the social structure and other specific characteristics of Southern Africa. Commenting on the new tactics of guerrilla movements in Southern Africa, the South African-born journalist Colin Legum wrote:

> There are signs of growing awareness both in South Africa and Rhodesia that the guerrilla movements have switched their tactics from open confrontation across the Zambesi river, and that they are infiltrating trained people to establish secret military camps inside South West Africa, Rhodesia and South Africa.
>
> Two trials now being held in Salisbury and Windhoek have produced some evidence of success inside Rhodesia and South West Africa. A recent trial in Petermaritzburg disclosed similar tactics by the African National Congress in South Africa.
>
> In the Windhoek trial—now being held under conditions of strict military security—eight supporters of the South West Africa People's Organization (SWAPO) are charged with promoting armed warfare.[24]

The trend toward armed struggle in Namibia, and in other parts of Southern Africa, has aroused concern in many quarters. Articles on guerrilla warfare in Southern Africa have appeared in magazines and newspapers in many parts of the world, but an accurate assessment of the war seems to elude both the sympathetic and the unsympathetic observer. Most observers seem pessimistic and feel that Southern African nationalist movements have not achieved internal cohesion or clarity of purpose. In the case of Namibia, they point out that South Africa has at its command an elaborate police apparatus as well as an impressive military capability.

While such a pessimistic picture is not entirely unwarranted, we believe that there are some positive aspects of the liberation struggle in Namibia. To begin with, lack of complete unity did not prevent the initiation and continuation of guerrilla activity in Namibia; now there is fundamental agreement among Namibian nationalists that recourse to armed struggle is the only effective means of liberating our country. Whatever differences exist among the nationalists, they are over issues of tactics. The ready acceptance of armed struggle to end white minority rule is what counts. A careful analysis of the history of guerrilla campaigns (in Algeria, Cuba, China, and Vietnam) reveals that triumphant movements invariably grew out of a cadre of sophisticated nationalists who understood both political and military affairs. We of the South West Africa People's Organization view guerrilla warfare as more of a political, rather than a military, undertaking. Given the present political situation in Namibia and in other parts of Southern Africa, political organization is the responsibility of well-trained cadres who must operate through underground channels. In addition to their military skills, the nationalist guerrilla forces must also have political skills in order to persuade their fellow Africans to join the struggle against pass laws, police brutality, and low wages, and to struggle for a more equitable distribution of land, the franchise, and skilled jobs. Trained guerrillas have systematically penetrated the Caprivi Zipfel since 1965 and have managed to become part of the local communities. Since the local population steadfastly refused to inform the South African security forces of the presence of freedom fighters, the South West African administration retaliated against the local inhabitants, as a result of which about four thousand of them fled to Zambia and several hundred went to Botswana between October and December 1968.[25] Furthermore, the two consecutive trials of SWAPO members in 1967–1968 and in 1969 revealed that most of the defendants had been recruited and trained locally by those Africans who had already been trained in guerrilla techniques elsewhere in the world. The second trial, involving eight SWAPO freedom fighters, took place in Windhoek from July 1 to August 22, 1969, and attracted large African crowds to the court sessions. It is probably due to the display of popular sympathy with the freedom fighters that the third trial of ten more SWAPO members, charged with participating in "terrorist" activities, is being held *in camera*.

The main problem we face at this stage is to cope with South Africa's counterinsurgency strategy, the basic aim of which is to halt SWAPO guerrilla activity at the earliest stage without allowing it to gain experience and a firm popular base. The large number of arrests in Namibia since 1966 under the provisions of the 1950 Suppression of Communism Act and the 1967 Terrorism Act is only part of a wide range of measures involved in such a counterinsurgency strategy.[26] One indication that this strategy has not been very successful is that the latest armed clashes between the South African and SWAPO forces occurred in the Grootfontein area (deep within the fortified Police Zone) between December 27 and 30, 1969.[27] Thus, even with the most favorable conditions, the South West African security forces have been unable to put a complete stop to guerrilla movement and activity.

Our fondest hope is that we shall be able to liberate Namibia, but we fully realize that this will involve determination, hard work, and real sacrifice. The South African government is incapable of making fundamental political concessions to African nationalism, yet it cannot repress the forces of African nationalism in Namibia indefinitely. Schemes such as "Bantustans" are illusory because they are designed to appeal to African traditionalists who now have little or no political influence among their people. Furthermore, such schemes will not fundamentally alter white oppression and exploitation in Namibia. Only the liberation of Namibia can change that.

We recognize that a liberation movement without sound theoretical guidelines will be unable to survive in the face of heavy odds. At worst, a movement devoid of theoretical guidelines or ideological content may degenerate either into vindictive racial fury or into ethnic chauvinism. Such guidelines are necessary to illustrate the manifest inadequacy of the political system that must be transformed while also defining normatively the nature of the political and economic systems in a liberated Namibia. The ideological guidelines thus provide the members of the movement with a set of values and a sense of direction, and they inspire the members to make the necessary sacrifices so that the movement can be a success.

International Implications of Namibian Nationalism

As we have suggested, the South African white minority suffers from its own history and psychology. White South Africa's long history of oppressing the African majority has led to the most debilitating and fearful neurosis which has found its expression in the "swamp theory." The "swamp theory" is one of the basic tenets of apartheid, for it postulates that any loosening of the whites' control over the African population must inevitably lead to total ruin of the white population of South Africa. This has led South African whites to seek security in the use, accumulation, and display of the instruments of physical force. Such a reactionary policy ignores the fact that white South Africans can no longer have exclusive access to firearms and to training in how to use them. The overwhelming majority of nations in the world are opposed to decadent systems of racism, imperialism and colonialism all of which characterize the present South African government. Africans of Namibia have received aid to continue their fight for national liberation and human dignity. Assistance has come from the independent African states as well as from Eastern European and Asian nations; such nations have already given us their moral and material support (in the form of technical skills, military training, and military and related supplies).

However, we are distressed that the American, British, and Western European governments have been so hospitable to the present South African regime. These governments are well disposed toward South Africa because continued white minority rule there is good for the profits of their nationals. South Africa provides Western investors with a large supply of cheap African labor, monopolistic concessions, and low tax rates.

American companies are now the most active foreign accomplices in the exploitation of Namibia's peoples and resources. The Tsumeb Corporation (owned primarily by American Metal Climax and Newmont Mining Corporation) is the second largest mining enterprise in Namibia (the largest is the Consolidated Diamond Mines of South West Africa Limited, which controls 98 per cent of Namibia's diamond industry). This corporation has owned and operated the Kombat mine since 1962, and also has mining claims at Okarusu, Gross Otavi, Horasib, and Tsumeb West. In addition, the corporation has acquired a large interest in a concession of roughly three thousand square miles in the area around its mine and it has been conducting geological surveys there on which active exploration has been in progress.[28] The corporation began an expansion program entailing a capital expenditure of about $23.8 million to construct a new copper smelter, a lead smelter and refinery, a sulphuric acid plant, and an arsenic plant. In addition, the germanium plant was considerably enlarged.[29] By 1964 the Tsumeb Corporation was exporting $29.5 million worth of minerals annually.[30] In 1968 the corporation was granted another concession to operate the Matchless mine, located thirty miles west of Windhoek. Recent investigations have revealed large deposits of copper and sulphur.[31] Meanwhile, an American businessman, Sam Collins, has been dredging up about one thousand carats of diamonds each day from the ocean bottom off the coast of Namibia.[32]

Anticipating a possible oil embargo, the South African government has granted large concessions for oil prospecting to a number of Western oil companies. Of the principal North American companies engaged in this oil hunt in Namibia, the Etosha Petroleum Company, which is a subsidiary of the Texan Eastern Transmission Company, has the biggest concession; it covers an area of about seventy-five thousand square miles. The others are the Chicago-based Artnell Exploration Company, and the Trans-American Mining Company, a Canadian corporation which is the authorized agent of an American syndicate composed of Charles Payson, Julius Fleischmann, Richard Cowell, Winton Guest, and the Waterford Oil Company.[33] Early in 1969 the Teledyne Exploration Company of Texas shipped a substantial amount of seismic equipment and a team of experts and technicians into Namibia in order to carry out seismic surveys for the Etosha Petroleum Company.[34] Caltex has been granted the concession for offshore oil prospecting along the "skeleton coast."[35]

Regarding the low tax rates accorded the corporations in Namibia, we find, for example, that the Consolidated Diamond Mines with an authorized capital of $14.67 million made a total profit of $516.6 million between 1943 and 1962 out of which it paid only $147 million (28.5 percent) in taxes.[36] Thus its net profit for that period was $369.6 million. By 1956 the diamond industry had increased its annual output to 1.6 million carats which by 1965 was valued at $98 million.[37] The Tsumeb Corporation, which bought the Tsumeb mine for $2.8 million in 1946, made a profit of $196 million between 1948 and 1961 out of which it paid only $49 million (25 per cent) in taxes.[38]

That these corporations have taken full advantage of the apartheid policies is illustrated by the fact that in the mining industry the white workers' average yearly wage in 1962 was $3,432 whereas the wage of the African worker was only $284.[39] Virtually all these companies comply fully with the legal provisions whereby Africans in Namibia are barred from advancing to the better paying positions.

We of SWAPO are pleased by the growth of groups in the West which share our ideals and are disturbed by the policies of Western governments which make our task all the more difficult. Members of such groups need not be overly pessimistic. The useful thing for them to do is to assist our liberation movement by collecting funds for us which we can use to purchase clothing, canned food, tents, medicine, vehicles, weapons, and communications equipment. They should do their utmost to get the Western nations to withdraw their support of apartheid. Finally, we of SWAPO must still expand our military training program, construct a sound administrative infrastructure, and develop a suitable and lasting ideology for our liberation movement.

PART THREE

The Former High Commission Territories

Country Profiles

BOTSWANA

Political situation
On September 30, 1966, Botswana, the former British High Commission Territory of Bechuanaland, became an independent republic within the Commonwealth of Nations. The president, Sir Seretse Khama, is the leader of the ruling Democratic Party. The vice president is Q. K. J. Masire.

The legislature consists of a National Assembly with thirty-six members and a House of Chiefs. Thirty-one representatives are elected by universal suffrage, four are specially elected, and the attorney general is an *ex officio* member. The president is elected by the National Assembly.

The opposition parties are the Pan-Africanist Botswana People's Party led by Philip G. Matante, Motsamai Mpho's Botswana Independence Party, and Dr. Kenneth Koma's Botswana National Front.

Demographic situation
Area: 222,000 square miles
Population: 580,000 (1968), including 4,000 whites
Capital: Gaborone, 18,000 inhabitants (1968)

Economic situation
Gross national product: $34,000,000 (1966)
Per capita income: $60 (1966)
Currency: South African Rand, 1R = $1.40
Principal products: cattle products, asbestos, manganese

LESOTHO

Political situation
On October 4, 1966, Lesotho, the former British High Commission Territory of Basutoland, became an independent constitutional monarchy within the Commonwealth of Nations. The king is Motlotlehi Moshoeshoe II. The prime minister is Chief Leabua Jonathan, who heads the ruling party, the Basutoland National Party.

The parliament consists of a Senate and National Assembly. The Senate is comprised of twenty-two principal chiefs and ward chiefs and eleven other senators nominated by the king. The National Assembly consists of sixty members elected by universal adult suffrage.

The opposition parties are the royalist Marematlou Freedom party, led by Seth Makotoko, which supports the king and the Pan-Africanist Basutoland Congress Party led by Ntsu Mokhehle. Following the general elections of January 27, 1970, there was a *coup d'état* led by Chief Jonathan. Since that time there has been a suspension of formal political activity.

Demographic situation
Area: 11,716 square miles
Population: 1,000,000 (1968), including 2,000 whites and 1,000 Asians and coloreds
Capital: Maseru, 9,000 inhabitants (1966)

Economic situation
Gross national product: $49,000,000 (1966)
Per capita income: $60 (1966)
Currency: South African Rand, 1R = $1.40
Principal products: wool, mohair, diamonds

SWAZILAND

Political situation
On September 6, 1968, Swaziland, a former British High Commission Territory, became an independent constitutional monarchy within the Commonwealth of Nations. The king is Sobhuza II. The prime minister, Prince Makhosini Dlamini, is the head of the ruling party, the Imbokodvo National Movement. The major opposition party is the Ngwane National Liberatory Congress.

There is a bicameral legislature. The House of Assembly has twenty-four elected members, and six members nominated by the king. The Senate has six members appointed by the king, and six appointed by the House of Assembly. All elected seats are held by the Imbokodvo National Movement.

Demographic situation
Area: 6,705 square miles
Population: 400,000 (1968), including 8,000 whites
Capital: Mbabane, 14,000 inhabitants (1968)

Economic situation
Gross national produce: $107,000,000 (1966)
Per capita income: $290 (1966)
Currency: South African Rand, 1R = $1.40
Principal products: iron ore, asbestos, sugar, timber, citrus fruits

1

The History of the Anglo-South African Conflict over the Proposed Incorporation of the High Commission Territories

RICHARD P. STEVENS

Introduction

On September 3, 1963, the late Dr. Hendrik F. Verwoerd, prime minister of the Republic of South Africa, formally altered the direction of his government's policy toward the British High Commission Territories, otherwise known as the protectorates of Basutoland, Bechuanaland, and Swaziland. Speaking in Pretoria, Dr. Verwoerd announced his wholehearted approval of the constitutional developments occurring in the territories which, he assumed, "should also ultimately lead to fully independent states in these Territories."[1] Although the prime minister had stated the previous year that the "incorporation of the High Commission Territories into South Africa was neither possible nor wise,"[2] he had not officially admitted that the abandonment of a policy pursued since the inception of the Union of South Africa in 1909, which called for the incorporation of the territories, necessitated acceptance of their political independence. But in his 1963 speech before the Transvaal National party congress, the prime minister stated that incorporation was contrary to his government's policy of separate development. Instead, he urged that these territories avoid multiracial constitutions and adopt South Africa's political philosophy. Such a course, he stated, would leave the way open for a territorial exchange between the protectorates and ethnically related groups within the Republic, it would promise economic development in coordination with the Republic's economy, and, finally, it would enable the protectorates to participate in some kind of Southern African consultative body dealing with mutual interests.

Placed against the backdrop of historical Afrikaner interests in Basutoland, Bechuanaland, and Swaziland both before and after the South Africa Act of 1909, Dr. Verwoerd's official shift from a policy involving years of political and diplomatic pressures might at first appear contradictory and indicative of a change in the basic political philosophy of South Africa. But South African acceptance of, and indeed insistence upon, early independence for the High Commission Territories merely reflected the capacity of the Republic to adjust to postwar realities without losing sight of its fundamental objectives. After the National party's victory in 1948, the Republic's departure from the Commonwealth in 1961, and a succession of condemnations of its racial policies by the United Nations, it was manifestly impossible for any British government to acquiesce in the transfer of the Territories to the Republic. It was not impossible, however, for South Africa to achieve the substance of her traditional interests through friendly support of independent governments in the Territories. In the first instance, this meant assurances that the Territories would not permit themselves to become bases for hostile operations against the Republic, and, in the second instance, this meant that they would work in harmony with South Africa's economic and racial policies.

If South Africa's present policy toward the former High Commission Territories is to be fully understood, it is necessary to analyze the history of Anglo–South African discussions on the question of their transfer both before and after the Act of Union. Such a discussion will not only highlight those South African priorities which continue to influence interstate relations in Southern Africa but will also point out the contradictions and legacy of British policy. Last but not least, the type of response of the African elite and masses, both inside and outside the Union, to the Anglo–South African negotiations and pressures sheds considerable light upon the quality and uniqueness of policies presently pursued by the independent governments of Lesotho, Botswana, and Swaziland as they endeavor to retain their freedom as members of the world community.

The Early History of the High Commission Territories

Although the emergence of Basutoland (Lesotho), Bechuanaland (Botswana), and Swaziland as recognized national entities must ultimately be traced to the seventeenth: and eighteenth-century African migrations into Southern Africa, the consolidation of these various clans and tribes into coherent groupings can, in great part, be attributed to the external pressures radiating from expansionist Zulu and Afrikaner (or Boer) communities as well as to the imperatives of British imperial policy. In each instance Afrikaner pressures led the chiefs to appeal for British protection. Reluctant as Britain usually was in the first instance to take on new responsibilities, a combination of missionary pressures, business interests, and strategic considerations invariably turned the tide in favor of protection. The result was that three isolated clusters of African tribes survived the upheavals of the Zulu wars and the ever-expanding control of Afrikaner and English settlers.

It was fear of Afrikaner domination which induced Chief Moshoeshoe, the father of the Basuto nation, to seek British protection for his people as early as 1843. In 1845 the Cape government recognized the tribe of the Basuto as "a friend and ally." All the land between the Orange and Caledon rivers from their source and beyond the Caledon to a distance of twenty-five or thirty miles was recognized as Basuto territory. Subsequent refusal by Moshoeshoe to accept revisions of his borders led to hostilities both with the Cape Colony and with the Afrikaners of the Orange Free State. When Basutoland was at last declared British territory in 1868, its administration was entrusted to the self-governing Cape Colony in 1871. After serious problems and disaffection on both sides, however, the responsibility for administration was resumed by Britain in 1884 when a resident commissioner, subject to the high commissioner of the Cape Colony, assumed control.[3]

A growing number of incursions on the part of Afrikaner trekkers from the Transvaal also threatened the Bechuana tribes further to the northwest. In 1882 the Afrikaner mini-republics of Goshen and Stellaland, forerunners perhaps of additional filibuster settlements, were created, thus suggesting the possibility of future Afrikaner expansion.[4] But when Germany became interested in South West Africa in 1884 and showed that, as Cecil Rhodes had warned, it posed a threat to Britain's continental interests, Great Britain became involved. Fearing a link between German territory on the Atlantic and the Afrikaner settlements in the interior, Britain at last responded to the pleas of the Cape Colony representatives and of the Bechuana chiefs.[5]

In 1885 all the Bechuana region south of the Molopo River was declared to be "British territory" and was incorporated into Cape Colony in 1895, while the area north of the Molopo River up to 22 degrees south latitude was vaguely shown "as remaining under Her Majesty's protection."[6] In 1891 it was formally brought under the administration of the British High Commission, but Britain contented itself with allowing Rhodes' British South Africa Company to show the flag and virtually to represent its imperial interests in the area. Therefore, not only was the company able to obtain grants of land for a railway to the north along the eastern perimeter of the protectorate but also a white settlement was established beyond the Kalahari Desert at Ghanzi to act as a check on German expansion from South West Africa. As the company went on to make preparations to bring the whole protectorate under its control, chiefs and missionaries protested in vain to London where Rhodes had a large and effective lobby. The Colonial Office not only refused, in 1895, to promise relief to chiefs Khama, Sebele, and Bathoen but also the three chiefs urged to settle with the company as soon as possible in order to obtain the most favorable terms.[7] Had it not been for the precipitate action of Rhodes' agent, Dr. Jameson, in launching his ill-fated raid of January 18, 1896, against Johannesburg from territory ceded by the Bechuana chiefs to the company, the British government undoubtedly would have acquiesced to total company control. However, the Jameson raid proved too much for British sensibilities. Unwilling to provoke war with the South African Republic (as the Transvaal was then known), Britain rescinded transfer of the administration of the eastern region to the company, reaffirming and strengthening its control of the protectorate by the Proclamation of 1896.[8]

Swaziland, too, had long been the object of Afrikaner encroachment. Speculators and concession hunters had brought Swaziland within the sphere of influence of the Transvaal by the early 1880s. But ill feeling between the Afrikaners and the Swazi chief, Mbandzeni, led to an appeal for British protection. Britain hesitated, however, to extend its own jurisdiction over an area which was isolated from its other territories. Fortunately for the Swazi, domestic problems prevented the Transvaal from occupying this area which was so vital for the Transvaal's expansion to the Indian Ocean. By the conventions of 1881 and 1884, Britain and the Transvaal settled for a mutual guarantee of Swaziland's independence, although these conventions reduced the Swazi territory by one half. In 1890 a provisional government, consisting of representatives of Swaziland, Britain, and the Transvaal was established with the consent of the Swazi. This government lasted until 1894 when Britain granted certain governmental rights to the Transvaal provided that Swazi law and specified agricultural and grazing rights were respected. This arrangement lasted until the outbreak of the Anglo-Boer War in 1899, when the Transvaal special commissioner formally handed over his authority to the Swazi queen regent. After the war the country was administered by a special commissioner under the British governor of the Transvaal until late 1906. After that date Swaziland came under the British high commissioner at the Cape, who by then was already responsible for administering Basutoland and Bechuanaland.

Formal British assumption of sovereignty (Basutoland), protection (Bechuanaland), or jurisdiction (Swaziland) would bind these three diverse territories under the administrative control of the high commissioner acting through local resident commissioners until 1963, when the post of high commissioner was abolished. Considering the diversity of problems posed by the respective geographic settings and economies of the three territories, such an administrative system frequently seemed to have all of the disadvantages and few of the advantages normally associated with colonial rule. But whatever the weakness of the structure, it was indeed only the high commissioner who interposed a British presence between the territories and their covetous neighbor. Since each of the territories had previously experienced the rigors of control by the provinces of the Union of South Africa, criticism of British rule was generally temperate, if not altogether muted.

The Formation of the Union of South Africa

The possibility that the territories would be incorporated in the proposed Union of South Africa was very real in 1908, when delegates of the Cape Colony, Natal, the Orange Free State, and the Transvaal met in the National Convention at Durban to devise a constitution which presumably would be consistent with the promise of British liberalism. The assumption that the problems of Southern Africa could be solved only with the creation of a central national government embracing the four South African colonies as well as the three protectorates was basic to the Selborne Memorandum of January 7, 1907, which set the stage for the national convention of the following year.[9] Aside from purely political considerations, the three territories were almost totally dependent on the adjacent South African colonies for their markets and employment. Moreover, the territories were already part of a customs convention which had been established in 1903 and which abolished all tariffs among the territories, Southern Rhodesia, and the four South African colonies. Thus it was no surprise that the question of the incorporation of the territories by the proposed union was a matter of considerable interest both before and during the national convention. It was pointed out by several Cape delegates, however, that the question of the protectorates' transfer would be adversely affected by the rejection of the Cape's "civilization franchise"[10] for the Union. The adoption of this franchise, it was argued, alone would permit Britain to absolve itself of its obligations toward the territories.[11] Other delegates, such as the former Boer general, Jan Christiaan Smuts, while recognizing that the franchise provisions must influence the British attitude toward possible transfer of the territories, were unwilling to apply the Cape formula to the Union and called for British "trust" in the Union government since it would "most impressively bring home to South Africans their solemn duties."[12]

The British government, however, had no more reason to trust the good judgment of the defeated Boer republics in 1908 than it had in 1906. At that time, while conferring responsible government on the Transvaal and the Orange Free State, the imperial government announced that "pending any grant of representation to natives, no native territory now administered by the Governor or High Commissioner will be placed under the control of the new Responsible Governments."[13] The example of Natal's notorious administration of Zululand also provided little reason for the British government to believe that the territories would fare particularly well if incorporated directly into the Union. British refusal to transfer the territories to the two former Afrikaner republics meant a direct condemnation of the radical policies espoused by those two republics. According to the late Lord Hailey, this British rebuke led to the strong and persistent demand for transfer of the territories. After union, said Lord Hailey, this insistence would become a symbol of the growing ascendancy of the Afrikaner element. The continued separate existence of the territories would be seen as glaring proof that South Africa must strive to become totally independent of Great Britain.[14]

Although no effort was made during the national convention to ascertain the views of the inhabitants of the protectorates regarding possible transfer, adequate proof was forthcoming that Africans not only in the protectorates but also in the South African colonies felt that such an incorporation would not be in the interests of all Africans. Remembering only too well their own unpleasant rule by the Cape, a delegation of Basuto chiefs visited England seeking assurances that Basutoland would not be incorporated in the proposed union. Should some change in status be inevitable, they asked that their existing government be permitted to continue functioning and that guarantees be given that none of their land be alienated.[15] The Bechuana chiefs also voiced their opposition to incorporation in the proposed union.[16] In response, the Colonial Office merely said that in the event of union the Basuto should be prepared eventually to come under the control of South Africa.[17] In 1910 Lord Selborne, the high commissioner, gave the same reply when he informed the Bechuana chiefs that while transfer was not imminent, "in the natural course of things it would take place some day."[18] A number of petitions dealing with the High Commission Territories were also placed before the national convention by South African colored organizations. The African political organization in Cape Town voiced its concern lest the territories be transferred to the Union without the prior agreement of their respective chiefs and councillors.[19] While no official cognizance was taken of these petitions by the convention, they served to suggest the feeling of many both inside and outside the proposed union that the interests of all nonwhites were better served by the maintenance of the British sovereignty over the territories.

Sensing that the incorporation of the protectorates could not be achieved simultaneously with union, General Smuts accepted this policy as only a temporary delay. Thus he set out to achieve the second best arrangement, entailing an understanding with the imperial government stipulating that not only the process by which transfer could occur but also the actual transfer need not be specifically approved by the British parliament. Failure to provide for the future transfer of the protectorates at the Union's inception would of necessity involve the British parliament at a later date, with the corresponding likelihood of increased opposition to the scheme.

The national convention's decision to draw up a set of conditions as a schedule to the Act of Union was at least in part based upon formal and informal British advice to the delegates. Lord Selborne advised the convention that the British government had "obligations of the greatest possible weight" to the tribes of Basutoland and Bechuanaland and only slightly less so to the Swazi.[20] While confirming British recognition of African opposition to transfer, Selborne also confessed his belief that "there is no doubt that it is to the permanent interest of those tribes and of the Imperial Government, no less than the South African Government, that the transfer should take place."[21] The high commissioner went on to support suggestions that "the constitution should empower the British Government to transfer the Protectorates to the Union on conditions to be embodied in the Constitution and consistent with the obligations of the British Government."[22]

While, on the one hand, some convention delegates considered British refusal to turn over control of the territories promptly a humiliating affront, General J. B. M. Hertzog (later prime minister of the Union), on the other hand, initially opposed the transfer of the protectorates for financial and security reasons. He argued that if the Union took over the administration of the protectorates, Britain would then have no commitment to defend South Africa against external foes or internal disorder. Moreover, he felt that since Britain would insist upon enforcing the conditions of transfer, the imperial factor would not be removed from South Africa.[23]

The final decisions relative to the High Commission Territories were embodied in Section 151 of the South Africa Act and a schedule to that act. Although a compromise, Section 151 still stirred further debate in London. The British government took pains to indicate that the provisions in the draft bill of Union regulating transfer were purely "permissive."[24] According to the under secretary of state for the colonies, the schedule

> does not bring transfer one hour nearer. In fact, in so far as it goes, . . . it makes it somewhat more difficult. . . . a form of government is proposed to be set up which will prevent that sudden break from one form of government to another. . . . in the long distant years it well may be when these Protectorates are transferred, instead of having a sudden transfer from the control from the High Commissioner's office . . . to a Government direct from a Parliament without any antecedent machinery, you will have the transition so gradual that I hope and believe that the natives will never know from anything that occurs to them that the transition has been effected.[25]

It does not appear that the government felt embarrassed that this gradual transition would constitute a violation of past promises. Other arguments advanced by the prime minister, Mr. Herbert H. Asquith, and the under secretary for the colonies, Lt. Col. J. E. B. Seely, stressed that no transfer could occur "unless the King, with the advice of the Privy Council—that is, the Cabinet here—agrees"[26] and that "the wishes of the natives in the territories will be most carefully considered before any transfer takes place."[27] Speaking in the House of Lords, the colonial secretary, Lord Crewe, also defended Section 151. He asserted that the protectorates had come under British administration voluntarily and that such a trust could not be turned over to another nation without guarantees. While stating that the government was in no hurry to hand over these areas, he added that "it does not seem conceivable that for an indefinite future these areas should remain administered from here and that the new South African Union should have no lot or part in their administration."[28] The very existence of the schedule, said Lord Crewe, "undoubtedly contemplates their being possibly handed over at some time to be fixed by agreement."[29] Discussion in the House of Lords also led Lord Crewe to admit that "consultation" with the African chiefs was not tantamount to giving the right of veto to the proposed transfer.[30] It was implied, even by the former colonial secretary (Alfred Lyttleton), that Africans could not form a reasonably sound opinion as to where their future lay.[31] This judgment was reinforced by England's highest ecclesiastical official, the archbishop of Canterbury, who, while regretting the color bar in the proposed union, stated he would not oppose it. He regarded the color bar as a series of ". . . restrictions and limitations which corresponded to those we impose on children . . . ."[32]

The South Africa Act of 1909, as amended by Britain and accepted by the various South African Governments, clearly indicated that the newly created union would be an extensive one, peacefully absorbing the High Commission Territories, Southern Rhodesia, and perhaps the other British colonies and protectorates in Central and East Africa. The preamble to the act proclaimed that "it is expedient to provide for the eventual admission into the Union or transfer to the Union of such parts of South Africa as are not originally included therein,"[33] and this objective was reinforced legislatively by section 151, which stated:

> The King, with the advice of the Privy Council, may on addresses from the Houses of Parliament of the Union, transfer to the Union the government of any territories, other than the territories administered by the British South Africa Company, belonging to or under the protection of His Majesty, and inhabited wholly or in part by natives, and upon such transfer the Governor-General-in-Council may undertake the government of such territory upon the terms and conditions embodied in the Schedule to this Act.[34]

The schedule itself, with its twenty-five articles, then went on in some detail to provide for the method of government after the transfer had been effected; this method of government purportedly would ensure that the inhabitants of the territories would not be in any worse position after the transfer. But whatever the official position (which in itself seemed ominous enough as far as the protectorates were concerned), there was evidence to suggest that if transfer should occur, nothing could really prevent the Union from imposing its will upon the territories. Writing to General Smuts after the promulgation of the act and in words which that South African leader later made his own. Mr. Gert C. Oliver[35] would say of the protectorates:

> These parts and other portions within the Union devoted to Natives comprise some of the richest regions of South Africa, which are really suitable for a white population. Would it not be possible gradually and gently to include these regions in the Union and to

> make provision for the different Native races in such portions of the former German territories as are not so suitable for a white population? . . .
> . . . is it possible to cherish a more beautiful image than a South Africa populated up to the Zambesi with a strong white nation . . .?
> And, in aiming at this ideal, proper steps will have to be taken to protect the white population against the Natives. I make bold to say that with a strong force of aeroplanes and airships as part of our Defence Force, we have nothing to fear.[36]

The Incorporation Question, 1909–1939

Following the passage of the South Africa Act of 1909, the question of the transfer of the territories was informally raised with ever increasing insistence by the Union government. On March 12, 1913, Prime Minister Louis Botha wrote to the British High Commissioner Lord Gladstone, suggesting that both Bechuanaland and Swaziland be transferred as soon as possible.[37] After the close of World War I, (on June 18, 1919), Prime Minister Botha wrote a memorandum (presumably to Lord Milner) setting forth the reasons for immediate transfer of Swaziland to the Union. Chief among these reasons were the importance of Swaziland to the opening up of the Transvaal's coal resources and the belief that the Swazis were "physically of an inferior type [who], . . . more than most other native tribes, continue to lean on the whites."[38] Because of this dependence and the presence of a white community, the Union envoys saw Swaziland as an excellent testing ground "to put into practice the Schedule system of administration, and thereby gain valuable experience to guide it in the eventual administration of the other territories."[39]

Again in 1924, Prime Minister Hertzog reopened the question of the transfer of Bechuanaland and Swaziland by requesting the high commissioner in Pretoria to ascertain the feelings of the British government on the subject. In reply, the secretary of state for the dominions, Mr. Amery, indicated that the British government was somewhat less than enthusiastic about the prospect of transfer. Whereas the Union prime minister had referred to the expressed desires of whites in the territories, Mr. Amery stated that the main British concern was not the attitude of the whites but rather of the Africans.[40] The secretary went on to suggest that a formal petition to Parliament, given the expressed opposition to transfer on the part of the Swazis, might well result in an unfavorable reception. Should such a proposal be rejected by the Swazis, the secretary suggested that it might not be possible to renew the question for many years to come.[41]

British coolness toward Prime Minister Hertzog's suggestion added to the growing Anglo–South African estrangement. Although in 1909 British statesmen had clearly expected that the protectorates would one day be transferred to the Union, notwithstanding their explicit obligations involving "consultation" with the inhabitants, events quickly disproved the naïve predictions of many that Cape "liberalism" would prevail in the Union. Instead, by 1924 not only was the Cape non-white franchise under attack but also efforts were under way to adopt a policy of even greater racial segregation. To implement these measures of increased segregation, it appeared that the incorporation of the territories was indispensable. Under these circumstances, any adverse change in the status of the territories would be construed by the British public as an approbation of the Union's racial policies. Although the British government would not explicitly condemn these racial policies, it thereafter stressed with greater insistence the seriousness of past promises to consult the inhabitants of the territories. While South Africa deeply resented the British position, the Union government hesitated to draw attention to the real basis of British reluctance. Instead, Prime Minister Hertzog stated that he would not press for transfer unless "the people—natives as well as Europeans—are prepared and desire to come in."[42] Still, these remarks only lightly concealed Union resentment at British refusal to transfer the territories. This refusal not only prevented the total application of racial policies pursued by the majority party, but served to keep intact a contrary social and political philosophy.

As the British interpretation of "consultation" thus took on a more literal significance, the Union government endeavored to shift the grounds of discussion. In 1919 General Botha had indicated this approach when he suggested that incorporation "would enable the Union Government to spend money on the development of the Territory, [*i.e.*, Swaziland] which is very badly wanted."[43] By 1924 the position was more fully stated by Prime Minister Hertzog, who observed that

> internal development under present conditions in these territories is not possible owing to the fact that their resources are so limited and considering the intimate geographical connexion of these territories with the Union, their incorporation with the latter has become essential to their own development and, as it seems to me, is fast becoming essential to the development, through railways and irrigation, of the Union itself.[44]

The question of the transfer of the High Commission Territories was vitally affected by the Statute of Westminster, which was adopted by the British Parliament in 1931; the statute formally debarred the British government from any interference in, or even expression of opinion about, Dominion concerns. Shortly thereafter, the South African Parliament adopted this statute by means of the 1934 Status of the Union Act, which affirmed the status of the Union as a sovereign independent state.[45] South Africa's total independence was subsequently confirmed in 1937, when the highest court in the Union ruled (in *Ndhlwana* v. *Hofmeyr*) that, after the passage of the Statute of Westminster, no court had the power to pass judgment on whether the Union had adopted the procedure laid down in the 1909 act relative to the franchise. Although the Status of the Union Act expressly provided that nothing in the act was to affect the provisions of section 151 of the 1909 act, it was obvious that sovereign power could not be legally fettered and thus the schedule could be nullified at any time.[46]

Therefore, unless the provisions of the schedule were embodied in a treaty between the Union and the United Kingdom, there could be no guarantee that the provisions of the schedule regarding the administration of the incorporated territories would be implemented. Under these circumstances it was natural that the British government should advise Prime Minister Smuts in 1933 that "before any question of transfer could be considered it would be necessary to ascertain:—(a) What the Union Government would propose to substitute for the provision relating to the power of disallowance. . . . And (b) What alternative form of security could be provided."[47] The new Anglo-South African relationship defined by the Statute of Westminster also necessitated the separation of the office of high commissioner from that of governor-general, the latter office now representing solely the crown and not the British government. Only in this way could the protectorates remain a British responsibility. While the move left the inhabitants of the protectorates outside the Union, it did not give them the advantages of the regular British colonial service. For now, in addition to his usual functions, His Majesty's high commissioner to South Africa remained responsible for the administration of Basutoland, Bechuanaland, and Swaziland.

Since the office of high commissioner fell under the Commonwealth Relations Office and not under the Colonial Office, the territories were placed in the anomalous position of being worse off than other British colonies and protectorates since these other dependencies could theoretically evolve toward independence. The High Commission Territories remained in a political limbo without prospects for political change other than in the direction of incorporation into South Africa. Even the development of local government was therefore twenty to forty years behind the times as compared with other British African territories.

However paradoxical the Union government's expression of concern for the backward economic condition of the High Commission Territories was, it undoubtedly influenced the British decision in 1933 to send Sir Alan Pim to report on their condition. Sir Alan's findings confirmed what so many had long known: British protection had left the territories to stagnate, and they were weighed down by poverty, ignorance, and disease. The customs union had primarily benefited South Africa, and during the depression Bechuanaland could not export its cattle to South Africa, ostensibly for veterinary reasons. Tribal society, meanwhile, had been disastrously affected by economic and political dislocations. No longer required to submit to traditional tests of fitness for office, chiefs drew their authority from the alien British administration which was unable to replace those traditional controls which it had consciously destroyed.[48] Tribal institutions were judged incapable of meeting modern needs without guidance, and the British policy "of non-interference, of proffering alliance, of leaving two parallel governments to work in a state of detachment unknown in tropical Africa" was seen as a serious weakness.[49]

Public attention both in Britain and South Africa was dramatically focused on the High Commission Territories in 1933, when the acting high commissioner, Vice Admiral Edward Evans, deposed Tshekedi Khama, who was the acting regent of the Bamangwato tribe in Bechuanaland, for exceeding his powers by administering corporal punishment to a white who offended the morals of the Bamangwato.[59] This punitive action, which also involved the overland dispatch of a naval detachment from Simonstown (near Cape Town) to the protectorate, was regarded as a disproportionate response and could well be interpreted by the Africans of Bechuanaland either as an indication of the high commissioner's sympathies for the racial policies of South Africa or of the extent to which British policy was responsive to white sensibilities in the Union. Although the incident caused the British government to be ridiculed in all quarters, it also caused considerable resentment among South African whites against Tshekedi and the protectorate.[51] The fact that mineral concessions had recently been secured by whites in areas of the Bechuanaland protectorate which were previously closed to them gave additional weight to these demands as did the petitions of whites who lived in the white enclaves along the railway.[52] Citing these arguments as well as complications associated with locust and disease control, problems resulting from different native policies, and the importance of the Union market for territorial cattle and labor, Prime Minister Hertzog reiterated his government's belief that "the time has come for the Union to assume responsibility in connection with these territories and to take them over,"[53] and he suggested that if transfer were delayed, difficulties would arise for the inhabitants of the territories especially with regard to their rights and privileges in the Union.[54]

Replying to various notes received from the South African prime minister over the next two years, the secretary of state for dominion affairs, Mr. J. H. Thomas, presented Prime Minister Hertzog with an *aide-mémoire* on May 15, 1935. Secretary Thomas recalled that the British government had promised to Parliament that the transfer of the High Commission Territories would not take place until their inhabitants had been consulted and until Parliament had been given an opportunity to express its views. In terms of these pledges, Mr. Thomas ventured the opinion that the time was not ripe for consulting the Africans since all information indicated "that at present native opinion in the Territories is very strongly opposed to transfer."[55] He believed that in the ensuing years the policy of both governments "should be directed to bringing about a situation in which, if transfer were to become a matter of practical politics, it could be effected with the full acquiescence of the populations concerned."[56]

The conflicting interpretation put on the policy of cooperation suggested in Secretary Thomas' *aide-mémoire* provided a major theme in discussions on the territories up to 1939. In a speech in the South African House of Assembly on June 16, 1936, Prime Minister Hertzog claimed that the British government had committed itself through the 1935 *aide-mémoire* to instruct officials "gradually to allow the natives to feel and to know that their ultimate destination was in the Union."[57] In the same speech, he claimed that Great Britain had also accepted the idea that the Territories "would be handed over after a few years, not at the same time, but one after the other," with Swaziland probably first on the list.[58]

Mr. Thomas' successor as dominions secretary, Malcolm MacDonald, contradicted this interpretation of the British position in a speech delivered in the House of Commons on July 16, 1936, but brushed over the matter by asserting that Prime Minister Hertzog's pronouncements were "to be read as an expression of his personal hope that, if the policy agreed to in the *aide-mémoire* is loyally carried out by both Governments, a position would, within a few years, be created which would permit the transfer . . . with the good will of their populations."[59] Continued debate on the degree to which Britain supposedly would encourage favorable attitudes toward the Union proved inconclusive, but it is significant that the high commissioner, Sir William Clark, apparently construed Secretary Thomas' remarks in much the same way as Prime Minister Hertzog did. In his *aide-mémoire* of July 1, 1935, Sir William informed the South African government that "it will then be the duty of officials in the Territories to expound to the chiefs and peoples the extent of the benefits which they may be receiving through the good will of the Union."[60] In pursuance of this object, the high commissioner suggested that the Union and the administration of the territories devise a program of cooperation. Territorial representation on various South African control boards and the financial association of the Union with territorial development schemes which were now under way, largely as the outcome of Sir Alan Pim's critical reports, were seen as useful devices to help bring about the proper climate of opinion.[61]

But this suggestion that South Africa financially contribute to such schemes was viewed with alarm by the inhabitants of the territories. Prime Minister Hertzog's announcement in the House of Assembly of a recurrent grant of £35,000 "to bring about a state of goodwill among the natives as soon as possible"[62] seemed an adequate basis for this distrust. Consequently, when the South African offer was communicated to the African authorities in the territories by their resident commissioners, accompanied by "assurances" "that they would incur no liability by accepting Union money," it became obvious that such "assurances" were not enough to dispel their fear of what might happen if their areas should eventually be incorporated in the Union.[63] In all three territories, the Africans suspected that poor whites and so-called "redundant" Africans from South Africa would covet their land, that they would no longer be allowed to keep their arms, and that they would be subject to the South African pass laws which would limit their freedom of movement.[64]

Prime Minister Hertzog's arguments justifying the proposed expenditure only increased this anxiety. The prime minister argued that such expenditure would merely be an investment in its future territory, since it was his understanding that Britain would very shortly transfer Swaziland to the Union.[65] Notwithstanding the repeated promise of the British authorities that the territories would not compromise their political future by accepting these South African funds, the chiefs unanimously rejected the proposal. The South African government had to withdraw its offer of funds and Prime Minister Hertzog again stated that the transfer would take more time.[66]

One of the more outspoken African opponents of transfer who was able to influence British public opinion was Acting Regent Tshekedi Khama. In 1935 he published a pamphlet, *Statement to the British People and Parliament*, in which he charged that the transfer of the protectorate administration from the British to the Union government would constitute a breach of previous agreements guaranteeing the rights of the African inhabitants. Should incorporation occur, he claimed, then the unsympathetic policy which the Union government had adopted toward Africans would certainly also be applied in the protectorates. That the Union had seen fit to sever its connection with the British Privy Council as a court of final appeal for the Commonwealth and empire was an indication that the South African government would deprive Africans of all legal safeguards.[67]

But South Africa's position was not without its champions even in British "liberal" circles. Some cited the economic stranglehold of the Union over the protectorates or the obvious impoverishment of the protectorates as justification of transfer. Lord Lugard, the marquess of Lothian, Sir Edward Grigg, the earl of Selborne, and Mr. L. S. Amery, M.P., suggested that a transfer be worked out by stages through a restructuring of the administration of the three territories so that, when the moment was propitious, the resulting transfer "would be imperceptible to the natives."[68] Lionel Curtis, who was a close associate of Lord Milner and who helped to form the Union, argued that faith in the whites of South Africa was necessary if they were ever to be able to come to terms with their situation. "To develop coherent relations of White and Black Society," argued Curtis, "is impossible so long as territories the size of Wales, Belgium and France, embedded in the Union, are beyond its control."[69] He professed to see in the changing attitudes of young Afrikaners a dissatisfaction with the traditional African policies of the Union. Their progressive attitude, he prophesied, would one day dominate Union policy—but only if the external pressure of British control over the territories were removed.[70] Small wonder it was that Africans inside and outside the Union found it increasingly difficult to decide which was their more dangerous enemy: avowed National party segregationists or liberal English compromisers.

During the course of parliamentary debates and continued Anglo-South African exchanges of correspondence regarding the intent and interpretation of the 1935 British *aide-mémoire*, Mr. MacDonald suggested that the Union government officially set down the terms to be observed in the event of transfer "so that the peoples of the territories may appreciate the conditions under which the territories would be governed."[71] Such a step, it was suggested, would be particularly helpful because the Statute of Westminster and the Status of the Union Act probably made the safeguards embodied in the schedule inoperative.[72] Prime Minister Hertzog replied to this suggestion on December 29, 1937, by asserting that, in the event of incorporation, the intentions of the schedule to the South Africa Act would be strictly observed since the Union government had "never contemplated any other form of administration for the Territories in question than that outlined in the Schedule to the South Africa Act."[73] Even so, the prime minister stressed that "the only real security on which the inhabitants of the Territories could rely by virtue of, or rather, in spite of, the. . . [Schedule], would be a security based upon a sense of responsibility towards, and understanding of, the native peoples, which would determine every decision of the Union Government."[74] At the same time he stressed that the British government must understand that the "policy and administration relating to the native peoples of South Africa is and must remain a matter '*of purely domestic concern*,' "[75] and went on to complain about misconceptions prevalent in Britain concerning South Africa's racial policies. He urged that "intelligent propaganda" both in the High Commission Territories and the United Kingdom be utilized to correct these misconceptions. In particular, the prime minister suggested that relations could be improved if all official vacancies in the territories were to be filled after consultation with the Union government, an obvious criticism directed at the recent appointment of Charles Arden-Clarke as resident commissioner of Bechuanaland.[76] Mr. Arden-Clarke's appointment, representing as it did the introduction of some sixteen years' experience with indirect rule in Nigeria, was undoubtedly seen as a dangerous precedent, and the prime minister called for officials "more conversant with South African problems."[77] Prime Minister Hertzog regretted that the effort "to discourage the agitation against joining . . . the Union . . . has so far met with very little success"[78] and expressed confidence that an active effort "on the part of officials in the Territories to counteract any attempt to prejudice the minds of the native inhabitants against the Union and actively do their duty to inculcate friendly feelings . . . towards the Union" would have positive results within a very short time.[79]

In its reply, the British government confirmed that it agreed with "the view expressed by General Hertzog in a speech in London in May, 1935, that Section 151 of the South Africa Act . . . has a meaning and intention" but reiterated its previous pledges to Parliament and to the inhabitants of the Territories.[80] Reviewing the progress in Anglo-South African cooperation over the previous three years, Mr. MacDonald informed the House of Commons on March 29, 1938, that agreement had been reached to establish a standing Joint Advisory Conference, composed of the three resident commissioners, the Union secretary for native affairs, and two other Union officials. He also noted that the Union government had agreed to the preparation of memoranda involving all apsects of transfer "for the information of the native and European inhabitants of the territories."[81]

The Joint Advisory Conference made its first report in February 1939. Although neither the report nor the promised memoranda was made public until 1952, the report contained a useful summary of all existing forms of cooperation between the Union and the British administration in the territories. No fewer than fifteen types of cooperation were enumerated, including the free services of Union judges, cooperation in the training of white policemen, the collection of customs duties, Union control of currency and most rail, motor, airway, post, and telegraphic services. If the British were apprehensive that South African involvement indeed constituted an abdication of British responsibility, it was not evident in the report. The conference affirmed "the essential economic unity of the Territories and the Union"[82] and concluded that "developmental work has to some extent been retained by political boundaries and limited financial resources" notwithstanding the increase of loans and grants both from the Imperial Treasury and from the Colonial Development Fund.[83]

The Incorporation Issue, 1939–1966

The outbreak of World War II not only delayed publication of the 1939 Union memorandum and the Joint Advisory Conference report, but led to the decision to leave in abeyance the question of transfer. Meanwhile, the Union government's announcement that the paramountcy of African interests in African areas would be maintained led many influential British "liberals," such as Mr. L. S. Amery, to argue that there was no longer an adequate reason for further postponement of transfer since such a policy coincided with British policy for the protectorates.[84] That independence might be another possible alternative was not suggested.

The National party victory of 1948 which elevated Dr. Daniel F. Malan to power as prime minister of South Africa revived discussion on the question of transfer. His decision to reopen the subject perhaps reflected South African confiddence that recent disturbances and serious challenges to law and order in Basutoland and Bechuanaland would convince Britain of its inability to govern the territories effectively. In the former territory, an increase in ritual murders (*diretlo*) from three in 1941 to twenty in 1948 led to the execution of six highly placed Basuto. An expert British investigation revealed that the secondary causes of these murders were almost entirely political and resulted from the insecurity following upon attempted, but ineffective, piecemeal reforms of the chieftaincy.[85] Trouble in Bechuanaland stemmed from the decision in 1948 of Seretse Khama, chief-designate of the Bamangwato and the nephew of Tshekedi Khama, to marry an English woman. Although there was good reason for the matter to cause serious tribal wrangling on constitutional and traditional lines, the issue also served to attract the attention of South Africans to the state of affairs in Bechuanaland. At a time when apartheid had become a crucial election issue in South Africa, a mixed marriage on the border of the Union was seen as an intolerable affront to that philosophy of race relations. Even the leader of the Opposition, Field Marshal Smuts, went so far as to warn that if the British administration would allow Seretse to become chief of the Bamangwato, it would undoubtedly cause the National party government to "demand the incorporation of Bechuanaland and possibly even threaten to blockade the Territories. His own Party [the United party] would be unable to oppose such a move because of the emotions aroused."[86] In any event, despite a subsequent decision by the Bamangwato tribe in favor of Seretse as chief with his white wife as queen, the British government ignored this decisive majority. Such disdain for African opinion, claimed *The Times*, made British promises to consult African opinion in the territories rather hollow.[87]

Although Dr. Malan did not allude to these events in Basutoland and Bechuanaland as justifications for transfer, he did inform the House of Assembly on April 13, 1950, that almost forty years had gone by since Great Britain had taken practical measures to transfer the territories to South Africa. Continued failure to achieve some progress, he warned, might necessitate initiation of formal action by the Union Parliament requesting transfer.[88] On May 4, 1950, the prime minister stated in the South African Senate that if the High Commission Territories were not transferred before too long, the South African government would be justified in treating the protectorates and their African inhabitants as foreign areas and persons and thus presumably not eligible to receive certain economic benefits that they had hitherto received from the union of South Africa.[89]

In early 1951 Dr. Malan pressed the Union position harder on the occasion of a visit to South Africa and the territories by the British secretary of state for Commonwealth relations, Mr. Patrick Gordon-Walker. While Dr. Malan admitted that the time was inopportune for a formal approach to the British government, such inopportuneness arose from the small majority which Prime Minister Attlee's second ministry commanded in the House of Commons rather than from any South African scruples about the attitude of the inhabitants of the territories. The prime minister invited comparison between the measures taken by the Union government to promote economic development and self-government in its African reserves with "any other native administration in Southern Africa."[90] He reproached Britain for its obvious mistrust of the Union's capacity to promote and protect African interests, and he expressed indignation that South Africa should be made to bear the burden of an intolerable affront to its self-respect as a nation:

> South Africa is an independent country and recognized as such. Constitutionally she stands on a footing of equality with the other members of the Commonwealth and with other independent nations. But in one vital respect she differs from them all, and that is, that within her embrace, and even actually within her borders, she is compelled to harbour territories, entirely dependent upon her economically and largely also for their defence, but belonging to and governed by another country.[91]

Britain could, of course, argue that movement across the borders of the protectorates was a two-way traffic. Should the Union try to blockade the territories, its own farmers and employers would be deeply affected. Still, Britain had no reason to hold the territories permanently. Not only were they a source of recurring expense but they also inhibited closer British relations with South Africa. Given the unanimous opposition of the African inhabitants to transfer and the consolidation of the power of the South African National party, transfer would both stir deep resentment in the territories and impair British relations with Africans in the British colonies to the north. Even then, the decision to install Mr. Kwame Nkrumah as Leader for Government Business in the Gold Coast deeply shocked Dr. Malan, who condemned the step as one which might "radically change the 'whole complexion and character' of the Commonwealth."[92] In response to secretary Gordon-Walker's defense of Gold Coast developments as being totally in keeping with the recognized tradition of the British Empire, Dr. Malan turned the question to the future of the High Commission Territories. However anxious he might be to settle the problem by agreement, the prime minister warned that he might have to make it an election issue. An African veto on transfer, said Dr. Malan, would never be acceptable.[93]

Within weeks after Mr. Churchill's Conservative government took office in October 1951, Dr. Malan again warned that unless transfer took place before too long, he would treat the inhabitants of the territories as foreigners. Shortly thereafter, the two governments agreed to publish the extensive correspondence relating to the transfer.[94] Speaking before the Orange Free State National Party Conference in 1953, the prime minister said that the problems of transfer must be settled within the next five years without any prior commitments that Africans should thereafter have a voice in South African affairs. "We cannot," he asserted, "accept conditions of this nature. . . . So far as self-government for the Natives is concerned, England should come to learn from us, not we from England."[95] With some logic, the prime minister asked how Great Britain could force unwilling Africans in Southern Rhodesia, Northern Rhodesia, and Nyasaland into the Central African Federation and at the same time insist that Africans have veto power over the transfer of the protectorates. He was disturbed that Mr. Nkrumah had now become the prime minister of the Gold Coast and warned that the "forcing" of self-government onto Africans was disastrous. Such a policy in his view, was counterproductive because "anyone with common sense" could foresee that if it were applied to the remainder of British Africa, the whites there would be forced out of the continent. He pointed out that the Africans of Northern Rhodesia were insisting that they be granted self-government as well.[96] There was all the more reason, then, that the High Commission Territories should be incorporated before this dangerous infection crept further south.

In 1954 the Union House of Assembly resolved that the transfer of the territories "should take place as soon as possible" and that negotiations should be resumed.[97] This was followed by an assurance from Prime Minister Strijdom the following year that "when the Protectorates were incorporated, the territories would be accorded the same sympathetic treatment which had always been accorded Native territories in the Union," a promise which gave small comfort to the inhabitants of the protectorates.[98] At the same time, however, the new prime minister gave indication of change in the South African approach to the question. In August 1955 the Afrikaans Sunday paper, *Dagbreek en Sondagnuus*, "suggested that South Africa should no longer insist on transfer but should try to co-operate with Britain in developing the Territories as Bantu homelands."[99] Since Prime Minister Strijdom belonged to the

Board of Directors of this newspaper, it seems reasonable to assume that such an important *détente* would not have been proposed had he objected.[100]

In 1956 the publication of the Tomlinson Commission Report on "separate development" revealed that all three territories were theoretically to be incorporated in the proposed South African Bantustan system. Although Dr. Verwoerd, who was then the minister for native affairs, denied in a speech before the House of Assembly on May 14, 1956, that their inclusion was a basic requirement for the success of his policy,[101] some of the maps in the report clearly indicated that transfer of the territories would permit the carrying out of the Bantustan project.[102] Without the territories, the Bantustan system would remain a patently unconvincing project and, with the exception of the Transkei, could hardly advance much beyond the drawing board. The commission pointed out that, even if all the land promised in 1936 were added to the reserves, only 13 percent of the country would be set aside for the African population. However, if the High Commission Territories were included in South Africa, and if they were added to existing reserves, the percentage would amount to nearly 45.[103]

As prime minister, Dr. Verwoerd spoke again of the transfer of the protectorates. On May 4, 1959, in a speech delivered in the House of Assembly, he pointed out that the transfer of these three territories to the Union would be advantageous to all concerned and might well entail the exchange of land among the white and African areas. The term "incorporation," noted the prime minister, did not imply that the Union coveted the land of the Africans in the protectorates. In fact, said Prime Minister Verwoerd, South Africa was helping its own Africans to manage more and more of their own affairs.[104] On November 12, 1958, in his address to the congress of the Transvaal National party in Pretoria, he took the position that the future prosperity of the three High Commission Territories was linked with that of the Union and that the system of administration the British government used there was not too dissimilar to the system proposed by the ruling National party in South Africa. Dr. Verwoerd asserted that the Union's policy of border industry for the African areas of the Union would be an economic boon to the protectorates, and he claimed that the British government was not taking advantage of these economic gains for its African wards by not agreeing to the incorporation of the protectorates. He suggested that the Union government serve as a guardian of the High Commission Territories until they became self-governing areas and pointed out that his government put forth its request for the incorporation only because it hoped to have friendly, rather than hostile, neighbors.[105]

In short, the prime minister was "saying two things at the same time: that South Africa could not establish Bantustans unless she has the territories; and, the inhabitants of the territories need not fear South Africa since she was following the enlightened policy of establishing Bantustans."[106]

But it was four years later, in September 1962, that Dr. Verwoerd finally implied that incorporation was incompatible with the British policy of granting self-government to these three African territories.[107] Although "this candid admission of reality had never been matched by any of Dr. Verwoerd's predecessors as Prime Minister, and it clearly revealed his inability to conceive of full independence for the Bantustans and by implication for the High Commission territories as part of that scheme."[108] The prime minister simultaneously attacked the opposition United party for its continued quest of transfer despite the many changes which had rendered that object unobtainable.[109]

Dr. Verwoerd's assessment of the impracticability of transfer stemmed from at least four major considerations. First, the traditional territorial resistance to incorporation by the chiefs had been transformed or escalated into modern articulate expressions of territorial nationalism.[110] Second, the nationalist parties of the territories had succeeded in internationalizing the problem of the High Commission Territories both at the United Nations and in various foreign capitals. Third, as a result of these and other pressures, Britain gave concrete evidence of its decision not to implement the transfer. Basutoland was granted greater self-government in the constitution of 1959, and the territories were transferred to the Colonial Office on December 1, 1961, under the British high commissioner to South Africa as high commissioner of the three territories. Finally, in the words of the retired high commissioner, Sir John Maud, since 1961 South Africa had known "that Great Britain . . . [was] in a unique position to help or harm the Republic"[111] and there was an understanding that South Africa's "behaviour towards these Territories . . . [was] now the principal touchstone whereby Great Britain . . . [could] judge how good a friend South Africa . . . [was] to her."[112]

By offering to "guide" the territories to political independence and economic prosperity in his famous speech in Pretoria on September 3, 1963, Dr. Verwoerd was varying the half-century-old policy aimed at bringing the territories under South African political control. With incorporation out of the question, the National party government now saw new opportunities to achieve the same end. Border posts, passport control, curtailment of railway passenger service, air flight restrictions, and repatriation of workers from the protectorates were all simultaneously employed in 1963 to demonstrate South Africa's ability to affect adversely life in the territories. But alternating with these displays of force, Dr. Verwoerd showed that he could cooperate with any government in the territories which sought South African friendship. Friendly relations, he said, were in accord with the Republic's policy of separate development. In 1964, with the prospect at hand of the final removal of the imperial factor from Southern African politics, the prime minister expressed confidence that independent governments would be better guarantors of their own interests than the British government.[113]

The subsequent elections which brought Seretse Khama to power as prime minister of Bechuanaland, Chief Leabua Jonathan to power as prime minister of Basutoland and King Sobhuza's Imbokodvo party to power in Swaziland were seen as a total vindication of South Africa's new diplomacy. In each instance the territorial party which had received South Africa's overt or covert support had not only gained power but seemed to have won a major point with the electorate by stressing its ability to come to terms realistically with the Republic. Whether such an entente would primarily promote the welfare and independence of the new states or enable South Africa to secure the substance of its traditional interests in the former protectorates remained to be seen as Lesotho, Botswana, and Swaziland joined the ranks of the world's independent nations.

2

Botswana

RICHARD DALE

Introduction

Within the course of the last century, the Bechuanaland Protectorate (as Botswana was known until it became independent on September 30, 1966) proved to be the gateway from the British possessions in South Africa to Rhodesia as well as a territorial impediment to German expansion in Southern and Central Africa.[1] Its geographical location, rather than its natural and/or human resources,[2] made it a strategic area in terms of the colonization of Southern Africa. As Dr. Anthony Sillery of the Taylor Institution of Oxford University (and former Resident Commissioner of the Bechuanaland Protectorate) has suggested, Bechuanaland was

> . . . a country poor in itself but situated in a position of strategic importance in the Scramble for Africa. It was reluctantly occupied by Great Britain under international and Colonial pressures on a basis of minimal responsibility. The British Government's clearly expressed intention in 1885 [the year in which the protectorate was proclaimed] was merely to hold the frontiers against intruders . . . and to abstain from administration or any other activity.[3]

Except at the point where Zambia and Botswana have a common, albeit undefined, border in the middle of the Zambesi River, the Republic of Botswana is completely enveloped by South West Africa, Rhodesia, and South Africa. Because of its border with Zambia—which has recently been the object of contention between the governments of Botswana and South Africa—Botswana is the only one of the three former British High Commission Territories in Southern Africa to have a common frontier with Black Africa; the other two erstwhile Protectorates, Lesotho and Swaziland, share borders with South Africa and (in the case of Swaziland) Mozambique, both of which are ruled by white minorities.

Not only is Botswana encircled by states or territories which are still governed by whites, but also, like several other states in Southern Africa, it is completely landlocked. This landlocked condition limits the kinds of policies that the decision-makers of Botswana can pursue, especially in terms of the patterns of communications and trade. As a small power located in the epicenter of Southern Africa, Botswana is subject to the inducements as well as pressures (overt and covert) of its more powerful neighboring states, while at the same time Black Africa to the north serves as a reminder that the Batswana are members of a larger, continental grouping whose goals and values they share.

In his analysis of small state behavior, David Vital suggested that

> The strength and weakness of [such] states and their longterm viability must . . . be examined not in terms of current, typical international practice, still less in terms legal and moral rights. It is the capacity of the [small] state to withstand stress . . . and its ability to pursue a policy of its own devising . . . that are the key criteria.[4]

Therefore, it would be appropriate to examine first the type of nexuses existing among the three white-controlled neighboring states and territories —those states that have the capacity to create conditions of stress for Botswana—and Botswana before analyzing the techniques that the political leaders of the Republic of Botswana have devised for withstanding latent and manifest stress, on the one hand, and for pursuing their own preferred values and goals, on the other hand.

THE SOUTH AFRICAN LEGACY

The British newspaper correspondent, Mr. Douglas Brown, once waggishly described Great Britain as ". . . Afrikanerdom's mother-in-law."[5] If such a simile be an acceptable one, then it might also be appropriate to regard South Africa as the "mother-in-law" of the Batswana of the Bechuanaland Protectorate until 1961 when South Africa left the Commonwealth of Nations. That is to say, although the Bechuanaland Protectorate was under *de jure* British rule until 1966, it was under *de facto* South African rule until the early 1960's. The South African legacy is surely as important in Botswana today as the British legacy is and it might even be a more important one.

Indeed, as Professor Richard P. Stevens has already shown in another chapter, the South African government initially expected after the the formation of the Union that, in due course, it would receive the British patrimony of the three High Commission Territories.[6] Such an expectation, moreover, was embodied in Section 151 of the 1909 South Africa Act and was continued on in the Constitution of the Republic which was adopted in 1961. Surprisingly enough, the 1961 republican constitution was not amended to take cognizance of the independence of one or more of the three British protectorates in Southern Africa until 1969. At that time, the South Africa Act was amended to delete all references to a possible incorporation of the former High Commission Territories. In particular, the South Africa Act Amendment Act (No. 26 of 1969) repealed Sections 150 (referring to Rhodesia) and 151 (referring to the High Commission Territories) of that Act and the Schedule to that Act (which dealt with the mode in which the incorporation of the protectorates was to have taken place).[7]

The most remarkable point about Act No. 26 of 1969 was that it was gazetted about *thirty months after* Botswana became independent. A suggestion to amend the constitution came from a former backbencher of the parliamentary National Party, Mr. J. A. F. Nel, who represented a Cape constituency in the House of Assembly from 1953 until 1966. In a letter (of February 28, 1968) to the influential Cape Afrikaans newspaper, *Die Burger*, Mr. Nel suggested that the time had come to repeal these two Sections and the Schedule to the South Africa Act. Approximately six months later, on September 18, 1968, Prime Minister B. J. Vorster told the Orange Free State Congress of the National Party meeting in Bloemfontein that the government intended to amend the constitution to delete any reference in it to incorporation of the erstwhile Southern African protectorates (and of Rhodesia as well). Such an amendment to the South Africa Act was regarded by the government as part and parcel of what has been described as its "outward policy" of trying to win friends and to influence statesmen in black Africa.[8]

A second strand of the web of relationships between South Africa and the Bechuanaland Protectorate concerned the site of the administrative headquarters of the Protectorate. Unlike either of the two other former High Commission territories, Bechuanaland until very recently had its administrative capital outside its borders—in Mafeking, Cape Province. From 1885 until 1895, the capital of the protectorate was Vyrburg, and it thereafter moved north along the line of rail to Mafeking, where it remained until it moved north once again along the railway line to Gaborone in 1965, the year in which the protectorate achieved internal self-government. The headquarters of the protectorate administration were located on the outskirts of Mafeking in an enclave known as the Imperial Reserve, which is now the site of the Tswana Territorial Authority offices.[9]

Such an arrangement was, of course, economically beneficial to Mafeking in terms of the employment of its local citizens as well as in terms of the profit the town derived from the sale of public utilities to the Imperial Reserve. In addition, a certain percentage of the salaries and wages of the employees of the protectorate administration was spent in Mafeking itself and thus provided an economic multiplier for the commercial life of Mafeking. Conversely, when the administrative capital was transferred to Gaborone, there was a corresponding constriction of commercial activity in Mafeking.[10] The maintenance of an extraterritorial capital for seventy years in South Africa was a constant reminder of the essential parsimony of British colonial policy in Bechuanaland. Even though the British understood only too well the political and economic costs of keeping the capital in Mafeking, the problem was the lack of funds for moving.[11] Currently, funds that would hitherto have been spent in Mafeking are being diverted to Gaborone, although many of the whites who live in Gaborone continue to shop in Mafeking and other areas in South Africa.[12] In addition, a significant number of whites (Britons as well as South Africans) who have retired from British government service chose to move to South Africa, where many of them are able to secure a job while on pension; thus, funds earned from service in Botswana are spent in South Africa rather than in Botswana.[13]

In the third place, the administration of the Bechuanaland Protectorate was, to some extent sub-contracted to locally recruited (meaning South African) persons, a policy which, in retrospect, perhaps created as many problems as it was intended to solve. In general, it may be said that the elites of the British colonial service recruited very largely by Major Sir Ralph D. Furse,[14] did not make their mark in Bechuanaland until after the end of World War II. The proportion of locally recruited South African whites in the Bechuanaland civil service diminished in the period since 1945 as more and more Britons were brought over to serve.[15] South Africans could serve as full-fledged members of H. M. colonial service during most of this time since South Africa was a member of the Commonwealth. Presumably, it was less expensive for H. M. government to use locally recruited South Africans to administer Bechuanaland than to staff the entire administration, from top to bottom, with British civil servants (with all the travel expenses and home leave time that would entail). The difficulty with using South African whites rather than Britons was that all too often, in the eyes of the Batswana, the South Africans had internalized, rather than rejected, those norms and attitudes associated with a *baasskap* (white supremacy) approach to white-African relations. South African racial attitudes and stereotypes thus enjoyed a type of extraterritoriality in Bechuanaland as long as these South Africans were in the employ of the protectorate administration, or so the argument ran.[16]

The argument seems rather persuasive and is accepted by many Batswana. Yet the matter is not quite so simple. There is the very difficult question of the distribution of racial attitudes among South African whites in the protectorate administration. Indeed, it would be an egregious error to assume that *all* South African whites held attitudes which were more appropriate to a *baasskap* society than to a non-racial one (which was the preferred type of social organization in Bechuanaland). Some South Africans may well have joined the British colonial service because they preferred the more liberal policy of the British government in Africa to that pursued in South Africa. It would seem that these persons, however, tended to be located at the upper echelons of the protectorate administration. Those South Africans whose racial attitudes grieved the Batswana tended to cluster at the lower levels of the protectorate administration and these persons all too often had skills which were considered absolutely vital to the continued functioning of the administration and could not easily be replaced from Britons recruited in the metropole.[17]

Conversely, the racial attitudes of some Britons in the colonial service were not always the preferred ones, for those Britons who had served long years in the Protectorate, worked alongside South Africans, traveled and took holidays in South Africa, and had their children educated in South African boarding schools were not always immune to such attitudes. The Batswana are quite sensitive to racial attitudes and can detect any sign of officiousness, condescension, and other attitudes redolent of *baasskap*; indeed, such antipathy to racial arrogance and to any philosophies of racial superiority is clearly manifested in the debates of the National Assembly. This antipathy is by no means the exclusive concern of the opposition Botswana Peoples' Party; it is shared by members of the governing Botswana Democratic Party.[18]

As long as South Africa remained in the Commonwealth, questions could be raised (although not always answered definitively) about the impact of South African racial attitudes on the Britons who were responsible for the administration of the protectorate. The anxiety stemmed from the position which the three High Commission territories occupied on the British table of organization and chain of command for the overall governance of the empire. In the case of the Bechuanaland Protectorate, not only was its headquarters located within the boundaries of the then Union of South Africa but also its top administrator, termed the Resident Commissioner, reported directly to the British High Commissioner (that is, Ambassador) in Pretoria who, in turn, reported to the Secretary of State for Commonwealth Relations. The Southern African protectorates were thus cheek by jowl with the Commonwealth Relations Office, rather than the Colonial Office. It was feared that the interests of the Batswana would be subordinated to the interests of cordial Anglo-South African relations.[19]

The nature of this triangular relationship and the stresses involved were made palpably obvious in the *cause célèbre* of Sir Seretse Khama, who, as heir-designate to the Chieftainship of the Bamangwato (the largest single ethnic unit in the Protectorate), chose to marry a British woman in 1948 against the wishes of his uncle, the late Tshekedi Khama, who served as the Regent of the tribe. This marriage crossed the color line and ruffled the sensibilities of many whites in South Africa. The nature of the whites' feeling was described by the late Field Marshal Jan C. Smuts in a letter to Winston Churchill in these terms:

> People, both in South Africa and Rhodesia, are as a whole united in their opinion against Seretse's marriage to a white woman. Indeed, in both countries miscegenation of this kind is legally criminal and would certainly be fatal to any claim to the chieftainship.
>
> Should the British Government ignore this sentiment in South Africa, public opinion here would harden behind [Prime Minister Daniel F.] Malan's claim for the annexation of the Protectorates to the Union, and in case this claim were refused, the extreme course of declaring South Africa a republic would at once become a live issue.
>
> . . . .
>
> . . . you will see that the Seretse case in its full implications is full of dynamite, and I think it would be a mistake to exploit British feelings in favour of Seretse to an extent which may damage the relations of South Africa to the Commonwealth and the Commonwealth itself.[20]

Sir Seretse, shortly before Field Marshal Smuts wrote this letter, had been declared a prohibited immigrant in South Africa, and he was kept in that status from 1949 until 1964.[21] As well as being anathema to the South African government, he was also banished by the British government from the Protectorate from 1950 until 1956 because of his marriage and his strained relations with his uncle, Tshekedi.[22] The Seretse affair was very time-consuming from the point of view of the protectorate administration, and it was felt that much greater progress in the economic (if not political) development of the territory could have been made had not so much of the civil servants'

time been devoted to dealing with this delicate and emotionally charged matter.[23]

The fourth kind of relationship between the Protectorate and the Union entailed the education of the Batswana, and, consequently, the political socialization of the present elite of Botswana. To refer once again to Mr. Brown's "mother-in-law" simile, South Africa, rather than the metropole, was the nation where most Africans received their secondary and university educations. Rare indeed were those Batswana who were educated abroad in the British Isles. Those Batswana who went to South Africa for a secondary education attended missionary schools, such as the well-known Tiger Kloof Institution (which is south of Vryburg). Indeed, as late as 1945, there were no secondary schools at all in the Protectorate, and Africans (as well as whites) who wished to pursue post-primary studies had to go to Rhodesia, the Union, or to the United Kingdom.[24]

Moreover, the pupils usually prepared themselves for South African, rather than British, examinations. Only recently have secondary school students in Botswana begun to use the Cambridge school certificate type examinations.[25] Children of white civil servants—especially expatriate ones—still do attend South African boarding schools (although some go to British "public schools"), and it is not uncommon for Africans to be enrolled in the non-residential University of South Africa (located in Pretoria) which is a correspondence university. For a while, the University of South Africa acted as the "mother-in-law" of Pius XII College (now called the University of Botswana, Lesotho, and Swaziland) in Roma, Lesotho in that students at that college would receive their bachelor's degrees from the University of South Africa. This relationship, however, has since been terminated.[26]

THE SMALL AND THE MIGHTY

President Khama of Botswana, in his maiden speech before the General Assembly of the United Nations on September 24, 1969, acknowledged that his nation was very much a ". . . part of Southern Africa and that the harsh facts of history and geography cannot be obliterated overnight."[27] For his nation to maintain its identity, meet its minimum international obligations, and cope with the perennial problems of poverty that beset his people, it was necessary for Botswana to come to grips with these "harsh facts" and, as Mr. Vital pointed out earlier, ". . . to pursue a policy of its own devising. . . ."[28]

Thus what Botswana needed to do was to follow these four maxims: (1) multilateralize the Southern African region by bargaining in concert with other black African states so that it would not have to face its powerful neighbor alone and without allies; (2) studiously avoid any kind of activities that would probably be regarded as legitimizing or condoning the system of apartheid in South Africa; (3) actively seek aid from non-South African sources which would diversify the pattern of aid and thus mollify to some extent the "harsh facts of history and geography;" and (4) prevent any diplomatic and economic isolation that might result from being closeted next to South Africa in Southern Africa. In short, Botswana needed diplomatic, political, and economic leverage in order to put distance between itself and its "mother-in-law."

Ever since 1910, Botswana had been a party to a customs agreement which included South Africa, Swaziland, and Lesotho (Basutoland as it was then called). This union provided for a customs-free area in Southern Africa except for alcoholic beverages and stipulated that the South African treasury was responsible for collecting duty on items that entered the customs area and for paying a proportion of the income it received to its partners.[29] At the time of its independence, the Republic of Botswana received 0.27622 per cent per annum of the revenue from the customs union as compared with 98.68903 per cent per annum for South Africa, 0.14900 per cent per annum for Swaziland, and 0.88575 per cent per annum for Lesotho. Even though this appeared to be a miniscule proportion for Botswana, it took on added significance when viewed in terms of Botswana's ordinary revenue. During 1965–1966, for example, revenue from this source constituted 21 per cent of Botswana's ordinary revenue.[30]

On the very first day of its independence, Botswana made it clear that it was interested, not in dissociating itself from the 1910 customs agreement, but rather in redressing what its economists regarded as the imbalances in that agreement.[31] A similar statement of intent was made almost two years later by the Government.[32] One of the major drawbacks of the existing customs union was that

> The actual tariffs levied are determined by South African interests. High protective duties imposed to protect South African industry tend to diminish the total revenue collected and therefore that part accruing to the Botswana Exchequer. In such cases the diversion of customers from cheaper overseas imports to more expensive South African manufactures results in a transfer of spending power from Botswana consumers to South African producers.[33]

Another detrimental aspect of the customs union was that, except in the case of alcoholic beverages, Botswana could not levy any duty itself on imports from South Africa and consequently the free trade area, with its external tariff, would preclude the possibility of Botswana's establishing any tariffs of its own to protect any of its nascent industries from being undercut by cheaper South African goods. This could have a deleterious effect on developing any viable industrial sector in the Botswana economy.[34] Moreover, it was felt that less than three-tenths of one per cent of the total customs revenue was hardly a generous figure.[35] "A Customs Union between a rich and a poor nation," claimed the economic planners in Gaborone, "normally produces a polarity of economic development, with the better endowed areas growing at the expense of the poor areas."[36] Therefore, they asserted, "In recognition of this process, it is necessary to make some provision for the automatic redistribution of resources towards the poorer partner."[37]

Finally, one of the more glaring inequities in the customs union was the manner in which decisions were made, decisions which affected the economic welfare of all the members of the union. There was nothing in the text of the original agreement about the decision-making process; indeed, the agreement was signed by Lord Gladstone no less than four times for each of the four parties involved; once as governor-general of South Africa, and three times as high commissioner for each of the three Southern African protectorates.[38] From 1910 until 1969, decisions were made unilaterally in a multilateral organization, and there was no provision in the 1910 agreement which would allow for multilateral decision-making.[39] The style of decision-making in the customs union was clearly illustrated when the South African government, without attempting to secure the approval of the governments of the three erstwhile High Commission territories, unilaterally levied a sales tax in 1969. Such a sales tax was, of course, passed on to consumers in the customs union, and the Botswana government rebuked the South African government for this action.[40]

On December 11, 1969, representatives of the four contracting parties signed a new customs agreement which goes a long way toward meeting Botswana's earlier objections to the existing agreement. In sum, South Africa will now share more of its economic power with its three African neighbors, and that power can be canalized and neutralized to a greater extent than heretofore. This agreement has been aptly described by the South African journalist, Mr. Clive Cowley (the editor of *The Windhoek Advertiser*), as ". . .the only multilateral instrument for trade in a region which is otherwise a spider's web of bilateral relationships."[41] The agreement is, of course, an integral part of what has been termed the "outward policy" of the Vorster Government and no doubt South Africa was prepared to pay a price for such a quadripartite treaty.

Indeed, there may have been some extremely hard bargaining before the agreement was signed, for one (unnamed) Botswana spokesman has been quoted as saying that "If the South Africans had not, in the Customs talks, recognised that our claims were just and based on reality, we would have left the Customs Union in due course."[42] Such a statement would, in all probability, have been regarded as idle talk had Botswana not been able to turn to its two black partners in the customs union for help in negotiations.

The 1969 customs agreement institutionalizes the practice of consultation and thus establishes a Customs Union Commission, which is a quadripartite body that meets at least once a year, if not more often. Moreover, it permits the three smaller states, in consultation with all the other contracting parties, to erect protective tariffs so that they can proceed apace with their industrial development. The industries so protected need to be designated as such, and the protective tariffs are not expected to be valid beyond eight years. Presumably this would be long enough for small-scale manufacturing plants to become fully operational in Botswana. Lesotho, and Swaziland. A new method for determining the allocation of customs revenues among the four governments was included in the agreement and was made retroactive to April 1, 1969.[43] The difference between the 1910 and the 1969 agreements is striking when one compares the amounts South Africa was expected to allocate to its three partners. If the formula used in the 1910 agreement is utilized, South Africa would have paid the three former protectorates a total of $6.6578 million in the year 1969–1970. Now the new figure, according to the South African Deputy Minister of Finance, will be a total of $23.039 million.[44] In the case of Botswana, the minister of finance who signed the agreement for Botswana estimated that the new agreement would more than double the amount Botswana would receive from the customs pool for 1969–1970. The new formula, he said, would assure the government of Botswana an annual income ". . . approximately equal to 18 per cent of the value of Botswana's imports and production of dutiable goods."[45]

Thus a most important precedent was set for the multilateralization of Southern Africa, and the lilliputian states of Botswana, Lesotho, and Swaziland were able to arrive at a satisfactory *modus operandi* with the South African Gulliver. True, such an agreement could be regarded as a great victory for South African diplomacy, as another example of the success of the "outward policy." But the success of the "outward policy"

need not necessarily be viewed as one which involves zero-sum games, that is, arrangements in which there must be both victor and vanquished. It could just as well entail non-zero-sum games, that is, arrangements which are mutually beneficial.[46] Perhaps one might formulate the hypothesis that the greater the number of non-zero-sum games between Botswana and South Africa—provided they did not violate the second, third, and fourth maxims suggested earlier in this section—the greater its opportunity of modulating South African power in Southern Africa. As Professor Robert A. Dahl of Yale University has suggested, "The likelihood of peaceful adjustment to a conflict is increased if there exist *institutional* arrangements that encourage *consultation, negotiation*, the exploration of alternatives, and the search for *mutually beneficial* solutions."[47]

There still remains, after the quadripartite customs agreement, an area of discontent between the two nations, one that would offer yet another opportunity for what might be termed "Lilliputian bloc" negotiations with South Africa. This concerns the multilateralization of the Rand currency area and, once again, entails the sharing (and consequent dilution) of South Africa's awesome economic power. Accordingly, the Botswana government is interested in restructuring the institutions of the Rand currency area in such a way that the Lilliputians will have

> A direct say in exchange control and other fiscal policies designed to protect rand currency and boost the economy of Southern Africa as a whole.
>
> A share of the interest on securities held in the South African Reserve Bank.
>
> The right to raise capital on the common money market with Government bonds and Treasury bills. Financial institutions would be compelled to invest a prescribed part of their assets in them as with South African Government stock.[48]

In addition, the economists in Gaborone are quite disconcerted that their government is not drawing any interest on the reserves it has sent to South Africa to cover the Rands circulating in Botswana; that interest is said to amount to $0.14 million. Finally, Botswana officials are not entitled to membership on the Board of the South African reserve bank.[49] Presumably negotiations between South Africa and the three former protectorates will, in time, result in an agreement which will meet most, if not all, of the complaints of South Africa's three neighboring black states. Botswana recently issued its own bonds, which were handled by the two commercial banks (Barclays Bank and the Standard Bank) in the nation. The $4.2 million thus raised will be ploughed into economic development. These bonds, which pay 7½ per cent (tax-free) over a 22 year period or 5½ per cent (tax-free) over a 5 year period, were significant, for they marked the first time that one of the three Lilliputians had ever gone to the Rand currency area for funds on a commercial basis. It is reported that South African financial institutions participated in the fund-raising venture.[50]

A HAVEN IN THE MIDST OF SOUTHERN AFRICA

Earlier it was suggested that the second maxim of Botswana's statecraft was to avoid any and all types of behavior that could reasonably be construed as giving aid, support, or legitimation to the policy of *apartheid* in South Africa. Naturally the obverse of this maxim is for Botswana to reaffirm, by word and deed, the nonracial character of its own society and the belief that such a society is the type which deviates least from the norms accepted (in theory, although not always in practice) by the rest of the world community. Hence, one set of norms (racialism as institutionalized by *apartheid*) is excoriated, whereas another set (nonracialism) is praised and accepted. In practice, therefore, Botswana must not only repudiate apartheid but also must be seen acting against this system practiced by its southern neighbor. Botswana must be seen by all and sundry to be a votary of nonracialism. It can do so by devising appropriate policy guidelines in four crucial areas, namely, in its (1) diplomacy with South Africa; (2) its attitude toward African nationalist guerrillas who are anxious to topple the white minority governments in Pretoria, Windhoek, and Salisbury; (3) its attitude toward political refugees from nearby South Africa, South West Africa, Rhodesia, and Angola; and (4) its relationships with the Rhodesian government now in power.

Botswana's statesmen have developed a rather sophisticated and subtle policy in their transactions with their South African counterparts and the South African Department of Foreign Affairs. This policy is cheap, effective, and does not compromise either the ideals of the Botswana decision-makers (many of whom received their secondary education in South Africa and have experienced racism first-hand) or the standing of Botswana in the rest of the African community of states. Botswana's diplomacy relative to South Africa contains three principal elements: (1) recognition of South Africa, but refusal to exchange diplomatic missions unless there is complete equality of treatment of both Botswana's and South Africa's diplomats in each other's nation;[51] (2) frequent commutation between Gaborone and Pretoria by airplane; and (3) constant use of the telephone.

In terms of the first element, Botswana not only avoids legitimating apartheid but also saves itself the expense of maintaining two embassies (one in Pretoria and the other in Cape Town—the standard practice because South Africa has both a legislative and an administrative capital) in South Africa. By following such a policy, it is free to concentrate its diplomatic corps where it needs it the most (in terms of access to black Africa, the United Nations, the Commonwealth of Nations, and the major aid donors). Moreover, it can avoid the calumny that some African states have heaped upon Malawi for exchanging diplomats with South Africa. Here again, Botswana's policy is in line with that followed by the two other former protectorates, Lesotho and Swaziland.

The second element of Botswana statecraft is really the logical outcome of the first since it is a useful surrogate for embassies in Pretoria, Cape Town, and Gaborone. It also can be the thin edge of the diplomatic wedge because when a Botswana diplomatic team—often composed of senior civil servants and ministers—travels to South Africa, the South African government will avoid discriminating against the Africans in the team, especially because it wishes to win friends and influence neighbors. Hence, the mission from Gaborone will receive the *same* social amenities, *irrespective* of race. Yet this *ad hoc* equality of treatment only serves to remind Africans in South Africa[52] and the government of Botswana[53] that the rigors of apartheid still are borne by the Africans in South Africa and by ordinary Batswana who either visit or work in South Africa. When the South African government extended its hospitality to the president of Botswana by arranging for him to stay in the otherwise all-white Johannesburg general hospital, the appreciation of the people of Botswana for this act was conveyed by the vice-president of Botswana to South Africa. Yet some South African whites—belonging to the *verkrampte* wing of the ruling National Party—found this gesture odious. Their incivility was rebuked by Prime Minister Vorster.[54]

For the run-of-the-mill diplomatic exchange between the two neighbors, the telephone is deemed quite adequate and naturally does not give rise to questions of the proper social etiquette, especially when it involves questions of race relationships. It might still be used when hard or delicate negotiations are involved, but obviously it would be redundant when important South African dignitaries (such as Foreign Minister Dr. Muller or other cabinet ministers or diplomats) visit Botswana.[55]

A closely related topic is the treatment that Botswana has meted out to African nationalist guerrillas who are regarded as "terrorists" in the south and "freedom fighters" in the north. The Bechuanaland Protectorate (and later, Botswana) was an important conduit from the white south to the black north because of its strategic location astride the Zambesi River, which is, after all, the gateway to Zambia. The Protectorate thus served as one of the most crucial, if not the most crucial, links in the "underground railway" of Southern Africa, especially because of the generally benign attitude of the British proconsuls in the Protectorate and in Northern Rhodesia (as Zambia was known in the early 1960's).

Those responsible for the security of the state in South Africa were particularly alarmed at what they regarded as the lax attitude shown by the British authorities in the Bechuanaland Protectorate towards this clandestine railroad, and the South Africans were markedly anxious about the egress from South Africa via Bechuanaland of persons they regarded as saboteurs, persons who would presumably return later as armed guerrillas to South Africa.[56] Naturally, these South Africans perceived Botswana as a link in the chain that began with the escape of wanted African nationalists (and their white colleagues) from South Africa, that led through Botswana onto what has been labeled the "freedom ferry"[57] at Kazungula (a border spot in Botswana that has been dubbed the "checkpoint Charlie"[58] of Southern Africa after the noted border post in West Berlin), and thence onwards to Black Africa, guerrilla instruction in Africa and/or in the Sino-Soviet bloc, and return to South Africa via Tanzania, Zambia, and Botswana.

This South African anxiety has diminished somewhat after Botswana became independent, but surfaced once again during the general election campaign in South Africa in 1970. Although far more subtle than the 1929 general election campaign, which centered on the "black peril,"[59] the 1970 campaign did include references to Botswana's decision to establish diplomatic relations with the Soviet Union[60] and to construct (with American foreign aid) an all-weather road to Kazungula with the express purpose of forging stronger communications and trade links with the Republic of Zambia.

In the heat of this campaign, one member of the South African Cabinet made quite clear his aversion to the *démarche* of the Botswana government with respect to the Soviet Union.[61] As the South Africans appeared to perceive it, the Soviet Union would be encamped virtually on their back stoep. Furthermore, the Soviet Union and its allies were known to be the logistical patrons of African nationalist guerrillas.[62] *Ergo*, this diplomatic move (by Botswana's High Commissioner in London) was tantamount to escalating the guerrilla war against South Africa, or so some South Africans might well have thought.

In the case of the road from the town of Nata to Kazungula[63] and the attendant question of the Zambian-Botswana border,[64] the anxiety was even more obvious. Like almost all other newly emergent African states, Botswana inherited its frontiers from the colonial powers with very little basic readjustment. Indeed, relations between Botswana and South Africa, and between Botswana and South West Africa, had been quite amicable with respect to border demarcation.[65]

But this cordiality did not extend to the matter of the Botswana-Zambia frontier which was also claimed to be the border between the Caprivi Zipfel (of South West Africa) and Rhodesia. The South African position was that there was no common border between the two black states,[66] whereas the opposing view[67] was that there was a common, albeit undefined, border between the two states which would allow one to pass from Botswana to Zambia without even so much as touching Rhodesia or the Caprivi Zipfel. Hence, if deemed necessary, a bridge could be constructed across the confluence of the Zambesi and Chobe Rivers. Judging from his recent remarks in the House of Assembly, the South African foreign minister has no objection whatsoever to the road which will lead up to the Chobe River.[68]

The problem would seem to be a twofold one. In the first place, it is hoped in Botswana that such a road from Nata to Kazungula and the improved ferry facilities (or even a bridge)[69] may, in the course of time, substantially improve Botswana-Zambian trade. If such were not the case, it would be difficult to explain the meaning of the recent round of bilateral trade talks in Gaborone and Lusaka.[70] Botswana may increase the value of its imports from Zambia (although the goods need not necessarily be of Zambian manufacture) and this, in turn, could adversely affect the volume of South African exports to Botswana. Yet given the size and elasticity of the domestic market in South Africa, it is doubtful that such a restructuring of trade between South Africa and Botswana would be a meaningful challenge to the defense of South African national interests. It would be an economic pinprick and not much more.

In the second place, the white South Africans are apprehensive about the improved road and ferry lest they facilitate an increased infiltration of African nationalist guerrillas.[71] This, rather than the trade links between Botswana and Zambia, appears to be the most meaningful challenge for them. They perceive it as a threat in light of their two-front counterinsurgency campaign. On the one hand, South African paramilitary units are engaged in action along the Zambesi Valley in Rhodesia—and South African policemen have already been killed there—and, on the other hand, the authorities in Pretoria are concerned about internal security in South West Africa, for there already has been armed conflict in that territory.[72] Thus far, such fears appear to be unfounded, although there is really nothing to stop a massive guerrilla incursion into Botswana (which, of course, the Rhodesian security forces would notice immediately, assuming their electronic gear and intelligence networks are fully operational). Rhodesian soldiers and policemen could easily photograph such guerrillas (from the air or from their own territory) if the guerrillas chose to cross the Zambesi here so blatantly, and, from the safety of the southern bank of the Zambesi, lay down quite a mortar, machine gun, or small arms enfilading fire.

Therefore, ordinary military logic would dictate against the guerrillas using such an obvious route of infiltration. The more serious problem, from the point of view of Botswana, is the possibility that they would cross the Zambesi and traverse Botswana in a westerly direction parallel to the southern boundary of the Caprivi Zipfel which would allow them to launch hit-and-run raids into the Caprivi. This would be extremely serious because it would call for an even larger Botswana Mobile Police Unit (a tactical striking force) to interdict and capture the guerrillas[73] and because it might even tempt the South African military or paramilitary forces to engage in hot pursuit of the guerrillas from the Caprivi into Botswana. Such hot pursuit could conceivably result in an extremely ugly incident, such as the Sakiet Sidi Youssef one in which the French air force bombed this Tunisian village (on February 8, 1958) during the course of the Algerian war.

The Botswana police force, which is a paramilitary force (for Botswana has no army), has been quite vigilant and effective so far in protecting the territorial integrity of the nation. Indeed, they have not engaged in any firefights with the guerrillas and are hoping that this state of mutual tolerance will continue. If the guerrillas throw their arms away before they are captured or surrender, they are regarded as illegal immigrants. If they are found with weapons, they are charged with illegal possession of firearms.[74] Botswana has no laws as harsh as the Terrorism Act in South Africa (perhaps because it is not against the goals of the liberation movements), but it nevertheless has been legally able to cope with the guerrilla problem so far. Indeed, while the British were the paramount power in Bechuanaland the Legislative Assembly enacted a statute to prevent persons from using the Protectorate as a base of operations against neighboring states.[75]

Furthermore, the government is empowered to declare persons ". . . who would endanger the peace and security of Botswana" prohibited immigrants and to imprison them for four years and/or to fine them $5,600, according to the provisions of the Immigration (Consolidation) (Further Amendment) Act No. 37 of 1968.[76] Finally, Botswana has requested the Organization of African Unity to insure that its territorial integrity and sovereignty are not in any way compromised by the various liberation units which might wish either to operate from Botswana or to traverse Botswana, and it seems to have received the necessary assurances from that Organization.[77] As the 1970 operations in Cambodia have shown, nations that are regarded (by more powerful states) as places of asylum for the enemy may be singled out as military targets. If, for example, the time ever came when the guerrillas could violate the sovereignty of Botswana with impunity, the government of Botswana might, on the one hand, be subjected either to South African or Rhodesian retaliation (the extent of retaliation presumably being linked to the intensity and immediacy of the perceived threat) and might, on the other hand, conceivably become the political hostage of guerrilla groups. The power of *Al Fatah*, the Palestine liberation movement, is not unimpressive, especially in Jordan. Doubtless, President Khama does not envy the position of King Hussein in Amman.

Yet Botswana has prided itself as a haven in the midst of Southern Africa, an oasis of sorts for *bona fide* refugees, both for those in transit to the north and for those who wish to stay and to make their living in Botswana. There were approximately 1,000 to 1,200 such transients from either South Africa or South West Africa during the British rule in the 1960s,[78] while the number of refugees in independent Botswana is placed at roughly 4,000 at the present time.[79] The overwhelming majority of these 4,000 are essentially apolitical Africans who have fled from the scene of fighting between African nationalist guerrilla units and Portuguese forces in southeastern Angola. These Angolans have arrived within the last two years; prior to that time, the number of refugees in Botswana was said to be somewhat less than 200 persons.[80] These 200 were presumably all congregated in the Francistown area.[81]

Since independence, the government of Botswana has made an attempt to cope with the refugee situation in a systematic and even-handed manner. On the one hand, it has made the position of the *bona fide* political refugee inviolable in terms of extradition to South Africa. The Extradition (Republic of South Africa) Order, 1969, which became operational in early May, 1969, stipulates explicitly that "Extradition *may be refused* if the offence in respect of which it is requested is *regarded by the requested Party* as a political offence or as an offence connected with a political offence."[82] This normalized the relationship between the two republics without compromising Botswana's position on political asylum for opponents of apartheid; yet it would allow for extradition of non-political offenses. On the other hand, the Khama government indicated its willingness to subscribe to international norms covering the treatment of refugees. In early January, 1969, it deposited instruments of accession to the Final Act and Convention Relating to the Status of Refugees of the 1951 United Nations Conference on the Status of Refugees and Stateless Persons and to the 1967 Protocol Relating to the Status of Refugees.[83] In addition, at the present time, there is a representative of the United Nations High Commission for Refugees resident in Gaborone.[84]

Having examined briefly the policies towards South Africa, African guerrillas, and political refugees, it would be fitting to end this section with an analysis of Botswana's relations with the Smith government in Rhodesia. At the outset, it is worth recalling that there are historical legacies which affect Botswana's policy regarding Rhodesia just as there are comparable legacies in the case of Botswana's foreign policy toward South Africa. Not long after the National party acceeded to office in Pretoria in 1948, the Rhodesians, perhaps piqued by the persistence with which the South African government requested the transfer of the High Commission Territories to the Union, saw fit to lay claim to at least part of the Bechuanaland Protectorate.[85] The Union government, however, took umbrage at this claim, asserting that Rhodesia had no standing in the issue.[86] However, at the time, it was thought that the Batswana would have preferred to have their nation absorbed by Rhodesia rather than by the Union because they found the racial policies of the former less oppressive than those of the latter.[87] The question, of course, never really became a pressing one, and the claims of Rhodesia were quietly dispensed with thereafter, except insofar as certain white farmers in the white enclaves adjoining Rhodesia—the Tuli block and the Tati Concession—have evinced an interest in having their areas detached from Bechuanaland and linked to Rhodesia. This the government has refused to do, for it would not tolerate secessionist movements.[88]

At the time the Smith government unilaterally declared its independence from the United Kingdom (on November 11, 1965), the British were still the sovereign power in Bechuanaland and were responsible for the conduct of the foreign affairs of the protectorate. Thus the British initiated policy toward Rhodesia, and the Khama government, once the protectorate became independent the subsequent September, continued that policy —with the exception of broadcasts into Rhodesia. That policy was to forbid the passage of arms and ammunition through Bechuanaland en route to Rhodesia,[89] to terminate the British postal order service between Bechuanaland and Rhodesia,[90] and to establish a radio broadcasting station outside Francistown in order to beam British broadcasts into nearby Rhodesia.

This Central African Relay Station[91] (also known as the Diplomatic Wireless Service Transmitting Station or as simply the "bush radio"), which was established by the British Foreign Office, proved to be a rather expensive exercise in foreign policy, for it cost the British taxpayers $1.775 million to build and maintain from 1965 until it was closed down in late March, 1968. Later in 1968, the British Government made a gift of the equipment at the "bush radio" to the Botswana government which had earlier furnished policemen to guard the station. These policemen, in turn, had replaced different British army units (the Gloucestershires, the Irish Fusiliers, and the South Wales Borderers) which were stationed there. Military and paramilitary units were used to guard the relay station because sabotage was feared. Earlier, in 1963, during the peak of the refugee exodus, an airplane which was intended to fly two very important South African refugees (who would have been defendants in the Rivonia Trial had they not managed to escape from jail in Johannesburg) was blown up at Francistown. The authorities never found out who destroyed the airplane,[92] and it was likely that the British feared the same thing would happen to the "bush radio." The station was guarded against possible sympathizers of the Smith government. During the time the station was operating, nothing dramatic happened, and the Rhodesians simply jammed the broadcasts.

Once the British closed down the station, the Botswana government did not continue the broadcasting policy of the British, and the matter lapsed. President Khama indicated his antipathy to recognizing what his government regarded as an illegal regime. In this the government has adopted a policy different from the one it employs for South Africa. It recognizes the regime in Pretoria, but not the one in Salisbury because the latter entailed what is regarded as an illegal seizure of power.[93] The declaration of a republic in Rhodesia following a referendum there in 1970 further strengthened the resolve of the government in Gaborone to withold recognition.[94] In addition, Botswana takes an extremely dim view of the presence of South African paramilitary forces in Rhodesia, for it hopes to avoid a further escalation of violence in the Zambesi valley. It has therefore requested, rather unsuccessfully it should be added, that the Vorster government remove these policemen from Rhodesia.[95]

Naturally, Botswana is anxious to preserve its territorial integrity and is just as concerned about the violation of its sovereignty by Rhodesian security forces which may be in hot pursuit of African nationalist guerrillas who may be operating in the Wankie area of Rhodesia.[96] Since it does not recognize Rhodesia, there is naturally the diplomatic problem of lodging a complaint with a government that does not legally exist, at least in the eyes of the plaintiff. Presumably the complaint can be left with the British government which is still regarded, in theory at least, as responsible for Rhodesia.

To a very limited extent, Botswana participates in the sanctions authorized against the Smith government by the United Nations, and it has placed a limited embargo on the purchase of Rhodesian tobacco and beer; this prohibition does not apply to the Chobe area of Botswana which may still continue to import these two products from Rhodesia.[97] This will make some dent in the Rhodesian economy, for Botswana is estimated to have purchased $2.38 million worth of tobacco, beer, and non-alcoholic beverages from Rhodesia in 1968, for example.[98] However, indications are that Botswana, at least in the short run, will not be able to do too much more in the way of economic sanctions against the Salisbury government lest it jeopardize its economic growth. It has told the United Nations of this dilemma.[99]

Furthermore, Botswana is dependent upon the Rhodesian railway[100] that traverses its eastern boundary and that links it to its overseas markets via the South African harbors in Durban, Port Elizabeth, and Cape Town. When he took command of the newly independent Republic of Botswana, President Khama assured the Rhodesian authorities that his government would not interfere with the operation of this railroad.[101] Indeed, the Khama government (out of necessity, no doubt) treats the Rhodesia Railways as a surrogate Rhodesian government, and the Botswana officials carry out their business with their opposite numbers in the Rhodesia Railways in Bulawayo. Yet the relationship between the government and people of Botswana and the Rhodesia railways has not been a consistently cordial, friendly one. There seems to be bitterness, fear, and rancor—all of which have become more apparent since independence.[102]

The Rhodesian position involves anxiety about possible nationalization of the 394 miles of the railroad that lie in Botswana, a disinclination to invest large sums of money in this line that connects Bulawayo with Mafeking, and a feeling that the white railway staff are harassed by the Batswana. The Rhodesians are apprehensive since their sole rail connection with South Africa is via a third nation, and there has been a long-standing desire to forge a rail link directly between Rhodesia and the neighboring Transvaal province of South Africa. The situation is further complicated by the fact that the Botwsana government does not recognize the Smith government, and this adds to the Rhodesian bitterness. Recently, Prime Minister Smith announced that his government would go ahead with plans to close the rail gap between his nation and South Africa by building the necessary railway link between the two railway systems at Beit bridge.

Conversely, the Rhodesia railway is an irritant for many in Botswana who charge that its personnel indulge in racial discrimination in the course of their duties, and the Batswana are only too aware of their economic dependency on that railroad, a railroad over which they have no significant political control. In addition, even were the government in Gaborone to purchase (or perhaps even to nationalize with full and prompt compensation) all the line of rail and related equipment, including an adequate supply of rolling stock, there are presently no Batswana technically qualified to take over the operation of the railroad. However, it is possible that the Khama government will choose to purchase the railway (assuming the necessary loans could be raised) and then contract on the international market for the necessary skilled personnel. This, of course, is mere conjecture, but it might be pointed out that in late January, 1970 four Canadian railway experts (one of whom was the vice president of the Canadian National Railways) visited Botswana to investigate the operation of the railway there. They were expected to present a report to the Botswana government.

The situation is particularly vexing for Botswana because of the grim realities of the economics of transport, the long distances involved, the low population density of Botswana, the amount of freight and passengers involved, and the very high costs of building alternative transportation networks. If, for example, the Rhodesia Railways no longer saw fit to rail goods from Rhodesia to South Africa via Botswana (but preferred the Beit Bridge link, irrespective of cost), the government would be faced with some extremely difficult decisions. It could decide to reroute the line that goes from Francistown to Bulawayo in such a way as to direct it northwest all the way to Kazungula. This would be indeed a most expensive undertaking and would doubtless entail the construction of a bridge across the Chobe and Zambesi Rivers over to Zambia. At present, the government has made it clear that it is not seeking to build a railway to Kazungula. An alternative would be to improve the road south of Kazungula to such an extent that it could take large truck traffic from Zambia, or, if trade with Rhodesia were still deemed to be essential, to upgrade what is usually called the north-south road (which runs parallel to the railway line). But, barring unforseen circumstances, it is likely that the current *modus operandi* between the Republic of Botswana and the Rhodesia Railway will continue; the alternatives are prohibitively expensive at the present time.

NEIGHBORS AND PATRONS

As the previous discussion of the dependence of Botswana on the Rhodesia Railway has intimated, the third maxim of statecraft for Botswana concerns maximizing the number of aid donors or patrons in order to diminish its need to rely on either Rhodesia or South Africa for its economic livelihood. Its reliance on these two neighbors is illustrated, of course, by the nature of the transportation network which links it to Rhodesia and South Africa and also by the large number of Batswana who need to seek work on the mines and white-owned farms of South Africa. Rural poverty is the specter that constantly haunts the Batswana, and the specter appears all the more frequently in times of drought, especially since Botswana's economy is so closely tied to beef cattle production. It is a nation of small ranchers, for the most part, rather than a nation of agriculturalists.[103]

Naturally, the first order of business is to increase appreciably the standard of living and *per capita* income of the Batswana so that more of them can rise above the poverty datum line.[104] Obviously, cleaning out the Augean stable of poverty is no easy or inexpensive task and entails sacrifices both for the Batswana and for those who wish to help with funds or skilled manpower. The United Kingdom bears considerable moral responsibility for the economic development of its former ward, and both H. M. government and private British organizations have played, and continue to play, a significant, and even crucial, role in assisting the Batswana in this task. In general, relations between Gaborone and London have been friendly, especially since independence was achieved through negotiation and without violence, and the British ministry of overseas development continues to supply substantial amounts of both development and maintenance aid, both in terms of funds and personnel.[105]

Thanks to recent discoveries of diamonds, nickel, and copper in the northern portion of the nation, it is quite likely that the government will be able to balance its own budget by the end of the first half of 1972.[106] The mining developments have been, of course, a marvelous serendipity for Botswana and will add the much needed thrust toward economic modernization. Yet the Botswana leaders, even though they may have proved to be most adept at securing foreign credits, recognize that the economy is still a pastoral one and that the country must improve its record in agricultural production. There will not be enough jobs in the infant mining industry to go around, and therefore the average Motswana must look to the soil and to the pasture for his livelihood.[107]

Thus, from the long-range point of view, one of the most significant developments has been the founding of the Botswana agricultural college just north of the capital on the road to Mochudi. This was built with the help of British funds.[108] There is still a desperate need for more Batswana agricultural demonstrators and for localization of the veterinary service. The British have proved to be particularly helpful to the Batswana ranchers in terms of foot-and-mouth vaccines, which have been developed at Pirbright laboratories,[109] while the United States has been able to help in the field of funds and rural youth programs such as the 4-H clubs.[110]

The government in Gaborone has sought to tap as many sources of aid as possible, and the number and types of governments and private groups which have responded so far is impressive. Most of the nation's patrons, however, are principally Western or non-Sino-Soviet bloc nations.[111] The Botswana government has established diplomatic relations with both the Soviet Union and Czechoslovakia, but neither Eastern bloc nation has given aid in any significant amount to Botswana.

Like other newly emerging nations, Botswana has turned to the United Nations and its related agencies for technical and financial assistance, and to date, it has proved most adept at securing aid. Indeed, the United Nations Development Program has both a resident representative and an office in Gaborone.[112] This type of multilateral aid is not only useful in and of itself but also is significant in terms of acting as a counterweight to South African assistance.

This is not to suggest that officials in Gaborone reject private South African aid, but rather that they would feel more comfortable if they were less economically dependent upon South Africa. Indeed, they are reminded of the close relationship that exists between the two countries by the annual exodus of migrant workers (who spend at least part of their incomes in South Africa),[113] ownership of some areas in the nation by absentee South African citizens[114] or companies,[115] the extent of their considerable trade with South Africa, and the presence of South African-owned or operated enterprises in their country.

At a time when tempers can get short about real

or imagined slights or racial discrimination and when frustration about the speed of localization (a term which is often a euphemism for Africanization) becomes all too apparent, apprehension about the profile of South Africa and South Africans is understandable. The optimum strategy is, of course, to nudge South Africa out of a favored nation position (which it has hitherto enjoyed for historical and geographical reasons) into one which is both competitive and compatible with other prospective aid donors and/or those who wish to conduct business in Botswana.

It would be unrealistic to expect that Botswana would dispense with South African aid,[116] provided that that aid is competitive with other types of aid readily available. South African aid, furthermore, is not likely to be especially large in view of the other demands on the South African budget, such as national defense and the increased concern about the economic development of African areas in the republic, such as the Transkei. South African aid will, in the future, probably come more from the private sector than from the public sector, for the former is better able to maintain a competitive position on the commercial marketplace. One can reasonably expect that, in the years to come, various South African church groups will support the medical and educational programs of their missions in Botswana and that certain highly motivated white South Africans, such as those in the S.A.V.S. (South African Voluntary Service), will give of their time and skills. But such programs will not be of a very large magnitude. In all likelihood, British and American volunteers will appear in larger numbers and stay for longer tours of duty than the South Africans. Finally, one can anticipate that certain types of aid—for example, the enrollment of Batswana in the non-residential University of South Africa and the technical advice available from South African scientific institutions such as the famous veterinary research laboratories at Onderstepoort—will continue because the benefits so outweigh the costs.

Along with a gradual displacement of the South African aid donors over time, perhaps one can look forward to two other aid developments. Both would stem from Washington, D.C. and both are related to the totality of Southern Africa. The first development can be interpreted in light of the foreign aid report of the former American ambassador to Addis Ababa, Mr. Edward M. Korry. The Korry Report stressed the importance of regional foreign aid as compared with foreign aid to single nations.[117] Thus the American assistance for the Botswana-Zambia road is an example of the promotion of intra-African, regional trade (which would, of course, benefit two black African states). In addition, the United States government has also supported a regional program for the three former High Commission Territories and Malawi which is based in Limbe, Malawi and handles personnel training and testing for all four governments.[118] This may mark the beginning of a whole new approach to solving the intractable problem of the marked economic dependence of these four small states on the colossus of the south, the Republic of South Africa.

The second development, though, is much less advanced at the present time and could, in time, have a synergistic effect on all other American public aid. It simply involves a partial or complete redirection of American private investment in Southern Africa to those areas most in need of it. In a press conference held in Gaborone, Congressman Charles C. Diggs of Michigan, Chairman of the Subcommittee on Africa of the Committee on Foreign Affairs of the U.S. House of Representatives, suggested that the three former British protectorates in Southern Africa ought to "have a piece of the action."[119] He wanted American businessmen ". . . to share with these three countries some of the benefits of investment, most of which now goes to the Republic of South Africa."[120] Steps have been taken to insure the safety of American private investment in Botswana,[121] and, if the mineral developments there prove as attractive as some would hope, it is conceivable that the Batswana will get that "piece of the action." Given the hostility in some circles in the United States to investment in South Africa and Portuguese Africa, even a small redirection of American investment to Botswana would doubtless be welcomed in Gaborone and in black Africa as well on both political and economic grounds.

A NATION IN SEARCH OF A ROLE

Turning to the fifth and final maxim of Botswana's statecraft, one can understand why Botswana has made an effort to avoid the political discomfiture that comes from being wedged into Southern Africa alongside Rhodesia and South Africa. Indeed, the Vice President of Botswana, Mr. Quett K. J. Masire, once claimed, on a visit to Lusaka, that he was happy ". . . to breathe in fresh air" there.[122] He completed the metaphor by observing that the Batswana had ". . . apartheid breathing over our shoulders and U.D.I. breathing down our necks."[123] In order to get more of this fresh air, Botswana has had to build windows. These windows now open on the wider world, a world with which the Batswana can identify.

The Batswana have become more cosmopolitan and their first ambassador to the United States and permanent representative at the United Nations, the late Professor Z. K. Matthews, reflected this cosmopolitanism. One of the most admired and sophisticated Africans of his time, Ambassador Matthews opened innumerable windows for the Batswana. A former treason trialist in South Africa, he won the respect of the South Africans as well as of other delegations from Africa at the United Nations. Indeed, some of the African diplomats there were his former students at Fort Hare, and this facilitated Botswana's entry into the world of African affairs.

With independence, of course, came admission to continental and universal organizations, such as the Organization of African Unity, the United Nations, and the Commonwealth of Nations, and this, in turn, called for the development of diplomatic missions abroad, the exchange of resident ambassadors and high commissioners, and the establishment of a small diplomatic corps right in Gaborone.[124] This corps, however, does not accurately reflect the full extent of its diplomatic interests and contacts, for Botswana makes considerable use of non-resident ambassadors and has a reciprocal agreement with Malta regarding consular work.[125] In this way, it can spread its very limited diplomatic resources even further, and its diplomats stationed in the United Kingdom and the United States can have full access to the other Commonwealth high commissioners and to the permanent missions at the United Nations. Finally, it is represented on the African continent by a high commissioner in Lusaka, who also is accredited to Tanzania, Malawi, Kenya, Uganda, and Ethiopia.

These diplomats and diplomatic missions, even though they may be small in number, are of tremendous significance to Botswana, for they keep the windows to Africa, to the Commonwealth, to the United Nations wide open. Naturally enough, these diplomatic channels serve as conduits for foreign aid, yet they also serve to remind the rest of the world that Botswana has all the attributes and perquisites of sovereignty. With this diplomatic apparatus, Botswana can bargain; it need not be a mere mendicant. This is especially important for a nation such as Botswana which has, until the last decade, not received much in British beneficence. Until that decade, British colonial rule in Bechuanaland could be characterized by Daniel P. Moynihan's aphorism of "benign neglect."

In addition to the diplomatic corps, Botswana can gain recognition and a sense of belonging, especially to its fellow nations in Southern and Central Africa, by the skillful use of state visits which are replete with all the panoply of statehood, such as motorcades, speeches, and inspecting a guard of honor. Since independence, Botswana has played host to visits by President Kaunda of Zambia[126] and by Vice President Moi of Kenya,[127] and President Khama has been the guest of President Banda of Malawi,[128] while

Vice President Masire has proved to be one of the most peripatetic men in the cabinet and in the entire nation. He is a person of relentless energy and enthusiasm and a man who enjoys projecting an attractive image for Botswana all across the globe.

At this point, it would be worthwhile to try to assess the types of contributions that Botswana can make to Southern Africa and to the wider world. It would not be unfair to say that Botswana is a nation in search of a role, for it is a nation which is still gaining experience in international affairs. Its role could vary with diplomatic age, and indeed Botswana could develop an entire repertoire of roles. Its president, Sir Seretse Khama, has the education, the tact, the bearing, and the dignity to be an African for all seasons, and his nation, in turn, could be all things to all men. For some, it is a haven of non-racialism in a region in which racialism is regarded as a way of life, while for others it is a halfway house on the journey to exile or training as a guerrilla. Some see it as a forward base of operations for the ensuing liberation or overthrow of the white south, while others regard it as a target for Sino-Soviet bloc infiltration. Some see it as a hostage of the white south, while others look upon it as a prize to be won in the new diplomacy of South Africa. Some see it as a constant threat to the forces of law, order, and western Christian civilization, while others envisage it as Walden Pond of racial tranquility and trust, where white and non-white can contribute to the all-consuming task of nation-building.

The role, then, may be in the eye of the beholder. It depends on who is doing the viewing: a "freedom fighter," a "terrorist," a *verligte* South African white, a *verkrampte* South African white, a white South African exile, a white supporter of Prime Minister Smith, a Peace Corps volunteer, a white who identifies completely with the Batswana and who speaks of the Batswana in the first person plural (such as Lady Naomi Mitchison who is a member of the Bakgatla tribe which lives around Mochudi[129]), a sophisticated African school teacher in Soweto who has cousins in Botswana, an embittered, frustrated African nationalist sympathiser in Port Elizabeth, a Sino-Soviet bloc diplomat, or a British journalist. If one stood long enough in front of the President Hotel in Gaborone, interviewing all and sundry, he would get a variety of answers to his question, what is Botswana's role?

Indeed, Botswana has several roles to play, but the most important one is an interlocutory one. That is, Botswana is located in such a geopolitical and strategic position in Southern Africa that it can best serve as the locus of a dialogue between the whites of the south and the blacks of the north. Such a role, moreover, has official sanction in Botswana, for it is symbolized in its flag with its horizontal bars of blue, black, and white, the blue representing the blue of the sky and the color of water (the most precious commodity there), while the black represents the majority population of the new republic, and the white the minority population. It has been suggested, moreover, that Botswana could serve as the political Switzerland of Southern Africa.[130]

Some years ago, the African political elite in South Africa regarded the (now defunct) Natives' Representative Council—a body on which the late Ambassador Matthews served at one time—as a "toy telephone" because, although the Africans were speaking through the telephone, they claimed the whites were not listening.[131] Had they listened, the entire political complexion of Southern Africa might well be radically different today. Still, Botswana can serve as that telephone, and instead of a "toy telephone," it could become a "hot line" between north and south. Its vital role, then, would be to help avoid the situation so well depicted by the famous contemporary white South African author, Alan Paton, in the classically beautiful lines of his celebrated novel, *Cry, the Beloved Country*:

> It was [the African priest] Msimangu who had said . . . I have one great fear in my heart, that one day when they [*i.e.*, the white South Africans] turn to loving they will find we [*i.e.*, the black South Africans] are turned to hating.[132]

As part of its interlocutory role, Botswana can try to keep the whites of the region and of the world from loving too little and too late, while striving to keep the blacks of the region and of the continent from hating too much. This newly conceived nation has more than enough work to do, and if it could succeed in its interlocutory role, it might even win the Nobel Peace Prize—if nations were eligible for such an honor!

3

Lesotho

RICHARD F. WEISFELDER

Introduction: An Election and a *Coup d'État*

Although many journalists acknowledged that the opposition Basutoland Congress Party (BCP)[1] retained a slim chance of success in the 1970 Lesotho general election, almost all made Prime Minister Leabua Jonathan's Basotho National party (BNP) the odds-on favorite to duplicate its 1965 electoral triumph, probably with an increased parliamentary majority.[2] Throughout the campaign Chief Jonathan asserted, with characteristic braggadocio, that his BNP would sweep all sixty constituencies on the January 27th polling date. The Basotho people, he assumed, had almost universally recognized the necessity of continuing his government's basic "bread and butter" policy of "friendly relations and mutual cooperation with South Africa."[3]

Despite such prognostications of overwhelming victory, the prime minister repeatedly felt compelled to warn that any constituencies foolhardy enough to return opposition candidates would be placed low on the list for future government aid and development projects.[4] Jonathan's veiled threats against members of the judiciary and civil service, who allegedly "subjected themselves to political influences in their work," might also have suggested that the opposition remained more viable than he cared to admit, even to himself.[5] Chief Jonathan expressed his belief in the need for opposition "to keep the Government on its toes" and his distaste for contrived unanimity.[6] Nevertheless he toyed with the idea that a *de facto* one-party system, emerging from a stupendous BNP electoral mandate, might be institutionalized in Lesotho's constitution.[7] Using the full weight of the government communications and information media, the BNP leadership heatedly denounced the opposition parties as groups dominated by alien and subversive, communist influences.[8]

Prime Minister Jonathan's deep ambivalence toward this supposedly moribund opposition was quite apparent in his statement that

> I am a democrat, and a great believer in parliamentary democracy, where there is an opposition. But that opposition must be loyal and constructive; nobody can stomach one that is subversive. The Basotho people are very angry with the performance of the opposition and say it is subversive.[9]

On January 28th early newspaper accounts described the previous day's polling as "the quietest election anyone could wish for," a view corroborated by Radio Lesotho, the government broadcasting station.[10] Initial returns from the hotly contested constituencies in northern Lesotho buoyed BNP confidence in a smashing triumph as the National Party gained several seats previously held by the BCP.[11] Such jubilation was premature since later results showed that Ntsu Mokhehle's Congress party had made even more impressive inroads into supposedly "safe" BNP mountain strongholds throughout the country. By noon on Friday, January 30th, Mr. Mokhehle claimed victory for the BCP in at least thirty-three National Assembly seats, thereby making him the new prime minister of Lesotho. Certain government officials conceded that Mokhehle's figures were probably accurate, but the official tally of results showed the BNP and BCP tied at twenty-three seats each with the outcomes in the remaining fourteen constituencies still to be determined.[12] The BCP had taken a substantial lead over the BNP in the popular vote totals for the forty-six officially declared seats.[13]

No further election results were to be broadcast on Radio Lesotho. At three o'clock that afternoon Prime Minister Leabua Jonathan went on the air to inform the Basotho people that he and his ministers had proclaimed a "state of emergency" and suspended the constitution. Jonathan contradicted earlier statements about the tranquility of the election and now asserted that he had acted "to protect not only the liberty of the individual, but also law and order."[14] He alledged that

> An atmosphere of fear and threats of violence was spread throughout the country by the opposition on the eve of the elections. On the election day the elections were marred by actual acts of violence all over the country.[15]

At a press conference the following day, Chief Jonathan declared the 1970 general election invalid and openly admitted that he had seized power by means that might appear undemocratic. While claiming the support of a majority of the Basotho, the prime minister argued that the swing of voters to the Congress party, approaching 60 percent in some constituencies, could not have happened legitimately in Lesotho or, for that matter, anywhere else. He stated that the substance of this free election had been debased by the alleged acts of violence and intimidation inspired by the opposition parties.[16] Not surprisingly, this "democrat and great believer in parliamentary democracy" had now recognized the suspended constitution to be a "foreign and hybrid" importation unsuitable for the Basotho.[17] In a statement echoing notions of "African personality", or possibly "separate development," Jonathan promised that the new constitution being drafted for Lesotho would

> be made to measure to our way of life and our conception of democracy. Democracy is not an exportable and importable product. It is native to a people. It is a product of their way of life and traditions.[18]

Subsequently, Chief Jonathan explained the nature of his doubts about the compatibility of Western concepts of democracy with African problems. He observed that "democracy in the West does not seem to provide the means whereby the very concept of democracy can be protected."[19] His government, he said, had acted to protect Basotho democracy "against the threat of international communism and its agents in Lesotho."[20]

Tarring political opponents with the Communist brush has long been a favorite BNP technique. From the founding of their party to the present day, Chief Jonathan and his followers have maintained a relentless barrage of accusations that the Congress party and Marematlou Freedom party (MFP) have "an allegiance to communism" and are "puppet political parties" of Peking and Moscow "acting in accordance with the wishes and desires of their communist masters."[21] In September 1968 the Lesotho government had publicly announced its intention of enacting legislation to suppress communism while the prime minister pointedly warned the opposition "to mend their ways."[22] However, Jonathan did not follow up either the proposed legislation or his less specific hints of taking "strong measures" against subversive opposition.[23] Speaking at a press conference in December, 1969, he expressed confidence that the Basotho would freely "reject communism and all it represents," making such legislation unnecessary.[24] When their inflated expectations of a massive popular endorsement for the incumbent government and its policies were so rudely shattered by the election results, the BNP leadership at once justified its drastic steps in terms of Communist machinations.

Emergency regulations giving comprehensive

powers to the government were quickly promulgated by order of Prime Minister Jonathan. The immediate targets of the regime were: first, the opposition leaders who were promptly detained for an indefinite period; second, opposition publications which were completely banned; third, incoming mail from communist sources which was confiscated; and fourth, the Communist party which was finally outlawed. In announcing his Suppression of Communism Order, Chief Jonathan made it abundantly clear that he had more in mind than the dissolution and obliteration of the insignificant Communist Party of Lesotho, which had entered one notably unsuccessful candidate in the 1970 election.[25] The order provided for the arrest and indefinite detention of any person who "shall perform any act that furthers or *is likely to further* the objects of communism."[26] No definition of communism was included to clarify this incredibly vague phraseology and, in fact, the more detailed prohibitions in subsections of the order increased rather than limited its comprehensiveness. Section 2a, an almost exact copy of section 8a of the notorious South African General Law Amendment Act of 1962, states that

> "no person shall advocate, advise, defend or encourage the achievement of *any* such object [i.e., of communism] or any act or *omission* which is calculated to further the achievement of any such objective."[27]

Clearly one could easily contravene this order without having even the remotest connection to an organized Communist movement or the vaguest understanding of Communist ideologies. Since judicial processes in Lesotho had ground to a halt with the suspension of the constitution, the interpretation of this order remained solely in the hands of the government. The order thus provided a justification for the possible detention or expulsion from the country of virtually all dissenting voices.

If Chief Jonathan had expected the hitherto sympathetic South African English language and "Bantu" press to accept his explanations for his unconstitutional seizure of power, he was to be sorely disappointed. The African weekly *Post* described Jonathan as "a man who wouldn't take 'no' for an answer," and launched a direct, scathing attack in an editorial entitled "Political Thuggery." It stated that:

> No amount of verbal camouflage about "law and order" and "preserving the freedom of the individual" can disguise that the Prime Minister of Lesotho has behaved like a political thug defending his territory against a rival by jailing Mr. Ntsu Mokhehle and declaring a state of emergency.[28]

More wryly, the *Rand Daily Mail* remarked that Chief Jonathan's

> discovery of democracy's defects was made in the nick of time. It coincided precisely, it seems, with his realization that he had just lost the election. At that point he found it necessary to nullify the result and imprison opponents.[29]

Although some reporters for these newspapers attempted to justify Jonathan's actions or else to reserve judgement pending investigation of his claims, the majority of articles were bluntly critical of the Lesotho regime. In fact, Jonathan felt sufficiently threatened to lash out against the South African press

> for involving itself in Lesotho's domestic affairs and publishing exaggerated and inflammatory reports obviously in an attempt to discourage the peace, order and calm that prevail here.[30]

Even the Afrikaans language Nationalist press appeared initially stunned by the realization that the Republic's staunchest and most highly touted black African friend was now leading an illegal regime in the heart of Southern Africa. According to several Afrikaans papers, senior South African officials seconded to the Lesotho government had attempted to persuade Chief Jonathan to effect a peaceful transfer of power to Mr. Mokhehle and his militant, pan-Africanist oriented Congress party.[31] Such reports implied that the South African leaders would rather have tolerated a duly elected Mokhehle regime, compelled by economic and geographic circumstances to get along with the Republic, than face constant embarrassment from a chronically unstable and unpopular Jonathan government. Chief Jonathan's coup, coming in the midst of a vigorous South African general election campaign, played into the hands of Prime Minister Vorster's United Party and *Herstigte Nasionale* party opponents. Both groups found new support for their fears of constant instability in the proposed, self-governing Bantustans and for their skepticism regarding the Republic's new "outward" foreign policy.[32] Nevertheless, by stating that South Africa would behave "as though nothing has happened in Lesotho," Prime Minister Vorster extended *de facto*, if not *de jure*, recognition to Chief Jonathan's regime.[33] Mr. Vorster also expressed the opinion that Chief Jonathan had firm justification for his actions, specifically,

> from what I have heard of the Basutoland Congress Party, I feel obliged to agree with Chief Jonathan that it was a communistic

> undermining influence, because the leader of the opposition was a Peking communist, and this was proved over and over again in the past.[34]

Similar statements from the South African Broadcasting Corporation and such papers as *Die Transvaler* gave the unsteady regime in Lesotho much needed breathing space and assurance.[35]

This remarkable series of events in Lesotho's recent experience has promoted a wide range of diverse interpretations. Some observers have reiterated opinions that Jonathan was a stooge or a puppet of Pretoria, albeit one "who has the effrontery to pull his own strings."[36] Many felt that Lesotho's prime minister had become power-hungry, corrupt, megalomanic, or else a rather pathetic Gilbertian figure. Others echoed Dr. A. J. van Wyk's contention that Western forms of democracy were simply inappropriate for Lesotho and all African societies, which were perceived as intrinsically and inevitably authoritarian.[37] Somewhat more optimistically, John Torres argued that Jonathan had squandered Lesotho's unique assets of high literacy and national unity and had "allowed democracy to fail because he refused to give it a chance" in a context where "it could have worked."[38]

None of these opinions adequately explains the roots of Lesotho's basic and virtually inevitable political instability. More appropriate answers can be discerned in Lesotho's complete dependence upon the Republic of South Africa and in the apparent absence of any substantive solutions to its problems so long as certain paradoxes engendered by the apartheid system prevail. This lack of capacity to devise efficacious policies and programs coincides with the harsh reality that faulty political judgment will not only be harmful, but also quite fatal, to large numbers of citizens in a country so desperately impoverished as Lesotho. The major Basotho political parties proffer significantly divergent approaches for dealing with the country's monumental economic and social problems. Hence the stakes of political power are very high indeed. The persistent tendency of all groups to view their own strategies as the only possible way out of this impasse and to reject their opponents' policies as capricious invitations to certain disaster is strongly reinforced. A basic presumption of this chapter is that any Basotho leader, however capable, dedicated or sincere a democrat would be sorely tempted to resort to authoritarian expedients not unlike those implemented by Chief Jonathan. It is no coincidence that Lesotho's two most recent general elections have both resulted in defeat for incumbent parties.

The National Party Government versus Lesotho's Material Environment

The ceremony, glitter and pageantry which heralded the independence of the kingdom of Lesotho on October 4, 1966, could not conceal the very precarious future that lay ahead of this tiny new state surrounded by three provinces of the Republic of South Africa. In his independence message, Prime Minister Leabua Jonathan effectively summed up the legacy of a century of British protection by remarking, "Our only assets are our people, our land and our spirit."[39] Even this statement seemed optimistic!

Ranked by area, population, or domestic productivity, Lesotho would fall among the smallest and poorest states of Africa and the world—in marked contrast to its South African neighbor.[40] At independence a *de jure* population of 976,000 Basotho generating a gross domestic product of approximately $51 million inhabited the 11,716 square miles which constitute this drought-stricken, badly eroded, mountain, and highland plateau country.[41] Comparable figures for South Africa revealed that the Republic had a population 20 times, an area 40 times, and a gross domestic product 189 times greater than that of Lesotho.[42]

While Lesotho's relatively small population comprised too narrow a domestic market to promote any substantial economic growth, there were, paradoxically, far too many Basotho to be supported by the hopelessly limited capacity of the country's dominant productive sector, subsistence agriculture. Domestic employment opportunities in government, missions, schools, and trading establishments provided jobs for no more than 16,000 to 18,000 persons, or less than 10 per cent of the available wage labor force.[43] Since this new state lacked even a single factory or preliminary processing and sorting enterprise—to say nothing of a modern industrial infrastructure—it was vital that the landless, impoverished Basotho peasants be permitted to seek work as unskilled laborers in the booming agricultural, mining and manufacturing areas of the Republic of South Africa. In 1966 at least 117,000 Basotho—namely, 15 per cent of the *de jure* population and including 40 per cent of all working age males, were "temporarily" resident in South Africa as migrant laborers.[44] If those Basotho who were absent for longer than five years and those who concealed Lesotho citizenship to retain their jobs "permanently" in South Africa had been counted, the total number of migrants could have been in the range of 250,000 to 300,000 persons.[45]

It takes little imagination to perceive the enervating effect that this perennial exodus of the most ambitious and adventuresome segments of the adult male population has had on Lesotho's subsistence agricultural economy. The mass migration, accelerating since the 1870s, has been a primary cause of the stifling "inferiority complex" or "slave mentality" which has led many Basotho to think of South Africa as the "place of work" and to regard prospects for development and self-help in Lesotho skeptically and suspiciously.[46] Pressure on land and for available domestic employment opportunities has been increasing during the past decade due to a population growth rate in the vicinity of 2½ to 3 per cent per annum that shows no sign of abating.[47]

Chief Jonathan could not by a stroke of the pen undo the disastrous effects of British policies of parsimony, convenient *laissez faire* and hesitant paternalism which had characterized colonial rule in Basutoland and permitted the territory to drift toward complete economic stagnation and dependence upon South Africa.[48] Although Jonathan's options for dealing directly and effectively with the problems of overpopulation, land hunger, labor migration, and extreme poverty remain severely limited, a number of possibilities bear discussion.

Acquisition of additional territory through adjustment of national boundaries with South Africa might initially seem a totally implausible or fruitless mode of action. However, the Basotho have nurtured a deep sense of national grievance since the Convention of Aliwal North of 1869 forced them to surrender vast tracts of fertile farmland along the northern and western borders of Lesotho to the Orange Free State Boers. Effective Congress party mobilization of popular sentiment on this issue prior to the abortive 1970 general election led Chief Jonathan to transform the long neglected National party pledge to seek "return of the conquered territory" into a promise of "immediate" negotiations with the Republic.[49] The South African government under the late Dr. Verwoerd had indicated that some border adjustments with Lesotho might be possible. Nevertheless it is virtually certain that Dr. Verwoerd and his supporters had no intention of surrendering thriving Orange Free State border towns in the "conquered territory" like Zastron, Ladybrand, and Ficksburg, or any of the prosperous Afrikaner farmlands around them. More likely, they considered the possible transfer of inhospitable reserves such as Witzieshoek, whose peoples are culturally, ethnically and historically Basotho.

In exchange for these few hundred square miles of unproductive territory, Lesotho would undoubtedly be asked to assume political responsibility for the 1.2 million kindred Southern Sotho people living in the Republic, who have no traditional home other than the Orange Free State and southern Transvaal areas reserved for whites.[50] If this "unallocated" mass of Africans could be incorporated in a Lesotho, slightly larger in area, the South African regime would have resolved a major anomaly in its blueprint for "separate development." Thus in Dr. Verwoerd's words, "the present difficulty of establishing. . .one large Sotho. . .area in Southern Africa would fall away."[51] Such a merger of all Southern Sotho groups into a larger Basotho nation, even if sweetened by a choice piece of Orange Free State territory, would be a Pyrrhic victory at best, if accomplished on South African terms. The basic problems of overpopulation, land hunger, and labor migration would hardly be solved by greatly enlarging the *de jure* population of Lesotho, particularly in an arrangement smacking of "Bantustan" status. Not surprisingly, Prime Minister Jonathan has not been too specific about his strategy for recovering the "conquered territories" and has described the issue as a "very delicate matter."[52] Like German reunification, the "conquered territories" becomes a convenient, highly charged election issue, but not a realistic escape route from contemporary problems.

The National party government has become acutely aware of the difficulties inherent in raising living standards while simultaneously paying the economic and social costs of feeding, educating, and providing a host of other social services for constantly increasing numbers of people. In a speech on development fund estimates, Prime Minister Jonathan suggested that private citizens and groups consider the serious implications of rapid population growth, but he has been unable to confront the issue directly with a government-sponsored birth control program.[53] Large families are traditional among the Basotho for a variety of cultural, economic, and social reasons, so that even benign attempts to limit them could prove very unpopular. This preference is strongly reinforced by the conservative brand of Roman Catholicism widely practiced in Lesotho, which happens to provide the primary electoral base of the ruling BNP. The extent of Chief Jonathan's dilemma is reflected in an article from the BNP journal, *Nketu*, which advocated "legislation to ban the importation of contraceptives into Lesotho" and remarked that "conjugal love is . . . an act of free will, intended to endure and grow by means of the *joys* and *sorrows* of daily life."[54] South Africa's obvious double standard in disseminating birth control information and devices to Africans while encouraging a white "population explosion" has led more radical Basotho to portray birth control wryly as a subtle method of genocide perpetrated against African peoples.

Permanent migration of excess rural population to urban areas has been a common escape valve in situations similar to that of Lesotho. However, the South African theory of apartheid or "separate development" seeks to reverse this process. Workers from Lesotho are classified as "foreign Bantu" in the Republic and have less flexibility in obtaining employment than their black South African counterparts. Hence the ability of Chief Jonathan's government not only to keep open access to vital jobs, but to permit the number of Basotho working in the Republic to increase, might be seen as a minor accomplishment.[55] Yet this situation reflects a failure to create domestic occupational alternatives or to check the debilitating impact of the migrant labor system. Even if permanent resettlement of migrants in South Africa were possible, it is highly unlikely that the prime minister of Lesotho could voluntarily consent to an efflux of large numbers of young, motivated citizens, especially to a society in which racial oppression is the norm!

In the last analysis, Chief Jonathan and his National party have accepted the limitations imposed by current boundaries, rapid population growth, and labor migration. They have concluded that the only feasible method of attacking Lesotho's vicious circle of impoverishment is rapid economic development with a strong emphasis on industrialization. Their solution depends upon a dynamic reconstruction of Lesotho's stagnant economy, full mobilization of all national resources, and substantial external assistance, which taken together would create the requisite capital, jobs, consumer goods, and social services for political stability and genuine independence. The government had no illusions that the process would be easy or of short duration. As the minister of finance, Chief P. N. Peete, recently put it

> We placed our cards on the table and have started playing. No man with a head on his shoulders can expect us to have managed to satisfy the people who elected us within a short period. We shall not have accomplished much even after twenty or twenty-two years, but the few things we have accomplished speak for us.[56]

The 1970 election results proved that a majority of Basotho were dissatisfied with five years of BNP leadership and far too impatient to accept the long slow process forecast by Chief Peete.

To evaluate Chief Jonathan's stewardship over Lesotho's various resources, one must understand his perceptions of the South African role in the development of his country. The prime minister and the BNP, along with the vast majority of Basotho, have repeatedly and emphatically denounced "the policy of racial discrimination practiced in the Republic of South Africa as being contrary to fundamental Human Rights."[57] Nevertheless, Jonathan has argued that Lesotho's geographical and economic vulnerability compels the Basotho to exploit the existing power configuration of Southern Africa rather than to engage in fruitless, self-destructive confrontation.

In Jonathan's view, Lesotho can most effectively contribute to what must be a long-term struggle for African freedom in South Africa by becoming a model of stable, dynamic, nonracial development in the heart of the Republic. To use his words, "I will set my own house in order first, before going to help other people put their house in order."[58] Therefore, he has urged the Basotho "to take advantage of the fact that the country which surrounds us is the most highly industrialized and richest in Africa" and has actively sought South African financial aid, technical assistance, and private capital.[59] Since independence Lesotho has received substantial budget aid from Great Britain, loans and grants from numerous other Western sources, Peace Corps volunteers and a variety of technical assistance schemes from countries as diverse as West Germany, Sweden, Israel, South Korea, and Taiwan. Despite this aid, Chief Jonathan has recognized that only South Africa might possibly have sufficient motivation and the capability to deliver the level of assistance needed to assault Lesotho's economic impasse.

In his eagerness to create a climate of mutual confidence conducive to rapid expansion of existing economic relationships with the Republic, Jonathan may have sacrificed vital room for political maneuver at home. As a result, opposition parties have monopolized the field in articulating popular grievances against the treatment of Basotho migrants and other citizens of Lesotho in the Republic. The BNP leadership has accepted parliamentary motions from opposition members of the National Assembly calling for government action in the following areas: (1) improvement of migrant wages and conditions of service; (2) relaxation of strict South African passport and influx control procedures; (3) protection for Basotho summarily deported from the Republic; and (4) an end to arbitrary, humiliating treatment of Basotho by South African border guards and other officials.

However, the fear of undermining South African confidence and/or of pricing Basotho migrants out of the labor market has kept Jonathan's government from strenuous protests or from attacks on the "domestic" policies of the Republic. Given Pretoria's obvious desire to cooperate with its black neighbors and its marked preference for his regime, Chief Jonathan could have risked far more vocal support for redress of these deeply felt grievances. The Lesotho government's recognition of the desirability of access to employment opportunities in the Republic need not have rendered it so vulnerable to identification with the South African policies that yield low wages, degrading racial discrimination and, all too frequently, death or disability for Basotho workers.

Upon assuming power, the National party found almost no established guidelines or priorities for economic development and few reliable statistics upon which planning could be based. To be sure, numerous economic study missions had visited colonial Basutoland, but their recommendations had generally been shopping lists of stopgap measures and isolated projects lacking coherence. Even these rudimentary suggestions were ignored or only partially implemented by an understaffed colonial administration which was entirely pessimistic about the potential for development and primarily concerned with maintaining order and a balanced budget.[60] Chief Jonathan's government has not yet fully overcome this liability, although more comprehensive statistical data are now being gathered, a Central Planning Office has been established, and a medium range development plan was in preparation at the time of the *coup*.

The creation of an effective communications infrastructure has assumed an urgent priority, both as a requisite for industrial and agricultural development and as a means of buttressing the very weak regulative capacities of the central government and administration. At independence, it was possible to reach the remote eastern mountain districts of Mokhotlong and Qacha's Nek, directly only by horseback or light aircraft and indirectly, after a long drive via the Republic of South Africa. Even in the populous western "lowlands,"[61] the main flows of commercial traffic still do not focus on any centralized marketing and distribution center in Lesotho, but rather move people and products back and forth between missions or stores at the ends of rugged mountain feeder roads and the nearest South African railhead. The economic benefits from the exchange of Lesotho's primary agricultural products, migrant labor and foreign aid subsidies for processed food, clothing, and manufactured goods continue to accrue to the prosperous South African border towns, each serving its own segment of the rural Lesotho hinterland.

One of the initial acts of the BNP government in 1965 was to pilot through Parliament a controversial International Development Association loan of $4.1 million for construction of Lesotho's first paved highway, a 67 mile stretch linking northern lowland districts with the national capital at Maseru. Road Project Alpha—or the Leabua Jonathan Highway, as it was named upon completion—was considered a waste of funds by the opposition parties since it improved the existing dirt roads in the lowlands rather than opening up the remote mountain areas of the interior. Although the government has earmarked as much as $2.5 million in 1968–1969 for engineering surveys and actual road construction, its expenditures still remain inadequate to overcome past neglect and almost impossible terrain. The majority of secondary roads are being hewn out of rocky hillsides by villagers, often women, working with picks and shovels on "self-help" or "food-for-work" schemes. Payment is in the form of grain and powdered foods contributed by overseas agencies for famine relief. Opposition charges that such projects represent "forced labor" or involve "political favoritism" in recruitment of workers are less telling than the fact that the roads produced have often been too precipitious or punctuated with sharp rocks to fulfill their purpose of opening new areas to economical motor transport.[62]

In a further attempt to improve internal and external communications, the government negotiated a $450,000 loan from the Post Office Savings Bank for renovation and extension of the decrepit telephone system and for expansion of postal services. A $100,000 independence gift from the United States for a radio transmitter permitted the establishment of Radio Lesotho, the first nationwide, domestic radio service other than the improvised police and mission networks.[63] Named "Radio Leabua" by his critics, this state-operated station has consciously been used to augment the weak informational capacities of government, but especially to explain, justify and promote the policies of the ruling National party to the exclusion of opposition viewpoints.[64] The government borrowed $225,000 from the Standard Bank Development Corporation to provide reliable electric power, a requisite for attracting industrial investment, to the town of Maseru, the University of Botswana, Lesotho, and Swaziland at Roma and the major mission stations at Mazenod and Morija.[65] To the dismay of the opposition, which urged development of domestic hydroelectric power potential and feared increased dependence on the Republic, the new electricity was to be purchased from the existing South African ESCOM power grid.

None of these improvements in internal communications could obviate the fact that virtually all of Lesotho's links to the outside world would remain totally dependent upon access to the railway, airline, postal and telecommunications services of the Republic. South African corporations continued to dominate such basic components of domestic infrastructure as labor recruitment and banking. South African newspapers and radio networks were still the primary sources of information for many Basotho.

Since independence, Chief Jonathan has sought to augment the regulative capabilities of the central administration over the myriad of widely dispersed and inaccessible villages that constitute

Lesotho. Consequently, he assigned each assistant minister responsibility for the political affairs of a specific district and directed the enactment of legislation which permitted greater governmental supervision of the administrative activities of the traditional chiefs. At the same time, he expanded the budget and manpower of the Lesotho Mounted Police, assigning top priorities to the paramilitary Police Mobile Unit, which in lieu of an army, is responsible for internal security, and to the new Stock Theft Unit which deals with the chronic problem of livestock stolen from South African farmers or fellow Basotho. Even the upgraded force of 1,300 men has been hard pressed to cope with its tasks. However, the Congress party could make political capital by questioning the government's motive in maintaining one policeman for every six hundred Basotho when there was only one physician for every twenty-five thousand persons, and of spending 12.8 per cent of the current budget on police as compared with only 9.0 per cent on health.[66] Suppression of stock theft may have won Chief Jonathan friends in South Africa, but the arbitrary, unsympathetic methods of the Basotho police and their visible collaboration with South African officials created emnity, particularly in mountain, cattle-grazing areas.[67] Some observers have attributed the stunning BNP reversals in mountain constituencies to this factor alone![68]

A survey of the BNP government's successes and failures in each of Lesotho's resource sectors must begin with agriculture to which Chief Jonathan has repeatedly assigned top priority. If Lesotho is to produce any sort of domestic surplus to finance development and to create a market for locally manufactured goods, a substantial portion of that surplus must derive from agricultural activity. The agricultural sector supplies 65.3 per cent of the gross domestic product and 71.2 per cent of exports in addition to providing the primary means of livelihood for 85 per cent of the resident population.[69] Ironically, it would seem that governmental activity in this crucial sphere has been least changed by the advent of independence.

The overwhelming battle against poor agricultural techniques, low productivity and the limitations of the existing land tenure patterns continues unabated with all of the same manpower and capital liabilities that have prevented marked successes in the past. More emphasis has been placed on community development, "self-help" and "food-for-work" projects, but considerable effort goes to well established ventures such as progressive farming, agricultural experimentation, training of agricultural extension agents, soil conservation and improvement of the quality of livestock and the wool clip. Physical disasters like the severe drought of 1968 can undo hard-won gains and have far-reaching political ramifications; heavy BNP electoral losses occurred in the southern and mountain regions that had been most seriously affected.

In 1968 Jonathan announced a new policy of intensive agricultural development in selected promising areas of Lesotho, thus permitting concentration of government resources for maximum short-term return.[70] While this policy may be more sound economically than the old strategy of wide dispersal of agricultural improvement resources, it could well produce severe political repercussions in those areas where existing agricultural services were *reduced*.[71] The BNP captured two former BCP constituencies in the Peka area which had been promised a $1.6 million, five-year agricultural scheme and had already received assistance from neighboring South African farmers who lent tractors to plow land hardened by drought.[72] But the heavy government setbacks in less favored mountain areas demonstrate the political risks involved in this approach.

Lesotho has only two known natural resources which could generate revenue for industrial growth—namely, diamonds and mountain water with vast hydroelectric potential. Under colonial rule, commercial mining was not tried because of prevailing pessimism about the extent of the deposits. The Ox-Bow hydroelectric scheme never left the preliminary planning stages because of British reluctance to confront the delicate political issues involved in selling water and power to South Africa. By 1969, Chief Jonathan had reached agreement in principle with the South African government on joint development of Lesotho's hydroelectric resources and was able to announce a $1.7 million grant from the United Nations Development Program for advanced feasibility studies.[73] A state diamond prospecting concession was awarded to Rio Tinto Zinc Company and further negotiations were proceeding with the Lonrho group of companies.[74]

But, again, the political costs of these long term ventures were high. The Congress party has been extremely critical of agreements which appeared to them to increase dependence upon South Africa and upon South African private capital; they felt that the major beneficiary of these projects was South Africa and not Lesotho. This explanation must have impressed the hundreds of Basotho diamond prospectors displaced from their diggings at Letseng-la-Terae by South African machines and technicians. The 1970 general election results for the two mountain constituencies including both the diamond mining and Ox-Bow areas were never reported, but if recent violent resistance to Jonathan's *coup* from these regions is any indication, the BCP must have won handily.

From the enthusiastic commentary in *Koena News* and *Nketu* on each of Lesotho's new "industries," one might think that another Johannesburg was in the making at Maseru. Because only 0.8 per cent of Lesotho's gross domestic product was generated by the manufacturing sector in 1965–1966, any progress was indeed noteworthy.[75] With the advice of Anton Rupert, the Afrikaner tobacco magnate who is Jonathan's leading industrial consultant, the Lesotho National Development Corporation was created in 1967 to facilitate the attraction and capitalization of industrial concerns.[76] Directed by a Rupert associate, Wynand van Graan, the Corporation has overseen the establishment of almost a dozen industrial ventures, now either in operation or in varying stages of planning and construction.[77] Among them are a $1.5 million Holiday Inn and casino aimed at the tourist trade, a $210,000 Mobil garage and mechanics training center, a brewery, a maize mill, a tire-retreading plant and pottery, paint, carpet and candle factories. However impressive these efforts have been compared with past inertia, their impact on the economy remains negligible and the total number of new jobs created has, even by the most optimistic estimates, been no more than 600—with most of them concentrated in Maseru. One wonders if all the publicity might be counterproductive when disappointed Basotho are no more successful at finding work than in the past.

Effective utilization of human resources has been a particularly troublesome problem for the National party leadership. Vigorous competition between Catholic and Protestant mission educational systems produced a literacy rate alleged to reach the relatively high level of 60 to 70 per cent. Still, most Basotho lack the skills and functional literacy required if they are to be effective producers in the civil service, the school systems, agriculture, and industry. Although education has remained the largest item in recurrent budget, accounting for 21.6 per cent of expenditure, Chief Jonathan has begun to question the relevance of the educational product to the manpower needs of the society.[78] However, because of the South African context, it would be difficult for the government to move from classical, academic education toward more technically oriented programs without being accused of having adopted the Republic's hated Bantu education format. Formal education and, even more important, the widespread, informal experiences of life in South Africa, are responsible for the high level of Basotho political consciousness and the unrealistic expectations that must inevitably create unrest and disillusionment, given Lesotho's rudimentary economic capacities.

Since many of the best educated Basotho within the civil service sympathize with the more radical Congress party, Chief Jonathan has been reluctant to depend upon persons who may be disloyal to, or subvert, his policies. Instead of "Africanizing" rapidly, the prime minister has often placed increased responsibilities on the 175-odd expatriate officials remaining in the civil service.[79] To the dismay of the opposition, he has readily accepted and encouraged the loan of South African officials to fill key positions under a technical assistance program whereby the government of the Republic of South Africa continues to pay their salaries. In 1968 there were sixty-seven South Africans, many of them Afrikaners, holding such politically sensitive positions as chief justice of Lesotho, director of public prosecutions, chief legal draftsman, district magistrate, chief electoral officer and director of Radio Lesotho. There is no way of knowing the impact of these officials on the average Mosotho, but it seems highly probable that their presence, regardless of their impartiality, would lend credence to the Congress party view of Chief Jonathan and his regime as "puppets" of or "sell-outs" to South Africa.[80]

A glance at Lesotho's financial position and resources will quickly explain the pattern of insufficiency observed in all other sectors and demonstrate Jonathan's very limited range of alternatives. For the year 1965–1966 per capita income was estimated at roughtly $64.[81] Since that time, population growth appears to have been outrunning sluggish increases in productivity, so that in the words of Chief Peete, "the *per capita* income of our people is not increasing and in real terms, it may even be falling."[82] As a result, it is virtually impossible for the government to extract additional revenues from its own population for either recurrent expenditure or for development, and it is even difficult to collect existing taxes. During the past few years the recurrent expenditure of government has been approximately two and a half times greater than territorial revenues. In other words, there has been an annual deficit in revenue equal to more than half the total budget. Recurrent expenditure has been increasing at a rate of 23.5 per cent per annum with almost 50 per cent of all expenditures going to wages and salaries, to say nothing of other non-developmental administrative costs.

Trade data for Lesotho depict an equally dismal situation, with imports currently five times greater in value than exports and a whopping $27.4 million trade deficit that grows larger each year.[83] A measure of South Africa's economic leverage over its enclave neighbor can be ascertained from the fact that Lesotho's annual imports are equivalent in value to 60 per cent of its gross domestic product. Put more simply, Lesotho must import to survive and lacks reserves to withstand even a brief trade stoppage. Geographical circumstances dictate that all of Lesotho's imports and exports must pass through South Africa, and, indeed, 90 per cent of this trade is with the Republic itself.[84] Wages of migrant laborers remitted to Lesotho, variously estimated as from $6.2 million to $11.2 million per year, represent a significant proportion of national income and an important means of redressing a part of the trade deficit.[85] Since trade with Lesotho comprises an insignificant portion of South African economic activity and Basotho workers could, with some difficulty, be replaced, even a hint of partial curtailment of these vital outlets by Pretoria would immediately exert tremendous political pressure on Lesotho.

The depressing figures cited above suggest that for the foreseeable future Lesotho will require external assistance not only for purposes of long-range development but also to permit the maintenance of essential domestic services at their present low levels. Great Britain has provided the bulk of such support since independence with grants-in-aid totaling $32 million over the three-year period from 1967–1968 to 1969–1970.[86] Throughout his tenure in office, Chief Jonathan (who also serves as foreign minister) has tried to combat the world-wide shrinkage in foreign aid funds by personal diplomacy which has taken him on frequent trips to North America, Western Europe, and Asia in a desperate search for assistance. The opposition has criticized him for behaving like a perennial mendicant with homburg in hand, but he has not been deterred from his quest.

Although the government vigorously publicizes even small bits of assistance, it is difficult to arrive at dollar totals for aid ranging from $4.2 million worth of famine relief supplied by the World Food Program to less quantifiable inputs such as visits by teams of South African surgeons to perform operations otherwise unavailable in Lesotho. The South African contribution is also obscure since it is given in the form of technical assistance and also comes from a variety of private sources rather than in bloc grants. Lesotho has joined a large number of international organizations—such as the International Monetary Fund, the International Bank for Reconstruction and Development, and UNESCO—in order to gain access to grants and loans.

One further set of restraints on Lesotho's ability to shape its own financial and economic policies must be considered. Lesotho, along with Botswana and Swaziland, is part of the Rand currency area and belongs to a customs union with the Republic of South Africa. In the past, these linkages have compelled the three former High Commission Territories to accept monetary and tariff policies reflecting Pretoria's interests, often to the detriment of their own fragile economies. For example, the South African decision to institute a purchase tax in 1969 was made without prior consultation of its "partners" in the customs union despite the serious impact of the tax upon their economies and the living standards of their low income populations.[87] Although all three countries soon felt compelled to levy a purchase tax of their own, the South African decision galvanized them to collaborate in demanding a radical revision of the customs agreement and monetary relationships.[88]

A new Customs Union Agreement was signed on December 11, 1969, which (1) provided for regular joint discussions concerning customs, excise and sales duties; (2) required South Africa to consult with the other members before making fiscal changes that could alter these revenues; (3) allotted significantly increased shares of the revenue pool to Lesotho, Botswana, and Swaziland; and (4) permitted these three countries to protect their infant industries by levying additional duties on goods imported from within the customs union.[89] Lesotho's estimated share of the revenue for 1969–1970 rose from $2.7 to $7.0 million under the new agreement, a considerable fillip for the country's beleaguered budget.[90] Nevertheless, South Africa clearly remains the senior partner in these arrangements. Lesotho, Botswana, and Swaziland cannot expect to gain more than a small voice in shaping financial and monetary policies for the whole customs union, but they have little other choice given the prohibitive costs of establishing their own currencies and customs arrangements.

This survey of the resources, options, and policies of Lesotho under Chief Jonathan's leadership has attempted to demonstrate the omnipresence of the South African variable in almost all "domestic" policy issues and decisions in Lesotho. The short-term political costs of difficult, long-term development decisions have been exacerbated by the intrusion of complicating South African racial issues. Nevertheless, the domestic political configuration in which Jonathan operated must also be briefly examined to comprehend the bizarre 1970 election and *coup*.

POLITICAL AND IDEOLOGICAL CONSTRAINTS ON THE NATIONAL PARTY

WELTANSCHAUUNG

Paradoxically, one of the initial assets of the National party government was its deceptive appearance of fragility and vulnerability which led major opponents to underestimate its capacity for skillful maneuver and its tenacious will to prevail. Although Chief Jonathan and other BNP leaders suffered embarrassing defeats in their own constituencies during the pre-independence general election of 1965, the National party eked out a narrow 42.6 per cent plurality that yielded a two-seat majority in the National Assembly, the lower house of parliament.[91] However marginal, this election victory was no fluke.

While lacking a highly rationalized modern party organization, the BNP had effective access to the ordinary villager at the grass roots level through two sympathetic, broadly based, interest structures: the lower echelons of chieftainship and the Roman Catholic mission system.[92] A substantial portion of the BNP leadership has been recruited among the lesser chiefs who furnished a traditional basis of legitimacy which is particularly valuable in remote mountain areas where popular support for the powers and prerogatives of local chiefs and headmen have been least eroded. The scarcely concealed preference of most expatriate priests for the conservative BNP has helped to mold a receptive phalanx of supporters among the many Catholic and non-Catholic Basotho benefiting from the educational, informational, religious and social services of the relatively prosperous Catholic mission stations. Whereas Catholics comprise 34 per cent of Lesotho's population, the leadership of the BNP has been predominantly Catholic with almost half of the party's National Assembly delegation consisting of former teachers in the Catholic school system, newly recruited as party activists. Established in 1959 to combat the alleged challenge of the Congress party to the traditional way of life and basic Christian values, the National party also found strong support among women, who were generally more attached to the existing moral and social fabric and concerned lest the vital flow of money and goods from Basotho working in South Africa be disrupted.

Because of these origins, recruitment patterns and institutional sources of strength, the BNP leadership consistently adopted non-revolutionary strategies emphasizing gradual, peaceful reform within the limits of established domestic and international patterns of authority. "Realism" for Chief Jonathan refers to objectives that can be attained without sacrificing Basotho national traditions embodied in the existing structures of chieftainship, churches, and village communities. Since the democratic legitimacy of the BNP government was weakened by its minimal plurality, its *status quo* oriented commitments assumed increased importance, thereby limiting Jonathan's freedom of action.

So long as the National party faced constant BCP criticism and harassment in the National Assembly, it could not risk being perpetually at loggerheads with the Senate, Lesotho's upper house of parliament where traditional interests are represented.[93] This body, composed of the twenty-two principal chiefs of Lesotho and eleven nominees of King Moshoeshoe II, could embarrass the government through its power to delay and amend legislation, but more importantly, could undermine any BNP pretensions of defending traditional values. The price of winning the inconstant support of a majority of senators away from the royalist Marematlou Freedom party apparently included the "temporary" return of powers previously held by BCP controlled district councils to chiefs and indefinite delay of proposals for the restructuring of local government. Despite substantial opposition in the Senate, the BNP leadership did push through legislation increasing governmental supervisory and disciplinary powers over traditional administration and effectively reducing certain prerogatives of the king. While the government may have gained some additional levers over political enemies, it could not hope to enforce an end to abuses of power, inefficiency, and drunkenness among chiefs without seriously undermining its own power base.

The dependence of the BNP leadership on significant elements of traditional legitimacy has also precluded any radical resolution of the bewildering and endless struggle between the government and King Moshoeshoe II.[94] Chief Jonathan has on numerous occasions threatened to force the king's abdication or hinted that the institution of monarchy itself might be destroyed unless Moshoeshoe II ended his persistent quest for substantial executive powers and accepted a limited "constitutional" role. But even after the 1970 *coup*, the prime minister could not depose his royal cousin, Moshoeshoe II, without risking a serious confrontation with chiefs of all ranks who perceived that such an action ultimately challenged their own hereditary status and privileges. Hence Chief Jonathan has felt compelled to reassure the nation that Lesotho would remain a constitutional monarchy. He also had to limit his reprisals against the king's alleged involvement in the 1970 general election campaign to sending the monarch on an extended, enforced "vacation" in The Hague under strict governmental supervision, or in effect, into temporary exile.[95]

The broad scope of Chief Jonathan's emergency regulations, the detention of opposition leaders after the coup, and exaggerated government rhetoric about the imminent dangers of communist-inspired subversion might create the impression that there were no residual limits on permissible treatment of political opponents. To be sure, the facile stereotypes which are commonly held by expatriate Roman Catholic priests and white South Africans and which equate radical, reformist movements with doctrinaire communism have provided the National party with a ready-made scapegoat. However, use of such rationalizations for BNP policies and the coup cannot override deep popular awareness that all of the leading political actors are Basotho sharing a common national heritage. Arbitrary or irrevocable actions against opposition leaders, in blatant contempt for Basotho traditions of free speech and judicious compromise between political opponents, would be offensive to Jonathan's supporters in the Catholic Church and chieftainship. The prime minister's willingness to negotiate with Ntsu Mokhehle, despite all that has been said and done, becomes more explicable when interpreted as a necessary step to retain credibility among his own following.[96]

In defining its strategy regarding South Africa, the National party has justified working within the limits of existing political, economic and social relationships as the only "realistic" tactic for promoting the rapid development of Lesotho and an ultimate end to apartheid in the Republic. However, Chief Jonathan, in marked contrast to President Sir Seretse Khama of Botswana, has gone far beyond mere coexistence with South Africa. Lesotho's prime minister has eagerly solicited, accepted, and applauded financial and technical assistance to both the BNP and the government from a variety of private and public South African sources. Unfortunately for the National party, such support was hardly sufficient to have any long-term, to say nothing of immediate, impact on the omnipresent problems of land hunger, domestic unemployment, and meagre agricultural or mineral endowments. The government's very visible reliance upon South African legal officials and constant threats to expel "meddlesome" South African political refugees lent credence to the opposition view that apartheid was being extended to Lesotho rather than challenged by an alternative non-racial pattern. Cynical Basotho could easily be convinced that Chief Jonathan's "realism" was scarcely different from Bantustan status and meant acquiescence to a condition of permanent inferiority in return for continued South African support of the traditionally-oriented BNP and a few economic dregs from the master's table. Evidently large numbers of Basotho in 1970 preferred poverty with pride to the apparent alternative of poverty with hat-in-hand deference to white racism.

Further afield, Chief Jonathan has maintained Lesotho's pre-independence alignment with the Western world and categorically rejected any possibility of diplomatic relations with the Eastern-bloc nations. At the OAU, the government has attempted to promote an understanding of Lesotho's difficult situation and has urged African nations to refrain from interference in Southern African relationships, particularly with emerging patterns of regional economic cooperation.[97] Lesotho's stance at the United Nations has been characterized by hard-line resistance to admission of Communist China, advocacy of dialogue rather than sanctions against residual colonialism in Africa, and convenient absence from votes on questions involving South Africa. Chief Jonathan has cultivated bilateral links with Botswana, Ghana, Kenya, Nigeria, Swaziland, and Zambia and developed a particularly close relationship with Dr. Banda's government in Malawi, which has provided organizational training for BNP youth in its Young Pioneers. The only militant note in Jonathan's foreign policy appears in his frequent and vigorous demands that Great Britain "take immediate steps" against Mr. Ian Smith's Rhodesian regime which

> must stand condemned . . . for its continued insults to the world community and utter disregard for constitutionality and any form of legality.[98]

In criticising Rhodesia, the prime minister experienced the rare luxury of identifying with black nationalist demands without compromising any vital domestic economic or political relationships. Ironically, Jonathan's own *coup* brought these words back to haunt him through the initial British refusal to recognize his regime!

The limited capacity of the National Party government to cope with the prodigious array of material and political problems has been further strained by the heavy concentration of decision-making powers in the hands of the prime minister and a few overburdened colleagues. Chiefs Majara, 'Maseribane, and Peete—three ministers with remarkably similar political backgrounds, beliefs and interests—comprise the inner core of the cabinet together with Chief Jonathan, who has retained personal control of the sensitive portfolios for foreign affairs, defense, and internal security. The influence of these men over the BNP has been augmented by the need for strict discipline to maintain power, given such a minimal parliamentary majority. Patronage and the panoply of government prerogatives have also been effectively manipulated to emphasize the high costs of possible exclusion from power in a country with so few appealing alternatives. Therefore, the cabinet leadership could generally enforce its judgments upon the party rank and file in the National Assembly without giving enough attention to dissenting voices. For example, BNP backbenchers publicly warned of the dangers of neglecting supposedly safe mountain constituencies when allocating development funds.[99]

Nevertheless, Chief Jonathan and his like-minded associates continued to concentrate their efforts on winning northern lowland constituencies where BCP candidates had defeated prominent BNP politicians in the 1965 general election. Similarly, the BNP journal, *Nketu*, sounded complaints during the 1970 election campaign that the party leadership had arbitrarily replaced candidates selected by local constituents with their own nominees.[100] However, the National party leaders apparently allowed contrived accolades at officially arranged meetings and visible accoutrements of power, such as armed police escorts, sycophantic bureaucratic functionaries and slick limousines, to distort their awareness of actual grass roots opinions and frustrations. But even more crucial, an experienced, well-organized radical movement waited in the wings to exploit the inevitable failings of a government with virtually no viable options.

THE CONGRESS PARTY: A RADICAL, PAN-AFRICANIST ALTERNATIVE?

Throughout five years in opposition since losing the 1965 general election, the Congress party has mounted a relentless, comprehensive attack on almost every aspect of Lesotho government operations under National party rule. Both in parliament and at countless political rallies, BCP spokesmen have severely criticized the government for alleged inefficiency, incompetence, and corruption and they have attempted to identify the myriad of specific flaws perceived in its decisions and programs. Most of these deficiencies have also been portrayed in a more sinister perspective as aspects of a BNP "sell-out" or "betrayal" of the Basotho to South Africa. When not accusing Chief Jonathan of deliberately serving South African or other Western interests, Ntsu Mokhehle has more charitably attributed the defects of the BNP regime to its lack of a distinctive political philosophy or ideology. In a speech to the National Assembly the BCP leader observed that

> our Government so far . . . has not been able to acquire a philosophy of its own. A Government without a political philosophy is like a ship or a plane without a compass. A nation like that is likely to be directed this and that way by the gentle breezes or the whirlwinds blowing from the countries that have a philosophy guiding their administrations.[101]

Mr. Mokhehle clearly felt that the BNP policies of gradual change within limits of the domestic and international status quo had the disastrous effect of making Lesotho increasingly more dependent, subservient and vulnerable, particularly to the purposive apartheid philosophy and arrangements of the Republic. In the BCP view, Jonathan's earthy emphasis on "the kingdom of the stomach" has trapped the Prime Minister in "the political dust of the time," namely in agreements failing to provide commensurate long-term benefits for Lesotho.[102]

As an alternative to Chief Jonathan's ad hoc approach, the Congress party has attempted to relate Lesotho's economic and political dilemmas in the Southern African context to a broad, general reaction of peoples of the "Third World" against "imperialist" or "neo-colonialist" forces of foreign domination and racial oppression. Mr. Mokhehle and his followers believe that only the complete revolutionary transformation of the whole economic, social and political structure of apartheid into an egalitarian, non-racial format can break the fetters which hold the Basotho in involuntary submission. A Congress Party government in Lesotho, linked through close, Pan-Africanist, fraternal bonds to the independent black African states would expect to serve as a lever to promote more rapid change in South Africa. Ntsu Mokhehle has indicated that he would accept a somewhat slower domestic rate of economic growth to reduce Lesotho's overall dependence;[103] yet he is clearly not willing to sacrifice the Basotho people in any premature, suicidal engagement with South Africa. While hopes of imminent revolution and talk of fraternal solidarity with "freedom fighters" may be ideologically satisfying, the BCP leader would, in practice, have to tread a very thin line between challenging the Republic and unduly antagonizing it with the subsequent risk of economic strangulation.

Widespread Basotho fears of possible Mokhehle "adventurism" were undoubtedly instrumental in his 1965 electoral setback and account for a new softer, "more reasonable" BCP line to convince the voters that a Mokhehle government could "get along" with South Africa.[104] Although Mokhehle's style might differ markedly from Jonathan's, his substantive policy conclusions would be constrained by the same set of unsatisfactory options. Non-alignment in the international sphere would not obviate the necessity of dealing with South Africa; neither would "Africanization" or restructuring of the domestic power configuration make self-help economic development efforts any less marginal.

Immediately after the 1965 general election, the BCP had high hopes of bringing down the inexperienced BNP government "of shepherds and herd-boys" and of forcing a new election.[105] When Chief Jonathan proved a tougher politician than expected, Mokhehle entered a tactical alliance with King Moshoeshoe II and elements of the MFP on the assumption that Great Britain would not grant independence to a demonstrably unpopular, minority government. Evidently the BCP leadership underestimated the extent to which the British desire to extricate themselves from Lesotho would work in favor of the incumbent government. Ntsu Mokhehle refused to sign the independence agreement, boycotted the independence celebrations and continued to support King Moshoeshoe II's agitation for increased executive powers.

After a brief flirtation with violent confrontation, leading to several deaths in December 1966 and ruinously expensive litigation, Mr. Mokhehle appeared to turn back to the electoral struggle as the most promising method of achieving his objectives. In Parliament, the Congress party frequently used the tactic of proposing a government of national unity to portray Chief Jonathan's egocentric, boastful style as the root cause of political disharmony. At the same time, the BCP argued that the National Party government was beyond saving and so unpopular that its policies had to be opposed at every juncture in Parliament and in the villages. When Mr. Mokhehle was arrested in his hour of electoral triumph, he rejected violent resistance and urged his followers to remain calm and peaceful, a suggestion he has strongly reiterated since serious outbreaks of fighting in mountain areas.[106] The BCP leader most certainly feared that attempts to overthrow Chief Jonathan by force could result in greatly increased South African influence and even *sub rosa* support to Lesotho's outmanned security forces.[107] From his jail cell, Mokhehle seemed to believe that some sort of negotiated arrangement was possible, particularly while the British continued to withhold vital budgetary assistance from Chief Jonathan's government.

To win the 1970 general election the Congress party had to overcome the substantial advantages of the incumbent BNP government which (1) monopolized the official domestic news media, (2) received sympathetic treatment from the South African press and radio networks, (3) used the resources of the state for partisan purposes, (4) controlled the electoral apparatus, and (5) imposed a heavy financial burden on would-be contestants by requiring each to supply a $280 deposit. Yet the BCP could counter with well-known, experienced leaders, long active in district and national politics, and a modern, if poorly funded, party organization modeled after Kwame Nkrumah's Convention People's party. Without the responsibilities of government, BCP activists could devote full time to campaigning at the grass roots level. Indeed only a token Congress party contingent attended the 1969 National Assembly sessions because the BCP representatives personally supervised registration of voters while their BNP counterparts remained in Maseru to constitute the necessary legislative quorum.

The Congress party base of power is rooted among common people in the lowland towns and along the main roads where modern communications and contacts with the outside world are most intense. Protestants, teachers, civil servants, wage laborers, unemployed workers, and individuals with long, often bitter, experiences of life and politics in South Africa constitute the inner core of BCP supporters. By 1970 the Congress party apparently remedied prior weaknesses in the mountain areas and assembled a broad coalition of the dissatisfied and discontented to supplement its ideologically committed, Pan-Africanist base. To be sure, the BCP had experienced some factionalism and splintering due to the pressures of life in opposition and the dominant personality Ntsu Mokhehle. However, these struggles within the leadership were not translated to the party rank and file. In 1970 the BCP had regained some of the broad support which characterized its spirited emergence in 1952 as a national front against racial discrimination and other inequities of colonial rule.[108] Only now, the unifying element had become Chief Jonathan's relationships with South African racialism!

Under a Congress Party government, one could expect rapid Africanization in upper level civil service positions and generally more effective use of trained and experienced manpower which, temporarily at least, would be sympathetic to the objectives and style of this new regime. Although Ntsu Mokhehle would be compelled to maintain existing patterns of labor migration and trade, he could, no doubt, create a stir in South Africa by seeking diplomatic exchanges and aid from Eastern bloc countries to balance or partially replace links with the Republic. Political refugees might again be welcome in Lesotho. Representatives of Mokhehle's government at the OAU and the UN could call for increased pressure on the South African redoubt, but certainly not for sanctions which would have a horrendous immediate impact on Lesotho.

Still the basic material and political problems would remain virtually unchanged. Domestic self-help projects and available foreign aid, even from new sources, would be unlikely to have much greater impact under Mr. Mokhehle than under Chief Jonathan. Confrontation with traditional elements in the Senate and with the monarchy, to say nothing of the BNP opposition, could easily create serious domestic repercussions. Indeed the successful South African revolution (required to fulfill the BCP vision) seems no closer than that day when an economically and politically viable Lesotho (based on South African assistance) would permit the BNP leadership to play a genuinely independent role. Meanwhile, Mr. Mokhehle, bound by the realities of economic dependence, might well have to face the same sort of rising tide of popular discontent that undermined Chief Jonathan's electoral base.

THE PARADOXES OF ROYALIST POLITICS

Although the role of the monarchy in Lesotho has been at issue constantly for the past ten years, King Moshoeshoe II has failed to parlay popular respect for the institution of monarchy into a successful royalist political movement.[109] The young, Oxford-educated king has never been able to reconcile his political ambitions and desire for real executive power with his preference for hereditary permanence and security in office. He is reputed to be a progressive thinker on basic social issues and has directly expressed his fears that Lesotho under Chief Jonathan's government is in danger of "being swallowed whole" by South Africa.[110] Nevertheless, his demands for increased powers have been justified in terms of traditional prerogatives, roles of monarchs in other countries, protection of Lesotho against arbitrary rule, and the potential stabilizing force of the monarchy, rather than by any specific, substantive policy goals.

Because his constitutional position required him to remain above politics, Moshoeshoe II has been unable to provide the direct, continuous leadership required to build a viable, royalist political bloc. However, he has been sufficiently active on select public occasions and has operated behind the scenes to such an extent that he remains perenially at odds with his elected prime minister. When forced to choose between politics and his throne, the king has invariably declined the challenge to abdicate and become a full-time politician. Instead, he has temporarily resigned himself to subordination to the wishes of "his government" while waiting for a renewed opportunity to achieve his goal.

The Marematlou Freedom party and its various offshoots comprise a tentative, and now hopelessly splintered, amalgam of individuals and groups sharing just one general unifying element, namely, a common belief that the king should play a major role in shaping Lesotho's destiny. Only the very ambiguity of this conception permitted principal chiefs, modern politicians alienated from the BCP, and a host of other extremely independent personalities, representative of the whole ideological spectrum, to work together, however briefly. With Moshoeshoe II unable to play a decisive role, the MFP lacked both the organization and sense of purpose to hold to any distinctive middle-of-the-road position after its disappointing performance in the 1965 general election. The

lure of power and patronage and the many advantages of being on the winning side prompted numerous MFP supporters, especially among the principal chiefs, to align themselves with the BNP government. Factional struggles within the MFP leadership further sapped whatever vitality remained, so that the party could not field a full slate of candidates in the 1970 general election and polled only 5.3 per cent of the vote in the forty-six declared constituencies.

It is possible, if unlikely, that King Moshoeshoe II might reemerge from his exile in The Hague as a figure of national reconciliation relatively uncompromised by recent events. Within an exceedingly fluid situation, the MFP might also get an unexpected infusion of new life from disgruntled supporters of the major parties. But it seems far more probable that Moshoeshoe II will be asked to legitimize an agreement worked out between Mokhehle and Jonathan or be required to accept arrangements dictated by the ultimate victor, whether BNP or BCP. Neither group seems likely to allow the king to reap the political rewards from its own bitter struggles. Similarly, the MFP lacks the organizational and ideological base from which to create a cohesive alternative to its larger rivals or the numerical strength to hold the balance of power between them. Like other minor parties, its influence will depend primarily on the creativity and effectiveness of individual leaders fortunate enough to be included in negotiations between the BCP and BNP.

PROSPECTS FOR THE FUTURE

After Chief Jonathan's coup Lesotho tottered on the brink of anarchy as the BNP government was sorely pressed to maintain order with its rudimentary, paramilitary police mobile unit. The loyalty of the police, and especially of its conservative British officers, was absolutely vital to the survival of the regime. Skirmishes between police and bands of poorly armed dissidents occurred in many widely dispersed areas, the worst of which took place at the Kao diamond diggings where at least 100 Basotho were killed shortly after King Moshoeshoe II was exiled.[111] Chief Jonathan's administrative difficulties were unquestionably compounded by an extensive purge of supposed opposition sympathizers from positions in all governmental agencies and departments including the police. Perhaps the most telling blow to his regime was the temporary suspension of British budgetary assistance until June 12th when the Lesotho government finally met Great Britain's criteria for renewed recognition, namely, effective control of the country and obedience from a majority of Basotho.[112] The extent of the immediate financial pinch was reflected in frantic attempts to speed up collection of taxes, in the reduction of teachers' salaries, and in suspension of many development projects.[113]

Both the unprecedented scale of violence and the spectre of impending economic chaos prompted Chief Jonathan to renew his efforts to reach a negotiated settlement with Mr. Mokhehle and other opposition leaders. Preliminary talks produced some encouraging results until the re-establishment of British recognition apparently reduced the prime minister's political and economic incentives to compromise. Ntsu Mokhehle had agreed to disregard the results of the abortive election and to press ahead with discussions on the establishment of some sort of government of national unity which would participate in the drafting of a new constitution.[114] The Congress party leader and his deputy also issued a strong statement calling upon BCP supporters to refrain from use of force or violence and asking those wanted by the police to surrender immediately.[115] Mr. Mokhehle's brother, Shakhane, and the BCP secretary general, Koenyama Chakela, were among the first to comply. Nevertheless, full agreement among the protagonists seems increasingly improbable now that Chief Jonathan has ostensibly regained international respectability and attained a somewhat firmer grasp on power without being compelled to make any substantial concessions, such as allowing opponents a place in a "national" government. Indeed the BNP leadership has felt secure enough to consider King Moshoeshoe II's early return to Lesotho.[116]

It is possible that the horror generated by the deaths of hundreds of Basotho in fratricidal conflict and by having confronted the abyss of economic catastrophe will eventually create overwhelming pressure for a genuine and permanent political compromise in the interests of Basotho national unity. But one must remember that, in the past, desperation has produced recrimination and has enhanced, rather than limited, the level of Basotho political competition. In this light, it seems far more probable that any resolution of the present crisis would be perceived, by at least some of the participants, as only a temporary expedient permitting them to live to fight another day and not as a binding commitment to a new common purpose. As Ntsu Mokhehle remarked in a recent interview,

> In Lesotho we have a saying: "When the ram withdraws it is not retreating, but gathering power for its next attack." This is exactly what we are doing by making these concessions.[117]

Evaluation of the overall impact of recent events on Lesotho's prospects for the future would be a highly speculative venture at this time. However, one cannot escape the conclusion that the already minimal capacities of the Lesotho government and administrative structure have been weakened further. Attention and funds have been diverted from the rudimentary economic development ventures causing at least some retrogression which will not be easily overcome. Confidence of potential private and public sources of capital in Lesotho's chances for orderly growth must be severely strained. To compound these problems, a severe drought, causing failure of as much as 60 per cent of the 1970 summer harvest in many areas, will force the government to devote its energies to emergency relief measures often at the expense of long-term priorities. Should Chief Jonathan proceed with rapid implementation of proposals aimed at boosting productivity through restructuring of the land tenure system, he might immediately overextend his meagre regulative capacities and face renewed unrest even among BNP supporters.[118] Thus the political leadership emerging from the current crisis faces, if anything, a more difficult task than in the past and will remain highly vulnerable to pressures from a fully mobilized and frustrated population.

Since Lesotho is so desperately poor and destined by geography to be dependent on South Africa in any event, the tiny kingdom seems unlikely to attract the massive foreign aid from East or West that might begin to resolve basic problems. The enclave state is also far too inaccessible and vulnerable to be important to African liberation movements in the initial stages of an assault on South Africa, although Lesotho's rough terrain could, in the long-term, be of crucial significance. Lesotho has too few options and requires far too much assistance to become a genuine showpiece for Mr. Vorster's "outward" foreign policy. In all respects, Botswana, Malawi, Swaziland, and Zambia seem to be much more valuable and highly sought after prizes in the South African power game. Hence Lesotho must rely on typically negative resources. Its lone asset is its irritant value, since a perpetually unstable regime within the borders of South Africa would obviously be embarrassing and undermine the credibility of the Republic's current diplomatic offensive. But such advantages are likely to produce only minimum palliative responses and not any fundamental breakthroughs toward solving Lesotho's problems.

To say the least the Kingdom of Lesotho has an inauspicious future!

4

Swaziland

CHRISTIAN P. POTHOLM*

No lake so still but that it has its wave,
no circle so perfect but that it has its blur.
I would change things for you if I could—as
I can't you must take them as they are.
attributed to Confucius

* The author is indebted for the thorough reading and careful analysis provided by Richard Willey, Richard Dale, Richard Morgan, John Donovan, and His Excellency, Mboni D'Amini.

General Introduction

This chapter is designed to look at Swaziland in two ways. On the one hand, we shall present the reader with an introduction to the political and economic status of Swaziland as an entity; on the other, we shall analyze the interaction of Swaziland with the international subsystem of Southern Africa and, to a certain extent, with other units in the larger international or global system. By way of conclusion, we shall make several predictions concerning the future of Swaziland and that of the subsystem.[1]

As used in this chapter, we are taking the term *international subsystem* to mean

> a pattern of relations among basic units in world politics which exhibits a particular degree of regularity and intensity of relations as well as awareness of interdependence among the participating units.[2]

That there is a distinctive Southern African subsystem involving at least nine units which encompass 2 million square miles and over 40 million persons and exhibiting a discernible structure, a pervasive and identifiable texture, and high levels of political and economic interaction has been well documented elsewhere.[3] Although this subsystem is itself embedded in the larger global political system and its units remain susceptible to great power intervention, in recent years it has demonstrated an increasing degree of political and economic independence from both the rest of Africa and the dominant actors in the international arena. The subsystem is presently distinguished by a hierarchical power configuration under South African hegemony and is generally characterized by a prevailing ethos of white domination. It contains nearly 90 percent of the Europeans in Africa and includes five units (South Africa, South West Africa, Rhodesia, Angola, and Mozambique) under their direct control and four

(Malawi, Botswana, Lesotho, and Swaziland) under their considerable influence. This is not the context within which the four African-led states would prefer to live but it is currently the one from which they cannot escape.

Swaziland is the smallest territorial and population unit in Southern Africa. Surrounded on three sides by the Republic of South Africa and on the fourth by the Portuguese territory of Mozambique, its 6,000 square miles are dwarfed by the 470,000 square miles of South Africa, the 480,000 square miles of Angola, and the nearly 300,000 square miles of Mozambique. Further, its 400,000 inhabitants also make it the least populated unit of Southern Africa. By comparison, there are 18 million persons in South Africa, 7 million in Mozambique, and 5 million in both Angola and Rhodesia. Even Lesotho has twice the area and population of Swaziland while Botswana has sixty times the area and half again as much population. The overwhelming majority of its inhabitants are Swazis, with only eighteen thousand Eurafricans and non-Swazi Africans and nine thousand Europeans in residence.[4]

The demographic homogeneity of Swaziland is a direct result of its convoluted history. We know little about the origins of the Swazi as a people except that after centuries of southward migrations with other Bantu-speaking peoples they emerged as a distinct group during the early 1800s.[5] A series of warrior-kings—Nggwane III, Ndvungunge, Sobhuza I, and Mswati—led the Swazis to victories over some of the local peoples but, faced with the rise of Zulu power and the steadily intensifying pressure of the various Boer republics, the Swazis sought the protection of Great Britain. Great Britain was not particularly anxious to assume direct responsibility for them and instead—in 1881 and 1884—signed a series of conventions with the South African Republic, which recognized the independence of Swaziland but which also enabled South Africa to incorporate three-fourths of the territory claimed by the Swazis. Britain later acknowledged the Boer control over Swaziland until the outbreak of the second Anglo-Boer war in 1899. Upon its conclusion, in what was initially regarded as a holding action, Great Britain administered the territory—first through the governor of the Transvaal and later through the office of the high commissioner for Basutoland, Bechuanaland, and Swaziland. After the South African Act of Union, it was generally accepted that at some future point these three territories would come under South African control.

The history of Swazi opposition to such plans and South African frustration with British ambivalence is long and convoluted.[6] For most of the 1920s and 1930s Swaziland was a more or less forgotten backwater of Britain's empire. When the National party won the 1948 general elections in South Africa, established a republic in 1961, and withdrew South Africa from the Commonwealth, Great Britain no longer cared to consider incorporation of the three territories and set about encouraging economic and political development within each territory with the ultimate aim of independence.

The British resident commissioner in Swaziland, Brian (later Sir Brian) Marwick, felt that the political future of the territory lay not with the Swazi traditionalists or the European settlers but with the "modern" political parties which developed in the 1960s. Faced with these major challenges, the Swazi leadership—led by Ngywenyama, or king, Sobhuza II—reacted strongly and sought to assert their own claim to political primacy. In the process they found that they shared many areas of agreement with the European settlers in Swaziland, who also feared a loss of political power in the face of the new political movements and the coming independence of the territory.

As this chapter is not designed to trace the intricate and often ironic struggle for control of Swaziland in any detail, the interested reader should consult the variety of works on this subject.[7] At the same time some recapitulation of events is necessary if the complex relationship between Swaziland and the subsystem of Southern Africa is to become clear. It is particularly important to appreciate the substantial areas of agreement shared by the present rulers of South Africa and Swaziland.

The first political party in Swaziland appeared early in 1960. Led by a Zulu, Mr. J. J. Nquku, the Swaziland Progressive party (SPP) stood for a nonracial society and a one-man, one-vote constitution and voiced a strong commitment to Pan-Africanism. Initially, it attracted many detribalized Swazis, including Dr. Ambrose Zwane and Mr. Dumisa Dlamini, but personality clashes soon splintered the movement and, led by Dr. Zwane, a majority of its members broke away to form their own party, later named the Ngwane National Liberatory Congress (NNLC). The NNLC proved to be the most resourceful and popular of the "modern" parties and soon established a major foothold in the fledgling labor movement in the country. Standing for immediate independence, African majority rule, militant Pan-Africanism, and the liberation of Southern Africa, the NNLC formed the backbone of the initial opposition to the Swazi traditional hierarchy and the white settlers.

A more moderate party advocating a constitutional monarchy with a qualified franchise arrangement and a non-racial society was formed in March 1962. The multiracial Swaziland Democratic party (SDP) was initially led by Simon Nxumalo and Vincent Rozwadowski and later by Dr. Allen Nxumalo. Essentially, it was a coalition of Europeans and Swazis who feared the militancy of the Pan-African-oriented parties even though they also opposed the demands of the Swazi traditionalists and the European settlers for exclusive control over the political life of Swaziland.

Other parties also sprang up and, although they lacked widespread membership, served to fragment the detribalized Swazis and to dissipate their energies in factional disputes. In April 1962, for example, Mr. O. M. Mabusa formed yet another Swaziland Progressive party and eventually claimed the title, "Joint Alliance of Swaziland Political Parties," despite the fact that its membership seldom exceeded twenty-five. Other splinter parties included the Swaziland Freedom party of Mr. Winston Madlala, the Mbandzeni party of Mr. Clifford Nkosi, and the National Convention party of Dr. George Msibi.

As soon as the British administration began constitutional talks with all parties, it became clear that the traditionalists led by Sobhuza II and the Europeans were not willing to accept a one-man, one-vote constitution. Instead, they advocated that the membership of the territory-wide legislature be evenly divided between Europeans (chosen by a European roll) and Swazis (chosen by the traditional *tinkhundla* method of local acclamation which meant, in effect, nomination by the tribal authorities). So strenuously did these two groups oppose alternative proposals that the constitutional talks dragged on inconclusively for three years and included two high-level conferences in London.

Exasperated, but seemingly cognizant of the existing political realities, the British authorities eventually imposed a compromise constitution on January 7, 1964. This constitution provided for a three-track arrangement for election to the legislature. Eight members of that body were to be elected by the Europeans on their own roll, eight by the *tinkhundla* method, and eight by a national roll open to voters of both races. This solution pleased no one, but once the traditionalists and their European allies discovered they could not change the form of the constitution, they worked diligently and realistically to circumvent its spirit.

For the Swazi monarchy this was a critical period. The traditionalists could have accepted their one-third of the legislative seats and maintained an important, if not primary, position for the Ngywenyama. Instead, they risked the prestige and power of the monarchy by forming an alliance with the European settlers and challenging the political parties on their own terms. Given the advantages of the traditionalists' loyalty to the Ngywenyama, the existing tribal network, and financial support available to the monarchy, this course of action was not foolhardy, but it did involve considerable risk should the traditionalists fail to compete successfully with the political parties. The traditionalists then formed their own party, the Imbokodvo National Movement, under the nominal control of Prince Makhosini but in reality under the command of the Ngywenyama and his closest advisers in the Swazi National Council. Together with the United Swaziland Association (USA), the Imbokodvo contested the eight national roll seats with a half-dozen other parties.

The USA group was an interesting phenomenon. Led by European settlers such as Willie Meyer and R. P. Stephens, the group sought to share power directly with the traditionalists as a means of maintaining white supremacy in Swaziland while giving the appearance of a "partnership." The USA party enjoyed the support of most Europeans in Swaziland even though another, more moderate European party, the Swaziland Independence Front (SIF), was also formed.

The USA-Imbokodvo alliance was strikingly successful. Despite a hastily formed "coalition" of the other political parties and well-substantiated charges of Swazi collaboration with Europeans (both within Swaziland and South Africa), the modern parties were decisively defeated in the elections of June 1964.[8] The Swazi tribal hierarchy nominated all the members chosen by the *tinkhundla* method. The USA party swept all the European roll seats. Most important, the Imbokodvo-USA alliance won every seat on the national roll, garnering 89 percent of the popular vote.

Yet the game was not played out. When the traditionalists discovered that the monarchy remained the central symbolic referent for the Swazi people and that, despite their rhetoric and ideology, the other political parties enjoyed minimal grass roots support, they moved quickly to disengage themselves from the European settlers and to reabsorb the "detribalized" Swazis who had opposed them. No sooner had the new legislative council met than the traditionalists attacked the existing constitution as "racist" and demanded a new one-man, one-vote arrangement without reserved seats for any racial group. Next, the Imbokodvo forces rejected a USA motion which would have given those South Africans living in Swaziland the right to vote beyond the British-imposed deadline of December 31, 1965. As the Imbokodvo began to change its stance, more and more detribalized Swazis joined it, sometimes as a body (the SDP merged with the

Imbokodvo early in 1965), but more often as individuals.[9]

For their part the USA leaders were bewildered and chagrined and, at the constitutional talks which followed the Imbokodvo declarations, fixated on the fifty-fifty sharing of power formula. When these suggestions were brushed aside by both the Swazis and the British, the USA party fell apart as a political force and did not contest the 1967 elections.

The new constitution, finally issued on February 22, 1967, was a highly significant document for it institutionalized the changed political configurations in Swaziland and recognized the primacy of the Ngywenyama, Sobhuza II.[10] It recognized Sobhuza II as king of Swaziland (instead of the more parochial king of the Swazis) and vested the country's mineral wealth and Swazi national land in his person in trust for the Swazi nation. The composition of the bicameral legislature also reflected his power. The assembly consists of twenty-four members elected by adult suffrage from eight three-member constituencies and six members nominated by the Ngywenyama. The Senate has twelve members, six of whom are nominated by the Ngywenyama and six by the house. It is the Ngywenyama, moreover, who retains the right to appoint the prime minister and cabinet.

Under the new constitution, national elections were held during June 1967, and once again the Imbokodvo National Movement emerged victorious. With the previous demise or absorption of the USA, SDP, and SIF, the Imbokodvo was challenged only by the NNLC and two fragments of the original SPP. The Imbokodvo candidates won every seat in the assembly with a popular vote of nearly 80 percent. Only the NNLC ran well, taking over 20 percent of the popular vote. Dr. Zwane of the NNLC quite rightly claimed that the electoral arrangement of three-man consituency hurt its showing due to the large rural majorities which inundated the NNLC strength in the urban and periurban areas. Still, for all its importance as an alternative party and its contribution to the political life of Swaziland, the NNLC does not pose a credible threat to the present preeminent position of the Imbokodvo or the Ngywenyama.

Much depends, however, on Sobhuza II who was sworn in as head of state of the independent kingdom of Swaziland on September 6, 1968. His presence extends throughout the country and he has gained the respect and support of all racial and tribal groups within the country. Yet succession may prove to be a time of severe testing for the political system, for although Sobhuza II is vigorous and alert he is over seventy years old. Traditionally, the new Ngywenyama has been chosen by the Queen Mother and the royal family council after the death of the king. Because of the importance of the institution of kingship in the Swazi political system, the next interregnum could entail a concerted struggle for power—both within the royal family and later between the new Ngywenyama and the leaders of the Imbokodvo—because it is difficult to imagine the next monarch having the same degree of control over the tribal hierarchy and the Imbokodvo as Sobhuza II now does. For the present, however, it is the Ngywenyama who most strongly influences the entire political system.

The economic situation continues to provide a major support for the present regime and for the entire political system. Unlike many of the surrounding countries, Swaziland enjoys relative economic viability based on a balanced economy of agricultural, mining, and industrial factors. In terms of agricultural potential, Swaziland is blessed with a wide variety of topographical and temperature zones which permit the raising of many diverse crops. In the 3,000-foot highveld are the largest man-made forests in Africa, which yield over $12 million in revenues annually.[11] The 1,000 to 2,000-foot middleveld is the center of a modest but expanding citrus and pineapple industry, while the 500-foot lowveld has over 70,000 acres under irrigation devoted primarily to the growing of sugar, cotton, and rice. Sugar is the most important of these products with exports valued at over $15 million. Agricultural products, primarily those produced on large plantations, account for 50 percent of the national export revenues.[12]

Mineral wealth, while by no means a cure-all, has aided in the process of economic development by attracting foreign capital, by improving the physical infrastructure of the country, and by spawning subsidiary industries. Iron ore and asbestos are the major sources of revenue, with the Ngwenya iron ore complex earning $18 million and the Havelock asbestos mine $9 million in 1968. There are also extensive coal fields in Swaziland and smaller amounts of gold, kaolin, tin, and pyrophyllite.

The industrial sector of the economy has undergone rapid expansion in recent years. There is now a full range of physical infrastructures, including a nationwide tarred road net, a 137-mile railroad linking Swaziland with the port of Lourenço Marques in Mozambique, and an aerial cable car linking the asbestos mine at Havelock with a railhead in Barberton, South Africa. Swaziland has extensive hydroelectric facilities and may become a net exporter of electricity in the near future. There is a modern, well-equipped industrial park at Matsapa and most of the export commodities are processed in Swaziland prior to shipment. There are two sugar mills and a pulp mill as well as plants for the manufacture of cement, chocolate candy, and packaging material. As will be seen in the section on transaction flows, the economy of Swaziland is heavily dependent on outside capital, both public and private. Tourism is a major source of revenue with over one hundred thousand visitors in 1966. There are two small, but appealing, game parks at Mlilwane and Ehlane, a gambling casino, and a major resort complex in the Ezulwini valley.

As a result of its balanced economy, Swaziland has enjoyed a favorable balance of trade since 1962, although until 1970 the government budget has had to be balanced by annual British grants-in-aid.[13] The gross national product exceeds $100 million and the per capita income is $250, one of the highest in Africa. This is not to say that the economic life of Swaziland is without difficulties. A majority of the Swazis are still tied directly to the land through subsistence agriculture and, with a population increase of nearly 3 percent annually, the Swaziland economy must continue to grow rapidly if the present boom is to be maintained. Also, the southern section of Swaziland has not fully participated in the last decade of growth. On balance, however, these are prosperous times in Swaziland and most Swazis—when comparing themselves to their neighbors in Lesotho, the Transkei, and Mozambique—are content with their economic lot even though a tide of rising expectations may change that.

What emerges, then, from this brief overview of Swaziland in 1970 is a picture of a small, isolated, and landlocked country experiencing modest but perceptible economic growth and ruled by a traditional political elite who, led by their monarch, have readily adapted to a modern political environment. Deeply aware of their own sense of nationhood and historically conservative with regard to change, the Swazi leadership seems anxious to work within the context of Southern Africa. Weak and vulnerable, lacking even an army, the Swazis seem unlikely to challenge the existing order in the area. In addition to the impetus for this position provided by their heritage and their history, there are clearly many discernible pressures engendered by the number and intensity of their contacts with other members of the subsystem. It is to these links and fetters that we now turn.

Interaction with the Subsystem

Against this domestic background, Swaziland as a unit interacts with other units in the Southern African subsystem. In the analysis which follows, we have attempted to rank, in a rough hierarchy of contacts, the other actors within the subsystem which seem to influence most clearly Swaziland's principal decision-makers and most readily structure their options and their perceptions. This section does not pretend to be a complete transaction flow analysis. We should like to be able to present such an analysis and believe that it should be attempted in the future despite the many handicaps to the approach present in Southern Africa.[14] At this juncture we are not seeking to register the precise flows but, rather, to suggest the major directions of flows in order to ascertain which ones seem to impinge most directly on Swazi international and domestic decision-making. Whenever the data have been available, we have summarized such aspects of interaction as the overall quality and quantity of those flows as well as their intensity and patterns. We have thus considered the flow of imports to and exports from Swaziland; the size and level of its diplomatic missions; the amounts and sources of its technical assistance, foreign aid, and private foreign investment; the types and levels of its communications with the surrounding units; the termini of its primary physical infrastructure routes; and the relative size of its armed forces compared with those units which surround it.

What emerges from such an analysis is a great deal of support for the proposition that South Africa dominates the economic, communicative, and military posture of Swaziland (and by extension enjoys significant political leverage over the country's decision-makers). Great Britain, which used to be the primary political factor in Swaziland, is no longer an integral part of the subsystem and its influence is diminishing rapidly. However, Mozambique, which a decade ago was hardly a factor in the affairs of Swaziland, is increasingly important, both in terms of transaction flows and, more important perhaps, in terms of possible future political pressure. The other two former High Commission Territories, Botswana and Lesotho, while sharing a common historical experience and somewhat similar relations *vis à vis* the principal actors in Southern Africa, do not currently interact with Swaziland except diplomatically. Rhodesia, South West Africa, and Angola, although clearly part of the Southern African complex, have virtually no contact with Swaziland. Instead, two trans-systemic groups—states of black Africa and the states of Japan, the United States, Sweden, and the Federal Republic of Germany—are increasing their contacts with Swaziland, the former psychologically and diplomatically, the latter diplomatically and economically. We shall consider each of these in turn.

SOUTH AFRICA

The relationship between South Africa and Swaziland is a complex one. Other writers have characterized the relationship as one between patron and client or captor and hostage.[15] This may have been the case in the past. Presently, however, the relationship is clearly one of coexistence—even cooperation—and economic integration. Primarily because the present leaders of Swaziland feel they cannot change the present political configurations in Southern Africa and instead hope to use the South African presence to help maintain themselves in power, and because South Africa now has a growing interest in helping to maintain a group of black-led but weak and conservative-minded states as political insulation against the rest of black Africa, this relationship now borders on symbiosis.[16] In terms of the relative importance of each partner, however, the symbiosis more resembles that of the tick bird and the rhinoceros rather than the more conventional type represented by algae and fungi living together as lichen. Because South Africa looms so large in the affairs of Swaziland we have divided their relations into three major categories: economic, political and paramilitary.

Economic interaction. South Africa is currently the single most important factor in the economic life of Swaziland. Swaziland, along with Botswana and Lesotho, belongs to a customs union with South Africa and shares its currency, the South African Rand (one Rand = $1.40). From 1910 until 1965, Swaziland received 0.149 percent of the total customs duties and excise taxes while from 1965 until 1970, Swaziland received 0.53033 percent. This amounted to over $4 million annually and represented fully 20 percent of the government's ordinary income.[17] On March 1, 1970, a new customs agreement between South Africa, Botswana, Swaziland and Lesotho went into effect. The central feature of the new agreement is its customs pool. Each country's share is based on a complicated formula (involving the production and consumption of excisable and sales duty goods) rather than as formerly, upon a fixed percentage of revenues. It is estimated that Swaziland's yearly share will double to over $10 million, enabling the country to have a balanced budget in 1970–1971. Furthermore, Article 6 of the agreement provides protection for some of Swaziland's infant industries. The South African Reserve Bank provides central banking facilities for Swaziland, and South African monetary and fiscal policy thus has a most direct and influential bearing on the total economic life of Swaziland.[18] It is instructive that Swaziland does not participate in any policy formulation on these latter matters. In 1969, Swaziland joined the International Monetary Fund and the World Bank.

In terms of trade, an interesting pattern has developed. 80 percent of Swaziland's imports come from South Africa, mostly in the form of foodstuffs and manufactured goods, while a majority of Swaziland's exports go to nations other than South Africa. In 1967, for example, Swaziland exported $8.8 million worth of goods to South Africa and imported items valued at over $30 million.[19] Swaziland enjoys access to markets in South Africa, but its wool, meat, cotton and citrus are entered under a strict quota system.

Swaziland is also a net exporter of labor to South Africa with six thousand workers on contract. Together with the twenty thousand Swazis who are resident in South Africa on a less structured basis, they remit over $100,000 annually. Thus Swaziland's dependence on the South African labor market does not approximate that of neighboring Lesotho or Botswana, although for Swazis living in the southern portion of the country it is a matter of considerable importance. In terms of foreign aid, South Africa currently provides little except some technical assistance, but it may be expected that as the British disengage from Southern Africa, South Africa may secure additional economic leverage. South Arifcan leaders long have maintained the economic future of all these former High Commission Territories lies with South Africa, not Great Britain:

> It is common knowledge that these Territories are economically linked to, and dependent upon, South Africa. Great Britain might guide them to political freedom, but she is almost powerless to regulate the ultimate economic situation or to achieve the economic viability of these areas for their people.[20]

Private venture capital emanating from South Africa is also of great economic relevance to Swaziland. Drawn by lower corporation tax rates, a growing consumer market, a stable political situation, and an opportunity to avoid what remains of the African boycott against South African goods, many South African firms have established subsidiary plants and corporations—Swaziland Warehouse, Swaziland Milling Company Limited, Tracar Limited, Moshal, Gensser and Marshall and Diesel Services—to name but a few. Until independence the British Commonwealth Development Corporation was the principal underwriter of Swaziland's economic development. Now that task will fall to such industrial giants as the South African–based Anglo-American Corporation which has already played such a vital role in the development of the iron ore–railroad complex in Swaziland.[21]

Prior to 1964 and the completion of the Swaziland railroad linking the country with the Mozambican port of Lourenço Marques, Swaziland transportation links (road net, bus lines, and the cable car system) terminated in South Africa.[22] Even though the railroad has served to some extent to alter the direction of certain aspects of Swaziland's communications network (iron ore and sugar are now principally exported through Mozambique), South Africa still stands astride most of Swaziland's links with the rest of the world. All international telephone traffic is routed through Johannesburg while telex operations are handled in Pretoria. Most mail is moved through South Africa. South Africa controls all flights over its airspace and Swaziland's principal air links are from Matsapa to Durban and Johannesburg. Thus, while it is conceivable that forthcoming events could alter the economic and communications connections between South Africa and Swaziland, it seems highly unlikely that these could be severed easily or rapidly, if at all.[23] For the foreseeable future, moreover, indications are that the economic life of Swaziland will become even more firmly bound up with that of South Africa.

Political interaction. The levels of political interaction between South Africa and Swaziland are more difficult to assess. South Africa has sought to maintain conservative leaders in Botswana, Lesotho, and Swaziland.[24] At the same time there is little evidence to suggest that the present government of Swaziland is a "puppet" regime or that, because it follows a certain course of action, South Africa is intervening directly and continually in its political life. As Professor David Baldwin has so lucidly pointed out, "influence" and "intervention" are complex concepts in political analysis and one should carefully distinguish the fact that nation A wants nation B to take action X from the fact that B does X. Often there is no causal connection between A's wish and B's action since getting nation B "to do what it would have done anyway can hardly be considered intervention."[25] Too often political analysts of the Southern African situation have overlooked what seems to be a genuine confluence of interest between the government of South Africa and the leaders of Swaziland.

Two areas of agreement, the question of refugees and the question of revolutionary change, stand out. South Africa, for example, does not wish to see her refugees using Swaziland as base for activity against South Africa. Similarly, while the government of Swaziland is willing to accept genuine political refugees from apartheid, it views their presence with less than enthusiasm because: (1) the Swazi government objects to their political activities within Swaziland, particularly their support for the NNLC; (2) the Swazis more generally resent the refugees' occupying many of the skilled and semiskilled jobs in the economy; and (3) many Europeans in Swaziland regard the political activities of the refugees as threatening the economic boom by scaring off potential investors and the Swaziland government has

accepted this view.[26] It is not surprising, then, that many African refugees have not hesitated, wherever possible, to leave Swaziland for Botswana, Zambia, and Tanzania. South Africa looks with favor on these developments but it would seem that at most South Africa is able to reinforce behavior which the government of Swaziland would have exhibited anyway.

In the case of revolutionary change there is also a commonality of interest. South Africa fears a radical, revolutionary-oriented regime in Swaziland. At the same time the present government of Swaziland also dreads such a regime: first, because it would replace the present elites in power; second, because it would jeopardize the flow of investment capital which the Swazis see as essential to their economic development. Despite their serious objection to apartheid and to the plight of Africans in South Africa, the present Swazi leadership sees itself threatened by any revolutionary activity just as surely as South Africa does. It is not by chance, therefore, or by South African pressure alone, that the government of Swaziland has gone on record as being both willing and anxious to accept South African aid to combat any armed attempt to overthrow the government or to use Swaziland as a base against South Africa.[27]

Moreover, Professor K. J. Holsti, in an incisive essay on intervention and influence, has shown six ways in which nations can influence each other in the process of interaction: by the use of persuasion, the offer of rewards, the granting of rewards, the threat of punishment, nonviolent punishment, and the use of force.[28] Such analysis helps to explain the symbiotic nature of the South African–Swaziland relationship even while it indicates the narrower and less cogent alternatives available to the smaller, weaker unit.

Both units rely heavily on the first category of persuasion. South Africa, through both formal and informal channels, may seek to influence Swazi behavior and since the advent of South Africa's new stance on foreign policy Swaziland may be able to appeal to South Africa's sense of "good neighbors." It is widely believed that South Africa's Prime Minister B. J. Vorster has been a guest at King Sobhuza's hunting lodge and South Africa has gone out of its way to preserve the semblance, if not the substance, of consultation between the two states. South Africa has also offered to provide civil servants, recruited and paid by the South African government. South Africa enjoys a quantitative and qualitative advantage in the second and third areas—offer of rewards and granting of rewards. We have already mentioned economic aid. Another major reward could be Swazi control over the three hundred and fifty thousand affiliates of the Swazi nation who have lived in South Africa since the partitions of the nineteenth century. Such control could be offered, with or without territory, perhaps for a *quid pro quo* such as the disenfranchisement of the Europeans in Swaziland, thus creating a semblance of a Bantustan which already enjoys international status. Swaziland, too, has rewards to offer, particularly diplomatic ones. Within the Commonwealth of Nations, the Organization of African Unity, and the United Nations, Swaziland could—in conjunction with Lesotho, Botswana, and Malawi—offer diplomatic support, providing countervailing influence to other black African states, even a link to the rest of black Africa.

By the same token both units could threaten punishment. South Africa has a wider range of options, but in a war of nerves Swaziland could allow the anti–South African exile groups access to its territory and could even ask for a United Nations presence to guarantee its territorial integrity. These threats, while not totally credible at the present time, could severely undercut the aura of legitimacy which South Africa is seeking to create as a cover over the entire subsystem. Depending upon circumstances and the mood of the South African government, Swazi threats could have some effect on South African policy. Swaziland could threaten to serve as a base for anti–South African propaganda or to ignore revolutionaries in transit to the Republic, withdraw from the customs union (thereby denying South Africa $30 million worth of foreign exchange annually) and declare its intractable opposition to South Africa in its present form and denounce the entire subsystem as a guise for white supremacy and exploitation.

South Africa, however, maintains greater leverage in the area of nonviolent punishment. It could repatriate Swazi workers, cut off most of Swaziland's lines of communication with the outside world, leaving only the narrow Lourenço Marques corridor, prohibit investment in Swaziland by its nationals, force Swaziland out of the customs union, eliminate trade with Swaziland (at substantial cost to South African manufacturers), and seal its borders with Swaziland. On balance, the rhinoceros could probably live without the tick-bird more easily than the reverse.

Professor Holsti's last category—namely, the use of force—indicates some of the very subtle interactions which appear possible in the Southern African context. South Africa has overwhelming military superiority and could occupy, even pacify, Swaziland within twenty-four hours since Swaziland lacks even a modest army, depending instead on a six hundred-man police force.[29] Swaziland represents no military threat to South Africa and, unlike Botswana, cannot at the present time even serve as a conduit for outside forces bent on the disruption of the status quo. At the same time we would argue that South Africa's overwhelming military superiority is most difficult to translate into effective power.[30] Barring a massive invasion of South Africa through Swaziland, a South African threat to invade Swaziland lacks credibility. South Africa has survived and prospered because the superpowers have both lacked the inclination and have not had their hands forced. The implications of the physical occupation of Swaziland might well change all that. What seems much more likely, however, is that South Africa will use its power sparingly, selectively, and in paramilitary ways to insure future Swazi docility. Given the international situation, this course of action is probably more functional and, as the past has indicated, at least as effective. It is worthy of a separate category of analysis.

Paramilitary interaction. Unlike the unequal but essentially two-way interaction between Swaziland and South Africa on the economic, political, and diplomatic levels, the paramilitary flows run entirely from South Africa to Swaziland. Because of its military weakness and overall vulnerability, the territorial integrity of Swaziland has often been violated and boundary permeability remains an essential ingredient in the present situation. Support for these propositions is not lacking. Even when the British government had primary responsibility for the internal security of Swaziland, its frontiers were often breached by South Africans in pursuit of refugees and exiles. Precise details are difficult to obtain in many instances, as such penetrations are either not known or are ignored by the government of Swaziland. Yet they occurred and continue to occur. For example, on May 5, 1965, two South African police—one in civilian clothes, the other in uniform—appeared in the commercial center of Manzini. When approached by the Swazi police they admitted they were "unofficially investigating." They were allowed to remain overnight and to proceed to South Africa without hindrance. The incident graphically indicated the ease with which South African security forces could operate deep within Swaziland. Six months later South African agents again crossed over the border and succeeded in inducing a junior Swazi police officer at Bunya to turn over Mr. Enoch Mduli whom they took back to South Africa. When the affair became known, the South African government, under strong British pressure, reluctantly returned the prisoner and put the entire incident down to "over-enthusiam and ignorance."[31]

A far more serious incident occurred on the night of May 8–9, 1965, when sixty-five refugees from Mozambique disappeared from the capital of Mbabane. Apparently lured into South African territory by agents posing as FRELIMO personnel and promising safe passage to the (then) Bechuanaland Protectorate and Zambia, the refugees left Swaziland. Once inside the Republic, however, the bus carrying the refugees stopped at the Middleburg police station. Apparently, the South African police then loaded the refugees on railroad cars and shipped them to Mozambique. When the British government protested, the Portuguese and South African authorities denied any involvement in the affair although the Portuguese did not contradict the statement that the refugees were in their hands. Mr. Mario Mondlane, the leader of the Mozambique refugees in Swaziland, bitterly denounced the kidnappings and complained about the lack of protection. Indeed, in retrospect his complaint seems to have been well founded because on the night of August 27–28, 1965, he too disappeared.[32]

While such blatant and large-scale operations are not often undertaken, we believe that surveillance of refugees inside Swaziland by South African security personnel was widespread until Swaziland received its independence and there is little evidence to suggest that South African penetration has diminished since that time. In fact, the government of Swaziland has repeatedly warned refugees not to engage in political activities and has threatened to deport them to their country of origin.[33]

South Africa, then, presently possesses a considerable capability to intervene selectively in the domestic affairs of Swaziland. This power is probably of far greater significance than any threat to occupy the country physically because it enables South Africa to obtain many of its international goals with minimum international repercussions.

In short, Swaziland is vulnerable to South African political, economic, and diplomatic pressure, even though physical incorporation within South Africa is no longer seriously considered by the Republic.[34] While the present government of Swaziland retains some political and diplomatic leverage with South Africa, the Republic is still the dominant power in the relationship. South Africa's goal of insulating itself from most of black Africa will probably spare Swaziland overt direct interference and may well produce some economic and political payoffs for Swaziland.[35] Given the present context of Southern Africa, the Swazis will even be encouraged to exist as an entirely separate, independent entity. As Charles de Gaulle has written, however, "*Le souveraineté, c'est quelque chose.*"[36]

GREAT BRITAIN

While important in its history, South Africa did not always loom so large in the affairs of Swaziland. For most of the twentieth century it was Great Britain which provided the bulk of military and political guidance and support. Once incorporation of the three High Commission Territories became unfeasible, however, Great Britain initiated two new policies with regard to Southern Africa. First, a decision was made to grant independence to the three territories and to provide substantial economic aid (at least to Swaziland). Second, Great Britain gradually disengaged herself militarily from the Southern African context. The steady but persistent withdrawal of British military force from the area has greatly, if undramatically, altered the military balance in that arena for it has been South African power which has flowed into the vacuum left by the British removal.[37]

From the point of view of the Swazis, most critical of these withdrawals was the exit of those British troops stationed at Matsapa. Flown in during a general strike in May–June 1963, the First Gordon Highlands Brigade gave Great Britain a strategic reserve in Southern Africa and some leverage against South Africa and Rhodesia as well as against dissident groups within Swaziland and Lesotho. The Highlanders were later replaced by a battalion of the North Lancashire Royal Regiment in 1964, which was succeeded in turn by a battalion of the Royal Gloucester Regiment in 1965 and by the Irish Fusiliers in 1966. This garrison was stationed between Manzini and Mbabane near Swaziland's only airfield and was widely regarded as a firm British commitment to the area—at least until they were withdrawn in November 1966. One could well argue that the credibility of their possible use was drastically undercut by Great Britain's unwillingness or inability to use them against the breakaway Rhodesian regime of Ian Smith. But their removal—when coupled with the withdrawal of the special police contingent guarding the BBC relay station at Francistown, Botswana, in 1968—seemed to underscore for the Swazis and other groups in Southern Africa that military reality lay not in London but in Pretoria. Even if British forces were asked to return, South African permission for overflights would have to be secured. The Swazis in general and the present government in particular would like to have a British counterweight present in Southern Africa but have decided that this is not to be and it makes little sense for them to formulate policy as if there were.

Economically and diplomatically, there is a considerable amount of interaction between Great Britain and Swaziland. Swaziland is a member of the Commonwealth and is a signatory to the Commonwealth Sugar Agreement. Two-thirds of Swaziland's sugar (its most valuable export), 100,000 short tons a year, is sent to

Great Britain at prices above the world market, while one-third is sold on the open market.[38] Until 1970 Great Britain paid between $3 million and $4 million annually in order to balance the Swazi budget and since 1944 (and primarily after 1961), the British government has provided over $95 million worth of economic assistance through the Colonial and (later) Commonwealth Development Corporation. Much of the present prosperity of Swaziland rests on the results of the earlier inputs of aid.

At the same time Great Britain seems reluctant to continue such aid into the future. British refusal to compensate the Swazis for land alienated by the Europeans during the nineteenth century and increasing talk of "austerity" indicate that Great Britain is in the process of reducing its aid to its former dependencies in Southern Africa and that future aid for sustained economic development will have to come primarily from private sources or from new international donors. While important, British private investment in Swaziland nowhere approaches the magnitude of South African investment. Given its own financial weakness, Great Britain is unable to continue to underwrite the development of Swaziland. Swaziland has already sought alternative sources of public aid (Sweden, for example, responded with $125,000 last year) but, given the present low levels of United States foreign aid and the unwillingness of the Swazis to seek aid from Communist countries, the situation does not look very promising. Great Britain has decided to keep a strong diplomatic presence in Swaziland through its high commissioner. This may be an important factor in Swazi calculations for the future but it is a factor which may well diminish the further Swaziland gets from independence and the more tightly it is bound up in the context of Southern Africa. Thus it would appear that while during the colonial period Swaziland was linked, through Great Britain, to the international system, new links and patterns of interaction will now have to be formed.

MOZAMBIQUE

If South Africa is currently the most important unit interacting with Swaziland and if Great Britain's role in the entire area of Southern Africa is diminishing, then it is the Portuguese territory of Mozambique which could prove critical to the future course of events in Swaziland and in the subsystem generally. If present levels of interaction between Swaziland and Mozambique are low relative to those between South Africa and Swaziland, they are nevertheless high relative to all the other units in the subsystem.

For example, the Swaziland railroad terminates at the port of Lourenço Marques. With the completion of the railroad in 1964, the patterns of Swazi trade—at least in certain export commodities—were reversed and Swaziland could trade internationally without going through South Africa. Over 2.5 million tons of cargo, primarily sugar and iron ore, are exported through Mozambique and the traffiic is increasing yearly.[39] While there is talk of extending the 140-mile rail link in the other direction—that is, to South Africa—the existence of an alternate line of communication for Swaziland's vital exports does give the Swazi decision-makers some alternatives to total economic and communications dependence on South Africa. Given the Portuguese control of Mozambique, however, this is difficult to translate into political leverage *vis à vis* South Africa even while it is of considerable economic import.

Also, although the trade transaction flows are almost entirely unilateral, there are other aspects to the interconnections between Swaziland and Mozambique. Historically, Mozambique has been to Swaziland as Swaziland has been to South Africa—more moderate racially, less aware politically, and more backward economically. Thus more migrant workers from Mozambique are in Swaziland than Swazi workers are in South Africa. In fact, 13 percent of the African work force in Swaziland is foreign-born, and most the of laborers on the sugar plantations are from southern Mozambique.[40] Portugal maintains an ambassador in Mbabane and contacts, including trade missions, have increased severalfold since independence. Like South Africa, Portugal has put pressure on Swaziland to curb the activities of Mozambique refugees and has offered to help patrol the joint Swaziland-Mozambique border.

As long as Portugal controls Mozambique, Swaziland can expect to retain some economic leverage against South Africa (at least for some exports and imports) but no encouragement for any disruption of the political status quo. Diplomatic contacts, joint use of lines of communication, and economic interaction will all grow in numbers and intensity in the years ahead, but any political alteration must await the coming to power of an African government and one bent on a radical change in the status quo at that. Mozambique is in many ways a key swing unit in the subsystem of Southern Africa. As long as the Portuguese control that unit, the forces of the status quo in neighboring countries of Swaziland, Rhodesia, and Malawi are supported. Given its strategic location, topography, and control over major lines of communications, Mozambique in other hands would alter the complexion of Southern Africa generally as well as putting increasing pressure on the leadership of Swaziland and Malawi to support the liberation of Southern Africa. We shall return to this aspect in the "future" section of this chapter and in the concluding chapter of this book.

THE OTHER FORMER HIGH COMMISSION TERRITORIES: LESOTHO AND BOTSWANA

One of the most interesting aspects to emerge from this study of Swaziland's interaction with its international environment is the relative paucity of its links with Botswana and Lesotho. For six decades, it is true, Swaziland, Basutoland, and the Bechuanaland Protectorate were grouped together as the High Commission Territories under British protection, and most works dealing with them have accented the similarity of their relationships with South Africa and Great Britain. In point of fact, all they share is a somewhat similar colonial experience and common weakness.[41] Their primary linkages are diplomatic and symbolic. There is virtually no trade among them and no population exchanges.

There are some areas of cooperation and a possibility of others. The three territories share a single university—the University of Botswana, Lesotho, and Swaziland at Roma, Lesotho—and they periodically hold conferences on common problems such as public service or health. All three have cooperated diplomatically at the UN and at various OAU meetings but, generally speaking, this cooperation is of a sporadic, ad hoc nature and there are little ongoing contact or extranational institutions to coordinate policy or to chart a common strategy for Southern Africa. This could change in the future. The three territories have over three hundred thousand persons at work in South Africa and could formulate a common policy to forestall the reductions which may be forthcoming if the various Bantustans in the Republic can provide alternative sources of manpower. Also, as South Africa currently controls the customs union, the three territories could work closely together in seeking greater participation in the monetary and fiscal decision-making process—particularly if the union is expanded into a common market or free trade zone.[42] All this lies in the future, however. At the present time the low levels of interaction, the increasing vulnerability, and the unfavorable geographical positions of the three territories militate against any concerted action. At the same time these very factors demand a solution based on united effort if the levels of dependency currently prevalent *vis à vis* the subsystem are to be reduced.

THE OTHERS: BLACK AFRICA

We turn now to the rest of black Africa, the countries beyond the subsystem of Southern Africa. We do so by summarizing Swazi contact and interaction with Angola, South West Africa, Rhodesia, and Malawi. Swaziland has no economic, diplomatic, or political relations with the first three and only minor contact with Malawi (exchange of soccer teams and trade delegations). Its relations with the rest of black Africa are also characterized not so much by economic or political interaction as by symbolic reinforcement and diplomatic contact. These are important to the Swazis but they do not impinge very directly on the Southern African subsystem. Prior to independence, the Imbokodvo leadership sought to establish contacts with black Africa and to assert Swaziland's independence from South Africa. In late 1964 and early 1965, Dr. George Msibi and Prime Minister Prince Makhosini visited Ethiopia, Nigeria, and Ghana while Simon Nxumalo, an emissary of the Ngywenyama, went to Zambia, Tanzania, Kenya, and the Congo (Kinshasa). Little came of these visits except an invitation to attend the OAU conference in Accra, Ghana, during October 1965 and an awareness on the part of the Swazi hierarchy that Pan-Africanism was not *ipso facto* anathema to them. At the OAU meeting the Swazi delegation, along with the representatives of the ruling Bechuanaland Democratic party and the Basutoland National party, was castigated by the secretary-general of the OAU, Diallo Telli, for too close cooperation with South Africa.[43]

Stung by the allegations that they were puppets of South Africa and not the true representatives of their people, the three delegations drafted a common statement asserting that

> these parties are unequivocally dedicated to the course of freeing their respective peoples from the humiliating yoke of colonialism, neo-colonialism and economic exploitation. These parties, further, affirm the unshakeable determination of the parties to the establishment of non-racial societies in Bechuanaland, Basutoland and Swaziland and complete opposition to the policy of apartheid.[44]

While this statement only partially mollified the more militant of the African delegations, it did mark the beginning of a long and concerted effort on the part of all three governments to be accepted in Africa north of the Zambezi. It became tremendously important to the Swazis, in particular, to be accepted as genuine Africans with an independent image and the government has been careful to explain its seeming economic and diplomatic support of South Africa by stressing that Swaziland has no alternative. For the present such explanations seem to satisfy most African leaders, and the Swazis now enjoy widespread understanding of their predicament. In the future, however, should the struggle simmering along the northern edges of the subsystem heat up or spread, there would be increased pressure on the Swazis to do more than verbally condemn apartheid. At that time the Swazis would be forced to decide exactly where they stood, although for the moment the economic and military weakness of most African states seems to rule out "wars of conquest or liberation" as viable policy alternatives.[45]

Beyond the psychological and some diplomatic links to the north, there are few quantifiable interactions between Swaziland and any of the African states north of the subsystem.[46] That the future might hold such ties seems clear, however. During June 1969 Prime Minister Makhosini and the minister of commerce, industry, and mines, Mr. Simon Nxumalo, visited Uganda, Kenya, and Tanzania to seek admission into the East African Economic Community and to conclude specific agreements for the sale of citrus and coal and for the purchase of maize, tea, coffee, and soda ash. Of interest was the apparent understanding that no goods of South African origin would be re-exported to Kenya.[47] Also, during 1969 Swaziland began to export small quantities of refined sugar to Zambia and Malawi.

THE OTHERS: BEYOND AFRICA

Despite the psychological importance of its ties with black Africa, it would seem that outside of its subsystem Swaziland is likely to interact more consistently and intensely in the coming years with non-African units than with African ones. Of its six diplomatic missions, for example, only one (at the United Nations) is directed toward Africa; the other five) United States, Great Britain, Canada, France, and Belgium) are designed to encourage non-African participation in order to further Swaziland's economic growth and diplomacy. Moreover, Swaziland has avoided ties of any kind with Communist countries.[48]

The contacts between Swaziland and these non-African countries are currently of minor but growing importance. The United States, for example, is represented by a chargé d'affaires in Swaziland and a small contingent of Peace Corps volunteers, and private American sources provide modest support for the multiracial Waterford school and for the nearly twenty Swazi students in the United States. American investment in Swaziland is virtually nonexistent except through South African subsidiaries of American firms, and even here the amounts are very modest. Japanese firms have a long-term contract to purchase Swaziland's iron ore, and Japan would like to increase its trade with Swaziland in particular and with the entire subsystem in general. West Germany and the Republic of China apparently seek diplomatic support *vis à vis* their Communist opposites and some economic interchange. For its part, Swaziland's major goals are investment capital, scholarship aid, and grants-in-aid.

Swaziland and the Future

In view of the domestic political and economic situation in Swaziland, the quality and quantity of its interaction with the Southern African subsystem, and its limited contacts with the international system as a whole, can we chart the course of its future? Prediction is always risky, but some tentative predictions seem in order.

The first is that barring any major inputs from outside the subsystems the present status quo of European domination will continue. Not only is Swaziland's ability to alter the subsystem severely circumscribed but, also, it is difficult to foresee any substantial change in the dynamics of the Swazi domestic political situation which would result in its principal decision makers working for such an alteration. The power and authority of the monarchy, the hold of tradition over most of the population, the Swazi's long tradition of international passivity, and the conservative nature of both the elite and the counterelite all reinforce the status quo. Not only is the NNLC hard pressed to expand its support, but its leadership is cognizant of the realities of Southern Africa despite its flamboyant rhetoric. In addition, South Africa's policy of "live and let live" (albeit within specific limits) with regard to all three former High Commission Territories is a powerful force for the maintenance of the status quo, preventing rapid buildup of antisystematic pressures and enabling the present leadership of Botswana, Lesotho, and Swaziland to rationalize their commitment to the status quo.[49] Even should such a policy be reversed, the Swaziland government seems the least likely of the three to challenge the existing order in Southern Africa.

It seems much more likely that economic, political, and even military bonds with South Africa will grow, influenced by the very character of the subsystem itself. Professor Karl Kaiser has postulated a series of subsystem typologies based on the nature of their interactions. Most relevant for an analysis of Swaziland's interaction with the subsystem members (particilarly South Africa, Lesotho, and Botswana) are what he terms the transnational and international regional subsystems. The transnational model is based on a pattern in which "relations between national systems are handled and decided upon by non-governmental elite and pursued directly between social, economic and political forces in the participating societies."[50] Presently, Swazi interaction with the subsystem exhibits discernible aspects of both patterns.

Swazi migrant workers, European plantation owners, and corporation managers interact with their counterparts in South Africa while entrepreneurs feed their produce into transnational markets without governmental interference. The common customs union and lack of currency restrictions encourage at least economic linkage of the transnational type. Politically, too, there has been appreciable interaction and feedback between South Africans and the Imbokodvo, members of the USA party and Europeans in South Africa, and the NNLC and the now-banned African National Congress in South Africa.

At the same time fundamental assumptions about the nature of human collectivities (that is, nonracial or multiracial versus separation of races), the juridical independence of each unit, the existence of different citizenships as defined by governmental agencies, and the many types of economic, political, and military interactions which take place solely through governmental agencies are all ingredients of the international model presently found in Southern Africa. In short, the present interactional relationship is hybrid in character and likely to remain so. It may well be that the present situation will eventually evolve into a true "security community" characterized by a comprehensive regional system or quasi-federation, with high levels of economic integration (of both a transnational and international type) and political cooperation (with nonmembers of the subsystem) but with separate and distinct domestic societies founded on quite different assumptions.[51] We shall return to considerations of this nature in the final chapter of this book.

The second prediction is a corollary of the first. The fundamental stability in Southern Africa and the preservation of the status quo depends on the relative absence of outside force. Therefore, much depends on the outcome of the present struggle for Rhodesia (Zimbabwe) and Mozambique. For Swaziland, the situation in Mozambique in particular is of great import. A change in government in Rhodesia, the attainment of African rule, even the coming to power of leaders bent on the radical reorganization of the subsystem would be of far less consequence than would similar phenomena in Mozambique. Should such developments take place in Mozambique, Swaziland would be thrown at once onto the horns of a dilemma. With the opening up of a major sanctuary bordering on the Republic of South Africa and the availability of ports and transportation facilities for a thrust from outside the subsystem, Swaziland would have to choose sides, thereby risking an armed invasion by either or both sides, or at the very least becoming a battleground for paramilitary or guerrilla sorties. South Africa might limit its response to the use of indirect forces or specific, one-time "gamma" raids or it might react with a spasm response of outright occupation. The forces in Mozambique might use Swaziland as a transit area, a sanctuary, or, if the Swazis proved too hostile, a conquered zone. Quite obviously, none of these possibilities is desirable or even acceptable to the Swazis.

However unlikely these scenarios might seem in 1970, they hold great dread for the Swazis. What it boils down to is this: The cause of liberation of Southern Africa and the radical reconstruction of the subsystem are not—at least to the Swazis—worth the price of economic or political dislocation, let alone the possibility of becoming an international battleground. While such a situation may be forced on Swaziland as it has been on other small, weak countries in the past and while those persons in other African states and other parts of the world may condemn the Swazi position of *de facto* neutrality, as long as the government of Swaziland has options it will support the status quo in preference to the development of a revolutionary situation with its concomitant turmoil and danger.

PART FOUR

Angola and Mozambique

Country Profiles

ANGOLA

Political situation

Angola is currently a province of Portugal with a governor-general and seven representatives in the *Assembleia Nacional* in Lisbon. The local Legislative Council, which has both elected and nominated members, advises the governor-general.

There are several underground liberation organizations which are now engaged in guerrilla warfare against the Portuguese in Angola. These include the *Movimento Popular de Libertação de Angola* (MPLA) of Agostinho Neto, the *Govêrno Revolucionário de Angola no Exilio* (GRAE) of Holden Roberto, and the *União Nacional para a Independência Total de Angola* (UNITA) of Jonas Savimbi.

Demographic situation

Area: 481,352 square miles
Population: 5,225,000 (1966), including 250,000 whites
Capital: Luanda, 280,000 inhabitants (1966)

Economic situation

Gross national product: $909,000,000 (1966)
Per capita income: $170 (1966)
Currency: Escudo, 28.89 escudos = U.S. $1.00
Principal products: coffee, diamonds, sisal, fishmeal, cotton, iron ore, and sugar

---

MOZAMBIQUE

Political situation

Mozambique is currently governed by the Portuguese governor-general, Dr. Baltazar Rebelo de Sousa. Seven elected representatives are also sent to the *Assembleia Nacional* in Portugal. There is a local Legislative Council, which has both elected and nominated members, whose major function is to advise the governor-general.

The *Frente de Libertação de Moçambique* (FRELIMO) provides the major underground opposition. FRELIMO is opposed by the *Comité Revolucionário de Moçambique* (COREMO), headed by Paulo Gumane.

Demographic situation

Area: 302,329 square miles
Population: 7,040,000 (1966), including 130,000 whites and 50,000 Asians and coloreds
Capital: Lourenço Marques, 180,000 inhabitants (1966)

Economic situation

Gross national product: $704,000,000 (1966)
Per capita income: $100 (1966)
Currency: Escudo, 29.0 escudos = $1.00
Principal products: cotton, cashew nuts, sugar, copra, tea, and sisal

1

Portugal and Africa: A Historical Survey (1482–1961)

ANTONIO DA SILVA REGO

Introduction

The history of Angola and Mozambique may be looked at from two main points of view: either as distinct units, independent from one another, or as a whole, both subject to the same political concepts and to the same factors of change. In this short survey of their history (1482–1961) they will be considered as a whole, for indeed both have experienced the same periods of prosperity and of decadence. Being ruled from Lisbon, they differed only in geographical environment and, to a certain extent, in the composition of their populations. Angola is situated on the west coast and Mozambique on the east coast of Africa. Angola had only whites and Africans; Mozambique, on the contrary, was peopled by whites, Africans, Indians, and Arabs. A common feature to both were the mulattoes or half-castes. The Africans of Angola and Mozambique belonged mostly to the Bantu-speaking tribes, but Islam, which was absent from Angola, played an important part in Mozambique.

The history of Angola may be divided somewhat differently from the history of Mozambique. Considered as a whole, it may be arranged along the following lines: first, from the end of the fifteenth century to the middle of the eighteenth century; second, from the middle of this century to the Berlin Conference (1885); third, from the Berlin Conference to 1895; and fourth, from 1895 to 1961. The first part considers the beginnings of both settlements, Angola being more or less dependent on Brazil and Mozambique being entirely dependent on India. The second part deals with the evolution of both toward modern life, deeply influenced by slavery. The following years (1885–1895) play a most important part in Portuguese African history, for they were fraught with international dangers which were overcome only in 1895. The last part already belongs to modern and contemporary history. The *ad quem* date (1961) is chosen because it was the year when the calm and peaceful Angolan life was suddenly disturbed by terrorism and subversion.[1a]

From the End of the Fifteenth Century to the Middle of the Eighteenth Century

PRELUDE TO ANGOLA

It is generally accepted that the occupation of Ceuta in North Africa in 1415 marks the beginning of the Portuguese overseas expansion. As the years went by, the Portuguese were increasingly attracted by the riches of the East and consequently continued their southward voyages along the African seaboard. In April 1482 they sailed for the first time into the large estuary of the Congo River. Would such a mighty waterway lead into the famous kingdom of Prester John, about which Europe heard so much and knew so little?

Friendly relations were finally established with the local chief, and it appears that the Portuguese were quite satisfied with this. For the European newcomers, the chief was a real king and as such was duly respected and honored. Once converted to Christianity, there was no other name for him, for king he was, according to the Portuguese, and king he would remain until our own days. The relations between the Portuguese and the Congolese became more intimate primarily during the reign of the Congolese King Afonso I. His letters to the Portuguese kings showed how learned and sincere he was.[1b] His efforts to copy the Portuguese social organization met, in fact, with so much success that they were to be remembered many centuries after. The Portuguese kings, in return, conducted their relations with the Congo monarch on the basis of equality, commerce being the principal source of their mutual understanding. In spite of the fact that there was a wide gap between European and African ways of life, the Portuguese did not change their former attitude toward the Congo. However, they were to pursue a different policy regarding Angola. The prestige that the Congo kingdom enjoyed for centuries was due entirely to the Portuguese, for there was nothing about the Congo to recommend such prestige to the neighboring chiefs.

PRELUDE TO MOZAMBIQUE

Once in the Indian Ocean, the Portuguese felt compelled to reach India. It was Vasco da Gama who first called at different ports of the territory now known as Mozambique. He crossed the Cape of Good Hope in November 1497 and called at Inhamgane, Quelimane, Kilwa, Mombasa, and Malindi. In 1500 Pedro Alvares Cabral called at Sofala and established a factory at Mozambique Island. This island attracted Portuguese attention from the beginning as it was situated near the monsoon limits and thus appeared the best spot in which to wait for the opportunity to sail to India. From the island the Portuguese soon passed to the mainland.

Sofala was then a port often frequented by the Arabs who exported great quantities of gold from it. The Portuguese, faithful to their anti-Islamic policy inherited from the eighth century, decided to dispute the Arab gold monopoly. The first gold sent to Portugal was melted into one of the best Portuguese art treasures, the Belem monstrance, attributed to Gil Vicente (which can still be admired at the Ancient Art Museum in Lisbon). In the beginning Sofala and Mozambique Island were thus the main places under Portuguese control. Delagoa Bay had been visited by them in 1502, but was to remain half abandoned for many years to come. During the first half of the sixteenth century, Sofala was the main economic base which the Portuguese held on the African side of the Indian Ocean, while Mozambique Island constantly increased in political importance, owing chiefly to its strategic location.[2]

The Portuguese appeared satisfied with their coastal settlements. However, they knew of the existence of a great empire situated in the interior —the Monomotapa. It was visited in 1514–1515 by a Portuguese convict, Antonio Fernandes, who also traveled through territory which is now in Rhodesia.[3] Stories about its riches were numerous but access to them appeared rather difficult. The Portuguese, always on the trail opened by the Arabs, followed them into the different markets scattered along the Zambezi River.

THE PORTUGUESE IN ANGOLA

Portuguese commercial relations with the Congo chief attracted the attention of the Dongo monarch whose territory was situated to the south. The Congolese, in his opinion, were being favored by the foreigners' presence, which he also desired for himself and his people—the *Mbundu* (the conquerors). His name was Ngola, which was later applied to the whole territory as Angola. In 1519 Ngola sent messengers to the Congo to contact the Portuguese and entice them to come down to his kingdom. His demand for missionaries was accompanied by some silver bracelets, thus hinting that there was silver in his territory. He was shrewd enough to know that the Portuguese were motivated in their overseas expansion both by religious zeal and economic interest. King Manuel of Portugal took an interest in the area and the next year (1520) sent Manuel Pacheco and Baltazar de Castro with particular instructions to carry on a complete economic survey of the West African coast down to the Cape of Good Hope. Baltazar de Castro had the opportunity of visiting the Ngola's village, where he was forced to spend some six years in semiconfinement. He could thus ascertain that there were no silver mines at all, despite what the silver bracelets had previousy hinted. On his return to Lisbon, he presented an interesting report regarding his own experiences, but tales die hard and he was not fully believed. Silver was still sought in Angola, particularly in the Cambambe region, until the beginning of the seventeenth century.

King Manuel died in 1521 and was succeeded by his son, King John III, who devoted most of his attention to India and Brazil. The commerce of Angola was conducted mainly through the merchants established at São Tomé where slaves were their main export. Meanwhile, the two African kingdoms, Congo and Dongo, continued their petty intrigues and differences which led to a fierce battle along the banks of the Dande River. The Mbundu won the day once again, but apparently did not succeed in attracting Portuguese attention. The new Ngola of Mbundu repeated the demand for missionaries which resulted in the first Jesuit mission being sent in 1559, accompanied by Paulo Dias de Novais, who served as ambassador. They arrived at Luanda Island on May 3, 1560.

On reaching Luanda, they once again found out that the chief was a different person. Consequently, they were ill received and the new Mbundu *soba* (paramount chief) did not allow them to leave at once and kept them in what might be termed "fixed residence." The Jesuits' letters show that they were treated almost as badly as if they were slaves. Paulo Dias de Novias, however, was sent back to Portugal five years later, taking along with him a few presents for the Portuguese king. The difficulties that he and the Jesuits encountered convinced them that Angola should be treated differently than the Congo kingdom.

He managed to convince the Portuguese court of the need for such measures and in 1571 obtained a *donataria* or donation charter, thus becoming "lord proprietor" of two large tracts of land—one for himself and his heirs and the other for himself during his lifetime to be assumed by the crown immediately after his death.[4]

He set out as governor, captain major, and conqueror. This time, besides being accompanied by Jesuit missionaries, he took along with him a full expedition of some seven hundred men. They arrived at Luanda Island on February 20, 1575. Their first relations with the Mbundu were quite cordial. Next year (1576), the Portuguese settled on the mainland, founding the city of Luanda. In spite of being officially the "conqueror," Paulo Dias de Novais had no interest at all in waging war against the Mbundu, for he had invested his own family's fortune in the scheme and naturally wanted to defray the expenses as soon as possible. The Mbundu, however, came to suspect the real intentions of the newcomers and became violent. This was the beginning of a new phase in Mbundu-Portuguese relations. By the end of September 1580 the Portuguese started military operations against the Mbundu Ngola. The Cuanza River was the waterway chosen for such penetration into the interior. Paulo Dias de Novais died in 1589 and was buried at Massangano, the farthest inland post he was able to occupy.[5]

WAS ANGOLA WORTH KEEPING?

After Novais' death the Portuguese crown wondered whether Angola was indeed worth keeping. In fact, the practical results obtained thus far were not very substantial. Moreover, Portuguese holdings in Brazil and the East were already so vast and the Portuguese so few in number that such a question became quite relevant. An investigation was conducted in Angola by Domingos de Abreu e Brito, who left Lisbon in 1590 and returned a year later. His report may be considered overly optimistic regarding the economic possibilities of Angola. Admittedly, had his report been pessimistic, the Portuguese would have soon departed. According to Abreu e Brito, however, Angola was worth keeping since a great number of slaves could be drawn from its territory. Economic prospects were also very good since there were indeed silver mines. Finally, the territorial conquest was felt to be quite easy, for some thousand men would be able to manage it.[6] The consequences of such a conquest would be truly far reaching, for it would enable the Portuguese in Angola to link up with those of East Africa established at the Monomotapa. This was, in any case, an old dream of the Portuguese who had been severely tried by the navigation around the Cape. In addition, a trans-African road would enable them to receive news from India twice a year.

THE PORTUGUESE IN MONOMOTAPA

The "empire" of Monomotapa continued to stir Portuguese imaginations. The Arabs had free access to it and had amassed huge profits. The "emperor" was suspicious about the Portuguese. Afterward, however, he entered into contact with them and even allowed the appointment of a certain *capitão das portas* (captain of the gates) to have control over the Portuguese in the gold zone. This "captain of the gates" resided at Massapa. The Monomotapa and other paramount chiefs received a curious kind of taxes called *curvas* (curves) which allowed Portuguese traders to circulate in the interior with relative security.

In 1559 an event took place at the town of Inhambane which was to play a fundamental role in Portuguese East Africa. A son of the paramount chief of Tungue was converted to Christianity, and it appeared that a new era was to begin. Rumors circulated that even the Monomotapa himself would be ready to take the same step. On being informed of this, the viceroy of India, Constantino de Bragança, at once sent a religious mission, headed by Gonçalo da Silveira, a Jesuit of noble descent. The Tungue paramount chief was easily baptized and the Monomotapa followed suit. The Arabs, however, managed to convince him that the water poured on his head had a magic influence, which would make him fall entirely under the foreigners' influence. The Monomotapa also disliked the tenets preached by Gonçalo da Silveira and allowed the Arabs to dispose of him as they liked. Consequently, he was murdered on March 15, 1561.[7]

These events led to the armed intervention of Portugal into the Monomotapa. Francisco Barreto, a former governor of India, was sent to avenge Father Silveira's death. His efforts were continued by others, such as Vasco Fernandes Homem and Diogo Simões Madeira. The Monomotapa was also harassed by his own African enemies and decided to make friends with the Portuguese, going so far as to allow two of his sons to be baptized at Tete. This stirred Portuguese imaginations. In 1609 Nuno Alvares Pereira arrived with some three hundred men as "governor general of the conquest of the silver mines." These mines, however, could not be found. Simões Madeira, held responsible for all this overoptimism, ended his career by disappearing into the jungle. However, after receiving baptism, the Monomotapa finally signed a most favorable agreement with the Portuguese in 1629, by which he promised to have the "captain of the gates" as his adviser, to grant religious freedom to his subjects, and to send away the Moslem traders. Two years later, in 1631, Dom Filipe, as he was then called, received the habit or the insignia of the military order of Christ. The Monomotapa territory was thus influenced markedly by the Portuguese, particularly after the defeat of Capranzine who sought the throne for himself. By 1633 a great colonization scheme for the Monomotapa and other Portuguese East African areas was devised in Lisbon, but somehow or other it was not implemented. Indeed, conditions did not favor such schemes. Portugal was preparing to regain full independence from Spain by the national revolution of 1640. For nearly three decades to come, the Portuguese would have their hands full with other problems, for Spain was always threatening a new invasion and it was not until 1668 that Portugal became free from that nightmare.

ANGOLA AND THE DUTCH

From 1641 to 1648 the towns of Luanda and Benguela were occupied by the Dutch West Indies Company. Sugar was then the main support of the Brazilian economy, both for the Portuguese and for the Dutch.[8] The sugar factories needed slaves and these were found mainly in Africa. The Portuguese imported their slaves from Angola and consequently they were in a favorable position to compete with the Dutch. The Dutch company had some reasons to dispute the possession of Brazilian territory by the Portuguese, as Portugal and the Netherlands were technically enemies. In 1640, however, the Portuguese managed to shake off the bonds which linked them to Spain.[9] The Dutch in Brazil were duly notified and the Portuguese hoped that the old friendly relations would soon be resumed. But the Dutch Governor Moritz of Nassau already had plans regarding Angola. Before receiving official news about the Portuguese revolution, he dispatched a fleet to Angola and with little difficulty became master of the two main towns of Luanda and Benguela. The Portuguese retreated towards the interior and managed to secure free passage along the Cuanza River by means of their forts at Massangano, Muxima, and Cambambe. Massangano became the capital of Portuguese Angola from 1641 to 1648.

The effect of the Dutch occupation of Luanda and Benguela was immediately felt in Brazil as the Dutch there could have as many slaves as they thought necessary. The Portuguese, in turn, were unable to get slaves in sufficient numbers with the result that the Dutch West Indies Company enjoyed a most favorable position. Its sugar shares became just as important as those of spices. Slowly, the Portuguese came to realize that Angola was essential to the maintenance of Brazil. Either they would reoccupy Luanda and Benguela or they would lose both Brazil and Angola. The Dutch West Indies Company did not share this opinion, and they treated the two colonies separately. In 1648 the Portuguese managed to reconquer these two towns, thus closing the Angola slave market to the Dutch Brazilian sugar factories. A year later the Dutch company was forced to abandon its Brazilian adventure.

ANGOLA AND MOZAMBIQUE AND THE PENETRATION OF THE INTERIOR

A common feature of the Portuguese expansion was that it took place mainly along the seaboard. The interior did not attract them at once. From the beginning the two African rivers, Zaire [Congo] and Zambezi, however, captured their attention. In spite of the first experience with the Zaire which led them to the "capital" where the paramount chief lived, the Portuguese were to establish themselves in Luanda and later in Benguela, both coastal places. These two main bases were used to explore the interior territory. On the eastern coast, first Sofala and then Mozambique Island became stopping places on the way to India, although the Zambezi, exactly like the Zaire, pointed a natural way into the interior.

The area of Angola of the eighteenth century and even part of the nineteenth was very small indeed. It consisted of two so-called "kingdoms": the kingdom of Angola and the kingdom of Benguela. The first was bordered by the Cuanza River at the south and the Dande River at the north. To the interior it went as far as the places of São José do Encoge and Pundo-Andongo, thus including the old kingdom of Dongo or Ndongo. Between the Cuanza and the Cuvo Rivers there stretched the Quissama region, which was quite independent and whose chiefs often differed in their sympathy toward the Luanda authorities. The Benguela kingdom was situated between the Cuvo River on the north and the town of Benguela on the south. To the interior it reached Quilengues at the south and hence its undefined border went up to and included Caconda (which was founded about 1682) and reached the Cuvo, following it to the Atlantic Ocean. When compared with contemporary Angola, it was a very tiny Angola indeed. The communications between Luanda and Benguela by land were both dangerous and long, for the Quissama region seldom offered a safe passage. As for Mozambique, the situation was very similar to the one just described in Angola. The capital of the Portuguese settlements was Mozambique Island, Sofala remaining for many years the southernmost port frequented and owned by the Portuguese, for Delagoa Bay became a normal port of call to the Portuguese merchant ships only in 1544.

The Zambezi, however, was an exception to this coastal policy. The waterway was so attractive that the Portuguese followed it to its possible limits. The Portuguese of the east coast decided to link up with their compatriots in Angola and to reach the headwaters of the Zambezi.[10] There is another reason for such an inward rush. The Portuguese had settled at Sofala because of its gold market. The Arab merchants, however, moved away from this market and tried to bring the precious metal to a new market at Angoche. The Portuguese were aware of this change and tried to cope with the problem by going to Sena first and then to Tete, from which they could control the gold route toward Angoche. Thus Sena and Tete were normally frequented from the middle of the sixteenth century. At that time the Portuguese also started visiting several trade fairs in the interior, mainly at Manica and Zumbo.

Naturally, all this movement led to the scattering of several Portuguese adventurers through all these regions. Left to themselves, they had to depend on their own initiative. They married local women and even obtained or acquired tracts of land from the local African chiefs which they administered and owned according to the prevailing customs. This is the origin of the *prazo* system. It may be useful to remember that at first there were two main divisions of land in Portuguese East Africa: *crown lands*, which belonged officially to the Portuguese crown, and *free people's lands*, which were the property of paramount chiefs. Effective Portuguese authority was exercised mainly along the littoral and on the Zambezi basin. Quelimane, Sena, and Tete were the main *crown lands* along the Zambezi.

The *prazos* resulted from the adaptation of Portuguese legislation governing land ownership to local African conditions. The Portuguese settlers, once in possession of pieces of land given them by local chiefs or otherwise acquired, wished to be recognized as legitimate owners according to their own custom. However, after the Portuguese gained a firm foothold in the Monomotapa, it became evident that the government could not control so vast a territory ceded by the "emperor." In March 1618 the first official documents regarding the distribution of land appeared. In this way the *sesmaria* legislation also came to be enforced in Zambézia. Soon thereafter a new government department was established at Sena in charge of all these land problems. The system took roots for all the Portuguese who bought lands came to Sena in order to register them. The real *prazos* granted by the crown came under fixed rules—for example, they were given almost exclusively to either orphan or abandoned girls as dowries so that their husbands might devote themselves to agriculture. The lease was ordinarily for "three lives" only, and on the expiring of this *prazo* (time limit) the land would return to the crown which was the real owner.

Because of prevailing conditions, there were many abuses connected with the *prazo* system. First of all, the owners enjoyed practically unlimited powers. They were, in fact, real overlords having the power of life and death over all the inhabitants of *prazo*. They could impose taxes at will, they could admit any person to the *prazo* and they could expel anyone without trial. Such powers were also entrusted to the African owners of land, although under the control of the paramount chiefs. The Portuguese saw these conditions as necessary to attract settlers. The misdeeds and oppression were so great, however, that very soon the government concluded that it was necessary to limit such powers. For example during the seventeenth and eighteenth centuries news reached Mozambique Island about the selling of slaves by the *prazo* owners. How could the owners be justly punished? The first step was to introduce within the system a certain administration of justice. But how?

These abuses were a constant source of anxiety for the central authorities. This state of affairs continued up to the end of the nineteenth century and into the twentieth century. This explains the long and meticulous list of legislation enacted in order to introduce peace, order, progress, and law in such a system for to the ordinary man the terms *prazo* life and oppressive life became nearly synonyms.[12]

PORTUGUESE-AFRICAN FEUDALISM

Portuguese expansion began with the premise that it required more men than were then living in the metropole. These new men were to be found overseas in Africa, in Asia, or in Latin America. This same feeling was shared by all the Portuguese wherever they settled in Angola, in Brazil, in India, and so on.[13] In Africa they soon realized that it was impossible to bring all local chiefs under their control. Because of their belief in the divine origin of power, the Portuguese felt that African rulers, by the mere fact that they held power, had received it from God. Hence the Portuguese bestowed names of kings on them all.

The capital of Angola was Luanda and the governor-general lived there. Benguela was the capital of the other "kingdom," but its governor was subject to the one in Luanda. The African paramount chiefs around Luanda and Benguela were divided into two groups: the friendly ones, who recognized the supreme power of the Portuguese (although at times they acted and governed themselves at will); and the hostile ones, who waged war against them and who did not allow the foreigners to pass through their own territories for trading or other purposes unless they complied with certain conditions (such as the paying of certain taxes, the recognition of their own subordination to local ordinances, the declaration of all articles for sale, and so on).

Portuguese influence varied according to both the distance between them and the villages of the local chiefs and to the relations maintained between the chiefs and the Portuguese. Many neighboring chiefs and even some from afar, once they assumed power, used to go to Luanda to be recognized as chiefs by the Portuguese. On such occasions the governor-general used to bestow several gifts on them. If a chief was unjustly attacked by a neighbor, he then appealed to Luanda for help. The governor-general would listen to him and order an army to be raised composed mainly of friendly troops. A few Portuguese officers would then take the field at the head of such an army and march to punish the miscreant. Once this was accomplished, the army would be disbanded, the officers would return to Luanda, and everything would continue as before. The friendly chiefs would go on ruling themselves as independent lords of their own lands and subjects. Some would live according to local traditions and customs, for the Portuguese did not feel justified in imposing the rule of European international law on them.

One of the most interesting documents relating to this curious situation is the instruction given on February 12, 1676, to the governor-general of Angola, Aires de Saldanha e Meneses. After his arrival at Luanda, he was ordered to prepare a report describing the relations to be maintained with the paramount chiefs. The report also specified which chiefs were obedient to the Portuguese and which were not, and the motives underlying such attitudes. Particular care was taken toward those who would come to Luanda to demand "investiture" from the governor-general.

According to this same document, the Portuguese would be allowed to wage war only under one of the following conditions: (1) when a paramount chief attacked another who was protected by the Portuguese; (2) when there was an obstruction to legitimate trade; (3) when a chief favored Portugal's enemies; and (4) when there were impediments to the preaching of the Gospel.[14] In Portuguese East Africa conditions were much the same. This was the only way the Portuguese could deal with the local chiefs for they had no manpower to do otherwise. Their traders and missionaries would occasionally go to the interior and gather useful information, but they knew that the territories through which they traveled were not subject to Portuguese law. This lasted almost until the Conference of Berlin in 1885.

From the Middle of the Eighteenth Century to the Berlin Conference

The eighteenth century was a century of slavery, a century in which the domination of the white race over nonwhite races was firmly established, a century of imperialism, a century which quite candidly admitted that the colonies should contribute to the motherland's welfare and prosperity. For example, the treaties negotiated at Utrecht in 1713 dealt with European and overseas affairs.[15] England managed to check the ambitions of France, obtaining at the same time the possession of Gibraltar and the much coveted *asiento* (slave monopoly), which it was to maintain for quite a good number of years. Slavery was then generally accepted and few would dare to question its morality.

THE MARQUIS OF POMBAL AND PORTUGUESE OVERSEAS POLICY

The eighteenth century, as far as Portuguese history is concerned, may be divided into two different parts: the first, up to 1750; and the second, from this date until 1800. In 1750 the reign of Dom José I (1350–1777) began; his prime minister, the future Marquis of Pombal, pursued his own colonial policy. Until then the "plantations" or colonies were more or less grouped by two, one being ancillary to the other. This colonial dualism was found in Angola-Brazil, Guinea-Cape Verde; Mozambique-India; and Timor-Macao.

The Marquis of Pombal tried to change this dualism so that the colonies were oriented toward the mother country. He followed the general trend of asserting the full authority of the crown over all the overseas possessions. He had been a diplomat in London and in Vienna and thus had the opportunity to get a clear insight into the European ideas about the overseas "plantations." The Marquis returned to Portugal with lofty ideals, such as civilization, progress, society, agriculture, industry, and the like. Further, he transmitted his own conviction to those around him, particularly the governors whom he later sent to Angola and Mozambique.

ANGOLA

From 1764 to 1772 Angola was ruled by one of the best "Pombalian" governors, Francisco Inocêncio de Sousa Coutinho, who wrote several reports which are still read today with interest. He wanted to make Angola into a second Brazil, and he directed his attention mainly to the southeast highlands where he established several European settlements. His colonizing efforts, however, were not continued by his successors, and by the end of the century all the settlements were practically left to themselves. One of his best measures was the introduction of "paid labor." Although he permitted slavery, he was rather reluctant to allow the shipment of slaves to Brazil or elsewhere. Angola, he said, was really worth as much as Brazil. This governor followed the ideas common to his epoch, but adapted them to the Portuguese situation. Whereas England opposed the establishment of industries overseas, Sousa Coutinho endeavored to found an iron factory in Angola. His enthusiasm for the scheme was approved by the Marquis of Pombal, but his efforts met with very meagre success.[16]

The French Revolution made a deep impact on Portugal, both at home and overseas. The royal family took refuge in Brazil in 1807 and Portugal endured three French invasions. In 1820 a liberal revolution occurred and in 1822 Brazil became independent—curiously enough not from the Portuguese crown, but from the Portuguese government.

The independence of Brazil deeply impressed the Portuguese in Angola. In the past there had been so many and varied contacts between Bahia and other Brazilian ports with Luanda and Benguela that many merchants on both sides of the Atlantic thought that the two countries could not long remain as separate units. This was the origin of a proposed Brazilian confederation—the *União Brazilica*—composed of Angola, Mozambique, and Brazil. The dream, however, vanished when confronted with realities. Direct communications between Luanda-Benguela and Lisbon increased. With the different problems resulting from the abolition of the slave trade Portuguese Africa could think of little else.

MOZAMBIQUE

As we observed earlier, Mozambique depended on India. A decree of April 19, 1752, severed the two, and Portuguese East Africa adopted a captaincy-general form of government, just like Angola. This situation lasted until May 24, 1822, when a law changed the captains-general into governors.

The Marquis of Pombal tried to reorganize the trade and ordered that Mozambique Island should become an ordinary port of call for all the ships going to, and returning from, the East. At the same time all Portuguese were granted commercial freedom. The "Pombalian" governor of Mozambique who may be compared to Sousa Coutinho (in Angola) was Baltazar Pereira do Lago, who ruled from 1765 to 1779. When he left Mozambique, he wrote an interesting report in which he mentioned the following places which had been occupied by the Portuguese: Lourenço Marques, Inhambane, Sofala, Quiteve, Bazaruto Islands, Luabo, Quelimane, Tete, Zimbaué, Dambarare, Sena, Manica, Zumbo, and Abutua. The simple mention of these names suggests how different the Mozambique of the eighteenth century was from the present one. During this period the Portuguese forts or settlements were very often attacked by the local chiefs. The main assaults took place from 1833 onwards. Lourenço Marques, Inhambane, and Sofala were the main targets. Most of these attacks and sieges were attempts at robbery and showed how weak the Portuguese were scattered all along the seaboard. At the beginning of the nineteenth century Portuguese East Africa had no fixed name as yet. It was not officially known as "Mozambique." Was it "Provincia de Sena," "Rios de Sena," "Provincia Africana do Sul"? The capital was indeed "Mozambique" Island. This adds more difficulty to the reading of old chronicles and documents.

THE ABOLITION OF SLAVERY

After the independence of the thirteen American colonies, the British attitude toward slavery changed so much that many people wondered whether the enthusiasm for the abolition of the slave traffic was based solely on purely humanitarian reasons. The abolition campaign was an ever-recurring problem because in Europe it became evident that sooner or later the traffic would be abolished and the greedy hoped to enrich themselves at any cost while there was still time.

In 1807 England enacted a law abolishing slavery. Three years later, on February 19, 1810, Portugal and Great Britain signed a solemn treaty of friendship and alliance. According to Article 10 of that treaty, the prince regent of Portugal resolved "to cooperate with His Britannic Majesty in the cause of humanity and justice, by adopting the most efficacious means for bringing about a gradual abolition of the slave trade throughout the whole of His dominions." Yet the same article allowed the Portuguese "the right of purchasing and trading in slaves within the African dominions of the Crown of Portugal." Five years later—on January 22, 1815—the two nations signed a treaty in Vienna, Article 1 of which stipulated that "it shall not be lawful for any of the subjects of the Crown of Portugal to purchase slaves, or to carry on the slave-trade on any part of the coast of Africa to the northward of the Equator." Moreover, an additional convention to the 1815 treaty was signed in London on July 28, 1817, which aimed to prevent their respective subjects from carrying on an illicit slave trade. The Portuguese continued to enjoy permission to carry on their slave business on their dominions south of the Equator, according to Article 2 of the convention, while Article 3 provided that both the British and Portuguese were to have the right, under certain conditions, to "visit such merchant vessels of the two Nations, as may be suspected, upon reasonable grounds, of having slaves on board acquired by an illicit traffic." According to Article 5 two mixed commissions, "formed of an equal number of individuals of the two Nations" were to be established, one in Portuguese, and the other in British territory to deal with the vessels detained and charged by the warships.[17]

This happened before the independence of Brazil in 1822. After this date, the interpretation of the treaties varied: while the British claimed that the Portuguese were no longer entitled to send slaves to Brazil, the Portuguese denied such an assertion. On December 19, 1836, the Portuguese overseas minister, Sá da Bandeira, settled the question by issuing a decree which forbade the exportation and importation of slaves. The reaction in the overseas Portuguese territories was unfavorable and both Angola and Mozambique showed signs of unrest. The British government knew what was happening in Africa and insisted that a new treaty was necessary to deal with the situation. The Portuguese government agreed in principle, but could not accept the British conditions. On July 10, 1839, Lord Palmerston and Lord John Russell presented a bill before the House of Commons which ordered the capture of all Portuguese ships engaged in the traffic. After several readings, it was finally passed on August 8, 1839. Several members of the House of Lords opposed it, such as Lord Wellington who was the former commander-in-chief of an Anglo-Portuguese army which fought against the French from 1808–1814.

The reaction to Sá da Bandeira's decree was rather violent in Angola and Mozambique. Some Portuguese even suspected that Great Britain itself was behind the antislavery movements. One of the counterproposals put forth by the Portuguese government before agreeing to any new treaty was that Britain would promise to defend the territorial integrity of the Portuguese possessions in Africa. Sá da Bandeira went so far as to send a memorandum to the British ambassador in Lisbon, Lord Howard de Walden, requesting the assistance of the British navy in case of any rebellion in Angola or Mozambique. However, the British never agreed to this request.

The Portuguese reaction to Lord Palmerston's bill was hardly cordial. The stalemate continued for some time and finally a new agreement was signed on July 3, 1842. The agreement provided, *inter alia*, that the two nations' navies, if provided with special instructions, might visit and search "such vessels of the two nations" suspected of being engaged in the slave traffic. It was also agreed that two or more mixed commissions should be established to deal with the vessels thus detained.[18] They were set up in Luanda and Cape Town. Great Britain, France, Portugal, the United States, and other countries sent gunboats to patrol the African shores to stop any illegal shipment of slaves. Portuguese authorities, however, continued to suspect the real motives behind Britain's dispatch of cruisers. Were the British only acting out of humanitarian concerns? In fact, they seemed keen to seize any slave ship and send the slaves caught on board to Jamaica. The Portuguese thought that it was much better to keep the African slaves in Africa than to ship them elsewhere.

In 1855 Sá de Bandeira ordered the occupation of Ambriz, a port through which many shipments of slaves were sent. He did so because the Portuguese government was accused of negligence in this area. Britain interfered again and made it quite clear that its government would not allow any other Portuguese expansion northward. The Mixed Commission at Luanda lasted until July 4, 1870, when the final meeting was held. Actually it did little and there was no logical reason for its existence.[19]

Officially, Britain had opposed slavery ever since 1807 and had incurred heavy expenses to keep several warships engaged in the antislavery campaign. Yet it was the British capitalists who fostered most of the traffic. Sá da Bandeira therefore responded to Lord Palmerston's bill in the booklet *O Tratado da Escravatura e o Bill de Lord Palmerston* (*The Slave-Trade Treaty and the Bill of Lord Palmerston*) in which he proved that slaves were being bought in Africa mainly with British manufactures and that British merchants in Rio de Janeiro were the main supporters of the traffic in the country. Similar allegations were never denied by the British government, although they questioned the veracity of other Portuguese charges.

Today there is a tendency to castigate the slave buyer more than the slave seller, because if there were no buyers sellers would have to abandon their "business." But the African seller should not be forgotten. Unlike the Arabs on the east coast the Europeans on the west coast of Africa did not need to go far into the interior to get their slaves. They always had them at hand, brought by the Africans. By the beginning of the nineteenth century (actually in 1829), an African chief plainly informed the Portuguese authorities that if the Portuguese crown was going to take no interest in slaves, then it would be better to abandon Angola to any other nation, for buyers from other nations were not lacking.[20]

PORTUGUESE AFRICAN TRAVELERS AND CARTOGRAPHY

From the sixteenth century on, the Portuguese wished to find a trans-African route between Angola and Mozambique. The Zambezi appeared to be that way, but although it was followed up to Zumbo and even farther, it did not turn out to lead across the continent. Sousa Coutinho, the Angolan governor, avowed that he would reach the Sena River on the east coast, but his efforts were fruitless. In 1789 Dr. Lacerda e Almeida, who was well known for his Brazilian explorations, headed an expedition sent to the interior of Africa to find a passage to Angola. Having left Tete, he reached the *zimbaoé* of the Cazembe paramount chief where he died on October 18 of the same year. The chaplain of the expedition, Father Francisco Joáo Pinto, took charge of the enterprise, but the Cazembe paramount chief kept the Portuguese for several months and finally did not allow them to continue their voyage, declaring that the way ahead was unsafe.

From 1802 to 1814 two *pumbeiros* (commercial travelers), acting on the orders of the director of the Cassange fair, completed a trip across Africa. They reached Tete and returned after having been detained at various places. This feat was performed by two Portuguese African slaves, Pedro Joáo Baptista and Amaro José. In July 1815 the Luanda authorities set up a "native foot company" to undertake several voyages between Angola and Mozambique, and Pedro Joáo Baptista was appointed its captain. It seems, however, that the company could not carry on the task. Later, in 1831, two Portuguese officers, Major José Maria Correia Monteiro, governor of Tete, and Antonio Candido Pedro Gamito, captain of Sena, went westwards from Tete, reaching Lunda, then an independent kingdom, but had to return to Tete, for they were not allowed to continue their expedition. Yet several Portuguese had regular contacts with the Lunda Muata Ianwo, including the explorer Joaquim Rodrigues Graça, who in 1843 was given the task of trying to reach the sources of the Sena River. However, he was unable to do so.

At the beginning of April 1852, three Arab traders arrived at Benguela, having crossed Africa from Zanzibar. The Portuguese António Francisco da Silva Porto, who was established at Bié and was already well known for his travels, accompanied them back to the Zambezi and ordered his men to follow the traders down to Mozambique. It may be remembered that from 1840 to 1873 David Livingstone carried on his well-known explorations. He was not well disposed toward the Portuguese and tried to minimize their African accomplishments and expeditions, yet he could not hide the fact that he had been helped by several Portuguese. Nevertheless, he disregarded the feat of the two *pumbeiros* Pedro Joáo Baptista and Amaro José because they were "slaves."

In 1877 began the era of great crossings of Africa by the Portuguese. In November 1877 Captain Serpa Pinto set out from Benguela for Caconda where he spent several months. The next February he left Caconda and reached Durban, South Africa, in March 1879. A few months before, in September 1877, the explorers Hermenegildo Capelo and Roberto Ivens had also left from Benguela on a large exploration of the Angolan territory. A few years later they completed a full crossing from Angola to Mozambique. Having left Moçâmedes in April 1884, they reached Quelimane in June 1885. By then the Berlin Conference was already over; its final resolutions were passed on February 26 of this year.[21]

INTERNATIONAL QUESTIONS

This was a period of several international disputes. There were six: one with France, one with the South African Republic, and four with Britain. They are particularly relevant to the study of the Portuguese presence in Africa, as all had something to do with the Portuguese colonial policy.

The question of the barque Charles & Georges. In 1857 the Portuguese authorities at Mozambique were notified that the French barque *Charles & Georges* was maneuvering north of the island in order to take a gang of slaves aboard. She was boarded by the Portuguese who found such a cargo. The case was duly tried in Mozambique and the captain of the barque was convicted. The French, however, were not satisfied and, on their appeal, the case was brought for a new trial in Lisbon.

At the time French public opinion was very hostile to Portugal because of the treatment which the Sisters of the Poor had met in Lisbon.[22] Imperial France insisted upon pressing the issue and Portugal, abandoned to itself (for no other nation would dare to defend its interests against Napoleon III), made a last appeal by proposing submission of the case to an international arbitration court. The French government retorted that such an arbitration would be accepted only for the purpose of establishing the amount of the indemnity to be paid by Portugal. In the face of this, the Portuguese government decided to bow down to what was in effect an *ultimatum*, since Admiral Lavaud was then commanding a French naval division sent to the Tagus River in Portugal. Consequently, the Portuguese government paid the entire amount demanded by the French, thus ending the affair in January 1859.

The Bolama question. The territory of Guinea was first reached by the Portuguese in 1446 and soon after it was frequented by traders. In November 1791 a British humanitarian association sought to discover whether the Africans could progress by means of work and legitimate trade. According to prearranged plans, over two hundred English men, women, and children disembarked at Bolama, Guinea. The Portuguese did not object to the enterprise, for the island was practically uninhabited. The expedition was not successful because the tropical climate claimed a very heavy toll of the colonists' lives. The head of the colony, Philip Beaver, and those who had survived decided to abandon the project and returned to England in November 1793. In 1828 the Portuguese authorities established a small fort at Bolama. The British government protested and claimed sovereignty over not only this island but also over the neighboring territories. The Portuguese disputed the claims and for several years the Bolama question was a source of disagreement between Lisbon and London. In 1860 the British decided to annex the island to their colony of Sierra Leone.[23] Portugal, however, protested and proposed that the question be submitted to international arbitration. Britain so agreed in 1868 and Ulysses Grant, president of the United States, was selected to arbitrate the case. He decided on April 21, 1870, in favor of the Portuguese.

The Anglo-Portuguese case on Lourenço Marques. Lourenço Marques (Delagoa Bay) remained half forgotten during most of the eighteenth century. William Bolts, who had served under the British East India Company, decided to offer his knowledge and experience to the Austrian Asiatic Company of Trieste whose directors, acting on his advice, sent the ship *Giuseppe and Thereza* to Delagoa Bay where they established a factory in March 1777. It appeared that the Portuguese had no intention of asserting their right to the bay, but the Austrian adventure ended four years later, in 1781, and in the beginning of 1782 a Portuguese fort was erected there to avoid further diplomatic incidents.

Yet incidents soon occurred. In 1821, when the fort was nearly abandoned and when Portugal was torn by internal disputes between absolutists and liberalists, the British government decided to occupy Delagoa Bay and sent Captain R. Owen who did so in 1822. The Portuguese authorities protested as best as they could, but to no avail. In 1860 the British authorities went further and declared that the whole of the territory situated south of the bay as well as the Elephants' and Inhaca's Islands also belonged to Great Britain. Once again Portugal proposed international arbitration. Once more Britain agreed. This time the chosen arbitrator was Marie Edme Patrice de Macmahon, the president of the Third French Republic. His decision of July 24, 1875, supported the Portuguese claims.

The Portuguese–South African dispute over Lourenço Marques. After the occupation of Cape Town by Great Britain because of the Napoleonic Wars, many Dutch settlers, unsatisfied with local conditions, marched northward in search of new lands where they would be their own masters. Between 1836 and 1837 several different treks took place. One of them, led by Louis Trichardt, went as far east as Delagoa Bay. As a result of this Boer exodus, three new states were born: the Transvaal, the Orange Free State, and Natal. In 1843 several English colonists settled in Natal which later fell completely under British influence. The other two states continued their individual Boer way of life. Years later, in 1852, the Boers and British signed the Sand River Convention which granted the Transvaal a certain degree of independence. Two years later the Orange Free State obtained the same recognition as a result of the Bloemfontein Convention.

The Boers were very interested in Delagoa Bay since it was their main outlet to the sea. They also knew that the bay was coveted by Britain and that London and Lisbon were engaged in a dispute over its status. What would become of the Transvaal if the British were to occupy it one day? Because there was as yet no definite frontier agreement, the Transvaal president, Marthinus

Pretorius, wrote to the governor-general of Mozambique in September 1864, asking him "as a great favour" to settle the question. The Portuguese appreciated the Boers' anxiety, but did not comply with their wishes at once. When the news spread that Portugal and Britain had finally decided to submit the Delagoa Bay question to international arbitration, President Pretorius acted on his own and on April 29, 1868, issued a proclamation annexing the whole territory along Delagoa Bay. Portugal immediately protested and President Pretorius willingly accepted proposals for the negotiation of a treaty. Indeed, a Portuguese-Transvaalian treaty was duly signed in July 1869, which demarcated the boundary between Mozambique and the Transvaal.

The Anglo-Portuguese dispute on Ambriz, Molembo, and Cabinda. From the beginning of the Portuguese presence in Angola, the Portuguese authorities believed that Ambriz, Molembo, and Cabinda fell within their sphere of influence. In the eighteenth century when the slave trade was very active different factories were set up in these regions. Consequently, doubts arose as to Portuguese sovereignty over the territories situated between the latitudes of 5° 12′ and the 8° S.

In 1723 a few British traders disembarked at Cabinda and claimed it as a British colony. In 1779 the Portuguese began fortifying the place, but several years later a French naval squadron destroyed the fortifications. Following an official protest, Portugal and France signed a convention on January 30, 1786, in Madrid, in which the Portuguese rights on Cabinda were fully recognized. In 1791 the Ambriz paramount chief publicly avowed obedience to the Portuguese authorities and sent his representatives the next year to Luanda to become a vassal of the Portuguese crown.

The British government recognized these facts in different treaties signed in 1810, 1815, and 1817. Until September 11, 1846, the British considered that the Portuguese held legitimate rights to all these territories. However, on November 24, 1846, the British ambassador in Lisbon informed the Portuguese government that his government intended to reserve its rights in the territories situated between the latitudes of 5° 12′ and 8° S. Thus began the Anglo-Portuguese dispute.

The port of Ambriz was frequented by foreign slavers. Since the Portuguese government was accused of negligence in its territories, Sá da Bandeira ordered its military occupation in 1855. Great Britain did not accept the occupation and indicated the possibility of direct intervention in case of any further action north of Ambriz. The status quo remained until the 1884 Zaire Treaty between Portugal and England.

The Zaire question and treaty. Leopold II, king of the Belgians from 1865 to 1909, conceived the

idea of convening an international conference in order to "open to civilization the only part of our globe which it has not yet penetrated." The conference which took place on September 12, 13, and 14, 1876, was attended by representatives from Germany, Austria-Hungary, Belgium, France, Great Britain, Italy, and Russia. Portugal had not been invited.

The conference may be described as the origin of the general movements now known as the "rush for Africa" or the "scramble for Africa." In 1877 the International African Association held a second meeting in Brussels. Portugal, although invited, did not send a representative. Later, another African organization was formed, the *Comité d'Etudes du Haut Congo* (Committee for the Study of the Upper Congo). It was virtually a private company, headed by King Leopold himself, and it was evident that its claims were more economic than philanthropic. As the years went by, the scramble for Africa continually increased. While France had at her disposal the services of a splendid explorer, Savorgnan de Brazza, whose exploits became known all over Europe, the committee engaged the services of Henry M. Stanley, well known for his African travels. Meanwhile, rumors spread that the International African Association was about to found something called a Free Congo State.

The rumors were not without foundation and the British government saw a need to act. Under such pressing conditions, Britain and Portugal negotiated and signed a treaty on February 26, 1884, known as the Zaire Treaty, according to which Portugal would retain political control of the mouth of the Zaire River and England would participate with Portugal in its trade. The treaty, however, pleased nobody and the other European powers did not accept the idea of Portuguese-English control over the Zaire.

From the Berlin Conference (1885) to 1895

This period is indeed very short, but nevertheless it is of some importance to Portuguese Africa, for it marks the beginning of a new historical era—it was never the same after.

THE BERLIN CONFERENCE

The Berlin Conference began on November 15, 1884, and ended on February 24, 1885, one year after the signature of the Zaire Treaty. The participating nations were Germany, Austria-Hungary, Belgium, Denmark, Spain, the United States of America, France, Great Britain, Italy, Netherlands, Portugal, Russia, Sweden, Norway, and

Turkey. The Zaire Treaty was attacked by nearly everyone at the conference. The British delegates gave the impression that Great Britain had not ratified it and that Portugal was entirely to blame for it.

One of the most important resolutions approved by the conference concerned the effective occupation of colonial territories. According to this doctrine, such occupation was restricted to the littoral regions. Afterward, however, Britain insisted that it also meant the interior ones. In fact, this resolution meant a virtual annexation of Africa by all the colonial powers. The resolution was accepted by Portugal with difficulty, for it meant the adoption of an entirely new colonial policy. The Portuguese-African feudalism had to give way to another form of occupation and influence. All this entailed heavy expenses and, what was more, numerous military forces, demands which Portugal was not in a position to meet.

EUROPEAN PLANS FOR AFRICA

Once begun, the scramble for Africa necessarily produced several international clashes. There were four schools of thought regarding Africa. The Portuguese desired to link Angola to Mozambique. Cecil Rhodes, the British founder of the Rhodesias, planned to build a railway between the Cape and Cairo. France had carried on its African expansion in such a grand scale that it also dreamt of a trans-African corridor between Dakar, West Africa, and Djibouti, on the Red Sea. Finally, Germany, a late arrival on the African scene, had been so successful in its settlements on the west and east coasts of Africa that its politicians, merchants, and travelers expected that the Cameroons in West Africa would be linked with German East Africa. It is obvious that all four plans clearly conflicted with one another. Consequently, none was completely carried out, although the one which most nearly succeeded was the British one.

As previously noted, Serpa Pinto traversed Africa in 1877. In 1881 the Geographical Society of Lisbon prepared a vast plan by which the area between Angola and Mozambique would be gradually occupied by "civilizing stations." A leaflet containing the plan along with a map describing in pink the region where stations would be located was widely distributed. It became known at once as the "rosy map" (*mapa cor de rosa*).

THE EFFECTIVE OCCUPATION OF PORTUGUESE AFRICA

After the Berlin Conference, it became evident that Portugal had to do something to achieve the effective occupation of what was called Portuguese Africa in order to defend the "historical rights" which had been discussed so often in international meetings. Lord Salisbury scoffed at such "archaeological rights" and insisted on practical and concrete assertions of Portuguese sovereignty. Such sovereignty was asserted in three ways: (1) exploration; (2) military action; and (3) treaties with local rulers.

In addition to the travels already mentioned, the one which deserves special mention is that of Major Henrique Dias de Carvalho to the Lunda. Begun in 1884, just before the Berlin Conference, it was crowned with complete success and opened up the different rivers which were considered the best waterways to the interior: the Cuang, the Cuando, the Cubango, the Cuilo, the Kunene, the Cutato, the Cuvo, the Loge, and the Zaire.

According to Bello de Almeida's interesting book *Meio Seculo de Lutas no Ultramar* (Half a Century of Fighting Overseas), published by the Geographical Society of Lisbon in 1937, there were military actions in Angola annually between 1872 and 1919 except for the years 1873, 1875–1884, 1887, 1888, 1894, 1899, and 1917. In Portuguese Guinea from 1871 to 1919 only the following were peaceful years: 1872–1879, 1881, 1883, 1885, 1887–1888, 1893, 1896, 1898, 1903, 1905, 1906, 1910–1911, and 1916; and in Mozambique: 1870–1877, 1879–1883, 1886, 1890, 1892–1893, 1901, 1903, 1905–1907, 1909, and 1911. The rest of the years involved one or more Portuguese military campaigns. Taken together, these campaigns represent a tremendous effort to achieve the effective occupation prescribed by the Berlin Conference.

THE ULTIMATUM OF JANUARY 11, 1890

The ultimatum sent by Great Britain to Portugal on January 11, 1890, was the cruelest blow suffered by the Portuguese nation in the nineteenth century. It was not the first, but it was the most severe one and one which was widely and deeply resented. It all started with the "rosy map" which we mentioned earlier. The British South Africa Company in Rhodesia had no northern boundaries; consequently, it wanted to expand as far north as possible. Great Britain supported such designs and Lord Salisbury was very annoyed with the rosy map. On the one hand, he maintained that effective occupation of an African territory was a prerequisite for the assertion of sovereignty. On the other hand he was reluctant to allow the Portuguese to occupy the territory which they had previously claimed for themselves. The British cabinet was aware of the Franco-Portuguese and German-Portuguese agreements. These gave rise to legitimate suspicions so that finally the British decided to shatter the Portuguese dream of the rosy map.

The necessary pretext was easily found. Dr. David Livingstone had brought over two hundred

Africans, the Macololos, with him to Tete and the Portuguese government sent them to the borders of the Shire River. Little by little, the Macololos succeeded in ruling over the neighboring tribes. In 1884 their chief, Melaure, committed several atrocities against Africans and Europeans, including the British; this called for military action. The Macololos were backed, however, by the British African Lakes Company Limited. On November 8, 1889, the Macololos under the British flag attacked the Portuguese. Several days later, Leiutenant João de Azevedo Coutinho moved his small gunboat toward Chicomo, the village of the Macololos, and easily brought it to heel. On December 8, 1889, Melaure acknowledged the legitimate authority of the Portuguese and declared that he had always been fair to the Portuguese.

The Portuguese regarded the Macololo affair as closed, but the British certainly did not. The British government duly informed the Portuguese government on December 18 that the Macololos were a friendly people and accordingly under British protection. At the same time several demands were sent to Lisbon which the Portuguese could not accept. The Portuguese government, backed by the whole nation, tried every possible means to avoid the approaching disaster. The last attempt was an appeal once more to international arbitration. Great Britain had not as yet forgotten the Bolama (1870) and Lourenço Marques (1875) decisions. This time the Portuguese proposal was ignored and on January 11, 1890, the British ultimatum came.

After this blow, Portugal was rent by domestic confusion and disorder. The Republican party unsuccessfully tried to overthrow the monarchical regime on January 31, 1891. Meanwhile, Anglo-Portuguese negotiations were being carried out and ended on June 11, 1891, with the signing of a treaty. During the negotiations, the British minister in Lisbon advised the Portuguese government that the paramount chief, the Gungunhana, in Mozambique was so powerful that the Portuguese forces would not be able to cope with him. The best procedure, in his opinion, would be to recognize the chief's independence under the joint supervision of both Great Britain and Portugal. The suggestion, however, was declined by the Portuguese.

The British advice, however, was sincere. In 1894 the Gungunhana and his allies began hostilities against the Portuguese, attacking Lourenço Marques. The British South Africa Company was backing the rebels who were well armed and who apparently wanted to push the Portuguese into the sea. By the first months of 1895, several foreign newspapermen had gathered in Lourenço Marques. Simultaneously, hostilities broke out at different regions. The Portuguese coped with the situation as best as they could. On February 2, 1895, a battle was fought at Marracuene, some thirty kilometers from Lourenço Marques; on September 8, 1895, a clash took place at Magul; on November 8, 1895, the main battle of the whole campaign took place at Coolela. After this, Gungunhana's army was utterly dispersed and the campaign was over. What is more, it had been much easier than the Portuguese had anticipated. Finally, by the end of 1895, a telegram reached Europe announcing that Gungunhana had been taken prisoner during a sudden raid on his kraal at Chaimite on December 29, 1895. After 1895 the Portuguese in Africa could also devote themselves to peaceful pursuits despite various campaigns which lasted until the end of World War I.

After the ultimatum of January 11, 1890, and before the treaty of June 11, 1891, Portuguese Africa continued to be threatened by the British South Africa Company. This led the Portuguese government to grant several administrative powers to two chartered companies in the districts of Cabo Delgado, Niassa, Manica, and Sofala. The first two districts were under the Niassa Company and the second two under the Mozambique Company. The two companies were thus entitled to act as agents of the state in their respective regions. This led to the formation of a new Mozambique Company, whose charter was signed by the government on May 17, 1897.

By this charter, the new Mozambique Company undertook to construct a railway line from Beira to the Rhodesian frontier, the responsibility for which had been given to Portugal under the Anglo-Portuguese agreements of 1891. As a result, two new British companies—the Beira Railway Limited and the Beira Works Limited—cooperated with the Portuguese. Beira remained under the influence of the British until on January 1 and 10, 1949, when the port and the Beira railway, respectively, reverted to the Portuguese government.

Portuguese Africa between 1895 and 1961

MORE DIFFICULTIES AHEAD

The defeat of Gunganhana had indeed made 1895 a magnificent year, yet it did not improve the domestic situation in Portugal. The nation was deeply split between monarchists and republicans and the monarchists themselves were divided. There was an annual deficit in the national budget. Loans were rather easy to obtain from foreigners but interest charges still had to be paid. The difficult state of Portuguese finances was known all over Europe. It is against this background that one must examine the Anglo-German agreement of 1898, by which the Portuguese overseas possessions would be divided between the two powers in the event that Portugal became bankrupt. This division was stipulated in a secret clause which soon came to the attention of the Lisbon government.

Fortunately for Portugal, the next year Great Britain became engaged in the second Anglo-Boer War. In 1899 Portugal and Great Britain signed a secret treaty at Windsor, which nullified the previous Anglo-German agreement of 1898. In October 1910 a Republic was declared in Portugal, but the difficulties continued. Once again Britain and Germany came to terms over the division of the Portuguese colonies. Fortunately for Portugal, a few months later England was at grips with Germany in another war. To these two wars Portugal perhaps owes the integrity of her overseas territories.

After World War I, conditions in Portugal improved somewhat, but it was evident that the different political parties were unable to cope with the situation. This explains the origin of the national revolution of May 26, 1926, followed by a dictatorship which ended in 1933 when a new constitution was promulgated.

THE MANUAL LABOR QUESTION OF SÃO TOMÉ AND PRINCIPE

The question of manual labor in São Tomé and Principe dates back to 1842 with the antislavery treaty between Portugal and Great Britain. The archipelago of São Tomé and Principe needed workers who were sent from Angola in accordance with Portuguese and international law. The British, however, found fault with such procedure. Little by little an anti-Portuguese campaign was taken up by the cocoa companies in Great Britain. The competition offered by São Tomé and Principe to their interests in Nigeria and Ghana was well known. Consequently, some British writers suggested that one of the best ways to protect British cocoa was to impose on the Portuguese colony of São Tomé legislation as favorable as possible for the workers and unfavorable to the employers.[24] In fact, Portuguese observers were puzzled as to why São Tomé and Principe—two tiny islands—were so often attacked by international cocoa dealers for William Cadbury, head of the British firm Cadbury Brothers Limited, ultimately became the most outspoken opponent of São Tomé's cocoa. The Portuguese case was ably defended by a São Tomé planter, Francisco Mantero.[25] Nevertheless, the campaign led by the British firm lasted several years more.

THE BENGUELA RAILWAY COMPANY

At the end of the nineteenth century, Tanganyika Concessions Limited, while prospecting in Katanga in the Congo, came to the conclusion that a route to the Atlantic was badly needed. It was Robert Williams, one of its administrators, who took the initiative for building a Benguela-Katanga railway. At first, some in Portugal were suspicious of Williams because he also belonged to the British South Africa Company which, under the leadership of Cecil Rhodes, had adopted an anti-Portuguese policy. Finally, however, Robert Williams was granted a ninety-nine-year concession by the Portuguese. The building of the line began in March 1907 and it was completed in June 1929—1,348 kilometers from Lobito to Teixeira de Sousa—and was linked to the Katanga railway on July 5, 1931. By means of this Benguela railway Katanga, Zambia, and Rhodesia have free access to the Atlantic Ocean.

THE COLONIAL ACT OF 1930

In 1930 Professor Antonio de Oliveira Salazar, then minister of overseas affairs, was instrumental in the preparation of the Colonial Act, Article 2 of which states: ". . . the organic essence of the Portuguese Nation belongs the historic function of possessing and colonizing overseas dominions and of civilizing the native populations inhabiting [such dominions]. . . . The Portuguese Colonial Empire, each of its colonies, and the mother country are linked by solidarity." Of course, differences exist between the civilized and the noncivilized persons of the empire. This is particularly stressed in Articles 15 and 22. According to Article 15, "The State guarantees the physical protection and the defence of the natives, according to the principles of humanity and sovereignty, the legal dispositions herein contained and the international conventions which are actually or in future may be in force." Article 22 provides that "in the colonies the state of evolution of the native peoples shall be duly attended to, and there will be special statutes for them in such a way that, under the influence of Portuguese private and public law, there will be set up juridical regimes of contemporation towards their usages, individual, familiar and social customs not opposed to Morals or the tenets of humanity."

The colonies were to be governed by means of special legislation, which provided for administrative decentralization and economic autonomy. Each colony would prepare its own budget, subect to the approval of the Colonial Office. In case of need the mother country would render financial assistance to the colonies. There was only one national government. In this way the Colonial Act may be considered the beginning of a new chapter in Portuguese overseas history. The notion of empire was very much alive for there were the British and the French empires, among others. While these two were based mainly on differences between mother country and overseas possessions, the Portuguese empire was understood to constitute a whole entity, temporarily dissociated by special legislation but subject always to a deep and complete feeling of integration. In 1933 the Colonial Act was embodied in the Fundamental Constitution of the nation when dictatorship ended its days, thus beginning the ordinary constitutional life. Because of Portugal's preference for integration, Minister of Overseas Affairs Adriano Moreira abolished the Natives Statute on September 6, 1961, thus erasing the last difference between metropolitan and overseas Portuguese.

CONCLUSION

Today Portuguese Africa occupies a very important place in world news. It all began on March 15, 1961, when the ancient and peaceful colony of Angola realized that it had been invaded. And as time went on, war also erupted in Portuguese Guinea and Mozambique. Premier Salazar decided to resist at all costs and by all means. After eight years of hardships and sufferings, his successor Professor Marcelo Caetano has expressed the same convictions. It seems that this decision is backed by the whole nation.

Portugal was a very tiny nation at the beginning of her overseas expansion. Underpopulated, it undertook a task far greater than its resources. Portugal thus needed other peoples to help it to carry out this "mission"—if it may be called that. This tendency revealed itself in Brazil, in Africa, in India, and elsewhere. Portugal was also a very poor country. The poor have their own qualities, indeed, but they also have their defects. These assets and liabilities were part and parcel of the Portuguese character. The attitude of the Portuguese toward money was not always as it should have been. The same may be true as regards their attitude toward the workers—the Africans. Although they intermingled freely with them, they also did oppress them on many occasions. The Portuguese chronicles bear open testimony to this. It was not, of course, an official policy, but the central government was so far away that it could not correct each act of abuse.

Up to the middle of the eighteenth century, Angola and Brazil were deeply linked with one another. Brazil needed slaves while Angola could easily furnish them. The Angola governor Sousa Coutinho was not content with the situation and hoped that Angola might one day become a second Brazil. Mozambique, in turn, was linked to India up to the same period. The Marquis of Pombal severed the ties between the two, but this measure hardly improved the situation.

It has often been said that history is the politics of the past and that politics, in turn, deals with the history of the present. This explains why I prefer not to deal with the "history of the present" since such history goes under the name of "politics." But certainly this "history of the present" will occupy an important place in any future essay on "Portugal and Africa: A Historical Survey."

2

*Portugal in Angola: A Living Colonialism?**

DOUGLAS L. WHEELER

Introduction

> But there is one thought which every white man . . . thinks when he sees a black army marching past. "How much longer can we go on kidding these people? How long before they turn their guns in the other direction?"
>
> —George Orwell, in "Marrakech," 1939[1]

George Orwell penned these lines in a 1939 essay on his brief observations of French colonialism in Morocco. The questions he asked then might well be applied today to the situation in Angola (or in Portuguese Africa in general), where a kind of European colonialism survives. Why have the Angolan black masses not followed the example of masses in independent Africa? Why do many Angolans not participate in insurgency against Portugal? Indeed, why is Portugal still in Africa?

The enigma of Portugal in Africa in 1970, an example of the weakest of the colonial powers lasting the longest, is a problem which requires more than an explanation of pre-1961 Portuguese policy. Literature published in the years 1959–1962, when Angola began to attract world attention, clearly outlined background causes for the explosive 1961 insurgency in northern Angola. In an article published in 1960, the American authority Professor James Duffy discussed "The Dual Reality" of Portuguese Africa.[2] In Portuguese Africa, he wrote, there were two conflicting images of the situation: on the one hand, in the writings of David Livingstone, Cecil Rhodes, H. W. Nevinson, J. H. Harris, Basil Davidson (and Thomas Okuma later), these territories were pictured as a slave camp; on the other hand, there was an opposing image: that of a multiracial paradise, portrayed in the works of Gilberto Freyre, Adriano Moreira, F. C. C. Egerton, and others.[3] Nearly a decade following the 1961 events in Angola, such stereotyped images provide only a limited understanding of the present reality.

* The author is indebted to the University of New Hampshire for a grant and a leave of absence from teaching duties, 1966–1967, in order to conduct research in Angola.

Something has occurred in the meantime which conflicts with the conclusions of knowledgeable observers, including Professor Duffy, that a Portuguese collapse was imminent and that African nationalism would soon triumph.

Recent articles on Angola, Portugal's largest and most profitable African possession, suggest that since 1961 little has changed except economic conditions and that force and repression are really the only effective means of Portuguese survival.[4] While other writers have acknowledged that Portugal has passed reforms, or "pseudo-reforms," these are depicted as deception schemes or as ineffective.[5] This present chapter will attempt to present evidence which suggests that a careful study of Portuguese activities reveals complex official responses, in some ways more flexible than many observers thought possible. This should not surprise students of the writings of Frantz Fanon, who, in his *The Wretched of the Earth* (1961), discussed the concessions granted by colonial powers as a useful means by which colonial rulers, Portugal included, could arouse a response of loyalty among African masses and thereby sabotage a budding nationalist movement.[6] As we shall see, this counterrevolutionary process is a feature of the current Angolan scene.

This chapter will outline the major factors which influence the internal situation in Angola and which will affect the role of Angola in the context of Southern Africa. Particular attention will be paid to the role of various European interest groups, the Portuguese expeditionary army in Angola, European attitudes, and the role of the Lisbon government. First, a summary of the Angolan political background is necessary.

The Voice of Angola Crying in the Wilderness[7]

Although the detailed political history of the territory is yet to be written, it is possible to make several general conclusions about the political legacies of Portuguese rule. First, disunity. In the violence of 1961 a struggling Angolan nationalism emerged in the form of numerous fragmented and disunited movements. But, even long before this, in the nineteenth century, Angolan protonationalists could rarely present united fronts. Modern Angolan nationalism has its origins in the feverish journalism of Luanda *assimilados* [or évolués] many of them *mestiços* (mulattoes), who debated the autonomy and independence of Angola in the 1870–1922 period before official censorship was thorough and well entrenched.[8] Angolan nationalism, therefore, is as old as or older than nationalism in the Gold Coast or in Senegal. Despite early origins, Angolan nationalist agitation and protest were always plagued by particularly restrictive conditions. Operating mainly in the capital of Luanda, political activists in the nineteenth century were isolated, found little support outside a circle of urban *assimilados* and radical Portuguese exiles, and usually suffered from periodic government repression in the form of deportation, censorship, imprisonment, threats from a hostile settler community, poverty, and a debilitating climate. Even before the post-1926 dictatorship in Portugal, Angolan politics experienced official intervention by the governors-general; a Draconian tradition of repression tended to weaken, fragment, and isolate political activity.

Besides the restrictiveness of Angolan politics, there was also the fact that political development atrophied due to failures of liberalism and democracy in the metropole, the low level of education, and the pressing demands of economic development in Angola. During the turbulent period of the Republic in Portugal (1910–1926), several governors and high commissioners acted as authoritarian rulers. The military dictatorship of 1926, in fact, based its authoritarian legislation in part on the foundations of republican legislation and action in Angola and in Portugal during the period from 1911 to 1921. Despite the frustration felt by aspiring *assimilados* who regarded the period of the Republic as a time for political, social, and economic advancement in Angola, the authoritarian reaction after 1926 did bring stability and managed to win over a small group of loyal *assimilados* to the official Portuguese position. This group of *assimilados*, mainly *mestiços* by race such as António de Assis Júnior,[9] professed loyalty to Portugal and assumed a kind of cultural leadership as writers and westernized Angolans, "caught between two fires,"[10]—that is, between native African and Portuguese cultures.

After a series of official purges, deportations, and a political moratorium during 1922–1942, Angolan nationalism entered the post-World War II era with a number of liabilities. The dictatorship forbade political organizations other than the one official, legal party of the metropole: the *União Nacional*, created in 1930 as Dr. António de Oliveira Salazar (premier, 1932–1968) consolidated his power from the post of minister of finance. Thus those Angolan groups interested in politics were obliged to go underground. In the struggle for membership and strength, these parties tended to be divided racially, regionally, and culturally. These organizations emerged in the following types: Portuguese settler organizations, separatist ethnic groups of black Africans (that is, Bakongo, Bazombo, and so on), urban *assimilado* (in part *mestiço*) parties, African nationalist groups such as the UPA (*União das Populações de Angola*), with regional bases of support yet having national or territorial appeals.[11] As was the case during the dissenting *assimilado* journalism of 1870–1922, the mulatto *assimilado*, usually better educated than most other Angolan nationalists, often found himself in a cultural and political no man's land. Such a position, "caught" between Portuguese nationalism and black African nationalism, elicited responses of increased ideological radicalism (largely leftist); such beliefs were not accepted by the majority of other Angolan political groups.

By 1961 it was clear that no broad coalition or united front party of Angolan nationalists had emerged. Political fragmentation increased as many groups went into exile abroad. Within Angola, legitimate political activity remained highly restricted and colonial in nature. A government reacted hostilely to considerable agitation and organizing by some parties in the 1958 presidential elections when a substantial portion of the European communities of Angola and Mozambique voted for the opposition candidate, General Humberto Delgado; again active politics were repressed. The political system was still characterized by the three following features: first, a system of formal and informal patronage, where organizations ceremoniously sought concessions from Lisbon's highest representative, the governor-general; second, an authoritarian hierarchy, with virtual omnipotence of the Lisbon officials and their high-level staffs and a concentration of power at Luanda, the capital; and third, institutionalized patriotism, with public professions of patriotism representing a *sine qua non* for individual acceptance and for institutions' admittance to the system of bureaucratic spoils.

Although the political system by 1961 had undergone little change and appeared to be stable largely because of the weight of the Portuguese government's system of control, nevertheless the economic system was being transformed. It is easy to attribute most changes which appeared after 1961 to a Portuguese reaction to the explosion of 1961. Yet if one analyzes the contemporary newspapers, books, and articles of the 1955–1960 era, it is evident that improvements in Angolan education, welfare, and the economy were slowly taking place before the African insurgency of February and March 1961. The government slowly increased the number of schools and trained more teachers and Portugal encouraged the establishment of more light industry in Angola and the development of the petroleum industry.[12]

These changes, nevertheless, were gradual and slow. Many Africans perceived only that Angola had become, in effect, a "white man's colony" during the past generation. Especially since World War II, with increased white immigration and competition, Angola increasingly became a more closely controlled appendage of metropolitan Portugal. Luanda as a city resembled a suburb of Lisbon. Between 1940 and 1960 the Portuguese population of the territory grew from 44,083 to 172,529.* Portuguese investment in Angola greatly expanded its control over certain industries. Perhaps more important, black and brown Angolans in the towns now faced intense competition for jobs and places in the few schools from the new Portuguese arrivals. As Angolans increasingly migrated to the Belgian Congo, Northern Rhodesia, South West Africa, and South Africa for better-paying jobs, they learned new things, experienced new ideas, and gained a bitter perspective on the situation in Angola. In short, though some economic conditions had improved by 1961, African discontent rose to a dangerous level.

Violent African action occurred in early 1961. Directed first against government installations in Luanda, and later against individual Portuguese settlers and their families in the coffee country in northern Angola, this violence cost the lives of hundreds of Portuguese and unknown thousands of Africans. While a number of Africans were murdered by Angolan nationalists when they refused to join the insurgents many others were killed in both unofficial and official Portuguese operations during 1961 and 1962.[13] The isolation of Angola was forever shattered and news of the territory now appeared in headlines in the world press. The stage for this sudden eventuality was set by the action of a member of the Portuguese opposition movement, Captain Henrique Galvão, a former high official in Angola. In late January 1961, Galvão, with a handful of revolutionaries (not all Portuguese), captured the Portuguese ocean liner, *Santa Maria*.[14] Though Galvão's plan of reaching Angola and seizing it as a base for attacking the Salazar regime in Portugal failed, his act attracted considerable attention both to Portugal and to Portuguese Africa. As the first Portuguese army reinforcements began to arrive in Angola in March 1961, Angola was no longer an obscure name on the map of Africa, and the traditional isolation was over.

The Legacies of 1961

The Portuguese forces managed to crush insurgent activity in Luanda and, in the months following the attacks in northern Angola, they were able to recapture and reoccupy many areas in the Congo district. Their main strategies of counterattack were traditional: the dispatch of an armed expedition of European troops, the reinforcement of European militia units, and an intensified build-

* It was estimated in 1969 that the white population of Angola was over three hundred thousand.

up of military facilities and communications. From the Portuguese point of view, several explanations for the African insurgency were offered: some said it was "foreign terrorism";[15] "an international conspiracy,"[16] opined the leading daily paper of Angola. Nonetheless, there were other weapons in the Portuguese arsenal of counterattack, for the Lisbon regime did not respond simply by securing frontiers, reinforcing border patrols and armies, and keeping out foreign influences as would seem to be logical in light of the published explanations for the African-directed violence of 1961.

The government response was reflected in part by the appointment of a new minister for overseas, Dr. Adriano Moreira, a well-known scholar and administrator. Dr. Moreira undertook extensive reforms in overseas legislation in the latter half of 1961. A decree of September 1961 abolished the *indigenato* laws, which were the cornerstone of the assimilation policy of Portugal for several decades.[17] Instead of having the Angolan (or other Portuguese African) population classified and given rights according to their achievement of a Lisbon-decreed standard of Portuguese culture, now (in theory at least) all Angolans were Portuguese citizens. Thus the term *assimilado*, meaning the non-European who had qualified as a Portuguese citizen, was no longer current. Dr. Moreira and his staff also arranged the passage of legislative reforms in the fields of labor, forced agricultural crop quotas (the decree of May 2, 1961, against compulsory cotton crop growing),[18] conditions for foreign capital investment in Portuguese Africa, economic development plans, and increased African opportunities for health, education, and welfare.[19] In the political realm, local autonomy was (in theory, at least) also increased during 1961 to 1963 by new regulations. Elected representation, mainly from the European population of Angola, was increased by government decrees for two bodies: the Legislative Council and the Economic and Social Council in Luanda. Furthermore, Angola's elected representatives to the national parliament in Lisbon (the National Assembly) were increased from three to seven as a result of the Overseas Organic Law of 1963, and elected membership in the Legislative Council was increased from twenty-one to thirty-four. Still, both in Luanda and in Lisbon these bodies did not enjoy a great deal of decision-making power as the official executive, usually appointed in Lisbon, retained many of the important legislative powers.[20] Nevertheless, by 1969 the Legislative Council in Luanda had acquired some of the characteristics of a minor provincial parliament, despite the fact that it met infrequently and was not wholly representative of the Angolan population.[21]

These Portuguese reforms in some ways were complicated and even neutralized by another new Lisbon policy, that of increased Portuguese immigration to Angola. The government position which supported greatly increased Portuguese immigration was founded on two suppositions: first, that more European settlers would strengthen the Portuguese position in Angola; and, second, that new settlers would bring new skills to an underdeveloped, backward country. In the opinion of some observers, however, these suppositions were nullified by several facts: in the history of Angola, and indeed of much of European-dominated Southern Africa, an increase of settlers may improve a military and demographic position but erode race relations; furthermore, a considerable number of the new arrivals from Portugal were illiterate farmers who needed an education in skills relevant to the Angolan situation. While the government debated the form of the increased immigration, reflecting an old debate over selected or unselected immigration programs, increased immigration was a definite political and economic commitment with important historic precedents.

There was more to Lisbon's response than legislative reforms and increased immigration; Lisbon now began to strengthen the effort to win allies abroad and within Portuguese Africa. In NATO, in the United Nations, and in bilateral relations with the Western powers, Portugal conducted a campaign to defend her position in Africa by stressing anew Portugal's control of areas considered by many to be strategic to Western defense in case of war, Portugal's record as an anti-Communist state, and the foreign elements involved in the African nationalist movements.[22]

The most interesting—and perhaps the most decisive, ultimately—of efforts to improve her "image" was the campaign within Angola. Portugal began a verbal defense of her position within Angola by an appeal to the African masses. This program had psychological and social characteristics. In those areas where known insurgent activity occurred, the army's "psycho-social" units produced propaganda and counterpropaganda to secure or regain the loyality of the Africans. In Angola, in general, the army and other agencies reinforced the psychological warfare program with social programs which included improvements in wages, welfare, and medical, religious, and educational facilities. Clearly, Portuguese leaders were well versed in the theory of guerrilla and counterguerrilla warfare and their new *Realpolitik* included a new attention to the loyalty of African masses.[23]

Para o Prêto Ver?

It was significant that official statements now laid

more emphasis on African welfare than on patriotic rhetoric as before. In short, instead of the nineteenth-century aphorism of *para o inglês ver* (for the Englishman to see), reflecting Portugal's ancient effort to impress her ancient ally and gain its confidence, now a more appropriate motto in post-1961 Angola might have been: *para o prêto ver* (for the black man to see). At high levels in the Angolan and Portuguese administrations there was an effort to make the campaign to change Angola into a new "Brazil" seem both possible and sincerely desired by all, despite the strongly European-centered character of Angolan towns.[24]

The new government campaign of influencing the attitudes of the black masses was in part the result of a belated realization that the events of 1961 had demonstrated the existence of serious discontent and that Portugal would lose Angola if she lost the loyalty of most Africans. At the same time it was obvious that at least three major Angolan nationalist parties were also appealing to the majority of black Africans. Many Portuguese leaders, and not a few settlers, sincerely believed that an African revolutionary success was *not* inevitable and that the outcome depended in many ways on how Portugal acted in response to the tragic days of 1961. Men in Lisbon and Luanda believed, then, that well-executed reforms would elicit loyalty from the Africans. They also tended to feel that independence in neighboring African states to the north and east had proved so unsuccessful and disappointing that Portugal, by means of reforms, could compete for the loyalty of the Africans.

How have the reform laws been implemented since 1961? This is a most controversial issue because there is at present little reliable evidence. Clearly, there is still a gap between theory and practice in Angolan administration. A perennial and persistent problem in Angolan history has been the failure to execute laws well or justly. The execution of these laws depends on many factors, not the least important of which is the conduct of the local Portuguese official who could well say with his Spanish counterpart in seventeenth-century Spanish American colonies, "I will obey but not fulfill the laws" (free translation from *obedezco pero no cumplo*). Then too, there is more evident reform in the towns than in the isolated and backward rural areas. The electoral reforms appeared to be carried out, but the regime closely supervised the elections in 1964 and 1967. As usual, security forces carefully controlled any individuals or groups suspected of acting as nationalists or as opponents of the present government. Police intervention often appeared to be a constant factor which influenced the attitudes of Angolans of all colors toward the post-1961 measures.

There was some evidence that the government would make an effort to enforce the law to protect African interests in economic spheres. One case in point was reported in a public announcement and news item published in the major daily paper of Luanda in late 1966.[25] A certain Portuguese, aged twenty-nine, was henceforth prohibited by the government from residing in Angola because he attempted to cheat Africans in a cattle sale and because he told the Africans that the government would take their cattle without compensation. It was also commonly known in Luanda during late 1966, when I visited there, that the government was playing a similar protective role in labor questions. To what extent such action by Lisbon is either consciously idealistic or counterrevolutionary is still unclear.

At least in some areas of Angola, the black African was better off than before 1961, but this statement should be qualified. In political life there seemed to be little improvement for the black African over the preinsurgency situation. Although on paper he was no longer an *indigena* (native) and, therefore, theoretically enjoyed the rights of a Portuguese citizen, this 1961 reform was being implemented very slowly. Civil registration was a prerequisite for the franchise in Angola and there was a lag in registration, so that probably only a small portion of the African masses had more political rights by the end of the decade.[26] Some would argue that this is true, yet it was not so strange since Portuguese themselves did not enjoy many *political* rights under the present regime.

This political restriction did not greatly change upon the removal from power of Dr. Salazar in September 1968.[27] Following a massive stroke which paralyzed him, Dr. Salazar was replaced as premier of Portugal by order of the president of the Republic, Admiral Américo Thomaz. Professor of a law faculty like his predecessor, Dr. Marcelo Caetano became the appointed replacement for Dr. Salazar. During the first months of his term in office, Dr. Caetano undertook certain reforms in Lisbon: censorship was relaxed, certain members of the exiled opposition were allowed to return to Portugal, political discussion meetings were allowed by the police, and, for the first time, Portuguese women were given full franchise rights. While these measures gave some new freedom to the Europeans in Angola, it was uncertain how they affected the political lot of the African majority.

In the field of education the government committed more funds to improve opportunities for Africans. Primary school facilities were rapidly expanded after 1961, and in 1964 the government made four years of education compulsory. Again, the execution of the new measures was uneven. There was a serious bottleneck in the educational system after the first few grades; many Africans dropped out and never reached secondary levels. By the fourth year few Africans survived the exams and fees. Although official statistics on education were neither completely reliable nor current, it appeared in late 1967 that only one out of five Angolan children had places in schools (out of a million children of school age), and that of these only 12 percent continued on to the next grade.[28] Rural Africans enjoyed fewer opportunities for education since rural areas lacked qualified teachers and facilities. Still, the educational picture by 1969 was significantly brighter than in 1961–1962.

A White Man's Colony?

If Lisbon was attempting to launch a counterrevolution by means of reforms designed to win black African loyalty and if the result were uncertain,[29] what was the position of the European settlers? The crisis of 1961, referred to colloquially in Angola as *a confusão* (confusing period), had an important impact upon the Portuguese residents of Angola: it tended to unite them behind the Lisbon government against the threat and fear of black African nationalism. After the initial panic caused by the slaughter of whites north of Luanda beginning on March 14–15, 1961, numbers of settlers fled to the capital and prepared to return to Portugal. Some sent their families on ships and planes. As the crisis subsided and as Portugal came to contain the insurgency to frontier areas by 1962–1963, many settlers renewed their confidence in Angola and began to return. By 1964 about ten thousand Portuguese immigrants a year were settling in the territory. Organizing and agitating for political autonomy by settlers were now curtailed both by the police activity and by the 1961 crisis and its aftermath of unity behind the aroused government leadership. Demands by the settlers for greater economic freedoms, however, did continue unabated throughout the decade; some of the more bitter settler grievances involved the tight credit and loan practices, low wages, restriction of local Angolan industry so as to safeguard Portuguese domestic industries in manufacturing and foodstuffs, and strict currency and investment laws which favored the metropole over the provinces.

Economic advances tended to muffle the settlers' political complaints. By the end of the decade the increased exploitation of large oil and iron reserves was beginning to provide new sources of revenue. The building industry was flourishing and wages rising. The Angolan economic boom

conditions benefited the European settler more than the African in many cases; indeed, some Europeans saw the post-1961 economy as a kind of miracle influencing all sectors of the Portuguese community. When a new reserve of petroleum was discovered at offshore Cabinda in 1966, more foreign investment entered Angola and the government urged more Portuguese reinvestment in the country;[30] Portuguese businessmen now found it more difficult to withdraw their capital from Angola due to new government laws. As the weak economy now got a much needed transfusion of capital the market grew in size. Besides an increasing African population and more immigrants, the market was expanded by the presence of over fifty thousand troops in the Portuguese overseas expeditionary forces.

Have the racial attitudes of the Portuguese settlers influenced the course of the Portuguese counterrevolution? Richard Hammond's conclusion on the subject, in 1966, based mainly on secondary printed sources,[31] were in part borne out by my first hand observations in Angola. Miscegenation in the general settler population—as opposed to off-duty miscegenation by the Portuguese troops—by the late 1960s was decreasing and appeared to have little bearing on individual race attitudes. While official public segregation had largely disappeared by then, traditional social attitudes remained and a type of economic segregation prevailed; in Luanda I saw the cafés and restaurants and hotels filled with whites and a few *mestiços*; often, the only black Africans visible were servants or waiters. Partly out of fear and partly out of ignorance, the majority of Portuguese residents who were not government officials openly expressed a conscious white superiority over blacks. It is evident that the 1961 crisis caused a white-backlash psychology among certain circles, and that as late as 1966, in the midst of Luanda, certain Europeans were prepared for a sudden African rising. Some carried firearms in their cars, while others had private stocks of arms cached for emergencies. I particularly recall being harangued by a white Portuguese citizen near the Commercial Association of Luanda in 1966; his main point was that even *if* the black man got freedom in Angola he did not have the *capability* to rule himself. This gesturing man with his deterministic philosophy might indeed have made Lisbon liberals wince. In Angola, however his attitude was not atypical.

With such racial attitudes, Portuguese settlers did not favor Lisbon-appointed officials who were too "generous" with the African population. Certain settler groups held serious reservations about the government programs for the "psychosocial" rehabilitation of *ex-terroristas* (ex-nationalists, now returned to Angola). Governor-General Silvino Silvério Marques (who was in office from 1962 until 1966) was unpopular with certain urban leaders because of what some called his "appeasement" measures; settlers feared that many of the "rehabilitated" nationalists, who now professed loyalty to Portugal, were in actual fact double agents or disguised saboteurs. Some felt this governor had encouraged African nationalism by his lenient policies. Such a hostile attitude is illustrated by one joke popular among the settlers in late 1966, namely, that this handshaking and friendly governor was so friendly to black Africans that his hands turned black as a result and that he was reluctant to shake hands with the whites in Lobito while on a tour. The Portuguese army also came under settler criticism in this period for it was accused of being too soft on the Africans and failing to end the guerrilla war on the northern and eastern frontiers. Settlers were not reassured when a new front was opened by Angolan insurgents in eastern Angola in 1966. By late 1968 several units of the MPLA ('Popular Movement for the Liberation of Angola') had established small bases in the remote sections of eastern Angola, an area with only a sparse Portuguese settlement.[32] The new governor-general, Lt. Col. C. A. Rebocho Vaz, appeared to have more settler support than his predecessor. In late 1966, when Rebocho Vaz was about to arrive to take over the post of Lisbon's proconsul in Angola, settlers from the Uige district (where the governor-to-be had served with distinction several years before) hired a plane and dropped laudatory leaflets over Luanda. The small red papers hailed the governor's appointment and promised support for his programs.

Despite their latent discontent, the settlers could do little to improve their position. While they enjoyed more economic freedom than before, they desired even more. What little political freedom there was appeared to be only token since the settlers had little control over the important decisions made in Luanda and Lisbon. Lisbon had lessened the power of the governor-general by appointing a commanding general for Angola who answered only to Lisbon on military matters, a prerogative once held by the governor. In a sense, the settlers were caught between the threat of African nationalism and the substantial Portuguese army in Angola. As long as the settlers' militias remained subordinate and the settlers' organizations inactive, little change seemed likely.

African Elites and Masses

While the pace of Portuguese assimilation increased after 1961, the emerging middle class of *assimilados* (in the cultural rather than the legal sense) was still politically and economically subordinate to the European community. The old *assimilado* organizations—the *Liga Nacional Africana* (National African League) and the *Associçao de Beneficencia e Cultural de Angola* (Welfare & Cultural Society)—lacked political effectiveness and were largely social welfare clubs of *mestiços* and some Africans in the Luanda area. While this Angolan elite enjoyed more opportunities in jobs and education—many of the leaders of the LNA, for example, had high school educations and were civil servants—few of their sons received any higher education. In the late 1960s in the newly established branch of Lisbon University in Luanda, the *Estudos Gerais Universitários* (General University Studies), there were few *mestiços* and even fewer Africans out of a student body of six hundred to eight hundred.[33] At this new university, securely enmeshed in the traditional Portuguese educational structure, the curriculum included mainly science, agronomy, and medicine. While introductory sociology was taught, the government was slow to permit the teaching of economics, a subject often considered politically sensitive to the regime in Lisbon.

If there was some improvement in the social position of the *assimilado* after 1961, a major development was in the expansion of opportunities in business and in better jobs and higher wages. For the African elite, able to get more education, the new economic boom was important. But for the African masses, now increasingly emigrating to Angolan cities and towns, the major problems continued to be lack of education, unemployment, and poor health. While more jobs were available than before 1961, the economy was not producing jobs fast enough to keep abreast of the population increases and the greater numbers of school-leavers. Cost of living rose with wages. New foreign enterprises could aid in economic development: West German, Japanese, South African, and American firms increased their investment commitments in the 1960s and thus created more jobs, higher wages, and better conditions.

The issue of land allocation continued to be a vital one for many Africans living outside towns. Although the land issue in Angola had never been as great a problem as it has been in South Africa and Rhodesia, in selected regions African grievances have been serious. Among the post-1961 reforms which affected African rural life was a revision of land ownership laws and an increase in areas set aside for African ownership. The government realized that a major Bakongo grievance which fed the fires of March 1961 was resentment felt toward European land ownership patterns in northern Angola. Often unable to acquire more land in the 1950s, the Bakongo saw the newly arrived Portuguese farmers and shopkeepers buying up the best farm lands near roads and in valleys.[34] Again, the actual impact of new land ownership laws is uncertain, for even by 1966 it was difficult for Africans in some areas to secure clear title to new lands.[35]

Many Angolans lived in great poverty. Here there was a stark contrast between underdeveloped Angola and industrialized South Africa. Angolans had fewer possessions than their South African brothers. While one sees almost no African-owned automobiles in Angola, in South Africa African ownership of automobiles is common. Poverty was especially visible in town life. In Angola the outstanding example of the African urban slum is the African section of Luanda, popularly known as the *musseques* (in the Kimbundu language "sandy places"). For over a generation this African shanty town built of makeshift materials and often without plumbing, running water, or sewers, has grown into a major community, several hundred thousand in population. Although the Luandan *musseques* are inhabited mainly by black Africans, a small number of Portuguese live there, just as they live interspersed with Africans on Luanda Island, which is located off the capital's harbor.[36] While there is more multiracial harmony in Luanda than in most other Southern African cities, this factor appears to have little influence on the brewing political crisis.

What of the perennial labor question? The Rural Labor Code of 1963 was designed by Lisbon to abolish finally African forced labor and to improve labor conditions for Africans outside the modern economy. In 1962–1963 Lisbon established in Luanda the *Instituto do Trabalho, Previdência e Acção Social* (Institute of Labor, Welfare and Social Action), headed by a distinguished Portuguese scholar, Sr. Afonso Mendes. The *Instituto*, supported by government funds, had several roles: it served as a watchdog over labor conditions (fining European employers for labor abuses), as sponsor of social welfare programs for African workers, as the administrator of a program (initiated in 1962–1963) to integrate Angolan labor and management into the metropolitan corporative system. In such a system, the government supervises the relations between labor and management. Despite its good intentions and its modern planning methods, the *Instituto* was still faced with problems which plagued previous leaders in Angola: continued abuses in labor activities, a small budget with which to effect improvements, and an African population still beset by infant mortality, emigration to outlying territories, and a subsistence economy psychology. Though forced labor was technically a thing of the past, many of the same labor problems remained.[37]

The black man in Angola usually occupies the lowest rung in every sphere of life. While there is little overt racial discrimination and no segregation (many "Right of Admission Reserved" signs disappeared during the 1960s), poverty and the lack of education often keep the African from enjoying many advantages already enjoyed by Portuguese. Although there is definitely a poor white class in Angola (farmers, waiters, servants), Africans, nevertheless, form the poorest strata in society. In Angola even though poor whites labor alongside black Africans (a very rare occurrence in much of Southern Africa), beggars are black, not white.[38] As noted earlier, the new Portuguese arrivals from Portugal tend to take jobs held before by black Africans: taxi drivers, bus drivers, waiters, artisans, barbers, and cooks.

The African in Angolan towns has observed how the atmosphere has become increasingly European. Luanda's suburbs in the upper section of the city resemble suburbs in Lisbon and Oporto. Posters in public places tell onlookers that "Angola is Portugal," a reminder of the prevailing belief. Even traditional Creole culture—a mixture of African and European—has been eroding under new European pressures. For example, *Carnaval*, the annual Luandan Creole celebration (similar to the "Carnaval" in Rio de Janeiro, Brazil) has become Europeanized to such an extent that older Luanda residents consider it almost unrecognizable compared to its pre-1940 heyday.[39] While the government has made an attempt to unite racial communities under the banner of Portuguese patriotism, such an effort in some ways is offset by the growing dominance of a Portuguese style of life which excludes respect for, or even knowledge of, African history and culture.

In the Angolan army, Africans have been given more opportunities to advance beyond the enlisted ranks. The army in the territory has 80 to 85 percent European and 15 to 20 percent African troops. This racial ratio was the reverse before 1958–1959, when Portugal began to build up large European-staffed security forces in anticipation of African nationalist activity.[40] Army service has advantages for the African recruit which he cannot find in some other occupations: steady wages, education to learn to read and write Portuguese (if he is illiterate), training in skills useful in civilian life, and benefits for his family. In the 1960s, however, it was difficult for an African to achieve a high military rank. One source claims that as of 1966 the highest officer rank attained by an African in Angola was captain.[41] The government continued its effort to promote interracial harmony by such measures as integrating all armed forces units and giving attention to such details as engraving on the

Luanda tombstones of all troops who fell in the guerrilla war since 1961 the inscription: "[Died] For Angola."

With the lack of reliable evidence and the difficulty of holding frank discussions with Africans *within* Angola, it is no wonder that we know little of the attitude of the mass of Angolans. Over 5 million strong, they live much as they lived before 1961; although life has improved for some and forced labor has been abolished, it is probable that discontent is strong among many. For some, fatalism has become a way of life. For every Angolan who has fled to the Congo, Zambia, or elsewhere, there are eight or nine inside Angola still struggling for a living. The superiority of Portuguese firepower and the existence of a police state atmosphere are sufficient reasons for a cautious peasant attitude. Meanwhile, the struggle for the allegiance of the Angolan masses continues, with Portugal on the one side and Angolan exiled nationalists on the other. While most Angolan peasants may not be exactly what Frantz Fanon considered antirevolutionary anathema and what he described as "an undivided mass, still living in the middle ages, endlessly marking time"[42], it is still true that many black Angolans are not joining African nationalist groups at this time.

The Portuguese Counterrevolution

The 1961 crisis shook Portugal almost as much as it shook Angola. It forced the government, however much it might be denied now, to take a new perspective and to effect changes which were long overdue. The 1961 crisis acted as a catalyst, a force lacking in the Portuguese experience during 1939–1945 when the other colonial powers were transfigured and devastated by World War II. In many ways *a confusão* in Angola was a concentrated form of a World War II awakening which spurred economic development and material progress and brought some reform. What seemed missing in this case was significant political reform, because Portuguese national determination, as exemplified by Dr. Salazar's regime in Lisbon, rallied and reinforced the effort to keep "political unity," a euphemism for continued colonial and national sovereignty in Africa. The regime attempted to mobilize the Portuguese populace with visions of a wartime crisis, national sacrfice for the sake of preserving historic legacies, and anti-Communistic fervor. By 1964 Portugal was fielding the largest overseas force in her history. As Dr. Adriano Moreira described it, Portugal now experienced "the greatest call to arms in Portuguese history."[43] No plans for decolonization were discussed and the ultimate goal seemed to be Portuguese paramountcy.

Several factors in Portugal and in Angola precluded an easy transition to decolonization. First, there was the increased economic value of Angola to Portugal. The discoveries of rich iron and oil reserves and the increasing investment commitments of international companies complicated the economic interests of Portugal. While in 1962 Richard Hammond could postulate that the withdrawal from Portuguese Africa would have consequences that were "serious but short of catastrophic,"[44] by 1969–1970 it seemed that this judgment was somewhat of an understatement. Vested economic interests in Portugal, some of which played a role in the division of political power following Dr. Salazar's passing from power in 1968, appeared more determined than ever to pressure Lisbon into maintaining the status quo overseas.[45]

Certain observers, including African nationalists, believed the new economic bonds were even more complex than this. Radical exiled Angolans feared the worst. In a polemical yet carefully documented book published in Brazil in 1967, Dr. Américo Boavida, a medical director for the MPLA in eastern Angola, suggested another factor complicating decolonization.[46] In the angry tradition of Angolan protest writings of the late nineteenth century, Boavida suggested that Angolans are victims of a "system of exploitation and of rapine without parallel in the history of colonialism."[47] Curiously enough, he asserted, Portugal was not the sole villain in its own house because it was a "vassal" of large international monopoly companies, international corporations, and cartels, such as Diamang (which holds the diamond monopoly in Angola) and Tanganyika Concessions Limited. Increasingly, he believed, Angola was tied to foreign industrial powers in the West, while Portugal, an economic parasite reaping some profits, was not the "ultimate threat to the sovereignty of the Angolan people." Instead, the threat was new foreign capital invested since 1961. Boavida went on to state that for the Angolan revolution—viewed largely through MPLA-colored glasses, in his case—the most revolutionary Angolans would be not rural workers but the "urban proletariat," a group which under the restrictive circumstances of Portuguese control had little communication with exiled nationalists. Boavida attacked not the Portuguese people, but the army and what he called "the system."[48]

This radical nationalist clearly appreciated the importance of the Portuguese counterrevolution. In his verbal attacks on "colonial reformism" and "pseudo-reformism" in Angola, he suggests that this post-1961 reformism made the leader of Portugal (at that time Dr. Salazar) "an even more dangerous enemy for the Angolan people."[49]

Besides domestic reforms and international pressures to maintain Portuguese control in Angola, there are Portuguese counterpressures on her African neighbors. These were included in Portugal's foreign policy in Africa and were meant to accomplish several objectives. In the short run, Portugal hoped to relieve hostile frontier pressures between the Congo (Brazzaville) and the Congo (Kinshasa) and Angola and also between Zambia and Angola. Portugal's long-run objectives were less clear, but it is probable that counterpressures were brought to bear partially to force the independent black states to the north and east to recognize Portuguese control as more than a temporary phenomenon. Such counterpressures took many forms: an informal alliance with the secessionist regime of Moise Tshombe of Katanga during 1960–1963 (when Portugal aided and even supplied white mercenaries in eastern Angola in the struggle against United Nations intervention); the supplying and harboring of white mercenaries later in 1964–1966 in their struggle both for and against the central government of the Congo; the temporary closing of the Benguela Railway to copper shipments from the Congo and Zambia in retaliation for Angolan nationalist attacks on the railway in 1966–1967; the selective bombing of the Zambian border area along the Angolan and Mozambican borders during 1968 in retaliation for Zambia's aid to Angolan nationalists; the secret police activity of the Portuguese in the independent neighboring states and capitals; implicit threats to deal severely with Zambia in case of further support for Angolan and Mozambique nationalists;[50] and, finally, Portugal's policy toward secessionist Biafra and the Biafran-Nigerian civil war in 1967–1969. Although the objectives of Biafran policy were not clear, this commitment to Biafra involved little more than landing rights in Lisbon and São Tomé for Biafran relief flights, some sympathy from the Portuguese academic community,[51] the publication of pro-Biafra materials, and some humanitarian contributions. If the government's objectives in its Biafran policy were uncertain, it was clear nevertheless that more conservative Portuguese leaders hoped that Biafran success would divide and therefore weaken black African nationalism in independent Africa.

These counterpressures did produce occasional concessions and relief for Portugal in the outlying African states. At times such Portuguese acts limited Congolese and Zambian aid to Angolan nationalists. One of the more notable developments prompted by Portuguese counterpressures occurred in Zambia in 1967–1969. President Kenneth Kaunda began to deny officially that any African insurgents enjoyed his support. He canceled the visa of a leading Angolan nationalist, Jonas Savimbi of UNITA (Union for the Total Independence of Angola) who was conducting operations in eastern Angola. Savimbi was then forced to leave for Cairo.[52] Nevertheless, whatever the short-range value of these counterpressures, which are closely tied to Portugal's counterinsurgency methods within Angola, it is difficult to believe that they could be a long-range panacea for African nationalist activity.

Indeed, in surveying the total results of Portugal's counterrevolutionary activity in Angola, the most difficult distinctions in the present situation are those between short- and long-range effects on the Angolan masses. Portugal's counterrevolution has employed flexible means especially in short-range activities—such as counterinsurgency, counterpressures on neighboring territories, internal reforms in economic and social spheres, and a persistent propaganda campaign. Nevertheless, the long-range plans for the future always come up against the stark fact that Lisbon has not prepared for a smooth devolution of political power.

Through the Angolan Glass Darkly

By the end of the 1960s, observers of the Angolan scene were hard put to set forth a timetable of decisive change, especially in the political realm. While the military situation became more complex than a stalemate described by Professor Ronald H. Chilcote in 1967,[53] it was not yet moving toward an African nationalist victory. Professor John Marcum wrote in 1969 that a long costly struggle between Portugal and the nationalists was ahead.[54] Clearly, the prophets of doom for both sides—at least in the short run—were proved wrong.

Despite the difficulty of predicting a timetable, it was certain that important Portuguese leaders were not counting on an easy military victory; some believed that even successful military activity against what they termed the *terroristas* was not the final answer to post-1961 problems. The present governor-general of Angola, when he served as governor of the war-ravaged Uige district, was quoted in a Portuguese book in 1963 as saying that Portugal will "win" in Angola only with "a radical transformation of the social environment."[55] This high official was probably saying that unless the social status of the African improved and until the social attitudes of the dominant white society were "transformed," in effect, a long-range victory would be impossible.

In the unpredictability of the Angolan situation, there are many variables. First are the attitudes and actions of the black Angolan masses; so far many have remained quiescent. Second are the capacity and willingness of Portuguese officials in Angola to execute reforms. Third are the attitudes and actions of Portuguese settlers. Fourth is the activity of the exiled Angolan nationalists. Finally, there is what might be termed the Lisbon factor,[56] or the policy of the government of Portugal, which is now under the leadership of Dr. Marcello Caetano, former minister for the colonies.

While it is possible that the decisive action leading to decolonization in Angola will occur in Africa, it is also conceivable that a decision by Lisbon could rapidly alter the situation. Certainly, the cabinet which took office in September 1968 brought some changes, and even though there was a protest sit-in in a Catholic Church in Lisbon on New Year's Day 1969 and rising oppositionist protest against the three wars in Africa, the direction of Dr. Caetano's policy still could not be safely charted by outside observers. For the policy depended in part on the strength of the new prime minister. Did he have the popular support required to override the wishes of the army command and the economic interests who stood for the status quo? Could he become for Portugal in Portuguese Africa what De Gaulle had been for France in Algeria? These highly sensitive political questions regarding the Lisbon factor could not be easily answered.

In late 1970 several developments led some observers to believe that the Caetano Government was about to alter the relationship between Lisbon and Portuguese Africa. Caetano made speeches in which he denied much of the Salazarist rhetoric for remaining in Africa, and stated that Portugal remained essentially to protect the persons and property of Portuguese citizens, of all races. Slated for National Assembly debate in March 1971 was a proposed constitutional revision which would give widened powers to Angola and Mozambique as "autonomous states," not "overseas provinces." As of the time of writing, the outcome of the debate or the meaning of such proposed changes remained unclear.

Portugal continues to control Angola. If the present policies have supported what the Portuguese have referred to as "continuity," this is no sure guarantee of future success. The events of 1961 shattered many illusions both in the Portuguese camp and in the African one. The sustained Portuguese will, insofar as it is expressed through the national leadership, is seemingly intransigent. At the same time the Angolan nationalists declare their faith in "the irrevocable march of history."[57] Neither position inspires much predictability regarding the future of Angola but both the illuminate the nature of the struggle. Several variants of nationalism are in conflict, and time will test them both in their struggle for the mastery of the country.

3

Mozambique: The African Nationalist Response to Portuguese Imperialism and Underdevelopment

RONALD H. CHILCOTE

In this chapter we are concerned with stages of Portuguese imperialism in Mozambique. We examine the structure of imperialism, especially the relation of the metropole to its outlying territory and to foreign influences which tend to dominate the whole imperial complex. In this system the metropole maintains monopoly power, resulting in misuses and misdirection of available resources.[1] Such a pattern has prevailed since the fifteenth century. It can be understood by noting differences between rulers and ruled, taking account of the contradictions inherent in colonial policy, and examining the revolutionary response to Portuguese imperialism. Thus we focus on forms of African protest and resistance among the black masses. We consider early African associational activity as well as the formation and evolution of exile nationalist organizations. Briefly, we review the continuing guerrilla war against the Portuguese and speculate on its course. Finally, we assess Mozambique's role within Southern Africa, examine relations with neighboring nations, notably South Africa, and offer some perspective on the future.

Patterns of Continuity

Three stages have characterized Portuguese imperialism and control in East Africa.[2] Initially in the fifteenth and early sixteenth centuries, Portuguese imperialism and control was based on a system of barter or purchase of one commodity for another. Exploitation was limited to domination over the exchange of commodities—principally ivory and gold—along the coast for the spice trade of Asia. Through control of the major ports and other coastal points, the Portuguese secured their position in Mozambique and challenged the Arab hegemony over trade with the African interior. The capture of Sofala ensured Portuguese commercial ties with the African kingdoms which ruled the interior. This imperialism of exchange was reinforced by technologically superior military weaponry, essentially artillery, which was used in the burning of Mombasa and the bombardment of other strategic points.

A shift from an imperialism of exchange to an imperialism of extraction accompanied Portuguese overseas expansion at a time when other European nations could not compete. This shift involved expanding control beyond the forts along a littoral and systematically conquering the extensive hinterlands. Rather than simply enforcing the advantageous exchange of primary products, the Portuguese moved to seize control of their extraction. During the last half of the sixteenth century, penetration up the Zambezi River valley resulted in the seizure of the ports of Tete and Sena from Arab and mixed Arab-African traders. Treaties between the Portuguese and the Monomotapa, hereditary chief of the interior, precipitated intertribal conflict between him and the subchiefs of his federation. This dissension resulted in raids on the Portuguese settlements and occasional disruption of trade routes, but disunity among the Africans also ensured a continued Portuguese presence in the area.

The imperialism of extraction remained intact until the late nineteenth century, in spite of Portugal's incorporation into the Spanish kingdom from 1580 to 1640 and the rise of Dutch influence and seizure of many Portuguese possessions which brought an end to the spice empire. Northeast Brazilian sugar saved Portuguese prosperity as Portuguese imperialism shifted from Asia to Latin America.[3] But the demand for labor on the Brazilian plantations motivated traders in Mozambique to turn from gold and ivory to slaves as the major export. Additionally, efforts to settle Mozambique focused on the system of *prazos* or land concessions whereby large estates were settled by owners authorized by the Portuguese crown.

With the division of Africa by the West European powers in the late nineteenth century, Portuguese imperialism evolved from an extractive to a "transformer" imperialism. This new imperialism, based on technological superiority, was part of the general thrust of European expansion in the Third World. Its motive force was industrialization, and it demanded large quantities of raw materials from the outlying colonial territories in return for which it provided manufactured goods. Portugal, caught up in the "scramble" for Africa, found it necessary to consolidate the remnants of its empire. What took shape became the foundation for the Portuguese domination in Mozambique today.

The implementation of the new economic imperialism involved two schemes. The first, adopted from an English and Dutch experiment, introduced the system of chartered companies to Mozambique. In 1891 the northern district of Cabo Delgado was granted to the Niassa Company, and an area between the Save and Zambezi Rivers was given to the Mozambique Company. A year later another concession went to the Zambézia Company.[4] A second scheme involved the effective occupation of territory and the subduing by military force of the African populations. For decades military expeditions had been sent against African insurgents in many parts of the colony, but not until about 1895 was Portugal able to claim any success. Under Mousinho de Albuquerque and António Ennes, the Portuguese finally succeeded in pacifying the Gaza region north of Lourenço Marques. However, as late as 1918 the Portuguese were still waging "pacification" campaigns.

In more recent decades Portugal maintained control over the territory through the establishment in the Limpopo and Zambézia valleys of planned agricultural communities run by Portuguese immigrants. After the nationalist outbreak in late 1964, a government resettlement plan moved several hundred thousand Africans to new, guarded villages where they would be isolated from the guerrilla activity. Further hegemony over the territory was assured by attraction of foreign capital, to build infrastructure—power, transportation, and so forth—as a foundation for both mineral extraction and agricultural production as well as an incipient industrial base; the key to such development was the construction of one of Africa's largest dams at Cabora Bassa on the Zambezi.[5] Foreign capital also plays a massive role in the exploitation of the territory's resources. The foreign corporations provide the capital which the government lacks, and in return they are assured conditions of stability and profitability through the maintenance of a colonial administration and a military force; the profits are shared between the corporations and the regime.[6]

THE STRUCTURE OF IMPERIALISM IN MOZAMBIQUE

Compared to the rest of Western Europe, Portugal today remains a poor and underdeveloped nation. Yet the remnants of the old empire continue to be maintained under Portuguese hegemony. One reason for this apparent contradiction is the fervent Portuguese nationalism based on historical traditions, symbols, and experience. Pervading that nationalism is a mystique of imperial destiny that for centuries has caught the imagination of Portuguese policymakers. Accordingly, Portugal's mariners not only discovered the world but fulfilled a special mission to transmit Catholicism and other Portuguese values to the tropical world. Nationhood was conceived as a pan-Lusitanian community stretching around the world and embracing many races into a cultural unity.[7]

A more important and fundamental reason for Portuguese continuity in Mozambique and elsewhere, however, is attributable to economics and the influence of England in the underdevelopment of Portugal. In 1703, during its extraction stage of imperialism, Portugal signed the Methuen treaty with England. Free entry was granted to British cloth, and in exchange Portuguese wine was given preferential entry into England. With the expansion of vineyards, cereal production declined; with the entry of British goods, a perennial trade deficit developed. And Portugal's textile industry stagnated.[8] The result was disastrous, for Portugal itself became a satellite to the English metropolis. The Marquis of Pombal, prime minister of Portugal in 1755, declared:

> The English had firmly bound the nation into a state of dependence. They had conquered it without the inconvenience of a conquest. . . . England had become mistress of the entire commerce of Portugal, and all the trade of the country was carried on by her agents. The English were at the same time furnishers and the retailers of all the necessities of life that the country required. Having a monopoly of everything, no business was carried on but through their hands.[9]

English dominance in Portuguese economic and political life prevailed through the nineteenth and well into the twentieth century. With the advent of the new imperialism, the establishment of charter companies in Mozambique was distinguished by a predominance of British capital in the nineteenth century.[10] The pattern of Anglo-Portuguese financial relationships today is somewhat similar, which partially explains the continued, if not still predominant, British interest in Mozambique. Within Portugal foreign capital penetration, notably British, is well advanced; British influence is ever present. Anglo-Scottish families, resident for generations in northern Oporto, dominate much of the commercial and industrial life there. English capital holds a monopoly over bus and train transportation as well as over the country's telephone system and about 30 percent of the insurance firms, and there are strong interests in shipbuilding and electrical goods.[11] Thus there has been an apparent close interconnection in the economy and the sociopolitical structure between Portuguese and English interests. One might expect relations of the two nations' ruling elites and governing classes also to be closely linked, although to date we have scanty empirical evidence for such a supposition.

Autocratic control characterizes the privileged few who comprise Portugal's ruling oligarchy. Long supported with concessions by the conservative and stable regime (1928–1968) of dictator Dr. António de Oliveria Salazar and present Prime Minister Dr. Marcelo Caetano, this ruling group has played a prominent role in economic activities. The nation's perspectives on development are in large measure shaped by the interests of this group which has gravitated toward joint participation with foreign investors, frequently British and South African, in capital ventures within Mozambique. The group itself is a traditional, socially exclusive, intermarrying elite which pervades the power structure through control of "interlocking directorships which link banks, industries, and insurance houses" and through "an all-embracing network of cartels [which] overlays the whole economy and ensures monopoly profit-levels from it."[12] The consolidation of economic power is represented by perhaps not more than eleven families, among which are the M. Pinto de Azevedo group which controls a large segment of the textile industry; the Pinto Basto family, prominent in shipping; the Espírito Santo family, associated with a bank chain and luxury hotels; and the De Mello family. In agriculture the four largest Portuguese landowners—Poser de Andrade, Santos Jorge, the Duke of Cadaval, and the Duke of Palmeta—hold nearly a quarter million acres, the equivalent of land held by some fifty thousand small farmers.[13] Considerable economic wealth is retained by the Bragança family which was ousted from monarchist power in 1910, and, of course, the Roman Catholic Church controls substantial property and other holdings throughout Portugal and the empire.

Although in the past the political suppression of the dictatorship often tended to obscure the relationship between the regime and the oligarchy, close ties between the two have prevailed, closely linking politics and economics. In 1958, forty-two ministers and former ministers, four ambassadors, and four governors or former governors occupied 116 positions on the boards of directors of the nation's largest enterprises.[14] This pattern was still in effect in 1969 when Alberto Franco Nogueira, who had been Portugal's foreign affairs minister for eight years, resigned to campaign for a seat in the National Assembly. Not only did he win his seat, representing the Lisbon district, but Nogueira was appointed to the Overseas Council, a policymaking body, as a regular member and also as the administrator to the board of directors of the Benguela Railway.[15] In monarchist circles, the Bragança family's political interests are manifested through the semiofficial *Causa Monárquica* which has established a network of advisory committees throughout Portugal and the overseas territories, including Mozambique. The close ties between the Roman Catholic Church and the state have been assured by a conservative majority led by Cardinal Patriarch Manuel Gonçalves Cerejeira, a close friend of the late Dr. Salazar. In fact, the regime traditionally has recruited cabinet ministers and other officials from the conservative Catholic *Centro Académico da Democracia Cristã* (CADC) in Coimbra. In Mozambique some dissent against the regime was voiced by the former bishop of Beira, the late Sebastião Soares de Resende, an author of several books and publisher of the "liberal" newspaper, *Diário de Moçambique*, who was concerned with the exploitation of the African worker. Resende, however, "conceived of an independent Mozambique only within a community of Portuguese interests, cultural, religious, and economic. His intention was to liberalize policy rather than to change it radically. But when finally his opinions began to annoy the Salazar regime, he was ordered by the Vatican to stop publishing them."[16]

The structure and character of the elitist Portuguese power structure extends to Mozambique where the population, according to a Portuguese source, is stratified into three distinct socioeconomic levels. At the top is a minority, estimated at between 2 and 3 percent of the population, comprised of European whites, Asians, mulattoes, and a few black Africans concentrated in urban areas and in the agricultural and mining developments. This extension of Portugal's ruling class is "a Westernized minority, and almost all of them are urbanized. They are employed in modern activities . . . , the State deriving a greater proportion of its public revenue from it." At the second level is a minority—about 3½ percent of the population—composed of various races but predominantly Africans of rural origin who have "detribalized themselves, thus abandoning, at least partially, the cultural and social habits of their origin. They turn, in general, into a salaried (proletariat)." The third level is made up of the mass of Africans, mostly peasants living under a subsistence economy and governed by traditional law.[17]

MANIFESTATIONS OF IMPERIALISM IN MOZAMBIQUE

Portuguese imperialism in Mozambique has been principally characterized by ideology, technological orientations, and exploitative labor practices.

Portugal's official ideology is corporativism, drawn from the experience of Italian, German, and French fascism. Theoretically, the state was to act as an arbiter between conflicting interest groups organized into corporations of employers and workers, but in practice the corporations are not fully operative.[18] This basic structure is shrouded in bureaucratic machinery through which the regime mobilizes institutional support. This machinery encompasses the various branches of government, including the ministries, the National Assembly, the Chamber of Corporations, the *União Nacional*, and related political, economic, and social agencies.

Within this framework it has been almost impossible for the opposition in Mozambique to participate in politics. While candidates often campaigned against the Salazar regime, none won an election. For the first elections under the Caetano government, seven opposition members (two lawyers, a secondary school teacher, an economist, a businessman, an office clerk, and a student) declared their candidacy in September 1969 but were promptly disqualified on the grounds that they did not offer proof of Portuguese origin.[19] Roughly 96 percent of the 82,539 registered voters (less than 1 percent of the total estimated population of 7 million) cast ballots in the October elections and the *União Nacional* slate, which had campaigned in favor of Portugal's continued policies in Africa, was duly elected. Of the seven new deputies, one was a representative in the Mozambique Economic and Social Council, another was president of the Association of Landowners of Beira, and a third was a practicing lawyer.[20]

The institutional and ideological façade is kept in place by a machinery of repression maintained by the military and police forces. The army, which absorbs 90 percent of the military budget, is the most important of the armed forces and maintains a force of more than fifty thousand men in Mozambique. High military officials customarily occupy the posts of governor-general and district governor. In fact, normally about 30 percent of the cabinet posts are assigned to military officers (who held four of fifteen posts in the Caetano government which was named in March 1969).[21] Supporting the regime are also at least five different paramilitary forces, including the feared secret police known as the *Direcão Geral de Segurança* and formerly as *Polícia Internacional e de Defesa do Estado* (PIDE).[22] PIDE was established on the German model, and its leadership was trained by the Gestapo during the thirties and by Italians sent to Portugal by Mussolini during the Spanish Civil War. It was established in Mozambique about 1961, and it has been particularly active since the outbreak of the guerrilla struggle in late 1964.

Historically, technology has served as a basis for Portuguese imperialism in Mozambique. During the early centuries of the empire, the imperialism of exchange was reinforced by the development of superior artillery as a technological means of violence to assure dominance over the outlying possessions. In shifting from exchange to extraction (which involved the domination of the hinterland), the Portuguese were able to gain control of raw material sources and markets through treaty arrangements and over centuries to maintain a certain hegemony through the use of sporadic colonization schemes and Roman Catholic missionaries who penetrated, and remained in, the interior. Technology to some extent and certainly the systematic use of violence through military expeditions, armed with superior weaponry, aided the Portuguese cause. Yet the Portuguese were relatively unsuccessful despite disorder in the African kingdoms.[23] During the implementation of newer forms of imperialism in the late nineteenth century, technological superiority was applied to colonial reality—to the need to exploit human and natural resources and to justify the Portuguese presence in the territory.

Exploitative labor practices have also characterized Portuguese imperialism in Mozambique. It was not until the eighteenth century that the slave trade became the principal commerce for the Portuguese on the east coast of Africa, although they had earlier traded in slaves as had the Arabs and Africans before them.[24] Slavery, of course, was the earliest and most conspicuous form of labor exploitation employed by the Portuguese, but forced labor during recent times has been somewhat obscured by Portuguese officialdom and the relative isolation of Mozambique.[25] The systematic use of forced labor and the human oppression involved in its use are reflected in wages and working conditions, forcible displacement of literally hundreds of thousands of persons, and widespread migration and emigration of Africans. Many forms of labor exploitation have been employed: correctional labor for Africans who have violated some criminal or labor code; obligatory labor imposed by the government when voluntary workers are insufficient to carry out public works projects; contract labor for "idle" Africans; and voluntary labor for workers who contract directly with the employers rather than being recruited by the regime. The result is African subservience to the Portuguese patron. According to Professor Duffy, "Whether the African has been an export commodity, a domestic slave, a *liberto*, *contratado*, or *voluntário*, his fundamental relationship with the Portuguese has remained the same—that of a servant."[26] Labor exploitation has resulted in displacement of most male workers. After a year of direct observation in Mozambique, anthropologist Marvin Harris noted: "It can be said with absolute certainty . . . that less than five percent of the mature, able-bodied males in southern Mozambique are legally entitled to remain within the confines of their homesteads."[27]

The observations of Duffy and Harris were made prior to Portugal's signing the international labor conventions of 1959 and the abolishment of old labor codes in favor of a new code, decreed in 1962, and revoking of the native statute which officially divided the Mozambican population into "civilized" and "native" groupings.[28] Reflecting on his earlier study and the legislative changes of the early sixties, Harris later observed that "there is not the slightest prospect that the *de facto* juridical and political distinctions between the former *indigenas* or their descendants and the former civilized or their descendants is about to be abolished."[29] He noted that the survival of the old system was evident in the process by which new identity documents were issued and that Portuguese administrators maintained almost absolute control over the African's social and economic life.

Two other aspects of labor exploitation deserve mention. First is the pattern of labor migration to South Africa, based on agreements worked out with the Portuguese government. The arrangement was initiated with the Mozambique-Transvaal Convention of 1909; this convention and subsequent ones provided labor for the South African mines while roughly half of South Africa's commercial traffic was to flow through Lourenço Marques. In 1909 some seventy-five thousand Africans were contracted and the number annually varied from sixty-five thousand to one hundred thousand thereafter.[30] The South African government pays the Portuguese government for each recruit, permits the Portuguese to continue taxing the African while residing abroad, and turns over about half the recruit's wages to the Portuguese until he is repatriated within the maximum contract time of eighteen months. During the half century from 1902 until the early fifties more than eighty thousand African recruits died while working the South African mines, according to official figures.[31]

The second aspect of labor exploitation is a system of legally forced cultivation among African producers north of the Zambezi. Until 1961 private companies with concessions in the principal cotton-growing zones were charged with supervising the farming of more than a half million African farmers in order to guarantee Portugal large supplies of cotton. Under the system Africans were given seed, assigned quotas of cotton to be produced on their land, and required to sell their crop to the companies at fixed prices, well below market levels. Critics charged that such a system coerced Africans to produce cotton on land forcibly converted from the subsistence economy; further, it ensured the privileged position of the cotton concessionaires and the compulsory supply of Mozambican cotton to Portugal at prices lower than world market. Legislation in 1961 abolished the compulsory cultivation of cotton and terminated the cotton concessions in August 1966. Little evidence is available on the impact of these changes, but cotton production in the north was reportedly in decline and this was attributable partially to increased guerrilla activity in the region.[32]

The Revolutionary Response to Portuguese Imperialism

An African perspective of Mozambique is gleaned from the many cases of resistance, sporadic and organized rebellions, and protest through semi-official channels, and the emergent nationalist struggle against the Portuguese presence in the territory. An indication of early difficulties in Mozambique was evident during the seventeenth century when the Arabs challenged the Portuguese grip on the coastal trade and provoked uprisings at Mombasa, Zanzibar, and other strategic points. Portuguese sovereignty north of Cabo Delgado was destroyed, and the loss of Mombasa demonstrated the futility of the attempt to convert the Swahili coast to Christianity, for, according to a major historian of the period, the Muslims "were unassailable."[33] In the interior, where traditionally the Arab had dominated the trade with the African kingdoms, the Portuguese encountered hostility.

In the early seventeenth century the Monomotapa, Gatsi Rusere, seems to have used the Portuguese to consolidate his power and put down rebellious rivals; then, failing to receive any tribute from the Portugese, he began to raid their camps and briefly denied them their silver mines and disrupted the gold trade. About 1613 a rebellious chief Chombe and an African force, equipped for the first time with firearms, nearly cut off the lower Zambesi from the interior Portuguese settlements at Tete and nearby areas. Toward the end of the century, Changamire, a minor chieftain, routed the Monomotapa's army and turned against the Portuguese settlements of the interior, destroying Dambarare and ending Portuguese political influence beyond the present Mozambican borders.[34]

The Portuguese established the *prazo* system in an effort to strengthen their tenuous hold on the interior and in the process replaced the African chiefs with a class of large estate owners who wielded absolute power and authority over their African subjects and who subsequently tended to operate independent of royal control. In several instances *prazo* owners confronted Portuguese authority. During several decades of the last half of the nineteenth century, for example, Joaquim José da Cruz or Nhaúde and his son, António Vicente or Bonga, established headquarters at Massangano and levied tolls on all traffic along the Zambezi, defeated several Portuguese expeditions sent to dislodge them, destroyed the town of Tete, and gained control of a large expanse of territory. Not until 1888 did the Portuguese succeed in capturing Massangano and the rebels from East Africa.[35]

Another challenge to the Portuguese during the nineteenth century was the invasion by several Ngoni tribes into the Gaza region. Eventually, they besieged the fortress at Lourenço Marques, just south of the Gaza, attacked Inhambane in 1834 and Sofala two years later, overran the *prazos* south of the Zambezi, and occupied large expanses of claimed Portuguese territory, establishing a kingdom that stretched from the Zambezi to south of the Limpopo. Official relations were maintained with the Portugese, although late in the century there were numerous African raids on their settlements and demands for tribute. About 1884 Gungunhana emerged as leader of the African kingdom; pragmatically, he cooperated with the increasingly active Portuguese while at the same time looking to the British as a potential ally. After a British ultimatum in January 1890 and a final agreement in 1891 which limited Portuguese control to its present territory, Gungunhana apparently consented to British protection over his dominions in return for ceding both Beira and the mouth of the Limpopo to the British South Africa Company. Rebellion ensued and eventually the Portuguese, under António Ennes, won major victories in late 1895, defeating the Gaza force at its capital Manjacaze and capturing Gungunhana; not until August 1897 with the death of Gungunhana's great military leader, however, was the Gaza region declared "pacified."[36]

African protest in Mozambique evolved from the early experience of Portuguese colonialism and imperialism. Mass forced labor, discrimination and exploitation, and omnipresent foreign capital provided the common experience of fear and reaction and the basis for coherence among different ethnic groupings. There evolved the "simple psychological rejection of the colonizer and his culture . . . an attitude bound up with the cultural tradition of the group, its past struggles with the Portuguese and present experience of subjection."[37] The late Dr. Eduardo Mondlane, the African nationalist hero and martyr, noted the expression of African revulsion to Portuguese culture through traditional oral expression—songs, dances, carvings, and the like. According to an African saying, for example, "When the whites came to our country we had the land, and they had the bible; now we have the bible, and they have the land." An African song ridicules the manners of the Portuguese who insist upon the African greeting them with *bom dia* or good day. The Makonde wood carving depicts a madonna holding a demon.[38]

Traditionally, under Portuguese rule, the black Mozambicans were divided into an illiterate mass of peasant subsistence farmers and migrant laborers and a privileged minority of *assimilados* (or "civilized" nonwhites, the majority of whom were mulatto) who were granted citizenship because they could read, write, and speak Portuguese fluently, were self-supporting, and were well behaved with a certain educational background. An *assimilado*, however, never achieved equal status with fellow white citizens, for he generally held an inferior economic position due to wage differentials and he was forced to carry an identity card.[39] Within these two groupings latent manifestations of protest and resistance surfaced in a variety of ways.

ORGANIZED MASS AFRICAN PROTEST AND RESISTANCE

While anticolonialism had traditionally been manifested through art forms, protest among the mass of disenfranchised blacks was crystallized into the cooperative movement which was organized by peasants in northern Mozambique in the 1950s. At first the movement strove to improve economic conditions for peasant farmers through the rationalization of cultivation and the sale of agricultural produce, but Portuguese authorities placed restrictions on its activities, imposed taxes on it, and kept its meetings under surveillance. The consequence was hostility and the beginnings of some politicalization in the area around Mueda where a major demonstration took place during 1960, culminating in the Portuguese massacre of five hundred protesting black Africans.[40] One of the leaders of the Makonde peoples of the north was Mzee Lázaro Kavandame, who became politically active about 1957. In 1963 he joined Mozambican nationalists in Dar es Salaam where he became a member of the central committee of the *Frente de Libertação de Moçambique* (FRELIMO), led by Mondlane at the time. He also became FRELIMO's provincial secretary of the district of Cabo Delgado.[41]

Another form of mass black resistance involved organized active resistance in urban areas, especially after World War II. There had been occasional protest as a result of poor working conditions by African stevedores in Lourenço Marques during the late 1930s. Outside of the corporative labor unions, in which membership rarely was extended to assimilated blacks, there was no organized outlet to protest against the poverty of the urban proletariat. This explains the reoccurrence of strikes during 1947 and an abortive uprising in Lourenço Marques during 1948 which resulted in the deportation to São Tomé and imprisonment of several hundred Africans. Another strike in 1956 ended with the death of forty-nine stevedores. Again in 1963 dock strikes at Lourenço Marques, Beira, and Nacala were suppressed by authorities who had apparently failed to pay a promised wage increase. The brutal response of the Portuguese to these spontaneous and localized developments prompted the African opposition to abandon strike tactics as an effective political weapon.[42]

ORGANIZED *Assimilado* PROTEST AND RESISTANCE

Assimilado protest and resistance were manifested in two ways. One was through journalism and other literary forms. The protest press was represented by the weekly, *O Brado Africano*, established in the early 1920s as one of the first African newspapers on the continent, although it succumbed to the regime's system of press censorship. Through poetry the *assimilado* and the mulatto revealed their alienation from colonial values and ideas and sought an identification in which "the foreign culture was being assimilated and being radically transformed by African realities, although the process engendered bitter conflicts for the individuals." [see footnote 43 for reference,—Eds.] During the first decades of the present century, there were isolated poetic outbursts of sorrow and despair, as shown, for example, in the writing of Rui de Noronha (1909–1943): "If God is just and good, why do I know evil and injustice?" Or his hopes for freedom: "Wake up! Your sleep is deeper than the earth. . . Listen to the voice of progress, that other Nazarene who holds out his hand to you and says 'Africa, get up and go!' " Political consciousness and a new national dimension appear in the poetry after World War II. Poetry assumes a subversive role and exerts a liberating revolutionary impact as in the lines of the poet, José Craveirinha, who angrily attacks Portuguese exploitation: "from the hunger of Mozambique I will give you the remnants of your greed." Poets like Craveirinha, Noémia de Sousa, Rui Nogar, and Malangatana Gowenha Valente contributed to a consciousness in which Africa is reaffirmed as the motherland, and the black man is called upon to revolt on behalf of the suffering and exploited Mozambicans.[43]

Assimilado protest also took root in associational activity. One of the earliest associations was the *Grêmio Africano*. Established in the early 1920s for mulattoes and other racially mixed peoples, it later evolved into the *Associação Africana*. During the 1930s a radical faction of black Africans broke away to form an *Instituto Negrófilo* after the *Associação*'s leadership had become subservient to an alarmed colonial regime. Later, under government pressure, the

Instituto was renamed the *Centro Associativo dos Negros de Moçambique*. Another grouping, the *Associação dos Naturais de Moçambique*, originally founded on behalf of whites born in Mozambique, encouraged membership of other racial groups in the 1950s and supported a policy of social integration between whites and blacks, leaned toward independence from Portugal and launched a scholarship program to support education for Africans. Eventually, the government intervened and replaced the leadership, thereby ending the association's effectiveness and "with its demise as a multi-racial nucleus may have gone all the hopes for a racially tolerant Mozambique."[44] In 1949 Eduardo Mondlane and other Mozambican students who had been attending school in South Africa formed a *Núcleo dos Estudantes Africanos Secundários de Moçambique* (*NESAM*) which was an offshoot of the *Centro Associativo*. NESAM engaged in political activities in an effort to socialize and radicalize black secondary school students while at the same time it established a nationwide network of communications which after 1964 was employed in the FRELIMO's underground throughout Mozambique.[45]

During the late 1950s there evolved a political opposition to Portuguese policy in Mozambique, which was manifested sometimes openly but usually clandestinely. One of the movements which was viewed suspiciously by authorities was the *Movimento Democrático de Moçambique* established by white Mozambicans who in April 1961 petitioned the dictatorship to grant civic rights for all Africans, end forced labor, and make available more education for Africans. In November 1961 this movement—whose membership included leading lawyers, doctors, and businessmen—called for a boycott of elections, thus prompting cancellation of elections, suppression of the party, and the arrest of many of its leaders.[46] Other movements opposed to the regime and known to exist at one time or another during the 1960s were the *Movimento Democrata Africano*, an political organization in Zambézia; the *Partido de Libertação de Moçambique* (*PLM*), whose two African leaders were imprisoned in 1962 after acknowledging charges they had founded their party in South Africa; the *Partido Socialista Católico*, an African movement in Inhambane; and the *União Progressiva de Moçambique* (UPM) an organization in Manica and Sofala which advocated self-determination for the territory in a manifesto issued in 1961 and demanded equality for the African.[47] Other black organizations included the *Núcleo Negrófico de Manica e Sofala* and the *União Makonde de Moçambique*, active in Pôrto Amélia.[48]

FORMATION AND EVOLUTION OF EXILED NATIONALIST ORGANIZATIONS

Disenchanted intellectuals, migrant workers, and others eventually joined in the formation of several nationalist movements outside Mozambique; their principal objective was immediate independence for the territory, either through negotiation or militant struggle. The first of these movements was the *União Democrática Nacional de Moçambique* (UDENAMO), established in Salisbury, Rhodesia, on October 2, 1960.[49] A second organization, the Mozambique African National Union (MANU), was formed in Mombasa, Kenya, during February 1961 as an amalgamation of several small groups including the *União Makonde de Moçambique*; MANU was supported by the Kenya African National Union (KANU) and the Tanganyika African National Union (TANU).[50] A third organization was established in present-day Malawi by exiled Africans from the Tete region and was known as the *União Africana de Moçambique Independente* (UNAMI).[51]

During 1961 and after the independence of Tanganyika, all three nationalist organizations moved their headquarters to Dar es Salaam, and on June 25, 1962, they joined together into the *Frente de Libertação de Moçambique* under the leadership of Mondlane, who had been relatively isolated from the nationalist developments but had been sympathetic to the UDENAMO.[52] The aims of the party were defined in a program of action and principles at the first congress of FRELIMO held in Dar es Salaam on September 23 to 28, 1962. The congress condemned Portuguese colonialism and political, economic, and social oppression as well as Portugal's unwillingness to recognize Mozambican independence. A series of resolutions called for a consolidation of the organizational structure of FRELIMO, unity among Mozambicans, promotion of literacy programs and the establishment of schools and trade unions, student, youth, and women's organizations, preparation of self-defense for the people, cooperation with nationalist groups in Angola, Portuguese Guinea, and the Cape Verde Islands, and the seeking of diplomatic, moral, and material support for the freedom and independence struggle in Mozambique.[53]

Faced with a diverse leadership and a variety of ideological tendencies, Mondlane began the arduous task of building a cohesive, effective organization. From the time he assumed leadership of the nationalist cause until his death seven years later, he matured rapidly as a revolutionary and political leader. Two phases marked his career as head of the nationalist forces: first, the preparatory period from September 1962 until September 1964 in which the *Frente* was consolidated and its cadres mobilized and trained in preparation for war; and, second, the experience of armed struggle after September 1964 which produced an articulation of clear perspectives on Mozambique as an independent nation.

During the preparatory period, he directed attention "to create conditions for a successful armed struggle . . . , to prepare the population inside Mozambique . . . , to recruit and train people for the responsibilities which such a struggle would impose."[54] Essentially, there were four objectives. First, to establish an underground organization within the territory, utilizing the forces of the combined exiled parties as well as the NESAM communications network and the cooperative movement in the north. Through this network Mozambicans were recruited into the party ranks and organized into cells and an effort was made to raise the general level of political consciousness throughout the territory. A second objective was the formation and training of military forces. Some two hundred Mozambicans received early training in Algeria during 1963, and a training camp was set up in the village of Bagamoyo in southern Tanganyika; their training involved military and political education and the rudimentary learning of Portuguese and attainment of literacy—their task was to socialize and mobilize the population within Mozambique for the revolutionary struggle.[55] A third objective was to raise the educational level of Mozambican exiles and refugees, and a secondary school, the *Instituto Moçambicano*, was established in 1963 under the directorship of Mondlane's American wife Janet; eventually, it accommodated 120 students.[56] The fourth objective was the mobilization of world opinion against the Portuguese, and party offices were opened in Algiers, Cairo, and Lusaka for this purpose.

The experience of armed revolutionary struggle within Mozambique sharpened Mondlane's perspective on goals after independence. A few months after the commencement of the guerrilla war, he defined Mozambican nationalism as "characterized by the development of attitudes, activities, and more or less structured programs aimed at the mobilization of forces for the attainment of self-government and independence." He argued that national consciousness among individuals and groups as well as the specific goals of self-government and independence could be attained through the political and military programs of his party. Along with independence, however, there must be established "more or less permanent political structures for the pursuit of national objectives in cooperation with other African nations!"[57] At this point he seemed purposefully vague on the developmental aims of his movement within a national context, apparent evidence, perhaps, of political immaturity and lack of sophistication due to inexperience. Nationalists claimed that the necessary details would be worked out through the revolutionary experience itself, and events proved them correct in their assessment, for soon both FRELIMO and Mondlane were offering explicit perspectives on the future.

It became obvious that "the battle against tribalism and regionalism is as important as the battle against colonialism, such a battle being the safeguard of our national unity and our liberty."[58] Furthermore, the purpose of the struggle was "first and foremost aimed at building a new Mozambique. . . . We are fighting with arms in our hands, because in order to build the Mozambique that we want we must first destroy the Portuguese colonial system."[59] After several years of battle and having secured the control of liberated areas, FRELIMO found itself burdened with administrative services no longer provided by the Portuguese. At first, according to Mondlane, the nationalists were unprepared to cope with the material needs of the people and were unable to provide food, medical service, and education.[60]

With this crisis, the political, economic, cultural, and social structure of the "new" Mozambique was clearly envisaged. Politically, the future Mozambique would follow the pattern of one-party democracy being established in liberated areas. The congress was the supreme organ of the party, constituted of elected representatives of the people. The congress elects the central committee of forty members which assumes "total responsibility for directing the liberation struggle" and "combined legislative, judicial, and executive powers," while below the congress are provincial councils, district councils, and cells.[61] Economic reorganization concerned rationalization of agricultural production to provide food supplies for both the army and the people. As a result, there was more land "under cultivation today than there was during the colonial administration"; farmers were given technical advice as well as basic tools like hoes, and the cooperative movement "reappeared rapidly and spontaneously after the colonial forces had been expelled."[62] FRELIMO was studying various agricultural methods to improve yields and to develop varieties of certain crops to ensure a surplus for eventual export. Further, the party was concerned with the problem of importing clothes, agricultural implements, and other necessities which were in inadequate supply; methods of producing these items within the country were being studied. In the cultural sector, a primary school program was under way in the liberated areas. Despite inadequately trained personnel, health centers were established and as a result "the population is now better served than it ever was under the Portuguese, when there was no organized free medical service."[63]

That FRELIMO had made substantial progress in the military struggle and in the implementation of its programs in liberated areas was symbolized by the holding of the party's second congress during July 1968. Especially remarkable was the fact that the congress was held in Niassa province, attended by the party executive and military leadership as well as by outside observers, and yet there was no interference by the Portuguese who claimed to control the area. A series of resolutions was approved as a guide to the future. These reaffirmed the commitment to armed struggle and the development of liberated zones. The resolutions constituted a synthesis of perspectives evolving from the struggle iself.[64]

Although the nationalists had claimed success and many accomplishments, they had also encountered very serious difficulties. The formation of FRELIMO had brought together a leadership representative of the many geographical regions of Mozambique, but personal ambition, lack of discipline, and differing ideological tendencies undermined the semblance of unity and leadership cohesiveness in the early years of activity. Among the original leaders were Paulo José Gumane, deputy secretary-general of FRELIMO in 1962 until his expulsion in December;[65] Lázaro Kavandame, provincial secretary for Cabo Delgado, who later defected to the Portuguese; David J. M. Mabunda, secretary-general of FRELIMO in 1962 until his expulsion later in the year;[66] Lawrence Mallinga Millinga, originally from the MANU who was also expelled;[67] Leo Milas (alias Leo Aldridge), at first publicity secretary and later secretary for defense security for FRELIMO until he was exposed for his American background and personal ambitions which resulted in expulsions of several other leaders;[68] and Mathew Michinji Mmole, formerly president of MANU and treasurer of FRELIMO in 1962 until his expulsion in the same year.[69] However, group leadership remained under Mondlane's direction, including such notable figures as Marcelino dos Santos. He was a poet educated in Lisbon and Paris. Originally, he was a member of UDENAMO and secretary-general of the *Conferênca das Organizações Nacionalistas das Colónias Portuguesas* (CONCP), the intra-Portuguese African nationalist organization in Rabat to which the FRELIMO was affiliated. Later, he became FRELIMO secretary for external affairs and secretary for the department of political affairs.[70] Besides Santos there were Reverend Uria Simango, a founder of UDENAMO and the vice president of FRELIMO, and Jaime Sigauke, originally affiliated with UDENAMO and later FRELIMO secretary for international organization in Mozambique.[71] Sigauke was the victim of an assassination on July 13, 1966, as was Mondlane three years later. These assassinations led to the temporary formation of a revolutionary presidential council of Simango, Santos, and Samora Moises Machel. That Mondlane's death had produced repercussions in the FRELIMO leadership was evidenced by reports of dissension between Simango, on the one side, and Santos and Machel, on the other.[72] Simango was eventually expelled at a FRELIMO central committee meeting of May 9 to 14, 1970; Machel emerged as president and Santos as vice-president.

Another problem in FRELIMO's early years was factionalization within the coalition party, which led to rival nationalist organizations. Several schisms developed. Well before the front's establishment, one of the founders of UDENAMO, Hlomulo Chitofo Gwambe, had announced the liberation of Mozambique through military struggle; for this, and because he was believed to be a Portuguese agent, he was expelled by the newly independent Tanganyika and subsequently was excluded from the FRELIMO central commitee.[73] Ostracized, he formed the *Comité Secreto da Restauraçao da UDENAMO* in Kampala, Uganda; later, he reformed the UDENAMO under a modified name, the *União Democrática Nacional de Monomotapa* (UDENAMO-Monomotapa).[74] The expulsion from FRELIMO of former UDENAMO, MANU, and UNAMI leaders in mid-1962 and in December 1962 resulted in the formation of several new organizations, including another UDENAMO the *União Democrática Nacional de Moçambique* (UDENAMO-Moçambique), established in Cairo by Gumane and Mabunda; and a reorganized MANU under Mmole.

At Kampala on May 20, 1963, the UDENAMO-Monomotapa, MANU, and the Mozambique African National Congress (MANC or MANCO), led by Sebastene Sigauke, coalesced into a front known as the *Frente Unida Anti-Imperialista Popular Africana de Moçambique* (FUNIPAMO).[75] Another expulsion of six members of the FRELIMO central committee culminated in the formation of the Mozambique Revolutionary Council (MORECO) during 1964. In early 1964 MORECO joined UDENAMO-Moçambique and, after initiation of unity talks in March, the two UDENAMO groups, MANU, and MANCO formed a new coalition in June called *Comité Revolucionário de Moçambique* (COREMO) with headquarters in Lusaka, Zambia, and a foreign office in Cairo.[76] Gwambe was named president, a post he retained until his expulsion in 1967 (he was succeeded by Paulo José Gumane). After his expulsion he formed another organization, the *Partido Popular de Moçambique* (PAPOMO). Another splinter group broke from the COREMO to become the *União Nacional Africana da Rombézia* (*UNAR*), with headquarters in Blantyre, Malawi.[77]

THE GUERRILLA WAR:
IN RETROSPECT

The struggle in Mozambique began on September 25, 1964, and was initiated by FRELIMO militants, although a rival group formed in the Sudan by the expelled Leo Milas, the Mozambique African National Union (MANU-Khartoum), claimed to have initiated the military struggle on August 28, 1964.[78] Although the COREMO had attempted military action in Tete during 1964, apparently without success, major direction of the war was maintained by FRELIMO.

At the outset of the war, FRELIMO attacked several military outposts in Cabo Delgado Province and later extended the struggle into the provinces of Niassa, Zambézia, and Tete by the end of 1964. FRELIMO then consolidated its strength in Niassa and Cabo Delgado provinces by withdrawing forces from Zambézia and Tete. While the Portuguese had anticipated the uprising, their forces were limited to guarding urban centers, garrisons, and strategic points throughout northern Mozambique. Throughout 1965 and most of 1966 a stalemate ensued, and beginning in late 1966 a series of nationalist attacks badly damaged a number of Portuguese bases. During 1967 nationalist forces reached the Lurio River and surrounded Pôrto Amélia, the capital of Cabo Delgado Province. In Niassa they moved southward, gaining control of the Catur zone between the provinces of Zambézia and Tete. With large portions of Cabo Delgado and Niassa provinces under their control, the nationalists turned attention to Tete Province and began full military operations there in March 1968. Tete was important because of its considerable economic resources and the Zambezi River, where the Portuguese planned to build the Cabora Bassa dam while encouraging white farmers to settle in the region. During late 1969 sporadic guerrilla activities were reported in Tete, with the mining of roads and attacks on Portuguese bases, including Diaca, Nangade, Mutamba dos Macones, Chiwaya, Nambude, and many others.[79] While these guerrilla activities were to continue thereafter, the Portuguese initiated an intensive campaign during October and November 1970 to halt FRELIMO infiltration and to destroy their bases in Tete, Niassa, and Cabo Delgado. Although this campaign did not achieve these objectives, it served to open areas for the building of new roads and airfields, thereby strengthening the Portuguese position.

Portuguese official sources, while admitting some guerrilla infiltration in the area, stressed the cooperation of local civil authorities in the protection of the population as well as action by government troops against guerrillas attempting to penetrate security lines. The Portuguese were aided by four major considerations: first, a fairly well-equipped army, trained in counterinsurgency techniques through Portugal's participation in the North Atlantic Treaty Organization (NATO); second, the presence of South African troops in Tete province at Chicoa, Chioco, Mague and Zumbo along the Zambezi River specifically to defend the Cabora Bassa project; third, the extensive use of propaganda and psychological warfare to win over the African populations; and, fourth, the relocation of Africans into protected villages, utilizing the strategic hamlet principle employed by American forces in Vietnam.[80]

Although they faced superior Portuguese manpower and arms, the Mozambican guerrillas benefited from guerrilla tactics which consisted of the use of ambush and occasional hit-and-run assaults against Portuguese forces which are confined to the towns and which are widely deployed throughout the heavily wooded terrain of the north. Portuguese troop detachments were ambushed as they moved from post to post, resulting in their gradual demoralization while improving African morale. Unfamiliar with the terrain, the Portuguese also frequently resorted to intimidation and terrorism as well as bombing raids on villages and suspected guerrilla camps. These forms of retaliation and the relocation of Africans into protected villages surely increased hostility among the people.[81]

In its liberation struggle, the FRELIMO combined warfare with political organization. While recruiting Africans into the guerrilla army, the FRELIMO simultaneously set up a local administration to fill the vacuum left by the colonial administration and to ensure the reconstruction of the liberated areas. The objective was the participation of the people as a whole and the breakdown of the barriers between a guerrilla force supplied from outside the country and a passive peasantry. Through their participation, the masses would theoretically shape the revolution in their own image. At the same time the FRELIMO relegated policy decisions to the central committee, although the meetings of the military command were normally presided over by an executive party officer to ensure close coordination of political and military decisions.[82]

The Prospects for Mozambique

The continued Portuguese presence in Mozambique was dependent, first, on the containment of black Africans by means of resettlement villages throughout the area and maintenance of a stalemate in the guerrilla war, and, second, on the economic development of the territory through land concessions to white farmers and large agricultural enterprise as well as extraction of minerals, including petroleum and iron ore. Achievement of these objectives was conditional upon unity within the empire and strong ties with Western Europe and the United States as well as well as with allied forces—namely, South Africa and Rhodesia—within Southern Africa.

Within the empire the developments in the metropolitan complex largely determined the direction of overseas domination. A class of landowners and industrialists ruled Portugal in concert with foreign interests and through a network of cartels and interlocking directorships. For more than four decades that ruling class quietly accepted the dictatorship, first under Salazar and now under Caetano, for the simple reason that it protected its vested interests and assured political and economic stability. The dictatorship also maintained a hold in Africa through a colonial administrative network, large armed forces, and security forces. The death of Salazar symbolized a break with the past, but it was likely that the mystique of the regime at home and in Africa would carry on.

While political opposition was increasingly evident in the metropole and there were divisions within the traditional props of the regime—the Church, the army, and the ruling class itself—economic interests served to consolidate the regime. In recent years the Portuguese oligarchy began to look outward at rapidly expanding Western European markets and economic integration. The immediate result was Portugal's entry into an economic alliance of nations, the European Free Trade Association (EFTA), headed by its oldest ally, Great Britain. The ties abroad also were solidified in the NATO alliance, which assured financial support and training for the armed forces within Portugal. Relations with the Western European nations and with the United States were cemented with a treaty arrangement which allowed the maintenance of U.S. military bases and a French missile tracking station in the Azores as well as West German military involvement at an air base in the southern province of Beja.[83]

With the establishment of economic development plans during the 1950s and 1960s, Portuguese capital began to flow in increasing amounts to the overseas territories.[84] While such capital was oriented to the retention of Mozambique within the imperial setting and the assurance of close integrated ties between Portugal's oligarchy and the economic and administrative elites of the colony, there was some evidence of separatism, a disenchantment with the regime, a hope for autonomy if not independence, and a willingness to consider involvement in a Southern African economic and political community.[85]

Mozambique was most closely tied to South Africa, which is economically dominant in the region of Southern Africa. The recruitment of African labor for work in the Witwatersrand mines, the transit of goods through the port of Lourenço Marques, a natural gas pipeline from an area near Lourenço Marques to the Witwatersrand, petroleum exploration in Mozambique, and the Cabora Bassa hydroelectric scheme were indications of the close ties between the two. South African confidence in the Portuguese determination to stay in Mozambique was attested by the sending of soldiers to defend the Cabora Bassa project.[86] Also not to be overlooked was the fact that the pattern of heavy foregin investment (60 percent British, and 10 percent U.S.) in South Africa paralleled that in Mozambique.[87]

Ties with Rhodesia were also close since Mozambique provided the natural outlets for Rhodesian trade. Rhodesian trade filtered through Beira, the nearest port to Salisbury and Bulawayo, and a major river, roads, and railways from Rhodesia reached the Mozambican coast. Some 10 percent of Mozambican income derived from the transit trade to and from Rhodesia. Although Portugal had not formally recognized the Rhodesian government, it was clear that an independent Rhodesia was viewed as "a new bastion of white supremacy and an addition to white imperialism in southern Africa."[88] In 1965 a commercial agreement between Rhodesia and Portugal was signed, and thereafter efforts were made to expand trade. In the same year a secret agreement among Portugal, Rhodesia, and South Africa provided for the common defense of Southern Africa against "nationalist and Communist subversion."[89]

Among the other Southern African states, Malawi signed agreements with Portugal providing for the construction of a railway to the Mozambique port of Nacala. In September 1969 Swaziland sent a trade mission to Lourenço Marques to explore the possibility of increasing imports from Mozambique. Zambia, which had cut its links with Rhodesia in an effort to extricate itself from that nation's absolute control, had directed some of its copper exports through Beira via Malawi. Relations with Zambia, however, were cooled by the occasional bombing of Mozambican nationalists along the Zambian border and the location of several national liberation movements within Zambia.[90] In mid-1969 Zambia's delegate to the United Nations presented the Lusaka Manifesto clarifying his nation's role in Southern Africa. On Portugal's role in Mozambique, it stated: "No decree of the Portuguese dictator, nor legislation passed by any parliament in Portugal, can make Africa part of Europe."[91]

The African nationalist response to the Portuguese in Mozambique was also influenced by other African liberation movements and independent African nations. Ties with other movements fighting in Portuguese Africa were maintained through the CONCP which included the *Movimento Popular de Libertação de Angola* (MPLA) with headquarters in Lusaka and the *Partido Africano da Independência da Guiné e Cabo Verde* (PAIGC) with headquarters in Conakry. Marcelino dos Santos of FRELIMO headed the CONCP during its early existence, and the second meeting of the CONCP was held from October 3 to 8, 1965, in Dar es Salaam.[92] FRELIMO also supported such other liberation movements as the African National Congress (ANC) of South Africa and the Zimbabwe African People's Union (ZAPU) of Rhodesia.[93]

FRELIMO was recognized as the major Mozambican liberation movement by the African Liberation Committee of the Organization of African Unity (OAU) and was strongly supported by Tanzania and other OAU members. Zambia had given its support to COREMO in Lusaka.[94] FRELIMO also established links with the Third World through such organizations as the Afro-Asian Peoples' Solidarity Organization, the Tricontinental Congress in Havana, and the World Council of Peace. Among the nations with which the FRELIMO had established relations were North Korea, North Vietnam, and Cuba. It also maintained a delegate at the United Nations, and in a petition late in 1969 FRELIMO requested the creation of a special development and aid fund for the struggle in Mozambique, invited the Special Committee to visit the liberated zones of the territory, and urged the Security Council to take measures to force the Portuguese government to comply with its obligations under the UN Charter and resolutions, to take a strong stand against South Africa's "increasing intervention in Portugal's colonial war" and to appeal to Portugal's NATO allies to halt military and financial aid.[95]

Diplomatic efforts at the United Nations, however, served generally to focus world attention on the struggle against the Portuguese in Mozambique. Because of Portugal's military and economic treaty relations in Western Europe and strong ties to the United States, it appeared highly improbable that sanctions would ever be applied against Portugal on behalf of the African struggle for independence. In the face of Portuguese intransigence, the Mozambican nationalists had accepted militant and revolutionary alternatives. Through their revolution they had confronted the complex political, economic, and social problems in liberated zones. Consciously aware of the legacy of underdevelopment created by Portuguese colonialism and imperialism, they desired to reshape Mozambican society and to mobilize all Africans to work for national independence, unity, and development.

4

African Nationalism and Guerrilla Warfare in Angola and Mozambique

MAINA D. KAGOMBE

Development of the Armed Struggle against Portugal in Africa

The armed struggle against Portugal in Africa is being waged by the following political groups: in Angola, the Angolan Revolutionary Government in Exile (GRAE), the Popular Movement for the Liberation of Angola (MPLA), and the National Union for the Total Independence of Angola (UNITA); in Mozambique, the Mozambique Liberation Front (FRELIMO) and the Revolutionary Committee of Mozambique (COREMO).

GRAE has gone through many changes. It was originally formed in 1954 outside Angola under the name of *União Populações do Norte de Angola*. However, the movement changed its name in 1958 to the *União das Populções de Angola* (UPA) under the chairmanship of Holden Roberto. At the time, the party reflected the dominance of one ethnic group, the Bakongo, who numbered over half a million; many of them lived in Leopoldville, the Congo, as migrant workers. It should be pointed out that when Africa was partitioned by the European countries in 1884–1885, the Bakongo people were divided, some living in Angola and others in the Belgian and French Congos. The UPA became more active, for most members were Bakongo who had migrated from Angola to search for jobs and, because of frustrations from being in exile, felt the need to go back to a liberated Angola. It was for this reason that Portuguese authorities accused the UPA of being Communist inspired and importing revolution to Angola from the outside. However, the UPA chairman, Holden Roberto, was born in San Salvador, a peasant community in northern Angola. The party currently has a paper, issued every two weeks, known as *La Nation Angolaise*, which is written in Kimbundu, Kikongo, Portuguese, and French. The UPA has been accused of being anti-white[1] because it has no white members, but the party is anticolonial rather than anti-white. Richard Mathews of the *New York Times* reported in September 1961:

> I, as white, was warmly welcomed. This was true in villages as well as later among the rebel troops. Holden Roberto and his colleagues had told me in numerous interviews that they were not leading an anti-European movement. The revolution is not anti-white; it is simply—and brutally—anti-Portuguese.[2]

The UPA condemned oppression, racial discrimination, forced labor, the use of napalm against civilians by the Portuguese, and deportations to Lisbon and to Angolan concentration camps. Its program points out that a common experience exists among the Angolan people, maintaining that what antagonisms exist are aggravated day by day by racial discrimination, the inequality of the socioeconomic system, and cynical exploitation and oppression without precedent in colonial history.[3] Although the UPA has been referred to as an ethnic rather than a national political party, its actions and attitudes reflect the aspirations of the whole African population:

> Each village should select an individual to be responsible for the transmission of information and receipt of UPA commands. Such a person was to express opinions "not according to his own views, but the views of the whole population." There was to be no stealing by UPA soldiers. No item seized from the Portuguese should be kept. There should be cooperation and mutual respect between old and young. All the money the people could lay their hands on should be sent to UPA in Leopoldville, "because if we do not have money our work for independence cannot continue."[4]

In April 1962 the *Frente Nacional de Libertação de Angola* (FNLA), *Partido Democrático de Angola* (PDA), and UPA united to form GRAE. Holden Roberto became the president and Jonas M. Savimbi became foreign minister. Savimbi was one of the Ovimbundu students sent to Lisbon in September 1958 for further studies by the United Church of Christ. He had refused to join MPLA in February 1961 unless MPLA and UPA got together.[5] However, Roberto, on his way to the United Nations General Assembly in 1961, persuaded Savimbi to leave his studies in Lausanne and join him at the Belgrade Conference of Non-Aligned States. Savimbi put the liberation and struggle of his country above his studies and joined the UPA in Leopoldville. He became secretary-general and Roberto retained the chairmanship. Roberto and Savimbi submitted their memorandum to the UN General Assembly,

requesting the right of self-determination for the Angolan people.[6]

In July 1964 Savimbi ended his association with GRAE and formed his own political party, the *União Nacional para a Independência Total de Angola* (UNITA) in March 1966. This was a southern Angola-oriented movement that aimed at working inside Angola itself rather than operating in exile like GRAE. Roberto was accused of monopolizing the revolutionary movement and decision-making as if they were his business alone and of ignoring non-Western sources of support.

With over one thousand guerrillas operating from Alto Chicapa north of the Benguela Railway to regions near the Caprivi Zipfel in Namibia and as far west as the outlying regions of Guimbundu country beyond Luso, Savimbi attacked Taixeira de Sousa. The attack, in March 1967, cut off the Benguela Railway which transported copper from Zambia and the Congo. Because of the importance of the railway, the Congo, Zambia, and even Tanzania felt the repercussions of the UNITA guerrilla attack. Zambia then refused to renew Savimbi's resident permit, and he left for Cairo.[7] Savimbi responded to the action taken by the Zambian government and lack of recognition by the Organization of African Unity (OAU) by proclaiming self-reliance and saying: "We don't need the help of anybody to lead our people to true independence."[8] He charged the MPLA with interfering and sending their guerrillas to a territory already held by the UNITA under the chief of staff, Kapesi Fundanga, and chief of operations, Jose Kalundungu, ex-GRAE commander.

In 1966 Roberto and Savimbi met in Lusaka under the auspices of President Kaunda of Zambia. Savimbi had spent three months inside Angola but negotiations were not fruitful because Roberto wanted UNITA individuals to go back to GRAE but not as members of UNITA.

The Popular Movement for the Liberation of Angola (MPLA) was founded in December 1956.[9] Its first president was Ilidio Tome Alves Machado, born in Luanda in 1915. Its secretary-general from 1956 to 1962 was Viriato da Cruz, who learned his politics inside Angola until 1959 when he left the country rather than be arrested. He was arrested in Lisbon in May 1959 and sent back to a Luanda prison. Machado "remains one of the most respected of the Angolan leaders"[10] although he is still restricted to a remote Cape Verde island. In 1958 the *Movimento de Independencia Nacional de Angola* (MINA) was formed and later fused with MPLA.

From the beginning, MPLA appealed to the

intellectuals and city dwellers such as Dr. Agostinho Neto, a physician and poet and president of MPLA until his arrest in June 1960, and Mario de Andrade, a sophisticated and prolific writer, who studied in the University of Paris and later assumed the MPLA presidency (April 1961) upon the arrest of Dr. Neto. When Dr. Neto was arrested in June 1960, hundreds of his patients, friends, and indigenous people joined to protest his arrest. Over thirty of them were shot in cold blood, over two hundred were wounded, and two villages were demolished. These incidents received no coverage by the news media.[11]

These atrocities committed by the Portuguese police compelled MPLA leaders to go into exile. Viriato da Cruz later described the situation as the "waves of arrests in Luanda, beginning in March 1959." On December 1, 1959, Cruz sent a telegram to UN Secretary-General Dag Hammarskjold, asking him to use his office to make the Portuguese government "put an end to constant atrocities and cruel assassinations against the African peoples of Guinea and Angola, set free political prisoners, [and] cease preparations for armed repression."[12]

In February 1960 President Sékou Touré of Guinea invited MPLA to establish its main headquarters in Conakry. It was from Conakry that MPLA launched a program to unite all exiled Angolan nationalists in the task of attacking the last bastions of Portuguese fascism in Angola. The program included these five objectives:

1. the right of self-determination for the people of Angola;
2. political amnesty for all political prisoners;
3. civil liberties, namely the legal rights to form political parties and establish solid guarantees for their effective exercise;
4. withdrawal of armed forces and military bases from Angolan territory;
5. a round-table conference between representatives of all political parties in Angola and the Portuguese government to discuss a peaceful settlement of colonial rule in Angola in the interest of both parties.[13]

Premier Salazar categorically rejected the MPLA appeal program and MPLA turned to armed struggle since its peaceful negotiations were rebuffed. Andrade (then acting president of MPLA) declared, "There can be no question of engaging in negotiations with the Portuguese Government as long as the Fascist regime of Dr. Salazar, enemy of the expression of the essential freedoms and of the right of self-determination, is in power. Our fight has already put the regime of Dr. Salazar on the way to the place it naturally belongs—the tomb."[14]

In October 1961 the MPLA moved to the neighboring independent state of the Congo (Kinshasha) to facilitate its activities against Portugal. In February 1961 the MPLA led attacks on the house of detention, the civil prison in San Paulo, a broadcasting station, and a military barracks. During the burial of about two dozen policemen, another attack was made and followed by a third at the Luanda prison in the Angolan capital. These incidents coincided with the successful hijacking of the *Santa Maria* by Captain Henrique Galvão. Later, the UPA invaded northern Angola from the Congo (Kinshasa) and directed the attacks against the Portuguese settlers, government officials, and Portuguese African loyalists.

The Portuguese responded by rushing as many troops to Angola as could be spared. On February 9, 1961, foreign newsmen reported that about two-hundred thousand Africans fled from Angola to the Congo (Kinshasa) and in the 1961 UN Security Council debate it was stated that about thirty thousand Africans were massacred by the Portuguese troops.[15] On February 5, 1961, more than three thousand Africans were killed. The African nationalists later reorganized and began operations in the northern part of Angola.

In July 1962 Dr. Neto, who had become the martyred symbol of Angolan nationalism, escaped from house arrest in Portugal. During his absence from the MPLA, he had been made honorary president. On his way home he stopped at Rabat, Conakry, and Kinshasha where he initiated unity talks between the Angolan nationalists—the *Frente Nacional de Libertação de Angola* (FNLA)—and MPLA in August 1962.[16]

As mentioned earlier, FNLA came into existence as a result of the merger of the UPA and the *Partido Democrático de Angola* (PDA). FNLA was to function under the direction of a national council composed of ten (later fifteen) representatives from each movement. David Livromentos (PDA) was named national president and Holden Roberto assumed the chairmanship of the executive committee. The aim of the FNLA was the freedom of Angola under a democratic government, agrarian reform and a policy of nonalignment.

The conversion of FNLA into provisional Government in Exile (GRAE) was aimed at making it the undisputed government of Angola when independence was won, as was the case when the Algerian provisional government in 1962 became the *de facto* government of Algeria, and of combatting the growing strength of the MPLA which was building "a mass following among the very people upon whose support the UPA was built," the Angolan refugees and migrant workers in Congo (Kinshasha).[17]

In June 1962 President Kwame Nkrumah of Ghana convened a conference of the African freedom fighters at the Kwame Nkrumah Institute for Ideological Training at Winneba, Ghana. The aim of the conference was to unify the liberation forces and at the same time create a joint military command to strengthen the freedom forces against imperialism and to stop factionalism among the African leaders.

Dr. Neto was regarded as the last hope for merging the two parties, FNLA and MPLA. Early in August, while still uncommitted to either party, he developed a formula for unity and asked the two parties to accept his three preferences. One was rapid "fusion" by stages into a single movement, the second was "close collaboration" in political-military action under a common body, and the third was President Nkrumah's July 1962 proposal of a joint military command of all Angolan forces.[18]

These three suggestions were not agreeable to FNLA, and Roberto was blamed for causing Angolan disunity:

> No national liberation struggle has ever prospered under an exile leadership which laid premature claim to a monopoly of decision and control. One has the impression, in short, that Mr. Holden [Roberto] is trying to cut up his elephant before shooting it.[19]

With all this confusion, Dr. Neto gave up trying to unite the two parties (FNLA and MPLA) and identified himself with MPLA as the organization which ". . . had 'best known how to interpret the meaning of Angolan nationalism' and had struggled for 'national unity and against all sorts of discrimination,' whether 'racial, regional, ideological, or otherwise.' "[20]

Holden Roberto defended himself and his party as being free from intellectual leadership (referring to MPLA) and refused to be

> seduced by the rank verbiage of a kind of anticolonialist in lounging robes, the kind who makes his appearance in a capital often far from his native land and puts forth beautiful anticolonialist theories inspired by ideas which are completely un-African, the kind who calls himself progressive and proclaims himself the great revolutionary, but never takes off his lounging slippers.[21]

The MPLA, previously regarded as reformist, became increasingly radical. This created confusion in the OAU. Should it revoke the UPA recognition, recognize both the GRAE and the MPLA, or neither? The MPLA seemed the better organized of the two, and its headquarters were moved to Congo (Brazzaville) as a result of the closing of the MPLA in Kinshasa office in 1963 by the Congolese government which favored GRAE. Dr. Neto, now the president of MPLA, declared that he and the MPLA were now ". . . the victims of 'American imperialism' acting through the intermediary of . . . [the] Congolese government. . . ."[22] Since 1964 the MPLA has launched raids into Angola and has established not only schools and camps but also medical clinics in the liberated area as well as carrying on the continually escalating conflict.

Prior to formation of the Mozambique Liberation Front, known as FRELIMO (*Frente de Libertação de Moçambique*), in June 1962, African associations in Mozambique were primarily interested in the cultural and social welfare of the Mozambicans. When these associations became more nationalistic, the government harassed and arrested the leaders, replaced them with more docile Africans, and put the organizations under the control of the colonial administration. FRELIMO was born out of a fusion of the exiled political parties, such as the Mozambique African Nationalist Union (MANU), *União Democrática Nacional de Moçambique* (UDENAMO), and Mozambique African National Congress (MANC). The MANU leaders acquired their political experience by organizing their fellow Mozambicans who were working in other East African countries. Among such leaders, for example, were MANU president Mathew Mmole and Mallinga Mallinga, its secretary-general, who organized UDENAMO for Mozambicans working in either Rhodesia or Malawi. Its headquarters were then in Salisbury. Adelino Gwambe defected from the Portuguese Secret Police Force (PIDE) in Mozambique to join UDENAMO. In 1959 he visited his colleagues in MANU at Dar es Salaam and, while there with Baltazar Changonga, president of the Malawi-based Mozambique National Independence party, decided to form a coalition of a united national political party to liberate Moazmbique as a whole.

This coalition of leaders helped form the Mozambique Liberation Front, an ad hoc committee with the responsibility of holding elections. In the first election, Dr. Eduardo Mondlane became president; Uria Simango, vice-president; David Makunda, secretary-general; and Leo Milas, publicity secretary. The headquarters of FRELIMO remained in Dar es Salaam where the election was held.

In early 1963 internal friction occurred in FRELIMO when Leo Milas, the former publicity secretary, alleged that Dr. Mondlane and the FRELIMO were tools of American imperialism. This allegation was followed by organized opposition in Cairo by the former secretary-general, David Makunda, and his deputy, Paulo Gumane, who had broken with FRELIMO. In June 1965 FRELIMO individuals founded another party in

Lusaka, Zambia. This party became known as the *Comité Revolucionário de Moçambique* (COREMO). The members of COREMO elected Adelino Gwambe as their first president; but in 1966 he was expelled from the party because of his militancy. However, COREMO was reorganized in May 1966 when Paulo Gumane assumed its presidency. The headquarters of COREMO are in Lusaka.

FRELIMO maintains a military force of ten thousand. It began its hit-and-run raids while in Tanzania, and later it moved inside and occupied Mozambique territory. From its bases there it continued fighting and started training its armed forces. The area controlled by FRELIMO consists of the northern uplands of the Niassa district, which stretch westward from the border of Tanzania and Mozambique to Lake Nyasa; eastward to the Makonde plateau; and northeastward to the Cabo Delgado district. In this liberated area a new approach to agriculture and new types of crops (ground nuts, for instance) for both domestic consumption and export are being developed.

In the field of education, FRELIMO has established the Mozambique Institute in Dar es Salaam, originally supported by $100,000 donated by various organizations from the U.S. and Western Europe, Scandinavian countries, and Eastern Europe.[23] The institute provides Mozambican students with fundamental educational skills and will even prepare some of them for college education overseas. One of the branches of the institute conducts nurses' training programs, technical training, and teacher training. The other branches of the institute conduct elementary schools for youngsters. Most pupils are taught in an outdoors school because of a lack of indoor facilities.

Because of FRELIMO's concern for education, COREMO accused FRELIMO of emphasizing education and administration at the expense of guerrilla tactics. The institute is attacked for being supported and run by Americans, Europeans and, to make matters worse, Portuguese teachers. COREMO has also alleged that FRELIMO is infiltrated by Portuguese sympathizers. The latter criticism might have validity, but as for the former, one wonders how an ideology or morality can be developed without education. It is important to educate African people in order to decolonize their minds which have been assimilated or are in a state of hopelessness.[24]

Revolutionary Theory and the Models for Guerrilla Action

Dr. Frantz Fanon, concerned with the state of African liberation movements, challenged Africans when he concluded that "the great danger which threatens Africa is the absence of ideology."[25] His observation is a very astute one, for despite the common and continuing experience of colonialism in unifying African peoples against imperialism, without ideology there can be neither a frame of reference nor a common denominator of beliefs and values with which to carry on the political and social revolution which is vital for all African peoples. That is, ideology will formulate and generate collective actions and practices of individuals and create new ideas with broader meanings of communal solidarity to direct human consciousness and social conduct of guerrilla warfare in a frame of mind of Pan-Africanism and African ancestry. Therefore, our collective consciousness will determine our social existence.

Thus, it is necessary for Africans to develop and share a common ideology of armed struggle.[26] Such an ideology might posit that there are three stages of an African revolution: first, organizing and educating the people; second, mobilizing the masses; and, third, armed struggle itself. In the first stage, what Mao Tse-tung calls "self-defense units"[27] must be organized and developed among the people on a voluntary basis from the genuine and potential revolutionaries dedicated to eradicating all forms of oppression and exploitation by colonial regimes. A member of such an organization must be well versed in African political and cultural traditions while also believing strongly in the efficacy of modern science and technology and in the need to modernize African societies. Similarly, adult education facilitates the development of a more sophisticated communications network and must precede training in art and science or guerrilla warfare.

In the second stage, the main objective is to politicize and arouse the masses,[28] to make people aware of both their needs and those rights which they are denied by the colonial regime. Terms such as *majority rule*, *stolen land*, and *Uhuru* have been used successfully to achieve this goal. Nationalist leaders must not only preach to the masses but must also demonstrate their convictions by concrete actions. Political organizations must involve the people in daily political activity. The national political party has to be both a mass movement and, if possible, a structured organization. By "structured," I mean placing political personnel according to guerrilla structures from the bottom to the top. This should be done in regional representation as well as in urban and rural areas.

A guerrilla fighter should not forget that people's support is the generating power of defeating the enemy and "political mobilization is the most fundamental."[29] Therefore, once the masses of the people are politicized and informed about the forms of colonial exploitation—such as forced labor, corporal punishment, inequality of salaries, and limitation of political rights—the nationalist leaders have to forecast the type of society they will offer after defeat of the enemy: a true system of government that will be responsive to the masses and reflect their aspirations and needs. It should be a system based on agrarian reform, a planned economy, industrialization, and social justice; in other words, it will "provide a new social synthesis in which the advanced technical society is achieved without the appalling evils and deep cleavages of capitalist industrial society."[30]

The third stage is where "all the people of both sexes from the age of sixteen to forty-five must be organized into self-defense units the basis of which is voluntary service. As a first step they must procure arms, then they must be given both military and political training."[31] The responsibilities of these units are local community duties, securing information from the colonial troops, detecting traitors, and preventing the spread of enemy propaganda. This may mean destroying leaflets and watering down the news or information and above all cautioning the people against such colonial agents.

At this point the liberation movement reaches a takeoff point. Of course, if the guerrilla expects loyalty and cooperation from the masses, the masses expect from freedom fighters sincerity in their actions, success, and sacrifice. Ché Guevara puts it this way in describing Camilo's qualities that must characterize a successful guerrilla: ". . . a faculty for precise and rapid analysis of situations and forehanded thought about problems to be resolved in the future."[32] The guerrillas have to give promises to the people and impart to them the conviction that they can triumph over the enemy.

Despite the ethnic rivalries promoted by the imperialists, a war for national liberation can create the most favorable conditions for the resolving of tribal and social antagonisms. By aiming at the total destruction of the colonial structures, such a war accelerates the building of nations and the development of a revolutionary force which will defeat the imperialist forces. In winning over the people for a war of national liberation emphasis should be placed on three things: the present condition of life under the colonial rule; the style of the precolonial past; and the anticipated style of life in the postrevolutionary society. The guerrillas have to cope with those problems that the masses perceive as most salient. For example, giving a copy of a tract by Mao Tsetung to a mother does not mean anything to her because she needs food for her child. Concrete projects such as clinics, child care centers, nursery schools, food for school pupils, self-help projects, and cooperatives are more appropriate means to deal with the sufferings of an oppressed people than the propagation of revolutionary ideas unaccompanied by social action.

Having aroused the social consciousness of the masses, freedom fighters will be in a strong position to sustain the armed struggle. Here the armed struggle may have to take two or three forms: (1) fighting from foreign soil; (2) fighting within the urban areas; and (3) fighting in the rural areas.

The freedom fighters have to be organized in the following general types of units. First, a squad, made up of nine to eleven men armed with two to five rifles, accompanied by a leader and an assistant leader. The other members of the squad could be armed with sticks, knives, swords, spears, or homemade guns. Second, a platoon, made up of two or four squads with a leader and an assistant. However, if the platoon is to act on its own, it should be assigned a political officer to carry on the propaganda work. The platoon may have arms proportionate to its relative strength, the weather, and the situation of the people.[33] Although tactics are the practical means used to achieve strategic objectives and they have to be flexible, some strategies should not change. The freedom fighter selects the tactics applicable to the situation: when to attack and withdraw or when to take the initiative or to hold his ground. Timing is also important, especially when the enemy can use airplanes for retaliation during the day. Night raids are a necessity in such a situation.

Before the onset of the armed revolution, the size of the guerrilla force is not absolutely crucial; for example, the Cuban revolution was led by less than a dozen men. Rather, the important things are cooperation, involvement, and efficiency. The party structure and the guerrilla army will have to be built as the war goes on. Differing here with with the idea of Regis Debray that the guerrilla force should be independent from the party, I would submit that the guerrilla should be under the direction of the party and should not function as a separate entity because the objective of guerrilla warfare is—in Angola and Mozambique—to free these countries. Freeing a country entails, in part, establishing a government. As such, the political party is very crucial, and if it is to run the government it should start its role during the first stage of guerrilla warfare. Cuba under Fidel Castro or China under Mao are good examples.[34] Castro was a military leader as well as a political party leader even though the party was not clearly established early in the Cuban revolutionary struggle. Mao, on the other hand, is a political organizer and military theoretician. Debray's point has some validity when he says, "in the absence of a single command, there is no clear strategy of armed struggle. In the absence of a clear strategy, no plan of action."[35] This does not mean that a political leader controls all guerrilla actions. There must be some autonomy within the guerrilla operations, yet general policy has to come from the chairman of the political party who should also be well versed in military matters.

Under certain circumstances fighting can start from foreign soil. For example, FRELIMO headquarters are in Dar es Salaam and those of COREMO are in Lusaka. MPLA has its headquarters in Brazzaville while UPA's are in Kinshasa. In West Africa we have the *Partido Africano da Independência da Guiné e Cabo Verde* (PAIGC) fighting in Guinea (Bissau) based in Conakry and the *Frente para a Libertação e Indepêndencia da Guiné Portuguesa* (FLING) based in Dakar. All these are very important in giving the African nationalist guerrilla a base from which to launch attacks. The lack of such facilities, particularly in South Africa and even in Namibia, creates some obstacles. However, a liberation movement is not worth the name until it has occupied, or has a foothold in, the territory it is trying to capture.

The first signs of the onset of a war of national liberation may appear in the form of a strike. It may then move to widespread resistance, which can be violent or nonviolent.[36] The next stage in the war to liberate a country may be the highly organized guerrilla technique of attacking and holding a given territory. During this time the people may not have either uniforms or weapons. As in the case of the Kenyan Mau Mau, the lack of weapons is not an impediment because the Mau Mau were able to supply their own guerrillas with the enemy's weapons as a result of hit-and-run raids.[37] Therefore, the Mau Mau valued arms very highly because they were so scarce. These weapons were originally obtained by using pangas and spears or homemade guns as the only weapons in the hit-and-run foray. During the Mau Mau uprising, most of the attacks and battles were fought at night because the British troops could use land rovers and helicopters in the countryside during the day. Urban guerrilla warfare means using highly explosive dynamite at strategic positions as well as attacking particular individuals. This developed in the city of Nairobi where strikes and boycotts took place. It is interesting that the Mau Mau started from the city (Nairobi), moved to the populated countryside (in the Central Province and Rift Valley Province), and, finally, went into the forests and mountains (Aberdares and Mount Kenya) where they remained until after independence. This was necessary to readjust to British troop maneuvers and African traitors.

I am not suggesting that the guerrillas in Mozambique should imitate the tactics of the Mau Mau or of the Algerian FLN or that they should follow the teachings of Mao or Debray, Ché Guevara, or the Viet Cong; however, those movements and men do provide a number of models. At the same time, the style of guerrilla warfare depends on the climate and terrain of the area concerned, and I disagree with those who say that a revolution can be "duplicated." I would say, rather, that it is "adapted." And, if it is adapted, it has to be a "new type," for if it uses the same tactics as another guerrilla movement, its moves will be easily anticipated by the enemy. The guerrillas will be met by counterinsurgency. Consequently, the guerrilla army needs not only fighters, supporters and technicians, but also tacticians and theoreticians. As with the PAIGC, it is necessary to

> reinforce political work and propaganda within the enemy's armed forces. Write posters, pamphlets, letters. Draw slogans on the roads. Establish cautious links with the enemy personnel who want to contact us. Act audaciously and with great initiative in this way. . . . Do everything possible to help the enemy soldiers to desert. Assure them of security so as to encourage their deserting. Carry out political work among Africans who are still in enemy service, whether civilian or military. Persuade these brothers to change direction so as to serve the party within enemy ranks or desert with arms and ammunition to our units.[38]

What the freedom fighters in Southern Africa need is an African country prepared to allow its soil to be used not only as a base (Tanzania, Zambia, Guinea, and the Congo [Brazzaville] have done this). They also need to strengthen their armed forces and, particularly, to acquire not only radar but effective anti-aircraft weapons because they are subject to retaliatory attacks by either Portugal, Rhodesia, or South Africa. The freedom fighters have to get down to the business of fighting the enemy—not making mere noise and quarreling among themselves in the host countries. Although a change of government in the host nation may adversely affect the liberation movement, as in the Congo (Kinshasa) under Moise Tshombe, it can also greatly improve the guerrillas' chances of success, as did the fortunes of MPLA during the government of Patrice Lumumba.

Although it is important to establish bases on foreign soil, a liberation movement must have a base in its home territory. Most of the African wars against the Portuguese are being waged from domestic bases. UPA, MPLA, FRELIMO, and particularly PAIGC have become effective revolutionary movements because they are fighting inside the territories (PAIGC controls nearly two-thirds of the territory). Furthermore, they have not only established primary schools, clinics, and cooperatives, but are also administering the liberated areas and training military forces within the occupied land. This is a great achievement. However, the work is not yet completed. The goal is not merely to maintain the territories now held, but rather to liberate Guinea (Bissau), Angola, and Mozambique as a whole, and to wipe out the remaining traces of alien rule on African soil.

Guerrilla warfare in Guinea (Bissau) has passed through the two stages mentioned earlier and has begun to enter the third one. PAIGC is fighting with uniforms, using heavy weapons, and raiding the Portuguese military installations. They are also adopting Mau Mau, FLN, Cuban, and particularly Viet Cong techniques such as destroying bridges, disrupting communications, uprooting railroad tracks, and putting the Portuguese army on the permanent defensive. These techniques may exhaust the enemy and prevent his expansion as well as impede his operations, which may mean Portuguese expulsion from Guinea (Bissau).

In Kenya the Kikuyu had faith in the Mau Mau fighters. When they happened to pass through a given area, no one dared to inform the British forces because informers feared the consequences. To maintain the necessary secrecy and loyalty of the Kikuyu, the use of oaths was significant and such oaths sustained the morale of the Mau Mau. Didan Kimathi, the Mau Mau general, like Castro, was not originally familiar with Mao Tse-tung's theories of guerrilla warfare.[39] His principles of guerrilla warfare were invented on the spot out of his experience and in conformity to his situation. Jomo Kenyatta's book, *Facing Mount Kenya*, contained inspirations and ideas which were later used to develop the Mau Mau as well as extensive descriptions of traditional legend, mythology, and religion.[40] For example, Kikuyus were convinced that "the God of Kikuyu never sleeps" and would bring independence if they fought for it. Kenyatta's book also asserted that God is on the side of the oppressed. I remember being told, that, with the help of charms, bullets directed at Mau Mau fighters would be converted into water. Secrecy and commitment were tremendous. Even when a Mau Mau guerrilla was threatened with death, he never would divulge Mau Mau secrets. They would hold their heads higher, grab the soil in their hand, and die that way. Many were shot in cold blood but grabbing the soil of the fatherland while dying means recapturing and retaining the land stolen by the Europeans. The interesting thing was that although the Mau Mau forest fighters held these ancestral beliefs, they also believed in the importance of material and arms.

Mau Mau then reached intermediate stages—starting with the first and second and proceeding to the third stage within the territory they were contesting for—without foreign supplies or any sort of diplomatic or foreign help. This transformation to the third stage was brought about by Kimathi between 1950 and 1954, and continued after his arrest and death.

The Future of Armed Struggle for Liberation in "Portuguese" Africa

As the foregoing analysis indicates, we have reached a point of departure. Swift and drastic actions must be taken in Angola, Mozambique, Guinea (Bissau), and the rest of Africa or the future of white-black relations in these territories and in other African territories will suffer. These territories have been under Portuguese domination for over four centuries. Yet the Western allies of Portugal do not understand that the Portuguese whites still prefer to look back to yesterday when the European people were the paramount political and economic force in the world. They do not understand that they should act before whites are dragged into a blood bath that may do irreparable harm to racial harmony in Africa and in the Pan-African world. How unfortunate that "Lisbon can cloud the hopeful sunrise of [independence] tomorrow by an illogical and psychopathic commitment to policies never moral and now no longer viable!"[41]

We Africans are asking the Western world and the United States in particular to come to our aid and stop supporting Portugal, our enemy—that is, to stop supplying NATO arms of all kinds and to stop investing in these countries, specifically, in projects that strengthen the dying Portuguese colonialism in Africa. If the Western world does not do this, it will regret it when Africa turns its back against the West at the conclusion of the liberation struggle.

Students and academicians in the Western world could help the situation by influencing their representatives to speak up against Portuguese colonialism and by persuading the U.S. government to put pressure on Lisbon.[42] Representative Charles Diggs, chairman of the subcommittee on Africa, who has encouraged freedom fighters and those informed about the liberation struggle to testify, is a good example to the American people.

European countries—namely, Great Britain and France—should end their hypocritical policies. They have already given up most of their colonial empires in Africa. Why do they encourage Portugal to retain its so-called "overseas provinces"? Could they not follow the example of the Scandinavian countries in aiding the African struggle? West Germany and Japan should also reconsider their positions and stop their profitable trade with our enemies.[43] Furthermore, the NATO allies should stop collaborating with Portugal to manufacture anti-guerrilla combat planes which are tested in Africa:

> Originally, the G-91 was built for the U.S. Air Force in West German factories under an Italian license. Later on, the Luftwaffe used them. With an Italian airframe, a British engine, a French undercarriage, and Dutch electronic equipment, the Fiat G-91 is particularly suitable for 'counter insurgency operations' because it requires a relatively short runway.[44]

This type of assistance is very serious because it does nothing more than prolong the war that is coming to an end. The allies of Portugal also forget that guerrilla warfare has no time limit. Either there is complete independence or the guerrilla warfare will continue indefinitely.

I believe that the blacks in the United States not only have a role to play in this war of liberation, but an obligation to take action. Their refusal to do so and to identify with the guerrillas who are fighting against the Portuguese in Africa would be interpreted by their brothers and sisters in Africa as a betrayal and a disservice to Africa and its ancestors. African descendants in the United States have the most immediate skills that African guerrillas need. Many of them fought in World War II, the Korean War, and now in Vietnam. Africa needs all these skills in fighting and eradicating colonialism and imperialism on the continent. In return, the Afro-Americans should expect not only identity with, but a right to settle in, the territories which they assisted in liberating—and elsewhere in Africa, if they so choose. As for the question of the possibility of Afro-Americans losing their U.S. citizenship by joining in the revolution, I believe that Pan-Africanism is a spirit of awareness, a movement of ideas that knows no geographical boundary or citizenship. Those blacks in America who choose to take part in the fight against Portugal in Africa, I believe, are brave enough and have reached the level of true nationalist revolutionaries, and the threat of the U.S. taking away their citizenship should be subordinated to the priority of liberating Africa.

African governments, individually and within the OAU liberation committee, have to help guerrillas by giving them shelter and training as well as providing them with support and diplomatic recognition. They should also offer the use of their missions abroad to disseminate information and to help students from these nongoverning territories spread their propaganda and organize those friends who would like to help. However, above and beyond all this assistance, unity among the freedom fighters is vital in order to avoid wasting energy on internal strife rather than forging together in a united front. Finally, they should remember that whether they get help from outside or not, they have to fight their own war to its final conclusion.

PART FIVE

The Former Central African Federation and Southern Africa

Country Profiles

MALAWI

Political situation
On July 6, 1966, Malawi became an independent republic within the Commonwealth of Nations. Dr. Hastings Kamuzu Banda is the president. Malawi has a unicameral legislature and full adult suffrage. There is a single party, the Malawi Congress Party.

Demographic situation
Area: 45,747 square miles
Population: 4,043,910 (1966), including 9,000 Europeans and 10,500 Asians
Capital: Zomba, 19,616 inhabitants (1966)

Economic situation
Gross national product: $206,000,000 (1966)
Per capita income: $50 (1966)
Currency: pound sterling, £1 = $2.40
Principal products: tea, tobacco, ground nuts, fish

RHODESIA (ZIMBABWE)

Political situation
On November 11, 1965, Rhodesia declared its independence from Great Britain by means of the Unilateral Declaration of Independence (UDI). Ian Smith is prime minister. Under Rhodesia's (1969) constitution, there is a 23-member Senate and a 66-member House of Assembly.

The Rhodesian Front party (RF) is the ruling party. White opposition is provided by the Rhodesian National Party.

There are several African opposition parties. The African United People's Party, led by Percy Mkudo, has thirteen seats in the House of Assembly. The Zimbabwe African People's Union (ZAPU) and the Zimbabwe African Nationalist Union (ZANU), which is led by Reverend Ndabaningi Sithole, are the liberation parties and have been banned.

Demographic situation
Area: 150,333 square miles
Population: 4,530,000 (1967), including 228,000 whites, 14,000 coloreds, and 8,000 Asians
Capital: Salisbury, 358,000 inhabitants (1967)

Economic situation
Gross national product: $915,000,000 (1966)
Per capita income: $210 (1966)
Currency: dollar, R$1 = $1.40
Principal products: tobacco, chrome, nickel, asbestos, sugar, copper, pig iron

---

ZAMBIA

Political situation
On October 24, 1964, Zambia became an independent republic within the Commonwealth of Nations. The president is Kenneth David Kaunda, who heads the ruling United National Independent Party (UNIP). There is a unicameral National Assembly with 75 elected members. The major opposition party is the African National Congress (ANC), which is led by Harry N. Kumbula.

Demographic situation
Area: 290,586 square miles
Population: 3,894,400 (1967), including 79,400 whites
Capital: Lusaka, 151,800 inhabitants (1967)

Economic situation
Gross national product: $704,000,000 (1966)
Per capita income: $180 (1966)
Currency: kwacha, 1K = $1.40
Principal products: copper, peanuts, corn, cotton

1

Malawi and the Southern African Complex

SAMUEL W. SPECK, JR.

Internal Affairs

MALAWI SOCIETY

Although a ministate approximating the size of Portugal, Malawi's population density nevertheless exceeds that of its southern neighbors and most other African countries.[1] By European standards this density is quite modest but, given the nature of the Malawi economy, population and land pressures are severe. Most of the people and economic development are centered in the southern and, to a lesser degree, the central regions, giving rise to the characterization of the northern region as the "dead North."

Malawi's population, unlike that of Lesotho or Swaziland, is ethnically heterogeneous. At the same time, even though it is composed of a number of different African peoples, no single group dominates numerically, economically, or politically, and it has never had a problem of ethnic divisiveness such as that experienced by Uganda or Nigeria.

For the most part, its traditional political systems have been small and relatively weak. None covers more than one of Malawi's present twenty-three administrative districts and most a great deal less. Using Professor David E. Apter's typology, most of the traditional political systems could be classified as nonhierarchical and noninstrumental.[2]

Admittedly, there are some ethnic and regional tensions, but the significance is not in their existence, but in their relative unimportance in Malawi politics. As Clyde Sanger has rightly observed, "The degree to which Malawi had achieved national unity before independence . . . has few parallels in Africa."[3] There have been many reasons for this pervasive sense of national solidarity. Some have their roots in the nuances of the country's history and cultural heritage; others developed only recently. The absence of large, strong traditional political systems, the colonial administration of the country as a single unit not permitting any traditionalist enclaves, extensive labor emigration, the prevalence of mission-introduced Christianity, linguistic unity, and, finally, the single-party modern political structure have all played a part in the creation of this national unity.[4]

Although small in actual numbers, the Europeans and Asians who first entered Malawi under British rule continue to play an important role in the country's national life.[5] Europeans largely dominate private trade and industry and control the production of tea, which is one of the two principal export crops. As elsewhere in Africa, Asians rule the African wholesale and retail trade market, with similar, although lesser, attendant tensions between them and would-be African entrepreneurs supported by the government.[6]

THE ECONOMY

Malawi has one of the lowest per capita gross domestic products of any African state, reflecting both its limited natural endowments and its long neglect by imperial Britain.[7] As Griff Jones sardonically reflects,

> The years of occupation were remarkable, in the early phase, for a neglect which stung Johnston to call Nyasaland the Cinderella of the colonies; and in the middle years until the second war, for a disinterest which allowed merely the solvency of the administration; and in the final period, for a benevolent stupidity which encouraged development by imposed unpopular arrangements without the determination to sustain imposition.[8]

Economic development has long been crippled by internal and external transportation problems.[9] The railway presently extends less than halfway up the country and the area beyond that is separated from its other transport artery, Lake Malawi, by a sheer escarpment. Since independence the government has taken steps toward partially alleviating this problem by allocating sizeable funds to improve internal roads, but even good roads will not eliminate the high costs involved in moving products to market. Since the Shire River silted and was closed to river traffic soon after the establishment of the protectorate, nearly everything that Malawi imports or exports must travel by rail through Mozambique from the port of Beira. With the completion of the Malawi section in 1970, Malawi obtained a second access route through Mozambique to the ocean at Ncala, thereby speeding up the movement and possibly lowering somewhat the cost of transport, but certainly not reducing the country's dependency on good relations with Portugal.

With little exploitable mineral resources, nearly all wealth up to now has been produced by agriculture and the sale of migrant labor. The country's chief agricultural exports are shown in Table 1.[10] The general improvement found in

Table 1. Malawi Agricultural Exports, 1964–1968 ($U.S. '000)[a]

Product	1964	1965	1966	1967	1968
Tobacco	10,274	12,312	10,850	10,142	12,684
Tea	8,011	9,043	10,671	10,778	11,640
Peanuts	2,671	3,934	3,089	8,242	5,539
Cotton	2,321	2,590	2,602	1,661	1,529
Peas and beans	1,831	2,230	1,498	1,834	1034
Corn	571	41	1,884	3,934	3,610
Other	1,930	2,352	2,604	3,110	4,234
Total	27,609	32,502	33,198	39,701	40,270

[a] Republic of Malawi. National Statistical Office, *Balance of Payments (1968)* (Zomba: Malawi Government Printer, 1969), p. 23.

agricultural production since independence has been the result of energetic efforts by both the government and the ruling Malawi Congress party. Two developments of particular importance are not shown in the above table. In the last half decade Malawi has moved from being almost totally dependent on imported sugar, raw cotton, and basic cotton textiles to self-sufficiency and a likelihood of surplus for export in all three. For the most part, however, increased agricultural output has come from more vigorous application of traditional farming methods rather than from the introduction of new agricultural technology. Since these traditional methods rapidly deplete soil fertility, Malawi's future productivity is being seriously threatened.

Because of their relative domestic poverty, Malawians have long been economically dependent on selling their labor in one form or another in foreign markets. At first, this took the form of slaves sold through indigenous peoples to Arab traders for export to the Middle East; later, as members of the King's African Rifles, they fought British wars in East Africa and Southeast Asia. Today about half of all Malawians employed in wage labor work outside the country.[11] About two-thirds of these emigrant laborers work in Rhodesia, with most of the remainder going to South Africa. Their wage remissions along with the money and goods they bring with them upon their return home comprise one of Malawi's principal exports.[12]

THE POLITY

The preindependence legacy. Although as a British protectorate Malawi had had a legislative council and an executive council since 1907, Africans were not permitted to sit on the former until 1949 and on the latter until 1959. Both bodies, in fact, were dominated by official majorities until late 1961 when an African nonofficial majority gained control of the legislative council.

Despite their overwhelming numbers and the administration's acknowledgement that the colony would always be primarily an African country, Africans never meaningfully participated in national political life until Malawi was on the verge of independence. Hence Malawians came to independence with less experience in participating in modern political structures than in many other African states.

Beneath the central administration, British rule was characterized by an enduring commitment to the so-called "chiefs." *Évolués* were systematically discouraged from participation in local governance.[13] The commitment to the chiefs, however, was never one to traditional systems *in toto*, but mainly to the real and imagined roles of the chiefs within them.[14]

In the founding years of the protectorate and under direct rule the government had implicitly relied on the chiefs out of expediency. Then, under the officially designated indirect rule of the 1930s, traditional political systems came to be regarded as having an intrinsic and explicit value of their own. After World War II the indirect rule system, commonly referred to as native administration, was judged incapable of promoting social development, and the commitment to the chiefs reverted simply to expediency. By this time it was not that the administration could not find any other representative agents of the people, but that it feared the ones that were so increasingly and obviously available—the nationalist *évolués*. It then became a matter of waiting until "more moderate commoners" could be found.[15] Until these "more moderate commoners" turned up, the local political structures were to be manipulated to reinforce the power of the chiefs; such a policy was followed until the British decided to scrap the Central African Federation and to recognize Malawi's demand for self-determination in 1961.

African reaction to British rule through the years took a number of different forms. During the initial period of "pacification" it assumed the character of overt violence led by traditional African leaders. Then it appeared in the guise of religious separatism and African associations until after World War II when a monolithic, protectorate-wide political party became the principal vehicle of nationalism.[16]

The direct antecedent of the present ruling party, the Malawi Congress party (MCP), the African National Congress (ANC) was first founded in 1944 by a group of civil servants and small businessmen, many of whom had had experience in various African and educational associations. Recognized by the administration in 1946 "as representing various African associations in Nyasaland,"[17] the congress progressively fell out

of favor with the government as it succeeded in uniting traditionalists and *évolués* until the government withdrew its recognition in 1957.

Despite an infusion of some younger leaders, the congress still lacked a charismatic national figure and disciplined party structure and as a result remained basically weak. Recognizing these weaknesses, two of the most articulate and radical of the younger leaders, H. B. Masauko Chipembere and W. M. Kanyama Chiume, prevailed upon Dr. Hastings Kamuzu Banda, who had been absent over forty years from the country, to return home and assume party leadership. Dr. Banda returned in July 1958 to become the "kind of hero to be hero-worshipped" that Chipembere had asserted was needed if the political struggle were to succeed.[18]

Dr. Banda was elected president-general of the congress on August 1, 1958, on his condition that he should have the sole discretion in the appointment of the other officers and executive committee members, and thereafter he was the authoritative leader of Malawi nationalism. Under his able leadership party finances, organization, membership, and discipline greatly improved and African nationalism rose precipitately. After a number of local incidents involving congress members, apparent deadlock between the congress and the government over constitutional advancement, and finally rumors of a plot to massacre Europeans which later proved unfounded, the government declared an emergency on March 3, 1959, banned the congress, and detained many of its leaders.

Despite the decimation of its leadership with detention of some 1,300 persons in the emergency and continued intimidation by the administration, Malawi nationalism did not subside. Toward the end of September 1960 a new Malawi Congress Party (MCP) appeared as successor to the banned ANC. The MCP began to publish a newspaper, and Africans flocked into the party. When Dr. Banda was released from detention in April 1960, he resumed the task of party leadership where he had left off—only now he was even stronger, having visibly suffered for his people's freedom. By early 1961 the party had a large block of offices in Blantyre-Limbe, a fleet of over a dozen land rovers, and claimed to have a membership of a million members. The country's first direct election involving Africans was held in August 1961 under a new constitution brought into effect a month earlier. The MCP won an overwhelming vote of confidence, taking all twenty of the lower roll seats and also unexpectedly winning two of the eight upper roll constituencies. With this victory the MCP gained control of the legislative council and policy-making authority on most internal issues. Since this election the party's leadership of the country—if not Dr. Banda's leadership of the party—has remained unchallenged.[19]

Much about the development of Malawi nationalism was common to most African states, but nationalism in Malawi was perhaps more pervasive with more genuine support in rural areas than was frequently the case elsewhere. And, unlike most of its neighbors in East and Central Africa and the former High Commission Territories, Malawi party politics evolved from the start through a strictly one-party structure where support for the party was a ". . . moral norm, not just a matter of opinion."[20]

Postindependence political dynamics. Since the achievement of independence, the MCP and its auxiliaries have continued to dominate the Malawi political system which has few other major associational structures. The military remains under the control of white officers, and many of the most important bureaucratic posts are still in the hands of expatriates. Although Dr. Banda has encouraged Africanization—at the national level, at least—it has been at the comparatively leisurely pace which he has regarded as necessary to maintain bureaucratic efficiency, it not political stability.[21] Cooperatives and trade union organizations remain comparatively weak, even by African standards—a condition that is at least partially attributable to the character of the economy.

The MCP was patterned after Nkrumah's Convention People's party in the days when Dr. Banda, who had lived in Ghana from 1953 to 1958, was one of President Nkrumah's leading protégés. Like most African political parties of extraparliamentary origin, it is a highly centralized, disciplined organization. Its formal structure is depicted in Table 2.[22]

Table 2. Malawi Congress Party Organization

Annual Party Congress
Life President
National Executive Committee
Regional Executive Committees
District Executive Committees
Sub-District Executive Committees
Branch Executive Committees
Branch Membership

Yet, as with so many one-party systems, the MCP still has an element of duality in its structure. From branch through district levels it is for the most part a democratic structure, permitting a wide latitude of views and accommodating open and often highly competitive leadership recruitment. But beyond the district level is another story.[23]

Formally, the annual delegates' conference is the party's highest authority for making basic policy and electing the party president. In practice, Dr. Banda, who was elected life president of the party in 1960, dominates party life. Efforts are made to promote and protect his charisma by setting him apart from other Malawi leaders: his photographs are emphasized in the press; Kamuzu Day has replaced the Queen's Birthday as a national patriotic celebration; party branches are encouraged to sponsor delegations to send off and welcome the returning president when he travels abroad but are discouraged from doing the same for other leaders. At political meetings the crowds are to sing songs only to honor Kamuzu and not other leaders. A beneficently paternalistic leader, he is self-portrayed as "a father, grandfather, uncle [and] granduncle to every child and infant from Karonga to Nsanje and from Mchinji to Nkota Kota."[24]

As party leader, Dr. Banda holds the supreme executive power as advised by the central executive committee which he appoints and which serves at his pleasure. More informally, he also dominates the recruitment of regional party leadership. Ever since the September 1960 Nkota Kota conference, where he was elected party president, he has exercised his prerogative of personally selecting the party's parliamentary nominees. He also holds—and has frequently used—the authority to purge recalcitrant local party organizations whose cadres select delegates to national party conferences. Through his control over the appointment of the editor of the *Malawi News*, he commands the party press. All of this does not mean that Dr. Banda acts without consultation or popular support. But few party leaders in Africa exercise more power within their respective parties than he does. One of Dr. Banda's closest lieutenants told the author: "We feel that he should be allowed to do pretty much as he sees fit, so long as he has the support of the people."

According to the party discipline,

> the Leagues of Malawi Women and Youth are integral parts of the M.C.P. The Leagues are wings of the Mother Body, the M.C.P., and their duty is to help the Mother Body to function and to obey and not to criticize or to argue.[25]

Organizationally, both leagues essentially replicate the parent body. Functionally, the Women's League serves as a special channel of communication between the party and the women. Probably its most important role has been the social uplifting of women through increased dissemination of new ideas among them in a fashion reminiscent of American county extension programs.

During the struggle for independence, Youth Leaguers served as party messengers, informants, and police who, through persuasion and intimidation, enforced party directives and discipline in the villages. When internal self-government was obtained and independence drew nearer, the need for these activities seemed to diminish, and in 1963 the Young Pioneer movement was launched. The Young Pioneers, who were to remain a special group within the Youth League, were to be trained at camps about the country in agricultural work to stimulate interest in rural life and to spur the agrarian revolution requisite for long-range national development.[26] With the breach in party and government in late 1964 (which will be discussed later), the Youth League once again emphasized its police role, and after the crisis the Young Pioneers assumed the role of a police reserve with members receiving twenty hours of basic rifle training.[27] Moreover, Dr. Banda forbade the police to arrest Young Pioneers or to release people arrested by them without his sanction.[28] To the Youth Leaguers and Young Pioneers, who had largely remained loyal to Dr. Banda in the 1964 internal upheaval, fell chiefly the responsibility of seeking out the disloyal.

Malawi gained independence July 6, 1964, under a constitution which structured the government on the British parliamentary model. On its second anniversary of independence, it became a republic but the parliament (known as the National Assembly) remained essentially as before. There were no new elections, but the maximum five-year life of parliament was extended to 1971 to run concurrent with the new office of president. Malawi officially became a one-party state, although the constitution allowed up to five non-Africans to be appointed to parliament to represent non-African opinion, and Dr. Banda duly made these appointments, much as the governor had done prior to 1956.

The president is both head of state and head of government, combining the positions formerly held by the governor and prime minister. As a temporary expedient, in 1966 Dr. Banda was elected president by the parliament. Hereafter, the president will be nominated by an electoral college comprising the elected government and party officials of the national, regional, and district levels and elected by a simple yes-no vote of the people.[29]

The present National Assembly was chosen by an election just prior to independence in 1964. All candidates were returned without opposition so that in reality no elections were held. Indeed, except for some township council posts, no formal elections have been held at the national or local level since 1961.

The principal challenge to Dr. Banda's leadership came in late 1964 when a group of his most articulate and influential lieutenants, including nearly all of the university-educated members of his cabinet, dramatically split with him over a series of issues. A majority of his cabinet ministers was dismissed or resigned in protest, and subsequently over a third of the country's district MCP committees were dissolved and successors appointed by the prime minister.[30]

Thereafter, the dissident ministers and a number of their followers fled to Zambia and Tanzania. In early 1965 Masauko Chipembere led an abortive insurrection against the government and since 1965 small insurgent bands have periodically undertaken to infiltrate the country; the most notorious attempt was in October 1967, in which the rebel and former minister of home affairs, Yatuta Chisiza, was shot by government troops in the rugged bush country northwest of the capital.

According to most accounts, the initial cleavage stemmed from Dr. Banda's paternalistic attitude toward and unwillingness to share decision-making authority with those who had initially brought him back to lead the nationalist movement, his conservative approach to Africanization of the civil service and compensation of African civil servants, certain other of his domestic policies (such as the unpopular imposition of hospital fees), and his positive, if not friendly, orientation toward the white-dominated regimes to the east and south. Although there is no doubt that these issues precipitated the internal crisis, there are also indications that at least Chipembere as early as 1961 was building a personal power base, particularly in the civil service and among local party and district council cadres, and that Dr. Banda was fully aware of this. But whether a primary cause or a principal pretext, it is significant for our subsequent analysis that conflict over Malawi's role in the Southern African nexus has created tension within the ruling MCP since independence.

The near coup of 1964 has left an enduring legacy in Malawi politics. Internally, Dr. Banda further tightened his grip on party and government affairs while simultaneously moving to assuage some of the domestic grievances raised by the dissidents.[31] As one might expect, there has also been a subsequent stress on weeding out the allegedly "disloyal" Malawians and dramatizing unity as fact and goal. Internationally, the sanctuary, and at times encouragement, that the rebels have received from Tanzania and Zambia exacerbated Malawi's relationship with these two nations. This, plus the loss of pan-Africanist pressure from the departed dissidents, has probably contributed to Malawi's cordial relations with the white-dominated nations and colonies in Southern Africa. In summary, the domestic crisis of 1964 was at least partially caused by, and has had a continuing impact on, Malawi's international relations.

External Relations

HISTORICAL TIES

Since its colonial beginnings, Malawi's development has been intimately related to East, and particularly Southern, Africa, Indeed, its very founding as a British protectorate was predicated on the anticipated growth of such a relationship.[32] To understand the nature of Malawi's rapidly developing ties with Southern Africa it is important that they be seen in this perspective. What they represent is far less a break from the past than an extension of it. Truly, Malawi has always been caught up in the Southern African complex.

From precolonial days when commerce was linked to the sea by footpaths across northern Mozambique, Malawi has depended largely on Mozambique for access to world markets. After the 1870s the Shire and Zambezi Rivers became the principal commercial arteries, succeeded after World War I by the railway. At the close of World War II, the Central African Airways Corporation was established to consolidate and develop Central African air service with most of the flights from Nyasaland connecting with Southern Rhodesia.

As early as 1903 the South African Witwatersrand mines entered into an agreement for recruiting Nyasaland labor, labor literally forced to leave the country in search of work to pay government-imposed hut taxes.[33] By 1935 over 45 percent of the northern region's adult male population was estimated to be employed abroad, largely in Southern Africa.[34] A decade later 65 percent were described as absentees, and the country as a whole was dependent on Southern Africa for the employment of the majority of its wage-earning labor force.[35] Malawi had been drawn into the Southern African nexus to such an extent that for some ethnic groups like the Lakeshore Tonga a stint on the mines of the Witwatersrand became incorporated into tribal coming-of-age ritual.

Although Southern Africa has been the principal employer of Malawi wage labor for at least the last half century, the development of other direct economic ties are of a more recent vintage. Until World War II nearly all other Malawi exports went to the United Kingdom, with some going to Germany. The war, however, altered trade patterns when Malawi began sending products to South Africa and Southern Rhodesia, so that by the beginning of the 1950s about one-sixth of all Malawi exports were finding Southern African markets, mostly in Southern Rhodesia.[36] In the postwar years Malawi also began importing Southern African goods in increasing amounts, and Southern Rhodesian coins became legal tender in Malawi along with those of the United Kingdom.[37]

Pressures for some kind of formal union with neighboring countries have a long history in Malawi.[38] As early as 1917 the head of a leading missionary society urged union with some other territory, preferably Northern Rhodesia.[39] An even larger union was proposed in the 1920s, and a commission was appointed to investigate the possibilities of an association of Nyasaland, Northern Rhodesia, and the three East African territories. The commission recommended, however, that the status quo be maintained until Africans were further developed and could determine their own destiny.[40] In the 1930s the question was raised once again and another commission was appointed, this time to consider the feasibility of closer association among Nyasaland, Northern Rhodesia, and Southern Rhodesia.[41] The commission reported that economic interdependence made closer association desirable and ultimately inevitable, but it stated that overwhelming African opposition in the northern territories, differences in levels of economic and political development between them and Southern Rhodesia, and the latter's harsher native policies precluded immediate closer association.[42]

THE FEDERATION OF RHODESIA AND NYASALAND

After World War II the white settler population in the two Rhodesias and Nyasaland, augmented by an influx of immigrants from Europe and South Africa, again pressed for union. Commencing in 1951, a series of conferences on union were held and in September 1953 the three territories were federated. Great Britain's acceptance of a union which it had earlier rejected was predicated on several factors. British colonial policy had become committed to more rapid development of the colonies and the British government hoped to create a larger Central African economic unit presumably more capable of attracting outside capital and engendering self-sustained growth. In this scheme of things, Malawi was to provide a stable supply of labor for Northern Rhodesian mines and Southern Rhodesian farms and factories, in return for which the federation would subsidize the Nyasaland economy and particularly its social services, thus relieving Great Britain of this burden. Accepting Malawi in the federation was part of Great Britain's price for allowing the settlers in the other two territories to join. In the face of pervasive African opposition in the two northern territories, it was rationalized that once the economic benefits of federation materialized, the bulk of African opposition to the forced marriage would melt away.[43] A second and more covert element in the British policy reversal represented a response to the 1948 National party victory in South Africa. The Central African Federation was a device for containing National party influence south of the Limpopo River. A Southern Rhodesia federated northward could be expected to remain more economically and politically independent of South Africa. Indeed, federation might even provide an alternative model for future development in South Africa.[44]

The federal government assumed responsibility for external relations to the extent permitted by the United Kingdom and for a number of other matters of special importance to the settler population. Objects of particular concern to the African population such as African education, agriculture, feeder roads, and local government remained territorial responsibilities. In part, this division of power was made in deference to African fears over federation. But the arrangement also facilitated the allocation of more resources for services to the whites than would have been politically expedient had the expenditures for white and African services not fallen under different governments.

Although Nyasaland had a larger population than either of the two other federal territories, it always had less than a fifth of the representation in the federal parliament, and Nyasaland's minuscule settler population dominated the recruitment of nearly all those seats—even most of the ones nominally held by Africans.[45] Again, despite its larger population, Nyasaland was by law allocated less than half of Southern Rhodesia's share of the monies borrowed and taxes collected by the federal government.[46]

By 1961 the federation was dead—a victim, more than anything else, of intransigent Malawi nationalism. Federal ties with Southern Rhodesia had never gained African confidence in Malawi because, despite its promise, federation was always politically and economically subservient to the interests of Southern Rhodesian whites, and the federation operated in such a way as to retard African political, if not economic, advancement.[47]

Although federation proved short-lived, it was not without long-range consequences. Politically, its imposition had a catalytic influence on Malawi Africans, doing more to promote the growth of African nationalism than probably any other single factor. Economically, it caused Malawi to shift much of its import trade from other countries to Southern Rhodesia.[48] The political implications ultimately destroyed the formal political links implied in the federation, but many of the economic ties remained after the federation's demise. If prior to federation Malawi was already being pulled economically into the Southern African nexus through the export of its labor, the federation forged yet another economic link in the chain.

ECONOMIC RELATIONS WITH SOUTHERN AFRICA SINCE INDEPENDENCE

The trade links that Malawi evolved with Southern Africa during federation have undergone significant reorientation since independence. In the final days of federation, Malawi concluded a trade agreement with Rhodesia providing for largely free entry of Rhodesian goods in return for an annual fiscal payment from Rhodesia of 10 percent of the net value of trade in specified categories. Since by 1964 about 39 percent of Malawi imports came from Rhodesia, this payment contributed substantially to Malawi's balance of payments. In response to Rhodesia's unilateral declaration of independence, however, Malawi abrogated the agreement but thereafter allowed Rhodesian goods to enter at Commonwealth preferential rates.[49] Malawi minister of education and leader of its delegation at the United Nations, Mr. Alec Nyasasulu, explained:

> To attempt to cut off all economic ties with Rhodesia would do *us* far more harm than it would do to Rhodesia if other sources of supplies, other means of carrying on our essential export trade are not available, but we can and will reduce those ties.[50]

As is indicated in Table 3, this is approximately what has happened. Since Rhodesia unilaterally proclaimed its independence, Malawi's trade with Rhodesia has sharply declined relative to its total trade. The real reason for this commercial disengagement, however, resides less in the political crisis precipitated by the Smith regime than in the character of the economic links forged in federation. Federation had allowed Rhodesia to expand its secondary industries rapidly to supply the protected markets in Malawi and Zambia. Since independence Malawi had followed the path of most newly independent African states and sought to develop its own secondary industries, both to provide more jobs locally and to improve its historically precarious

Table 3. Malawi Trade with Rhodesia as a Percentage of Total Malawi Trade, 1964–1968[a]

Year	Imports from Rhodesia	Exports to Rhodesia
1964	39%	16%
1965	38%	10%
1966	23%	6%
1967	21%	4%
1968	18%	5%

[a] Republic of Malawi. Department of Census and Statistics, *Annual Statement of External Trade, 1968* (Zomba: Malawi Government Printer, n.d), pp. 1, 5.

balance-of-payments position. The independence issue aside, it was inevitable that Malawi trade with Rhodesia would stabilize or decline as it developed its own import-substituting secondary industries.[51]

But while Malawi trade with Rhodesia has been declining, its imports from—and very recently its exports to—South Africa have been rising (see Table 4). This does not represent a shift of trade in competitive products from Rhodesia to South Africa. Rather, South Africa has increasingly become a supplier of capital goods for Malawi in a way that Rhodesia was not and could not have been because Rhodesia lacked and still lacks the economy either to produce such heavy goods or, equally important, to provide the credit to finance their export. Malawi's increasing purchases from South Africa are the result of Malawi's rising demand for capital goods and South Africa's new willingness to finance development projects in black-dominated countries with loans tied to the purchase of South African goods.[52]

Table 4. Malawi Trade with South Africa as a Percentage of Total Malawi Trade, 1964–1968[a]

Year	*Imports from South Africa*	*Exports to South Africa*
1964	6%	5%
1965	5%	4%–
1966	7%	3%+
1967	8%	3%
1968	11%	4%

[a] Republic of Malawi. Department of Census and Statistics, *Annua Statement of External Trade, 1968* (Zomba: Malawi Government Printer, n.d.), p. 5.

This new trade relationship was formally recognized and promoted in March 1967 when the two countries signed a trade agreement providing for mutual preferential tariff treatment and a commitment of South African assistance to Malawi economic development. In addition to its intrinsic importance, the agreement has particular symbolic significance because it represented the first trade agreement South Africa had signed with an independent black African state.[53] This latter aspect was not lost to the member states of the Organization of African Unity whose spokesmen responded helplessly at the Kinshasa summit conference in September 1967 by denouncing maneuvers by South Africa "aimed at seducing certain independent African States by economic and financial offers."[54] By August 1968 the South African foreign minister, Dr. Hilgard Muller, visited Malawi and spoke, in perhaps historically relevant terms, of a new "co-prosperity" partnership.[55]

Malawi's trade with Mozambique has never been extensive and in recent years has, if anything, declined in relative terms. Nevertheless, Malawi and Mozambique are being drawn closer together not only through the expansion of communications links, but also through both increased Portuguese investment in Malawi (which President Banda has assiduously courted) and the projected development of the Cabora Bassa hydroelectric scheme which will serve a power grid stretching from Malawi to South Africa.

Increased ties between Malawi and Southern Africa are also manifested in other ways such as new communications patterns. Rather than connect its railway to the Tanzam railway, Malawi has opted to develop a second line to the sea through Mozambique. And understandably so, for the latter was much shorter and cheaper and could be completed by mid-1970, whereas the Tanzam link was years away. With the introduction of Air Malawi flights to Johannesburg in 1968 and South African Airways flights to Blantyre in 1969, Malawi became the principal communications link between its beleaguered southern neighbors and the rest of black Africa.

At the first flush of independence, Malawi encountered internal pressures, particularly from some of its more radical elements, to discourage labor emigration to Southern Africa. But economic realities quickly prevailed over histrionics, and since then Malawi's relations with Rhodesia and South Africa have been based on a clearly discerned interest to protect its access to the Southern African labor market; for many years African labor will remain Malawi's third largest export. Although about two-thirds of Malawi emigrant labor goes to Rhodesia and only about a fifth to South Africa, more than half of the laborers' remittances to Malawi come from those working in South Africa and thus—at least in this regard—South Africa is the most important market for Malawi labor.[56] In 1967 Malawi negotiated its first formal labor agreement with South Africa, which protected and even promised to expand this market.[57] Malawi's mild and cautious attitude toward Rhodesia has been at least partially determined by its fear that Rhodesia might force Malawi workers to return home—either as an act of political leverage or because of a boycott-engendered economic recession in Rhodesia. Indeed, the Smith regime ominously threatened to repatriate Malawians and, in fact, some Malawians have been sent home because of increased unemployment in Rhodesia.[58]

The fact that Rhodesia and South Africa could very likely topple the Malawi government if they expelled large numbers of Malawi workers does not perforce mean that the export of Malawi labor is solely dependent on the altruism of these two countries. It should be pointed out that foreign labor tends to provide both Rhodesia and South

Africa with a more stable work force and with a means to check internal inflationary tendencies.

From a political perspective, the high percentage of foreign labor in the urban areas of these two countries has unquestionably been an important contributing factor, particularly in Rhodesia, to the difficulty African nationalist movements have had in organizing effectively.[59] Were Rhodesia to replace foreign African labor with Rhodesian Africans, it would serve as a stimulus to African nationalism there. Finally, it is improbable that any successor to Dr. Banda would be more congenial to white interests in Southern Africa. By far the greatest actual pressures for the repatriation of Malawi labor have come from localization demands in Zambia and Tanzania, and Malawi cannot help but question whether it would find black governments in Rhodesia and South Africa as receptive to Malawi labor as the present white-controlled ones.

Although Malawi is developing new economic relations with Southern Africa, its currency devaluation—simultaneous with that of the British pound—dramatically revealed just how tied the Malawi economy is to that of Great Britain. While Malawi's trade with South Africa is rising, it still imports nearly three times as much from, and exports ten times as much to, the United Kingdom.[60] And, although South Africa is becoming an important source of loan capital, Malawi still depends on the United Kingdom for some $7 million annually to balance its recurrent budget account and for more loan capital than from any other national source.[61]

THE POLITICS OF ECONOMIC NECESSITY: THE BRIDGE AND THE LAAGER

We have already observed that the abortive 1964 coup was at least partially the result of internal conflict over what Malawi's posture as an independent nation should be toward black and white Africa.

In both foreign and domestic policy fields, Dr. Banda has always been much more of a realist and a pragmatist than many of his more ideologically oriented fellow African leaders, urging his countrymen not to be "swayed by doctrines, theories, and impractical idealism."[62] If his foreign policy has made him, to use his own characterization, "the Number One Unpopular Man in Africa" among the OAU nations and a real statesman in the eyes of many Southern African whites,[63] it is not because he has sold out the interests of his own country but precisely the opposite—that he has placed Malawi national self-interest above other and particularly pan-African values. As he colorfully puts it, Malawi will "align itself even with the Devil" to help its own people, and this means, according to the former minister of natural resources, Gomile Kumtumanji, putting the interest of the country first and the OAU last.[64] Vociferously pro-West, his policies have been relatively consistent and overt. Indeed, it has been the unapologetic blatancy of Malawi's relations with white-dominated Southern African regimes as much as these relations *per se* that has infuriated the leaders of other African states.

Malawi foreign policy is self-defined as discretionary nonalignment. With particular reference to Southern Africa, it operates on the premise that

> Relations between Malawi as a nation or state and any other country or state in Africa, must not be governed or influenced by the race or colour of those now in control of the affairs of any country.
>
> Relations between Malawi as a nation or a state, and any other country or state in Africa, must not be governed or influenced by the internal policies of such country or state.
>
> The only criterion in this matter must be the existence between Malawi and the countries concerned of some sphere or spheres of mutual interest whereby both countries may benefit from a common association. If this realistic policy is to be fulfilled we must remain free in our friends and to recognize our enemies.[65]

Repeatedly, the president has referred to his country as playing the role of bridge between black and white Africa, a role that he believes will gain greater acceptance in black Africa once the member states of the OAU recognize that resolutions and even trained African nationalist guerrillas will not bring down the entrenched white regimes.[66] At least at one point, however, he has revealingly depicted Malawi's role somewhat differently. Malawi is not merely a bridge but "*a laager around southern Africa.*"[67] In other words, Malawi will help insulate Southern African states, black and white, from revolutionary influences in return, one presumes, for trade and assistance in economic development.

Prior to UDI, Malawi took a relatively ambivalent, yet stronger stand against Rhodesia than it has subsequently. At the 1964 OAU summit conference in Cairo, Dr. Banda endorsed anti-Rhodesian resolutions, although even then he publicly announced Malawi's inability to subscribe fully to them. At this time Malawi was appointed along with Tanzania to provide good offices to help the two nationalist parties in Rhodesia, the Zimbabwe African People's Union (ZAPU) and the Zimbabwe African National Union (ZANU) to unite. A year later, however, the OAU supplanted this committee with a larger one in which Malawi did not participate. In August 1965 Emperor Haile Selassie of Ethiopia and Dr. Banda issued a joint communiqué at the end of the former's visit to Malawi, asserting their agreement on the need for the liberation of Rhodesia and their support of OAU efforts to that end. But by the time of the OAU's summit meeting in October 1965, Malawi was no longer willing to endorse the anti-Rhodesian resolutions of the OAU since these resolutions had escalated to the point of openly condoning the use of force to establish African majority rule in Rhodesia. Understandably, Malawi was omitted from the committee of five appointed to implement these resolutions. At this point the growing tensions between Malawi and some other Organization members broke out into a conflict over the seating of Malawi on the eleven-member Liberation Committee. In September 1965 Dr. Banda had said that he would not assist the Liberation Committee until such time as it moved from Tanzania, and now Tanzania blocked Malawi's nomination, charging that Malawi was "in collusion with the Portuguese in Mozambique."[68]

After the 1965 OAU summit at Accra the schism between the Organization and Malawi over the Rhodesia issue further widened when the Organization's Rhodesia Committee called for an Algerian-type guerrilla war against the Rhodesia Front government. Malawi openly spurned the Organization's demand that members break off diplomatic relations with the United Kingdom if the British government failed to bring down the Smith regime by December 15, 1965, it steadfastly rejected force as a means of overcoming UDI, and it refused to subscribe to Organization demands for a total trade boycott. Whereas the OAU continued its attempt to reconcile the two Rhodesian African nationalist movements, Malawi presently entertained a delegation of the United People's party which held seats in the Rhodesian parliament and which was regarded as treasonable by most African states, and Dr. Banda subsequently banned ZAPU, the principal representative of Rhodesian African nationalist interests.[69]

In the United Nations, Malawi has usually abstained from voting on General Assembly resolutions dealing with Rhodesia, although it did support that organization's initial action and has generally endorsed Commonwealth proposals on Rhodesia.

Malawi's unwillingness to abet revolution in Rhodesia is in part attributable to the country's economic interdependence with Southern Africa. It is also a product of the close ties Malawi maintains with Great Britain. The legacy of the abortive 1964 coup is another contributory factor. Because of the asylum, if not encouragement, that Zambia and particularly Tanzania gave to the Malawi rebels the Banda government has feared that OAU aid that was supposed to be channeled to Rhodesian guerrillas through the Liberation Committee headquartered in Tanzania might instead go to Malawi guerrillas. Tanzania, on the other hand, cannot forgive Malawi's lack of pan-African zeal as manifested particularly in Malawi's cordial relationship with Portugal while African nationalist guerrillas were waging war in northern Mozambique. Finally, the prolonged boycott of Rhodesia has served Malawi interests, temporarily increasing its trade with Zambia and allowing it to capture some of Rhodesia's tobacco market.

Malawi's growing political ties with South Africa and Portugal are indicated in many ways: the establishment of diplomatic relations; the exchange of high-ranking visitors, including a visit of both the Portuguese and South African foreign ministers to Malawi; the increased cordiality with which each country is treated in the other's press; and, of course, the growing communication, trade, and investment links. As a part of this pattern, Malawi has refused to join the African bloc's attacks on Portugal and on South Africa at annual meetings of the heads of state of East and Central Africa, the OAU, and the United Nations. Habitually, its delegate has abstained from voting on resolutions supporting boycotts of South African or Portuguese goods or urging the United Nations to assume control in South West Africa. Along with its fellow black states south of the Zambezi, it voted against expelling South Africa from the United Nations Committee on Trade and Development.

These expanding political relations with South Africa and Portugal are based principally upon economic necessity, but Dr. Banda also believes that since violence against South Africa is unlikely to succeed, the "bluff and bluster" of the OAU merely increases the fears of the whites and makes them less willing to recognize African humanity and rights. Addressing a state banquet for visiting President Tsiranana of Malagasy in April 1969, he explained:

> The White people of South Africa and Rhodesia are afraid of Africans. We will not cure them of apartheid by boycotting them or denouncing them at a distance. We have to let them come here and mix with us and let them see how it is to live under Black Government. This is an honest, sincere, religious belief about *apartheid*. We African leaders will help Africans in South Africa much better if we let Whites come in and see how Black, Brown, and White people live together.[70]

Following this logic, the president regards it as a real victory for Malawi that its African diplomats were the first to be accorded full and equal diplomatic treatment by the South African government; to him this represents a breach in apartheid. Once the South African regime begins to treat foreign African leaders as equals, presumably it will be more difficult to deny the rights of its own black people.[71] To many African leaders, of course, all of this is but a fatuous rationalization for economic self-interest.

The increased liaison with South Africa and Portugal may have undermined Malawi's security to the extent that it has alienated its intellectuals, encouraged Tanzania and Zambia to collaborate with Malawi insurgents, and isolated it from black states north of the Zambezi. Yet there is little reason to think that the average peasant really cares about all of this very much so long as progress is being made at home, and in some very direct ways the new relationship with Southern Africa has enhanced the Banda government's security.[72] Now Portuguese troops seemingly stand sentry just across the border when President Banda travels abroad and he is able to warn Tanzania that " 'if war breaks out—apart from the bravery and ability of our soldiers, we will have allies across the borders—we will have to welcome them.' "[73] Finally, Dr. Banda has been able to obtain from South Africa something he has deemed of particular political value and which has seemingly been unavailable elsewhere—funding for moving the country's capital from its southern to central region.[74]

MALAWI AND BLACK AFRICA

Malawi's relative isolation in the OAU and elsewhere has already been noted. Dr. Banda has not attended an OAU summit meeting since 1965 (when Kwame Nkrumah sent his Russian Ilyushin to pick him up) and the Malawi delegation has frequently been absent from ministerial meetings. When its isolation has not been manifested by its absence, it has been dramatized by its votes. Not only has its position on Southern African problems often set it apart but so have its uncompromisingly pro-Israel and caustically anti-Arab policies.[75]

Malawi's estrangement from black Africa, however, is far from complete. Closer ties have been developing with the three former High Commission Territories and Malagasy, relieving Malawi's sense of isolation. Perhaps more than anyone else President Jomo Kenyatta of Kenya, Dr. Banda's long-time personal friend, has at various points helped the Malawi president to refurbish and maintain his credentials as a bona fide African nationalist, and through this personal friendship between the two leaders Malawi has maintained closer and more cordial relations with Kenya than with any other major African state.

Conclusions

Independent Malawi has largely been the art and craft of its singular leader, Dr. Hastings Kamuzu Banda. Although he is in his late sixties, there is no heir apparent and purposely so. Thus it is difficult to project Malawi's course very far into the future. Dr. Banda's passing from leadership could result in a dramatic shift in Malawi's orientation if the president's departure were followed by internal dissension which allowed the expatriate rebels to return and, with their presently quiescent internal allies, to assume power. But among the expatriate rebels, only Chipembere has had any independent and widespread following and, his health problems aside, he has many implacable enemies who, because they have much to lose, would probably see to it that he never lived to rule the country.

An African nationalist victory in the northern half of Mozambique cutting off Malawi's access to ports could also lead to a redirection in Malawi's policies, but such a victory is unlikely in the very near future unless the Mozambique insurgents receive appreciably more outside assistance than they have up to now.

These possibilities aside, Dr. Banda's successors are likely to continue to be attracted by the economic gravity of Southern Africa. Although Dr. Banda has an aristocratic and authoritarian demeanor, the strength of his administration inheres in its peasant base. His supporters are found in the Youth League, which does not attract the university-bound African youth; the Women's League; much of the traditional leadership; the functionaries in the party apparatus; and, of course, the common peasant. His detractors are also found in all of these groups, but they come especially from the civil service and intelligentsia. The bias is evident when President Banda rhetorically asks and answers what he understands by practical democracy in Malawi:

> To do the best for my people. And when I say "for my people," . . . I do not mean clerks in the offices here in Blantyre and Zomba. I mean the ordinary people in the villages—farmers. I must create a situation for them in which they find not only peace and tranquility, but have something to eat, something to put on their back, on their wives' heads, and if possible, shoes.[76]

It is also made clear when he lauds the Young Pioneers, saying,

> You are more important than they [the students at the University of Malawi] are because you have produced something. They are noth-

ing but parasites. You are superior to them. Can they live without eating? But you can live without books.[77]

It has been submitted that Malawi's position in the Southern African nexus is best conceptualized by the mixed metaphors of a bridge and a laager. The two roles are not easily compatible. Serving as a buffer for white-dominated regimes south of the Zambezi makes it difficult for Malawi to be taken seriously to the north, but at this stage Malawi serves increasingly as one of the principal communications, if not diplomatic, links between north and south.

Malawi the laager is not Malawi the puppet. In the parlance of game theory, Malawi's involvement in the Southern African nexus is not a zero-sum game situation born of total dependency for, as we have seen, Malawi also holds important inducements in its relations *vis à vis* Southern African white regimes.[78] Besides helping to deflect revolutionary thrusts from the north and providing new outlets for South African products and investment, good relations with Malawi enhance the legitimacy of the South African government, at least in the West, and thereby contribute to the psychic security of the *verligte* Afrikaners in a way that relations with the geographically captive former High Commission territories do not.

That Malawi has been increasingly attracted into the Southern African orbit is a result, above all else, of economic factors. But its strong ties to Great Britain and the legacy of the 1964 near *coup* are also important.

Malawi can be expected to disengage from Southern Africa only when disengagement would no longer jeopardize it economically or threaten it politically, and that is not likely for some time. As Dr. Banda has said, one must "have a sense of patience."[79]

2

Rhodesia and Interstate Relationships in Southern Africa

JAMES P. BARBER

On November 11, 1965, Mr. Ian Smith, the Rhodesian prime minister, unilaterally declared his country independent of the United Kingdom. Since then Rhodesia has been at the center of a major international controversy not merely because UDI (Unilateral Declaration of Independence) was illegal but because most nations have interpreted it as an act of racism, an attempt by a white minority to perpetuate its rule over a black majority. At the United Nations and at meetings of the Commonwealth, Britain has been urged to overthrow the Smith government by the use of military force, but, although Britain bitterly denounced Mr. Smith and his colleagues, she has refused to use force. Instead, she has organized economic sanctions against Rhodesia through the United Nations.

Even from this brief summary it can be seen that the Rhodesian crisis has had important implications for the whole international community, but in this chapter we shall concentrate on Rhodesia's relations with Zambia and its Southern African neighbors and on developments within Rhodesia which are relevant to these relations.

Although the concentration on Rhodesia must necessarily produce a particular and somewhat narrow view of interstate relationships in Southern Africa, it is possible, by drawing on Rhodesian examples, to examine: first, the emergence and identification of a Southern African bloc of states; second, the nature of the relationships between these states; third, the factors which have strengthened the relationships; and, finally, the forces which challenge the relationships.

In analyzing these topics it will become obvious that the relationships are in no way fixed or static. They are constantly under change, partly from internal developments in Southern Africa and partly from external challenges.

Britain, Rhodesia, and the Southern African Bloc

There now exists a bloc of states in Southern Africa in which the four most powerful states—the Republic of South Africa and South West Africa, the Portuguese territories of Angola and Mozambique, and Rhodesia—are under white control. South Africa, because of her economic and military strength, is clearly the leader of the bloc. Clustered around the white states are smaller black-controlled states which, from choice or weakness, accept a subordinate status. Although this structure now gives an impression of strength and stability it is in fact very new. As recently as 1960, the year of Sharpeville and Prime Minister Harold Macmillan's "Wind of Change" speech, the white states of the sub-continent appeared to be exposed and vulnerable to the black nationalist movements which were rapidly replacing the Western European colonial regimes in West and East Africa. It would have appeared foolhardy then to predict that by the mid-1960s a white-controlled South Africa would emerge as the dominant partner in a state system embracing the whole of Southern Africa and including a white-controlled Rhodesia and two Portuguese colonial territories. It would have appeared foolhardy because then it seemed unlikely that Portugal could retain her colonial possessions while more powerful Western European states were abandoning theirs, and because it was widely assumed that the colonial withdrawal could benefit only black nationalism. Black nationalism was seen both as an irresistible force and as the rightful inheritor of the states that had been carved out of Africa. In Southern Africa subsequent events have belied these assumptions. Although black rulers have taken control in some small and relatively poor states, in the Portuguese territories, in Rhodesia, and in South Africa the white rulers have consolidated their positions. In South Africa's case the Republic has spread its influence across the whole subcontinent.

The white rulers have taken advantage of the new situation created in Southern Africa by the British colonial withdrawal. The British withdrawal took place quickly in the mid-1960s, first with the breakup of the Central African Federation and the grant of independence to two of the component territories, Northern Rhodesia (now Zambia) and Nyasaland (now Malawi), and then later with the grant of independence to the three High Commission Territories of Bechuanaland (now Botswana), Basutoland (now Lesotho), and Swaziland. On achieving independence all these states came under black governments. The only British possession not to be granted independence was Rhodesia. In constitutional terms Rhodesia has always been an exception in that Britain claimed it as a colony, but granted a white settler government virtual self-government in internal affairs including the right to recruit its own civil service and armed forces. Unlike every other British colony, there was no direct British administrative or military presence in Rhodesia. Yet in external affairs the British claimed the same responsibility for Rhodesia as they claimed for their other territories. The British presence, bringing with it the strengths and interests of a major world power, had excluded the possibility of a separate Southern African bloc emerging or of South Africa holding a dominant position in the subcontinent.

The British withdrawal created the conditions for a reorganization of relationships in Southern Africa, and Mr. Smith's actions have been especially important in underlining the implications of the withdrawal. His actions, in particular, revealed the determination of the white rulers to confirm their own positions. UDI and the resistance to sanctions have been assertions of white strength and determination.

The Commitment to White Rule

The South African and Portuguese decision to support Rhodesia in her fight against international sanctions has revealed the strength of fellow feeling among the three white governments. All three have been bitterly attacked in the international community as racist regimes, and the strength of these attacks has tended to weld the three governments together. They do not, however, share ideological or political traditions. The National government in South Africa with its strong commitment to apartheid is particularly conscious of these differences. They view with apprehension the integrationist ideas of the Portuguese and the pattern of multiracial government which has been developed in Rhodesia, where even today black men sit in the parliament. Among the governments of Southern Africa these distinctions are very real, and there is a temptation therefore to search for binding ties within the Southern African bloc in terms of geography, communications systems, and economic relationships. Plainly, these material links are important and for the small, economically weak states of Lesotho, Swaziland, and Botswana, they may be all important, leaving them no real choice but to accept a subordinate relationship with their white neighbors.

UDI has confirmed the strength of these material ties but it has also revealed the strength of a major ideological tie—the right of white minorities to rule African majorities. Although both the

South Africans and the Portuguese are committed to continued white rule within their own borders, neither have welcomed the emphasis upon white minority government which the Rhodesian crisis has produced. To remove international pressures, South Africa and Portugal have both attempted to create acceptable images of themselves—the Portuguese by emphasizing their policy of integration, the South Africans by their Bantustan policy and by trying to establish good relations with black states. In fashioning these new images, they did not want to be identified merely with a "white power" bloc. Dr. Verwoerd stated the case for South Africa in 1963. Speaking about Rhodesia, he refused to distinguish it from the other neighboring states. He said: "When consultative relationships developed between the Republic of South Africa and any other state, whether Black or mixed or White in Southern Africa, then naturally we would be able to co-operate with Southern Rhodesia as well."[1] Dr. Verwoerd dismissed any idea of a political union between Rhodesia and South Africa and said that South Africa's aim was cooperation and friendship with all the states of Southern Africa. There must be considerable doubt whether the Portuguese and the South Africans could, in fact, have built more acceptable international images for themselves but UDI, by reemphasizing the continued commitment to white minority rule, has made a difficult task even more difficult. The South Africans and Portuguese have continually found themselves isolated in refusing to take action against the Smith government. For example, when a republic was declared in Rhodesia in March 1970, all other states except South Africa and Portugal broke their final consular ties with Rhodesia.

There were other reasons why the South Africans in particular disliked UDI. Two cardinal features of South Africa's foreign policy since 1945 have been the insistence on noninterference in a country's internal affairs and a very legalistic interpretation of interstate relations. Whatever else may be said about it, UDI was illegal and the South Africans have implicated themselves at least partly in this illegality by offering their sympathy and help to the Rhodesians. And this help has involved South African action inside Rhodesia—notably sending police units to the Zambezi valley—which can be interpreted as interference in another state's internal affairs. The British complained to the South Africans on these very grounds. Added to the legal niceties, UDI has meant that renewed international antagonism and action has been directed against white Southern Africa. Therefore, there were strong reasons for the South Africans and Portuguese to oppose UDI and yet they both gave Rhodesia their support. Dr. Verwoerd advised against UDI: he disliked its consequences; he hoped for a quick negotiated settlement between Britain and Rhodesia, but he confessed that:

> the declaration of independence in Rhodesia, with whom bonds of friendship and economic ties have grown through the years, has created a situation from which the Republic cannot escape. We have blood relations over the border. However others may feel or act towards their kith and kin when their international interests are at stake, South Africans on the whole cannot cold shoulder theirs.[2]

For Dr. Verwoerd and the vast majority of white South Africans it was emotion as well as logic which dictated support for the Rhodesian cause. Logic dictated they should not abandon the Rhodesians because any action which succeeded against Rhodesia might next be turned against South Africa. Emotion dictated support for another white minority. In terms of their own convictions, and the strong emotional convictions of their followers, it would be unthinkable for the South African or Portuguese government to participate in the overthrow of the white minority of Rhodesia or even to stand aside while they saw it happen. The white governments of Southern Africa are motivated by the firm conviction that the white race, by virtue of its superior skills and even by divine providence, has the right to rule and "uplift" the other races of Southern Africa. It was on this—as well as the calculation that South Africa and Portugal were unlikely to support economic sanctions—that Mr. Smith gambled when he anticipated support from his white neighbors. The Portuguese and South Africans disliked UDI but they disliked even more the prospect of a white government being overthrown by international action or internal revolution.

Events within Rhodesia have further strengthened the commitment to white rule in Southern Africa. In South Africa there was never any doubt that the whites' aim was to retain exclusive control of the central government; until UDI there was doubt in Rhodesia. Now that doubt has disappeared. Although the disparity in the ratio of white to nonwhite[3] makes it impossible for Rhodesia to emulate South Africa entirely, the imprint of apartheid is now firmly upon Rhodesia. Whereas before racial distinctions were clothed in social habits and norms of behavior, now they are increasingly spelled out in legislation. For example, the African Urban Areas Accommodation and Registration Act, by which municipalities and towns can prohibit African servants from having their wives and children live with them on white premises, is now energetically prosecuted. In

October 1968 this legislation was applied to seven Salisbury suburbs affecting about three thousand Africans who were forced to find new accommodations. Another example is the Land Tenure Act which comes into force in 1970 with the new republican constitution. There has always been a division of land holding between the races under the Land Apportionment Act but the new act, which divides Rhodesia's land area equally between the 5 million Africans and the quarter-million whites, will increase the government's powers by giving it the right to dictate whether members of the one race may occupy or reside in land or buildings within the other race's area. Among the protests against the new legislation was one from the Roman Catholic Church, which has a large number of multiracial churches, missions, and schools spread over the country. The Roman Catholic bishops stated:

> Henceforth the Church shall merely be tolerated and may be permitted to exercise her mission only within such limits as Government Ministers see fit to determine. . . . Priests and nuns and teaching brothers may have to be segregated in their communities, according to their racial origins. The liberty of the Church to move freely among the people has been set aside in principle . . . .[4]

In Rhodesia today there is a bold assertion that racial distinction, and as much racial separation as can be achieved while preserving the white-dominated economic structure, are "natural" and "good." Africans are seen as "tribal men" who are best represented by chiefs and not by politicians.

In the early 1960s there appeared to be at least a chance that Rhodesia might achieve a *modus vivendi* between the black nationalism to the north and the white nationalism of the Republic. Although throughout this century Rhodesia had been under white control, lip service was paid to Cecil Rhodes' dictum of "equal rights for all civilized men south of the Zambezi." The claim was that the right to political participation depended not upon race but upon a test of civilization,[5] and that although the white man ruled *now* there was no reason why in the distant future black men should not control the government. It was argued that Rhodesia could offer a halfway house between black and white nationalism and this was one of the arguments advanced for the establishment of the Central African Federation in 1953.[6] The claim was that, in addition to its obvious economic advantages, the federation would demonstrate that racial cooperation in government could be achieved and would draw Rhodesia away from an Afrikaner dominated South Africa.

The Central African Federation lasted only ten years—from 1953 through 1963. The decision to break it up was taken by the British government against the opposition of almost all the white politicians in Central Africa. The decision came after sustained criticism of the federation in Britain and often bitter African opposition to it in Central Africa itself. The African nationalist leaders preached that the whites of Central Africa had no real intention of sharing political power, and still less of handing over control to Africans. They said that men like Lord Malvern and Sir Roy Welensky, the two premiers of the federation, were as dedicated to permanent white rule as any of the Afrikaners of South Africa. This is no place to examine the validity of these charges but, with the breakup of the federation and the subsequent internal political development in each of the member states, even the illusion of a middle path was abandoned. In the two northern territories of the old federation—Zambia and Malawi[7] —black nationalism triumphed while in Rhodesia a new powerful white nationalism emerged.

The Rhodesian election of December 1962 mirrored the federal failure to achieve compromise. It was the first election under a new constitution and clearly distinguished the contestants for political power. The constitution was so designed that, although Africans would sit in Rhodesia's Parliament for the first time, the white members would form a large majority. There were two electoral rolls, an upper or "A" roll which was European-dominated and had control of fifty seats, and a lower or "B" roll which was mainly African and had control of fifteen seats. What it meant initially was that there were fifty "white" seats and fifteen "black" ones. It was anticipated that over the years, with economic and social developments, an increasing number of Africans would obtain "A" roll qualifications and thereby more political influence. These complex franchise arrangements were aimed at ensuring that, although political control would be kept in "responsible hands," slowly and steadily an increasing number of Africans would be enfranchised. In blunter terms, the constitution was designed to retain white rule for the present, but to give increased African participation which could lead either to "nonracial" parties emerging or to African majority rule at an unspecified future date. The reactions to this constitution drew the lines of Rhodesia's political development during the 1960s.

The African nationalist leaders[8] rejected the constitution because it offered too little for Africans and left political power in white hands. They decided to boycott the election and to concentrate their energies on overthrowing the constitution by rallying international support and by militant activity inside Rhodesia. This was one extreme in a situation which became increasingly polarized.[9]

The other extreme was provided by the Rhodesian Front, a party which was formed only six months before the election to rally together the more reactionary whites. Before the formation of the new party the right wing had been in disarray and appeared to have little chance of winning an election, but from the beginning the Rhodesian Front was a well organized and efficient party.[10] It quickly attracted to itself those who felt most threatened by African advancement, the farmers and the white artisans. The party was determined to retain white control and so it opposed the new constitution because, in its opinion, the constitution gave Africans too much immediately and, even more seriously, endangered long-term white control. However, unlike the African nationalists, the Rhodesian Front decided to fight the election, to frustrate the new constitution by working inside it. The party could afford to do this because the electorate was predominantly white. In 1962 on the "A" or upper roll there were 86,720 Europeans in a total roll of 91,072. The Rhodesian Front has never attempted to mobilize African support. It has kept itself exclusively white, and so when its turn came to rule it asked the African majority not to participate but to obey.

Opposing the Rhodesian Front at the election was the ruling United Federal Party (UFP) which preached racial partnership and which, although led by whites, had some African support. Within the context of Rhodesia the UFP offered a middle path aiming at a form of racial cooperation, and it went into the election a strong favorite. In any event it was the white supremacists' party, the Rhodesian Front, which won. It was this victory which eventually led to UDI.

At a later election in 1965 the Rhodesian Front consolidated its hold by winning all 50 "white" seats while the middle party, the old UFP, collapsed and disintegrated. After the 1965 election the political battlefield was left to the two extreme parties: the African nationalists, who were determined to overthrow white supremacy and establish black rule by working outside the constitution, and the Rhodesian Front, using the powers of government to counter the African nationalist threat and to entrench white rule. At least in the short run, it is the white-dominated government with its efficient, ruthless use of government powers and emergency legislation which has triumphed.

The African nationalist movement in Rhodesia had fertile soil in which to grow. Rhodesia could not be isolated from developments elsewhere in Africa and, as news spread of the increasing success of nationalist movements in other parts of the continent and as the Africans grew increasingly resentful at racial discrimination, nationalist activity grew in Rhodesia. The nationalist leaders appealed to the great mass of Rhodesian Africans, who they claimed were both underprivileged and discriminated against because of their race. They based their appeal both on political issues, like the claim for "one man, one vote," and on social and economic conditions, such as wages and land holding, in which whites enjoyed obvious advantages. There was no absence of discontent on which an African nationalist movement could be built, but the problem remained how the movement could be made into an effective political force.

The nationalist leaders faced enormous difficulties. They and their followers had no previous experience with political parties. There were major problems of organization and communication, especially in the rural areas where the bulk of African population lived. Among the leaders there were uncertainty and often disputes about what tactics should be used to achieve their stated goal of majority government. All the difficulties mentioned were substantial, but they had been overcome by African nationalist parties in other British territories. The great distinction was that in Rhodesia the African nationalists faced one additional hazard which has so far proved critical. In the other territories the nationalists' pressure was directed against a British government which had committed itself to withdrawal from Africa. The uncertainties were simply "how" and "when" the withdrawal would take place. In contrast, the African nationalists of Rhodesia faced a white settler government which was determined to resist the nationalists with all its resources. The nationalists used techniques similar to those used in other territories—appeals for international support, mass demonstrations, boycotts, and disruption of government activities. In the early 1960s these tactics had considerable success. The nationalist leaders attracted large numbers of African followers, organized successful demonstrations, and gained international attention. Although the nationalist leaders in Rhodesia were never outstanding in terms of organizational ability or militancy, in the early years of the 1960s they appeared to be a genuine threat to the white government. The government responded by banning the nationalist parties, restricting public meetings, imprisoning leaders and by establishing an effective police informer system.

By such steps the white government suppressed the African nationalist parties, but the nationalists had gravely weakened their own position by a deep internal split. This came in July 1963 when a group led by the Reverend Ndabaningi Sithole broke away from the Zimbabwe African People's Union (ZAPU) to form a new party, the Zimbabwe African National Union (ZANU). Mr. Joshua Nkomo, the leader of ZAPU, rallied a majority of his supporters against the new party, but he failed to heal the breach. A deep and bitter division resulted in which supporters of the rival parties abused and intimidated each other. In the latter half of 1963 the nationalists dissipated their energies fighting each other, while the Rhodesian government seized the opportunity by claiming that the preservation of order obliged it to suppress the two parties. The government did this very effectively. There may still be some form of underground nationalist movement within Rhodesia, but even this seems doubtful. Today there is no overt sign of nationalist organizations within the country. The leaders, including Nkomo and Sithole, are in prison or restriction camps with no chance of early release. In February 1969 Sithole, who was already being detained without trial, was sentenced to six years' imprisonment for incitement to murder Ian Smith. The accusation was that Sithole had smuggled letters from his prison cell instructing a "Mr. X" to murder Smith.[11] Apart from this dramatic incident, the main activity of the African nationalists since UDI has been outside Rhodesia in organizing the guerrilla fighters.

The Rhodesian government's commitment to permanent white rule was also made plain in its protracted but fruitless negotiations with the British government.[12] The British government laid down six principles which they said must be met in any settlement.[13] In the broadest terms, these principles aimed at the removal of racial discrimination and at "unimpeded progress toward majority rule." The negotiations failed not because of any defect of constitutional engineering but because Mr. Smith and his colleagues were not prepared to accept these principles. Mr. Smith has sometimes hidden his opposition behind a smokescreen of vague phrases and disputes over constitutional details but the aims of his government were finally made plain in constitutional proposals which were published in May 1969[14] and which received strong support from the predominantly white electorate in June of that year. The proposals came after heated and often bitter discussions within the ruling Rhodesian Front party. The Rhodesian Front had been formed with largely negative aims—to counter British interference, to prevent majority rule, and to oppose multiracial government. It has always been easy to identify what the Rhodesian Front disliked but when it came to the positive task of constructing a new constitution there was considerable internal party conflict. A division arose between those who, like Mr. Smith, supported continued African representation in Parliament, and those who opposed it. The group which opposed Mr. Smith was led by two cabinet ministers, Mr. William Harper and Lord Graham. The split reached a crisis when the party congress of September 6, 1968, accepted by only 217 votes to 206 (with 70 delegates abstaining) the new constitutional proposals introduced by Mr. Smith. This was the only serious overt challenge to Mr. Smith's leadership in the whole period since UDI. Mr. Smith dismissed Mr. Harper and Lord Graham from the cabinet and soon restored his firm hold on the party.

Mr. Smith introduced his constitutional proposals when all attempts at a compromise solution with Britain or with other groups inside Rhodesia had been abandoned by the Rhodesian Front party.[15] There was no pretense that the proposals represented an objective or broad-based view. It was a constitution *of* the ruling party *for* the ruling party. Although Mr. Smith had stood out for African representation in Parliament, this did not imply that white minority control would be abandoned. Mr. Smith's position is that he is prepared to give Africans some representation in Parliament, probably because he hopes to retain the good will of conservative African forces such as the chiefs by giving them an outlet for their political ambitions, but he is determined that Africans will never control the Rhodesian government. He will give them a voice but no power. While speaking in support of the proposals, Mr. Smith came out openly against majority rule and emphasized that white rule must be preserved. He said "that he believed the white man was so superior in skills and knowledge that he could see the gap between whites and Africans widening, not narrowing."[16] He was elaborating the principle which was contained in the opening sentence of the introduction to the proposals: "The Government of Rhodesia believe that the present constitution is no longer acceptable to the people of Rhodesia because it contains a number of objectionable features, the principal ones being that it provides for eventual African rule and, inevitably, the domination of one race by another and that it does not guarantee that government will be retained in responsible hands."[17]

Under the new constitution the main legislative body is a 66-member House of Assembly consisting of 50 whites elected by the white electorate, 8 Africans elected by the African electorate, and 8 other Africans elected by four tribal electoral colleges. The idea of electoral rolls based on qualifications, not race, has been abandoned for straight racial rolls. There is provision for an increase in African members up to half the total membership of the House of Assembly, but it seems unlikely or even impossible that this could ever happen. The number of seats given to each race is dependent upon their income tax contributions. As the whites are by far the richest section of the the community, they pay the bulk of the income tax and are likely to go on doing so unless there is a social and economic revolution in Rhodesia. The Rhodesian government's argument is that those who pay for government should have the say in how the money is spent. This simplistic view, which ignores the complexities of the country's economic structure including the African's contribution to indirect tax, is obviously attractive for the white minority. The figures speak for themselves. At present, African pay about 1 percent of total personal income tax. However, under the new constitution 24 percent of the seats in the House of Assembly are occupied by African members and so it is only when the African contribution to income tax rises above 24 percent that they can hope for more seats.

In reality, the new constitution perpetuates white rule. As in other parliamentary systems, the executive government is drawn from the majority party in the legislature which means that whites will continue to dominate the government. The blacks have some representation but will always be in a parliamentary minority.

In the first election under the new constitution, held in April 1970, four parties contested the seats. These were the governing Rhodesian Front led by by Mr. Smith; the Center Party led by Mr. Pat Bashford which attempts to gain the support of both white and black "moderates"; the National People's Union led by Mr. Gordon Chavanduka which is an African party fighing for the African seats; and an extreme right-wing white party, the Conservative Alliance, led by Mr. Robin James. While these parties represent a wide range of political opinion, the election was a foregone conclusion because of the Rhodesian Front's strength among the white electorate. In December 1968 the Rhodesian Front had the remarkably high proportion of 18,000 full party members in a white electorate of about 90,000 people.[18]

In the 1970 election the Rhodesian Front won all fifty of the "white" seats and so continued as the governing party. In contrast to its success among the white electorate, the Rhodesian Front did not even nominate candidates to contest the African seats. Although the Center Party gained almost 25 percent of the votes cast for the sixteen white seats it contested, it failed to win any of these seats, while the Republican Alliance failed badly with thirteen of its fourteen candidates losing their deposits. The only opposition to the Rhodesian Front will lie in the eight elected Africans members, seven of whom are Center Party members. For the future it will be interesting to see if any of the Rhodesian Front's rivals of the 1970 election will survive. Even the future of the Center party must be in doubt, for can a party which has been led by whites hold together when all its parliamentary representatives are Africans?

The new constitution contains a Declaration of Rights but no court will have the right to declare a law invalid because it is inconsistent with the declaration. Preventive detention without trial and restriction without trial are authorized "in the interests of national defence, public safety or public order," and laws controlling communications media are to be extended to permit control of newspapers and other publications.

In this constitution the powers of the government have been increased at the expense of the individual. For those who share the Rhodesian Front government's commitment to preserving white rule, the increase of government powers follows automatically. If individuals have to be imprisoned without trial, if an accused has to be forced to give evidence against himself, if racial distinctions have to be emphasized more sharply than ever, these things may be unpleasant and personally disagreeable but they may be necessary to defend the central commitment to white rule. To imprison an individual without trial, or to make an accused give evidence against himself would be seen as a breach of fundamental rights in Western European society. But these are not seen as fundamental by the white political rulers of Rhodesia for they have a different yardstick of what is fundamental—the preservation of white rule. All else is measured by that criterion.

To preserve itself, the Rhodesian Front government is forced to deny the franchise to a majority of Rhodesians and it is forced to take exceptional powers because it is surrounded by opponents who reject its principles. In the normal run of events, the Rhodesian government can anticipate internal African opposition, guerrilla activity across its borders, persistent international antagonism and long term economic sanctions. With so many opponents the Rhodesian Front's position is chronically insecure. It cannot afford political magnanimity. As A. P. Thornton has observed,

> They resent grave statements on the inevitable development of Africans in Africa, or Africa for the Africans, for they do not share the detachment and cannot admit the inevitablity. Such views menace their own security, to preserve which is, and must always be, their first duty. . . . To such men, therefore, liberalism is an irrelevance at best. At worst, it is a subversive activity.[19]

The white Rhodesians have developed an elaborate rationalization to justify continued white supremacy. They argue that not only do they have skills and experience which enable them to rule more expertly and more peacefully than their black countrymen but also they are upholding Christian Western civilization against forces which are trying to undermine it. The forces are variously identified as "Communists," "black nationalists," "liberal," and "internationalist." The white Rhodesians claim that to give way to these forces would be a disaster not only for Rhodesia but also for Western civilization in general.

Outside Southern Africa it is easy to dismiss these arguments as simplistic rationalizations to preserve the privileges of a racial minority. But it would be a mistake to dismiss them too lightly, for they are widely believed in Southern Africa, and it is belief, not logical analysis, which counts in such a situation. Across Southern Africa the white minorities are bound together by the belief in the justice of their cause and so the bonds of geography, economic resources, and communications systems are increasingly reinforced by this ideological commitment. For those white Southern Africans who see themselves as crusaders defending the Christian civilization, the Rhodesians have been riding at the head, carrying the banners.

With these convictions, the whites of Rhodesia now identify themselves as part of a distinct white Southern African group. In the past most white Rhodesians saw themselves as "British." They held on to the symbols of the crown and the flag to give them an identity in an alien continent and to distinguish them not only from black Africans but from the white Afrikaners, who were seen as political rivals, and from the Portuguese who were seen as "inferior" Europeans. But with Britain's withdrawal from its African colonies and with its commitment to majority rule, the white Rhodesians have thrown off the old identity. Now they see themselves principally as white Southern Africans with close and friendly relations with their Portuguese and Afrikaner allies and hostile to any, including the British, who challenge the whites' position. The new self image plainly revealed itself in June 1969 when more than 80 per cent of the predominantly white electorate voted to break the ties with the British monarchy and become a republic.

Drawing the Boundary Lines of Southern Africa

The Rhodesian UDI has temporarily, at least, drawn clear boundary lines around the Southern African bloc. This has been demonstrated both in the strengthening of economic interdependence and in the guerrilla fighting which has spread across the northern frontiers of the bloc. Zambia's reaction to UDI has been critical in demarcating the bloc. The Zambians, in refusing to accept UDI, drew the bloc's northern border along the Zambezi River which divides Rhodesia from Zambia rather than farther north.

The drawing of a clear boundary line is another feature of UDI which the South Africans disliked but were forced to accept. In its "outward policy" the South African government had hoped to retain a flexible situation in which it would seek co-operation in Africa without fixing geographical limits. A few months before UDI, Dr. Hilgard Muller, the South African foreign minister, said: "I believe the time has come when all the territories in Southern Africa will co-operate in all matters of common interest with a view to tackling their common problems and solving them in the interests of all the inhabitants of each particular territory." When Dr. Muller was asked what he meant by "Southern Africa," he replied: "I draw the line very vaguely. I even include the Congo (Leopoldville). I am explaining my view as to the future and I do not think the hon. member can expect me in these circumstances to draw a very clear line of demarcation."[20]

When UDI came, Rhodesia's neighbors had no choice but to make clear their reactions toward it.[21] It would be exaggerating the point to suggest that a sympathetic response to UDI became the chief distinguishing characteristic of the states which formed the Southern African bloc, but it became one of the characteristics. Those who were prepared to support Rhodesia, or at least acquiesce in its action, were the members of the bloc. Those states, notably Zambia, which opposed UDI thereby opted out.

Zambia's reaction to UDI was to try to reduce her ties with and dependence on Rhodesia. This was demonstrated in the way Zambia has cut trade with her southern neighbor. In 1965 Zambia imported goods worth about $99.5 million from Rhodesia. In 1966 she cut this to $65 million and in 1967 to $45 million.[22] Zambia's exports to Rhodesia fell from $15.26 million in 1965 to $7.0 million in 1967.[23] Zambia took these steps mainly to demonstrate her opposition to continued white minority rule, but also to conform, as far as she felt able, with the United Nations' call for economic sanctions. President Kaunda of Zambia has had little faith that sanctions could bring down the Smith government but he is certainly not prepared to aid that government in any way. Throughout this century Zambia has had strong economic links with Rhodesia. These links were further strengthened during the federation period. Joint power and communications systems were developed, and Zambia became an important market for Rhodesia's manufactured goods. Even the break-up of the federation did not destroy this relationship for Zambia's copper still passed along the line of rail through Rhodesia, Zambia still relied upon Rhodesian coal for its smelters, shared power with Rhodesia from the Kariba Dam, and the two had a common air service. There were, therefore, very strong inducements for Zambia to retain her links with Rhodesia whatever the political developments. Zambia was seen as a "natural" part of Southern Africa. But while economic benefits were sufficient to induce Dr. Banda, the president of Malawi, to retain and even strengthen his country's ties with the white states of Southern Africa, President Kaunda refused to do so. After UDI, he deliberately set out to end Zambia's economic reliance upon Rhodesia. Indeed, Zambia has been in the vanguard of those states which have sought to overthrow Prime Minister Smith's control in Rhodesia.

One paradoxical result of Zambia's break with Rhodesia has been to increase her trade with South Africa. In the short term, South Africa offered an alternative source of supply for goods which Rhodesia previously provided. For example, in 1967 South Africa was Zambia's chief supplier of goods with exports valued at $86.3 million.[24] Although in the short term Zambia continues to rely on economic links with its white southern neighbors, President Kaunda's aim is to reorient Zambia's economy and supply routes.

As alternatives to its previous reliance on Rhodesia, Zambia has developed her own resources in coal and hydroelectric power, she has purchased manufactured goods from other sources and, what is probably most significant, she has redirected supply and communications routes through Tanzania. An oil pipeline has already been constructed and plans have been made for a new rail link to the Tanzanian coast which will be built with Communist Chinese aid. When he opened the oil pipeline, President Kaunda emphasized the political background to the economic decision. He said:

> We are land locked; we are surrounded on the east, south, and west by regimes basically opposed, if not hostile, to the fundamental principles upon which our policies are based; our communications to the north and north-east, which provide the only reliable lifeline, still have a capacity which falls below the requirements of the nation. . . . The pipeline therefore removes one of our greatest sources of hardship.[25]

Zambia has not yet—and perhaps never can—cut herself off completely from the white states of Southern Africa, but her recent efforts have demonstrated how she has given primacy to the political decision. Since UDI, the Zambian government has decided that it is neither safe nor honorable to rely upon the white states of Southern Africa and, therefore, at considerable expense and inconvenience she is reorienting herself toward East Africa.

While Zambia has drawn away to the north, Rhodesia's response to sanctions has been to strengthen further its economic and communications ties with the South. For protection, she has tucked herself into Southern Africa. She has countered sanctions, in part, by finding loopholes and, in part, by reorienting her economy. In both, Rhodesia has relied upon her Southern African neighbors. To find the loopholes she has used the banking, commercial, and transport facilities of her neighbors. For example, transfers of money in and out of Rhodesia are made simply by using South African banks. Also, in developing markets for her new products, she has relied upon her neighbors both in what they are prepared to absorb within their own economies and in what they are prepared to export and import for Rhodesia.

The trade figures between Rhodesia and its white neighbors have not been published since UDI, and it is impossible to quantify with any accuracy Rhodesia's trade to or through these countries. R. B. Sutcliffe has made a rough calculation based on a comparison of Rhodesia's export figures and the import figures claimed by countries importing from Rhodesia other than South Africa and Mozambique. According to this calculation, about 26 percent of Rhodesia's exports went to South Africa and Mozambique in 1965. The proportion rose to 35 per cent in 1966, to 65 percent in 1967, and Mr. Sutcliffe estimated that it was as high as 85 percent by 1969.[26] A substantial part of this trade will simply be passing through Mozambique and South Africa as these two territories offer "middle man" facilities to circumvent sanctions. As Mr. Sutcliffe emphasized, these can only be taken as rough figures but they do indicate the importance of Rhodesia's white neighbors in countering sanctions. This help is openly acknowledged in Rhodesia and admitted in the neighboring states. When UDI was declared, Dr. Verwoerd stated: "I need not go into details, but anyone will realize that maintaining regular relations, especially economic relations, with a neighbouring state means everything to a state which is isolated, as Rhodesia is to-day."[27]

South Africa and Portugal were not prepared to support economic sanctions because of their commitment to white rule and because they realized that if sanctions were effective against Rhodesia they would be next in line. As they saw it, in helping Rhodesia they were directly helping themselves.

Sanctions have been applied in three stages.[28] The first stage came immediately after UDI when Britain, calling for support through the United Nations, applied sanctions against specific parts of the Rhodesian economy, such as denying Rhodesia access to the capital market and refusing to buy her tobacco and sugar. These sanctions failed to produce the results Prime Minister Harold Wilson had hoped for and so, in December 1966, after the failure of constitutional negotiations between Wilson and Smith aboard a British warship, H.M.S. *Tiger*, the Security Council imposed selected mandatory sanctions. Again, when these sanctions failed to produce the desired political result, there was a further escalation in May 1968 when the Security Council resolved on comprehensive santions against Rhodesia. (There were exceptions for imports into Rhodesia of goods required for medical, educational, and humanitarian purposes.)

Sanctions have certainly hurt Rhodesia. In some sectors of the economy, and notably European farming, where contributions to the Gross Domestic Product fell from 13 percent to 8.9 percent between 1965 and 1968, their impact has been severe. Also Rhodesia's prospects of long-term economic growth have been adversely affected. Professor Robert McKinnnell states that there were already signs of weakness in Rhodesia's economic growth before UDI and that sanctions have intensified these weaknesses. He writes: "One is led to conclude that the forces that stimulated the growth of the Rhodesian economy in the past have either diminished or disappeared, or even been reversed, partly by events prior to November 1965, partly by UDI itself."[29]

Despite these adverse effects, sanctions have not achieved the political result hoped for and anticipated by the British. The British were too optimistic in their assessment of the impact of sanctions and too naïve in their analysis of the relationship between economic pressures and political change. It was because they believed that as soon as economic pressure was felt in Rhodesia there would be a retreat from the path paved by the Rhodesian Front that the British applied sanctions piece by piece. This gave the white Rhodesians a breathing space in which to regain their morale and reorganize their economy. By a continuation of skilled economic management within Rhodesia, help from their Southern African neighbors, and "leaks" within the international sanctions, the white Rhodesians have survived. They have demonstrated the strength of their political commitment to white rule and at the same time the resilience of the Southern African economy, for it is the Southern African economy as a whole and not just Rhodesia's that has been organized to defeat sanctions.

The development of trading and communications systems in Southern Africa since UDI has further strengthened South Africa's predominant position in the subcontinent. South Africa's importance was reflected in the negotiations between Britain and Rhodesia which followed UDI. In these negotiations, which aimed at reaching a constitutional settlement, South Africa was used by both sides as a channel of communication and a potential source of pressure on the other side. South Africa has been seen as the fulcrum around which negotiations over the future of Southern Africa must turn. Although this has enhanced the Republic's prestige, it has failed to achieve the reconciliation it desired. This point must be stressed because, although Rhodesia now relies heavily on South Africa, the relationship is an international relationship in which both sides claim sovereignty within their own borders. This was made plain in June 1969 when the Rhodesian government held a referendum to gain support for new constitutional proposals which included the establishment of a republic. There were press reports of South African and Portuguese disquiet because they wanted to avoid a new outburst of international indignation against Southern Africa.[30] Mr. Smith brushed these reports aside as a "travesty of the truth" and went on to explain how he saw Rhodesia's relationship with South Africa. He said that

> I have maintained closer association with the South African Government than any Prime Minister previously in our history. I can assure you that I have been kept completely in the picture as far as the feelings of these governments are concerned. They don't interfere in our affairs and we don't interfere in theirs, but we do think aloud together.[31]

As sanctions have dragged on without achieving their aims, it has become increasingly obvious that the only way to make them fully effective would be to impose sanctions against the whole of the economic bloc of Southern Africa. This Britain has refused to do. Therefore, Britain has found herself in the paradoxical position of continuing as South Africa's chief trading partner and source of capital investment while at the same time leading the imposition of sanctions against Rhodesia. The two positions are incompatible, but Britain has decided that the cost and practical difficulties of an economic war with the whole of Southern Africa are too great. Mr. George Brown, then Britain's foreign secretary, said bluntly that Britain "cannot and will not now contemplate an economic war with South Africa."[32]

The Military Confrontation

The division of Africa at the Zambezi River is most dramatically and tragically demonstrated by the outbreak of guerrilla warfare. On the one side sit forces of the white governments of South Africa and Rhodesia. On the other are the guerrilla forces of the African nationalists determined to penetrate and overthrow the white redoubt.

Although divisions remain among the nationalists, and in particular between the Zimbabwe African People's Union (ZAPU) and the Zimbabwe African National Union (ZANU), there is general agreement that the purpose of the struggle is to overthrow the white rulers of Southern Africa. The nationalist guerrilla fighters draw their main support from the Organization of African Unity, from individual African countries—notably Tanzania and Zambia—and from some Communist powers. By mid-1969 Communist China, with its vast experience of revolutionary war, seemed to be emerging as potentially the most powerful external supporter. President Nyerere of Tanzania explained the acceptance of Chinese support by saying that

> Only the Western world can help solve the problem of Southern Africa with the minimum of violence. We still appeal for that. . . . If all this fails we shall be compelled to take arms from the East, and we shall be accused of being Communists.
>
> To us China is a friend in need.[33]

The response to the challenge of the guerrilla fighters in Rhodesia has again demonstrated the interdependence of the Southern African states and their recognition of common interests. None of the Southern African states is prepared to help the guerrilla fighters because they see them as a threat to the established order which they accept. The white states are actively fighting the guerrillas while the small black states, again pleading their weakness, have refused to help or encourage them. When guerrilla fighters were pursued from Rhodesia across the border into Botswana they were arrested as illegal immigrants. A Botswana government spokesman said: "Our President, Sir Seretse Khama, has repeatedly made it clear that his Government will not allow Botswana to be used as a stepping stone for subversive activities against its neighbouring states, no matter how unacceptable to Botswana the policies of these states might be."[34]

The fighting which has flared up along the Zambezi since UDI is only part of a larger black-white confrontation which stretches across Angola and Mozambique and at times has penetrated into South West Africa. On both sides of the military struggle there is a tacit understanding that an attack upon one part of white Southern Africa is an attack upon the whole. This has led to significant alliances and pooling of resources. In September 1967 the leaders of the African National Congress (ANC) of South Africa and the Zimbabwe African People's Union (ZAPU) of Rhodesia asked the Organization of African Unity (OAU) for its support in "the struggle which is already raging for liberation." They asked for recognition that a full-scale war was being waged and that prisoners should be treated under the terms of the Geneva Convention. The OAU had already established a Liberation Committee in 1963 to help liberate the white states of Southern Africa, and when the organization met in 1967 it allocated $2 million of its $3.1 million budget to the "freedom fighters" of Angola, Mozambique, Rhodesia, South Africa, and South West Africa and set up a new military committee to help them.[35] Earlier, the ANC and ZAPU had combined their forces in guerrilla fighting in the Wankie area of Rhodesia. In a joint statement Messrs. J. R. D. Chikerema, vice president of ZAPU, and Oliver Tambo of the ANC said that their combined orces had marched into Rhodesia "as Comrades-in-arms on a common route, each bound to its destination. It is the determination of these Combined Forces to fight the common settler enemy to the finish. . . ."

On the other side of the border, South African forces have openly been sent to support the Rhodesians against the guerrillas. When the British government, still claiming to be the legal authority for Rhodesia, objected to this, Mr. B. J. Vorster, the South African prime minister, replied that these troops had been sent because it would be folly to wait until the "terrorists" came to South Africa.[37] On another occasion he told a National party rally:

> We sent our policemen to Rhodesia to fight terrorists who were destined for South Africa. This action has nothing whatsoever to do with the Rhodesian issue—all we are doing is pulling our own chestnuts out of the fire.[38]

So far the fighting has been fierce, but on a small scale. In general, the government forces seem to have had the better of the guerrillas. Accurate figures of casualities are difficult to obtain but, according to Mr. Jack Howman, the Rhodesian minister for external affairs, 160 guerrillas had been killed by the end of 1968 as compared with 12 members of the Rhodesian security forces.[39] Reports from African nationalist sources give very much higher figures for government losses. For example, *Spotlight*, an ANC publication, claimed that 157 Rhodesian and South African troops had been killed by April

1968[40] and a ZAPU-ANC statement of April 10, 1968, said:

> On April 5 there were six white fascist officers quietly buried in Zimbabwe. They were deprived of military burial in order to conceal the losses suffered by the fascist troops. The dead bodies of the South African soldiers are carried from Karoi to the Wankie mortuary. From there they are flown to the Caprivi Strip military air base and from the Caprivi Strip the bodies are flown to South Africa. On March 4, there were 42 fascist corpses transported from the Caprivi Strip to Dundee in South Africa.[41]

The African nationalists have almost certainly exaggerated both their successes and the extent of the fighting. In mounting their operations, they have faced considerable difficulties in finding "officer material" recruits[42] and in gaining sufficient external backing. African states have been prepared to give them vocal support but no more, while the OAU's Liberation Committee has suffered from internal squabbles and lack of support from member states. Zdenek Cervenka, writing of the committee's difficulties during 1967 and 1968, stated: "Activity has increasingly been paralysed, on the one hand by the failure of the members to agree on what movements should be recognised, where arms should be bought and the general strategy to be applied, and on the other hand by the reluctance of African States which are not members of the Committee to pay their assessments."[43]

It is difficult to assess the significance of the present guerrilla fighting in Rhodesia, for while so far it has been on a relatively small scale the potential danger for white Southern Africa could be enormous. The guerrillas face so many difficulties that it is easy enough to imagine their efforts petering out. They may fail to organize themselves efficiently, or their morale may crack, or they may receive insufficient external support, or they may be decisively defeated by the forces of the white governments. These are some of the difficulties the guerrillas face but, according to some commentators (including President Kaunda of Zambia), the issues are so strongly felt and so fundamental to human dignity that the struggle will never be abandoned. The battle lines are drawn for a major racial conflict which will consume the whole of Africa. In February 1968 President Kaunda said that a major "conflagration" was impending in Central and Southern Africa and he warned Mr. Smith that "while you may escape punishment, your children cannot escape it. They will pay very heavily for your misbehaviour today."[44]

The Lessons Drawn from Rhodesia's UDI

Speculation about Southern Africa's future is now based upon assumptions which are very different from those held ten years ago. In 1960 there was a general belief that the white rulers would have to accept rapid and major changes or fall before the combined forces of international antagonism and African nationalism within Southern Africa. There are few who now accept this. Today the white rulers of Southern Africa seem to be firmly entrenched, their position almost impregnable, at least in the short term. African nationalism is no longer seen as an irresistible force. Of course, present assumptions may also prove wrong, but it is these assumptions which dictate existing relations in Southern Africa and the international response to developments there.

Since UDI, Rhodesia has been a testing ground for many of the forces which claim a share in shaping the political future of Southern Africa. These forces include the white rulers of Rhodesia, backed by South Africa and Portugal; the African tribal chiefs; the African nationalists, supported by the OAU, other African states, and some Communist countries; the Western powers, still mainly represented by the United Kingdom; and the international community as a whole, which through the United Nations claims that racial discrimination and the denial of individual rights in Southern Africa are matters of international concern and should be eradicated for international peace and harmony. In evaluating the effectiveness of these forces, we have seen Rhodesia as a microcosm of all "white" Southern Africa. A brief survey of some of the conclusions which we have already noted will underline their significance.

The limitations of British influence in Southern Africa have been cruelly exposed by the events which have followed UDI. This includes the important implication that attempts to persuade the white rulers to accept increasing African participation through peaceful constitutional means have failed. Both in South Africa and Rhodesia, Britain relied upon constitutional devices to achieve racial cooperation and to blunt the edge of white domination.[45] In both cases constitutional arrangements have been thrown aside when they have threatened continued white control. The most recent failure in Rhodesia has confirmed the view that the white rulers will never agree to African political advancement by peaceful constitutional means.

One alternative to peaceful constitutional change has been the attempt to force the hand of the white Rhodesians by applying international economic sanctions.[46] Their failure to bring down the Smith government in Rhodesia has been seen as a demonstration that this means of achieving political change is ineffective for South Africa as a whole. The rhetorical question has been put: If sanctions are ineffective against a small country like Rhodesia, how could they ever be effective against a rich, powerful state like South Africa? The conclusion is clear and must be emphasized. In the early 1960s sanctions were seen as an obvious and powerful weapon which could be used against the white rulers of Southern Africa.[47] There was considerable pressure on the major Western powers to apply sanctions directly against the Republic of South Africa. It was argued that the effective imposition of sanctions would force the South African government to change its racial policies. With the failure of sanctions against Rhodesia, that pressure has virtually disappeared.

Among the reasons advanced for the failure of sanctions is the accusation that the economically advanced states have not been sufficiently involved or interested to ensure that the United Nations decisions have been carried out effectively. The implication is that both East and West are prepared to denounce the white rulers of Southern Africa, but are not prepared to take effective action against them. African nationalist leaders have seen the failure of economic sanctions as an example of this. They never believed that economic sanctions could be effective, and from the beginning urged Britain to use force against Smith's government. They see their doubts about sanctions fully justified by subsequent events—the continued direct and indirect trade with Rhodesia,[48] the refusal of Portugal and South Africa to comply with United Nations resolutions, and the refusal of other states to apply sanctions against Portugal and South Africa. As a result of this, the nationalist leaders, who previously placed so much faith in mobilizing international opinion and international action against Southern Africa,[49] have become increasingly disillusioned.

The message which African nationalist leaders now preach is that armed force is the only way to overthrow the Smith government. Because Britain refuses to use force and because the African states have failed to persuade the United Nations to use force, the nationalists have accepted that it can only be done by organizing guerrilla warfare themselves. But, as already noted, the nationalist guerrilla effort has not yet brought any tangible success. There has not been a general rising to support the guerrillas, the African chiefs in Rhodesia—granted increased rewards and responsibilities—have remained loyal to Prime Minister Smith, and the African members of Rhodesia's armed forces have so far fought vigorously against the guerrillas. John Worrall, the *Guardian* reporter, wrote about the African troops of the Rhodesian African Rifles who had been fighting in northwestern Matabeleland:

> Without the loyalty and fighting ability of these rugged troops, Rhodesia might be in a parlous state. . . . Since the guerrilla incursions plunged them into action, they are fighting, killing, wounding or capturing African nationalists who could be tribal brothers or close relatives—and doing it without mercy or compunction.
>
> There have been reports of mutinies and desertions. But when I visited the African troops I found no evidence of this.[50]

One of the possible explanations for the absence of African militancy inside the country is that while many Africans are sympathetic to the nationalists' aims at present, they fear the government more than they support the nationalists. The Rhodesian government keeps a stranglehold on African political activity by means of severe legislation, skilled intelligence and police work, the arbitrary arrest and imprisonment of African leaders without trial, and a general aggressive determination to suppress any African dissent. To those who are not committed to the retention of white control this appears harsh and indefensible, but so far it has worked and while it continues to work it is difficult to imagine Mr. Smith abandoning it.

Again, implications for the whole of Southern Africa have been drawn from the Rhodesian experience. An increased respect for the toughness and military strength of the white governments and their ability to suppress African opposition is apparent. This ranges from Dr. Banda, who asserted that the South African and Rhodesian air forces could destroy all the major towns of Central and East Africa at will, to the nationalist leaders who, while confident of final victory, accept that a long, bitter struggle lies ahead.

A further conclusion is that general African risings, spontaneous or otherwise, cannot be expected. The Reverend Ndabaningi Sithole drew up instructions for action by his ZANU followers when UDI was declared. He called the instructions an "historic document"[51] but it seems more realistic to regard them as a pointless gesture, for the instructions were entirely ignored when UDI came. For example, the instructions state in part:

> 5. When the Government declares unilateral independence, all Africans must stop paying dipping fees, cattle fees, dog fees, and poll tax until an African Government is fully established in Zimbabwe.
>
> 6. Town residents must stop paying rents from the day unilateral independence is proclaimed.

7. Every man must have axes, bows and arrows, and other instruments ready to oppose physically unilateral independence and ACT as soon as unilateral independence is declared.
8. All African parents must withdraw their children from school as soon as illegal independence is declared.[52]

None of these things occurred and it seems that, other than drawing up these instructions, ZANU did nothing to make them occur. ZAPU was equally inactive. The lack of action shattered the illusion that somehow, almost miraculously, there would be spontaneous African uprisings.

The lessons drawn so far from the Rhodesian crisis seem to point to one conclusion: that at present the white rulers are virtually impregnable. The failure of the British, the ineffectiveness of the United Nations sanctions, the containment of African guerrilla activity, and the absence of an internal African revolt have created, or at least reinforced, a general assumption that the white rule in Southern Africa will continue indefinitely.

Perhaps an even clearer way of showing the importance of the lessons drawn from the Rhodesian crisis is to try to imagine what very different lessons would have been drawn if UDI had not succeeded. If, for example, at UDI there had been an African uprising, everyone, including the whites of South Africa, would now be expecting a similar uprising in the Republic. Or, if economic sanctions had brought down Mr. Smith, international pressure on the Western powers for sanctions against the Portuguese territories and South Africa would have been enormous.

Therefore, developments in Rhodesia have helped to create an assumption of white strength. But how accurate will this assumption be, especially in relation to Rhodesia? It has already been noted that UDI and its consequences have had severe drawbacks as well as advantages for the whites of Southern Africa. For example, it has been pointed out how renewed international antagonism has been unleashed against Southern Africa and how Rhodesia's actions have made interstate relationships less flexible. There must also be considerable doubt about the ability of Rhodesia's small white population to retain its position of supremacy over the long term. Again only speculation is possible, but when the limits within which Mr. Smith works are examined, the apparently secure position starts to look tenuous. Can the quarter-million whites hold down indefinitely an African population which is now almost 5 million and growing fast? Will African troops and police always be prepared to shoot persons of their own race, whose ambition is to gain greater political rights for Africans? Will Africans always be prepared to inform on their fellows? The weakness of Mr. Smith's position is that to retain white control in Rhodesia he has to place heavy reliance upon cooperation from black Africans. This is quite unlike Mr. Vorster's position, with his much larger white population, and could be the Achilles heel of white Rhodesia.

This view of white Rhodesia's potential weakness is shared by Major General R. J. Putterill, who commanded the Rhodesian army immediately before and after UDI. He protested against the Rhodesian Front's new constitution because, he said, "it is my firm belief that the security of the country is being endangered by this new constitution. Every serviceman knows it is vital in counter-insurgency operations to maintain the good-will and cooperation of all Rhodesians."[51] He believed that the new constitution could only increase racial division among Rhodesians, and thereby be a danger to the state.

The potential internal weakness of the white Rhodesians' position must be related to the continued international antagonism which Rhodesia attracts both to itself and to the white minority governments of Southern Africa. Those who plan to overthrow Mr. Smith must aim to combine this internal African discontent with continued external pressure. So far the international antagonism has been ineffective and the white Rhodesians are apt to dismiss it as mere rhetoric, but the bitter antagonism persists and as long as it does the possibility remains that it will be translated into positive and effective action. Certainly, the verbal protests are as strong as ever. In a manifesto drawn up after a meeting at Lusaka in April 1969, fourteen East and Central African leaders declared:

> On the objective of liberation. . . , we can neither surrender nor compromise. We have always preferred and we still prefer, to achieve it without physical violence. We would prefer to negotiate rather than destroy, to talk rather than kill. We do not advocate violence; we advocate an end to the violence against human dignity which is now being perpetrated by the oppressors of Africa. . . . But while peaceful progress is blocked by actions of those at present in power in the States of Southern Africa, we have no choice but to give to the peoples of those territories all the support of which we are capable in their struggle against their oppressors. This is why the signatory states participate in the movement for the liberation of Africa, under the aegis of the Organisation of African Unity.[54]

Conclusion

In conclusion, we return to the four points which we suggested would emerge from an examination of developments in Rhodesia.

1. *The emergence and identification of a distinct bloc of states in Southern Africa.* As the British colonial authorities have withdrawn, the white rulers of Southern Africa—and, in particular, the rulers of South Africa—have seized the opportunity to extend their influence and authority. Rhodesia has emphasized and consolidated the development both in its internal politics, where a white minority government is entrenched in power, and in its acceptance of a subordinate relationship with South Africa. The identity of the Southern African bloc has been confirmed by the reactions of its members to the attacks made against the white Rhodesians. Members of the bloc have refused to support either African nationalist guerrilla activity or international sanctions and, in the case of the white states, have actively opposed these external threats. In distinguishing the geographical limits of the bloc, Zambia's reactions have been especially important. Under President Kaunda it has set out to break its old links with Rhodesia, and in so doing has drawn the boundary line of the Southern African bloc along the Zambezi River.

2. *Characteristics of the relationships.* The relationships among the Southern African states are based upon the conceived interests of these states. These interests are partly determined by the obvious factor of geographical proximity, and of shared economic and communications systems. But added to these material ties is the ideological commitment to white minority rule in the most powerful states of the bloc. An elaborate rationalization has been developed to explain and defend the continuation of white minority rule. Again the Rhodesian crisis has helped to identify and emphasize these characteristics.

3. *The forces which strengthen the relationships.* Those forces which support the characteristics mentioned in (2) above help to strengthen existing relationships. In Rhodesia's case, the success of the white minority government in holding on to power and suppressing the internal African nationalist movement has further strengthened the acceptance of and commitment to white rule. Furthermore, Rhodesia's success in gaining support from her neighbors to counter economic and military threats has helped to strengthen the existing economic and communications links between the states and has given the Southern African bloc a confidence in its ability to withstand external pressure. The foundation for the strength and confidence of the bloc rests on the Republic of South Africa's economic and military strength.

4. *The forces which challenge the relationships.* The Rhodesian crisis has revealed not only the strength of the interstate relationships in Southern Africa but also the range of forces which challenge the relationship. First, there is internal discontent which, although so far successfully repressed by the white Rhodesians, must always be a potential danger. To continue to rule at all, the white Rhodesians must place tight restrictions on African political activity and so accept a "police state" atmosphere. Second, there is the challenge of the international community in general, specifically translated into the application of sanctions against Rhodesia. There is no sign of international antagonism declining, although so far it has not been translated into effective action. Finally, there is the military challenge of the African nationalist guerrillas supported by the Organization of African Unity and by Communist states. The Rhodesian crisis has, therefore, identified the contestants in the long-term struggle which lies ahead for Southern Africa.

3

Zambia's Policy toward Southern Africa

VERNON J. MWAANGA

For some time many persons have seen the problems of Southern Africa as divisible into separate categories—namely, apartheid in South Africa and South West Africa (Namibia), minority rule in Rhodesia (Zimbabwe) and Portugese colonialism in Angola and Mozambique. During the past five years events have challenged this view. Some of these developments are:

1. The continued expansion of South Africa's military, economic, and political influence into Rhodesia, Angola, and Mozambique.
2. The demise of British authority in Rhodesia.
3. The resurgence of aggression by the Portuguese soldiers stationed in Angola and Mozambique.
4. The continued acts of sabotage, espionage, and military aggression by the Portuguese, Rhodesian, and South African forces against the independent African states to the north, especially Zambia, Tanzania, and the Congo (Kinshasa).
5. The introduction of no fewer than 2,700 South African troops in Rhodesia,[1] and
6. The coordinated efforts of some of the African nationalist movements such as the Zimbabwe African People's Union (ZAPU) and the African National Congress (ANC).

It is in this context that the heads of state from East and Central Africa adopted the historic *Manifesto on Southern Africa* at their Fifth Summit Conference held at Lusaka between April 14 and 17, 1969. This declaration was later endorsed by the Organization of African Unity (OAU) and later adopted by the United Nations General Assembly. Because that manifesto underlines Zambia's attitude toward her southern neighbors, I shall quote extensively from it:

> To talk of the liberation of Africa is thus to say two things. First, that the peoples in the territories still under colonial rule shall be free to determine for themselves their own institutions of self-government. Secondly, that

the individuals in Southern Africa shall be freed from an environment poisoned by the propaganda of racialism, and given an opportunity to be men—not white men, brown men, yellow men, or black men.

Thus the liberation of Africa for which we are struggling does not mean a reverse racialism. Nor is it an aspect of African Imperialism. As far as we are concerned the present boundaries of the States of Southern Africa are the boundaries of what will be free and independent African States. There is no question of our seeking or accepting any alterations to our own boundaries at the expense of these future free African nations.

On the objective of liberation as thus defined, we can neither surrender nor compromise. We have always preferred, and we still prefer, to achieve it without physical violence. We would prefer to negotiate rather than destroy, to talk rather than kill. We do not advocate violence, we advocate an end to the violence against human dignity which is now being perpetrated by the oppressors of Africa. If peaceful progress to emancipation were possible, or if changed circumstances were to make it possible in the future, we would urge our brothers in the resistance movements to use peaceful methods of struggle even at the cost of some compromise on the timing of change. But while peaceful progress is blocked by actions of those at present in power in the States of Southern Africa, we have no choice but to give to the peoples of those territories all the support of which we are capable in their struggle against their oppressors. This is why the signatory states participate in the movement for the liberation of Africa under the aegis of the Organization of African Unity. However, the obstacle to change is not the same in all the countries of Southern Africa, and it follows, therefore, that the possibility of continuing the struggle through peaceful means varies from one country to another.[2]

The manifesto was prompted by a general desire to find a peaceful solution to the problem of colonialism in Africa. I regard the manifesto as one of the most important documents produced on the question of human freedom since the Universal Declaration of Human Rights and the United Nations Charter.

For a long time many diplomats, especially those at the United Nations, have felt that African representatives have been interested only in using force or violence to resolve the problems of Southern Africa. The manifesto demonstrates beyond doubt, however, that the overwhelming concern of the African countries is to find a peaceful solution to those problems and to enable people of all races to live in peace and harmony in the area. Reactions to the manifesto differed. Judging from the private talks among the African group at the United Nations prior to the adoption of the manifesto in the General Assembly, it is clear that a number of African countries were not enthusiastic about the manifesto and felt that it was unnecessarily weak. It also turned out that two or three countries had not endorsed the manifesto in Addis Ababa for this same reason. The reaction of the liberation movements to the manifesto remains unclear; some of them felt that they ought to have been consulted before the manifesto was made public.

Zambia's Policy toward Rhodesia (Zimbabwe)

The usurpation of power in Rhodesia by the 220,000 white settlers, in defiance of the United Kingdom and against the wishes of 4 million Africans, is a violent act against the principles of democracy, the Charter of the United Nations, and, indeed, against civilized conduct. Unlike other historic rebellions, such as the one which brought about the emergence of the United States of America, the Unilateral Declaration of Independence (UDI) in Rhodesia, on Nov. 11, 1965, was in pursuit of the narrow interests of a tiny minority bent on surpressing the liberties and freedoms of the majority of the people of the colony. A British minister of state said,

> In Rhodesia the illegal régime remains in power. . . . It remains in power, a tyranny, unashamedly based on racial doctrines. All tyrannies are odious, but at the present time in history those based on racial doctrines are the most odious and the most dangerous. To deny anyone his political rights is to depart from justice. But to do these things on the basis of bogus theories of racial supremacy is to depart from reason as well.[3]

After the Declaration of Independence by the Smith government, the president of the Republic of Zambia appealed to the British government to take immediate steps, including the use of force, to topple the illegal regime, to restore normality, and to prepare the area for majority rule and eventual independence. Indeed, the government of Zambia offered the British military the use of its territory to cope with the grave situation in Rhodesia. The Zambian government was satisfied that the action of November 11, 1965, was perpetrated by a small group of white racists and that had Great Britain taken punitive measures at once, the rebels would have surrendered with little loss of life. The call for the use of force was made not because Zambia wanted to see the loss of life and property in Rhodesia but rather because the eventual consolidation of the illegal act and the establishment of full apartheid would lead to a second rebellion by the African majority in Zimbabwe which would result in even greater loss of life. Moreover, it became clear that the Smith regime would not and could not contain the crisis within its own borders, for the last few years have seen grave violations of Zambia's territory and airspace by the Rhodesian armed forces. Innocent Zambian lives have been lost as a result of unprovoked attacks on Zambia. Scores of Rhodesian saboteurs and infiltrators have been sent to Zambia to create civil disorder; fortunately, the security forces of Zambia have successfully dealt with this challenge.

While this ugly situation was unfolding, the British prime minister, Mr. Harold Wilson, sought to accommodate the rebels. Having promised the world that the Rhodesian crisis would be only of short duration, he then went to great lengths in order to find any *modus vivendi* with the rebels. After four years of this shameful British policy of duplicity and connivance, we in Zambia still find ourselves confronting several battalions of Rhodesian troops across our borders.

In the meantime scores of innocent Zimbabwians, whose only fault is their claim for the inalienable right of freedom and self-determination, have been brutally killed by the Smith government, thousands of others are in prisons, and hundreds of thousands are detained or restricted. Meanwhile, the British have contented themselves with the following:

1. An ineffectual attempt at legal and diplomatic isolation of Rhodesia (it should be remembered that Rhodesia's diplomatic relations with Portugal and South Africa are more than adequate for her present dealings with the outside world).

2. A nearly meaningless resignation of the governor, Sir Humphry Gibbs (the post has not been abolished and the door is therefore still open for the British government to appoint another governor), and the unimpressive recall of the administering power's mission from Salisbury (the representative of the British government in Salisbury had been as powerless as the former governor since UDI).

United Nations economic sanctions against Rhodesia resemble those of the League of Nations against Italy in 1936 when Ethiopia was a victim of Mussolini's unprovoked aggression. By its Resolution 232 (1966), the Security Council determined that the situation in Rhodesia constituted a threat to international peace and security and, *inter alia*, decided that all member states of the United Nations should impose mandatory sanctions—including a ban on the import of certain commodities originating in Rhodesia and on the export to Rhodesia of oil or oil products, arms and military equipment, aircraft and motor vehicles or equipment and materials for the manufacturing, assembly, or maintenance of such commodities.[4] And then, on May 29, 1968, the Security Council condemned Rhodesia for its measures of political repression—including arrests, detentions, trials, and executions—which violated the fundamental freedom and rights of the people of Rhodesia.[5] The Security Council urged the government of the United Kingdom to take all possible measures to stop such actions and to suppress the rebellion in Rhodesia so that the African majority there could enjoy those rights set forth in the Charter of the United Nations. The sanctions were to be expanded to cover almost all import and export commodities. The Security Council forbade members of the United Nations to invest in Rhodesia, to travel to Rhodesia, and called upon them not to recognize Rhodesian passports. There was also a call for the withdrawal of all consular and trade representation in Rhodesia. A committee of the Security Council was established to supervise the sanctions policy.

On November 7, 1968, the General Assembly adopted Resolution 2383 (XXIII), operative paragraph 5 of which called upon the government of the United Kingdom to use force to put an immediate end to the illegal Smith regime and referred to the efforts of Zambia and the Democratic Republic of the Congo who had offered the use of their territories and airspace for this purpose.[6]

Despite all these solemn declarations of intent, life went on as usual in Rhodesia—continued suppression, executions, arrests and detentions, a state of continuous emergency, and the continued presence of South African forces. Furthermore, there was a clandestine but effective export of Rhodesian products with the full support of Portugal and South Africa in contravention of Articles 25 and 41 of the United Nations Charter. Imports continued to flow through South Africa and the Portuguese colony of Mozambique from Japan, France, West Germany, Italy, and even from the United Kingdom herself.

Throughout this period the Zambian government has consistently opposed any government not based on the consent of the people, whatever their color. The so-called referendum on the establishment of a republic and the acceptance of a new constitution held by the Smith regime on June 20, 1969 was no more than a stratagem to try to convince the outside world that the actions of the rebels had the backing of the people of Rhodesia. Africans have had virtually no say in an issue which is of the utmost importance for the future of their country.

The Rhodesian situation cannot be considered apart from the whole crisis of Southern Africa. First, since the outbreak of the revolt, Rhodesia has relied on South African troops to supplement her thin defense against the African majority. Second, South Africa and Portugal have consistently thwarted United Nations sanctions intended to bring down the Smith regime. The present Ian Smith regime represents 220,000 whites who are controlling by force the African population now estimated at 5 million. Three-quarters of these whites have been in the country for less than twenty years and the original settler population moved up from South Africa around 1890 and seized the territory by force of arms after major wars against the local inhabitants. Thus, in effect, most Europeans represent an alien occupation of the country. Because self-government was given to the whites in the 1920s, the problem of ending colonial rule was more difficult for Britain in Rhodesia than in other countries. The Europeans had experience in the legislation of repression, a certain amount of industrialization, trade relationships abroad, and their own armed forces. Thus they felt strong enough to reject those British proposals for independence, which included increasing participation of the African majority, and finally seized independence on their own terms in 1965. Discrimination and repression were widespread before Ian Smith's Unilateral Declaration of Independence. The major African political parties—the Zimbabwe People's Union (ZAPU) and the Zimbabwe African National Union (ZANU)—were banned and the leadership detained or imprisoned. Emergency regulations such as the Law and Order Maintenance Act and the Unlawful Organizations Act were put into force and forbade African gatherings, meetings, or demonstrations and permitted detention without charges, trials, or appeals. The constitution adopted by referendum in 1969 was more overtly discriminatory than the previous one and was specifically drafted to exclude the possibility of majority rule even at some unspecified future date. The emergency regulations, in effect, mean rule by police and not by law. Further, the Land Apportionment Act was recently revised to provide roughly 44 million acres of land to Europeans and 45 million acres to Africans, with 6 million vested in the European head of state.

What this means, in practice, is illustrated by a recent land case. The small Tangwena tribal group lived on its ancestral land in a mountainous district near the Mozambique border and had no other home. The land was in an area "owned" by a white rancher and had been declared a white area in the Land Apportionment Act. However, no move was made against the thousand-odd members of the Tangwena tribe until five years ago, and since then they have resisted eviction by all legal means. On July 22, 1969, the Appellate Division of the High Court in Salisbury, Rhodesia, unanimously upheld the chief's contention that his people were entitled to stay. The government's response was a proclamation ordering the chief to quit the land by August 31, 1969. On September 18, 1969, police and troops moved into handcuff the chief, and later a bulldozer moved in to demolish the compound. Press accounts indicate that the people have returned only to be moved out once again. The final result is not in doubt, for a sufficient number of Tangwena tribesmen were detained or imprisoned to enforce the government mandate.[7]

With no legal defense left, it is no wonder that the African majority have resorted to other means to continue their struggle for majority rule.

Zambia's Policy toward the Portuguese-Held Territories of Angola and Mozambique

When Zambia became independent in 1964, the territories of Angola and Mozambique were already in a state of turmoil. African leaders in these territories, having been deprived of their inalienable rights by the oppressive government of Dr. António Salazar and having been denied the right to discuss their territories' political future, had decided to organize their people in 1961 to rise against the oppressors. During that year over one thousand five hundred Portuguese were killed and one hundred administrative posts and towns and over three districts within thirty miles of Angola's capital, Luanda, were overrun. The economy of Angola was paralyzed. In 1964, the Africans of Mozambique also rose against the Portuguese colonial administration. But because Zambia (or Northern Rhodesia, as it was known at that time) was also under colonial rule, the only result of this uprising (to Zambia) was a continuous influx of refugees.

The position changed, however, with the attainment of independence. As the nationalist organizations operating in both Angola and Mozambique began to achieve greater military success, the Portuguese began to change their attitude toward the neighboring independent states—in particular, Zambia, Tanzania, and the Congo (Kinshasa). Thus, between the end of 1966 and June 1969, Portuguese forces based in Angola and Mozambique made no fewer than sixty military incursions into Zambia. There were nine such incursions in the Western Province (formerly known as Barotse Province), three in the Central Province, one in the Southern Province, twelve in the North Western Province, and ten in the Eastern Province. Apart from these, the Portuguese airforce violated Zambian airspace seventy-five times. As a result of these incursions many Zambian lives were lost, considerable property was damaged, and several cases of kidnapping were recorded. Zambia protested to the United Nations about these unprovoked acts of aggression on several occasions, the last one being the formal complaint made to the Security Council on July 18, 1968, which resulted in a strong censure of Portugal by the Security Council.

In the course of that debate in the Security Council, Zambia called attention to Article 2 of the Charter of the United Nations, which requires that all members refrain from the threat or use of force against the territorial integrity or political independence of any state. Clearly, Portugal's aggression against Zambia was in contravention of that article.

In various pronouncements, Zambia has reiterated its faith in the policy of good neighborliness. Indeed, on many occasions Zambia advised the Portuguese government that it should not blame its tragic failures in Angola and Mozambique on its neighbors. Zambia pointed out that the answer to its colonial problems lay in the granting of freedom and independence to the peoples of Angola and Mozambique. Instead of liberalizing its policies, Portugal now maintains about one hundred and fifty thousand troops in Africa. In addition, South Africa has continued to intervene on the side of the Portuguese against the indigenous people of Angola and Mozambique as it has in Rhodesia.[8] The cost of maintaining its troops in Africa for the period of 1965 to 1967 totaled some 44 percent of the total public expenditure, and since, 50 percent of the annual income. In 1969, out of a budget of about 25 billion escudos, approximately 11 billion escudos were earmarked for defense and security.[9] The absurd and tragic nature of these heavy expenditures is surpassed only by the resulting senseless loss of lives, and the stagnation of the economies of both Portugal and its colonies.

Zambia believes that if Portugal has interests it wishes to preserve in these territories, they must be guaranteed by the indigenous peoples of the territories. The same is true for Portuguese nationals who have no home other than Angola or Mozambique. Inasmuch as we in Zambia believe in a policy of nonracialism and abhor segregation, we are convinced that the future of these colonial countries depends on equality between the races. Today in Zambia there are hundreds of thousands of refugees from Angola and Mozambique. These men, women, and children are entitled to a safe home just as much as our own nationals; they are entitled to the same freedoms and opportunities that we enjoy in independence. We have an obligation to help them attain these objectives and we believe that their struggle for self-determination, human rights, and independence is supremely legitimate.

Zambia's Policy toward Namibia

By its Resolution 2145 (XXI) of October 27, 1966, the General Assembly of the United Nations terminated the mandate of South Africa over South West Africa and on May 19, 1967, it established the United Nations Council for South West Africa to administer the territory and entrusted it with certain specific responsibilities for that territory. After considering the first report of the United Nations Council for South West Africa, the General Assembly resolved on December 16, 1967, to request the council "to fulfil by every available means the mandate entrusted to it by the General Assembly."[10]

On June 12, 1968, the General Assembly adopted Resolution 2372 (XXII) which stated that South West Africa should be known as "Namibia," and that the United Nations Council for Namibia should perform the following functions:

1. Coordinate foreign technical and financial assistance to Namibia.
2. Help organize an administrative training program for Namibians.
3. Assist in the issuing of travel documents to Namibians to enable them to travel abroad.

Despite all these decisions by the United Nations General Assembly (which recognized the Council for Namibia as the formal government of the territory until its people attained independence), the government of South Africa violated each and every one of them as well as those of the United Nations Security Council which had also decided that Namibia was an international territory. While the General Assembly (in its Resolution 2145 [XXI] of October 27, 1966) called upon the government of South Africa to refrain and desist from any constitutional, administrative, or political action which would tend to alter the present international status of Namibia, the South African government ignored that call and went ahead with the establishment of so-called homelands or "Bantustans" in Namibia. Indeed, on May 27, 1968, the president of the United Nations Council for Namibia informed the President of the Security Council that the South

African government was proceeding with legislation designed to secure parliamentary approval of that scheme. As a consequence, the South African government proceeded to remove by force many Africans from their original homes despite their resistance to these moves. Approximately 59,000 Damaras and 24,000 Hereros have been affected by this inhuman action.[11]

In the South African act (called the Development of Self-Government for Native Nations in South West Africa Act, 1968), six African areas have been designated as homelands: Damaraland, Hereroland, Kaokoland, Okavangoland, Eastern Caprivi, and Ovamboland. The act further provided for the establishment of a legislative council and an executive council and other quasi-constitutional arrangements. Naturally, however, the ultimate legislative and executive powers remain vested in the state president of South Africa. To implement this odious act on October 2, 1968, the South African government promulgated the constitution of the legislative council for Ovamboland with an executive council headed by a chief councillor.

In the face of this blatant defiance of the United Nations by the South African authorities, the Council for Namibia appealed to the Security Council to take effective measures against South Africa. The council felt that apartheid in Namibia was calculated to destroy the unity of the African people and the territorial integrity of Namibia. Thus it viewed with great concern South Africa's illegal arrests, trials, and convictions of Namibian nationalists in flagrant defiance of the United Nations. All efforts by the Council for Namibia, the General Assembly, and the Security Council failed to secure the release and repatriation of these persons. Meanwhile, the Security Council decided on August 12, 1969, that the government of South Africa should "withdraw its administration from the territory immediately and in any case before 4 October, 1969."[12] That date has gone by and South Africa still illegally remains the administrative authority there.

Because of its special status as a United Nations territory, Namibia must be viewed in a somewhat different light than the other territories in Southern Africa. To us in Zambia, Namibia is one of the greatest challenges to the United Nations, an organization in which we very firmly believe. The United Nations General Assembly cannot sit idly by while its decisions are being flouted; nor can the Security Council—especially after its decision of August 12, 1969—fail to recognize the grave threat to its authority involved in the refusal of South Africa to comply with that resolution.

It may be useful at this point to see what the Lusaka Manifesto has to say about Namibia:

> South West Africa remains in the clutches of the most ruthless minority government in Africa. Its people continue to be oppressed and those who advocate even peaceful progress to independence continue to be persecuted. The world has an obligation to use its strength to enforce the decision which all the countries co-operated in making. If they do this there is hope that the change can be effected without great violence. If they fail, then sooner or later the people of South West Africa will take the law into their own hands. The people have been patient beyond belief, but one day their patience will be exhausted. Africa, at least, will then be unable to deny their call for help.[13]

As I pointed out earlier, Zambia cannot stand idly by while fellow Africans across the Zambezi River are being cruelly mistreated. Already it has absorbed hundreds of refugees from Namibia. Nevertheless, it does not believe that the only role it can play is that of perpetual host to those unfortunate persons, not can it condone the acts of aggression being committed by South Africa. It is for these reasons that the Republic of Zambia is among those countries which feel strongly that to enhance the status of the United Nations and to reassert the authority of the Security Council, South Africa should be made to leave the territory immediately. Since all earlier efforts at persuasion have failed, the only course left involves the use of Chapter VII of the Charter—namely, full and comprehensive mandatory sanctions.

Zambia's Attitude toward South Africa

The entire complex of Southern Africa centers around South Africa. This subject is especially difficult because Zambia and Africa in particular and the world at large may sooner or later be enveloped by the flames of racism. When the Charter of the United Nations was signed, hardly anybody realized that within two decades the composition of the members of the United Nations Organization would be so radically different. Zambia does not believe that race, power, and wealth are more important than man, nor does she believe that ideology is more important than man. On the contrary, she believes that power and wealth should be so used as to assist man to fully realize himself. In South Africa the greatest obstacle to the attainment of this goal has undoubtedly been color prejudice.

South Africa is the most criticized country in the United Nations and in the world because of its continued defiance of all important United Nations decisions pertaining to free choice, self-determination, and human rights. It is quite remarkable that African states have continued to believe in the art of persuasion as a solution to these grave problems rather than resorting to other more aggressive methods. The Charter of the United Nations and the Declaration of Human Rights are clear manifestations of what we should expect to occur in South Africa and in other colonial territories. We have been patient enough to continue with the struggle of liberation through persuasion instead of pursuing policies that could lead to quite widespread violence. By continuing this policy, we have given oppressed people hope that someday world opinion will force these administering powers to hand over political control to them.

Apartheid is a dangerous, insidious form of racial hatred which is destructive to all who come in contact with it. Zambia and the United Nations (especially the Security Council) have a special responsibility to eliminate it in Southern Africa. Apartheid would not be so successful in South Africa were it not for the covert and overt support the South African system has received from major Western European powers whose citizens have invested heavily in South Africa. In my view, the situation in South Africa is so terrible, so inhuman, that ordinary Western Europeans and Americans would recoil with horror if they really understood the amount of suffering caused by apartheid. It is not enough to declare a commitment to the principles of democracy, to reject racism, or simply (in the words of the Preamble to the United Nations Charter) "to reaffirm faith in fundamental human rights, in the dignity and worth of the human person, [and] in the equal rights of men and women and of nations large and small." The major powers of the world must be firmly committed to these principles in both theory and practice. When there is need to demonstrate such commitments in practice, the United States, the United Kingdom, France, and the Soviet Union must have the courage to exercise their authority to right the wrongs of their fellow men. Leadership in world affairs should be genuine, responsible, and in the interests of those oppressed. The great powers must face up to the need to act in Southern Africa in order to prevent the racial holocaust which is developing and to liberate the African majority from their oppressors.

Prospects for the Future

And so it must be clear that events of the past will have a significant bearing on the future of Zambia. Therefore, relations between Zambia and Southern Africa should be clearly divided into two categories: (1) relations with white minority regimes; and (2) relations with Southern African independent hostage states (Botswana, Swaziland, and Lesotho).[14]

Zambia has not only been preoccupied with stability and progress for herself, but also has been conscious of her international obligations as a member of the United Nations and as a member of other international and regional organizations which together form, in my view, a huge complex machinery for the preservation of stability, peace, and security for the entire world. Zambia's peace, progress, and stability provide a good counterpoint to the minority regimes in Southern Africa which derive strength from African instability and weakness. These regimes claim that our errors and blunders are sufficient justification for their holding on to what power they possess and for crimes they commit against humanity in the name of "Western civilization," Christianity, and democracy. Because of Zambia's strategic geographical location and because of the determination of the white minority regime to break Zambia's economic back, the road to Zambia's survival should be acknowledged as long and arduous. Under these circumstances Zambia's close cooperation with the African states to the north is imperative. She must depend on the friendship and support of these states if she is to maintain her present policy towards the minority regimes. African independent states in Southern Africa (Botswana, Swaziland, and Lesotho) are an asset not only to Zambia but also to the rest of independent Africa. They are an asset because they serve to extend the boundaries of freedom and reduce the areas of tension and because they show how multiracial states can work.

Zambia's policy toward the three former High Commission Territories has been one of friendship and understanding. Needless to say, Zambia has not always applauded all their policies. Although I have emphasized the importance of independent Southern Africa, its effectiveness and capability to contribute positively to the struggle against minority regimes will largely depend upon its internal strength, economic independence, and degree of self-reliance. Independent Africa to the north must, therefore, show more tolerance and understanding toward these states and spare no efforts to build favorable conditions.

In conclusion, *Southern Africa with its center in South Africa forms the biggest problem for Zambia in her African policies*. It is a dilemma and a challenge. The unholy alliance of South Africa, Rhodesia, and Portugal has shown its determination to rule Southern Africa in perpetuity. I submit that the United States, the United Kingdom, West Germany, France, Japan, the Soviet Union, and Italy have the means and ability to act decisively to wreck the evil system of colonialism in Southern Africa. Unless they convince South Africa, Portugal, and Rhodesia to alter their policies and do so now, Southern Africa will not escape a racial holocaust which will probably permanently divide the races at a time when we are struggling to achieve universal racial harmony.

PART SIX

Influence Vectors

1

The Organization of African Unity and the Liberation of Southern Africa

YASHPAL TANDON

In May 1963 the Summit Conference of Independent African States, meeting in Addis Ababa, Ethiopia to establish the Organization of African Unity (OAU) resolved to speed up the liberation of African peoples still under foreign or white domination, a task it considered "imperious and urgent."[1] Now, eight years later, Southern Africa remains about the only major African area which has not yet been liberated from such domination. Pockets of colonial remnants exist in the north—such as Portuguese Guinea and French territory of the Afars and Issas—but it is in Southern Africa where the colonial and racial regimes have taken their last-ditch stand.

The situation in Southern Africa is rapidly developing into a situation of armed conflict. Both the OAU and South Africa act as if they were belligerents. Thus South Africa's Prime Minister B. J. Vorster declared on November 9, 1966, that "these terrorists are coming here to wage war and kill. I have given orders to deal with them as one does in war."[2] Similarly, the Council of Ministers of the OAU meeting in Algiers in September 1968 demanded "the right of freedom fighters in colonial territories when captured to be treated as prisoners of war under the Red Cross Geneva Convention of 1949."[3] But the conflict is recognized as a state of war by both parties only insofar as it suits their interests. For example, African freedom fighters captured by Portugal, Rhodesia, and South Africa are not dealt with as "prisoners of war."

This chapter examines the conflict from the perspective of the OAU. It will describe the OAU's response to the challenge posed by Southern Africa and will evaluate the OAU's strategy of liberation.

The Structural and Political Framework of the OAU's Strategy of Liberation

What is strategy? Karl von Clausewitz, in his classic *On War*, defined it as

> the use of the engagement to attain the object of war. . . . It must therefore give an aim to the whole military action. This aim must be in accord with the object of war. In other words, strategy develops the plan of war, and to the aforesaid aim links the series of acts which are to lead to it; that is, it plans the separate campaigns and arranges the engagements to be fought in each of them.[4]

Who determines the strategy in Africa's war of liberation against the South? It is often assumed that the Liberation Committee of the Organization of African Unity determines this strategy. To be effective, a strategy requires not only a high command that clearly understands the objectives of war but also channels of communication with soldiers at the front. As von Clausewitz has pointed out, "Strategy must accompany the army to the field in order to arrange particulars on the spot, and to make modifications in the general plan which constantly become necessary. Strategy can therefore never take its hand from its work for a moment."[5] Such a hierarchical relationship does not exist between the OAU and the Mozambican or Angolan guerrilla fighting the Portuguese troops. The guerrilla takes his orders not from the OAU but rather from the high command of his political party—or movement, as it is often called. If the movement itself were to take its orders from the OAU, the hierarchical relationship would be complete. But this is not the case. All liberation movements in Southern Africa are autonomous, often competing, bodies organized in semipolitical, semimilitary structures. What we have, then, is not a monolithic organization that determines Africa's liberation strategy, but rather a complicated, indeed very complex, set of relationships between largely atomized liberation movements, loosely linked together by a single general objective—namely, terminating colonial rule and racial dominance and, hopefully, assuming power for themselves in the liberated territories.

What, then, is the function of the Organization of African Unity, and especially of its Liberation Committee? And what is the relationship between the Organization and the liberation movements? The Liberation Committee is really a "coordinating committee." That was what it was called when it was established at the very first meeting of the independent African states at Addis Ababa in May 1963 which launched the OAU. But what is it supposed to coordinate? In a war between coalitions of states, the coordinating body usually consists of the high commands of the allies on each side. The important question facing allies is how to divide the theater of operations among themselves in a mutually linked strategy. The Liberation Committee of the OAU does not consist of the high commands of the various armies that are supposed to be waging war in the various theaters of operation. It is not the usual type of coordinating body. It consists of representatives of independent African states whose armed forces themselves are not directly participating in combat operations against Portugal, South Africa, and Rhodesia. These states are Algeria, Ethiopia, the Congo (Kinshasa), Guinea, Nigeria, Senegal, Somalia, Uganda, Tanzania, United Arab Republic (UAR), and Zambia.[6]

Its executive secretariat is not staffed by military personnel but by civilians. Its present executive secretary is a young Tanzanian whose military expertise or lack thereof was not even an issue in his appointment to the post because the Liberation Committee is not really a military body. The committee is supposed to coordinate the policies of independent African states toward liberation and not the military strategies of the high commands of the various liberation moements. Its terms of reference, formally unchanged since 1963, are that it is "responsible for harmonizing the assistance from African States and for managing the Special Fund to be set up for that purpose."[7]

However, from the terms of reference alone it is not easy to determine the relations between the OAU and the liberation movements. "Assistance" can take many other forms besides the financial aid clearly implied in the terms. We shall discuss this question of relationship later when we analyze the strategy of liberation; for the moment it would be advisable to concentrate on the political environment that determines this strategy.

The Liberation Committee can act only on the basis of the policies that the sovereign states of Africa have toward liberation. Like the United Nations, the OAU is an intergovernmental organization that has neither a will of its own nor a capacity to enforce a collective will. Hence to understand the OAU's strategy of liberation one must turn to the strategies of liberation of its individual member states. Of particular significance are the policies of states in the neighborhood of the fighting fronts, and that are thus the likeliest to be affected by the war. For example, Algeria and the UAR are certainly influential in giving the OAU a degree of militancy, but they are rather far from the theaters of operations in Southern Africa and may not necessarily or sufficiently appreciate some of the subtleties of strategy that only Malawi or Lesotho can fully understand.

Of the three former British High Commission Territories—now the sovereign states of Botswana Lesotho, and Swaziland—Lesotho is a total enclave within South Africa and Swaziland shares a border with Mozambique. Botswana shares one border with Rhodesia but that, in the present circumstances (with a minority regime in Rhodesia), does not leave her any better off than her two sister African nations. Botswana is prevented from having a common border with Zambia by South African-held Caprivi Zipfel of South West Africa that juts fingerlike between the two states.

The economic integration among Botswana, Lesotho, and Swaziland and South Africa will be covered in other chapters in this book. But the implications of this integration for the OAU and its strategy of liberation is a concern of this chapter, and it would therefore be useful to highlight some aspects of this integration. The present annual per capita incomes of Botswana, Lesotho, and Swaziland are $70, $61, and $224, respectively, compared to $602 for South Africa. But that is a level of income sustained by British annual grants-in-aid (which still continue after independence) and repatriation of funds from migrant laborers from these three states who are working in South African mines. It is widely agreed that South Africa would find it impossible to replace this labor from domestic sources, but Botswana, Lesotho, and Swaziland cannot really afford to withdraw it from South Africa either. On the contrary, what they want is more favorable terms for their labor. Furthermore, the three territories have no control over what in other less developed countries is a major source of government revenue and a powerful instrument of economic policy—namely, customs duties. All imports come through South African ports. Botswana, Lesotho, and Swaziland and South Africa form a customs union which until recently allowed the three states a precisely calculated 1.31097 percent of the total customs and South Africa the remaining 98.68903 percent. In theory, Botswana, Lesotho, and Swaziland have a large South African market for their manufactured products; in practice, only South Africa can afford to operate efficiently and on a large scale. Swaziland's road haulage is undertaken by South African railways; Botswana's railways are operated by Rhodesian railways which are linked with South African railways. Most of Botswana's, Lesotho's, and Swaziland's external links—telephone, telegraph, international air service—operate through South Africa. Some of the key civil service and judicial posts in these states are or were manned by South African whites.[8]

Botswana, Lesotho, and Swaziland would have constituted no special problem for the OAU if they were integral parts of South Africa. They would have been regarded as yet another colonial area whose liberation it was OAU's task to assist. But as sovereign member states of the OAU, the three are a source of vulnerability for the whole Organization. One might instead have expected them to be a source of strength for the OAU. As pockets of independent African states within Southern Africa, they might have been expected to provide the bases for an assault on South Africa. That, however, is not the case—not, at least, in the foreseeable future.

Botswana, Lesotho, and Swaziland have rightly been referred to as South Africa's "hostages."[9] Any false move—by not only these three states but also by the OAU—could lead to the economic and political strangulation of the "hostages." The degree to which a policy of blackmail by South Africa will have an effect on the OAU will depend, of course, on the sensitiveness of the OAU to the question of the independence of its three members. In a moment of future crisis between South Africa and the OAU, the latter has the alternative of either slackening its offensive to save Botswana, Lesotho, and Swaziland, or sacrificing them on the altar of an eventual liberation for Southern Africa. So far, however, the dilemma has not materialized, but its potential can be skillfully exploited by South Africa, even if such a tack would really be an awkward instrument of policy.

Furthermore, as full members of the OAU, Botswana, Lesotho, and Swaziland are—in theory at least—privy to the deliberations of the Organization in all matters, including liberation. South Africa's pressure has helped to bring into power conservative governments in the three countries. Lesotho's Prime Minister Jonathan's advice to his electors "to think of your stomachs" has wider implications that can be quite serious for the effectiveness of the OAU's strategy of liberation.[10] In any case, since the three countries are so thoroughly penetrated by South African interests, official personnel, and spies, it would be remarkable if South Africa did not get access to classified documents of the OAU.

At one time South Africa did make vague threats of annexing Botswana, Lesotho, and Swaziland. But annexation, even from South Africa's point of view, would have been a mistake. Their independence ensures that the black governments are responsible for whatever takes place within their territories. If Lesotho will not allow refugees from South Africa to operate from her territory, the responsibility for this policy is Lesotho's and not South Africa's. Independent Botswana, Lesotho, and Swaziland are in this sense even better for South Africa than they were under the British. The late South African prime minister, Dr. H. F. Verwoerd, sensed this as early as June 5, 1964, when he told the South African Senate that he wished

> to challenge . . . the supposition . . . that once these territories become independent it must necessarily be accompanied by hostility. . . .
> . . . I personally believe that their becoming independent will perhaps afford us a better

> opportunity not for a hostile relationship but the contrary! The independence of these High Commission territories will mean that the people themselves will become responsible for their future existence and they will have to consider what is in their interest. As long as Britain is the overlord they could even be hostile towards us and reckon that anything they lose here in the form of employment or revenue will be made up by Britain.[11]

Malawi is in a comparable position to the three former High Commission Territories, but it is not identical. Both Malawi and Zambia were parts of the former Central African Federation. Both had, and still have, considerable economic links with Rhodesia, South Africa, and the Portuguese colonies of Angola and Mozambique. But while Zambia is attempting to loosen her dependence on Southern Africa and looking forward to building bridges with Eastern Africa, Malawi is only strengthening her ties with the white-dominated countries in the South. As an earlier study suggested,

> Between 1957 and 1965 Malawi's imports from South Africa and Rhodesia have increased from 15 percent of total imports to 41 percent, although exports to these countries have only slowly increased from 4 percent to 7 percent. South Africa is prepared to come to Malawi's economic assistance when necessary, and irrespective of whether the projects for which Malawi seeks assistance has [*sic*] economic merits or not. Thus when all the Western countries refused to give Malawi assistance to transfer its capital from Blantyre to Lilongwe South Africa moved in with a generous £4.7 million. Furthermore, South Africa has facilitated more than ever before the entry of Malawian immigrant labour into South Africa. . . .
> South Africa calls this relationship with Malawi as [*sic*] "partnership for prosperity." Malawi calls it a "relationship between equals." But [they] are most certainly distorting the existing reality and the future reality to come. There is no doubt that it is a growing partnership between unequals, whose inequality too is growing.[12]

Malawi's policy of increasing ties with South Africa may be dictated by economic necessity. But it is also significantly a conscious choice by its president. Historians would perhaps continue to argue about the degree of choice that President H. Kamuzu Banda had in directing the course of his nation, but there is no question that he has drawn Malawi more into the orbit of South Africa, and with a greater alacrity, than he need have done. From a distance it is difficult to be certain but, like President Kaunda, Dr. Banda could have taken a more independent line with South Africa than he has so far. Undoubtedly, such a line would have imposed considerable sacrifice on the people of Malawi, but a joint program of action by Malawi and Zambia to build links with the North and reduce them with the South would in the long run have provided relief from the initial difficulties of separation from South Africa. Now, in fact, Malawi is more dependent on South Africa and Portugal than she ever was before. Even Botswana, Lesotho, and Swaziland, although they are far closer to the South African sphere of interest than Malawi, have not exchanged diplomatic missions with South Africa as Malawi has done.

Malawi's *rapprochement* with South Africa might have been excused by most other African states for, although they do not share the plight of Malawi, Botswana, Lesotho, and Swaziland, they are not unsympathetic to them. Even the Tanzanian president, Julius Nyerere, observed that

> all independent Africa . . . calls for the complete trade boycott of South Africa and Southern Rhodesia. But if Lesotho or Botswana tried to implement it they would be condemned to complete economic collapse—and might even be militarily occupied by South Africa as well. In neither case could the rest of Africa do anything effective to help. The job of these two countries is to survive, with as little cooperation as is consistent with that survival. We can ask that they should not embrace the racialist states which surround them; we can ask that they should do everything possible to assert the principle of human dignity. But we should not ask them to commit suicide.[13]

What is of greater concern for the OAU, howhowever, is that the economic importance of Malawi, Botswana, Lesotho, and Swaziland is a basis for a whole new strategy for the liberation of Southern Africa. The two essential aspects of this strategy are peaceful coexistence with "white power" and liberation by negotiation. President Banda's enemies point out that he has accepted colonialism and racism as well as the discrimination against black African peoples inherent in these policies. He denies this vigorously. His is a policy of short-term compromise with the existing reality in the hope that it will ultimately change through persuasion and example.

> Negotiate [*sic*], round table talks for peace between white and black must be the aim. At roundtable negotiation, not at gun-point. . . . Leave Rhodesia to Smith and Wilson. Like Nigeria, leave it alone.[14]

It would seem that President Banda's strategy for liberation is based on a combination of considerations. The first is a recognition of the futility of a policy of sanctions:

> African States north of the Zambezi must stop thinking they can solve the problem of South Africa by shouts and threats in Addis Ababa, London or New York. . . . South Africa has been isolated and boycotted for years now. She is thriving on boycotts and isolation.[15]

The second is the hope that through demonstrating the ability of the Africans to govern themselves, South Africa might be persuaded to trust Africans with power:

> Let the white people of South Africa visit us and see for themselves how things are in countries under Black Governments and run by Black people.[16]

What gives this strategy a chance of survival is not only President Banda's strong espousal of it but also the powerful economic inducements that South Africa can offer to draw more states into her sphere of influence, such as the Malagasy Republic.

The alternative to Dr. H. Kamuzu Banda's strategy of liberation is the power strategy, advocated by President Nyerere of Tanzania. It is based on the assumption that South Africa, Rhodesia, and Portugal are beyond persuasion and that the only language they understand is the language of violence. All else follows logically from this assumption. It follows that the main thrust for liberation will come from the guns of the nationalist soldiers. And therefore the function of the rest of the African states is to provide moral and material assistance to those nationalists engaged in war with white power. Thus international diplomacy should aim at putting pressure on states such as the United States, the United Kingdom, and the Soviet Union to impose economic, political, and even military sanctions against Rhodesia, Portugal, and South Africa. All this comes out clearly in the following three statements made by the Tanzanian president:

> The struggle for freedom must go on. Our preference, and that of every true African patriot, has always been for peaceful methods of struggle. We abhor the sufferings and the terror, and the sheer waste, which are involved in violent upheavals, and believe that peaceful progress is worth some sacrifice in terms of time. But when the door of peaceful progress to freedom is slammed shut, and bolted, then the struggle must take other forms; we cannot surrender.[17]
>
> The only choice available is a violent struggle for freedom or continued acquiescence in slavery. The peoples of all the Portuguese colonies have chosen; they are fighting. . . . Neighbouring territories give moral support to the freedom fighters. . . .[18]
>
> Colonialiam and racialism and, indeed, their ramifications have ceased to be merely anomalies. They are serious and real world liabilities, and we must expect the United Nations to address itself methodocally and to apply its energies diligently to the unfinished task in these areas.[19]

Tanzania's line is, by and large, supported by her other two neighbors close to the battleline, Zambia and the Congo (Kinshasa). Of the three states Zambia is the most vulnerable, but certainly less so than Malawi or Botswana, Lesotho, or Swaziland. Both Zambia and Malawi have about the same population, 4 million each, but while the gross national product of Zambia was $880 million in 1966, that of Malawi was only $156 million. Furthermore, Malawi is much smaller in size and its southern half is almost totally surrounded by the Portuguese territory of Mozambique. Zambia's borders, however, are also vulnerable. She shares thousands of miles of borders with Mozambique, Rhodesia, Angola, South Africa, and South West Africa, and the latter includes the dangerous Caprivi Zipfel which might well become a site for South Africa's missile, and possibly nuclear, bases in the future.

Zambia is vulnerable and yet Pan-African. In the Southern African context, it is easy to be either one or the other, but to be both is to walk a tightrope. Malawi and the former High Commission Territories have chosen to dilute their Pan-Africanism in proportion to their vulnerability. Zambia has chosen to walk the tightrope. The implications are hazardous. Pan-African loyalties demand that the freedom fighters of Southern Africa be given moral and material support which, in turn, exposes the country to reprisals by South Africa, Rhodesia, and Portugal. Zambia, in fact, has recently come under attack from Portuguese intruders.

Zambia responds with calculated security risks. These risks may not prove to be calculated after all, should the white regimes decide to assume a more aggressive posture than heretofore. But Zambia would wish to avoid a confrontation while still giving some kind of assistance to the freedom fighters. Officially, she takes the line, therefore, that she does not encourage or provide facilities for training guerrillas for operation against Southern Africa. The limit of her "official" assistance is to provide passage through Zambia for refugees fleeing from Southern Africa. It is almost certain that Zambia does not have training bases for guerrillas. However, she does have bases from which guerrillas (trained outside Zambia) can launch their assaults on the territories. The guerrillas, on entering Zambia, have to surrender their arms to the Zambian ministry of internal affairs, which releases the arms only on application from the guerrillas. One consequence of this is that the Zambian government can control guerrilla activities and allow only those it approves. But another implication of this policy is that Zambia cannot now easily deny knowledge of these operations, and since these operations would appear to have had official blessings, South Africa gains a "legal" basis for a policy of hot pursuit.

Tanzania and the Congo (Kinshasa) are less vulnerable than Zambia and can therefore afford to adopt a bolder policy. Each shares a border with a Portuguese colony, and although this certainly exposes them to a certain degree of risk of reprisals by the Portuguese forces, the risk is much less than that of Zambia. Tanzania's militancy is greater than that of the Congo. The latter aids only the moderate wing of the Angolan liberation movements— namely, *Frente Nacional de Libertação de Angola* (FNLA)—while Tanzania, besides actively helping the Angolan liberation movement, *Frente de Libertação de Moçambique* (FRELIMO), is the headquarters of most of the other liberation movements, including the two South African ones—namely, the African National Congress and the Pan-Africanist Congress. Within Africa itself, Tanzania most certainly has the largest number of guerrilla training camps and arms depots—alleged to be as many as forty.[20] Furthermore, her close association with Communist China puts her in contact with not only a major external arms supplier but also the leading radical Communist state. Tanzania, the South African deputy minister of police, Mr. S. L. Muller, is reported to have claimed, poses "the greatest potential threat to the Republic [of South Africa]."[21]

OAU'S Current Strategy of Liberation

In the existing balance of power which fundamentally favors the white-controlled nations of Southern Africa, it can be argued that a prudent government would pursue a conciliatory approach in the hope that the opposing regimes may be persuaded to relax their racial and colonial policies. But this is really an unworkable strategy. To what extent President Banda sincerely believes this strategy will produce the desired results and to what extent he is using this strategy to cover up his own policy of compromise that the economic weakness of his country probably demands is difficult to know. But there is now general agreement among most observers of the South African scene that it is unlikely that South Africa will ever yield as a result of persuasion alone. President Banda's efforts, however honest and hopeful, are unlikely to convince the whites of Southern Africa to relinquish their power. On the contrary, his acceptance of South Africa's economic aid and the extension of South Africa's defensive perimeter to include Malawi—as well as Rhodesia, South West Africa, Botswana, Lesotho, and Swaziland—might be interpreted by the Pretoria government as evidence of the success of its diplomacy and thus serve to increase its confidence in its ability to preserve white power indefinitely.

In the long run, the militant line would appear to be the only realistic strategy in the present context of Southern Africa. The Organization of African Unity, therefore, has chosen this line as its policy. This policy precludes coexistence with the white regimes and is consistent with the Organization's objectives as stated in its charter. Thus there is a diplomatic alliance in the OAU between the more militant states such as Tanzania, Algeria, and the United Arab Republic and the usually more moderate states such as Ethiopia and Liberia as well as the conservative French-speaking African states.

What are the implications of this strategy in terms of the OAU's relations with the liberation movements and with countries such as Malawi, the Malagasy Republic, Botswana, Lesotho, and Swaziland?

The accommodative relations between Malawi and the former High Commission Territories, on the one hand, and South Africa, on the other hand, confront the OAU with "the-enemies-within" type of situation that is not without historical precedent. Given a powerful adversary, it is obvious that unity should be an essential element of an opposing strategy. When, however, such unity is compromised by short-term or immediate considerations of states prepared to ally themselves with the adversary, then the question is: What should be done with such states? Should sanctions be imposed against those that will not join in the united front against a common adversary? There are individuals who would subscribe to the view that the task of dealing with "the enemies within" takes priority over that of dealing with "the enemies without." The logical extension of this policy would be to attempt to subvert existing regimes in Malawi, Botswana, Lesotho, Swaziland, the Malagasy Republic, and such other noncooperative regimes in order to put like-minded revolutionary governments into power.

But no African state is prepared to adopt such a policy—at least officially. The legal fiction of sovereignty, according to which states are forbidden to interfere in each other's affairs, is only a small part of the explanation. The other part of the explanation lies in the fact that a revolutionary doctrine which calls for the subversion of African regimes alleged to be under the domination of one or the other external power would further split an already divided continent. Instead of fighting merely Portugal, Rhodesia, and South Africa, African states might also start fighting each other. Therefore, strictly pragmatic considerations dictate that the OAU adopt a policy of coexistence with states that adopt a similar policy *vis à vis* the regimes of Southern Africa. Once again, President Nyerere defined the limits of the relations with such African states:

> We must be ready to co-operate with all African states in African affairs regardless of our opinion of their internal—or even their external policies. Only where a free African state is betraying the liberation of Africa or deliberately and avoidably damaging the degree of co-operation which already exists, has Africa, or any African state, the right to protest. And even then we should make our protests as one brother to another—in private and in a fraternal spirit.[22]

The deviant states may be tolerated but they cannot be allowed to sabotage the joint strategy. They are a security risk for the OAU, for in this war of liberation they could pass on information regarding the movements and actions of the OAU and the liberation forces to the enemies. Therefore, such states, despite their full membership in the Organization, are kept in the dark about the details of the strategy. Furthermore, their nationals are not allowed to work in the Liberation Committee. In February 1969, for example, the OAU Council of Ministers passed a resolution which authorized the Liberation Committee to

> reserve the right, in order to continue safeguarding the secrecy of its work, not to circulate documents to those Member States who have diplomatic relations with Portugal and the regimes of Pretoria and Salisbury.[23]

When Malawi's proposed inclusion in the Liberation Committee was considered several years ago, Tanzania threatened to leave the committee, President Nyerere charging that

> Malawi is in collusion with the Portuguese in Mozambique to sabotage the work of the Liberation Committee, and if she is admitted into membership, Tanzania would find it difficult to continue as a member. . . .[24]

Keeping the deviant states away from the secrets of the Liberation Commission does not imply, however, that they are abandoned to their own fate. The Organization is quite concerned about the possible threat that South Africa poses to their security and independence—particularly in the cases of Botswana, Lesotho, and Swaziland. The OAU has warned South Africa that "any attempt to annex or encroach upon the territorial integrity of these three Territories shall be considered an act of aggression," and it has sought, without success, "to secure a guarantee by the United Nations for the territorial integrity, independence and sovereignty of these territories."[25] However, as we mentioned earlier, it is also to South Africa's advantage that these territories remain—or at least are seen to remain—independent. For the time being, South Africa can get all it wants from these three countries without formally annexing them. The OAU's attitude toward the deviant states is similar to any parent's attitude toward wayward children: they must be protected but they must not be allowed to damage the family's interests.

What can be said, then, of the OAU's relations with the various national liberation movements? As the Liberation Committee's terms of reference imply, liberation is primarily the task of the liberation movements and of the people of the territories themselves and not of the OAU. The latter will provide moral and material assistance to the movements wherever possible, but it is not the OAU's function to fight battles for them. Proposals for the raising of volunteer armies are sometimes heard in individual countries such as Algeria, Tanzania, and Uganda, but these have been proposals by individuals or by political parties.[26] So far no government has seriously supported such a proposal. In fact, so far there is no evidence of any extranational volunteers from independent African states fighting in the unliberated areas. It is possible that if the combat zone expands and there are incursions into neighboring territories by the Portuguese, Rhodesian, or South African troops, the people of these areas might feel themselves threatened and thus be driven to join actively in the fighting. But for the present this seems unlikely.

The OAU can help the liberation movements in four ways. First, it can recognize them and thus give them international respectability; second, it can attempt to bring together rival nationalist parties in a common front; third, it can coordinate material support given them by individual member states of the OAU; and, finally, it can fight their diplomatic battles in the world at large and in the United Nations.

As regards the first function, the OAU has no standard practice on recognition of the liberation movements. The only limitation that applies is to refuse to recognize those African political parties in Rhodesia, Mozambique, Angola, South West Africa, and South Africa that have adopted President Banda's policy of "compromise and settlement through negotiations." When Mr. Percy Mkudu, the leader of Rhodesia's African parliamentary opposition party (United People's party), came to Addis Ababa in February 1969 to persuade the OAU Council of Ministers to give him a hearing, the council agreed but condemned his conciliatory approach to the problem of Rhodesia. In a strongly worded statement, the council denounced "the latest manoeuvres of certain so-called African opposition leaders who are trying to convince others that it is still possible to negotiate with the rebel regime."[27]

This stance of the OAU would appear to have been justified by subsequent events. Three months after Mr. Mkudu's futile attempts to get the OAU to accept a negotiated settlement of the Rhodesian problem, the Smith government in Rhodesia introduced a new constitution that broke the colony's last formal links with the British crown and created a new apartheid-type political structure in Rhodesia. Those Rhodesian African nationalists who had hoped that the Smith regime might still be open to persuasion are now facing increasing hostility and exploitation by the Rhodesian whites. No conciliatory approach has been successful.

Whether the intransigent policies of Rhodesia, South Africa, and Portugal will eventually induce all African nationalists to follow the hard line proposed by the OAU is difficult to say. One may hazard the guess, however, that white power will always be able to attract enough moderate African nationalists who, in turn, will be granted symbolic representation in these white-dominated political systems at some future date.

While recognition by the OAU is thus limited to movements that have chosen active struggle as their instrument of liberation, it is not necessarily the more militant movements that automatically receive OAU's blessings. Among other factors that are just as significant as the militancy of the liberation movements are their efficiency, whether or not they have headquarters within their own national territory, the location of their foreign headquarters, the influence of their patron states in the councils of the OAU, their financial position, and their contact with external powers, such as the United States, the Soviet Union, and Communist China. A combination of any of these factors could change the fortunes of a liberation movement in its relations with the OAU.

To give but one example, in August 1963 the OAU gave exclusive recognition to the Angolan liberation movement and its government in exile, *Governo Revolucionário de Angola no Exilo* (GRAE), on a unanimous recommendation of the Liberation Committee. A number of states followed this OAU action with individual recognition of GRAE. Its president, Holden Roberto, went to Peking in 1964 and was seated as a full delegate at the Cairo Heads of State meeting of the OAU in July 1964. In the meantime, however, the fortunes of its rival, *Movimento Popular de Libertação de Angola* (MPLA), changed. The revolution in the Congo (Brazzaville) in August 1963 and the overthrow of President Youlou put into power a government sympathetic to MPLA, and thus the MPLA acquired a base for building up its strength. In the Congo (Kinshasa), on the other hand, the Adoula government which favored the GRAE was replaced in July 1964 by the Tshombe government. Messrs. Tshombe and Roberto had strained relations, and the GRAE began to lose its hold over the African nationalist movement in Angola.[28]

The Liberation Committee of the OAU thereupon set up a three-nation conciliation committee (the Congo [Brazzaville], Ghana, and the UAR) to attempt to bring together the GRAE and MPLA. The Congo (Brazzaville) and Ghana, however, were basically inclined toward the MPLA, and the committee's efforts at conciliation failed. In a special session at Dar es Salaam in November 1964, the Liberation Committee decided to withdreaw its exclusive recognition of the GRAE and to give assistance to both the movements. But the OAU's Council of Ministers, meeting at Nairobi in March 1965, did not accept the committee's recommendations and decided once again to attempt to bring together the GRAE and MPLA through the efforts of the three-nation conciliation committee. In June 1965, however, the GRAE's Minister of Defense Alexander Toty attempted an unsuccessful coup within the movement. This action was taken by the committee as evidence of the GRAE's internal divisions and it decided to increase its aid to the MPLA without, however, totally cutting off the GRAE. But as the GRAE became increasingly known for its American connections, it became less popular with the OAU. In February 1968 the Council of Ministers finally passed a resolution recommending that the Heads of State and Government

> review the status of the Government in exile of Angola [that is, the GRAE] as this status could not only lead some liberation movements to complacency but also diminishes their dynamism and vigor in the struggle.[29]

Although the recommendation specifically applied to the GRAE, it appeared as if the council were making a general case against all recognitions. The council, it seemed, had finally realized that the OAU's policy of recognizing only one of the factions as the legitimate standard-bearer of the liberation struggle in a given country—and, by implication, the only recipient of OAU's aid—had proved disastrous. The members of the Liberation Committee did not always agree as to which faction should receive the blessings of the Organization. One Liberation Committee formula which transferred the primary responsibility of recognizing and aiding liberation fighters to "neighboring countries" (that is, Tanzania, Malawi, and Zambia for Mozambique; the Congo [Kinshasa] and the Congo [Brazzaville] for Angola and Cabinda; Guinea and Senegal for Portugese Guinea; and Ethiopia for French Somaliland) was not very effective. The "neighboring states" had vested interests and sympathies for particular groups. Thus, for example, in the case of Portuguese Guinea, Senegal backed the *Frente para a Libertação e Independência da Guiné Protuguesa* (FLING) and Guinea supported the *Partido Africano da Independência da Guiné e Cabo Verde* (PAIGC). Often a group that was not recognized proved more effective than the one that was, and the Liberation Committee had to reverse its order of recognition. Decisions of the committee were sometimes undermined by individual states which gave support to parties less favored by the committee. Furthermore, the committee's policy of giving aid to favored movements sometimes intensified the conflict between the rival movements, leading to bitter struggles for power within the movements as well as within the Liberation Committee.

But recognition, however unsuccessful as a policy, was still eagerly sought after by the liberation movements since it not only helped them to secure material assistance from the OAU, but also was thought to give them an increased legitimacy in the eyes of their followers and their foreign patrons. To get OAU recognition, the movements often exaggerated their successes on the battlefield, and poached on each other's captured territories or took each other's men as "rebel prisoners." To prevent this, the Liberation Committee started sending commissions of military experts on frequent visits to the various theaters of operation to assess the performance of the various movements and to advise the Liberation Committee as to how much aid it should give these movements.

The second major function of the OAU is the establishment of mediation bodies to resolve the disputes between rival factions of liberation movements and to persuade them to present a common front against the enemy. The most persistent factionalism occurred in the Angolan and Rhodesian liberation movements. Two mediatory bodies were set up for Angola, one in July 1964 composed of the Congo (Brazzaville), Ghana, and the UAR,[30] and the other in February 1968 composed of the Congo (Brazzaville) and the Congo (Kinshasa).[31] Three conciliation commissions were appointed to mediate between the Zimbabwe African National Union (ZANU) and the Zimbabwe African People's Union (ZAPU) of Rhodesia, one in July 1964 composed of Malawi and Tanzania;[32] a second in June 1965 composed of Malawi, Zambia, Tanzania, Uganda, Kenya, and Ethiopia;[33] and a third in September 1968 composed of Tanzania, Kenya, and Zambia.[34]

The OAU's efforts to persuade rival liberation movements to bury their differences have largely failed. Where does the fault lie? There was no lack of conciliatory efforts by the OAU and hence it can hardly be blamed for the failure. Some of the blame might be laid at the doorstep of the white-controlled regimes in Southern Africa, for they have often exploited the differences and helped perpetuate them. Long imprisonments or house-arrests of Rhodesian and South African nationalists have kept the leaders physically apart and thus prevented them from meeting and resolving their differences.

But the main blame must lie with the nationalist leaders themselves. Although differences usually disappear in the face of a common foe, they have nevertheless persisted in the liberation movements. Some of these differences are rooted in the ideologies and political styles of the various movements. For example, in South Africa the ANC is less militant and vociferous than the PAC. The latter, furthermore, restricts its membership to black nationalists whereas the former admits all South Africans, irrespective of race, who are opposed to the present regime. But differences in ideology, in mode of operation, or in connections with foreign powers do not provide a complete explanation of their factionalism. These differences assume an exaggerated importance in the daily lives of members of the rival organizations. But, at the back of it all, there is a power struggle going on for control of the territories once they have been liberated. Liberation may not even be achieved in the lifetime of the present leaders but, insofar as it is the only goal their movements are fighting for, the question of what happens after liberation is a perfectly legitimate one.

The OAU is not in a position to smooth over these differences since it is not a supranational agency which can impose its will on the movements and any help the OAU can give along these lines will remain marginal. What the liberation movements need is dynamic leadership, similar to that the late Dr. Eduardo Mondlane provided for the Mozambique liberation movements. These movements were badly fragmented until Dr. Mondlane assumed leadership and unified them in the name of *Frente de Libertaçao de Moçambique* (FRELIMO)—Liberation Front for Moazmbique. But he was assassinated in February 1969, and this has split the FRELIMO once again between an allegedly Moscow-oriented group and a Peking-oriented group.[35] Who killed Mondlane is uncertain. If he was assassinated by the Portuguese, this would be further evidence of the divisive influence of colonial nations on the liberation movements. If he was assassinated by a member of an incipient splinter group within FRELIMO, then the situation is much more serious, for it would indicate that the liberation movements have not yet achieved that degree of organization necessary to wage war against Portugal.

The third and main function of the OAU is to coordinate assistance to the liberation movements. However, not all aid passes through the OAU. There is nothing in the OAU charter to forbid the liberation movements from obtaining assistance from whatever source they can; they can do so without going through the OAU channels. This is particularly the case with regard to aid obtained from extra-African sources. Most liberation movements have their own contacts in the Soviet Union, Communist China, the United States, and Europe (especially Scandinavia). The Swedish government, for example, makes a direct annual grant of $115,000 to the Mozambique Institute in Dar es Salaam which is run by Dr. Eduardo Mondlane's American widow. This institute trains students to assume fundamental civic responsibilities in the liberated areas of Mozambique in addition to giving them the requisite political and military education for the liberation struggle.

The amount of aid that liberation movements receive from the OAU and from foreign sources is difficult to estimate not only because their records are secret but also because this assistance may vary from year to year. According to one apparently reliable source,[36] the amount of assistance promised to the various countries by the OAU itself during the last two years was as follows:

	1967–1968	*1968–1969*
Rhodesia	$300,000	$240,000
Portuguese Guinea	$216,000	$331,200
Mozambique	$264,000	$348,000
Angola	$180,000	$120,000
South Africa	$120,000	$86,400
South West Africa	$72,000	$48,000
Others	$36,000	$36,000
Total	$1,188,000	$1,209,600
Administration and Propaganda	$168,000	$146,400
	$1,356,000	$1,356,000

If the figures are right, they indicate that the OAU has favored those movements that have fared better than others in the battlefield—namely, FRELIMO in Mozambique and PAIGC in Portuguese Guinea. The figures also reveal that the amount of aid given South African liberation movements is small, thus illustrating the basic OAU strategy of helping to liberate Rhodesia, Angola, and Mozambique first before going on to liberate South Africa and South West Africa. Although this strategy seems correct to an outside observer, there is some question as to whether it is supported by all the liberation movements, particularly those in South Africa. It is reasonable to assume that each liberation movement is primarily concerned with success in its own theater of operations. Therefore, it must seek alternative sources of logistical and financial support if it receives only a small share of the Organization's liberation budget.

Like the United Nations, the OAU has its financial problems. The financial difficulties of the United Nations do not stem from the poverty of its members, but rather from political differences among them regarding the proper use of these funds.[37] Members of the OAU also have their political differences, but their inability to provide adequate financial support for the OAU is just as serious a liability as their political differences. They all need development capital for national economies, and they all rely on foreign aid (even to balance their annual budgets, in many cases). Therefore, it requires a considerable devotion to the cause of Pan-Africanism if these states are to support the OAU at the expense of their own national development. Thus the budgets of the OAU are really quite small. In 1967–1968 the OAU had a regular budget of $2.915 million reduced to $2.3 million in 1968–1969. By comparison, the regular budget of the United Nations was $129.237 million for 1967 and $141.619 million for 1968. This comparison is an invidious one except that it illustrates the relative magnitude of the OAU's activities, and the relative poverty of its members. The OAU has many more financial defaulters than the United Nations. Out of a total membership of thirty-three states in 1965, twenty-four had not yet paid their dues as of October 1965, according to a report by the secretary-general of the OAU.[38]

The Liberation Fund, like the United Nations' peacekeeping fund, is not part of the regular budget; but this Fund suffers from the general impecunity of the OAU members, just as the regular budget does. Every meeting of the OAU Assembly of Heads of State and Government and of the Council of Ministers has passed a resolution asking the defaulting members to pay their dues to the Liberation Fund. During its February 1969 meeting at Addis Ababa, the Council of Ministers requested the administrative secretary-general,

Mr. Diallo Telli, and a subcommittee of the Advisory Committee on Budgetary Matters to investigate why certain member states had not yet made their contribution to this fund.[39]

The Administrative Committee has not yet reported its findings, but it is clear that the Liberation Committee is facing a serious financial crisis. Consequently, the Liberation Committee is not even able to meet its commitments to the liberation movements. There is a wide discrepancy between what is promised to these movements and what they finally receive. Thus, according to the source mentioned above, the PAIGC of Portuguese Guinea and Cape Verde was promised $216,000 in 1967–1968 but received only $45,000 in the first six months.[40] Other figures for the same period are as follows:

	Allocated	*Given*
FRELIMO	$264,000	$28,322
MPLA	$88,800	$11,172
GRAE	$90,000	$23,335
PAC	$40,000	$4,160
ANC	$80,000	$3,940
SWAPO	$72,000	$6,235
Total	$634,800	$77,164

Another possible consequence of the Liberation Committee's financial crisis is that its budget may well be cut in future to the point where it does not exceed the sums allocated to it by member states.

Both the liberation movements' access to foreign sources of aid (which is in most cases more than aid provided by the OAU) and the OAU's general financial crisis will naturally affect the influence the OAU can exert over the movements. To the extent that the movements secure financial aid from sources other than the OAU, they are free to flaunt its decisions, particularly if their respective strategies of operation conflict. However, they cannot completely do without the support of neighboring states which provide them with bases from which to launch their assaults and to which they can retreat when pursued by South African, Rhodesian, or Portuguese forces. Thus the attitudes and policies of the neighboring states are more important to the liberation movements than those of the OAU. A movement that is able to secure outside funds as well as a base of operations from a sympathetic neighbor, such as Holden Roberto's *Frente Nacional de Libertação de Angola* (FNLA), which is alleged to receive financial aid from sources in theUnited States and which uses the Congo (Kinshasa) as its base, is virtually immune from OAU pressures.

Now we come to the fourth and final function of the OAU with regard to liberation. This is to fight the liberation battle in the international diplomatic area. The strategy of this battle is to persuade other nations to cooperate in general economic, diplomatic, and military sanctions against all the Southern African white-dominated regimes. Thus, although there might be differences in the types of tactics used against Rhodesia, Portugal, South West Africa, and South Africa, the basic OAU strategy remains the same. In the case of Rhodesia, the OAU still contends that the British government has "primary responsibility" for settling the problem, just as in the case of South West Africa it asserts that the United Nations has the final responsibility for what was once a League of Nations mandated territory.

But it has become increasingly clear that the legal fictions of British responsibility for Rhodesia and of United Nations responsibility for South West Africa are no substitute for more powerful economic (and possibly military) sanctions against Rhodesia and South Africa than have so far been taken by the United Nations. From the very beginning of the Rhodesian crisis in November 1965 and increasingly since the failure of the United Nations to establish an effective presence in South West Africa,[41] the majority of African states have asserted in the United Nations that that body must now invoke the military provisions of Chapter VII of the United Nations Charter[42] against the regimes of these two territories. This policy is also reflected in many OAU resolutions on these questions.

Ever since 1963 the OAU has maintained a semi-permanent caucusing group in the United Nations —comprising the permanent representatives of Liberia, Malagasy, Senegal, and Tunisia—to represent the African case on the liberation of Southern Africa to the other members of the Organization. Until recently, the Council of Ministers and the Assembly of Heads of State and Government almost routinely congratulated this committee every year for its work and advised it to continue. This might appear incongruous since no member of this group has great enthusiasm for the Liberation Committee (Tunisia, in fact, asked that it be disbanded at one time) and one of the members (Malagasy) is increasingly adopting an accommodationist approach toward Southern Africa. Lately, however, the OAU has kept rather quiet about this group, but so far it has neither disbanded nor replaced it. It has probably terminated *sine die*.

The OAU's diplomacy on behalf of the liberation movement has not produced the expected results. The combined votes of the African states, in conjunction with those of Asian and Latin American states, were able to secure the formal termination of South Africa's mandate over South West Africa and the consequent internationalization of the territory under United Nations jurisdiction, but they were unable to persuade the United States, the United Kingdom, and France to impose military sanctions against South Africa. The Soviet Union alone, even if it were so disposed, could not have imposed these sanctions. In the case of Rhodesia, an effective diplomatic entente between the United States and the United Kingdom in the United Nations has kept the problem firmly in the latter's hands. It was only with Great Britain's consent that the United Nations Security Council was able to pass a resolution imposing selective mandatory sanctions against Rhodesia. The African states unsuccessfully attempted to have comprehensive sanctions (including an embargo on oil) imposed against Rhodesia.[43]

The OAU has been more successful in expelling South Africa, but not Portugal, from international organizations. Thus South Africa was expelled from the International Labor Organization (ILO) and the Food and Agricultural Organization (FAO) in 1964, and from the World Health Organization (WHO), International Civil Aviation Organization (ICAO), and the United Nations Educational, Scientific and Cultural Organization (UNESCO) in 1965. But these expulsions did not adversely affect South Africa's economy or the morale of its white population. South Africa, once a member of the Commission for Technical Cooperation in Africa South of the Sahara (CCTA), was expelled from it in 1963 and was not allowed to become a member of the Economic Commission for Africa (ECA), but with a quarter of Africa firmly within its economic sphere of influence, South Africa has not only survived exclusion from the ECA but is threatening to absorb in its fold some of the members of the ECA, such as Malawi.

The Post-Rhodesia Disillusion in the OAU

The Organization, ever since the Unilateral Declaration of Independence in Rhodesia, has fallen into a sullen mood of despair. None of its major objectives appears to have been achieved, although it may seem too early to expect results. Nonetheless, nobody expected the white Rhodesians to show such determined tenacity. Compared to South Africa, about which few African states had any illusions, Rhodesia seemed a tractable problem. But time proved only to be on the side of the illegal regime. The OAU felt let down by the British who adamantly refused to heed African advice to use force to terminate the rebellion.

Comparisons were made between British resort to force in Aden and in former British Guiana and its refusal to do so in Rhodesia. The only plausible explanation for this inconsistency was that the British were unable to use force where their "kith and kin" were the culprits. Some African states construed British inaction over Rhodesia as evidence of British complicity in the illegal seizure of power by the Smith government which seemed to enjoy the support of British business interests in South Africa. While some African states contemplated breaking off relations with the United Kingdom because of the Rhodesian issue (as was the case with Tanzania and seven other African states) and also leaving the Commonwealth (or expelling the British from that organization), most states realized that their economic dependence on the United Kingdom made it impossible for them to do so.

The weaknesses of the OAU were further compounded by a spate of military *coups d'état* in Western Africa in 1966, followed by a lengthy civil war in Nigeria which immobilized one of the potentially most powerful states in Africa. The *coups d'état* not only got rid of such radical Pan-Africanist leaders as Kwame Nkrumah, but also created an atmosphere of internal instability and political uncertainty in these countries. From now on the new military regimes concentrated more on national consolidation than on Pan-African ventures. For a vast majority of OAU members, OAU resolutions on Pan-African problems, such as liberation, represented mainly an affirmation of their Pan-African ideals rather than a serious dedication to fight for them. They could not afford to do much more than pay lip service to these ideals because they had more urgent domestic priorities.

Thus the burden of liberation was increasingly assumed by a few dedicated states and the liberation movements themselves. Tanzania seemed to have more than its share of the burden; it provided the site for the headquarters of the Liberation Committee, the first chairman and executive secretary of the committee, and an operational base for most of the liberation movements. Several OAU member states accused Tanzania of mismanaging the Liberation Committee, and Tanzania refuted these charges by accusing these states of not doing enough for the cause of liberation. The French-speaking African states were heavily criticized; such criticism usually was in the form of innuendoes suggesting that, since these states were still virtual dependents of France (which had vested business interests in South Africa), they were under French pressure not to contribute money to the Liberation Fund. Tanzania's critics claimed that the Liberation Committee did not operate efficiently and alleged that its Tanzanian executive secretary was spending committee funds for nonessential purchases.[44]

These mutual recriminations were considered at the last Addis Ababa meeting of the Council of

Ministers in February 1969. In an attempt to satisfy both sides, the council authorized an investigation into the matter under the supervision of the administrative secretary-general and the Advisory Committee on Budgetary Matters. According to the terms of reference established by the Council of Ministers, the administrative secretary-general was to

> 1. Investigate the root cause of noncontribution by Member States to the Special Fund and the reasons . . . for the loss of enthusiasm in the Liberation Committee.
>
> 2. Examine the problems confronting the Liberation Committee and present such recommendation as would help the Committee in the execution of its assignment.
>
> 3. Invite the attention of the Executive Secretariat of the Liberation Committee to the need for adoption of an improved accounting system.
>
> 4. Investigate the problems which beset the functioning of the Executive Secretariat.[45]

There were member states, such as Tunisia, which, in fact, suggested that the Liberation Committee should be disbanded altogether. The decision to investigate the operations of the Liberation Committee meant that the committee was given the opportunity to justify its existence and possibly to improve its operations.

Much more debilitating for the OAU, though, is the increasing self-doubt about the efficacy of the strategy of liberation. At its September 1967 meeting, the Council of Ministers recommended that the Assembly of Heads of State and Government "devise a new strategy for the liberation of African territories still under foreign domination."[46] The council repeated this recommendation in February 1969 when, having noted that "little progress has been made in the liberation struggle during the period from September 1968 to February 1969," it suggested that "a review of the strategy in the conduct of the armed struggle should be effected."[47] Accordingly, the Assembly of Heads of State and Government decided in September 1969 to appoint a committee of seven member states—namely, Algeria, Central African Republic, Ethiopia, Kenya, Morocco, Senegal, and Sierra Leone—"to conduct a study, after consultations with the Liberation Movements and all Member States of the OAU on the mandate, the structure and the composition of the Coordinating Committee for the Liberation of Africa."[48]

What are the possibilities of the OAU revising its strategy of liberation? Is the OAU now likely to consider adopting the more conciliatory approach toward Southern Africa that President Banda and others recommend? Or is it likely to

continue with what appears to be the presently ineffective strategy?

Prospects for the Liberation Struggle

The present doubts of the OAU about the efficacy of its strategy of liberation stem from an incorrect analysis of the nature of the challenge posed by the white-controlled states of Southern Africa as well as from false expectations of a relatively fast response to this challenge. The attempts of the Organization to explain its shortcomings, especially those of the Liberation Committee, have been concerned mainly with the search for convenient scapegoats and therefore have been somewhat superficial.

This is not to suggest that the organization of the Liberation Committee does not need improvement. Its executive secretariat certainly needs an overhauling, and so do its methods of acquiring and disposing of funds and logistical assistance. Even if the institutional weaknesses are convenient scapegoats, they are nonetheless a source of genuine concern among the member states, and institutional improvements would certainly help to kindle greater enthusiasm for the work of the Liberation Committee.

However, organizational reforms alone will not solve the problem of liberation. The difficulties the OAU faces are, in fact, much more complex. The first difficulty is the African politico-economic situation. Since the OAU is only an intergovernmental organization and thus cannot impose upon its member states those sacrifices which the latter are not prepared to make, it is evident that the "failures" of the OAU are ultimately due to the fact that most of its member states are too preoccupied with problems of nation-building to be able to devote sufficient time and funds for extranational problems.

While African states have scarce resources to deploy in the struggle for the liberation of Southern Africa, the white-controlled regimes of this area control formidable resources with which to respond to the challenge of the OAU and the liberation movements. South Africa has built a powerful neofascist state, a state in which human beings are methodically categorized into various racial groups and their behavior regulated accordingly. Any deviation from this pattern, even by the whites, results in a merciless application of "corrective measures" that range from police surveillance of interracial sexual contacts to confinement in prisons which have sophisticated instruments of torture to elicit confessions from even the most stubborn and courageous. The

African population is placed under a tightly controlled economic system that is designed to ensure their continual dependence and vulnerability for what the South African regime hopes will be an eternity.

With an ever-expanding economy (the benefits of which are disproportionately enjoyed by the minority white population), South Africa can afford to spend a great deal on defense. The phenomenal expansion of defense expenditures is suggested by the following figures. In 1960–1961 the total defense expenditure was $85.8 million; in 1961–1962 it rose to $144 million; in 1962–1963 it increased to $156 million; in 1964–1965 (two years later) it had risen to $252 million; and still two years later (in 1966–1967) it grew to $307.02 million. The defense budget for 1967–1968 was $307.2 million.[49] These figures are for South Africa only. Portugal spent $249.5 million in 1968 on national defense,[50] while the Rhodesian budgetary allocation for defense has rise from $26.64 million in the year prior to UDI to $33.6 million in 1967–1968 and $35.28 million in 1968–1969.[51]

Thus the balance of power in Southern Africa—for the present, at least—rests with the white-controlled states. South Africa has a very wide range of strategic alternatives. It has used both threats of force against its African neighbors, on the one hand, and, on the other hand, has invited them to join its "co-prosperity sphere." For example, in October 1967, Prime Minister Vorster warned President Kaunda of Zambia to

> stop this braggadocio and develop your country, because in that way it will be to the benefit of your people and the whole of Southern Africa. It you want to try violence, as you have advised other States in Africa, we will hit you so hard that you will never forget it.[52]

The threat was later changed to a sweet invitation to "come to my prosperous parlor" when, exactly a year later (in October 1968), the South African minister of defense, Mr. P. W. Botha, stated the conditions for joining the rich men's club:

> President Kaunda does not have to look for weapons against South Africa. If he wants to seek true friendship, all he needs to do is to keep the terrorists out of his country and to join Southern Africa in building a strong force against the Communist campaign aimed at enslaving his own country with the rest of Southern Africa.[53]

The entente of South Africa, Rhodesia, and Portugal has a formidable number of men and weapons in its defense and security system. Thus Rhodesia can mobilize a regular army of 3,400 men (all but 1,000 of whom are whites) and as many as 10,000 territorial reserves. It has one squadron each of Hunter fighters, Vampire fighters, Camberra light bombers, and Alouette helicopters.[54] In 1966–1967 the number of Portuguese troops was estimated to be about 55,000 men in Angola and about 52,000 men in Mozambique.[55] But it is the South African defense force which is the most formidable of all. In its defense white paper submitted to the parliament on June 3, 1964, the government indicated that South Africa could mobilize 14,926 officers and men of the permanent force, 51,487 commandos, and 16,527 men of the Citizen Force.[56] In July 1965 Commandant R. C. Hiemstra disclosed that, in the event of a conventional war, the South African army alone could mobilize 100,000 men and 80,000 commandos.[57] What is perhaps more relevant is the significant reorganization of the defense system to enable South Africa to reduce its dependence on foreign powers for arms. For example, South Africa claims it can now produce the 7.62-mm. R1 automatic rifle; an improved version of the FN (the standard rifle of NATO forces); Italian jet aircraft; and small, 4-inch air-to-ground missiles. Nonetheless, it still continues to get significant support from other states, especially from France, from which it purchased three submarines of the Daphne class. On February 22, 1967, Defense Minister Botha declared that South Africa's northern frontiers were protected by a radar complex which would provide an early warning system against enemy aircraft, and that the South African coasts were protected by the installation of the Decca navigational system at a cost of $8.4 million.[58] In addition, South Africa has rapidly been building reservoirs of "oil mines" in case the United Nations ever imposes oil sanctions. In October 1968 South Africa was reported to have launched its first guided missile from St. Lucia missile testing site, a military base north of Durban.[59]

By comparison, the armies of the other states in Africa are not only small but also poorly equipped and meagerly financed. Figures for defence expenditures in independent African states are not always readily available. It is obvious from the available sources that these states not only spend small amounts for defense and security but also cannot afford any larger amounts for the foreseeable future. The statistics on p. 259 illustrate the point.[60]

More relevant still is the fact that while almost the entire budgetary allocation of South Africa for defense and security is spent on measures against external intervention or internal revolution, a very tiny proportion of the independent African states' budget goes toward fighting the white regimes in Southern Africa.

	1966		1967		1968	
	Total Expenditure (in $ million)	*Expenditure on law and order (in $ million)*	*Total Expenditure (in $ million)*	*Expenditure on law and order (in $ million)*	*Total Expenditure (in $ million)*	*Expenditure on law and order (in $ million)*
Kenya	175	9.05	193	12.5	252.95	17.36
Sudan	226.5	47	262	55	312.28	50.96
Tanzania	113	19.5	127	20	200.73	30
Uganda	129.5	12.5	146	12	162.87	14.76

The entire OAU budget for liberation is less than $1.2 million. If one adds this sum to the amount that the liberation movements secure from non-OAU sources, the total cannot come to more than $7 million to $10 million (as compared with South Africa's budget of $307.2 million in 1967–1968). The movement which has the largest single guerrilla contingent in Southern Africa is the FRELIMO in Mozambique, which claims to have mobilized something like ten thousand men (as compared with fifty-two thousand Portuguese troops in Mozambique). Most other liberation movements have much smaller guerrilla forces. Furthermore, the movements are almost wholly dependent on foreign sources for their arms and even for basic supplies like army boots. The flow of supplies is both sporadic and uncertain, and these supplies are unevenly and unsystematically distributed among the various movements.

It would be easy to conclude from these comparative statistics that the fight for liberation is hopeless from the very start. "In six hours," Lesotho Prime Minister Jonathan is reported to have said, "South Africa forces would be in Cairo."[61] In fact, the very basis of the Banda-Jonathan strategy of compromise is the unquestionable military superiority of white Southern African armed forces.

Since power is the ultimate arbiter of relations among states, it would appear that military superiority of the white states in Southern Africa would have the effect of forcing the OAU to reappraise its strategy of liberation along the lines indicated by President Banda. Is it likely that the OAU would reassess its strategy of liberation?

Despite the OAU's present disillusioned mood, it is unlikely to undertake a radical revision of its liberation strategy. Most African states and most of the liberation movements are far too committed to liberation to abandon it so easily. Even if the struggle has only begun, it is unlikely that the OAU would adopt an accommodationist strategy. The struggle will probably be intensified.

The likely result of the recent setbacks suffered by the OAU is that it will gradually recognize that there is no easy or quick solution to the problem of liberation and that the struggle will indeed be a long and protracted one. Thirty years ago, when China was fighting Japan, Mao Tse-tung criticized those of his compatriots who, expecting a quick victory, fell into despair (much like the OAU now) when that quick victory did not materialize. He argued that

> the exponents of quick victory, however, do not realize that war is a contest of strength, and that before a certain change has taken place in the relative strength of the belligerents, there is no basis for trying to fight strategically decisive battles and shorten the road to liberation. Were their ideas to be put in practice, we should inevitably run our heads into a brick wall. Or perhaps they are just talking for their own pleasure without really intending to put their ideas into practice. In the end Mr. Reality will come and pour a bucket of cold water over these chatterers, showing them up as mere windbags who want to get things cheap, to have gains without pains.[62]

Mao Tse-tung had to contend not only with those who expected a quick victory, but also with those who argued for a compromise with the enemy because of his overwhelming strength. He called the latter group theorists of "national subjugation."

> The theorists of national subjugation, who see nothing but the contrast between the enemy's strength and our weakness, used to say, "Resistance will mean subjugation."[63]

Karl von Clausewitz was the theorist par excellence of the conventional war; Mao Tse-tung is the theorist of a new type of war, the people's war. Those like President Banda who argue that armed superiority is the supreme arbiter of the conflict see the struggle primarily in conventional terms. The theory that "weapons decide everything," claimed Mao Tse-tung,

> constitutes a mechanical approach to the question of war and a subjective and one-sided view. Our view is opposed to this; we see not only weapons but also people. Weapons are an important factor in war, but not the decisive factor; it is people, not things, that are decisive. The contest of strength is not only a contest of military and economic power, but also a contest of human power and morale.[64]

An analysis of China's struggle against Japan not only provides historical perspective for an analysis of the current liberation struggle in Southern Africa, but also a set of standards with which to evaluate the African struggle. The initial comparison between the forces of the liberation movements and of their white opponents in Southern Africa does, of course, engender a sense of defeatism. But most guerrilla wars have begun with small bands of men fighting against much stronger enemy forces. Discussing urban guerrilla warfare and the balance of power between the guerrillas and the government, Regis Debray has taken the position that

> city terrorism cannot assume any decisive role, and it entails certain dangers of political order. But if it is subordinate to the fundamental struggle, the struggle in the countryside, it has, from the military point of view, strategic value; it immobilizes thousands of enemy soldiers, it ties up most of the repressive mechanism in unrewarding tasks of protecting factories, bridges, electric generators, public buildings, highways, oil pipe-lines —these can keep busy as much as three-quarters of the army. The government must, since it is the government, protect everywhere the interests of property owners; the *guerrilleros* don't have to protect anything anywhere. They have no dead weight. Therefore the relation of forces cannot be measured in purely arithmetical terms. In Cuba, for example, Batista could never utilize more than 10,000 out of his 50,000 men against the guerrillas at any one time. And the Rebel Army, its chief tells us, became invincible when it reached a ratio of one to 500.[65]

This ratio of armed forces of 1:500 between the government and the guerrillas presupposes that the guerrillas are well organized and suitably equipped. Inefficient organization, insufficient arms, and inadequate logistics are some of the main deficiencies of the present liberation movements in Africa. Most of these movements have still not won the complete support of their own peoples. A belief in the invincibility of the white man, a myth which was skillfully cultivated during the colonial era and is still widely held by the rural people, inhibits the latter from giving the guerrillas the support they badly need to make their operations effective. The economic dependence of most Africans in Southern Africa on the whites makes them incapable of supporting a full-scale revolt that might entail the destruction of the existing economic system on which they depend for their present livelihood.

Yet it is very likely that as the conflict continues the guerrillas will be able to overcome their present disadvantages while those of their enemies will become more apparent. Again, Mao's description of China in 1938 would be apposite for Southern Africa at the present time:

> The fact is that the disparity between the enemy's strength and our own is now so great that the enemy's shortcomings have not developed and for the time being cannot develop to a degree sufficient to offset his strength, while our advantages have not developed and, for the time being, cannot develop to a degree sufficient to compensate for our weakness. Therefore there can as yet be no balance, only imbalance.[66]

The current disillusionment in the OAU is due to the imbalance of power in Southern Africa. But this imbalance is not likely to persist indefinitely. Although it is true that South Africa is not on the verge of violent revolution, as many proponents of African liberation imagine, nevertheless, South Africa has changed remarkably over the years. A "Herrenvolk democracy," Professor van den Berghe has observed, has changed into an "albinocratic tyranny"[67] so that it is not only the Africans who are victims of this tyranny but increasingly the whites as well. Social strains must ultimately appear in a political system that combines a high degree of economic development with rigid social controls.[68] As the people prosper in an affluent society, they value freedom and leisure more. In the South African context, the whites may succeed for a time in preventing Africans from securing well-paid and respectable jobs in factories, in mines, and in the professions, but the demands of a prospering economy may later force them to employ Africans in these jobs. If and when this development occurs, the task of imposing controls over the Africans will become even more difficult than it is now. The whites may themselves become divided on the question of how best to tackle this problem, just as they are presently divided between the *verligtes* and the *verkramptes* on the issue of the relationship with African governments in the north.[69] A discussion about the future developments in South Africa takes us into the speculative realm but the point is that with time the internal contradictions of apartheid will become more evident. Therefore, even before the liberation movements will have attained parity in arms and manpower with the white regimes of Southern Africa, the balance of power might shift in their favor. It is these movements which will have to fight the real battles; the Organization of African Unity will only play an essentially peripheral role in this struggle, just as it has in the past.

However, the OAU's record is not all one of failures. Without the Organization to cement some degree of unity among its member states, they most certainly would have been in much greater disarray. Mistakes have, of course, been made in the tactical handling of many of the issues, such as the precipitate decision in November 1965 to break off diplomatic relations with the United Kingdom over the Rhodesian crisis; but, by and large, the OAU has helped to coordinate widely disparate views on the challenging problems posed by Southern Africa. If it has not produced effective results, it has at least provided a common forum for members to deliberate together on the implications of the trends of events in the continent. No state, after the OAU meetings, can plead ignorance of these implications as a basis of its policies. In the arena of international diplomacy, the OAU has not been able to make the United Nations adopt the course of action it has proposed, but at least it has been able to keep the issues alive. The battle has not been lost simply through silence, and as long as defeat is not openly and unequivocally conceded, the war cannot be said to have been lost.

2

The Exile Condition and Revolutionary Effectiveness: Southern African Liberation Movements

JOHN A. MARCUM

The central political fact about contemporary Southern Africa has been the ability of its white minorities to impose or perpetuate their rule over preponderant African majorities. The 1960s brought an anticlimactic end to a half century of legal nonwhite political protest in South Africa[1] and witnessed the suppression of all African nationalist movements within South West Africa, Rhodesia, and the Portuguese territories.[2] Denied hope for nonviolent change, African nationalists, where not wholly crushed, went underground and turned to revolutionary goals and strategies.[3] They could not, however, match the technical skill and means of European defenders of the status quo, especially the European security police, equipped with modern electronic devices for radio detection or wire tapping and aided by networks of paid informers. Given the overwhelming odds against them, hundreds of Southern African political leaders and youthful followers went abroad during the 1960s in search of external assistance, if not external deliverance.[4]

Banned and at least partially dismantled inside, political movements took on new lives outside. Their external leadership viewed exile as transitory and generally expected that the prevailing "winds of change" would assure a triumphal repatriation within just a few pan-African years.[5]

The southerly progress of African independence, however, ground to a halt as it met the resilient counterthrust of white power evident, for example, in Katangese secession and Rhodesian UDI. Exile ranks grew and expectations of an early return home receded. By the end of the decade a score of African liberation movements confronted the necessity of surviving a prolonged period of exile.

If these movements were ever to attain revolutionary goals, however, they had to do much more than simply survive. Their leaders and militants had to overcome the initial shock of displacement and had to deal successfully with a broad range of environmental, existential, and technical problems. As clustered or condensed into three aggregates, these problems represent the principal focus and structural outline of the analysis which follows. Sequentially, they concern the need for and nature of efforts by Southern African exiles seeking political power through revolution to

1. *Contend realistically with a new external environment* that offers some moral and material assistance but also presents new frustrations and invites overdependency and wasted motion;

2. *Cope with the particular perceptual and behavioral problems* that normally arise under such conditions and, to varying degrees, impair the political effectiveness of exiles and refugees; and

3. *Organize and effect a return, by guerrilla and/or underground action*, to the political life of their respective countries, a return which is, in the final analysis, the only way to prevent political exile from becoming a voluntary or involuntary "escape" into political irrelevance.

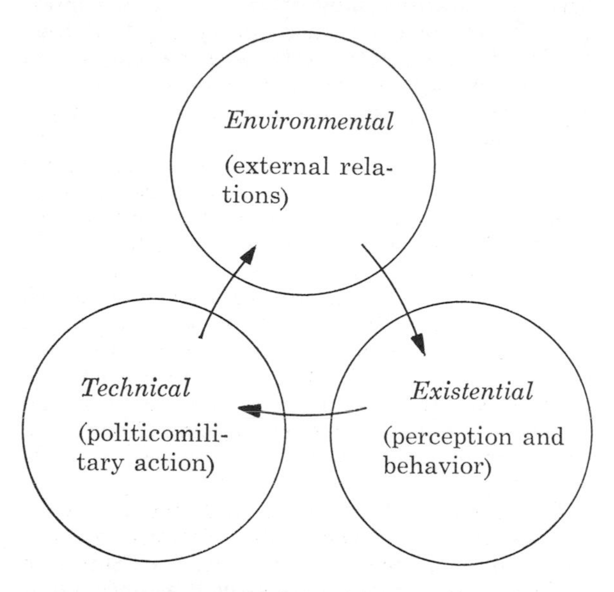

Aggregate Problems Confronting Revolutionary Exiles

The Struggle Outside: Deliverance or Dependency?

Southern Africa's liberation movements have had to contend with the "objective conditions" of a superficially responsive but often manipulative and debilitating exile environment. Success in efforts to obtain moral and material assistance within differing segments of political community "outside," however, is generally considered crucial to exile hopes for a successful return home. Yet such recognition and aid are of unequal, sometimes questionable, importance, depending upon their source and extent. Moreover, because they face perceptual and behavioral problems (as discussed in the section below), African exiles often prove susceptible to external involvements that tend, in turn, to perpetuate, aggravate, or compound these same difficulties. Outsiders who "respond" to the exile's plight, often without fully realizing it, foster escapist hopes for improbable peaceful solutions, encourage energy dispersion into "diplomatic" travel and lobbying, or indulge self-delusions by recognizing exile "governments" and holding "freedom-fighter" conferences; in sum, they make it easier for exiles to escape from reality into a "pretend world" of aimless wheel-spinning. External powers also react to and "use" conflict-prone exile movements in the alien context of American-Soviet, Sino-Soviet or Arab-Israeli disputes and thus ensnarl them in new quarrels that further dissipate energy and fragment loyalties.

Perhaps the most systematic way to assess whether or how external relationships have enhanced the revolutionary, goal-related capacity of Southern African exiles or, conversely, have encouraged exile tendencies toward debilitating overdependence and malfunction is to examine these relationships, beginning with the broadest level of community at which the exiles seek recognition and moving systematically to the narrowest level. This means starting with the United Nations and concluding with the revolutionary group's own home constituency.

OUTSIDE COMMUNITY: THE UNITED NATIONS

During the 1950s African independence movements generally sought to utilize the world forum of the United Nations and its trusteeship concepts (as provided for in chapters XI and XII of the United Nations Charter) in campaigns to terminate colonial rule and they eventually obtained a broad moral condemnation of colonialism and racism (apartheid, in particular) along with expressions of support for the principle of self-determination. The debates, and the resolutions that regularly poured forth from them, helped to reinforce nationalist militancy and, by means of public pressure, to induce political concessions to Africans living in British, French, and Belgian territories.

As haphazard decolonization came up against the hard-core resistance of European rule in Southern Africa, however, it gradually became clear that moral suasion would not be enough to produce change in that region. Though United Nations resolutions could, at the most nearly universal level of institutionalized community, legitimize African aspirations for equality and independence, they could not muster supportive pressure for the attainment of these goals without the cooperation of major Western powers. In a gloomy introduction to his annual report to the Twenty-first General Assembly in 1966, Secretary-General U Thant noted that the "most conspicuous and acquiescent mass violation of human rights and fundamental freedoms" in the world persisted in South Africa with no sign of improving "despite repeated appeals by the Security Council and the General Assembly." He recalled that in the year previous the General Assembly had concluded that only "universally applied economic sanctions" might achieve a peaceful solution, and went on to express a personal opinion that "the main trading partners of South Africa [had] a special responsibliity as well as the means to persuade the South African government to abandon its present course." The import of the secretary-general's message was clear. International charity—for example, pledges of something over $100,000 to a trust fund for legal assistance, relief and education for victims (mainly refugees) of apartheid (which he duly cited)—would leave the "basic problem unresolved" and neither donor nor exile recipient should allow himself to be deluded into thinking otherwise.[6]

Indeed, the ineffectiveness of action initiated through the United Nations was being dramatized at that time by the dispute over South West Africa, the one Southern African issue widely thought to be susceptible of a United Nations solution. On July 18, 1966, after nearly six years of contentious proceedings, the International Court of Justice dismissed, without ruling on its merits, an Ethiopian-Liberian case that charged South Africa with violating the terms of its League of Nations mandate.[7] Following the Court's judicial, if injudicious, escape from decision, Afro-Asian states pushed through the General Assembly a resolution that "terminated" South Africa's mandate, created a Council for South West Africa "to administer" the territory "until independence" (set for June 1968), and requested the Security Council to take "appropriate measures" to enable the new council to carry out its functions.[8] Inasmuch as four permanent members of the Security Council—namely France, the Soviet Union, the United Kingdom, and the United States—did not support the resolution, it was predictable that the Security Council would not take such "appropriate measures."

Nevertheless, the General Assembly instructed the new territorial council to seek the unlikely cooperation of Pretoria, in the absence of which it was "to proceed to South West Africa with a view to . . . taking over administration of the Territory."[9] When Pretoria did, in fact, defy it and deny it entry into South West Africa, the council issued brave statements of intent, but pushed itself no closer to a confrontation than a commercial air flight to Zambia.[10]

Demonstrating that political exiles have no monopoly on collective self-delusion, the diplomats of the General Assembly next attempted to assuage frustrations by "doing something." Without being able to consult the inhabitants of South West Africa, whose political servitude was plainly not considered by any major power to justify the risks or sacrifices of a real collision with South Africa, the General Assembly renamed the territory Namibia, after a largely uninhabited coastal desert.[11]

One result of this false motion, and equally ineffective gestures concerning Rhodesia (economic sanctions) and Portuguese Africa (political censure) has been a sharp decline in the value attached to the United Nations by Southern Africans and others as a forum for the airing of disputes and grievances. Whereas in the 1950s Southern Africans hopefully sought United Nations intervention—in some instances proposing that they be placed under United Nations trusteeship—[12] as the 1960s drew to a close, most Southern Africans were presenting only *pro forma* protests to the world body.

For the record and for the psychological solace that it provides, some Southern Africans continue to argue their case in the United Nations. Few top leaders now make the trip to New York, however, and expect little and spend less time when they do. When a new exile petitioner, Benjamin Pinto-Bull, head of a Dakar-based exile-émigré movement from Guinea (Bissau), showed up in New York in 1968 in search of a United Nations "solution," the obvious and dated futility of his quest served to label him as an exile out of touch with the realities of world politics.[13]

To those desirous of external deliverance from colonial rule, then, the United Nations has been able to offer a symbolic legitimation of Southern African revolutionary aims as well as an implicit endorsement of revolutionary action. But, as time has passed, the world organization has demonstrated that, in the absence of support from its more powerful members, it is unable to promote and support such aims and action with any real effectiveness. Increasingly, therefore, realism has required that revolution-oriented Africans see the United Nations as not much more than a politically harmless (and thus useful) arena in which to relieve psychic tensions through rhetoric. For South West Africans, at least, overreliance upon United Nations political and legal processes has proved to be a demoralizing, dead end strategy. By appearing, but yet failing, to confront South African power, the collective membership of the world body raised false hopes and inhibited nationalist initiative, only finally to leave exiled Namibians further from power and thus more frustrated and dependent than they had been before the United Nations assumed responsibility for their cause.

OUTSIDE COMMUNITY: THE WESTERN POWERS

Western, and in particular, American policy with regard to Southern Africa has had a similarly negative impact that can be summed up in an old nursery rhyme:

> Mother, may I go out to swim?
> Yes, my darling daughter
> Hang your clothes on a hickory limb
> But don't go near the water.

Western governments have misleadingly appeared (at least to Africans) to manifest serious intentions of responsive action by making "hickory limb" statements in condemnation of colonialism and apartheid and in favor of self-determination and racial justice. But for a variety of reasons, including economic investments in South Africa,[14] military bases in the Azores,[15] and fear of "Communist" political alternatives, they have always stopped at water's edge short of taking the action that would be necessary to give effect to their statements. By developing nuclear facilities and oil resources, by offering technological and managerial training to South African whites, by helping these whites to automate industry and transportation and thereby to reduce (though not eliminate) their reliance on skilled African manpower, and, above all, by refusing to support proposed United Nations sanctions, Western powers have built and nourished a relationship with Southern Africa that is fundamentally antirevolutionary.[16]

In general, "Third World" revolutionaries seeking "radical redistribution of political and economic power to overcome centuries of political oppression and crushing poverty"[17] have been viewed with apprehension by most Western powers, especially by the United States. Even though such revolutions may arise out of indigenous grievances and aspirations, nevertheless they are often perceived in terms of a stark cold war perspective. "Wars of liberation" that enjoy Soviet or Chinese support tend to be seen indiscriminately and simplistically as part of a well-coordinated, worldwide Communist conspiracy. As Richard J. Barnet of the Institute of Policy Studies in Washington, D.C., has put it: "The essence of the argument is that guerrillas in Vietnam, Thailand, Peru, Guatemala, and Angola are all part of the same army."[18] An extreme illustration of this sort of thinking on the part of an influential southern legislator is Senator Strom Thurmond's statement welcoming the assassination of the American-educated Mozambican revolutionary, Dr. Eduardo Mondlane, in February 1969 as a blow against communism.[19]

Attitudes like those of Senator Thurmond are vigorously promoted in the United States by groups such as the American-African Affairs Association (AAAA).[20] And even a top policymaker with reputedly moderate or "dovish" views concerning the Vietnamese war, such as former Under-Secretary of State George W. Ball, has persistently and publicly argued against American policies that would be congenial to the interests of Southern African liberation movements.[21]

By 1967 Southern African exiles found that American private (largely church) and government scholarship programs that had been opened for them early in the decade were closing down.[22] Of some usefulness to nationalist groups if only because of the patronage it involved, these and other Western educational programs, which excluded military, security, or intelligence training available elsewhere, never compensated for the inadequacies of Western policy. Nevertheless, these programs did offer some politically oriented, former and/or prospective nationalist leaders an opportunity to acquire new analytic tools, professional skills, and personal security, and thus rendered them more effective persons or potentially more formidable political strategists. This positive impact was largely offset, however, by a softening context of affluence and undisciplined individualism and an unsettling (if familiar) threat of white racism, both of which suffused their American experience. The political (as distinct from personal) value of their education was also undermined by the ease with which they could integrate (escape) into black American communities.[23]

Fund-raising tours in the United States by exiled leaders were invariably disappointing, and bitterly so because of the visible affluence of the society which failed to respond. Although some private groups, notably the American Committee on Africa (ACOA), argued the exiles' collective cause and even managed to raise enough money to contribute an occasional Land Rover,[24] probably no private American assistance was at any time quantitatively important, let alone decisive, for any Southern African exile movement. The value of private aid, moreover, was further reduced in 1966–1967, when disclosures about activities of the Central Intelligence Agency (CIA) revealed that supposed distinctions between "private" and "public" had in some instances been blurred—for example, the operations of the United States National Student Association (USNSA).[25]

The gap between principle and practice in

American policy and the unlikelihood of substantial American moral or material support for Southern African revolution were only reluctantly and slowly perceived by some exiles (or most American sympathizers), who then came to feel that they had been rejected, isolated, and wronged. Their reaction sometimes took the form of an aggressive and energy-consuming anti-Americanism which served as a common denominator among them. Partly because it was rare and meager and not likely to become really significant, American endorsement or even presumed assistance became a liability (possibly even in terms of self-image) for an exile group such as the *União das Populações de Angola* (UPA). American professions of sympathy came to evoke skepticism—if not cynicism—and all ties with Americans became suspect. Charges of covert American assistance (which were impossible to prove or disprove) became a convenient weapon with which to discredit a rival.

Future help given by militant Afro-American or New Left organizations with sufficiently revolutionary credentials might be an exception to this generalization. The ability of such groups to assist must be limited, however, by the preoccupying nature of their political action commitments within the United States.[26] Moreover, as Susan Sontag has pointed out with reference to the Cuban revolution, many American (white) radicals are devoted to releasing "new energies" of often hedonistic "individual life-history" and "private passion." They counsel retreat from "the rough, dehumanizing embrace" of such "corporate life-killers" as the army and may be "positively counterrevolutionary" from the perspective of those who seek revolution through disciplined, collective action. Southern African exiles are unlikely to be rendered more effective societal revolutionaries by close association with individualistic revolutionaries who can afford voluntary poverty and the values of "spontaneity, gaiety, sensuality, and freaking out."[27] On the contrary, associations with such Americans may only encourage personal escape or intensify goal frustration.[28] And, given the ambiguous and precarious visa status of most Southern Africans in the United States, compounded insecurity may be an inevitable result of any associations that attract the attention of the Federal Bureau of Investigation (FBI).

Self-interest requires that Southern African exiles both perceive and accept the fact that appreciable help from the West is improbable.[29] It also suggests that they must realistically assess the likelihood of increased American intervention —economic, technological, military—on the side of the status quo. How much may their rhetorical denunciations of the United States and their international alliances influence American decisions in this regard? Africans are probably inclined to answer "very little," though it is possibly still in the interest of exile groups to control their anger and to project an image of nationalist independence in order to reinforce the voices of those persons in the post-Vietnam war period who may be expected to argue that the United States should not assume an "anti-Communist" mission as "Guardian at the Gates"[30] of Southern Africa.

OUTSIDE COMMUNITY: THE COMMUNIST POWERS

Solid supporters of the need for revolutionary action in Southern Africa, members of the "socialist camp" have in important ways related more affirmatively to the exile dilemma and have offered a variety of revolutionary models that reflect diverse experiences and divergent interpretations of Marxist-Leninist ideology. To the extent that the increased polycentrism of the Communist community in recent years has enabled them to select from a variety of theory, strategy, and assistance, Southern African exiles have found increasing utility in what this community has to offer.

The Soviet Union has long-standing ties with political protest movements in Southern Africa through its early association with the South African Communist party (SACP) and the Portuguese Communist party (PCP), which was once active in Angola (principally in Luanda).[31] These predominantly white organizations eventually merged or allied with the African National Congress (ANC) of South Africa[32] and the *Movimento Popular de Libertação de Angola* (MPLA),[33] respectively, and these, in turn, have enjoyed Soviet endorsement. In United Nations debates, international conferences, and the press and radio, the Soviet Union has consistently backed the Southern African revolutionary cause, although it has refrained from direct or decisive intervention by means of collective action to enforce United Nations resolutions on South West Africa or by means of direct air, naval, or other logistical support (as distinct from training and arms) for African guerrilla units moving into the area. The Soviet Union has also provided a broad range of scholarships and, in contrast to the United States and other Western countries, it has actively encouraged recipients to be politically active and to maintain ties with their sponsoring liberation movements while studying in Soviet institutions.

The Soviets stress a need for political spade work and a "sober and objective" analysis of social conditions prevailing in a given country *before* launching an armed struggle.[34] They regard careful planning, attention to organization, propaganda, and mass political education and flexibility—that is, the capacity to alternate between violent and nonviolent action as warranted by circumstances—as crucial. They also attach considerable importance to external aid. Though Soviet or pro-Soviet writers counsel that revolution "must arise and develop" from conditions within a country and "cannot be exported," they feel that the "external factor" is of "growing importance."[35] From the vantage point of a liberation movement, however, such emphasis on the importance of external aid poses a serious question. Does it not serve to foster external dependency and possibly to focus attention on "diplomatic" lobbying to the detriment of internal organization?

The Chinese offer a revolutionary model or faith that differs in important respects from that of the Soviet Union. In particular, the Chinese approach has the therapeutic merit of offering hope even to those most frustrated by the curse of exile.[36] Though the imperialists may appear to have terrifying power, Marshal Lin Piao has said the history of the "peoples' war" in China demonstrates that the growth of revolutionary forces "from weak and small beginnings into strong and large forces is a universal law of development of the class struggle." Though there will be ups and downs, revolutionaries "should despise the enemy strategically and take full account of him tactically" and should "dare to win" because no force can alter the general trend toward inevitable victory.[37]

Stressing the need for "peoples' wars," as distinct from variegated Soviet strategy, Lin Piao has asserted that even as poorly armed "amateurs," well-trained peasants can defeat heavily armed "professionals." He has argued for guerrilla self-reliance, placing less emphasis on the "external factor."[38] Therefore, revolutionaries "must be prepared to carry on the fight independently, even when all material aid from outside is cut off." They should not blame others, or history, for their fate. He urges that they "independently ponder and solve problems of revolution in [their] own country" and not become dependent on foreign aid, "even though this be aid from socialist countries which persist in revolution."[39]

There are other Communist models. Cuba offers a guerrilla "success story" and a Castro-Debray recipe for almost "instant revolution"—that is, the thesis that rebels should begin with military rather than political action and should then build a mass movement from the military nucleus (*foco*) and not the reverse.[40] Yugoslavia and Vietnam, both small and thus unintimidating countries like Cuba, also offer models of successful guerrilla warfare (Partisans and Viet Cong) and defiance of great powers. All three, along with North Korea, Czechoslovakia, and other Eastern European countries, have helped Southern Africans with training, technical advice, arms, or funds, within the limits of their means.[41]

If the multiplicity of models and sources of significant aid have tended to reduce the need to rely on any single source of Communist support and thus the danger of dependency upon a single benefactor, the sharp deterioration in Sino-Soviet relations during recent years has tended to offset this advantage. It has increasingly polarized already quarrelsome exile movements into two rival leagues. It has also introduced ideological discord, reinforced factionalism, and thereby undermined both collective purpose and organizational stability within some of these movements.

In general, those movements which have sought and received Soviet support are led by a relatively well-educated, multiracial, urbanized elite, with some exposure to, if not a sophisticated grasp of, Marxist-Leninist ideology.[42] There are currently six of these movements: the *Frente de Libertação de Moçambique* (FRELIMO): *Movimento Popular de Libertação de Angola* (MPLA); *Partido Africano da Independência da Guiné e Cabo Verde* (PAIGC); African National Congress (ANC, South Africa); Zimbabwe African People's Union (ZAPU, Rhodesia);[43] and South West Africa People's Organization (SWAPO).[44] In keeping with the Soviet formula for a three-way alliance of socialist countries, liberation movements, and "revolutionary and progressive movements" in capitalist countries, the Soviet-oriented World Peace Council and Afro-Asian People's Solidarity Organization jointly convened an international conference on Southern Africa at Khartoum, Sudan in January 1969, in order to launch a worldwide drive in support of these six movements.[45] Thus Soviet policy has laid stress upon the "external factor." In the view of a British participant, the Khartoum meeting "emphasised that what is now required is a big expansion of international solidarity." "The African people," he continued, "are expecting that in the West in particular there will now be a new interest and understanding which will be translated into active solidarity and practical aid."[46] To the MPLA of Angola, the conference raised "hopes" that it would "be the starting point for a vast and irreversible process that will channel dynamic support and the largest possible volume of international aid to the people fighting in Angola, Guinea-Bissau, Mozambique, Zimbabwe, South Africa and Namibia."[47]

Excluded from the Khartoum gathering, the Chinese excoriated it as one dominated by the Soviet "revisionist renegade clique" and the Hsinhua News Agency (in London) carried denunciations of the meeting by rival movements that enjoy Chinese favor: the *Comité Revolucion-*

ário de Moçambique (COREMO); *União Nacional para a Independência Total de Angola* (UNITA); Zimbabwe African National Union (ZANU) and Pan-Africanist Congress (PAC, South Africa).[48] Also associated with this group of Chinese-endorsed movements is the South West Africa National Union (SWANU), dismissed by *Pravda* as "virtually paid agents of Peking. . . ."[49]

In the past, Chinese support—probably financially and materially less significant than that of the Soviets—has gone to a broad array of exiles, including some who were also enjoying Soviet assistance.[50] The leaders of those groups now most favored by Peking, however, whether by default (no Soviet ties) or affinity, often appear to be more uniracial (or nonwhite), less well educated (except for very top leadership), and products of African peasant or labor (as distinct from intellectual) protest.

Increasingly, then, liberation movements have been called upon to choose either Moscow or Peking. As Sino-Soviet competition deepened, it perpetuated cleavages among exiles, who denounced each other and each others' benefactors as "revisionists" or "adventurists" and who found themselves drawn into international disputes which were unrelated to their own struggles. The ANC publicly approved, whereas the PAC condemned, the Soviet occupation of Czechoslovakia in 1968.[51] According to Chinese-oriented analysis, "Moscow inclined movements" even came to consider Afro-American militants visiting Africa as "a potential threat to continuous collaboration [by these movements] with their white friends in the Soviet Union and elsewhere in Eastern Europe."[52] Attempts to escape from making such a choice sometimes failed and led only to self-deflating behavior and embarrassment, as when an exile group's representatives in Peking were prevailed upon to denounce a Soviet-sponsored meeting that same group was scheduled to attend.[53]

Probably, neither Soviet nor Chinese aid in weapons or finance was of such magnitude as to permit selected recipients to realize their full revolutionary potential.[54] And, with the exception of some Yugoslav aid, all Communist help was given directly, thus assuring the donor of direct political influence. If the Soviet Union or China—or the United States, for that matter—was interested in strengthening independent nationalist movements or Africa's collective capacity for southern liberation to the exclusion of building selective client relationships, it could channel assistance through and thereby strengthen the available multilateral, Pan-African machinery of the Organization of African Unity (OAU). Such an extra-African input might be made directly to the OAU or to a parallel United Nations or special ad hoc international fund functioning in cooperation with the OAU. If made to the OAU, it might be made contingent upon OAU reforms in order to assure greater efficiency, consistency, and equity, including regularized procedures for the determination of revolutionary merit and for the distribution of assistance to liberation movements.

Should feuding between Moscow and Peking intensify competition for influence among Southern African exiles, one of two possibilities is likely. Either one of the two leagues of exile movements, plausibly the one relatively heavily aided by the Soviet Union, would resolve the issue by eclipsing the other, or all movements would risk a serious deflection of their energy into self-defeating, internecine conflict such as has long plagued the Angolans.[55] For Southern Africa's exiles, fate seems to have concocted a bitter irony: those who aid them also use and divide them and thus largely fail, in the final count, to help them overcome the distractions and dissensions of exile.

OUTSIDE COMMUNITY: THE AFRO-ASIAN NATIONS

By and large, the Third World has shared a common colonial or racial experience in its relations with the European world. Afro-Asians in general accept the necessity, and hence the legitimacy, of revolution in Southern Africa. Oratorical enthusiasm, however, has exceeded supportive action and has further obscured external reality for the exile.

As a political-psychological force, Afro-Asian "solidarity" reached its apogee at the time of the Bandung Conference of 1955 and declined thereafter.[56] The Pan-African context proved to be a more significant legitimizing and supporting force. Collective African backing for revolutionary action came first through the medium of the Pan-African Freedom Movement for East, Central and Southern Africa (1958–1963) and its Coordinating Freedom Council. Though the latter dispensed only about $3,000 a year to a given exile movement, it did establish the principle of collective responsibility for the political liberation of Southern Africa.[57]

The responsibility was projected from the regional to the continental plane with the creation of the OAU in May 1963. An OAU Liberation Committee then assumed the function of translating a general Pan-African consensus about the need for revolution into an endorsement of, and aid to, particular Southern African movements.[58]

The Liberation Committee became an important arbiter within revolutionary exile politics.[59] In mid-1963 it recognized the Angolan Government in Exile (GRAE), founded in 1962 by Holden Roberto's *Frente Nacional de Libertação de Angola*, as directing the "only real fighting front in Angola" and recommended that all African or foreign aid to the Angolans be channeled through the government of the Congo (Kinshasa) and earmarked for the FNLA exclusively.[60] A year later, however, the OAU reversed itself, granted aid to both the MPLA and the GRAE, and, finally, in 1969, the OAU Liberation Committee recommended that the OAU Council of Ministers not only withdraw its recognition of, but suspend all further assistance to, the GRAE/FNLA.[61] As for the third Angolan movement, UNITA, the OAU never did extend recognition and this cost UNITA prestige, publicity, and funds, even if it left UNITA intact with a highly self-reliant strategy.[62] UNITA'S president, Jonas Savimbi, eventually denounced the OAU as unfair and biased in favor of the MPLA which, he charged, was using OAU weapons "to massacre" unarmed civilians (presumably UNITA supporters).[63]

Actually, from the beginning the OAU Liberation Committee failed both to attain the professional competence and to muster the funds expected of it.[64] After over half a decade of OAU mismanagement and unrealistic Pan-African expectations, in the words of a seasoned journalist, African guerrilla movements concluded that bilateral aid from the Soviets, Chinese, and others was "vastly more important" than aid from the OAU.[65] An organization such as FRELIMO, for example, received only about 20 percent of its external support from the OAU. On the other hand, OAU backing came to coincide with that extended by the Soviet Union (except for some OAU help to the FNLA, PAC, and ZANU), so that the "external factor" came to weigh heavily in favor of the Khartoum Conference alliance of six.

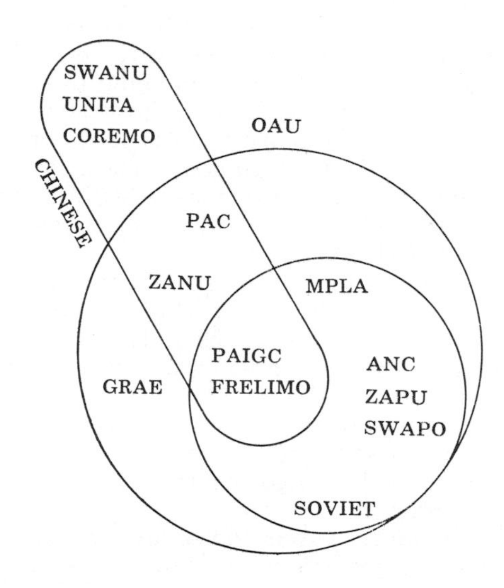

When confronted with the OAU as a dispenser of Pan-African legitimacy, African exile movements were more self-assertive than when dealing with non-African benefactors. They sometimes responded like labor to management. In 1964, for instance, a group of liberation movements in Dar es Salaam (headquarters of the OAU Liberation Committee) established an ephemeral Union of Non-Independent African States (UNIAS) to engage in collective bargaining with the OAU and to bolster their self-image.[66]

More important, certain liberation movements leagued together and pooled their prestige and bargaining power on the basis of one movement per country. Thus the *Conferência das Organizações Nacionalistas das Colónias Portuguesas* (CONCP), allying the MPLA, FRELIMO, PAIGC, and a small *Comité de Libertação de São Tomé e Príncipe* (CLSTP) achieved sufficient interterritorial cooperation to enable it to exert greater independent collective weight than the sum of its constituent parts. The prestige and intercession of CONCP partners, for example, probably helped the MPLA to win OAU support.[67] The CONCP parties then linked up with the ANC and ZAPU (namely, the Khartoum alliance) and, under a joint military command, the ANC and ZAPU embarked upon guerrilla operations in Rhodesia.[68] Occasionally, albeit in a less organized fashion, an anti-CONCP counterleague manifested itself, sometimes focused about the GRAE and the Congo (Kinshasa),[69] and at other times around Chinese efforts to counter Soviet influence.[70]

Asylum and aid provided by a single contiguous African state can be more important to a liberation movement than the aggregate of all the other external assistance it may receive. A friendly neighbor that both can and will furnish financial and logistical support can make an enormous difference in a movement's potential for revolutionary action. Nearby asylum, of course, may be less disorienting than asylum in Europe and the United States thousands of miles away. And recognition, military sanctuary, and arms transit rights granted by a contiguous state—for example, the Congo (Kinshasa) to the GRAE of Angola—may be of inestimable value to any given movement's guerrilla efforts.[71]

By refusing to recognize such a group, a contiguous state may prevent it from having access to home frontiers even when the OAU has given its approval to the group concerned.[72] An example of this has been the refusal of the Mobutu government of the Congo (Kinshasa) to grant transit and base rights to the MPLA in addition to the GRAE. Similarly, COREMO (unrecognized by the OAU) has been barred from access to northern Mozambique via Tanzania, the latter having sanctioned only FRELIMO activity on its soil. More systematically and completely than the British before them, the conservative, postindependence governments of Botswana, Lesotho, and Swaziland, whose countries remain economically and geographically dependent upon South Africa, prohibit liberation movement activity within their borders. They thereby deny South African exiles any contiguous base of operations.

Nevertheless, the importance of remaining on good terms with a government providing sanctuary can be overestimated. When the top leadership of UNITA was expelled from Zambia in 1967,[73] it readjusted its strategy, moved inside Angola, and concentrated henceforth on efforts to build and rely almost exclusively upon a political underground and militia within its own country.[74] Excessive reliance upon a sanctuary, it seemed, could entangle and confound exile politics with those of the host state (for example, GRAE in the Congo [Kinshasa]) and thus absorb energy and deflect action that might otherwise be focused on the real revolutionary target.[75] It should also be noted in passing that some recent revolutions—for example, those in China and Cuba—have been successful in the absence of an available contiguous sanctuary.

In sum, political exiles might find assistance or escape abroad, but they could find revolutionary fulfillment (an end to exile) only at home. Even in its most disinterested or generous form, external assistance remained ancillary.

When external involvements become a diversion from, or substitute for, primarily "internal" concerns, they simply increase the likelihood of enduring exile. What is not often taken into consideration is that these external relationships interact with and aggravate certain perceptual and behavioral problems normally associated with the human condition of exile. The result can be a serious reduction in political effectiveness and hence in prospects for revolutionary fulfillment.

The Struggle Outside: The Perceptual and Behavioral Problems of Exile Politics

For the exile who came from a crime-ridden South African township where he was already a propertyless, voteless "exile" subject to being "endorsed out" to a rural reserve or to arrest at the government's whim, exile abroad meant new trauma added to a previous state of distress and insecurity.[76] Thus, for South Africans whose socialization had taken place in a milieu of violence, anxiety, and indignity, exile posed a kind of double jeopardy and threatened to prove doubly debilitating.[77] Angolans and Mozambicans who had previously belonged to clandestine, secretive, and anxiety-plagued underground groups at home,[78] as well as Rhodesian Africans who had been politically frustrated by the "intractable whites" of Salisbury and London[79] were also very vulnerable to the new strains of exile.

There is a surprising lack of adequate comparative literature on exile politics as such.[80] Studies and observations of refugee behavior made for and by the Office of the United Nations High Commissioner for Refugees (UNHCR), however, may offer some insight into the psychological pitfalls and trials that confront exile political leaders.[81]

Such studies suggest that these leaders and their followers, especially when crowded together in impersonal refugee centres (Mbeya, Tanzania), communal dwellings (the "White House" of Francistown, Botswana), or military camps (Kinkuzu, the Congo [Kinshasa]), must have (or develop) a very high frustration tolerance. As persons of presumably highly goal-integrated behavior (*e.g.*, political) —as distinct from persons fleeing floods or pogroms—however, their response to the intrapyschic tension of being goal-frustrated (blocked from power and exiled) may be, at least initially, an increased effort at goal attainment.[82] At the outset, then, exile may not render behavior politically less functional, although the manner in which a refugee is received in a country of first asylum—with sympathy, apathy, or hostility—may also strongly condition the nature of both his initial and enduring response to exile.

Hostile reception in an expectedly friendly neighboring state can be especially devastating to morale. A refugee is not likely to be prepared for the possibility that he may be viewed as a potentially disruptive person who may make difficult, even "impossible" demands of his hosts by seeking their material assistance or involvment in his revanchist goals. Refugees belonging to political movements not recognized by host states may experience acute insecurity, isolation, or pressure to change political allegiance. Such may be the lot, for example, of militants of the MPLA arriving in the Congo (Kinshasa), which recognizes only the rival GRAE/FNLA.

The traumatic experience of South or South West Africans arriving at Francistown, Botswana, where they found themselves surrounded by hostile whites and fated to idle waiting and an uncertain future was inevitably more debilitating than was the transition for Angolan Bakongo moving into a sanctuary among their ethnic kin, the Congolese Bakongo, on the safe side of the Congo border.[83]

In due course, four types of dysfunctional behavior, as identified in clinical research on frustration by psychologist Norman R. F. Maier and incorporated in UNHCR studies by Dr. F. A. S. Jensen and others, could be anticipated:

personal aggression, regression, apathy, and compulsive repetition.[84]

1. *Aggression.* Whether they take the form of overt physical violence or antisocial action such as stealing (negative identity),[85] aggressive outbursts provide tension release. They may also disrupt organization, ruin discipline, and contribute to the factionalism, mutinies, and alcoholic and sexual indiscretions that endemically afflict exile movements. Illustrative of how aggressive behavior can destroy discipline is a (possibly embellished) description of life in a military training camp for South Africans in Tanzania. According to this account by a defector, trainees were flogged by "hose-pipe," imprisoned and shot on suspicion of disloyalty, "insensated" by weekend drinking of local brew, afflicted by venereal disease from a nearby "village of fifty pleasure women," and subject to nervous breakdowns.[86]

Another, less contentious illustration of the damage wrought to discipline by uncontrolled, aggressive outbursts is the following front-page story from a Zambian newspaper: "Freedom fighters did battle yesterday—against themselves. Fighting broke out in the offices of the Zimbabwe African National Union in Lusaka's refugee centre between ZANU officials. The police were called to break it up."[87]

2. *Regression.* Retreat from harsh reality and "adaptational levels of self-reliance"[88] may lead the exile back to less mature states of passive dependency or to escapist repudiation of personal responsibility—that is, the tendency to blame one's fate entirely on others, the *Blame Me on History* syndrome.[89] Thus the exile may indulge in self-pity and place unreasonable demands on third parties by assuming that they *could* easily change his situation if they *really* so wished or cared. Such an attitude is especially logical for those of the many Southern Africans who, in the words of a United Nations specialist on the subject, "left because they imagined, rightly or wrongly, that the rest of independent Africa was anxiously waiting to offer them whatever assistance they required."[90]

An exile may also evidence a reduced capacity for making responsible decisions or for handling money. He may seek escape in the false security of a fantasy world replete with expectations of deliverance by imminent and massive internal upheavals or external interventions.[91] The failure of such expectations to materialize may then be followed by a compulsive search for scapegoats (spies, traitors, foreign agents) to account for misfortune.[92] Moreover, anyone who challenges (and thus kicks at the crutch of) such comforting but distorted perception is liable to be denounced with tension-releasing violence. Criticism becomes intolerable.[93] In 1967 when Stokely Carmichael offered unsolicited, critical counsel to African liberation movements, at Dar es Salaam, he was promptly accused of "meaningless and arrogant demagoguery" for, among other things, "his disbelief of enemy casualties given by liberation movements" and his "lack of faith in the Organization [of] African Unity."[94]

For some exiles, then, there is a tendency toward emotional overreaction or regressive behavior and this can lead to a loss of that quality of personal "responsibleness" through which psychiatrist Viktor Frankl found it possible to overcome hopelessness or despair and to discover meaning even in the relatively more extreme and victimizing circumstances of a Nazi death camp.[95]

For liberation movements, behavioral patterns of overdependency may also mean lost opportunity. Although several of these movements control the requisite territory as well as access to that territory through a friendly member state of the Universal Postal Union and although these movements have surely been aware for some time of the rewards involved, none has established an independent postal system such as the one that earned valuable revenue and publicity for Biafra.[96]

3. *Apathy.* Barring a change of fortune or corrective therapy, a protracted period of frustration may lead to a terminal or "burned out" stage of numbed resignation or depression. In terms of political exiles this may result in desultory leadership, careless security, and imprudence. For instance, dispirited Southern African politicians and guerrilla trainees, feeling alone and forgotten, may (and do) find solace and retrieved identity by writing long, despondent, and, for the police who intercept them, informative letters back home. Or, as in the case of a defector from the ANC, they may write demoralized and damaging letters to an "anti-Communist" publication which will obligingly air their despair.[97] Others have found solace and sympathetic ears at hotel bars and diplomatic cocktail parties in Lusaka, Kinshasa, Dar es Salaam—and London.

4. *Compulsive repetition.* One other frequently observed dysfunctional characteristic of refugee behavior is that of "apparently insensate repetition of unproductive activity or persistence in a series of goal-frustrating attitudes."[98] This should be distinguished from a single-minded pursuit of an absolute goal/value (Max Weber's *Wertrationalität*), a pursuit that may appear subjectively to an external observer as irrational or fanatic yet which may be functional in terms of that goal. Compulsive repetition as used here refers to the persistent use of demonstrably self-defeating, short-range tactics. It refers to an inability to see, over time, that one has been locked into repetitious or fixated behavior that is "non-productive

in the goal oriented sense of the term,'' even in the presence of more promising avenues of conduct.[99] Repeatedly insulting those whom one really wishes (however grudgingly) to convert to one's own cause (or at least to neutralize) and compulsively and continuously running from one place or political movement to another (only to find that the same old problems reappear) may, of course, give a distressed person ''something to do.'' Habitually making (easily monitored) inter- or transcontinental telephone calls and issuing extravagant press statements may also serve to relieve tension temporarily. One *feels* as though he is responding to a situation. In terms of concrete political goals, however, this sense of progress is illusory and often costly.

If an exiled political leader is going to organize a serious challenge to something as formidable as white rule in Southern Africa, he and his followers cannot afford to allow exile psychology—even though it represents a normal response to an abnormal condition—to cloud perception, distort purpose, or misdirect action. To the extent that such exiles are able to perceive or permit themselves an awareness of tendencies toward such behavior, they may, of course, enhance their capacity to overcome them. The threatening self-doubts and insecurities of exile, however, tend to foster a mental block or resistance to the notion that it is normal for a person in acute distress to display some symptoms of abnormal behavior.[100]

A student of Latin American politics has observed that the common fate of most exiles is an ''oblivion'' that is hastened ''by ugly factional squabbles, increasingly irrelevant programs based on distorted information, and wishful thinking, and dissolving organizations as the exiles eventually become resigned to defeat and begin to make new homes abroad.''[101] This suggests that systematic efforts by political leaders to confront and understand, rather than to deny the existence of, the particular problems of exile might improve their capacity to build and maintain effective movements. It also suggests that they should seek to develop politically harmless mechanisms of tension release—that is, procedures and forums for ventilating frustrations within the confines of a movement and highly structured training and work programs that at least appear ''politically goal oriented.'' Beyond this, the leaders of such movements might be well advised to invest personnel and material resources in methodical analyses of refugee-exile behavior as it relates to their own specific goals and circumstances.

The need to overcome the psychological impediments of exile is seldom mentioned by either advocates of revolution or analysts of revolutionary prospects in Southern Africa. Nevertheless, this need is even more apparent when one reconsiders the environmental problems discussed earlier and how the external factors with which exiles must contend may further frustrate, mislead, or dominate their movements.

The Struggle Inside: Efficacy or Irrelevance?

Confronting and overcoming both the perceptual and behavioral problems of exile and the related dangers involved in external exile relationships constitute prerequisites to, but no guarantee of, success in efforts by African liberation movements to return via guerrilla and/or underground action to the political life of their own countries. To achieve this primordial goal, such movements need to attain levels of strategy, cohesion, and performance that might well defy most political movements anywhere—exile or not.

To begin with, they need to cope with a kind of inner defeatism induced by the overwhelming odds against them. Political reality, not just exile psychology, has presented them with a severe problem of self-justification in the form of a troubling half-suppressed doubt. After all, is it not possible that they constitute threats to established regimes just credible, audible, and visible enough to keep the latter alert so that they do not relax their oppression? Does the very existence of these movements not merely worsen the lot of those whom they would liberate? Certainly, Lisbon, Pretoria, and Salisbury have responded to them with radically increased counterinsurgency activity and intensified military, economic, and technical tripartite cooperation.[102]

It does not require—though this might help—a Tillichian ''leap of faith'' to assert otherwise. The fact that guerrilla fighting has gradually spread and persisted *inside* all three Portuguese territories, and that repeated incursions have been made into Rhodesia, and the Caprivi Zipfel gives some basis for a negative reply.[103] Even *The Star* (Johannesburg), which is disinclined to look favorably upon revolution, published an appraisal of Southern African guerrilla movements in 1968 which suggested that ''astute propaganda coupled with a few successes against the security forces'' might enable these movements to achieve popular support and thus become a real force. ''In the long run,'' *The Star* concluded, their ''potentially decisive asset'' is ''one which lies in the minds of the Whites themselves. If the present tendency to alienate the loyalties of local Africans continues, time can operate only in favour of the guer[r]illas.''[105]

Though it is difficult to assess the effectiveness of guerrilla action, let alone the potential of what is going on underground,[105] it is possible to suggest some of the factors that bear on the success or failure of exile efforts to mount revolutions in Southern Africa.[106] Emphasis is placed here upon those factors that might be expected to be the most difficult for exiles fully to perceive or master precisely because of the conditions and limitations of exile status as already discussed. Such factors may be broadly grouped under three headings: military, political, and social service functions.

1. *Military functions*. The manner in which a revolutionary armed force selects its members will have a strong bearing on its efficacy; this is often underestimated by those exiles who are prone to wishful thinking. Not everyone is born or reared to be a potential guerrilla. It is patent, for example that college graduates or "intellectuals" who weigh, argue, or agonize over decisions based on the relative merits of alternative courses of action must make very poor guerrillas.[107] Régis Debray has made this point both in his writing and in his own disastrous interlude as an intellectual companion of Cuban-Bolivian insurgents.[108]

In 1965 Communist insurgents in Venezuela reportedly recognized the folly of recruiting just any able-bodied man for guerrilla action: the kind of policy that has been followed by most, if not all, Southern African liberation movements.[109] According to police reports, "Venezuelan insurgents had been recruiting youths, mostly high school and university students, for their guerrilla forces. Many seemed to be attracted by the olive green uniforms, jaunty berets, sub-machine guns, and admiration of girl friends for daring young men." Motivated by revolutionary romanticism, perhaps one in four of the recruits was able to take the hard life in the mountain forests. Many, "hungry, bearded, and bedraggled from days and nights in rain and mud," gave themselves up. Others broke down after a few days and had to be sent home. These factors led local insurgent leaders to send fresh recruits to psychiatrists in hopes of weeding out those "unlikely to endure the hardships and dangers of guerrilla life."[110]

If rigorous screening was necessary for movements initiating operations inside a country, it was surely as necessary for those attempting to create the nucleus of a guerrilla force by recruiting among dislocated exiles abroad. Those volunteers (notably "intellectuals") found wanting, however, could be used in support functions and/or be held in reserve for action later on if the revolution developed to a more advanced stage which called for mass action.

A guerrilla force needs expert and intensive training. To live patiently hidden in forests or caves, enduring long periods of silence and inactivity broken by sudden, decisive action requires special learned attributes, particularly discipline. Such training, however, will be fully

effective only among those who have a high frustration tolerance and steeled purposefulness that may be especially rare among exiles and refugees. It was logical, for example, that a South African exile who could not tolerate rural isolation, a mere "two packets of a very unpalatable blend" of cigarettes per week, or "dry, hard, tasteless biscuits" would reject and flee from "sadists" who attempted to train him to withstand and function under harsh environmental pressures.[111] It is sometimes argued that in order to produce a sufficiently hardened core of skilled fighters, instruction and testing should be so severe as to bring trainees to the brink of assaulting their trainers.[112]

The earlier assumption of exiles that one needed only to give a Johannesburg, Salisbury, or Luanda schoolboy a rifle and some rudimentary drills and lectures and he would automatically become a guerrilla was indeed a costly delusion. More recently, Cuban, Chinese, North Korean, and other training coupled with the comparative study of the techniques of guerrilla warfare—such as Castro's use of caves in the Sierra Maestra and the Viet Cong's use of tunnels on the outskirts of Saigon—have done much to correct this easy-going approach to unconventional warfare. Because it has not, itself, had in-depth military training or experience, however, the top leadership of Southern Africa's liberation movements probably remains excessively dependent upon the counsel of outsiders who are necessarily inadequately conversant with some of the local factors that must shape a winning strategy.

In addition to good selection and training, a guerrilla force needs arms and ammunition, and it must acquire skill in capturing these from the enemy so as not to be entirely dependent upon an uninterrupted inflow of arms from outside. This force must also be supported by good intelligence work. Those directing guerrilla operations need to acquire a sound knowledge of social, economic, cultural, and topographical data concerning combat areas. They must be able to make realistic appraisals of the size, armament, morale, location, and routine of enemy forces. To be effective in such intelligence work, they need to make a conscious effort to free themselves from the emotional bias and wishful thinking that haunts exile politics.

Similarly, effective psychological warfare, which Southern African liberation movements have only rarely used, requires a degree of subtlety, manipulative skill, and sensitivity to enemy attitudes that is incompatible with aggressive-repressive exile behavior. Bombastic radio broadcasts from exile may provide for a release of tension, but they also help to unify the enemy.

Exiles can make purposeful use of broadcasts, underground papers, and leaflets in order to sow dissent and lower morale among the enemy only if they have overcome tendencies toward low frustration tolerance. It is the restrained rather than the boastfully exaggerated "war communiqué" that is most likely to prove worrisome and unsettling to the enemy. A claim that nearly one-third (over 1.5 million) of the Angolan population is "now living in liberated areas" (which suggests that Portuguese forces might soon be inundated) is, for example, at such variance with all reportorial evidence as to invite incredulity.[113]

2. *Political functions.* The "return" capability of exiled liberation movements will also depend upon their capacity for resolute, disciplined action to improve levels of political and politico-military performance. Self-reliant movements that have developed well-ordered structures and procedures and have defined, clarified, and differentiated leadership roles and responsibilities have a comparative advantage. In the words of Eqbal Ahmad, the guerrilla must concentrate on "out-administering" and isolating his enemy. He must be concerned with administrative structures and with meeting his obligations to the local populace. Otherwise, his action degenerates into "banditry."[114]

Indeed, the relative success of the PAIGC of Guinea (Bissau) is at least partly attributable to an emphasis upon political education and mobilization of the local peasantry.[115] Top PAIGC leadership, including its celebrated secretary-general, Amilcar Cabral,[116] spends considerable time within nationalist-held areas, explaining, orienting, directing, and identifying as participants and not as exiles.[117] By organizing schools and agricultural cooperatives, as well as local militia, the PAIGC structured an internal revolutionary force and popular following that has gradually eroded and isolated Portuguese authority (which is now limited mainly to coastal towns and islands). Movements such as FRELIMO and the MPLA, which have not yet had comparable success, and the ANC which has had little visible success, in transferring the locus of their activity back into their own countries, have nevertheless similarly emphasized organizational structure. It appears therefore, that they may be less apt than others to collapse or to lapse into inactivity in case their top leadership is incapacitated or absent. For the MPLA to operate simultaneously in widely separated geographic areas of Angola (Cabinda, Nambuangongo-Dembos, Moxico, and Cuando-Cubango) in spite of being barred from a logistical base in the Congo (Kinshasa) of itself constitutes a considerable organizational achievement.[118]

If a "communications gap" is not to isolate exiles from what is being thought and done by their countrymen at home and vice versa,[119] one of the principal functions of exile political structure must be to develop and maintain underground links with supporters inside the home country. This means not only that they must acquire the technical means to transmit information from outside—coded radio messages or courier systems—but also that they must be psychologically prepared to receive, evaluate, and utilize information, however depressing, concerning changing conditions, including shifting popular grievances.

Exile (and later internal guerrilla) organizational strength may depend to some extent upon ethnic and class representation; thus the leadership must recognize and face up to communal differences and conflicts. Such differences within the "revolutionary constituency" are grounded in history, ethnicity, culture, class structure, and geography, and they constitute very real obstacles to united action. Exile or internal leadership, for example, may be reluctant to take account of rivalry or tension between the Shona and Ndebele in Rhodesia, Western Cape and Johannesburg Africans in South Africa, or *assimilados* and rural peasants in the Portuguese territories. These cleavages still remain and are more apt to disrupt and fragment insurgent groups when they are defensively and dogmatically denied than when they are acknowledged and accommodated. In 1970 just such unattended ethnic differences erupted and tore Rhodesia's ZAPU asunder.[120]

The quality, popularity, and charisma of exile leadership constitute yet another set of important variables. This leadership must develop a reputation for courage and integrity, which is to suggest that it must share the risks of the *maquis*. It must also display a capacity to rise above the sterile, fratricidal quarrels of exile. The experience of recent years suggests that many of those leaders exiled in urban centers abroad lack adequate perception of the need to identify with the aspirations of peasants at home and of the need to avoid the alienating (regressive) behavior associated with intellectual posturing, big cars, luxury hotels, and expensive women.[121] It also points to another prevalent weakness, nepotism—scholarships, sinecures, and internal security posts for kin and friend.

Political effectiveness also demands that exile leaders come to realize that the indignities and anxieties of exile naturally engender wars of epithets and charges of embezzlement, treason, collusion with "agents of imperialism," "revisionism," or "adventurism." Indeed, these indignities and anxieties may be largely responsible for a salient pattern of desertions, suspensions, exclusions, and even executions.[122] They may also militate against sound (as contrasted with tyrannical) security systems and practices which are sorely needed to cut down on the damage done by assassins and informers. Impoverished and despairing exiles or guerrillas have been easy prey for security police, Portugal's PIDE, and both Rhodesia and South Africa's Special Branch.[123]

3. *Social service functions*. Less obviously or immediately than military and political functions, social services may help exiles increase their insurgency capabilities. Considered at the psychological level, the therapeutic value of releasing and channeling exile energy into such creative activity is a very positive factor. In addition, of course, the establishment of a health service may favorably influence the loyalty of émigré and refugee communities along border areas through which guerrillas move:[124] and the insurgents may depend to some extent upon people in these areas for funds (taxation), food (requisition), or recruits (draft). Similarly, educational services for refugees help to build political support, prepare future leadership for the country whose liberation is being sought, and promote personal security and creativity within the exile community.[125]

Within internal guerrilla military zones it is essential for morale that there be both medics and medicine. Within nationalist-held areas it is important to codify law and to create agricultural cooperatives and public services (schools and health clinics). Movements such as FRELIMO (which operates in northern Mozambique) are thereby able to contribute to the *élan* of their insurgents and, as a protogovernment, to demonstrate a responsiveness to popular needs. If "liberators" have no time for such concerns during the armed struggle there is little assurance that they will have later when they have inherited the problems and perquisites of office. The issue is whether or not an insurgent movement increasingly surmounts exile *and* presents itself as a credible alternative to the status quo. Unless it convinces its own people and perhaps some external communities that it does, it will not be able to mobilize durable, winning support.

Conclusion

Political exiles face many problems. In the case of Southern Africans, widespread external sympathy for their aims has in some measure aggravated these problems. International charity and United Nations pronouncements about the moral imperative of liberation have, in fact, probably rendered some of them—especially those who had earlier been victims of South African apartheid—more dependent, more self-indulgent, and less effectual. Furthermore, the gap between rhetoric and action in Western policy, in particular, has contributed to unrealistic expectations of international action followed by crippling disillusionment. Even the non-Western assistance that has been offered has often been divisive or quantitatively inadequate.

A political exile can seek escape from such a predicament by "opting out"—that is, by either integrating into or creating a separate fantasy realm within a foreign country. Or, of course, he may defect and return home to collaborate with his former adversaries, as in the dramatic case of FRELIMO's ranking Makonde (key northern border community) elder, Lázarus Kavandame.[126] Alternatively, he can pursue revolutionary goals by "opting back"—that is, by attempting to return from exile by means of a *maquis* or underground to his own country. If the case of South Africa illustrates how international sympathy and assistance may not always improve his prospects for successfully "opting back," the southern Sudan, by way of contrast, suggests that the absence of such support may sometimes improve those prospects. The southern Sudanese rebellion against Arabization has not been recognized as legitimate at any level of the external community (the United Nations, Western, Communist, or Afro-Asian powers). Nevertheless, the *Anyanya* (southern Sudanese guerrillas) have sustained a surprisingly effective insurrection against great odds with only a thin layer of educated leadership and with a minimum of outside support.[127] They have created their own revolutionary legitimacy, achieved more unity than most African exile-guerrilla movements, and fought on, if perhaps in vain, against well-equipped, well-trained, and numerically superior forces. They have done this knowing that, with the possible exception of Israel,[128] they can rely on help from no one but themselves.

Certainly, an overreliance on external aid has undercut the effectiveness of Southern African liberation movements. As the South African writer Lewis Nkosi has noted, liberation movements have not been focusing adequately on "the outstanding issues" facing them: how to act so as to overcome apathy, develop political consciousness, and mobilize a national struggle within their home constituencies.[129] To what extent might this failure be remedied through a better understanding of, or more adequate response to, the vulnerable condition of exile? This is a question that political exiles struggling to become effective revolutionaries need to ask themselves.

3

Southern Africa: Towards a New Commonwealth?

ESCHEL M. RHOODIE

What may turn out to be the most significant political and economic development in sub-Saharan Africa since European colonial disengagement is presently occurring in Southern Africa. Little is known in the United States about this development since Southern Africa is an area which has hitherto mostly been studied piecemeal and not in a regional context. When it is brought together, Southern Africa can be much larger than the sum of its parts.

Geographically, it is no small region of Africa. Angola, South West Africa, South Africa, Botswana, Lesotho, Swaziland, Rhodesia, Malawi, and Mozambique comprise an area of just over 2 million square miles, as contrasted with the United States' 3½ million square miles, and it is nearly as richly endowed. Practically every known mineral is to be found within its confines, particularly gold, diamonds, uranium, vast reserves of coal and iron ore (on which a modern industrial economy must be based), as well as copper, platinum, chrome, and asbestos in enormous quantities. Among them the nine countries produce more than 50 percent of the mineral output of Africa.[1] In population, the nine already have something over 45 million people (1970) but by the turn of the century they will have close to 100 million.[2]

Southern Africa is the only region in Africa which has a permanent white population, a nation in its own right, with roots in Africa going back to the seventeenth century.[3] It contains the only industrially developed country in Africa; in fact, the only real industrial complex south of Milan is in the triangle of Johannesburg, Pretoria, and Vereeniging.[4] The area also has the last remaining provinces in Africa of a Western European power (Portugal) and the only area where newly independent black African states rub shoulders with a white-controlled country.

Sociopolitically, all of this represents an explosive combination if what happened elsewhere in Africa between black and Arab, between black and white, and between Indian and black is any indication. In debates at the General Assembly of the United Nations, the region is, therefore, frequently identified as a threat to world peace. But when the facts and fallacies are sorted out, little remains of any physical threat; the economic prosperity is impressive, while the political outlook compared to black Africa is becoming increasingly good.[5] During the past five years important developments, which would normally have served to highlight this state of affairs, have been obscured by the publicity of lurid events in Ghana, the Sudan, Nigeria, Tanzania, the Congo (Kinshasa), and the United Arab Republic.

Southern Africa, therefore, deserves a fresh appraisal. It has, of course, always been worthy of appraisal because of the harmonious coexistence between the black and white states of this region, because of their joint efforts to establish a greater Southern Africa with close political and economic cooperation, and because of the vision of a common market now supported by responsible people in each of the nine states. Regrettably, it has always been the spectacular in Africa or the ugly isolated incident which has attracted American attention. There was little interest in the slow unfolding of a carefully nurtured policy when elsewhere in Africa *coups* followed upon violent uprisings with incredible speed. Even in scholarly works it has mostly been West, North, and East Africa which attracted the attention.[6]

Cabora Bassa is a name which is still unknown to the vast majority of Americans, and the decision of the Portuguese and South African governments in September 1969 to proceed with the Cabora Bassa hydroelectric project on the Zambezi River in Mozambique received almost no publicity in the press of the United States. Yet it represents a development in Southern Africa with important political implications. Cabora Bassa illustrates, as does no other individual project, the rapid growth of political and economic regionalism in Southern Africa, a movement toward closer economic cooperation perhaps of no less significance for Africa than the European Common Market is for Western Europe. It is tangible evidence of international cooperation between black and white states in a region of Africa which has the human and socioeconomic potential to become comparable to the European Common Market.

In brief, the Cabora Bassa project involves the construction of a huge dam on the lower Zambezi River with a megawatt power output twice that of the much-vaunted Aswan Dam on the Nile. Unlike the Aswan Dam, which was built by the Soviets, the Cabora Bassa project will be built by a consortium of companies from three West European states headed by a South African concern.[7] The cost of $350 million will be borne by Portugal and South Africa.[8] Cabora Bassa will eventually irrigate an area of Mozambique large enough to support a million newcomers, but its benefits will also be shared by other states. For Malawi it means not only a spurt in industrialization but also the wherewithal to develop the vast deposits of aluminium ore around Mount Mlanje. It will aid industrialization in Rhodesia and, through the purchase of material and equipment for the dam, boost its payments position. South Africa will have more electricity available for its rapid economic growth (now second only to Japan) but eventually the power from Cabora Bassa will flow into a grid linking all the countries of the South. For Zambia, politically the odd one out in Southern Africa, it means cheaper power and the first real outlet to the sea, since the Zambezi River will then be open to shipping—albeit for smaller vessels—all the way from the Indian Ocean to the dam. As the *Rand Daily Mail* stated editorially, "The signing of the Cabora Bassa contract . . . is yet another pointer to Africa's bright prospects when people of enterprise, faith and goodwill come together to build for the future."[9]

Ten years ago a project such as Cobora Bassa was simply not practical politics. The year 1960 was the so-called "Africa Year" when more than a dozen African states became independent and when black nationalism was still considered the irresistible factor in African political development for the next decade.[10] At that stage any talk of regional cooperation between the black and white states of Southern Africa to the extent of forming a common market would have been ridiculed. The extent of cooperation in economic and political spheres between black and white states may then have been foreseen, but it was certainly not anticipated that it would develop so rapidly and so favorably as it did during the past five years. Such has been the pace of development in Southern Africa that it has become a talking point in international circles, and such is the vision of the seventies that trade missions, tourists, and investors from New Zealand to Canada and from Argentina to Japan are descending on South Africa at an embarrassing rate.[11]

The possibility of a common market for Southern Africa which would link the nine black and white states depends on two important factors. These two are the Republic of South Africa's policy of establishing separate states for its various Bantu (black African)[12] nations (called "separate development" in South Africa and apartheid in the United States) and the development of sound political and economic relations with the neighboring and nearby black states (Lesotho, Botswana,

Swaziland, and Malawi) which became independent during 1964–1968. As far as the first factor is concerned, the South African government and most of the white electorate as well as the majority of those Bantu who have been able to express an opinion on the matter by way of the ballot box[13] consider South Africa to be inhabited by different black, Bantu-speaking nations and by a white nation and feel that they should seek their political destiny or the exercise of their nationalism, whether black or white, separate from each other. From the geopolitical and constitutional points of view, the government aims at the orderly and ethnocentric development of the Bantu into nationally autonomous communities, each settled geopolitically in its own territory[14] and associating with the white states on a basis of peaceful coexistence, preferably according to the model of the Commonwealth of Nations or the West European community of states.[15] In terms of this policy, at least two other Bantu territories may receive independence in the next decade (the Transkei in South Africa and Ovamboland in South West Africa), followed by other Bantu nations. Thus the entire map of South Africa may have to be redrawn to indicate the new nation states.[16]

The Transkei and Ovamboland both already have legislative assemblies, the right of taxation, several autonomous ministries (including education, economic affairs, and justice), their own national anthem, and their own flag, while the Transkei has already had two general elections. Success in implementing the policy of separate development will simply increase the number of sovereign communities in Southern Africa. Undoubtedly, there will be political and economic problems with such a balkanization, but they do not begin to compare with the racial stresses and political strains which a failure of separate development will bring to the only country able to coordinate and sustain this drive toward a commonwealth or common market for Southern Africa.[17] Equally, should South Africa's foreign policy of friendly coexistence and cooperation with neighboring black states (the second factor) be rejected, the chances of Southern Africa drawing together and of a collective endeavor of developing the region for the benefit of black and white would be drastically reduced, just as they would for a similar movement in North America without the assistance and cooperation of the United States.

When the late prime minister of South Africa, Dr. H. F. Verwoerd, predicted in 1961 that one day there might be a common market for Southern Africa, he was subjected to strong criticism and even ridicule. He saw the ultimate geopolitical arrangements of the states comprising Southern Africa, and possibly including Zambia, as a commonwealth or community of Southern African states where the leaders could meet on the basis of full equality and "in which no state would lord it over another."[18] In this commonwealth, he said, political independence and economic interdependence would serve as the cornerstones of governmental relationships between member states.[19] Such a common market, or any advanced form of regional economic cooperation in Southern Africa, coupled with friendly political coexistence, is bound to come as a surprise to most foreign observers, who predicted only five to ten years ago that once the neighboring colonial territories of Bechuanaland, Basutoland, Swaziland, Nyasaland, and Northern Rhodesia gained independence from Britain, South Africa would be totally isolated from the rest of Africa.[20] Furthermore, the irresistible wave of black nationalism would then be washing the shores of white South Africa, with an almost certain outbreak of hostilities. The establishment of such a common market would undoubtedly be a major setback to the Organization of African Unity and to the bulk of the Afro-Asian and Communist countries which have been politically and militarily active in their efforts to upset South Africa, Rhodesia, and Portugal. It would also reflect poorly on several American organizations (such as the African-American Institute, the Presbyterian and Methodist churches, and the American Committee on Africa) which for some years have considered this area a "threat to world peace" in which conflict between black and white was inevitable and which, therefore required foreign (particularly United Nations) armed intervention as well as the withdrawal of all American support, both official and private. Any continuation of the present trend in Southern Africa would even deprive the American Committee on Africa of its *raison d'être*.[21]

Since Dr. Verwoerd's original pronouncement, the concept of a common market for Southern Africa has certainly gained ground. Today, only a few years after Dr. Verwoerd's death, it is shared not only by a great many South African politicians, diplomats, government officials, university professors, economists, and students of differing political views, but also by an even greater number of South Africans in all walks of life. It also has support in Malawi, Rhodesia, Mozambique, Angola, South West Africa, Lesotho, Botswana, Swaziland, and even Zambia.[22] In 1965 the South African minister of planning supported this objective in his address to a national symposium on the subject of a common market,[23] and two years later President Banda of Malawi openly expressed his wish to see the nations of Southern Africa hold a round table conference to discuss this matter. In Rhodesia, and even in

Mozambique and Angola, the plan was advocated in government circles, while in 1967 Lesotho's special economic adviser, Professor Denis Cowen, also pleaded for a common market.[24] In 1969 the South African minister of finance, Dr. Nicolas (Nico) Diederichs, said that the formation of trade blocs such as the European Common Market greatly stimulated European trade and that if South Africa wished to make any headway it would have to create close economic relations with Southern Africa. A Southern African trade bloc was one such possibility.[25]

But Dr. Verwoerd also appears to be vindicated posthumously in his other major objective—namely, to weld the countries of Southern Africa into a consortium of states with a relatively common foreign policy and with close cooperation in many other fields. Southern Africa is, for example, beginning to show the semblance of a united front against the increasing militancy of the Organization of African Unity (OAU) and talks of sanctions against the Republic of South Africa on the part of the United Nations. It is pressing ahead with its own projects in Rhodesia, Angola, Mozambique, South Africa, and Swaziland to find, refine, and stockpile oil, which is the one commodity always mentioned in talk of sanctions, and it is closing its ranks against terrorist infiltration from member states of the OAU.

For the first time independent black states are coming into contact with the white-controlled Republic of South Africa. Instead of generating ideological sparks, as was generally predicted outside South Africa, a remarkable degree of cooperation is being achieved. A trade pact has been signed with Malawi, and the first black diplomat from Malawi arrived in South Africa in 1968. Further afield, South Africa has established cordial relations with the Malagasy Republic. Not only have their officials visited South Africa for talks, but an air link has been set up between the two countries. On February 8, 1970, the French Bank in South Africa and other French companies joined South African trading houses in setting up a special company called INSERCO to promote trade with Malagasy in cooperation with the Commercial Bank of Malagasy. In October 1969 Malagasy gave a warm and cordial reception to a forty-man white trade mission from South Africa.[26] On April 9, 1969, in Blantyre, Malawi, President Philibert Tsiranana of Malagasy joined President Banda in stating his belief in cooperation with South Africa and in condemning any policy leading to boycott or isolation of South Africa. This is not an isolated case of increasing contact between South Africa and other black states further afield. Gambia's prime minister, Sir Dawda Jawara, has made an open bid for South African trade and tourists.[27] South African trade with black Africa in general has been up a healthy 10 to 15 percent each year during 1966–1970 and continues to increase even with the more militant states of the OAU.[28]

South Africa's diplomatic campaign to normalize relations with Black African states is lately directed principally towards former French territories in Africa. The approach was given added point in September 1970 by the South African government's offer to conclude a mutual nonaggression treaty with any other state in the continent. The dividends began to come in on 16 November, when President Houphouet-Boigny of the Ivory Coast, speaking at a rally in Zomba, urged his fellow Black African leaders to abandon such "ridiculous" measures as denying aircraft landing rights to South Africa and to open instead a diplomatic dialogue with Pretoria. He was supported by President Banda, and his words were echoed in the following weeks by spokesmen not only in Lesotho, Malagasy, Upper Volta, Niger, Dahomey and Togo, but also in the Gambia, Kenya and even Ghana. Most striking of all was the stand taken by the prime minister of Ghana, Dr. Busia, who bluntly warned his fellow Africans, later in November, that neither partial economic embargoes nor guerrilla warfare would destroy White rule in South Africa. "Sending a few people across the border is sending them to slaughter," he said; instead of sending guerrilla fighters, the OAU should send delegates to Pretoria to discuss the problem of *apartheid* reasonably.

Hydroelectric projects, such as the massive Cabora Bassa dam in Mozambique which will link nine of the ten countries of Southern Africa in a power grid, are now under construction. Frequent discussions between black states and South Africa on the development of water resources of Southern Africa are taking place.[29] During February 1970 no less than fifty representatives from eight countries in Southern Africa met in Lourenço Marques, Mozambique under the auspices of the Southern Africa Regional Council for the Conservation and Utilization of the Soil (SARCCUS) for a symposium on "Water for Progress" in which the development of the water resources for Southern Africa was discussed and plans were laid for future cooperation. Discussions in Pretoria among senior cabinet ministers of Botswana, Lesotho, and Swaziland and South Africa on the question of the renegotiation of the customs union which links the four countries took place in a cordial spirit resulting in rapid agreement. As a result, an extra $23.8 million will flow into the hard-pressed economies of these three states. The new agreement was welcomed by all the states concerned as proof of regional cooperation in Southern Africa despite political differences. The new customs union, signed on December 11, 1969, provides for the duty-free movement of locally produced goods within the union and the establishment of an executive organ for intergovernmental consultation.[30] These three African states have also followed a policy at the United Nations and at the Organization of African Unity which runs contrary to the line militant members of the Afro-Asian world had preferred.[31] Their leaders (and those of Malawi) have made it clear that they are resolutely opposed to the OAU's crusade to "liberate" South Africa, South West Africa, Rhodesia, Mozambique, or Angola. Botswana has cracked down hard on so-called "freedom fighters" en route to South West Africa.[32]

Lesotho has put a stop to efforts of the Basuto Communist party to aid affiliated groups in their efforts to attack South Africa.[33] Swaziland has warned that it would act resolutely against any terrorists on their way to South Africa and would permit South African forces to act against these would-be "liberators."[34]

All four countries have forecast the exchange of diplomats with South Africa. Although Malawi already has its own diplomatic mission in Pretoria, the three former British protectorates are so close to Pretoria that they consider establishing a mission at present an unnecessary expenditure. As the prime minister of Swaziland observed: "If my officials or my ministers want to discuss matters with South Africa, we just take a car or 'plane to Johannesburg and the whole matter can be dealt with in an hour or two," and he added that "missions are very expensive. At the moment we are trying to be conservative."[35]

By their forthright opposition to communism and militant Pan-Africanism, these states also removed, almost with one stroke, the remaining obstacles to full cooperation with the white-controlled states of the South. At the meetings of the General Assembly of the United Nations in 1966, Malawi became the first African state to refuse to join the walkout which the Afro-Asians and the Communists stage whenever the South African delegate steps up to the rostrum to speak. During a meeting of Commonwealth representatives in London in September 1967, these four countries sparked a dramatic upheaval by breaking the solid front of Commonwealth and African hostility towards Rhodesia for the first time, suggesting that a compromise be reached with Prime Minister Ian Smith. The visit to South Africa of the prime ministers of Lesotho, the president of Botswana, and cabinet ministers from Malawi took place in an obvious spirit of good will, as did the visit of South Africa's foreign minister to Malawi. The official statements issued at the time called for the closest cooperation in the political and economic sphere.[36] A white parliamentary delegation from South Africa was given a standing ovation when its members entered the Malawi House of Representatives, led by the speaker of the South African House of Assembly. This was the first visit of its kind to a black state.[37]

Trade, scientific, and government delegations of cabinet rank from Malawi, Zambia, Rhodesia, Angola, Mozambique, Botswana, Lesotho, and Swaziland have been arriving in South Africa and vice versa. A road is being constructed through South West Africa which will, in one year's time, link Cape Town and Luanda, the port city and capital of Angola. From Mozambique a gas pipeline is being laid to Johannesburg. South African and foreign-owned companies based in South Africa are spreading all over the subcontinent. In South West Africa eighteen companies are active in mining alone and forty-four in mineral prospecting.[38]

All over Southern Africa, on the Kunene River in Angola, the Zambezi River in Rhodesia, and the Orange River in South Africa, hydroelectric projects are being started which involved cooperation of *all* the governments before construction could begin. When Mozambique completes the Lourenço Marques–Beira road project in 1971 (at a cost of $20 million), it will add the last leg of a spectacular V-shaped land route through a third of the African continent, running a distance of 4,500 miles from Beira to Cape Town and then to Luanda.[39]

Close relationships exist and are growing daily between the Portuguese provinces of Angola and Mozambique, on the one hand, and Rhodesia and South Africa, on the other hand. Portuguese and Mozambican business organizations have joined the Afrikaans Trade Institute in Johannesburg in the formation of a new economic committee to boost trade.[40] When an eighty-man trade delegation from South Africa visited Angola in June 1969, the governor of Angola forecast an increasing trade with South Africa and South African capital investment in Angola.[41] The late Prime Minister Salazar of Portugal and his successor, Dr. F. M. Caetano, stressed the role of Mozambique and Angola in this developing relationship with Malawi, Rhodesia, and South Africa.[42] Currently, Malawi and Portugal are working on a new railway link costing $16 million.[43] During his visit to the Rhodesian trade fair in Lourenço Marques, Rhodesia's minister of commerce and industry pleaded for a limited free trade area in Southern Africa which would include his country and the Portuguese provinces as a forerunner to a common market.[44]

Suffice it to say that these countries are all pressing rapidly ahead for the improvement of trade (South Africa's 1965 trade agreement with Rhodesia which favors South Africa above all other countries is an example) in the provision of power (the natural gas line being constructed between Mozambique and Johannesburg), hydroelectric projects (such as on the Kunene River between Angola and South West Africa), communications (the new road to link Luanda, capital of Angola, with Cape Town), and scientific and technical research. South African funds and technical expertise are also being put to use in these countries: in harbor developments in Mozambique, in the search for copper in Angola, in industrial projects in Rhodesia and Swaziland, in economic development (railways, harbors, and power) in South West Africa, in the construction of a new capital in Malawi, and in mining in Zambia and in the development of Madagascar's tourist industry and communications.

Leaving aside for the moment the very close economic ties which exist between the former British protectorates (Botswana, Lesotho, Swaziland) and South Africa (a relationship which is really an advanced form of economic union), it is important to note that South West Africa has now become so dependent upon South Africa for a sustained high rate of growth that without the Republic's assistance it would be unable to survive for more than three to six months.[45] Not even the United States or the Soviet Union could lend sufficient help to keep an "independent" South West Africa going. Money alone is not sufficient. The absence, for example, of coal in economic quantities means that South West Africa is totally dependent on the Republic for power which turns the wheels of industry, lights the towns, keeps the telephone system going, and drives the pumps that provide water—the life blood of arid South West Africa. The only commercial harbor, Walvis Bay, is constitutionally and legally a part of the Republic; since 1878 it has been part of the Cape Province.[46] South Africa also provides teachers, engineers, technicians, physicians, and scientists for South West Africa, and its per capita aid to South West Africa is the highest ever provided by any country to a dependent territory. The implementation of the recommendations of the Odendaal Commission also calls in the coming years for annual expenditure equivalent to the total operating costs of the United Nations.[47]

Rhodesia, locked in bitter economic struggle with Britain and Zambia, is now dependent on "normal trade" with South Africa, Angola, and Mozambique for its survival. The United Nations General Assembly had voted for economic sanctions (including an oil blockade) against Rhodesia, but both Portugal and South Africa refused to go along with sanctions; instead, the South African prime minister declared that his country would continue its "normal trade" with Rhodesia. With the benefit of the 1965 trade agreement—which, in any case, favored South Africa—this normal trade enabled Rhodesia to survive economically, and the additional trade with Portugal has kept the country going ever since. Trade apart, the British action against Rhodesia has forced that country politically and economically into the South African orbit. Capital investment from South African sources and technical assistance in the form of men, machines, and expertise have helped to diversify the Rhodesian economy. Rhodesian and South African police patrol the borders with Zambia to intercept guerrillas who may be heading for South Africa. Rhodesia may have voted in 1922 not to become part of South Africa, but today the ties between the two cover almost every field: sports, culture, economics, and politics.[48]

Thus all over Southern Africa—in Malawi, Rhodesia, Angola, Swaziland, Botswana, Lesotho, and Mozambique—South African trade, capital, skills, and technical assistance are contributing to economic growth and regional cooperation which, it is generally conceded among economists, holds out the best hope for the people of Africa. In the words of Mr. W. W. Rostow, presidential assistant during the Johnson administration, "It is, I believe, one of the most important, if unnoticed, transitions in policy . . . that we are now actively supporting the building of *regional institutions* and *regional cooperation* in Latin America, Asia and Africa as well as in Europe."[49] South Africa has the same objective. Three outstanding examples come to mind. All have to do with water which, in semiarid Southern Africa, is the most important factor of economic life. First, the development of the vast inland delta formed by the Okavango River (where it sweeps into the Okavango swamps of northern Botswana) could boost Botswana's industrial and economic development to a degree which no amount of foreign aid could do in a lifetime. The Okavango delta plan calls for damming of the river to develop electricity and for the construction of a four hundred-mile pipeline to bring water to the huge industrial complex around Johannesburg. But, in order to succeed, South Africa's cooperation and willingness to purchase the water and power are necessary. Second, for Lesotho, landlocked by South Africa, the Oxbow River project can mean "white gold" for an impoverished mountain state, provided South Africa agrees to buy the water.[50] South Africa has already indicated its willingness to cooperate in this project on the Oxbow River. The electricity would be fed into the South African power grid and water would be led by pipeline to the industrial heart of South Africa where, if the pace of consumption is maintained, water would eventually be as valuable as gold, fully earning the description "white gold." Third, the Cabora Bassa project in Mozambique will result in a power grid which could cover the whole of Southern Africa, linking the Kariba and Orange River hydroelectric projects and providing water to nine nations.[51] Here, again, only South Africa's cooperation as the primary purchaser of power has brought this massive project, which is the fourth largest in the world, to the production stage.

The countries of Southern Africa are also mak ing headway in a number of fields where the rest of Africa is experiencing numerous setbacks: the eradication of poverty, illiteracy, and disease. Perhaps nowhere outside the United States and Canada is the economic development of non-whites proceeding at a more rapid pace. A 95 percent rate of literacy in South Africa for people of all races is only a decade away, while in health services South Africa is perhaps twenty years ahead of most of Africa.[52]

In short, Southern Africa is experiencing socio-economic and political changes which are slowly, but surely, drawing the various states in this region into a closer orbit. Regional cooperation in various fields is proceeding apace in the search for and in the stockpiling of oil; in the use and conservation of soil and water; in the exploitation of international rivers; in improving communications and planning for a power grid to blanket Southern Africa; in the boosting of bilateral trade: and in the eradication of stock disease. In fact, what is taking place is the birth of a strong regionalism in which racial affairs are of secondary importance.

Increasing contact between black and white states is leading to increasing appreciation of each other's domestic political problems, and there is a blurring of old animosities. The new capital city of Malawi is being designed by white men from South Africa. In Lesotho white physicians and nurses from South Africa are providing meaningful foreign aid.[53] Students from South Africa have formed a volunteer Peace Corps for service in Southern Africa.[54] White farmers of South Africa crossed the border into Lesotho to plow the fields of Basuto farmers as a gesture of friendship. The black president of Botswana was treated as a VIP in a white hospital in Johannesburg.[55]

Clearly, a new political and economic relationship is being fashioned in Southern Africa which may set this area completely apart from the rest of Africa. *Destined to become perhaps the most significant political and economic development in sub-Saharan Africa since European colonial disengagement, this trend will make it possible for small and numerically weak African states such as Lesotho and Botswana as well as the embryonic states of the Transkei (South Africa) and Ovamboland (South West Africa) to enjoy untrammeled political independence even when not economically viable.* One of the major arguments against South Africa's policy of separate development has always been the question of economic viability. In the foregoing pattern, however, economic viability is clearly not a *sine qua non* for self-determination.

Ideological differences are no longer a bar to political and economic cooperation. This point was also made in the joint statement issued by the prime minister of South Africa and the prime minister of Lesotho after their meeting in Cape Town on January 10, 1967. The *coup d'état* by Chief Leabua Jonathan, prime minister of Lesotho, following the confusion after the annulment of the country's second general election in February 1970, does not materially change Lesotho's attitude toward South Africa, or *vice versa*. Nor will the opposition Congress party in Lesotho (whose leaders were imprisoned) seek to change the special relationship in any material way. The secretary-general of the Congress party said in London on February 6, 1970, that the party, if in power, would work closely with South Africa.[56]

Suddenly, Dr. Verwoerd's vision is no longer regarded as a political pipedream. Even the most anti–South African neighbors and newspapers have now conceded that instead it has become a distinct possibility. Old political opponents are suddenly showing their support of this ideal. Notable is the address of former Natal University President Horwood to the Economic Association of Southern Africa in March 1969 and the attitude of Laurence Gandar, principal critic of Dr. Verwoerd and editor of the *Rand Daily Mail*, winner of the American Newspaper Union's award for 1968.[57] Writing in the March 1970 issue of *Harper's Magazine*, the deputy editor of *The Economist*, Norman Macrae, noted that South Africa "could help to spread a sort of co-prosperity sphere" for Southern Africa.[58]

This development is taking place in an area which I have called *The Third Africa* (embracing all the countries in Africa south of the Congo [Kinshasa] and Tanzania) to set it apart from Arab (North) Africa and black (East, West, and Central) Africa. The Third Africa is a name with historical basis. It was North Africa which first felt the influence of Europe, followed by the West African areas, and finally Southern Africa in the seventeenth and eighteenth centuries.

The Third Africa is an area of over two million square miles (twice the size of Western Europe) and even though it has a population of only some 45 million people, in terms of economic productivity, stability of government, and socioeconomic progress, it overshadows the rest of the African continent with its 260 million people and 7 million square miles of land. The Republic of South Africa alone accounts for more than one-fifth of the gross national product of the entire African continent. If allowed to proceed unhindered, developments in this area could conceivably lead to the creation of a new multinational giant, a Europe of Africa, which may then exercise a profound influence on economic and political developments in all of Africa. Could this be one of the reasons why the militant and socialist groups in Africa (and at the United Nations) often go to such lengths to see the Republic of South Africa fail in its domestic program or in its foreign policy for Southern Africa?[59]

Since Ghana received its independence from the United Kingdom in 1957, a great number of other African territories have become sovereign independent states. Some of the new countries had fewer people than an average city in the United States; almost ten years later the annual budget of some such as Togo and Gabon was still less than that of a large university in America or in Great Britain.[60] For some ten years, West and East appeared to be outbidding each other for the favor of these new nations and for their voting support in the General Assembly of the United Nations. Whether the big powers are happy with the result of their efforts is doubtful, and apparently the honeymoon is coming to an end. Easy handouts to African nations which squander millions of dollars on palaces and private bank accounts and whose leaders kick the shins of the donor nation are unlikely to be tolerated by the Nixon administration.

Despite massive doses of foreign aid and a liberal amount of cheek-turning on the part of the donor countries, Western-style democracy and political stability for most of Arab and black Africa are becoming more and more of a dream. In Nigeria, the Congo (Kinshasa), Ghana, Guinea, Uganda, Rwanda, Burundi, Sudan, and Algeria, to name but a few countries, both East and West have had disappointments and serious setbacks—in different ways, of course. What the West had hoped would take place in Africa—namely, political stability, economic progress, cooperation with neighboring states, maintenance of democratic institutions, and a better deal for the average man—did not materialize. Certainly "independence" is no longer considered the same as decolonization and the magic event that solves all ills.[61] Wars, revolutions, *coups d'état*, and other convulsions claimed the lives of hundreds of thousands, while millions were left homeless, and two million have become refugees. Fortunately, what both Chinese and Soviet Communists had hoped would happen has so far also failed to materialize.[62]

In the remaining part of the African continent—namely, the states and territories lying to the south of the Congo (Kinshasa) and Tanzania—the predictions of Western statesmen, editors, professors, and businessmen have also proved erroneous.[63] Whereas misery and turmoil followed independence in so many Arab and black African states, economic progress, certainly stability, as well as cordial relations between black and white states have become part of a new way of life in the Third Africa. It was in this respect that these persons have substantially miscalculated. Since 1948 the world has experienced more than ninety-eight revolutions, *coups*, wars, and civil wars. During 1960–1970 no less than twenty-seven governments in Africa were subject to a *coup d'état*. In 1966 alone seven governments were overthrown by force of arms. Yet, barring Lesotho and the Portuguese provinces, not one of these wars or revolutions has occurred in the Third Africa, and even in the case of Mozambique and Angola there was no bona fide rebellion by the local inhabitants since the guerrilla attacks were led by foreigners (across the borders) from the Congo (Kinshasa) and Tanzania. Because the guerrillas were mostly foreigners with foreign aid and support, mainly from Red China and the Soviet Union,[64] and because fewer than 1 percent of the local population participated, the definition of civil war cannot be applied to the guerrilla and terrorist incursions into Angola or Mozambique.[65] However, the state of affairs elsewhere in the world (or Africa) did not discourage those prophets who predicted doom for Southern Africa. For the past twenty years some of the more responsible newspapers and many self-styled experts on African affairs in the West have predicted chaos, strife, and political turmoil for South Africa.[66] Exactly the opposite has taken place. "There is at present no real 'South African revolution' or 'war of liberation' in progress," wrote Norman Macrae in *Harper's Magazine*, while Dr. C. W. de Kiewiet now sees strength in South Africa's position instead of the weaknesses he predicted in 1948.[67]

The southern mass of Africa is, by and large, enjoying a rising standard of living, a higher per capita income than any other African state, barring oil-rich Libya, and unparalleled economic growth. In most areas political stability is equal to that enjoyed by the countries of Western Europe. Certainly governments in Southern Africa remain in power for longer periods than in Western Europe; South Africa has had only seven prime ministers in sixty years, and continuity is assured by a well-established civil service. That this is the case can also be shown, for example, by the flow of hundreds of millions of dollars in stock and business ventures into a country such as South Africa during 1968–1969. No one invests on this scale in a politically unstable country.[68] In addition, the outlook is not only for continued prosperity but also for increasing cooperation between the black states of Malawi, Botswana, Lesotho, Swaziland (and lately Gambia and Malagasy), on the one hand, and the white-controlled states of South Africa, Angola, Rhodesia, and Mozambique, on the other hand. When Zambia reassesses its position in Southern Africa and ends its suicidal economic war against Rhodesia, this African state (which has close ties with South Africa) could enjoy economic prosperity in a Southern African consortium of nations which its present neighbor, Tanzania, could never help it to obtain.

Yet if the idea of closer ties in Southern Africa is to develop or, indeed, if there is to be an improvement of relations between the countries of the South and those of the militant North, then all must look to Zambia, which has a vital role to play. Geography, politics, history, and everybody's hopes for the future put Zambia in this key position. This does not mean that Zambia's membership is a prerequisite for a successful consortium of Southern African states (or for the successful functioning of the new regionalism), but this nation represents a bridge between the states of Central Africa (and those further north) with those of the South. Therefore, it is the keystone for building a bigger, more successful, and more stable Southern African community of nations.

The events of the past two years, however, have shown that Zambia today is neither a bridge nor a keystone. Political relations with the South are bad. Yet no matter now hard Zambia tries, it remains as much part of the militant North as of the economically powerful South. Economically, Zambia is virtually tied to the South and economic factors are increasingly important in determining the nature of political attitudes in Africa. Its lines of communication go south; its vast copper industry is in large measure controlled by the South; its sixty thousand whites, on whom so much of its economic growth presently depends, come mainly from the South; and Zambia has considerable trade with South Africa. But politically Zambia today wants to look north. It is fiercely anti-Rhodesian and fiercely anti-Portuguese. It works closely with the OAU and closely with Tanzania. Accordingly, it wishes to end its economic dependence on the South. It has already joined itself by an oil pipeline to Dar es Salaam and, with Red Chinese help, it hopes to build the Tanzam railway. It does so to escape the South's economic embrace.

The recent uproar over the white judiciary in Zambia was very disturbing, and at one point even undermined the minimal confidence which South African and Rhodesian whites have in Zambia. Not only was Zambia's dedication to the rule of law jeopardized by the hounding of its white judges, but it was an ugly indication of the government's xenophobia when it came to the whites of the South.[69] President Kaunda's public admission that his handling of the crisis was a mistake and his plea to the white judges to return has helped put things right again, but one still has one's doubts. The Zambian government must be criticized for its emotional outbursts against the South when it is so inordinately economically dependent on the South. Zambia continued to buy more goods from South Africa than from any other country and in 1968 increased its South African purchases by $4 million to a total of $94 million. In the face of President Kaunda's emotional tirades against the South, his nationalization of mines built up largely by South African funds, and his ever closer cooperation with the Red Chinese (who are now building three new radio transmitters in Zambia and training the programers and announcers),[70] the South nonetheless remained calm and continued to stress the benefits of cooperation with a region which includes both white and black states.

The countries in the South are sitting on top of the greatest treasure chest the world has ever known—gold, uranium, diamonds, copper, platinum, chrome, asbestos, iron, vanadium, and a host of other minerals; these metals are essential for the industrial progress of the West. Moreover, the nations of Southern Africa are sparsely populated; their food-producing potential (in a world facing serious food shortages in Africa, Asia, and Latin America) is also tremendous.[71] Elsewhere in Africa, virtually every single attempt at regional economic cooperation, in the form of some closely integrated economic bloc, has had serious economic or political setbacks; however, the southern tier of the continent has made some remarkable progress in this field. Here a powerful economic alliance is slowly, but surely, being forged not only between the white-controlled states but also between these states and their black neighbors.

The Third Africa includes the only country in Africa which the United Nations considers an industrially developed state—namely, the Republic of South Africa—and it represents America's principal trading bloc in Africa. South Africa is the recipient of 50 percent of all private American investment in Africa. To the West this is indeed one of the most critical areas in the world. The entire industrial system of the West would be adversely affected and long-term Western strategy imperiled if the Third Africa failed to continue its production of strategic minerals and metals or if it fell prey either to communism or to the same disorder and strife which have beset the far greater majority of other African states and regions.[72] The strategic significance of Southern Africa has been recently stressed by E. S. Virpsha in a lengthy article in *N.A.T.O.'s Fifteen Nations* and also by American strategists, particularly after the closing of the Suez Canal caused a mass of American shipping to be diverted to South African harbors.[73]

What has been occurring lately in Southern Africa has not been lost on politicians or on the more responsible press of the West. In New York, London, Geneva, Rome, and Sydney reports have appeared referring to "the new sweet winds of change" in Southern Africa.[74] But what these reports have not revealed is the scope and depth of this change—a change for which South Africa has consistently labored, but which has constantly been ignored or played down by the same news agencies until events made it impossible to continue to do so. The 1968 annual report of the Commonwealth Development Corporation contained the first official British praise for South Africa's assistance to neighboring black states, although such assistance had already been given for many years.[75]

Admittedly, South Africa dominates the Third Africa just as the United States dominates the Western hemisphere. For example, the total gross domestic product of Swaziland, Lesotho and Botswana is only 1 percent of that of South Africa (see Table 1). Rhodesia, whose need for oil has become a matter of world importance, consumes only a little more oil than the city of Cape Town. South West Africa's national income is only 1.9 percent of that of South Africa. But the important fact is that South Africa has been using this power to assist neighboring states, and virtually every such state has publicly acknowledged the fact that not the slightest political pressure has been put on it.

Table 1. Area, Population and Gross Domestic Product of the Countries of Southern Africa, 1967

COUNTRIES	Area (in square miles)	Population[a] (in millions)	Population per square mile	Gross Domestic Product Per capita (dollars)	Gross Domestic Product Total (in million dollars)
SOUTHERN AFRICA:[b]					
Republic of South Africa	471,445	17,867	38	596	12,627
Zambia	290,587	3,710	13	267	1,052
Mozambique	302,250	6,956	23	150	1,041
Rhodesia	150,952	4,330	29	222	1,007
Angola	481,350	5,154	11	164	844
South West Africa	318,261	0.589	2	560	329
Malawi	36,100[c]	3,940	109	50	208
Swaziland	6,704	0.375	56	196	73
Lesotho	11,716	0.838	72	78	67
Botswana	222,000[c]	0.559	3	94	54
TOTAL SOUTHERN AFRICA	2,291,365	44,318	19	237.7	17,302
AFRICA	11,699,000	309,295	26	131.6	41,600

Source: The data given in this table are derived from diverse sources and hence are not strictly comparable. These sources are: United Nations, *Statistical Yearbook*, 20th ed. (1969), Table 190, p. 585; and *Africa, Economic Growth Trends* (Washington, D.C.: Statistics and Reports Division, Office of Program and Policy Coordination, Agency for International Development, January 1968), p. 17.

[a] Midyear estimates for 1965.

[b] Countries are given in order of the size of their gross domestic product.

[c] Excluding inland water areas.

Swaziland's minister of finance stated in Parliament in March 1969 that South Africa is expected to help his country complete two ambitious projects—namely, the purchase of power from a newly planned giant thermal power station and the construction of a $14 million, 93-mile rail link between the eastern part of the Transvaal Province of South Africa and Swaziland. This assistance, he pointed out, was promised after negotiations between the two governments.[76]

Having outlined political developments in Southern Africa, which suggest, first, that ideological differences are no longer a bar to cooperation and to mutually satisfactory relations between white and nonwhite states and, second, that common interests and economic objectives, rather than racial attitudes, are paramount, we can now turn to the subject of the need for, as well as the possibilities of, a common market for Southern Africa. Since South Africa dominates the subcontinent economically to the same extent that the U.S.A. dominates Latin America and Canada, the economic possibilities of such a market need to be examined primarily from the point of view of the Republic of South Africa.[77]

In South Africa this topic has been the subject of several systematic and comprehensive studies by leading economists and Africanists.[78] Assuming that the present political and constitutional policies of creating separate statehoods for the different black groups in South Africa and South West Africa continue to be applied, but on a larger scale and at an increased tempo, the end of the next decade or two may see a Southern Africa of some sixteen countries in place of the present ten.[79] What are the chances, then, for a common market or some sort of economic union?

Generally speaking, there are five schools of thought.

First. There are those who advocate a common market for Southern Africa or for parts of Southern Africa primarily for political reasons—that is, they see in this advocacy a means of assuring the neighboring states, which are considerably underdeveloped compared with South Africa, of South Africa's political goodwill and bona fides in the question of interstate and race relations. The economic considerations are either played down or the political objectives are considered to be of such importance by them that the economics will have to adjust to politics. The political umbrella for this common market is often seen as a commonwealth of nations for Southern Africa. Their argument is that only a closely knit economic union among all the countries in the South will enable the region to stave off the political pressures by the Organization of African Unity upon the weaker neighboring black states, the cooperation and good will of whom South Africa requires in order to break out of its relative isolation in Africa; these neighboring states are intended to serve as a buffer area between the more militant North and the white South. The economic problems (which will be dealt with later) and the price for such cooperation will have to be faced and met in the interest of the political objective. This argument is found in some lower and higher echelons of government service, in newspaper editorials, in speeches by the representatives of (not all) the United party and the Progressive party and by political scientists at universities, and it also has considerable support among theorists in the National party.

Second. Another group maintains that because of the inherent instability of the newly independent African states and because of the imcompatibility between black and white people, a policy of full economic cooperation and technological integration with neighboring African states will not succeed. They point to the Central African Federation (composed of Southern Rhodesia, Nyasaland, and Northern Rhodesia) which fell apart because of nationalist and racial attitudes (and not because of economic factors); two of the federation's ex-members, Rhodesia and Zambia, are now at economic war. Their plea is based on hard-line self-interest which would call for only that measure of cooperation where the benefits accrue primarily to South Africa. This school has scattered support among politicians in all parties, particularly among right-wing groups such as Dr. Albert Hertzog's *Herstigte Nasionale* party (not to be confused with the National party, the government party), right-wing newspapers, a number of economists and political scientists (for purely pragmatic reasons), and economists and politicians who maintain that South Africa should confine its economic cooperation to the states south of the Limpopo River. In this region, South Africa can exercise considerable economic and political power (which is more difficult to do in the northern areas which are either further removed from South Africa or part of the existing Portuguese Commonwealth) because the countries in this region are so dependent on South African aid and markets for their future development as to constitute no political threat.

Third. A group of agroeconomists, political scientists, geographers, and economists advocate a special free trade area for the entire South. Such an area will be characterized by coordinated economic planning which will ensure that the economic development of the smaller and poorer countries will benefit these countries as well as the entire region. This school is fairly popular and includes Drs. P. Smit and E. J. van der Merwe of the Africa Institute in Pretoria.[80] Because of the far more realistic economic targets which they set, more attention will be paid to their suggestions and arguments later on in this chapter. They have wide support among economists at the universities.

Fourth. A fourth school represented by the Bureau for Economic Policy and Analysis in Pretoria[81]—whose associates consist of economists at all the leading Afrikaans-medium universities and who have wide support both at the public, university, and government level—is opposed to a common market, but it suggests a policy of closest economic cooperation in which each participating member would maintain control over the nature and extent of its participation in the system. Their view of cooperation entails: (1) technological integration; (2) economic cooperation, particularly in the industrial field; and (3) political independence. In many respects their economic arguments resemble those of the third group.

Fifth. The present National party government favors close economic cooperation and supports the principle of a common market, but for the moment regards economic cooperation as a means of ensuring political stability in Southern Africa. Political integration is not the ultimate objective as it is in the case of the Western European model of the common market. The government considers that South Africa is in a favorable position to furnish leadership in the economic development of Southern Africa, yet the point has not been reached where a common market can be made a definite objective. What South Africa should do, government spokesmen maintain, is to take every opportunity of encouraging a more effective intraregional marketing system of goods and greater economic cooperation among all the countries.[82] Planning for a common market now would be premature. The government nonetheless realizes that there is a continuous need for new approaches to, and instruments for, economic advancement of the less developed areas in Southern Africa with a view to maximizing the spill-over advantages they enjoy from their proximity to the Republic.[83] The government's policy, therefore, is basically in line with the economic arguments of the groups represented by Drs. Smit and van der Merwe and the Bureau for Economic Policy.

Obviously, cooperation on a regional basis can provide many advantages for Southern Africa. Not only is intraregional cooperation of great political importance to South Africa, but also because Southern Africa is the only region in Africa where a modern industrial economy is adjacent to, and closely interwoven with, a number of undeveloped economies, closer economic links will be to the mutual advantage of all participants. South Africa's minister of planning, Dr. Jan Haak, has stressed the fact that South Africa is interested only in seeing economic progress and stability in its neighboring countries and has no designs on the independence or freedom of action of its neighbors. This view was repeated by Dr. Riekert, economic adviser to the prime minister and chairman of the government's economic advisory council, during his address to the South African Institute of Race Relations.[84] It is also echoed by private industry in South Africa and by the student community. Stellenbosch University has formed its own permanent peace corps to render aid on a voluntary basis. Students from the universities in Cape Town, Johannesburg, and Grahamstown have built schools, hospitals, and clinics in Swaziland and Lesotho.

A number of developments suggest that private industry is also taking the government's attitude seriously. For example, to keep abreast of the overall expansion of Southern Africa, the Botswana government has formulated plans for the launching of a mining and industrial infrastructure embracing a five-year program and capital expenditure of between $35 and $42 million. However, when the Botswana government approached Britain for assistance, no aid was forthcoming. A group of leading South African companies then prepared a blueprint for the creation of a water and electricity supply corporation which could form the keystone of the new infrastructure. This proposal calls for a seven-year program involving a capital expenditure of about $60 million which can be financed by South African companies and banks.[85]

The third and fourth schools are primarily responsible for the study and debate on the question of a common market and for analyzing government policy in the economic and technological spheres toward the states of Southern Africa. Both the first and second groups do not actively participate in this study or debate; they confine themselves to commenting on or reacting to statements by the other groups. For this reason, we have concentrated in this chapter on the attitude of the government and the findings and proposals of the third and fourth groups.

Before proceeding to summarize the proposals which the third and fourth groups believe embody the best hope for effective economic cooperation in Southern Africa and thus improve chances of a common market, we need to explore briefly the presently existing state of economic and technological cooperation among the countries of Southern Africa and the intraregional trade pattern.

The latest reliable statistics on intraregional trade (see Table 2) are only for 1963. During this period the countries forming part of the Third Africa enjoyed an intraregional trade of $771 million, a figure which the Bureau for Economic Policy and Analysis estimated to be $911 million in 1964.[86] Although this is small compared with South Africa's trade with the rest of the world, the January 1963 United Nations *Economic Bulletin for Africa* revealed that this figure of $771 million represented 70 percent of the total recorded intra-African trade. The figure for 1970 is probably much higher. For strategic reasons, however, South Africa no longer reveals statistics of the trade with individual African countries. However, during the period 1963–1969, South Africa's total trade with the countries in Southern Africa has shown significant increases, sometimes by as much as 10 percent—as in 1968 and 1969—so that these 1963 statistics need to be taken as showing only about 50 to 60 percent of the current intraregional trade for Southern Africa. For example, South Africa's visible exports of manufactured items, minerals, and foodstuffs to all African states in 1969 amounted to $358 million and imports of goods and services to $161 million, a total of $519 million.[87]

As can be seen from Table 2, intraregional trade between the Republic and the two Portuguese territories, Rhodesia, Zambia, and Malawi did not assume large proportions in 1964. However,

Table 2. Southern Africa: Intraregional Trade
Southern Africa: Merchandise Imports and Exports, 1964 in Thousands of Dollars

Exports / Imports	South Africa	Rhodesia	Malawi	Zambia	Angola	Mozambique	Botswana	Lesotho	Swaziland	South West Africa	Rest of World	Total
South Africa	X	83,851.6	1,524.6	45,236.8	3,014.2	25,600	6,531	21,294	22,078	176,400	1,208,250.4	1,593,781
Rhodesia	30,737	X	20,242.6	114,051	631.4	3,269	5,549.6	9.8	134.4	168	237,112.4	411,905.2
Malawi	2,185.4	4,566.8	X	1,281	—	347.2	8.4	—	12.6	1.4	25,396	33,798.8
Zambia	28,368.2	15,110.2	1,360.8	X	19.6	86.8	142.8	—	5.6	47.6	444,043.6	489,185.2
Angola	1,831.2	156.8	9.8	326.6	X	2,991.8	—	—	—	—	216,458.2	221,810.4
Mozambique	9,916.2	3,855.6	644	72.8	3,451	X	—	—	210	—	96,875.8	115,025.4
Botswana	5,696.6	921.2	—	435.4	—	—	X	—	—	—	7,189.0	14,242.2
Lesotho	6,916	4.2	—	—	—	—	—	X	—	—	359.8	7,280
Swaziland	13,662.6	182	—	133	—	103.6	—	—	X	—	17,691.8	31,773
South West Africa	105,676.2	156.8	—	60.2	—	—	—	—	—	X	122,129	228,022.2
Rest of World	2,126,833.8	201,140.8	16,067.8	59,620.4	171,073	137,361	828.8	2,356.2	4,159.4	19,383.0	X	2,738,824.2
Total	2,331,823.2	309,946	39,849.6	221,253.2	178,189.2	169,759.8	13,060.6	23,660	26,600	196,000	2,375,506	5,885,647.6

Source: G. M. E. Leistner, "Economic Co-operation in Southern Africa," *Tegnikon* (Pretoria), March, 1967, p. 22.

following Rhodesia's declaration of independence, the bilateral trade pacts between South Africa and Rhodesia and between South Africa and Malawi in 1965 and 1967, respectively, increased the trade between these countries, and South Africa soon replaced the United Kingdom as the major trading partner of both Rhodesia and Malawi and, in 1968, Zambia. The nine countries of Southern Africa have signed a total of sixteen bilateral trade agreements with each other, as indicated in Table 3:

Table 3. Illustration of Bilateral Agreements among the Countries in Southern Africa

	Republic of South Africa	*Botswana Lesotho Swaziland*	*Rhodesia*	*Malawi*	*Zambia*	*Mozambique*	*Angola*
Republic of South Africa		×	×	×		×	×
Botswana							
Lesotho	×						
Swaziland							
Rhodesia	×						
Malawi	×					×	×
Zambia							
Mozambique	×		×			×	×
Angola	×		×			×	×

Source: Lombard, Stadler, and van der Merwe, *op. cit.*, Table 6, p. 47.

Furthermore, as Drs. Smit and van der Merwe have recently pointed out,

> The Republic supplies most of the goods and services imported into South West Africa and the B.L.S. countries [*i.e.*, Botswana, Lesotho, and Swaziland], and it buys a fairly large part of their exports. This pattern can largely be attributed to the close economic ties with these four countries. They form a customs union with the Republic and use the same monetary unit while there is also free movement of capital between them and reasonably free movement of labour. These countries' infra-structures are also closely bound up with that of the Republic (for example, their transportation and communications systems and their South African-based banking institutions).
>
> Moreover, these countries' agricultural and mineral products which form the basis of their economic activities, are to a very large extent marketed as an integral part of those of South Africa. The South African Wool Board makes no distinction between the domestic wool clip and that of Lesotho. Diamonds from South West Africa and Lesotho are purchased by the Central Selling Organization located in the Republic; beef carcasses and slaughtered stock from South West Africa, Swaziland and Botswana are exported to South Africa under controlled marketing schemes, administered by the South African Livestock and Meat Industries Control Board. South Africa has an agreement with Swaziland under which all butter, tobacco, wattle, citrus and cotton surpluses in the latter are bought by or marketed through the different South African Control Boards.[88]

In addition to the bilateral trade and provision of services, there is also a significant flow of unskilled African labor from other countries in Southern Africa to the Republic. There are approximately 530,000 registered foreign African workers employed in South Africa (see Table 4).

Table 4. Estimated Total Employment, Earnings and Remittances of Foreign African Workers in the Republic of South Africa, 1964

	Total Number of Workers	*Earnings in Millions of Dollars*	*Remittances in Millions of Dollars*
Mozambique	135,000	53.2	10.3
Rhodesia	27,000	10.0	1.5
Angola	11,000	4.7	0.9
Zambia	13,000	5.0	0.8
South West Africa	2,000	0.8	0.1
Malawi	82,000	30.8	5.7
Swaziland	18,000	6.3	1.1
Lesotho	164,000	58.3	10.2
Botswana	52,000	18.3	3.2
Other African Countries	26,000	11.2	2.3
Total	530,000	188.6	36.1

Source: G.M.E. Leistner, "Foreign Bantu Workers," pp. 49, 51–52. The data for Malawi are based on Smit and van der Merwe, *op. cit.* Table 3, p. 287.

Of this total 504,000 are from other states in Southern Africa, the rest being from Tanzania and other East and Central African states. Migrant laborers of Lesotho (164,000), Mozambique (135,000), Malawi (82,000), and Botswana (52,000) thus form the bulk of the migrant labor force.[89]

The significance of these labor movements to South Africa, observed Drs. Smit and van der Merwe, is the fact that most of the other countries are unable to employ the majority of their own labor force. As Dr. G. M. E. Leistner, a distinguished economist at the University of South Africa, has pointed out, ". . . apart from South Africa, Rhodesia is the only country in the region which is able to employ a substantial portion of its labour force (41 per cent) whereas only 5 percent of the Basotho find work at home as compared with about one-fifth in the case of Botswana, Swaziland, and Zambia, and one-seventh in Malawi."[90]

The migrant labor system to South Africa, therefore, acts as a safety valve for economically developing areas where excessive unemployment creates both economic and political pressures. An analysis of the earnings of migrant workers clearly reveals that the smaller states in Southern Africa (particularly Lesotho, Malawi, and Swaziland) benefit economically as much from this system as does South Africa. Of the $188.6 million earned in South Africa by migrant labor in 1964, some $36.4 million was remitted to the nations of origin of the migrant labor force—a significant amount by African standards.

By 1967 about three hundred thousand laborers from the three former British protectorates worked in South Africa and their income of some $85.4 million represented about one-quarter of the gross national product of the three countries. In the case of Lesotho, one-fifth of whose population worked in South Africa, the one-fifth earned a total of $58.8 million as compared with $78 million for the remainder of Lesotho.[91] In 1967 the total wage bill that South African employers paid to foreign African workers totaled $210 million and the total in remittances sent home by the workers came to $35 million.[92] An important aspect is that the countries in Southern Africa also benefit from the general knowledge and technical skills the migrant workers acquire in South Africa. Some leave home as unskilled labor and return as crane, bulldozer, mechanical saw, and hoist operators, able to read and write. It is difficult to estimate the cost of training such a worker, but since the number of workers is so great it may save the various countries millions of dollars per annum. In a sociological context the migrant system has great disadvantages. The long absence from wives leads to a rise in homosexuality and an increase in prostitution and contributes to the breakup of the family unit, sociologically the backbone of Bantu society.

Yet it is a voluntary system and one which, apart from the benefits mentioned, spreads knowledge of other people, races, societies, and developments throughout Southern Africa. This, in turn, leads to a better understanding of different points of view and an appreciation of the lack of hostility in Southern Africa.

The basic need of Malawi, Rhodesia, Botswana, Swaziland, and Lesotho for sufficient capital for development purposes is at least partially overcome by their proximity to South Africa (and the special historical relationship). As Drs. Smit and van der Merwe pointed out:

> Domestic savings are on the whole not large enough to meet the requirements of more rapid economic development.
>
> South Africa already plays a significant role in respect of providing capital to its neighbours. At the end of 1964 the Republic had invested R333 million [$466 million] in the former Federation of Rhodesia and Nyasaland. Since then South Africa lent R5 million [$7 million] to Rhodesia in 1965 for specific projects, including the Chiredzi Dam, the Mbezi-Chiredzi Railway, the Kyle Dam Canals, electric power supply and an airport at Chiredzi. In the same year the South African Reserve Bank also lent R2 million [$2.8 million] to Rhodesia to provide it with funds to meet its external obligations. The government has lent R8 million [$11.2 million] to Malawi for the construction of Lilongwe, the new capital, while the South African Industrial Development Corporation provided R6 million [$8.4 million] for the erection of a sugar mill and about R11 million [$15.4 million] for the extension of the railway line to the port of Nacala. The I.D.C. has also financed a R5.3 million [$7.4 million] sugar mill in Mozambique and lent R5 million [$7 million] for harnessing the waters of the Cunene River in Angola. Moreover, of the estimated private investment of R70 to R80 million [$98 to $112 million] in Swaziland between 1960 and 1966, enterprises located in the Republic accounted for about one-third. In addition, the South African government has also created a R5 million [$7 million] fund this year [1968] to promote co-operation with African states.[93]

However, the most important capital aid to date was the South African government's decision to underwrite the Cabora Bassa project in Mozambique to the extent of $98 million during the first five years through the purchase of electricity. At the end of 1967 total South African government and private investment in Southern Africa totaled about $910 million, a figure which by 1969 was probably close to $1.3 billion. An important point in South African government policy on aid to Southern Africa is its determination not to compete with Western European, Sino-Soviet, or American aid to African states because this could introduce a political note in what is in fact regional economic cooperation. Thus funds are not allocated to projects already in progress.[94]

In the field of technical cooperation, Drs. Smit and van der Merwe have provided the following examples:

> Because of corresponding climate, soil, plant growth and mineral-bearing geological formations, there are many similarities in the spheres of agriculture and mining between South Africa and the other countries of Southern Africa. In the technical field, South Africa is the most advanced of this group of countries and furthermore with the development of the Bantu Homelands has gained valuable experience in the reclamation of economically retarded areas. The results of research on common problems by research organizations such as Onderstepoort [Veterinary Institute], the Bureau of Standards, the C.S.I.R. [Council for Scientific and Industrial Research], the S.A. Institute for Medical Research, agricultural research stations, etc. are available to these countries and can help increase production.
>
> South Africa is already co-operating closely with the countries of Southern Africa in combatting diseases such as foot and mouth, lung sickness, malaria, etc. Technical aid, as in the improvement of the cattle herds of Botswana, Angola, Mozambique and Malawi is also being provided at present, while South African scientists have also been of assistance in other spheres in connection with development projects.[95]

In addition to these examples, we can also point to the aid rendered by the South African Broadcasting Corporation (Radio South Africa) to Malawi and Lesotho. South African Airways furnishes technical assistance, crews, and maintenance equipment to the fledgling air services of Botswana, Swaziland, Lesotho, and Malagasy. Research at no less than twenty-six institutes varying from building research to food and personnel are carried out in South Africa and research results are either channeled directly to the surrounding states or are available on request.[96] Excepting Zambia, all states of Southern Africa also cooperate in the Southern African Regional Commission for the Conservation and Utilization of the Soil (SARCCUS). In this way

even the technically less endowed countries share in the experience and expertise of South Africa. Cabinet ministers from South Africa, during their visits to neighboring states, have drawn attention to the many fields in which South Africa was prepared to render aid (such as physical planning, mining, health, or housing) and have also pointed out how much aid was already being given in order to encourage further cooperation.[97]

Another important factor which contributes to regional cooperation is the question of political stability. Dr. P. J. Riekert, the chairman of South Africa's economic advisory council, dealt with this aspect at some length in his address to the 1970 annual meeting of the South African Institute of Race Relations. Referring to Professor Simon Kuznets' views on economic growth (that "clearly some minimum political stability is necessary. . . . One could hardly expect much economic growth under conditions of political turmoil, riots and unpredictable changes in regimes"),[98] Dr. Riekert said that the relationship between economic development and political stability is quite relevant to the situation in Southern Africa where there is a marked dualism, similar to the rest of the world, between the economic situation of a prosperous and rapidly advancing minority and that of a majority which has only recently begun to emerge from a stagnant, subsistence level of existence.[99] The prospect of achieving the required stability, said Dr. Riekert, is much more favorable in Southern Africa than in any other part of the developing world. He said that

> This is so not only on account of the Republic's relatively great economic power, which enables her to afford the facilities required to maintain internal security and deter foreign aggression, but also because of the more positive reason that the proximity of the other countries in Southern Africa to a dynamically growing economy such as the Republic appreciably improves their chances to achieve economic development and the concomitant improvements in the material welfare of their inhabitants. This, in turn, enhances the probability that Governments in the other countries will be able to maintain at least that minimum degree of stability necessary to sustain their economic development.[100]

Dr. Riekert pointed out that without the attraction of the Republic of South Africa's dynamic economy for foreign investors and without South Africa's entrepreneurs and the savings generated and reinvested inside the Republic as well as in some of these countries,

> the less developed parts of the sub-continent would in all likelihood have had little chance of attracting investment capital in any case, so that the actual impact of the polarization effect, for example, must not be overrated. The fact remains that the less developed parts of the sub-continent have even under comparatively *laissez faire* conditions benefited very substantially from the various spill-over advantages flowing from their proximity to the Republic, such as a near-by and accessible market not only for their goods, but also for their surplus labor; participation in the Republic's overseas marketing for a number of primary products; the expertise and financial backing of large South African mining companies for the exploration and development of their mineral resources, the use of the Rand as their monetary unit without any contribution to the stability of this currency, and so on.[101]

Having examined the most important aspects of technological, scientific, economic, and political cooperation existing among the states of Southern Africa,[102] we can now proceed to summarize the views of Drs. Smit and van der Merwe (the spokesman for group three) as they relate to the concept of economic cooperation among the countries of Southern Africa, the question of a common market, and the considerations which must be borne in mind when fashioning the instruments of the proposed free trade area.

According to Drs. Smit and van der Merwe, a common market is, strictly speaking, only possible if all participating countries are more or less on the same level of economic development (as in the case of Western Europe). A Western European type common market for Southern Africa is therefore ruled out for the immediate future. In contrast to Western Europe, they point out, the various Southern African states are at widely different levels of economic development and lack competitive productive patterns. However, a fairly advanced form of economic union exists among South West Africa, Lesotho, Botswana, Swaziland, and the Republic of South Africa. For this reason, they argue, a special free trade area based on systematic economic cooperation for the whole region has a much better chance of success:

> A free trade area with reasonably free movement of *certain goods* within the region, without restricting individual countries too much in respect of domestic policy and trade, appears to be far more acceptable. Nevertheless, this will only be possible if the participating countries can reach agreement on a pattern of the degree of specialization to be permitted between the countries concerned. In Southern Africa, where many countries are still in the initial development planning stage such a pattern of specialization will be easier than in countries with long-established economies. Thorough co-ordinated planning can channel the economic development of these countries in specific directions.[103]

Although the 1970 customs union agreement between South Africa and the three former High Commission Territories indicates that rapid strides are being made toward eliminating obstacles in the way of a true common market among Lesotho, Swaziland, Botswana, and South Africa, Drs. Smit and van der Merwe quite rightly found that obstacles in the case of the remaining areas are both political and economic and are equally difficult to surmount. According to them, the factors which still impede trade with the Portuguese territories, Malawi, and Zambia are essentially four:[104]

First. Mozambique and Angola as overseas provinces are already part of the Portuguese free trade area, while, as former British dependencies, Zambia and Malawi share in the advantages of Commonwealth preferential tariffs. The close historical links between Zambia and Malawi (both were also members of the Central African Federation set up by Britain) do not favor the establishment of closer economic ties with South Africa. It is from the former metropole, Great Britain, that most of the development capital and grants are obtained.

Second. "Transport facilities were established to provide for the needs of trade with overseas countries, and not with a view to interregional trade in Southern Africa."[105]

Third. The variety of revenue-earning exports are limited to a few items. In the case of Zambia, copper accounted for 90.3 percent of all exports in 1965. This is a dominant pattern not only in Southern Africa (barring, of course, the Republic of South Africa and Rhodesia) but in all of Africa.

Fourth. The problem of too limited a range of exports, they observe,

> is intensified by the physical characteristics of the countries in Southern Africa that are responsible for production structures, particularly in the primary sector, which are more *competitive* with, than *complementary* to, that of the Republic of South Africa. For instance, South Africa is a net exporter of maize, and so are Angola, Rhodesia, Zambia and Malawi. Similarly, iron ore is exported by Angola, Rhodesia and South Africa; sugar is exported by Rhodesia, Mozambique, Angola

and the Republic. South Africa is largely self-sufficient in its sisal requirements, and hence does not import the surplus production of Mozambique and Angola. Numerous other examples could be quoted.

In general South Africa's resources are such that they provide little scope for greatly increased imports of primary products from these countries, which, again are highly dependent on these products for their economic development. Nevertheless, the Republic offers a significant market for tropical and sub-tropical products such as coffee, tea, rice, cashew nuts, hardwoods and cotton. Moreover the Republic does not produce enough wheat and meat for its own needs. Aluminium, lead, zinc, tin and particularly petroleum are mineral products which can also be imported from these countries rather than other foreign countris. Further investigation would, without doubt, also reveal other primary products which could be traded intraregionally.

Industrially these countries are, as yet, not far advanced. Consequently, it is difficult to determine, without detailed study, the prospects for an enlarged and more diversified intraregional flow of trade in manufactured products. . . . On the other hand, the Republic [of South Africa] is in a favourable position to provide manufactured, including capital, goods to these countries.[106]

Considering the various aspects of the economies of Southern African nations, Drs. Smit and van der Merwe argue that the only way to improve interstate trade in Southern Africa is by way of bilateral trade pacts.

> The trade agreements concluded with Rhodesia, Angola and Mozambique in 1964, and that with Malawi in 1967, are logical steps in this direction. It may, however, also be to the mutual advantage of the countries concerned (particularly in view of the small surpluses sometimes available for export) to devise regional marketing schemes for certain agricultural products, such as that with South West Africa and the B.L.S. countries [*i.e.*, Botswana, Lesotho, and Swaziland]. Indeed, an arrangement with Rhodesia and Mozambique was included in the trade agreements of 1964, whereby the citrus products of these two countries are marketed, together with those of South Africa, by the South African Citrus Board. The South African Banana Control Board also distributes bananas from Mozambique on a quota basis in the local market of the Republic [of South Africa].[107]

If we examine the argument of the fourth group, the Bureau for Economic Policy and Analysis in Pretoria, we find general agreement with the previous school (which favors a free trade area based on bilateral trade agreements) as to the chances of a common market for Southern Africa. Writing in *The Concept of Economic Co-operation in Southern Africa*, the bureau's research team states that the immediate target must be an increased intraregional flow of goods and decreased labor migration and extraregional trade, although it admits that

> at first sight it would seem that the achievement of . . . [this] target . . . is extremely idealistic, especially in view of the fact that three-quarters of the existing trade of the subcontinent is with trading partners outside the group. On the other hand, it is quite true that this large gap is an indication of the potential growth of inter-regional [*sic, i.e.*, intraregional] trade through the diversion of the extra-regional movement of goods and services. It is, however, hardly likely that this diversion of trade towards the members of the group will come about within the institutional arrangement of a so-called "common market" on lines similar to that of the European Economic Community.[108]

Furthermore, the bureau has pointed out that, in terms of economic theory, customs unions are worthwhile when they involve nations whose products are competitive until the union is formed and whose products may become less so and increasingly complementary following the formation of the union. Moreover, economic theory suggests that there cannot be too great a disparity among the member states of a customs union with respect to their economic development and maturation. In Southern Africa, then, the building of a customs union would not be apposite in terms of these lessons from economic theory.[109] Consequently, the bureau does not endorse the idea of a union and points out that

> what is needed is more diversification and the development of greater competitiveness in the various member states. This would . . . require the opposite of a common market and . . . [would require] certain protection of the industrial possibilities of the various regions. The protection would, however, have to take place within a broad overall plan for the subregion as a whole, with the very positive co-operation of the Republic of South Africa.[110]

The bureau comes out strongly in favor of upgrading the economic infrastructure of the component states of Southern Africa as a prelude to subsequent industrial development. Of course, the Republic of South Africa would play an important role in this process by providing both funds and expertise when requested to do so by the underdeveloped states in the region.[111]

Thus it appears that even though both schools reject the notion of a common market, the third school (represented by Drs. Smit and van der Merwe) views a common market as a future possibility, beginning with the maximum feasible number of bilateral trade agreements; the fourth school (represented by the bureau) rejects the common market idea even as a future development. Both the third and fourth schools agree on the impracticality of a common market fashioned on Western European lines, having the twin objectives of both economic and political integration. Indeed, the bureau asserted that its

> basic point of departure . . . was that the maximum measure of political sovereignty would, for the foreseeable future, have to be maintained and even developed among the . . . states in the [Southern African] group. . . . this political sovereignty could not be maintained on the basis of economic and technological isolation. Since [*sic*] full integration in the sense of relinquishing control over the functional participation in trade, finance and communication would also destroy . . . [the] idea of self-determination, we have suggested the principle of co-operation which was defined as that system in which each participating member would still retain control over the nature of . . . [its] participation in the system.[112]

However, neither the bureau nor anyone else for that matter believes that there must be an absence of controls over the supranational economic institutions which may emerge from regional cooperation. It is here that Dr. Verwoerd's concept of a commonwealth of states is germane because economic planning could be undertaken, for example, by a commonwealth economic directorate. The bureau recognizes such a possibility and concedes that there would have to be at least a partial limitation of the customary unilateral controls and that controls which are essentially political in nature should not be applied to the primary sector of the economy and should be permitted only in the secondary and tertiary sectors. Moreover, the bureau is cognizant of the central role of the free enterprise system and the concomitant importance of the quest for profits when it comes to regional economic development and cooperation.[113] With respect to the development of a regional economic infrastructure, the economists of the bureau have observed that

> the extent of political sovereignty would have to be severely limited by the technological nature of the processes. The cost differences between small micro units of power generation, irrigation projects and tele-communication [*sic*] systems, railway connections and even roads. . . and that of the giant units . . . would be such that the political authorities would, economically speaking, have very little choice between the one and the other. If their take-off into sustained industrial growth should materialize in practice, and a measure of self-respecting and satisfying political self-determination is to be achieved in this sphere, sovereignty would have to be relinquished in the field of technical co-operation. In this way, . . . [we could strive for] (1) *technological integration*, (2) *economic co-operation particularly in the industrial field*, and (3) *political independence*.[114]

On the subject of the development of regional services and the exploitation of regional natural resources there is very broad agreement. Both the third and fourth schools stress the great importance of the development of communications and power on a regional basis, seeing them as the principal technological requisites for any form of regional economic cooperation. Thoughtful research and analysis of the problems and possibilities of closer economic cooperation are particularly evident in the work of Drs. P. Smit and E. J. van der Merwe of the Africa Institute even though they did not stress technological integration as a takeoff point to the extent that the Bureau for Economic Policy did. "It is generally accepted that a modern physical infrastructure (traffic and communications network, power supply, etc.) is a prerequisite for economic growth," they wrote.[115] They also believe however, that the nature of the social infrastructure is of equal importance because a well-educated and/or technically competent and physically healthy population is a critical element in long-term economic advancement.[116]

In the scope of this chapter, however, we can only refer to the transport of goods, power, water supplies, and technical cooperation.

Drs. Smit and van der Merwe rightly stress that "underdevelopment and poor transport systems are usually closely related. Although the total population of Africa comprises 8.5% of the total world population, Africa provides only 1.8% of the world's rail freight."[117] They also point out that "Southern Africa consists of a few '*economic islands*' (the Southern Transvaal region, [the] Salisbury/Bulawayo area, and the Zambian Copperbelt), and farflung, relatively undeveloped areas with low population densities."[118] There is only a light railroad freight traffic among these three aforementioned developed areas because most African railway systems were originally developed with the sole purpose of carrying freight to the nearest harbor for shipment to the metropole—in this case, Great Britain. Thus, although there is a rail link between South Africa and Umtali, Rhodesia, the former is primarily dependent on coastal shipping for access to its markets adjacent to Umtali in central and northern Mozambique.[119] Therefore, Drs. Smit and van der Merwe recognize that the objective of increased bilateral trade cannot be achieved unless the communications system for handling this trade is vastly improved. Here again South Africa could play an important role because

> transport systems usually have to be built on a large scale and consequently big capital outlay is necessary. South Africa possesses the necessary heavy machinery and knowledge of similar environmental conditions to compete favourably with overseas companies. The construction and major share in the financing of the Swaziland railway line [to Mozambique], for example, has been made possible by South African companies.[120]

As in the case of transportation, South Africa is sufficiently developed and has a large enough consumer market to play a constructive role in the exploitation of the water and power resources of the sub-continent. The resources are there, but the cost of exploitation is such that only through cooperation between the various countries is there any hope for utilizing these resources on an economic basis. The mere fact that most of the major rivers of Southern Africa—such as the Zambezi, Limpopo, Kunene, Orange, and Usutu—are international rivers, forming boundaries, calls for careful planning in their development.[121] Most students of the subject, such as Drs. Smit and van der Merwe, agree that "no matter how essential the provision of cheap electrical power and water might be for development, the underdeveloped countries cannot undertake large projects to meet their own requirements and . . . such projects will only be feasible if markets for water and especially power are found *outside* the boundaries of the countries where the schemes are undertaken."[122] The tremendous increase in South Africa's consumption of electricity (the per capita use of generated units now equals that of Western Europe) during the past decade and the anticipated doubling of power requirements by 1980 has made it clear that a large enough market exists in South Africa to spur on the development of projects elsewhere in Southern Africa.[123] During the past decade units generated by South Africa's Electricity Supply Commission (ESCOM) have increased by about 8 percent annually.

To meet the demand for the future, South Africa will spend about $2.8 billion during the next two decades on the construction of power stations.[124] Currently, South Africa generates about 57 percent of all electricity produced in all of Africa. Bearing in mind the available hydroelectric resources and the need to provide power to the subcontinent for the development of the entire region, South African planners have drawn up a far-sighted program to link all of the subcontinent in a power grid. This is a further aid in the development of power projects elsewhere since in this way power generated outside South Africa can be delivered into the grid. South Africa, because of its need for more power, will form the principal market.[125] "The provision of cheap power," wrote Drs. Smit and van der Merwe, "will be a great stimulus for the development of these countries and South Africa can purchase the power until such time as the countries have themselves developed to the stage where they can take large quantities of power and South Africa's needs are large enough for it to utilize economically its own nuclear power stations."[126]

Water is also in ever increasing demand in South Africa, where the growth of population and the development of industries are such that by 1990 (that is, in twenty years' time) more than twice the present amount of water will be required. Within three decades, allowing for maximum development of local sources, South Africa will face a shortage of 27 percent in the country's water supply.[127] Thus, much the same way as in the case of electricity, South Africa forms a ready market for water supply projects in adjacent states. Therefore, many of the projects currently under way or in an advanced stage of planning include the supply not only of electricity but also of water to South Africa; examples include the Oxbow project in Lesotho and the plan to dam the Okavango in Botswana.

The nine major projects currently under construction or in the blueprint stage in Southern Africa are as follows: first, there is the Orange River hydroelectric project in South Africa which will cost $700 million and which will also benefit Botswana and South West Africa; second, there is the Cabora Bassa scheme in Mozambique on the Zambezi River which will cost about $364 million; third, there is the Oxbow scheme on the Madibamatso River in the Lesotho Highlands which is estimated to cost $44.8 million; fourth, there is a hydroelectric project on the Kunene River in South West Africa which will include a regulating dam at Matala and will be financed jointly by

South Africa and Portugal; fifth, there are plans to build a dam at Eriksson's Drift in South West Africa to divert water to Ovamboland as well as plans for a hydroelectric project at the Ruancana Falls; sixth, there is the Limpopo River dam, near Beit Bridge, which will be financed by South Africa; seventh, there are plans for damming the rivers of Swaziland for the purpose of generating electricity; eighth, there is the Kafue hydroelectric scheme near Lusaka, Zambia, which will cost an estimated $98 million; and, ninth, there is the Okavango River project in Botswana, which was mentioned previously.[128]

Reviewing various studies and discussions on the question of closer economic cooperation, the editor of the well-known South African journal, *News Check*, came to these conclusions which seem representative of government and private opinion on this subject:

> It is beguiling to look upon Southern Africa as a Common Market or a Free Trade Area, and this must surely come in time. But at present Southafrica's [*sic*] neighbours primarily need to build up their own industries—and to do this behind protective barriers. Free trade for the moment would only benefit Southafrica [*sic*], for thus, with its dominant position, it would take all things unto itself. In view of its long-term interest, however, Southafrica [*sic*] would be wise to be reticent in using its economic power. It should be prepared to buy from neighbours, give them a chance, and not force its goods upon them. So can Southern Africa move to a situation where all its component nations are developed, and then the great logic of modern economics will begin: developed nations simply do far better business with each other than with undeveloped nations, and this is the prize for which Southern Africa should reach out. When all-round development is attained, Southern Africa will indeed be on to something big. It will have a market of the dimensions necessary to sustain true mass production, its market will be big enough for competitive disciplines to have a fully beneficial effect. This is worth working for.
>
> Economically then, Southern Africa should see itself far more in the light of a Development Community. Where trade has brought Europe together, so can the goal of development bring Southern Africa together. Development is the one aim that all its people have in common, and it should be the guiding strand. This puts a heavy burden on Southafrica [*sic*], but if it wishes to make anything of the Southern African concept at all, then it must be willing to withhold its potential dominance. And that is only right.
>
> What applies in the economic sphere, applies equally in the political. The withholding of economic dominance is directly related to the chief political prerequisite which makes a new kind of Southern Africa possible. That is the principle of independence and its corollaries of respect for nations and of non-interference in others' affairs.[129]

The key, however, is development—development of Southern Africa's resources, of its people's skills, education, and standard of living—so that by the end of the century the regional development would be borne by 100 million people and not merely by the population of the economically advanced states of South Africa and Rhodesia or by Portugal. At the present rate of development, it may take another 343 years before the average black African catches up with his white counterpart in the United States in standard of living,[130] but in Southern Africa it could possibly be achieved in only thirty years. To reach this objective, Southern Africa requires more foreign capital investment and less foreign intervention in domestic political affairs. It also requires the assurance that the great powers—and particularly the United Nations—will not continue to turn a blind eye on the terrorist and guerrilla raids across international boundaries which are hindering developments in the South. Southern Africa needs to marshal its capital, manpower, mineral and hydroelectric resources in the best possible way. Clearly, the way to do this is by drawing closer together, thus giving Southern Africa a weight far greater than its individual nations have today.

As we have shown in this chapter, there have been some important economic studies on the possibilities of a Southern African common market. The *idea* is gaining headway and whatever form of economic cooperation it may take, more and more people are seeing the opportunity for the states of Southern Africa to build some kind of community of nations, an entity of independent countries coming together in their own interests and thereby improving race relations in a way which no amount of political rhetoric can accomplish.[131] Others are investing heavily in the growth of this new regionalism, as illustrated by the fact that the world's first comprehensive *Encyclopedia of Southern Africa* is being published in 1970 by the firm of *Nasionale Boekhandel* in Cape Town. The twenty-five volumes of this encyclopedia cost in the region of $4.2 million to prepare and publish.[132]

South Africa, the linchpin in the structure, is actively pursuing a policy of cooperation with the other African states.[133] As the influential editor of the Cape Town Afrikaans newspaper, *Die Burger*, observed in his address to the South Africa Club in London in October 1968,

> Our success or failure will probably remain in the balance for years of gruelling groundwork. This much, however, is obvious: South Africa can pack a lot of economic, technological and cultural power into her good-neighbour policy. What is more, there are almost daily signs that the idea is catching on at the expense of the isolationist mood which prevailed in the early 'sixties. . . .
>
> All this is now building up to something like a national endeavour, driven by a central creative idea which is flexible and adaptable enough to draw the interest and co-operation of divergent elements in South African society.[134]

Farther afield, the prospect of a community of nations of Southern Africa is truly exciting. It not only offers the individual states of Southern Africa an opportunity to get out of their shells and to share in something bigger, but it also guarantees the political stability of the region which, in turn, creates favorable conditions for their rapid economic growth. The West should support, rather than obstruct, South Africa by desisting from actions which may win a largely meaningless vote at the General Assembly of the United Nations and a favorable headline in the Afro-Asian press but which do not improve the outlook for a longer and better life for a single black African. Not very much can be accomplished in Southern Africa without the concurrence or assistance of South Africa or contrary to its will and national interests, yet much could be accomplished with its cooperation. *Tempora mutantur, nos et mutamur in illis.*[135]

4

The Military Balance in Southern Africa

CHARLES W. PETERSEN

In addition to the political and economic ingredients in the Southern African context, the military should not be overlooked. In view of the present guerrilla warfare in parts of the region, such an assessment should be of major import in establishing the range of possibilities for the future course of developments in the entire nexus south of the Zambezi River. This chapter will analyze the following six topics: (1) terrain and climatic considerations; (2) the logical combatants: the white-controlled areas; (3) the logical combatants: the African states; (4) the probable neutrals; (5) combat events, 1961–1969; and (6) the future course of armed struggle.

Terrain and Climatic Conditions

Proper utilization of terrain and climatic factors can be a major determinant of battlefield success. One of the most prominent guerrilla leaders in all history, Mao Tse-tung, stresses the need for secure base areas from which one's forces can strike out at the more numerous enemy. He states that mountains offer the best sanctuary for insurgents, particularly if they are extensive and allow room for maneuver. Next in desirability as a guerrilla base are river-lake-estuary regions. There high grasses can shield soldiers, and at the same time leave them free to strike out against water-borne commerce. Least desirable are the plains since they provide scanty cover except when the "green curtain" of summer vegetation covers the land.[1]

The western coast of Angola, South West Africa, and South Africa is mostly desert or semi-arid land. There are only two exceptions to this generalization. At the continent's southern tip, around Cape Town, there is a Mediterranean climate. Much farther north, in Cabinda and northern Angola, the low latitude wet and dry climate predominates. High temperatures throughout the year and an alternating wet and dry season are characteristic of this zone. The vegetation is composed of mixed savanna grasses and semideciduous trees. Such an area is well suited to guerrilla operations as events have already proved. Tree cover is heavy enough to provide protection against the limited airpower which the Portuguese use to patrol the extensive area. Should events lead to a major conventional war, the wet season in northern Angola could, indeed, hinder motorized troop and supply movements.[2]

The Namib Desert, the western valley of the Orange River, and the Great Karroo present a 1,500-mile stretch of land along Africa's southwest coast that is very arid. Such dry desert areas are poorly suited to guerrilla activity due to the lack of cover. In the days of Lawrence of Arabia or the Boer commandos this was not especially consequential. Nowadays, with air reconnaissance and accurate strike capability, small bands operating without heavy antiaircraft weapons are at a severe disadvantage.

There are two stretches of land in this dry region, however, where guerrilla bands could successfully operate. One is the mountainous region along the Orange River between its confluence with the Atlantic and Aughrabies Falls, some three hundred miles into the heart of Cape Province. In this rugged landscape, guerrilla bands would be hard to find, but they themselves would have difficulty living off the land. Also, they would be so far from any major inhabited area as to pose little threat to the government. The other area is Ovamboland. In northern South West Africa, this region has considerable growth of thick semitropical forest. Such heavy and tangled vegetation provides an excellent shield for roving bands against hostile reconnaissance aircraft. Due to the inhospitable terrain and government policy, few whites inhabit Ovamboland, and the Africans there might be expected to provide at least food for revolutionary groups.[3] Finally, the proximity of friendly Zambia would give guerrillas the same type of staging and training sanctuary which the Viet Cong presently enjoys in Cambodia.[4]

Should events escalate to the point of conventional war, the terrain of southwestern Africa, with the exception of the Orange River and Ovamboland areas, would lend itself to a mobile form of combat. Armor, artillery, and airpower would dominate the fast-changing battlefield, much as they did in North Africa in 1941 or in Sinai in 1966. Even if Angola proved untenable, the white regimes could set up a defense in depth behind the Kunene River along the Angola–South West Africa border or along the Orange River in South Africa. The only drawback from the defensive point of view is the inconstant depth of these

waterways. At times raging torrents, both streams on other occasions deteriorate to fordable rivulets. Present efforts by the South African government to harness and control the Orange and its tributaries more closely could eventually keep the river's depth more constant and thereby serve as a major invasion barrier.[5]

The central region of Southern Africa also has a diversity of climate and terrain. Most of interior Angola, Rhodesia, and Zambia is covered with forest or grassland. As in northern Angola, there is a dry season followed by a wet one. From May through October there are less than 5 inches of rainfall. Then, for the rest of the year, precipitation increases markedly, with anywhere from 10 to 40 inches falling during the period. If the rainy season is particularly prolonged, grass grows very high in the Zambezi and other river valleys. This aids infiltrators from Zambia and facilitates surreptitious movement of small armed groups from one area to another. The region is well above sea level, being part of the Central African Plateau. Scrubby mapani bush covers much of the uncultivated areas and grows thickly enough to provide effective cover. Mixed in with the mapani is thorn growth which can be a severe irritant to lightly clad patrol forces.[6]

To the southwest of Rhodesia lies semiarid Botswana. About two-thirds of this dry country is covered with scrubby acacia and commiphora growth. The north and northeast is somewhat less arid, particularly from November through April, but its most dominant feature, the Okavango Basin, is an unhealthy area. This marshy region just south of the Zambezi River has never been developed, due partially to the apparent lack of minerals and prevalent tsetse fly which is a deterrent to ranching. Roads in Botswana are very limited, and those in existence would better be called tracks. During the rainy season they are washed out as freshets suddenly arise and tear across the dry landscape. The Okavango Swamp seems to be the only area in the country suitable for a guerrilla base.

It is along the eastern coast of Southern Africa that terrain and climate considerations seem most conducive to revolutionary warfare. Along the entire coast of Mozambique it is humid and tropical. During the rainy season from November through April, much of this area receives as much rainfall as the Congo Basin and rarely less than 40 inches. Vegetation grows profusely and land must be closely cultivated or it returns to jungle. Thousands of acres near the coast have been brought to useful productivity and plantations of sisal, cotton, and cashew nuts dot the countryside.

Further inland, the natural vegetation changes to a mixture of savanna and forested land. In some areas, such as the high tableland near Lake Malawi, the land is quite hospitable. Much of the interior is forbidding bush, however, and has never attracted much European settlement. The tsetse fly is a persistent hazard to livestock. Dirt roads and sandy tracks penetrate most areas, but these become impassable during the rainy season and often wash away entirely. Already, determined guerrillas operate extensively in this rough terrain, aided by a sanctuary in nearby Tanzania.

Moving south into the eastern region of South Africa and Swaziland, a gradual shift in terrain and climate may be noted. This area has four distinct seasons, with warm summers and cold winters. Mixed forests, at times coniferous and at others broadleaf deciduous, are found. The Drakensberg Mountains are bleak and unforested at the higher elevations. Cold and frost are not restricted to the mountain zones. During the winter months many parts of the interior plateau are frequently hit by sharp frosts.[7]

Should Mozambique pass from European control, an invasion from the area of Lourenço Marques into South Africa's eastern coastal belt might be possible. This coastal belt, which varies from three to thirty miles wide, is one of the most fertile stretches of land in the whole country. It extends from Mozambique to Cape Town and, besides being agriculturally important, contains excellent seaports. South African defensive efforts, however, would be facilitated by the narrowness of the plain, proximity to the sea and supporting naval gunfire, and a number of small rivers which flow down from the Drakensberg into the sea. Unless opposing African forces possessed overwhelming numerical superiority, it is doubtful that such an invasion would succeed, although if the Europeans were defeated loss of the coastal belt would cut off the great inland mountains and tableland from the sea and thus seriously threaten continued European rule.

Should conventional warfare break out on a major scale, it is also conceivable that African states might launch a direct assault from Zambia through Rhodesia and into the northern districts of South Africa. The road and rail systems in Rhodesia are extensive and could support the movement of large military forces. Aircraft from Zambia could effectively support such a drive, while the superiority of South Africa's navy would be of little consequence for such an inland campaign. Several facts on the debit side for invading forces should be noted, however. The northern Transvaal, which would have to be crossed, is dry and scrubby. Only one railroad line leads southward from Beit Bridge, Rhodesia, into the Transvaal. Two major rivers, the Zambezi and Limpopo, and a number of smaller ones would have to be crossed by invaders, probably in the face of determined resistance from the ground and air. Obviously, it would be a substantial undertaking and one which could be successfully accomplished only by well-trained and well-equipped soldiers.

As long as the African states continue to lack resources for such a direct frontal thrust, they may concentrate their military efforts on guerrilla activity in eastern South Africa. To initiate such warfare will not be easy, however. Parts of the Drakensberg Mountains are sparsely inhabited but they are cold and guerrilla fires could easily be spotted. The climate is much warmer in the sparsely populated northern Transvaal, but that area is also only minutes away in flying time from major airfields. Then, too, successful new mining ventures, such as that of the Palabora Mining Company at Loolekop, are bringing about the development of roads and reducing the isolation of the region.[8]

For a successful staging area, guerrillas need isolation, cover from aircraft, and a sympathetic local populace. No area in eastern South Africa seems to possess all these attributes. In summary, climate and terrain will indeed have an effect on the military events in Southern Africa. Guerrilla operations could be carried on with relative ease in much of the Portuguese territories and Rhodesia, but in South West Africa and South Africa only a few isolated regions seem conducive to partisan operations. A large-scale conventional assault on the South is not likely to be mounted in the near future, but it should not be ruled out as a possibility if the African states to the North gain in strength and unity.

Should such a major invasion materialize, it is interesting to speculate about its possible course. Invaders would do well to avoid the dry west coast, with its poor roads, supply problems, and vulnerability to air attack from South Africa's superior air force. A direct assault from Tanzania down along the east coast would entail having to cross a dozen easily defended rivers and having to contend with naval gunfire from the South African and Portuguese fleets. Thus the assault with the highest probability of success would most likely come from Zambia, through Rhodesia, and into the heart of the Witwatersrand and into Lourenço Marques. Invaders would have to negotiate difficult crossings of the Zambezi and Limpopo Rivers, but with close air support from Zambian bases this would not be impossible. If the attack were launched by surprise, there seems little doubt that the Zambezi at least could be crossed, resistance brushed aside, and the heartland of Rhodesia opened to invading columns. Before white Rhodesia could be mobilized and other European reinforcements arrive, it is possible that the country could be overrun. Continuance of the attack across the Limpopo would be more difficult and chances for success problematical, since a forewarned South Africa could rally powerful defensive forces. Nevertheless, African victory would be possible, given sufficient manpower, weaponry, air support, and well-timed harassing attacks by guerrilla bands in European rear areas.[9]

The Logical Combatants: The White-Controlled Areas

SOUTH AFRICA

At one time South Africa did not need a large military establishment. The region was far from world trouble spots, and it could rely on Great Britain for military protection against attack. Times have changed and with them alliances. In a confrontation with black Africa, South Africa feels that Great Britain would not support it. Therefore, South Africa has found it necessary to build up a powerful independent military establishment to safeguard its position. The magnitude of this military growth is graphically indicated by a few statistics. From 1960 to 1964 the South African military expenditure grew by almost 500 percent (from $61.6 million to $294 million).[10] In 1966 the nation spent $400 million on the military. This was three times the Moroccan and five times the Algerian defense budgets.[11] Should a major showdown occur, it is this nation's military might which would be the single most important determinant regarding continued white control of South Africa. For that reason each branch of that nation's military deserves separate comment.

The navy operates principally from the former Royal Navy base at Simonston near Cape Town where there are both a full dockyard and repair facilities. There are also good docking and support facilities at cities all along the coast from Walvis Bay in South West Africa to Durban. As of 1965 South African naval personnel consisted of 270 officers and 2,700 enlisted men. While many senior officers studied in British defense colleges, all training is now carried out in South Africa. Major training centers are maintained at Simonston, Wingfield, and Gordons Bay in the Cape Peninsula, Saldanha Bay on the west coast, and at Durban. Besides instruction in basic seamanship at all these centers, Saldanha Bay offers a degree in military science. The latest innovation was the establishment of a torpedo and antisubmarine school at Simonston in 1967.[12]

The navy has no heavy gun ships or aircraft carriers, but concentrates on vessels of the escort type.[13] Its pride are the three "President" class antisubmarine frigates which were completed in the early 1960s. They were built in Glasgow yards, along the same design as the Royal Navy's "Witby" class frigates of the late 1950s. Although British policy was already turning against South Africa at the time these vessels were constructed, the desire to provide shipyard employment apparently outweighed ideological considerations. Nomenclature for these vessels was drawn from the pages of the nation's history—*President Kruger*, *President Pretorius*, and *President Steyn*. Primarily designed for the detection and destruction of the most modern types of submarine, these vessels are of all-welded construction to save weight. Their geared turbine-propelling machinery will push them to a speed of 31 knots, which would be impossible for most submarines to outrun. Each ship has two Limbo three-barreled depth-bomb mortars plus two 4.5-inch twin gun mounts as well as lighter antiaircraft armament.

Backing up the "President" frigates are a number of older escort vessels. Three of these are former British "W" class destroyers which were built in Scotland during World War II. Purchased from Great Britain ten years ago, they were rechristened *Jan van Riebeeck*, *Simon van der Stel*, and *Vrystaat*. The former two vessels each carry two Westland Wasp helicopters, significantly increasing their reconnaissance and antisubmarine capability. These two ships also bear four 21-inch torpedo tubes which give them an offensive capability against even larger naval units. All three vessels carry 4-inch main batteries and 40-mm. Bofors flak defense. With a maximum speed of over 31 knots, they provide a powerful strike force when combined with the "President" class vessels. They could easily conduct raids on the harbors of many black African countries.

Considerably slower, but nevertheless effective, naval units are the two former "Loch" class frigates *Good Hope* and *Transvaal*. They were built in Scotland late in World War II and immediately presented to South Africa. They carry 4-inch main batteries, 40-mm. Bofors, and Squid triple-barreled depth-charge mortars. Designed for convoy protection, their fuel tanks allow them to cover 9,500 miles at 12-knot convoy speed. In case of war, they would be ideal for protection of merchant ships bringing supplies to South Africa. Their guns would also be useful for supporting troops on shore, but their relatively slow maximum speed of 18 knots makes them unsuitable for raiding operations northward. The *Good Hope* serves as a training vessel, and one further "Loch" class ship, the *Natal*, has had all weapons removed and is classified as a survey ship.

Three submarines are presently being built in French yards for South Africa. These vessels are of the "Daphne" class and are designed for conventional torpedo attack. Each ship has twelve

21.7-inch torpedo tubes; eight of these are in the bow while four are in the stern. France has been building submarines of this class since the early 1960s, and when South Africa takes possession of the three vessels under construction they will provide a formidable addition to her offensive capability.

It is recognized that mines could provide a threat to South Africa's ports and sealanes. To counter this threat, the navy built up a considerable minesweeper force. Most powerful of the minesweepers are two former British vessels of the "Algerine" class. These ships, the *Bloemfontein* and *Pietermaritzburg*, are almost thirty years old now but still perform active service. While the *Bloemfontein*'s 4-inch and Bofors guns have been dismantled and the *Pietermaritzburg* serves as a midshipmen's training vessel, both could be quickly reconverted to ocean minesweeping service should the situation demand this.

Less powerful, but more modern and numerous, are ten "Ton" class coastal minesweepers. These craft were built in Britain during the late 1950s and are capable of dealing with either contact- or influence-type mines. They bear only light antiaircraft armament and are suitable for sweeping along the continent's south shore or coastal convoying, but not midocean work. They are named after South African cities: *Durban*, *East London*, *Johannesburg*, *Kaapstad*, *Kimberley*, *Mosselbaai*, *Port Elizabeth*, *Pretoria*, *Walvisbaai*, and *Windhoek*.

Rounding out the nation's navy are several types of harbor defense craft. There are two formerly British boom defense vessels of the "Bar" class. These small ships are designed to place protective nets across harbor entrances to impede the entrance of submarines. Named *Somerset* and *Fleur*, these small craft provide security for anchored merchant vessels. Five seaward defense boats—*Gelderland*, *Haerlem*, *Nautilus*, *Osterland*, and *Rijger*—add to this capability. They are also designed to detect and destroy submersibles in the approaches to ports. Their small size and shallow draft enable them to probe inshore waters in search of midget submarines. They were built in Britain in the period from 1953 to 1957.

Overall, the South African navy is powerful enough to protect the country's shoreline against most probable adversaries in Africa. A shore-based Decca radar navigational system is developed which can pinpoint the location of an offshore vessel to within twenty-five yards. This should be a substantial help to the navy in protecting the coast against raiders or ships bringing in infiltrators. For offensive purposes, the nation's fast frigates and destroyers could raid enemy harbors farther north and provide gunfire support for army ground troops or raiding parties.

The South African army is small, but highly professional. The number of men in active service varies slightly from month to month but is usually around nineteen thousand to twenty thousand. The army is well equipped and France has become a major supplier of military hardware. The United States and Great Britain have placed an arms embargo on the country, but South Africa manufactures 140 different varieties of ammunition and armaments and suffers little from the embargo. Some of the armaments manufactured locally are the entire range of infantry weapons and a considerable quantity of electronic equipment.[14]

The army has not taken part in regular warfare since World War II, but in recent years the defense command has given increasing attention to counterinsurgency techniques, while not neglecting plans against a conventional invasion. In 1968 a major exercise in unconventional warfare was carried out on the Rhodesian border. Several thousand troops were involved, as well as tactical aircraft of the South African Air Force. Such a maneuver not only gave excellent practice in anti-infiltration procedure but also, since it was well publicized, gave warning to invaders that they will be met by a trained and ready defending force.[15]

The army has five thousand five hundred to five thousand seven hundred career soldiers and the remainder of men in active service are called Citizen Force trainees. From thirteen thousand to seventeen thousand of these trainees are on active duty at any given time. The Citizen Force is similar to the British Territorial Army or the United States Army Reserve. These men spend three months of very comprehensive training, similar to the basic and advanced infantry courses of the United States Army. Then they go on to six more months of more specialized training or posting to a garrison somewhere in the country. Thereafter, they are required to spend four years on active reserve status with frequent meetings and drills. This is a shorter time in service than the American draftee spends, but the nation's severe shortage of white labor in industry demands that as few men as possible be tied up in military service. At the same time the system has led to a sizeable buildup of reserve manpower. A reliable estimate notes that the nation now has one hundred and forty-five thousand men trained for military service, and that twenty thousand of them could be in the field within an hour.[16]

South Africa also has the Commando Force, an organization somewhat similar to the American National Guard. This force provides security in the rural areas. Its members put in a week or two of full-time training each year and this is supplemented by periodic weekend drills. A special school for commandos has been established at Bloemfontein and different units are brought here to improve their training. There are about 51,500 men in the Commando Force, divided into 210 separate units. Each unit averages about two hundred and fifty men and is a highly mobile strike force, with its own infantry and armored car section and attached air support. The Air Commandos are organized into twelve squadrons with about two hundred and fifty aircraft, some privately owned.[17] The fast-moving commando units with their armored cars seem ideally suited to stamp out small-scale rebellion, and with air reconnaissance they have the capability to follow and harry a pedestrian enemy to extinction. Such was actually the case in 1961 in Pondoland.[18]

Mention should be made of South Africa's large police establishment. The nation has nearly thirty thousand active police and six thousand reservists. They possess 430 riot trucks and 80 armored cars to increase their mobility.[19] The police are synchronized with the regular military through legislative action, and this symbiotic relationship maximizes the counterinsurgency potential of the government.[20] Through their ubiquitous presence and the continual nature of their contact and coverage of a limited area, the police are able to maintain close surveillance over Africans and Europeans alike. They are aided by an informer system which is quite extensive. The ratio of police to civilian population is about 1:535 in South Africa. This compares unfavorably with United States figures of 1:430 but very favorably to the figures throughout the rest of Africa.[21]

The South African Air Force (SAAF) is a powerful fighting force which should be able to support ground forces, defend its home territory, and carry out missions deep into enemy regions. The mainstays of the air force are the two Sabre Mk. 6 interceptor squadrons with about thirty-eight planes which operate out of Waterkloof Air Station on the outskirts of Pretoria. These 600-mph aircraft are armed with 30-mm. cannon and machine guns and are suitable for interceptor or ground support roles in combat. With the addition of auxiliary fuel tanks to fuselage or wings, the Sabre has a combat radius of over 600 miles. Many of the Sabre pilots and ground crews are combat veterans, since No. 2 squadron fought with the United Nations in Korea. "The Flying Cheetahs" racked up over two thousand sorties in three years of action and veterans of this organization, numbering over eight hundred pilots and ground personnel, provide a valuable combat-seasoned nucleus for the newer airmen.[22]

Less numerous, but even more modern, is the SAAF's squadron of 16 Mirage IIIC fighter-bombers which were purchased from France. These aircraft, especially when vectored in by

slower propeller planes, are well suited to support ground troops, for the Mirage proved itself as a potent weapon during the 1967 Arab-Israeli War. Besides having pinpoint strike capability, the speedy jets were able to take a tremendous number of hits from light antiaircraft defenses and still return safely to base.[23] These aircraft either mount conventional cannon or the Nord AS.30 tactical air-to-surface missile, which is manufactured in France. This missile uses a pilot-operated radio-command guidance system and carries a 550-pound high-explosive warhead. It has a range of 7.5 miles.[24]

An airfield has been strategically built in the Caprivi Zipfel from which these planes could fly into Zambia, Botswana, or Angola. Construction of this airfield would seem to be in violation of the mandate's prohibition against militarizing South West Africa but, as world opinion has turned so sharply against South Africa anyway, Pretoria reasoned that strategic considerations outweighed adverse foreign opinion.[25]

Long-range air reconnaissance is provided by a squadron of seven Shackleton propeller planes. These slow but reliable craft are used for training purposes during peacetime. Their long air endurance and slow speed would give them the capability to provide cover for merchant ships far out in the Atlantic and Indian Oceans in wartime. From bases in Angola they could range far north into the Gulf of Guinea to provide reconnaissance for naval forays into that region. They could also carry mines for deposition off Matadi, Takoradi, or other African ports. The air force also has eighteen Buccaneer reconnaissance aircraft for patrol duties.[26]

The Air Commando forces which operate in support of rural ground detachments are mainly equipped with Harvard aircraft. These single-engined propeller planes are relatively slow, but are excellent for ground support or reconnaissance for faster jets. The Air Commandos operate six to eight squadrons of these aircraft with two hundred aircraft in active service. Three hundred more Harvards are kept in storage and many of these could be brought into service should the need arise. Each Harvard is fitted with bomb holders for eight 191-pound fragmentation bombs; thus they represent a powerful antiguerrilla deterrent. With such a large number of planes of one type available, South Africa has little to fear from a spare parts embargo from overseas, for most of its older planes could be cannibalized.[27]

South Africa has begun to build its own aircraft industry. At Dempton Park, about thirty miles from Pretoria, the Atlas Aircraft Corporation has constructed a major plant and skilled workers have been lured from many parts of the world. A multipurpose jet aircraft called the Impala is being produced. The Impala is small and technically simple; when it comes into service in large numbers it will probably replace the Harvards used by the Air Commandos. Thus it is significant that South Africa now has an independent aircraft industry and does not have to rely on purchases from abroad.[28]

In summary, South Africa possesses a large, modern military force. The configurations of defense forces are geared either to anti-insurgent activity or to blocking any major push from the North for, in addition to the regular forces, there are large and well-trained commando units and a sizeable police force. Even if Rhodesia and the Portuguese provinces should come under African control, South Africa would remain a formidable opponent.

RHODESIA

Landlocked Rhodesia has only about 220,000 whites and 4 million Africans. Through its UDI decision and subsequent elections, the European electorate has clearly indicated its desire to continue the status quo of "civilized government," segregated neighborhoods, and minority control by Europeans. Under such control the African populace has shown increasing restiveness and the government has been forced to build up the armed forces since 1965.[29]

Rhodesia maintains a regular army of 3,400 men. About one thousand soldiers are Africans; the rest are whites. The regular army is composed of three major units—the Rhodesian African Rifles, the Rhodesian Light Infantry, and the Special Air Services. The latter unit is a small, elite counterguerrilla detachment which can be brought by helicopter anywhere in the country within a very short time. The African regulars are all in the Rhodesian African Rifles which was considered a strong fighting force during World War II. In more recent years morale problems have developed within the unit and in April 1966 a mutiny occurred. It was quickly suppressed but some question persists as to the reliability of these soldiers. Upward mobility is limited for African soldiers even in this unit, as official policy states that all officers must be European. The Rhodesian Light Infantry was formed in 1960 and is an all-white outfit.

Backing up the regular army are four battalions of active Territorial Reserves. Four second-line battalions bring the total reserve force to eight thousand. Europeans are conscripted for nine months of military service, followed by three years in the active Territorial Reserves. They then pass on to inactive status and will not be called back into service except in national emergency.[30]

The Rhodesian police, which go by the misleading name of the British South Africa Police (BSAP), number about 6,400 regulars and 28,500 reservists. Whites account for about one-third of the regulars and three-fourths of the reservists. With increasing unrest in the country, there is a modest buildup of police forces under way and armored cars are now among the equipment of some detachments. The BSAP carries out recruiting activities in South Africa, apparently with the blessing of the National party government there.[31]

When Prime Minister Sir Roy Welensky ordered a partial callup of the nation's reserves in 1961, it placed a severe strain on the economy and administration. Now, under sanctions, Prime Minister Ian Smith will certainly be reluctant to disrupt the economy with a major mobilization unless the most severe crisis develops. South Africa recognizes the manpower problems of her northern neighbor and, as mentioned earlier, has been willing to help. As a consequence of talks between Rhodesian and South African military officers on common problems, the latter had furnished considerable direct military support for counterinsurgency service in Rhodesia by late 1968.[32] This policy is likely to continue as the major political parties in South Africa agree on helping Rhodesia. Sir de Villiers Graaff, the leader of the opposition in South Africa, has stated publicly that Rhodesia "is fighting as much for South Africa's survival as their own," while Prime Minister John Vorster has observed that "we are good friends and good friends do not need an agreement. Good friends know what their duty is when the neighbor's house is on fire. We shall act in any country where we are asked to act by the government of that country."[33]

Being landlocked, Rhodesia has no navy but the nation maintains an air force. For troop-carrying purposes there are both helicopters and fixed-wing aircraft. The helicopters—apparently, there are less than a dozen—are French-produced Alouettes. The fixed-wing aircraft are twelve Aer-Macchi-Lockheed types which were shipped in from Italy in defiance of sanctions. These small troop carriers are designed to land in a limited area—such as a highway or patch of open savanna land. They supplement the helicopters for moving the Special Air Services detachments of the army into trouble spots with dispatch.[34]

The air force also exhibits potent striking power. There are twelve British-made Hawker Hunter jet fighters. These swept-wing aircraft may be used as fighter-bombers for ground support since they carry a varied armament. This usually consists of four 30-mm. Aden cannons and two 500-pound bombs. With minor adjustments this plane can also carry air-to-air missiles, which South Africa may manufacture in the near future. If they are subjected to hard wartime usage, the Hunters could run into a shortage of spare parts for their Rolls-Royce turbojet engines if Britain continues to maintain sanctions. For strategic bombing purposes there are fifteen Canberra jets. Manufactured by English Electric and powered by twin Rolls-Royce turbojets, these planes could also have spare parts and engine replacement problems. However, the Canberra was produced in large numbers and sold to many countries by the British, and it is probable that these items can be procured elsewhere. The Canberra can operate at altitudes of over 50,000 feet, has a level speed in excess of 640 mph, and a range of 3,000 miles. The Hunters and Canberras, if used as a unified strike force, have the capability of dealing a severe blow to any military or civilian target as far north as the equator. Should Rhodesia itself be overrun, these aircraft could continue to operate from Portuguese or South African bases. The total strength of the Rhodesian Air Force is 900 men and 75 aircraft.[35]

Thus Rhodesia has a small but compact military force. Two percent of the white population is presently in the armed service and a full 18 percent would be called into army and police units in case of full mobilization. Rhodesia is maintaining more of its whites in service than neighboring South Africa, where the number in active service is about 1 percent and would increase to 5 percent under mobilization.[36] There is some use of African manpower in the Rhodesian army and police force, but recent recruiting for both organizations has focused primarily on enlarging European participation.

PORTUGAL

As a member of the North Atlantic Treaty Organization (NATO), Portugal is committed to share in the defense of Western Europe. Increasingly since 1961, however, it has been forced to employ most of its armed forces in defense of its overseas provinces. These efforts have succeeded in keeping all the provinces except those in India. At the same time Portugal has reduced its military presence in Europe and in the metropolitan islands. The decrease of the regular army in these areas has been supplanted by several paramilitary organizations. The *Polícia Internacional e de Defesa do Estado* (PIDE) (International Police for the Defense of the State) is a secret police force patterned on the German Gestapo. Its leadership was trained by the Germans and Italians during the 1930s. The PIDE operates effectively throughout Portugal with an efficient informer system. Its director is usually an army officer, insuring close cooperation with the regular military. The *Policia de Seguranca Publica* (PSP) (Police for Public Security) and the *Guarda Nacional Republicana* (GNR) (National Republican Guard) operate in urban and rural areas respectively.

The *Legião Portuguesa* (Portuguese Legion), *Guarda Fiscal* (Fiscal Guard), and *Polícia Judiciária* (Judiciary Police) are other paramilitary organizations which help maintain internal security.[37]

Portugal is spending a large percentage of its national budget on defense, particularly in support of the military in Africa. In 1969, 40 percent of the national budget was earmarked for that purpose.[38] Such an expenditure makes sense only if one considers the economic potential of Portuguese Africa. Apparently encouraged by Lisbon's determined stand in Angola and Mozambique, foreign firms have poured in heavy capital investment to tap the resources of both provinces. The West German firm of Krupp has signed a $65 million contract for iron ore extraction in Angola. The American Tenneco Angola Inc. has indicated a willingness to expend large sums in development of a 260,000-acre sulphur concession. If the Cabora Bassa dam project succeeds in providing 4 million additional acres of irrigated land in Mozambique, as many experts say it will, the economic expansion of the African provinces will become agricultural as well as mineral.[39]

In mainland Portugal, opposition to the war seems to have found little expression. There are several reasons for this. Military losses have been rather low. From 1961 until 1965 less than five hundred soldiers lost their lives overseas, and the rate of casualties has increased only slightly since then. Portugal's press is controlled and the citizens receive only that news from Africa which is likely to encourage their nationalistic spirit. Increased income to servicemen's families has boosted morale. Finally, the hostility of some of Portugal's former friends as well as international organizations has hardened the Portuguese stand as it has that of South Africa and Rhodesia.[40]

Estimates of Portuguese army strength vary, but apparently there are about sixty-two thousand soldiers fighting for Lisbon in Angola and a slightly smaller number engaged in Mozambique. Thus three out of every four soldiers wearing the Portuguese uniform are committed to Africa.[41] This massive buildup of forces has taken place entirely during the last ten years.

There were only about 1,000 white troops in all Angola in 1958–1959. The suddenness of the 1961 revolt and its devastating effectiveness[42] convinced Portuguese planners that the tedious movement of soldiers by sea was not always satisfactory. For troop airlift purposes, as well as generally to improve communications, the government established *Transportes Aeros Portugueses*, a private airline under government auspices designed to link the territories to the metropole and to facilitate the transfer of reserve forces to any troubled region.

The Portuguese army makes considerable use of African troops in Angola and Mozambique, although the percentage of blacks to whites in the military has dropped sharply since the infusion of large numbers of whites in the past few years. Though many units are all-white, racial prejudice does not seem to be overt in the forces. Several Africans have reached officer ranks in the army and command their own detachments. Men recruited from the Kwanhama tribe of southern Angola are reputed to have performed especially useful service along the Congo border.[43]

Morale among Portuguese troops seems to have remained relatively high for a number of reasons. Draftees serve for twenty-four months, only part of which is spent in Africa. There is a 25 percent bonus for combat duty, which looks very good to those habitually accustomed to low wages. The opportunity to travel away from one's own Portuguese village and to visit Africa is appealing. Offsetting these advantages, however, are the possibilities of injury or death, tedious patrol operations, and the debilitating effects of tropical diseases which seem to hit many soldiers unaccustomed to the area.[44]

In addition to preventing the incursion of terrorists from neighboring states and to maintaining internal security, the army is expected to serve as a source of manpower for the colonization of Portuguese Africa. A number of incentives are offered soldiers who are due for discharge soon in order to encourage them to remain in Africa as civilians. The concept of the soldier-colonist may be traced throughout history, from the Roman legionnaire to the American frontiersman. So far only a small number of men have elected to stay in Africa when their service was completed. Soldiers everywhere seem to like to return to the traditional home after a period of service and the Portuguese are no exception.[45]

Both Angola and Mozambique have extensive coastline and river systems. For that reason Lisbon's navy will play a vital role in combating further insurgency and particularly outright invasion from the north. In 1950 naval personnel numbered 6,920. In response to increased pressures in Asia, Africa, and NATO, there has been a great increase in naval personnel since that time. Today there are 1,400 officers and 13,600 enlisted men in the navy and attached marines. The navy may be broken down for purposes of description into two groups—the heavy vessels and the inshore patrol group.[46]

The former group is composed of eighteen ocean escort vessels and seven submarines. Three of the latter are of the British "S" class and were built in 1945. Purchased by the Portuguese, they were renamed *Narval*, *Nautilo*, and *Neptune*. They each carry twelve torpedoes, fired from bow tubes and specifically designed for offensive operations in confined waters. Four much larger submarines of the "Daphne" class are presently being constructed for Portugal at the Dubigeon-Normandie shipyard in Nantes, France. They are joining the Portuguese navy in the 1968–1970 period. In the event of a major confrontation, the Portuguese and South African submarine forces could seriously endanger the movement of supplies into Mombasa, Dar es Salaam, and the other black African ports.

Among the ocean escort vessels, the most modern are four "Comadante" class fast frigates. Completed in the period 1967–1969, these multipurpose warships carry three 3.9-inch and two 40-mm. guns, six 21.7-inch torpedo tubes, and antisubmarine armament. Their 4,500-mile cruising radius at 15 knots would enable them to spend long periods at sea without refueling.

Only slightly older than these ships are the three fast frigates of the "Almirante" class. They were built in the mid-1960s and are very similar to the "Dealey" type escort ships of the United States navy. They carry four 3-inch guns, two Bofors four-barreled mortars, two depth-charge throwers, and six tubes for antisubmarine torpedoes.

During the mid-1950s the fast antisubmarine frigate *Pero Escobar* was built in Italy for the Portuguese navy. Modernized in recent years, this vessel carries sophisticated antisubmarine weaponry, new torpedo tubes, and light guns.

There are three destroyers in the Portuguese navy. The oldest of them is the *Vouga*, which was constructed in Great Britain during the latter days of the Great Depression. Despite its age, this ship is a sound combat unit, for it underwent extensive refitting and modernization in 1946–1949 and again in 1957. It carries sonar and radar equipment for the detection of submarines as well as Squid and conventional depth-charge apparatus. Somewhat newer are the *Diogo Cao* and *Corte Real*. These ships of the "John C. Butler" class saw a considerable amount of combat with the United States navy in the latter days of World War II. They were given to Portugal in 1957. Their 5-inch main batteries are the heaviest in the Portuguese navy and could be useful in support of ground troops along the African coastline.

From 1959 to 1961 Lisbon purchased four "Bay" class frigates from Great Britain. These vessels were launched in the last months of World War II. Following the conclusion of the war, Britain found herself with an excess of escort vessels and sold quite a number of them, usually at a fraction of their cost. These four frigates—the *Alvares Cabral*, *D. Francisco de Almeida*, *Pacheco Pereira*, and *Vasco de Gama*—are primarily designed for antiaircraft work and are heavily armed for that purpose. With depth-charge throwers and hedgehog, they are also capable of dealing with submarines. The hedgehog is a mortar apparatus which can fire sixteen small depth charges in a pattern from the escort ship. If one of the depth charges hits a submarine, it explodes and breaks the ship's hull. If none hit, there are no explosions and the sonar operator on the escort vessel is able to continue tracking the underwater enemy without the underwater turbulence caused by conventional depth charges which explode at a prearranged depth whether they are near the enemy or not.[47]

Very similar to the "Bay" class ships are two former British frigates of the "River" class. Named *Diogo Gomes* and *Nuno Tristão* by their new owners, these ships were refitted in 1959 and no expense was spared to make them formidable combat vessels. Their new Squid triple-barreled depth-charge mortars are considered particularly effective antisubmarine weapons.

The oldest frigate in the Portuguese navy is the *S. Cristovao*. She carries heavy armament: four 4.7-inch main guns, eight antiaircraft batteries, depth-charge throwers, and the capacity for laying 40 mines. This ship is nearly forty years old now, however, and has not been modernized. Another vessel of the same type, the *Afonso de Albuquerque*, was lost during the Indian invasion of Goa in 1961.

The second group of Portugal's vessels may be classified as the inshore patrol group. These ships are smaller than the units previously described and are capable of operating very close to the African shore and in the major rivers. Many are already on patrol duty in the Zambezi and other waterways. Most powerful of the inshore group are fourteen patrol vessels in the 300 to 375-ton category. Eight of these ships were built under the United States Mutual Defense Assistance Program from 1954 to 1958. They were constructed in French and Portuguese shipyards. The other six were purchased from the United States in 1948. They were built during World War II as part of a very numerous group of small coastal escort vessels called "submarine chasers." They are well-armed little craft with the hedgehog antisubmarine device. Considerably smaller, and capable of penetrating far up the African rivers due to their shallow draft, are thirty patrol launches. Most of these craft were built in the 1960s in Portugal, Great Britain, and the Federal Republic of Germany. Lightly armed and with small crews, they are inexpensive to produce and operate. Several were lost during the Indian invasion of Goa.

Should the presence of mines along the coast of Angola and Mozambique become a problem, the navy has eighteen vessels expressly designed to combat such a menace. Two of these are ex-British minesweeping trawlers, purchased from that country shortly after World War II. Four are large enough to be classified as ocean minesweepers. These were built in the United States during the mid-1950s and then given to Portugal under the Mutual Defense Assistance Program. The other twelve were also transfered from—or their construction in Portugal financed by—the United States. It is a rather powerful minesweeping armada, which should be able to keep the ports of Southern Africa open in case of major hostilities.

For offensive purposes, Portugal has a fleet of forty-five landing craft. While most of these are small, four are 500-ton vessels. These craft could transport Portuguese marines far up the coast of East Africa or up the Congo River for raiding operations. They are unarmed but could be escorted by heavier vessels or armament could be added. Most of these landing craft are less than ten years old and were constructed in Portuguese yards.

Rounding out the navy are a diversity of vessels, some of which might see action in Southern Africa. The *Cacheu* is a 672-ton Canadian-built minesweeper, now reclassified as a corvette. There are five survey ships, all old escort vessels with armament removed. Five fishery protection launches are well suited for inshore patrol work. For training there is the ex-German three-masted sailing ship *Sagres*, a sister ship of the *Eagle*, now in use by the U.S. Coast Guard. The old auxiliary gunboat *Dio*, built in 1929, is also used for training purposes. Two large tankers supply the navy with petroleum.

Portugal is the strongest maritime power on the African continent, and if aided by the South African navy, her ships could control the southern oceans in any conventional warfare situation involving the African states. She would also probably support the army in riverine operations and is capable of raiding efforts farther north in Africa.

While Portugal has a long and often glorious tradition of the sea, the nation does not have an imposing historical record in the air because of its lack of involvement on any major scale in the two world wars. At the same time membership in NATO has resulted in acquisition of many aircraft from the United States at advantageous terms. Though the nation's air force dates back to 1912, it only became an independent branch of the armed forces with equal status with the army and navy in 1952. By 1966 the air force had 13,500 members and 250 aircraft. The aircraft are a varied assortment, mainly produced during the 1950s and purchased from a variety of foreign suppliers.

The air force does not possess a strong strategic bombing capability but instead has concentrated on reconnaissance, transport, fighter, and fighter-bomber types. In the reconnaissance field there is a squadron of P2V-5 Neptune patrol planes. These American-made craft are ideal for long-range convoy protection, minelaying or observation missions. The military air transport service still uses a great many Douglas C-47 twin-engined propeller planes. There are also some more modern transport aircraft, such as the American-made C-54s and DC-6s and the French Noratlases. For short-range transport service there is a helicopter squadron. Fighter strength is composed of two squadrons of F-86 sabre jets manufactured by the North American Aviation Company in the United States. They are supplemented by two squadrons of Fiat G-91R aircraft made in Italy, which can double as ground-support bombing aircraft.[48]

The Logical Combatants: The African States

TANZANIA

Tanzania has been among the most outspoken African countries in the demand for an end to European domination in Southern Africa. The last decade has proven that polemics, international censure, sanctions, and arms embargoes will not secure this goal. In the face of the European power in Southern Africa, it appears that only the armed forces of Tanzania and of her sister states, along with an uprising of Africans in the South, could begin to challenge the status quo. History has shown that the East African has martial potential. During World War I many Africans from German East Africa fought well with General Paul von Lettow-Vorbeck against a vastly superior British force. Then during World War II many served in the King's African Rifles in a variety of campaigns. East African soldiers particularly distinguished themselves in years of rugged combat against the Japanese in Burma.[49]

When the traditional British garrison pulled out of Tanzania with the advent of independence in 1961, several infantry battalions were raised with the assistance of those British officers who were retained. In January 1964, however, two battalions revolted, protesting the low pay and slow pace of Africanization of officer corps. The First Battalion of the Tanganyika Rifles took control of all major government buildings, the airport, and the main broadcasting station in Dar es Salaam. It was a delicate situation but government promises to repatriate all the British officers calmed the mutineers and many returned to their barracks. The confused nature of the situation and official hesitation were noted by the troops, however, and they began making excessive demands concerning pay and living quarters. Chaos mounted and President Julius Nyerere was forced to call for help from British troops. Royal Marine Commandos were brought in by helicopter and quickly disarmed the First Battalion at Dar es Salaam. Then they flew to Tabora and Nachingwea to pacify the Second Battalion which had also mutinied.[50]

A major reorganization of the armed forces was begun at once. The old battalions were dissolved and the Tanzania People's Defense Force, half of which was recruited from the National Youth Service, took over the maintenance of order. By 1966 the soldiers were grouped in four battalions, three on the mainland and one in Zanzibar. Expatriate personnel, including Chinese Communists, have directed training.[51] Steady progress is being made and the army now numbers about two thousand. The influence of professional soldiers who served under the British has been balanced by an infusion of new recruits who achieved maturity since independence. While foreign officers are instrumental in training the new forces, Africans are in command.

On January 28, 1964, twenty-nine-year-old Brigadier Sam Hagai Sarakikya was sworn in as commander of the Tanganyika Military Forces. A brief description of his career is indicative of the pace of Africanization. The brigadier, son of a policeman, received his initial education at the Old Moshi and Tabora secondary schools. In 1958 he appeared before the first selection board for Tanganyikans wishing to enter the army, and in the following year he entered the prestigious Royal Military Academy at Sandhurst, England. In 1961 he was commissioned in the King's African Rifles, transferring to the Tanganyika Rifles shortly before independence. In 1963 he attended an all-arms course at the School of Infantry in Westminster, England. Though intelligent and ambitious, he has never taken part in a war nor have most of his soldiers. He is now in command of the nation's army.[52]

While Tanzania's army has potential, it is the Israeli-trained police force which presently seems best prepared to react in any immediate national crisis. There are about six thousand police in active service, and an elite unit has recently been formed which has extensive paramilitary capabilities. With the state of the army's readiness still somewhat in doubt, this small and well-trained police force is one of the strongest pillars of the government.[53]

Tanzania has not developed its naval forces to any appreciable extent. The navy did have four ex-German KW type coastal patrol boats which were given to Tanzania by the Federal Republic of Germany in 1965. However, this modest naval force has been turned over to a private enterprise, the Southern Engineering Company of Mombasa,[54] and the government does not seem to be encouraging maritime expansion.

The air force is also in an embryonic stage. The Federal Republic of Germany furnished some instructors until 1965 and since then Canada has assisted in a small aerial buildup. Tanzania now possesses four Caribou, eight Otter, and six Beaver aircraft.[55] All are small Canadian-built types which could be utilized to move troops into forward bush landing strips. They are totally unsuitable for offensive or defensive action against armed fighter aircraft, however. It is conceivable that once Tanzania's supply of pilots has been expanded, more military aircraft will be acquired.

Thus Tanzania is moving ahead boldly and in some ways successfully. The army is not yet a major fighting force and the air force and navy will have to be considerably strengthened before they would present any meaningful threat to European-dominated Southern Africa.

ZAMBIA

Jutting deep into Southern Africa, Zambia presents a promising staging area for guerrilla or conventional attack on Rhodesia or the Portuguese territories. At present the nation is too beset with a variety of problems even to consider a major military confrontation. The smelters of the Copperbelt could not run without coal from Wankie in Rhodesia. In 1965 Zambia imported 60 percent of its consumer goods from south of the Zambezi. Perhaps most serious from the standpoint of internal security is the Barotseland problem. In this area some of the Lozi ruling class are demanding secession from Zambia. Private police forces are maintained by the Litunga (paramount chief) there and secessionist activities seem to be encouraged by the South African secret service.[56] Should there actually be a revolt in Barotseland, Zambia might be hard pressed to suppress it. If Rhodesian forces launched a preemptive strike at Lusaka concurrently, as President Kaunda is said to fear,[57] Zambia's very existence could be at stake.

To prepare for eventualities, the nation is building up its armed forces. In 1965, $19.6 million was earmarked for defense purposes in an eighteen-month financial planning program. Many new barracks are being erected at Broken Hill, Lusaka, and Ndola. Extensions and improvements to many of the country's police stations are being undertaken.[58] Yet Zambia maintains only small regular military forces. Prior to the dissolution of the Central African Federation in 1963, the region supported two regular infantry battalions—the Northern Rhodesian Rifles and the King's African Rifles. By 1966 the army had been increased to three battalions, one armored

car squadron, one howitzer battery, and support units. About three thousand soldiers fill the ranks of these units.[59] These modest forces are typical of black Africa. In the United States the ratio of military to civilian population is 15:1,000. In the Maghreb it is 5:1,000, but in black Africa it is less than 1:1,000.[60]

Zambia is making preliminary moves to build up a riverine force. A landing craft tank (LCT), the *Bastion*, was purchased from Britain in 1966 and personnel are being recruited to man it. With an experienced crew, a vessel of this type could ferry very large numbers of soldiers across the Zambezi in a short time if given protection from air attack.[61]

The Zambian air force does not as yet have combat capability. It does have eighteen aircraft, but two are Chipmunk trainers and the other sixteen are transports. These transports—four twin-engined Caribous, six single-engined Beavers four Dakotas, and two Pembrokes—will facilitate troop movement and supply, but without fighter support they will be easy prey for intercepting enemies.[62]

Not only are the armed forces of Zambia weak, but they still depend on expatriate personnel in many of the specialized fields such as communications, maintenance, and heavy weapons. The services have yet to prove themselves in combat, and the loyalty of the Barotse and expatriates would be in question in a major war. To defend the country from air attack, President Kaunda is seeking to obtain ground-to-air missiles from Britain. Such sophisticated weaponry is difficult to service and to operate, so if such acquisitions are made it seems likely that additional foreign personnel would have to be imported.[63] Until Zambia can build up an all-African military establishment of greater size, the nation will be able to do little to force African government upon the countries to the South.[64]

THE CONGO (KINSHASA)

The problems which have beset the vast Republic of the Congo since independence have been overwhelming. Two hundred different tribes, with thirty-eight languages, have defied attempts at unification. Disunity has led to two military coups. Expropriation of foreign property has resulted in a marked reduction in European and American investment in the country's mines and forests.

One of the major reasons for the chaos is the weakness (and unreliability) of the army. Belgian colonial administrators never envisioned the building of a regular Congolese army. The twenty-five thousand-man *Force Publique*, with less than one thousand Belgian officers, was an internal police force not intended for operations outside the Congo. No African could hold even the lowest noncommissioned rank in this force.[65]

With independence there was a rush to Africanize the armed forces, and traditional discipline and loyalties were lost. Belgian officers left the country and soldiers often elected their new leaders. Politics played a big part in military appointments and corruption was not unknown. The logistical system is very weak, and many troops lived off the land. They often bring their wives, concubines, and children along with them to a region and get involved in local politics. There are few incentives for the serious career soldier. There is no logical progression in the ranks and no provision for pensions after a certain period of service.

Not all factors are discouraging, however. The army is rather large—about thirty thousand men—and could be rather swiftly expanded. Five thousand soldiers have received paracommando training from experienced Israeli officers since 1963. They provide an elite corps which would be a serious threat to any enemy.[66]

Municipal police for local law enforcement and *gendarmerie* at the provincial level assist the army in maintaining internal security. Although the police number fifteen thousand, they have not demonstrated sufficient ability to keep order without the aid of the army and even of foreign mercenaries. When one considers the substantial role an efficient and equitable police force can perform in nation-building, it is to be hoped that the Congo national government will be able to give greater assistance to the development of its police force.[67]

While the Republic of the Congo has no navy, there is a former Belgian naval base at Banana by the mouth of the Congo River. The country is developing a promising air force. Its 125 aircraft were acquired largely as the result of aid from the United States and Italy. There are nine B-26K twin-engined bombers, manufactured in the United States during the late 1940s. These aircraft proved excellent for ground support and medium-range interdiction in Korea, and more recently during the Congo's campaigns against various dissidents and separatists. The air force has considerable transport capability, with eight Alouette III helicopters, four C-54s, and twelve C-47s. There are a wide variety of aircraft for training purposes.[68]

The air force operates from two fine bases built by the Belgians—Kitona (near the mouth of the Congo) and Kamina (in Katanga)—and a number of lesser installations. Both of the big bases have runways that can take modern jet bombers should such be acquired. At Kitona there are permanent billets for two thousand troops and unlimited bivouac space for others nearly.[69] Thus it could serve as an excellent staging area for paratrooper invasion of Angola.

On balance, however, there is little danger to the white-controlled states of Southern Africa from the contiguous states of Tanzania, Zambia, or the Republic of the Congo. If all the African countries north of the Zambezi River could join together, they would muster considerable military force. Naval units would include ten destroyer-type vessels, thirteen submarines, and about seventy-five smaller vessels—such as torpedo boats, minesweepers, and armed launches. By far the largest part of this force would be Egyptian.[70]

Likewise, if these countries were working together, they could form a sizeable army. Egypt, Algeria, Senegal, Nigeria and the Sudan all have large military establishments and a group of experienced soldiers. By 1963 these countries could put nearly two hundred thousand soldiers into the field.[71] Egypt, Algeria, and Nigeria have received excellent weaponry—including armor, artillery, radar, and missiles—from the Communist bloc.

Formidable obstacles exist to thwart such an alliance, however. Egypt, which would contribute almost all the naval strength, is very much tied down in the Near East, while Nigeria and the Sudan are troubled by dissident minorities which have taken up arms against the central government. Politicians in West Africa frequently limit the size of their armies, due to the tendency of the latter to overthrow the established government. In the period from 1960 to 1963, for example, France intervened twelve times in former colonies to maintain order or to support a threatened president.[72] Many African politicians apparently prefer to rely on French military support rather than to build up their own potentially dangerous army. While this may be sound domestic politics, it will not help defeat the whites to the South unless metropolitan France drastically changes its foreign policy. Thus it would appear that unless there is a significant reversal of present trends, it is most unlikely that the African states can put sufficient conventional forces into the Southern African theater to challenge seriously the white-dominated regimes there.

THE EXILE MOVEMENTS

It is thus from within and from guerrilla exile groups that the present governments of Southern Africa may expect the greatest danger. Within South Africa, Rhodesia, and the Portuguese provinces, the Africans vastly outnumber the Europeans. In South Africa the ratio is 4:1; in Rhodesia it is 10:1; in Angola and Mozambique it is 25:1. If this African superiority in numbers can be organized, inspired, and activated, it could well topple the Europeans from power. Presently, this is a large order.

Police and security forces have been so ubiquitous in Southern Africa that the headquarters for liberation movements of necessity have been established in friendly neighboring countries. Considerable numbers of exiles from the South have been organized by these leadership nuclei and their armed incursions into Rhodesia, Angola, and Mozambique are placing heavy pressure upon the governments there. They have not succeeded in mobilizing the great majority of Africans to arise in revolt, however, for reasons which are examined in other chapters of this book. In our opinion, only if such internal rebellion breaks out on a broad scale is it foreseeable that Southern Africa will revert to African control.

The Probable Neutrals

A number of states, because of their geographical location, might be expected to play an important role in a military showdown. They probably will not play such a role, however, for a variety of reasons; other chapters in this book examine their levels of dependence and options available to their leaders. This brief description is designed to be suggestive rather than exhaustive.

Lesotho, Botswana, and Swaziland are not economically self-sufficient. Their leaders are faced with the iron priorities of their geographical and economic connections with South Africa and are under pressure from both the Organization of African Unity and the opposition parties in each of the territories to confirm their allegiance to the goal of liberation in Southern Africa.[73]

Botswana is in an especially difficult position for its strategic position between Zambia and South Africa could be used as a "lifeline" by "freedom fighters." Sir Seretse Khama has been under fire from Organization of African Unity militants for his moderate and neutral stance. Yet arid Botswana is in need of South African technical assistance and investment. These could be cut off very quickly should Sir Seretse adopt a more revolutionary stance. If such economic actions did not convince Botswana to change its posture, a South African military invasion, with crushingly superior force, could be envisioned.[74]

Since independence in 1964, Malawi has shown more desire to cooperate with its white neighbors than with other African states. Whether the country has adopted this position out of consideration for its transport facilities under Portuguese control, its migrant workers in Rhodesia, its irritation over Tanzanian support for exiles from Malawi, or a combination of all three factors, the result has been a very pro-European stance.[75] Its pragmatic president, Dr. H. Kamuzu Banda, is attempting to develop his country's armed forces. Strangely enough, women are a bulwark of the nation's defense. Their five thousand-member force is officially called the Amazon Army of Malawi. On field work the girls wear khaki uniforms of shirts and shorts modeled after the Women's Army of Israel. They train in hand-to-hand combat, marksmanship, and jungle fighting. President Banda has emancipated the women of his nation from near-feudal serfdom, and they are considered very loyal to him and the new state as a result.[76] The army is not make up entirely of women. The all-male Malawi Rifles and the mobile police force are patterned closely along British lines and are considered efficient units. A military attaché and 150 soldiers from South Africa are presently training these forces.[77]

Clearly, Botswana, Lesotho, Swaziland, and Malawi are in a difficult position. With their economies closely tied to their European-dominated neighbors, they are reluctant to serve as *entrepôts* for various "freedom fighters." At the same time, being African themselves, the leaders of these nations are under pressure from further north to support the various exile groups. In case of a major war, it is doubtful that they would join in an attack on the white fortress, except in the unlikely event that it was about to fall and they wished to be numbered among the victors.

Combat Events, 1961–1969

REVOLT IN ANGOLA

After years of inactivity, many Africans of Angola rose in March and April 1961 to attack whites. Scores of administrative posts and settlements over three districts of northern Angola were wiped out, over one thousand five hundred whites were killed, the economy of the area was devastated, and many observers believed that Portugal's days in Africa were over. The small army units in Angola, numbering about eight thousand men, seemed unable to defeat the guerrilla forces.

Lisbon reacted decisively. Troopships and planes poured a steady stream of reinforcements into the province and a counteroffensive against those northern towns held by the insurgents began with a vengeance. Four hundred thousand Angolans fled as refugees to the Congo (Kinshasa), where they were granted sanctuary and for a time allowed to conduct military training for incursions back into their homeland. Some guerrilla fighters remained in hiding in the wild bush region of eastern Angola. Despite their failure to oust the whites, the Africans had proved that they meant to fight for control of the country. At this stage of the revolt, nationalist elements had some three thousand to eight thousand men in the field in Angola, with considerable reserves in the Congo.[78]

As time passed the Africans seemed unable to maintain the thrust of their early success. There were many reasons for this. The powerful Portuguese reinforcements convinced many wavering Africans that the time had not yet come to forsake their established way of life and to join the guerrillas. Some reforms of existing injustices encouraged this view. Among the revolutionaries there was little agreement concerning the common struggle or future. Mr. Holden Roberto, leader of the *Govêrno Revolucionário de Angola no Exílio* (GRAE) (Revolutionary Government in Exile of Angola), a coalition of the two major anti-Portuguese groups proved unable to keep a unified organization of all Angolan émigrés in the Congo. At least a dozen exile groups appeared in Kinshasa and Brazzaville, each with slightly different goals or methods, and revolutionary strength became fragmented. Finally, some form began to emerge from this maze and two other major organizations appeared besides GRAE. Under Dr. Agostinho Neto, the *Movimento Popular de Libertação de Angola* (MPLA) (Popular Movement for the Liberation of Angola) worked from Brazzaville and initially concentrated its military strength against Cabinda. Mr. Jonas Savimbi and the *União Nacional para e Independência Total de Angola* (UNITA) (National Union for the Total Independence of Angola) began operating in 1966 from Zambian territory against eastern Angola and the Benguela Railway.[79] The Congolese and Zambian bases for these organizations did not prove entirely secure, as Portuguese pressure or shifts in power (particularly in the Congo) made the plotting émigrés an embarrassment to their hosts. A chronic shortage of funds has also plagued all the revolutionary groups.

Despite these problems, the Africans have been able to keep up some almost continuous military pressure on their enemies from the inception of hostilities in 1961 until the present time. A few examples will illustrate the nature of their operations. On Christmas Day 1966, UNITA guerrillas raided the town of Teixeira de Sousa and bloody combat ensued. In mid-1967 they derailed several trains on the Benguela Railroad. GRAE adherents have kept up a steady string of small but deadly ambushes in the North. These military actions have not by any means been confined to the immediate border regions. Many occur in the Dembos Forest, only forty miles east of Luanda. MPLA guerrillas have been successful in ambushing enemy forces and sabotaging roads, bridges, and river barges along the upper Zambezi and Lunguenvungue Rivers. They also range widely over the sparsely populated grasslands of eastern Angola, at times sparring with Portuguese patrols. This area, near the Zambian border, seems completely out of Portuguese control, as single European battalions patrol wild country the size of Portugal itself.[80]

Though Portuguese troops are spread thin over the country, the insurgents have not succeeded in seriously threatening them. Relations between guerrillas of the varying groups have been so poor that combined operations, which might bring very promising results, are rarely attempted. Between the Congo border and Luanda relations between GRAE and MPLA forces have been so strained that rival bands have fought each other rather than the common enemy. The recent discovery of oil in Cabinda by Gulf Oil Company has led to a local economic boom that is enticing Cabindan refugees back from the Congo. The renewed loyalty of tribal chief Alfredo Tati and his nine hundred-man militia is also strengthening the Portuguese presence in this region. Many former Angolan refugees, now back from the Congo, have been resettled in planned communities. Though negligible militarily, this renewed allegiance to Portugal by some Africans reflects discouragement at the immediate prospects for guerrilla success.[81]

COMBAT EVENTS IN MOZAMBIQUE

Beginning in 1962, a group of young revolutionaries from Mozambique began working for the independence of their country. Operating from Tanzania, they infiltrated cadres southward for eighteen months and then commenced military operations against the Portuguese. Strong leadership for the freedom movement—called *Frente de Libertação de Moçambique* (FRELIMO) (Movement for the Liberation of Mozambique)—was furnished by the late Dr. Eduardo Mondlane, a well-educated African social scientist and nationalist. Dr. Mondlane brought together, with only few exceptions, a wide variety of gifted but individualistic Mozambicans and has apparently succeeded in establishing a protostate in the northern sectors of Mozambique.

Portuguese countermeasures against the guerrillas have succeeded in their containment, but hardly in their destruction. Plagued already by heavy troop commitments in Guinea (Bissau) and Angola, Lisbon can spare no more than fifty thousand to sixty thousand soldiers for Mozambique and this is not enough to control the country effectively. This is not surprising for the United States army, with over five hundred thousand troops, cannot maintain effective control over an area one-fifth its size in Vietnam. Portuguese countermeasures include the use of scorched earth zones along the Rovuma River, and along the parallel Messalu and Montepuez Rivers to the south. Lisbon's soldiers continue to hold all important centers, but have lost control of much of the hinterland in Niassa and Cabo Delgado provinces. Although pushed back into the fastness of jungle and bush, the guerrilla forces continue to exist even though they must struggle hard for sheer survival against Portuguese patrols and air strikes. The guerrillas have used mines manufactured in Communist China to harass the movement of Europeans and supplies, and the mines have caused considerable losses. The Portuguese navy patrols actively along both the shores of Lake Malawi and the Indian Ocean. Battles on land, sea, or lake tend to be quick and decisive, with ambush and surprise widely utilized by both sides.[82]

FRELIMO has grown to a strength of eight thousand to ten thousand and retains sufficient control of some hinterland areas of northern Mozambique to keep up its own governmental and educational system. Agricultural cooperatives are marketing cashew nuts in Tanzania in exchange for food for guerrilla forces. A start has been made in codifying a new set of laws in the liberated areas. Such actions would not have taken place were the region not rather solidly under insurgent control.

Despite this achievement, however, FRELIMO has not succeeded in initiating major guerrilla activity in any areas besides the North. Occasional ambushes and harassing attacks against the Portuguese in the Tete province have not delayed construction of the huge Cabora Bassa dam project. Portugal's *Policia Internacional e de Defesa do Estado* (PIDE) (International and State Defense Police) has secretly penetrated the liberation movement and many Africans are in its service. In 1964 and 1965 FRELIMO's fledgling underground apparatus in Lourenço Marques was smashed by the police. In July 1966 Mr. Jaime Sigauke, an important FRELIMO official, was assassinated by a European in Lusaka. Early in 1969 Dr. Eduardo Mondlane himself fell victim to assassination. Whether the event was perpetrated by PIDE or rival Africans is not yet known. A rival revolutionary organization called *Comité Revolucionário de Moçambique* (COREMO) (Revolutionary Committee of Mozambique) operates from Zambia. It advocates smuggling agents into the major cities of Mozambique to form revolutionary cells. At a prearranged time these cells will launch a unified rebellion against the Europeans. COREMO considers FRELIMO's open guerrilla warfare in Niassa and Cabo Delgado provinces excessively costly in terms of African lives and unlikely to free the entire country.[83]

Lisbon is obviously worried by the situation in its African provinces. Liberation movements defy destruction, despite the heavy commitment of European troops and massive military expenditures. In Angola and Mozambique the insurgents are still confined to isolated areas, however, and their power is not clearly expanding. Unless the

"freedom fighters" can gain more unity, it is difficult to foresee further appreciable expansion of their territory. A lengthy stalemate could ensue, with international developments or a change in government in metropolitan Portugal eventually the critical factor for a major change in the situation.

GUERRILLA ACTIVITY IN RHODESIA (ZIMBABWE)

Since defiant white settlers unilaterally declared their independence in 1965, Rhodesia's Africans have been restive. British efforts to impose majority rule caused a wide divergence of opinion in the mother country and were unsuccessful.[84] Rhodesia has managed to withstand the impositions of sanctions, even though the economy has not escaped unscathed. In the early part of the decade, African resistance to the status quo took the form of isolated destruction of tobacco sheds, injuring of cattle, and an army mutiny. These incidents, while disturbing, did not seem overly consequential and an increasing flow of white immigrants from Britain joined Ian Smith's rebel government.

In August 1967, however, there was a serious outbreak of guerrilla violence. Many Africans headed north to friendly Zambia, received training there, and returned home to fight for liberation. For three weeks insurgent groups seriously harassed white infantry and police in the Wankie district. At times the Europeans were pinned down and could not evacuate their wounded. White officers lost their lives in Rhodesia for the first time since the Ndebele rebellion of 1896.[85] Rhodesian Hawker Hunter jets joined the fray and used rockets and possibly napalm to set fire to grasslands and to burn out the guerrillas. Finally, Prime Minister Ian Smith had to summon South African assistance.[86]

This was not slow in arriving. South Africa seems willing to expend both currency and lives to prevent an African takeover of her northern neighbor. Three hundred South African troops and police were rushed northward and against such powerful reinforcements the guerrillas, who numbered between eighty and two hundred, were at a serious disadvantage. Some fled to Botswana or Zambia; others were killed or captured.[87]

Despite the abortive nature of this action, it seriously frightened the governments in both Salisbury and Pretoria, and South Africa has maintained its military presence in its neighboring country since this time. These South Africans have been active in patrolling the "Zambezi Line" to prevent the infiltration of men and arms from the North. The South African air force is also making high-altitude photoreconnaissance flights over Zambia and southern Tanzania, possibly for photointerpretive or mapping purposes.[88] As long as Pretoria is willing to keep up this support, African guerrilla activity in Rhodesia seems to have limited prospects, unless its tempo can be greatly increased.

Despite this strong resistance, African nationalist fighters are still keeping up the pressure. Two African organizations have been formed for the purpose of ousting Rhodesia's white rulers. The Zimbabwe African People's Union (ZAPU) has a solid working relationship with the African National Congress (ANC), a South African party-in-exile. Recruits for ZAPU receive military training at Ilala near Dar es Salaam or at Morogoro in Tanzania.[89] The Zimbabwe African National Union (ZANU) receives Communist Chinese financial support and sends some of its adherents to that country for training. ZANU has gravitated toward alliance with the Pan-Africanist Congress, another South African exile group, but the two organisations do not have as close a relationship as ZAPU and ANC appear to have built. The rank and file of both organizations are either recruited inside Rhodesia or among Africans who have slipped out of the country. Efforts to recruit educated Rhodesian Africans from the British universities have at times met with strong resistance. In late 1968 an attack occurred on a nationalist recruiting officer in a London suburb; the attackers were apparently African students who resented excessive persuasion to return to the fight in their homeland. Zambia has also shown increased irritation at the strong-arm tactics employed by ZAPU and ZANU in recruiting exiled African Rhodesians for training as guerrillas. On October 15, 1968, the minister of home affairs confirmed reports that fifty-two ZAPU and ZANU members had been arrested and expelled to Tanzania because of such actions.[90]

Despite such setbacks, ZAPU and, to a lesser extent, ZANU continue to infiltrate small bands into their homeland. Many cross the Zambezi River to the west of Lake Kariba through the Wankie Game Reserve, from where they fan out to the west and south. Others cross the Zambezi further east, below the Kariba Dam, into the Zambezi Valley and on to the prosperous farming areas of Karoi and Sinoai.[91] Most of the incursions seem to be of the hit-and-run variety, with guerrillas fading back into Zambia when hard pressed. The nationalists carry weapons of Communist manufacture; the rapid nature of many of their movements precludes the possession of armaments heavier than mortars. These indirect-fire weapons can be broken into three parts and carried by a team of men at least twenty miles in a day. In its reports of guerrilla casualties, the Rhodesian government tacitly admitted that the scale of combat was rising until 1969. Salisbury claimed 20 guerrillas killed in 1966, 25 in 1967, and over 100 in the first ten months of 1968. It also admitted that thirteen members of the government forces lost their lives; African nationalist claims listed hundreds of white Rhodesians as casualties.[92] This combat is likely to continue and possibly intensify, but prospects for a major African success against the Europeans seem limited for the present.

THE STRUGGLE IN SOUTH WEST AFRICA (NAMIBIA)

Barren, underpopulated South West Africa has been under white domination for over three-quarters of a century. South Africa has over the past two decades shown an increasing determination to administer this territory. Those Africans from South West Africa who desired independence hoped, until 1966, that United Nations pressure and international sanctions against South Africa might persuade that country to leave its small northwestern neighbor alone to work out a future.

In the early 1960s, as the South African government continued its stubborn control of South West Africa, many Africans slipped out of their homeland and received guerrilla training at Kongwa in Tanzania. Some went as far as Algeria, the United Arab Republic, and North Korea for the same purpose. A few managed to set up a clandestine center at Ongulumbashe, Ovamboland (the northern sector of South West Africa), right "under the noses" of the occupying power. The revolutionaries gained strength by uniting under a single organization called the South West Africa People's Organization (SWAPO). They received generous amounts of small arms from the Sino-Soviet bloc.[93]

The first major confrontation between nationalists and South African police occurred on August 26, 1966. The police ferreted out the clandestine training center at Ongulumbashe, Ovamboland, and attacked it by helicopter. The insurgents had apparently been forewarned but decided to stick it out and hold their ground. This proved costly as the police killed two Africans and captured nine. About a month later SWAPO guerrillas proved that they could take the offensive. On September 26, 1966, they attacked the administrative post of Oshikango, used by the South African commissioner for part of Ovamboland. They claim to have killed an unspecified number of South African soldiers and to have caused some $28,000 damage to the post.[94]

South Africa was worried by these incidents and counterattacked on both the military and legal fronts. Vigorous search-and-capture missions throughout the territory resulted in the capture of many dissident Africans. The South African parliament passed a measure called the Terrorism Act in mid-1967. It provided harsh penalties (even death), trial by a judge without jury, indefinite detention for suspects, and other strongly repressive measures designed to deter and combat terrorism in the four South African provinces and in South West Africa. Despite much adverse foreign reaction to this legislation, it has been firmly implemented. Thirty-seven guerrillas were placed on trial in 1967 and it is thought that some two hundred and fifty more are being detained as suspects.[95]

The main burden of South West Africa's defense falls upon police forces. The territory has been divided into two zones according to the racial composition of the populace. The Police Zone is the white-inhabited southern and central sector of the country. The Non-Police Zone is the African-occupied northern region. In the Police Zone there are 594 policemen, 323 of whom are white; this is enough men to provide rather full coverage for the scanty population. In this rough country of the Non-Police Zone there are only twenty-four policemen, half of whom are whites. Obviously, this is not a defense in depth in the north, but seems rather a clever plan to keep the government presence there to a minimum. South Africa has developed a very close rapport with the Ovambos, who live in northern South West Africa, and particularly with their chiefs. The usual racial frictions which arose in most of Southern Africa did not appear in Ovamboland, as few whites ever entered the area. Thus many of its Africans see nothing distasteful about the very indirect European rule under whose auspices they live, and have shown little enthusiasm for joining the guerrillas. On December 29, 1966, a group of guerrillas attempted to assassinate Chief Jacky Ashipala, an Ovambo chief who continues to favor a Bantustan policy for his people. The attempt misfired, but it does indicate the nationalist realization that many Africans will have to be threatened or eliminated if the status quo is to change.[96]

While the police forces and the loyalty or non-involvement of the majority of Africans are South West Africa's major defenses, several others are also worthy of mention. Launches are patrolling the Zambezi River to control illegal crossings into the Caprivi Zipfel from Zambia. On May 18, 1967, police from such a launch boarded a small passenger vessel, exchanging fire with and killing a guerrilla leader. A modern airfield has been constructed in the Caprivi Zipfel; there are a number of bush landing strips; more are in the planning stages. Thus air support can be speedily directed in anywhere in Ovamboland. The army's Regiment Windhoek, which has its administrative headquarters in the capital, is immediately available to combat any major "freedom fighter" incursion which is beyond the capability of the police.[97] Thus it is likely that South Africa will be able to contain SWAPO activity in South West Africa, though it probably cannot halt it completely.

REVOLUTIONARY ACTIVITY IN SOUTH AFRICA

It is this country with its apartheid philosophy which presents the greatest challenge to—and at the same time the greatest opportunity for—the African revolutionary. The opportunity lies in the fact that if the white South Africans can be overthrown, certainly their partners in Rhodesia and the Portuguese territories will quickly fall. It is South Africa which is the very symbol, backbone, and arsenal of white resistance to African majority rule.

Bringing about this change will be a very difficult task. The Afrikaner—and to a lesser extent the English-speaking white—gains strength from his isolation in world opinion. He is convinced on historic, religious, and economic grounds that his paternalistic attitude toward the African is both wise and justified.[98] The government maintains an able military establishment to reinforce its policy and division among the Africans is encouraged by a fostering of tribal and ethnic, rather than national, consciousness.[99]

To most Africans, apartheid and separate development are merely crude disguises for subjugation of their race. They have been remarkably docile in accepting the whites' rule, but in the past nine years signs of violence have begun to appear. The first major confrontation took place in 1960 when police killed seventy-two Africans who were demonstrating at Sharpeville (outside Vereeniging in the Transvaal) against the Pass Laws. This "Sharpeville Massacre" shocked the world,[100] and was followed by increasing restiveness among South Africa's Africans. The government reacted by banning the two major African political organizations—the long-established African National Congress (ANC) and the recently formed Pan-Africanist Congress (PAC)—and arresting hundreds of their members and sympathizers. The result was a complete denial of any lawful means of protest against the existing government by the Africans. The ruthless actions of the National party leaders made a turn to violence seem inevitable.

In late 1961 a revolutionary organization called *Umkonto We Sizwe* (Spear of the Nation) was formed as an outgrowth of the banned ANC. One of its members, Nelson Mandela, succeeded in escaping to East Africa where he was warmly received and promised support by many newly independent countries. The Spear of the Nation viewed sabotage as the best way to hamstring the nation's economy and force social and political change. It commenced operations on December 16, 1961, with coordinated attacks against government buildings in Johannesburg, Durban, and Port Elizabeth. Further sabotage was carried out over the following months, but the group was dealt a heavy blow by the arrest of seventeen key members by the police at Rivonia, near Johannesburg, in July 1963. The police may have been tipped off by the remarkably efficient informer system which the authorities have developed in African townships.[101] Though Spear of the Nation may still exist, its sabotage activity has come to an end and any members are apparently dormant.

Concurrent with the rise of Spear of the Nation, another revolutionary group called *Poqo* ("alone" or "pure") appeared. Instead of adopting a sabotage policy, it carried out numerous acts of terrorist assault and murder against whites and African sympathizers. Its adherents were mainly from western Cape Province and belonged to the PAC before that organization was forced into exile or underground. Though *Poqo* succeeded in causing a good deal of concern from 1961 to 1963, a police crackdown has resulted in effectively suppressing the organization. By June 13, 1963, over three thousand *Poqo* members had been arrested, of whom 124 were sentenced to death for murder.[102]

A third group, called the African Resistance Movement, also arose during the early 1960s as a protest against government absolutism. It was composed mainly of young liberal Europeans; most of them were students or professional men. This group planned to sabotage the country's economy through concentrated disruption of communications and power facilities. Its members caused considerable damage to railroad installations and pylons carrying electric wires, especially around Cape Town. Most of its members were arrested by the police in 1964, although some of its principal adherents succeeded in fleeing the country.[103]

With the practical destruction of all three serious revolutionary groups, South Africa's National Party government has apparently suppressed sabotage and guerrilla activity in the country. The government believes that all terrorist groups have been dealt a knockout blow. Exile groups such as the PAC and the ANC claim that the harsh laws, mass arrests, and severe sentences meted out to insurgents are signs of increasing unrest and government desperation in its repression. The truth is probably somewhere in between. While dissatisfaction exists among a sizeable portion of South Africa's African inhabitants, the development of a major threat to the government by subversive organizations has not as yet successfully taken place.

The Future Course of Armed Struggle

Clearly, armed conflict will continue in Southern Africa and it will increase in intensity. A number of factors may be cited to support this contention. There was some hope that Portugal's new prime minister, Dr. Marcello Caetano, might relax the authoritarian rule of his predecessor, Dr. António de Oliveira Salazar, in the African provinces. Liberal Portuguese have been disappointed, however, as Dr. Caetano has firmly stated his conviction of Portugal's "right and duty" to remain in Africa. He raised settler morale by a personal inspection tour of all three African provinces, something Salazar had never done.[104] South Africa continues to show willingness to work closely with Portugal on both military and economic levels, and this powerful support should increase Lisbon's conviction that the overseas provinces can be held.[105] The liberation groups, such as FRELIMO and MPLA, have been heartened by some military successes and the support of the struggle by contiguous countries, but they lack the strength to make further gains.

In Rhodesia the failure of sanctions[106] and of guerrilla raids have convinced the white inhabitants that their position can be maintained. South African support has bolstered Rhodesia and the "Zambezi line" is largely successful in curbing nationalist infiltration from Zambia. While incursions will continue, they should be containable.

South Africa has successfully driven most revolutionaries underground or into exile. Yet there are foreseeable factors which could cause a renewal of terrorist activity. Among these would be major foreign intervention, a severe depression, or the eviction of the Portuguese from Angola and Mozambique or the Europeans from Rhodesia. Though none of these possibilities should be ruled out over the long term, they do not appear likely to happen immediately.[107]

Among the independent nations of Central and Northern Africa, the military potential for a major attack against the white-ruled states in Southern Africa seems to be lacking. This situation is subject to change, however. If the Congo (Kinshasa), Zambia, and Tanzania succeed in solving internal problems, developing their transportation networks, and increasing the size and effectiveness of their armed forces, they could conceivably launch a powerful offensive against the South. If this were supported by Nigeria, Eygpt, Algeria, and other African states, chances of success would improve. However, the troubled circumstances and weak economies of each of these areas preclude such intervention for years to come.

Thus the fight at present must continue to be carried on by African liberation movements, with headquarters in exile, operating within the

European-controlled countries. Already, they have made inroads into Angola and Mozambique, effectively control some areas there, and have forced Rhodesia and South Africa to expend huge sums on defense and security. Insurgent leadership often tends to be divided with regard to strategy, tactics, and goals. Only if there can be greater unity, more participation by the African populace, and greater outside support, can revolutionary activity make much headway. At present, the day of a major African invasion of the South, which would be met and aided by an uprising of other Africans, still seems both distant and problematic.

PART SEVEN

Conclusion

1

Toward the Millennium

CHRISTIAN P. POTHOLM*

It is not the purpose of this concluding chapter to summarize the preceding essays and previous arguments. Instead, it is intended that this chapter will utilize them, as well as other works on Southern Africa, in order to extrapolate a set of possible scenarios relevant for the last three decades of the twentieth century. There are, of course, too many variables present in the context of the region to enable us to make precise predications but we hope that the creation and exploration of a number of scenarios dealing with the future of the southern one-sixth of the African continent may offer a worthwhile opportunity for "thinking about the unthinkable." As Edgar Brookes has written, those dealing with the Southern African area have too often simplified the situation:

> The temptation is to take one of the extreme views—either that the white man must maintain his predominance, or that he must be handed over, by force and bloodshed if need be, to the African majority.[1]

The textual richness of Southern Africa contains a wide range of possibilities, particularly when the potential exogenous inputs are added to an analysis of the region. Moreover, this is a propitious time to explore these possibilities for, as the preceding chapters of this book indicate, we are now in a halfway, twilight period when it seems too late for peaceful evolution to African majority rule and too early for a revolution of significant magnitude (however inspired and generated) to reorder the subsystem radically. It is a matter of great import, therefore, to indicate the possible courses of future events and to underscore the variety of options open to the principal decision-makers in the coming years—both those within the subsystem and in the wider world.

In making our projections about the area, we have accepted the premise of Larry W. Bowman that there is a definable subsystem operative in

* The author wishes to thank Larry W. Bowman, Gary Gappert, Richard Dale, John Donovan, El Morgan and Glen Johnson for their many provocative comments on this chapter.

Southern Africa.[2] Currently, it includes nine units with a combined population of 45 million persons and an area of 2 million square miles. Viewed in systemic terms, there are relatively high levels of political and economic interaction among the units, a discernible hierarchical power configuration under South African hegemony, and a prevailing ethos of white domination.[3] Thus, while transaction flows determine the extent of the operative subsystem, the racial power configurations and the ethos determine the texture of the system. It is, therefore, held that any fundamental alteration in the subsystem would involve either or both of the following: one, a shift to African majority rule both within individual units and over the subsystem as a whole thus changing its texture; and, two, a reorientation of the existing transaction flows so that, in terms of interaction, the geographical region no longer would constitute a distinctive community. In either case, the alteration of South Africa or a pronounced reduction in its role in systemic maintenance is of crucial importance because it is currently the core of the subsystem.[4]

In examining the future possibilities for the area, we have arrived at a set of nine primary scenarios, each with a number of variations. We hope that the tripartite analysis of each will provide meaningful directions for future research and reflection by scholars as well as by political and economic practitioners. Each scenario is divided into three parts: *configurations* (or what would happen if the scenario were actualized), *assumptions* (or what would have to happen for the scenario to be actualized), and *appraisal* (or the author's estimate of the probability of those assumptions being actualized). It should be noted that because of limits of space the appraisal section is designed to be suggestive rather than exhaustive. Therefore, emphasis is placed on the configurations and assumptions rather than on the author's personal conclusions, leaving the reader to make his own appraisals on the basis of the entire book. There are two major categories into which the nine scenarios fall—namely, those which do not involve a fundamental alteration of the subsystem (scenarios 1–3) and those which do (scenarios 4–9). It is to the first of these groups that we now turn.

Preservation of the Systemic Status Quo

SCENARIO I: CONTINUATION OF THE PRESENT SUBSYSTEM

Configurations:

(1) The present stalemate in Portuguese Africa between the 100,000-man Portuguese army and the 6,000 to 7,000 Africans bent on overthrowing their colonial apparatus will continue.[5] The African nationalist movement remains fragmented. In Angola, for example, such groups as the *Movimento Popular de Libertação de Angola* (MPLA), *União Nacional Para a Independência Total de Angola* (UNITA), and *Govêrno Revolucionário de Angola no Exilo* (GRAE) operate separately. There are relatively low levels of violence in both Angola and Mozambique.[6]

(2) The quasi-vassal status of Lesotho, Botswana, Swaziland, and Malawi remains constant or intensifies. There is increasing economic interdependence within the subsystem.

(3) African exiles continue to mount hit-and-run raids into Rhodesia (Zimbabwe) and South West Africa (Namibia). These are not sufficient to enable Africans to take control of these units, but despite the asymmetrical balance of forces in Southern Africa favoring the defense, the Europeans in these areas cannot construct a totally impregnable perimeter.

(4) South Africa remains a safe zone under firm European control. Internal African opposition is tightly controlled or broken up.[7]

Assumptions:

(1) The principal Portuguese decision-makers maintain their commitment to Portugal's "overseas provinces." Despite the heavy cost (over 40 percent of the national budget), Portugal is able to maintain itself in Africa.[8]

(2) The existing African governments in Lesotho, Botswana, Swaziland, and Malawi continue their support for the subsystem or, if they are replaced by counterelites, these perceive only limited opportunities for changing the subsystem.

(3) Whether due to the lack of a sanctuary, arms, manpower, will, organization, or external support, African nationalist movements are unable to take over any units in the subsystem. African states north of the Zambezi and the Organization of African Unity continue to make the liberation of Southern Africa—particularly South Africa—a low-priority item.[9]

(4) Europeans bent on the continuation of white supremacy are able to maintain their control over South Africa and continue their informal, *de facto* alliance with Portugal and Rhodesia. It should be noted that the Rhodesian Unilateral Declaration of Independence (UDI) is both a symbol of, and a major contribution to, European intransigence toward African majority rule in Southern Africa.

(5) There is a lack of Great Power (here taken to mean the United States, Soviet Union, France, Great Britain, and the People's Republic of China) intervention on the side of those forces bent on

the alteration of the subsystem or continued tacit support for the maintenance of the status quo. There is, for example, no enforced economic boycott against South Africa and not all powers acquiesce to the arms embargo against it.

Appraisal:
In terms of probability, this scenario seems to be the one most likely to correspond to reality during the next few years. All evidence now available indicates that the defensive strength of the subsystem is of sufficient magnitude to prevent the forceful alteration of the subsystem. Moreover, it is difficult to imagine why or how exogenous forces of sufficient power to alter the system could be made to intervene in the near future. In short, this is where Southern Africa is now and where it is likely to remain over the near term.

SCENARIO II: EXPANSION OF THE SUBSYSTEM

Configurations:
(1) The stalemate outlined in Scenario I will continue in Portuguese Africa and/or the African nationalist threat to these areas will be reduced.

(2) In terms of increased transaction flows, particularly growing economic ties and political influence, the subsystem expands north of the Zambezi to include such additional units as Zambia and the Congo (Kinshasa). South Africa, for example, has already replaced Rhodesia as Zambia's primary supplier of imports and has also conducted intelligence and paramilitary operations in such areas as Barotseland and the Congo (Kinshasa).[10]

(3) While the raids of the African freedom fighter–guerrillas (hereafter referred to as FFGs) continue, their impact is blunted, both by counterinsurgency operations and by political strategies involving the increased fragmentation of Southern Africa.[11] Bantustans such as Zululand, Vendaland, and the Transkei obtain the *de jure* "independence." The Odendaal Report is implemented in South West Africa and Rhodesia is subdivided into European and African areas. This process leads to the development of a "race federation" in which large numbers of Africans imagine that they have a substantial stake in the status quo, even though *de facto* political, economic, and military control rests with Europeans. This type of political "net" is extended to units north of the Zambezi.

(4) South Africa increases its economic, political, and diplomatic power. Its gross national product (now over $1 billion) grows at a rate of 4 to 5 percent yearly and thus provides a wide range of politicomilitary options including significant nuclear and chemical-biological capabilities in the 1980s.[12] Through the use of economic rewards and military threats, South Africa undermines its opposition within the Organization of African Unity and the United Nations. During 1969, for example, South Africa undertook informal and/or secret talks with Mauritius, the Malagasy Republic, Gabon, Senegal, Chad, and the Ivory Coast.[13] The South African domestic situation remains quiescent.

Assumptions:
(1) Portugal continues its commitment to Southern Africa, or South Africa, with Portuguese settler support, and develops the capability to maintain the status quo in Portuguese Africa.

(2) African-led states in the area remain committed to the subsystem in its existing form or, if they become opposed to it, they are not able to significantly alter it.

(3) The various African exile movements are unable to mount a sustained offensive against the white-controlled areas and neither the OAU nor any new inter-African organization is able to generate rising force levels.[14]

(4) The South African government continues its "forward strategy" despite internal European opposition and is able to maintain a credible counterforce deterrence *vis à vis* Africa north of the Zambezi. Thus African states on the periphery of the expanding subsystem are made to believe that the benefits (economic and technical) or potential costs (South African aid to secessionist movements, threatened coups, sabotage, assassinations, even military intervention) outweigh advantages in attempting to alter the subsystem. South Africa is able to win peace for the expanding subsystem by threatening the domestic security of its antagonists and/or providing rewards to its supporters.

(5) The Great Powers remain neutral or aid in the maintenance of the subsystem through increased trade and tacit support for South African (and systemic) expansion. Particularly with regard to the West, South Africa is able to use its strategic position and economic attractions to insure Great Power neutrality. Also, the current *détente* between the United States and the Soviet Union dampens Great Power rivalry in this area.[15]

Appraisal:
Today this scenario may well seem to be the wave of the future, especially in light of the serious internal difficulties experienced by many independent African states and the strong avoidance reaction toward any new commitments to Africa shown by the Great Powers. At the same time there are some increasingly formidable obstacles to the expansion of the subsystem. In the first place, there is substantial opposition to expansion within the European community of South Africa.[16]

Second, South Africa's professed "good neighbor" policy rules out most overt forms of military pressure such as occupation and any attempt to utilize such pressure would likely be counterproductive. Even more important, new lines of communication which are now developing (such as the Tanzam railroad) seem likely to diminish the appeal of too close cooperation over time. In terms of transaction flows, East Africa is rapidly evolving into a subsystem of its own. Thus, while it is possible to imagine Tanzania coming under control of a government more highly disposed toward the subsystem, one which might reduce Tanzanian support for the Southern African exile groups, it would probably not reverse Tanzania's patterns of trade with East Africa. Therefore, it seems likely that although South Africa may well attempt to actualize Scenario II, the limits of statecraft suggest that this strategy will at best provide an aura of legitimacy for the present system rather than to expand it.

SCENARIO III: REDUCTION OF THE SUBSYSTEM

Just as the subsystem might be expanded so, too, it might be reduced in size without fundamentally altering the nature of the system. The reduction of the size of the subsystem could take place under two sets of conditions: first, through peaceful transition; second, through a state of intensified siege. In the former situation, just as Zambia has attempted to reduce its participation in the subsystem since 1965, so Malawi, for example, could decide to reorient many of its transactions toward East Africa. Far more likely to affect the subsystem, however, is the attempt of various African exile groups to deprive the subsystem of units by overthrowing the existing governments in Angola, Rhodesia, and Mozambique. It is on this second course of action that we wish to concentrate in this scenario.

Configurations:

(1) The defense in Southern Africa loses ground relative to the offensive. Although the South African heartland remains secure, the series of "brush fire wars" or "wars of national liberation" intensify, ultimately depriving the system of units. Under heavy pressure, Portugal decides to grant independence to its African areas in the hope of a "Brazilian" solution whereby the new states remain members of the informal Lusotropical cultural and economic community. This is not presently in the offing for the government of Premier Marcelo Caetano and the ruling National Union party (which holds all 130 seats in the Portuguese Parliament) has thus far resisted this alternative. At the same time, during the 1969 parliamentary elections some Socialists and liberal Catholics began calling for "negotiation" and "self-determination" for the "overseas provinces." A series of military defeats in Africa could hasten the reevaluation process.

(2) The loss of units, however, does not have a cumulative effect on the subsystem and it continues—despite its truncated state—to remain under South African economic and military hegemony and retains its ethos of European supremacy. In this context, the question arises: How many and which units could the subsystem lose without being fundamentally altered? From an analysis of the previous chapters, it would appear that the subsystem could lose Angola and Malawi without endangering the entire system, but the loss of Mozambique in its entirety would pose a grave threat to a continuation of the system.[17] Of the four African-run states, Botswana is probably of the greatest strategic consequence.[18]

(3) The number of FFGs operative in Southern Africa multiplies. In addition to taking over several units, these African groups intensify their military pressure on the remaining portions of the system, and there is a gradual escalation of antisystemic violence throughout the area.[19]

(4) Despite its mounting difficulties, South Africa is able to maintain itself and at least some of the auxiliary units (such as Rhodesia, Lesotho, and South West Africa). It is also able to "manage" the conflicts along the northern perimeter of the subsystem. Its core value of "white supremacy" remains intact.

Assumptions:

(1) If Portugal withdraws its armed forces from Southern Africa, this withdrawal cannot be compensated for by Portuguese settler refusal to accept African majority rule (*à la* UDI) and South African attempts to preserve the status quo. It is conceivable, however, that Portuguese settlers with South African support could maintain themselves in a partitioned Mozambique, holding the area south of Beira or along the Zambezi.

(2) While some African leaders in the subsystem support a radical restructuring of the system, some do not (or are prevented from doing do) and thereby continue to provide the remaining portion of the subsystem with political insulation.

(3) While able to take control of some units, African nationalist movements cannot take over all European-controlled areas.

(4) South African Europeans remain willing to pay the increasingly high costs of systemic maintenance, the "ticket of admission." A garrison-type state (similar to the situation in Israel since 1967) evolves in which South Africa is able to prevent large-scale insurgency in South Africa and at least some other units such as South West

Africa but cannot maintain the entire subsystem. The South African–centered subsystem is thus reduced in size and scope but not terminated.

(5) Great Power neutrality, or at least non-decisive intervention, continues. For example, the United States and Great Britain still allow their citizens to invest in South Africa and the Soviet Union continues to supply the bulk of the material for the antisystemic FFGs but neither "aid" is decisive.[20]

Appraisal:
There is not a great deal of evidence to suggest that Southern Africa is likely to move from Scenario I to Scenario III in the near future. Over time (5 to 10 years), however, Scenario III could well come to pass. Curiously enough, a good deal could depend upon subsequent events in Guinea (Bissau). Here the African nationalist movement led by Amilcar Cabral, the *Partido Africano da Independência da Guiné e Cabo Verde* (PAIGC), has made impressive inroads into Portuguese strength.[21] Here the FFG's control nearly two-thirds of the country and seem close to victory. An African takeover of Guinea could have a substantial psychological impact on Portuguese thinking and could encourage a substantial re-evaluation of their position in Southern Africa. At the very least the PAIGC movement provides the most promising model for self-generated revolution within the units of the subsystem. As matters now stand, the viability of the various African nationalist movements in Angola and Mozambique depends upon a coordination of effort and a gradual buildup of organizational cadres as much as upon either external support or systemic counterforce.[22] Were this achieved, Scenario III could loom as most probable, and the one most likely to be actualized during the intermediate period.

Fundamental Alteration of the Subsystem

The first three scenarios outlined above would result in the preservation of the heart of the subsystem and its prevailing ethos of white domination even though the size of the subsystem would vary depending upon the scenario actualized. We now turn to the set of six scenarios which would result in a fundamental alteration of the subsystem.

SCENARIO IV: SELF-GENERATED, PEACEFUL ALTERATION OF THE SUBSYSTEM TO:

(A) African Majority Rule

(B) Genuine Sharing of Power (on the order of 50–50 percent)

Either of the above options connected with Scenario IV would lead to a fundamental alteration of the subsystem. In Scenarios IV through VIII, there will be little effort made to separate the variables likely to produce A rather than B or vice versa simply because both A and B lead to a fundamental alteration and either option is most difficult to predict save in the existential moment when the choice is present. Currently, *meaningful* sharing of power is just as unacceptable to most Europeans within the subsystem as is African majority rule and just as likely to produce severe opposition. Similarly, meaningful sharing of power is the very least African nationalist movements will consider and then probably only if there are no alternatives. Therefore, in terms of domestic politics in each of the systemic units, we shall concentrate on the transition to African majority rule. For analytical purposes, however, options A and B do seem to have relevance for those scenarios which stem from exogenous inputs into the system and they will be considered in those contexts.

Configurations:
(1) The present government of Portugal accepts a policy of African majority rule or is replaced by a government which does.

(2) African majority rule continues in Lesotho, Botswana, Swaziland, and Malawi, perhaps coupled with a change in government (for example, the Ngwane National Liberatory Congress in Swaziland or the Basutoland Congress party in Lesotho).

(3) African nationalist movements in the yet-to-be-liberated areas accept the peaceful transition to African majority rule:
(*a*) with formal or informal safeguards for Europeans and other non-Africans.
(*b*) without formal or informal safeguards for Europeans and other non-Africans.

(4) South African, Rhodesian, and Portuguese Europeans accept the principle of majority rule and turn over power to an elected body based on one man, one vote (perhaps through a series of constitutions). This is done with or without formal or informal safeguards for Europeans and non-Africans.

Assumptions:
(1) The Portuguese government is willing to change its basic colonial policy and to convince, or force, its European settlers to accept such a decision, or simply to abandon them.

(2) African leaders in the states presently under

their control would be willing or could be forced to accept the alteration of the subsystem.[23]

(3) African nationalist groups, particularly those in exile, are willing to eschew violence against Europeans and to accept the position that, Frantz Fanon aside, a *Götterdammerung* solution is not necessary to compensate for past injustices through the catharsis of violence.

(4) Europeans, particularly those in South Africa, are willing to give up the core values of white supremacy which they have heretofore demanded for three centuries. A peaceful transition to majority rule would also demand that the "peacemakers" in the European community be able to deliver their constituency. The extreme reaction of many European settlers in Kenya during the mid-1950s and in Angola during 1961 indicate the extent to which this element is crucial if Scenario IV is to be actualized.

(5) Same as assumption (5), Scenario III.

Appraisal:
Of all the scenarios under review, this is judged the one least likely to develop. Even if assumptions 1, 2, 3, and 5 were met (which seems highly doubtful), assumption 4 seems most improbable. At best, the Europeans in Angola, Mozambique, and South Africa seem willing only to create an illusion of eventual power sharing (such as the theoretical outcome of the recently adopted Rhodesian constitution). Most are unwilling to accept even that.[24] European intransigence since World War II has also prompted an African reaction of significant magnitude. In South Africa, for example, attempts at peaceful change initiated by Africans have been so unsuccessful and their repression so severe that it is difficult to imagine Africans having enough faith in the scenario even to attempt to bring about peaceful change.[25] Thus,

> Deprived of reasonable hope for peaceful change, Southern Africans are abandoning moral persuasion as ineffective. They are resorting increasingly to violence in their efforts to end minority rule.[26]

Irrespective of the reasons for the African change in attitude (and/or resignation), the change is of little systemic consequence for it is the goal, not the process, which is so steadfastly being resisted south of the Zambezi. In any case, it is our view that there is virtually no chance for a fundamental alteration of the subsystem by peaceful means. Whether exogenously or internally generated, if meaningful change is to come to the subsystem, it will have to be accompanied by the use of force.

SCENARIO V: EXOGENOUSLY INDUCED ALTERATION OF THE SUBSYSTEM: LOW LEVELS OF COERCION

A and B options

Configurations:
(1) Same as configuration (1), Scenario IV.

(2) Same as configuration (2), Scenario IV.

(3) Same as configuration (3), Scenario IV, except "more or less peaceful" replaces "peaceful."

(4) Same as configuration (4), Scenario IV, except for the addition of the phrase "or are forced to accept" after "accept."

(5) Exogenous units from outside the subsystem—including the United States, most countries in Western Europe, and others—combine to put nonviolent pressure on the European-controlled governments in Southern Africa in order to induce them to alter their policies. This is done by cutting off diplomatic relations, eliminating trade and withdrawing investments, and curtailing all contacts with the governments in question, culminating in as severe a state of isolation as is possible without the use of violence.[27]

Assumptions:
(1) Same as assumption (1), Scenario IV, except that the phrase "or are made" is added after "willing."

(2) Same as assumption (2), Scenario IV.

(3) Same as assumption (3), Scenario IV.

(4) Same as assumption (4), Scenario IV, except that the phrase "or are forced" is inserted after "willing."

(5) Those countries of sufficient economic, diplomatic, and political importance to the maintenance of the subsystem are willing to combine (openly or covertly) in order to alter the subsystem and are willing to pay the costs of systemic alteration. In the case of the United States, the economic costs of such a strategy should be neither exaggerated nor underestimated. American private investment in Portugal amounts to under $100 million, with slightly more in the Portuguese territories in Africa, particularly Cabinda.[28] American private investment in South Africa is approximately $800 million.[29] This amounts to but 1.1 percent of total United States foreign investment (but 11 percent of South Africa's investment), and 1 percent of U.S. trade (but the United States provides 17.7 percent of South Africa's imports and takes 11.3 percent of South Africa's exports).[30] By way of comparison, already two-thirds of American investment in Africa is in countries north of the Zambezi.[31] The citizens of Great Britain have over $3 billion invested in South Africa, and this amounts to nearly 60 percent of all foreign investment in

South Africa. Other countries in Western Europe provide an additional 16 percent, and France is also a key unit in any economic strategies, with investment levels rapidly approaching those of the United States. In addition, France has become the major supplier of South African weapons and weapons systems.

(6) Economic and diplomatic pressure is translatable into political change without the use of violence.

Appraisal:

This scenario is often suggested by those who wish to see the subsystem altered but who eschew the use of "violence" (here equated with middle and high levels of coercion). Exponents of this scenario rightly maintain that since the strategy has not been implemented in any meaningful way, we do not know if it would work. Certainly the halfhearted and easily circumvented sanctions against Rhodesia and the "boycott" and arms embargo against South Africa do not constitute a bona fide test of such a strategy. Likewise, pressures on Portugal have been minimal.[32] Present indications of its feasibility, however, are at best mixed. We know, for example, that South Africa, the strongest of the units, is not self-sufficient.[33] At the same time the history of economic sanctions and diplomatic pressure divorced from the threat or use of force does little to inspire faith in such a strategy.[34] Finally, there is the complicating factor of the subsystem's mixed population. Any severe economic dislocation would seem to have its most adverse impact—at least, in the short run—on the non-Europeans within the system although this should not be used to rationalize ignoring the scenario.

In any case, whatever its intrinsic appeal, Scenario V is not likely to be actualized. Despite its pacific aura (which might encourage some of the Great Powers to adopt it as a policy goal), it seems most likely that middle-range coercion would have to be utilized in order to enforce it once it were adopted. As long as South Africa in particular and Southern Africa in general has products the rest of the world needs or wants, the temptation to undercut whatever collective steps are taken must be taken into account. And it is likely that South Africa would not allow economic pressure to build up (say, perhaps, through a blockade) without an attempt to defeat such action. Thus it seems most plausible that even were Scenario V to develop, it would probably quickly escalate into a Scenario VI situation, or one where the exogenous powers would have to resort to middle-range coercion (or the direct use of force) to enforce the steps taken. Either force would have to be used or the sanctions would be circumvented. In either case Scenario V would be eclipsed.

SCENARIO VI: EXOGENOUSLY INDUCED ALTERATION OF THE SUBSYSTEM: MIDDLE-RANGE COERCION

A and B options

Configurations:

(1) Same as configuration (1), Scenario IV.

(2) Same as configuration (2), Scenario IV.

(3) Same as configuration (3), Scenario V.

(4) Same as configuration (4), Scenario V.

(5) Exogenous powers combine to threaten or actually to use force to alter the subsystem. This includes such acts as a forceful maintenance of an economic blockade, a series of "surgical" air-strikes against military targets, and massive support for exile movements including advisers.[35] In short, "middle-range coercion" is taken to mean all acts short of a full-scale invasion of Southern Africa by the Great Powers. This use of force leads to African majority rule or to meaningful sharing of power within the subsystem.

Assumptions:

(1) Same as assumption (1), Scenario V.

(2) Same as assumption (2), Scenario IV.

(3) African nationalist groups participate in, or at least do not hinder, the application of the middle-range forms of coercion by the exogenous forces.

(4) Same as assumption (4), Scenario V.

(5) Exogenous forces are willing to combine for the purposes of altering the subsystem and willing both to threaten the use of force and to apply it if necessary. Middle-range coercion might not have to be used if the ruling elites in Southern Africa thought it would be used and were not willing to risk its consequences. However, an essential part of this assumption deals with the currently "incredible" aspects to its use. Therefore, it is assumed that some forms of middle-range coercion would have to be used to convince the powers in question to alter the subsystem. There are a number of combinations possible:

(a) the United States and the principal countries of Western Europe operating in concert, the Soviet Union remaining neutral;

(b) the United States, principal Western European Powers, and the Soviet Union combining;

(c) the United States and the Soviet Union acting together, with Western Europe neutral;

(d) the United States neutral, the Soviet Union working in concert with other powers;

(e) the United States and Western European countries neutral, the Soviet Union the primary actor.

(6) Middle-range coercion is translatable into political change leading to African control of the subsystem.

Appraisal:
The crucial assumptions of Scenario VI involve the combination of at least some of the Great Powers and rest on the premise that medium-range coercion would convince the Europeans within the subsystem to give up their preeminent position. It is difficult to see these criteria being met in the foreseeable future. In the first place, there is no question that both the United States and the Soviet Union display something of an avoidance reaction with regard to Africa, and the current *détente* between the two may, as Immanuel Wallerstein has suggested, jeopardize the short-term chances of either intervening in Southern Africa.[36]

However, all this could change during the latter two decades of this century. The Soviet Union could be drawn into the situation by its small but increasing commitment to the African exile movements. Their success in one or more units could either encourage the Soviet Union to intervene more directly or force its hand to do so. This latter possibility might occur, for example, if China drastically increased its involvement.[37] For its part, the United States may well be faced in the 1980s or 1990s with a need to decide for or against major systemic alteration in Southern Africa. This could develop quite apart from Soviet or Chinese designs. The gradual political mobilization of black Americans and their increasing concern with Southern Africa could create a situation in which the United States could no longer avoid direct intervention.[38] In fact, there are signs that the hesitant first steps toward a reappraisal of American foreign policy are already taking place, although most of the weight continues to be on the side of those who favor the maintenance of the status quo.[39]

Other events could also trigger Great Power intervention:

(1) To date, there has been very little concerted pressure put on the Great Powers by the African states. The Organization of African Unity, despite its rhetoric to the contrary, has not been united on the desirability, let alone the feasibility, of maximum support for a forceful alteration of the status quo in Southern Africa.[40] General agreement when coupled with cohesive action (such as the threat to nationalize all the foreign holdings of all countries which did not join in the "crusade") could pressure one or more of the Great Powers into action and thereby force the hands of others.

(2) The United Nations might decide to undertake direct action in pursuance of the General Assembly Resolution 2145 (XXI) of October 27, 1966, which terminated South African control over Namibia.

(3) Under Scenario II or III, South Africa might make a miscalculation (or be goaded into one) which would involve a direct South African attack on Tanzania or Zambia, thereby providing the impetus for joint action of the type outlined in (1) and (2).

(4) A large-scale, "spasm" revolt in Rhodesia or South Africa leading to a bloody repression (involving the loss of thousands of African lives) could provide the needed stimulus to force action on the part of the Great Powers.[41]

These events would not, in and of themselves, guarantee Great Power intervention, but they would substantially increase the probability of such action.

Assuming that force can be brought to bear by the Great Powers, how much would then be required to get the Europeans in Southern Africa to give up their core values? At this point we simply do not know how tough they really are. To date, those Europeans have proven themselves to be extremely powerful in dealing with unarmed civilians bent on passive resistance and in attacking minuscule, disorganized, poorly armed groups of FFGs. What they have not done is face anything like the coercion of the levels outlined in Scenario V or VI. South Africa, it is true, is a powerful factor in the Southern African context but hardly comparable to France, Great Britain, the United States, and the Soviet Union. Assuming these countries are willing to undertake such action, it seems likely that they could unravel the fabric of white domination quite quickly. Moreover, were there to be exogenous inputs resulting in middle-range coercion, it seems unlikely that there would be a replay of the long-draw-out second Anglo-Boer War. Given the urbanized, industrialized character of European South Africa, the security of the South African political system is predicated on domestic tranquility which, in turn, depends upon African passivity. To date, much of this passivity has been due to the African's view that armed revolt is doomed to failure. With outside intervention this passivity could no longer be assured.

On balance, then, while Scenario VI seems improbable over the short and intermediate term, it could well develop by century's end. With one or more of the Portuguese areas under African control, rising levels of violence along the perimeter of the remaining portions of the subsystem, limited inputs of force could impinge directly upon the South African heartland with reasonable chances of success. We believe that it is unlikely that the Great Powers will see the century out without coming under intense pressure to make a choice with regard to Southern Africa. They could, of course, opt to preserve the subsystem, in which case it would probably be maintained (as suggested in Scenario VIII). If they do choose the path of systemic alteration, however, it is difficult to imagine them failing. In such a situation, Scenario VI has a great deal of appeal, for it offers a definite chance for success without massive bloodshed and enables the Great Powers to exercise some control over events. One could well argue that

> It is far wiser to embark upon a studied program of political and economic measures, combined with quiet and persistent pressures, than to risk a certain confrontation, triggered by unpredictable events, at times and places of no one's choosing.[42]

Along with Scenario III, Scenario VI appears to be a distinct possibility over the long term, although it is perhaps less likely to happen than the former.

SCENARIO VII: EXOGENOUSLY INDUCED ALTERATION OF THE SUBSYSTEM: HIGH LEVELS OF COERCION

A and B options

Configurations:

(1) Same as configuration (1), Scenario IV.

(2) Same as configuration (2), Scenario IV.

(3) Same as configuration (3), Scenario V.

(4) Same as configuration (4), Scenario V, except that the European power structure does not give up its core values until faced with high levels of coercion, perhaps including an invasion of South Africa proper. This "conversion" could take place at three different points in time:

(a) immediately after the initial invasion by African exile groups in conjunction with at least some of the Great Powers;

(b) after a substantial portion of South Africa has been physically occupied and severe pressure is exerted on the rest (perhaps the destruction of the entire Witwatersrand industrial complex);

(c) after a *Götterdammerung* situation in which perhaps 20 percent of the European population were killed and most of South Africa devastated.

(5) Same as configuration (5), Scenario VI.

Assumptions:

(1) Same as assumption (1), Scenario IV.

(2) Same as assumption (2), Scenario IV.

(3) African nationalist groups, both within and outside the subsystem, accept the need to use high levels of coercion even if that coercion is applied by exogenous forces and even if it entails substantial African casualties, both as a result of the combat itself and of European reprisals.

(4) While European decision-makers resist giving up their core values when confronted with low and middle levels of coercion, they would do so when faced with high levels of coercion.

(5) Same as assumption (5), Scenario VI, except that the Great Powers are willing to use massive amounts of force, including an armed invasion, to alter the subsystem.

(6) Same as assumption (6), Scenario VI.

Appraisal:

Is time, as Ernest Gross has suggested, running toward chaos in Southern Africa?[43] Is the Southern African subsystem to be drowned in a storm of fire and blood? While this solution might have appeal for some, there are few indications that the leaders of the Great Powers, the European power structure, and many Africans would opt for such a solution.[44] It is possible that Scenario VI could slide into that twilight area where it blends with Scenario VII, but it seems unlikely that this scenario would be a chosen course of action. In fact, were the Great Powers to become so engaged, they (at least the Western powers) would come under severe domestic pressure to disengage, particularly if South Africa held out for a long period of time or if there were not widespread, internal African support for the high levels of coercion. In such a situation, the Great Powers might be forced to withdraw, leaving South Africa battered but intact (similar to the state of Prussia after the Seven Years' War). This outcome, of course, would lead to a Scenario III situation rather than to a Scenario VII one.

On balance, Scenario VII seems unlikely to materialize. Great Power intervention in a Scenario V or VI situation would require far less unanimity and involve far fewer costs than those entailed in Scenario VII. Further, it seems that an "all African" army of liberation, without at least substantial Great Power support, could not overcome South African persistence. More important, we contend that the subsystem itself would be drastically altered as a result of the coercion utilized in Scenario VI. Europeans in the area have gotten an enormous amount of mileage out of their "tough" heritage and *laager* mentality. No one doubts the efficacy of these aspects in the nineteenth century. But today, while the urbanized, industrialized, literate European society is in a better position to defeat internal opposition, it is far more vulnerable to severe exogenous pressure. The credibility of its threat to "fight to the death" in the face of such opposition as outlined in Scenario VI is open to serious question, if not outright disbelief.

SCENARIO VIII: SELF-GENERATED, VIOLENT ALTERATION OF THE SUBSYSTEM
A and B options

Configurations:

(1) The defense loses ground relative to the offensive, forfeiting a number of units in the process. The Portuguese territories come under African control and these newly won areas serve as staging areas for the liberation of the rest of the subcontinent.

(2) The loss of units has a cumulatively dysfunctional impact on the subsystem.

(3) There is a geometric multiplication of FFGs and a steadily increasing flow of arms to them. The African nationalist groups are able to generate their own revolutions and overcome their initial weakness *vis à vis* the subsystem ("that is what struggle means, turning weakness into strength").[45]

(4) Although South Africa is able to hold out longest and for a time prop up European regimes in Rhodesia and southern Mozambique, eventually the entire subsystem comes under African majority rule or a meaningful sharing of power. As in Scenario VII, this "conversion" could take place at three different stages:

(a) when South Africa is the remaining unit;

(b) after a portion of its territory is taken over by African nationalists;

(c) after the devastation of much of the country.

Assumptions:

(1) Same as assumption (1), Scenario III.

(2) African leaders in Swaziland, Lesotho, Botswana, and Malawi either support the alteration of the subsystem or cannot prevent it.

(3) African exile leaders are able to expand their operations, coordinate their activities, and sustain a twenty- to thirty-year movement.

(4) Europeans in Southern Africa are either unable or unwilling to pay the increasingly high costs of systemic maintenance and are forced to accept the fundamental alteration of the subsystem.

(5) The Great Powers indirectly support the African movements, remain neutral, or, if they are in favor of the *status quo*, are unable to prevent its alteration.

Appraisal:

This scenario has a great deal of attraction for African exile groups ("We did it ourselves"), some African governments ("We helped them to do it"), and some exogenous forces ("We are happy to see it come to pass, but we didn't want to be involved"). It is also based on the realistic assumption that the subsystem is powerful enough to resist a conventional assault by the other African countries.[46] At the same time this scenario definitely depends on African strength, will, and determination, the opportunity to broaden support, *and* the ability to translate this growth into antisystemic pressure culminating in its overthrow. And here the evidence, although fragmentary, suggests that this is quite an assumption. There are virtually no data to indicate that African liberation movements will be able to do more than reduce the scope of the subsystem and change the character of some of its units. This is in line with Scenario III and is plausible. But the intrinsic power of South Africa, the nature of its terrain, and the general handicaps associated with the development of a revolutionary movement within the country all militate against the Africans being able to overthrow it *without* substantial exogenous inputs of the type outlined in Scenario VI. There is no evidence that the African movements have, *or are devleoping*, the capability to overthrow the South African heartland. South Africa is not all-powerful and could not simultaneously hold Angola, Mozambique, and Rhodesia as well as its own territory, but it seems well able to maintain itself, South West Africa (at least the portion south of the Police Zone), Lesotho, and probably Swaziland and southern Mozambique.[47] Scenario VIII, therefore, seems a remote possibility at best.

SCENARIO IX: TERMINATION OF THE PRESENT SUBSYSTEM

As defined in the current literature, a subsystem needs at least three units.[48] Given this definition, it is possible to conceive of a situation in which the subsystem itself comes to an end due to a lack of members since the South African core retains its separate texture as outlined in the introduction to this chapter and other units such as Angola, Rhodesia, and Mozambique change the patterns of their economic, communications, and political interaction to include East or Central Africa.

Configurations:

(1) Angola and Mozambique become independent and, rather than remain part of the subsystem, reorient their transaction flows toward Central (Angola) and East (Mozambique) Africa.

(2) This change in status encourages the FFGs to redouble their efforts against Rhodesia and Rhodesia is eventually pulled away from Southern Africa and integrated into East Africa. South West Africa is also liberated and joined to Angola in terms of transactions.

(3) The enclave states of Botswana and Swaziland as well as Malawi also remove themselves from the system, Botswana linking itself to Zambia and Central Africa, Malawi and Swaziland to East Africa.

(4) South Africa, however, together with Lesotho, remains under European control but, in terms of the definition, the susbystem of Southern Africa is terminated.

Assumptions:
(1) Same as configuration (1), Scenario IV.

(2) Same as configuration (2), Scenario IV, with the addition that the units in question are willing and able to reorient their interactions more or less to exclude South Africa.

(3) African exiles are able to take over Rhodesia and South West Africa and choose to reorient the newly liberated areas.

(4) South Africa is strong enough to survive and to control Lesotho, but is not strong enough to prevent the *de facto* breakup of the subsystem.

(5) The Great Powers either encourage or do not actively discourage the breakup of the subsystem or cannot prevent it.

Appraisal:
This scenario is not without relevance for, as outlined in Scenario VIII, South Africa seems powerful enough to prevent its own destruction, barring Great Power intervention, but is not strong enough to prevent the eventual reduction of the subsystem. At the same time, in terms of definition, it seems most unlikely that the system would be reduced to two units since South Africa could maintain itself, Lesotho, and at least the southern portion of South West Africa. Thus Scenario III, not Scenario IX, would be the outcome.

Conclusion
It would, therefore, appear that Southern Africa is heading in the following directions: Over the short term (5 years), Scenario I is the one most likely to occur. Over the intermediate term (10–15 years), Scenario III seems the most probable (although Scenario II cannot be totally ruled out). In the late 1980s and 1990s, however, systemic alteration is clearly possible. If certain assumptions are valid—most notably, the direct involvement of black Americans in foreign policy formulation for the Southern African area and/or substantial Soviet or Chinese intervention into the area—Scenario VI takes on great importance. Without Great Power intervention, however, only Scenario III seems feasible.

Thus, with the approach of the twenty-first century, the odds seem to be that, without Great Power intervention, at least a truncated version of the subsystem will continue to exist under South African domination. The number of its client states will depend upon such factors as African determination to reduce the subsystem, Portuguese intransigence, and the relative "neutrality" of the Great Powers as much as upon the intrinsic economic and military powers of South Africa itself.

Notes

PART ONE CHAPTER 1

1. John A. Marcum, *The Angolan Revolution. Volume 1. The Anatomy of an Explosion (1950–1962)* (Cambridge and London: M.I.T. Press, 1969), pp. vii–viii. See also Paul M. Whitaker, "The Revolutions of 'Portuguese' Africa," *Journal of Modern African Studies*, vol. 8, no. 1 (April 1970), p. 17, n. 3. For a more general discussion see Myron Weiner, "Political Interviewing," in Robert E. Ward *et al.*, *Studying Politics Abroad: Field Research in the Developing Areas*. Sponsored by the Committee on Comparative Politics of the Social Science Research Council (Boston, Toronto: Little, Brown, 1964), pp. 103–133.

2. See James S. Coleman, "Documentary Research," in Ward, *op. cit.*, pp. 79–102.

3. See Peter Duignan, *Handbook of American Resources for African Studies*. Hoover Institution Bibliographical Series no. 29 (Stanford: Hoover Institution on War, Revolution, and Peace, 1966), pp. 14–17, for a description of the CAMP.

4. "History," *South African Digest* (Pretoria), vol. 15, no. 29 (week ended July 19, 1968), p. 14; and "Wide Interest in Africana Reprints," *The Star* (Johannesburg), May 7, 1969, second city late ed., p. 6, cols. 8–9.

5. See Thomas G. Karis, "The South African Treason Trial," *Political Science Quarterly*, vol. 76, no. 2 (June 1961), pp. 117–140; and Thomas G. Karis, *The Treason Trial: A Guide to the Microfilm Record of the Trial*. Hoover Institution Bibliographical Series no. 23 (Stanford: Hoover Institution on War, Revolution, and Peace, 1965). Some insightful work on African nationalism in South Africa has utilized these and similar documents. See Edward Feit, *South Africa: The Dynamics of the African National Congress*. Issued under the auspices of the Institute of Race Relations, London (London, New York, Ibadan: Oxford University Press, 1962); and Edward Feit, "Urban Revolt in South Africa: A Case Study," *Journal of Modern African Studies*, vol. 8, no. 1 (April 1970), pp. 55–72.

6. See Thomas G. Karis, "South Africa," in Gwendolen M. Carter (ed.), *Five African States: Responses to Diversity* (Ithaca: Cornell University Press, 1963), p. 553; and Gwendolen M. Carter, *The Politics of Inequality: South Africa since 1948*, rev. ed. (New York: Frederick A. Praeger, 1959), pp. 43–44, 70–71. Such newspapers have been utilized in two thoughtful studies: Jeffrey Butler, "South Africa and the High Commission Territories: The Ganyile Case, 1971," in Gwendolen M. Carter (ed.), *Politics in Africa: 7 Cases* (New York, Chicago, Burlingame [Calif.]: Harcourt, Brace & World, 1966), pp. 245–283; and Edward Feit, *African Opposition in South Africa: The Failure of Passive Resistance* (Stanford: Hoover Institution on War, Revolution, and Peace, 1967).

7. See Shirley B. Smith, *The Formation and Functioning of the Trusteeship Council Procedure for Examining Petitions* (Boston: Boston University, unpublished M.A. thesis, 1957).

8. See Thomas Hodgkin, "A Note on the Language of African Nationalism," in Kenneth Kirkwood (ed.), *African Affairs Number One*. St. Antony's Papers, no. 10 (Carbondale: Southern Illinois University Press, 1961), pp. 22–40.

9. "Cataloguing of League Files," *The New York Times*, February 1, 1966, late city edition, p. 2, col. 6 and *Guide des Archives de la Société des Nations, 1919–1946*. Rédaction provisoire (Geneva: Bibliotheque des Nations Unies, Section des Collections Historiques, 1969). This will, of course, facilitate research in the League of Nations archives especially regarding the mandate system in South West Africa, *e.g.*, Rita Hinch, "The League of Nations Mandate System and South West Africa" (Ann Arbor: University of Michigan, Ph.D. dissertation in progress). Letter to the author from Miss Hinch, dated April 2, 1971.

10. "Secret of Ambassador's 'Rearm against Hitler' Warning," *The Times* (London), December 30, 1967, late London ed., p. 1, cols. 1–6.

11. For some studies which utilized these archives, see Richard Victor Pierard, *The German Colonial Society, 1882–1914* (Iowa City: State University of Iowa, unpublished Ph.D. dissertation, 1964); Jan Henrik Esterhuyse, *South West Africa, 1880–1894: The Establishment of German Authority in South West Africa* (Cape Town: C. Struik, 1968); Helmut Bley, *South-West Africa under German Rule, 1894–1914* (Evanston: Northwestern University Press, 1971); and Horst Drechsler, *Südwestafrika unter deutscher Kolonialherrschaft: Der Kampf der Herero und Nama gegen den deutschen Imperialismus (1884–1915)* (Berlin: Academie Verlag, 1966).

12. Ronald H. Chilcote, *Emerging Nationalism in Portuguese Africa: A Bibliography of Documentary*

Ephemera through 1965. Hoover Institution Bibliographic Series no. 39 (Stanford: Hoover Institution on War, Revolution, and Peace, 1969).

13. Letters to the author from Mr. Guy Arnold, director of the Africa Bureau, dated May 5, 1970, and from Mr. Hans E. Panofsky, Curator of Africana at Northwestern University, dated May 18, 1970.

14. See Robert A. Lystad, "Research Opportunities in the Social Sciences and Humanities in Sudan, Ethiopia, South Africa, Lesotho, and Swaziland," *African Studies Bulletin*, vol. 12, no. 2 (September 1969), pp. 111–129; and Joan Ells, "Newspapers and Periodicals on Africa in Microform," *African Studies Bulletin*, vol. 12, no. 2 (September 1969), pp. 193–209.

15. Paulus Mohome and John B. Webster (compilers), *A Bibliography on Bechuanaland*. Occasional Bibliography no. 5 (Syracuse: Syracuse University, Maxwell School of Citizenship and Public Affairs, Program of Eastern African Studies, Bibliographic Section, 1966); John B. Webster, Paulus Mohome, and Catherine M. Todd (compilers), *A Supplement to a Bibliography on Bechuanaland*. Occasional Bibliography no. 12 (Syracuse: Syracuse University, Maxwell School of Citizenship and Public Affairs, Program of Eastern African Studies, Bibliographic Section, 1968); John B. Webster and Paulus Mohome (compilers), *A Bibliography on Lesotho*. Occasional Bibliography no. 9 (Syracuse: Syracuse University, Maxwell School of Citizenship and Public Affairs, Program of Eastern African Studies, Bibliographic Section, 1968); Edward E. Brown, Carol A. Fisher, and John B. Webster (compilers), *A Bibliography of Malawi*. Eastern Africa Bibliographical Series no. 1 (Syracuse: Syracuse University, Maxwell Graduate School, Eastern African Studies Program, 1965); and John B. Webster and Paulus Mohome (compilers), *A Bibliography on Swaziland*. Occasional Bibliography no. 10 (Syracuse: Syracuse University, Maxwell School of Citizenship and Public Affairs, Program of Eastern African Studies, Bibliographic Section, 1968).

16. For a list of these bibliographies see C. Struik, *Africa Book Bulletin* (Cape Town), no. 58 (May 1968), *Supplement*, pp. 1–4; and no. 60 (n.d.), p. 1.

17. Michael A. Samuels, "Report of Historical Research in Angola," *African Studies Bulletin*, vol. 11, no. 3 (December 1968), pp. 245–247; Roger K. Tangri, "Political Change in Colonial Malawi: A Bibliographic Essay," *African Studies Bulletin*, vol. 11, no. 3 (December 1968), pp. 269–285; Ronald H. Chilcote, "Nationalist Documents on Portuguese Guine and Cape Verde Islands and Mocambique," *African Studies Bulletin*, vol. 10, no. 1 (April 1967), pp. 22–42; and Reuben Musiker, "Bibliographical Progress in South Africa, 1967–1968," *African Studies Bulletin*, vol. 12, no. 3 (December 1969), pp. 305–314.

18. Fourth revised edition (Cape Town, Amsterdam: A. A. Balkema, 1965).

19. Compiled by the Ferdinand Postma Library, Potchefstroom University for C.H.E., Potchefstroom, South Africa. To date, ten supplements have been issued, the latest being for 1968.

20. Pretoria: University of South Africa, 1966.

21. Monica Wilson, "South Africa," *International Social Science Journal* (Paris), vol. 13, no. 2 (1961), pp. 225–244.

22. Pierre L. van den Berghe, "Current Studies and Research Centres: Some Trends in Unpublished Social Science Research in South Africa," *International Social Science Journal*, vol. 14, no. 4 (1962), pp. 723–732.

23. Leonard M. Thompson, "Afrikaner Nationalist Historiography and the Policy of Apartheid," *Journal of African History*, vol. 3, no. 1 (1962), pp. 125–141. See also his "South Africa" in Robin W. Winks (ed.), *The Historiography of the British Empire-Commonwealth: Trends, Interpretations, and Resources* (Durham, N. C.: Duke University Press, 1966), pp. 212–236. The Afrikaner point of view is ably presented in F. A. van Jaarsveld, *The Afrikaner's Interpretation of South African History* (Cape Town: Simondium, 1964).

24. Deryck van der H. Schreuder, "History on the Veld: Towards a New Dawn?" *African Affairs* (London), vol. 68, no. 271 (April 1969), pp. 149–159.

25. Leslie Rubin, "South Africa and Her Immediate Neighbors: A Bibliographic Essay," *African Forum*, vol. 2, no. 2 (Fall 1966), pp. 78–84.

26. Salisbury: University College of Rhodesia and Nyasaland, Department of Government, 1965.

27. By the African Section of the Library of Congress. (Washington, D.C.: Library of Congress, 1965.)

28. Cape Town: Longmans, Green, 1956.

29. Prior to the annual listing of theses on Africa, SCOLMA had issued *Theses on Africa Accepted by Universities in the United Kingdom and Ireland* (Cambridge: W. Heffer & Sons, 1964).

30. Robert Collison (compiler), *The Scolma Directory of Libraries and Special Collections on Africa*, 2nd ed. (Hamden, Conn.: Archon Books, 1967).

31. Oxford: Bodleian Library, 1968.

32. Published for the Institute of Commonwealth Studies, University of London (London: The Athlone Press, 1957).

33. See Liselotte Hofmann (compiler), *United States and Canadian Publications on Africa in 1965*. Hoover Institution Bibliographical Series no. 34 (Stanford: Hoover Institution on War, Revolution, and Peace, 1967).

34. For a listing of these guides see Duignan, *op. cit.*, pp. 47–48.

35. The African Bibliographic Center in Washington, D.C., issues the monthly publication, *A Current Bibliography on African Affairs*, as well as special bibliographic series.

36. Boston University. Libraries, *List of French Doctoral Dissertations on Africa, 1884–1961*. Compiled by Marion Dinstel (Boston: G. K. Hall, 1966).

37. See John B. Webster, "Toward an International Automated Bibliographic System for Africana." Paper prepared for delivery at the Eleventh Annual Meeting of the African Studies Association, Los Angeles, Calif., October 16–19, 1968; and Alan R. Taylor, "Report on the Activities of the Archives-Libraries Committee for the Year, 1967," *African Studies Bulletin*, vol. 11, no. 2 (September 1968), pp. 214–216.

38. This analysis of the Africa Institute draws on the following sources: "Africa—All about the Continent," *Bantu* (Pretoria), vol. 15, no. 11 (November 1968), pp. 2–8; Africa Institute, *Annual Report, 1969* (Pretoria: Africa Institute, n.d.); P. F. D. Weiss, "Africa Institute: Field of Work Outlined by Director" (letter to the editor), *The Star*, November 22, 1966, first stop press ed., p. 12, cols. 4–5; and P. F. D. Weiss, "The Africa Institute: No Links with Government" (letter to the editor),

The Star, January 27, 1967, city late ed., p. 13, cols. 2–4.

39. P. Smit, G. M. E. Leistner, A. J. van Wyk, and E. J. van der Merwe, *Lesotho* (Pretoria: Africa Institute, 1969); *Swaziland on the Eve of Independence*. Occasional Papers of the Africa Institute of South Africa no. 4 (Pretoria: Africa Institute of South Africa, 1968); and A. J. van Wyk, *Swaziland: A Political Study*. Communications of the Africa Institute No. 9 (Pretoria: Africa Institute of South Africa, 1969); G. M. E. Leistner and P. Smit, *Swaziland: Resources and Development*. Communications of the Africa Institute no. 8 (Pretoria: Africa Institute of South Africa, 1969); P. Smit, *Botswana: Resources and Development*. Communications of the Africa Institute no. 13 (Pretoria: Africa Institute of South Africa, 1970); F. R. Metrowich, *Rhodesia: Birth of a Nation* (Pretoria: Africa Institute of South Africa, 1969); and P. Smit, *Current Trends of Development in Malawi*. Occasional paper no. 2 (Pretoria: Africa Institute of South Africa, n.d.).

40. This discussion of the South African Institute of Race Relations is based on South African Institute of Race Relations (Inc.), *39th Annual Report, 1967–1968* (Johannesburg: South African Institute of Race Relations, n.d.) and Quintin Whyte, "South African Institute of Race Relations: Suid-Afrikaanse Instituut vir Rasseverhoudings," *Race* (London), vol. 10, no. 1 (July 1968), pp. 103–105. See also Marshall Lee, "Aggrey's Black and White Melody Lingers On: Race Group Plays Fortissimo," *The Star*, January 25, 1969, city late sport ed., p. 11, cols. 1–9.

41. For a partial listing of some of the publications sponsored by the institute, consult Wilson, *op. cit.*, pp. 232–244.

42. A. L. Müller, *Minority Interests: The Political Economy of the Coloured and Indian Communities in South Africa* (Johannesburg: South African Institute of Race Relations, 1968); Muriel Horrell, *South Africa's Workers: Their Organizations and the Patterns of Employment* (Johannesburg: South African Institute of Race Relations, 1969); and Muriel Horrell, *The African Reserves of South Africa* (Johannesburg: South African Institute of Race Relations, 1969).

43. This discussion of the South African Institute of International Affairs is based on Edwin S. Munger, *Notes on the Formation of South African Foreign Policy* (Pasadena: Grant Dahlstrom/Castle Press, 1965), pp. 51–52; and South African Institute of International Affairs, *The South African Institute of International Affairs* (Johannesburg: South African Institute of International Affairs, 1969). The author would like to thank Miss C. Daphne Saul, Librarian of the Institute, for furnishing him with materials on the Institute.

44. Sir Charles Dundas and Dr. Hugh Ashton, *Problem Territories of Southern Africa: Basutoland, Bechuanaland Protectorate, Swaziland* (Johannesburg: South African Institute of International Affairs, 1952); Eric Rosenthal, *South African Diplomats Abroad: The S.A. Department of External Affairs* (Johannesburg: South African Institute of International Affairs, 1949); Ben Cockram, *Problems of Southern Africa* (Johannesburg: South African Institute of International Affairs, 1963); Sir Charles Dundas, *South-West Africa: The Factual Background* (Johannesburg: South African Institute of International Affairs, 1946); Harold M. Glass, *South African Policy towards Basutoland* (Johannesburg: The South African Institute of International Affairs, 1966); and R. B. Ballinger, *South Africa and the United Nations: Myth and Reality* (Johannesburg: South African Institute of International Affairs, 1963).

45. *Suid-Afrika in die Veranderde Wêreld: Referate Gelewer by Geleentheid van die Eerste Simposium oor die Internasionale Politiek, Potchefstroom, 31 Augustus 1967* (Potchefstroom: Sentrum vir Internasionale Politiek, 1968); *Suid-Afrika in 'n Onveilige Wêreld: Referate Gelewer van die Tweede Simposium oor die Internasionale Politiek, Potchefstroom, 23 Augustus 1968* (Potchefstroom: Sentrum vir Internasionale Politiek, 1968); and G. S. Labuschagne, *Suid-Afrika en Afrika: Die Staatkundige Verhouding in die Tydperk 1945–1966* (Potchefstroom: Sentrum vir Internasionale Politiek, 1969); *Suid-Afrika en Suider Afrika: Die Republiek se Ontwikkelende Betrekkinge met Sy Buurstate* (Potchefstroom: Sentrum vir Internasionale Politiek, 1970); and *Suid-Afrika in Uitwaartse Beweging: Referate Gelewer by Geleentheid van die Derde Simposium oor Internasionale Politiek, Potchefstroom, 22 Augustus 1969* (Potchefstroom: Sentrum vir Internasionale Politiek, 1970).

46. "Council of the Institute," *SAIPA: Journal for Public Administration* (Pretoria), vol. 5, no. 1 (December 1969), p. 62.

47. This discussion of the Abe Bailey Institute draws on the following sources: Abe Bailey Institute of Inter-Racial Studies, *First Annual Report, 1968* (Randebosch: Abe Bailey Institute of Inter-Racial Studies, 1968); H. W. van der Merwe, "Abe Bailey Institute of Inter-Racial Studies," *Race*, vol. 10, no. 2 (October 1968), pp. 212–214; "Survey Findings: Not Much Contact of Races," *The Star*, October 30, 1968, second city late ed., p. 30, cols. 5–6; "Several Trends of Interest," *The Star*, October 30, 1968, second city late ed., p. 30, col. 6; "Survey of S.A. 'Elite' Launched," *The Star*, December 22, 1968, city late ed., p. 11, cols. 5–6; and Abe Bailey Institute of Inter-Racial Studies, *Second Annual Report, 1969* (Rondebosch: Abe Bailey Institute of Inter-Racial Studies, 1969). The author would like to thank Professor van der Merwe for supplying him with material on the Institute.

48. See the series of five articles by Patrick Laurence entitled "Politics: What the White Man Thinks" in *The Star*, May 12, 1969, second city late ed., p. 8, cols. 2–5; May 13, 1969, second city late ed., p. 10, cols. 4–7; May 14, 1969, second city late ed., p. 6, cols. 5–9; May 15, 1969, second city late ed., p. 8, cols. 7–9; and May 16, 1969, second city late ed., p. 8, cols. 4–7. These five articles are based on research conducted by the firm of Media and Communications Research in Johannesburg. For the work of the firm of Market Research Africa (Pty.), Ltd., see "Gallup Type Poll of Voters," *The Star*, January 19, 1970, second city late ed., p. 1, col. 9. See also Christopher Orpen, "Just How Prejudiced Are White South Africans," *New Nation* (Pretoria), vol. 4, no. 7 (February, 1971), pp. 10–12.

49. See the series of four articles by Patrick Laurence entitled "Soweto," in *The Star*, April 28, 1969, second city late ed., p. 10, cols. 6–9; April 29, 1969, second city late ed., p. 9, cols. 8–9; April 30, 1969, second city late ed., p. 10, cols. 4–5; and May 1, 1969, second city late ed., p. 29, cols. 4–6. These four articles are based on research conducted by the two Johannesburg firms of International Consumer Research and Media and Communications Research. See also J. C. de Ridder, *The Personality*

of the Urban African in South Africa: A Thematic Apperception Test Study (London: Routledge & Kegan Paul, 1961).

50. See E. A. Brett, *African Attitudes: A Study of the Social, Racial and Political Attitudes of Some Middle Class Africans*. Fact Paper no. 14 (Johannesburg: South African Institute of Race Relations, 1963); and "If Africans Were in Power . . . Black on White: A Special Survey," *The Star*, January 2, 1969, second city late ed., p. 11, cols. 1–4.

51. See "Organization To Take Monthly Opinion Polls," *The Star*, August 15, 1968, second city late ed., p. 3, cols. 2–3; "Poll Shows Up Ignorance of S.A. Voters: Some Don't Even Know Mr. Vorster," *The Star*, December 5, 1969, second city late ed., p. 12, cols. 1–5; and H. Lever, "The Johannesburg Station Explosion and Ethnic Attitudes," *Public Opinion Quarterly*, vol. 33, no. 2 (Summer 1969), pp. 180–189. A standard work in this field is I. D. MacCrone, *Race Attitudes in South Africa: Historical, Experimental and Psychological Studies* (Johannesburg: Witwatersrand Press, 1937, 1957 reprint).

52. See Cyril A. Rogers and C. Frantz, *Racial Themes in Southern Rhodesia: The Attitudes and Behavior of the White Population* (New Haven and London: Yale University Press, 1962).

53. Gabriel A. Almond and Sidney Verba, *The Civic Culture: Political Attitudes and Democracy in Five Nations* (Princeton, N.J.: Princeton University Press, 1963). See also Lucian W. Pye and Sidney Verba (eds.), *Political Culture and Political Development*. Studies in Political Development no. 5 (Princeton, N.J.: Princeton University Press, 1965).

54. This analysis of the bureau is based on "The South African Bureau of Racial Affairs," *Bantu*, vol. 16, no. 5 (May 1969), pp. 20–25. For a more extensive account of the bureau see Edwin S. Munger, *Africa Field Reports, 1952–1961* (Cape Town: C. Struik, 1961), pp. 503–550.

55. This account of the institute is based on Philip Mason, "Ten Years of The Institute," *Race*, vol. 10, no. 2 (October 1968), pp. 193–202; and a letter to the author from Mr. Hans E. Panofsky, Curator of Africana at Northwestern University, dated May 18, 1970.

56. *Angola: A Symposium: Views of a Revolt* (London: Oxford University Press, 1962) and David Birmingham, *The Portuguese Conquest of Angola* (London: Oxford University Press, 1965); R. W. Imishue, *South West Africa: An International Problem* (London: Pall Mall Press, 1965); S. Pienaar and Anthony Sampson, *South Africa: Two Views of Separate Development* (London: Oxford University Press, 1960); Z. J. De Beer, *Multi-Racial South Africa: The Reconciliation of Forces* (London: Oxford University Press, 1961); Peter Calvocoressi, *South Africa and World Opinion* (London: Oxford University Press, 1961); Edward Feit, *South Africa: The Dynamics of the African National Congress* (London: Oxford University Press, 1962); Christopher R. Hill, *Bantustans: The Fragmentation of South Africa* (London: Oxford University Press, 1964); Edwin S. Munger, *Afrikaner and African Nationalism: South African Parallels and Parameters* (London: Oxford University Press, 1967); Philip Mason, *The Birth of a Dilemma: The Conquest and Settlement of Rhodesia* (London: Oxford University Press, 1958); James P. Barber, *Rhodesia: The Road to Rebellion* (London: Oxford University Press, 1967); Edwin S. Munger, *Bechuanaland: Pan-African Outpost or Bantu Homeland?* (London: Oxford University Press, 1965); J. E. Spence, *Lesotho: The Politics of Dependence* (London: Oxford University Press, 1968); Richard Gray, *The Two Nations: Aspects of the Development of Race Relations in the Rhodesias and Nyasaland* (London: Oxford University Press, 1960); and Philip Mason, *Year of Decision: Rhodesia and Nyasaland in 1960* (London: Oxford University Press, 1960).

57. G. V. Doxey, *The High Commission Territories and the Republic of South Africa*. Chatham House Memoranda (London: Distributed for the Royal Institute of International Affairs by the Oxford University Press, 1963); J. E. Spence, *Republic Under Pressure: A Study of South African Foreign Policy*. Chatham House Essays no. 9 (London: Oxford University Press, 1965); and Dennis Austin, *Britain and South Africa* (London: Oxford University Press, 1966).

58. See Col. Donald H. Humphries, *The East African Liberation Movement*. Adelphi Papers no. 16 (London: Institute for Strategic Studies, 1965); and David Wood, *The Armed Forces of African States*. Adelphi Papers no. 27 (London: Institute for Strategic Studies, 1966). Recently the Royal United Service Institution in London sponsored two studies on Southern Africa. See J. E. Spence, *The Strategic Significance of Southern Africa* (London: Royal United Service Institution, 1970) and Rear-Admiral Morgan-Giles, D.S.O., O.B.E., G.M., M.P. (Chairman), *The Cape Route: Report of a Seminar Held at the Royal United Service Institution on Wednesday, 25 February 1970* (London: Royal United Service Institution, 1970).

59. For a published account of the activities of this organization, see Harold Soref and Ian Greig, *The Puppeteers* (London: Tandem Books, 1965), pp. 12–29. Examples of some of its literature are Rosalynde Ainslie and Dorothy Robinson, *The Collaborators* (London: Anti-Apartheid Movement, 1963) and Abdul S. Minty, *South Africa's Defence Strategy* (London: Anti-Apartheid Movement, 1969).

60. Examples of such pamphlets include *Rhodesia: Why Minority Rule Survives* (London: Published for the International Defence and Aid Fund by Christian Action Publications, 1969); Alexander Hepple, *South Africa: Workers under Apartheid* (London: Published for the International Defence and Aid Fund by Christian Action Publications, 1969); and *South Africa: The BOSS Law* (London: Published for the International Defense and Aid Fund by Christian Action Publications, 1969).

61. On the work of the South Africa Foundation see Colin and Margaret Legum, *South Africa: Crisis for the West* (New York, London: Frederick A. Praeger, 1964), pp. 112–116, 245–246. Until July 1969 the London office of the foundation published a monthly journal entitled *Perspective*. Presently, it publishes *South Africa International* and *South African Press Review*, both of which appear monthly.

62. For published accounts of the activities of the Africa Bureau, consult Soref and Greig, *op. cit.*, pp. 63–76; and Michael Scott, *A Time to Speak* (London: Faber & Faber, 1958), pp. 269–296.

63. Isobel Edwards, *Basutoland Enquiry* (London: Africa Bureau, n.d.); Tshekedi Khama, *Bechuanaland and South Africa* (London: Africa Bureau, 1955); Tshekedi Khama, *Political Change in African Society: A*

Study of the Development of Representative Government (London: Africa Bureau, 1956); and Isobel Edwards, *Protectorates or Native Reserves? A Political and Constitutional Survey of the High Commission Territories in South Africa—Basutoland, Bechuanaland and Swaziland* (London: Africa Bureau, n.d.).

64. See Sandor (pseudonym), *The Coming Struggle for South Africa*. Fabian Tract no. 345 (London: Fabian Society, 1963); and Fabian Society, *The Unprotected Protectorates: Basutoland, Bechuanaland, Swaziland*. Fabian Research Series no. 250 (London: Fabian Society, 1965).

65. See Soref and Greig, *op. cit.*, pp. 30–39. Examples of their literature include Mary Benson, *The Badge of Slavery* (*The Pass Laws of South Africa*) (London: Christian Action, n.d.); Suzanne Cronje, *Witness in the Dark: Police Torture and Brutality in South Africa* (London: Christian Action, n.d.); and The Right Reverend Ambrose Reeves, *South Africa: Let the Facts Speak* (London: Christian Action, 1962).

66. Waldemar A. Nielsen, *African Battleline: American Policy Choices in Southern Africa* (New York and Evanston: Harper & Row 1965).

67. Thomas G. Karis, *South Africa: The End Is Not Yet*. Headline Series no. 176 (New York: Foreign Policy Association, 1966).

68. James Duffy, *Portugal's African Territories: Present Realities*. Occasional Paper no. 1 (New York: Carnegie Endowment for International Peace, 1962); Richard J. Hammond, *Portugal's African Problem: Some Economic Facets*. Occasional Paper no. 2 (New York: Carnegie Endowment for International Peace, 1962); Particia Wohlgemuth, "The Portuguese Territories and the United Nations," *International Conciliation*, no. 545 (November, 1963), pp. 3–68. Ralph Zacklin, "Challenge of Rhodesia: Toward an International Policy," *International Conciliation*, no. 575 (November, 1969), pp. 5–70; and Amelia C. Leiss (ed.), *Apartheid and United Nations Collective Measures: An Analysis* (New York: Carnegie Endowment for International Peace, 1965).

69. Irving Kaplan *et al.*, *Area Handbook for the Republic of South Africa*. D. A. Pam. no. 550–93 (Washington, D.C.: USGPO, 1971); Allison Butler Herrick *et al.*, *Area Handbook for Angola*. D.A. Pam. no. 550–59 (Washington, D.C.: USGPO, 1967); Allison Butler Herrick *et al.*, *Area Handbook for Mozambique*. D.A. Pam. no. 550–64 (Washington, D.C.: USGPO, 1969); and Irving Kaplan *et al.*, *Area Handbook for Zambia*. D.A. Pam. no. 550–75 (Washington, D.C.: USGPO, 1969).

70. United States. Congress. House of Representatives. Committee on Foreign Affairs. Subcommittee on Africa, *United States–South African Relations: Hearings*. 4 parts. Eighty-ninth Congress. Second session (Washington, D.C.: USGPO, 1966); United States. Congress. House of Representatives. Committee on Foreign Affairs. Subcommittee on Africa, *United States–South African Relations: Hearing*. Ninetieth Congress. First session (Washington, D.C.: USGPO, 1967); United States. Congress. House of Representatives. Committee on Foreign Affairs. Subcommittee on Africa, *South Africa and United States Foreign Policy: Hearings*. Ninety-first Congress, First session (Washington, D.C.: USGPO, 1969); Hon. Charles C. Diggs, Jr. and Hon. Lester Wolff, *Report of a Special Study Mission to Southern Africa, August 10–30, 1969*. Ninety-first Congress. First session (Washington, D.C.: USGPO, 1969); and United States. Congress. House of Representatives. Committee on Foreign Affairs. Subcommittee on Africa, *Rhodesia and United States Foreign Policy: Hearings*. Ninety-first Congress. First session. (Washington, D.C.: USGPO, 1969).

71. David M. Abshire and Michael A. Samuels (eds.), *Portuguese Africa: A Handbook* (New York, Washington, London: Frederick A. Praeger, 1969).

72. Rita M. Cassidy, *Financial Administration in Basutoland, 1884–1900*. Papers in International Studies no. 7 (Athens, Ohio: Ohio University Center for International Studies, 1967); Richard F. Weisfelder, *Defining National Purpose in Lesotho*. Papers in International Studies. Africa Series no. 3 (Athens, Ohio: Ohio University Center for International Studies, Africa Program, 1969); Norman H. Pollock, *The Struggle Against Sleeping Sickness in Nyasaland and Northern Rhodesia, 1900–1922*. Papers in International Studies. Africa Series no. 5 (Athens, Ohio: Ohio University Center for International Studies, Africa Program, 1969); and Richard Dale, *Botswana and Its Southern Neighbor: The Patterns of Linkage and the Options in Statecraft*. Papers in International Studies. Africa Series no. 6 (Athens, Ohio: Ohio University Center for International Studies, Africa Program, 1970).

73. Charles Burton Marshall, *Crisis over Rhodesia: A Skeptical View*. Studies in International Affairs no. 3. Washington Center of Foreign Policy Research, School of Advanced International Studies, The Johns Hopkins University (Baltimore: Johns Hopkins Press, 1967).

74. Gary Gappert (ed.), *South African Dilemmas: Some Dynamics of a Static State*. Occasional Paper no. 18 (Syracuse: Syracuse University, Maxwell School of Citizenship and Public Affairs, Program of Eastern African Studies, n.d.).

75. Ernest A. Gross *et al.*, *Ethiopia and Liberia vs. South Africa: The South West Africa Cases*. Occasional Paper no. 5 (Los Angeles: University of California, Los Angeles, African Studies Center, 1968); and Martin Legassick, *The National Union of South African Students: Ethnic Cleavage and Ethnic Integration in the Universities*. Occasional Paper no. 4 (Los Angeles: University of California, Los Angeles, African Studies Center, 1967).

76. Alan C. G. Best, *The Swaziland Railway: A Study in Politico-Economic Geography* (East Lansing, Mich.: Michigan State University, African Studies Center in cooperation with the Office of International Programs, 1966).

77. Edward Callan, *Albert John Luthuli and the South African Race Conflict*, rev. ed. Monograph Series on Social and Cultural Change no. 1 (Kalamazoo, Mich.: Institute of International and Area Studies and School of Graduate Studies, 1965).

78. See George W. Shepherd, Jr., "The Center on International Race Relations, University of Denver," *Race*, vol. 11, no. 2 (October, 1969), pp. 228–229; Elizabeth Landis, *Namibia: The Beginning of Disengagement*. Studies in Race and Nations, vol. 2, no. 1 (1970–1971) (Denver: University of Denver, Graduate School of International Studies, Center on International Race Relations, 1970); and James R. Scarritt and John L. Hatter, *Racial and Ethnic Conflict in Zambia*. Studies in Race and Nations, vol. 2, no. 2 (1970–1971) (Denver:

University of Denver, Graduate School of Graduate Studies, Center on International Race Relations, 1970).

79. J. M. Tinley, *South African Food and Agriculture in World War II*. Studies on Food, Agriculture, and World War II. Food Research Institute, Stanford University (Stanford: Stanford University Press, 1954); and S. Daniel Neumark, *Economic Influences on the South African Frontier, 1652–1836*. Miscellaneous Publication no. 12. Food Research Institute, Stanford University (Stanford: Stanford University Press, 1957).

80. Hector Menteith Robertson, *South Africa: Economic and Political Aspects*. Duke University Commonwealth Studies Center Publication no. 2. Published for the Duke University Commonwealth Studies Center (Durham, N.C.: Duke University Press; London: Cambridge University Press, 1957).

81. Heinz Hartmann, *Enterprise and Politics in South Africa* (Princeton, N.J.: Princeton University, Department of Economics, Industrial Relations Section, 1962).

82. Items listed in *A Bibliography of Selected Rand Publications. Africa*. SB-1001 (Santa Monica, Calif.: Rand Corporation, 1968) include the following: B. F. Massell and R. W. M. Johnson, *African Agriculture in Rhodesia: An Econometric Study*. R-443-RC, June, 1966; S. Enke, *The Federation of Rhodesia and Nyasaland: A Case Study in Economic Development*. P-1616, February, 1959; and V. J. Croizat, *The Economic Development of South Africa in Its Political Context*. P-3534, February, 1967.

83. According to its *Report to the Members, 1968* (Croton-on-Hudson, N.Y.: Hudson Institute, 1968), p. 9, the institute received funds from the Sprague Electric Company to investigate "the economic viability of Botswana and its African and international implications." Earlier, it had sponsored a study by Jean M. Ingersoll, *Historical Examples of Ecological Disaster: Famine in Russia, 1921–22; Famine in Bechuanaland, 1965*. HI-518-RR/A1 (Croton-on-Hudson: Hudson Institute, 1965). Other studies bearing on Southern African affairs are Michael E. Sherman, *Racial War in Africa: A Peacekeeping Scenario*. HI-1121/2-RR (Croton-on-Hudson: Hudson Institute, 1968) and *Angola: Some Views of Development Prospects*. 2 vols. HI-1278-RR/I and HI-1278-RR/II (Croton-on-Hudson: Hudson Institute, 1969).

84. This account is based on American-African Affairs Association, *1969 Program; Report, September, 1965–December, 1968* (New York: American-African Affairs Association, n.d.).

85. Examples of such reports include the following: Daniel T. Brigham, *Blueprint for Conflict* (New York: American-African Affairs Association, 1969); Walter Darnell Jacobs, *South Africa Looks Outward* (New York: American-African Affairs Association, 1968); Thomas Molnar, *Spotlight on South West Africa* (New York: American-African Affairs Association, 1966); Walter Darnell Jacobs, *A Constitution for Rhodesia: An Analysis Submitted to the American-African Affairs Association* (New York: American-African Affairs Association, 1968); and James Jackson Kilpatrick, *A Special Study of the Portuguese Provinces: A Place for Pioneers* (New York: American-African Affairs Association, 1968).

86. Examples of its publications include the following: Collin Gonze, George M, Houser, and Perry Sturges, *South African Crisis and United States Policy*. Africa Today Pamphlet no. 5 (New York: American Committee on Africa, 1962); *Action against Apartheid* (New York: American Committee on Africa, 1960); Marvin Harris, *Portugal's African "Wards": A First-Hand Report on Labor and Education in Mozambique* (New York: The American Committee on Africa, 1958); and Winifred Courtney (ed.), *South West Africa: The UN's Stepchild*, 2nd ed. (New York: American Committee on Africa, 1960).

87. See United States. Congress. House of Representatives. Committee on Foreign Affairs. Subcommittee on Africa. *United States–South African Relations: Hearings*. 4 parts. Eighty-ninth Congress. Second session (Washington, D.C.: USGPO, 1966), part 1, pp. 190–211; and United States. Congress. House of Representatives. Committee on Foreign Affairs. Subcommittee on Africa, *Rhodesia and United States Foreign Policy: Hearings*. Ninety-first Congress. First session (Washington, D.C.: USGPO, 1969), pp. 70–100.

88. See United States Congress. House of Representatives. Committee on Foreign Relations. Subcommittee on Africa, *United States–South African Relations: Hearings*. 4 parts. Eighty-ninth Congress. Second session (Washington, D.C.: USGPO, 1966), part 1, pp. 71–80.

89. Jane W. Jacqz, *Development Needs in Botswana and Lesotho: Report of a Conference on United States Assistance to Botswana and Lesotho Sponsored by the African-American Institute at AAI Headquarters, New York City, June 29, 1967* (New York: African-American Institute, 1967); and Jane W. Jacqz, *Refugee Students from Southern Africa: Report of a Workshop on the Training and Utilization of Refugee Students from Southern Africa Sponsored by the African-American Institute and Syracuse University at Lubin House, New York City, April 18–19, 1967* (New York: African-American Institute, 1967).

90. Harvey Glickman, "Political Science," in Robert A. Lystad (ed.), *The African World: A Survey of Social Research* (New York, Washington, London: Frederick A. Praeger, 1965), pp. 131–165.

91. Henry L. Bretton, "Political Science Field Research in Africa," *Comparative Politics*, vol. 2, no. 3 (April, 1970), pp. 413–443. See also Klaus Knorr, "Social Science Research Abroad: Problems and Remedies," *World Politics*, vol. 19, no. 3 (April, 1967), pp. 465–485.

92. See Larry W. Bowman, "The Subordinate State System of Southern Africa," *International Studies Quarterly*, vol. 12, no. 3 (September, 1968), pp. 231–261.

93. Much of the literature on international subsystems is ably surveyed in a special issue of *International Studies Quarterly*, vol. 13, no. 4 (December, 1969), which is devoted to this topic. See also I. William Zartman, "Africa as a Subordinate State System in International Relations," *International Organization*, vol. 21, no. 3 (Summer, 1967), pp. 545–564; Joseph S. Nye, "Comparative Regional Integration: Concept and Measurement," *International Organization*, vol. 22, no. 4 (Autumn, 1968), pp. 855–880; Karl Kaiser, "The Interaction of Regional Subsystems: Some Preliminary Notes on Recurrent Patterns and the Role of Superpowers," *World Politics*, vol. 21, no. 1 (October, 1968), pp. 84–107; Roger D. Hanson, "Regional Integration: Reflections on a Decade of Theoretical Efforts," *World Politics*, vol. 21, no. 2 (January, 1969), pp. 242–271; and Michael Haas, "International Subsystems: Stability

and Polarity," *American Political Science Review*, vol. 64, no. 1 (March, 1970), pp. 98–123.

94. For a discussion of the advantages and disadvantages of this type of study, consult Herbert H. Hyman, "Research Design," in Ward, *op. cit.*, pp. 173–181.

95. This matter is analyzed in Edmund H. Dale, "Some Geographical Aspects of African Land-Locked States," *Annals of the American Geographers*, vol. 58, no. 3 (September, 1968), pp. 485–505.

96. See T. J. D. Fair, G. Murdoch, and H. M. Jones, *Development in Swaziland: A Regional Analysis* (Johannesburg: Witwatersrand University Press, 1969); and Charles F. Schmidt, *South Africa and the Former High Commission Territories: Political Independence in an Interacting Space Economy* (Carbondale: Southern Illinois University, unpublished M.A. thesis, 1969).

97. William Buchanan and Hadley Cantril, *How Nations See Each Other: A Study in Public Opinion*. Prepared under the auspices of the United Nations Educational, Scientific and Cultural Organization (Urbana: University of Illinois Press, 1953).

98. Walter Lippmann, *Public Opinion*, (New York: The Macmillan Company, 1960), p. 81. The book was originally published in 1922.

99. See Dr. William Hudson, Dr. Gideon Francois Jacobs, and Dr. Simon Biesheuvel, *Anatomy of South Africa: A Scientific Study of Present Day Attitudes* (Cape Town, Johannesburg: Purnell & Sons S.A., 1966).

100. See L. Bloom, A. R. C. De Crespigny, and J. E. Spence, "An Inter-Disciplinary Study of the Social, Moral and Political Attitudes of White and Non-White South African University Students," *Journal of Social Psychology*, vol. 54, first half (June 1961), pp. 3–12.

101. Jacques G. Rapoport, "The Participation of Ministates in International Affairs," *Proceedings of the American Society of International Law at Its Sixty-Second Annual Meeting Held at Washington, D.C., April 25–27, 1968* (Washington, D.C.: American Society of International Law, 1968), pp. 155–163; Patricia Wohlgemuth Blair, *The Ministate Dilemma*. Occasional Paper no. 6. Rev. ed. (New York: Carnegie Endowment for International Peace, 1968); and David Vital, *The Inequality of States: A Study of the Small Power in International Relations* (Oxford: Clarendon Press, 1967).

102. Colin de B. Webb, "The Foreign Policy of the Union of South Africa," in Joseph E. Black and Kenneth W. Thompson (eds.), *Foreign Policies in a World of Change* (New York: Harper & Row, 1963), pp. 425–449; J. E. Spence, "Tradition and Change in South African Foreign Policy," *Journal of Commonwealth Political Studies* (Leicester, England), vol. 1, no. 2 (July, 1963), pp. 136–152; J. E. Spence, *Republic under Pressure*; J. E. Spence, "South Africa's 'New Look' Foreign Policy," *The World Today* (London), vol. 24, no. 4 (April, 1968), pp. 137–145; S. F. du Toit, *Home and Abroad* (Cape Town: Nasionale Boekhandel, 1969); Rosenthal *South African Diplomats*; and Munger, *Notes on the Formation of South African Foreign Policy*.

103. The most recent studies of South African foreign policy are Amry Vandenbosch, *South Africa and the World: The Foreign Policy of Apartheid* (Lexington: The University Press of Kentucky, 1970) and Gail-Maryse Cockram, *Vorster's Foreign Policy* (Pretoria and Cape Town: H & R Academia [Pty.] Ltd., 1970).

104. See George S. Gilley, *The Foreign Policy of the Kingdom of Lesotho, 1966–1969* (Carbondale: Southern Illinois University, unpublished M.A. thesis, 1969).

105. Austin, *op. cit.*

106. Sanford David Greenberg, *United States Policy toward the Republic of South Africa, 1945–1964* (Cambridge, Mass.: Harvard University, unpublished Ph.D. dissertation, 1965); William A. Hance (ed.), *Southern Africa and the United States* (New York and London: Columbia University Press, 1968); and John Seiler, "Making Southern African Policy in the Nixon Administration." Paper prepared for delivery at the thirteenth annual meeting of the African Studies Association, Boston, October 21–24, 1970.

107. Two of the more recent works are Solomon Israel Slonim, *South West Africa and the United Nations: A Struggle over International Accountability* (New York: Columbia University, unpublished Ph.D. dissertation, 1967) and Alden Colt Small, *The United Nations and South West Africa: A Study in Parliamentary Diplomacy* (Medford, Mass.: Fletcher School of Law and Diplomacy, unpublished Ph.D. dissertation, 1970).

108. H. M. Moolman (compiler), *How They Hate Us: South Africa, and in Particular the Afrikaners, Their Church, Culture and Leaders, under Fire in the World Press* (Pretoria, Johannesburg, Klerksdorp: Voortrekkerpers, 1965); and Madeline Green Kalb, *The Soviet View of the Union of South Africa* (New York: Columbia University, unpublished M.A. thesis, 1959).

109. On the anti–South African lobby, consult Soref and Greig, *op. cit.*, pp. 9–108; on the pro–South African lobby, consult Legum, *op. cit.*, pp. 246–251.

110. See J. D. Stewart, *British Pressure Groups: Their Role in Relation to the House of Commons* (Oxford: Clarendon Press, 1958); Joseph Frankel, *The Making of Foreign Policy: An Analysis of Decision-Making* (London, New York, Toronto: Oxford University Press, 1963); Richard C. Snyder, H. W. Bruck, and Burton Sapin (eds.), *Foreign Policy Decision-Making: An Approach to the Study of International Politics* (New York: The Free Press of Glencoe, 1962); and Lester W. Milbrath, "Interest Groups and Foreign Policy," in James N. Rosenau (ed.), *Domestic Sources of Foreign Policy*. Published for the Princeton Center of International Studies (New York: The Free Press; London: Collier-Macmillan, 1967), pp. 231–251.

111. See Colin Leys, *European Politics in Southern Rhodesia* (Oxford: Clarendon Press, 1959), pp. 98–130; and P. B. Harris, *Interest Groups in South African Politics*. University College of Rhodesia, Department of Political Science Monographs in Political Science no. 1 (Salisbury: University College of Rhodesia, 1968).

112. Leo Kuper, *An African Bourgeoisie: Race, Class, and Politics in South Africa* (New Haven and London: Yale University Press, 1965).

113. The clipping files of the *Cape Times* were used by Professor Thompson's research assistant to help him write a profile of the Afrikaner political elite. See Leonard M. Thompson, *Politics in the Republic of South Africa* (Boston and Toronto: Little, Brown, 1966), pp. 114–120, especially p. 115, n. 36. Two guides which do contain biographies of Africans are Eric Rosenthal (compiler), *Southern African Dictionary of National Biography* (London and New York: Frederick Warne & Co., 1966) and W. J. de Kock (editor-in-chief), *Dictionary of South African Biography*. Published for the National Council for Social Research, Department of

Higher Education (Cape Town: Nasionale Boekhandel Beperk, 1968).

114. This was the 1953 general election. See Carter, *The Politics of Inequality*, pp. 9–10, 145–217. See also Andrew Johnson Milnor, *The Election of 1948 in the Union of South Africa, with Special Reference to the Origin and Development of the Reunited National Party* (Durham, N.C.: Duke University, unpublished M.A. thesis, 1959).

115. See Newell M. Stultz and Jeffrey Butler, "The South African General Election of 1961," *Political Science Quarterly*, vol. 78, no. 1 (March 1963), pp. 86–110; Newell M. Stultz, *The Electoral Revival of the National Party in South Africa, 1934–1948* (Boston: Boston University, unpublished Ph.D. dissertation, 1965); Leys, *op. cit.*, pp. 190–240; and Pieter Schalk Joubert, *Partypolitieke Groepering in Suidwes-Afrika sedert 1915* (Bloemfontein: University of the Orange Free State, unpublished M.A. thesis, 1959).

116. Archibald Peter Hunter, *The Reorientation of Educational Policy in South Africa since 1948* (Los Angeles: University of California, Los Angeles, unpublished Ed.D. dissertation, 1963); and Deborah Lavin, "The Dilemma of Christian-National Education in South Africa," *The World Today*, vol. 21, no. 10 (October 1965), pp. 428–438. Also consult F. E. Auerbach, *The Power of Prejudice in South African Education: An Enquiry into History Textbooks and Syllabuses in the Transvaal High Schools of South Africa* (Cape Town, Amsterdam: A. A. Balkema, 1965).

117. Legassick, *The National Union of South African Students*; and Martin Legassick and John Shingler, "South Africa," in Donald K. Emmerson (ed.), *Students and Politics in Developing Nations* (New York, Washington, London: Frederick A. Praeger, 1968), pp. 103–145.

118. Muriel Horrell (compiler), *Bantu Education to 1968* (Johannesburg: South African Institute of Race Relations, 1968).

119. Alexander Kerr, *Fort Hare, 1915–48: The Evolution of an African College* (London: C. Hurst & Co., 1968).

120. "South African Missionary Institutions: Tiger Kloof," *The South African Outlook* (Lovedale, Cape Province), vol. 85, no. 1013 (September 1, 1955), pp. 137–139.

121. John Day, *International Nationalism: The Extra-Territorial Relations of Southern Rhodesian African Nationalists* (London: Routledge & Kegan Paul; New York: Humanities Press, 1967).

122. Marcum, *op. cit.*

123. Eduardo Mondlane, *The Struggle for Mozambique* (Harmondsworth, Middlesex, England: Penguin Books, 1969).

124. The newest work in this field is *The Rise of African Nationalism in South Africa: The African National Congress, 1912–1952* (Berkeley: University of California Press, 1971).

125. Ruth First, *South West Africa* (Baltimore: Penguin Books, 1963).

126. John Joseph Grotpeter, *Political Leadership and Political Development in the High Commission Territories* (St. Louis: Washington University, unpublished Ph.D. dissertation, 1965).

127. Robert I. Rotberg, *The Rise of Nationalism in Central Africa: The Making of Malawi and Zambia, 1873–1964* (Cambridge, Mass.: Harvard University Press, 1965).

128. Barnett F. Baron, *Southern African Student Exiles: The Functions of Politics* (New Haven: Yale University, unpublished Ph.D. dissertation, 1969); and Margaret Legum, "Problems of Asylum for Southern African Refugees," in Sven Hamrell (ed.), *Refugee Problems in Africa* (Uppsala, Sweden: Scandinavian Institute of African Studies, 1967), pp. 54–64.

129. See Mondlane, *op. cit.*; A. J. Venter, *The Terror Fighters: A Profile of Guerrilla Warfare in Southern Africa* (Cape Town, Johannesburg: Purnell & Sons, 1969); Russell Warren Howe, "War in Southern Africa," *Foreign Affairs*, vol. 48, no. 1 (October 1969), pp. 150–165; and Muriel Horrell, *Terrorism in Southern Africa* (Johannesburg: South African Institute of Race Relations, 1968).

130. See Kenneth W. Grundy, "Ideology and Insurrection: The Theory of Guerrilla Warfare in Africa." Paper prepared for delivery at the annual convention of the International Studies Association, San Francisco, Calif., March 27–29, 1969; and Harry Eckstein (ed.), *Internal War: Problems and Approaches* (New York: The Free Press of Glencoe; London: Collier-Macmillan, 1964).

131. A particularly valuable point of departure, especially for comparative analysis, would be William P. Snyder, *The Politics of British Defense Policy, 1945–1962*. A publication of the Mershon Center for Education in National Security (Columbus: Ohio State University Press, 1964).

132. See George Armstrong Kelly, *Lost Soldiers: The French Army and Empire in Crisis, 1947–1962* (Cambridge, Mass.: M.I.T. Press, 1965); and John Steward Ambler, *Soldiers against the State: The French Army in Politics* (Garden City, N.Y.: Doubleday, Anchor Books, 1968).

133. See Walter Darnell Jacobs, "The Military and Politics in Rhodesia." Paper prepared for delivery at the Tenth Annual Meeting of the African Studies Association, New York, N.Y., November 1–4, 1967.

134. See Douglas L. Wheeler, "The Portuguese Army in Angola," *Journal of Modern African Studies*, vol. 7, no. 3 (October 1969), pp. 425–439.

135. See Christian P. Potholm, "The Multiple Roles of the Police as Seen in the African Context," *Journal of Developing Areas*, vol. 3, no. 2 (January 1969), pp. 139–158.

136. Consult Raymond A. Moore, Jr., "The Peaceful Uses of Military Forces in Underdeveloped Areas: A Review Essay," *Journal of Developing Areas*, vol. 4, no. 1 (October 1969), pp. 112–119.

PART TWO CHAPTER 1

1. We are aware that the term "nonwhite" may be offensive to many, yet it is the only convenient collective description of the African, colored, and Asian population groups. The official estimated population figures in June 1966 were as follows:

Whites	3,481,000
Africans	12,465,000
Coloreds	1,805,000
Asians	547,000
Total	18,298,000

2. There is a fair body of literature on the historical development of Afrikaner nationalism, but much of it is in Afrikaans. A good general treatment in English is William Henry Vatcher's *White Laager: The Rise of Afrikaner Nationalism* (New York, Washington, London: Frederick A. Praeger, 1965), and from the Afrikaner's point of view, there is the useful work of F. A. van Jaarsveld, *The Afrikaner's Interpretation of History* (Cape Town: Simondium, 1964). Narrower in scope is F. A. van Jaarsveld's *The Awakening of Afrikaner Nationalism—1868–1881* (Cape Town: Human & Rousseau, 1961). A perceptive synoptic view of Afrikaner nationalism is provided by Edwin S. Munger, *Afrikaner and African Nationalism: South African Parallels and Parameters* (London: Oxford University Press, 1967).

3. The difficulties involved in defining nationalism are well known (see Rupert Emerson, *From Empire to Nation* [Boston: Beacon Press, 1962], pp. 89–92); and the attempt is not made here. It seems sufficient to indicate that nationalism is used in this chapter as Hans Kohn describes it. (See Hans Kohn, *Nationalism* [New York: Van Nostrand, 1955], pp. 9–10.) From the Afrikaner's point of view, possibly the most sophisticated statement of nationalism is contained in N. P. van Wyk Louw, *Liberale Nasionalisme* (Cape Town: Nasionale Boekhandel, 1958), especially pp. 102–106.

4. "Afrikaans is a highly stream-lined version of the 17th century Dutch brought to South Africa by its first permanent settlers. It is a very flexible medium of expression in all fields, technical as well as literary. . . . In its short span of life as a language it has developed a literature in poetry and prose, the best of which compares favourably with that of older literatures." E. G. Malherbe, "Bilingualism in Education," in *Bilingualism in Education: Report on International Seminar* (Aberystwyth, Wales: HMSO, 1965), p. 9.

5. Dr. P. J. Meyer, "Nasionalisme: Die Onsigbare Vlam," in F. A. van Jaarsveld and G. D. Scholtz (eds.), *Die Republiek van Suid-Afrika: Agtergrond, Onstaan en Toekoms* (Johannesburg: Voortrekkerpers, 1966), p. 289 (the translation is the author's).

6. van Jaarsveld, *The Awakening of Afrikaner Nationalism*, p. 13.

7. *Ibid.*, p. 3.

8. As quoted in Vatcher, *op. cit.*, p. 24.

9. As quoted in van Jaarsveld, *The Awakening of Afrikaner Nationalism*, p. 110.

10. Vatcher, *op. cit.*, p. 24.

11. *Ibid.*

12. Emerson, *op. cit.*, p. 170.

13. E. P. du Plessis, *'n Volk Staan Op* (Cape Town: Human & Rousseau, 1964), p. 16.

14. As quoted in *ibid.* (the translation is the author's).

15. As quoted in *ibid.*, p. 70 (the translation is the author's).

16. According to the South African Jewish Board of Deputies there were an estimated one hundred and twenty-five thousand Jews in South Africa in 1969. For a history of South African Jewry, see Gustav Saron and Louis Hotz (eds.), *The Jews of South Africa* (London: Oxford University Press, 1955), and for an illuminating account of Afrikaner-Jewish relations, see "Afrikaners and Jews—A Frank Discussion," *New Nation* (Pretoria), vol. 2, no. 9 (April 1969), pp. 1–3, 5–6.

17. Agitation for an industrial color bar started soon after union, and the first major legislative enactment in this regard was the Mines and Works Act of 1911.

18. D. W. Krüger, *The Making of a Nation: A History of the Union of South Africa, 1910–1961* (Johannesburg, London: The Macmillan Company, 1969), p. 65.

19. *Ibid.*, pp. 69–70.

20. As quoted in D. W. Krüger (ed.), *South African Parties and Policies, 1910–1960: A Select Source Book* (London: Bowes & Bowes, 1960), pp. 69–70.

21. Ivor Jennings, *The British Commonwealth of Nations* (London: Hutchinson University Library, 1967), p. 192.

22. As quoted in Vatcher, *op. cit.*, pp. 55–56.

23. In any event, the policies of both major parties varied only in degree in their commitment to segregation and paternalism. See D. W. Krüger (ed.), *South African Parties and Policies*, pp. 45–94.

24. As quoted in M. C. E. van Schoor, "Die Herlewing van die Republikeinse Ideaal, 1962–1961," in Van Jaarsveld and Scholtz, *op. cit.*, p. 173 (the translation is the author's).

25. In fact, after about 1962 Dr. Verwoerd's authority was buttressed by charisma, something which he encouraged himself. Thus after the first attempt on his life he avowed seeing the hand of the Almighty in his survival. See Munger, *Afrikaner and African Nationalism*, p. 59.

26. After Dr. Verwoerd's death, Anthony Delius wrote that "Dr. Verwoerd stands as the great intellectual formulator, and propagandist of *apartheid*. . . ." A.R.D. [Anthony R. Delius], "New Premier Will Differ in Style," *The Cape Times* (Cape Town), September 14, 1966, late final ed., p. 12, cols. 8–9. Delius was here echoing most appraisals of Dr. Verwoerd.

27. Munger, *Afrikaner and African Nationalism*, p. 59.

28. The homeland policy entails the granting of some measure of self-government to South Africa's major black African "tribes" or "nations" in the areas reserved for their occupation and ownership. The end result of the process has been stated by government spokesmen to be independence. See Paul Ginewski, *Bantustans: A Trek towards the Future* (Cape Town: Human & Rousseau, 1961); Christopher R. Hill, *Bantustans: The Fragmentation of South Africa*. Issued under the auspices of the Institute of Race Relations, London (London, New York: Oxford University Press, 1964); and Gwendolen M. Carter, Thomas Karis, and Newell M. Stultz, *South Africa's Transkei: The Politics of Domestic Colonialism* (Evanston, Ill.: Northwestern University Press, 1967).

29. See Denis Worrall, "Mr. Vorster and the Right," *New Nation*, vol. 3, no. 4 (November 1969), pp. 9, 12, 20.

30. Some idea of the improvement in the Afrikaner's economic position is indicated in the table below. It reflects the Afrikaner's share (in percentage terms) of the income from the private sector of the economy. The increase since 1964 has been quite dramatic.

	1938/39 %	1948/49 %	1954/55 %	1963/65 %
Mining	1	1	1	10
Manufacturing	3	6	6	10
Commerce	8	25	26	31
Transport	—	9	14	14
Liquor and services	—	20	30	30
Professions	—	16	20	27

Financial	5	6	10	21
Diverse	—	27	35	36
Agricultural, Forestry and Fishing	87	85	84	83
Total	—	24.8	25.4	26.3

Source: Afrikaanse Handelsinstituut.

31. For a description of the *South African Observer* and its editor, see Edwin S. Munger, *African Field Reports—1952–1961* (Cape Town: C. Struik, 1961), p. 490.

32. "No Comfort for Forces of Conservatism," *S.A. Observer*, vol. 11, no. 12 (August 1966), p. 2.

33. "A Sad Day for South Africa," *S.A. Observer*, vol. 10, no. 2 (September 1964), p. 1.

34. C. P. Beyers, "Vorster in Phase with Liberal Establishment," *S.A. Observer*, vol. 13, no. 11 (September 1968), p. 3.

35. Schalk Pienaar, "Die Begrip van Nasionale Eenheid," *Die Beeld*, February 16, 1969, p. 10, col. 4. Italics added (the translation is the author's).

36. The *S.A. Observer* of March 1969, as a result of Dr. Hertzog's ouster, wrote: "Today, we see it [the National party] losing its character, its idealism and its gains of the past. . . . What we are actually witnessing is its very nationalism and conservatism being pushed out by those who have the audacity still to proclaim themselves Nationalists."

37. Ownership of the Afrikaans press is divided between two major companies. Nasionale Press with headquarters in Cape Town owns *Die Burger* (Cape Town), *Die Oosterlig* (Port Elizabeth), *Die Volksblad* (Bloemfontein), and *Die Beeld* (national Sunday). Afrikaanse Press with headquarters in Johannesburg owns *Die Vaderland* (Johannesburg), *Hoofstad* (Pretoria), *Dagbreek en Landstem* (national midweek). *Die Transvaler* (Johannesburg) is owned by Voortrekker Press, which is also a major shareholder of *Die Nataller* (Durban). The two big companies also own magazines and all three are leading book publishers.

38. South Africans (and particularly white South Africans) are great sports lovers, and anti-apartheid groups in countries with which South Africa has sporting relations have applied pressure on their governments and sporting bodies to end their association with South Africa as a protest against racial discrimination. The two major games as far as white South Africans are concerned are rugby and cricket, and South Africa has developed strong rugby and cricket ties with the British, the Australians, and the New Zealanders. The late inclusion of a former South Africa colored, now resident in Britain, on a British cricket team to tour South Africa in late 1968 led to cancellation of the tour as a result of the South African government's refusal to admit the colored player. As he had not originally been selected, there was a suggestion that political factors later influenced the British cricketing body. The possible inclusion of a Maori player in a New Zealand rugby tour of South Africa in 1967 led to the cancellation of the tour when Dr. Verwoerd in 1965 said South Africa would not admit a team with a Maori. Mr. Vorster reversed government policy in a speech in parliament in April 1967 and at the time of writing (November 1969) a New Zealand rugby tour of South Africa is scheduled to take place in 1970. It is likely to include Maori players.

39. The South African parliament has a five-year term, and the last general election took place in March 1966. A few days later Mr. Vorster announced that the election would take place on April 22, 1970.

40. One can only guess at the strength of the HNP. At the time of writing few commentators give the party more than two seats. Most acknowledge that it has a potential for growth. Ideological considerations aside, after twenty-one years of rule there is a considerable "grievance vote" within Afrikanerdom which would abstain rather than vote for the United Party, and which welcomes the establishment of the HNP. The HNP is also exploiting the socioeconomic differences which have emerged within Afrikaner nationalism by presenting social and economic policies with a strong *petit bourgeois* content.

41. Gwendolen M. Carter (ed.), *Five African States: Responses to Diversity* (Ithaca: Cornell University Press, 1963). Nowhere in this work is the relationship between government and diversity explained, and nowhere is there an explanation of what is expected of a response to diversity if it is to be successful. (See Denis Worrall, "The Problem of Diversity and a Comparison of Responses to It in Ghana and Nigeria," in C. J. Swanevelder (ed.), *Viewpoints on Africa*, Special Publication no. 3 [Stellenbosch: Society for the Teaching of Geography, 1966], pp. 37–49.)

42. Gabriel Almond and James S. Coleman, *The Politics of the Developing Areas* (Princeton, N.J.: Princeton University Press, 1960).

43. Pierre L. van den Berghe's *South Africa: A Study in Conflict* (Middletown: Wesleyan University Press, 1965) is a very good example.

44. See K. L. Roskam, *Apartheid and Discrimination* (Leyden: A. W. Sythoff, 1960), for numerous illustrations of this.

45. The restrictions imposed in terms of the Suppression of Communism Act (1950) affect rights relating to travel, association, expression, and choice of occupation and residence. The greater involvement of nonwhites is reflected in the following figures abstracted from official sources:

Total number of persons banned (i.e., restricted) since 1950

126 Whites
829 Nonwhites

Banned persons: refers to individuals or organizations whose rights—generally of movement and association—have been curtailed in varying degree in terms of the Suppression of Communism Act.

Banning orders: refers to the order of the minister of justice advising individuals or organizations that restrictions on their freedom are deemed to be in the interests of state security.

Listed persons: refers to a list of persons deemed by the minister of justice to be Communists and who consequently are subject to varying restrictions by administrative order.

Banning orders still in force
50 Whites
283 Nonwhites

Listed persons
166 Whites
235 Nonwhites

Source: various government gazettes.

46. The homeland policy, for example, apparently has some effect on black African politicization. (See Leo Kuper, "The Political Situation of Non-Whites in South Africa," in William Hance [ed.], *Southern Africa and the United States* [New York: Columbia University Press, 1968], p. 103.)

47. David E. Apter, "System, Process, and the Politics of Economic Development," in Jason L. Finkle and Richard W. Gable (eds.), *Politcal Development and Social Change* (New York: John Wiley & Son, 1966), pp. 441–457.

48. *Ibid.*, p. 444.

49. *Ibid.*

50. *Ibid.*

51. *Ibid.*, p. 445.

52. *Ibid.*

53. *Ibid.*

54. *Ibid.*

55. See L. M. Thompson, *The Unification of South Africa, 1902–1910* (Oxford: The Clarendon Press, 1960).

56. Gwendolen M. Carter, *The Politics of Inequality: South Africa since 1948*, rev. ed. (New York: Frederick A. Praeger, 1959), p. 32.

57. See Vatcher, *op. cit.*, pp. 76–88.

58. As quoted in J. Albert Coetzee, *Nasieskap en Politieke Groepering* (Pretoria: Transvaalse Uitgewers-maatskappy, 1969), p. 291 (the translation is the author's).

59. *Ibid.*

60. As quoted in *ibid.*, p. 292 (the translation is the author's).

61. Krüger, *The Making of a Nation*, p. 191.

62. Du Plessis, *op. cit.*, p. 104.

63. As quoted in *ibid.*, p. 113.

64. The predominant role of the National party within what was (and is) formally a very religious community is to be explained in terms of the fundamental tenet of Calvinism that everything is subordinated to God's will. As a consequence the separation of church and party is purely institutional.

65. Until recently, leading politicians (generally ministers) have served on the directorates of the different newspaper companies. However, the decision of the present prime minister in October 1967 to relinquish his position with Afrikaanse Press (soon after his election he was made chairman of the board) presumably because it associated him too closely with the National party in the Transvaal at a time when the competition between the Cape Nasionale Press–owned *Die Beeld* and Afrikaanse Press' *Dagbreek* was at its height, raised doubts about the validity of this practice. It resulted in the leader of the National party in the Cape announcing that he would continue to serve as a director of Nasionale Press but would forfeit any remuneration.

66. Krüger, *The Making of a Nation*, p. 205; Vatcher, *op. cit.*, p. 63; Coetzee, *op. cit.*, p. 298.

67. Krüger, *The Making of a Nation*, p. 206.

68. The issue as far as General Hertzog was concerned was between involvement in the war on the side of Great Britain and neutrality. He did not see Great Britain's and South Africa's interests as identical and therefore declared for neutrality. General Smuts won the debate with a vote of 80 to 67. The governor-general judged circumstances in the country unsuitable for a peaceful general election, refused General Hertzog's request for a dissolution of parliament and a general election, and asked General Smuts to form a cabinet.

69. Krüger, *The Making of a Nation*, p. 206.

70. Carter, *The Politics of Inequality*, p. 34.

71. Krüger, *The Making of a Nation*, p. 215.

72. *Ibid.*, pp. 215–216.

73. As quoted in Krüger, *South African Parties and Policies*, p. 96.

74. Carter, *The Politics of Inequality*, p. 166.

75. As quoted in *ibid.*

76. The fact that the National party did not opt for a republic outside the Commonwealth of Nations and a republican form of government modelled on the early Boer republics is generally interpreted as a concession to English-speaking South Africans.

77. In the decade following the 1948 general election, the National party government introduced the following important (as far as black Africans are concerned) legislative enactments:

The Prohibition of Mixed Marriages Act, 1949
The Group Areas Act, 1950
The Native Building Workers Act, 1951
The Bantu Authorities Act, 1951
The Natives (Abolition of Passes and Co-ordination of Documents) Act, 1952
The Bantu Education Act, 1953
The Reservation of Separate Amenities Act, 1953
The Group Areas Development Act, 1955
The Group Areas Act, 1957
The Bantu Investment Corporation Act, 1959
The Extension of University Education Act, 1959
The Promotion of Bantu Self-Government Act, 1959

78. Mimeographed newsletter of the Afrikaanse Handelsinstituut, Pretoria, n.d.

79. One illustration of this is the difference in response which met the protest of the so-called "Pretoria thirteen academics" in 1955 and the protest of Afrikaans judges and academicians against the legislation setting up the Bureau for State Security in 1969. The 1955 dissidents, who opposed the government's plan to reconstitute the Senate (upper chamber of the South African parliament), so as to obtain the two-thirds majority required by the constitution for the removal of the coloreds from the common voters' roll, were ridiculed in cartoons and their integrity impugned in editorials. In 1969 the protesters enjoyed a very favorable Afrikaans press and were largely responsible for the appointment of a commission to inquire into the objections.

80. This is a point not always appreciated by observers of the South African political scene. Not only do Afrikaners form a sizable minority within the United party (one would estimate it to be about 15 percent), but the Christian Institute, a body of Afrikaans churchmen who support the ecumenical movement, adopts a liberal (in the South African context) position on race relations.

81. See Denis Worrall, "Mr. Vorster," *New Nation*, vol. 3, no. 3 (October 1969), pp. 4–6; and Edwin S. Munger, "South Africa: Are There Silver Linings?," *Foreign Affairs*, vol. 47, no. 2 (January 1969), pp. 375–386.

82. *Program van Beginsels* (Pretoria: *Herstigte Nasionale Party*, n.d.), p. 2.

83. *Ibid.*, p. 1 (the translation is the author's).

CHAPTER 2

1. Jean Ziegler, *La Contre-Révolution en Afrique* (Paris: Payot, 1963).
2. As quoted in Nathan M. Shamuyarira, *Crisis in Rhodesia* (London: Andre Deutsch, 1965), pp. 30–31.
3. Leo Kuper, "The Political Situation of Non-Whites in South Africa," in William Hance (ed.), *Southern Africa and the United States* (New York: Columbia University Press, 1968), pp. 91–92 and Shamuyarira, *op. cit.*, p. 32.
4. Shamuyarira, *op. cit.*, p. 38.
5. Nelson Mandela, *No Easy Walk to Freedom* (New York: Basic Books, 1965), p. 18 and Albert Luthuli, *Let My People Go* (New York: McGraw-Hill, 1962), p. 108.
6. Mary Benson, *The African Patriots: The Story of the African National Congress of South Africa* (London: Faber and Faber, 1963), pp. 102–103, 142.
7. *Ibid.*, pp. 102, 104.
8. *Ibid.*, pp. 105–107, 109.
9. *Ibid.*, p.109.
10. Colin Legum and Margaret Legum, *The Bitter Choice* (Cleveland: World Publishing Co., 1968), pp. 75–99.
11. The information on Dr. Xuma has been drawn from Benson, *op. cit.*, pp. 95–99, 138–139, and 157–158.
12. Benson, *op. cit.*, p. 157.
13. *Ibid.*
14. *Ibid.*
15. *Ibid.*
16. As quoted in Edward Feit, *South Africa: The Dynamics of the African National Congress* (New York: Oxford University Press, 1962), p. 2.
17. Mandela, *op. cit.*, pp. 82–83.
18. Feit, *op. cit.*, pp. 27–29.
19. *Ibid.*, p. 28.
20. Shamuyarira, *op. cit.*, pp. 45–46.
21. *Ibid.*, p. 50.
22. Mandela, *op. cit.*, p. 39.
23. Luthuli, *op. cit.*, p. 113.
24. Vulindlela Mtshali, *Rhodesia: Background to Conflict* (New York: Hawthorne Books, 1967), p. 118.
25. John Day, "Southern Rhodesian African Nationalists and the 1961 Constitution," *Journal of Modern African Studies*, vol. 7, no. 2 (July, 1969), pp. 226–227.
26. Mtshali, *op. cit.*, p. 115.
27. Day, *op. cit.*, p. 230.
28. *Ibid.*, pp. 221, 233–234.
29. Waldermar A. Nielsen, *African Battleline: American Policy Choices in Southern Africa* (New York: Harper & Row, 1965), p. 75.
30. Kuper, *op. cit.*, p. 93. This account of the rebellion draws on that given by Edward Roux, *Time Longer Than Rope: A History of the Black Man's Struggle for Freedom in South Africa*, 2nd ed. (Madison: University of Wisconsin Press, 1964), pp. 87–100.
31. Benson, *op. cit.*, p. 19.
32. As quoted in Roux, *op. cit.*, p. 94.
33. *Ibid.*, p. 96.
34. *Ibid.*
35. *Ibid.*
36. For a detailed account of the early Communist role in the African nationalist struggle in South Africa see *Ibid.*, pp. 198–286.
37. *Ibid.*, p. 211.
38. *Ibid.*, p. 211–214.
39. *Ibid.*, p. 226.
40. *Ibid.*, p. 227.
41. Colin Legum and Margaret Legum, *South Africa: Crisis for the West* (New York: Frederick A. Praeger, 1964), p. 182.
42. Benson, *op. cit.*, pp. 198–199.
43. Legum, *The Bitter Choice*, p. 84.
44. Mandela, *op. cit.*, p. 82.
45. *Ibid.*, p. 179.
46. *Ibid.*
47. *Ibid.*
48. *Ibid.*, p. 181.
49. Legum, *The Bitter Choice*, p. 111–112.
50. Benson, *op. cit.*, p. 233.
51. Mandela, *op. cit.*, p. 166.
52. Legum, *South Africa: Crisis for the West*, p. 181–182.
53. As quoted in Legum, *The Bitter Choice*, p. 112.
54. As quoted in *Ibid.*, p. 113.
55. Marion Friedmann, (ed.), *I Will Still Be Moved* (Chicago: Quadrangle Books, 1963), p. 92.
56. *Ibid.*, p. 93.
57. *Ibid.*
58. Legum, *South Africa: Crisis for the West*, p. 180.
59. Legum, *The Bitter Choice*, p. 116.
60. Leonard Thompson, *Politics in the Republic of South Africa* (Boston: Little, Brown, 1966), pp. 181–182.
61. Mandela, *op. cit.*, p. 164. See also Govan Mbeki, *South Africa: The Peasant's Revolt* (Baltimore: Penguin Books, 1964).
62. As quoted in Mandela, *op. cit.*, p. 169.
63. *Ibid.*, p. 163.
64. *Ibid.*, p. 172.
65. Shamuyarira, *op. cit.*, p. 72.
66. *Ibid.*, chap. 10; Theodore Bull (ed.), *Rhodesia: Crisis of Color* (Chicago: Quadrangle Books, 1967), pp. 126–127.
67. It is extremely difficult to obtain an accurate picture of developments in Zimbabwe and South Africa regarding the guerrilla movements. ANC publishes its own newsletters in the form of *Sechaba* (printed in Dar es Salaam), *Spotlight on South Africa*, and *Mayibuye* (both printed in Lusaka). ZAPU puts out two newspapers by the same name—*Zimbabwe Review* (one a weekly newssheet published in Lusaka, the other a bi-monthly magazine printed in London). ZANU has a weekly newspaper, *Zimbabwe News*, published in Lusaka. With the exception of *Spotlight on Africa* these newspapers and magazines are not distributed widely in the United States. Congressman Charles Diggs, in commenting on the task of ascertaining the true state of affairs in Zimbabwe and South Africa, stated: "In the existing situation in Rhodesia, public claims by both leaders of the freedom movements and the Rhodesian authorities are often exaggerated and should be carefully scrutinized to verify their accuracy" (U.S. Congress, Committee on Foreign Affairs, *Report of Special Study Mission to Southern Africa*, August 10–30, 1969, by Hon. Charles C. Diggs and Hon. Lester L. Wolff, 91st Cong., 1st sess., October 10, 1969, p. 10 [hereafter cited as the Diggs–Wolff Report]). Many of the accounts on the use of violence in South Africa and Zimbabwe have been written from the perspective of the South African and Rhodesian governments. Those who might be expected to emphasize internal developments in the guerrilla movement may be reluctant to do so. It is interesting to

note that the Diggs-Wolff Report reveals very little detailed current information on the guerrilla tactics or achievements of ZAPU-ANC or ZANU.

68. Central Africa Research, *The Military Strengths in Southern Africa* (London: Central Africa Research Office, August 10, 1968), p. 6.

69. Matthew Nkoana, "Southern Africa: Internal Problems of the New Phase," *New African* (London), vol. 8, no. 1 (1969), p. 12.

70. *Ibid.*

71. *Ibid.*, p. 13.

72. *Spotlight on South Africa*, March 21, 1969, p. 2.

73. Russell Warren Howe, "War in Southern Africa," *Foreign Affairs*, vol. 48, no. 1 (October 1969), p. 151.

74. Central Africa Research, *op. cit.*, p. 6. See also Alan Rake, "Black Guerrillas in Rhodesia," *Africa Report*, vol. 13, no. 9 (December 1968), pp. 23–25.

75. Central African Research, *op. cit.*, p. 6.

76. Howe, *op. cit.*, p. 156.

77. South Africa. Parliament. House of Assembly, *Debates*, no. 17 (June 2–6, 1969), col. 7095 (June 2, 1969).

78. David R. Smock, "The Forgotten Rhodesians," *Foreign Affairs*, vol. 47, no. 3 (April 1969), p. 538.

79. United Nations, *Special Committee on the Policies of Apartheid of the Government of the Republic of South Africa*, Summary Record of the First Part of the One Hundred and Sixth Meeting, February 19, 1969, A/AC. 115/SR.106, p. 4.

80. Nkoana, *op. cit.*, p. 13.

81. "Un Combattant du Zimbabwe Raconte . . .," *AfricAsia* (Paris), no. 2 (November 23, 1969), pp. 30–32.

82. Howe, *op. cit.*, p. 157.

83. In his book *On War*, Clausewitz listed the following conditions for success in guerrilla warfare: (1) the war must be carried on in the interior of the country; (2) the war cannot hinge on a single battle; (3) the theater of war must extend over a considerable area; (4) the national character must support the war; (5) the country must be irregular, difficult, inaccessible. During the Chinese revolutionary struggle "winning the support of the population was considered a major objective of the communists." (Peter Paret and John W. Shy, *Guerrillas in the 1960's* [New York: Frederick A. Praeger, 1962], pp. 13 and 26.) The same importance was attached to gaining the confidence and support of the population by Fidel Castro and Che Guevara.

84. Howe, *op. cit.*, pp. 150–151.

85. Central Africa Research, *op. cit.*, p. 6.

86. Mandela, *op. cit.*, p. 80. For a more detailed account of the 1956 treason trials see Helen Joseph, *If This Be Treason* (London: Andre Deutsch, 1963) and Anthony Sampson, *The Treason Cage* (London: Heinemann, 1958).

87. D. A. Leonard, "Proscribed Ideals (The State v. Duma Nokwe and 11 Others)," in Friedmann, *op. cit.*, p. 100.

88. As quoted in *ibid.*, p. 103.

89. For the relevant passages of S. 263 see *Ibid.*, pp. 103–104.

90. Mandela, *op. cit.*, p. 125.

91. Duma Nokwe, "An African Barrister," in Friedmann, *op. cit.*, p. 74.

92. This account of Nokwe's life is based on Nokwe, *op. cit.*, pp. 72–75.

93. *Ibid.*, p. 75.

94. Mandela, *op. cit.*, p. 162.

95. United Nations, *Report of the Special Committee on the Policies of Apartheid of the Government of the Republic of South Africa.* General Assembly Official Records. 24th Session. Supplement no. 25(A/7625/Rev. 1) (New York: United Nations, 1969), p. 75.

96. *Ibid.*, p. 66.

97. *Ibid.*, pp. 66–67.

98. *Spotlight on Africa*, March 5, 1969, p. 3.

99. United Nations, *Report of the Special Committee on the Policies of Apartheid*, p. 7; *Chronique Politique Africaine* (Paris, 1969), p. 116.

100. *Chronique Politique Africanine* (1969), p. 115.

101. "South Africa Drops Trial of 22 Blacks and Rearrests Them under Another Act," *The New York Times*, February 17, 1970, late city ed., p. 4, cols. 3–8.

102. Muriel Horrell (compiler), *A Survey of Race Relations in South Africa, 1969* (Johannesburg: South African Institute of Race Relations, 1970), p. 63.

103. *Annual Report of the Commissioner of the South African Police for the Period 1 July 1966 to 30 June 1967.* R.P. 40/1968 (Pretoria: The Government Printer, 1968), p. 4.

104. "Wholesale Arrests," (editorial) *Rand Daily Mail* (Johannesburg), April 14, 1969, morning final ed., p. 12, cols. 7–9.

105. Mtshali, *op. cit.*, p. 125.

106. Central Africa Research, *op. cit.*, p. 6, and *Chronique Politique Africaine* (1969), p. 111.

107. Shamuyarira, *op. cit.*, p. 188.

108. Mtshali, *op. cit.*, pp. 125–127.

109. *Ibid.*

110. Diggs–Wolff Report, p. 11.

111. Edwin S. Munger, *Afrikaner and African Nationalism* (New York: Oxford University Press, 1967), pp. 92–93.

112. Diggs–Wolff Report, p. 13.

113. For a glimpse into the internal power struggle in PAC see Nkoana, *op. cit.*, p. 14.

114. Nielsen, *op. cit.*, p. 49.

115. Richard Gibson, "African Unity and Afro-Americans," *Liberator* (London), vol. 8, no. 8 (August 1968), p. 17.

CHAPTER 3

1. Hence the debate in the early 1960s over the wisdom of coercive action by the United Nations against South Africa. See Colin and Margaret Legum, *South Africa: Crisis for the West* (London: Pall Mall Press, 1964), pp. 256–310.

2. For this reference to South Africa's traditional economic and cultural links with Britain, see D. W. Krüger, *The Making of a Nation: A History of the Union of South Africa, 1910–1961* (Johannesburg: Macmillan South Africa, 1969), p. 329.

3. "The survival of the white man was linked to the issue of the republic by the person of Verwoerd who, as the visible symbol of both, converted many waverers. [Macmillan's 'wind of change' speech] . . . was the last straw. It destroyed the image of Britain in South Africa and the republic was the natural result." *Ibid.*

4. Willem van Heerden, "Coming to Terms with Africa," *Perspective* (London), vol. 6, no. 9 (June 1969), p. 10.

5. *Ibid.*

6. See his Graduation Day address at the University of Pretoria in March 1957. The full text is printed in "Union's Africa Policy," *Fact Paper no. 33* (Pretoria: State Information Office, April 1957).

7. *Ibid.*, p. 9. In the 1950s South African authorities periodically attempted to interest the Western powers in the establishment of a South Atlantic Treaty Organization.

8. A speech delivered in November 1963 as quoted in "Foreign Affairs: The Louw Era," *Background to South African and World News* (Johannesburg), August 1968, p. [3].

9. The noted editor of *Die Burger*, Piet Cillié, clearly assessed the mood of that time when he wrote:

> In that notable year the tides of "freedom" and independence were flooding the continent. Storms of disapproval and agitation raged round our heads. We were due for a fundamental constitutional change which had been resisted to the last by the great majority of English-speaking Whites. To friend and foe alike we seemed a house badly divided, doomed to fall by external force and internal upheaval. Hostile forces worked out timetables for destroying the existing order, and there was talk of ships and men for blockades and invasion.

Piet Cillié, "Vision of the Seventies: Evolving Relationships in Southern Africa," *Report from South Africa* (London), January 1969, p. 8.

Larry Bowman scathingly observed that "scholars, politicians, governments, and citizens have all contributed to the litter of discarded assumptions and expectations about the area." (Larry Bowman, "The Subordinate State System of Southern Africa," *International Studies Quarterly*, vol. 12, no. 3 [September 1968], p. 234.)

10. Between 1960 and 1968 this expenditure increased from $61.6 million to $354.2 million per annum. Total armed forces now number 38,200 regular personnel plus a further 32,000 in reserve. (See *The Military Balance, 1968–9* [London: Institute for Strategic Studies, 1968], p. 51.)

11. "We have never relished the idea of being insular —an Israel in Africa, an ox-wagon *laager* or fortress. The *laager* serves its purpose in emergency but can never be a way of life. It can be dispensed with once a nation has proved itself strong and worthy to be accepted as a power to live with." (Cillié, *op. cit.*, p. 8.)

12. See J. E. Spence, *Lesotho: The Politics of Dependence*. Published for the Institute of Race Relations, London (London: Oxford University Press, 1968), pp. 65–67.

13. But the evidence suggests that the improvements brought about by white enterprise were slow to "spill over" into the African agricultural areas. (See L. P. Green and T. J. D. Fair, "Preparing for Swaziland's Economic Growth," *Optima* [Johannesburg], vol. 10, no. 4 [October 1960], pp. 203–204.)

14. It is estimated that about 15 percent of the Swazi adult male population is at work in the Republic in any one year. This contrasts favorably with the figures of 43 percent and 20 percent for Lesotho and Botswana respectively. (See J. E. Spence, "British Policy Towards the High Commission Territories," *The Journal of Modern African Studies*, vol. 2, no. 2 [July 1964], pp. 234–235.)

15. Colin Eglin, a Progressive party leader, in his address to the Sixth Annual Conference of the Botswana Democratic party in Gaborone in March 1967 observed that "the more you deal with us, trade with us, forge and preserve links between the Republic and the rest of Africa, the greater the chances are that South Africans will think again about race relations. I speak as a lifelong opponent of racialism in South Africa." (*Forging Links in Africa* [Cape Town: Progressive party, 1967], p. 11.)

16. Noel Mostert, "Africa: New Nations and New Alignments," *The Reporter*, vol. 36, no. 13 (June 29, 1967), p. 28.

17. This pact provides for the export to South Africa of certain Malawi commodities, notably tea, free of customs duties or at South Africa's most favored-nation tariff.

18. As quoted in "The Devil's Disciple," *Background to South African and World News*, July 1968, p. [1]. President Banda asserted that "for Malawi, regional co-operation means co-operation with all countries in Southern Africa regardless of the colour . . . of those who are . . . in control of their government, . . . regardless of their political views or their ideologies" (as quoted in "The Devil's Disciple," p. [2]).

19. After signing the trade agreement, Mr. Aleke Banda, the Malawian minister of development planning, commented that "politics and trade" were "completely separate matters." As quoted in *ibid.*, p. [2].

20. This line will also link Malawi with the Cabora Bassa hydroelectric scheme in neighboring Mozambique, the power from which, it is claimed, will enable Malawi to exploit its bauxite deposits on Mount Mlanje. The work of construction is being undertaken by a South African consortium, using South African resources and contractors.

21. Prime Minister Jonathan, in a speech of September 25, 1967, at the United Nations, opposed the use of force in the context of the Rhodesian crisis. He asserted that "the people of Lesotho and the Africans of South Africa would be the first to suffer the consequences— 'consequences that would not befall those who from a safe distance urge us to adopt impossible policies.' " As quoted in "News in Brief: Southern Africa: Lesotho: Jonathan Appeals to the U.N. for Understanding," *Africa Report*, vol. 12, no. 8 [November 1967], p. 42.)

22. Bowman, *op. cit.*, p. 246.

23. There are some 73,000 Malawians employed in South Africa. Although this is substantially fewer than either Lesotho (280,000) or Mozambique (220,000), it is nevertheless a significant measure of the Republic's political leverage in relation to its northern neighbor. (*Ibid.*, p. 241.)

24. Mozambique has for over sixty years been a major supplier of African labor to South Africa's mining industry; in return, in terms of a labor convention signed in 1909, the Portuguese port of Lourenço Marques is guaranteed 47.5 percent of the Witwatersrand's import-export traffic. (*Ibid.*, p. 240.)

25. As quoted in "The Portuguese and the Ultimate Target," *Background to South African and World News*, March 1969, p. [1].

26. *Ibid.*, pp. [1–2].

27. *Ibid.*, p. [2].

28. As quoted in *ibid.*, p. [3].

29. One such opponent asserted that "Indeed, a bilateral military agreement between South Africa and Moçambique is widely assumed to exist; considerable pressure has been put on the South African authorities to help the Portuguese in Angola; and the air-field now in use in the Caprivi Strip (bordering Angola and South West Africa) is reportedly for use by both the South African and Portuguese air forces." (Rosalynde Ainslie, *The Unholy Alliance: Salazar, Verwoerd, Welensky* [London: Anti-Apartheid Movement, Council for Freedom in Portugal and the Colonies, and the Movement for Colonial Freedom, n.d.], p. 6.)

The FRELIMO leader, the late Dr. Eduardo Mondlane, alleged that "the apartheid regime . . . is deeply involved —it has many of its military officers fighting in Mozambique." (*The Nationalist* [Dar es Salaam], July 1968, as quoted in Abdul S. Minty, *South Africa's Defence Strategy* [London: Anti-Apartheid Movement, 1969], p. 10.)

30. "The Portuguese and the Ultimate Target," p. [2].

31. As quoted in *ibid.*, p. [1]. The military expenditures of South Africa and Portugal are as follows:

	Portugal	*South Africa*
Estimated gross national product	$4.4 billion	$13.1 billion
Military budget	$302 million	$354 million
Army: total strength	182,500	28,000
total when fully mobilized	500,000	70,000
Percentage of gross national product devoted to the military	6.7 percent	2.7 percent

Two-thirds of Portugal's military budget is spent in its African colonies. (*The Military Balance, 1968–9*, pp. 27, 51.)

32. As quoted in "The Portugese and the Ultimate Target," p. [1].

33. As quoted in *ibid.*, p. [1]. His views were subsequently incorporated in a resolution passed by the Cape congress of the United party in September 1968 (*ibid.*, p. [2]).

34. As quoted in *ibid.*, p. [2]. He warned of the danger that the Republic could have "devilish powers on our borders. . . . Then it will be a case of not only Portuguese soldiers fighting but our own young men, who will then withdraw from the economic sphere to form a phalanx on our northern borders." (As quoted in *ibid.*, p. [2].)

35. As quoted in *ibid.*, p. [3]. This stress on the strategic significance of South Africa to the Western Alliance occurs repeatedly in ministerial statements and serves both as a justification of Portugese–South African cooperation in the area and a criticism of the NATO powers' unwillingness to support and encourage this policy publicly.

36. See R. B. Sutcliffe, "The Political Economy of Rhodesian Sanctions," *Journal of Commonwealth Political Studies* (Leicester, England), vol. 7, no. 2 (July 1969), p. 124.

37. In late September 1968, in an address to the annual congress of the Natal National Party, Prime Minister Vorster asserted that the

> the time will come when Zambia and South Africa will understand each other. We will understand each other, not only because of good relationships and everything that will flow from these relationships, but because of the need for Southern Africa to be kept free of Communist infiltration.
>
> We will be obliged to close our ranks—and here I include Zambia—to save Southern Africa from the destruction and infection of Communism.

(As quoted in "S.A. and Zambia: Understanding Will Come," *The Star* [Johannesburg], September 24, 1968, second city late edition, p. 7, cols. 1–2.)

38. See Bowman, *op. cit.*, p. 245.

39. *Ibid.*, p. 244.

40. *Ibid.*, pp. 244–245.

41. In a speech before the House of Assembly on April 3, 1968, Mr. P. W. Botha, the minister of defense, emphasized that his government regarded facilitating terrorism as an act of provocation which could "lead to severe retaliation for the sake of self-respect and peace." In the same speech, he cited Israel's raids on terrorist camps in Jordan as a threatening analogy which Zambia would do well to take into account. (South Africa. Parliament. House of Assembly, *Debates*, vol. 23, col. 3328.)

42. "Zambia: Pawn or Primer?" *Background to South African and World News*, September 1968, p. [3].

43. South Africa. Parliament. House of Assembly, *Debates*, vol. 24, cols. 6322–6323. N.B. in this context Dr. Muller's statement to the House of Assembly on May 7th, 1969:

> It is totally wrong to think that South Africa is in a state of war with the rest of the world, or part of it. There is continual contact between other countries and us by means of South Africa's representatives in the principal cities of the world who negotiate and discuss matters with their counterparts whenever necessary, particularly in London, Washington, Paris and even at the U.N. Often we negotiate directly with governments, although we do not have official diplomatic relations with them.

(South Africa. Parliament. House of Assembly, *Debates*, vol. 26, col. 5446.)

44. See Edwin S. Munger, "South Africa: Are There Silver Linings?", *Foreign Affairs*, vol. 42, no. 2 (January 1969), p. 385.

45. As quoted in "Vorster Tells World: We'll Lead Africa," *The Star*, November 4, 1968, second city late edition, p. 7, cols. 1–2. Mr. Piet Cillie has written that

> It [the "outward" policy] appeals to a deep-seated and idealistic sense of calling which has always characterised some of our best Afrikaner elements— a basically religious belief that the White people have been placed at the lower end of Africa for purposes transcending their own existence. With Africa and the world in its present state, we tend to the belief that Black Africa desperately needs us, and that the world needs us in Africa in many ways.

(Cillié, *op. cit.*, p. 9.)

46. Hilgard Muller, "South Africa and the World," *Report from South Africa*, December 1969, p. 8.

47. "The stronger we are, the less they can touch us . . . this is our guarantee for the future." (A speech by

Mr. Dirk Uys, Minister of Agriculture, in August 1968, as quoted in Minty, *op. cit.*, p. 12.)

48. "Interview with John Vorster, Prime Minister of the Republic of South Africa: The Story of Race and Progress in Africa's Richest Nation." *U.S. News & World Report*, vol. 61, no. 20 (November 14, 1966), p. 105.

49. All three governments have passed stringent legislation to limit the political activity of refugee elements from the Republic.

50. Mr. Vorster's speech as quoted in "Zambia: Pawn or Primer?", p. [1].

51. Zambia's demand that South African aid to Rhodesia be stopped otherwise "active measures with friends . . . [would be taken] . . . to defend her territory" evoked the following response from Mr. Vorster:

> I dare him to carry out his threats. We will hit him so hard that he will never forget it. . . . South Africa's standpoint is clear. We do not wish to fight with anyone, nor do we consider using violence against anyone, but South Africa, small as she is, will answer any country wishing to use violence against her in the only way that such violence can be answered.

As quoted in *ibid.*, p. [2].

52. Mr. P. W. Botha, the minister of defense, declared that

> President Kaunda is looking for weapons against South Africa in England. There is no need for him to look for weapons against Southern Africa if he wants to be realistic and desires true friendship. All he needs to do is to keep the terrorists out of his country and join Southern Africa in building up a strong force against the Communist campaign aimed at enslaving his country together with the rest of Southern Africa. . . . Projectiles can't save Zambia from economic disaster and chaos, but sensible statesmanship can guarantee Zambia a new life.

As quoted in *ibid.*, p. [3]

53. Furthermore, an attempt to alter Zambian policy in this way might have serious repercussions in domestic politics and expose President Kaunda to attack from extreme left-wing elements in his own party.

54. The Afrikaner industrialist, Dr. Anton Rupert, claimed that "If they do not eat, we do not sleep." As quoted in Cillié, *op. cit.*, p. 9.

55. In a speech to the Malawi Congress party in 1967, President Banda claimed, "They [South Africa] will not wait to be invaded. First they will cross their borders to meet the enemy wherever he is likely to appear on the principle that attack is the best form of defence." (As quoted in Minty, *op. cit.*, p. 13.) In April 1968 the Swazi premier, Prince Dhlamini, asserted that "if terrorists come to Swaziland, they would not just come to mess up us alone. They would be here on their way through Swaziland to its neighbouring countries, and naturally in those circumstances South Africa would come to our aid." (As quoted in "Zambia: Pawn or Primer?", p. [1].)

56. This might be interpreted as a South African variation on the oft-quoted theme that the real threat to world peace lies in the ever-widening gap between the rich, white and poor, nonwhite states. Newspaper comment in South Africa has particularly stressed this aspect of the policy: "It is only too clear, then, that over the years a dangerous situation could develop . . . in a world where the rich tend to get richer and the poor poorer. To attain . . . an equilibrium—and peace for Southern Africa—the poorer people must progress." ("Muller Moves to Aid Africa," *News Check* [Johannesburg], vol. 6, no. 45 [May 17, 1968], p. 18.)

57. South Africa. Parliament. House of Assembly, *Debates* (speech of the prime minister), vol. 17 col. 2606 (September 21, 1966).

58. Bowman, *op. cit.*, pp. 259–260 (italics in the original).

59. *Ibid.*, p. 259.

60. See John Day, "The Rhodesian African Nationalists and the Commonwealth African States," *Journal of Commonwealth Political Studies*, vol. 7, no. 2 (July 1969), pp. 132–144.

CHAPTER 4

1. Faye Pye, "Aspects of the Psychology of South African Women," *Race* (London), vol. 7, no. 2 (October 1965), pp. 123–130.

2. See O. Mannoni, *Prospero and Caliban: The Psychology of Colonization*, 2nd ed. Translated by Pamela Powesland with a foreword by Philip Mason (New York, Washington: Frederick A. Praeger, 1964), p. 120.

3. Cyril A. Rogers and C. Frantz, *Racial Themes in Southern Rhodesia: The Attitudes of the White Population* (New Haven and London: Yale University Press, 1962), pp. 123–124.

4. William Shakespeare, *Love's Labour's Lost*, Act IV, Scene III, lines 254–255.

5. Muriel Horrell (compiler), *A Survey of Race Relations in South Africa, 1968* (Johannesburg: South African Institute of Race Relations, 1969), p. 36.

6. Roger Bastide, "Dusky Venus, Black Apollo," *Race*, vol. 3, no. 1 (November 1961), pp. 10–18.

7. *The Future of South Africa: A study of British Christians*. Published for the British Council of Churches (London: SCM Press, 1965), p. 92.

8. The Christian Institute of Southern Africa was founded in 1963. "Its aim is to build meaningful and functional bridges of fellowship and understanding between Christians, irrespective of their race or denomination. Prominent among those who joined were certain ministers and members of the Dutch Reformed Churches." (Muriel Horrell [compiler], *A Survey of Race Relations in South Africa, 1966* [Johannesburg: South African Institute of Race Relations, 1967], p. 28.)

"Conservative Dutch Reformed Church adherents have resented this Institute's multi-racial and multi-denominational nature and, as described in previous years, have actively discouraged membership of it." (Muriel Horrell [compiler], *A Survey of Race Relations in South Africa, 1967* [Johannesburg: South African Institute of Race Relations, 1968], p. 10.)

9. The fact that white South Africans have created their problem for themselves does not entitle us to say that there is no problem. As Leo Kuper argues (in "The Heightening of Racial Tension," *Race*, vol. 2, no. 1 [November, 1960], pp. 24–32), if South Africans had actively wished to create racial tension they could hardly have used more effective methods than they have.

10. See J. P. McDonagh, "External Investment in South Africa: Opportunities and Risks," in *Africa*

South of the Congo (London: Royal African Society, 1968), pp. 22–34.

11. Information about the armed services is hard to gather and newspapers are often reluctant to publish such information because of the very extensive prohibitions contained in the Defence Amendment Act No. 85 of 1967. The best estimate I have been able to obtain is that there are (July 1969) two hundred to two hundred and twenty South African police in Rhodesia.

12. See Igor Kopytoff, "Socialism and Traditional African Societies," in William H. Friedland and Carl G. Rosberg, Jr. (eds.), *African Socialism.* Published for the Hoover Institution on War, Revolution, and Peace (Stanford: Stanford University Press, 1964), pp. 53–62.

13. As Max Gluckman says in his classic discussion, *Custom and Conflict in Africa* (Oxford: Blackwell, 1966), pp. 27–53 (though he does not use the term *intercalary role* here).

14. For a more detailed account see Christopher R. Hill, *Bantustans: The Fragmentation of South Africa.* Issued under the auspices of the Institute of Race Relations, London (London, New York: Oxford University Press, 1964), pp. 81–83, 111–112.

15. Developments in Botswana are described by J. H. Proctor in "The House of Chiefs and the Political Development of Botswana," *Journal of Modern African Studies*, vol. 6, no. 1 (May 1968), pp. 59–79.

16. It won 28 of the 45 elected seats at the October 1968 elections. (Horrell (compiler), *Survey of Race Relations . . . 1968*, p. 142.)

17. Hill, *Bantustans*, pp. 62–63.

18. Philip Mayer, "Labour Migrancy and the Social Network," in *Problems of Transition.* Proceedings of the Social Sciences Research Conference, 1962, edited by J. F. Holleman and others (Pietermaritzburg: Natal University Press, 1964), pp. 21–51.

19. Under the Physical Planning and Utilization of Resources Act, no. 88, of 1967.

20. For example, the target population of Mdantsane, a township near East London, "is 25,000. The official population figure is 58,000. Unofficially, 70,000 people live there." South Africa. Parliament. House of Assembly, *Debates*, weekly ed. no. 1, col. 144 (Feb. 4, 1969) (Speech of Dr. J. H. Moolman).

21. Horrell (compiler), *Survey of Race Relations . . . 1968*, p. 71. Africans must carry passes recording their permission to be in the white area, which is normally given only for the purpose of employment. An offense is committed if the owner cannot produce his pass, or if it is not in order.

22. South Africa, *Summary of the Report of the Commission for the Socio-Economic Development of the Bantu Areas within the Union of South Africa.* U.G. 61/1955 (Pretoria: Government Printer, 1955), p. 114.

23. South Africa. Parliament. House of Assembly, *Debates*, vol. 22, cols. 850–851 (February 20, 1968).

24. Permanent Committee for the Location of Industry and the Development of Border Areas, *Report of Activities for the Period 1st. January, 1967 to 31st. December, 1967.* Published as a supplement to *Commerce and Industry* (Johannesburg), June 1968, pp. 538–543; and Horrell, *Survey of Race Relations . . . 1968*, pp. 96, 98.

25. Horrell (compiler), *Survey of Race Relations . . . 1968*, pp. 143–144.

26. A summary of recent developments in the Ciskei and Tswana homelands may be found in *ibid.*, pp. 146–147.

27. H. Bhengu, "What It Means To Be an Urban African," a paper delivered at the Natal Conference of the South African Institute of Race Relations, Pietermaritzburg, November 8, 1958.

28. Jonty Driver, "Alan Paton's Hofmeyr," *Race*, vol. 6, no. 4 (April 1965), p. 277.

29. Professor Gwendolen M. Carter, in her 1966 Hoernlé Memorial Lecture to the South African Institute of Race Relations, *Separate Development: The Challenge of the Transkei* (Johannesburg: South African Institute of Race Relations, 1966), p. 14, suggested that separate territorial development might be worthy of consideration if resources were drastically reallocated between the races and if the settlement were reached after genuine and extensive interracial discussion. The argument is repeated in Gwendolen M. Carter, Thomas Karis, and Newell M. Stultz, *South Africa's Transkei: the Politics of Domestic Colonialism* (Evanston, Ill.: Northwestern University Press, 1967), p. 181.

30. See G. Naudé, "Banning in South Africa: A Technique of Repression," in Christopher R. Hill (ed.), *Rights and Wrongs: Some Essays on Human Rights.* Published for Amnesty International (Harmondsworth: Penguin Books, 1969), pp. 51–78.

31. Herbert Blumer, "Industrialisation and Race Relations," in Guy Hunter (ed.), *Industrialisation and Race Relations: A Symposium.* Issued under the auspices of the Institute of Race Relations, London (London, New York: Oxford University Press, 1965), pp. 220–253.

32. Professor Blumer includes as "political" such factors as the threat of Negro boycott in the southern United States, leading to reformed employment practices, and this, of course, is a response to an economic threat. But this does not weaken his thesis, which is that such responses do not grow out of the industrialization process *per se.*

33. Blumer, *op. cit.*, p. 252.

34. Two whites, 14 coloreds, and 81 Africans were executed in 1967. South Africa. Parliament. House of Assembly, *Debates*, vol. 23, cols. 3209–3210. (April 2, 1968).

CHAPTER 5

1. See Philip Noel-Baker, "Science and Disarmament," *UNESCO Courier* (Paris), 20th year (August–September 1967), pp. 10–21, 58–63.

2. International Court of Justice, *Reports of Judgments, Advisory Opinions and Orders. South West Africa Cases* (*Ethiopia* v. *South Africa; Liberia* v. *South Africa*). *Second Phase. Judgment of 18 July 1966* (n.p.: International Court of Justice, n.d.), p. 36 (hereafter cited as International Court of Justice, *1966 Judgment*).

3. *Ibid.*, p. 19.

4. Quoted in International Court of Justice, *Reports of Judgments, Advisory Opinions and Orders. International Status of South-West Africa. Advisory Opinion of July 11th 1950* (Leyden: A. W. Sijthoff's, n.d.), p. 134.

5. One passage reads as follows: "Another argument which requires consideration is that *in so far as the Court's view leads to the conclusion that there is now no entity to claim the due performance of the Mandate*, it must be unacceptable." (International Court of Justice, *Judgment 1966*, p. 36 [italics added]).

6. This fact was admitted by the Ethiopian delegate at the United Nations, Mr. Yifru. (United Nations, General Assembly, *Official Records*, 21st sess., 1414th Plenary Meeting, September 23, 1966, p. 3 [hereafter cited as UNGAOR, 21st sess., with plenary meeting number, date, and page].)

7. International Court of Justice, *1966 Judgment*, pp. 320–322 and 330, respectively.

8. "The World Court's Decision on South West Africa: A Symposium of the Section of International and Comparative Law at the Annual Meeting in Montreal on August 8, 1966," *The International Lawyer*, vol. 1, no. 1 (October 1966), p. 38.

9. International Court of Justice, *Pleadings, Oral Arguments, Documents. South West Africa Cases (Ethiopia* v. *South Africa; Liberia* v. *South Africa) 1966*, vol. 9, p. 110 [hereafter cited as International Court of Justice, *Pleadings, Oral Arguments, Documents* with volume number].

10. *Ibid.* vol. 8, p. 278.

11. *Ibid.*, vol. 8, pp. 279–280.

12. *Ibid.* vol. 9, p. 53.

13. International Court of Justice, *1966 Judgment*, p. 9.

14. International Court of Justice, *Reports of Judgments, Advisory Opinions and Orders. South West Africa Cases (Ethiopia* v. *South Africa; Liberia* v. *South Africa). Order of 29 November 1965* (n.p.: International Court of Justice, n.d.), p. 10.

15. International Court of Justice, *Pleadings, Oral Arguments, Documents*, vol. 9, p. 21.

16. United Nations, *Resolutions Adopted by the General Assembly during Its Fifth Special Session, 21 April—13 June 1967. Supplement No. 1. (A/6657)* (New York: United Nations, 1967), p. 1.

17. "The Goldberg Moth, The African Flame" (editorial), *Chicago Tribune*, October 14, 1966, sports final edition, sec. 1. p. 22, col. 2.

18. UNGAOR, 21st sess., 1414th Plenary Meeting, September 23, 1966, p. 3.

19. UNGAOR, 21st sess., 1417th Plenary Meeting, September 26, 1966, p. 19.

20. UNGAOR, 21st sess., 1419th Plenary Meeting, September 27, 1966, p. 13.

21. UNGAOR, 21st sess., 1425th Plenary Meeting, September 30, 1966, p. 6.

22. UNGAOR, 21st sess., 1427th Plenary Meeting, October 3, 1966, p. 7.

23. UNGAOR, 21st sess., 1429th Plenary Meeting, October 4, 1966, p. 7.

24. *Ibid.*, p. 17.

25. UNGAOR, 21st sess., 1431st Plenary Meeting, October 5, 1966, p. 1.

26. *Ibid.*, p. 3.

27. UNGAOR, 21st sess., 1414th Plenary Meeting, September 23, 1966, p. 8.

28. *Ibid.*, p. 10.

29. *Ibid.*, pp. 14–15.

30. UNGAOR, 21st sess., 1419th Plenary Meeting, September 27, 1966, p. 9.

31. *Ibid.*, p. 21.

32. UNGAOR, 21st sess., 1425th Plenary Meeting, September 30. 1966, p. 1.

33. *Ibid.*, p. 6.

34. UNGAOR, 21st sess., 1427th Plenary Meeting, October 3, 1966, p. 6.

35. UNGAOR, 21st sess., 1429th Plenary Meeting, October 4, 1966, p. 16.

36. UNGAOR, 21st sess., 1433d Plenary Meeting, October 7, 1966, p. 7.

37. *Ibid.*, p. 8.

38. The 16th General Assembly of the United Nations adopted a resolution in 1961 calling for the appointment of a committee of seven persons (from the Philippines, Mexico, Brazil, Burma, Norway, Somalia, and Togo) who were instructed, in consultation with the government of South Africa, to visit South West Africa and to inquire into a number of matters there. The South African government invited the chairman (Dr. Victorio Carpio) and the vice-chairman (Dr. Salvador Martinez de Alva) of the committee to come to South Africa for discussions, but it was made clear that the invitation was without prejudice to the position which South Africa had consistently taken on the juridical issue. The committee decided on April 13, 1962, to accept the invitation, and Dr. Carpio and Dr. de Alva arrived in Pretoria on May 5. At South Africa's invitation they made a tour of South West Africa from May 9 to May 19 and visited remote areas in the north of the territory, including the Herero, Damara, Ovambo, and Bushmen homelands. In Windhoek, they had talks with representatives of various racial groups, organizations, and political parties and thereafter visited the Transkei in order to study the South African policy of separate development. After this visit on May 23, the *Rand Daily Mail* (a newspaper violently opposed to the government's policy of separate development) and other newspapers (such as *Die Transvaler* and *Die Vaderland*) quoted Dr. Carpio as having stated publicly that he "would like to see apartheid succeed," as it was ". . . contrary to what I thought." ("No Race Has All Wisdom, Says Carpio," *Rand Daily Mail* (Johannesburg), May 24, 1962, p. 1, cols. 1–2.)

Subsequently, on May 26, a joint communiqué was issued in which Dr. Carpio and Dr. de Alva had expressed appreciation of the "free and uninhibited opportunities" extended to them to meet with all sections of the population of South West Africa, and they stated that they had found no evidence that the situation in South West Africa was a threat to international peace and security, nor had they found any signs of militarization in the territory or evidence that the indigenous population was being exterminated.

Ten days after the joint communiqué, Dr. Carpio claimed that he had taken no part in drafting the document. At a series of meetings of the Special Committee at the end of July, heated exchanges took place between Dr. Carpio and Dr. de Alva, the latter maintaining that Dr. Carpio, although ill in bed at the time, had been shown the draft communiqué and that it had his full approval. In fact, two senior members of the UN Secretariat who accompanied the two gentlemen confirmed this statement. Furthermore, the original document contains the amendments in Dr. Carpio's own handwriting in the form in which they were ultimately published.

39. The Liberian motion was passed by a vote of 67 to 1 (South Africa); the United States delegations did not participate in this vote. (United Nations, *Official Records of the General Assembly. Sixteenth sess. Plenary Meetings. Verbatim Record of Meetings. 19 September–18 October 1961* [n.p.: United Nations, n.d.], vol. 1, pp. 395, 403, 406.)

40. United Nations. General Assembly, *Provisional*

Verbatim Record of the 1439th Plenary Meeting. A/PV 1439, October 12, 1966, p. 106.

41. United Nations, *Official Records of the Second Part of the First Session of the General Assembly. Fourth Committee. Trusteeship. Part I. Summary Record of Meetings. 1 November–12 December 1946* (Lake Success, N.Y.: United Nations, n.d.), Annex 13, pp. 199–235 (especially pp. 232–234) and Annex 13a, pp. 235–244 (especially pp. 241–242) [hereafter cited as United Nations, *O.R. 2nd Pt. 1st sess. G.A., 4th Comm., Pt. I, S.R.M.*].

42. "Transvaal Val Afro-Asiatiese Lande in V.V.O. Skerp Aan," *Die Burger* (Cape Town), October 5, 1966, laaste uitgawe, p. 13, cols. 1–3.

43. "Damaras Sê: V.V.O. Moet Suidwes Los," *Die Burger*, January 5, 1967, p. 9, col. 1.

44. "Kleurlinge Wil Niks van V.V.—Sending Weet Nie," *Die Suidwester* (Windhoek), April 5, 1968, p. 3, cols. 1–2.

45. "Vorster Praat Skerp: 'Weste Sal vir of teen S.A. Moet Kies,' " *Die Burger*, June 12, 1967, p. 3, col. 1. (The translation is the author's.)

46. "Lidmaatskap: Premier Stel Saak oor die V.V.O.," *Die Suidwester*, September 27, 1967, p. 1, cols. 7–8. (The translation is the author's.)

47. George Louis Beer, *African Questions at the Paris Peace Conference with Papers on Egypt, Mesopotamia, and the Colonial Settlement.* Edited with introduction, annexes, and additional notes by Louis Herbert Gray (New York: The Macmillan Company, 1923), pp. 443–444.

48. Ray Vicker, "Disputed Territory: UN Is Eager To Control South West Africa But Could It Keep The Economy Operating?", *Wall Street Journal*, November 1, 1963, Eastern edition, p. 12, cols. 4–5.

49. United Nations, *O.R. 2nd Pt. 1st sess. G.A., 4th Comm., Pt. I, S.R.M.*, Annexes 16a and 16b, pp. 257–262.

50. Great Britain. Central Office of Information. Reference Division, *Russia, China and the West.* RF.P. 5815/68 (New York: Issued by the Reference Division of the British Information Services, 1968), p. 47 [hereafter cited as *Russia, China, and the West*].

51. Eschel M. Rhoodie, *The Third Africa* (Cape Town: Nasionale Boekhandel, 1968), p. 23.

52. *Ibid.*

53. *Russia, China, and the West*, p. 69.

54. *Ibid.*, p. 70.

55. "Total Sanctions Would Not Destroy S. Africa," *The Cape Argus* (Cape Town), July 12, 1966, city late edition, p. 15, cols. 1–2.

56. Ian D. Smith, *Speech to the Nation by the Prime Minister the Hon. I. D. Smith.* For the Record no. 4 (Salisbury: Ministry of Information, Immigration, and Tourism, 1968), p. 9.

57. "Pipeline Dreams," *The Cape Argus* (Cape Town), March 26, 1969, p. 22, col. 7.

58. "More Gas Finds Are Probable," *The Cape Argus*, March 26, 1969, p. 1, cols. 1–2.

59. Amelia C. Leiss (ed.), *Apartheid and United Nations Collective Measures: An Analysis* (New York: Carnegie Endowment for International Peace, 1965).

60. Field Marshal Lord Montgomery, "Any Invasion of S.A. Must Fail, Says Monty," *Sunday Times* (Johannesburg), March 29, 1964, p. 15, cols. 1–8.

61. Rhoodie, *op. cit.*, p. 52.

62. Republic of South Africa, *Report of the Commission of Enquiry into South West Africa Affairs 1962–1963.* R.P. no. 12/1964 (Pretoria: Government Printer, 1964). [Hereafter cited as *The Odendaal Report.*]

63. South Africa. Parliament. House of Assembly, *Debates*, vol. 22, cols. 1196–1197.

64. Act no. 54 of 1968, sec. 2.

65. *Ibid.*, sec. 4–6.

66. *Ibid.*, sec. 11.

67. *Ibid.*, sec. 5 and 8 and Schedule.

68. The "split tariff" implied two separate tariff systems—one for the Republic for goods railed to De Aar and one for South West Africa for commodities railed from De Aar to South West Africa, this actually worked out at a higher tariff than one over the same distance in the Republic.

69. *The Odendaal Report*, p. 245.

70. *Ibid.*, p. 127.

71. South Africa, *Memorandum. Decisions by the Government on the Financial and Administrative Relations Between the Republic and South West Africa.* W.P. NN-'68 (Pretoria: Government Printer, 1968), p. 5.

72. "Suidwes Nou Nader Getrek," *Die Suidwester*, August 30, 1967, p. 1, cols. 2–3. (The translation is the author's.)

73. South Africa. Department of Foreign Affairs, *South West Africa: Measures Taken To Combat Terrorism [Text of Letter Dated 15th February, 1968, and Annexures, Addressed to the Secretary-General of the United Nations by the South African Minister of Foreign Affairs].* (Pretoria: Government Printer, 1968), p. 3.

74. *Ibid.*, p. 12.

75. *Ibid.*

76. *Ibid.*, p. 13.

77. *Ibid.*, p. 7.

78. *Ibid.*, p. 5.

79. South Africa. Parliament. House of Assembly, *Debates*, vol. 23, col. 4118 (statement of the deputy minister of police, April 25, 1968).

80. *Ibid.*, col. 3328 (April 3, 1968).

CHAPTER 6

1. Eschel M. Rhoodie, *South West: The Last Frontier in Africa* (New York: Twin Circle, 1967), p. 52.

2. J. P. van S. Bruwer, *South West Africa: The Disputed Land* (Cape Town: Nasionale Boekhandel Beperk, 1966), pp. 2–3.

3. Ruth First, *South West Africa* (Baltimore: Penguin Books, 1963), p. 62.

4. Bruwer, *op. cit.*, pp. 4–5.

5. "Statement by Toivo Hermon Ja Toivo Delivered in Open Court on February 1, 1968," in *Erosion of the Rule of Law in South Africa* (Geneva: International Commission of Jurists, 1968), Appendix 1, p. 55.

6. United Nations. Security Council, *Report by the Secretary-General in Pursuance of Resolution 269 (1969) Adopted by the Security Council at Its 1497th Meeting on 12 August 1969 concerning the situation in Namibia.* Doc. no. S/9463. October 3, 1969 (n.p.: United Nations, 1969), p. 84.

7. Rhoodie, *op. cit.*, p. 121.

8. John H. Wellington, *South West Africa and Its Human Issues* (Oxford: Clarendon Press, 1967), p. 184.

9. First, *op. cit.*, p. 66 and Rhoodie, *op. cit.*, p. 128.

10. J. H. Esterhuyse, *South West Africa, 1880–1894: The Establishment of German Authority in South West*

Africa (Cape Town: C. Struik, [Pty.] Ltd., 1968), pp. 30–33.

11. "A General Order," (editorial), *Cape Times* (Cape Town), July 14, 1915, daily ed., p. 6, cols. 6–7.
12. As quoted in First, *op. cit.*, p. 78.
13. Rhoodie, *op. cit.*, p. 95 and Wellington, *op. cit.*, p. 205.
14. Karl W. Deutsch, "The Theoretical Basis of Data Programs," in Richard L. Merritt and Stein Rokkan (eds.), *Comparing Nations: The Use of Quantitative Data in Cross-National Research* (New Haven and London: Yale University Press, 1966), pp. 45–46.
15. *South West Africa Survey, 1967* (Pretoria: Department of Foreign Affairs, 1967), p. 24. See also United Nations. Security Council, *op. cit.*, pp. 153–155.
16. First, *op. cit.*, pp. 197–198.
17. *Ibid.*, pp. 209–210, 261.
18. *Ibid.*, p. 196.
19. *Ibid.*, pp. 209–211.
20. "Windhoek Riots—Appeal to International Court by Ethiopia and Liberia," *Keesing's Contemporary Archives* (Keynsham, Bristol, England), vol. 13 (1961–1962), p. 18231.
21. First, *op. cit.*, pp. 206–207.
22. "Meeting Banned, " *Africa Digest* (London), vol. 10, no. 2 (February, 1964), p. 141.
23. "Southern Africa: Black Man's War," *The Economist* (London), vol. 231, no. 6559 (May 10, 1969), p. 32.
24. Colin Legum, "South Africa Steps Up Secret War on Guerrillas," *The Observer* (London), June 8, 1969, p. 7, cols. 4–6.
25. "The Plight of Namibian Refugees in Zambia," *Namibia News* (London), vol. 2, nos. 4–6 (April-June 1969), p. 4.
26. "Measures and Counter-Measures," *Namibia News*, vol. 2, nos. 4–6 (April-June 1969), pp. 2–3.
27. "Stop Press," *Namibia News*, vol. 3, nos. 1–3 (January-March 1970), p. 17.
28. United Nations. General Assembly. 19th sess. *Implications of the Activities of the Mining Industry and of the Other International Companies Having Interests in South West Africa: Report of the Special Committee on the Situation with Regard to the Implementation of the Declaration on the Granting of Independence to Colonial Countries and Peoples*. Document A/5840. January 5, 1965 (New York: United Nations, 1965), Annex, pp. 34, 66, 72 [hereafter cited as United Nations, *Mining Industry in South West Africa*].
29. *Ibid.*, Annex, p. 72.
30. Wellington, *op. cit.*, p. 113.
31. "Old-Timer To Reopen," *South African Digest* (Pretoria), week ended October 11, 1968, pp. 3–4.
32. Rhoodie, *op. cit.*, p. 79.
33. United Nations, *Mining Industry in South West Africa*, Annex, pp. 81–82.
34. "Nuwe Fase in Olie-Soektog," *Die Suidwes Afrikaner* (Windhoek), April 18, 1969, p. 3, cols. 1–7.
35. *Summary of Press Reports on South West Africa*, Office of the United Nations Commissioner for Namibia (New York), June 18, 1968, p. 1.
36. United Nations, *Mining Industry in South West Africa*, Annex, pp. 37, 43.
37. Wellington, *op. cit.*, pp. 112.
38. United Nations, *Mining Industry in South West Africa*. Annex, pp. 68, 71.
39. *Ibid.*, Annex, p. 147.

PART THREE CHAPTER 1

1. Dr. H. F. Verwoerd, *I. Crisis in World Conscience. II. The Road to Freedom for Basutoland, Bechuanaland, Swaziland*. Fact Paper no. 107 (Pretoria: South African Government, Department of Information, 1964), p. 12.
2. "Republic and Protectorates: We Will Never Link—Premier," *Rand Daily Mail* (Johannesburg), September 5, 1962, p. 1, col. 9 and p. 2, col. 4.
3. G. Tylden, *The Rise of the Basuto* (Cape Town: Juta, 1950), p. 186.
4. Cecil Headlam, "The Race for the Interior, 1881–1895," in Eric A. Walker (ed.), *The Cambridge History of the British Empire*, vol. 8, *South Africa, Rhodesia and the High Commission Territories*, 2nd ed. (Cambridge: Cambridge University Press, 1963), p. 519.
5. Lord William Malcolm Hailey, *Native Administration in the British African Territories*, Part V. *The High Commission Territories: Basutoland, The Bechuanaland Protectorate and Swaziland* (London: HMSO, 1953), p. 190.
6. As quoted in *ibid.*, p. 192.
7. Anthony Sillery, *The Bechuanaland Protectorate* (Cape Town, London, New York: Oxford University Press, 1952), p. 70.
8. *Ibid.*, p. 78.
9. William Waldegrave Palmer Selborne, 2nd Earl of Selborne, *The Selborne Memorandum . . .* (London. Humphrey Milford, Oxford University Press, 1925), pp. 7–25. See Alan R. Booth, "Lord Selborne and the British Protectorates, 1908–1910," *Journal of African History*, vol. 10, no. 1 (1969), p. 134. Professor Alan R. Booth has cogently argued that Lord Selborne had second thoughts on the advisability of transfer even as the memorandum was being issued. This change in attitude resulted from a greater knowledge of the Basuto who had clearly articulated their opposition to incorporation through the National Council. Through his own investigation and reports from Reverend Jacottet in Basutoland, Lord Selborne had concluded that transfer would directly result in rebellion. (Booth, *op. cit.*, pp. 134–137.)
10. By an order-in-council effective July 1, 1853, the British government approved a constitution for the Cape Colony conferring the franchise without regard to color upon all those earning £50 per annum. (See T. R. H. Davenport, "The Consolidation of a New Society: The Cape Colony" in Monica Wilson and Leonard M. Thompson [eds.], *The Oxford History of South Africa* [New York, Oxford: Oxford University Press, 1969], vol. 1, pp. 323–324.)
11. Eric A. Walker, *A History of Southern Africa* (London: Longmans, Green, 1965), p. 533.
12. As quoted in Leonard M. Thompson, *Unification of South Africa, 1902–1910* (Oxford: Clarendon Press, 1960), p. 124.
13. As quoted in Sir Charles Dundas and Hugh Ashton, *Problem Territories of Southern Africa* (Johannesburg: South African Institute of International Affairs, 1952), p. 30.
14. Lord William Malcolm Hailey, *The Republic of South Africa and the High Commission Territories* (London: Oxford University Press, 1963), pp. 25–26.
15. Sir Godfrey Lagden, *The Basutos*. 2 vols. (New York: D. Appleton, 1910), vol. 2, p. 623.

16. Hailey, *Native Administration in the British African Territories*, Part V, p. 207.
17. Lagden, *op. cit.*, vol. 2, p. 623.
18. Great Britain, *Colonial Reports (Bechuanaland)*, No. 652 (1909–1910) (London: HMSO, 1911), p. 12.
19. Thompson, *op. cit.*, p. 214.
20. As quoted in Ibid., pp. 271–272. While formally endorsing transfer under the right conditions, Lord Selborne had decided against transfer with or without provision for African franchise. Therefore, subsequent South African rejection of a Union franchise for non-whites served as a convenient reason to defer transfer. (Booth, *op. cit.*, p. 142.)
21. As quoted in Thompson, *op. cit.*, p. 272.
22. *Ibid.*
23. *Ibid.*, p. 276.
24. Great Britain. Parliament. House of Commons, *Debates*, [5th series], vol. 9, col. 957 (August 16, 1909).
25. *Ibid.*, cols. 957–958 (August 16, 1909).
26. *Ibid.*, col. 1012 (August 16, 1909) (speech of Prime Minister Asquith).
27. *Ibid.*, col. 1649 (August 19, 1909) (speech of Lt. Col. Seely).
28. Great Britain. Parliament. House of Lords, *Debates*, [5th series], vol. 2, cols. 762–763 (July 27, 1909). Quotation from col. 763.
29. *Ibid.*, col. 763 (July 27, 1909).
30. *Ibid.*, col. 830 (August 3, 1909).
31. Great Britain. Parliament. House of Commons, *Debates* [5th series], vol. 9, col. 967 (August 16, 1909).
32. Great Britain. Parliament. House of Lords, *Debates* [5th series], vol. 2, cols. 788–791 (July 27, 1909). Quotation from col. 790.
33. G. W. Eybers (ed.), *Select Constitutional Documents Illustrating South African History 1795–1910* (London: George Routledge & Sons, 1918), p. 521.
34. Great Britain. Office of Commonwealth Relations, *Basutoland, the Bechuanaland Protectorate and Swaziland: History of Discussions with the Union of South Africa, 1909–1939*. Cmd. 8707 (London: HMSO, 1952), p. 121 [hereafter cited as Cmd. 8707].
35. Mr. Gert C. Olivier (1837–1922) was a farmer in the Cape Colony (where he owned a large ostrich farm). He had been active in Cape politics as a mayor of Oudsthoorn, a member of the Municipal Council, and a member of the District Council. (See Jan Christiaan Smuts, *Selections from the Smuts Papers*. Edited by W. K. Hancock and Jean van der Poel. 4 vols. [Cambridge, England: Cambridge University Press, 1966], vol. 4, p. 364.)
36. Letter from Mr. Gert C. Olivier to General Smuts dated November 18, 1918. Translated from the Dutch and published in *ibid.* vol. 4, pp. 16–20. Quotation from p. 20.
37. Cmd. 8707, p. 13.
38. *Ibid.*, p. 14.
39. *Ibid.*
40. *Ibid.*, p. 19.
41. *Ibid.*, p. 18.
42. *Ibid.*, p. 17.
43. *Ibid.*, p. 14.
44. *Ibid.*, p. 15.
45. Walker, *A History of Southern Africa*, pp. 636–637.
46. Richard C. Fitzgerald, "South Africa and the High Commission Territories," *World Affairs* (London), vol. 4, no. 3 (July 1950), pp. 310–311.
47. Cmd. 8707, p. 56.
48. Margery Perham and Lionel Curtis, *The Protectorates of South Africa: The Question of Their Transfer to the Union* (London: Oxford University Press, 1935), p. 21.
49. Great Britain. Commission on Financial and Economic Position of Basutoland, *Report*. Cmd. 4907 (London, HMSO, 1935), p. 49.
50. See Mary Benson, *Tshekedi Khama* (London: Faber and Faber, 1960), pp. 90–111.
51. Hailey, *Republic of South Africa*, p. 66.
52. Walker, *A History of Southern Africa*, p. 661.
53. Cmd. 8707, p. 44.
54. *Ibid.*, p. 48.
55. *Ibid.*, pp. 53–54.
56. *Ibid.*, p. 54.
57. South Africa. Parliament. House of Assembly, *Debates*, vol. 27, col. 6257.
58. *Ibid.*
59. Great Britain. Parliament. House of Commons, *Debates*, 5th series, vol. 314, col. 2239.
60. Cmd. 8707, p. 59.
61. *Ibid.*, p. 63.
62. South Africa. Parliament. House of Assembly, *Debates*, vol. 27, cols. 6257–6258 (June 16, 1936).
63. Walker, *A History of Southern Africa*, p. 663.
64. *Ibid.*
65. *Ibid.*
66. *Ibid.*, p. 664.
67. Excerpts from this pamphlet are published in S. M. Gabatswane, *Introduction to the Bechuanaland Protectorate History and Administration* (Kanye, Botswana: S. M. Gabatswane, 1957), pp. 40, 42.
68. As quoted in Benson, *op. cit.*, p. 118.
69. Perham and Curtis, *op. cit.*, p. 49.
70. *Ibid.*, pp. 70–71.
71. Great Britain. Parliament. House of Commons, *Debates*, 5th series, vol. 333, col. 1809 (March 29, 1938).
72. Cmd. 8707, p. 79.
73. *Ibid.*, pp. 81–82.
74. *Ibid.*, p. 84.
75. *Ibid.* (Italics in the original.)
76. *Ibid.*, pp. 85–86.
77. *Ibid.*, p. 86.
78. *Ibid.*
79. *Ibid.*
80. Great Britain. Parliament. House of Commons, *Debates*, 5th series, vol. 333, cols. 1808–1809 (March 29, 1938). Quotation from col. 1808 (speech of Mr. MacDonald).
81. *Ibid.*, cols. 1809–1810. Quotation from col. 1810.
82. Cmd. 8707, pp. 90–98. Quotation from p. 92.
83. *Ibid.*, p. 92.
84. J. E. Spence, "British Policy Towards the High Commission Territories," *Journal of Modern African Studies*, vol. 2, no. 2 (July 1964), p. 242.
85. Great Britain, *Report on the Recent Outbreak of "Diretlo" Murders in Basutoland*, Cmd. 8209 (London: HMSO, 1951), pp. 221ff.
86. Benson, *op. cit.*, p. 200.
87. "The Protectorates" (editorial), *The Times* (London), April 15, 1950, late London ed., p. 7, cols. 2–3.
88. South Africa. Parliament. House of Assembly, *Debates*, vol. 71, col. 4192.
89. South Africa. Parliament. Senate, *Debates, 1950*, vol. 2, cols. 1944–1945.

90. Nicholas Mansergh (ed.), *Documents and Speeches on British Commonwealth Affairs, 1931–1952*. Issued under the auspices of the Royal Institute of International Affairs. 2 vols. (London, New York, Toronto: Oxford University Press, 1953), vol. 2, pp. 928–929. Quotation from p. 929.

91. *Ibid.* vol. 2, pp. 928–929. Quotation from p. 929.

92. Walker, *A History of Southern Africa*, p. 825.

93. *Ibid.*

94. *Ibid.*, pp. 852–853.

95. As quoted in *ibid.*, p. 853.

96. *Ibid.*

97. South Africa. Parliament. House of Assembly, *Debates*, vol 85, cols. 3769, 3972.

98. "Strijdom says Claim for Protectorates Won't Be Abandoned: 'Clearly Envisaged in South Africa Act,' " *Rand Daily Mail*, September 14, 1955, p. 1, cols. 4–5.

99. "South Africa and the High Commission Territories," *African Institute International Bulletin* (Pretoria), vol. 2, no. 1 (January 1964), p. 11.

100. *Ibid.*

101. South Africa, Parliament. House of Assembly, *Debates*, vol. 91, col. 5309.

102. Union of South Africa, *Summary of the Report of the Commission for the Socio-Economic Development of the Bantu Areas within the Union of South Africa*. U.G. 61/1955 (Pretoria: Government Printer, 1955). The summary consists of fifty-one chapters, innumerable tables, and an atlas of sixty-four maps.

103. William H. Vatcher, *White Laager: The Rise of Afrikaner Nationalism* (New York, Washington, London: Frederick A. Praeger, 1965), pp. 152–155.

104. South Africa. Parliament. House of Assembly, *Debates*, vol. 101, cols. 5254–5257.

105. "Verwoerd at Nat. Congress: Pleads for Protectorates, But Keeps Off Republican Election," *The Star* (Johannesburg), November 13, 1958, city late edition, p. 4, cols. 3–5 and *Die Transvaler* (Johannesburg), November 13, 1958, as translated and quoted in "South Africa and the High Commission Territories," p. 11.

106. Leo Marquand, *The Peoples and Policies of South Africa*, 3d ed. (London: Oxford University Press, 1962), p. 266.

107. "South Africa and the High Commission Territories," p. 11.

108. *Ibid.*, pp. 11–12.

109. See Richard P. Stevens, *Lesotho, Botswana, and Swaziland: The Former High Commission Territories in Southern Africa* (New York, Washington, London: Frederick A. Praeger, 1967), pp. 59–60 on the founding of the Basutoland National Congress.

110. Sir John Maud, "The Challenge of the High Commission Territories," *African Affairs* (London), vol. 43, no. 251 (April 1964), p. 96.

111. *Ibid.*

112. See Stevens, *op. cit.*, p. 10.

CHAPTER 2

1. The writer wishes to thank his co-editor (Professor Christian P. Potholm), Mr. Q. Neil Parsons of the Dept. of History of the University of Zambia, and Mr. Christopher S. Dambe (formerly First Secretary of the Embassy of the Republic of Botswana in Washington, D.C.), for reading and commenting upon an earlier draft of this chapter. In addition, he would like to express his gratitude to the American Philosophical Society for a grant to travel to Southern Africa in the summer of 1970 and to the Trustees of the Smuts Archive Trust for permission to use the Smuts Archive.

2. It should be pointed out that gold was found in Bechuanaland approximately twenty years before it was discovered at the Witwatersrand in South Africa. Gold was located in the Tati area (near Francistown) in 1866. See "Monarch Mine Offered for Sale: Big Part Played in Progress of Bechuanaland," *The Star* (Johannesburg), October 7, 1948, city late ed., p. 14, col. 3.

3. Anthony Sillery, *Founding a Protectorate: History of Bechuanaland, 1885–1895*. Studies in African History, Anthropology, and Ethnology no. 3 (London, The Hague, Paris: Mouton & Co., 1965), p. 235.

4. David Vital, *The Inequality of States: A Study of the Small Power in International Relations* (Oxford: Clarendon Press, 1967), p. 4.

5. Douglas Brown, *Against the World: Attitudes of White South Africa* (Garden City, N.Y.: Doubleday & Company, Inc., Anchor Books ed., 1969), p. 236.

6. See also Ronald Hyam, "African Interests and the South Africa Act, 1908–1910," *The Historical Journal* (London), vol. 13, no. 1 (March, 1970), pp. 85–105.

7. Henry John May, *The South African Constitution*. 3rd ed. (Cape Town and Johannesburg: Juta & Co., Limited, 1955), pp. 19, 517, and 626–631 and South Africa, *Government Gazette*, vol. 46, no. 2341 (April 2, 1969), pp. 1–2.

8. J. A. F. Nel, "Dié Artikels Pas Nie in Grondwet," (letter to the editor), *Die Burger* (Cape Town), February 28, 1968, laaste uitgawe, p. 12, cols. 7–8; "Amend S.A. Constitution Call by Former M.P.," *The Star*, March 1, 1968, city late ed., p. 21, col. 1; and "Take-over Clause in Act To Be Dropped," *The Star*, September 18, 1968, 2nd city late ed., p. 13, cols. 1–2.

9. This matter is examined in greater detail in Richard Dale, "The Tale of Two Towns (Mafeking and Gaberones) and the Political Modernization of Botswana," *SAIPA: Journal for Public Administration* (Pretoria), vol. 4, no. 2 (March, 1969), pp. 130–144.

10. Personal interview with Mr. A. M. Zietsman, retired Town Clerk of Mafeking, in Mafeking on August 28, 1970.

11. Great Britain. Commission on Financial and Economic Position of the Bechuanaland Protectorate, *Financial and Economic Position of the Bechuanaland Protectorate*. Cmd. 4368 (London: H.M.S.O., 1933), pp. 50 and 148–149.

12. Alan C. G. Best, "Gaberone [*sic*]: Problems and Prospects of a New Capital," *The Geographical Review*, vol. 60, no. 1 (January, 1970), p. 13.

13. This is a theme one constantly encounters in the social columns of the *Mafeking Mail and Botswana Guardian* (hereafter cited as *Mafeking Mail*), the weekly newspaper which circulates both in Mafeking and throughout Botswana. Naturally, a Motswana would find the prospect of retiring in South Africa less attractive than either a Briton or a white South African, neither of whom is subject to the indignities of *apartheid*. Part of the problem of retired civil servants may be due to the amount of cash needed to acquire a farm in Botswana as well as to the need to find subsequent employment to supplement one's pension.

14. See Robert Heussler, *Yesterday's Rulers: The*

Making of the British Colonial Service (Syracuse: Syracuse University Press, 1963), pp. 130–219, for an analysis of Major Sir Ralph D. Furse's contribution to the recruitment and training of the British colonial service.

15. Personal interview with Sir R. Peter Fawcus, retired former H. M. Commissioner of the Bechuanaland Protectorate, in London on June 23, 1970. Hereafter cited as Fawcus interview.

16. See Edwin S. Munger, *Bechuanaland: Pan-African Outpost or Bantu Homeland?* Issued under the auspices of the Institute of Race Relations, London (London, New York: Oxford University Press, 1965), pp. 46–48.

17. Fawcus interview.

18. See "Govt. Will Act against Racialism—Masisi," *Mafeking Mail*, March 26, 1970, p. 3, cols. 2–3; "Move To Condemn D.R.C. Rejected by Assembly," *Mafeking Mail*, April 3, 1970, p. 1, cols. 1–2; "Private Sector Attacked in Assembly," *Mafeking Mail*, April 10, 1970; and "Tuli Block Farmers under Fire," *Mafeking Mail*, July 17, 1970, p. 2, cols. 3–4.

19. See Jack Halpern, *South Africa's Hostages: Basutoland, Bechuanaland and Swaziland* (Baltimore: Penguin Books, 1965), pp. 57–58 and Anthony Sillery, "The British Protectorates in Africa—II," *The Fortnightly* (London), vol. 177 (n.s. vol. 171), no. 1021 (n.s.) (January, 1952), p. 27.

20. Copy of a letter from Field Marshal Jan C. Smuts to Winston Churchill dated March 16, 1950. The Smuts Archive (J. W. Jagger Library, University of Cape Town), vol. 95, no. 180.

21. The manner in which the ban on Sir Seretse was lifted by the South African government was rather unusual and embarrassed Sir R. Peter Fawcus, the Queen's Commissioner at the time, since neither he nor the British government was officially notified when the South African minister of the interior withdrew the ban on Sir Seretse on October 21, 1964. "Union Bans Seretse and His Wife," *The Star*, November 1, 1949, city late ed., p. 1, col. 5; "Verwoerd Talks of Khama Visit: Sends His Personal Congratulations," *The Star*, March 4, 1965, city late ed., p. 1, cols. 2–4; "In Bechuanaland . . . Verwoerd Statement Causes Astonishment," *The Star*, March 5, 1965, city late ed., p. 3, cols. 4–6; and "Seretse Decision: Why S.A. Kept Mum," *The Star*, March 26, 1965, 1st stop press ed., p. 1, col. 1.

22. See M. D. W. Jeffreys, "Seretse's Exile and Return: The Legal Issues," *The Forum* (Johannesburg), vol. 5, no. 8 (November, 1956), pp. 42–43.

23. Fawcus interview.

24. Lord Harlech, "Basutoland, Bechuanaland and Swaziland," *United Empire* (London), vol. 36, no. 2 (March-April, 1945), pp. 52–53. It should be noted that Tiger Kloof (which is the *Alma Mater* of probably more of the Batswana elite than any other South African secondary school) received subventions from the Department of Education of the Cape Province. See South Africa. Department of Bantu Administration and Development, *The Tribes of the Vryburg District*. By P.-L. Breutz. Ethnological Publications no. 46 (Pretoria: The Government Printer, 1959), p. 49.

25. The shift took place in the early 1960's just prior to independence. Compare Great Britain. Commonwealth Relations Office, *Bechuanaland Protectorate: Report for the Year 1960* (London: H.M.S.O., 1963), p. 53 and Great Britain. Colonial Office, *Bechuanaland Protectorate: Report for the Years 1961–1962* (London: H.M.S.O., 1964), pp. 51–52. See also Great Britain. Parliament. House of Commons, *Debates*, 5th series, vol. 685, cols. 145–146 (written answers) (December 3, 1963) on the matter of South African textbooks used in the Bechuanaland Protectorate schools.

26. "University Opens in Maseru," *The Star*, October 10, 1964, city late sport ed., p. 11, col. 3 and "Britain To Aid Expansion Plans of Basuto University," *The Times* (London), May 25, 1965, late London ed., p. 11, cols. 3–4.

27. Extracts for this speech are published in Sir Seretse Khama, "Outlook for Botswana," *The Journal of Modern African Studies*, vol. 8, no. 1 (April, 1970), pp. 123–128. The quotation is from p. 125 of these extracts. For the full text of the speech, consult Sir Seretse Khama, K.B.E., President of the Republic of Botswana, *Address to the General Assembly of the United Nations, September, 1969* (Gaborone: The Government Printer, n.d.).

28. Vital, *op. cit.*, p. 4.

29. Articles I, II, and III of "Customs Agreement: Union of South Africa—Territories of Basutoland, Swaziland, and the Bechuanaland Protectorate, 1910," in Bechuanaland Protectorate, *Orders in Council and High Commissioner's Proclamations and Notices Issued from the 9th May, 1891, to the 30th June, 1914*. Edited by M. Williams (Mafeking: Mafeking Mail, Printers, 1915), pp. 367–368. Hereafter cited as Bechuanaland Protectorate, *Orders, Proclamations, and Notices, 1891–1914*.

30. Peter Robson, "Economic Integration in Southern Africa," *The Journal of Modern African Studies*, vol. 5, no. 4 (December, 1967), p. 474, table 2 and p. 470, table 1, respectively.

31. "Botswana Seeks New S.A. Customs Pact," *The Star*, September 30, 1966, city late ed., p. 21, cols. 4–6.

32. Botswana, *National Development Plan, 1968–73* (Gaborone: The Government Printer, 1968), p. 12.

33. Botswana, *Transitional Plan for Social and Economic Development* (Gaborone: The Government Printer, 1966), p. 10. Hereafter cited as Botswana, *Transitional Plan*.

34. Robson, *op. cit.*, p. 486.

35. *Ibid.*, pp. 486–488.

36. Botswana, *Transitional Plan*, p. 10.

37. *Ibid.*

38. "Customs Agreement: Union of South Africa—Territories of Basutoland, Swaziland, and the Bechuanaland Protectorate, 1910," in Bechuanaland Protectorate, *Orders, Proclamations, and Notices, 1891–1914*, p. 369.

39. See Robson, *op. cit.*, p. 486.

40. "Botswana Upset by S.A. Action," *The Star*, April 25, 1969, 2nd city late ed., p. 1, col. 9.

41. Clive Cowley, "Document Binds 10 Countries," *The Star*, November 11, 1969, 2nd city late ed., p. 44, cols. 5–9.

42. Quoted in "Cash and Customs Dealings with S.A.: Black States Seek a Bigger Say: New Look at Rand Tie-Up," *The Star*, September 1, 1969, 2nd city late ed., p. 1, cols. 4–5 and p. 3, col. 5.

43. Articles 6, 7, 14, and 20 of "Agreement between the Government of the Republic of Botswana, the Government of the Kingdom of Lesotho, the Government of the Republic of South Africa and the Government of

the Kingdom of Swaziland Terminating the Customs Agreement of 1910 and Concluding a New Customs Agreement, Together with a Memorandum of Understanding Relating Thereto," in Botswana, *Government Gazette*, vol. 7, no. 64 (December 12, 1969), pp. E.640–E.341, E.343–E.345, and E.347–E.348.

44. "Customs Union Agreement Tabled in Cape Town: Levy Rights of Botswana, Lesotho and Swaziland," *Southern Africa* (London), vol. 82 (February 28, 1970), p. 131 and South Africa. Parliament. House of Assembly, *Debates*, no. 3 (February 16–20, 1970), col. 1326 (February 18, 1970) (speeches of Mr. A. Hopewell and the deputy minister of finance).

45. "Minister's Statement on Customs Union Agreement," *Therisanyo/Consultation* (Gaborone), vol. 8, no. 2 (February, 1970), p. 7.

46. For an application of game theory to the bilateral relationships between Botswana and South Africa, consult Richard Dale, *Botswana and Its Southern Neighbor: The Patterns of Linkage and the Options in Statecraft.* Papers in International Studies. Africa series no. 6 (Athens, Ohio: Ohio University Center for International Studies, Africa Program, 1970), pp. 6–21.

47. Robert A. Dahl, *Modern Political Analysis*. 2nd ed. (Englewood Cliffs, N.J.: Prentice-Hall, Inc., 1970), p. 62 (italics added).

48. "Cash and Customs Dealings with S.A.: Black States Seek a Bigger Say: New Look at Rand Tie-Up," *The Star*, September 1, 1969, 2nd city late ed., p. 1, cols. 4–5 and p. 3, col. 5.

49. Botswana, *Transitional Plan*, p. 10.

50. "Botswana: General," *Standard Bank Review* (London), April, 1970, p. 30; "Botswana: Finance," *Barclays Overseas Review* (London), May, 1970, p. 44; "Botswana: Bond Issue," *Standard Bank Review*, July, 1970, p. 34; and "Botswana: Finance," *Barclays Overseas Review*, July, 1970, p. 39.

51. President Khama stated his position quite unmistakably when he declared that Botswana would ". . . decline to consider the exchange of diplomatic representatives with South Africa until we are confident that South Africa can fully guarantee that Botswana's representatives will in *all respects*, at *all times* and in *all places* be treated in the *same way* as diplomats from other countries." Sir Seretse Khama, *Botswana's Foreign Policy: Address by His Excellency the President to the Botswana Democratic Party Conference at Molepolole, on Saturday 28th March, 1970* (Gaborone: Government Printer, 1970), p. 5 (italics added).

52. This point was forcefully brought home to white South Africa by an African journalist who writes the informative column "Window on the Townships" in *The Star* under the pseudonym of Mhloli. His remarks are worth quoting at some length:

> Soweto Africans [that is, those who live in the sprawling African townships in Johannesburg] applaud the Government for trying to establish harmonious relations with other African states. At the same time they are asking two questions.
>
> The first is why the Government reserves red-carpet treatment for Africans from other states while according none of it to leaders of the African community here. Soweto residents are wondering whether it has ever occurred to the Government that if it treated local Africans with the same respect as it treats those from abroad, there would be a great improvement in race relationships here.
>
> The second question is whether the admittedly admirable attitude of the Government towards other African states will ever yield impressive dividends unless it is accompanied by a parallel improvement in the cordiality between the Government and Africans of this country.

Mhloli, "Red Carpets and Deep Questions," *The Star*, April 3, 1967, city late ed., p. 20, cols. 8–9.

53. See Clive Cowley, "Sore Points on the Borders," *The Star*, January 20, 1969, 2nd city late ed., p. 18, cols. 8–9.

54. " 'Outwards' Policy Is for Safety—Vorster: Answers to Nationalist Doubters," *The Star*, September 12, 1968, 2nd city late ed., p. 1, cols. 2–3 and p. 3, col. 3 and "Botswana's Thanks to S. Africa," *The Star*, October 21, 1968, 2nd city late ed., p. 11, col. 3. Yet almost a year later, the former South African ambassador to the United Kingdom (who later became minister of mines and planning), Dr. Carel de Wet, declared that "It was well known that Sir Seretse regarded apartheid unfavourably but that same Black man, when he was sick, came to the 'apartheid police state' and said 'I'm sick, help me.' " As quoted in " 'A Duty To Be Friendly'—De Wet," *The Star*, December 5, 1969, 2nd city late ed., p. 21, col. 1. This remark did not go unnoticed in Botswana, and the government of Botswana charged that Dr. De Wet was ". . . surely not typical of his colleagues [in the South African cabinet] in appearing to wish to extract a political price for what Botswana has so far assumed was a Christian and humanitarian decision." As quoted in "Remark by De Wet Criticized," *The Star*, December 9, 1969, 2nd city late ed., p. 13, col. 7.

55. The writer was present in Gaborone during the independence celebrations and recalls having seen the South African foreign minister, Dr. Hilgard Muller, there during the ceremonies when Sir Seretse Khama was sworn in as the first President on the morning of September 30, 1966. Other subsequent visitors to Botswana included Mr. J. J. Fouché (the current president of South Africa, who visited Botswana while minister of agricultural technical services in 1967) and Mr. A. F. B. Burger (formerly head of the African division of the department of foreign affairs and now the South African ambassador to France).

56. See "100 Trainee Saboteurs Fly North This Week: Police Tell How Bechuanaland Is Being Used," *The Star*, August 26, 1963, 2nd stop press ed., p. 1, cols. 2–3.

57. "Freedom Ferry: Zambesi Crossing Last Hurdle for Refugees," *The Star*, September 23, 1964, city late ed., p. 28, cols. 7–9 and p. 29, cols. 1–3.

58. *Ibid.*

59. See J. S. M. Simpson, "The Black Manifesto Election—Part 1," *The Star*, June 11, 1969, 2nd city late ed., p. 38, cols. 5–7 and J. S. M. Simpson, "The Black Manifesto Election: Part 2: 'Equal Rights' Stampeded White Voters," *The Star*, June 12, 1969, 2nd city late ed., p. 44, cols. 6–9 and p. 45, cols. 1–3.

60. "Soviet Envoy to Zambia May Fill Post: Botswana-Soviet Link: S.A. Alert: No Resident Ambassador," *The Star*, March 11, 1970, 2nd city late ed., p. 1, cols. 2–3 and p. 14, col. 3.

61. The anxiety was not confined to the ruling

National Party; it was also shared by the opposition United Party. For the views of the National Party, consult "Nats Worried by Red Link with Botswana: Subversion Fear," *The Star*, March 12, 1970, 1st city late ed., p. 5, cols. 5–7 and "Red Link: Botswana Warned," *The Star*, April 8, 1970, 2nd city late ed., p. 7, col. 3. The United Party position (as stated by one of its leading frontbenchers) is given in Marais Steyn, "Russian Presence in Botswana Is Warning for S.A.," *The Star*, March 17, 1970, 2nd city late ed., p. 20, col. 9. This anxiety was not diminished when it became known in South Africa that two persons who were alleged to be Communists—a Briton, John R. Syson, and the son of the late Botswana Ambassador to the United States, Joe Matthews—were thought to have considerable access to, and influence with, President Khama. See "Questions about Botswana," *News/Check* (Johannesburg), vol. 8, no. 26 (June 26—July 9, 1970), p. 9, for an exposition of this point of view. Finally, it should be remembered that the South African government was extremely worried about the Soviet presence in Southern Africa, especially after the South African police captured a Soviet K.G.B. agent, Yuri R. Loginov, in Johannesburg in late 1967. See "Spy Swoop Drama on Rand: Arrested K.G.B. Man on 'Special Mission' to S.A.," *The Star*, September 9, 1967, city late sport ed., p. 1, cols. 1–3 and p. 3, cols. 4–6.

62. On August 27, 1970, the writer attended a fair in Pretoria, where he saw an exhibit of arms and equipment of Sino-Soviet manufacture which had been seized from captured African nationalist guerrillas. This exhibit appeared to be quite popular with the white South Africans who were visiting the fair then and no doubt had the desired effect on the South African electorate.

63. The road, which will connect Francistown, Botswana with Livingstone, Zambia, is reported to cost $6.3 million, while the link between Nata and Kazungula (the border point) will cost $2.52 million. The government of the United States will furnish $6 million for the project. See "Haskins Calls for Spending Curb: Encouraging Report by Dr. Masire," *Mafeking Mail*, March 20, 1970, p. 1, cols. 1–2 and p. 2, col. 5; "S.A. Upset by Proposed Zambia Road Link: But Botswana Enthusiastic," *Mafeking Mail*, April 17, 1970, p. 1, cols. 3–4; and John Edlin, "Four Nations Line Up To Do Battle over the Pinpoint Frontier," *The Star*, June 18, 1970, 2nd city late ed., p. 42, cols. 3–6.

64. Three of the documents bearing on this question are published in "Botswana-Zambia Border Claim," *Bulletin of the Africa Institute of South Africa* (Pretoria), vol. 8, no. 5 (June, 1970), pp. 196–197.

65. On the Botswana-South West African border, see W. S. Barnard, "Die Oosgrens van Suidwes-Afrika," *Journal for Geography* (Stellenbosch), vol. 1, no. 9 (September, 1961), pp. 23–25, 27–31, and 33–34 and "Compensation for Tribal Families," *The Star*, August 2, 1967, city late ed., p. 7, cols. 2–3. On the Botswana-South African border, consult "No Moving Because of Boundaries," *The Star*, June 27, 1968, 2nd city late ed., p. 23, cols. 6–7 and "Joint Boundary," *The Star*, March 6, 1969, 2nd city late ed., p. 11, col. 1.

66. Arnold Benjamin, "Middle of Nowhere," *The Star*, April 18, 1970, city late sport ed., p. 11, cols. 6–9.

67. The statement of the Botswana government, issued on April 14, 1970, is published in "South Africa-Botswana Exchanges: Proposed Trans-Zambezi Highway Creates Disturbing Discord," *Southern Africa*, vol. 82 (May 2, 1970), p. 247. The case for Botswana is set forth in Neville Rubin, "Botswana's Last Exit to Freedom," *Venture* (London), vol. 22, no. 8 (September, 1970), pp. 21–25. The government of the United States is taking a neutral stance toward both the Botswana and the South African governments on this matter even though it is supplying the funds for the road. See "Zambesi Row: U.S. Stays Out," *The Star*, June 2, 1970, 2nd city late ed., p. 4, cols. 7–9.

68. South Africa. Parliament. House of Assembly, *Debates*, no. 7 (August 31–September 4, 1970), col. 3279 (September 3, 1970).

69. Neither the American nor the Botswana governments is entertaining the idea of constructing a bridge from Botswana to Zambia. See "How Can a Pinpoint Support a Bridge?" *The Star*, April 4, 1970, stop press ed., p. 5, cols. 7–9 and "Botswana Denial of Link with Zambia," *The Star*, April 13, 1970, 2nd city late ed., p. 20, cols. 4–6.

70. For details, consult "Ministerial Trade Talks in Zambia," *Botswana Daily News* (Gaborone), August 6, 1970, p. 1; "More Botswana-Zambia Talks This Month," *Botswana Daily News*, August 10, 1970, p. 2; and "Botswana-Zambia Trade Talks Started," *Botswana Daily News*, August 27, 1970, p. 1.

71. "Diplomatic Crisis over Botswana Road Issue," *The Star*, April 21, 1970, 2nd city late ed., p. 32, cols. 3–6.

72. See Richard Dale, "South African Counter-insurgency Operations in South West Africa." Paper prepared for delivery at the eleventh annual meeting of the African Studies Association, Los Angeles, October 16–19, 1968.

73. By 1968, the government of Botswana doubled the size of its police force, according to President Khama. Botswana. Parliament. National Assembly, *Official Report* (*Hansard 23*), pp. 1–2 (January 8, 1968).

74. Personal interview with a senior official of the Botswana government in Gaborone, August 20, 1970, on a not-for-attribution basis.

75. "The Prevention of Violence Abroad Act, 1963," in Bechuanaland Protectorate, *Statute Law, vol. 47, 1963* (n.p.: n.p., n.d.), pp. 347–358. The penalties included a maximum of three years in prison and a maximum fine of $1,400.

76. "The Immigration (Consolidation) (Further Amendment Act), 1968," in Botswana, *Government Gazette*, vol. 6, no. 23 (May, 3, 1968), pp. B.217–B.218.

77. "O.A.U. 'Freedom Fighters' Will Avoid Botswana: Sovereignty To Be Respected," *The Star*, September 17, 1967, city late ed., p. 5, cols. 2–3.

78. See footnote 74, *supra*.

79. "Refugees in Botswana: A Policy of Resettlement," *Kutlwano* (Gaborone), vol. 9, no. 7 (July, 1970), p. [15].

80. *Ibid.*

81. "Botswana To Make Refugees Citizens," *The Star*, September 27, 1967, city late ed., p. 9, cols. 5–6.

82. Article 3 of "Statutory Instrument No. 56 of 1969. The Extradition Act, 1968. The Extradition (Republic of South Africa) Order, 1969 . . . ," in Botswana, *Government Gazette*, vol. 7, no. 18 (May 2, 1969), p. D.156 (italics added).

83. See Botswana, *Government Gazette*, vol. 7, no. 5 (February 7, 1969), pp. E.75–E.139 for the text of these documents.

84. Botswana, *List of Diplomatic and Consular Missions and International Organisations*, March, 1970 (n.p.: n.p., n.d.), p. 9. Hereafter cited as Botswana, *Diplomatic List*.

85. "Rhodesian Concern over Future of Bechuanaland," *The Star*, November 1, 1949, city late ed., p. 5, cols. 4–5.

86. "Dr. Malan Tells Rhodesia Protectorates Concern Only Britain and Union," *The Star*, December 22, 1949, city late ed., p. 5, cols. 3–4.

87. "Bechuanaland Is Strongly Opposed to Incorporation: If No Choice, Residents Would Prefer To Be under Rhodesia," *The Star*, September 5, 1951, city late ed., p. 3, cols. 1–2.

88. Halpern, *op. cit.*, p. 331 and Richard P. Stevens, *Lesotho, Botswana, & Swaziland: The Former High Commission Territories in Southern Africa* (London: Pall Mall Press, 1967), p. 148. See "Seretse Khama's 'Stay On and Help' Appeal: 'Let Bechuanaland Be Multi-Racial Success,' He Says," *The Star*, November 23, 1963, city late sport ed., p. 3, cols. 1–2, for the views of Sir Seretse on the Tuli Block.

89. "B. P. Bans Arms Shipments to Rhodesia," *Mafeking Mail*, November 19, 1965, p. 1, cols. 1–2. Similarly, there was a ban against transporting oil through the Protectorate to Rhodesia. See J. E. Spence, "The Implications of the Rhodesia Issue for the Former High Commission Territories," *Journal of Commonwealth Political Studies* (Leicester, England), vol. 7, no. 2 (July, 1969), p. 105.

90. "Postal Orders Stopped," *Mafeking Mail*, November 26, 1965, p. 1, col. 4.

91. This account of the Central African Relay Station is based on the following sources: Great Britain. Parliament. House of Commons, *Debates*, 5th series, vol. 723, col. 19 (oral answers) (January 25, 1966) and vol. 764, cols. 201–202 (written answers) (May 13, 1968); "Bush Radio Sabotage Feared: British Troops Were 'Forced' on Seretse," *The Star*, December 27, 1965, city late ed., p. 1, cols. 4–6; "B.B.C. Station Is 'Military Base' Now," *The Star*, May 10, 1966, 2nd stop press ed., p. 19, cols. 1–2; "Khama Again Urged To Stop Broadcasts," *The Star*, October 12, 1966, city late ed., p. 13, cols. 2–4; "Troops To Pull Out," *The Star*, May 9, 1967, city late ed., p. 11, col. 1; "British Troops Quit 'Bush Radio' Patrol," *The Star*, August 10, 1967, city late ed., p. 7, cols. 1–3; "Francistown 'Bush Radio' To Close," *The Star*, city late ed., April 1, 1968, p. 10, col. 7; and "B.B.C. 'Bush' Radio," *The Star*, May 30, 1968, 2nd city late ed., p. 8, col. 9.

92. These matters were raised on the floor of the Protectorate Legislative Council. See Bechuanaland Protectorate. Legislative Council, *Official Report* (*Hansard 11*), pp. 46–47 (questions for oral answer) (August 26, 1964).

93. Consult "Khama and Rhodesia," *The Star*, February 1, 1966, city late ed., p. 3, cols. 1–3 for an explanation of the difference between South Africa and Rhodesia.

94. "Botswana's Stand on Rhodesia—H.E.," *Botswana Daily News*, March 2, 1970, p. 1.

95. "Police in Rhodesia: Seretse: Ask S.A. To Quit," *The Star*, January 10, 1969, 2nd city late ed., p. 1, cols. 8–9.

96. See Botswana. Parliament. National Assembly, *Official Report* (*Hansard 23*), pp. 27–29 (questions for oral answer) (January 9, 1968) and "Rhodesians 'Fired at Our Men'," *The Star*, July 9, 1970, 2nd city late ed., p. 3, col. 1.

97. According to "Statutory Instrument No. 2 of 1970. Exportation and Importation Restriction Proclamation (Chapter 162). Import Control (Beer and Tobacco) Regulations, 1970," in Botswana, *Government Gazette*, vol. 8, no. 3 (January 9, 1970), p. D.2. The ban went into effect on March 1, 1970.

98. "Botswana Beer Ban Will Hit Rhodesia," *The Star*, January 13, 1970, 2nd city late ed., p. 5, cols. 4–6.

99. "Botswana's Plea to U.N.: 'We Need Links with Rhodesia'," *The Star*, April 30, 1970, 2nd city late ed., p. 7, cols. 4–6.

100. See P. Smit, "Botswana Railway Line," *Bulletin of the Africa Institute of South Africa*, vol. 8, no. 7 (August, 1970), pp. 273–280.

101. "Won't Touch Rail Line: A Promise from Sir Seretse," *The Star*, October 6, 1966, 1st stop press ed., p. 9, cols. 4–6.

102. The subsequent account of the relationship between Botswana and the Rhodesian railway authorities is drawn from the following sources: Rhodesia. Parliament, *Parliamentary Debates. Official Report. Unrevised*, vol. 75, no. 8 (September 3, 1969), cols. 618–695; "Penal Code Amended: Rhodesia-Botswana Train Discrimination," *The Star*, August 22, 1969, 2nd city late ed., p. 13, cols. 7–9; "Botswana To Run Rail Link?" *The Star*, September 4, 1969, 2nd city late ed., p. 21, col. 6; "No Nationalization Plans: Rhodesian Fears over Railway Are Groundless," *The Star*, September 20, 1969, city late sport ed., p. 4, cols. 6–9; "S.A. to Rhodesia Soon? Rail Link Gets Green Signal," *The Star*, June 18, 1970, 2nd city late ed., p. 9, cols. 1–3; "Beitbridge Rail Link Is Certain: Ian Smith's View," *The Star*, August 19, 1970, city ed., p. 23, cols. 4–6; Smit, *op. cit.*, pp. 273–280; "Railway Line through Botswana To End?" *Mafeking Mail*, September 12, 1969, p. 1, cols. 1–2; "Railmen from Canada," *Mafeking Mail*, January 30, 1970, p. 6, col. 3; "Haskins Calls for Spending Curb: Encouraging Report by Dr. Masire," *Mafeking Mail*, March 20, 1970, p. 1, cols. 1–2 and p. 2, col 5; and "Private Sector Attacked in Assembly," *Mafeking Mail*, April 10, 1970, p. 2, cols. 3–4.

103. The full dimensions of this poverty are analyzed in P. M. Landell-Mills, "Rural Incomes and Urban Wage Rates," *Botswana Notes and Records* (Gaborone), vol. 2 (n.d.), pp. 79–84. For an account of the appalling effects of prolonged drought, consult Jean M. Ingersoll, *Historical Examples of Ecological Disaster: Famine in Russia, 1921–22. Famine in Bechuanaland, 1965.* HI-518-RR/A1 (Croton-on-Hudson, N.Y.: Hudson Institute, Inc., 1965), pp. 55–73.

104. It is anticipated that the *per capita* income will rise to $84 by 1972. *Barclays Overseas Survey, 1970: A Survey of Trade and Economic Conditions during 1969 in the Territories in Which the Bank and Its Subsidiaries Are Represented* (London: Barclays Bank DCO, n.d.), p. 34.

105. The relations between the two nations were not improved by the decision of the newly-elected Conservative government in 1970 to sell arms to South Africa. See "Khama Hesitant on S.A. Arms Sales," *Mafeking Mail*, August 14, 1970, p. 1, col. 3. During the calendar year 1969, the British Ministry of Overseas Development furnished $11.696 million in foreign aid, along with 255

persons (excluding volunteers), to Botswana. "Aid from Britain," *Mafeking Mail*, August 21, 1970, p. 7, col. 1.

106. "Botswana on Way to Independence," *The Star*, March 19, 1970, 2nd city late ed., p. 8, cols. 7–9.

107. See "3,000 Will Get Jobs, Khama Forecasts," *Mafeking Mail*, August 1, 1969, p. 2, cols. 4–5 and "Search for Minerals Continues," *Mafeking Mail*, June 19, 1970, p. 1, col. 3.

108. This assistance was provided in large measure by the United Kingdom Freedom from Hunger Campaign. Consult Hugh Tristram, "Botswana's £1 Million Agricultural Scheme: U.K. Freedom from Hunger Committee Provide £500,000," *African Development* (London), vol. 1, no. 11 (1967), pp. 11–13.

109. See "Britain To Market F & M Vaccine," *Mafeking Mail*, August 25, 1961, p. 9, cols. 1–2.

110. See "Better Citizens through 4-B Clubs," *Kutlwano*, vol. 7, no. 12 (December, 1968), pp. 4–5.

111. At present, Botswana is receiving development aid from the United Kingdom, private British organizations (such as the U.K. Freedom from Hunger Campaign and Oxfam), the United States, private American groups, the Netherlands, Denmark, and Sweden. For details, see Botswana, *Estimates for the Development Fund, 1969–70* (Gaborone: The Government Printer, n.d.), p. 2 and Jane W. Jacqz, *Development Needs in Botswana and Lesotho* . . . (New York: African-American Institute, 1967), pp. 38–50.

112. Botswana, *Diplomatic List*, p. 9.

113. See G. M. E. Leistner, "Foreign Bantu Workers in South Africa: Their Present Position in the Economy," *The South African Journal of Economics* (Johannesburg), vol. 35, no. 1 (March, 1967), pp. 30–56 for details.

114. An examination of the list of title deeds for holdings in the Gaborone/Lobatse blocks showed that only a handful of Botswana citizens own land there. The land in these blocks, other than that held by companies with mixed shareholding, is largely owned by expatriates, mostly South Africans. However, in the period from September 1970 to March 1971, the Botswana did increase their holdings in the blocks. Personal interview with Mr. G. M. Myers, Legal Adviser (Land), in Gaborone on August 21, 1970, and letter to the writer from Mr. Myers, dated March 3, 1971.

115. The most obvious example of this is the Tati Company which sold 220,000 acres of rural land and 1,600 acres of urban land and also donated 115,000 acres of rural land and 2,000 acres of urban land to the Republic of Botswana. The Botswana government paid $0.42 million for this land; the British government made the necessary grant to the Botswana government for the purchase of this land. "58-Year-Old Tati Regime Comes to an End," *Mafeking Mail*, September 19, 1969, p. 2, cols. 3–4; "R300,000 Paid to Tati Company," *Mafeking Mail*, October 3, 1969, p. 2, cols. 3–4; and "More Aid from U.K.," *Mafeking Mail*, October 17, 1969, p. 1, col. 5.

116. For details, consult G. M. E. Leistner, *South Africa's Development Aid to African States*. Occasional Papers of the Africa Institute no. 28 (Pretoria: Africa Institute of South Africa, 1970), p. 26.

117. Waldemar A. Nielsen, *The Great Powers and Africa*. Published for the Council on Foreign Relations (New York, Washington, London: Praeger Publishers, 1969), pp. 393–394.

118. "Regional Training Centre for African Countries Opened in Malawi," *Mafeking Mail*, January 30, 1970, p. 6, cols. 1–2.

119. As quoted in "Diggs Plan for Ex-Protectorates," *The Star*, August 22, 1969, 2nd city late ed., p. 7, cols. 2–4.

120. As quoted in *ibid*.

121. Consult "(Treaty Series No. 12 (1969)). An Agreement between the Government of the United States of America and the Government of the Republic of Botswana Relating to Investment Guarantees. Gaberone, 12th January, 1968. Presented to Parliament by the Minister of State, February, 1969" in Botswana, *Government Gazette*, vol. 7, no. 5 (February 7, 1969), pp. E.157–E.160.

122. As quoted in "Tswanas Find 'Clean' Air in Zambia," *The Star*, August 17, 1967, city late ed., p. 11, cols. 4–5.

123. As quoted in *ibid*.

124. See Botswana, *Diplomatic List*, pp. 3–9 and 11–13.

125. Consult "(Treaty Series No. 14 (1969)). Exchange of Notes between the High Commissioner for Botswana and the High Commissioner for Malta Concerning an Agreement for the Reciprocal Performance of Consular Functions. London, 13th January, 1967 to 25th January, 1968. Presented to Parliament by the Minister of State, February, 1969" in Botswana, *Government Gazette*, vol. 7, no. 7 (February 14, 1969), pp. E. 179–E.194.

126. See "A State Welcome for a State Visitor," *Kutlwano*, vol. 7, no. 7 (July, 1968), pp. 9–24.

127. See "Around the Country—A Big Welcome for Mr. Moi," *Kutlwano*, vol. 9, no. 9 (September, 1970), p. 29.

128. See "Special Guests to Malawi's First Republic Anniversary Celebrations: His Excellency Sir Seretse Khama, President of the Republic of Botswana, and Lady Khama," *This Is Malawi* (Blantyre), vol. 3, no. 8 (August, 1967), pp. 9–10.

129. Lady Mitchison's "adopted son," Chief Linchwe II, is now the Botswana Ambassador to the United States. An example of her identification with the Bakgatla is " 'What Are We Like?' ," *Kutlwano*, vol. 8, no. 5 (May, 1969), pp. 8–9.

130. This was suggested by Wilf Nussey in "Bechuanaland: A Role Like the Swiss," *The Star*, March 22, 1965, city late ed., p. 20, cols. 8–9.

131. The phrase was coined by Councillor P. R. Mosaka in 1946. For excerpts from the speech in which he used the term, see C. M. Tatz, *Shadow and Substance in South Africa: A Study in Land and Franchise Policies Affecting Africans, 1910–1960* (Pietermaritzburg: University of Natal Press, 1962), p. 116.

132. Alan Paton, *Cry, the Beloved Country* (New York: Charles Scribner's Sons, 1948), p. 276.

CHAPTER 3

1. The Congress party has retained its preindependence name since it does not recognize independence under Chief Jonathan's government as "genuine independence."

2. This assessment is based on press coverage of the election campaign from all major English-language South African newspapers.

3. Similar comments appeared on several occasions, most notably the following: "Chief Jonathan Hints at

Possibility of One-Party State," *The Star* (Johannesburg), November 17, 1969, 2nd city late ed., p. 7, cols. 2–3; and "Can't Change Neighbours: Will Stay Friendly to S.A.—Jonathan," *The Star*, December 12, 1969, 1st city late ed., p. 4, cols. 6–8.

4. "Government Will Support Its Supporters First: Chief Jonathan," *Koena News* (Maseru), October 17, 1969, pp. 1–2. See also Anthony Rider, "Support Me or Else . . . Jonathan," *Rand Daily Mail* (Johannesburg), October 25, 1969, morning final ed., p. 5, cols. 1–2; and "Lesotho Goes to the Polls," *Financial Mail* (Johannesburg), vol. 35, no. 3 (January 23, 1970), p. 182.

5. "Jonathan Warns Lesotho Judiciary," *The Friend* (Bloemfontein), January 8, 1970, city late ed., p. 3, col. 2; and "Jonathan Planning Major Changes," *Eastern Province Herald* (Port Elizabeth), December 18, 1969, p. 2, col. 8.

6. "Chief Jonathan Address [*sic*] Press Conference in Maseru," *Koena News*, December 15, 1969, p. 1.

7. "Chief Jonathan Hints at Possibility of One-Party State," *The Star*, November 17, 1969, 2nd city late ed, p. 7, cols. 2–3.

8. Anthony Rider, "'Red Flirting in Lesotho' Charge," *Rand Daily Mail*, November 6, 1969, morning final ed., p. 5, cols. 1–4.

9. Quoted in "Jonathan Hints at One Party State," *The Friend*, November 18, 1969, city late ed., p. 13, col. 8.

10. "300,000 Have Voted in Lesotho," *The Friend*, January 28, 1970, city late ed., p. 1, cols. 1–3; and Ralph Cohen, "World Lo[a]th To Accept Premier's Story," *Eastern Province Herald*, February 9, 1970, p. 3, cols. 1–3.

11. "B.N.P. Gains on B.C.P.," *Rand Daily Mail*, January 29, 1970, morning final ed., p. 10, col. 5. See also "1970 General Election Results," *Nketu Oa Mara* (Maseru), vol. 6, no. 9 (February 27, 1970), pp. 11–16.

12. "One Seat Decides Neck-and-Neck Election: Winners-Opposition Claim in Lesotho: Few Results To Come," *The Star*, January 30, 1970, 2nd city late ed., p. 1, cols. 2–3 and "Lesotho Emergency: S.A. Whites Are Urged To Leave the Country," *Rand Daily Mail*, January 31, 1970, morning final ed., p. 1, cols. 2–4 and p. 3, cols. 4–7.

13. Conflicting statistics have been published, but only the degree of the BCP margin is at issue. Noel Harford reported that the BNP received 83,000 votes as against 143,000 for the opposition in these forty-six constituencies. (See Noel Harford, "Lesotho—and the Cattle Thefts That Caused the Government To Lose Vital Election Votes," *The Argus*(Cape Town), February 7, 1970, late sport ed., weekend magazine, p. 1, cols. 1–7.) This approximate ratio is confirmed by Matthew White's statement that the BNP gained only 37 percent of the vote. (See Matthew White, "Paying the Price of His Own Dictatorship: Chief Jonathan Is Facing a Bleak Future," *The Star*, February 6, 1970, 2nd city late ed., p. 14, cols. 7–9. The following summary totals for the forty-six seats are derived from "1970 General Election Results," *Nketu Oa Mara*, vol. 6, no. 9 (February 27, 1970), pp. 11–16.

Parties	*Votes*	*Percentage*
Basotho National Party (BNP)	104,537	43.8%
Basutoland Congress Party (BCP)	119,998	50.3
Marematlou Freedom Party (MFP)	12,666	5.3
United Democratic Party (UDP)	345	.2
Independents	940	.4
Total	238,486	100.0%

14. Quoted in "Lesotho Placed Under State of Emergency," *Nketu Oa Mara*, vol. 6, no. 5 (January 30, 1970), p. 5.

15. *Ibid.*

16. "I Have Now Seized Power, Says Jonathan: More Opponents Will Be Held," *The Star*, January 31, 1970, city late sport ed., p. 1, cols. 4–6; Desmond Blow, "Jonathan: I Have Seized Power," *Sunday Times* (Johannesburg), February 1, 1970, p. 1, cols. 7–9, and p. 8, col. 6; and "Leabua Admits Grabbing Power," *The World* (Johannesburg), February 2, 1970, stop press ed., p. 2, col. 5. To be sure, isolated incidents of disruption or confrontation with the police were reported, but none serious or widespread enough to render the election as a whole suspect. Most of the events listed in evidence by Jonathan occurred in constituencies won by the BNP.

17. See Jonathan's statement in footnote 9; and "Premier Jonathan Broadcasts to the Nation," *Koena News*, February 2, 1970, pp. 1–2.

18. "Premier Jonathan Broadcasts to the Nation," *Koena News*, February 2, 1970, p. 1.

19. Quoted in "Jonathan: Reds the Enemy: 'I Acted To Avert Bloodshed'," *The Cape Times* (Cape Town), February 4, 1970, peninsula ed., p. 1, cols. 2–3 and p. 3, col. 4.

20. Quoted in "Our Fight Is Against Communism—Chief Jonathan, *Koena News*, February 4, 1970, p. 2.

21. "Masses Support Jonathan on South Africa," *Koena News*, July 28, 1968, p. 1.

22. "Communism To Be Suppressed," *Lesotho Times* (Maseru), September 6, 1968, p. 7, col. 3.

23. See Clive Cowley, "Impatient with Opposition: Jonathan in the Saddle," *The Cape Argus* (Cape Town), October 25, 1968, city late ed., p. 20, cols. 8–9.

24. "Press Statement by the Honourable the Prime Minister During Press Conference on Monday, 15th December 1969," *Nketu Oa Mara*, vol. 5, no. 51 (December 19, 1969), p. 3.

25. "Communists Had Part in Lesotho's Election Malpractices—Chief Jonathan," *Koena News*, February 9, 1970, p. 1.

26. "The Suppression of Communism Order 1970," *Lesotho Government Gazette*, vol. 5, no. 11, Legal Notice no. 7 of 1970 (Maseru: Government Printer) (February 9, 1970), p. 100 (Italics added.)

27. *Ibid.* (Italics added.)

28. See "Political Thuggery," (editorial), *Post* (Johannesburg), February 1, 1970, late Reef ed., p. 7, cols. 1–2 and "The Day Jonathan Wouldn't Take 'No' for an Answer," *Post*, February 1, 1970, late Reef ed., p. 3, cols. 1–4.

29. "The Nick of Time," (editorial) *Rand Daily Mail*, February 5, 1970, morning final ed., p. 10, cols. 7–9.

30. "Keep Out of Our Domestic Affairs—Chief Jonathan Warns S.A. Press," *Koena News*, February 4, 1970, p. 1.

31. Stanley Uys, "Lesotho Puts Nats in Hot Spot:

Jonathan's Coup Imperils Bantustan Self-Govt. Policy," *Sunday Times* (Johannesburg), February 1, 1970, p. 1, cols. 2–3 and p. 2, cols. 4–5. See also Dan van der Vat, "Why Lesotho Is Worrying Vorster," *The Times* (London), February 2, 1970, late London ed., p. 8, cols. 2–3 and Stanley Uys, "Lesotho: S.A.'s Enclave of Unrest," *Sunday Times*, February 15, 1970, p. 16, cols. 6–9.

32. Stanley Uys, "Lesotho Puts Nats in Hot Spot: Jonathan's Coup Imperils Bantustan Self-Govt. Policy," *Sunday Times*, February 1, 1970, p. 1, cols. 2–3 and p. 2, cols. 4–5 and "Lesotho Proves Me Right—Graaff," *The Friend*, February 3, 1970, city late ed., p. 6, col. 8.

33. Quoted in Stanley Uys, "Lesotho: S.A.'s Enclave of Unrest," *Sunday Times*, February 15, 1970, p. 16, cols. 6–9.

34. *Ibid.* See also "Virtual S.A. Recognition of Jonathan," *Rand Daily Mail*, February 7, 1970, morning final ed., p. 4, cols. 7–9.

35. See "Power at Any Price," (editorial) *Rand Daily Mail*, February 2, 1970, morning final ed., p. 10, cols. 7–9.

36. For a view of Jonathan's coup from a Western African perspective, see "Leabua Jonathan's Only Way Out," *New Nigerian* (Kaduna), February 13, 1970, p. 5. The opposition parties in Lesotho constantly played on such images as "betrayal" and "sell-out" to South Africa.

37. See Harald Pakendorf, "Lesotho Goes 'African,' " *South African Financial Gazette* (Johannesburg), February 6, 1970, national ed., p. 8, cols. 1–2; and A. J. van Wyk, *Lesotho: A Political Study*, Communications of the Africa Institute no. 7 (Pretoria: Africa Institute of South Africa, 1967), pp. 58–61.

38. John Torres, "Leabua's Crisis: The Failure in Lesotho," *The Daily News* (Durban), February 18, 1970, city late ed., p. 14, cols. 6–9.

39. "Prime Minister's Message," in *Lesotho: Land of Rolling Mountains and Running Streams* (Maseru: Lesotho Department of Information, 1966), p. 1.

40. For an interesting attempt to define "smallness," see Burton Benedict, ed., *Problems of Smaller Territories*, Commonwealth Papers no. 10, Institute of Commonwealth Studies, University of London (London: Athlone Press, 1967), especially "Introduction," pp. 1–10.

41. For population data see Lesotho. Bureau of Statistics, *1966 Census—Preliminary Results* (mimeographed). Two versions of the national accounts of Lesotho have been published which give slightly divergent information due to differing estimates and modes of computation. They are E. J. van der Merwe, *Lesotho: National Accounts, 1954/55–1965/66* (Pretoria. Africa Institute of South Africa, 1969); and Lesotho. Bureau of Statistics, *Lesotho: National Accounts—1964/5 and 1965/6* (Maseru, n.d.). The former gives 1965–66 gross domestic product as R35,962,100 (p. 17); the latter, as R37,425,700 (p. 1).

42. van der Merwe, *op. cit.*, p. 2, Table 1. Recent data indicate a widening of the economic diffential with the South African gross domestic product now approximately 250 times greater than that of Lesotho.

43. Walter Elkan, *Report to the Government of Basutoland on the Manpower Situation* (Geneva: International Labor Organization, 1964), p. 14. Allowance has been made for expansion of the labor force immediately prior to independence.

44. Lesotho. Bureau of Statistics, *1966 Census—Preliminary Results* (mimeographed), pp. 1–2.

45. G. M. E. Leistner, *Lesotho: Economic Structure and Growth*, Communications of the Africa Institute no. 5 (Pretoria: Africa Institute of South Africa, 1966), p. 4, especially footnote 12.

46. This and other sociological resultants of labor migration are discussed in Sandra Wallman, *Take Out Hunger: Two Case Studies of Rural Development in Basutoland*. London School of Economics Monographs in Social Anthropology no. 39 (London: The Athlone Press, University of London; New York: Humanities Press, 1969). Charles Mofeli, leader of the United Democratic party of Lesotho commented extensively on the persistence of a "slave mentality" in recent parliamentary debates. See Lesotho. *Parliamentary Debates of the National Assembly* (*Hansard*), *Official Report of the Second Meeting, Third Session* (unrevised), *October 3, 1969*, vol. 3/2, nos. 2–5, pp. 172–192, especially p. 174. [Hereafter cited as *National Assembly Debates*. Since session, meeting, and volume numbering is often confusing and jumbled in these unedited debates, dates and pages must be regarded as definitive for reference purposes.]

47. Economic planning in Lesotho has been based on continuation of this high rate of growth. See Basutoland, Government, *The Framework of the Economic and Financial Policies of the Government of Basutoland, 1967–1972* (Mazenod: Mazenod Institute, 1966), p. 16 [hereafter cited as *Framework of Economic and Financial Policies*].

48. For a brief survey of the colonial backgrounds, see J. E. Spence, *Lesotho: The Politics of Dependence*. Published for the Institute of Race Relations (London, New York, Toronto: Oxford University Press, 1968), chap. 2, especially pp. 13–22.

49. "Jonathan on 'Conquered Territory,' " *The Friend*, November 14, 1969, city late ed., p. 1, col. 5; and "B.N.P. Wants Return of Conquered Territory," *Koena News*, November 12, 1969, p. 1.

50. See J. A. Lombard, J. J. Stadler, and P. J. van der Merwe, *The Concept of Economic Co-operation in Southern Africa*, Publication no. 1 (Pretoria: Bureau for Economic Policy and Analysis, 1969), especially pp. 14–26. For data on the area's *de jure* as compared with *de facto* populations and gross domestic products as compared with incomes of the *de jure* populations of the countries of Southern Africa, see p. 22, Table 1; Table 2, a foldout chart between pp. 22 and 23; and Table 4, a foldout chart between pp. 28 and 29.

51. *Ibid.*, quoted on p. 20.

52. Quoted in "Can Change Friends—Not Neighbours: Jonathan Affirms Good Relations with S.A.," *The Friend*, December 16, 1969, city late ed., p. 5, cols. 4–5.

53. Lesotho. Parliament. National Assembly, *Debates*, March 20, 1968, vol. 1, no. 23, pp. 12–13.

54. "Not Shocked by Papal Decision," *Nketu Oa Mara*, vol. 4, no. 34 (August 23, 1968), p. 14 (italics added).

55. The average number of Basotho employed in mines in South Africa rose from 54,960 in 1964 to 72,606 in 1968. See Lesotho. Parliament. National Assembly, *Debates*, March 24, 1969, vol. 1, nos. 21–24, p. 8.

56. Lesotho. Parliament. National Assembly, *Debates*, February 25, 1969, vol. 1, nos. 2–6, p. 48.

57. *Manifesto of the Basuto National Party* (n.p., 1965), p. 3.
58. Speech of Chief Leabua Jonathan, made at Peka, Lesotho, on April 25, 1965, and translated from a recording (unpublished).
59. "Jonathan Reaffirms 'Friendly' Policy," *The Friend*, July 29, 1968, city late ed., p. 9, cols. 4–6.
60. For a thorough discussion of such survey missions see Basutoland Government, *Framework of Economic and Social Policies*, pp. 3–11.
61. "Lowlands" in local parlance refers to land between five thousand and seven thousand feet above sea level!
62. The data on conditions of self-help roads are derived from personal correspondence with a reliable observer in Lesotho. For a detailed survey of government road projects, see Lesotho. Parliament. National Assembly, *Debates*, March 20, 1968, vol. 1, no. 23, pp. 14–18.
63. It had, of course, been possible to receive various South African Broadcasting Corporation (SABC) services and a host of short-wave broadcasts including Voice of America, the BBC, Radio Moscow, and Radio Peking.
64. Chief Jonathan contends that only the government represents the will of the nation and that "divisive" dissident views should not be presented.
65. All of these places fall within a twenty-five-mile radius. For further detail see Lesotho. Parliament. National Assembly, *Debates*, March 13, 1968, vol. 1, no. 18, p. 16.
66. Data in this section are derived from a speech by Koenyama Chakela, a leading BCP spokesman, in Lesotho. Parliament. National Assembly, *Debates*, April 1, 1968, vol. 1, no. 31, p. 12; and from statistics in Lesotho. Parliament. National Assembly, *Debates*, March 18, 1969, vol. 1, nos. 16–20, p. 61.
67. Evidence of the South African role can be found in Lesotho. Parliament. National Assembly, *Debates*, March 1, 1968, vol. 1, no. 11, p. 4.
68. See Noel Harford, "Lesotho—and the Cattle Thefts That Caused the Government To Lose Vital Election Votes," *The Argus*, February 7, 1970, late sport ed., weekend magazine, p. 1, cols. 1–7.
69. See van der Merwe, *op. cit.*, p. 13, Table 18; and Lesotho. Bureau of Statistics, *Lesotho: National Accounts*, p. 4, Table 6.
70. Lesotho. Parliament. National Assembly, *Debates*, February 19, 1968, vol. 1, no. 2, p. 24.
71. *Ibid.*
72. "R 1 Million Peka to St. Monica's Agricultural Scheme Announced," *Koena News*, October 17, 1969, p. 1.
73. Lesotho. Parliament. National Assembly, *Debates*, February 23, 1968, vol. 1, no. 6, pp. 1–4 and Lesotho. Parliament. National Assembly, *Debates*, March 24, 1969, vol. 1, nos. 21–24, p. 6.
74. Lesotho. Parliament. National Assembly, *Debates*, March 24, 1969, vol. 1, nos. 21–24, p. 6.
75. Lesotho. Bureau of Statistics, *Lesotho: National Accounts*, p. 4, Table 6.
76. Lesotho. Parliament. National Assembly, *Debates*, March 13, 1968, vol. 1, no. 18, p. 7.
77. The information in this section is derived from bits and pieces in *Koena News*, *Nketu*, and *Debates* since 1968.
78. Lesotho. Parliament. National Assembly, *Debates*, March 18, 1969, vol. 1, nos. 16–20, p. 61. See also Chief Jonathan's comments on the weakness of teacher training institutions and the failings of the University of Botswana, Lesotho and Swaziland at Roma in Lesotho. Parliament. National Assembly, *Debates*, March 24, 1969, vol. 1, nos. 21–24, pp. 17–18.
79. The data in this section are derived from Lesotho. Parliament. National Assembly, *Debates*, February 27, 1968, vol. 1, no. 4, p. 2; Ken Owen, "Outward Policy at Work—1: S. Africans Help Run Lesotho," *The Star*, March 10, 1969, 2nd city late ed., p. 18, cols. 8–9; and various articles in *Koena News*.
80. Mokhehle's views are spelled out in Ken Owen, "Outward Policy at Work—2: Conflict of Need and Pride," *The Star*, March 11, 1969, 2nd city late ed., p. 18, cols. 8–9.
81. Lesotho. Bureau of Statistics, *Lesotho: National Accounts*, pp. 6–7, Table 7.
82. Lesotho. Parliament. National Assembly, *Debates*, March 13, 1968, vol. 1, no. 18, p. 24. The remaining data in this paragraph come from the same budget speech, pp. 4–35.
83. "Trade Gap in Lesotho Worsens," *The Friend*, December 2, 1968, city late ed., p. 1, col. 2.
84. Derived from data in Lombard, Stadler, and van der Merwe, *op. cit.*, Table 5, a foldout chart between pp. 32 and 33.
85. See van der Merwe, *op. cit.*, p. 78, Table 46; and Lesotho. Bureau of Statistics, *Lesotho: National Accounts*, p. 1, Table 1.
86. Lesotho. Parliament. National Assembly, *Debates*, March 13, 1968, Vol. 1, no. 18, p. 27.
87. Clive Cowley, "This Is No Way to Treat a Neighbour," *The Daily News*, June 26, 1969, city late ed., p. 20, cols. 8–9.
88. "S.A.'s Black Neighbours Plan Pact," *Cape Argus*, September 1, 1969, city late ed., p. 1, cols. 1–2.
89. "Customs Union Agreement," *Lesotho Government Gazette*, vol. 4, no. 58 (Maseru: Government Printer), pp. 937–950.
90. "New Customs Unit More Favorable to Lesotho: Hon. Peete," *Koena News*, December 17, 1969, p. 1.
91. The results of the 1965 general elections were as follows:

Party	Votes	Percent	seats
Basutoland National Party (BNP)	108,169	41.6	31
Basutoland Congress Party (BCP)	102,974	39.6	25
Marematlou Freedom Party (MFP)	43,085	16.6	4
Marema Tlou Party (MTP)	5,697	2.2	—
Independents	79	—	—
	260,004	100.0	60

Source: polling station reports

92. For a survey of the history and bases of support of the BNP and analysis of the 1965 general election, see Spence, *op. cit.*, chapter 3, pp. 29–54; Richard P. Stevens, *Lesotho, Botswana and Swaziland: The Former High Commission Territories in Southern Africa* (New York, Washington, London: Frederick A. Praeger, 1967), Chapters 4–5, pp. 53–97, especially pp. 54–56, 62, 84–88; Richard F. Weisfelder, "Power Struggle in Lesotho,"

Africa Report, vol. 12, no. 1 (January 1967) especially pp. 10–12 (hereafter cited as "Power Struggle"); and Richard F. Weisfelder, *Defining National Purpose in Lesotho*, Papers in International Studies, Africa series, No. 3 (Athens, Ohio: Ohio University Center for International Studies, 1969), pp. 15–17 (hereafter cited as *Defining National Purpose*).

93. A perceptive discussion of the role of the senate appears in W. J. A. Macartney, "African Westminster? The Parliament of Lesotho," *Parliamentary Affairs* (London), vol. 23, no. 2 (Spring 1970), pp. 133–137.

94. For a more detailed analysis of the pre-independence struggles and immediate post-independence developments, see Spence, *op. cit.*, pp. 47–54; Stevens, *op. cit.*, pp. 85–97; and Weisfelder, "Power Struggle," pp. 5–6, 12–13. Moshoeshoe's title was changed from "Paramount Chief" to "King" when Lesotho became independent.

95. "King's Exile Is a Blow to Lesotho," *The Star*, April 1, 1970, 2nd city late ed., p. 17, cols. 1–2.

96. "S. Africans Assured of Protection: Vital Maseru Peace Talks: Second Meeting To Follow Soon," *The Star*, April 9, 1970, 2nd city late ed., p. 1, cols. 2–4 and p. 32, cols. 7–9.

97. "The Prime Minister's Speech on the Occasion of the Official Raising of the Flag of the Organization for African Unity, on 11th March, 1970," *Nketu Oa Mara*, vol. 6, no. 11 (March 13, 1970), p. 6.

98. Quoted in "Premier Jonathan's Message Given Wide Publicity," *Koena News*, November 12, 1968, p. 1. See also "Premier Jonathan Says Rhodesian Referendum Is an Insult to Africa," *Koena News*, June 17, 1969, p. 1.

99. See Mr. N. Betsetsa's speech in Lesotho. Parliament. National Assembly, *Debates*, March 24, 1969, vol. 1, nos. 21–24, p. 30.

100. "Parties Grappling with Rivalries in Nomination Contests," *Nketu Oa Mara*, vol. 5, no. 47 (November 21, 1969), pp. 6–8; "Nomination Day," *Nketu Oa Mara*, vol. 5, no. 48 (November 28, 1969), pp. 1–2; and "Freedom of Choice Is in Danger in Lesotho," *Nketu Oa Mara*, vol. 5, no. 52 (December 26, 1969), pp. 2–6.

101. Lesotho. Parliament. National Assembly, *Debates*, February 20, 1968, vol. 1, no. 3, p. 32.

102. *Ibid.*, p. 31. See also "Lesotho Goes to the Polls," *Financial Mail*, vol. 35, no. 3 (January 23, 1970), p. 182.

103. "Lesotho Goes to the Polls," *Financial Mail*, vol. 35, no. 3 (January 23, 1970), p. 182.

104. Numerous South African journalists have remarked that "fiery" Ntsu Mokhehle seems to have mellowed with time and become "more realistic" in his thinking about the Republic.

105. A useful survey of BCP tactics in parliament can be found in Macartney, *op. cit.*, pp. 127–140. For a more general analysis of BCP strategy since the 1965 election, see Spence, *op. cit.*, pp. 41–54; Stevens, *op. cit.*, pp. 85–97; and Weisfelder, "Power Struggle," pp. 5–6, 12–13.

106. "Lesotho Rebels Told To Surrender," *Rand Daily Mail*, April 30, 1970, morning final ed., p. 14, cols. 1–3.

107. One South African correspondent contended that the Republic provided financial support for Lesotho's paramilitary police mobile unit. See Marion Heslop, "S.A. Is Helping Lesotho Unit, Says Official," *Sunday Times*, April 26, 1970, p. 3, cols. 1–2.

108. For historical materials on the development of the BCP, see Stevens, *op. cit.*, pp. 59–85.

109. For the historical backgrounds of royalist politics and an analysis of the recent roles of the king and the MFP, see Macartney, *op. cit.*, pp. 133–137; Spence, *op. cit.*, Chapter 3, pp. 29–54; Stevens, *op. cit.*, pp. 53–55, 63–64, 67–97; and Weisfelder, "Power Struggle," pp. 5–6, 12–13; and J. H. Proctor, "Building a Constitutional Monarchy in Lesotho," *Civilisations* (Brussels), vol. 19, no. 1 (1969), pp. 64–85.

110. Address of the Paramount Chief Moshoeshoe II at Teyateyaneng, Lesotho, May, 1966, unpublished translation from Sesotho.

111. "Fight in Lesotho: 150 Die in Clashes," *The Friend*, April 8, 1970, city late ed., p. 1, cols. 1–3.

112. "U.K. Recognized Regime: Lesotho Aid Just in Time," *The Star*, June 12, 1970, 2nd city late ed., p. 5, cols. 5–7.

113. "Lesotho Books Won't Balance," *The Star*, April 24, 1970, 2nd city late ed., p. 22, cols. 8–9.

114. Noel Harford, "For a Number of Reasons . . . It Is Talking Time in Lesotho," *The Star*, April 27, 1970, 2nd city late ed., p. 20, cols. 7–9.

115. "Lesotho Rebels Told To Surrender," *Rand Daily Mail*, April 30, 1970, morning final ed., p. 14, cols. 1–3.

116. "Lesotho King May Return," *The Friend*, July 1, 1970, city late ed., p. 1, col. 4. King Moshoeshoe II was permitted to return to Lesotho on December 4, 1970, after capitulating to Chief Jonathon's terms.

117. "Mokhehle Interview: B.C.P. Will Support Jonathan Coalition," *The Friend*, May 9, 1970, city late ed., p. 1, cols. 5–7.

118. The food shortage and possibility of reform of the land tenure system are discussed in "Farming System for Change: Lesotho Famine: Call for Food," *The Star*, June 11, 1970, 2nd city late ed., p. 13, cols. 1–3.

CHAPTER 4

1. For a holistic analysis of the future of the entire subsystem of Southern Africa, see the concluding chapter of this book.

2. Karl Kaiser, "The Interaction of Regional Subsystems," *World Politics*, vol. 21, no. 1 (October 1968), p. 86.

3. See Larry W. Bowman's perceptive "The Subordinate State System of Southern Africa," *International Studies Quarterly*, vol. 12, no. 3 (September 1968), pp. 231–261; Richard Dale's introductory chapter in this book; and Eschel M. Rhoodie, *The Third Africa* (New York and Cape Town: Twin Circle, 1968). Curiously enough, Southern Africa is not even classified as an international region of study in Bruce M. Russett's *International Regions and theInternational System* (New York: Rand McNally, 1967). "Structure" and "texture" are defined respectively as "[the] basic features of the patterns of relationship among and between the units of the system" and "[the] broad characteristics of the environment—material, political, ideological—in which those relationships function." (Michael Brecher, "The Subordinate State System of Southern Asia," *World Politics*, vol. 15, no. 2 [January 1963], pp. 213–235.)

4. The Europeans are a dominant factor in the economy, however. Although they constitute only 2.5 percent of the population, they comprise 10 percent of

the labor force, own nearly 40 percent of all land in Swaziland, and control most of the commerical enterprises in the country. (Great Britain. Colonial Office, *Swaziland 1966* [London: HMSO, 1968], pp. 1–9.)

5. For a more detailed description see Hilda Kuper's four works: *An African Aristocracy: Rank Among the Swazis* (London: Oxford University Press, 1947); *The Uniform of Color* (Johannesburg: University of Witwatersrand Press, 1947); *The Swazis: A South African Kingdom* (New York: Holt, Rinehart & Winston, 1963); and "The Swazis of Swaziland" in J. L. Gibbs (ed.), *Peoples of Africa* (New York: Holt, Rinehart & Winston, 1965), pp. 479–511. See also Brian Marwick, *Abantu Bakwa Ngwane* (Cape Town: University of Cape Town Press, 1939) and *The Swazis* (Cambridge, England: Cambridge University Press, 1940).

6. See Richard P. Steven's chapter in this book as well as such earlier works as Eric A. Walker, *A History of Southern Africa*, rev. ed. (London: Longmans, Green, 1965); C. Dundas and H. Ashton, *Problem Territories of Southern Africa* (Cape Town: South African Institute of International Affairs, 1952); Lord Hailey, *The Republic of South Africa and the High Commission Territories* (London: Oxford University Press, 1963); Margery Perham and Lionel Curtis, *The Protectorates of South Africa: The Question of Their Transfer to the Union* (London: Oxford University Press, 1935); G. V. Doxey, *The High Commission Territories and the Republic of South Africa*. Chatham House Memoranda (London: Distributed for the Royal Institute of International Affairs by the Oxford University Press, 1963); and South Africa, *Negotiations Regarding the Transfer to the Union of South Africa of the Government of Basutoland, the Bechuanaland Protectorate and Swaziland, 1910–1939* (Pretoria: Government Printer, 1953).

7. Richard P. Stevens, "Swaziland Political Development," *Journal of Modern African Studies*, vol. 1, no. 3 (September 1963), pp. 327–350; Christian P. Potholm, "Changing Political Configurations in Swaziland," *Journal of Modern African Studies*, vol. 4, no. 3 (November 1966), pp. 313–322; and "Swaziland in Transition to Independence," *Africa Report*, vol. 12, no. 6 (June 1967), pp. 49–54; Richard P. Stevens, *Lesotho, Botswana, and Swaziland: The Former High Commission Territories in Southern Africa* (New York: Frederick A. Praeger, 1968); and Jack Halpern, *South Africa's Hostages: Basutoland, Bechuanaland, and Swaziland* (Baltimore: Penguin Books, 1965).

8. Alistair Sparks, "Secret Advice for 'Free Tribalism': Swazi 'Bantustan' Bid: Fight U.K. Charter, Chief Told," *Rand Daily Mail* (Johannesburg), October 1, 1963, p. 1, cols. 3–4 and p. 2, col. 9; and Ngwane National Liberatory Congress, press release, January 26, 1965, p. 2.

9. Arthur Khosa, Dumisa Dlamini, Simon Nxumalo, Dr. Allen Nxumalo, and Leo Lovell, for example, were all early opponents of the Imbokodvo who were later given positions of authority within it. As of July 1, 1969, the cabinet consisted of the following members:

Prime minister	Makhosini Dlamini
Deputy prime minister	Mfundza Sukati
Minister of finance	Leo Lovell
Minister of works, power, and communication	Polycarp Dlamini
Minister of local administration	Mfanasibili Dlamini
Minister of agriculture	A. K. Hlophe
Minister of health	Dr. Allen Nxumalo
Minister of education	A. B. Gamede
Minister of commerce, industry, and mines	Simon Nxumalo
Minister of foreign affairs	Zonke Khumalo
Minister of public service	E. S. Dhladhla

10. For an analysis of the Swaziland situation which places the rise of the Nggywenyama in the context of political development, see Christian P. Potholm, "The Ngywenyama of Swaziland: The Dynamics of Political Adaptation," in René Lemarchand (ed.), *Kingship in Africa* (forthcoming).

11. *Swaziland 1966*, p. 30.

12. The government has in recent years encouraged Swazi farmers to produce cash crops and to increase their output of the subsistence products such as maize and sorghum which are currently imported on balance.

13. Exports in 1966 exceeded $69 million while imports totaled only $37 million (*Swaziland 1966*, pp. 30–31).

14. The presence of Swaziland, Lesotho, and Botswana in a customs union with South Africa and sharing a common currency (the Rand), for example, inhibits a precise analysis of the monetary transactions which flow among all four.

15. See Halpern, *op. cit.*; Ben Cockram, "The Protectorates: An International Problem," *Optima* (Johannesburg), vol. 13, no. 4 (December 1963), pp. 177–183; and Alan Gray, "Three 'Islands' in South Africa," *New Commonwealth* (London), vol. 39, no. 7 (July 1961), pp. 431–435.

16. "In many ways, a ring of black states economically beholden to South Africa can provide a far better protective cushion against the north than the odd arc of white colonies which, being colonies, tend to invite attention and trouble." Alistair Sparks, "A Time for Detente? South Africa: A View from Within," *Africa Report*, vol. 12, no. 3 (March 1967), p. 40.

17. Swaziland, *Recurrent Budget Estimates for the Financial Year 1969/70* (Mbabane: Government Printer, 1967), p. 7. *The Standard Bank Review* (London), January 1970, p. 30, puts the figure at over $10 million.

18. See Great Britain, *The Development of the Swaziland Economy* (London: HMSO, 1965); and Peter Robson, "Economic Integration in Southern Africa," *Journal of Modern African Studies*, vol. 5, no. 4 (December 1967), pp. 469–490. In April 1969, for example, South Africa instituted a sales tax imposed at the factory or place of origin. This was carried directly to the Swazi consumers. Increases in prices went as high as 20 percent on such items as soap and matches.

19 D. A. Beale, "Customs Deal," (letter to the editor), *Times of Swaziland* (Mbabane), April 18, 1969, p. 9, col. 1. Of $47.6 million worth of imports in 1968, $43.4 million were from South Africa. Swaziland, *Post Independence Development Plan* [Mbabane: Government Printer, 1969], pp. 66–67).

20. Dr. H. F. Verwoerd, *I. Crisis in World Conscience. II. The Road to Freedom for Basutoland, Bechuanaland, Swaziland*. Fact Paper no. 107 (Pretoria: South Africa. Department of Information, 1964), p. 12 [hereafter cited as *Crisis*].

21. The proposed hydroelectric facilities and power

grid, for example, are currently estimated at a cost of $750 million. The relative importance of private investment should be seen in perspective. Recently, the firms of Anglo-American and the De Beers group announced plans to invest $28 million to develop the AKI diamond pipe in Botswana. This amount is greater than the total annual budget of Botswana.

22. Alan C. G. Best, *The Swaziland Railroad: A Study in Politico-Economic Geography* (East Lansing: Michigan State University, African Studies Center, 1966).

23. After the Rhodesian UDI, Zambia made a concerted effort to cut off trade with that country. Yet it was South Africa which moved in to supply much of Zambia's imports as Zambian–South African trade doubled from 1966 to 1967. For example, air traffic between South Africa and Swaziland involves over four hundred persons per month and is expected to double shortly. ("Phenomenal Swazi Air Success," *The Times of Swaziland*, April 25, 1969, p. 13, cols. 1–2.)

24. See footnote 10 of this chapter, Part One, and Part Three, Chapters 3 and 4.

25. David A. Baldwin, "Foreign Aid, Intervention and Influence," *World Politics*, vol. 21, no. 3 (April 1969), p. 429.

26. Before and after independence, "localization," not Africanization, was the crucial issue within the various governmental bureaucracies. The percentage of non-Swazi African wage earners has declined from 16 percent of the work force in 1964 to 9 percent in 1967.

27. " 'We Would Expect Aid from S.A.': Swazi Premier on Terrorist Threat," *The Star* (Johannesburg), April 8, 1968, city late ed., p. 21, cols. 2–3. It is instructive, however, that in the context of the United Nations and the Swaziland independence celebrations the prime minister, Prince Makhosini, in an interview with the author on September 23, 1968, maintained that he had been "misquoted." At the presen ttime it is not entirely clear exactly what he did say.

28. K. J. Holsti, "Influence," *Background*, vol. 7, no. 4 (February 1964), pp. 179–190, 190–193.

29. See the section on "Influence Vectors" in this book.

30. The inherent shackles on American military might in Vietnam are illustrative of similar constraints in Southern Africa.

31. " 'Enthusiasm' Led to Swazi Kidnap Case," *The Star*, November 4, 1965, city late ed., p. 3, cols. 7–8.

32. For an analysis of a comparable series of events in Basutoland which received far greater publicity, see Jeffrey Butler, "South Africa and the High Commission Territories: The Ganyile Case, 1961," in Gwendolen M. Carter (ed.), *Politics in Africa: 7 Cases* (New York: Harcourt, Brace & World, 1966), pp. 245–283. Dr. Verwoerd called the incident "a mistake" (*Crisis*, p. 11). He did not state that such incidents would not occur again.

33. Rob Hancock, "Sukati Tells Refugees: 'No Nonsense Here,' " *Times of Swaziland*, January 12, 1968, p. 1, cols. 3–5.

34. We would argue, for example, that the present Bantustans are likely to evolve—however slowly and hesistantly—toward the status (*vis à vis* South Africa) of Lesotho or Swaziland rather than vice versa.

35. Much of this remains conjecture, however, for there are no definite plans to enlarge Swaziland by turning over territory to it even though this might prove feasible in the future.

36. "Sovereignty is something else." Quoted in Thomas Hodgkin, "The New West African State System," *University of Toronto Quarterly*, vol. 31, no. 3 (October 1961), pp. 74–82.

37. See Richard Dale, "South African Counterinsurgency Operations in South West Africa," a paper prepared for delivery at the eleventh annual meeting of the African Studies Association, Los Angeles, October 16–19, 1968.

38. Swaziland has entered into exploratory talks with Malawi and Mauritius in an attempt to develop a common policy for the export of sugar.

39. The flows of material, however, are almost entirely outward from Swaziland rather than into Swaziland.

40. Swaziland, *Swaziland 1969* (Mbabane: Government Printer, 1969), p. 11.

41. Even here, however, the relatively large numbers of European settlers in Swaziland and the general per capita income of three or four times that of the other two territories reduced the sense of commonality even more.

42. Robson, *op. cit.*, pp. 482–490.

43. *Joint Memorandum by the Leaders of the Elected Governments of Basutoland, Bechuanaland Protectorate and Swaziland to the Heads of African States* (Accra: mimeographed, October 25, 1965), p. 1.

44. *Ibid.*, p. 2.

45. I. William Zartman, "Africa as a Subordinate State System in International Relations," *International Organization*, vol. 21, no. 3 (Summer 1967), pp. 545–564.

46. In 1965 Zambia and Swaziland signed an agreement whereby Swaziland would ship 25,000 beef carcasses yearly to Zambia. This is one of its very few such transactions with all of black Africa.

47. "Bid to Join East African Market," *Times of Swaziland*, June 6, 1969, p. 1, cols. 4–6.

48. Fifty-three countries were invited to attend the independence celebrations in Swaziland. Rhodesia, Greece, and all Communist states were conspicuously absent.

49. There is, of course, opposition to the present foreign policy within the National party, but it represents a decidedly minority position. See Patrick O'Meara, "Tensions in the Nationalist Party," *Africa Report*, vol. 14, no. 2 (February 1969), pp. 24, 41–45.

50. Kaiser, *op. cit.*, p. 90.

51. *Ibid.*, p. 92.

PART FOUR CHAPTER 1

1a. Portuguese Africa is composed of Angola, Mozambique, Portuguese Guinea, and the archipelagos of Cape Verde, São Tomé and Principe. This essay focuses mainly on Angola and Mozambique.

1b. Afonso I's correspondence was published by António Brasio in vols. 1 and 2 of his *Monumenta Missionaria Africana* (Lisbon, Agência Geral do Ultramar, 1952, 1953).

2. On April 20, 1530, the factory of Sofala received a most interesting *regimento* (royal instructions) which touched upon practically every economic and political aspect, such as commerce, maintenance of good relations with local and neighboring authorities, geographical exploration of the interior, gathering of information

relating to possible communications with the Prester John kingdom, conversion of the Africans to Christianity, setting of good examples by the Portuguese to all those who would contact them, and so on. This *regimento* is to be found in the National Archives of the Torre do Tombo, *Caixa* (box) 18, Peculio II. Vid. *O Regimento de Sofala*. See António Brasio, *Portugal em Africa* (Lisbon: Ediçõs Cosmos, 1948), pp. 5–9.

3. See Alexandre Lobato, *A Expansão Portuguesa em Moçambique de 1408 a 1530*, 3 vols., 1 and 2 being edited by Agência Geral do Ultramar, Lisbon, 1954, and 3 by Centro de Estudos Históricos Ultramarinos, Lisbon, 1960. Hugh Tracey published this *regimento*. His conclusions were discussed by W. A. Godlonton and V. W. Hiller in the *Transactions of the Rhodesia Scientific Association*, vol. 40, no. 1 (April 1945).

4. See the donation charter in Brasio, *Monumenta Missionaria*, vol. 3, pp. 36–51. Paul Dias de Novais and his family were to own a territory stretching over thirty-five leagues south of the Cuanza River. The northern part, from the Cuanza River to the boundaries of the Congo River, would constitute the royal colony. See David Birmingham, *Trade and Conflict in Angola. The Mbundu and Their Neighbours under the Influence of the Portuguese 1483–1790* (Oxford: Clarendon Press, 1966), p. 46.

5. In 1580 the Portuguese crown was joined to the Habsburgs who then ruled Spain. The situation lasted until December 1640. Portuguese overseas administration had been conducted along decentralized lines, while Spain followed an opposite policy of centralization mainly during the reign of Phillip II (Phillip I of Portugal). This explains why Novais' powers were rather reduced after 1580.

6. This report is to be found in the National Library of Lisbon. Its title is "Sumario e descripção de Angola e o descobrimento da Ilha de Oanda e da grandeza das capitanias do Estado do Brasil." (Alfredo de Albuquerque Felner, *Um Inquérito à Vida Administrativa e Económica de Angola e do Brasil* [Coimbra: Imprensa da Universidade, 1933].)

7. The way Gonçalo da Silveira faced his death became a legend. He is now considered as the first Catholic martyr of Rhodesia.

8. The Dutch used to buy their Eastern spices in Lisbon; after 1580, however, due to the personal union between Portugal and Spain, and because of their hostility toward the Habsburgs, they were deprived of such use of the Portuguese ports and had to look for other sources of supply. This led them to the Indies themselves. The Dutch East Indies Company and the Dutch West Indies Company bore testimony to their enterprising spirit. The first worked in the Indian Ocean while the second operated in the Atlantic. After a few unsuccessful attempts, the Dutch managed to establish themselves at Pernambuco in northern Brazil in 1630, where they were to stay until 1649, when the Dutch West Indies Company abandoned the post. See C. R. Boxer, *Salvador de Sá and the Struggle for Brazil and Angola, 1602–1686* (London: University of London, 1952).

9. The period 1641–1648 is coupled in my book, *A Dupla Restauração de Angola* (Lisbon: Agência Geral das Colónias, 1948).

10. The Zambezi has its origin at the Caombra mountains in Rhodesia, a few miles from Angola. From Rhodesia it flows first into Angola, where it receives several tributary rivers, then it returns to Rhodesia where it passes in Victoria Falls. It continues its course toward the Indian Ocean, entering Portuguese East Africa through Zumbo, Chicoa, and Tete, then entering into the Indian Ocean.

11. *Sesmari* meant an uncultivated or abandoned piece of land which was granted or leased on very favorable conditions. The system was very ancient in Portugal. See the words *prazo* and *sesmaria* in the *Elucidário das Palavras, Termos e Frases que hoje Regularmente se Ignoram: Obra Indispensável, para Entender sem Erro os Documentos mais Raros e Preciosos que entre Nós se Conservam*. 2 vols. (Porto-Lisbon: Livraria Civilização, 1966).

12. The *prazo* system has been the subject of much discussion. Practically all works on Mozambique touch on this problem. The book by Alexandre Lobato, *Evolução Administrativa e Económica de Moçambique 1752–1763* (Lisbon: Agência Geral do Ultramar, 1967), pp. 25–26, should be consulted. The same author has dwelt on the same subject in *Colonização Senhorial da Zambézia e Outros Estudos* (Lisbon: Junta de Investigações do Ultramar, 1962), pp. 97–116. See also James Duffy, *Portuguese Africa* (Cambridge, Mass.: Harvard University Press, 1961), pp. 82–89. Allan Isaacman has recently published "The Prazos da Coroa 1752–1830—A Functional Analysis of the Political System," in *Studia* (Lisbon), April 1969, pp. 149–178.

13. I find it rather difficult to agree with the statement made by David Birmingham in *The Portuguese Conquest of Angola* (London: Oxford University Press, 1965). This writer says: "The first incentive to the Portuguese to conquer a colony in Angola was the hope of acquiring lands suitable for European settlement similar to those which were being settled in Brazil." (pp. 1–2). These were indeed the instructions given to Paulo Dias de Novais and to the Brazil captains or "donatários." In spite of them, however, Portugal was from the beginning, and would remain for centuries, an under-populated country.

14. This important document was published in the *Arquivo das Colónias* (Lisbon: Arquivo Histórico Colonial) July-December, 1918, pp. 60–73, 124–136, 188–192.

15. One may consult Gaston Zeller, *Les Temps Modernes* (Paris: Hacette, 1965), pp. 81–108.

16. *Arquivo de Angola* (Luanda: Instituto de Investigação Cientifica de Angola) January-October 1953, pp. 39–42.

17. José Ferreira Borges de Castro, *Collecção dos Tratados, Convenções, Contratos e Actos Publicos Celerados entre a Coroa de Portugal e as mais Potencias desde 1640 até ao Presente* (Lisbon: Imprensa Nacional, 1857), vol. 4, pp. 396–415.

18. *Ibid.*, vol. 6, pp. 374–479.

19. One may read the record of the meeting in *Boletim Official da Provincia de Angola* (Luanda), no. 29, July 16, 1870, p. 432.

20. Ralph Delgado, *A Famosa e Histórica Benguela* (Benguela; Ed. Ções Cosmus, 1940), Dec. 23.

21. A. Teixeira da Mota, *A Cartografia Antiga da Africa Central e a Travessia entre Angola e Moçambique 1500–1860* (Lourenço Marques: Imprensa Nacional, 1964), pp. 113 ff.

22. A few French Sisters of the Poor arrived in Lisbon

by the end of October 1857 in order to help their Portuguese colleagues. They were badly received and even scorned by the people of Lisbon who were under the influence of Freemasonry. They left Portugal in June 1862.

23. Philip Beaver, the head of the expedition, wrote a most interesting *African Memoranda relative to an Attempt to Establish a British Settlement on the Island of Bolama on the Western Coast of Africa in the Year 1792* (London: Armstrong, 1805).

24. C. de Lanoy, *La Réglémentation du Travail dans l'Afrique Centrale*, an offprint of the *Bulletin de Colonisation Comparée* (Brussels), July 1910.

25. *Manual Labour in S. Thomé and Principe* (Lisbon: Imprensa Nacional, 1910).

CHAPTER 2

1. George Orwell, "Marrakech," *New Writing* (London: Christmas, 1939), as reprinted in Sonia Orwell and Ian Angus (eds.), *The Collected Essays, Journalism and Letters of George Orwell*. 4 vols. (New York: Harcourt, Brace & World, 1968), vol. 1, pp. 387–393.

2. James Duffy, "The Dual Reality of Portuguese Africa," *Centennial Review*, vol. 4, no. 4 (Fall 1960), pp. 450–464.

3. See F. C. C. Egerton, *Angola in Perspective* (London: Kegan, Routledge & Paul, 1957); Gilberto Freyre, *Portuguese Integration in the Tropics* (Lisbon: n. p., 1960); and Adriano Moreira, *Portugal's Stand in Africa* (New York: University Publishers, 1962).

4. Basil Davidson in his new introduction to a new edition of H. W. Nevinson's *A Modern Slavery* (New York: Schocken Books, 1967), pp. vii–xix; Stanley Meisler, "Portuguese Africa," *Atlantic Monthly*, vol. 223, no. 1 (January 1969), pp. 14–22; Thomas Okuma, *Angola in Ferment* (Boston: Beacon Press, 1962).

5. Marvin Harris, "Race, Conflict and Reform in Mozambique," in Stanley Diamond and Fred G. Burke (eds.), *The Transformation of East Africa* (New York: Basic Books, 1966), pp. 156–183; Robert Davezies, *Les Angolais* (Paris: Les Editions Minuit, 1965).

6. Frantz Fanon, *The Wretched of the Earth* (New York: Grove Press, 1961), pp. 141–142, 149. On the nature of Portuguese reforms after 1961, especially the abolition of forced labor, see Giovanni Giovannini, "Can Colonialism Make It?", *Atlas*, vol. 9, no. 6 (June, 1965), pp. 353–359.

7. "The Voice of Angola Crying in the Wilderness" is a translation of the title of a remarkable written protest by Angolans published as *Voz d'Angola Clamando No Deserto, Offerecida Aos Amigos da Verdade Pelos Naturaes* (Lisbon: n. p., 1901).

8. Douglas L. Wheeler, "Angola Is Whose House? Early Stirrings of Angolan Nationalism and Protest, 1822–1910," *African Historical Studies*, vol. 2, no. 1 (1969), pp. 1–22.

9. On Assis Junior as a novelist of Angola, see Mario António, *Luanda, "ilha" crioula* (Lisbon: Agência-Geraldo Ultramar, 1968), pp. 123–128.

10. António de Assis Júnior, *Relato dos Acontecimentos de Dala, Tande, e Lucala*, 2 vols. (Luanda: Tipografia Mamã Tita, 1917–1918). vol. 2, pp. 55–56.

11. For a thorough analysis of the emergence of Angolan nationalism in the 1950s and the events of 1961–1962, see John Marcum, *The Angolan Revolution,*

Volume I: The Anatomy of An Explosion (1950–1962) (Cambridge, Mass: M.I.T. Press, 1969).

12. Walter Marques, *Problemas do Desenvolvimento Económico de Angola*. 2 vols. (Luanda: Lito-Tipo, Lda., 1964), vol. 1, pp. 269–336.

13. A recent book published in Portugal has stated that "injustices" were committed by "civilians" (militia) in Luanda. (Pereira da Costa, *Um Mes de Terrorismo* [*Angola–Março-Abril de 1961*] [Lisbon: Editorial Polis, 1969], p. 88.)

14. Henrique Galvao, *Santa Maria: My Crusade for Portugal* (Cleveland: World Publishing Co., 1962); Henry A. Zeiger, *The Seizing of the Santa Maria* (New York: Popular Library, 1961).

15. This phrase is from Rodrigues Júnior, *Angola. Terra de Portugal* (Lisbon: n. p., 1961), p. 16.

16. This phrase is from *A Provincia de Angola* (Luanda), March 11, 1961.

17. For the text of this important decree, see Adriano Moreira, *Portugal's Stand in Africa*, pp. 225–261 (Decree no. 43,893 of September 6, 1961).

18. *Ibid.*, p. 195, citing the abolition of compulsory growing of cotton (Decree no. 43,637 of May 2, 1961).

19. Douglas L. Wheeler, "Reflections on Angola," *Africa Report*, vol. 12. no. 8 (November 1967), pp. 58–62.

20. United Nations, General Assembly, *Working Paper of Special Committee on the Situation with regard to the Implementation of the Declaration on the Granting of Independence to Colonial Countries and Peoples: Territories Under Portuguese Administration*, A/AC. 109/L.126 (New York: United Nations, June 9, 1964), pp. 6–23; A/AC. 109/L.451/Add.1 (New York: United Nations, March 27, 1968), pp. 1–6.

21. The duration of Legislative Council (Legco) sessions cannot exceed three months and members of the Legco cannot propose legislation which involves increases in expenditures or decreases in revenue as set by previous decrees. The continuation of this sort of regulation betrays the "antiparliamentary" philosophy of the Lisbon regime.

22. Franco Nogueira, *Terceiro Mundo* (Luanda: n. p., 1967): Moreira, *op. cit.*

23. Amadeu Da Silva Carvalho, "Presença das Forças Armadas em Angola," *Ultramar* (Lisbon), vol. 5, no. 15, Número Especial (1964), pp. 190–192.

24. James Duffy, *Portugal in Africa* (Cambridge, Mass.: Harvard University Press, 1962), pp. 191–206; Wheeler, "Reflections on Angola," p. 60.

25. As cited in *A Província de Angola* (Luanda), October 23, 1966.

26. Allison Butler Herrick *et al.*, *Area Handbook for Angola*, DA Pamphlet no. 550–59 (Washington, D.C.: USGPO, 1967), pp. 203–207.

27. "Portugal: Dr. Salazar Incapacited by Grave Illness: Dr. Caefano Appointed Prime Minister: Cabinet Reorganization: New Government Policy," *Keesings Contemporary Archives* (London), (October 5–12, 1968), p. 22960 and Richard Elder, "Lisbon Considers Chief's Successor: New York Doctor to Treat Salazar, Near Death," *New York Times*, September 18, 1968, late city ed., p. 3, cols. 1–3.

28. Michael Samuels, "The New Look in Angolan Education," *Africa Report*, vol. 12, no. 8 (November 1967), pp. 63–66.

29. David J. Paine, "The War In Angola," *Sunday*

Herald Traveler (Boston), September 14, 1969, p. 42. A Portuguese "senior intelligence officer" was quoted recently as saying that the military situation was "stable," but that "we can't get rid of them" (the nationalists).

30. "Angola at Tantalysing Stage in Quest for Oil," *The Star* (Johannesburg), October 25, 1966, city late ed., p. 24, cols. 6–9; information gathered by the author while in Luanda, September-December 1966.

31. Richard J. Hammond, "Race Attitudes and Policies in Portuguese Africa in the Nineteenth and Twentieth Centuries," *Race* (London), vol. 9, no. 2 (October 1967), pp. 205–216.

32. Donald Barnett, "Angola: Report From Hanoi II," *Ramparts*, vol. 7, no. 10 (April 1969), pp. 49–54.

33. Samuels, *op. cit.*, p. 66.

34. Clifford Parsons, "The Makings of a Revolt," in Philip Mason (ed.), *Angola: A Symposium: Views of a Revolt* (London: Oxford University Press, 1962), pp. 58–66; Helio Felgas, *História do Congo Português* (Carmona, Luanda: Empresa Gráfica do Uige, 1958), pp. 190–198; Hélio Felgas, *As Populações Nativas do Norte de Angola*, 2nd ed. (Lisbon: Tipografía da LCGG, 1965), pp. 106–108.

35. Herrick, *op. cit.*, pp. 277–282.

36. José De Sousa Bettencourt, "Subsidio para o Estudo Sociológica da população de Luanda," *Boletim do Instituto de Investigação Cientifica de Angola* (Luanda), vol. 2, no. 1 (1965), pp. 83–130.

37. Antunes Valente and J. Eduardo Carvalhal, "Acção Social No Trabalho Em Angola," *Ultramar* (Lisbon), vol. 5, no. 15, Número Especial (1964), pp. 93–110.

38. Beggars in Angolan towns are often black boys, with congenital deformities. In Portugal, on the other hand, beggars are invariably afflicted Portuguese men and women, officially registered with the government and carrying numbered collection boxes.

39. Information gathered by author during his visit to Angola in 1966; see Oscar Ribas, *Izomba. Associativismo e Recreio* (Luanda: Tipografía Angolana, 1965), pp. 43–61.

40. Douglas L. Wheeler, "The Portuguese Army in Angola: Its Changing Character and Role," *Journal of Modern African Studies*, vol. 7, no. 3 (September 1969), pp. 425–439.

41. Herrick, *op. cit.*, pp. 378–385.

42. Fanon, *op. cit.*, p. 147.

43. Moreira, *op. cit.*, p. vi.

44. Richard J. Hammond, *Portugal's African Problem: Some Economic Facets*. Occasional Paper no. 2 (New York: Carnegie Endowment for International Peace, 1962), p. 36

45. William A. Hance, "Three Economies," *Africa Report*, vol. 12, no. 8 (November 1967), pp. 23–27.

46. Américo Boavida, *Angola: Cinco Séculos de Exploração Portuguesa* (Rio de Janeiro: Editòra Civilização Brasileira, 1967).

47. *Ibid.*, p. 84.

48. *Ibid.*, p. 127.

49. *Ibid.*, p. 8, from preface by Manuel Urbano Rodrigues.

50. "Zambia—Portugal: Villages Bombed," *Africa Research Bulletin: Political, Social, and Cultural Series* (Exeter, England), vol. 5, no. 4 (May 15, 1968), p. 1051; "Zambia—Portugal: Further Border Incidents," *Africa Research Bulletin: Political, Social, and Cultural Series*, vol. 5, no. 12 (January 15, 1969), p. 1276.

51. See the recent monograph by a Portuguese scholar, Eduardo dos Santos, *A Questão do Biafra* (Oporto, Portugal: Portucalense Editora, 1968); a well-known scholar of African affairs, dos Santos shows considerable sympathy for the Biafran cause.

52. John Marcum, "Three Revolutions," *Africa Report*, vol. 12, no. 8 (November 1967), p. 14.

53. Ronald H. Chilcote, *Portuguese Africa* (Englewood Cliffs, N.J.: Prentice-Hall, 1967), pp. 81, 128.

54. Marcum, *The Angolan Revolution*, vol. 1, p. 319; Marcum, "Three Revolutions," pp. 9, 16–17.

55. As quoted in Artur Maciel, *Angola Heroica. 120 Dias Com Os Nossos Soldados*, 3rd ed. (Lisbon: Livraria Bertrand, 1963), p. 280.

56. Wheeler, "Reflections on Angola," p. 62.

57. Boavida, *op. cit.*, p. vi, preface. For a fairly typical semiofficial view of traditional Portuguese values and interpretations of their role in Portuguese Africa, see the essay by Dr. Alexandre Lobato, "Permanence and Change in Overseas Portuguese Thought," in Raymond S. Sayers (ed.), *Portugal and Brazil in Transition* (Minneapolis: University of Minnesota Press, 1968), pp. 93–107, translated and condensed by Douglas L. Wheeler.

CHAPTER 3

1. Supporting this perspective of Portuguese Africa are James Duffy, *Portuguese Africa* (Cambridge, Mass.: Harvard University Press, 1959) and *Portugal in Africa* (Harmondsworth, Middlesex, England, and Baltimore: Penguin Books, 1962); and Ronald H. Chilcote, *Portuguese Africa* (Englewood Cliffs, N.J.: Prentice-Hall, 1967).

2. J. A. Hobson is generally regarded as the originator of the conception of imperialism (see his classic *Imperialism: A Study* [Ann Arbor: University of Michigan Press, 1965], originally published by George Allen & Unwin, 1902, and revised in 1938) and Lenin's analysis (*Imperialism: The Highest Stage of Capitalism* [New York: International Publishers, 1938]) was largely drawn from Hobson. Howard Sherman, an economist at the University of California, Riverside, makes the point that Marx foreshadowed both men with his prediction of the dominance of monopolies and awareness of finance capital and the credit mechanism (from Howard Sherman, chap. 8, "Imperialism," p. 2, of a forthcoming study of political economy). Lenin, however, dates modern imperialism as late as the last decade of the nineteenth century and associates imperialism with the phenomenon of monopoly capitalism which became predominant in the United States and Western Europe. For a detailed analysis of monopoly capitalism, see Paul A. Baran and Paul M. Sweezy, *Monopoly Capital* (New York: Monthly Review, 1966). For the present essay we view imperialism in a broader context and interpret Portuguese imperialism through three phases of history: the imperialism of exchange, extraction, and industrialization or development. The analysis generally follows that of Perry Anderson, "Portugal and the End of Ultra-Colonialism," *New Left Review*, Part I in 15 (May-June 1962), pp. 84–102; Part II in 16 (July-August 1962), pp. 88–123; Part III in 17 (Winter 1962), pp. 85–114. These articles in revised form are also published in *Le*

Portugal et la Fin de l'Ultra-Colonialisme (Paris: François Maspero, 1963).

3. The development of the sugar industry in northeast Brazil and its repercussions upon the Portuguese empire are fully and critically examined by Celso Furtado, *Formação económica do Brasil*, 4th ed. (Rio de Janeiro: Editôra Fundo de Cultura, 1961) (translated and published by the University of California Press in 1963 as *The Economic Growth of Brazil*), and Caio Prado, Jr., *The Colonial Background of Modern Brazil* (Berkeley and Los Angeles: University of California Press, 1969).

4. A generally useful and detailed account of the Portuguese economic troubles and the establishment of the charter companies is Richard J. Hammond, *Portugal and Africa, 1815–1910: A Study in Uneconomic Imperialism* (Stanford: Stanford University Press, 1966), especially chap. 7, "Concessions and Concession Hunters," pp. 210–223.

5. South Africa would be the largest consumer of Cabora Bassa power which would also be transmitted to Rhodesia and Malawi. The project is critically assessed by Eduardo Mondlane in *The Struggle for Mozambique* (Baltimore: Penguin Books, 1969), pp. 97–98. According to Mondlane, "The plan draws South Africa closer to Portugal and gives her an important stake in the future of Mozambique" (p. 98).

6. U.S. capital is prominent in the distribution of pharmaceutical goods and sewing machines as well as the exploration, exploitation, and distribution of petroleum (the U.S. firms include Caltex Oil, Mobil Oil Southern Africa, Mozambique Gulf Oil Company, Mozambique Pan American Oil Company, Sunray, Clark and Skelly Consortium, and the Hunt Oil Company). British interests control Sena Sugar Estates, the most highly capitalized company, which exports about 60 percent of the annual sugar yield. Foreign capital dominates the majority of the eighteen sisal companies while the seventeen large tea companies are represented by substantial British capital. Concessions of large tracts of land have been granted to a few foreigners for the establishment of modern cattle ranches. Among extractive industries, coal is mined by a predominantly Belgian company. Of the five commercial banks, one was British-owned, another South African. In the insurance field, nine of twenty-three companies were in foreign hands.

7. An excellent example of this Portuguese view is expressed by a long-time supporter of the regime, António Júlio de Castro Fernandes, *The Presence of the Portuguese in Africa* (Lisbon: Secretariado Nacional da Informação, 1961).

8. Anderson, "Portugal and the End of Ultra-Colonialism," Part I, p. 95.

9. Quoted in André Gunder Frank, *Capitalism and Underdevelopment in Latin America: Historical Studies of Chile and Brazil* (New York and London: Monthly Review Press, 1967), p. 156.

10. See Richard J. Hammond, "Economic Imperialism: Sidelights on a Stereotype," *Journal of Economic History*, vol. 21 no. 4 (December 1961), p. 592. Hammond, however, suggests that the chartered companies were speculative and unsuccessful enterprises, and he minimizes the imperialist intentions of the British capitalist.

11. Anderson, "Portugal and the End of Ultra-Colonialism," Part I, p. 88.

12. Quoted in *ibid.*, p. 87. An obvious case of a Portuguese cartel is the *Companhia União Fabril* (CUF) which controls iron and steel, cement, the majority of dockyards and shipping firms, and a variety of related industries. In Portuguese Guinea a CUF subsidiary held absolute dominance over the private economy, a major factor in Portugal's continued presence in that enclave.

13. Information based on data in the archives of the *Registo Predial* and reported in Peter Fryer and Patricia McGowan Pinheiro, *Oldest Ally: A Portrait of Salazar's Portugal* (London: Dennis Dobson, 1961), p. 146.

14. Although perhaps not entirely accurate, these data from a generally unreliable source give an indication of the interpenetration of the Portuguese economic and political elites; cited in *The Case Against Salazar* (Prague: International Union of Students, n.d.), p. 26.

15. *Diário de Noticias* (Lisbon), October 17, 1969, and *Diário de Luanda* (Luanda), October 27, 1969. Nogueira maintained that Portugal's true interests lay in retaining and developing the overseas territories and that there should be no change in the nation's overseas policies, a view shared by some high military authorities and rightist members of the single ruling party, the *União Nacional*.

16. Mondlane, *The Struggle for Mozambique*, p. 73. See "*Diário de Moçambique* Suspended Again," *Mozambique Revolution* (Dar es Salaam), 19 (June 1965), p. 9. The traditional order in Portugal and its impact on developments in Mozambique can be analyzed through examination of institutional strengths and weaknesses as well as the supports and countersupports to the regime; such an analysis is presented in Chilcote, *Portuguese Africa*, chap. 2, especially pp. 30–41.

17. This paragraph is based on Junta de Investigação do Ultramar, *Promoção Social em Moçambique* (Lisbon, 1964), as quoted in Mondlane, *The Struggle for Mozambique*, pp. 38–39.

18. In the late 1950s the first of the corporations was formally established, but they seem to be ineffective and, except for the publication of theoretical works by advocates of the New State regime, there has been little systematic propagation of the fascist model. Anderson attributes this to the fact that "Catholicism is virulent and unchallenged, more so than in any other European country, even Spain. A developed fascist ideology is therefore unnecessary." (See Anderson, "Portugal and the End of Ultra-Colonialism," Part I, p. 89.)

19. *Diário de Notícias* (Lisbon), September 28, 1969.

20. *Diário* (Lourenço Marques), September 25, 1969.

21. Official note published in the press, March 27, 1969; see *Notícias de Portugal* (Lisbon), vol. 22 (March 29, 1969), pp. 3–4.

22. Press reports in late 1969 announced that the Caetano government had decided to abolish the PIDE. It appears that the old organization is to be retained under a different name, the *Direção Geral de Segurança*.

23. In a provocative paper Marvin Harris suggests that the Portuguese encountered substantial resistance from Guinea to Dahomey where there were "highly stratified, populous, well-organized native states capable of raising large armies, whose weaponry was based upon metallurgical techniques." Less organized and less developed Angola offered the possibility of an easy conquest, although "the Portuguese seriously miscalculated their military possibilities." Harris' comments apply as well to Mozambique. (See Marvin Harris,

"Portugal's Contribution to the Underdevelopment of Africa and Brazil," a paper presented to the University of California Colloquium, Riverside and Los Angeles, March 1968, pp. 5–7.)

24. C. R. Boxer, *Race Relations in the Portuguese Colonial Empire, 1415–1825* (Oxford: Clarendon Press, 1963), p. 55. See especially his chapter, "Moçambique and India," pp. 41–85.

25. Probably the most useful synthesis is James Duffy, *A Question of Slavery* (Oxford: Clarendon Press, 1967), especially chaps. 3 and 6 on Mozambique.

26. Duffy, *Portuguese Africa*, p. 131. The forms of forced labor are discussed in pp. 317–328 of this book.

27. Marvin Harris, *Portugal's African "Wards": A First-Hand Report on Labor and Education in Moçambique* (New York: American Committee on Africa, 1958), p. 25.

28. In 1959 Portugal signed both the International Labor Convention of 1955 and the Abolition of Forced Labor Convention of 1957. In 1960 the controversial sections of the 1928 Portuguese Native Labor Code were repealed. Labor reforms were instituted in 1961 and the 1954 *Estatuto de Indígenas* was abolished in the same year.

29. A full critique of the labor reforms is in Marvin Harris, "Raça, Conflito e Reforma em Moçambique," *Política Exterior Independente* (Rio de Janeiro), vol. 1, no. 3 (January 1966), pp. 9–39.

30. Duffy, *A Question of Slavery*, p. 155.

31. Harris, *Portugal's African "Wards,"* p. 27, bases his estimate on the *Anuário Moçambique*, 1917, 1940, 1940–1954. He also notes: "Real wages paid to mine workers are lower today than they were in 1896" (p. 27). A full discussion of forced labor appears in International Labor Organization, "Report of the Commission Appointed Under Article 26 of the Constitution of the International Labour Organisation to Examine the Complaint Filed by the Government of Ghana Concerning the Observance by the Government of Portugal of the Abolition of Forced Labour Convention, 1957 (No. 105)," *Official Bulletin* (Geneva), vol. 45, no. 2 (April 1962), supplement 2, pp. 1–253. A critical assessment of the commission's findings is by Reverend Malcolm McVeigh, "Some Observations on the Commission Report of the International Labor Organization Concerning Labor Practices in Portuguese Africa," (New York: American Committee on Africa, June 1962). The Portuguese view is in Secretariado Nacional de Informação, *The Ghana Complaint Against Portugal* (Lisbon: Secretariado Nacional de Informação, 1962).

32. Allison Butler Herrick *et al.*, *Area Handbook for Mozambique*. DA Pam. no. 550–64. (Washington, D.C.: USGPO, 1969), p. 217.

33. Eric Axelson, *Portuguese in South-East Africa, 1600–1700* (Johannesburg: Witwatersrand University Press, 1969), p. 96.

34. *Ibid.*, pp. 30–42, 178–185.

35. See M. D. D. Newitt and P. S. Garlake, "The 'Aringa' at Massangano," *Journal of African History*, vol. 8 (1967), pp. 133–156, for a useful summary account of the period and additional references. The most exhaustive account of the African resistance led by the Cruz family is in Filipe Gastão de Almeida de Eça, *História das guerras no Zambeze: Chicoa e Massangano (1807–1888)*. 2 vols. (Lisbon: Agência Geral do Ultramar, 1953).

36. One has to rely upon Portuguese memoirs for an account of the struggle. See António Ennes, *A guerra de Africa em 1895: memórias*. 2nd ed. (Lisbon: Gama, 1945), and his *Moçambique. relatório apresentado ao govêrno* (Lisbon: Agência Geral das Colónias, 1946); and Joaquim Mousinho de Albuquerque. *Mousinho de Albuquerque*, 2 vols. (Lisbon: Agência Geral das Colónias, 1934–1935) and his *A prisão do Gungunhana . . .* (Lourenço Marques: Typographia Nacional de Sampaio e Carvalho, 1896). Also Agência Geral das Colónias, *As campanhas de Moçambique em 1895* (Lisbon: Atica, 1947). There is a general account in P. R. Warhurst, *Anglo-Portuguese Relations in South-Central Africa, 1890–1900* (London: Longmans, 1962), chap. 3, "The Tragedy of Gungunhana," pp. 73–108. See Douglas Wheeler, "Gungunhana," in Norman Bennett (ed.), *Leadership in Eastern Africa* (Brookline, Mass.: Boston University Press, 1969), pp. 165–220.

37. Mondlane, *The Struggle for Mozambique*, p. 102.

38. *Ibid.*, pp. 23, 53, 103–104.

39. According to the 1950 census there were only 4,349 black (*negros*) *assimilados* in a total black population of 5.65 million; see Instituto Nacional de Estatística, *Anuário Estatístico de Ultramar, 1959* (Lisbon, 1960), pp. 32–33.

40. Mondlane, *The Struggle for Mozambique*, pp. 104, 117–118.

41. After the assassination of Dr. Mondlane in Dar es Salaam on February 3, 1969, Kavandame surrendered himself, apparently voluntarily, to Portuguese authorities. The official Portuguese note on the incident is in *Notícias de Portugal*, vol. 22 (April 5, 1969), pp. 2–3. A statement by FRELIMO announced that Kavandame had been implicated in the assassination of a nationalist military commander on December 22, 1968, and that he had been dismissed from the central committee on January 3, 1969, prior to his defection to the Portuguese. See "Press Statement on Lázaro Kavandame," *Mozambique Revolution* no. 38 (March-April, 1969), pp. 10–11.

42. For details on the stevedores' strike of August 27, 1963, see "The Stevedores' Strike: Paulo Baloi Murdered by the Portuguese Colonialists, 64 Stevedores in Machava Prison," *Mozambique Revolution* no. 1 (December 1963), p. 9.

43. These quotations and poetical excerpts are from a fascinating and powerful analysis of Mozambican revolutionary poetry which concludes with a critique of these poets: "None of them has given himself to the liberation struggle. For this very reason they are *before* the revolution, in spite of being contemporary with it." Quoted in "The Role of Poetry in the Mozambican Revolution," *Mozambique Revolution*, no. 37 (January–February 1969), pp. 23–31, and no. 38 (March-April 1969), pp. 17–32. Craveirinha as well as the short story writer Luís Bernardo Honwana are in prison, while Nogar and Malangatana were arrested in December 1964 and May 1965, respectively, and are closely watched in Mozambique. An example of Honwana's prose is in Mário de Andrade (ed.), *Prosa: páginas excolhidas* (Algiers), March 1968, pp. 283–295. Of the early poets, only Marcelino dos Santos, a leader of FRELIMO, joined the liberation struggle.

44. Eduardo C. Mondlane, "The Struggle for Independence in Mozambique," (Dar es Salaam: mimeographed, April 1963), p. 5.

45. Mondlane in *The Struggle for Mozambique*, pp. 113–114, devotes considerable detail to his involvement

in NESAM. Outside Mozambique, NESAM evolved into the *União Nacional dos Estudantes de Moçambique* (UNEMO) established in 1961. Mozambican students in Lisbon also associated with the *Liga Africana* in the early 1920s and the *Casa dos Estudantes do Império* (CEI) during the 1950s and 1960s until it was closed by the government in 1965. In 1951 African students formed a *Centro de Estudos Africanos* and through the *Clube dos Marítimos* established contact with sailors who came to Lisbon from Africa.

46. The *Movimento's* manifesto appeared in *Tribuna Livre*, no. 2 (June 1961), a clandestine opposition publication in Lisbon. See also *Est et Ouest* (Paris), no. 280 (June 15, 1962), p. 6.

47. The black leaders of the PLM, Diniz Mengame and Tomaz Betulane Nhantumbo, had founded the PLM about 1953 or 1954; it had been known also as the *Convenção do Povo de Moambçique*; see *Diário de Lisboa*, February 27, 1962. The other African movements above were identified in petitions to the United Nations. Also, see the UPM's "Primeiro Comunicado do Partido União Progressiva de Moçambique (Manica e Sofala)," *Portugal Democrático* (São Paulo), vol. 5 (June 1961), p. 6.

48. The Núcleo's president, S. Simango, was arrested by Portugese police in 1956 according to *Voice of Africa* (Accra), vol. 4 (May-June 1964), p. 32. The *União Makonde de Moçambique* incorporated blacks of the Makonde tribe of northern Mozambique and maintained ties with the Tanganyika African National Union (TANU), according to Edouard Bustin, *Guide des Partie Politiques Africains* . . . (Brussels: Editions CRISP—IPC, 1962), pp. 24–25.

49. An early document published by UDENAMO was "America, the Country Responsible for the Colonial Wars in Africa!" (Dar es Salaam: mimeographed, October 8, 1961). Also see hearings of petitioners (Gwambe, Bahule, Gumane, Simango, Murupa, Magaia, Marapendo, Mengwambe, Mahlayete, Nungu, Chapo, Numgaka, Ndimeni, Tembe, Matsoko, Ndeyo, Ngwenya) before the United Nations Special Committee on Territories under Portuguese Administration Established under General Assembly Resolution 1699 (XVI), A/AC. 108/SR. 22–25, 40, 41, Dar es Salaam and Accra, May 14–15 and June 1, 1962.

50. For background on MANU, see its hearings of petitioners (Mmole, Milinga, Viegas, Lala) before the United Nations Special Committee on Territories under Portuguese Administration Established under General Assembly Resolution 1699 (XVI), A/AC. 108/SR. 26–27, Dar es Salaam, August 26, 1962.

51. For background on UNAMI, see its hearings of petitioners before the United Nations Special Committee on Territories under Portuguese Administration Established under General Assembly Resolution 1699 (XVI), A/AC. 108/SR. 28, Dar es Salaam, August 21, 1962.

52. Mondlane had studied in Lisbon and then in the United States at Oberlin College and Northwestern University where he obtained his doctorate. He also served with the United Nations as a research officer and in 1961 joined the faculty of the Maxwell School of Graduate Studies at Syracuse University. After the formation of FRELIMO, Mondlane returned to Dar es Salaam where he led the movement until his assassination in February 1969. See Eduardo C. Mondlane, "Statement Before the U.N. Special Committee on Territories under Portuguese Administration Established under General Assembly Resolution 1699 (XVI), April 9–10, 1962, A/AC. 108/SR. 8–10; Ronald H. Chilcote, "Eduardo Mondlane and the Mozambique Struggle," *Africa Today*, vol. 12, no. 6 (November 1965), pp. 4–7, an interview with Mondlane in Dar es Salaam, July 27, 1965; and Helen Kitchen, "Conversation with Eduardo Mondlane," *Africa Report*, vol. 12, no. 8 (November 1967), pp. 31–32, 49–51.

53. Frente de Libertação de Moçambique, *1° Congresso. Documentos* (Dar es Salaam), September 23–28, 1962.

54. Mondlane, *The Struggle for Mozambique*, p. 126.

55. Originally, the army was organized into battalions, detachments, companies, and units under the direction of regional commands. In 1966 this structure was modified with the creation of a central command headed by the secretary for the department of defense, his assistant (political commissar of the army), and twelve other leaders.

56. The activities of the *Instituto Moçambicano* are described by Janet Mondlane in "The Mozambique Institute (Instituto Moçambicano)," (Dar es Salaam: mimeographed, 1963). In its early years the institute received support from the Ford Foundation, but this was terminated after protests from the Portuguese government.

57. The quotations in this paragraph are from Eduardo C. Mondlane, "The Development of Nationalism in Mozambique" (Dar es Salaam: mimeographed, December 1964).

58. Resolution of the FRELIMO Central Committee, Dar es Salaam, October 1966 as quoted in Mondlane, *The Struggle for Mozambique*, p. 164.

59. *Frente de Libertação de Moçambique*, "Message from the Central Committee to the Mozambican People," Dar es Salaam, September 25, 1967, as quoted in Mondlane, *The Struggle for Mozambique*, p. 163.

60. Mondlane, *The Struggle for Mozambique*, p. 167.

61. See the details of the party structure in *Frente de Libertação de Mozambique, Estatutos e programa* (Dar es Salaam, September 1963).

62. Mondlane, *The Struggle for Mozambique*, pp. 172–173.

63. *Ibid.*, pp. 173–183 (quotation from p. 181). In general, the accomplishments of the FRELIMO within liberated zones may be exaggerated. Details are covered by Mondlane, *The Struggle for Mozambique*, pp. 163–180 and also in "National Reconstruction," *Mozambique Revolution*, no. 40 (September 25, 1969), pp. 33–51.

64. See "Resolutions of the Central Committee," *Mozambique Revolution*, no. 35 (June-September 1968), pp. 4–7; and Mondlane, *The Struggle for Mozambique*, pp. 187–196. The resolutions are divided under the following headings: armed struggle, administration of liberated zones, national reconstruction, social affairs, and foreign policy.

65. Among Gumane's writings are "Mozambique Enslaved," *Review of International Affairs* (Belgrade), vol. 15 (April 5, 1964), pp. 9–10; and "Salazar's Misconceptions," *Voice of Africa*, vol. 4 (May-June 1964), pp. 23, 28.

66. Mallinga's views are in "Statement Made by Mr. Mallinga of MANU at the 26th Meeting of the United Nations Special Committee on Territories under Portuguese Administration Established under General

Assembly Resolution 1699 (XVI), held at Dar es Salaam on May 16, 1962, A/AC. 108/23.

67. An early view by Mabunda is his "Portuguese Colonization of Monomotapa (Mozambique)," *Voice of Africa*, vol. 2 (July 1962), pp. 23–24, 26.

68. See "Expulsion of Leo Milas from FRELIMO," *Mozambique Revolution* (Dar es Salaam), no. 9 (August 1964), pp. 4–5. Milas was expelled August 14, 1962.

69. The expulsion of many FRELIMO leaders during 1962 and 1963 is reviewed in *Frente Unida Anti-Imperialista Popular Africana de Moçambique*, "Memoranda Supporting Declaration of Dissolution of FRELIMO" (Kampala: mimeographed, May 27, 1963).

70. Marcelino dos Santos is without question one of the few eminent intellectuals within the FRELIMO, yet he has not written prolifically about the revolution. An exception is his "The Voice of the Awakened Continent," *World Marxist Review* (Prague), vol. 7, no. 1 (January 1964), pp. 55–57, and his views have been recorded in United Nations publications—see his "Statement . . . at the 52nd Meeting of the Special Committee, held at Rabat, Morocco, on June 15, 1962," New York, August 9, 1962, A/AC. 108/32.

71. Personal interview with Jaime Sigauke at Dar es Salaam, July 27, 1965; see also "A FRELIMO Top Leader Murdered in Lusaka [Zambial," *Information Bulletin* (Dar es Salaam), no. 2 (June-July 1966), p. 10. Simango's views have not been widely disseminated, but he presented a statement to the United Nations on June 7, 1962, while still a member of UDENAMO: see United Nations document A/AC. 109/SR. 69, pp. 12–14, for a summary of his statement.

72. According to the Portuguese bulletin *Notícias e Factos* (New York), November 5, 1969, Simango released a thirteen-page statement containing "a series of accusations" against Santos and Machel. He alleged that FRELIMO was divided by tribalism and regionalism and internal dissension. President Julius Nyerere of Tanzania was reportedly attempting to heal the differences. Prior to Dr. Mondlane's death, party dissension had been apparent. In Dar es Salaam during March 1968 rebellious students at the *Instituto Moçambicano* had forced the school's closing, and two months later a group of Mozambique Africans had raided the FRELIMO headquarters; the dissension was apparently caused by a young African Roman Catholic priest, Padre Mateus Gwenjere, who had escaped Mozambique to join the liberation movement but who had fallen out with Mondlane, according to Stanley Meisler, "Rebel Unit Split over Africa Goals: But Mozambique Leader Sees No Basic Problems," *Los Angeles Times*, June 30, 1968, final edition, section H, p. 3, col. 8, p. 4, col. 1, and p. 5, col. 8. The defection of Kavandame in April 1969 was followed in November by that of another member of the FRELIMO central committee, Alexandro Magno, according to a Portuguese report in *Notícias de Portugal*, vol. 23 (November 8, 1969), p. 2.

73. Gwambe's exclusion from FRELIMO may have been attributed to the fact that apparently he had earlier expelled Marcelino dos Santos from the UDENAMO. Gwambe's views on Mozambique are in "Dangers of New Colonialism in Mozambique," *Voice of Africa*, vol. 1 (November 1961), pp. 31–32. He also appeared before a United Nations investigating committee in Dar es Salaam on May 14, 1962, and his statement was recorded in document A/AC. 108/22.

74. Documents which describe these developments in detail include *Comité Secreto da Restauração de UDENAMO*, "Press Communiqué" (Kampala: mimeographed, May 14, 1963), and *União Democrática Nacional de Monomotapa*. Mozambique African National Union, and Mozambique African National Congress, "Declaration of Dissolution of FRELIMO" (Kampala: mimeographed, May 21, 1963).

75. For details on FUNIPAMO, see especially its "Draft Constitution and Rules" (Lampala: mimeographed, n.d.); "Declaration of Dissolution of FRELIMO" (Kampala: mimeographed, May 21, 1963); and "Memoranda Supporting Declaration of Dissolution of FRELIMO" (Kampala: mimeographed, May 27, 1963). Documents relevant to the activities of the UDENAMO-Mozambique include: *The UDENAMO at the United Nations* (Cairo: mimeographed, November 1963); *Constitution and Programme* (Cairo, 1963); and "Press Communiqué" (Cairo: mimeographed, August 22, 1963).

76. Documents on the formation of COREMO are its "Constituição," (Lusaka: mimeographed, 1965). Mondlane, in *The Struggle for Mozambique*, p. 131, claimed that the Lusaka and Cairo branches of COREMO "seem to be separated by ideological differences." As late as January, 1971 COREMO was reporting its military operations in Tete, Manilae Sofala, and Zambezi; see its official organ, *O Combatente* (Lusaka), vol. 4, no. 4 (January, 1971).

77. Mondlane, *The Struggle for Mozambique*, p. 131, alleged that "UNAR's programme aims at weakening the work of FRELIMO in the area between the two main rivers of north Mozambique, the Zambezi and the Rovuma."

78. The MANU-Khartoum was never significant and seems to have disappeared. Its position was stated in "The National Conference of MANU Held Successfully" (Khartoum: mimeographed, May 11, 1965). The personal story of Alberto-Joaquim Chipande, a guerrilla who participated in the September 25 uprising, is published in Mondlane, *The Struggle for Mozambique*, pp. 133–137; he describes the events culminating in the revolt. See the FRELIMO announcement of the revolt, "Proclamação ao povo Moçambicano," *Boletim Nacional* (Dar es Salaam), no. 13 (October 1964), pp. 2–3.

79. Details on FRELIMO's military operations in Mozambique are included in periodical communiqués and in various periodicals, including *Boletim de Informação* (issued monthly in Dar es Salaam since August 1963); *Boletim Nacional* (issued monthly in Dar es Salaam since September 1964); *Bulletin d'Information* (issued monthly in Algiers since January 1964); *Mozambique Revolution* (issued monthly in Dar es Salaam since December 1963 and also in New York City). Not reviewed by this writer but known to exist are *Voz da Revolução* and *25 de Setembro*, both issued by FRELIMO in Dar es Salaam.

80. Portuguese perspectives on the war, which are quite naturally very different from those of the nationalists, are revealed in military communiqués published in the Mozambican press. According to Mondlane in *The Struggle for Mozambique*, pp. 140–141, FRELIMO estimates of Portuguese casualties totaled nine thousand in the first three years of the war; he states that the Portuguese acknowledged four thousand casualties, including 378 soldiers killed as of mid-1967.

81. The advantages to the African guerrilla were identified and analyzed by Ayres d'Ornellas, *Colectanea das Suas Principais Obras Militares e Coloniais* (Lisbon: Agência Geral das Colonias, 1934), vol 2, pp. 169–171. Ornellas had been a military commander in the pacification campaigns at the turn of the century. A contemporary discussion of FRELIMO tactics and progress is in Glyn Hughs, "FRELIMO and the Mozambique War of Liberation," *Monthly Review*, vol. 20 no. 7 (December 1968), pp. 7–18.

82. Mondlane, *The Struggle for Mozambique*, p. 153. According to Regis Debray in *Revolution in the Revolution* (New York: Grove Press, 1967), p. 108, "A guerrilla force cannot develop on the military level if it does not become a political vanguard . . . the guerrilla movement, if it is to triumph militarily, must politically assemble around it the majority of the exploited classes." Drawing a fundamental lesson from the Cuban Revolution, Debray argues that the effectiveness of the guerrilla struggle is often dependent on the integration of the military and the political. Such a principle was not advocated by Lenin nor by Mao who placed their emphasis upon the revolutionary vanguard role of the party itself. Recent history, especially in Latin America, has demonstrated that traditional and well-established Marxist parties are less inclined to engage in revolutionary struggle. Thus the failure of the Bolivian Communist party to provide effective support to Ernesto "Ché" Guevara's guerrilla operations in Bolivia during 1967. The top FRELIMO leadership has tended to reside in Tanzania and periodically venture into northern Mozambique. If military decisions are dependent on this leadership, progress in the guerrilla war could be impeded by geographical distance and lack of familiarity with changing conditions in the field. The ultimate success of the guerrilla struggle may well depend on the full-time involvement of the FRELIMO political leadership in the military struggle.

83. A focus on U.S. policy is in Ronald H. Chilcote, "Angola or the Azores?" *New Republic* vol. 147 (July 30, 1962), pp. 21–22. Also see John Marcum, "Southern Africa and the United States Policy: A Consideration of Alternatives," in George W. Shepherd, Jr. (ed.), *Racial Influences on American Foreign Policy* (New York: Basic Books, 1970), pp. 186–219. Ties with the United States have resulted in involvement by the Central Intelligence Agency—namely, the supply of B-26 bombers to Portugal; see David Welsh, "Flyboys of the CIA," *Ramparts*, vol. 5, no. 6 (December 1966), pp. 11–18.

84. An up-to-date analysis of investments (domestic and foreign) in Mozambique is in "Activities of Foreign Economic and Other Interests Which are Impeding the Implementation of the Declaration on the Granting of Independence to Colonial Countries . . . ," (New York: United Nations Special Committee on the Situation with Regard to the Implementation of the Declaration on the Granting of Independence to Colonial Countries and Peoples, November 28, 1969), A/7752/Add. 1, especially pp. 48–96.

85. There is not much documentation on such manifestations in Mozambique. However, occasional reports from South Africa may be indicative. In an interesting analysis ("Portuguese Roots in Africa," *Optima* (Johannesburg), vol. 15, no. 1 [March 1965], p. 13) Austin Coates states: "Angola and Mozambique are not afraid of losing their Portuguese identity; it is Portugal who needs to be afraid of losing her identity in them." Edwin S. Munger (in "Mozambique: Uneasy Today, Uncertain Tomorrow," *American Universities Field Staff Reports Service*, Central Southern African series, vol. 9, no. 4 (1961), pp. 2, 18), considers three alternatives to the future of Mozambique, including the breakup of the territory with various regions going to Tanzania, Rhodesia, Malawi, and South Africa.

86. Mondlane, *The Struggle for Mozambique*, p. 162.

87. The dominant role of South Africa in the subordinate system of Southern Africa is fully discussed by Larry W. Bowman, "The Subordinate State System of Southern Africa," *International Studies Quarterly*, vol. 12, no. 3 (September 1968), pp. 231–261, especially pp. 238–240, 249 ff. on Mozambique.

88. Ralph Zacklin, "Challenge of Rhodesia," *International Conciliation*, 575 (November 1969), pp. 62–63.

89. "Une 'Entente' Aurait Eté Conclue entre le Portugal, l'Afrique du Sud et la Rhodésie pour la Défense de la Domination Blanche," *Le Monde* (Paris), September 14, 1965, dernière édition, p. 7, cols. 4–5 as translated in Mondlane, *The Struggle for Mozambique*, p. 202. The close ties between Portugal and Rhodesia appear to have been maintained, although an Associated Press dispatch reported that Portugal, bowing to British diplomatic pressures, was recalling its consul-general from Salisbury; reported in "Portugal to Sever Close Rhodesia Ties," *Los Angeles Times*, April 27, 1970, part 1, p. 4, cols. 2–3.

90. During July 1969 the United Nations Security Council censured Portugal for " . . . carrying out unprovoked raids against Zambia." See United Nations Security Council Resolution 268 (1969), July 28, 1969.

91. V. J. Mwaanga, "Letter Dated 28 July 1969 from the Permanent Representative of Zambia Addressed to the President of the Security Council" (New York: United Nations Security Council, July 28, 1969), S/9363.

92. A useful discussion of these nationalist movements is in John A. Marcum, "Three Revolutions," *Africa Report*, vol. 12, p. 6 (November 1967), pp. 8–22, and in his essay in the present volume.

93. "Statement, Support for the Movement ZAPU/ANC," *Mozambique Revolution*, no. 35 (June-September 1968), p. 22.

94. Immanuel Wallerstein, *The Politics of Unity: An Analysis of a Contemporary Social Movement* (New York: Random House, 1967), pp. 152–175.

95. Sharfudine Mohamed Khan, "Petition Submitted to the United Nations Fourth Committee" (New York: mimeographed, October 14, 1969).

CHAPTER 4

1. Joao Cabral, "Portugal's Rotting Empire," *The Nation*, vol. 192, no. 9 (March 1961), p. 183.

2. Richard Mathews, "A Visit to the Rebels of Angola," *The Reporter*, vol. 25, no. 5 (September 28, 1961), p. 41.

3. Patricia McGowan Pinheiro, "Politics of a Revolt," in *Angola: A Symposium: Views of a Revolt* (London: Oxford University Press, 1962), p. 116.

4. *Ibid.*, pp. 116–117.

5. John Marcum, *The Angolan Revolution: The Anatomy of an Explosion* (Cambridge, Mass.: M.I.T. Press, 1969), p. 138.

6. Ibid., p. 221.

7. John Marcum, "Three Revolutions," *Africa Report*, vol. 12, no. 8 (November 1967), p. 16.
8. *Ibid.*, p. 13.
9. MPLA was formed by leaders of various African organizations.
10. Ronald Segal, *Political Africa: A Who's Who of Personalities and Parties* (New York: Frederick A. Praeger, 1961), pp. 62–63.
11. James Duffy, *Portuguese Africa* (Cambridge, Mass.: Harvard University Press, 1959), p. 214.
12. The quotations in this paragraph are from Marcum, *Angolan Revolution*, pp. 36, 43.
13. Antonio De Figueiredo, "The Case Against Portugal," in *Angola: A Symposium: Views of a Revolt*, p. 56.
14. As quoted in *Ibid.*
15. *Ibid.*, p. 111.
16. Marcum, *Angolan Revolution*, p. 262.
17. *Ibid.*, pp. 145–146.
18. *Ibid.*, p. 263.
19. Basil Davidson, "Phase Two in Angola," *West Africa* (London), no. 2382 (January 26, 1963), p. 87.
20. Marcum, *Angolan Revolution*, p. 266.
21. As quoted in *Ibid.*, p. 308.
22. Marcum, "Three Revolutions," p. 12.
23. Helen Kitchen, "Conversation with Eduardo Mondlane," *Africa Report* vol. 12, no. 8 (November 1967), p. 50.
24. Conversation with Daniel Chirembas of Mozambique.
25. Frantz Fanon, *Toward the African Revolution* (New York: Grove Press, 1967), p. 186. See also his *The Wretched of the Earth* (New York: Grove Press, 1966), pp. 121–122 and *Black Skin, White Masks* (New York: Grove Press, 1967).
26. Kwame Nkrumah, *Revolutionary Warfare* (New York: International Publishers, 1968), p. 42.
27. Samuel B. Griffith (ed.), *Mao Tse-tung On Guerrilla Warfare* (New York: Frederick A. Praeger, 1961), p. 78.
28. Mao Tse-tung, *Selected Military Writings* (Peking: Foreign Language Press, 1963), p. 169.
29. *Ibid.*, p. 261.
30. Nkrumah, *op. cit.*, p. 28.
31. Griffith, *op. cit.*, p. 80.
32. Che Guevara, *Guerrilla Warfare* (New York: Monthly Review Press, 1961), p. 7.
33. Griffith, *op. cit.*, p. 46.
34. Maina Kagombe, "The Implications of Fidelism in the Western Hemisphere," *Pan-African Journal*, vol. 2, no. 1 (1969), pp. 26–45.
35. Regis Debray, *Revolution in the Revolution* (New York: Monthly Review Press, 1967), p. 75.
36. Amilcar Cabral, in a recent interview with the author, pointed out that the peaceful demonstration which he led in 1959 during a dock workers' strike was brutally crushed by the Portuguese and taught him that "power grows out of the barrel of a gun." Following this, he went into exile to organize the guerrillas and to return to the countryside for armed action.
37. The correct and objective history of the Mau Mau has yet to be written. I am writing here from my own experience of Mau Mau or from contact with participants. There are a few articles and books which might be of interest to the reader; Maina Kagombe, "Kikuyu Studies; A Case of Conflict and Violence," *Pan-African Journal*, vol. 3, no. 1 (1970), pp. 3–13; Carl Rosberg, Jr. and John Nottingham, *The Myth of "Mau-Mau": Nationalism in Kenya* (New York: Frederick A. Praeger, 1961); and Donald Barnett and Karari Njama. *Mau Mau from Within* (New York: Monthly Review Press, 1966).
38. As quoted in Basil Davidson, *The Liberation of Guiné* (Baltimore: Penguin Books, 1969), p. 127.
39. Debray, *op. cit.*, p. 20.
40. Jomo Kenyatta, *Facing Mount Kenya* (New York: Vintage Books, 1968).
41. Thomas Patrick Melady, *The White Man's Future in Black Africa* (New York: Macfadden-Bartell Corp., 1962), p. 172.
42. For a further expansion of these points see Maina Kagombe, "Does America Love Africa?", *Pan African Journal*, vol. 2, no. 1 (1969), p. 3–5.
43. West Germany, for example, has a bilateral agreement with Portugal allowing wounded soldiers from Angola, Mozambique, and Guinea to be treated in west German hospitals. See Basil Davidson, "Arms and the Portuguese: What Kinds of Aid Does Portugal Get From Its NATO Allies, and What Is Its Role in the Colonial Wars?" *Africa Report*, vol. 15, no. 5 (May 1970), p. 11.
44. *Ibid.*

PART FIVE CHAPTER 1

1. According to the 1966 population census, Malawi's population was 4,042,412, giving it a population density of 117 per square mile. Malawi, *Malawi 1968* (Blantyre: Malawi Department of Information, 1969), p. 12.
2. Hierarchical systems distribute authority along bureaucratic or military lines with subordinate authorities having power at the leader's pleasure. Malawi's traditional political systems are generally more pyramidal—that is, "each of the levels represents segmental groupings organized on the basis of kinship" and "for each segment the powers of the chief or the equivalent are more or less identical." Apter categorizes traditional value structures as instrumental and noninstrumental or consummatory. The former is "characterized by a large sector of intermediate ends separate from and independent of ultimate ends," while the latter involves "a close relationship between intermediate and ultimate ends." (David E. Apter, *The Politics of Modernization* [Chicago and London: University of Chicago Press, 1965], pp. 92–93, 85–87.)
3. Clyde Sanger, "Nyasaland Becomes Malawi: An Assessment," *Africa Report*, vol. 9, no. 8 (August 1964), p. 8; see also Guy Clutton-Brock, *Dawn in Nyasaland* (London: Hodder & Stoughton, 1959), p. 21.
4. For further discussion of this point see Samuel W. Speck, Jr., *African Local Governance in Malawi: Its Development and Politics under British Rule* (Cambridge, Mass.: Harvard University, unpublished Ph.D. dissertation, 1967), pp. 72–76.
5. Less than one-half of 1 percent of the population is non-African. According to the 1966 census there were some 10,880 Asians and 7,046 Europeans (*Malawi 1968*, p. 12).
6. Speck, *op. cit.*, pp. 32–35; "Asian Traders Advised to Help Africans," *Malawi News* (Limbe), August 26, 1969, p. 1, col. 3.
7. John G. Pike, *Malawi: A Political and Economic History* (New York: Frederick A. Praeger, 1968), p. 218.

8. Griff Jones, *Britain and Nyasaland* (London: George Allen & Unwin, 1964), p. 262.

9. See Pike, *op. cit.*, pp. 207–214, for a discussion of Malawi's acute transportation problems.

10. No mineral extractive industries of consequence have been developed, although the cheap electric power of the Cabora Bassa projects in Mozambique promises to make the mining of bauxite economically feasible.

11. Dr. Kamuzu Banda, "Why Malawi Ministers Visited S.A. and Portugal," supplement to *Malawi News*, March 31, 1967, p. 3, col. 1.

12. This is covered in the section of this Chapter headed "Economic Relations with Southern Africa since Independence."

13. *Evolué* is a useful French term which has recently come into usage in American social science writing. Literally, it means one who is "in advance" of his time or "has reached a certain advanced degree of civilization." (See *Larousse Classique* [Paris: Librarie Larousse, 1957], p. 435.) As applied here, *évolué* refers to an African who had attained literacy and other marks of Western culture and who favored emphasizing achievemental rather than ascriptive criteria in political recruitment and pragmatic rather than immemorial prescriptive norms in validating human behavior. See Apter, *op. cit.*, p. 83.

14. See Speck, *op. cit.*, pp. 461–463.

15. The central provincial commissioner, in his letter of May 4, 1955, advised the secretary for African affairs that "no matter how inefficient some Chiefs may be, we should nevertheless bolster them until such time as we have more moderate and balanced commoners available." (Secretariat SMP 11680, II, Malawi Archives, Zomba.)

16. See Speck, *op. cit.*, pp. 53–61; Robert I. Rotberg, *The Rise of Nationalism in Central Africa: The Making of Malawi and Zambia, 1873–1964* (Cambridge, Mass.: Harvard University Press, 1966); George Shepperson and Thomas Price, *Independent African: John Chilembwe and the Origins, setting, and significance of the Nyasaland Native Rising of 1915* (Edinburgh: Edinburgh University Press, 1958); George Shepperson, "Nyasaland and the Millennium," in Sylvia L. Thrupp (ed.), *Millennial Dreams in Action* (The Hague: Mouton, 1962), pp. 144–159; J. van Velsen, "Some Early Pressure Groups in Nyasaland," paper presented at Seventeenth Conference of Rhodes Livingstone Institute, Lusaka, Northern Rhodesia, 1963; Roger K. Tangri, "The Rise of Nationalism in Colonial Africa: The Case of Colonial Malawi," *Comparative Studies in Society and History*, vol. 10, no. 2 (January 1968), pp. 142–161.

17. Lord Hailey, *Native Administration in the British African Territories*, Part II (London: HMSO, 1950), p. 73.

18. Great Britain. Colonial Office, *Report of the Nyasaland Commission of Inquiry* (Devlin Report), Cmd. 814 (London: HMSO, 1959), pp. 12–13.

19. Five of the other upper roll seats were won by the settler-dominated United Federal Party and the other seat was won by an MCP-oriented independent. There was no appreciable opposition to the MCP among Africans.

20. Lucy Mair, *The Nyasaland Election of 1961* (London: Athlone Press, 1962), p. 38. See also "Minister Tells People To Grow Cash Crops," *Malawi News* (Limbe), August 22, 1969, p. 4, col. 4.

21. Malawi has one of the highest ratios of expatriate officers relative to the size of its army of any independent African state and Dr. Banda has indicated he envisages white control of the army and police for same years to come. (See J. M. Lee, *African Armies and Civil Order* [New York and Washington: Frederick A. Praeger, 1969], pp. 5, 13.)

22. See Maurice Duverger, *Political Parties*, 2nd rev. ed., translated by Barbara and Robert North (London: Methuen, 1959), p. xxiv.

23. See Aristide R. Zolberg, *Creating Political Order* (Chicago: Rand McNally, 1966), especially pp. 128–150, 157, for a discussion of a similar phenomenon in West African party structures.

24. "As Head, My People Come First," *Malawi News*, April 4, 1967, p. 1, col. 6.

25. Malawi Congress Party, *Rules and Regulations Governing the Discipline of the Malawi Congress Party* (Limbe: Malawi Press, 1962), p. 5.

26. "Dr. Banda Speaks to Young Pioneers," *The Times* (Blantyre), May 19, 1964, p. 3, col. 4.

27. Lee, *op. cit.*, p. 152.

28. "Police Cannot Arrest Pioneers," *The Times* (Blantyre), November 12, 1965, p. 1, col. 6.

29. Bridglal Pachai, "Constitutional Progress in Malawi," *Africa Quarterly* (New Delhi), vol. 6, no. 1 (April–June 1966), pp. 11–16.

30. For a discussion of the split which is sympathetic to the rebels, see Chimwene Wange [pseud.], "The Littlest Revolution," *Africa Today*, vol. 12, no. 4 (April 1965), pp. 5–9; and Rotberg, *The Rise of Nationalism in Central Africa*, pp. 317–321. For a critical view of Rotberg's interpretation see "Author Was Bias [*sic*]," *Malawi News*, April 15, 1966, p. 1, col. 2. The case against the rebels is well chronicled in the *Malawi News*. Pike, *op. cit.*, pp. 163–171, offers a moderately pro-Banda narrative of the crisis.

31. For a critical appraisal of Dr. Banda's reaction to the crisis see "Malawi Since Independence," *Bulletin of the International Commission of Jurists* (Geneva), no. 27 (September 1966) pp. 20–27. See also Henry J. Richardson III, "Malawi: Between White and Black Africa," *Africa Report*, vol. 15, no. 2 (February 1970), pp. 18–21.

32. A. J. Hanna, *The Beginnings of Nyasaland and North-Eastern Rhodesia, 1859–95* (Oxford: Clarendon Press, 1956), pp. 133–172.

33. Richard Gray, *The Two Nations: Aspects of the Development of Race Relations in the Rhodesias and Nyasaland* (London: Oxford University Press, 1960), p. 94.

34. *Ibid.*, p. 121.

35. *Ibid.*, pp. 120–127; William J. Barber, *The Economy of British Central Africa* (London: Oxford University Press, 1961), p. 80; and Lord Hailey, *op cit.*, p. 19.

36. See C. A. Baker, "Malawi's Exports: An Economic History," in B. Pachai, G. W. Smith, and R. K. Tangri (eds.), *Malawi Past and Present* (Blantyre: University of Malawi, 1968), pp. 77–94.

37. For additional examples of increased cooperation between Malawi and Southern Rhodesia, see A. J. Hanna, *The Story of the Rhodesias and Nyasaland* (London: Faber & Faber, 1960), p. 249.

38. For a discussion of these pressures see Robert I. Rotberg, "The Federation Movement in British East and Central Africa, 1889–1953," *Journal of Commonwealth Political Studies* (Leicester, England) vol. 2 (May 1964), pp. 141–160.

39. Norman H. Pollock, *Nyasaland and Northern*

Rhodesia, 1889–1924 (Philadelphia: University of Pennsylvania, unpublished Ph.D. dissertation, 1948), p. 457.

40. Gray, *op. cit.*, pp. 6–7, 37–38.

41. Great Britain. Rhodesia–Nyasaland Royal Commission, *Report*. Cmd. 5949 (London: HMSO, 1939) (The Bledisloe Report).

42. *Ibid.*, pp. 213–216.

43. See, for example, the statement of the colonial secretary, Oliver Lyttleton, as quoted in Jones, *op. cit.*, p. 145.

44. Rotberg, *The Rise of Nationalism in Central Africa*, pp. 155–156; Hanna, *The Story of the Rhodesias and Nyasaland*, p. 266; and Jones, *op. cit.*, p. 133.

45. Philip Mason, *Year of Decision: Rhodesia and Nyasaland in 1960* (London: Oxford University Press, 1960), p. 257.

46. W. V. Brelsford (ed.), *Handbook to the Federation of Rhodesia and Nyaslaand* (London: Cassell, 1960), pp. 678–679; see also Patrick Keatley, *The Politics of Partnership* (Baltimore: Penguin Books, 1963), p. 368.

47. See Keatley, *op. cit.*, pp. 337–384; Pike, *op. cit.*, p. 182; Arthur Hazelwood, "The Economics of Federation and Dissolution in Central Africa," in Arthur Hazelwood (ed.), *African Integration and Disintegration* (London: Oxford University Press, 1967), pp. 205–207.

48. Hazelwood, *op. cit.*, p. 217.

49. *Ibid.*, p. 244; "Rhodesian Trade Agreement Is Ended," *The Times* (Blantyre), November 19, 1965, p. 1, col. 2.

50. "Nyasulu Speaks at U.N. 21st Session of the General Assembly," *Malawi News*, October 18, 1966, p. 2, col. 7.

51. This trend was also accelerated by Malawi's move to devalue its currency while Rhodesia refused to follow the British example.

52. Among other projects, South Africa has financed an $8.4 million sugar factory on the understanding that at least 60 percent of all materials used in the mill construction be of South African origin, made over an $11 million loan to begin the new Malawi capital at Lilongwe on the condition that maximum use be made of South African contractors and materials, and extended in excess of $14 million credit to build the Malawi rail link to Mozambique on similar conditions. See "Agriculture, Forestry, and Fisheries," *Africa Research Bulletin: Economic, Financial, and Technical Series* (Exeter, England), vol. 3, no. 2 (March 31, 1966), p. 468 [hereafter cited as *ARBEFTS*]; "South Africa–Malawi: Loan for New Capital," *ARBEFTS*, vol. 5, no. 4 (May 31, 1968), p. 996; and "Malawi–South Africa: Rail Construction Loan," *ARBEFTS*, vol. 5, no. 4 (May 31, 1968), p. 1014.

53. "Malawi–South Africa, Trade Agreement," *ARBEFTS*, vol. 4, no. 2 (March 31, 1967), p. 690; and "Malawi–South Africa: Further Details of Trade Agreement," *ARBEFTS*, vol. 4, no. 3 (April 30, 1967), p. 710.

54. "Organization of African Unity (OAU)—Fourth Ordinary Session of the Assembly of Heads of State and Government," *Africa Research Bulletin: Political, Social, and Cultural Series* (Exeter, England), vol. 4, no. 9 (October 15, 1967), p. 854. [Hereafter cited as *ARBPSCS*.]

55. "South Africa–Malawi: Dr. Muller's Visit," *ARBPSCS*, vol. 5, no. 8 (September 15, 1968), p. 1144.

56. *Malawi, 1968*, p. 18; G. M. E. Leistner, "Foreign Bantu Workers in South Africa: Their Present Position in the Economy," *South African Journal of Economics* (Johannesburg), vol. 35, no. 1 (March 1967), p. 52.

57. "Malawi–South Africa: Increased Trade", *ARBEFTS*, vol. 5, no. 12 (January 31, 1969), p. 1221.

58. "U.K. Sanctions and Counter Measures," *ARBEFTS*, vol. 2, no. 11 (December 31, 1965), p. 402; and "Moves by Smith Regime," *ARBEFTS*, vol. 3, no. 3 (March 31, 1966), p. 461.

59. Davis M'Gabe, "Rhodesia's African Majority," *Africa Report*, vol. 12, no. 2 (February 1967), pp. 14–20.

60. Malawi. Department of Census and Statistics, *Annual Statement of External Trade, 1968*, pp. 1, 5.

61. *Republic of Malawi, Public Sector Financial Statistics, 1969* (Zomba: Government Printer, 1969), Table A.23.

62. "We Welcome Businessmen To Do Business," *Malawi News*, October 31, 1967, p. 2, col. 4.

63. "Africa's Most Unpopular Leaders Meet," *The Times* (Blantyre), May 16, 1967, p. 1, col. 1.

64. Dr. Kamuzu Banda, "President Speaks at Tea Association Annual Dinner," supplement to *Malawi News*, February 21, 1967, p. 4, col. 1.

65. *Malawi, 1968*, p. 5.

66. Dr. Kamuzu Banda, "Why Malawi Ministers Visited S.A. and Portugal," supplement to *Malawi News*, March 31, 1967, p. 4, cols. 1–4.

67. "Malawi—Diplomatic Relations with South Africa," *ARBPSCS*, vol. 4, no. 9 (October 15, 1967), p. 858 (italics added).

68. "Organization of African Unity—Summit Conference," *ARBPSCS*, vol. 2, no. 10 (November 16, 1965), p. 379.

69. "Rhodesia," *ARBPSCS*, vol. 3, no. 4 (May 16, 1966), p. 516.

70. "Madagascar—Malawi: President Tsiranana's Visit," *ARBPSCS*, vol. 6, no. 4 (May 15, 1969), p. 1374.

71. See "Malawi Mission Changes South African Minds," *Malawi News*, April 11, 1967, p. 1, col. 2.

72. See I. William Zartman, *International Relations in the New Africa* (Englewood Cliffs, N.J.: Prentice-Hall, 1966), p. 77.

73. " 'We Will Have Allies Across the Border,' " *Malawi News*, July 4, 1967, p. 1, col. 4.

74. There has been speculation that the Portuguese might eventually cede northern Mozambique to Malawi. After a visit of four Malawi government ministers to Lisbon in early 1968, the Portuguese foreign minister felt it necessary to deny that Portugal was contemplating transferring "Portuguese" territories to Malawi. Later, however, Dr. Banda alluded to Malawi's boundary as being the Indian Ocean. Malawi of course, may simply have been using Portugal in its heated boundary feud with Tanzania. See "Portuguese Overseas Territories," *ARBPSCS*, vol. 5, no. 3 (April 15, 1968), pp. 1020–1121; and "Malawi—U.R. Tanzania/Zambia: Statements on Boundary Dispute," *ARBPSCS*, vol. 5, no. 9 (October 15, 1968), p. 1178.

75. Malawi's closeness to Israel stems not only from the amount of aid that the latter has given to Malawi but also from the timing of it. When, for example, at the end of federation, the federal doctors largely withdrew from Malawi, threatening the country with a nearly complete breakdown in medical services, Israel stepped forward with interim medical staffing.

76. Dr. Kamuzu Banda, "President Speaks at Tea

Association Annual Dinner," supplement to *Malawi News*, February 21, 1967, p. 4, col. 4.

77. "Pioneers Are Superior to University Students," *Malawi News*, March 10, 1967, p. 1, col. 2.

78. A zero-sum game situation denotes an interaction between two actors in which one of them necessarily loses if the other gains. In a non-zero-sum game situation both players may benefit from the interaction, although possibly by different degrees.

79. Dr. Kamuzu Banda, "President Speaks at Tea Association Annual Dinner," supplement to *Malawi News*, February 21, 1967, p. 4, col. 4.

CHAPTER 2

1. South Africa. Parliament. House of Assembly, *Debates*, vol. 6, col. 4599 (April 23, 1963).

2. South African Permanent Mission to the United Nations, New York, Fact Sheets, *A Collection of Factual Summaries of the Views and Statements of the Government of the Republic of South Africa on Issues before the United Nations* (Pretoria: Government Printer, n.d.), p. 4.

3. Roughly 1:5 in South Africa and 1:19 in Rhodesia.

4. As quoted in "Catholic Pastoral's Warning on Race Legislation Trend: Rhodesian Hierarchy and Land Tenure Act, *Southern Africa* (London), vol. 82 (March 28, 1970), p. 180.

5. In relation to the franchise, "civilization" was defined in terms of property, income, and education. These were, of course, related to European achievements and standards which Africans did not share. In the words of Reverend Ndabaningi Sithole, an African nationalist leader, "to expect a man to qualify on what he hasn't, is really to expect him not to qualify at all." He added that "Qualified franchise in this country is virtually 'one man one vote for the white man.' " Rev. Ndabaningi Sithole, "Our Franchise: A Historical Background,' *The Central African Daily News* (Salisbury) April 4, 1962, 1st edition, p. 4, cols. 5–7.

6. There is an extensive literature on the federation. For contrasting views see Sir Roy Welensky, *4,000 Days* (London: Collins, 1964); C. Leys and C. Pratt (eds.), *A New Deal in Central Africa* (London: Heinemann, 1960); Lord Alport, *Sudden Assignment* (London: Hodder & Stoughton, 1965); P. Mason, *Year of Decision* (London: Oxford University Press, 1960); and P. Keatley, *The Politics of Partnership* (Baltimore: Penguin Books, 1963).

7. Malawi, unlike Zambia, later accepted a close relationship with the "white" states.

8. There have been several African nationalist parties, but all have been banned by the government. The main parties which have existed, with dates of banning are: African National Congress (1959), National Democratic party (1961), Zimbabwe African Peoples' Union (1963), and Zimbabwe African National Union (1963). "Zimbabwe" is the name African nationalists have given to Rhodesia.

9. For conflicting views of the nationalists' action see L. J. MacFarlane, "Justifying Rebellion: Black and White Nationalism in Rhodesia," *Journal of Commonwealth Political Studies* (Leicester, England) vol. 6, no. 1 (March, 1968), pp. 54–79; and Richard Brown, "A Comment on L. J. MacFarlane's 'Justifying Rebellion: Black and White Nationalism in Rhodesia'," *Journal of Commonwealth Political Studies*, vol. 6, no. 2 (July 1968), pp. 155–161.

10. For an account of its organization see Larry Bowman, "Strains in the Rhodesian Front," *Africa Report*, vol. 13, no. 9 (December 1968), pp. 16–20; and "Organisation, Power, and Decision-Making within the Rhodesian Front," *Journal of Commonwealth Political Studies*, vol. 7, no. 2 (July 1969), pp. 145–165.

11. "Six Year Sentence Passed on Sithole: ZANU Leader Found Guilty of Incitement to Murder Rhodesian Ministers," *Southern Africa*, vol. 81 (February 15, 1969), p. 102.

12. For accounts of the negotiations see James Barber, *Rhodesia: The Road to Rebellion* (London: Oxford University Press, 1967) and "Rhodesia: The Constitutional Conflict," *Journal of Modern African Studies*, vol. 4, no. 4 (December, 1966), pp. 457–469.

13. Five principles were laid down by the British in September 1965. These were: "(1) The principle and intention of unimpeded progress to majority rule, already explained in the 1961 Constitution, would have to be maintained and guaranteed. (2) There would also have to be guarantees against retrogressive amendments of the Constitution. (3) There would have to be immediate improvement in the political status of the African population. (4) There would have to be progress toward ending racial discrimination. (5) The British government would need to be satisfied that any basis proposed for independence was acceptable to the people of Rhodesia as a whole." (As quoted in Barber, *Road to Rebellion*, p. 301.) Mr. Harold Wilson, the British prime minister, announced a sixth principle to the House of Commons on January 25, 1966. This was "the need to ensure that, regardless of race, there is no oppression of majority by minority or of minority by majority" (Great Britain. Parliament. House of Commons, *Debates*, 5th Series, vol. 723, col. 42).

14. *Proposals for a New Constitution for Rhodesia* (Salisbury: Government Printer, May 1969). The proposals were supported by a 73 percent vote in a referendum on June 19, 1969. In the same referendum the declaration of a republic received 82 percent support.

15. For an account of the rejection of a constitutional settlement recommended by a commission in Rhodesia, see P. J. Harris, "The Failure of a Constitution: The Whaley Report, Rhodesia 1968," *International Affairs* (London), vol. 45, no. 2 (April 1969), pp. 234–245.

16. "Ian Smith Spells It Out: Votes for Some," *Daily Express* (London), June 6, 1969, p. 1, col. 7.

17. As quoted in "Rhodesia: New Constitution." *International Defence and Aid Fund Information Service. I. Political & Social* (London). no. 7 (January–July, 1969), p. 301.

18. Bowman, "Organization . . . within the Rhodesian Front," p. 146.

19. A. P. Thornton, *For the File an Empire* (London: The Macmillan Company, 1968), pp. 370–371.

20. South Africa. Parliament. House of Assembly, *Debates*, vol. 15, col. 7280 (June 4, 1965) for both quotations in this paragraph.

21. At least, that is how they perceived their position.

22. Colin Legum and John Drysdale (eds.), *Africa Contemporary Record: Annual Survey and Documents, 1969–1970* (Exeter, England: Africa Research Limited, 1970), p. B247.

23. *Ibid.*

24. "S.A. is Zambia's Chief Supplier," *The Star*, (Johan-

nesburg), August 7, 1968, 2nd city late ed., p. 31, cols. 8–9.

25. As quoted in "News in Brief: Zambia: Tazama Pipeline Opened," *Africa Report*, vol. 13, no. 8 (November 1968), pp. 26–27.

26. R. B. Sutcliffe, "The Political Economy of Rhodesian Sanctions," *Journal of Comonwealth Political Studies*, vol. 7, no. 2 (July 1969), pp. 113–125.

27. South Africa. Parliament. House of Assembly, *Debates*, vol. 16, col. 53 (January 25, 1966).

28. For this section I have drawn on Professor Robert McKinnell's article, "Sanctions and the Rhodesian Economy," *Journal of Modern African Studies*, vol. 7, no. 4 (December, 1969), pp. 559–581.

29. *Ibid.*, p. 574.

30. See "Rhodesia: Constitutional Referendum," "*Africa Research Bulletin: Political, Social, and Cultural Series* (Exeter, England), vol. 6, no. 6 (July 15, 1969), p. 1449.

31. As quoted in " 'Seig Heils' as Mr Smith seeks Public Support," *The Guardian* (London and Manchester), June 19, 1969, city ed., p. 3, cols. 3–7.

32. "Mr Brown Endorses US Vietnam Stand: Wide Policy Review in UN Speech," *The Times* (London), September 27, 1967, late London ed. p. 4, cols. 4–5.

33. Quoted in Patrick Keatley, "The Battle for Africa. III. The Chinese on the Right Track," in *The Guardian*, July 18, 1969, city ed., p. 11, cols. 4–7. In a series of five articles Keatley emphasized the increasing Chinese influence in Africa and especially in the confrontation with white Southern Africa.

34. As quoted in Ralph Cohen, "Terrorist Suspected by Botswana Police Patrol: 9 Held in Border Swoop: Charges of 'Illegal Entry'," *Rand Daily Mail* (Johannesburg), August 22, 1967, morning final ed., p. 1, cols. 1–2.

35. "South Africa: African Nationalist Guer[r]illas," *International Defence and Aid Fund Information Service. I. Political & Social*, no. 3 (October-December, 1967), p. 81.

36. "ANC-ZAPU Alliance," *Sechaba* (Dar-es-Salaam), vol. 1, no. 10 (October, 1967), p. 3.

37. "SA Help Veg in Rhod.: Premier Onthul: Rooi Spioen Hier Gevang," *Die Transvaler* (Johannesburg), September 9, 1967, p. 1, cols. 1–3.

38. As quoted in "S.A. Police Will Stay, Until . . .," *The Star*, September 12, 1968, 2nd city late ed., p. 21, cols. 5–7.

39. "Death Toll of 172 in Rhodesia," *The Times* December 27, 1968, late London ed., p. 4, col. 6.

40. According to "Rhodesia: African Nationalist Guer[r]illas," *International Defence and Aid Fund Information Service. I. Political & Social*, no. 5 (April–June 1968), p. 188.

41. As quoted in *ibid.*

42. Alan Rake, "Black Guerrillas in Rhodesia," *Africa Report* vol. 13, no. 9 (December, 1968) pp. 23–26.

43. Zdenek Cervenka, *The Organisation of African Unity and Its Charter* (London: C. Hurst, 1969), p. 18.

44. "Kaunda Warning to Rhodesia: 'Your Children Will Pay'," *The Times*, February 5, 1968, late London ed., p. 5, cols. 6–7.

45. For South Africa see Leonard M. Thompson, *Politics in the Republic of South Africa* (Boston and Toronto: Little, Brown, 1966). For Rhodesia see James Barber, *Rhodesia: The Road to Rebellion* (London: Oxford University Press, 1967).

46. For a discussion on the effect of sanctions see T. R. C. Curtin, "Rhodesian Economic Development under Sanctions," *African Affairs* (London), (April 1968) vol. 67, no. 267, pp. 100–110; and R. T. McKinnell, "Assessing the Economic Impact of Sanctions against Rhodesia," *African Affairs*, vol. 67, no. 268 (July 1968), pp. 227–232.

47. See Ronald Segal (ed.), *Sanctions against South Africa* (Baltimore: Penguin Books, 1964). For a less committed evaluation see Dennis Austin, *Britain and South Africa* (London: Oxford University Press, 1968).

48. For statistics of continuing direct trade with Rhodesia see McKinnell, "Rhodesian Economy," p. 578. McKinnell's figures are for direct trade and not the trade which is routed via South Africa and Portugal.

49. See John Day, *International Nationalism* (London: Routledge & Kegan Paul, 1968), for a description of the efforts made by the Rhodesian nationalists.

50. John Worrall, "Rhodesia's Faith in Black Troops: Africans Man the Zambezi Defence Line," *The Guardian*, April 26, 1968, city ed., p. 11, cols. 1–3.

51. Ndabaningi Sithole, *African Nationalism*. 2nd ed. (London: Oxford University Press, 1968), p. 43.

52. *Ibid.*, p. 42, capitalization in the original.

53. "Smith's Former Army Chief Turns Critic," *The Times*, June 2, 1969, late London ed., p. 4, cols. 6–7.

54. "The Future of Southern Africa," *The Guardian*, May 28, 1969, city ed., p. 6, cols. 1–4.

CHAPTER 3

1. According to "Southern Africa: Black Man's War," *The Economist* (London), vol. 231, no. 6559 (May 10, 1969), p. 31.

2. These passages are from the "Lusaka Manifesto on Southern Africa: Joint Statement by Thirteen Governments, Lusaka (April 1969), "as reprinted in Colin Legum and John Drysdale (eds.), *Africa Contemporary Record: Annual Survey and Documents, 1969–1970* (Exeter, England: Africa Research Limited, 1970), p. C42. The quoted passages constitute paragraphs 10–12 of this reprinted document.

3. Speech by Mr. Michael Stewart, foreign and Commonwealth secretary before the United Nations General Assembly, September 22, 1969 (United Nations. General Assembly. 24th Session. *Provisional Verbatim Record of the 1759th Meeting, September 22, 1969.* A/PV 1759, p. [*sic*] 33–35).

4. United Nations Security Council Resolution 232 (1966). (December 16, 1966).

5. United Nations Security Council Resolution 253 (1968). (May 29, 1968).

6. United Nations General Assembly Resolution 2383 (XXIII) (November 7, 1968).

7. "Police Escort Crowd to Camp after Protest at DC's Office: Tangwena Leaders Moved: Dawn Operation Evicts Inyanga Tribesmen," *The Chronicle* (Bulawayo), September 19, 1969, p. 1, col. 3.

8. Speech by Mr. E. H. K. Mudenda, Zambian minister of development and finance, before the United Nations General Assembly, September 23, 1969 (United Nations. General Assembly. 24th Session, *Provisional Verbatim Record of the 1762nd Meeting, September 23, 1969.* A/PV 1762, p. 28).

9. *Ibid.*, p. 31.

10. United Nations General Assembly Resolution 2325 (XXII) (December 16, 1967).

11. Letter dated May 27, 1968 from the President of the United Nations Council for South West Africa to the President of the Security Council. Doc. S/8600/Rev. 1, May 29, 1968 (United Nations. Security Council, *Official Records. 23rd Year. Supplement for April, May, and June, 1968* [New York: United Nations, 1969], pp. 172–174).

12. United Nations Security Council Resolution 269 (August 12, 1969).

13. "Lusaka Manifesto," in Legum and Drysdale, *op. cit.*, p. C44. The quoted passage is from paragraph 19 of this reprinted document.

14. Malawi is not considered a hostage state because of her geographical access to the African states to the north.

PART SIX CHAPTER 1

1. CIAS/Plen. 2/Rev. 2, A: Agenda Item II, Addis Ababa, May, 1963. (This is the standard documentary citation of the revised document number 2, presented for the second item at the Second Plenary Meeting of the Conference of Independent African States held at Addis Ababa in May 1963.)

2. "South and South West Africa: South African Police Deal with African Nationalist Infiltrators in South West Africa: Other Internal Security Developments," *Keesing's Contemporary Archives* (Bristol, England), vol. no. 16 (1967–1968), p. 21970.

3. CM/Res. 154 (XI), para. 4, Algiers, September 1968. (This is the standard documentary citation of Resolution 154 presented at the Eleventh Session of the OAU Council of Ministers held at Algiers in September 1968.)

4. Karl von Clausewitz, *War Politics and Power*. Translated and edited by Edward M. Collins (Chicago: Henry Regnery, 1965), p. 171.

5. *Ibid.*

6. CIAS/Plen. 2/Rev. 2, A: Agenda Item II, para. 11, Addis Ababa, May 1963; and AHG/Res. 38 (II), para. 7, Accra, October, 1965. The latter is the standard documentary citation of Resolution 38 presented at the second session of the OAU Assembly of Heads of State and Government. In May 1963, the committee consisted of nine members to which Somalia and Zambia were added in October 1965.

7. CIAS/Plen. 2/Rev. 2, A: Agenda Item II, para. 11, Addis Ababa, May 1963.

8. The above information is based on Jack Halpern, *South African Hostages: Basutoland, Bechuanaland and Swaziland* (Baltimore: Penguin Books, 1965), pp. 135–425, and on Peter Robson, "Economic Integration in Southern Africa," *Journal of Modern African Studies* vol. 5, no. 4 (December 1967), pp. 469–490.

9. This phrase is the title of Jack Halpern's book cited in footnote 8 *supra*.

10. J. E. Spence, *Lesotho: The Politics of Dependence* (London: Oxford University Press, 1968), p. 44.

11. South Africa. Parliament. Senate, Debates, *1964*, vol. 3, cols. 4702–4703.

12. Yashpal Tandon and T. M. Shaw, *Contrasting Attitudes and Behaviour Towards Southern Africa: Tanzania and Malawi*. University Social Science Committee Conference Papers (Makerere: mimeo, December 1968), p. 24.

13. Julius K. Nyerere, *Freedom and Socialism: Uhuru na Ujamaa: A Selection from Writings and Speeches, 1965–1967* (London, Oxford, New York: Oxford University Press 1968), p. 380.

14. *Daily Nation* (Nairobi), May 20, 1968, p. 20, col. 2.

15. "Mr Smith in South Africa," (editorial), *East African Standard* (Nairobi), July 30, 1968, p. 4, cols. 1–2.

16. *Ibid.*

17. Nyerere, *op. cit.*, p. 374.

18. *Ibid.*

19. Broadcast message to the United Nations, October 24, 1963, Julius K. Nyerere, *Freedom and Unity: Uhuru Na Umoja* (Dar es Salaam: Oxford University Press, 1967), p. 228.

20. "Black Liberators Made in Moscow," *Sunday Telegraph* (London), May 11, 1969, p. 6, cols. 1–6 and p. 7, cols. 1–7.

21. "South Africa—UR Tanzania: 'Greatest Potential Threat,' " *Africa Research Bulletin: Political, Social, and Cultural Series* (Exeter, England), vol. 5, no. 2 (March 15, 1968), p. 974.

22. Nyerere, *op. cit.*, pp. 379–380.

23. CM/Res. 175 (XII), para. 2, Addis Ababa, February, 1969.

24. "Liberation Committee," *Reporter* (Nairobi), vol. 4, no. 145 (November 5, 1965), pp. 12–13.

25. AHG/Res. 12 (I) Cairo, July 1964.

26. Only once, at the very inception of the OAU in May 1963, was any mention made of volunteers. The OAU resolved then "to promote, in each State, the transit of all material aid and the establishment of a body of *volunteers* in various fields, with a view to providing the various African national liberation movements with the assistance they need in the various sectors." (CIAS/Plen. 2/Rev. 2, A: Agenda Item II, para. 15, Addis Ababa, May 1963. Italics added.) There appears to have been no concrete action taken to raise such a body of volunteers.

27. CM/St. 2 (XII), para. 2, Addis Ababa, February 1969.

28. Immanuel Wallerstein, *Africa: The Politics of Unity* (New York: Random House, 1967), pp. 163–164.

29. CM/Res. 136 (X), para. 2, Addis Ababa, February 1968.

30. AHG/Res. 18 (I), Cairo, July 1964.

31. CM/Res. 137 (X), Addis Ababa, February 1969.

32. AHG/Res. 8 (I), Cairo, July 1964.

33. ECM/Res. 10 (V), Lagos, June 1965.

34. CM/Res. 153 (XI), Algiers, September 1968.

35. The allegedly Peking-oriented member of the triumvirate which governed FRELIMO, Reverend Uria Simango, was suspended from the group in November 1969, after he had made charges against his two colleagues, Foreign Minister Marcelino dos Santos and Defense Minister Samora Machal, accusing them of plotting to assassinate him.

36. "Africa's Warring Liberators," *Sunday Telegraph* (London); May 4, 1969, p. 6, cols. 1–2.

37. See, for instance, H. G. Nicholas, "The United Nations in Crisis," *International Affairs* (London), vol. 41, no. 3 (July 1965), pp. 441–450.

38. "Organization of African Unity: Accra Assembly of Heads of State and Government," *Keesing's Contemporary Archives*, vol. 15 (1965–1966), p. 21052.

39. See footnote 41 *infra*.

40. See footnote 36 *supra*.

41. On October 17, 1966, the General Assembly of the

United Nations terminated the South African mandate for South West Africa and on May 19, 1967, it created an eleven-member Council for South West Africa "to administer South West Africa until independence." On April 5, 1968, the council left New York, but went only as far as Lusaka, because it was denied entry into Windhoek by the South African government.

42. Chapter VII of the Charter deals with "Action With Respect to Threats to the Peace, Breaches of the Peace, and Acts of Aggression." It empowers the Security Council to determine a situation as threatening international peace, and to decide on measures or sanctions against the state or states responsible for the situation. These measures may be nonmilitary, such as a complete or partial interruption of economic relations and of rail, sea, air, postal, telegraphic, radio, and other means of communication, and the severance of diplomatic relations, or they may be military, including blockade, and other operations by air, sea, or land forces against the states committing breaches of the peace.

43. See Yashpal Tandon, "The Organization of African Unity as an Instrument and Forum of Protest," in Robert I. Rotberg and A. A. Mazrui (eds.), *Protest and Power in Black Africa* (New York: Oxford University Press, 1970) pp. 1153–1183.

44. Most of the above information is obtained through interviews with officials of the Organization of African Unity and cannot as yet be documented since the relevant documents are still classified as confidential.

45. CM/Res. 175 (XII), para. 5, Addis Ababa, February 1969.

46. CM/Res. 103 (IX), para. 6, Kinshasa, September 1967.

47. CM/Res. 175 (XII), para. 1, Addis Ababa, February 1969.

48. AHG/Dec. 41 (VI), Addis Ababa, September 1969.

49. Figures collected from Brian Bunting, *The Rise of the South African Reich* (Baltimore: Penguin Books, 1964), p. 299 and *Keesings' Contemporary Archives*. 1967–1968, 22116–22117.

50. *United Nations, Statistical Yearbook, 1968* (New York: United Nations, 1969), p. 681. The figure given is 7.2104 billion escudos for national defense out of a total national expenditure of 18.2434 billion escudos.

51. See Alan Rake, "Black Guerrillas in Rhodesia," *Africa Report*, vol. 13, no. 9 (December 1968), pp. 23–25.

52. "South Africa Threatens Zambia," *East African Standard* (Nairobi) October 16, 1967, p. 1, cols. 2–4.

53. "S.A. Missiles a Threat to Zambia," *East African Standard* (Nairobi) October 12, 1968, p. 4, cols. 3–4.

54. Rake, *op. cit.*, p. 24.

55. "Angola: Continued Guerrilla Activities in Northern and Eastern Areas," *Keesing's Contemporary Archives*, vol. 16 (1967–1968), p. 21965; and "Mozambique: Guerrilla Warfare in Northern Provinces: Detention of suspected Nationalists: Political Trials," *Keesing's Contemporary Archives*, vol. 16 (1967–1968), p. 21913.

56. "South Africa: Adoption of Defence Amendment Act: Expansion of Defence Forces: Purchases of Aircraft and Submarines from France," *Keesing's Contemporary Archives*, vol. 16 (1967–1968), p. 22116.

57. *Ibid.*

58. *Ibid.*, pp. 22116–22117.

59. Muriel Horrell (compiler), *A Survey of Race Relations in South Africa, 1968* (Johannesburg: South African Institute of Race Relations, 1969), p. 39.

60. *United Nations Statistical Yearbook, 1968*, pp. 623, 630, 631, 633.

61. "News in Brief: Lesotho: Jonathan on Kaunda," *Africa Report*, vol. 13, no. 1 (January 1968), p. 36.

62. *Selected Military Writings of Mao Tse-Tung* (Peking: Foreign Languages Press, 1963), p. 218.

63. *Ibid.*, p. 198.

64. *Ibid.*, p. 218.

65. Regis Debray, *Revolution in the Revolution?* (New York: Grove Press, 1967). pp. 75–76.

66. Mao Tse-tung, *op. cit.*, p. 209.

67. Pierre L. van den Berghe: "Albinocracy in South Africa: A Case Study in the Growth of Tyranny," *Journal of Asian and African Studies* (Leiden, Netherlands), vol. 1, no. 1 (January 1966), pp. 43–49.

68. Erik Allardt, "Reactions to Social and Political Change in a Developing Society," *International Journal of Comparative Sociology* (Leiden, Netherlands), vol. 7, no. 1–2 (March 1966), pp. 1–11.

69. The *verkramptes* (the "cramped") believe in the fundamentalist, "purified" version of Afrikaner movement, which allows no compromise—in principle or in practice—with African nationalism. The *verligtes* (the "enlightened"), led by the prime minister, Mr. Vorster, are more pragmatic, and are prepared to compromise, at least in practice, with independent African governments in the North, and treat them on the basis of legal equality.

CHAPTER 2

1. See Edward Feit, *African Opposition in South Africa: The Failure of Passive Resistance* (Stanford: Hoover Institution on War, Revolution and Peace, 1967); and Edward Roux, *Time Longer Than Rope: A History of the Black Man's Struggle for Freedom in South Africa*, 2nd ed. (Madison: University of Wisconsin Press, 1964).

2. See John A. Davis and James K. Baker (eds.), *Southern Africa in Transition* (New York: Frederick A. Praeger, 1966); and James Duffy, *Portugal in Africa* (Cambridge, Mass.: Harvard University Press, 1962).

3. See John Marcum, *The Angolan Revolution*. vol. 1—*The Anatomy of an Explosion, 1950–1962* (Cambridge, Mass.: M.I.T. Press, 1969), pp. 13–122.

4. This is not counting thousands of émigrés and, after 1961, war refugees who moved northward. In particular, Angolan refugees streamed into the Congo (Kinshasa) where by August 1969, according to the United Nations Office of the High Commissioner for Refugees, they numbered 370,000. Actual "political" refugees or exiles—*i.e.*, militants within nationalist movements or persons who had strong political views uncongenial to the *status quo*—from all of Southern Africa were at most a few thousand. (See Sven Hamrell [ed.], *Refugee Problems in Africa* [Uppsala, Sweden: Scandinavian Institute of African Studies, 1967]; also articles by Lars-Gunner Eriksson, T. F. Betts, Margaret Roberts, Kodwo E. Ankrah, and Oystein Opdahl on "Refugees in Africa" in *Venture* [London], vol. 19, No. 8 [September 1967], pp. 3–18.)

5. Representative of such optimism was the tone of the Fourth Conference of the Pan-African Freedom Movement for East and Central Africa (PAFMECA) at Addis Ababa in 1962, where a South African exile leader spoke enthusiastically of "lunging into the last phase of the

liberatory struggle." ("Africa: Southward March," *The Economist* [London], vol. 202, No. 6181 [February 10, 1962], p. 537).

6. "Introduction to the Annual Report of the Secretary-General on the Work of the Organization," *UN Monthly Chronicle*, vol. 3, no. 9 (October 1966), p. 113.

7. See Elizabeth S. Landis, "The South West Africa Cases: Remand to the United Nations," *Cornell Law Quarterly*, vol. 52, no. 5 (Spring II, 1967), pp. 627–671; and Ernest Gross *et al.*, *Ethiopia and Liberia vs. South Africa: The South West Africa Cases*, Occasional Paper no. 5 (Los Angeles: University of California, African Studies Center, 1968).

8. General Assembly Resolution 2248 (S-V), May 19, 1967.

9. General Assembly Resolution 2325 (XXII), December 16, 1967.

10. See "Issues before the 23rd General Assembly," *International Conciliation*, no. 569 (September 1968), p. 67.

11. General Assembly Resolution 2372 (XXII), June 12, 1968. The name Namibia was rejected by some South West African nationalists, notably Jariretundu Kozonguizi and the South West Africa National Union (SWANU). (See Richard Gibson, "A Hard Look at Africa's Liberation Movements—or a Study in Disunity" *Race Today* [London], vol. 1, no. 4 [August 1969], p. 111.)

12. In 1955, for example, the founders of the *União das Populações do Norte de Angola* (UPNA) sent a petition to the United Nations requesting that the area of the former Kongo kingdom ruled by Portugal as part of Angola be placed under a United Nations trusteeship administered by the United States. (See Marcum, *The Angolan Revolution*, p. 61).

13. See petition by Pinto-Bull, president of the *Frente de Luta Pela Independência Nacional da Guiné dita Portuguesa* (FLING), General Assembly (XXIII), A/AC. 109/Pet. 992.

14. See "Apartheid and Imperialism: A Study of U.S. Corporate Involvement in South Africa," *Africa Today*, vol. 17, no. 5 (September–October, 1970), pp. 1–42.

15. Portuguese threats to cancel American base rights in the Azores have barred any possibility of American support for United Nations sanctions designed to persuade Lisbon to implement self-determination in its African territories. By virtue of Portugal's refusal of a long-term renewal of the Azores base accord that expired on December 31, 1962, American use of the bases became dependent on Portugal's short-term pleasure. (Marcum, *The Angolan Revolution*, pp. 271–274.) Lisbon thus gained and maintained a strong influence over American policy *re* Angola and Mozambique, in spite of the fact that technological advance has reduced the need for such overseas bases as the Azores. In James Reston's words: "Washington needed the Azores as a ferry base in the last war for aircraft of limited range; it needs the Azores no longer, but the old arrangements go on." ("President Nixon's Military Reappraisal," *New York Times*, March 5, 1969 late city ed., p. 46, cols. 5–8.)

16. John Marcum, "Southern Africa and United States Policy: A Consideration of Alternatives," in George W. N. Shepherd, Jr. (ed.), *Racial Influence on American Foreign Policy* (New York: Basic Books, 1970), pp. 186–219.

17. Richard J. Barnet, *Intervention and Revolution: The United States in the Third World* (New York: World Publishing Co., 1968), p. 5.

18. *Ibid.*, p. 273.

19. Senator Thurmond quoted from an editorial in the Charleston *News and Courier* (February 5, 1969) that described Mondlane's murder as a "grave reverse for the Communists" and that concluded "for the present . . . the threat to a civilized region of Africa has ceased." (*Congressional Record*, 91st congr., 1st sess., vol. 115, no. 26 [February 7, 1969], p. E941.) For a contrary interpretation of Mondlane's death see John Marcum, "A Martyr for Mozambique," *Africa Report*, vol. 14, nos. 3 and 4 (March–April 1969), pp. 6–9.

20. Arguing that each side in the cold war "on whose outcome depends the future of all mankind for centuries to come, feels compelled to move into the vacuum left in Africa by the colonial powers," the AAAA publishes and distributes free literature supporting the present regimes in Southern Africa—nearly $33,000 worth in 1968 alone. See AAAA, *Report, September 1965–December 1968* (New York: AAAA, 1969), which notes that "all contributions to the American-African Affairs Association, Inc., are deductible from taxable income." In 1969 the AAAA published a thirty-four-page anti-Communist tract, *Blueprint for Conflict* by Col. Daniel T. Brigham, which describes the defense of "white-ruled" Southern Africa against black "terrorists" as part of a Western struggle against Red conspiracy.

21. See George W. Ball, *The Discipline of Power: Essentials of a Modern World Structure* (Boston: Little, Brown, 1968), pp. 245–259. An unheeded case for taking "moderate" initiatives to promote peaceful change in Southern Africa was made by the president of the African American Institute, Waldemar A. Nielsen, in *Africa Battleline: American Policy Choices in Southern Africa* (New York: Harper & Row, 1965). Senator Edward W. Brooke and Arthur J. Goldberg, among others, have argued for a much more forceful American policy. See George M. Daniels (ed.), *Southern Africa: A Time for Change* (New York: Friendship Press, 1969), especially pp. 6–7 and 22.

22. In the absence of the political change that had been widely anticipated, Southern African students could anticipate only arrest or demeaning collaboration with the Special Branch (police) if they returned home. They experienced great difficulty in obtaining visas for or jobs in African states such as Tanzania or Zambia. Consequently, many graduated into the growing ranks of a young, stranded, and frustrated exile community in the United States and Europe. (See Margaret Legum, "Problems of Asylum for Southern African Refugees," in Hamrell *op. cit.*, pp. 56–61.)

23. See "S. A. Refugees: Where Should They Go?" *Africa 1965* (London), no. 2 (January 22, 1965), pp. 1–2. In keeping with their own growing militancy, at least some politicized black Americans seemed increasingly to expect Southern African exiles to demonstrate an active revolutionary commitment to return home, not to settle in. Nonetheless, a detailed study of Southern African student exiles in the United States by Barnett F. Baron suggests that such expectations are unlikely to be realized. Baron has concluded that by providing previously politically active young men with new, nonpolitical means of fulfilling personal needs, American scholarship programs "may lead to the decline or deflection of political interest and involvement in individuals who come from a class that has historically

played a vanguard role in revolutionary change." The quotation is from Barnett F. Baron, *Southern African Student Exiles: The Functions of Politics* (New Haven: Yale University, unpublished Ph.D. dissertation, 1969), p. [2] (abstract).

24. Unlike the AAAA, the ACOA does not enjoy tax-deductible status.

25. Neil Sheehan, "A Student Group Concedes It Took Funds from C.I.A.," *New York Times*, February 14, 1967, late city ed., p. 1, col. 1. and p. 7, col. 1.

26. Groups such as the Congress on Racial Equality (CORE) and the Black Panthers have publicly offered sympathy and/or personnel to Southern African movements. See Eric Pace, "Mozambique Rebel Says Forces Aim to Block Dam," *New York Times*, January 23, 1969, late city ed., p. 3, cols. 5–7; and "African Patriotic Armed Struggle Grows in Strength," *Black Panther* (San Francisco), vol. 2, no. 23 (February 17, 1969), p. 14, cols. 1–5. New Left intellectuals have established a Liberation Support Movement (headquartered in Seattle, Washington) that has mounted a publicity and fund raising campaign on behalf of the MPLA of Angola.

27. Susan Sontag, "Some Thoughts on the Right Way (for Us) To Love the Cuban Revolution," *Ramparts*, vol. 7, no. 11 (April 1969), p. 14.

28. The West, like the East, is polycentric and the revolutionary cause has won a more positive governmental response in at least two Western areas: (1) Scandinavia (especially Sweden), where sympathy, scholarships, and trade boycotts represent a significant measure of popular concern though only modest material aid (Martin Lowenkopf, "Sweden and Africa," *Africa Report*, vol. 13, no. 7 October, 1968, pp. 64–65) and (2) Israel, which extends a modicum of technical aid and moral support to select exile leaders and movements for reasons of its own national interest. (See *Ma'ariv* [Tel Aviv], August 14, 1962; *Davar* [Tel Aviv], August 15, 1962 and Philippe Decraene, "Israël et les États d'Afrique Noire. II.—Le Poids des Considérations Politique," *Le Monde* (Paris), September 5, 1967, p. 3, cols. 1–4). The presence of a sizeable and affluent, though insecure, Jewish minority in South Africa has probably served to inhibit Israeli policy in this regard. Of the two, only Scandinavian approval can offer a net gain in revolutionary "legitimacy," for, to the extent that it becomes public, Israeli assistance must be balanced off against Arab disapproval and thus a loss in aid from such countries as Algeria and the United Arab Republic.

29. The leadership of at least one nationalist movement has expressed the opinion that in any case as a matter of principle one should not accept Western assistance. "It would not make sense, for example, if the MPLA went out to find allies among the imperialists who provide colonialist Portugal with substantial aid with which to wage war against our people. That would be incoherent." Agostinho Neto as quoted in Robert Davezies, *La Guerre d'Angola* (Bordeaux, France: Ducros, 1968), pp. 155–156.

30. The title of chap. 1 of Barnet, *op. cit.*

31. See V. Sidenko, "The Last African Colonies: Angola," *New Times* (Moscow), no. 50 (December 1960), p. 20; and "Africa Today: The Soviet View," *Mizan Newsletter* (London), vol. 4, no. 5 (April 1962), p. 3.

32. South African Communist Party, *The Road to South African Freedom* (London: Ellis Bowles, n.d.). See also the interview with Moses Kotane, treasurer-general of the ANC and former general secretary of the Communist party (1938–1950) in *The African Communist* (London), no. 35 (Fourth Quarter 1968), pp. 98–101.

33. Mário de Andrade, "Et les colonies de Salazar?" *Démocratie Nouvelle* (Paris), vol. 14, no. 9 (September 1960), p. 34; and Sidenko, *op. cit.*, p. 20.

34. They invoke Lenin's arguments against "left adventurism" (*viz.*, Maoism), *i.e.*, against plunging into "premature" revolutionary action without adequate preparation. (See V. I. Lenin, "Left-Wing Communism, an Infantile Disorder," *Selected Works*, vol. 3 [New York: International Publishers, 1967], pp. 373–374.) They hold that success in revolution depends upon convincing at least "a majority of the class conscious, thinking, and politically active workers" of the necessity for revolution to the point where they are in fact "prepared to die for it." And they maintain that the ruling classes must be experiencing a crisis of authority that renders them vulnerable to a well-organized bid for power. (Lenin, *op. cit.*, p. 392, and William J. Pomeroy [ed.], *Guerrilla Warfare and Marxism* [New York: International Publishers, 1968], pp. 21–24.)

35. Pomeroy, *op. cit.*, pp. 28–29, 39. Pomeroy argues that because the Organization of African Unity (OAU) has been hobbled by "reactionary and neo-imperialist influences within it," bilateral aid from socialist and "progressive" countries is vital (p. 29). "It is," he concludes, "a long step from the isolated ill-equipped Mau Mau movement of Kenya in the 1950's to the internationally aided and trained popular armies now in the field in southern Africa." "To a considerable extent," Africans have been "the beneficiar[ies] of the armed liberation struggles in Asia and in Latin America. They have been provided with lessons and advisers from all the victorious movements (Vietnam, Cuba, Algeria), and at the same time have probably had more direct assistance from socialist countries (the Soviet Union, China) than movements elsewhere in the past" (pp. 248–249).

36. Prepared to support assaults on "reactionary" governments in independent states as well as on colonial regimes, the Chinese have thus continued to endorse exiled revolutionaries whose causes have been deserted by the Soviets (and African states)—that is, the *Conseil National de Libération* (CNL) of the Congo (Kinshasa), the *Union des Populations Camerounaises* (UPC) of Cameroon, the Bechuanaland People's Party (BPP), and the Basutoland Congress Party (BCP). (See Hsinhua News Agency, *Daily Bulletin* [London], no. 3945 [November 19, 1968], no. 3967 [December 11, 1968], and no. 4019 [February 3, 1969].) These movements, however, have risked being even further isolated in their exile because of the exigencies of Chinese benefactors who require a *quid pro quo* of loyal, public alignment behind Peking in its numerous international quarrels, as reflected in the *Daily Bulletin* of the official Chinese Hsinhua News Agency (London). See also Colin Legum, "Africa and China, Symbolism and Substance," in S. M. Halpern (ed.), *Policies Toward China: Views from Six Continents* (New York: McGraw-Hill, 1965), pp. 389–436.

37. Lin Piao, "Long Live the Victory of People's War! In Commemoration of the 20th Anniversary of Victory in the Chinese People's War of Resistance Against Japan," *Peking Review* (Peking), vol. 8, no. 36 (September 3, 1965), p. 23. As against the Soviets who argue for a balanced mobilization of the cities and

countryside, Lin Piao had advocated the Chinese strategy of establishing revolutionary base areas in rural districts so as to encircle cities. In Southern Africa most Africans live in the countryside and most Europeans in the cities.

38. *Ibid.*, p. 27.

39. *Ibid.*, p. 22.

40. Régis Debray, *Revolution in the Revolution?* (New York: Monthly Review Press, 1967). For a critical view of this thesis by a South African, see Joe Slovo, "Latin America and the Ideas of Régis Debray," *The African Communist*, no. 33 (Second Quarter, 1968), pp. 37–54.

41. Ideologues associated with the Fourth International have also offered their counsel to Southern Africa's revolutionaries. See for example, *Sous le Drapeau du Socialisme*, published in Paris (1964–1966). The only Trotskyite movement in Southern Africa is the exiled Unity Movement of South Africa, also known as the African People's Democratic Union of Southern Africa (APDUSA). See I. B. Tabata, "South Africa Freedom Struggle," *International Socialist Review* (New York), vol. 26, no. 9 (Summer 1965), pp. 83–93.

42. The relevance of the October Revolution (1917) in the Soviet Union and of the "scientific theory of dialectical and historical materialism" to the struggle for Mozambique's independence is argued cogently by a leader of the Mozambique Liberation Front (FRELIMO), Marcelino dos Santos, in "The Revolutionary Perspective in Mozambique," *World Marxist Review* (Prague), vol. 11, no. 1 (January 1968), pp. 43–44.

43. A high incidence of student and teacher membership in the rival Zimbabwe African National Union (ZANU) suggests exceptions to the generalization made above about the nature of the movements in the Soviet-backed alliance. The association of some white liberals such as Garfield Todd with ZAPU, however, has fit this pattern.

44. SWAPO's inclusion in this lineup appears to be due more to the expediency of external selection—*e.g.* recognition by the Organization of African Unity (OAU) and the Soviets as the preeminent nationalist movement of South West Africa—than to the predilections of a social class or ideological affinity. SWAPO's leadership and militants are, after all, largely, though not exclusively, of rural Ovambo and Caprivi background.

The Soviets also support two other movements associated with these six: (1) the *Frente Patriòtica de Libertação Nacional* (FPLN) of Portugal whose strongest constituent is the pro-Soviet Portuguese Communist party (see *Pravda*, April 7, 1966) [Portuguese Maoists organized within a Marxist-Leninist Committee and a rival front, the *Frente de Acção Popular* (FAP), occasionally praised in the past by the MPLA's rivals, the *Frente Nacional de Libertação de Angola* (FNLA). See *Angola Informations* (Algiers), no. 17 (December 1965), p. 7]; and (2) the South African Communist party (SACP) (see "Message from the South African Communist Party to the 23rd Congress of the Communist Party of the Soviet Union," *The African Communist*, no. 25 [Second Quarter 1966], pp. 86–88).

45. See "Khartoum: A Report of the International Conference in Support of the Peoples of the Portuguese Colonies and Southern Africa: Khartoum, 18–20 January 1969," in *The African Communist*, no. 37 [Second Quarter 1969], pp. 13–24. According to *Pravda* (January 21, 1969), the Chinese sent a large group of correspondents to the Khartoum conference where they "carried out subversive activities" and "exerted every effort to undermine Africa's trust in the USSR." The conference decided to establish a Mobilization Committee in Cairo to coordinate activities related to the "liberation struggle" and to channel information and funds to the movements concerned. This move was widely viewed as a Soviet effort to bypass the coordinating machinery of the OAU's Liberation Committee and expand Soviet influence at the OAU's expense.

46. Jack Woddis, "The Khartoum Conference," *Liberation* (London), July–August 1969, p. 14; Woddis first presented this view in "Alliance in African People's Decisive Liberation Struggle," *Morning Star* (London), January 29, 1969, p. 2, cols. 1–4.

47. "Statement of the MPLA on the Khartoum Conference," *MPLA Informations* (Algiers), March 1969, p. 9.

48. These four groups charged that the conference was "calculated to control the Liberation struggle of the Portuguese colonies and southern Africa in order to further Soviet cooperation with the United States for their joint domination of the world." (Hsinhua News Agency, *Daily Bulletin*, no. 4008, January 23, 1969.) Such organizations as the Afro-Asian Journalists' Association in Peking echoed these allegations and denounced the Khartoum conference as an effort to "peddle" the "revisionist line of peaceful coexistence and U.N. intervention." (*Ibid.*, no. 4065, March 21, 1969.)

49. *Pravda*, March 5, 1967 as translated in "Notes on the News: Africa," *Mizan* (London), vol. 9, no. 3 (May–June, 1967), p. 142.

50. In cases like that of Guinea (Bissau) where only one movement possesses any revolutionary credentials (*viz.*, the PAIGC), both Chinese and Soviet approval is still possible. Where Chinese relations with a host country, such as Tanzania, are good, Peking may continue to funnel assistance through the government of that country to movements such as FRELIMO which are publicly linked to the Soviets although they reputedly contain elements friendly to Peking. Aid can be sent through the Tanzanian government in its capacity as a member (chairman) of the Liberation Committee of the Organization of African Unity.

51. The secretary-general of the ANC noted that "socialist countries are great supporters of the liberation struggles throughout the world," and declared that "the normalization of the situation in Czechoslovakia is the concern of the family of socialist countries and the peoples of the world." Accordingly, he said, "steps taken by the Warsaw Pact countries" were "justified." (*Mayibuye* [Dar es Salaam], vol. 2, no. 35 [September 27, 1968], p. 13.) The PAC condemned the "invasion of Czechoslovakia" as a "flagrant violation of the right of self-determination" committed under the leadership of the "Soviet revisionist clique." "Statement on Soviet Aggression," *PAC News and Views* [Dar es Salaam], no. 15 [August, 1968], p. 12.)

52. Gibson, "A Hard Look," pp. 111–112.

53. At a meeting in Peking in June, 1966, FRELIMO central committeemen, Armando Guebeza and João Mungwambe, denounced a Soviet-backed seminar on "Africa: National and Social Revolution," scheduled to take place in Cairo (Hsinhua News Agency, *Daily Bulletin*, no. 3083, June 27, 1966). In October, FRELIMO

was nonetheless a prominent participant in the Cairo Seminar. ("Africa-National and Social Revolution," *Mizan* [London], vol. 9, no. 2 [March-April 1967], pp. 58–67.)

Another case of externally induced inconsistency concerns the PAC and the Congo (Kinshasa). In November 1966, PAC offices in Cairo and Algiers issued statements backing Congolese anti-government "freedom fighters" (Hsinhua News Agency, *Daily Bulletin*, no. 3235, November 28, 1966 and no. 3236, November 29, 1966. Then in March 1967 the PAC's president, Potlako Leballo, visited Kinshasa, spoke at ceremonies organized by the GRAE/FNLA honoring the sixth anniversary of the Angolan uprising and expressed "admiration" for the "wisdom" and "farsightedness" of President Joseph Mobutu ("M. Potloko [*sic*] Parle au Nom des Combattants Africains," in supplement to *Le Progrès* [Kinshasa], April 2, 1967). In November of that same year, however, PAC offices once again endorsed Mao Tse-tung's position in support of anti-Mobutu rebels (Hsinhua News Agency, *Daily Bulletin*, no. 3594, November 28, 1967.)

54. Chinese assistance to the PAC (South Africa), for instance, is reported to have come in occasional grants of $10,000 or $20,000. (Matthew Nkoana, *Crisis in the Revolution* [London: Mafube, 1969] as quoted in Lewis Nkosi, "Crisis in the Revolution: Nkoana's version," *South Africa Bulletin* [Paris], no. 73 [March 1969], p. 6.)

55. See George Houser, "African Liberation Movements," *Africa Today*, vol. 14, no. 4 (August 1967), pp. 11–13; John Marcum, "Three Revolutions," *Africa Report*, vol. 12, no. 8 (November 1967), pp. 8–22; "Angolan Setback," *Africa 1965*, no. 10 (May 21, 1965), pp. 1–3; and "An Angolan Reminder," *Africa 1963* (London), no. 3 (February 1, 1963), pp. 1–2.

56. For Southern Africans such "solidarity" was given the *coup de grâce* in December 1961 when India, without consulting embattled Angolan nationalists, occupied Goa, released Portuguese troops to fight in Africa, and convincingly demonstrated the primacy of national over Afro-Asian interests. Realistically, other than rhetorical support at meetings like the Tricontinental conclave of revolutionaries at Havana in 1966, Southern African exiles could expect little concrete help at this broad, multicontinental level of the Third World community.

57. See "PAFMECSA Deplores Arms Build-up in S. Africa," *Tanganyika Standard* (Dar es Salaam). January 3, 1963, p. 2, cols. 4–7; Harvey Glickman, "Where Exiles Plan and Wait," *Africa Report*, vol. 8, no. 7 (July 1963), p. 3; and Richard Cox, *Pan-Africanism in Practice: PAFMECSA, 1958–1964* (London: Oxford University Press, 1964), p. 57.

58. A proposal by President Sékou Touré of Guinea that African states contribute the equivalent of 1 percent of their annual budget to an OAU Liberation Fund was bypassed in favor of voluntary contributions. The Liberation Committee (of originally nine, later eleven, states) was created to manage the fund and to harmonize assistance destined for liberation movements. (See "The Poetry of Action," *West Africa* [London], no. 2410 [August 10, 1963], p. 887.) For an analysis of the origins and activities of the Liberation Committee, see Immanuel Wallerstein, *Africa: The Politics of Unity* (New York: Random House, 1967), pp. 152–175.

59. On occasion it even came to influence or determine the outcome of a leadership struggle within a weak or divided movement—*viz.*, its recognition of Potlako Leballo as head of the PAC after he had been "ousted" by a contending party faction in 1969.

60. See "General Report of the Goodwill Mission of the Coordinating Committee for the Liberation of Africa to the Angola Nationalists" (Leopoldville: July 1963, mimeographed), adopted by the OAU Foreign Ministers meeting at Dakar, Senegal, in August 1963.

61. "L'O.U.A. Suspendrait Son Aide au G.R.A.E. de M. Roberto Holden," *Afrique Nouvelle* (Dakar), no. 1147 (July 31–August 6, 1969), p. 3, cols. 1–4. The Council of Ministers took the recommendation under advisement. Meanwhile the Liberation Committee funneled the bulk of its Angolan support to the MPLA.

62. In a statement addressed to the OAU Liberation Committee in 1968, UNITA claimed considerable success in political organizing and guerrilla action inside Angola "without outside assistance," but it implied that it might have achieved "much more" if it had had help from independent African states. It called upon the OAU committee to send a commission of inquiry inside to see "*who* is doing *what*" and promised a "hearty welcome," (UNITA, "Statement Addressed to the African Liberation Committee of the Organization of African Unity," *Kwacha-Angola* [London], no. 1 [January 1969], pp. 7–9.)

63. Charges made in a letter from Savimbi to Justin Bomboko, then foreign minister of the Congo (Kinshasa), from an undesignated place inside Angola, May 30, 1969.

64. See "OAU-Post Mortem," *Crisis and Change* (London), vol. 1, no. 1 (November–December, 1965), pp. 8–9; and Gibson, "A Hard Look," p. 110.

65. Russell Warren Howe, "African Guerrilla Funds Disputed," *Christian Science Monitor*, March 8, 1969, Eastern ed., p. 3, cols. 1–3; and "Southern Africa: Black Man's War," *The Economist*, vol. 231, no. 6559 (May 10, 1969), p. 32.

66. "Freedom Fighters Band Together," *West Africa*, no. 2431 (January 4, 1964), p. 26. This brief alliance, formed under the leadership of T. G. Silundika (ZAPU), stated that its aim was "to uphold the independence of the Liberation movements, protect their initiative to determine the struggle in their areas and to safeguard the interests of the Liberation struggle as a whole." (*Constitution, Union of Non-Independent African States* [1964, mimeograph], art. 2, para. d.) An abortive effort to relaunch this grouping was made by twelve exile parties at Accra, Ghana, in 1965. (See "Liberation Movements Regroup," *Africa 1966* [London], no. 4 [February 18, 1966], pp. 4–6.)

67. See *La Lutte de Libération Nationale dans les Colonies Portugaises* (Algiers: Information CONCP, 1967); and review by John Marcum in *Africa Report*, vol. 13, no. 7 (October 1968), pp. 73–75.

68. Alan Rake, "Black Guerrillas in Rhodesia," *Africa Report*, vol. 13, no. 9 (December 1968), pp. 23–25. There were also reports of cooperation between the MPLA and SWAPO in the southeastern corner of Angola. See "Communist-Backed Southern Africa Terrorist Onslaught," *Africa Institute Bulletin* (Pretoria), vol. 6, no. 5 (June 1968), pp. 130–148.

69. See John Marcum, "The Angolan Rebellion: Status Report," *Africa Report*, vol. 9, no. 2 (February 1964), pp. 2–7, for a discussion of the "Congo Alliance."

Benjamin Pinto-Bull of FLING claimed in 1968 that he had the *accord de principe* of Holden Roberto for the creation of a new, anti-CONCP alliance grouping the GRAE, COREMO, FLING, and an unnamed São Tomé movement. (*L'Action* [Tunis], April 17, 1968.) Before carrying out such an *accord de principe*, however, it seemed likely that Roberto would expect some tangible evidence of revolutionary activity on the part of FLING.

70. Visible evidence of such efforts can be seen in the joint statements made by a selected group of liberation movements to the Hsinhua News Agency, statements frequently involving denunciations of CONCP and other Soviet-backed groups.

71. It was Congolese *de jure* recognition in June 1963 that set off the chain reaction which led to collective OAU recognition and support of the GRAE two months later. Similarly, exclusive recognition and aid by the government of Guinea (Conakry) has been of substantial help in establishing Amilcar Cabral's PAIGC in its position of uncontested leadership of the Guinea (Bissau) revolution.

72. For an analysis of liberation movement–host state relations see Paul M. Whitaker, *Angola, Guinea, Mozambique. A Comparative Study of the International Relations of the Revolutionary Nationalist Liberation Movements of Portuguese Africa* (Cambridge: Harvard College, Department of Government, unpublished senior thesis, 1969), pp. 39–51.

73. "UNITA's 'Lost' without Dr. Savimbi," *Zambia News*, (Lusaka), August 13, 1967, p. 2.

74. UNITA President Jonas Savimbi reportedly has been leading these efforts from inside Angola. Only time will reveal their measure of success. ("Call for Friendship," *The Times of Zambia* (Lusaka), October 10, 1968, p. 1.) On UNITA strategy see Jorge Sangumba, "UNITA and Angola's Struggle for Independence," *The New African* (London), vol. 8, no. 1 (1969), pp. 6–8; and UNITA Central Committee, *Angola: Seventh Year* (London: UNITA, 1968).

75. On the other hand, permission to exercise authority within an émigré-refugee community of several hundred thousand Angolan Bakongo in the Lower Congo has offered the GRAE not only a safe mass support base but an (only partially utilized) opportunity to gain experience in governmental administration.

76. For a discussion of this previous state see Pierre van den Berghe, *South Africa: A Study in Conflict* (Middletown, Conn.: Wesleyan University Press, 1965); the analysis of a special Commission on Race Relations reporting to the Cape Synod of the Dutch Reformed Church, Report no. 6A entitled "The System of Migratory Labour in South Africa," and Report no. 7 entitled "The Family Life of Non-White Population Groups" (Cape Town, October 1965, mimeographed). On the need for more research into "the psychic and often physical trauma which result from constant deprivation, degradation and exploitation" of the African in South Africa, see Hoyt S. Alverson, *Urban-Industrialization among the "Bantu" in the Republic of South Africa*, Occasional Paper no. 1 (Johannesburg: University of Witwatersrand, African Studies Program, 1967), p. 64. See also J. C. de Ridder, *The Personality of the Urban African in South Africa* (London: Routledge & Kegan Paul, 1961); and K. Danziger, "The Psychological Future of an Oppressed Group," *Social Forces*, vol. 42, no. 1 (October 1963), pp. 31–40.

77. The concept as well as the problem of "internal exile," in addition to those of exile abroad, are discussed by an anti-Salazarist Portuguese writer, Pedro Bandeira (pseudonym), in "Letter from Lisbon," *New Leader*, vol. 48, no. 23 (November 22, 1965), pp. 6–10. A special class of "internal exiles" has been created within South Africa by a form of social "excommunication" known as banning. See G. Naudé, "Banning in South Africa: A Technique of Repression," in Christopher R. Hill (ed.), *Rights and Wrongs* (Baltimore: Penguin Books, 1969), pp. 51–78.

78. See Marcum, *The Angolan Revolution*, pp. 10, 23, 31, and *passim*.

79. See John Day, *International Nationalism: The Extra-territorial Relations of Southern Rhodesian African Nationalists* (London: Routledge & Kegan Paul, 1968), p. 120.

80. Finding it "strange" that exile politics have attracted "little attention from political scientists," the author of one of the few recent studies on the subject points out that the intensely polemical and partisan nature of such politics discourages many scholars: "Research into exile politics is an experience that tends to make one appreciative of the conditional, tenuous nature of 'facts.' " (Paul H. Lewis, *The Politics of Exile: Paraguay's Febrerista Party* [Durham, N.C.: University of North Carolina Press, 1968], p. xii.) See also Lewis J. Edinger, *German Exile Politics: The Social Democratic Executive Committee in the Nazi Era* (Berkeley: University of California Press, 1956). Supportive and illustrative data for such general analysis can be found in many historical chronicles of exile activities—*e.g.*, Bertram Wolfe's study of Russian exiles in *Three Who Made a Revolution. A Biographical History* (New York: Dial Press, 1961), *passim*. For Southern Africa, such data can be found in mimeographed exile bulletins that denounce rival movements with unmerciful violence and in the literature of intraparty conflict—*e.g.*, Matthew Nkoana's *Crisis in the Revolution* (London: Mafube, 1969). In *The Anatomy of Revolution* (New York: Vintage Books, 1952), p. 230, Crane Brinton notes that although what happens to émigrés "remains one of the most obscure parts of the sociology of revolution," the harshness of exile generally embitters, rigidifies, and narrows those who experience it.

81. In particular, Dr. F. A. S. Jensen, *Psychological Aspects of the Isolation of Refugees*, MHCR/304/63, GE. 63-17135, a paper presented to the Conference on Socially Handicapped Families (Paris: UNESCO, February 10–12, 1964); Dr. H. Strotzka, *Psychological Aspects of Integration*, MHCR/120/60 (Geneva: UNHCR, 1960); United Nations, General Assembly, Dr. H. Strotzka, *Report on the Mental Health of Refugees and in Particular of Special Cases in Austria, Germany, Greece, and Italy*, A/AC. 96/84 (September 9, 1960). The author is also indebted to UNHCR officials at Kinshasa and Geneva for sharing their insights into the problems of Southern African exiles.

82. Those Southern Africans who left on a whim or with vague notions of personal advantage, as well as those who left under duress (*e.g.*, fear of arrest), were more likely to show early signs of maladaptive behavior than those who left as the result of a reasoned political act. Of those politically oriented persons who left to get military training so as to fight, some later found that they could not endure the hardship and frustration of

their initial military option, came to view liberation as "hopeless," and chose to escape what had become intolerable psychic tension by changing goals—seeking scholarships and/or (temporary) integration into other societies, or returning to their own countries.

83. See Cato Aall, "Refugee Problems in Southern Africa," in Hamrell, *op. cit.*, p. 33.

84. See Norman R. F. Maier, *Frustration: The Study of Behavior Without a Goal* (Ann Arbor: University of Michigan Press, 1949).

85. Jensen, *op. cit.*, p. 14. The "negative identity" assumed by alienated young Africans living in South Africa's black township ghettos (internal exiles) has resulted in the rise of a tough underworld *tsotsi* caste, whose members vent their aggression on fellow Africans rather than on those responsible for African frustrations, the dominant white minority.

86. "An African's Story of a Terrorist Training Camp," *Intelligence Digest* (Cheltenham, Gloucestershire, England), vol. 31, no. 368 (July 1969), pp. 17–18.

87. "The Freedom Fighters Fall Out . . .," *Zambia News* (Lusaka), April 30, 1967, p. 1.

88. Jensen, *op. cit.*, p. 11. For a discussion of regression among concentration camp internees see Bruno Bettelheim, "Individual and Mass Behavior in Extreme Situations," *Journal of Abnormal and Social Psychology*, vol. 38, no. 4 (October 1943), pp. 444–447.

89. See Bloke Modisane's autobiographical *Blame Me on History* (London: Dutton, 1963).

90. T. Peter Omari (a Ghanaian sociologist and social affairs officer in the United Nations Economic Commission for Africa at Addis Ababa), "From Refugee to Emigré: African Solutions to the Refugee Problem," in Hamrell, *op. cit.*, p. 87.

91. In a report to the Eighth Argentine Congress on Mental Health of January 1965, Dr. Roberto Doria Medina, himself a Bolivian exile, noted that typically the political exile in Latin America is constantly waiting for an amnesty or the success of "his revolution." He works and longs "often in a mere wishful-thinking mood, because the very intensity of his daydreaming distorts the real facts for him." (*New York Times*, January 10, 1965.) Southern Africans have also been known to make unrealistic predictions—for example, the much publicized remarks in 1963 about an "imminent" uprising in South Africa attributed to the leader of the Pan-Africanist Congress (PAC) of South Africa ("Hint of Rising in S. Africa This Year: 'Time and Manner Being Discussed'," *The Times* [London], March 26, 1963 royal ed., p. 10, col. 3).

92. American political and military intervention in the Congo (Kinshasa) encouraged African tendencies toward conspiratorial interpretations of Western policies. (See "Those Yankees Are Not All Spies," *Africa 1965*, no. 4 [February 19, 1965], pp. 1–3.) Southern Africans have been conditioned in their own countries to expect the worst of all authority and to view any government with cynical suspicion. (See John Strong, "Emerging Ideological Patterns among Southern African Students," *Africa Today*, vol. 14, no. 4 [August 1967], pp. 14–17.) For a general discussion of suspiciousness and paranoia among displaced persons see Libuse Tyhurst, "Displacement and Migration: A Study in Social Psychiatry," *American Journal of Psychiatry*, vol. 107, no. 8 (February 1951), pp. 561–568.

93. An analyst sympathetic to the Chinese revolutionary model has commented on the inability of liberation movements to tolerate criticism. "To report . . . feuds and squabbles is sometimes held as inimical to the cause of African freedom, as though silence would alter the unpleasant reality. All too often, in any case, important developments within the liberation movements go unreported, even by the few veteran observers of the scene who indeed know what is happening. The present author holds the view that these contradictions can only be resolved through their airing in debate in the forums of Africa and the world, except where the lives of men engaged in military operations are concerned." (Gibson, "A Hard Look," p. 111.)

94. "Brother Carmichael—We Disagree," (editorial), *Spotlight on South Africa* (Dar es Salaam), vol. 5, no. 43 (November 3, 1967), pp. 1–2.

95. Viktor Frankl, *Man's Search for Meaning: An Introduction to Logotherapy* (New York: Washington Square Press, 1963).

96. Biafran stamps were printed by the Portuguese State Security Printers of Lisbon (David Lidman, "Biafra Producing Its Own Postage," *New York Times*, September 8, 1968, late city ed., section 2, p. 40D, cols. 5–8), and were sold in the world philatelic market.

97. "An African's Story of a Terrorist Training Camp," pp. 17–18.

98. Jensen, *op. cit.*, p. 12.

99. *Ibid.*, p. 10.

100. Dr. Doria Medina (see footnote 91) has pointed out that political exiles often suffer hallucinations and, lacking jobs and funds, manifest "pathological symptoms that make them bad mixers and lead them to self-ostracism." He has observed that such persons are naturally prone to feelings of "insecurity, loneliness, and hopelessness" and to "trigger cravings for revenge and hatreds that are discharged upon political opponents and part of the community when they return to positions of government." Speaking of Latin American exiles, he urged governments to open psychiatric centers and labor bureaus to help them pursue a constructive career abroad.

101. Lewis, *op. cit.*, p. xiii.

102. See Russell Warren Howe, "War in Southern Africa," *Foreign Affairs*, vol. 48, no. 1 (October, 1969), pp. 154–156, 162–165.

103. GRAE guerrillas have held a mountainous redoubt in northern Angola, known as "the Rotten Triangle," for nearly nine years. (See Pierre-Pascal Rossi, *Pour Une Guerre Oublée* [Paris: Julliard, 1969].)

104. Patrick Laurence, "Gaps in the Guer[r]illa's Strategy," *The Star* (Johannesburg), May 22, 1968, city late ed., p. 16, cols. 8–9. Peter Heldrew—in "Rhodesia: Fending off the Fearless," *The World Today* (London), vol. 25, no. 2 (February 1969), p. 77—suggests that rising unemployment and related crime rates might provide the spark to ignite the situation in Rhodesia, where "at present, while many Africans may be broadly nationalists in their sympathies, few are motivated to the level of active resistance to the regime."

105. Some press reports of a "vigorous" resurgence of ANC underground activity in South Africa have minimized its relationship with the ANC movement in exile and stressed its "purely indigenous growth." (*Los Angeles Times*, July 6, 1969.

106. Kwame Nkrumah has offered as a "practical guide" for such revolutions his *Handbook of Revolution-*

ary Warfare: a Guide to the Armed Phase of the African Revolution*. (New York: International Publishers, 1969.)

107. Noting the failure of students overseas to volunteer for guerrilla forces, even though "they are the ones who claim the loudest to be patriots" and the ones who "will benefit most from independence," a Rhodesian African nationalist writer has argued that students should be expected to accept a period of military service. In his view, presumably, even a marginal military contribution on their part would serve the principle of equity. (See Davis M'gabe, "The Beginning of Guerrilla Warfare," *Monthly Review*, vol. 20, no. 10 [March 1969], p. 46.) Nationalist representatives who attempted to recruit officer or medical personnel for guerrilla units from among exile students in the U.S. and Europe met considerable resistance. It is reported that "To combat resistance, [a] Rhodesian Students Trust [was] established in the United Kingdom to arrange scholarships without political ties." (Rake, *op. cit.*, p. 25.)

108. Debray, *op. cit.*

109. Some observers hostile to African nationalism have alleged that, because of a lack of popular support, liberation movements have been obliged to resort to the demoralizing practice of kidnapping in order to obtain guerrilla "volunteers." See "Guerrilla Dividends," *RSA World* (Pretoria), File 5, no. 3 (3rd issue, 1969), p. 35.

110. *New York Times*, July 18, 1965, p. 19.

111. "An African's Story of a Terrorist Training Camp," pp. 17–18. In late 1969 South African police sources reported the flight of three hundred to four hundred guerrilla trainees from nationalist camps in Tanzania to asylum in Nairobi, Kenya. "More and More Terrorists Leaving Camps," *The Windhoek Advertiser* (Windhoek), November 13, 1969, p. 4, cols. 5–6.

112. This opinion is held, for example, by such an experienced guerrilla war expert as the former *Washington Post* reporter, Sterling Seagrave.

113. Dr. Agostinho Neto, president of the MPLA, quoted from an interview by Hans-Dieter Bräuer, "This Is Victory," in *World Student News* (Prague), vol. 23, nos. 3 and 4 (1969), p. 25.

114. Eqbal Ahmad, "Revolutionary Warfare. How to Tell When the Rebels Have Won," *The Nation*, vol. 201, no. 5 (August 30, 1965), pp. 95–101.

115. For a discussion of PAIGC strategy and its focus upon internal rather than exile activities, see Basil Davidson, *The Liberation of Guiné: Aspects of an African Revolution* (Harmondsworth, Middlesex, England: Penguin Books, 1969); and Gérard Chaliand, *Armed Struggle in Africa: With the Guerrillas in "Portuguese" Guinea* (New York and London: Monthly Review Press, 1969). See also João Baptista Nunes Pereira Neto, "Movimentos Subversivos da Guinė, São Tomé e Principe," in *Cabo Verde, Guiné, São Tomé e Principe. Curso de Extensão Universitária. Ano Lectivo de 1965–66* (Lisbon: Instituto Superior de Ciências Sociais e Política Ultramarina, 1967), pp. 549–600; and William Zartman, "Guinea: The Quiet War Goes On," *Africa Report*, vol. 12, no. 8 (November 1967), pp. 67–72.,

116. See Ronald H. Chilcote, "The Political Thought of Amilcar Cabral," *Journal of Modern African Studies*, vol. 6, no. 3 (October 1968), pp. 373–388.

117. It has become common wisdom to argue that the measure of an African liberation movement lies in its

ability to educate and mobilize peasant masses for a guerrilla struggle and in its preparedness to move its own headquarters from a safe exile sanctuary back into its own country. See, for example, Chenhamo Chimutengwende, "The Rhodesian Crisis and the Liberation Movement," *Race Today*, vol. 1, no. 3 (July 1969), p. 71.

118. Citing his movement's program to politicize peasant communities inside Angola, Dr. Agostinho Neto has argued that even though none of the MPLA's rivals ("so-called Angolan parties abroad") suffer external difficulties on the order of those facing the MPLA, none of them is "developing effectively" like the MPLA. (Interview in Davezies, *op. cit.*, p. 153.)

119. See M'gabe, *op. cit.*, p. 41.

120. Richard Gibson, "Zimbabwe: Les Shonas contre les Matabélés," *Jeune Afrique* (Paris), no. 488 (May 12, 1970), p. 23. Fragmentation among South African exiles, the most urbanized of Southern Africans, has revealed the depths of latent ethnicity—as witness the creation of a Zulu-oriented exile movement in Nairobi in 1968. Formed in the main by defectors from the ANC and PAC and known as The National Liberation Front of Southern Africa (NLFSA), it declared itself for a separate Nguni-Zulu state. NLFSA, Press release (Nairobi, October 6, 1969).

121. According to Arslan Humbaraci (in "Dilemma of Salazar's Enemies," *Central African Mail* [Lusaka], November 13, 1964, magazine section, p. 3), by late 1964 Ghana's Bureau of African Affairs had come to the conclusion that most of the "freedom fighters" being trained in Ghana were "not serious" about their mission. Humbaraci said that a survey carried out by the OAU Liberation Committee showed a high incidence of desertion in guerrilla ranks. The article went on to say that liberation movements were "weakened by conference-mongering (notably in Europe), by seeking funds, and then using them for more comfortable living and further globe-trotting, and the game of distributing 'ministerial' and 'diplomatic' titles."

122. See Marcum, "Three Revolutions," pp. 11–12.

123. According to Norman Macrae (in "The Green Bay Tree," *The Economist*, vol. 227, no. 6514 [June 29–July 5, 1968], p. xiv), those "few brave lunatics" who manage to infiltrate into South Africa with intentions of sabotage are "promptly picked up by the South African police which has informers in every one [of their exile] camps as well as among most of the addressees to whom the saboteurs are supposed to come."

124. For example, the operations of the *Corpo Voluntário Angolano de Assistência dos Refugiados* (CVAAR/MPLA) and the *Servico de Assistência aos Refugiados de Angola* (SARA/GRAE) in the two Congo republics and Zambia and adjacent areas of Angola.

125. Notable among African initiatives to serve these ends are the Angolan Institute of Secondary Education and GRAE primary schools in the Congo (Kinshasa) and FRELIMO's Mozambique Institute in Dar es Salaam.

126. After giving himself up to the Portuguese in March 1969, Kavandame undertook to campaign among the Makonde, urging them to lay down their arms. (See "Mozambique: A Chief Surrenders," *Africa Confidential* [London], no. 8 [April 11, 1969], pp. 7–8.) In 1967 the Portuguese reportedly began encouraging defections among guerrillas moving into Mozambique from

Tanzania by offering to buy their arms, either directly or through village intermediaries: R30 for a mortar, R24 for a machine gun, R12 for a rifle. ("Guerrilla Dividends," p. 35.)

127. For an overview of the southern Sudan problem see George W. Shepherd, Jr., "National Integration and the Southern Sudan," *Journal of Modern African Studies*, vol. 4, no. 2 (October 1966), pp. 193–212; for a northern, pro-federalist analysis see Mohamed Omer Beshir, *The Southern Sudan: Background to Conflict* (New York: Frederick A. Praeger, 1968); Oliver Albino, *The Sudan: A Southern Viewpoint* (London: Oxford University Press, 1970); for reports on rebel action see Keith Kyle, "Sudan Officer: 'Only Political Formula Can End Fighting'," *The Christian Science Monitor*, April 30, 1966, Eastern ed., p. 13, cols. 1–5; and Lawrence Fellows, "6-Year Revolt in Sudan Leaves Untold Casualties," *New York Times*, April 15, 1968, late city ed., p. 1, col. 3 and p. 16, cols. 1–8.

128. See Decraene, *op. cit.*, p. 3, cols. 1–4; and "The Southern Sudan's Leaders," *Africa Confidential*, no. 14 (July 12, 1968), p. 7.

129. Lewis Nkosi argues that "the liberatory movement" of South Africa should be studying how to politicize the developing African urban middle class, or how to form links with "the more progressive elements" in the predominantly rural Bantustans so as to reorient their opposition to "Bantustan ideology" into a national political force. Also begging for analysis, he suggests, is the "possible role of the so-called 'lumpen proletariat' in urban South Africa—the tsotsi element which has proved under certain circumstances to be more daring than the so-called politically conscious urban workers." ("Crisis in the Revolution: Nkoana's Version," *South African Bulletin* [Paris], no. 73, March 1969).

CHAPTER 3

1. Paul Fordham, *The Geography of African Affairs* (Harmondsworth, Middlesex, England: Penguin Books, 1968), pp. 78–79. See also United Nations, *Statistical Yearbook 1968* (New York: United Nations, 1969), Table 54, p. 175.

2. Based on government and private company projections. For South Africa see "Population—Past, Present and Future," Standard Bank of South Africa *Annual Economic Review* (Johannesburg), July 1969, pp. 22–23; and *Data Southern Africa* (Pretoria: Africa Institute, 1969), p. 9.

3. See D. W. Krüger, *The Making of a Nation: A History of the Union of South Africa, 1910–1960* (New York: St. Martin's Press, 1969), p. 4. See also John Fisher, *The Afrikaners* (London: Cassell, 1969), p. 11.

4. John Davenport, " 'The Only Industrial Complex South of Milan': The Controversy over South Africa's Racial Policies Has Obscured the Achievements of Its Dynamic Economy," *Fortune*, vol. 74, no. 7 (December 1966), pp. 180–185, 236, 251–252.

5. David L. Niddrie, *South Africa: Nation or Nations?* (Princeton, N.J.: D. van Nostrand, 1968), pp. 166–168. See also "De Kolonels van Afrika," *Elseviers Magazine* (Amsterdam), vol. 26, no. 4 (January 24, 1970), pp. 29–45.

6. At the Institute of Social Studies at The Hague and at the Center for African Studies at the age-old Leiden University, three out of five available works in English deal only with West and East Africa, reflecting a trend found in most American universities.

7. "Scheme Will Dwarf Kariba and Aswan: Giant Contract for S.A.-Led Consortium: Cabora Bassa Decision," *The Star* (Johannesburg), September 3, 1969, stop press ed., p. 1, cols. 5–6 and p. 3, cols. 8–9.

8. "Cabora Bassa," *R.S.A. World* (Pretoria), file 5, no. 6 (1969), pp. 89–90.

9. "Africa's Hopes" (editorial), *Rand Daily Mail* (Johannesburg), September 6, 1969, first ed., p. 10, col. 1.

10. T. L. V. Blair, *Africa: A Profile* (London: Business Publications, 1965), p. 3; and Fritz Schatten, *Communism in Africa* (London: Allen & Unwin, 1966), p. 15.

11. In 1968 no less than twenty-two trade missions came from Great Britain, the Netherlands, South Korea, Nationalist China, Canada, Japan, Australia, New Zealand, France, West Germany, and other countries. In 1969 there were sixteen missions from Great Britain alone and thirteen planned for 1970. See "Thirteen Missions Coming," *South African Digest* (Pretoria), week ended February 6, 1970, p. 6.

12. The word *Bantu* is used in preference to *Africans*, which is misleading and erroneous when applied to the black inhabitants of South and East Africa. "Africans" include black as well as white, brown, and yellow people. Many of Africa's races and people come from Eurasia and some even come from the East. The white nation in South Africa, for example, has lived there for almost as many years as Americans have lived in the United States. Yet no scholar refers to Americans as "Europeans" (or "whites") although, ironically, the original inhabitants are not called Americans but "Indians." The word *Bantu* is a scholarly term and is ethnologically correct. It has the same meaning as Europeans in the sense that the Europeans of Europe include many nations such as the French, Germans, and Italians. Similarly, the Bantu of South Africa include different nations, such as the Zulu, Swazi, Xhosa, Tswana, and Sotho. Bantu is now used by many leading Africanists. See, for instance, George Peter Murdock, *Africa: Its People and Their Culture History* (New York: McGraw-Hill, 1959); Robert I. Rotberg, *A Political History of Tropical Africa* (New York: Harcourt, Brace & World, 1965); and Isaac Schapera (ed.), *The Bantu-Speaking Tribes of South Africa: An Ethnographical Survey*. Edited for the (South African) Inter-University Committee for African Studies (London: Routledge & Kegan Paul, 1937).

13. In the 1968 general election in the Transkei, the National Independence party (NIP) won 60 percent of the popular vote on a platform openly favoring separate development. In the current legislative assembly for the Transkei, the elected members of the NIP total 28 as against the Democratic Party's (Opposition) 14 and three independents. *State of South Africa: Economic, Financial and Statistical Year-Book for the Republic of South Africa, 1969* (Johannesburg: Da Gama Publishers, n.d.), p. 77.

14. For a detailed exposition of the policy, its objectives, problems, prospects, and progress, see N. J. Rhoodie, *Apartheid and Racial Partnership in Southern Africa . . .* (Pretoria, Cape Town: H. & R. Academia, 1969), particularly pp. 91, 356–357.

15. South Africa. Parliament. House of Assembly, *Debates*, vol. 99, cols. 65–66, 69 (January 23, 1959) and

vol. 101, cols. 6520–6521 (May 4, 1959); South Africa, *Memorandum Explaining the Background and Objectives of the Promotion of Bantu Self-Government Bill, 1959.* White Paper 3 (Pretoria: Government Printer, 1959), pp. 6–7; South Africa, *Progress through Separate Development* (New York: South African Information Service, 1968), p. 50; and A. N. Pelzer (ed.), *Verwoerd Speaks: Speeches, 1948–1966* (Johannesburg: APB Publishers, 1966), p. 512.

16. This was confirmed by the present prime minister of South Africa (Mr. B. J. Vorster) in a recent interview with Mr. Albert J. Meyers of *U.S. News & World Report*. "Interview with John Vorster, Prime Minister of the Republic of South Africa: The Story of Race and Progress in Africa's Richest Nation," *U.S. News & World Report*, vol. 61, no. 20 (November 14, 1966), pp. 94–96, 98, 100, 105. See also the map entitled "The Existing and Emerging States in Southern Africa" in J. A. Lombard, J. J. Stadler, and P. J. van der Merwe, *The Concept of Economic Co-operation in Southern Africa* (New York: Richard Abel, 1968), p. 15, and the population statistics in Table 2 of this chapter.

17. For expert testimony on the difficulties which a policy of integration would face, see the summary of oral evidence before the International Court of Justice in the cases of *Liberia* v. *South Africa* and *Ethiopia* v. *South Africa* by Professors Stefan Possony, Ernest van den Haag, D. C. Krogh, C. A. Manning, and others in South Africa. Department of Foreign Affairs, *South West Africa Survey, 1967* (Pretoria and Cape Town: Government Printer, 1967), Annexure D, pp. 154–190.

18. Pelzer, *op. cit.*, p. 364.

19. *Ibid.*, p. 283.

20. See Gwendolen M. Carter, *Independence for Africa* (New York: Frederick A. Praeger, 1961), p. 161.

21. See United States. Congress. House of Representatives. Committee on Foreign Affairs. Subcommittee on Africa, *United States–South African Relations: Hearings.* 4 parts. Eighty-ninth Congress, second session (Washington, D.C.: USGPO, 1966), Part I, pp. 71–80, 190–215; and Eschel M. Rhoodie, *The Paper Curtain* (Johannesburg: Voortrekkerpers, 1969), pp. 87–88, 99.

22. Zambia is included for good reasons. Since Rhodesia's declaration of independence, Zambia has shown no willingness to copoerate with Rhodesia or South Africa (except in matters of trade) and has, instead, concentrated all its efforts to improve its links with Tanzania. Politically, therefore, it is almost wholly an outsider. Nonetheless, it maintains cordial political relations with Botswana and, to a lesser extent, with Malawi and Lesotho, all member states of Southern Africa, while it is economically and geographically inescapably part of Southern Africa. It is linked by rail to Rhodesia and Mozambique and by road to Malawi and Mozambique. Its coal and electricity come from Rhodesia. See the address by Professor O. P. F. Horwood to the Economic Society of South Africa on March 19, 1969, entitled "Economic Co-operation in Southern Africa" (mimeographed), p. 5; and Lombard, Stadler, and van der Merwe, *op. cit.*, pp. 32–33.

23. See the verbatim text issued by the Department of Information, Pretoria, 1965; Nico Diedrichs, "Southern African Common Market: Many Obstacles Still Lie Ahead," *South African Financial Gazette* (Johannesburg), April 28, 1967, supplement, p. 1; and "The Problem of Aid: South Africa's Policy," Africa Institute *Bulletin* (Pretoria), vol. 3, no. 6 (June 1965), pp. 128–134.

24. Eschel M. Rhoodie, *The Third Africa* (New York: Twin Circle, 1968), pp. 213, 217–220.

25. Opening address to the Fourth Annual Congress of the South African Branch of the International Association of Students of Commerce and Trade, Cape Town, June 30, 1969. Verbatim text no. 89/69 (P) issued by the Department of Information, Pretoria.

26. See "South African Mission Is Off to Madagascar," *Rand Daily Mail*, September 8, 1969, first ed., p. 8, cols. 4–6; " 'After That, Who Knows What Can Follow?,' " *South Africa International* (London), February 1970, p. 1; and "Cabinet Ministers from Mauritius Arrive," *South Africa International*, February 1970, p. 1.

27. Al J. Venter, "Gambia Wants S.A. Trade and Tourists Says Jawara," *Sunday Times* (Johannesburg), January 25, 1970, p. 3, cols. 4–6.

28. Al J. Venter, "Greater Trade with Black States," *Sunday Times*, February 1, 1970, Business Times, p. 9, cols. 1–5.

29. See H. J. van Eck, "A Central Scheme for the Supply of Water in Southern Africa," *Tegnikon* (Pretoria), special edition, March 1967, p. 37; H. J. van Eck, "Industrial Development in the Republic of South Africa and Its Impact on Southern Africa," the Hendrik van der Bijl lecture at the University of Pretoria on May 19, 1967 (mimeographed); and "Transforming a Sub-Continent," *Standard Bank Review* (Johannesburg), no. 610 (January 1970), pp. 2–9.

30. Press statement no. 185/69 (P) issued by the Department of Information, Pretoria, August 27, 1969; and "New Customs Agreement: Treble Gain for S.A. Neighbours," *The Star*, February 18, 1970, 2nd city late ed., p. 13, cols. 2–4.

31. Eschel M. Rhoodie, *The Third Africa*, pp. 43–47, 191–192; and "Swaziland and South Africa," *Background to South African and World News* (London), October 1968, p. 3.

32. Eschel M. Rhoodie, *The Paper Curtain*, pp. 21–26, 44–46. See also "Swaziland and South Africa," p. 3.

33. F. R. Metrowich, *Africa and Communism: A Study of Success, Set-backs and Stooge States* (Johannesburg: Voortrekkerpers, 1967), pp. 219–220. See also "Ban on Red Literature," *African Express* (Amsterdam), March 12, 1970, p. 2.

34. Eschel M. Rhoodie, *The Paper Curtain*, pp. 21–26, and "Swaziland and South Africa," p. 3.

35. "Swazis Do Not Plan Closer Ties with S.A.," *The Star*, September 8, 1969, 2nd city late ed., p. 20, cols. 6–7.

36. The mimeographed texts of the statements by the prime minister of Lesotho, the president of Botswana, and the cabinet ministers of Malawi are available from the Press Liaison Division of the Department of Information, Pretoria. These statements stressed three points: first, ideological differences were no bar to cooperation; second, the countries would continue to seek closer cooperation with South Africa; and third, common interests dominated the talks. See the speeches by the ministers of finance of Botswana and Lesotho at the signing of the Customs Union Agreement among South Africa, Botswana, Lesotho, and Swaziland. These texts —nos. 381/69 (P) and 382 (P)—are available from the Department of Information, Pretoria.

37. "Rousing Welcome for S. Africans," *The Star*, July 30, 1969, 2nd city late ed., p. 7, cols. 8–9.
38. "They Are Sifting Riches from Sand," *South African Financial Gazette*, March 13, 1970, p. 6.
39. "Spectacular Road Link from Zambesi to Congo," *The Star*, August 27, 1969, 2nd city late ed., p. 35, cols. 2–4.
40. For trade links, tourism, and communications between South Africa and Mozambique, see *Mozambique*, Supplement to *Standard Bank Review* (Johannesburg), November 1968, pp. 11–20.
41. "Assurance to Investors: Angola Seeks Closer Ties with South Africa," *The Star*, June 4, 1969, 2nd city late ed., p. 21, cols. 7–9.
42. Dr. A. de Oliveira Salazar, "As I See Southern Africa," *Million* (Johannesburg), issue no. 2 (1968), p. 8; and "Africa—Portugal Stays," *R.S.A. World*, file 5, no. 7 (1969), pp. 104–105, 110.
43. "Lisbon Keen To Aid Malawi," *The Star*, March 3, 1969, stop press ed., p. 12, cols. 7–9.
44. "Trading Alliance Suggested," *Rand Daily Mail*, June 3, 1969, morning final ed. p. 21, col. 9.
45. Eschel M. Rhoodie, *South West Africa: The Last Frontier in Africa* (New York: Twin Circle, 1968), pp. 32, 35–36; South Africa. Department of Foreign Affairs, *South West Africa: South Africa's Reply to the Secretary-General of the United Nations (Security Council Resolution 269 of 1969)* (Pretoria: Government Printer, 1969), pp. 49–50; and Eschel M. Rhoodie, *The Third Africa*, pp. 156–158.
46. Eschel M. Rhoodie, *The Third Africa*, p. 158; M. C. van Zyl, "States and Colonies in South Africa, 1854–1902," in C. F. J. Muller (ed.), *Five Hundred Years: A History of South Africa* (Pretoria and Cape Town: H. & R. Academia, 1969), p. 274: and Thomas Molnar, *South West Africa: The Last Pioneer Country* (New York: Fleet Publishing, 1961), p. 61.
47. See Eschel M. Rhoodie, *South West Africa*, pp. 66, 230, 269.
48. Eschel M. Rhoodie, *The Third Africa*, pp. 162–168. See also "Rhodesia—Now and Tomorrow," *News Check* (Johannesburg), vol. 7, no. 44 (June 27–July 10, 1970), pp. 17–19.
49. W. W. Rostow, "Regionalism and World Order," *Department of State Bulletin*, vol. 57, no. 1464 (July 17, 1967), p. 67 (italics added).
50. N. Shand, *Report on the Regional Development of the Resources of Basutoland* (Cape Town: Government Printer, 1956), p. 23.
51. Van Eck, "A Central Scheme," p. 39, and "Transforming a Sub-Continent," p. 9.
52. See *Care* (Pretoria: Department of Information, 1969), pp. 15–27; and United Nations, *Statistical Yearbook, 1968* (20th issue) (New York: United Nations, 1969), Table 206, p. 701.
53. "Medical Aid to Lesotho," Africa Institute *Bulletin*, vol. 7, no. 2 (March 1969), pp. 43–46.
54. "Hulp aan Buurstate," South African Broadcasting Corporation *Bulletin* (Johannesburg), vol. 15, no. 11 (August 18, 1969), p. 3; and Ken Campbell, "Outward Looking Students at Work," *Rand Daily Mail*, November 13, 1969, 1st ed., p. 21, cols. 1–5.
55. Piet J. Cillié, "Evolving Relationships in Southern Africa: Vision of the Seventies," *Report from South Africa* (London), January 1969, pp. 7–9.
56. For the full text of the Lesotho–South African statement see Eschel M. Rhoodie, *The Third Africa*, p. 42. For the London statement of the Congress party, see " 'S. African Will Work with B.C.P.,' " *The Star*, February 6, 1970, 2nd city late ed., p. 15, cols. 6–7.
57. F. J. C. Cronjé, "Can a Free Trade Association Be Created in Southern Africa?", *Optima* (Johannesburg), vol. 15, no. 3 (September 1965), pp. 113–119; and O. P. F. Horwood, "Suider Afrika Begin Nouer Saamwerk," *Die Burger* (Cape Town), March 14, 1969, laaste vitgawe, p. 15, cols. 4–6.
58. Norman Macrae, "What Will Destroy Apartheid?", *Harper's Magazine*, vol. 240, no. 1438 (March 1970), p. 36.
59. See "People in Glass Houses: The UN Crusade against South Africa Is a Disgrace," *Barrons*, vol. 44, no. 52 (December 28, 1964), p. 1. This question is also examined in detail in Eschel M. Rhoodie, *The Paper Curtain*, chaps. 4–5.
60. S. H. Steinberg (ed.), *The Statesman's Yearbook: Statistical and Historical Annual of the States of the World for 1966–67* (London: The Macmillan Company 1966), pp. 1023, 1041.
61. See Stanislav Andreski, *The African Predicament: A Study in the Pathology of Modernisation* (London: Michael Joseph, 1969); and René Dumond, *False Start in Africa* (London: André Deutsch, 1966), pp. 78–86.
62. Schatten, *op. cit.*, p. 144; Metrowich, *op. cit.*; and Anthony Harrigan, *Red Star over Africa* (Cape Town: Nasionale Boekhandel, 1964).
63. Niddrie, *op. cit.*, pp. 3–4.
64. Al J. Venter, *The Terror Fighters: A Profile of Guerrilla Warfare in Southern Africa* (Cape Town, Johannesburg: Purnell & Sons, 1969), pp. 13–15, 29–31. See also P. K. Huibregtse, *Angola Is Anders* (The Hague: Forum Books, 1968), pp. 9–15, 58–82.
65. "Secrets of 'Black Freedom' Money: Africa's Warring Liberators—2," *Sunday Telegraph* (London), May 4, 1969, p. 6, cols. 1–6 and p. 7, cols. 1–6. See also Bernardo Teixeira, *The Fabric of Terror: Three Days in Angola* (New York: Devin-Adair, 1965), pp. 157–176; Thomas Molnar, *Africa: A Political Travelogue* (New York: Fleet Publishing, 1965), pp. 91–92; and P. K. Huibregtse, *Zo Is Mozambique* (The Hague: Forum Books, 1967), pp. 243–249.
66. For example, the *New York Times*, the *Observer* (London), *Dagens Nyheter* (Stockholm), and *Le Monde* (Paris), not to mention persons such as Thomas Karis, "South Africa," in Gwendolen M. Carter (ed.), *Five African States: Responses to Diversity* (Ithaca: Cornell University Press, 1963), pp. 471–616; John Hatch, *Africa To-day and To-morrow* (London: Dennis Dobson, 1962); Philip Mason, *An Essay on Racial Tension* (London: Hunt, 1954); Waldemar A. Nielsen, *African Battleline: American Policy Choices in Southern Africa.* Published for the Council on Foreign Relations (New York and Evanston: Harper & Row, 1965); and three members of the South African Communist Party (Ruth First, Govan Mbeki, and Brian Bunting) whose books are published by the African library of Penguin Books under the editorship of Ronald Segal.
67. Macrae, *op. cit.*, p. 30; and C. W. de Kiewiet, "The World and Pretoria," *Virginia Quarterly Review*, vol. 45, no. 1 (Winter 1969), pp. 15–18.
68. A. W. Smith, "Europe's Investors Flock Back to South Africa," *Sunday Times*, February 15, 1970, Business Times, p. 32, cols. 1–6. See also Niddrie, *op.*

cit., pp. 3–4, 77. Virtually every week, the *South African Financial Gazette* reports that a new company with foreign backing is established in South Africa or that there is a large expansion program of existing foreign companies. This is also borne out in reports of British, American, West German, French, Swiss, and Dutch banks operating in South Africa.

69. See "Zambia: The Wages of Radicalism," *News Check*, vol. 8, no. 5 (September 5–18, 1969), pp. 20–21.

70. "Chinese Radios for Zambia," *Sunday Telegraph*, September 21, 1969, p. 2, col. 8; and "Red China: Agitation, Propaganda, Contacts and Other Activities," *Monthly Review* (The Hague), no. 1 of 1970, pp. 7–8.

71. See *State of South Africa . . . 1969*, pp. 122–128. Except for Southern Africa and a few other independent states elsewhere in Africa, most African states face a crisis in food production in the decade ahead which is causing the gravest concern. See William and Paul Paddock, *Famine 1975! America's Decision: Who Will Survive?* (Boston: Little, Brown, 1967); and William A. Hance, "The Race between Population and Resources," *Africa Report*, vol. 13, no. 1 (January 1968), pp. 6–12.

72. See General S. L. A. Marshall, *South Africa: The Strategic View* (New York: American African Affairs Association, 1966); and *South Africa in World Strategy: Special Survey* (London: South African Embassy, 1969).

73. E. S. Virpsha, "Strategic Significance of Southern Africa," *N.A.T.O.'s Fifteen Nations* (Amsterdam), vol. 14, no. 1 (February-March 1969), pp. 100–107; and Anthony Harrigan, "Naval Defense of the Southern Oceans: The Soviet Threat in the South Atlantic and Indian Oceans," American Security Council *Washington Report*, August 18, 1969, pp. 1–4.

74. These words were first used by Robert Hallett, Africa correspondent for the *Christian Science Monitor*, in 1965. See also Venter, "Greater Trade with Black States," p. 9, cols. 1–5.

75. Published in London by the corporation.

76. Simon Sishayi Nxumalo, "Swaziland," *Optima*, vol. 19, no. 3 (September 1969), p. 154; "Mbabane Proposal: Hint on S.A. Aid for Swaziland," *The Star*, March 18, 1969, 2nd city late ed., p. 13, cols. 1–2; and "Developing Communications," *Background to South African and World News*, October 1968, p. 3.

77. For a brief review of South Africa's economic preeminence in Africa, see Jan Marais, "South Africa in Global Perspective," in *South African Progress 1969* (Cape Town: Afrikaanse Handelsinstituut, 1969), chap. 1.

78. See P. Smit and E. J. van der Merwe, "Economic Co-operation in Southern Africa," *Journal for Geography* (Stellenbosch), vol. 3, no. 3 (September 1968), pp. 279–294; Lombard, Stadler, and van der Merwe, *op. cit.*; Cronjé, *op. cit.*, pp. 113–119; A. F. Ewing, "Prospects for Economic Integration in Africa," *Journal of Modern African Studies* (London), vol. 5, no. 1 (January 1967), pp. 53–67; *South African Financial Gazette*, April 28, 1967, "Special Supplement on a Common Market for Southern Africa;" and various articles in *Tegnikon*, March 1967, special edition devoted to the topic of the development of the Bantu homelands and economic relations with neighboring states.

79. Probable new states in South Africa and South West Africa are Xhosaland, Ovamboland, North Sotholand, Tswanaland, and Zululand. See also J. A. Lombard, "Economic Co-operation in Southern Africa," *Tegnikon*, March 1967, p. 19.

80. Smit and van der Merwe, *op. cit.*, pp. 279–294.

81. The purposes of this bureau are stated in Lombard, Stadler, and van der Merwe, *op. cit.*, p. 7.

82. Senator O. P. F. Horwood's speech of February 12, 1970, before the South African Senate. South Africa. Parliament. Senate, *Debates*. Weekly English edition no. 2, cols. 258–265.

83. Dr. P. J. Riekert, "The Economy of the Republic," an address to the annual general meeting of the South African Institute of Race Relations, January 28, 1970. Mimeographed text No. 15/70 (P) issued by the Department of Information, Pretoria, p. 5.

84. Dr. Jan Haak's address to a symposium on a Southern African common market, Johannesburg, May 31, 1965. The text of the address, Bulletin 70/65 (k), is available from the Department of Information, Pretoria; Riekert, *op. cit.*, pp. 3–7.

85. Arne Pitlo, "Botswana's Big Blast-Off," *South African Financial Gazette*, August 1, 1969; and "Decision Soon on World Bank Botswana Loan," *South African Financial Gazette*, February 20, 1970, p. 5.

86. Lombard, Stadler, and van der Merwe, *op. cit.*, p. 33.

87. "Bigger Trade Volume," *South African Digest*, week ended January 30, 1970, p. 7.

88. Smit and van der Merwe, *op. cit.*, pp. 283–284. In most cases the production of these items is too small to justify separate overseas marketing. In the case of citrus fruit, for instance, all profits would be swallowed up by the so-called "dead freight" in ships. The fruit is shipped in refrigerated cargo holds of specific cubic size, meaning that a small consignment filling half the space costs the same as a full hold.

89. *Ibid.*, pp. 285–286. See Table 3 of this chapter. However, official estimates put the total number of of foreign Africans in South Africa at 836,000. See *Summary of the Report of the Commission for the Socio-Economic Development of the Bantu Areas within the Bantu Areas of the Union of South Africa.* U.G. 61/1955 (Pretoria: Government Printer, 1955), pp. 39–41; and G. Owen, *Summary of the Froneman Report* (Pretoria: Department of Bantu Administration, 1967), pp. 2, 42, 54–61.

90. G. M. E. Leistner, "Foreign Bantu Workers in South Africa: Their Present Position in the Economy," *South African Journal of Economics* (Johannesburg), vol. 35, no. 1 (March 1967), pp. 38–39.

91. Dr. Leistner's data for Malawi were updated by Drs. Smit and van der Merwe. See Smit and van der Merwe, *op. cit.*, p. 287. See also the address of the president of the South African Chamber of Mines as reported in "S.A. Gold Output, Pointer to Sales," *Rand Daily Mail*, June 25, 1969, 1st ed., p. 19, cols. 1–2.

92. "Migratory Labour," *Tempo* (Johannesburg), no. 68 (December 1968–January 1969), p. 3.

93. Smit and van der Merwe, *op. cit.*, p. 287. For a discussion of this newly created fund, see the speech of the deputy minister of finance during the second reading debate of the Economic Cooperation Promotion Loan Fund Bill. South Africa. Parliament. House of Assembly, *Debates*, vol. 23, cols. 5308–5309 (May 14, 1968).

94. See Diedrichs, *op. cit.*, p. 1.

95. Smit and van der Merwe, *op. cit.*, p. 293.

96. See W. Marshall Clark, "South Africa Has Made a Great Contribution to the African Continent," *Africa* (Johannesburg), vol. 1, no. 1 (May 1965), pp. 41–48.

97. Address by the minister of mines, Dr. Carel de Wet, to the Chamber of Mines of Rhodesia at Salisbury, Rhodesia, July 29, 1969, Press statement no. P.125/69 issued by the Department of Information, Pretoria.

98. Simon Kuznets, *Modern Economic Growth: Rate, Structure, and Spread* (New Haven and London: Yale University Press, 1966), p. 451.

99. Riekert, *op. cit.*, p. 3.

100. *Ibid.*

101. *Ibid.*, p. 4.

102. For further details consult Lombard, Stadler, and van der Merwe, *op. cit.*, pp. 44–49.

103. Smit and van der Merwe, *op. cit.*, p. 294 (italics in the original). See also Robert Haynes, "Economic Co-operation in Southern Africa," *South African Financial Gazette*, June 16, 1969, p. 8.

104. Smit and van der Merwe, *op. cit.*, pp. 284–285.

105. *Ibid.*, p. 284.

106. *Ibid.*, p. 285 (italics in the original).

107. *Ibid.*

108. Lombard, Stadler, and van der Merwe, *op. cit.*, pp. 34–35.

109. *Ibid.*, p. 35.

110. *Ibid.*

111. *Ibid.*, pp. 39–42.

112. *Ibid.*, p. 62.

113. *Ibid.*, pp. 62–63.

114. *Ibid.*, p. 63 (italics in the original).

115. Smit and van der Merwe, *op. cit.*, pp. 288–289.

116. *Ibid.*, p. 289.

117. *Ibid.*, See also C. Verbrugh, "Africa's Big Need Is Transport," *South African Financial Gazette*, April 28, 1967, supplement, p. 5.

118. Smit and van der Merwe, *op. cit.*, p. 289. See also L. P. Green and T. J. D. Fair, *Development in Africa: A Study in Regional Analysis with Special Reference to Southern Africa* (Johannesburg: Witwatersrand University Press, 1962), p. 51.

119. Smit and van der Merwe, *op. cit.*, pp. 289–290.

120. *Ibid.*, p. 290.

121. *Ibid.*, pp. 290–291.

122. *Ibid.*, p. 291 (italics in the original).

123. Van Eck, "A Central Scheme," p. 37, and "Transforming a Sub-Continent," p. 9.

124. Electricity Supply Commission, *46th Annual Report for 1968* (Johannesburg: Electricity Supply Commission, 1969), pp. 8–9. See also "Signs Point to Booming 1970," *South African Financial Gazette*, December 31, 1969, p. 5.

125. Smit and van der Merwe, *op. cit.*, pp. 291–292.

126. *Ibid.*, p. 292.

127. During 1948 South Africa spent only $5.74 million on the construction of dams, whereas it allocated $108.64 million for that purpose in 1970. See "Water Saving Plans," *South African Digest*, week ended March 6, 1970, p. 3.

128. Smit and van der Merwe, *op. cit.*, pp. 292–293.

129. Otto Krause, "Towards a Greater Southern Africa," *News Check*, vol. 6, no. 15 (October 20, 1967), pp. 17–18.

130. *South Africa: An African-Rooted Nation: Speech by Dr. H. Muller, Minister of Foreign Affairs of the Republic of South Africa, during a Dinner Given by the Africa Institute of South Africa in Pretoria on June 25, 1968.* Occasional Paper no. 5 (Pretoria: Africa Institute, 1968), p. 11.

131. See Willem van Heerden, "Coming to Terms with Africa," *Perspective* (London), vol. 6, no. 9 (June 1969), pp. 9–11.

132. "Ensiklopedie Nou Ter Perse," *Die Burger*, February 13, 1970, laaste vitgawe, p. 7, cols. 1–3.

133. Richard Pattee, "S.A. & Portugal," Africa Institute *Bulletin*, vol. 7, no. 6 (July 1969), pp. 238–239; Standard Bank of South Africa *Annual Economic Review*, July 1967, p. 9; and "SA Businessmen Share Managerial Know-How with Neighbouring African States," *South Africa International*, February 1970, p. 1.

134. Cillié, *op. cit.*, p. 9.

135. The times are changed and we with them (from the Latin).

CHAPTER 4

1. Mao Tse-tung, *Selected Works*. 5 vols. (New York: International Publishers, 1954), vol. 2, pp. 134–141.

2. The effect of a wet season on supply movements for a mechanized army is graphically depicted in Field Marshal The Viscount Slim's *Defeat into Victory* (New York: David McKay, 1961), pp. 417–432.

3. Richard Dale, "South African Counterinsurgency Operations in South West Africa," a paper prepared for delivery at the Eleventh Annual Meeting of the African Studies Association, Los Angeles, October 17, 1968, p. 11.

4. Richard Dale, "Ovamboland: 'Bantustan without Tears?' " *Africa Report*, vol. 14, no. 2 (February 1969), pp. 16–23.

5. Desmond C. Midgley, "The Orange River Development Project in South Africa," *Progress* (London), vol. 49, no. 278 (Autumn 1963), pp. 242–253.

6. Alan Rake, "Black Guerrillas in Rhodesia," *Africa Report*, vol. 13, no. 10 (December 1968), p. 25.

7. *State of the Union: Financial and Statistical Year-Book for the Union of South Africa* (Cape Town: Culemborg, 1957), pp. 25–27.

8. Palabora Mining Company Limited, *1968 Annual Report and Accounts* (n.p., 1969), pp. 8–18.

9. Perhaps the classic example of guerrilla activity in rear areas supporting a frontal drive by conventional forces occurred in Russia in the summer of 1944. The destruction of rail lines, bridges, and truck convoys by partisans greatly assisted the Red Army in destroying twenty-five German divisions. (Heinz Guderian, *Panzer Leader* [London: Michael Joseph, 1952], pp. 335–337.)

10. J. E. Spence and Elizabeth Thomas, *South Africa's Defense: The Problem of Internal Control*. Security Studies Paper no. 8 (Los Angeles: University of California, 1966), p. 10.

11. Christian P. Potholm, "After UDI: An Assessment of Southern Africa," *Journal of Asian and African Studies* (Leiden, Netherlands), vol. 2, nos. 3–4 (July and October 1967), p. 249.

12. "Guardians of the Coast," *South African Scope*, January 1969, p. 8.

13. All details concerning South Africa's navy are based on data in Raymond V. B. Blackman (ed.), *Jane's Fighting Ships, 1967–1968* (New York: McGraw-Hill, 1968), pp. 236–239.

14. Spence and Thomas, *op. cit.*, p. 11.

15. Russell Warren Howe, "Southern African Conflict Simmers on Many Fronts," *Christian Science*

Monitor, August 21, 1968, Eastern edition, p. 5, cols. 1–5.
16. *Ibid.*, and Edgar O'Ballance, "South Africa's Defence Problems . . .," *African World* (London), August 1965, pp. 4–5.
17. Spence and Thomas, *op. cit.*, p. 11.
18. Govan Mbeki, *South Africa: The Peasants' Revolt* (Baltimore: Penguin Books, 1964), pp. 111–134.
19. Spence and Thomas, *op. cit.*, p. 12.
20. Dale, "South African Counterinsurgency," p. 16.
21. For a detailed discussion of this matter and ratios for many African countries, see Christian P. Potholm, "The Multiple Roles of the Police as Seen in the African Context," *Journal of Developing Areas*, vol. 3, no. 2 (January 1969), pp. 139–157.
22. "Defense of the Free World: South Africa's Record," *South African Scope*, January 1965, p. 4; and Eric Linklater, *Our Men in Korea* (London: HMSO, 1952), p. 73.
23. David Kimche and Daniel Bawley, *The Sandstorm: The Arab-Israeli War of June 1967: Prelude and Aftermath* (New York: Stein & Day, 1968), pp. 178–181.
24. John W. R. Taylor (ed.), *Jane's All The World's Aircraft, 1966–1967* (London: Sampson Low, Marston, 1966), p. 416.
25. Ernest A. Gross, "The Coalescing Problem of Southern Africa," *Foreign Affairs*, vol. 46, no. 4 (July 1968), p. 747.
26. Spence and Thomas, *op. cit.*, p. 11; and Steven H. Steinberg (ed.), *Statesman's Yearbook, 1968–1969* (New York: St. Martin's Press, 1968), p. 1404.
27. Spence and Thomas, *op. cit.*, p. 11.
28. "Progress on Impalas," *South African Panorama* (Pretoria), vol. 13, no. 10 (October 1968), pp. 12–17; and Taylor, *op. cit.*, p. 118.
29. Larry W. Bowman, "Strains in the Rhodesian Front," *Africa Report*, vol. 13, no. 10 (December 1968), pp. 16–20.
30. Rake, *op. cit.*, pp. 24–25.
31. "Rhodesia Looks to S.A. for Police," *The Star* (Johannesburg), July 25, 1968, 2nd city late edition, p. 10, col. 9; and Rake, *op. cit.*, p. 24.
32. Peter Tonge, "Pretoria Anxious on Rhodesia," *Christian Science Monitor*, November 22, 1968, Eastern edition, p. 21, cols. 3–5.
33. *Ibid.*
34. Martin Legassick, "The Consequences of African Guerrilla Activity for South Africa's Relations with her Neighbours," a paper prepared for delivery at the Tenth Annual Meeting of the African Studies Association, New York, November 3, 1967, p. 16.
35. Steinberg, *op. cit.*, p. 561; and Paul H. Wilkinson, *Aircraft Engines of the World, 1960/61* (Washington: Paul H. Wilkinson, 1960), p. 279.
36. Legassick, "Consequences of African Guerrilla Activity," p. 17.
37. Ronald H. Chilcote, *Portuguese Africa* (Englewood Cliffs, N.J.: Prentice-Hall, 1967), pp. 31–32.
38. "News in Brief: Portuguese Africa: Policy under Review?" *Africa Report*, vol. 14, no. 1 (January 1969), p. 29.
39. For a graphic review of the economic growth of the two provinces, see Farrell Lines, *African News Digest*. Nearly every issue has commentary on the subject, but that of May 1966 is among the most interesting.
40. For a good defense of the Portuguese position, see Adriano Moreira, *Portugal's Stand in Africa* (New York: University Publishers, 1962), pp. v–viii, 23–43.
41. Douglas Wheeler, "Reflections on Angola," *Africa Report*, vol. 12, no. 9 (November 1967), p. 62; and *The Military Balance* (London: Institute for Strategic Studies, 1966), p. 26.
42. A good account of the early days of the rebellion may be found in Thomas Okuma, *Angola in Ferment* (Boston: Beacon Press, 1962), pp. 81–102.
43. Allison Butler Herrick *et al.*, *Area Handbook for Angola*, DA Pam. no. 550–59, USGPO, 1967), p. 383; and Okuma, *op. cit.*, pp. 68–69.
44. Douglas L. Wheeler, "The Portuguese Army in Angola," *Journal of Modern African Studies*, vol. 7, no. 3 (October 1969), p. 432.
45. Herrick, *op. cit.*, pp. 375–390.
46. All data concerning the Portuguese navy are derived from Blackman, *op. cit.*, pp. 226–233.
47. Friedrich Ruge, *Der Seekrieg: The German Navy's Story* (Annapolis: U.S. Naval Institute, 1957), p. 302.
48. Steinberg, *op. cit.*, p. 1364.
49. Slim, *op. cit.*, pp. 300–302; and James S. Coleman and Belmont Brice, Jr., "The Role of the Military in Sub-Saharan Africa" in John J. Johnson (ed.), *The Role of the Military in Underdeveloped Countries* (Princeton, N.J.: Princeton University Press, 1962), pp. 372–373.
50. A good description of these events may be found in Henry Bienen, *Tanzania: Party Transformation and Economic Development* (Princeton: Princeton University Press, 1967) pp. 363–381. See also Tanganyika Information Services, *January/February Events, 1964* (Dar es Salaam: Government Printing Office, 1964), pp. 33–34.
51. For details on the Chinese military presence see Colin Legum, "Why Tanganyika Accepted a Chinese Military Mission," *Africa Report*, vol. 9, no. 9 (October 1964), p. 16.
52. Tanganyika Information Services, *op. cit.*, pp. 9–10.
53. Potholm, "The Multiple Roles of the Police," pp. 11, 34.
54. Blackman, *op. cit.*, p. 264.
55. Steinberg, *op. cit.*, p. 498.
56. For a detailed account see Gerard L. Caplan, "Barotseland: The Secessionist Challenge to Zambia," *Journal of Modern African Studies*, vol. 6, no. 3 (October 1968), pp. 343–360.
57. Rake, *op. cit.*, p. 24.
58. "Zambian Development," *African News Digest*, vol. 6, no. 5 (June 1965), pp. 1–2.
59. George Weeks (compiler), "The Armies of Africa," *Africa Report*, vol. 8, no. 1 (January 1964), pp. 16–17.
60. Kenneth W. Grundy, "On Machiavelli and the Mercenaries," *Journal of Modern African Studies*, vol. 6, no. 3 (October 1968), pp. 295–310.
61. Details of the *Bastion* transaction are given in Blackman, *op. cit.*, pp. 321, 483.
62. Steinberg, *op. cit.*, p. 541.
63. Rake, *op. cit.*, p. 24.
64. Zambia's determination to extend majority rule over Southern Africa was reaffirmed by the "Manifesto on Southern Africa" issued on April 14–16, 1969, by the fifth Summit Conference of East and Central African States meeting at Lusaka. The test of this manifesto, sponsored by Vernon J. Mwaanga, Permanent Repres-

entative of the Republic of Zambia to the United Nations, is published in the *New York Times*, May 2, 1969, late city edition, p. 25, cols. 5–8.

65. T. R. Kanza, "The Problems of the Congo," *African Affairs* (London), vol. 67, no. 266 (January 1968), p. 57.

66. Details on the Congo's army are based on Weeks, *op. cit.*, pp. 7–8; and "The Congo: Three Years After Independence," *Africa Institute International Bulletin* (Pretoria), vol. 2, no. 3 (March 1964), pp. 84–86.

67. Potholm, "The Multiple Roles of the Police," pp. 5, 9.

68. Steinberg, *op. cit.*, p. 918. The need for training aircraft is obvious when one considers that Cuban exiles are presently manning many of the Congo's planes.

69. United States Army, *Area Handbook for the Republic of the Congo (Leopoldville)* (Washington: American University, 1962), pp. 645–646.

70. Blackman, *op. cit.*, pp. 74–75, 204.

71. Weeks, *op. cit.*, pp. 4–21.

72. "France's Military Role in Africa," *Africa Report*, vol. 9, no. 1 (January 1964), p. 10.

73. Christian P. Potholm, "The Protectorates, the O.A.U. and South Africa," *International Journal* (Toronto), vol. 22, no. 1 (Winter 1966–1967), p. 68.

74. For discussion of Botswana's difficult position see C. Edward Crowther, "South Africa's New Look: A *Détente Cordiale*?" *American Scholar*, vol. 37, no. 1 (Winter 1967–1968), pp. 47–58.

75. Potholm, "After UDI," p. 248.

76. Sidney Goldberg, "Africa's Amazon Army," *World Week*, vol. 46, no. 8 (March 25, 1965), p. 5.

77. Martin Legassick, "The Southern African Bloc: Integration for Defense or Expansion?" *Africa Today*, vol. 15, no. 5 (October–November 1968), p. 9.

78. Legassick, "Consequences of African Guerrilla Activity," p. 2.

79. An excellent description of the difficulties experienced in unifying the anti-Portuguese forces is found in John A. Marcum, "Three Revolutions," *Africa Report*, vol. 12, No. 9 (November 1967), pp. 9–17.

80. *Ibid.*, pp. 13–14.

81. *Ibid.*, p. 13; and Marvine Howe, "Portuguese Lands Weather Change in Regime," *New York Times*, January 24, 1969, late city edition, p. 69, cols. 4–8.

82. Legassick, "Consequences of African Guerrilla Activity," p. 2; Lawrence Fellows, "Portuguese Curb Guerrillas in Mozambique . . .," *New York Times*, November 21, 1966, late city edition, p. 1, cols. 3–6 and p. 8, cols. 4–8; and James M. Dodson, "Dynamics of Insurgency in Mozambique," *Africa Report*, vol. 12, no. 8 (November 1967), pp. 52–55.

83. Marcum, *op. cit.*, p. 20

84. David Winder, "Labour and Tories Split on Rhodesia," *Christian Science Monitor*, March 29, 1968, Eastern edition, p. 6, cols. 4–5.

85. An extremely interesting novel, based on fact, which catches the flavor of Rhodesia from the Ndebele rebellion to the Unilateral Declaration of Independence is W. A. Ballinger's *Call It Rhodesia* (New York: G. P. Putnam's Sons, 1969).

86. Legassick, "Consequences of African Guerrilla Activity," p. 3.

87. *Ibid.*

88. *Ibid.*, pp. 1–3; and "Southern African War," *Africa Digest* (London), vol. 15, no. 5 (October 1968), pp. 87–88.

89. Rake, *op. cit.*, p. 24.

90. "News in Brief: Zambia: Rhodesian Nationalists Expelled," *Africa Report*, vol. 14, no. 1 (January 1969), p. 26.

91. Rake, *op. cit.*, pp. 24–25.

92. *Ibid.* In 1969 African nationalist incursions into Rhodesia from Zambia were nonexistent. This seems to be largely due to tightened security by the Rhodesian army along the "Zambezi line" and disunity among the African opposition. For details see "Rhodesia: Sitting Pretty," *Africa Report*, vol. 14, no. 8 (December 1969), pp. 9–11.

93. Dale, "South African Counterinsurgency," pp. 9–10.

94. *Ibid.*, pp. 18–20.

95. *Ibid.*, pp. 21–25.

96. *Ibid.*, pp. 16–18, 20. For an interesting account of the watchfulness of an African chief over suspected troublemakers, see *Statement by Toivo Herman Ja Toivo* (New York: SWAPO office, April 1968), pp. 1–5.

97. Dale, "South African Counterinsurgency," pp. 18, 20–21.

98. Dennis Austin, *Britain and South Africa*. Issued under the auspices of the Royal Institute of International Affairs (London: Oxford University Press, 1966), pp. 4–5.

99. Mbeki, *op. cit.*, pp. 23–48.

100. Peter McGennis Bulwer, *Commonwealth History* (London: Blandford Press, 1967), p. 135.

101. Nelson Mandela, *No Easy Walk to Freedom: Articles, Speeches, and Trial Addresses* (New York: Basic Books, 1965), p. 175; and Thomas, *op. cit.*, p. 6.

102. Muriel Horrell, *Action, Reaction and Counteraction* (Johannesburg: South African Institute of Race Relations, 1963), pp. 40–45.

103. Spence and Thomas, *op. cit.*, pp. 7–8.

104. Marvine Howe, "Portugal at War: Hawks, Doves and Owls: How Long Can Portugal Hold Out in Africa and at Home?" vol. 14, no. 7 (November 1969), pp. 16–21.

105. For a description of Portuguese–South African cooperation see William A. Hance, "Three Economies," *Africa Report*, vol. 12, no. 9 (November 1967), pp. 23–30.

106. For an analysis of the Rhodesian strength in the face of economic adversity, see Otakar Hulec, "Some Aspects of the 1930s Depression in Rhodesia," *Journal of Modern African Studies*, vol. 7, no. 1 (April 1969), pp. 95–105.

107. The unlikelihood of United States involvement in the Southern African independence movements during the Nixon administration is succintly traced in Earl W. Foell, "Africa's Vanishing Act at the UN: Where Does the United States Stand on African Questions?", *Africa Report*, vol. 14, no. 7 (November 1969), pp. 31–33.

PART SEVEN CHAPTER 1

1. Edgar H. Brookes, *Apartheid: A Documentary Study of Modern South Africa* (London: Routledge & Kegan Paul, 1968), p. xxxvii. For the wide range of predictions and quasi-predictions see Vernon McKay, "The Range of Futures," Amelia C. Leiss (ed.), *Apartheid and United Nations Collective Measures* (New York: Carnegie Endowment for International Peace, 1968), pp. 45–72.

2. Larry W. Bowman, "The Subordinate State System of Southern Africa," *International Studies Quarterly*, vol. 12, no. 3 (September 1968), pp. 231–261. Zambia, which was once a tenth unit, is now withdrawing from the subsystem. To take but one example, during 1969, 40 per cent of Zambia's imported food came from the countries to the north as opposed to 4 percent in 1968 ("Zambia: Record Trade Surplus," *Standard Bank Review* [London], February 1970, p. 15).

3. Southern Africa contains nearly 90 percent of all Europeans in Africa. Five of its nine units are under their direct control while the remaining four are under their considerable influence. For an interesting analysis of the power relationships within South Africa, see Austin T. Turk, "The Futures of South Africa," *Social Forces*, vol. 45, no. 3 (March 1967), pp. 402–412.

4. Bowman, *op. cit.*, p. 260.

5. Figures on the numbers of opposing forces differ greatly. Russell Warren Howe puts them at 250,000 Portuguese and 26,000 Africans ("War in Southern Africa," *Foreign Affairs*, vol. 48, no. 1 [October 1969] pp. 150–165). This estimate seems highly inflated. See the chapters by Wheeler, Chilcote and Kagombe in this book as well as Douglas Wheeler, "The Portuguese Army in Angola," *Journal of Modern African Studies*, vol. 17, no. 3 (October 1969), pp. 425–439, and the November 1967 issue of *Africa Report*, vol. 12, no. 8, devoted to the Portuguese-controlled areas.

6. For example, *the New York Times* estimates that there were something on the order of three hundred Portuguese killed during 1968 (Richard Eder, "Portugal's Hazy African Wars Go on, with Only Stalemate in Sight," *New York Times*, August 6, 1969, late city ed., p. 3, cols. 1–6).

7. As Edward Feit has so dramatically underscored, even in the more fluid 1950s, African nationalist movements in South Africa had severe manpower, organizational, communications, and security problems (Edward Feit, *South Africa: The Dynamics of the African National Congress* [London: Oxford University Press, 1962] and *African Opposition in South Africa: The Failure of Passive Resistance* [Stanford: Hoover Institute, 1967]). At the height of African mobilization in the late 1950s, he estimates that the African National Congress had a membership of sixty to one-hundred thousand persons or 0.5 percent of the African population and the Pan-Africanist Congress twenty to thirty thousand or 0.15 percent (*African Opposition in South Africa*, p. 44). See also Leo Kuper, *Passive Resistance in South Africa* (New Haven: Yale University Press, 1957). In Rhodesia the African nationalist movement peaked somewhat later, in 1961. See John Day, "Southern Rhodesian African Nationalists and the 1961 Constitution," *Journal of Modern African Studies*, vol. 7, no. 2 (July 1969), pp. 221–247; his *International Nationalism: The Extra-Territorial Relations of Southern Rhodesia African Nationalists* (London: Routledge & Kegan Paul, 1967); and James Barber, *Rhodesia: The Road to Rebellion* (London: Oxford University Press, 1967), as well as Barber's chapter in this book. See also B. V. Mtshali, *Rhodesia: Background to Conflict* (New York: Hawthorn Books, 1967); Kenneth Young, *Rhodesia and Indepedence* (New York: Heinemann, 1967); and Douglas Reed, *The Battle for Rhodesia* (New York: Devin-Adair, 1967). Of particular interest is Frank Clements, *Rhodesia: A Study of the Deterioration of a White Society*, (New York: Frederick A. Praeger 1969).

8. Marvin Howe, "Portugal at War: Hawks, Doves and Owls: How Long Can Portugal Hold Out in Africa and at Home?" *Africa Report*, vol. 11, no. 7 (November 1969), pp. 16–21. The Portuguese have already displayed a remarkable tenacity. As James Duffy has written, "For four hundred and fifty years in Africa, the Portuguese have survived disease, native wars, neglect, and foreign attack, surely the most remarkable endurance record in colonial history" (James Duffy, *Portuguese Africa* [Cambridge, Mass.: Harvard University Press, 1961], p. 342). See also da Silva Rego's chapter in this book. For a comprehensive overview of the environmental context of Portuguese Africa, David N. Abshire and Michael A. Samuels (eds), *Portuguese Africa: A Handbook* (New York: Frederick A. Praeger, 1969). A more optimistic view of the African nationalist position is given in Paul M. Whitaker, "The Revolutions of Portuguese Africa," *Journal of Modern African Studies*, vol. 8, no. 1 (April 1970), pp. 15–35.

9. "Africa itself has given South Africa another generation of time" (C. W. deKiewiet, "The World and Pretoria," *Africa Report*, vol. 14, no. 2 [February 1969], p. 52). Similar points were made in Dennis Austin, "White Power?", *Journal of Commonwealth Political Studies*, vol. 6, no. 3 (July 1968), pp. 95–106; and Russell Warren Howe, "African Guerrilla Funds Disputed," *Christian Science Monitor*, March 8, 1969, Eastern ed., p. 3, cols. 1–3. See also Speck's chapter in this book.

10. Gerald L. Caplan, "Barotseland: The Secessionist Challenge to Zambia," *Journal of Modern African Studies*, vol. 6, no. 3 (October 1968). pp. 343–360; Immanuel Wallerstein, "Penetrating the Continent," *New Leader*, vol. 50, no. 19 (September 25, 1967), pp. 5–7; Mike Hoare, *Congo Mercenary* (London: Robert Hall, 1967). Imagine, for example, the setback to African exile groups which would result from a South African–inspired coup in Tanzania.

11. See chaps. by Spence, Hill and Stevens in this volume.

12. Chemical-biological research has gone on since 1963, according to J. J. le Roux, vice president of South Africa's National Council for Scientific and Industrial Research (Seymour M. Hersh, *Chemical and Biological Warfare* [Garden City, N.Y.: Doubleday, 1969], p. 255). South Africa exports to the rest of Africa (including Rhodesia) totalled $375 million in 1969, placing Africa in second place behind Great Britain ("South Africa: Direction of Foreign Trade, *Standard Bank Review* [October, 1970], p. [52]).

13. Ray Vicker, "Reaching Out: South Africa Launches Effort to find Friends, End its Pariah Status," *The Wall Street Journal*, September 22, 1969, Eastern ed., p. 1, col. 6 and p. 29, col. 2.

14. It is instructive that during 1968–1969 only Tanzania, Zambia, Algeria, and the Ivory Coast paid their assessments to the OAU Liberation Committee (Howe, "Africa Guerrilla Funds," p. 3). Dr. Yashpal Tandon, while somewhat more optimistic, nevertheless underscores some real difficulties in actualizing the OAU's stated goals in his chapter in this book.

15. Wallerstein, *op. cit.*, pp. 5–7. In addition to the leverage provided by its economic power, South Africa is currently enjoying favorable strategic focus. Since the closing of the Suez Canal in 1967, for example, over thirty-five thousand ships have passed the Cape of Good

Hope, eight thousand of which stopped in South African ports (Al J. Venter, "Two Years After Suez," *Panorama* [Pretoria], vol. 161, no. 6 [June 1969], p. 2). The South Africans undoubtedly plan to make use of their strategic position with the Cape of Good Hope as a "Southern Gibraltar" (*South Africa in World Strategy*: *Special Survey* [London: South African Embassy, 1969]).

16. Chap. by Worrall in this book.

17. Chap. by Petersen in this book.

18. Edwin S. Munger, *Bechuanaland: Pan-African Outpost or Bantu Homeland?* (London: Oxford University Press, 1965); and Richard Dale, *Botswana and Its Southern Neighbor: The Patterns of Linkage and the Options in Statecraft*. Papers in International Studies. Africa series no. 6 (Athens, Ohio: Ohio University Center for International Studies, Africa Program, 1970).

19. Alan Rake, for example, in his "Black Guerrillas in Rhodesia," (*Africa Report*, vol. 13, no. 9 [December 1968], pp. 23–25), indicates that the number of FFGs killed rose from twenty in 1960 to one hundred in 1968; 1969 and 1970 saw reduced fighting, however.

20. For an in-depth examination of the relative amounts of exogenous aid provided the various FFG groups, see Paul Whitaker, "Arms and the Nationalists: Where and on What Terms Do They Obtain Their Support and How Important is External Aid to their Revolution?" *Africa Report*, vol. 15, no. 5 (May, 1970), pp. 12–14.

21. Basil Davidson, *The Liberation of Guiné* (Baltimore: Penguin Books, 1969); and Ronald A. Chilcote, "The Political Thought of Amilcar Cabral," *Journal of Modern African Studies*, vol. 6, no. 3 (October, 1968), pp. 373–388.

22. The failure of the 1964 rebellion in the Congo (Kinshasa) to overthrow the central government clearly shows that supplies, slogans, and grievances are not enough to energize a successful revolution. Also germane to the Southern African context is competition among would-be revolutionary groups: John Marcum, *The Angolan Revolution*: *Volume I. The Anatomy of an Explosion (1950–1962)* (Cambridge, Mass.: M.I.T. Press, 1969), and his chapter in this book.

23. This assumption cannot be taken for granted. In the chap. on Swaziland, we indicated the substantial areas of agreement between the present leadership in Swaziland and their counterparts in South Africa. If it appeared that a fundamental alteration of the subsystem would threaten their political hegemony or their very existence they would oppose it. Similar analysis of Malawi, Lesotho, and Botswana are found in Speck's, Weisfelder's and Dale's chaps. An interesting perspective on this problem is to be found in Henry J. Richardson, "Malawi: Between Black and White Africa," *Africa Report*, vol. 15, no. 2 (February 1970), pp. 18–21.

24. The demise of the Liberal party in South Africa and the provisions of the new Rhodesian constitution are but the latest in a long series of indications that this is the case. See chaps. by Worrall, van der Merwe and Barber.

25. See chaps. by Reid, Hamutenya and Geingob, and Speck. As Arthur Wina has stated: "If the powers prevailing are absolutely indifferent to human values or moral precepts, then non-violence is likely to subject its followers to arrest or even to hanging," John A. Davis and James K. Baker (eds.), *Southern Africa in Transition* (New York: Frederick A. Praeger, 1966), p. 240.

26. John A. Marcum and Allard K. Lowenstein, "Force: Its Thrust and Prognosis," in *ibid.*, p. 247.

27. It is in this context and that of the next three scenarios that options A and B are of the greatest consequence. Option B, for example, would undoubtedly have wider support in Western Europe and the United States than Option A.

28. Hon. Charles C. Diggs, Jr. and Hon. Lester Wolff, *Report of a Special Study Mission to Southern Africa, August 10–30, 1969*. Ninety-first Congress. First session (Washington, D.C.: USGPO, 1969), p. 16.

29. *Ibid.*, p. 4.

30. William A. Hance, "The Case for and against United States Disengagement from South Africa," in William A. Hance (ed.), *Southern Africa and the United States* (New York: Columbia University Press, 1968), pp. 119–122.

31. These and the statistics which immediately follow are taken from Ernest A. Gross, "The Coalescing Problem of Southern Africa," *Foreign Affairs*, vol. 46, no. 4 (July 1968), p. 744.

32. The Portuguese, for example, have gotten almost unbelievable leverage out of the "strategic importance" of the Azores. It would seem obvious to anyone with even a rudimentary knowledge of airlift capabilities and geography that the Azores, however convenient, are in no way central to American military power. Likewise, the Portuguese presence in NATO is hardly essential to the defense of Western Europe. Yet both illusions seem to have persuaded the United States policymakers to reverse their earlier support for African majority rule in Angola (Marcum, *Angolan Revolution*, pp. 268–277).

33. Hance, "The case for and against United States Disengagement from South Africa," p. 117.

34. R. B. Sutcliffe, "The Political Economy of Rhodesian Sanctions," *Journal of Commonwealth Political Studies* (Leicester, England), vol. 7, no. 2 (July 1969), pp. 113–125; Ralph Zacklin, "Challenge on Rhodesia," *International Conciliation* no. 575 (November 1969), pp. 1–72; and Timothy Curtin and David Murray, *Economic Sanctions and Rhodesia* (London: Institute of Economic Affairs, 1967). Some are more hopeful: Colin and Margaret Legum, *South Africa, Crisis for the West* (New York: Frederick A. Praeger, 1964); Robert McKinnell, "Sanctions and the Rhodesian Economy," *Journal of Modern African Studies*, vol. 8, no. 4 (December 1969), pp. 559–582; and Ronald Segal (ed.), *Sanctions Against South Africa* (Baltimore: Penguin Books, 1964).

35. "Surgical" airstrikes—that is, sudden, effective, destructive attacks against military targets alone—might have a great deal of semantic and emotional appeal but they are likely to involve significant civilian casualties and, in the South African context, this means African as well as European. For the classic example of the usage of the term in policy formation, see Robert F. Kennedy, *Thirteen Days* (New York: Signet Books, 1969), pp. 33–46; Roger Hilsman. *To Move a Nation* (Garden City, N.Y.: Doubleday, 1964), pp. 157–229; Theodore C. Sorensen, *Kennedy* (New York: Harper & Row, 1965), pp. 667–718; Arthur M. Schlesinger, Jr., *A Thousand Days* (Boston: Houghton Mifflin, 1965), pp. 794–841; and Elie Abel, *The Missile Crisis* (New York: Bantam Books, 1966), pp. 43–75.

36. Wallerstein, *op. cit.*, pp. 5–7.

37. The last decade in Africa has witnessed a number of situations (the Congo, Cameroun, Nigeria, Biafra, and Southern Africa) in which the cost of exogenous involvement is very low and, in terms of the potential rewards, the temptation to intervene remains strong.

38. Consider the impact which six million American Jews have had on the American Middle East policy. There are 26 million black Americans. In this regard, it would seem to be in African and Afro-American interests to push for American involvement only if they feel that if the United States took sides, it would aid the liberation movements. If they judge that the United States would intervene on the side of (or continue to support) the *status quo*, they should push for United States neutrality. On the question of international intervention, see Legum, *op. cit.*, pp. 213–282; and William A. Hance, "Efforts to Alter the Future: Economic Action," in Leiss, *Apartheid and United Nations Collective Efforts*, pp. 95–130 and Amelia C. Leiss, "Efforts to Alter the Future: Military Measures," in Leiss, *Apartheid and United Nations Collective Measures*, pp. 131–153.

39. Diggs and Wolff, *op. cit.*; Waldemar A. Nielsen, *African Battle Line: American Policy Choices in Southern Africa* (New York: Harper & Row, 1965); and United States Congress, House of Representatives Committee on Foreign Affairs, *South Africa and United States Foreign Policy: Hearings*, Ninety-first Congress, First session (Washington, D.C.: United States Government Printing Office, 1969). See, for example, the policy statements of the newly formed Washington Task Force on African Affairs: Gary Gappert, *A Legislative Program for Disengagement from South Africa, an End to Support for Portugal's Colonialism, Aid for African States Besieged by Apartheid* (Washington, D.C.: Washington Task Force on African Affairs, n.d.).

40. Howe, "African Guerrilla Funds, "p. 3.

41. An alternative would be the situation created by the thousands of African refugees from Southern Africa "returning home," escorted by United Nations or OAU "shepherds."

42. Gross, *op. cit.*, p. 757. Another article predicting imminent escalation of the conflicts in the area is Tim Smith, "The Growing Racial Struggle in Southern Africa," *War/Peace Report*, vol. 9, no. 3 (March 1969), pp. 9–11.

43. Gross, *op. cit.*, p. 743.

44. How many Africans in South Africa, for example, would willingly choose a course of action in which European reprisals and direct action resulted in millions of dead? Would it be worth one hundred thousand dead to liberate the area? A million? Three million? We know of no studies which seriously deal with the casualty lists which would be engendered by a Scenario VII or VIII situation. They would be of enormous import (Leiss, *op. cit.*, confines her estimates to military casualties in the attacking forces and, in opinion, underestimates them).

45. Davidson, *op. cit.*, p. 13.

46. "The struggle is one that must be fought from within, making use of guerrilla tactics and based on a persuasive and popular underground movement. The independent states cannot help by direct military intervention but can give much more valuable assistance in the form of material and diplomatic support." (Eduardo Mondlane, *The Struggle for Mozambique* [Baltimore: Penguin Books, 1969], p. 211.)

47. See the assessment of South African strength found in J. E. Spence and Elizabeth Thomas, *South Africa's Defense: The Problem of Internal Control.* Security Studies Paper no. 8 (Los Angeles: University of California, 1966); Christian P. Potholm, "South Africa," *Four African Political Systems* (Englewood Cliffs, N.J.: Prentice-Hall, 1970), pp. 91–137; and Douglas Brown, *Against the World: A Study of White South African Attitudes* (London: William Collins Sons, 1966), as well as Petersen's chapter in this book.

48. Michael A. Brecher, "International Relations and Asian Studies: The Subordinate State System of Southern Asia," *World Politics*, vol. 15, no. 1 (January 1963), p. 220.

Suggested Readings on Southern Africa*

* This bibliography has been compiled by Dr. Doris Cruger Dale, Assistant Professor of Instructional Materials, Southern Illinois University, on the basis of the bibliographies submitted to the editors by the individual contributors. Additional titles have been added by the compiler in order to present a balanced list. The bibliography has been designed primarily to meet the needs of American upperclassmen and graduate students. It is a selective bibliography showing the wide range of materials available to students of Southern African affairs. Only material in the English language has been included, which therefore unfortunately eliminates much excellent material. Recency of publication date has also been used as a criterion for selection, although a few older titles of lasting value have been included. An attempt has been made to include materials representing many political points of view. All entries for books and documents have been verified in the *National Union Catalog* of the Library of Congress in order to facilitate interlibrary loan for students unable to obtain these materials in their own libraries.

BOOKS AND DOCUMENTS

Addicott, Len E. *Cry Angola!* London: SCM Press, 1962.

Ainslie, Rosalynde. *The Unholy Alliance: Salazar-Verwoerd-Welensky*. 2nd ed. London: Anti-Apartheid Movement, 1962.

American Society of African Culture. *Southern Africa in Transition*. Edited by John A. Davis and James K. Baker. New York: Frederick A. Praeger, 1966.

American University, Washington, D.C., Foreign Areas Studies Division. *Area Handbook for Angola*. Washington, D.C.: U.S. Government Printing Office, 1967.

Angola: A Symposium: Views of a Revolt. London: Oxford University Press, 1962.

Arrighi, G. *The Political Economy of Rhodesia*. The Hague: Mouton, 1967.

Ashton, Edmund Hugh. *The Basuto: A Social Study of Traditional and Modern Lesotho*. 2nd ed. London: Oxford University Press, 1967.

Austin, Dennis. *Britain and South Africa*. London: Oxford University Press, 1966.

Axelson, Eric Victor. *Portugal and the Scramble for Africa, 1875–1891*. Johannesburg: Witwatersrand University Press, 1967.

Baldwin, Robert E. *Economic Development and Export Growth: A Study of Northern Rhodesia, 1920–1960*. Berkeley: University of California Press, 1966.

Ballinger, Margaret. *From Union to Apartheid: A Trek to Isolation*. New York: Frederick A. Praeger, 1969.

Ballinger, Ronald B. *South Africa and the United Nations: Myth and Reality*. Johannesburg: South African Institute for International Affairs, 1963.

———. *South-West Africa: The Case Against the Union*. Johannesburg: South African Institute of Race Relations, 1961.

Barber, James P. *Rhodesia: The Road to Rebellion*. London: Oxford University Press, 1967.

Barker, Dudley. *Swaziland*. London: HMSO, 1965.

Bellwood, W. A. *Whither the Transkei?* London: Bailey Bros. & Swinfen, 1964.

Benson, Mary. *South Africa: The Struggle for a Birthright*. Rev. ed. of *The African Patriots*. New York: Minerva Press, 1969.

———. *Tshekedi Khama*. London: Faber & Faber, 1960.

Best, Alan C. G. *The Swaziland Railway: A Study in*

Politico-Economic Geography. East Lansing, Mich.: African Studies Center, Michigan State University, 1966.

Birmingham, David. *The Portuguese Conquest of Angola*. London: Oxford University Press, 1965.

———. *Trade and Conflict in Angola: The Mbundu and Their Neighbours under the Influence of the Portuguese, 1483–1790*. Oxford: Clarendon Press, 1966.

Botha, Jan François. *Verwoerd Is Dead*. Cape Town: Books of Africa, 1967.

Brookes, Edgar Harry. *Apartheid: A Documentary Study of Modern South Africa*. London: Routledge & Kegan Paul, 1968.

Brown, Douglas. *Against the World: Attitudes of White South Africa*. Garden City, N.Y.: Doubleday, 1969.

Bruwer, J. P. van S. *South West Africa: The Disputed Land*. Cape Town: Nasionale Boekhandel, 1966.

Bull, Theodore, ed. *Rhodesia: Crisis of Color*. Chicago: Quadrangle Books, 1968.

Bunting, Brian Percy. *The Rise of the South African Reich*. Rev. ed. Baltimore: Penguin Books, 1969.

Callan, Edward. *Albert John Luthuli and the South African Race Conflict*. Kalamazoo: Western Michigan Press, 1962.

Calvocoressi, Peter. *South Africa and World Opinion*. London: Oxford University Press, 1961.

The Cambridge History of the British Empire. Vol. 8—*South Africa, Rhodesia and the High Commission Territories*. 2nd ed. Cambridge: University Press, 1963.

Carroll, Faye. *South West Africa and the United Nations*. Lexington: University of Kentucky Press, 1967.

Carter, Gwendolen Margaret. *The Politics of Inequality: South Africa since 1948*. 3rd rev. ed. New York: Frederick A. Praeger, 1962.

———, Karis, Thomas, and Stultz, Newell M. *South Africa's Transkei: The Politics of Domestic Colonialism*. Evanston, Ill.: Northwestern University Press, 1967.

Cervenka, Zdenek. *The Organisation of African Unity and Its Charter*. 2nd ed. London: C. Hurst, 1969.

Chilcote, Ronald H. *Portuguese Africa*. Engelwood Cliffs, N.J.: Prentice-Hall, 1967.

Clements, Frank. *Rhodesia: A Study of the Deterioration of a White Society*. New York: Frederick A. Praeger, 1969.

Coates, Austin. *Basutoland*. London: HMSO, 1966.

Cockram, Gail-Maryse. *Vorster's Foreign Policy*. Pretoria: Academica, 1970.

Cox, Richard Hubert Francis. *Pan-Africanism in Practice: An East African Study: PAFMECSA, 1958–1964*. London: Oxford University Press, 1964.

Creighton, Thomas Richmond Mandell. *The Anatomy of Partnership: Southern Rhodesia and the Central African Federation*. London: Faber & Faber, 1960.

Dale, Richard. *Botswana and Its Southern Neighbor: The Patterns of Linkage and the Options in Statecraft*. Athens, Ohio: Ohio University Center for International Studies, Africa Program, 1970.

Davenport, T. R. H. *The Afrikaner Bond: The History of a South African Political Party, 1880–1911*. Cape Town: Oxford University Press, 1966.

Day, John. *International Nationalism: The Extraterritorial Relations of Southern Rhodesian African Nationalists*. London: Routledge & Kegan Paul, 1968.

Debenham, Frank. *Nyasaland: The Land of the Lake*. London: HMSO, 1955.

DeBlij, Harm J. *Africa South*. Evanston, Ill.: Northwestern University Press, 1962.

DeKiewiet, Cornelius William. *The Anatomy of South African Misery*. London: Oxford University Press, 1956.

De Ridder, Jacobus C. *The Personality of the Urban African in South Africa: A Thematic Apperception Test Study*. London: Routledge & Kegan Paul, 1961.

De Villiers, Dawid. *The Case for South Africa*. London: Tom Stacey, 1970.

Diggs, Charles C., and Wolff, Lester L. *Report of the Special Study Mission to Southern Africa, August 10–30, 1969*. Washington, D.C.: U.S. Government Printing Office, 1969.

Duffy, James. *Portugal in Africa*. Baltimore: Penguin Books, 1962.

———. *Portuguese Africa*. Cambridge, Mass.: Harvard University Press, 1961.

———. *A Question of Slavery*. Oxford: Clarendon Press, 1967.

———. *Shipwreck & Empire: Being an Account of Portuguese Maritime Disasters in a Century of Decline*. Cambridge, Mass.: Harvard University Press, 1955.

Duncan, Patrick. *South Africa's Rule of Violence*. London: Methuen, 1964.

Ehnmark, Anders, and Wästberg, Per. *Angola and Mozambique: The Case Against Portugal*. London: Pall Mall Press, 1963.

Esterhuyse, J. H. *South West Africa, 1880–1894: The Establishment of German Authority in South West Africa*. Cape Town: C. Struik, 1968.

Eybers, George von Welfling, ed. *Select Constitutional Documents Illustrating South African History, 1795–1910*. London: George Routledge & Sons, 1918; New York: Negro Universities Press, 1969 reprint.

Fair, Thomas J. D., Murdoch, G., and Jones, H. M. *Development in Swaziland: A Regional Analysis*. Johannesburg: Witwatersrand University Press, 1969.

Feit, Edward. *African Opposition in South Africa: The Failure of Passive Resistance*. Stanford: The Hoover Institution on War, Revolution, and Peace, 1967.

———. *South Africa: The Dynamics of the African National Congress*. New York: Oxford University Press, 1962.

First, Ruth. *South West Africa*. Baltimore: Penguin Books, 1963.

Fisher, John. *The Afrikaners*. London: Cassell, 1969.

Franklin, Harry. *Unholy Wedlock: The Failure of the Central African Federation*. London: George Allen & Unwin, 1963.

Friedmann, Marion Valerie, ed. *I Will Still Be Moved: Reports from South Africa*. Chicago: Quadrangle Books, 1963.

Frye, William R. *In Whitest Africa; the Dynamics of Apartheid*. Englewood Cliffs, N.J.: Prentice-Hall, 1968.

The Future of South Africa: A Study by British Christians. London: SCM Press, 1965.

Gann, Lewis H. *A History of Northern Rhodesia: Early Days to 1953*. London: Chatto & Windus, 1964.
Gilchrist, Sidney. *Angola Awake*. Toronto: Ryerson Press, 1968.
Giniewski, Paul. *Bantustans: A Trek towards the Future*. Cape Town: Human & Rousseau, 1961.
Glass, Harold Maurice. *South African Policy towards Basutoland*. Johannesburg: South African Institute of International Affairs, 1966.
Great Britain. High Commissioner for Basutoland, the Bechuanaland Protectorate, and Swaziland. *Basutoland, Bechuanaland Protectorate & Swaziland; Report of an Economic Survey Mission*. London: HMSO, 1960.
Great Britain. Office of Commonwealth Relations. *Basutoland, the Bechuanaland Protectorate and Swaziland: History of Discussions with the Union of South Africa, 1909–1939*. Cmd. 8707. London: HMSO, 1952.
Green, L. P., and Fair, T. J. D. *Development in Africa: A Study in Regional Analysis with Special Reference to Southern Africa*. Johannesburg: Witwatersrand University Press, 1962.
Gregory, Theodor Emanuel Gugenheim. *Ernest Oppenheimer and the Economic Development of Southern Africa*. Cape Town: Oxford University Press, 1962.
Hailey, William Malcolm. *Native Administration in the British African Territories*. 5 vols. London: HMSO, 1950–1953.
———. *The Republic of South Africa and the High Commission Territories*. London: Oxford University Press, 1963.
Hall, Richard Seymour. *The High Price of Principles: Kaunda and the White South*. New York: Africana Publishing Corp., 1969.
———. *Kaunda: Founder of Zambia*. London: Longmans 1965.
———. *Zambia*. New York: Frederick A. Praeger, 1965.
Halpern, Jack. *South Africa's Hostages: Basutoland, Bechuanaland and Swaziland*. Baltimore: Penguin Books, 1965.
Hammond, Richard James. *Portugal and Africa, 1815–1910: A Study in Uneconomic Imperialism*. Stanford, Calif.: Stanford University Press, 1966.
Hancock, William Keith. *Smuts*. 2 vols. Cambridge: University Press, 1962–1968.
Hanna, Alexander John. *The Story of the Rhodesias and Nyasaland*. 2nd ed. London: Faber & Faber, 1965.
Hepple, Alexander. *South Africa: A Political and Economic History*. New York: Frederick A. Praeger, 1966.
———. *Verwoerd*. Baltimore: Penguin Books, 1967.
Herrick, Allison Butler, *et al*. *Area Handbook for Mozambique*. Washington, D.C.: U.S. Government Printing Office, 1969.
Hill, Christopher R. *Bantustans: The Fragmentation of South Africa*. London: Oxford University Press, 1964.
Hole, Hugh Marshall. *The Making of Rhodesia*. London: Cass, 1967.
Horwitz, Ralph. *The Political Economy of South Africa*. New York: Frederick A. Praeger, 1967.
Houghton, D. Hobart. *The South African Economy*. 2nd ed. Cape Town: Oxford University Press, 1967.
Imishue, R. W. *South West Africa: An International Problem*. London: Pall Mall Press, 1965.
International Conference on Economic Sanctions against South Africa, London, 1964. *Sanctions against South Africa*. Edited by Ronald Segal. Baltimore: Penguin Books, 1964.
International Conference on South West Africa, Oxford, 1966. *South West Africa: Travesty of Trust*. Edited by Ronald Segal and Ruth First. London: Andre Deutsch, 1967.
Jones, Griffith Bevan. *Britain and Nyasaland*. London: George Allen & Unwin, 1964.
Joseph, Helen. *If This Be Treason*. London: Andre Deutsch, 1963.
Kaplan, Irving, *et al*. *Area Handbook for Zambia*. Washington, D.C.: U.S. Government Printing Office, 1969.
Kaunda, Kenneth David. *A Humanist in Africa: Letters to Colin M. Morris*. Nashville: Abingdon Press, 1966.
———. *Zambia: Independence and Beyond: The Speeches of Kenneth Kaunda*. Edited by Colin Legum. London: Nelson, 1966.
———. *Zambia Shall Be Free: An Autobiography*. New York: Frederick A. Praeger, 1963.
Kay, George. *A Social Geography of Zambia: A Survey of Population Patterns in a Developing Country*. London: University of London Press, 1967.
Keatley, Patrick. *The Politics of Partnership*. Baltimore: Penguin Books, 1963.
Krüger, D. W. *The Making of a Nation: A History of the Union of South Africa, 1910–1961*. Johannesburg: The Macmillan Company, 1969.
———, ed. *South African Parties and Policies, 1910–1960: A Select Source Book*. London: Bowes & Bowes, 1960.
Kuper, Hilda. *An African Aristocracy: Rank among the Swazi*. New York: Oxford University Press, 1947.
———. *The Swazi: A South African Kingdom*. New York: Holt, Rinehart & Winston, 1964.
———. *The Uniform of Colour: A Study of White-Black Relationships in Swaziland*. Johannesburg: Witwatersrand University Press, 1947.
Kuper, Leo. *An African Bourgeoisie: Race, Class, and Politics in South Africa*. New Haven: Yale University Press, 1965.
———. *Passive Resistance in South Africa*. New Haven: Yale University Press, 1957.
Landis, Elizabeth. *Namibia: The Beginning of Disengagement*. Studies in Race and Nations, vol. 2, no. 1, 1970–1971. Denver: University of Denver, 1970.
Legum, Colin, and Legum, Margaret. *The Bitter Choice: Eight South Africans' Resistance to Tyranny*. Cleveland: World Publishing Co., 1968.
———. *South Africa: Crisis for the West*. New York: Frederick A. Praeger, 1964.
Leiss, Amelia Catherine, ed. *Apartheid and United Nations Collective Measures: An Analysis*. New York: Carnegie Endowment for International Peace, 1965.
Leistner, G. M. E., and Smit, P. *Swaziland: Resources and Development*. Pretoria: Africa Institute, 1969.
Lessing, Doris May. *Going Home*. Rev. ed. London: Panther, 1968.
Lever, Henry. *Ethnic Attitudes of Johannesburg Youth*. Johannesburg: Witwatersrand University Press, 1968.

Leys, Colin. *European Politics in Southern Rhodesia.* Oxford: Clarendon Press, 1959.

Livermore, Harold Victor. *A New History of Portugal.* Cambridge: Cambridge University Press, 1966.

Lombard, Johannes Anthonie, Stadler, J. J., and van der Merwe, P. J. *The Concept of Economic Co-operation in Southern Africa.* Pretoria: Econburo, 1969.

Louw, Eric Hendrik. *The Case for South Africa, As Put Forth in the Public Statements of Eric H. Louw.* Edited and compiled by H. H. Biermann. New York: Macfadden Books, 1963.

Lowenstein, Allard K. *Brutal Mandate: A Journey to South West Africa.* New York: Macmillan, 1962.

Ludi, Gerard, and Grobbelaar, Blaar. *The Amazing Mr. Fischer.* Cape Town: Nasionale Boekhandel, 1966.

Luthuli, Albert John. *Let My People Go.* New York: McGraw-Hill, 1962.

Macmillan, William Miller. *Bantu, Boer, and Briton: The Making of the South African Native Problem.* Rev. and enl. ed. Oxford: Clarendon Press, 1963.

Mandela, Nelson. *No Easy Walk to Freedom: Articles, Speeches, and Trial Addresses.* New York: Basic Books, 1965.

Mansergh, Nicholas. *South Africa, 1906–1961: The Price of Magnanimity.* New York: Frederick A. Praeger, 1962.

Marcum, John. *The Angolan Revolution.* Vol. 1—*The Anatomy of an Explosion (1950–1962).* Cambridge, Mass.: M.I.T. Press, 1969.

Marks, Shula. *Reluctant Rebellion: The 1906–8 Disturbances in Natal.* Oxford: Clarendon Press, 1970.

Marquard, Leopold. *The Peoples and Policies of South Africa.* 4th ed. London: Oxford University Press, 1969.

———. *A Short History of South Africa.* New York: Frederick A. Praeger, 1968.

Marshall, Charles Burton. *Crisis Over Rhodesia: A Skeptical View.* Baltimore: Johns Hopkins Press, 1967.

Marwick, Brian Allan. *The Swazi: An Ethnographic Account of the Natives of the Swaziland Protectorate.* 2nd ed. London: Cass, 1966.

Mason, Philip. *The Birth of a Dilemma: The Conquest and Settlement of Rhodesia.* London: Oxford University Press, 1958.

———. *Year of Decision: Rhodesia and Nyasaland in 1960.* London: Oxford University Press, 1960.

Mbabane. Times of Swaziland. *Politics in Swaziland, 1960 to 1968: A Selection of Reports in the Times of Swaziland.* Edited by Sishayi Simon Ndwandwe. Johannesburg: University of the Witwatersrand, African Studies Programme, 1968.

Mbeki, Govan Archibald Mvunyelwa. *South Africa: The Peasants' Revolt.* Baltimore: Penguin Books, 1964.

Metrowich, F. R. *Rhodesia: Birth of a Nation.* Pretoria: Africa Institute, 1969.

Mitchison, Naomi (Haldane). *Return to the Fairy Hill.* London: Heinemann, 1966.

Modisane, Bloke. *Blame Me on History.* London: Thames & Hudson, 1963.

Molnar, Thomas Steven. *South West Africa: The Last Pioneer Country.* New York: Fleet Publishing, 1966.

Mondlane, Eduardo. *The Struggle for Mozambique.* Baltimore: Penguin Books, 1969.

Moreira, Adriano. *Portugal's Stand in Africa.* New York: University Publishers, 1962.

Morris, Colin M. *The Hour After Midnight: A Missionary's Experience of the Racial and Political Struggle in Northern Rhodesia.* London: Longmans, 1961.

Mtolo, Bruno Sipiwe. *The Road to the Left.* Durban: Drakensberg Press, 1966.

Mtshali, B. Vulindlela. *Rhodesia: Background to Conflict.* New York: Hawthorn Books, 1967.

Mulford, David C. *Zambia: The Politics of Independence, 1957–1964.* London: Oxford University Press, 1967.

Munger, Edwin S. *Afrikaner and African Nationalism: South African Parallels and Parameters.* London: Oxford University Press, 1967.

———. *Bechuanaland: Pan-African Outpost or Bantu Homeland?* London: Oxford University Press, 1965.

———. *Notes on the Formation of South African Foreign Policy.* Pasadena, Calif. Grant Dahlstrom/Castle Press, 1965.

Neame, Lawrence Elwin. *The History of Apartheid: The Story of the Colour War in South Africa.* London: Pall Mall Press, 1962.

Ngubane, Jordan K. *An African Explains Apartheid.* New York: Frederick A. Praeger, 1963.

Niddrie, David L. *South Africa: Nation or Nations?* Princeton, N.J.: Van Nostrand, 1968.

Nielsen, Waldemar A. *African Battleline: American Policy Choices in Southern Africa.* New York: Harper & Row, 1965.

Nogueira, Alberto Franco. *The Third World.* London: Johnson, 1967.

———. *The United Nations and Portugal: A Study of Anti-Colonialism.* London: Tandem Books, 1964.

Okuma, Thomas Masaji. *Angola in Ferment: The Background and Prospects of Angolan Nationalism.* Boston: Beacon Press, 1962.

Panikkar, Kavalam Madhusudan. *Angola in Flames.* New York: Asia Publishing House, 1962.

Paton, Alan. *The Long View.* Edited by Edward Callan. London: Pall Mall Press, 1968.

Pattee, Richard. *Portugal and the Portuguese World.* Milwaukee: Bruce, 1957.

Patterson, Sheila. *The Last Trek: A Study of the Boer People and the Afrikaner Nation.* London: Routledge & Kegan Paul, 1957.

Perham, Margery Freda, and Curtis, Lionel. *The Protectorates of South Africa: The Question of Their Transfer to the Union.* London: Oxford University Press, 1935.

Pietermaritzburg. University of Natal, Institute for Social Research, Durban. *Experiment in Swaziland: Report of the Swaziland Sample Survey, 1960.* Edited by J. F. Holleman. Cape Town: Oxford University Press, 1964.

Pike, John G., and Rimmington, G. T. *Malawi: A Geographical Study.* London: Oxford University Press, 1965.

Pike, John G. *Malawi: A Political and Economic History* New York: Frederick A. Praeger, 1968.

Portuguese Africa: A Handbook. Edited by David M. Abshire and Michael A. Samuels. New York: Frederick A. Praeger, 1969.

Potholm, Christian P. *Four African Political Systems.* Englewood Cliffs, N. J.: Prentice-Hall, 1970.

Ransford, Oliver. *The Rulers of Rhodesia from Earliest Times to the Referendum.* London: Murray, 1968.

Reed, Douglas. *The Battle for Rhodesia.* New York: Devin-Adair, 1967.

Refugee Problems in Africa. Edited by Sven Hamrell. Uppsala: Scandinavian Institute of African Studies, 1967.

Rego, Antonio da Silva. *Portuguese Colonization in the Sixteenth Century: A Study of the Royal Ordinances (Regimentos).* Johannesburg: Witwatersrand University Press, 1959.

Rhoodie, Eschel Mostert. *The Paper Curtain.* Johannesburg: Voortrekkerpers, 1969.

———. *South West: The Last Frontier in Africa.* Johannesburg: Voortrekkerpers, 1967.

———. *The Third Africa.* New York: Twin Circle, 1968.

Rhoodie, N. J., and Venter, H. J. *Apartheid; A Socio-Historical Exposition of the Origin and Development of the Apartheid Idea.* Cape Town: HAUM, 1960.

Rhoodie, N. J. *Apartheid and Racial Partnership in Southern Africa: A Sociological Comparison between Separate Ethno-National Development in South Africa and Racial Partnership in the Former Federation of Rhodesia and Nyasaland, with Special Reference to the Principles and Motives Involved in These Policy Systems.* Pretoria: Academica, 1969.

Rogers, Cyril A., and Frantz, C. *Racial Themes in Southern Rhodesia: The Attitudes and Behavior of the White Population.* New Haven: Yale University Press, 1962.

Rotberg, Robert I., and Mazrui, Ali A., eds. *Protest and Power in Black Africa.* New York: Oxford University Press, 1970.

Rotberg, Robert I. *The Rise of Nationalism in Central Africa: The Making of Malawi and Zambia, 1873–1964.* Cambridge, Mass.: Harvard University Press, 1965.

Roux, Edward. *Time Longer than Rope: A History of the Black Man's Struggle for Freedom in South Africa.* 2nd ed. Madison: University of Wisconsin Press, 1964.

Sampson, Anthony. *The Treason Cage: The Opposition on Trial in South Africa.* London: Heinemann, 1958.

Scarritt, James R., and Hatter, John L. *Racial and Ethnic Conflict in Zambia.* Studies in Race and Nations, vol. 2, no. 2, 1970–1971. Denver: University of Denver, 1970.

Shamuyarira, Nathan M. *Crisis in Rhodesia.* London: Andre Deutsch, 1965.

Sillery, Anthony. *The Bechuanaland Protectorate.* Cape Town: Oxford University Press, 1952.

———. *Founding a Protectorate: History of Bechuanaland, 1885–1895.* London: Mouton, 1965.

Sithole, Ndabaningi. *African Nationalism.* Cape Town: Oxford University Press, 1959.

Smith, Donald. *Rhodesia: The Problem.* London: R. Maxwell, 1969.

Smuts, Jan Christiaan. *Selections from the Smuts Papers.* Edited by W. K. Hancock and Jean van der Poel. 4 vols. Cambridge: University Press, 1966.

South Africa. Commission for the Socio-Economic Development of the Bantu Areas. *Summary of the Report.* U.G.61/1955. Pretoria: Government Printer, 1955.

South Africa. Department of Information. *Ethiopia and Liberia Versus South Africa: An Official Account of the Contentious Proceedings on South West Africa before the International Court of Justice at The Hague, 1960–1966.* 2nd ed. Pretoria: Department of Information, 1966.

South Africa Foundation. *South Africa in the Sixties: A Socio-Economic Survey.* Edited by H. T. Andrews and others. 2nd rev. ed. Johannesburg: Distributed by the Central News Agency, 1965.

Southern Africa and the United States. Edited by William A. Hance, with Leo Kuper, Vernon McKay, and Edwin S. Munger. New York: Columbia University Press, 1968.

Spence, C. F. *Moçambique: East African Province of Portugal.* Cape Town: Howard Timmins, 1963.

Spence, John Edward. *Lesotho: The Politics of Dependence.* London: Oxford University Press, 1968.

———. *Republic Under Pressure: A Study of South African Foreign Policy.* London: Oxford University Press, 1965.

———. *The Strategic Significance of Southern Africa.* London: Royal United Service Institution, 1970.

Stevens, Richard P. *Lesotho, Botswana, & Swaziland: The Former High Commission Territories in Southern Africa.* New York: Frederick A. Praeger, 1966.

Steward, Alexander. *The Sacred Trust: South West Africa.* Johannesburg: DaGama, 1963.

Strydom, Lauritz. *Rivonia Unmasked!* Johannesburg: Voortrekkerpers, 1965.

Tatz, Colin Martin. *Shadow and Substance in South Africa: A Study in Land and Franchise Policies Affecting Africans, 1910–1960.* Pietermaritzburg. University of Natal Press, 1962.

Teixeira, Bernardo. *The Fabric of Terror: Three Days in Angola.* New York: Devin-Adair, 1965.

Thompson, Cecil Harry, and Woodruff, Harry Wells. *Economic Development in Rhodesia and Nyasaland.* London: D. Dobson, 1954.

Thompson, Leonard Monteath. *Politics in the Republic of South Africa.* Boston: Little, Brown, 1966.

———. *The Unification of South Africa, 1906–1910.* Oxford: Clarendon Press, 1960.

Thompson, Vincent Bakpetu. *Africa and Unity: The Evolution of Pan-Africanism.* New York: Humanities Press, 1969.

Tindall, P. E. N. *A History of Central Africa.* New York: Frederick A. Praeger, 1967.

Todd, Judith. *Rhodesia.* London: MacGibbon & Kee, 1966.

Tshekedi Khama. *Bechuanaland and South Africa.* London: Africa Bureau, 1955.

Tylden, G. *The Rise of the Basuto.* Cape Town: Juta, 1950.

U.S. Congress. House of Representatives. Committee on Foreign Affairs. Subcommittee on Africa. *South Africa and United States Foreign Policy: Hearings.* 91st congr. 1st sess. Washington, D.C.: U.S. Government Printing Office, 1969.

———. *United States—South African Relations: Hearings.* 89th congr., 2nd sess. Parts 1–4. Washington, D.C.: U.S. Government Printing Office, 1966.

Van den Berghe, Pierre L. *South Africa: A Study in Conflict.* Middletown, Conn.: Wesleyan University Press, 1965.

Vandenbosch, Amry. *South Africa and the World: The Foreign Policy of Apartheid.* Lexington: University Press of Kentucky, 1970.

Van Jaarsveld, Floris Albertus. *The Afrikaner's Interpretation of South African History.* Cape Town: Simondium, 1964.

———. *The Awakening of Afrikaner Nationalism, 1868–1881.* Cape Town: Human & Rousseau, 1961.
Van Rensburg, Patrick. *Guilty Land.* London: Cape, 1962.
Van Wyk, Adam Johannes. *Lesotho: A Political Study.* Pretoria: Africa Institute, 1967.
Vatcher, William Henry, Jr. *White Laager: The Rise of Afrikaner Nationalism.* New York: Frederick A. Praeger, 1965.
Venter, Al J. *The Terror Fighters: A Profile of Guerrilla Warfare in Southern Africa.* Cape Town: Purnell, 1969.
Vermaak, Christopher Johann. *The Red Trap: Communism and Violence in South Africa.* Johannesburg: APB Publishers, 1966.
Verwoerd, Hendrik Frensch. *Verwoerd Speaks: Speeches 1948–1966.* Edited by A. N. Pelzer. Johannesburg: APB Publishers, 1966.
Walker, Eric Anderson. *A History of Southern Africa.* New impression with corrections. London: Longmans, 1962.
Weisfelder, Richard F. *Defining National Purpose in Lesotho.* Athens, Ohio: Ohio University Center for International Studies, Africa Program, 1969.
Welensky, Roland. *Welensky's 4000 Days: The Life and Death of the Federation of Rhodesia and Nyasaland.* New York: Roy Publishers, 1965.
Wellington, John H. *South West Africa and Its Human Issues.* Oxford: Clarendon Press, 1967.
Wills, Alfred John. *An Introduction to the History of Central Africa.* 2nd ed. London: Oxford University Press, 1967.
Wilson, Monica (Hunter), and Thompson, Leonard, eds. *The Oxford History of South Africa.* Vol. 1—*South Africa to 1870.* New York: Oxford University Press, 1969.
Wood, Anthony St. John. *Northern Rhodesia: The Human Background.* London: Pall Mall Press, 1961.
Young, Bertram Alfred. *Bechuanaland.* London: HMSO, 1966.
Young, Kenneth. *Rhodesia and Independence: A Study in British Colonial Policy.* Rev. ed. London: Dent, 1969.

ARTICLES IN PERIODICALS AND IN BOOKS

Austin, Dennis. "White Power?" *Journal of Commonwealth Political Studies* (Leicester, England), vol. 6, no. 2 (July 1968), pp. 95–106.
Barber, James. "The Impact of the Rhodesian Crisis on the Commonwealth." *Journal of Commonwealth Political Studies*, vol. 7, no. 2 (July 1969), pp. 83–95.
Bates, Robert H. "A Simulation Study of a Crisis in Southern Africa." *African Studies Review*, vol. 13, no. 2 (September 1970), pp. 253–264.
Best, Alan C. G. "Gaberone: Problems and Prospects of a New Capital." *The Geographical Review*, vol. 60, no. 1 (January 1970), pp. 1–14.
Booth, Alan R. "Lord Selborne and the British Protectorates, 1908–1910." *Journal of African History*, vol. 10, no. 1 (1969), pp. 133–148.
Boutros-Ghali, Boutros. "The Addis Ababa Charter." *International Conciliation*, no. 546 (January 1964). pp. 3–62.
Bowman, Larry W. "Organisation, Power, and Decision-Making Within the Rhodesian Front." *Journal of Commonwealth Political Studies*, vol. 7, no. 2 (July, 1969), pp. 145–165.
———. "Strains in the Rhodesian Front." *Africa Report*, vol. 13, no. 9 (December 1968), pp. 16–20.
———. "The Subordinate State System of Southern Africa." *International Studies Quarterly*, vol. 12, no. 3 (September 1968), pp. 231–261.
Caplan, Gerald L. "Barotseland: The Secessionist Challenge to Zambia." *Journal of Modern African Studies*, vol. 6, no. 3 (October 1968), pp. 343–360.
Carter, Gwendolen M. "Challenges to Minority Rule in Southern Africa," *International Journal* (Toronto), vol. 25, no. 3 (Summer 1970), pp. 486–496.
Cefkin, J. Leo. "The Rhodesian Question at the United Nations." *International Organization*, vol. 22, no. 3 (Summer 1968), pp. 649–669.
———. "United States Policy Towards the Rhodesia Rebellion." *Africa Today*, vol. 14, no. 5 (October 1967), pp. 14–17.
Chilcote, Ronald H. "Development and Nationalism in Brazil and Portuguese Africa." *Comparative Political Studies*, vol. 1, no. 4 (January 1969), pp. 501–525.
———. "Eduardo Mondlane and the Mozambique Struggle." *Africa Today*, vol. 12, no. 9 (November 1965), pp. 4–7.
———. "The Political Thought of Amilcar Cabral." *Journal of Modern African Studies*, vol. 6, no. 3 (October 1968), pp. 373–388.
Cilliers, S. P. "Border Industries: A South African Approach to the Problem of Under-Development." *Optima* (Johannesburg), vol. 19, no. 3 (September 1969), pp. 165–174.
Coates, Austin. "Portuguese Roots in Africa." *Optima*, vol. 15, no. 1 (March 1965), pp. 1–15.
Cronjé, F. J. C. "Can a Free Trade Association Be Created in Southern Africa?" *Optima* (Johannesburg), vol. 15, no. 3 (September 1965), pp. 113–119.
Curtin, T. R. C. "Total Sanctions and Economic Development in Rhodesia." *Journal of Commonwealth Political Studies* (Leicester, England), vol. 7, no. 2 (July 1969), pp. 126–131.
Dale, Richard. "The Implications of Botswana–South African Relations for American Foreign Policy." *Africa Today*, vol. 16, no. 1 (February–March 1969), pp. 8–12.
———. "Ovamboland: 'Bantustan Without Tears?' " *Africa Report*, vol. 14, no. 2 (February 1969), pp. 16–23.
———. "The Tale of Two Towns (Mafeking and Gaberones) and the Political Modernization of Botswana." *SAIPA: Journal for Public Administration* (Pretoria), vol. 4, no. 2 (March 1969), pp. 130–144.
D'Amato, Anthony A. "The Bantustan Proposals for South-West Africa." *Journal of Modern African Studies*, vol. 4, no. 2 (October 1966), pp. 177–192.
Davenport, Rodney. "African Townsmen? South African Natives (Urban Areas) Legislation Through the Years." *African Affairs* (London), vol. 68, no. 271 (April 1969), pp. 95–109.
Davidson, Basil. "An Inside Look at Angola's Fight for Freedom." *Africa Report*, vol. 15, no. 9 (December 1970), pp. 16–18.
———. "The Liberation Struggle in Angola and 'Portu-

guese' Guinea." *Africa Quarterly* (New Delhi), vol. 10, no. 1 (April–June 1970), pp. 25–31.

Davis, Jennifer. "Allies in Empire; Part I—U S Economic Involvement." *Africa Today*, vol. 17, no. 4 (July-August 1970), pp. 1–15.

Day, John. "The Rhodesian African Nationalists and the Commonwealth African States." *Journal of Commonwealth Political Studies*, vol. 7, no. 2 (July 1969), pp. 132–144.

———. "Southern Rhodesian African Nationalists and the 1961 Constitution." *Journal of Modern African Studies*, vol. 7, no. 2 (July 1969), pp. 221–247.

De Kiewiet, C. W. "Loneliness in the Beloved Country." *Foreign Affairs*, vol. 42, no. 3 (April 1964), pp. 413–427.

———. "South Africa's Gamble with History." *Virginia Quarterly Review*, vol. 41, no. 1 (Winter 1965), pp. 1–17.

———. "The World and Pretoria." *Virginia Quarterly Review*, vol. 45, no. 1 (Winter 1969), pp. 1–18.

Duffy, James. "Portugal in Africa." *Foreign Affairs*, vol. 39, no. 3 (April 1961), pp. 481–493.

Dugard, C. J. R. "South-West Africa and the Supremacy of the South African Parliament." *South African Law Journal* (Cape Town), vol. 86, pt. 2 (May 1969), pp. 194–204.

———. "The Revocation of the Mandate for South West Africa." *American Journal of International Law*, vol. 62, no. 1 (January 1968), pp. 78–97.

Du Toit, Brian M. "Afrikaners, Nationalists, and Apartheid." *Journal of Modern African Studies*, vol. 8, no. 4 (December 1970), pp. 531–551.

Eiselen, W. W. M. "Harmonious Multi-Community Development." *Optima*, vol. 9, no. 1 (March 1959), pp. 1–15.

Elias, Taslim Olawala. "The Charter of the Organization of African Unity." *American Journal of International Law*, vol. 59, no. 2 (April 1965), pp. 243–267.

Falk, Richard A. "The South West Africa Cases: An Appraisal." *International Organization*, vol. 21, no. 1 (Winter 1967), pp. 1–23.

Feit, Edward. "Community in a Quandary: The South African Jewish Community and 'Apartheid.' " *Race* (London), vol. 8, no. 4 (April 1967), pp. 395–408.

———. "Conflict and Cohesion in South Africa: A Theoretical Analysis of the Policy of 'Separate Development' and Its Implications." *Economic Development and Cultural Change*, vol. 14, no. 4 (July 1966), pp. 484–496.

———. "Urban Revolt in South Africa: A Case Study." *Journal of Modern African Studies*, vol. 8, no. 1 (April 1970), pp. 55–72.

Fitzgerald, Richard C. "South Africa and the High Commission Territories." *World Affairs* (London), vol. 4, no. 3 (July 1950), pp. 306–320.

Gibson, Richard. "A Hard Look at Africa's Liberation Movements—or a Study in Disunity." *Race Today* (London), vol. 1, no. 4 (August 1969), pp. 110–112.

Gross, Ernest A. "The Coalescing Problem of Southern Africa." *Foreign Affairs*, vol. 46, no. 4 (July 1968), pp. 743–757.

———. "The South West Africa Case: What Happened?" *Foreign Affairs*, vol. 45, no. 1 (October 1966,) pp. 36–48.

Grundy, Kenneth W. "Host Countries and the Southern African Liberation Struggle." *Africa Quarterly*, vol. 10, no. 1 (April–June 1970), pp. 15–24.

Gupta, Anirudha. "African Liberation Movements: A Bibliographical Survey." *Africa Quarterly*, vol. 10, no. 1 (April–June 1970), pp. 52–60.

Gutteridge, William F. "Africa's Armies and the Fortress of Southern Africa." *Commonwealth* (London), vol. 14, no. 5 (October 1970), pp. 179–184.

Hammond-Tooke, David. "Chieftainship in Transkeian Political Development." *Journal of Modern African Studies*, vol. 2, no. 4 (December 1964), pp. 513–529.

Hance, William A. "Three Economies." *Africa Report*, vol. 12, no. 8 (November 1967), pp. 23–30.

Hill, Christopher R. "UDI and South African Foreign Policy." *Journal of Commonwealth Political Studies*, vol. 7, no. 2 (July 1969), pp. 96–103.

Hoskyns, Catherine. "Trends and Developments in the Organization of African Unity." In *Yearbook of World Affairs, 1967*. London: Stevens & Sons, 1967, pp. 164–178.

Howe, Marvine. "Portugal at War: Hawks, Doves and Owls: How Long Can Portugal Hold Out in Africa and at Home?" *Africa Report*, vol. 14, no. 7 (November 1969), pp. 16–21.

Howe, Russell Warren. "War in Southern Africa." *Foreign Affairs*, vol. 48, no. 1 (October 1969), pp. 150–165.

Jackson, Dudley. "Income Differentials and Unbalanced Planning—The Case of Botswana." *Journal of Modern African Studies*, vol. 8, no. 4 (December 1970), pp. 553–562.

Karis, Thomas. "South Africa." In *Five African States: Reponses to Diversity*. Edited by Gwendolen Margaret Carter. Ithaca: Cornell University Press, 1963, pp. 471–616.

Kennan, George F. "Hazardous Courses in Southern Africa." *Foreign Affairs*, vol. 49, no. 2 (January 1971), pp. 218–236.

Krause, Otto. "Vorster and the Future of Nationalist Policy." *Optima*, vol. 16, no. 4 (December 1966), pp. 171–177.

Kuper, Hilda. "The Colonial Situation in Southern Africa." *Journal of Modern African Studies*, vol. 2, no. 2 (July 1964), pp. 149–164.

Kuper, Leo. "The Heightening of Racial Tension." *Race*, vol. 2, no. 1 (November 1960), pp. 24–32.

Lawrie, Gordon G. "South Africa's World Position." *Journal of Modern African Studies*, vol. 2, no. 1 (March 1964), pp. 41–54.

———. "What Will Change South Africa? Seeds that Await a New Political Climate." *Round Table*, (London), vol. 58, no. 229 (January 1968), pp. 41–55.

Legassick, Martin. "Bechuanaland: Road to the North." *Africa Today*, vol. 11, no. 4 (April 1964), pp. 7–9, 12.

———. "The Southern African Bloc: Integration for. Defense or Expansion?" *Africa Today*, vol. 15, no. 5 (October–November 1968), pp. 9–12.

Legum, Colin. "Independent Africa and the Liberation of the South." *Africa Quarterly*, vol. 10, no. 1 (April–June 1970), pp. 9–14.

Leistner, G. M. E. "Foreign Bantu Workers in South Africa: Their Present Position in the Economy." *South African Journal of Economics* (Johannesburg), vol. 35, no. 1 (March 1967), pp. 30–56.

Louis, William Roger. "The South West African Origins of the 'Sacred Trust,' 1914–1919." *African*

Affairs, vol. 66, no. 262 (January 1967), pp. 20–39.
Lovell, Colin Rhys. "Afrikaner Nationalism and Apartheid." *American Historical Review*, vol. 61, no. 2 (January 1956), pp. 308–330.
Macartney, W. J. A. "African Westminster? The Parliament of Lesotho." *Parliamentary Affairs* (London), vol. 23, no. 2 (Spring 1970), pp. 121–140.
———. "Botswana Goes to the Polls: Khama Government Retains Power in the Face of Lively Opposition and Paves Road to Economic Take-off." *Africa Report*, vol. 14, no. 8 (December, 1969), pp. 28–30.
———. "The Parliaments of Botswana, Lesotho, and Swaziland." *Parliamentarian* (London), vol. 50, no. 2 (April 1969), pp. 92–101.
McKinnell, Robert. "Sanctions and the Rhodesian Economy." *Journal of Modern African Studies*, vol. 7, no. 4 (December 1969), pp. 559–581.
Makonese, Philemon T. "ZAPU and the Liberation of Zimbabwe." *Africa Quarterly* (New Delhi), vol. 10, no. 1 (April–June 1970), pp. 40–51.
Manning, Charles A. W. "South Africa and the World: In Defense of Apartheid." *Foreign Affairs*, vol. 43, no. 1 (October 1964), pp. 135–149.
Marcum, John A. "The Angola Rebellion: Status Report." *Africa Report*, vol. 9, no. 2 (February 1964), pp. 3–7.
———. "A Martyr for Mozambique." *Africa Report*, vol. 14, nos. 3–4 (March-April 1969), pp. 6–9.
———. "Southern Africa and United States Policy: A Consideration of Alternatives." *Africa Today*, vol. 14, no. 5 (October 1967), pp. 5–13.
———. "Three Revolutions." *Africa Report*, vol. 12, no. 8 (November 1967), pp. 8–22.
Markakis, John. "The Organisation of African Unity: A Progress Report." *Journal of Modern African Studies*, vol. 4, no. 2 (October 1966), pp. 135–153.
Mason, Philip. "South Africa and the World: Some Maxims and Axioms." *Foreign Affairs*, vol. 43, no. 1 (October 1964), pp. 150–164.
Maud, John. "The Challenge of the High Commission Territories." *African Affairs*, vol. 63, no. 251 (April 1964), pp. 94–101.
Minter, William. "Allies in Empire: Part II—U.S. Military Involvement." *Africa Today*, vol. 17, no. 4 (July–August 1970), pp. 28–32.
———. "Allies in Empire: Part III—American Foreign Policy and Portuguese Colonialism." *Africa Today*, vol. 17, no. 4 (July–August 1970), pp. 34–36.
Mondlane, Eduardo C. "A Document for the History of African Nationalism: A FRELIMO 'White Paper.' " Translated and with notes by Douglas L. Wheeler. *African Historical Studies*, vol. 2, no. 2 (1969), pp. 319–333.
———. "The Kitwe Papers: Race Relations and Portuguese Colonial Policy, with Special Reference to Mozambique." *Africa Today*, vol, 15, no. 1 (February–March 1968), pp. 13–18.
Munger, Edwin S. "South Africa: Are There Silver Linings?" *Foreign Affairs*, vol. 47, no. 2 (January 1969), pp. 375–386.
Murray, David J. "The Future of Southern White Africa." *Current History*, vol. 56, no. 333 (May 1969), pp. 269–274, 305–306.
Naudé, G. "Banning in South Africa: A Technique of Repression." In *Rights and Wrongs: Some Essays on Human Rights*. Edited by Christopher R. Hill. Baltimore: Penguin Books, 1969, pp. 51–78.
Nieuwenhuysen, J. P. "Economic Policy in the Reserves Since the Tomlinson Report." *South African Journal of Economics*, vol. 32, no. 1 (March 1964), pp. 3–25.
———. "Prospects and Issues in the Development of the Reserves." *South African Journal of Economics*, vol. 32, no. 2 (June 1964), pp. 128–147.
Nixon, Charles R. "The Conflict of Nationalisms in South Africa." *World Politics*, vol. 11, no. 1 (October 1958), pp. 44–67.
Nogueira, Alberto Franco. "The View from Lisbon." *Africa Report*, vol. 12, no. 8 (November 1967), pp. 56–57.
Nyerere, Julius K. "Rhodesia in the Context of Southern Africa." *Foreign Affairs*, vol. 44, no. 3 (April 1966), pp. 373–386.
Pattee, Richard. "S. A. & Portugal." *Africa Institute Bulletin* (Pretoria), vol. 7, no. 6 (July 1969), pp. 226–245.
Patten, J. W. "Separate Development: A Look at the Facts." *Optima*, vol. 13, no. 1 (March 1963), pp. 17–23.
Pillay, P. D. "White Power in Southern Africa." *Africa Quarterly*, vol. 10, no. 1 (April–June 1970), pp. 32–39.
Pollock, Norman. "The Transkei: An Economic Backwater?" *African Affairs*, vol. 68, no. 272 (July 1969), pp. 250–256.
Potholm, Christian P. "After UDI: An Assessment of Southern Africa." *Journal of Asian and African Studies* (Leiden, Netherlands), vol. 2, nos. 3–4 (July and October 1967), pp. 245–250.
———. "Changing Political Configurations in Swaziland." *Journal of Modern African Studies*, vol. 4, no. 3 (November 1966), pp. 313–322.
———. "The Protectorates, The O.A.U. and South Africa." *International Journal* (Toronto), vol. 22, no. 1 (Winter 1966–1967), pp. 68–72.
———. "Swaziland in Transition to Independence." *Africa Report*, vol. 12, no. 6 (June 1967), pp. 49–54.
Proctor, J. H. "Building a Constitutional Monarchy in Lesotho." *Civilisations* (Brussels), vol. 19, no. 1 (1969), pp. 64–86.
———. "The House of Chiefs and the Political Development of Botswana." *Journal of Modern African Studies*, vol. 6, no. 1 (May 1968), pp. 59–79.
Rake, Alan. "Black Guerrillas in Rhodesia." *Africa Report*, vol. 13, no. 9 (December 1968), pp. 23–25.
Rasmussen, Thomas. "Political Competition and One-Party Dominance in Zambia." *Journal of Modern African Studies*, vol. 7, no. 3 (October 1969), pp. 407–424.
Richardson, Henry J., III. "Malawi: Between Black and White Africa." *Africa Report*, vol. 15, no. 2 (February 1970), pp. 18–21.
Rippon, Geoffrey. "South Africa and Naval Strategy: The Importance of South Africa." *Round Table*, no. 239 (July 1970), pp. 303–309.
Robson, Peter. "Economic Integration in Southern Africa." *Journal of Modern African Studies*, vol. 5, no. 4 (December 1967), pp. 469–490.
Sklar, Richard L. "On Returning 'To the Road of Legality' in Rhodesia." *Pan-African Journal*, vol. 1, no. 4 (Fall 1968), pp. 168–171.
Smit, P., and van der Merwe, E. J. "Economic Co-

operation in Southern Africa." *Journal for Geography* (Stellenbosch), vol. 3, no. 3 (September 1968), pp. 279–294.

Smith, Geoffrey. "England v. South Arica: The History of a Cricketing Tradition." *Round Table* (London), no. 239 (July 1970), pp. 311–316.

Snellen, I. Th. M. "Apartheid: Checks and Changes." *International Affairs* (London), vol. 43, no. 2 (April 1967), pp. 293–306.

"South Africa and the High Commission Territories." *Africa Institute International Bulletin* (Pretoria), vol. 2, no. 1 (January 1964), pp. 9–24.

Spence, J. E. "British Policy Towards the High Commission Territories." *Journal of Modern African Studies*, vol. 2, no. 2 (July 1964), pp. 221–246.

———. "The High Commission Territories with Special Reference to Swaziland." In *Problems of Smaller Territories*. Edited by Burton Benedict. London: Athlone Press, 1967, pp. 97–111.

———. "The Implications of the Rhodesia Issue for the Former High Commission Territories." *Journal of Commonwealth Political Studies*, vol 7, no. 2 (July 1969), pp. 104–112.

———. "The Political Implications of the Bantustan Policy." *Race*, vol. 3, no. 2 (May 1962), pp. 20–30.

———. "South Africa's 'New Look' Foreign Policy." *World Today* (London), vol. 24, no. 4 (April 1968), pp. 137–145.

———. "Tradition and Change in South African Foreign Policy." *Journal of Commonwealth Political Studies*, vol. 1, no. 2 (July 1963), pp. 136–152.

Spiro, Herbert J. "The Rhodesias and Nyasaland." In *Five African States: Responses to Diversity*. Edited by Gwendolen Margaret Carter. Ithaca: Cornell University Press, 1963, pp. 361–470.

Stevens, Richard P. "Bechuanaland: The Reconciliation of Traditional and Modern Forces." *Africa Report*, vol. 9, no. 4 (April 1964), pp. 15–17.

———. "The New Republic of Botswana." *Africa Report*, vol. 11, no. 7 (October 1966), pp. 15–19.

———. "Swaziland Political Development." *Journal of Modern African Studies*, vol. 1, no. 3 (September 1963), pp. 327–350.

Stultz, Newell M. "The Politics of Security: South Africa under Verwoerd, 1961–6." *Journal of Modern African Studies*, vol. 7, no. 1 (April 1969), pp. 3–20.

Sutcliffe, R. B. "The Political Economy of Rhodesian Sanctions." *Journal of Commonwealth Political Studies*, vol. 7, no. 2 (July 1969), pp. 113–125.

Tandon, Yashpal. "The Organization of African Unity as an Instrument and Forum of Protest." In *Protest and Power in Black Africa*. Edited by Robert I. Rotberg and Ali A. Mazrui. New York: Oxford University Press, 1970, pp. 1153–1183.

Thompson, Leonard M. "South Africa's Relations with Lesotho, Botwsana, and Swaziland." *African Forum*, vol. 2, no. 2 (Fall 1966), pp. 65–77.

Tiryakian, Edward A. "Sociological Realism: Partition for South Africa?" *Social Forces*, vol. 46, no. 2 (December 1967), pp. 208–221.

Trapido, Stanley. "Political Institutions and Afrikaner Social Structures in the Republic of South Africa." *American Political Science Review*, vol. 57, no. 1 (March 1963), pp. 75–87.

———. "The South African Party System." *Journal of Commonwealth Political Studies*, vol. 4, no. 2 (July 1966), pp. 83–93.

Turk, Austin T. "The Futures of South Africa." *Social Forces*, vol. 45, no. 3 (March 1967), pp. 402–412.

Umozurike, U. O. "International Law and Self-Determination in Namibia." *Journal of Modern African Studies*, vol. 8, no. 4 (December 1970), pp. 585–603.

Walshe, A. P. "Black American Thought and African Political Attitudes in South Africa." *Review of Politics*, vol. 32, no. 1 (January 1970), pp. 51–77.

———. "The Changing Content of Apartheid." *The Review of Politics*, vol. 25, no. 3 (July 1963), pp. 343–361.

———. "The Origins of African Political Consciousness in South Africa." *Journal of Modern African Studies* vol. 7, no. 4 (December 1969), pp. 583–610.

Ward, Michael. "Economic Independence for Lesotho?" *Journal of Modern African Studies*, vol. 5, no. 3 (November 1967), pp. 355–368.

Webb, Colin de B. "The Foreign Policy of the Union of South Africa." In *Foreign Policies in a World of Change*. Edited by Joseph E. Black and Kenneth W. Thomson. New York: Harper & Row, 1963, pp. 425–450.

Weisfelder, Richard. "Power Struggle in Lesotho." *Africa Report*, vol. 12, no. 1 (January 1967), pp. 5–13.

Welch, Claude E., Jr. "Constitutional Confusion in Swaziland." *Africa Report*, vol. 8, no. 4 (April 1963), pp. 7–9.

Welsh, David. "Urbanisation and the Solidarity of Afrikaner Nationalism." *Journal of Modern African Studies*, vol. 7, no. 2 (July 1969), pp. 265–276.

Wheeler, Douglas L. " 'Angola Is Whose House?' Early Stirrings of Angolan Nationalism and Protest, 1822–1910." *African Historical Studies*, vol. 2, no. 1 (1969), pp. 1–22.

———. "An Early Angolan Protest: The Radical Journalism of José de Fontes Pereira (1832–1891)." In *Protest and Power in Black Africa*. Edited by Robert I. Rotberg and Ali A. Mazrui. New York: Oxford University Press, 1970. pp. 854–874.

———. "Nineteenth-Century African Protest in Angola: Prince Nicolas of Kongo (1830?–1860)." *African Historical Studies*, vol. 1, no. 1 (1968), pp. 40–59.

———. "The Portuguese Army in Angola." *Journal of Modern African Studies*, vol. 7, no. 3 (October 1969), pp. 425–439.

———. "Reflections on Angola." *Africa Report*, vol. 12, no. 8 (November 1967), pp. 58–62.

———. "Thaw in Portugal." *Foreign Affairs*, vol. 48, no. 4 (July 1970), pp. 769–781.

Whitaker, Paul M. "Arms and the Nationalists: Where and on What Terms Do They Obtain Their Support and How Important is External Aid to Their Revolution?" *Africa Report*, vol. 15, no. 5 (May 1970), pp. 12–14.

———. "The Revolutions of 'Portuguese' Africa." *Journal of Modern African Studies*, vol. 8, no. 1 (April 1970), pp. 15–35.

Zacklin, Ralph. "Challenge of Rhodesia: Toward an International Public Policy." *International Conciliation*, no. 575 (November 1969), pp. 1–72.

Zwane, Timothy M. J. "The Struggle for Power in Swaziland." *Africa Today*, vol. 11, no. 5 (May 1964), pp. 4–6.

Index

Abreu e Brito, Domingos de, 159
Achkar, 74-75
Afonso I, King, 158
African National Congress (ANC), 9, 32-34, 36-40, 42-45, 229, 234, 250, 253, 255, 266-67, 269, 274, 314-16
Afrikaans, 20-21, 26
Afrikaners
  nationalism of, 19-30
    Christianity and, 26-27
    economics and, 21, 27
    language and, 20-21
    National party and, 21-22
    polarization and, 23-25
    political system and, 25-26
    South African polity and, 27-30
    Verwoerd and, 22-23
  race relations of, 59-68
Aggression, 271
Agriculture
  in Lesotho, 132
  in Malawi, 208
  in South West Africa, 81
  in Swaziland, 144-45
Ahmad, Eqbal, 274
Ake (U.N. representative), 74, 75
Albuquerque, Mousinho de, 184
Algeria, 246, 250
Almeida, Bello de, 168
Almeida, Dr. Francisco José, Lacerda e, 165
Almond, Gabriel A., 9
Amery, L. S., 102, 105-6
ANC (African National Congress of South Africa), 9, 32-34, 36-40, 42-45, 229, 234, 250, 253, 255, 266-67, 269, 274, 314-16
Andersson, Charles John, 85-87
Andrade, Mario de, 198
Andrade, Poser de, 185
Angola, 157-71, 80, 322
  bibliography of, 5
  guerrillas in, 196-99, 203-4, 283, 311-12
    defense against, 305-8
  investment in, 305
  Portugal and, 157-82, 305-6
    African elites and masses and, 178-80
    from Berlin Conference to 1895, 162-67
    from 1895-1961, 169-71
    from 18th century to Berlin Conference, 162-67
    from 15th to 18th century, 158-62
    guerrilla activity and, 196-99, 203-4
    political history of, 173-74
    post 1961 reforms, 174-77
    white residents of Angola and, 177-78
  refugees from, 118
  Rhodesia and, 281
  size of, 142
  South Africa and, 51-53, 238, 281, 292-93
  Swaziland and, 151
  terrain of, 298-99
  Zambia and, 237-38
Angolan Revolutionary Government in Exile (GRAE), 196-99, 252, 255, 268-70, 312, 322
Anti-Semitism in South Africa, 21, 27-28
Apartheid, 22-25, 59-68, 277-78
Apathy, 271
Apter, David E., 25, 207
Arden-Clarke, Charles, 105
Arkhurst (U.N. representative), 74
Ashipala, Chief Jacky, 315
Asquith, Herbert H., 101
Assis Júnior, António de, 173
Attlee, Clement, 107
Auguste (U.N. representative), 75
Azevedo, M. Pinto de, 185
Azevedo Countinho, Lt. João de, 169

Ba (U.N. representative), 75
Bakala (U.N. representative), 74
Baldwin, David, 147
Ball, George W., 265
Bambata, Chief, 35-36
Banda, H. Kamuzu, 123, 227, 231, 248-50, 252, 257, 259, 279
  on common market for Southern Africa, 278
  on economy of Malawi, 50-51
  election of (1958), 209-10
  military of, 311
  Organization of African Unity and, 217
  as party leader, 210-11
  Portugal and, 214
  as pragmatist, 215
  on Rhodesia, 216
  strength of, 217
Bandeira, Sá da, 164-65
Banjar (U.N. representative), 74
Baptista, Pedro Joáo, 165
Barber, James P., "Rhodesia and Interstate Relationships in Southern Africa," 219-32
Barnet, Richard J., 265
Barreto, Francisco, 160
Bashford, Pat, 225
Bastide, Roger, 60
Basto, Pinto, 185
Basutoland, *see* Lesotho
Bathoen, Chief, 99
Batista, Fulgencio, 260
Beaver, Philip, 166
Bechuanaland, *see* Botswana
Beer, G. L., 77
Benson, Mary, 10, 33
Bernstein, Lionel, 43
Bhangu, Hyacinth, 42
Bhengu, H., 66
Biafra, 70, 181
Blumer, Herbert, 68
Boavida, Américo, 180
Bolts, William, 166
Bonga, 188
Botha, Louis, 15, 102
Botha, P. W., 53, 84, 258
Botswana, 110-24, 140, 246-47, 249, 270, 311, 322
  bibliography of, 5
  diplomatic relations of, 116, 122-23
  economy of, 114-17, 121-22, 247, 285, 287
  geography of, 110-11
  Great Britain and, 121
  as High Commission Territory, 97-100, 102-3, 106, 109
  investment in, 122
  Lesotho and, 136
  Organization of African Unity and, 251
  Rhodesia and, 119-21, 229
  role of, 123-24
  South Africa and, 111-19, 121, 152, 250, 277, 282
    diplomatic relations between, 50, 116, 248
    economic dependency between, 50, 114-15, 121-22, 134, 146, 279-81, 287, 290-92
    nationalist guerrillas and, 117-19
    "outward" policy and, 49-50
    refugees and, 118-19
  Swaziland and, 142, 145, 151
  terrain of, 299
  U.S.S.R. and, 117, 121
  Zambia and, 117, 240
Bowman, Larry W., 11, 51, 58, 321
Bragança, Constantino de, 160
Brazza, Savorgnan de, 167
Brooks, Edgar H., 8, 321
Brown, Douglas, 111, 113
Brown, George, 228
Brown, S. E. D., 24
Busia, Kofi A., 279

Cabral, Amilcar, 274
Cabral, Pedro Alvares, 158
Cadaval, Duke of, 185
Cadbury, William, 170
Caetano, Marcelo, 171, 176, 182, 185, 194, 280, 316, 324
Capelo, Hermenegildo Capelo, 165
Capitalism in South Africa, 21, 27, 29
Carmichael, Stokely, 271
Carter, Gwendolen M., 26, 28
Carvalho, Maj. Henrique Dias de, 168
Castro, Baltazar de, 158
Castro, Fidel, 201, 267
Catholic Church
  in Lesotho, 135-36
  on Rhodesia, 222
  See also Christianity
Central African Federation, 5, 222, 286
Cerejeira, Cardinal Patriarch Manuel Gonçalves, 186
Cervenka, Zdenek, 230
Chakela, Koenyama, 140
Changonga, Baltazar, 199
Chavanduka, Gordon, 225
Chikerema, James, 32, 40, 229
Chilcote, Ronald H., 5, 181
  "Mozambique: The African Nationalist Response to Portuguese Imperialism and Underdevelopment" by, 183-95
Chimutengwende, Hasan, 41

China, 78-79, 136, 152, 229, 250, 259-60, 267-68
Chipembere, H. B. Masauko, 209, 211, 217
Chisiza, Dunduzu, 32
Chisiza, Yatuta, 211
Chitepo, Herbert, 34, 40
Chiume, W. M. Kanyama, 209
Chombe, Chief, 188
Chou En-lai, 78
Christianity
  Afrikaner nationalism and, 26-27, 226
  preservation of, 60-61, 226
  See also Catholic Church
Churchill, Winston, 113
City Youth League, 32-33, 37-38
Clark, Sir William, 104
Coetzee, J. Albert, 26
Coleman, James S., 25
Collins, Sam, 93
Common market for Southern Africa, 277-97
Communist parties, *see specific countries*
Compulsive repetition, 271-72
Congo, 78, 158-59, 236
Congo (Kinshasa), 249-50, 309-10
Congress party (Lesotho), 137-39
COREMO, 192-93, 196, 200, 202, 268-69, 313
Cowell, Richard, 93
Cowen, Denis, 279
Cowley, Clive, 114
Craveirinha, José, 189
Crewe, Lord, 101
Cruz, António Vicente da, 188
Cruz, Joaquim José da, 188
Cruz, Viriato da,197-98
Curtis, Lionel, 105
Customs union, 114-15, 134, 146, 247, 279-80

Dahl, Robert A., 115
Dale, Richard, "Botswana," 110-24
Data, 3-7
  collection of, 4-5
  retrieval of, 5-7
Davidson, Basil, 172
Day, John, 34-35
De Gaulle, Charles, 149
Debray, Régis, 201-2, 260, 267, 273
Decolonization, 4
Delgado, Cabo, 192
Delgado, Gen. Humberto, 174
Deutsch, Karl, 88
Diederichs, Nicolas, 279
Diggs, Charles C., Jr., 10, 122, 203
Dinizulu, Chief, 35-36
Diplomatic relations with South Africa, 50, 116, 248
Dlamini, Dumisa, 142

Dönges, T. E., 27
Driver, Jonty, 67
Duffy, James, 172-73, 187
Duignan, Peter, 6

Economic sanctions against Rhodesia, 227-28, 230-31, 236-37, 256, 281
Economics and Afrikaner nationalism, 21, 27
Economy
  of Botswana, 114-17, 121-22, 247, 285, 287
  of Lesotho, 128-34, 247, 285
  of Malawi, 208, 213-15, 249
  of South Africa, 247
  of South West Africa, 81-82, 285
  of Swaziland, 144-47, 149-50, 247, 285
  of Zambia, 249, 284
Education
  in Angola, 176-77
  FRELIMO and, 200
  in Lesotho, 133
  in South West Africa, 81
Egerton, F. C. C., 172
Egypt, 246, 250, 310
El Kony (U.N. representative), 75
El Mufti (U.N. representative), 75
Ennes, António, 184, 188
Ethiopia, 71-73, 250
Evans, Vice Adm. Edward, 103
Exile groups, 262-75, 310-11
  activities of, 263-70
    with Afro-Asian nations, 268-70
    with Communist powers, 266-68
    in United Nations, 263-65
    with Western powers, 265-66
  social service functions of, 275
  military functions of, 273-74
  perceptual and behavioral problems of, 270-72
  poltical functions of, 274-75
Expansionist policies of South Africa, 61

Fanon, Frantz, 173, 180, 200
Fear, 60-61
Fernandes, Antonio, 158
First, Ruth, 86, 90-91
Fleischmann, Julius, 93
Fouché, J., 7
Frankl, Viktor, 271
Fraser, Lt. Gen. C. A., 53
FRELIMO, 190-93, 195-96, 199-200, 202, 250, 254-55, 259, 267, 269, 274-75, 312-13, 316
Frewer, Louis B., 6
Freyre, Gilberto, 172

Friedmann, Marion, 38
Fundanga, Kapesi, 197
Furse, Maj. Sir Ralph D., 112

Gabon, 283
Gallin-Douathe (U.N. representative), 74
Galvão, Capt. Henrique, 174, 198
Gama, Vasco da, 158
Gambia, 279
Gamito, Antonio Candido Pedro, 165
Gandar, Laurence, 282
Gardiner, Robert, 50
Geingob, Gottfried H., "African Nationalism in Namibia" by, with Hidipo L. Hamutenya, 85-94
Gerdener, Theo, 53
Ghana, 136, 283
Gibbs, Sir Humphrey, 236
Gibson, Richard, 45
Gladstone, Lord, 102, 114
Goldberg, Arthur, 73
Goldberg, Nelson, 43
Goraseb, David, 77
Gordon-Walker, Patrick, 107
Graça, Joaquim Rodrigues, 165
GRAE (Angolan Revolutionary Government in Exile), 196-99, 252, 255, 268-70, 312, 322
Graham, Lord, 224
Grant, Ulysses, 166
Great Britain, 163
  Botswana and, 121
  Central African Federation and, 222
  High Commission Territories and, 97-109
    early history of, 98-99
    South Africa and, 99-109
    Verwoerd on, 97-98
    See also specific territories
  Lesotho and, 130, 134, 136-39
  Malawi and, 215
  Rhodesia and, 219-20, 224, 228, 230-32, 255-56
    Zambia and, 235-36
  slavery and, 163-65
  South Africa and, 228
    British language policy and, 20
    High Commission Territories and, 99-109, 112-13, 146
    National party and, 21-22
    Rhodesia and, 221
  Swaziland and, 142, 145, 149-50
  Tanzania and, 256
Green (trader), 87
Grigg, Sir Edward, *see* Selborne, Lord
Grimes (U.N. representative), 74
Gross, Ernest, 71, 329
Guerrilla activity, 298-317
  in Angola, 196-99, 203-4, 283, 311-12
    defense against, 305-8
  Botswana and, 117-19
  in Mozambique, 188-93, 196-99, 203-4, 283, 312-13
    defense against, 305-8
  neutrals in, 311
  in Rhodesia, 118, 229-32, 300, 313-14, 322
    defense against, 53, 304-5
  in South Africa, 91-92, 281, 315-16
    defense against, 301-4
  in South West Africa, 314-15, 322
  Tanzania and, 308-9
  terrain and climate conditions for, 298-301
  theory and models for, 200-203
  Vorster on, 245
  Zambia and, 249-50, 309
Guest, Winton, 93
Guevara, Ché, 201
Gumane, Paulo José, 192, 199-200
Gumede, J. T., 36-37
Guyana, 73
Gwambe, Adelino, 199-200
Gwambe, Hlomulo Chitofo, 192

Haak, Jan, 287
Haile Selassie, 216
Hailey, Lord, 100
Hammarskjold, Dag, 198
Hammond, Richard, 177, 180
Hamutenya, Hidipo L., "African Nationalism in Namibia" by, with Gottfried H. Geingob, 85-94
Hansards, 4
Harper, William, 224
Harris, J. H., 172
Harris, Marvin, 187
Health services in South West Africa, 81
Herero Council, 89-90
Hereros, 87, 90
Hertzog, Albert, 24, 30, 286
Hertzog, Gen. J. B. M., 22, 24, 26-28, 100, 102, 104-5
Hewitt, A. R., 6
Heybittel (trader), 87
Hiemstra, R. C., 258
High Commission Territories, 97-109
  early history of, 98-99
  South Africa and, 99-109, 112-13, 146
    1909-1939, 102-6
    1939-1966, 106-9
  Verwoerd on, 97-98
  See also specific territories

Hill, Christopher R., "The Future of Separate Development in South Africa," 59-68
Hirsch, M. I., 34-35
Holsti, K. J., 147-48
Homem, Vasco Fernandes, 160
Hopewell, Arthur, 8
Horrell, Muriel, 8
Horwood (university president), 282
Houphouët-Boigny, Félix, 279
Houser, George M., 11
Howe, Russell Warren, 40-41
Howman, Jack, 44, 229
Hussein, King of Jordan, 18
Hynning, Clifford J., 71

Ilboudo (U.N. representative), 74, 75
India, 28, 73, 88
Indonesia, 73
Industry
  in Lesotho, 133
  in South West Africa, 81
  in Swaziland, 144-45
Institutional sponsorship of research and publications, 7-11
International Court of Justice, 69-75, 91, 264
Investment
  in Angola, 305
  in Botswana, 122
  in Mozambique, 305
  in South Africa, 63, 65-67, 93-94, 194, 283-84
Ivens, Roberto, 165

Ja Toivo, Herman Toivo, 86, 89-90
Jacha, Aaron, 32
James, Robin, 225
Jameson, Sir Leander Starr, 99
Japan, 152
Jawara, Sir Dawda, 279
Jensen, F. A. S., 270
Jessup, Phillip C., 71
John III, King of Portugal, 159
Jonathan, Chief Leabua, 49-50, 109, 125-40, 247, 259, 282
Jones, Griff, 208
Jorge, Santos, 185
José, Amaro, 165
José I, Dom, 163

Kagombe, Maina D., "African Nationalism and Guerrilla Warfare in Angola and Mozambique," 196-204
Kaiser, Karl, 152
Kalundungu, José, 197
Kapwepwe (U.N. representative), 75
Kathrada, Ahmed, 42
Kaunda, Kenneth, 40, 123, 181, 197, 226, 230, 233
  Vorster and, 258
  white people in Zambia and, 284
  Zambian economy and, 54
Kavandame, Mzee Lázaro, 189, 192, 275
Kenya, 136
Kenyatta, Jomo, 203, 217
Kerina, Mburumba G., 90
Kgosana, Philip, 38
Khama, Sir Seretse, 10, 106, 109, 113 118-20, 123, 136, 229, 311
  South African ban of, 49
Khama, Tshekedi, 10, 103, 105
Kiewiet, C. W. de, 283
Kimathi, Didan, 203
Kironde (U. N. representative), 75
Klerk, Jan de, 7, 23
Korry, Edward M., 122
Kotane, Moses, 37
Kozonquizi, Jariretundu F., 90
Krüger, D. W., 27, 47
Kruger, Paul, 28
Kumtumanju, Gomile, 215
Kuper, Leo, 14
Kutako, Chief Hosea, 89-90
Kuznets, Simon, 291

Labor movement, 89
Labor party (South Africa), 22
Lago, Baltazar Pereira do, 163
Language and Afrikaner nationalism, 20-21
Lardner-Burke, Desmond, 40, 44
Lavaud, Adm., 166
League of African Rights, 37
League of Nations, 4, 70-71
Leballo, Potlako, 44
Legum, Colin, 38, 92
Leistner, G. M. E., 290
Lembede, Anton, 32-33
Leopold II, King of the Belgians, 167
Lesotho, 110, 125-40, 246-47, 249, 270, 311, 322
  bibliography of, 5
  Botswana and, 136
  Communist party in, 127
  Congress party and, 137-39
  customs agreement of, 114-15, 134, 146, 247, 279-80
  economy of, 128-34, 247, 285
    agriculture, 132
    education, 133
    industry, 133
    natural resources, 132
    trade, 133-34
  election in (1970), 125-28

Great Britain and, 130, 134, 136-39
as High Commission Territory, 97-100, 103, 106, 108-9
Malawi and, 136
National party and, 134-37
Organization of African Unity and, 251
Rhodesia and, 136
royalist politics in, 139
South Africa and, 127-28, 152, 250, 277, 280, 282
borders of, 129
diplomatic relations between, 50, 116, 248
economic relationship between, 49-50, 130-32, 134, 136, 281, 290-92
"outward" policy and, 49-50
Swaziland and, 136, 145, 151
Zambia and, 136, 240
Liberia, 71-73, 250
Lin Piao, 267
Lippmann, Walter, 12
Livingston, David, 165, 168, 172
Livromentos, David, 198
Lothian, Marquess of, 105
Louw, Eric H., 47-48, 76
Lugard, Lord, 62, 105
Lumumba, Patrice, 78, 202
Luthuli, Chief Albert, 32, 34
Lyautey, Louis Hubert Gonzalve, 62
Lyttleton, Alfred, 101

Mabunda, David J. M., 192
Mabusa, O. M., 143
MacDonald, Malcolm, 104-6
MacDonald, Ramsay, 21
Machado, Ilidio Tome Alevs, 197
Machel, Samora Moises, 192
McKinnell, Robert, 228
MacMahon, Marie Edmé Patrice de, 166
Macmillan, Harold, 47, 220
Macrae, Norman, 282-83
Madagascar, 281
Madlala, Winston, 143
Magwababa, Chief, 36
Maharero, Chief, 87
Maier, Norman R. F., 270
Majara, Chief, 136
Makhosini, Prince, 143, 151-52
Makunda, David, 199
Malagasy Republic, 54, 250, 279
Malan, Daniel F., 21-22, 26-27, 106-7, 113
Malawi, 31, 61, 122, 140, 207-18, 311, 322
bibliography of, 5
economy of, 208, 213-15, 249
Great Britain and, 215
historical ties of, 212
Lesotho and, 136
Mozambique and, 150, 212, 214
Organization of African Unity and, 215-16, 251
polity of, 208-12
postindependence, 210-12
preindependence, 208-10
Portugal and, 216-17
Rhodesia and, 212-16
society of, 207-8
South Africa and, 116, 212, 214-18, 248-50, 278-82, 287-93
"outward" policy and, 50-51, 57
Swaziland and, 151
Tanzania and, 215-16
Zambia and, 215
Malianga, Washington, 44
Malie, Julius, 42
Mallinga, Lawrence Mallinga, 192, 199
Malvern, Lord, 222
Mandela, Nelson, 32-34, 37-39, 42-43, 45, 315
Mandela, Winnie, 43
Manning, C. A. W., 72
Mannoni, O., 60
Mantero, Francisco, 170
Manuel, King of Portugal, 158-59
Mao Tse-tung, 201, 259-60, 298
Marais, Jan, 23
Marcum, John A., 1, 14, 181
"The Exile Condition and Revolutionary Effectiveness: Southern African Liberation Movements" by, 262-75
Marks, J. B., 37
Marques, Silvino Silvério, 178
Marshall, Gen. S. L. A., 76
Marwick, Sir Brian, 142
Maseribane, Chief, 136
Masire, Quett, 122-23
Matanzima, Kaiser, 77
Mathews, Richard, 197
Matthews, Z. K., 32, 122, 124
Mau Mau, 202
Maud, Sir John, 108
Mawema, Michael, 35
Mayer, Philip, 64
Mbandzeni, Chief, 99
Mbeki, Govan, 43
Mduli, Enoch, 148
Melaure, Chief, 169
Mendes, Sr. Afonso, 179
Meyer, J. P., 20
Meyer, Willie, 143
Mgonja (U.N. representative), 74
Milas, Leo, 192-93, 199
Military
of Congo (Kinshasa), 309-10
of Portugal, 305-8
of Rhodesia, 304-5

of South Africa, 301-4
of Tanzania, 308-9
of Zambia, 309
Milner, Lord, 102, 105
Mitchison, Lady Naomi, 123
Mkudu, Percy, 252
Mlangani, Raymond, 43
Mmole, Mathew Michinji, 192, 199
Mobilization system, 25-29
Modernizing autocracy, 25
Mokhehle, Ntsu, 13, 126-27, 136-40
Mokhehle, Shakhane, 140
Mondlane, Eduardo, 188-91, 199, 253-54, 265, 312-13
Mondlane, Janet, 191, 254
Mondlane, Mario, 149
Monteiro, Maj. José Maria Correia, 165
Montgomery, Field Marshal Lord, 79
Moreira, Adriano, 171-72, 175, 180
Moritz (governor of Nassau), 160
Moroka, James, 33-34
Moshoeshoe, Chief, 98
Moshoeshoe II, King, 135, 137-40
Moynihan, Daniel P., 123
Mozambique, 142, 157-71, 280, 322
guerrillas in, 283, 312-13
defense against, 305-8
investment in, 305
Malawi and, 150, 212, 214
Portugal and, 157-71, 183-95, 305-6
from Berlin Conference to 1895, 167-69, 184
discovery of Mozambique, 158
from 18th century to Berlin Conference, 162-67
from 1895-1961, 169-71
from 15th to 18th century, 160-62 183-84
guerrilla activity and, 188-93, 196-99, 203-4
imperialism and, 184-88
Rhodesia and, 150, 194, 227, 281
South Africa and, 51-53, 194, 238, 281-82, 290, 292-93
Swaziland and, 145, 150, 153
terrain of, 299-300
Zambia and, 237-38
MPLA (Popular Movement for the Liberation of Angola), 196-99, 202, 252, 255, 266-67, 269-70, 274, 312, 316, 322
Msibi, George, 143, 151
Mswati, King, 142
Mtshali, 35, 44
Mugabe, Robert, 44
Müller, A. L., 8
Muller, C. F. J., 5
Muller, Hilgard, 7, 52, 54, 76, 86, 116, 214, 226
Muller, S. L., 40, 250
Musgrave, Benjamin, 87
Musiker, Reuben, 5
Mveli, Chief, 36
Mwaanga, Vernon J., "Zambia's Policy toward Southern Africa," 234-41

Namas, 87
Namibia, *see* South West Africa
National Democratic party (Rhodesia), 34-35, 39
National party (Lesotho), 134-37
National party (South Africa)
apartheid and, 61-62, 66
growth of, 67
moderate policies of, 28-30
nationalism and, 21-22, 24-25, 28-30
National purity, 60
Nationalism
in Rhodesia, 31-45, 222-24
guerrillas and, 53, 118, 229-32, 300, 304-5, 313-14, 322
in South Africa, 4, 19-45
African, 31-45
Afrikaner, 19-30
guerrillas and, 91-92, 281, 301-4, 315-16
in South West Africa, 4, 85-94
ethnic group antagonisms and, 86-88
guerrilla actions and, 91-92, 314-15, 322
international implications of, 93-94
labor movement and, 89
organizational rivalry and, 90-91
students and, 88, 90
See also Guerrilla activity
Natural resources
in Lesotho, 132
in Swaziland, 144
Ndvungunge, King, 142
Nel, J. A. F., 111
Neto, Agostinho, 198-99, 312
Nevinson, H. W., 172
Nggwane III, King, 142
Ngubane, Jordan, 42
Nhaúde, 188
Nielsen, Waldemar A., 11, 35, 45
Nigeria, 70, 73, 136, 256, 310
Nkoana, Matthew, 40
Nkomo, Joshua, 32, 34-35, 39, 44, 57, 224
Nkosi, Clifford, 143
Nkosi, Lewis, 275
Nkrumah, Kwame, 107, 198-99, 210, 217, 256
Nogar, Rui, 189

Nogueira, Alberto Franco, 52, 185
Nokwe, Duma, 37, 42-43
Noronha, Rui de, 189
Novais, Paulo Dias de, 159
Nquku, J. J., 142
Nujoma, Sam, 89-90
Nxumalo, Allen, 143
Nxumalo, Simon, 143, 151-52
Nyasasulu, Alec, 213
Nyerere, Julius, 44, 63, 229, 248-49, 251, 308
Nzula, Albert, 37

O'Hara, Barratt, 10
Okuma, Thomas, 172
Oliver, Gert C., 101
OPO (Ovamboland People's Organization), 89-90
Organization of African Unity, 118, 245-61, 268-69, 278-79
  Banda and, 217
  Botswana and, 251
  future of, 257-61
  Lesotho and, 251
  liberation strategy of, 250-56
  Malawi and, 215-16, 251
  after Rhodesian independence, 256-57
  structural and political framework of, 245-50
Orwell, George, 172
"Outward" policy of South Africa, 46-58
  with Angola, 52-53
  with High Commission Territories, 49-50
  with Malawi, 50-51, 57
  with Mozambique, 51-53
  with Rhodesia, 53-54, 56
  risks of, 54-57
  with Zambia, 53-54, 56
Ovamboland, 80-81, 278
Ovamboland People's Organization (OPO), 89-90
Owen, R., 166

PAC (Pan-Africanist Congress), 36-39, 42, 44-45, 250, 253, 255, 268-69, 315-16
Pacheco, Manuel, 158
Pakistan, 73
Palmerston, Lord, 164-65
Palmeta, Duke of, 185
Pan-Africanist Congress (PAC), 36-39, 42, 44-45, 250, 253, 255, 268-69, 314-16
Passmore, Gloria C., 6
Paton, Alan, 8, 124
Payson, Charles, 93
Peete, Chief P. N., 130, 133, 136
Pereira, Nuno Alvares, 160
Peterson, Charles W., "The Military Balance in Southern Africa," 298-317
Pim, Sir Allen, 103-4
Pinto, Father Francisco Joáo, 165
Pinto, Serpa, 165, 168
Pinto-Bull, Benjamin, 264
Pirzada (U.N. representative), 74
Plesis, Wentzel C. du, 7
Plessis, L. J. du, 27
Polarization, 23-25
Pombal, Marquis, 163, 185
Popular Movement for the Liberation of Angola (MPLA), 196-99, 202, 252, 255, 266-67, 269-70, 274, 312, 316, 322
Poqo, 38-39, 43, 316
Portugal
  Angola and, 157-82, 305-6
    African elites and masses and, 178-80
    from Berlin Conference to 1895, 167-69
    from 1895-1961, 169-71
    from 18th century to Berlin Conference, 162-67
    from 15th to 18th century, 158-62
    guerrilla activity and, 196-99, 203-4
    political history of, 173-74
    post 1961 reforms, 174-77
    white residents of Angola and, 177-78
  Banda and, 214
  Malawi and, 216-17
  military of, 258, 305-8
  Mozambique and, 157-71, 183-95, 305-6
    from Berlin Conference to 1895, 167-69, 184
    discovery of Mozambique, 158
    from 18th century to Berlin Conference, 162-67
    from 1895-1961, 169-71
    from 15th to 18th century, 160-62, 183-84
    guerrilla activity and, 188-93, 196-99, 203-4
    imperialism and, 184-88
  Rhodesia and, 221
  sanctions against, 231
  South Africa and, 238
Possony, S. T., 73
Potholm, Christian P.
  "Swaziland" by, 141-53
  "Toward the Millennium" by, 321-31
Pratt, David, 23

Pretorius, Marthinus, 166-67
Purified National Party (South Africa), 22-23, 26
Putterill, Maj. Gen. R. J., 232

Race, South African policies of, 22-25, 59-68, 277-78
Rajuili, Rev., 42
Rebelo, Gen., 53
Rebocho Vaz, Lt. Col. C. A., 178
Reconciliation system, 25-29
Refugees, 118-19, 147, 150
Regression, 271
Reid, Inez Smith, "African Nationalism in South Africa and Zimbabwe," 31-45
Republic of South Africa, 260
  Angola and, 238, 281, 292-93
    "outward" policy and, 51-53
  anti-Semitism in, 21, 27-28
  bibliography of, 5
  Botswana and, 111-19, 121-22, 152, 250, 277, 282
    diplomatic relations between, 50, 116, 248
    economic dependency between, 50, 114-15, 121-22, 134, 146, 279-81, 287, 290-92
    nationalist guerrillas and, 117-19
    "outward" policy and, 49-50
    refugees and, 118-19
  capitalism in, 21, 27, 29
  common market for Southern Africa and, 277-97
  Communist party in, 36-38, 44
  customs agreement of, 114-15, 134, 247, 279-80
  economy of, 247
  expansionist policies of, 61
  Great Britain and, 228
    British language policy and, 20
    High Commission Territories and, 99-109, 112-13, 146
    National party and, 21-22
    Rhodesia and, 221
  guerrillas in, 91-92, 281, 315-16
    defense against, 301-4
  invasion route into, 300-301
  investment in, 63, 65-67, 93-94, 194, 283-84
  Lesotho and, 127-28, 152, 250, 277, 280, 282
    borders of, 129
    diplomatic relations between, 50, 116, 248
    economic relationship between, 49-50, 130-32, 134, 136, 281, 290-92
    "outward" policy and, 49-50
  Malawi and, 116, 212, 214-18, 248-50, 278-82, 287-93
    "outward" policy and, 50-51, 57
  military of, 258-59, 301-4
  Mozambique and, 194, 238, 281-82, 290, 292-93
    "outward" policy and, 51-53
  nationalism in, 4, 19-45
    African, 31-45
    Afrikaner, 19-30
    guerrillas and, 91-92, 281, 301-4, 315-16
  Organization of African Unity and, 251
  "outward" policy of, 46-58
    with Angola, 51-53
    with High Commission Territories, 49-50
    with Malawi, 50-51, 57
    with Mozambique, 51-53
    with Rhodesia, 53-54, 57
    risks of, 54-57
    with Zambia, 53-54, 56
  Portugal and, 238
  power of, 257-58
  race policies of, 22-25, 59-68, 277-78
  Rhodesia and, 221, 226-29, 238, 280-81, 287-90
    "outward" policy and, 53-54, 57
  right-wing in, 23
  sanctions against, 231, 256
  South African subsystem dominated by, 141, 220, 228, 322
  South West Africa and, 69-84, 238-39, 281, 292
    aftermath of International Court's decision on, 73-75
    economic progress of, 81
    financial arrangements for, 81-82
    legal aspects of, 70-71, 264
    nonwhite homelands and, 80-81
    political aspects of, 71-73
    self-determination and, 83
    South African membership in United Nations and, 75-77
    South West Africa's future and, 79-80
    strategic position of South West Africa and, 77-78
    terrorist infiltration and, 83-84
  Swaziland and, 142, 145-49, 152, 250, 278, 280-81
    diplomatic relations between, 50, 116, 245
    economic interaction between, 50, 146-47, 285, 290-92
    "outward" policy and, 49-50

paramilitary interaction between, 148-49
political interaction between, 147-48
terrain of, 298, 300
United States and, 93-94, 256
World War II and, 27-28
Zambia and, 227, 239-40, 248-50, 281, 287-89, 292-93
"outward" policy and, 53-54, 56
Resende, Sebastião Soares de, 186
Resha, Robert, 42
Reunited National party (South Africa), 27-30
Rhodes, Cecil, 98-99, 168, 170, 172, 222
Rhodesia, 142, 219-32, 285
Angola and, 281
bibliography of, 5
Botswana and, 119-21, 229
Great Britain and, 219-20, 224, 228, 230-32, 255-56
Zambia and, 235-36
guerrillas in, 53, 118, 229-32, 300, 304-5, 313-14, 322
Lesotho and, 136
Malawi and, 212-16
military of, 258, 304-5
Mozambique and, 150, 194, 227, 281
nationalism in, 31-45, 222-24
guerrillas and, 52, 118, 229-32, 300, 304-5, 313-14, 322
Portugal and, 221
sanctions against, 227-28, 230-31, 236-37, 356, 381
South Africa and, 53-54, 57, 221, 226-29, 238, 280-81, 287-90
South African invasion route through, 300
South African subsystem and, 200
Swaziland and, 151
terrain of, 299
white rule in, commitment to, 220-26, 252
Zambia and, 54, 226-27, 233, 235-37, 286
Rhoodie, Eschel M., 12, 78, 85, 87
"Southern Africa: Towards a New Commonwealth?" by, 276-97
Riekert, P. J., 287, 291
Roberto, Holden, 196-99, 252, 268, 311
Rostow, W. W., 281
Roux, Edward, 36
Royalists in Lesotho, 139
Rozwadowski, Vincent, 143
Rubin, Leslie, 6
Rupert, Anton, 23, 49, 133
Rusk, Dean, 78
Russell, Lord John, 164

Salazar, Antonio de Oliveira, 170, 171, 173, 176, 185, 194, 198, 237, 316
Saldanha e Meneses, Aires de, 162
Salisbury, Lord, 168
Samkange, Thompson, 32
Sandys, Duncan, 34
Sanger, Clyde, 207
Santo, Espírito, 185
Santos, Marcelino dos, 192, 195
Sarakikya, Sam Hagai, 308
Savimbi, Jonas, 181, 197, 269, 312
Scott, Rev. Michael, 10
Sebele, Chief, 99
Seely, Lt. Col. J. E. B., 101
Segal, Ronald, 41
Selborne, Lord, 100, 105
Shamuyarira, Nathan, 32, 44
Shiimi, Ushona, 81
Sigananda, Chief, 36
Sigauke, Jaime, 192, 313
Sigauke, Sebastene, 192
Sillery, Anthony, 110
Silundika, George, 34
Silva Porto, António Francisco da, 165
Silva Rego, Antonio da, "Portugal and Africa: A Historical Survey (1482-1961)," 157-71
Silverira, Gonçalo da, 160
Simango, Rev. Uria, 192, 199
Simbwaye, Bredan K., 91
Simões Madeira, Diogo, 160
Sislu, Walter, 32-33, 37, 42-43, 45
Sithole, Edson, 32
Sithole, Rev. Ndabaningi, 34-35, 39, 44, 223-24, 231
Slavery, 162-65
Slim, Taieb, 74
Smit, P., 286-87, 289-95
Smith, Harry, 35
Smith, Ian, 40, 44, 120, 219, 304
challenge to leadership of, 224
Kaunda and, 230
weakness of, 232
Smock, David, 41
Smuts, Jan Christiaan, 15, 22, 26-27, 33, 76, 100-101, 103
expansionist desires of, 47
on Seretse, 106, 113
Sobhuza I, King, 142
Sobhuza II, King, 142-44, 147
Sobukwe, Robert, 37-38, 43-45
Sontag, Susan, 266
Sousa, Noémia de, 189
Sousa Coutinho, Francisco Inocêncio de, 163, 165, 171

South West Africa, 69-84, 255
bibliography of, 5
economy of, 81-82, 285
geography of, 85-86
guerrillas in, 314-15, 322
nationalism in, 4, 85-94
South Africa and, *see* South Africa–South West Africa and
Swaziland and, 151
terrain of, 298-99
Zambia and, 238-39
South West African People's Organization (SWAPO), 9, 85-86, 90-92
Spear of the Nation, 39, 315-16
Speck, Samuel W., Jr., "Malawi and the Southern African Complex," 207-18
Spence, J. E., "South African Foreign Policy: The 'Outward Movement,' " 47-58
Spender, Sir Percy, 74
Stanley, Henry M., 167
Stephens, R. P., 143
Stevens, Richard P., 111
"The History of the Anglo-South African Conflict over the Proposed Incorporation of the High Commission Territories" by, 97-109
Strijdom, Johannes G., 28, 107
Sudan, 70, 310
Sutcliffe, R. B., 227
Suzman, Helen, 7-8
SWAPO (South West African People's Organization), 9, 85-86,90-92
Swaziland, 110-11, 140-53, 246-47, 249, 270, 311, 322
Angola and, 151
bibliography of, 5
Botswana and, 142, 145, 151
customs agreement of, 114-15, 134, 146, 247, 279-80
economy of, 144-47, 149-50, 247, 285
Great Britain and, 142, 145, 149-50
as High Commission Territory, 97, 99-100, 102-4, 109
Lesotho and, 136, 145, 151
Malawi and, 151
Mozambique and, 145, 150, 153
Organization of African Unity and, 251
political parties in, 142-44
Rhodesia and, 151
South Africa and, *see* South Africa–Swaziland and
South West Africa and, 151
terrain of, 300
United States and, 152
Zambia and, 240
Sweden, 150, 254

Takawira, Leopold, 35, 44
Tambo, Oliver, 32-33, 39, 42, 229
Tanaka (judge), 71
Tandon, Yashpal, 12
"The Organization of African Unity and the Liberation of Southern Africa," by, 245-61
Tantsi, Rev., 42
Tanzania, 39, 229
Great Britain and, 256
guerrillas and, 308-9
Malawi and, 215-16
militancy of, 249-50
military of, 308-9
Organization of African Unity and, 256
Zambia and, 227, 249, 284
Tati, Chief Alfredo, 312
Telli, Diallo, 151, 255
Terrain for guerrillas, 298-301
Thomas, J. H., 104
Thomaz, Américo, 176
Thompson, Leonard M., 6
Thornton, A. P., 225
Thurmond, Strom, 265
Todd, Garfield, 34
Togo, 283
Toit, Rev. S. J. du, 20
Torres, John, 128
Toty, Alexander, 252
Touré, Sékou, 198
Trade, 133-34, 145, 227-28
Tribes, 62-63, 70
Trichardt, Louis, 166
Tshombe, Moise, 181, 202, 252
Tsiranana, Philibert, 216, 279
Tunisia, 257

U Thant, 264
Uganda, 70
United Nations, 4, 33
exile groups and, 263-65
League of Nations mandates and, 70-71
Lesotho and, 136
Organization of African Unity and, 255
South African membership in, 75-77
South West Africa and, 69-70, 73-77
United States, 93-94, 122, 152, 256
U.S.S.R., 78, 117, 121, 256, 266-68

Valente, Malangatana Gowenha, 189
Van den Berghe, Pierre L., 6, 260
Van den Haag, E., 73
Van der H. Schreuder, Deryck, 6
Van der Merwe, E. J., 286-87, 289-95
Van der Merwe, Hendrik W., 8

Van der Merwe, Paul S., "South Africa and South West Africa," 69-84
Van Graan, Wynand, 133
Van Jaarsveld, F. A., 5, 20
Van S. Bruwer, J. P., 86
Van Wyk, A. J., 128
Van Wyk, Theo, 5
Vatcher, William H., 21
Vedder, Heinrich, 7
Verba, Sidney, 9
Verwoerd, Hendrik F., 22-23, 28-29, 60, 108-9
  on common market for Southern Africa, 278
  on High Commission Territories, 97-98, 247-48
  Lesotho and, 129
  on Rhodesia, 221, 227
Vicente, Gil, 158
Vicker, Ray, 78
Viljoen, Gerrit, 9
Villiers Graaff, Sir de, 7, 53, 304
Virpsha, E. S., 285
Vital, David, 111, 113
Von Clausewitz, Karl, 245-46, 259
Von Lettow-Vorbeck, Gen. Paul, 308
Vorster, B. J., 7, 23-24, 29, 41, 61, 67, 77, 80
  Botswana and, 116
  on guerrillas, 245
  on incorporation of territories, 111
  Kaunda and, 258
  Lesotho and, 127-28
  on "outward" policy, 55-56
  Portugal and, 52-53
  on Rhodesia, 53
  Sobhuza and, 147
  on South African troops in Rhodesia, 229, 304
  on Windhoek, 82

Walden, Lord Howard de, 164
Weber, Max, 271
Weisfelder, Richard F., "Lesotho," 125-40
Welensky, Sir Roy, 222, 304
Wellington, J. H., 87
Wellington, Lord, 164
Wessels, Albert, 23
Wet, Carel de, 79
Wet Nel, M. D. C. de, 7
Wheeler, Douglas L., "Portugal in Angola: A Living Colonialism," 172-82
Whitehead, Sir Edgar, 34-35
Williams, Robert, 170
Willson, F. M. G., 6
Wilson, Harold, 228, 236
Wilson, Monica, 6
Witbooi, Chief Hendrik, 87
World War II, 27-28
Worrall, Denis J., "Afrikaner Nationalism: A Contemporary Analysis," 19-30
Worrall, John, 231

Xuma, A. B., 33

Yifru (U. N. representative), 74
Youlou, 252

Zambia, 73, 140, 229, 234-41
  Angola and, 237-38
  Botswana and, 117, 240
  China and, 79
  economy of, 249, 284
  guerrillas and, 249-50, 309
  Lesotho and, 136, 240
  Malawi and, 215
  military of, 309
  Mozambique and, 237-38
  Rhodesia and, 54, 226-27, 233, 235-37, 286
  South Africa and, 53-54, 56, 227, 239-40, 248-50, 281, 287-89, 292-93
  South African invasion route through, 300
  South West Africa and, 238-39
  Swaziland and, 240
  Tanzania and, 227, 249, 284
  terrain of, 299
ZANU (Zimbabwe African National Union), 39-41, 44-45, 215, 224, 229, 231-32, 237, 253, 268-69, 314
ZAPU (Zimbabwe African People's Union), 39-41, 44-45, 215-16, 224, 229, 232, 234, 237, 253, 267, 269, 274, 314
Zimbabwe, *see* Rhodesia
Zimbabwe African National Union, *see* ZANU
Zimbabwe African People's Union, *see* ZAPU
Zwane, Ambrose, 142, 144